973.3 AME

The American Revolution

THE AMERICAN REVOLUTION
1764-1772

)

The American Revolution:
Writings from the Pamphlet Debate 1764–1772
is kept in print by a gift from

SIDNEY AND RUTH LAPIDUS

to the Guardians of American Letters Fund,
established by The Library of America
to ensure that every volume in the series
will be permanently available.

The American Revolution:
Writings from the Pamphlet Debate 1764–1772
is published with support from

THE BODMAN FOUNDATION

Contents

Preface   xiii
Introduction   xv

1. "Cato," *Thoughts on a Question of Importance Proposed
   to the Public, Whether It Is Probable That the Immense
   Extent of Territory Acquired by This Nation at the Late
   Peace, Will Operate Towards the Prosperity, or the Ruin
   of the Island of Great-Britain?* London, 1765   1

2. Francis Bernard, "Principles of Law and Polity, Applied
   to the Government of the British Colonies in America.
   Written in the Year 1764." From *Select Letters on the
   Trade and Government of America; and the Principles
   of Law and Polity, Applied to the American Colonies.*
   London, 1774   25

3. James Otis, *The Rights of the British Colonies Asserted
   and Proved.* Boston, 1764   41

4. [Stephen Hopkins], *The Rights of Colonies Examined.*
   Providence, 1765   121

5. [Martin Howard Jr.], *A Letter from a Gentleman at
   Halifax, to His Friend in Rhode-Island, Containing
   Remarks upon a Pamphlet, Entitled, The Rights of
   Colonies Examined.* Newport, 1765   143

6. [Thomas Whately], *The Regulations Lately Made
   Concerning the Colonies, and the Taxes Imposed upon
   Them, Considered.* London, 1765   163

7. [Daniel Dulany], *Considerations on the Propriety of
   Imposing Taxes in the British Colonies, for the Purpose
   of Raising a Revenue, by Act of Parliament.* Annapolis,
   1765   241

8. Richard Bland, *An Inquiry into the Rights of the British
   Colonies, Intended as an Answer to the Regulations Lately
   Made Concerning the Colonies, and the Taxes Imposed upon
   Them Considered. In a Letter Addressed to the Author of
   That Pamphlet.* Williamsburg, 1766   305

9. *The Examination of Doctor Benjamin Franklin, Before an August Assembly, Relating to the Repeal of the Stamp-Act, etc.* Philadelphia, 1766 331

10. [William Hicks], *The Nature and Extent of Parliamentary Power Considered; in Some Remarks upon Mr. Pitt's Speech in the House of Commons, Previous to the Repeal of the Stamp-Act: with an Introduction, Applicable to the Present Situation of the Colonies.* Philadelphia, 1768 363

11. [John Dickinson], *Letters from a Farmer in Pennsylvania, to the Inhabitants of the British Colonies.* Philadelphia, 1768 405

12. [Allan Ramsay], *Thoughts on the Origin and Nature of Government. Occasioned by the Late Disputes Between Great Britain and Her American Colonies: Written in the Year 1766.* London, 1768. 491

13. [Silas Downer], *A Discourse, Delivered in Providence, in the Colony of Rhode-Island, upon the 25th. Day of July, 1768. At the Dedication of the Tree of Liberty, from the Summer House in the Tree.* Providence, 1769 521

14. *An Inquiry into the Nature and Causes of the Present Disputes Between the British Colonies in America and Their Mother-Country; and Their Reciprocal Claims and Just Rights Impartially Examined, and Fairly Stated.* London, 1769 537

15. [John Joachim Zubly], *An Humble Enquiry into the Nature of the Dependency of the American Colonies upon the Parliament of Great-Britain, and the Right of Parliament to Lay Taxes on the Said Colonies. By a Freeholder of South-Carolina.* Charleston, 1769 577

16. [William Knox], *The Controversy Between Great Britain and Her Colonies Reviewed; the Several Pleas of the Colonies, in Support of Their Right to All the Liberties and Privileges of British Subjects, and to Exemption from the Legislative Authority of Parliament, Stated and Considered; and the Nature of Their Connection with, and Dependence on, Great Britain, Shewn, upon the Evidence of Historical Facts and Authentic Records.* London, 1769 613

17. Edward Bancroft, *Remarks on the Review of The Controversy Between Great Britain and Her Colonies. In*

Which the Errors of Its Author Are Exposed, and the Claims of the Colonies Vindicated, upon the Evidence of Historical Facts and Authentic Records. New London, 1771 667

18. Joseph Warren, *An Oration Delivered March 5th, 1772. At the Request of the Inhabitants of the Town of Boston; to Commemorate the Bloody Tragedy of the Fifth of March, 1770.* Boston, 1772 743

19. *The Votes and Proceedings of the Freeholders and Other Inhabitants of the Town of Boston, in Town Meeting Assembled, According to Law.* Boston, 1772 759

Chronology 791
Biographical Notes 825
Note on the Texts 831
Notes 849
Index 917

Preface

"What do We Mean by the Revolution? The War? That was no part of the Revolution. It was only an Effect and Consequence of it. The Revolution was in the Minds of the People, and this was effected, from 1760 to 1775, in the course of fifteen Years before a drop of blood was drawn at Lexington. The Records of thirteen Legislatures, the Pamphlets, Newspapers in all the Colonies ought to be consulted, during that Period, to ascertain the Steps by which the public Opinion was enlightened and informed concerning the Authority of Parliament over the Colonies."
—John Adams to Thomas Jefferson, 1815

BRITISH imperial reforms undertaken in the 1760s sparked one of the most consequential constitutional debates in Western history. Taken up between American colonists and Britons and among the colonists themselves, this debate was carried on largely in pamphlets—inexpensive booklets ranging in length from five thousand to twenty-five thousand words and printed on anywhere from ten to a hundred pages. Easy and cheap to manufacture, these pamphlets were ideal for rapid exchanges of arguments and counter-arguments. Pamphlets concerned with the American controversy from both sides of the Atlantic number well over a thousand, and they cover all of the significant issues of politics—the nature of power, liberty, representation, rights, constitutions, the division of authority between different spheres of government, and sovereignty. This Library of America volume, the first of a two-volume set, presents the most interesting and important of these works, with a preference in selection for pamphlets directly in dialogue with one another. By the time the debate traced here was over, the first British empire was in tatters, and Americans had not only clarified their understanding of the limits of public power, they had prepared the way for their grand experiment in republican self-government and constitution-making.

Introduction

IN 1763 Great Britain emerged from the Seven Years War—or the French and Indian War, as the American colonists called it—as the greatest and richest empire since the fall of Rome. From the Mediterranean to Manila, from Quebec to Havana, its armies and navies had been victorious, so much so that the British public concluded that its military forces were invincible. The Peace of Paris of 1763 compelled France to cede Senegal in West Africa and Dominica, Grenada, Tobago, and Saint Vincent and the Grenadines in the Caribbean to Britain; renounce all claims to compensation for British naval seizures during the war; destroy its fortifications at Dunkirk; return Minorca and other captured places to Britain; remove its armies from the German states of Hanover, Hesse, and Brunswick; and recognize British suzerainty over India. Most important, the treaty gave Britain undisputed dominance over the eastern half of North America. From the defeated Bourbon powers, France and Spain, Britain acquired huge expanses of territory in the New World—all of Canada, East and West Florida, and millions of fertile acres between the Appalachian Mountains and the Mississippi River. At the same time France turned over to Spain New Orleans and the vast territory of Louisiana in compensation for Spain's loss of the Floridas. Thus France, the most fearsome of Britain's enemies, was entirely removed from the North American continent.

The war's end left many American colonists feeling more British, more proud of their membership in the great Protestant empire, than ever before. They had celebrated the accession of the new king George III in 1760 with more enthusiasm than most of their fellow subjects at home three thousand miles away. And "home" for many colonists was still Great Britain. Although unprofessional provincial soldiers and sometimes haughty British regulars had often clashed during the war, the overwhelming victory over the Catholic Bourbon powers and, perhaps more important, Prime Minister William Pitt's policy of reimbursing the colonists for their financial expenditures, had helped to ease much of the colonists' anger at

British arrogance. Boston's liberal minister Jonathan Mayhew, who earlier had spoken out passionately against unlimited submission to the higher powers, now exulted in the outcome of the war. He, like many colonists, foresaw the growth of "a mighty empire (I do not mean an independent one) in numbers little inferior perhaps to the greatest in Europe, and in felicity to none."

Suddenly, however, the British government was faced with the imposing task of organizing and financing this huge empire, especially the colonies and territories on the North American continent. In the aftermath of the Seven Years War British officials found themselves forced to make long-postponed decisions concerning the North American colonies, decisions that would set in motion a chain of events that ultimately shattered this grand empire and created the United States of America.

The patchwork of territories now known as the first British Empire took shape over the course of the seventeenth century without the benefit of much in the way of central planning. The Crown simply chartered private companies, or granted proprietary rights to individuals, to create colonies that would promote the public interests of the realm. But by the second half of the century the English government began trying to exert tighter control over its colonies, principally through a series of Navigation Acts designed to channel colonial trade and shipping for the benefit of the mother country. The colonists were required to purchase manufactured goods made in Britain, and they were obliged to send to Britain certain enumerated commodities— exotic staples such as tobacco, rice, furs, and sugar—to satisfy its markets before selling them elsewhere. Since commerce remained the dominant business of the empire, its power was felt mainly at the seaports.

At the same time, however, royal officials and bureaucrats had not been content simply to supervise trade. They continually sought to exert greater control over the colonial governments in order to project the king's authority deeper into colonial society. At the end of the seventeenth century the Crown began taking back most of the proprietary and corporate grants it had issued and installing royal governors responsible for enforcing the Navigation Acts and carrying out Crown instructions. By 1760 only four colonies on the North

American continent had not been royalized: the proprietary colonies of Pennsylvania and Maryland, which were nonetheless still subject to all sorts of royal restrictions, and the corporate colonies of Connecticut and Rhode Island, which were deemed too small and insignificant to require restructuring. Thus by the early eighteenth century the empire had become essentially a royal empire, under the direct control of the Crown. While the navigation system had been authorized by statutes of Parliament, the administration of the empire was largely based on the Crown's prerogatives, the bundle of rights and powers adhering in the monarchy that historically gave it the authority to rule over the realm.

Undergirding these efforts was a theory of empire that held the colonies to be inferior to the mother country and that envisioned authority flowing smoothly down from the Crown through royal governors to royally commissioned justices of the peace in colonial towns and counties. To their great frustration, British bureaucrats were never able to make the actual operation of the empire fit this idealized image. There were too many diverse authorities and agencies responsible for colonial policy—a complex bureaucratic structure that reflected the ad hoc way in which the colonies had developed. The Board of Trade came closest to being a general supervisory body, but it lacked decision-making authority and shared power with several executive bodies, including the secretary of state for the Southern Department, the Treasury Department, and the Admiralty and the War Office. This hodgepodge of offices and conflicting jurisdictions bred confusion and inefficiency everywhere in the empire. Even in the empire's main business of trade regulation, the prevalence of loopholes and numerous opportunities for smuggling and corruption prevented effective enforcement of the Navigation Acts.

Of course, there was never a shortage of royal bureaucrats and sub-ministers eager to reform this ramshackle imperial structure and to expand the Crown's authority over the colonies. But enhancing crown power was difficult for the Whig aristocrats who were the king's chief ministers. As good Whigs, they were reluctant to be seen as openly supporting any enhancement of crown authority, which smacked of Toryism. Ever since the struggles against the Stuart kings in the seventeenth

xviii   INTRODUCTION

century, Whigs had stood for liberty and the rights of the people, embodied in Parliament, in opposition to Crown power. They had triumphed in the Glorious Revolution of 1688–89, when James II was ousted in favor of William, the Prince of Orange, and his wife, Mary, James's Protestant daughter, and Parliament enacted a Bill of Rights that circumscribed royal authority. With the death of Mary's sister Anne in 1714, the Whig leaders had brought over the Elector of Hanover and made him King George I of Great Britain in order to preserve a Protestant succession. This broke the hereditary line and created a threat to their regime from the Stuarts in exile in France, one expressed in the Jacobite risings of 1715 and 1745. The Tories, as traditional defenders of crown authority and presumed supporters of the Stuart claim to the throne, were proscribed from crown offices and regarded as traitors by many Whigs. It was an odd situation: the king's government was in the hands of Whig ministers who were supposedly fearful of the very royal power they themselves were exercising. Any attempt to reform the king's empire and strengthen royal authority was sure to alarm the Whigs in Parliament and to unite the opposition to the king's government. Consequently, ministries during the reigns of the first two Hanoverian monarchs, George I and George II, usually tried to keep imperial questions out of Parliament, where they could only cause trouble.

Under these complicated circumstances the empire had been allowed to grow haphazardly, and representative assemblies in each of the colonies had continually expanded their authority. Royal governors, whose tenure was tentative and always susceptible to the vagaries of politics in London, increasingly complained that it was impossible, as one of them put it, "to preserve the king's just prerogative, as every province is endeavoring to gain from the crown by adding to their privileges." While the governors had legal authority, they lacked much of the informal influence and patronage power that would have allowed them greater control over the assemblies and their constituents. Consequently, most colonists, especially those outside of the port towns, had not experienced much royal authority and by and large had been left free to pursue their own interests.

By the middle of the eighteenth century, however, British politicians and officials were faced with dynamic new developments that compelled them to think in fresh ways about the empire. The British colonies—there were twenty-two of them in the Western Hemisphere in 1760—were becoming too important to be treated as casually as they had been. The irrational and inefficient working relationship between the mother country and the colonies had to change, and for several reasons.

First, owing both to immigration and impressive birth rates, the population of the North American colonies was growing faster than any other people in the Western world, doubling roughly every twenty years. Between 1750 and 1770 the mainland colonists increased from one million to more than two million, and consequently became a more important part of the greater British world. In 1700 North Americans had represented only one out of twenty of the empire's population; by 1770 the colonists had come to represent one out of five. Farsighted provincials like Benjamin Franklin were predicting that sooner or later the center of the British Empire would have to shift to America. Moreover, this growing colonial population was on the move. Confined for more than a century to a several-hundred-mile-wide strip of territory along the Atlantic coast, the colonists were now pressing westward and putting increasing pressure on the Indians on the far side of the Appalachian Mountains—a situation that required some sort of imperial action.

At the same time the colonists' economy was rapidly expanding. In the years after 1745 colonial trade with Great Britain grew dramatically and became an increasingly important segment of the English and Scottish economies. Nearly half of all English shipping was engaged in American commerce. The North American mainland was absorbing twenty-five percent of English exports and Scottish commercial involvement with the colonies was expanding even more rapidly. From 1747 to 1765 the value of colonial exports to Britain doubled from about £700,000 to £1.5 million, while the value of colonial imports from Britain grew even faster. Indeed, from the late 1740s on, Americans imported about £500,000 more in goods from Britain than they were exporting, participating in what historians have called "a consumer revolution" as more and more middling Americans began purchasing luxuries—from tea and tea sets to silk handkerchiefs and feather mattresses—that hitherto had been the preserve of aristocrats. This resulted in massive trade deficits that were counterbalanced by the extension of huge amounts of English and Scottish credit to the colonists. By 1760 colonial debts to Britain amounted to £2 million; by 1772 they had jumped to £4 million, half of which was owed by spendthrift Virginians alone. Such important commercial developments could not help but capture the attention of imperial officials. When the Earl of Halifax took over the Board of Trade in 1748, he began some piecemeal efforts at imperial reform—efforts that were interrupted by the need for colonial cooperation during the Seven Years War.

The war brought home to many officials the extent to which the colonists were violating the Navigation Acts and colonial assemblies were stymieing the prerogative powers of the governors. It was the treaty of peace in 1763 ending the Seven Years War, however, that made some sort of imperial reform imperative. The newly acquired territory had to be organized, conflicting land claims had to be sorted out, and something had to be done to keep the conflicts between land-hungry white settlers and angry Indians from exploding into open warfare. In 1763 the Crown issued a proclamation that sought to confine white settlement to the east of a hastily drawn line along the Appalachian chain. It was a crude attempt at a solution, and many colonists, including George Washington, considered it to be only temporary.

Dealing with the enormous expenses facing the British government was a much more demanding problem. By 1763 the war debt totaled £137 million; its annual interest alone was £5 million, a huge figure when compared with an ordinary yearly British peacetime budget of £8 million. Taxpayers in England were protesting their heavy wartime burden, and there seemed little prospect of a peace dividend. Lord Jeffrey Amherst, commander in chief in North America, estimated that ten thousand troops would be needed to keep the peace with the Indians and the French left in Quebec and to deal with squatters, smugglers, and bandits in the newly acquired territories in the trans-Appalachian West. Since there were virtually no British inhabitants in the new acquisitions, the government could not rely on its traditional system of local militia defense and police to preserve order; royal troops and military posts in the wilderness would have to be maintained. The cost of doing this quickly climbed to over £300,000 a year.

Confronted with this wartime debt and these rising military expenses, the British government naturally looked to the North American colonies for new sources of revenue. After all, it seemed, the war had been fought in large part for their benefit. And with returning British soldiers bearing tales of American prosperity, the government presumed that the colonists could easily afford to help out the mother country in its time of need. Perhaps the navigation system could be tightened up in order to extract some revenue, and maybe some direct taxes, even a stamp duty, which some colonies themselves had occasionally used in the past as a source of revenue, could be levied on the colonists.

Even as the empire required reform the political situation in Britain was dramatically changing, marked by growing divisions among political elites and by the emergence of a new popular politics. Perhaps the most obvious development was the accession in 1760 of a new king, George III. Unlike his grandfather, George II, and his great-grandfather, George I, this twenty-two-year-old prince was a British-born "patriot king," determined to exert his right to rule in ways his German-born predecessors had not. The first two Hanoverian kings had been deeply indebted to the Whig oligarchies for making possible their accession to the Crown of Great Britain—a remarkable rise in stature for the electors of Hanover. Hence they allowed Whig ministers to rule without exercising much of their personal royal authority. George III was different. He wanted to appoint his own ministers, which he had every constitutional right to do, regardless of whether his choice of ministers had the support of Parliament. He even welcomed Tory gentry to his court for the first time since the Hanoverian accession.

George's naïve determination to be his own king unsettled English politics. At the beginning of his reign the young king appointed as prime minister his tutor and friend, Lord Bute, a Scottish aristocrat who had no political strength whatsoever in Parliament. Bute, who Samuel Johnson said had "his blood full of prerogative," lasted only a year, but in the minds of many English politicians his secret influence continued to pervade the government as George ran through a series of short-lived ministries. Not until Lord North in 1770 did George find a prime minister he liked who at the same time had the support of a majority in Parliament.

Ministerial office-holding in the 1760s could scarcely have been more chaotic and unstable. Between 1761 and 1768 six different individuals were appointed and dismissed as secretary of state for the Southern Department for reasons that had nothing to do with American affairs. The Board of Trade, which had only three presidents between 1730 and 1760, had no fewer than six between 1760 and 1766. The twenty years following George's accession to the throne produced twice as many county elections as the two decades preceding it. And so, at the very moment the empire badly needed to be re-formed, British politics were more confused and volatile than they had been at any time since George I had acceded to the throne in 1714.

Something else had changed by the 1760s. Contrary to earlier experience, the Crown's ministers now found that colonial issues were the one thing that could *divide* the opposition in Parliament. Inhibitions that had existed for decades against invoking parliamentary authority in formulating colonial policy now fell away. Strengthening the king's authority to run his empire was no longer feared as much as it had been in the past. A major overhaul of the empire, engineered by parliamentary means, was in the offing, and a half century of what Edmund Burke would famously call the "salutary neglect" of the colonies was coming to an end.

Gordon S. Wood

"Cato," Thoughts on a Question of Importance Proposed to the Public, Whether It Is Probable That the Immense Extent of Territory Acquired by This Nation at the Late Peace, Will Operate towards the Prosperity, or the Ruin of the Island of Great-Britain? London, 1765.

The acquisition of millions of acres of territory as a result of the Peace of Paris in 1763 did not please all Englishmen. Knowing they could not keep everything they had conquered, some Britons wanted to retain the rich sugar-producing French islands of Martinique and Guadeloupe and return to France the barren wastes of Canada. Following debates in the English press, in which Benjamin Franklin participated, the jealousy of the British sugar-producing islands and the prospect of new markets in North America for English manufactured goods convinced the government to keep Canada and return the two sugar islands to France. It was a fateful decision. Better to have given up Canada and faced again the combined frontier menace of the French and Indians, Thomas Hutchinson, the last civilian royal governor of Massachusetts, would remark in 1773. If Canada had remained in the hands of France, declared Hutchinson with the benefit of a decade of hindsight, "none of the spirit of opposition to the Mother Country would have yet appeared."

"Cato," the anonymous English author of this pamphlet, wrote with a sense of deep foreboding about Britain's immense acquisitions of what he took to be the virtually empty land of the New World. Not only anxious about the potential challenge posed by the development of trade and manufacturing in the colonies, he expressed a concern, shared by many other Britons in the 1760s and early 1770s, about the large numbers of British subjects migrating to the colonies. In some cases whole neighborhoods seemed to be pulling up stakes and sailing to America, leaving behind the depopulated countryside famously described by Oliver Goldsmith in his 1770 poem "The Deserted Village." Indeed, some British officials even contemplated a parliamentary ban on the exodus of people to America. Dr. Samuel Johnson especially came to lament the scale of such emigration, which, he warned, would not only diminish the society of Britain but would leave the migrating settlers scattered throughout the wilds of America bereft of all civilization. Although Cato's pamphlet suggested that the flight of Britons to the New World might act as a goad to reforming

British society, it also revealed that even before the American crisis erupted there existed in London a feeling that the vast extent of the colonies in the New World might turn out to be more of a curse than a blessing to the mother country.

THOUGHTS

ON

A Question of Importance

PROPOSED

To the PUBLIC,

Whether it is probable that the Immense Extent of Territory acquired by this Nation at the late Peace, will operate towards the Prosperity, or the Ruin of the Island of Great-Britain?

———————————

L O N D O N:

Printed and sold by J. DIXWELL, in *St. Martin's Lane*, near *Charing-Cross*.

———

MDCCLXV.

SIR,

A FTER the repeated Victories gained over the Minority, it is supposed that the two Houses of Parliament, and particularly that of the Commons, which hath nothing to do as a Court of Judicature, will employ themselves in concerting Measures for promoting the Good of the Nation. You ought to lose no Time in falling about this Work; for a quiet Interval, such as you now enjoy, is very rare in Countries where there is so much Liberty as we have at present; neither can it be expected to last long. This is the best Excuse that can be made for Ministers of State doing so little for the Public Benefit among us. The Duration of their Power is so uncertain, and its Extent so limited, even while they possess it, that few Designs of general Utility can be either projected or carried into Execution while it continues.

Your present Opportunity therefore is the more precious, and I hope will not be altogether lost. It is very probable, however, that with the best Intentions in the World, you may be misled. Proposals for new Laws will probably be made and supported chiefly by those who have particular Interest in them; and this may be done with so much Plausibility as to deceive Persons of the best understanding. With great Humility, therefore, I submit the Thoughts in the following Tract to Your Consideration, and that of the Publick. They arise from Attachment to no Party, and, so far as I can perceive, to no particular Interest. They have been generated by Reading and Reflexion on the History of other Nations, and a good deal of Attention paid to the Causes of Prosperity or Decay in several Cities and Counties of this Kingdom. I have generally found, that Bodies of Men, as well as private Persons, were incessantly pursuing after Things which proved prejudicial to them, after they had attained them. And in many Cases it was easy to see, after some Years Experience, that the Prosperity of Societies had been owing, in a great Measure, to a Circumstance or two, which all the while they were groaning under, and crying out against as an intolerable Grievance.

Filled with Reflections of this Kind, I leave you to judge what were my Sentiments of the violent Clamours against the late Peace. I began to think what Dominions the King of Great Britain now had, and what use he had for any more; and was soon led into a strong Suspicion, that, instead of having too little Land, he had by far too much. Whether in prosecuting those Reflections I have carried the Matter too great a Length, I shall not say, as we are all ready to run into Extremes. But one Thing is certain; that the Basis of all Deliberation on our Connection with the Colonies abroad, ought to be *Not*—how will they bring the greatest immediate Wealth into the Coffers of a few Merchants? Or how will they bring the greatest immediate Splendor to the City of London?—*But* how will they continue to promote the Population of the Island, and the Industry of the People of *Great Britain*?

I sincerely wish you a good Session of Parliament, and am,

> SIR,
> Your most obedient
> Humble Servant,
>
> CATO.

Thoughts on a Question, &c.

Whether is it probable that the Immense Extent of Territory acquired by this Nation at the late Peace, will operate towards the Prosperity, or the Ruin of the Island of Great-Britain?

I HAVE proposed this Question to the Public, because, after thinking upon it a good deal in the most cool and dispassionate Manner, my own Opinion is still, in a great Measure, undetermined. Let no Man imagine it is a Political or Party Question. I believe the Ministers of State, in negotiating the late Peace, acted as wisely and sincerely as any who have been before them employed in the like Work; subject however at the same time to the Errors and Prejudices which are inseparable from Humanity. I would not at this Moment give three Farthings, for my own particular Part, to determine which of the Parties, Majority or Minority should prevail. Neither do I think it is of any Importance to the Public, except in so far as every good Subject would wish, that His Majesty should partake a little of the Peace and Quiet which we so happily enjoy under his Government.

Having proposed the Question, no more should have been said upon it by me, were it not for the following Circumstance. Some perhaps who have given Credit to my Declaration, that it is not Politically intended, may still be so clear upon one Side, as to despise and count it Ridiculous. I shall therefore throw out a few general Reflections which have led me to look upon it, as, at least, Problematical; and I am sure if it be doubtful, no Man can deny that it is Important.

The Territory acquired is so immense, that it must make the Time of Acquisition a remarkable Æra of this Government, and produce a great Change in our Situation and Circumstances as a Society. As the smallest Member of a Natural Body affects the whole in some Degree; so every one Circumstance with regard to a Political Body, has some Influence upon every other. A Nation must accommodate itself some way or other, well or ill, to the whole Extent of its Territory. The most distant and desolate Part of the Dominions of any People, has some Relation to them, either as a Benefit or Burthen; otherwise it is not their's. Hence it follows, that any Acquisition would have produced some Change; and therefore so great an Acquisition, and that made all at once, must produce a very great one.

Men have often conjectured wrong, perhaps they have seldom conjectured right, as to the Effects of great Changes in a State or Government, till they felt them by Experience. The Spanish Monarchy, at the Time when it got Possession of the West Indies, was one of the most powerful, if not the most powerful and flourishing in Europe. Would not any Man at that Time have been reckoned disordered in his Judgment, who should have affirmed, that the Kingdom would be the worse for that Addition; and particularly that it would become *poor* by Means of the *Gold* and *Silver* Mines? Yet do we not know that it proved so in Fact; and that there is not now any Man of the least Political Reflection, but can explain for what Reasons it was, and behoved to be so? That solemn People believed that they should possess all Things without working, because they had plenty of Gold, which they had always hitherto seen sufficient to Purchase all Things. They only forgot, that as they could neither eat nor wear Gold, they must necessarily pay to such as would work for them, just in Proportion to the Abundance of Gold they possessed. Thus their Stock was soon exhausted, and would have been so, perhaps sooner, if it had been a thousand times greater than it was. When either a Person or People are ruined by *too much* of any thing that is good in a moderate Degree, the greater the Quantity, their Ruin comes on so much the more speedily.*

* It is probable this Observation will appear somewhat strange to many, because it is a little out of the common Road. But if they will reflect with Attention and Accuracy, they will find it conclusive in point of Reasoning, and confirmed by Experience, in innumerable Instances. Remember, the Supposition is, that the Excess is prejudicial; now does it not follow that the greater the Excess, the greater the Prejudice? Try this on every Subject, and it will be found to hold. If a man is tempted to Luxury, Softness, and Indulgence, by an affluent Fortune; the greater the Fortune, the more whimsical, extravagant, and endless his Desires. If a man happens to get more Applause than he is able to bear, the greater Quantity of Incense you offer to him, the sooner is his Head turned, and the greater is his Intoxication. If a General is incommoded in the Day of Battle by the very Numbers of his own Army, the greater the

I know it will be said (and perhaps every Reader is before-hand with me in thinking it) "We have not got more Money to make us idle, but more Land, which we may have an Opportunity to improve." But I must beg leave to ask, Is any Man sure that it is not possible to get too much Land, as well as too much Money? We have now from the Gulph of Florida to the North-Pole, at least with very little Exception; how far West I really do not know. What pity is it that we did not keep the whole Island of Cuba, and by another Year's War, take from the Spaniards all their Possessions in South-America? After we had done so, there would have remained still some more of the Globe to conquer. Is not the Lust of Conquest in a Nation as insatiable as the Lust of Gold in a Miser? And is it not much more hurtful? If any thinks otherwise, if he either thinks we have not enough, or not more than enough at present, let him explain clearly the Reasons of his Opinion, and what will be the probable Effect of the Acquisition upon the Society.

There is the greater need of Accuracy in this Matter, that I believe the Event, taking in all its Circumstances, is quite singular, the like never having happened before. Some Nations formerly have in the Course of a few Years, conquered great Tracts of Country; but they ordinarily obtained new Subjects as well as new Ground: Whereas our late Acquisition may be justly called mere Earth. Nay, though we had all that the Indians possess behind, as which we shall very soon have, it will be the same Thing; for they seem upon the Eve of either dwindling into nothing of themselves, or being exterminated by us.*

Multitude, the more inexpressible the Confusion; the more sudden and dreadful his Defeat.

* The Severities exercised upon the Indians, have certainly given much pain to Princes of humanity, among us, who hear of them, as they appear to have given to several of our Officers who were obliged by their Orders to commit them. The great absurdity of them in point of Policy will plainly appear, by comparing the State of these People with our own. There are three great Stages in the Progress of human Society. The First is, the Savage State, in which Men subsist by Hunting, and need by far the greatest Quantity of Ground. The Second, the Pastoral Life; which needs considerably less than the former, but still a good deal.—And the Last, is that of Agriculture and Commerce, which needs least of all. Now the Indians are in the first State; we are in the last; and yet we

Has it not been long ago agreed upon by Persons of Reason and Observation, that it is not the Extent of a Country, but the Number of Inhabitants in proportion to its Extent, that constitutes the Strength of a Nation? If I am not mistaken, it used to be affirmed in some such Proportion as this, that supposing ten Millions of People to inhabit one Country, and the same Number to inhabit another of double the Extent, the first State would be four times as powerful as the last. Is this Maxim now found to be false? Or, on what Account is it not applicable to our Case? If we take Great-Britain and its Colonies as one Body, I do not see what should hinder it to be applied. If we take them as separate Bodies in Alliance, from which Alliance we in this Nation hitherto derived great Advantages, I acknowledge it in Part. But my Question still remains; will these endless Tracts of Ground, in future Times, fill this Kingdom with Inhabitants, or depopulate it?

First, let us suppose Great-Britain and its Colonies as one Society.

I am very sensible that a Situation can be supposed, and that many Nations have been in such a Situation, as that occupying waste Grounds has tended to increase both their Number and Strength. It increases their Number without Question, because when the Means of Subsistence are made easy, the common People are encouraged to marry. But before it can increase their Strength, I apprehend two Conditions are essentially requisite. 1st. That the Land they have already be fully stocked, and likely to continue so. If this is not the Case, the Migration is unnecessary at least, if not hurtful. 2d. There is another Condition, not so commonly thought of, necessary to a People's increasing in Strength by settling more Land. What I mean is, that there be a plain and simple Taste of Life, so that Agriculture may support them comfortably. This was the Case with the Romans in the early Times of their Republick, as well

---

are never satisfied, but still driving them into Corners, and obliging them to cede vast Tracts, which are necessary to them, and which possessed by them, might be of some use to us, but which without them can be of no Service to us at all. This Cruelty however, it will be said, tho' undesirable, was necessary, because they would not let us alone. It is impossible to believe it. No Briton at this Time hath so much to say with them as Sir William Johnson; and it is evident he acquired his Influence, not by Cruelty, but by Honesty and Mercy.

as many other antient Nations. Now it must be considered, that they had very little either of Commerce or Manufactures; so that they soon became not only full, but overstocked; and having nothing but the Fruits of their own Ground to support them, they were obliged to send Colonies abroad. These Colonies went not to seek Wealth, but Food. So simple was their Taste of Life, that in the beginning of the Roman State, a Family was decently maintained upon one Acre and a Quarter of an Acre English. When Appius Clausus left the Sabines, he brought with him to Rome five thousand Sabine Families, to each of whom the above Quantity was assigned, and that Great Man had the immense Estate of fifteen Acres given to himself. How different from the late Grants of American Lands?

Let us carefully remember therefore, that it must be Manufacture and Commerce only, which can make a People numerous and prosperous, after Elegance and Luxury have been once introduced. Now it is at least very doubtful, whether a narrow be not more favourable than an extended Territory for their Advancement. There is less Necessity either of Manufactures or Commerce in an extended Territory, because the Multitude of common People, by whose Hands National Industry must be carried on, can easily find Support without them: Whereas when they are confined to their own Bounds, those who cannot be Husbandmen, are obliged to be Artificers. I believe Experience will confirm this Observation, whether we consider the State of Mankind in antient or modern Times.

But let us now suppose our Colonies separate Bodies in Alliance with us. It will probably be thought that these Settlements growing in Numbers, in the same Manner and from the same Causes, that all new planted Colonies do, their Commerce, which is confined to us, must be of great Benefit to this Island. And no doubt if they be serviceable at all, this is the single Light in which they can be so to us. How far they have been so hitherto, I do not enquire; but whether they will continue to be so, or not, seems to me very uncertain, for several Reasons.

1. They seem to threaten us with an Evil, not only dangerous or troublesome, but ruinous, viz. Depopulation. Settling small Colonies may do such Services as to Counterballance an inconsiderable Loss of People; but settling vast Tracts may

exhaust the Mother Country, and prove Destruction. Letting a little Blood may be not only harmless, but serviceable to the Body; and yet excessive Bleeding will kill as certainly as any Disease, to which it is liable. I shall not spend Time in enumerating the various Ways in which our Colonies drain us of People. Men of Rank or Wealth, who have obtained Grants of Lands, spare no pains to inveigle them away in Crowds to settle their several Possessions, because without People these Possessions are good for nothing. Multitudes go away of their own accord, allured by the enchanting Prospect of Wealth; and either never return at all, or return in a frail diseased State, unfit for Propagation. We suffer no inconsiderable Loss in the many thousands of Seamen and Soldiers, which must now be sent to all Parts of the known World, to annoy our Enemies in Time of War, and to protect our Friends in Time of Peace. If all the Men who died an untimely Death by Sickness, Famine or the Sword, in the Havannah Expedition, had been employed in some useful Occupation in Great Britain, they and their Posterity, would have been of greater Benefit to this Nation, than any two Islands in the West-Indies.

The farther Investigation of this I leave to every Reader, that he may compute the Numbers in his own Mind. Let me only observe, that in Proportion as the Number of Hands is lessened, the Price of Labour, and the first Cost of our exported Commodities must be increased; at the very same Time the Quantity of these Commodities must decrease, and the Gain upon them centering here, must be diminished by the two concurring Causes. If therefore a Trade to our foreign Plantations be highly profitable, we ought to be the more concerned, lest by driving the Matter too far, we leave next to no-body at home to trade with them. Every thing may be Evidence. Many a Gentleman has laid out so much Money in building an elegant Palace, that he has left himself no Estate on which he might possess and enjoy it.

2. The Advantage is in Danger of being lost another Way. Our Plantations are becoming so extensive, that it is probable they will speedily set up Manufactures of their own, and be our Rivals instead of our Customers. This Effect will be accelerated by the Circumstance formerly mentioned. Our Commodities will not be sufficient in Quantity for them to consume, and

they wil be too costly for them to purchase. That this must be the Case in some future Period, from the natural Course of Things, many Writers have confessed; but they have generally considered it as at a very great Distance, and therefore unworthy of Attention. There are however at this Time many Symptons of its being much nearer than we apprehended.

The only Thing by which it is retarded, is, that as Land is cheap in America, and Labour dear, it is a more immediate and sure Way for a Family to get Bread by cultivating the Ground, than by fabricating Goods, which may be brought on easy Terms from Great-Britain. But this will soon be at an End, both from the Numbers of People settled in Places near the Sea, and from the unsatiable Avarice of the Proprietors of Land, who already begin rather to suffer their vast Possessions to lie waste, than part with them but at a very great Profit. The Truth is, I have some Suspicion that it has been at an End in several of our Colonies for some Time, and that nothing stands in the Way but the Difficulties and Discouragements which attend the first setting up of Manufactures in every Country. Whenever Interest or Necessity therefore shall overcome these Difficulties, it is easy to foresee what an amazing and rapid Progress will be made in every Branch of Business, by an enterprizing and industrious People.

Is there not also a Confirmation of this from Experience. If any Credit may be given to our News-papers, many Tradesmen have of late gone from different Parts of the Kingdom to America. I think it was said no less than one hundred, of one Profession, from one Place, and at one Time.* It has also been affirmed, that several different Branches of Manufacture are already set up in New-England: And our Merchants at home (who, however little they understand of the Interest of the Public, understand their own immediate Interest well enough) are making dreadful outcries upon it. We are told it will be half a Million Sterling loss yearly to Great-Britain; and I can easily believe it will very soon be double that Sum. But what Remedy? Mention has been made of applying to Parliament to hinder the Exportation of Artificers. On which I must beg leave to ask, Will they go if it does not appear to be their

* Stocking-Weavers, from Nottingham.

Interest? And if it be their Interest, will you hinder them? Or if you would, how can you hinder them? I do not know whether the Parliament will pay any regard to these childish Complaints, or not; but I am sure that any Measures they could contrive for that purpose would be quite ineffectual.

3. I must examine another Circumstance in our Situation with regard to the Colonies; viz. Our exclusive Right to trade with them. It may be said, let them be as extensive as you please; let them set up as many Manufactures as they themselves please: Still their Trade will be valuable, and it is wholly confined to this Island, they are not permitted to carry on Business with any other Nation, but through the Medium of Great-Britain. But what signifies a Trade, if it come to be a losing Trade? And that, from some of the above Considerations, it may be sooner than we are aware of. Whenever they can supply themselves, with Manufactures they will have no need of us; most of the Luxuries and Delicacies of Life they can get nearer home from one another, and are indeed a kind of World in themselves.

Besides, I strongly suspect this Circumstance of our having an exclusive Right to trade with them, will operate slowly and silently indeed, but constantly, and at last fatally, to our own Prejudice. There is much selfishness in human Nature; and it will be, nay probably it has been, a Temptation to us not to make our Manufactures as good and as cheap as possible to procure voluntary Purchasers, because we think we can send them to those who are obliged to take them. Let no Man think this a slight Circumstance, or of no Moment. Baron Montesquieu has observed, in more places than one of his Spirit of Laws, that the moral Causes of the Thriving or Decay of a Nation, viz. such as arise from the Tempers or Principles of the People, the Spirit of their Constitution, or their Situation with regard to others, are unspeakably more powerful than occasional Causes, such as War, Famine and Pestilence; or their Contraries. The Reason is plain—The Effect of those which he calls Moral Causes, tho' Impracticable, is *Universal* and *Perpetual*. If therefore our exclusive Right to trade to our own Plantations, tempts us to trust or lean too much to it, it may sink under the Weight, and prove the Cause of our Destruction.

I think I have observed it asserted frequently by political Writers, when railing against the Government, that the Ballance of Trade is against us to every Nation, or almost every Nation in the World, except our own Plantations. These Writers indeed are a sort of Witnesses, to whose Testimony the least Credit is to be given of any People under the Sun; for when it answers their Purpose, they will not stick to Assert not only the grossest, but the most manifest Falshoods, as if they were quite superior to any sense of Shame upon Detection. With Regard to this, in particular, I am pretty certain the Ballance cannot be against us to Spain and Portugal, because they have been already ruined in the very Way that I suspect our Ruin to be approaching. But if the Ballance be against us with other Nations, it is probable our Plantations themselves are the Cause of it, by shewing us an easy Way of making a considerable Profit, so that now we are not at so great Pains to Work as well and as cheap, and as much, as our Neighbours about us.

This is naturally followed by another dangerous Consequence of our exclusive Trade. Our Merchants will import from other Nations what they can export to the British Plantations with Advantage. Such Commodities passing through our Hands make a great Appearance of Commerce, and yet add next to nothing to our Strength or Numbers; and not so much to our Wealth as may perhaps be supposed. This shews how it is at least possible, that our Possessions may have the same Effect upon us, that the Conquest of Mexico and Peru had upon the Spaniards. We may slacken our own Industry, and supply our Settlements by the Industry of others. Great Men and great Merchants who have Estates and Property abroad, may make a splendid Figure for a Time, while the Body of the Kingdom is gradually losing its Nourishment, and falling into an incurable Consumption.

An exclusive Trade is of far less Consequence than may be imagined. The Spirit of Commerce, says a late eminent Author, is of a very nice and delicate Nature—I add, it is of a very subtile and penetrating Nature. The Reason is the same for both. It is animated and conducted entirely by the Interest of Individuals: So that unless this happens to co-incide with the public good, one Part of the Nation must be indefatigable in bringing on the Ruin of the Whole. Wherever Interest leads, or seems to lead,

Trade will force its Way over all Obstructions; neither can it be almost by any Means forced to go another Way. We hear sometimes great Outcries against those mercenary Wretches, who, for the sake of private Gain, will suck the very Blood of the Poor, and riot in the Spoils of their Country.

Alas! you know little of Human Nature, if ever you expect to restrain the Plurality by such Arguments; or if you could hinder them from doing Ill, you will never make them do any Good. I remember not long ago, taking a Walk through the Streets of London, I was led to reflect what an endless Variety of Designs must be carried on uniformly to supply the Inhabitants of that vast City, with every Necessary, and every imaginable Conveniency of Life; and it immediately occurred, that nothing but mutual Interest could do it. Without this, ten thousand Legislators constantly employed could not devise the Means, and an hundred thousand Judges could not enforce the Execution. The Spirit of all Laws on the Police of a City, or the Commerce of a People, must be to make public and private Interest not only really, but apparently and evidently the same.

Hence it follows, that an exclusive Trade preserved by Force against the Inclination of the People concerned, cannot be carried very far, and cannot continue very long. While we serve our Plantations as well as other People, we may expect they will chearfully trade with us: So soon as we either will not, or cannot do this, they will use every possible Means to be supplied from another Quarter. The Spaniards have an exclusive Trade to their own Settlements; and yet, if I am rightly informed, there are few Branches from which we derive greater Profit, than an illicit Trade forced at the Hazard both of Life and Fortune, from our West India Islands to the Spanish Main. There have been lately some hideous Complaints against our Commanders of King's Ships for not encouraging this Trade. Would these Complainers be pleased that the Parliament should open a free Trade to all the World to our Plantations? They would certainly burn or pull down that Member of Parliament's House who should move for it. Now I desire to know what an honest Man in Spain would think of the Equity of this Procedure?

It appears indeed, from what I have said above, that I do not expect much Equity from them, and therefore it is not upon that Side that I propose to press the Argument. It is from the side of Interest. If we are so partial to ourselves, as to trample upon every Law and every national Engagement, when we hope to do it with Impunity or Profit, why should we expect others to be more honest than ourselves, or that our Colonies will continue to trade with us longer than it is their Interest to do so? For this Reason we should bend all our Force to the Improvement of our own Country, by increasing the Number, Sobriety and Industry of its Inhabitants. If there be any Defect here, the most valuable Settlements will do us no good; and if there be a visible Disproportion between our Colonies and our Ability to trade with them, upon just and equal Terms, the more they are enlarged, the sooner shall we be destroyed.

As I have all along professed the greatest Regard for the Parliament and Ministry, it will be thought, perhaps, that we may, without much Concern, leave the Care of the Public to them. Some Admirers of modern Improvements are apt to speak in very high Terms of the Discernment of this enlightened Age, as it is called. Such, it is not impossible, may be ready to say, "Great National Mistakes have indeed formerly been committed, but the Principles of Trade and Commerce, as well as Government, are now so well understood that they will not be repeated. While Individuals are pursuing their own Interest with unremitting Activity, the Legislature, ever watchful for the general Good, and presiding over the whole, will observe the first Appearance of any thing going against us, and take effectual Measures for turning it into its proper Channel." But though I see no Reason for impeaching the Character of those who now compose the Legislation or Administration, when compared with their Predecessors, yet it is uncertain whether they will endeavour, and more so, whether they will be able to prevent the injury we may suffer from unweildy Possessions. I have not built my Arguments upon the Treachery of particular Men, or even the Degeneracy of the present Age, but upon the Mistakes of Human Nature, and the αχμη, as it were, of our Constitution, to which we have been brought by the ordinary course of Things, and peculiar Disposition of Providence.

Bodies of Men, alas! are far from being so clear-sighted, as they themselves imagine. Immediate and seeming, or particular Interests, have ordinarily so powerful an Effect on the most uncorrupted Part of them, as bears down all other Considerations. How many Laws relating to Trade have been framed with a sincere Intention to promote it, and yet have, in Experience, proved hurtful to it; so that those who made them were obliged to repeal them? Perhaps if all the Laws on the Subject were enumerated, it might be shewn that the greater Part are prejudicial. All the exclusive Rights of Corporations, and Monopolies of private Companies, if they were necessary or useful at the Beginning, have long ceased to be so, and yet many of them still continue. They must also probably continue for Ages yet to come: such is the Spirit of the People. He would be a bad Minister; nay, it would be a bold Parliament, that should attempt to lay them open. There is nothing that appears to me more clear, than that the Restrictions we have laid our Sister Kingdom of Ireland under, are prejudicial to ourselves; and yet I would not be the Man who should propose to take them off in an English House of Commons.

Have not most Laws been made to satisfy the interested Demands of particular Persons, Classes and Counties? And have not the Clamour of the Mob, in favour of their supposed, been generally against their own real Interest? When the Woollen Trade was brought into this Country by People from Flanders, did not the Natives immediately cry out, that they came to eat the Bread out of their Mouths? Whereas it is now plain, they came to put it into the Mouths of them and their Posterity. What monstrous Outcries were made against the late Peace, because the Ministry gave back to the French some of the Places we had taken from them? And yet have we not much more behind than we know what to do with, or shall know for two hundred Years, tho', contrary to all Probability, we should be reaping Benefit by them all the while. I will yield to no Subject of his Majesty in Loyalty to my Prince, or Love to my Country; and yet I sincerely wish he had given them back all that we took, and a good deal of our own besides; provided we had brought all the People to Great Britain; and obliged our Enemies to pay the real Expence of the War, that these new Subjects might be put at first into a way of living. The French, had they attended to their own Interest, had as little to do to fight with us in America, as we had to fight with them in Germany; and if their Expulsion from so great a Part of it shall make them so wise, as to cultivate their own excellent Country, to fill their Land with People, and employ their People in Industry, future Historians will be able to demonstrate that they were Gainers by being beat.

However fully I am satisfy'd of the Truth of these Remarks, I have little hope that any Body of Men, even tho' they should assent to them, will have so much self government as to act steadily on the Principles to which they lead. We all agree in Speculation that a King may have too much Power, a Peerage too much Influence, a House of Commons too much Weight, and a Multitude too much Liberty, so as to overturn the very Constitution; and yet it is not to be expected that any one of them will refuse an Accession to their own Share when it is offered, or surrender it after they have obtained it.

But to keep close by the Subject of Commerce—How little Men in general understand the Nature of it, may be seen from this Circumstance; that many Nations have Laws still in force against the Exportation of Corn. Is not this infinitely absurd? What signifies any such Law. If we import more from any Nation than we send them, must we not pay the Ballance, or give up the Trade? I am persuaded it is scarcely possible to make any Law on the Subject of Trade, but what shall do more harm than good, excepting those which are directly intended for preventing Fraud. These are absolutely necessary and highly useful. Of the same Nature are all such Laws as tend to make our own Commodities cheap and plentiful—But those which aim only by Force or Prohibition to keep out the Commodities of other Nations, have an inherent Weakness in them, and seldom or never answer the End proposed.

There is an Assertion in some Part of the Writings of a well known living Author (David Hume) that it is a Mistake for trading Nations to look upon one another as Rivals, or as the opposite Weights in a Ballance; so that the Exaltation of one implies of necessity the Depression of the other. He says, he is persuaded of the contrary, and that the thriving of one Nation is a Benefit, instead of an Injury, to all that are about them. The Sentiment is undoubtedly noble and generous:—And I am persuaded that it is also perfectly just and true. We may soon be satisfied of it, by going back to the Original of all Traffick, and analysing it in the following plain and simple Manner. If there was but one Man in the Earth, he would be obliged to dig the Ground for his food, and dress it for his own Use; to patch together something or another for his cloathing; to build himself some shelter from the Weather;—that is to say— to be his own Gardiner, Cook, Taylor, Mason;—and in short every Thing to himself. If there were one or two more joined with him, they would find it convenient to distribute the common Labour, and every Man to do as much of some particular Branches as to serve the whole; and receive of the Labour of others for what he communicated of his own. Its Society increases: the same general Plan is carried on—And one City or Nation is to another in every Respect the same, as one Man to another in a very small Number. Therefore the Radical Principle of all Commerce is this: As much as one Person, Family, City or Nation provides by its own proper Labour and Application of the common Conveniencies of human Life, more than it uses itself, it will lay up or dispose of, and keep under some instituted Sign, such as Money, and is rich just to that Degree and no more. If it provides less than it uses, no Circumstance imaginable, and least of all extensive Possessions, will prevent it from being poor.

Now let me ask, does the Industry and Activity of one Nation hinder another from working diligently? Very far from it. It rather serves to excite them by Imitation. There cannot be the least Interference but when they are both employed in producing Commodities of the same Kind; and then to be sure upon the Supposition of equal natural Advantages, the most sober and diligent People will send them to Market cheapest, and carry away the Trade. But it is in vain to complain in this Case. The Remedy is only in ourselves: and the Commodities of Life are so various and innumerable, that every Country affords Opportunities to its Inhabitants of securing their own Prosperity, and contributing to that of the whole Earth. The only proper and just, and indeed the only effectual Way, of one Nation out-stripping another, is by out working them. When instead of this, we only endeavour to hinder them from working, or to destroy them, it seems to be little less absurd than the Measure of the Savage, who meeting a Man wiser than himself, put him to Death, that he might plunder him of his Wisdom.

Nothing appears to me more ridiculous and pusillanimous than what we meet with almost every Day in our News-papers, since the late Peace. If any French Ships are seen at Sea, immediately the Alarm is sounded, and the Ruin of Britain is at hand. *Capt. —— in his Passage met with —— French Ships in —— Latitude, and they seemed to be steering their Course for the Gulf of Darien, where, if they effect a Settlement they will carry away the whole Riches of South-America.—Great Preparations are making by the French for fishing this Season on the Banks of Newfoundland; and it is thought they will have more Ships in that Trade than ever they had before.—The French seem resolved to establish a Settlement and Forts on some Parts of the African Coast, and if they do, they will ingross the whole Negro Trade entirely to themselves.* When I read such Reflections as these, I sigh, and say to myself, Oh, my poor Country! Is there no Way of preserving thee from Destruction but by depriving the whole French Nation of their Senses? If this is the Case, why should we mince the matter? Let us aim a Blow at the Root. Let us rise as one Man, pass the Straits of Dover, and without staying to demolish Dunkirk, let us drive them all before us, young and old, Male and Female, and drown them in the Mediterranean Sea.

If this Discourse had not been drawn out to a greater Length than I intended, it might have been proper to have considered a little how the Matter has appeared in Fact. Every Person acquainted with History must acknowledge, that the Places in antient Times, remarkable for Trade, had but small Territories. Tyre had a very limited Territory. I cannot be precise as to its Extent, but am certain it was not greater than two or three Shires in England. Carthage, the Daughter of Tyre, had but little Room for several Ages; but growing rich and powerful by Commerce, she attempted to extend her Conquests, and by doing so, brought on her own Destruction. At this present Time, excepting France and England, the other Places in Europe where Trade flourishes, have but very narrow Limits. The Dutch, who as a Nation have deviated as little from the Maxims of sound Policy as any People on Earth, do not seem at all covetous of much Ground, or many distant Settlements; yet they are the richest People in Europe, and for their Numbers the strongest; just because these Numbers are inclosed in so narrow Bounds. They have indeed very valuable Settlements in the East Indies, from this single Circumstance, that they ingross the Spice Trade. But whatever it be to them, it seems to be granted by all who understand the Subject, that the East-India Trade is hurtful to the rest of Europe.

I fancy to myself that some of my Mercantile Readers will have long ago perceived that I am no Merchant, and therefore will be saying within themselves in the most contemptuous Manner, What has this Author to do with Trade? How can he take upon him to write upon a Subject he does not understand? I am sure if I was a Merchant, I should reckon myself utterly unqualified for speaking on the Question which stands at the Head of my Paper. Actual Merchants are so ingrossed by the Gain or Loss of their own particular Branches, that it is impossible for them to perceive the Hurt or Benefit of the whole Body. These proceed upon general principles, on which any Man of common Understanding may write clearly, and those who are not Traders themselves must be supposed to judge with the greatest Impartiality. A Man who is in the Middle of a Crowd, will not perceive so distinctly, half what is doing in five different Parts of it, or whither the whole is tending, as he who is removed at a little distance from it, and by his Situation above it. I remember Dr. Burnet says somewhere, that when the new-modelling the Government at the Revolution was upon the Tapis, of all who wrote or spoke on that Subject, none were so much bewilder'd as the Lawyers. He seems to be surpriz'd at this. But it was no Wonder at all. For Lawyers were so accustomed to think of the Force of particular Statutes, that they were every now and then saying, that such and such Measures were against Law: Than which nothing could be more ridiculous. For what signified all former Laws, when the Government was to be resettled from the very Foundation. It was easy to see, that if the Revolutioners were able to keep their Ground, they would justify themselves: Whereas if the banish'd Prince had recover'd Possession, he would have hanged as many as he pleased of his Opposers, though they had never broke a Law in their Lives, any otherwise than by sending him away.

To draw towards a Conclusion: I am desirous of having the Question examin'd with Care; and whether this insatiable Desire in our Nation of such extensive Territories, as must be measured by the Heavens, and probably never will be perambulated, be not like all selfish interested Affections in Individuals, Destruction to ourselves. If my Fears are quite groundless, so much the better for us and our Posterity: If otherwise, it were to be wish'd that the best Means were pointed out for retarding our Ruin as much as possible.

If any have been so far moved by what I have said as to wish me to proceed in mentioning these Means; I answer, let us be well convinced that the Danger is real, before we come to Particulars. In general however, the Remedies must be of the same Nature as are prescribed by Physicians, when the Patient is under a bad Habit, without any acute Disorder, that is to say, slow and alterative, but radical and fundamental. They must be such as have an Influence upon the Principles and Manners of the People, and the Cultivation of the Soil. The first is chiefly necessary, and will produce the other as its Effect. Yet Agriculture ought to be the Object of immediate Attention, as it will promote Health and Sobriety among those who are employed in it; Numbers of People to fill the Cities, and abundance of Provision for their daily Support. It is demonstrable that all our great Cities are supplied with Inhabitants from the Country, and therefore whatever tends to the depopulating of the distant Parts, will in the End prove Destruction not only to themselves, but the whole.

FINIS.

Francis Bernard, "Principles of Law and Polity, Applied to the Government of the British Colonies in America. Written in the Year 1764." From Select Letters on the Trade and Government of America; and the Principles of Law and Polity, Applied to the American Colonies. London, 1774.

By 1764 many current and former colonial officials were emphasizing the need to reform and tighten up the newly enlarged empire. That year an influential anonymously published treatise entitled *The Administration of the Colonies*, written by Thomas Pownall, who had held numerous positions in the colonies including the governorship of Massachusetts, observed that with the coming of peace there was a "general idea of some revolution of events, beyond the ordinary course of things; some general apprehension, of something new arising in the world; . . . something that is to be guarded against, on one hand, or that is to be carried to advantage on the other. There is an universal apprehension of some new crisis forming."

Francis Bernard was royal governor of Massachusetts Bay from 1760 to 1769, and for many American colonists he would come to symbolize much that was wrong with the governance of the British Empire. Although Bernard did not publish the ninety-seven point plan for the empire that follows until 1774 in London, he actually wrote it in 1764, in Boston. At that time he had a few copies printed in the provincial capital, which he sent for their private edification to several royal officials in London, including Lord Halifax, who by 1763 had become secretary of state for the Southern Department; Lord Hillsborough, president of the Board of Trade; and Lord Barrington, treasurer of the Royal Navy and Bernard's patron. Bernard's proposals represented the kinds of ideas for imperial reform that had long been circulating among second-level bureaucrats in the empire.

With British politics in the 1760s in disarray, as ministries rose and fell one after another, much of what stability existed in the British government came from such undersecretaries and sub-ministers as Thomas Whately, secretary to the Treasury and author of the Stamp Act, and John Pownall, secretary to the Board of Trade, who received a copy of Bernard's proposals in 1764. Not only did the relative permanence of these second-level bureaucrats mark the beginnings of a modern British civil service, their steady presence in the government gave what evenness there was to the implementation of the imperial reforms in the 1760s and 1770s. These bureaucrats often had a clearer sense of the problems facing imperial administrators in America than did their political superiors in the privy council, and, like Bernard, they had very definite ideas about what was needed to solve them.

SELECT
LETTERS
ON THE
TRADE and GOVERNMENT
OF
AMERICA;
AND THE
PRINCIPLES
OF
LAW and POLITY,
APPLIED TO THE
AMERICAN COLONIES.

Written by GOVERNOR BERNARD,
at BOSTON,
In the Years 1763, 4, 5, 6, 7, and 8.

LONDON,
Printed by W. BOWYER and J. NICHOLS.
MDCCLXXIV.

A VIEW of the present wealth, power, and extension of the *British Empire* is alarming as well as pleasing: we cannot but be concerned for the stability of a fabrick built on so disjoined foundations, and raised to so great a heighth; and must be convinced that it will require much political skill to secure its duration. The most obvious means to effect this, must be an Union of the several parts of this vast body, and especially a Connection between the *Seat of Empire* and its Dependencies; a Connection not created by temporary expedients, or supported by enforced subjection; but established upon fixed *Principles* of *Law* and *Polity*, and maintained by a regular, free, and equitable subordination. What are the principles which will best connect the Head and the Members of this great *Empire* is the subject of the present enquiry. They ought to be simple, plain, and certain, or they will not be suitable to their general purpose; they ought to be generally admitted, or they will not have their full effect; they must be such as will stand the test of reason, or they will not be generally admitted.

In this disputative age, and in a science of all the most disputative, it may seem a difficult task to attempt to settle a general theory for a business in which such a variety of passions, prejudices, and interests, are like to interpose. Sensible of this, and studious only of Truth and Utility, the writer has avoided declamation, and kept close to argument. He has reduced his whole subject into a set of propositions; beginning with first principles which are self-evident, proceeding to propositions capable of positive proof, and descending to hypotheses which are to be determined by degrees of probability only. This was intended to be a perfect chain; the avoiding of prolixity is the cause why it is not so: where any links shall appear to be wanting, the judicious reader will easily supply them. The advantages of this kind of writing are obvious: by seeing the principles and the reasoning of the arguments laid before him articulately, the reader can more precisely determine what to assent to, and what to deny; and the writer, if he should appear to be mistaken, will have the merit of contributing to his own conviction.

The present expectation, that a new Regulation of the *American* Governments will soon take place, probably arises more from the opinion the public has of the abilities of the present Ministry, than from any thing that has transpired from the Cabinet: it cannot be supposed that their penetration can overlook the necessity of such a Regulation, nor their public spirit fail to carry it into execution. But it may be a question, whether the present is a proper time for this work: more urgent business may stand before it; some preparatory steps may be required to precede it; caution and deliberation may retard it: but these will only serve to postpone. As we may expect that this Reformation, like all others, will be opposed by powerful prejudices, it may not be amiss to reason with them at leisure, and endeavour to take off their force before they become opposed to Government.

Principles of Law and Polity.

1. THE Kingdom of *Great Britain* is *imperial*; that is, Sovereign, and not subordinate to or dependent upon any earthly power.

2. In all *imperial* states there resides somewhere or other an absolute power, which we will call the *Sovereignty*.

3. The *Sovereignty* of *Great Britain* is in the *King in Parliament*; that is, in the King, acting with the advice and consent of the *Lords* and the *Commons* (by their Representatives), assembled in the *Parliament* of *Great Britain*.

4. The *King in Parliament* has the sole right of legislation, and the supreme superintendency of the government; and, in this plenitude of power, is absolute, uncontrolable, and accountable to none; and therefore, in a political sense, can do no wrong.

5. The Execution of the government is in the *King* alone, to be exercised according to the laws of the country, written and unwritten.

6. The exercise of this right is the *King's Prerogative*; and, whilst it is regulated by the laws, the *King* can do no wrong in such exercise.

7. The Laws are either unwritten, that is, rules of government immemorially admitted and approved; or written, that is, ordinances of the *Parliament*.

8. The *privileges* of the people are the right of having conjunctively, by their representatives, one third part of the sovereign legislative power, and of enjoying separately the protection and benefit of the laws.

9. The kingdom of *Great Britain* has, belonging to and depending upon it, divers external dominions and countries; all which, together with *Great Britain*, form the *British Empire*. Let, therefore, the *British Empire* signify the aggregate body of the *British* dominions, and the *Kingdom of Great Britain* the island which is the seat of the government.

10. The *King in Parliament*, is the sole and absolute Sovereign of the whole *British Empire*.

11. No members of the *British Empire*, other than the *Parliament* of *Great Britain*, can have a right to interfere in the

exercise of this Sovereignty, but by being admitted into the *Parliament*, as *Wales*, *Chester*, and *Durham* have been, and *Ireland* may be.

12. Such an union is not necessary to the generality of the *British* external dominions; but it may be expedient with most of them.

13. The external *British* dominions, without such an union, are subordinate to and dependent upon the *Kingdom* of *Great Britain*, and must derive from thence all their powers of legislation and jurisdiction.

14. Legislation is not necessary to an external and dependent government; jurisdiction is necessary and essential to it. Therefore,

15. A separate Legislation is not an absolute right of *British* subjects residing out of the seat of Empire; it may or may not be allowed, and has or has not been granted, according to the circumstances of the community.

16. Where it is granted or allowed, it must be exercised in subordination to the Sovereign power from whom it is derived.

17. No grant of the power of Legislation to a dependent government, whether it comes from the *King* alone, or from the *Parliament*, can preclude the *Parliament* of *Great Britain* from interfering in such dependent government, at such time and in such manner as they shall think fit. Because,

18. Though the *King* can do acts to bind himself and his successors, he cannot bind the *Parliament*; nor can the *Parliament* bind their successors, nor even themselves.

19. It is the *King's* prerogative to provide for the administration of justice in general, according to law.

20. In places to which the ordinary administration of justice does not extend, the *King* has a right to make extraordinary provision for it, so that such provision be as conformable to the laws as the case will permit. Nevertheless,

21. It is the right of the *Parliament*, by its supreme power of legislation and superintendency, to adjust and settle finally the powers and modes of jurisdiction. Therefore,

22. The new jurisdictions established by the *King*, until they are confirmed by *Parliament*, are only temporary provisions.

23. The *King* has a right to grant to private persons goods or lands which have been acquired by, or have fallen to the

general estate, so that such grants be agreeable to law; in which case, they are presumed to be beneficial to the community.

24. Such grants may be enquired into legally by the courts of law, and discretionally by the *Parliament*; and if they shall be found to be illegal, exorbitant, or prejudicial to the community, they may be avoided, upon a presumption that the *King* was deceived.

25. A grant upon a condition performed or to be performed, is a grant upon a valuable consideration: if the condition is performed, the grantee becomes a purchaser for value; if it is not performed, the grant is void.

26. Jurisdiction, being a matter of public trust, and not of private property, cannot be claimed as granted for a valuable consideration.

27. If a grantee professes to hold a jurisdiction as a property yielding profit, he proves that he ought not to hold it; as the profit must arise from something or other prejudicial to the public; for whose sake only jurisdictions are or ought to be created or exercised.

28. Where the *King* grants jurisdiction and lands in one grant, they are in law two separate grants, as they are to be judged by separate and distinct principles; and the grant of the one may be valid, and of the other void or voidable.

29. The rule that a *British* subject shall not be bound by laws, or liable to taxes, but what he has consented to by his representatives, must be confined to the inhabitants of *Great Britain* only; and is not strictly true even there.

30. The *Parliament* of *Great Britain*, as well from its rights of *Sovereignty* as from occasional exigences, has a right to make laws for, and impose taxes upon, its subjects in its external dominions, although they are not represented in such *Parliament*. But,

31. Taxes imposed upon the external dominions ought to be applied to the use of the people, from whom they are raised.

32. The *Parliament* of *Great Britain* has a right and a duty to take care to provide for the defence of the *American* colonies; especially as such colonies are unable to defend themselves.

33. The *Parliament* of *Great Britain* has a right and a duty to take care that provision be made for a sufficient support of the *American* governments. Because,

34. The support of the Government is one of the principal conditions upon which a colony is allowed the power of Legislation. Also, because

35. Some of the *American* Colonies have shewn themselves deficient in the support of their several Governments, both as to sufficiency and independency.

36. The Colonies ought, so far as they are able, to pay the charge of the support of their own Governments, and of their own defence.

37. The defence of the *American* Colonies, being now almost wholly a sea service, is connected with the defence of trade. Therefore,

38. Duties upon imports and exports, make the most proper funds for the expences of such defence. And

39. It being the proper business of the *Parliament* of *Great Britain*, to establish and determine the necessary regulations and restrictions of the trade of their external dominions; and the duties upon the *American* imports and exports being interwove with the regulations and restrictions of trade, the imposition of such Duties is, the proper business of the *Parliament*.

40. The port duties being most properly applicable to the defence of the Colonies, it remains that the support of the Governments be provided for by internal duties.

41. The fund for the defence of the country, and those for the support of the Governments, should be kept separate; because the former relates to the general whole of the country, and the latter to the particular divisions of it.

42. The fund for the defence of the country should be kept entire, because it must be applied to the defence of such parts as shall have most need of it, without any regard to the particular divisions of the country.

43. The several funds for the support of the Governments ought to be kept separate: otherwise money, raised by internal taxes in one Province, may be applied to the support of the Government of another; which seems not to be equitable.

44. Although the right of the *Parliament* of *Great Britain*, to raise taxes in any parts of the *British Empire*, is not to be disputed; yet it would be most adviseable to leave to the Provincial Legislatures the raising the internal taxes.

45. If the sums required were fixed, there would be no

inconvenience in letting the Provincial Legislature determine the manner in which they shall be raised.

46. It will be more agreeable to the people, that the necessary internal taxes should be raised by the Provincial Legislatures; as they will be most able to consult the particular convenience of their respective provinces. Whereas,

47. It may be difficult to form a general Parliamentary tax, so as to make it equally suitable to all Provinces.

48. It would make it more agreeable to the people; though the sum to be raised was prescribed, to leave the method of taxation to their own Legislature.

49. If the Provincial Legislatures should refuse to raise the sums required for the support of Government, or should insist upon doing it by improper means, the *Parliament* might then take the business into their own hands.

50. But it is most probable that the people would acquiesce in this measure, and would soon be reconciled to it, when they observed the good effects of a certain and adequate establishment for the support of Government. For

51. The want of such an establishment has had bad consequences in many of the Governments of the *American* colonies, and has contributed more than all other things put together, to contention in the legislature, and defect of justice in the courts of law. Therefore,

52. The establishment of a certain, sufficient, and independent Civil List, is not only expedient, but necessary to the welfare of the *American* Colonies.

53. Such an appointment will tend greatly to remove all the seeds of contention, and to promote a lasting harmony and good understanding between the Government and the People.

54. The People of the colonies ought not to object to such an appointment, because the support of Government is one of the terms upon which they have received the power of Legislation; and, if the Government is not supported, the Legislation must cease: and because

55. The Support of Government ought to be certain and sufficient; otherwise the execution of it will be uncertain, and its powers insufficient for its purposes.

56. The Government ought not to be dependent upon the people; and the particular means used in some of the Colonies

to keep their Governments dependent, and the use which has been made of such dependency, afford ample proofs that they ought not to be so.

57. The right of a people in a Legislative Colony, to judge of the expediency of extraordinary and contingent expences, does not conclude for the same right as to the ordinary and necessary expences; because

58. The former must be ever uncertain, the latter may be reduced to a certainty; the one concerns the welfare only of the colony, the other the very existence as a separate state.

59. The subjects of the *British Empire*, residing in its external dominions, are intitled to all the rights and privileges of *British* subjects, which they are capable of enjoying.

60. There are some rights and privileges which the *British* subjects, in the external dominions, are not equally capable of enjoying with those residing in *Great Britain*.

61. The right of having a share in the Imperial Legislature, is one of these incapacities in those external dominions, where a representation is impracticable.

62. A Representation of the *American* Colonies in the Imperial Legislature is not impracticable: and therefore

63. The propriety of a Representation of the *American* Colonies in the Imperial Legislature, must be determined by expediency only.

64. A Representation of the *American* Colonies, in the Imperial Legislature, is not necessary to establish the authority of the *Parliament* over the Colonies. But

65. It may be expedient for quieting disputes concerning such authority, and preventing a separation in future times.

66. The expediency of *American* Legislatures, does not arise from the want of their having Representatives in the Imperial Legislature.

67. If the *American* Colonies had Representatives in *Parliament*, still there would be an occasion for provincial Legislatures for their domestic œconomy, and the support of their Governments. But

68. All external Legislatures must be subject to, and dependent on, the Imperial Legislature: otherwise there would be an *Empire in* an *Empire*.

69. Some external States are incapable of a Legislature; which has often been the case of infant Colonies. Therefore,

70. The same form of Government is not equally proper to a Colony in its infant and in its mature state.

71. There may be a middle state between infancy and maturity, which may admit of a form of Government more proper for it than either of the extremes.

72. There is but one most perfect form of Government for Provinces arrived at maturity.

73. That is the most perfect form of Government for a *dependent* province, which approaches the nearest to that of the *sovereign* state, and differs from it as little as possible.

74. There is no such form of Government among the *American Colonies.* And therefore

75. Every *American* Government is capable of having its Constitution altered for the better.

76. The Grants of the powers of Governments to *American* colonies by charters, cannot be understood to be intended for other than their infant or growing states.

77. They cannot be intended for their mature state, that is, for perpetuity; because they are in many things unconstitutional and contrary to the very nature of a *British* Government. Therefore,

78. They must be considered as designed only as temporary means, for settling and bringing forward the peopling the colonies; which being effected, the cause of *the peculiarity* of their constitution ceases.

79. If the Charters can be pleaded against the authority of *Parliament,* they amount to an alienation of the dominions of *Great Britain,* and are, in effect, acts of dismembering the *British Empire,* and will operate as such, if care is not taken to prevent it.

80. To make the Government of a Province the most perfect, it is necessary to regard the Extension as well as the Constitution of it.

81. A Province should be so extended, that the honourable support of the Government should not be burthensome; and so confined, that the assembling the Legislature may not be inconvenient.

82. Where the Legislature can meet without inconvenience,

the larger a Province is, the more effectual will be the powers of its Government.

83. The notion which has heretofore prevailed, that the dividing *America* into many governments, and different modes of government, will be the means to prevent their uniting to revolt, is ill-founded; since, if the Governments were ever so much consolidated, it will be necessary to have so many distinct States, as to make an union to revolt impracticable. Whereas,

84. The splitting *America* into many small governments, weakens the governing power, and strengthens that of the people; and thereby makes revolting more probable and more practicable.

85. To prevent revolts in future times (for there is no room to fear them in the present) the most effectual means would be, to make the governments large and respectable, and balance the powers of them.

86. There is no Government in *America* at present, whose powers are properly balanced; there not being in any of them a real and distinct third Legislative power mediating between the *King* and the *People*, which is the peculiar excellence of the *British* Constitution.

87. The want of such a third Legislative power, adds weight to the popular, and lightens the royal scale: so as to destroy the balance between the *royal* and *popular* powers.

88. Although *America* is not now (and probably will not be for many years to come) ripe enough for an hereditary *Nobility*; yet it is now capable of a *Nobility* for life.

89. A *Nobility* appointed by the *King* for life, and made independent, would probably give strength and stability to the *American* governments, as effectually as an hereditary *Nobility* does to that of *Great Britain*.

90. The reformation of the *American* governments should not be controlled by the present boundaries of the colonies; as they were mostly settled upon partial, occasional, and accidental considerations, without any regard to a whole.

91. To settle the *American* governments to the greatest possible advantage, it will be necessary to reduce the number of them; in some places to unite and consolidate; in others to

separate and transfer; and in general to divide by natural boundaries instead of imaginary lines.

92. If there should be but one form of Government established for all the *North American* Provinces, it would greatly facilitate the reformation of them: since, if the mode of Government was every where the same, people would be more indifferent under what division they were ranged.

93. No objections ought to arise to the alteration of the boundaries of provinces from Proprietors, on account of their property only; since there is no occasion that it should in the least affect the boundaries of properties.

94. The present distinctions of one government being more free or more popular than another, tend to embarrass and to weaken the whole; and should not be allowed to subsist among people, subject to one *King* and one *Law*, and all equally fit for one form of Government.

95. The *American* colonies, in general, are at this time arrived at that state, which qualifies them to receive the most perfect form of government, which their situation and relation to *Great Britain* make them capable of.

96. The people of *North America*, at this time, expect a revisal and reformation of the *American* Governments, and are better disposed to submit to it than ever they were, or perhaps ever will be again.

97. This is therefore the proper and critical time to reform the *American* governments upon a general, constitutional, firm, and durable plan; and if it is not done now, it will probably every day grow more difficult, till at last it becomes impracticable.

James Otis, The Rights of the British Colonies Asserted and Proved. Boston, 1764.

In 1733 the British government had levied a prohibitory high duty of six pence a gallon on foreign molasses imported into the North American colonies. This had been designed to keep French West Indian molasses—a by-product of sugar refining used in the making of rum—out of the hands of the colonists in order to prevent them from developing a rum industry that would rival that of the British West Indian sugar planters. By contrast, France, fearing competition to its wine and brandy industry, had forbidden its colonial sugar planters from using their own surplus molasses to make rum. Hence the French planters always had lots of leftover molasses to sell. Since the high tariff had not kept foreign molasses out of the English colonies—the Americans being very efficient smugglers and rum producers—the British administration finally concluded in 1764 that lowering the tariff to three pence a gallon not only would make it revenue-generating but would eliminate the colonists' need to smuggle molasses and bribe customs officials. The former prohibitory tariff designed in 1733 to regulate colonial trade now suddenly appeared to resemble a tax.

This Sugar Act of 1764 and the accompanying new trade regulations signaled a change in the long-standing relationship between the mother country and America. These initial efforts at imperial reform stirred up a series of colonial protests and writings, of which this pamphlet by James Otis of Massachusetts was one of the most radical and far-reaching. Reprinted in London before the year was out, it was advertised there as "universally approved" of in the colonies and "highly necessary for the perusal of the members of both houses, and of such who chuse to make themselves masters of an argument so little understood, but of so great consequence to every British subject, and lover of constitutional Liberty."

Just as it was one of the most influential pamphlets of the early stages of the American crisis, Otis's *Rights* was also one of the most complicated and seemingly self-contradictory, here avowing that Parliament's "uncontrollable" power must be obeyed, there averring that no legislature, not even Parliament, could deprive individuals—and remarkably for his time, he makes clear he does not mean just white individuals—of their natural rights. The apparent contradiction disappears once it is understood that Otis conceived of Parliament in an old-fashioned, even medieval sense and in the same terms that Chief Justice Edward Coke had invoked in the seventeenth century. Parliament to Otis, as it was to Coke, was a court that discovered the law, not a legislature that willed it. Parliament was undoubtedly supreme, but, like any court administering the common law, it could never be arbitrary; as soon as it discovered any mistake it had made, it would correct it, just as Coke had corrected Parliament in Dr. Bonham's case when it had mistakenly made a man a judge in his own cause in violation of the common law.

At once outdated and visionary, clinging to a legal fiction at odds with the realities of eighteenth-century politics even as it argued for natural rights in a way that many regarded as dangerously revolutionary, Otis's *Rights* left its author vulnerable to criticism from all sides.

THE

RIGHTS

OF THE

Britiſh Colonies

Aſſerted and proved.

By James Otis, *Eſq*;

Hæc omnis regio et celſi plaga pinea montis
Cedat amicitiæ Teucrorum : et fœderis æquas
Dicamus leges, ſocióſque in regna vocemus.
Conſidant, ſi tantus amor, et mœnia condant.

Virg.

B O S T O N:

Printed and Sold by Edes and Gill, in Queen-Street.

M,DCC, LXIV.

INTRODUCTION
OF THE ORIGIN OF GOVERNMENT.

THE origin of *government* has in all ages no less perplexed the heads of lawyers and politicians, than the origin of *evil* has embarrassed divines and philosophers: And 'tis probable the world may receive a satisfactory solution on *both* those points of enquiry at the *same* time.

The various opinions on the origin of *government* have been reduced to four. 1. That dominion is founded in *Grace*. 2. On *force* or meer *power*. 3. On *compact*. 4. On *property*.

The first of these opinions is so absurd, and the world has paid so very dear for embracing it, especially under the administration of the *roman pontiffs*, that mankind seem at this day to be in a great measure cured of their madness in this particular; and the notion is pretty generally exploded, and hiss'd off the stage.

To those who lay the foundation of government in *force* and meer *brutal power*, it is objected; that, their system destroys all distinction between right and wrong; that it overturns all morality, and leaves it to every man to do what is right in his own eyes; that it leads directly to *scepticism*, and ends in *atheism*. When a man's will and pleasure is his only rule and guide, what safety can there be either for him or against him, but in the point of a sword?

On the other hand the gentlemen in favor of the *original compact* have been often told that *their* system is chimerical and unsupported by reason or experience. Questions like the following have been frequently asked them, and may be again.

"When and where was the original compact for introducing government into any society, or for creating a society, made? Who were present and parties to such compact? Who acted for infants and women, or who appointed guardians for them? Had these guardians power to bind both infants and women during life, and their posterity after them? Is it in nature or reason that a guardian should by his own act perpetuate his power over his ward, and bind him and his posterity in chains? Is not every man born as free by nature as his father? Has he not the same natural right to think and act and contract for himself? Is it possible for a man to have a natural right to make a slave of himself or of his posterity? Can a father supersede the laws of nature? What man is or ever was born free, if every man is not? What will there be to distinguish the next generation of men from their forefathers, that they should not have the same right to make original compacts as their ancestors had? If every man has such right, may there not be as many original compacts as there are men and women born or to be born? Are not women born as free as men? Would it not be infamous to assert that the ladies are all slaves by nature? If every man and woman born or to be born has, and will have, a right to be consulted, and must accede to the original compact before they can with any kind of justice be said to be bound by it, will not the compact be ever forming and never finished, ever making but never done? Can it with propriety be called a compact original or derivative, that is ever in treaty but never concluded?"

When it has been said that each man is bound as soon as he accedes, and that the consent may be either express or tacit, it has been asked, "What is a *tacit* consent or compact? Does it not appear plain that those who refuse their assent can not be bound? If one is at liberty to accede or not, is he not also at liberty to *recede* on the discovery of some intolerable fraud and abuse that has been palm'd upon him by the rest of the high contracting parties? Will not natural equity in several special cases rescind the original compacts of great men as effectualy as those of little men are rendered null and void in the ordinary course of a court of chancery?"

There are other questions which have been started, and a resolution of them demanded, which may perhaps be deemed indecent by those who hold the prerogatives of an earthly monarch, and even the power of a plantation government, so sacred as to think it little less than blasphemy to enquire into their origin and foundation: while the government of the supreme *ruler* of the universe is every day discussed with less ceremony and decency than the administration of a petty German prince. I hope the reader will consider that I am at present only mentioning such questions as have been put by high-flyers & others in church and state, who would exclude all compact between a Sovereign and his people, without offering my own sentiments upon them; this however I presume I may be allowed hereafter to do without offence. Those who want a full answer to them may consult Mr. Locke's discourses on government, M. De Vattel's law of nature and nations, and their own consciences.

"What state were Great-Britain, Ireland and the Plantations left in by the abdication of James II? Was it a state of nature or of civil government? If a state of civil government, where were the supreme legislative and executive powers from the abdication to the election of William and Mary? Could the Lords and Commons be called a complete parliament or supreme power without a King to head them? Did any law of the land or any original compact previous to the abdication provide, that on such an event, the supreme power should devolve on the two houses? Were not both houses so manifestly puzzled with the novelty and strangeness of the event, and so far from finding any act of parliament, book-case, or precedent to help them, that they disputed in solemn conferrence by what name to call the action, and at last gave it one, as new in our language and in that of parliament as the thing itself was in fact?"*

If on this memorable and very happy event the three kingdoms and the dominions fell back into a state of *nature*, it will be asked, "Whether every man and woman were not then equal? If so, had not every one of them a natural and equitable right to be consulted in the choice of a new king, or in the formation of a new original compact or government, if any new form had been made? Might not the nation at that time have rightfully changed the monarchy into a republic or any form, that might seem best? Could any change from a state of nature take place without universal consent, or at least without the consent of the *majority* of the individuals? Upon the principles of the original compact as commonly explained and understood, could a few hundred men who before the dissolution

---

* On King James's leaving the kingdom and *abdicating* the government, the lords would have the word *desertion* made use of, but the commons thought it was not comprehensive enough, for that the King might then have liberty of returning. The Scots rightly called it a forfeiture of the crown, & this in plain english is the sense of the term *abdication* as by the convention and every parliament since applied. See the history and debates of the convention, and the acts then made.

of the government had been called, and in fact were, lords, knights and gentlemen, have lawfully made that glorious deliverer and defender W. 3. rightful king?" Such an one he certainly was, and such have been all his illustrious successors to the present happy times; when we have the joy to see the sceptre sway'd in justice, wisdom and mercy, by our lawful Sovereign George the Third; a prince who glories in being a Briton born, and whom may God long preserve and prosper.

"If upon the abdication all were reduced to a state of nature, had not apple women and orange girls as good a right to give their respectable suffrages for a new king as the philosopher, courtier, petit maitre and politician? Were these and ten millions of others such ever more consulted on that occasion, than the multitude now are in the adjustment of that real modern farce, an election of a king of the Romans; which serves as a contrast to the grandeur of the antient republics, and shows the littleness of the modern German and some other gothic constitutions in their present degenerate state?

"In the election of W. 3, were the votes of Ireland and the plantations ever called for or once tho't of till the affair was settled? Did the lords and commons who happened to be then in and about Westminster represent, and act, for the individuals, not only of the three kingdoms, but for all the *freeborn and as yet unconquered possessors and proprietors of their own money-purchased, blood-purchased plantations, which, till lately, have been defended with little or no assistance from Great-Britain?* Were not those who did not vote in or for the new model at liberty upon the principles of the compact to remain in what some call the delectable state of nature, to which by the hypothesis they were reduced, or to join themselves to any other state, whose solemn league and covenant they could subscribe? Is it not a first principle of the original compact, that all who are bound should bind *themselves?* Will not common sense without much learning or study dictate obvious answers to all the above questions?—and, say the opposers of the original compact and of the natural equality and liberty of mankind, will not those answers infallibly show that the doctrine is a piece of *metaphysical* jargon and *systematical* nonsense?" Perhaps not.

With regard to the fourth opinion, that *dominion is founded in property*, what is it but playing with words? Dominion in one sense of the term is synonimous with property, so one cannot be called the foundation of the other, but as one *name* may appear to be the foundation or cause of another.

Property cannot be the foundation of dominion as synonimous with government; for on the supposition that property has a precarious existence antecedent to government, and tho' it is also admitted that the security of property is one end of government, but that of little estimation even in the view of a *miser* when life and liberty of locomotion and further accumulation are placed in competition, it must be a very absurd way of speaking to assert that *one* end of government is the foundation of government. If the ends of government are to be considered as its foundation, it cannot with truth or propriety be said that government is founded on any *one* of those ends; and therefore government is not founded on property or its security *alone*, but at least on something else in conjunction. It is however true in fact and *experience*, as the great, the incomparable *Harrington* has most abundantly demonstrated in his *Oceana*, and other divine writings, that Empire follows the balance of *property*: 'Tis also certain that *property* in fact generally *confers* power, tho' the possessor of it may not have much more wit than a mole or a musquash: And this is too often the cause, that riches are sought after, without the least concern about the right application of them. But is the fault in the riches, or the general law of nature, or the unworthy possessor? It will never follow from all this, that government is *rightfully* founded on *property*, alone. What shall we say then? Is not government founded on *grace*? No. Nor on *force*? No. Nor on *compact*? Nor *property*? Not altogether on either. Has it *any* solid foundation? any chief corner stone, but what accident, chance or confusion may lay one moment and destroy the next? I think it has an everlasting foundation in the *unchangeable will of* GOD, the author of nature, whose laws never vary. The same omniscient, omnipotent, infinitely good and gracious Creator of the universe, who has been pleased to make it necessary that what we call matter should *gravitate*, for the celestial bodies to roll round their axes, dance their orbits and perform their various revolutions in that beautiful order and concert, which we all admire, has made it *equally* necessary

that from *Adam* and *Eve* to these degenerate days, the different sexes should sweetly *attract* each other, form societies of
single families, of which *larger* bodies and communities are as
naturally, mechanically, and necessarily combined, as the dew
of Heaven and the soft distilling rain is collected by the all en-
liv'ning heat of the sun. *Government* is therefore most evidently
founded *on the necessities of our nature.* It is by no means an
arbitrary thing, depending merely on *compact* or *human will*
for its existence.

We come into the world forlorn and helpless; and if left
alone and to ourselves at any one period of our lives, we should
soon die in want, despair or destraction. So kind is that hand,
tho' little known or regarded, which feeds the rich and the
poor, the blind and the naked; and provides for the safety of
infants by the principle of parental love, and for that of men by
Government! We have a King, who neither slumbers nor
sleeps, but eternally watches for our good; whose rain falls on
the just and on the unjust: yet while they live, move, and have
their being in him, and cannot account for either, or for any
thing else, so stupid and wicked are some men, as to deny his
existence, blaspheme his most evident government, and disgrace their nature.

Let no Man think I am about to commence advocate for
despotism, because I affirm that government is founded on the
necessity of our natures; and that an original supreme Sovereign, absolute, and uncontroulable, *earthly* power *must* exist in
and preside over every society; from whose final decisions
there can be no appeal but directly to Heaven. It is therefore
originally and *ultimately* in the people. I say this supreme absolute power is *originally* and *ultimately* in the people; and
they never did in fact *freely*, nor can they *rightfully* make an
absolute, unlimited renunciation of this divine right.* It is ever
in the nature of the thing given in *trust*, and on a condition,

---

* The power of GOD almighty is the only power that can properly and strictly
be called supreme and absolute. In the order of nature immediately under
him, comes the power of a simple *democracy* or the power of the whole over
the whole. Subordinate to both these, are all other political powers, from that
of the French Monarque, to a petty constable.

the performance of which no mortal can dispence with; namely, that the person or persons on whom the sovereignty is confer'd by the people, shall *incessantly* consult *their* good. Tyranny of all kinds is to be abhor'd, whether it be in the hands of one, or of the few, or of the many.—And tho' "in the last age a generation of men sprung up that would flatter Princes with an opinion that *they* have a *divine right* to absolute power"; yet "slavery is so vile and miserable an estate of man, and so directly opposite to the generous temper and courage of our nation, that 'tis hard to be conceived that an *english-man*, much less a *gentleman*, should plead for it:"* Especially at a time when the finest writers of the most polite nations on the continent of *Europe*, are enraptured with the beauties of the civil constitution of *Great-Britain*; and envy her, no less for the *freedom* of her sons, than for her immense *wealth* and *military* glory.

But let the *origin* of government be placed where it may, the *end* of it is manifestly the good of *the whole*. *Salus populi suprema lex esto*, is of the law of nature, and part of that grand charter given the human race, (tho' too many of them are afraid to assert it,) by the only monarch in the universe, who has a clear and indisputable right to *absolute* power; because he is the *only* ONE who is *omniscient* as well as *omnipotent*.

It is evidently contrary to the first principles of reason, that supreme *unlimited* power should be in the hands of *one* man. It is the greatest "*idolatry*, begotten by *flattery*, on the body of *pride*," that could induce one to think that a *single mortal* should be able to hold so great a power, if ever so well inclined. Hence the origin of *deifying* princes: It was from the trick of gulling the vulgar into a belief that their tyrants were *omniscient*; and that it was therefore right, that they should be considered as *omnipotent*. Hence the *Dii majorum et minorum gentium*; the great, the monarchical, the little, Provincial subordinate and subaltern gods, demi-gods, and semidemi-gods, ancient and modern. Thus deities of all kinds were multiplied and increased in *abundance*; for every devil incarnate, who could enslave a people, acquired a title to *divinity*; and thus

* Mr. Locke.

the "rabble of the skies" was made up of locusts and catterpil-
lars; lions, tygers and harpies; and other devourers translated
from plaguing the earth!*

The *end* of government being the *good* of mankind, points
out its great duties: It is above all things to provide for the security, the quiet, and happy enjoyment of life, liberty, and
property. There is no one act which a government can have a
right to make, that does not tend to the advancement of the
security, tranquility and prosperity of the people. If life, liberty
and property could be enjoyed in as great perfection in *solitude*, as in *society*, there would be no need of government. But
the experience of ages has proved that such is the nature of
man, a weak, imperfect being; that the valuable ends of life
cannot be obtained, without the union and assistance of many.
Hence 'tis clear that men cannot live apart or independent of
each other: In solitude men would perish; and yet they cannot
live together without contests. These contests require some
arbitrator to determine them. The necessity of a common, indifferent and impartial judge, makes all men seek one; tho' few
find him in the *sovereign power*, of their respective states or any
where else in *subordination* to it.

Government is founded *immediately* on the necessities of
human nature, and *ultimately* on the will of God, the author
of nature; who has not left it to men in general to choose,
whether they will be members of society or not, but at the
hazard of their senses if not of their lives. Yet it is left to every
man as he comes of age to chuse *what society* he will continue
to belong to. Nay if one has a mind to turn *Hermit*, and after
he has been born, nursed, and brought up in the arms of society, and acquired the habits and passions of social life, is willing
to run the risque of starving alone, which is generally most
unavoidable in a state of hermitage, who shall hinder him? I
know of no human law, founded on the law of *nature*, to restrain him from separating himself from all the species, if he
can find it in his heart to leave them; unless it should be said, it

---

* Kingcraft and Priestcraft have fell out so often, that 'tis a wonder this grand
and ancient alliance is not broken off for ever. Happy for mankind will it be,
when such a separation shall take place.

is against the great law of *self-preservation*: But of this every man will think himself *his own judge*.

The few *Hermits* and *Misanthropes* that have ever existed, show that those states are *unnatural*. If we were to take out from them, those who have made great *worldly* gain of their *godly* hermitage, and those who have been under the madness of *enthusiasm*, or *disappointed* hopes in their *ambitious* projects, for the detriment of mankind; perhaps there might not be left ten from *Adam* to this day.

The form of government is by *nature* and by *right* so far left to the *individuals* of each society, that they may alter it from a simple democracy or government of all over all, to any other form they please. Such alteration may and ought to be made by express compact: But how seldom this right has been asserted, history will abundantly show. For once that it has been fairly settled by compact; *fraud, force* or *accident* have determined it an hundred times. As the people have gained upon tyrants, these have been obliged to relax, *only* till a fairer opportunity has put it in their power to encroach again.

But if every prince since *Nimrod* had been a tyrant, it would not prove a *right* to tyranize. There can be no prescription old enough to supersede the law of nature, and the grant of GOD almighty; who has given to all men a natural right to be *free*, and they have it ordinarily in their power to make themselves so, if they please.

Government having been proved to be necessary by the law of nature, it makes no difference in the thing to call it from a certain period, *civil*. This term can only relate to form, to additions to, or deviations from, the substance of government: This being founded in nature, the superstructures and the whole administration should be conformed to the law of universal reason. A supreme legislative and a supreme executive power, must be placed *somewhere* in every common-wealth: Where there is no other positive provision or compact to the contrary, those powers remain in the *whole body of the people*. It is also evident there can be but *one* best way of depositing those powers; but what that way is, mankind have been disputing in peace and in war more than five thousand years. If we could suppose the individuals of a community met to deliberate, whether it were best to keep those powers in *their own* hands, or dispose of them in *trust*, the following questions would occur— Whether those two great powers of *Legislation* and *Execution* should remain united? If so, whether in the hands of the many, or jointly or severally in the hands of a few, or jointly in some one individual? If both those powers are retained in the hands of the many, where nature seems to have placed them originally, the government is a simple *democracy*, or a government of all over all. This can be administred, only by establishing it as a first principle, that the votes of the majority shall be taken as the voice of the whole. If those powers are lodged in the hands of a few, the government is an *Aristocracy* or *Oligarchy.** Here too the first principles of a practicable administration is that the majority rules the whole. If those great powers are both lodged in the hands of one man, the government is a *simple Monarchy*, commonly, though falsly called *absolute*, if by that term is meant a right to do as one pleases.—*Sic volo, sic jubeo, stet pro ratione voluntas*, belongs not of right to any mortal man.

The same law of nature and of reason is equally obligatory on a *democracy*, an *aristocracy*, and a *monarchy*: Whenever the administrators, in any of those forms, deviate from truth, justice and equity, they verge towards tyranny, and are to be opposed; and if they prove incorrigible, they will be *deposed* by the people, if the people are not rendered too abject. Deposing the administrators of a *simple democracy* may sound oddly, but it is done every day, and in almost every vote. A. B. & C. for example, make a *democracy*. To day A & B are for so vile a measure as a standing army. To morrow B & C vote it out. This is as really deposing the former administrators, as setting up and making a new king is deposing the old one. *Democracy* in the one case, and *monarchy* in the other, still remain; all that is done is to change the administration.

The first principle and great end of government being to provide for the best good of all the people, this can be done only by a supreme legislative and executive ultimately in the

---

* For the sake of the unlettered reader 'tis noted, that Monarchy means the power of one great man; Aristocracy and Oligarchy that of a few; and Democracy that of all men.

people, or whole community, where GOD has placed it; but the inconveniencies, not to say impossibility, attending the consultations and operations of a large body of people, have made it necessary to transfer the power of the whole to a *few*: This necessity gave rise to deputation, proxy or a right of representation.

A Power of legislation, without a power of execution in the same or other hands, would be futile and vain: On the other hand, a power of execution, supreme or subordinate, without an *independent* legislature, would be perfect despotism.

The difficulties attending an universal congress, especially when society became large, have bro't men to consent to a delegation of the power of all: The weak and the wicked have too often been found in the same interest, and in most nations have not only bro't these powers *jointly*, into the hands of one, or some few, of their number; but made them *hereditary*, in the families of despotic nobles & princes.

The wiser and more virtuous states, have always provided that the representation of the people should be *numerous*. Nothing but life and liberty are *naturally* hereditable: this has never been considered by those, who have *tamely* given up both into the hands of a tyrannical Oligarchy or despotic Monarchy.

The analogy between the natural, or material, as it is called, and the moral world is very obvious; GOD himself appears to us at some times to cause the intervention or combination of a *number* of simple principles, tho' never when *one* will answer the end; gravitation and attraction have place in the revolution of the planets, because the one would fix them to a centre, and the other would carry them off indefinitely; so in the moral world, the first simple principle is *equality* and the power of the whole. This will answer in small numbers; so will a tolerably virtuous *Oligarchy* or a *Monarchy*. But when the society grows in bulk, none of them will answer well *singly*, and none worse than absolute monarchy. It becomes necessary therefore as numbers increase, to have those several powers properly combined; so as from the whole to produce that harmony of government so often talked of and wished for, but too seldom found in ancient or modern states. The grand political problem in all ages has been to invent the best combination or distribution of the supreme powers of legislation and execution. Those states have ever made the greatest figure, and have been most durable, in which those powers have not only been separated from each other, but placed each in more hands than one, or a few. The *Romans* are the most shining example; but they never had a balance between the senate and the people, and the want of this, is generally agreed by the few who know any thing of the matter, to have been the cause of their fall. The *British* constitution in theory and in the present administration of it, in general comes nearest the idea of perfection, of any that has been reduced to practice; and if the principles of it are adhered to, it will according to the infallible prediction of *Harrington*, always keep the *Britons* uppermost in *Europe*, 'till their *only* rival nation shall either embrace that perfect model of a common wealth given us by that author, or come as near it as *Great Britain* is. Then indeed and not till then, will that rival & our nation either be eternal confederates, or contend in greater earnest than they have ever yet done, till one of them shall sink under the power of the other, and rise no more.

Great Britain has at present, most evidently the advantage, and such opportunities of honest wealth and grandeur, as perhaps no state ever had before, at least not since the days of *Julius Cæsar*, the destroyer of the roman glory and grandeur; at a time when but for him and his adherents both might have been rendered immortal.

We have said that the form and mode of government is to be settled by *compact*, as it was rightfully done by the convention after the abdication of *James* II, and assented to by the first representative of the nation chosen afterwards, and by every parliament, and by almost every man ever since, but the bigots, to the indefeasible power of tyrants civil and ecclesiastic. There was neither time for, nor occasion to call the whole people together: If they had not liked the proceedings it was in their power to controul them; as it would be should the supreme legislative or executive powers ever again attempt to enslave them. The people will bear a great deal, before they will even murmur against their rulers: But when once they are thoroughly roused, and in earnest, against those who would be glad to enslave them, their power is *irresistible*.*

At the abdication of King *James*, every step was taken that

---

* See Mr. Locke on the Dissolution of Government.

natural justice and equity could require; and all was done that was possible at least in the wretched state in which he left the nation. Those very noble and worthy patriots, the lords spiritual and temporal of that day, and the principal persons of the commons, advised the prince, who in consequence thereof caused letters to be "written to the lords spiritual and temporal, being protestants, and other letters to the several counties, cities, universities, boroughs and cinque ports, for the choosing such persons to represent them as were of right to be sent to parliament, to meet at Westminster upon the 22d of January 1688, in order to such an establishment, as that their religion, laws and liberties might not again be in danger of being subverted." See W & M. sess. I. C. I.

Upon this elections were made, and thereupon the said lords spiritual and temporal and commons met, and proceeded to assert their rights and liberties, and to the election of the Prince and Princess of Orange to be King and Queen of England, France and Ireland, and the dominions thereto belonging. The kingdom of Scotland agreed in the same choice: These proceedings were drawn into the form of acts of parliament, and are the basis of the acts of union and succession since made, and which all together are the sure foundation of that indisputable right which his present Majesty has to the Crown of *Great-Britain* and the dominions thereto belonging; which right 'tis the greatest folly to doubt of, as well as the blackest treason to deny. The present establishment founded on the law of GOD, and of nature, was began by the convention, with a professed and real view, in all parts of the *British* empire, to put the liberties of the people out of the reach of arbitrary power in all times to come.

But the grandeur, as well as justice, equity and goodness of the proceedings of the nation on that memorable occasion, never have been nor can be so well represented as in the words of those great men who composed the convention; for which reason partly, but principally because they shew the rights of all British subjects, both at home and abroad, and should therefore be in as many hands as possible, I have transcribed the following clauses.

1 Wm. & M. sess. I. Chap. I preamble & sec I—entituled—
"An act for removing and preventing all questions and

disputes concerning the assembling and sitting of this present parliament."

For preventing all doubts and scruples which may in any wise arise concerning the meeting, sitting and proceeding of this present parliament; be it declared and enacted by the King's and Queen's most excellent Majesty's, by and with the advice and consent of the lords spiritual and temporal, and commons, now assembled, and by authority of the same:

IIdly. That the lords spiritual and temporal, and commons, convened at Westminster, the two and twentieth day of January A. D. 1688, and there sitting the 13th of February following, are the two houses of parliament, and so shall be and are hereby declared, enacted and adjudged to be, to all intents, constructions, and purposes whatsoever, notwithstanding any want of writ or writs of summons, or any other defect of form or default whatsoever, as if they had been summoned according to the usual form.

1 of W. & M. sess. 2. Chap. 2. sec. 3, 4, 5, 6, 11, 12.

"An act declaring the rights and liberties of the subject, and settling the succession of the Crown."

Whereas the lords spiritual and temporal, and commons, assembled at Westminster, lawfully, fully and freely representing all the estates of the people of this realm, did upon the 13th of February A.D. 1688, present unto their Majesties, then called and known by the names and stile of William and Mary, Prince and Princess of Orange, being present in their proper persons, a certain declaration in writing, made by the said lords and commons in the words following; viz.

Whereas the late King James the second, by the assistance of divers evil counsellors, judges, and ministers employed by him, did endeavour to subvert and extirpate the protestant religion, and the laws and liberties of this kingdom.

1. By assuming and exercising a power of dispensing with and suspending of laws, and the execution of laws, without consent of parliament.

2. By committing and prosecuting divers worthy prelates, for humbly petitioning to be excused from concuring to the said assumed power.

3. By issuing and causing to be executed a commission under

the great seal for erecting a court called, The court of commissioners for ecclesiastical causes.

4. By levying money for and to the use of the crown, by pretence of prerogative, for other time, and in other manner, than the same was granted by parliament.

5. By raising and keeping a standing army within this kingdom in time of peace, without consent of parliament, and quartering soldiers contrary to law.

6. By causing several good subjects, being protestants, to be disarmed, at the same time when papists were both armed and employed, contrary to law.

7. By violating the freedom of election of members to serve in parliament.

8. By prosecutions in the court of king's bench, for matters and causes cognizable only in parliament; and by divers other arbitrary and illegal courses.

9. And whereas of late years, partial, corrupt and unqualified persons, have been returned and served on juries in trials, and particularly divers jurors in trials for high treason, which were not freeholders.

10. And excessive bail hath been required of persons committed in criminal cases, to elude the benefit of the laws made for the liberty of the subjects.

11. And excessive fines have been imposed; and illegal and cruel punishments inflicted.

12. And several grants and promises made of fines and forfeitures, before any conviction or judgment against the persons, upon whom the same were to be levied.

All which are utterly and directly contrary to the known laws and statutes, and freedom of this realm—

And whereas the said late King *James* the second having abdicated the Government, and the throne being thereby vacant, his highness the prince of Orange (whom it hath pleased Almighty GOD to make the glorious instrument of delivering this kingdom from popery and arbitrary power) did (by the advice of the Lords spiritual and temporal, and divers principal persons of the commons) cause letters to be written to the lords spiritual and temporal, being protestants, and other letters to the several counties, cities, universities, boroughs, and cinque-ports, for the choosing of such persons to represent them, as were of right to be sent to parliament, to meet and sit at Westminster upon the two and twentieth of January in this year 1688, in order to such an establishment, as that their religion, laws and liberties might not again be in danger of being subverted. Upon which letters, elections having been accordingly made:

And thereupon the said lords spiritual and temporal and commons, pursuant to their respective letters and elections, being now assembled in a full and free representative of this nation, taking into their most serious consideration the best means for attaining the ends aforesaid; do in the first place (as their ancestors in like case have usually done) for the vindicating and asserting their ancient rights and liberties, declare,

1. That the pretended power of suspending of laws, or the execution of laws, by regal authority, without consent of parliament, is illegal.

2. That the pretended power of dispensing with laws, or the execution of laws, by regal authority, as it hath been assumed and exercised of late, is illegal.

3. That the commission for creating the late court of commissioners for ecclesiastical causes, and all other commissions and courts of like nature, are illegal and pernicious.

4. That levying money for or to the use of the crown, by pretence of prerogative, without grant of parliament, for longer time, or in other manner, than the same is or shall be granted, is illegal.

5. That it is the right of the subjects to petition the King; and all commitments and prosecutions for such petitioning are illegal.

6. That the raising or keeping a standing army within the kingdom in time of peace, unless it be with consent of parliament, is against law.

7. That the subjects which are protestants, may have arms for their defence, suitable to their conditions, and as allowed by law.

8. That election of members of parliament ought to be free.

9. That the freedom of speech, and debates, or proceedings in parliament, ought not to be impeached or questioned in any court or place out of parliament.

10. That excessive bail ought not to be required, nor excessive fines imposed; nor cruel and unusual punishments inflicted.

11. That jurors ought to be duly impannelled and returned; and jurors which pass upon mens trials for high treason, ought to be freeholders.

12. That all grants and promises of fines and forfeitures of particular persons before conviction, are illegal and void.

13. And that for redress of all grievances, and for the amending, strengthening, and preserving of the laws, parliaments ought to be held frequently.

And they do claim, demand, and insist upon all and singular the premises, as their undoubted rights and liberties; and that no declarations, judgments, doings, or proceedings, to the prejudice of the people in any of the said premises, ought in any wise to be drawn hereafter into consequence or example:

To which demand of their rights they are particularly encouraged by the declaration of his Highness the Prince of Orange, as being the only means for obtaining a full redress and remedy therein—

Having therefore an entire confidence, that his said Highness the Prince of Orange, will perfect the deliverance so far advanced by him, and will still preserve them from the violation of their rights, which they have here asserted, and from all other attempts upon their religion, rights and liberties.

II. The said Lords spiritual and temporal, and commons assembled at Westminster, do resolve that William & Mary Prince and Princess of Orange be, and be declared, King and Queen of England, France and Ireland, and the dominions thereunto belonging, to hold the crown and royal dignity of the said kingdoms and dominions to them the said Prince and Princess, during their lives, and the life of the survivor of them; and that the sole and full exercise of the regal power be only in, and executed by the said Prince of Orange, in the names of the said prince and princess, during their joint lives; and after their deceases, the said crown and royal dignity of the said kingdoms and dominions to be to the heirs of the body of the said princess; and for default of such issue, to the princess Anne of Denmark, and the heirs of her body; and for default of such issue, to the heirs of the body of the said prince of Orange.

And the Lords spiritual and temporal, and commons, do pray the said prince and princess to accept the same accordingly.

IV. Upon which their said Majesties did accept the crown and royal dignity of the kingdom of England, France and Ireland, and the dominions thereunto belonging, according to the resolutions and desire of the said lords and commons, contained in the said declaration.

V. And thereupon their Majesties were pleased, that the said Lords spiritual and temporal, and commons, being the two houses of parliament, should continue to sit, and with their Majesties royal concurrence, make effectual provision for the settlement of the religion, laws and liberties of this kingdom; so that the same for the future might not be in danger again of being subverted; to which the said lords spiritual and temporal, and commons, did agree and proceed to act accordingly.

VI. Now in pursuance of the premises, the said lords spiritual and temporal and commons, in parliament assembled, for the ratifying, confirming and establishing the said declaration, and the articles, clauses, matters and things therein contained, by the force of a law made in due form by authority of parliament, do pray that it may be declared and enacted, That all and singular the rights and liberties asserted and claimed in the said declaration, are the true, ancient and indubitable rights and liberties of the people of this kingdom, and so shall be esteemed, allowed, adjudged, deemed, and taken to be; and that all and every the particulars aforesaid, shall be firmly and strictly holden and observed, as they are expressed in the said declaration; and all officers and ministers whatsoever shall serve their Majesties and their successors according to the same in all times to come.

XI. All which their Majesties are contented and pleased shall be declared, enacted, and established by authority of this present parliament, and shall stand remain and be the law of this realm for ever; and the same are by their said Majesties, by and with the advice and consent of the Lords spiritual and temporal, and commons, in parliament assembled, and by the authority of the same, declared, enacted, and established accordingly.

XII. And be it further declared and enacted by the authority aforesaid, that from and after this present session of parliament, no dispensation by *non obstante* of or to any statute or any part thereof, shall be allowed; but that the same shall be held void and of no effect, except a dispensation be allowed in such statutes, and except in such cases as shall be specially provided for by one or more bill or bills to be passed during this present session of parliament.

12 & 13 of William 3d, Chap. 2. sec. 3 & 4.

"Whereas it is necessary that further provision be made for securing our religion, laws and liberties, after the death of his Majesty and the Princess Anne of Denmark, and in default of issue of the body of the said Princess, and of his Majesty respectively; it is enacted,

That after the said limitation shall take effect, judges commissions be made *quamdiu se bene gesserint*, and their salaries ascertained and established; but upon the address of both houses parliament, it may be lawful to remove them;

That no pardon under the great seal of England be pleaded to an impeachment by the commons in parliament.

Whereas the laws of England are the birth-right of the people thereof, and all the Kings and Queens, who shall ascend the throne of this realm, ought to administer the government of the same according to the said laws, and all their officers and ministers ought to serve them according to the same; all the laws and statutes of this realm for securing the established religion, and the rights and liberties of the people, and all other laws and statutes now in force, are by his Majesty with the advice and consent of the lords spiritual and temporal, and commons, ratified and confirmed."

I shall close this introduction with a passage from Mr. Locke.

"Tho', says he, in a constituted common wealth, standing upon its own basis, and acting according to its own nature, that is, acting for the preservation of the community, there can be but one supreme power which is the legislative, to which all the rest are and must be subordinate; yet the legislative being only a fiduciary power, to act for certain ends, there remains still, "*in the people, a supreme power to remove, or alter, the legislative when they find the legislative act contrary to the trust reposed in them.*" For all power given, with trust for the attaining

an end, being limited by that end, whenever that end is manifestly neglected, or opposed, the trust must necessarily be forfeited, and the power devolve into the hands of those who
gave it, who may place it anew where they shall think best, for
their safety and security. And thus the *community* perpetually
retains a supreme power of saving themselves from the attempts and designs of any body, even of their legislators whenever they shall be so foolish, or so wicked, as to lay and carry
on designs against the liberties and properties of the subject.
For no man or society of men having a power to deliver up
their preservation or consequently the means of it to the absolute will and arbitrary dominion of another; whenever any one
shall go about to bring them into such a slavish condition,
they will always have a right to preserve what they have not a
power to part with; and to *rid* themselves of *those* who invade
this fundamental, sacred and unalterable law of self preservation, for which they entered into society.

And thus the community may be said in this respect to be
always the supreme power, but not as considered under any
form of government, because this power of the people can
never take place, till the government be dissolved." Locke on
Government, B. II. C. 13.

This he says may be done, "from without by conquest; from
within, 1st. When the legislative is altered. Which is often by
the prince, but sometimes by the whole legislative. As by in-
vading the *property* of the subject, and making themselves arbitrary disposers of the lives, liberties and fortunes of the
people; reducing them to slavery under arbitrary power, they
put themselves into a state of war with the people, who are
thereupon absolved from any further obedience, and are left to
the common refuge which GOD hath provided for all men,
against force and violence. Whensoever therefore, the legislative shall transgress this fundamental rule of society; and either
by ambition, fear, folly or corruption, endeavour to gain
themselves, or put into the hands of any other an absolute
power over the lives, liberties and estates of the people, by this
breach of trust, they forfeit the power the *people* had put into
their hands for quite contrary ends, and it devolves to the *people*, who have a right to *resume* their original liberty, and by the

establishment of a *new* legislative (such as they shall think fit) provide for their own safety and security, which is the end for which they are in society." Idem Chap. 19.

OF COLONIES IN GENERAL.

THIS subject has never been very clearly and fully handled by any modern writer, that I have had the good fortune to meet with; and to do it justice, would require much greater abilities than I pretend to, and more leisure than I ever expect will fall to my share. Even the *English* writers and lawyers, have either intirely wav'd any consideration of the nature of *Colonies*, or very lightly touched upon it, for the people of England never discovered much concern for the prosperity of the *Colonies*, 'till the revolution; and even now some of their great men and writers, by their discourses of, and conduct towards them, consider them all rather as a parcel of *little insignificant conquered islands*, than as a very extensive settlement on the continent. Even their law-books and very dictionaries of law, in editions so late as 1750, speak of the *British* plantations abroad as consisting chiefly of islands; and they are reckoned up in some of them in this order—*Jamaica, Barbados, Virginia, Maryland, New-England, New-York, Carolina, Bermudas.* At the head of all these *Islands* (for there is no distinction made) stands *Jamaica*, in truth a *conquered* island; and as such, this and all the other little West-India islands deserve to be treated, for the conduct of their inhabitants and proprietors with regard to the Northern Colonies: Divers of these colonies are larger than all those islands together; and are well settled, not as the common people of *England* foolishly imagine, with a compound mongrel mixture of *English, Indian* and *Negro*, but with freeborn *British white* subjects, whose loyalty has never yet been suspected.

There is a man now living, or but lately dead, who once was a secretary of state; during whose *wonderful* conduct of national affairs, without knowing whether *Jamaica* lay in the Mediterranean, the Baltic, or in the Moon, letters were often received, directed to the Governor of the *island* of New-England. Which *island* of New-England is a part of the *continent* of North-America, comprehending two provinces and two colonies; and according to the *undoubted* bounds of their charters, containing more land than there is in the three kingdoms. But I must confine myself to matters of more importance than detecting the geographical blunders, or refuting the errors of dead, superannuated or any otherwise stupified secretaries of state, who are now all out of place.

If I were to define the *modern* Colonists, I should say, *they are the noble discoverers and settlers of a new world*; from whence as from an endless source, *wealth*, and *plenty*, the means of *power, grandeur* and *glory*, in a degree unknown to the hungry chiefs of former ages, have been pouring into *Europe* for 300 years past: In return for which those Colonists have received from the several states of *Europe*, except from *Great-Britain*, only since the revolution, nothing but ill-usage, slavery and chains, as fast as the riches of *their own* earning, could furnish the means of forging them.

A plantation or colony, is a settlement of subjects in a territory *disjoined* or *remote* from the mother country, and may be made by private adventurers or the public; but in both cases the Colonists are entitled to as *ample* rights, liberties and priviledges as the subjects of the mother country are, and in some respects *to more*.

OF THE NATURAL RIGHTS OF COLONISTS.

THOSE who expect to find any thing very satisfactory on this subject in particular, or with regard to the law of nature in general, in the writings of such authors as *Grotius* and *Pufendorf*, will find themselves much mistaken. It is their constant practice to establish the matter of right on the matter of *fact*: This the celebrated *Rousseau* expresly says of *Grotius*, and with the same reason he might have added an hundred others. "The learned researches into the laws of nature and nations are often nothing more than the history of ancient abuses, so that it is a ridiculous infatuation to be too fond of studying them."* "This was exactly the case with *Grotius*."† The sentiments on this subject have therefore

---

* Marquis D' A.
† Rousseau.

been chiefly drawn from the purer fountains of one or two of our *English* writers, particularly from Mr. *Locke*, to whom might be added a *few* of other nations; for I have seen but a few of any country, and of all I have seen, there are not ten worth reading. *Grotius* B. 3. C. 1. sec. 21. discoursing of confederates on unequal terms according to his manner says, "to the inequality in question may be referred some of those rights which are now called right of protection, right of patronage, and a right termed *mundiburgium*; as also that which mother cities had over their colonies among the Grecians. For as *Thucydides* says, those colonies enjoyed the same rights of liberty with the other cities, but they owed a *reverence* to the city whence they derived their origin, and were obliged to render her respect and certain expressions of honor, *so long as the colony was well treated.*" Grotius de jure belli, &c. B. 1. C. 3. 21.

"Hitherto also (says he) may be referred that separation which is made when people *by one consent*, go to form colonies. *For this is the original of a new and independent state. They are not content to be slaves, but to enjoy equal priviledges and freedom* says *Thucydides*. And King *Tullius* in Dion. Hali. says, *we look upon it to be neither truth nor justice, that mother cities ought of necessity and by the law of nature to rule over their colonies.*" B. 2. C. 9. sec. 10.

"Colonies, says Pufendorf, are settled in different methods. For either the colony continues a part of the common-wealth it was sent out from, or else is obliged to pay a dutiful respect to the mother common-wealth, and to be in readiness to defend and vindicate its honor, and so is united to it by a sort of unequal confederacy, or lastly is erected into a separate commonwealth, and assumes the same rights with the state it is descended from." Pufend. B. 8. C. 11. 6.

"Different common wealths may be formed out of one by common consent, by sending out colonies in the manner usual in old Greece. For the Romans afterwards when they sent a colony abroad, continued it under the jurisdiction of the mother commonwealth, or greater country. But the colonies planted by the Greeks, and after their method, constituted particular commonwealths, which were obliged only to pay a kind of deference and dutiful submission to the mother commonwealth." Pufend. B. 8. C. 12. sec. 5.

From which passages tis manifest that these two great men only state facts, and the opinions of others, without giving their own upon the subject: And all that can be collected from those facts or opinions, is, that Greece was more generous, and a better mother to her colonies than Rome. The conduct of Rome towards her colonies and the corruptions and oppressions tolerated in her provincial officers of all denominations, was one great cause of the downfall of that proud republic.

Dr. Strahan says, "there is a great affinity between the British colonies and those of the Spaniards and other nations, who have made settlements among the Indians in those parts: For the grants made by our Kings, of tracts of lands in that country, for the planting of colonies, and making settlements therein, appear to have been made in imitation of grants made by the Kings of Spain to the proprietors of lands in the Spanish colonies, upon the very same conditions, and in consideration of the same services to be performed by the grantees. So that the *government* of the Spanish colonies and the rights of the proprietors of lands therein, depending chiefly on the rules of civil and feudal law, as may be seen by the learned treatise of Solorzanus, *de indiarum jure*, the knowledge of the said laws must be of service likewise for determining any controversy that may arise touching the duties or forfeitures of the proprietors of lands in our English colonies." Pref. to translat. of Domat.

With submission to so great an authority as Dr. Strahan, tis humbly hoped that the British colonists do not hold their lands as well as liberties by so slippery a tenure as do the Spaniards and French. The will of the Prince is the only tenure by which *they* hold; and the government of the Spanish and French settlements is in every respect despotic.

'Tis well known that the first American grants were by the Bulls of the Popes. The Roman Pontiffs had for ages usurped the most abominable power over princes: They granted away the kingdoms of the earth with as little ceremony as a man would lease a sheep-cot. Now according to Dr. Strahans's logic, it may be inferred, that the canon law, and the Popes Bulls, must be of *service likewise, for determining any controversy that may arise, touching the duties or forfeitures of the proprietors of lands in the British colonies.* And indeed it must be owned, if we were to judge of some late proceedings* by this rule, we must allow that they savor more of modern Rome and the Inquisition, than of the common law of England and the constitution of Great-Britain.

In order to form an idea of the natural rights of the Colonists, I presume it will be granted that they are men, the common children of the same Creator with their brethren of Great-Britain. Nature has placed all such in a state of equality and perfect freedom, to act within the bounds of the laws of nature and reason, without consulting the will or regarding the humor, the passions or whims of any other man, unless they are formed into a society or body politic. This it must be confessed is rather an abstract way of considering men than agreeable to the real and general course of nature. The truth is, as has been shown, men come into the world and into society at the same instant. But this hinders not but that the natural and original rights of each individual may be illustrated and explained in this way better than in any other. We see here by the way a probability, that this abstract consideration of men, which has its use in reasoning on the principles of government, has insensibly led some of the greatest men to imagine, some real general state of nature, agreeable to this abstract conception, antecedent to and independent of society. This is certainly not the case in general, for most men become members of society from their birth, tho' seperate independent states are really in the condition of perfect freedom and equality with regard to each other; and so are any number of individuals who separate themselves from a society of which they have formerly been members, for ill treatment, or other good cause, with express design to found another. If in such case, there is a real interval, between the separation and the new conjunction, during such interval, the individuals are as much detached, and under the law of nature only, as would be two men who should chance to meet on a desolate island.

The Colonists are by the law of nature free born, as indeed all men are, white or black. No better reasons can be given, for enslaving those of any color than such as baron Montesquieu

* Of some American Courts of Admiralty, if the reader pleases.

has humorously given, as the foundation of that cruel slavery exercised over the poor Ethiopians; which threatens one day to reduce both Europe and America to the ignorance and barbarity of the darkest ages. Does it follow that tis right to enslave a man because he is black? Will short curl'd hair like wool, instead of christian hair, as tis called by those, whose hearts, are as hard as the nether millstone, help the argument? Can any logical inference in favour of slavery, be drawn from a flat nose, a long or a short face? Nothing better can be said in favor of a trade, that is the most shocking violation of the law of nature, has a direct tendency to diminish the idea of the inestimable value of liberty, and makes every dealer in it a tyrant, from the director of an African company to the petty chapman in needles and pins on the unhappy coast. It is a clear truth, that those who every day barter away other mens liberty, will soon care little for their own. To this cause must be imputed that ferosity, cruelty and brutal barbarity that has long marked the general character of the sugar-islanders. They can in general form no idea of government but that which in person, or by an overseer, the joint and several proper representative of a Creole,* and of the D——l, is exercised over ten thousands of their fellow men, born with the same right to freedom, and the sweet enjoyments of liberty and life, as their unrelenting task-masters, the overseers and planters.

Is it to be wondered at, if, when people of the stamp of a Creolian planter get into power, they will not stick for a little present gain, at making their own posterity, white as well as black, worse slaves if possible than those already mentioned.

There is nothing more evident says Mr. Locke, than "that creatures of the same species and rank promiscuously born to all the same advantages of nature, and the use of the same faculties, should also be equal one among another, without subordination and subjection, unless the master of them all should by any manifest declaration of his will set one above another, and confer on him by an evident and clear appointment, an

* Those in England who borrow the terms of the Spaniards, as well as their notions of government, apply this term to all Americans of European Extract; but the Northern colonists apply it only to the Islanders and others of such extract, under the Torrid Zone.

undoubted right to dominion and sovereignty." "The natural liberty of man is to be free from any superior power on earth, and not to be under the will or legislative authority of man, but only to have the law of nature for his rule." This is the liberty of independant states; this is the liberty of every man out of society, and who has a mind to live so; which liberty is only abridged in certain instances, not lost to those who are born in or voluntarily enter into society; this gift of God cannot be annihilated.

The Colonists being men, have a right to be considered as equally entitled to all the rights of nature with the Europeans, and they are not to be restrained, in the exercise of any of these rights, but for the evident good of the whole community.

By being or becoming members of society, they have not renounced their natural liberty in any greater degree than other good citizens, and if tis taken from them without their consent, they are so far enslaved.

They have an undoubted right to expect, that their best good will ever be consulted by their rulers, supreme and subordinate, without any partial views confined to the particular interest of one island or another. Neither the riches of Jamaica, nor the luxury of a metropolis, should ever have weight enough to break the balance of truth and justice. Truth and faith belong to men as men, from men, and if they are disappointed in their just expectations of them in one society, they will at least wish for them in another. If the love of truth and justice, the only spring of sound policy in any state, is not strong enough to prevent certain causes from taking place, the arts of fraud and force will not prevent the most fatal effects.

In the long run, those who fall on arbitrary measures, will meet with their deserved fate. The law of nature, was not of man's making, nor is it in his power to mend it, or alter its course. He can only perform and keep, or disobey and break it. The last is never done with impunity, even in this life, if it is any punishment for a man to feel himself depraved; to find himself degraded by his own folly and wickedness from the rank of a virtuous and good *man*, to that of a brute; or to be transformed from the friend, perhaps father of his country, to a devouring Lion or Tyger.

The unhappy revolutions which for ages have distressed the human race, have been all owing to the want of a little wisdom, common sense and integrity, in the administration of those, whom by their stations, God had in kindness to the world, rendered able to do a great deal, for the benefit of mankind, with the exertion of a small portion of private and public vertue.

OF THE POLITICAL AND CIVIL RIGHTS OF THE BRITISH COLONISTS.

HERE indeed opens to view a large field; but I must study brevity—Few people have extended their enquiries after the foundation of any of their rights, beyond a charter from the crown. There are others who think when they have got back to old *Magna Charta*, that they are at the beginning of all things. They imagine themselves on the borders of Chaos (and so indeed in some respects they are) and see creation rising out of the unformed mass, or from nothing. Hence, say they, spring all the rights of men and of citizens.—But liberty was better understood, and more fully enjoyed by our ancestors, before the coming in of the first Norman Tyrants than ever after, 'till it was found necessary, for the salvation of the kingdom, to combat the arbitrary and wicked proceedings of the Stuarts.

The present happy and most righteous establishment is justly built on the ruins, which those Princes bro't on their Family; and two of them on their own heads—The last of the name sacrificed three of the finest kingdoms in Europe, to the councils of bigotted old women, priests, and more weak and wicked ministers of state: He afterward went a grazing in the fields of St. Germains, and there died in disgrace and poverty, a terrible example of God's vengeance on arbitrary princes!

The deliverance under God wrought by the prince of Orange, afterwards deservedly made King Wm. 3d. was as joyful an event to the colonies as to Great-Britain: In some of them, steps were taken in his favour as soon as in England.

They all immediately acknowledged King William and Queen Mary as their lawful Sovereign. And such has been the zeal and loyalty of the colonies ever since for that establishment, and for the protestant succession in his present Majesty's illustrious family, that I believe there is not one man in an hundred (except in Canada) who does not think himself under the best national civil constitution in the world.

Their loyalty has been abundantly proved, especially in the late war. Their affection and reverence for their mother country is unquestionable. They yield the most chearful and ready obedience to her laws, particularly to the power of that august body the parliament of Great-Britain, the supreme legislative of the kingdom and its dominions. These I declare are my own sentiments of duty and loyalty. I also hold it clear that the act of Queen Anne, which makes it high treason to deny "that the King with and by the authority of parliament, is able to make laws and statutes of sufficient force and validity to *limit* and *bind* the crown, and the descent, limitation, inheritance and *government* thereof" is founded on the principles of liberty and the British constitution: And he that would palm the doctrine of unlimited passive obedience and non-resistance upon mankind, and thereby or by any other means serve the cause of the Pretender, is not only a fool and a knave, but a rebel against common sense, as well as the laws of God, of Nature, and his Country.

☞ —I also lay it down as one of the first principles from whence I intend to deduce the civil rights of the British colonies, that all of them are subject to, and dependent on Great-Britain; and that therefore as over subordinate governments, the parliament of Great-Britain has an undoubted power and lawful authority to make acts for the general good, that by naming them, shall and ought to be equally binding, as upon the subjects of Great-Britain within the realm. This principle, I presume will be readily granted on the other side the atlantic. It has been practiced upon for twenty years to my knowledge, in the province of the *Massachusetts-Bay*; and I have ever received it, that it has been so from the beginning, in this and the sister provinces, thro' the continent.*

---

* This however was formally declared as to Ireland, but so lately as the reign of G. I. Upon the old principles of conquest the Irish could not have so much to say for an exemption, as the unconquered Colonists.

I am aware, some will think it is time for me to retreat, after having expressed the power of the British parliament in quite so strong terms. But 'tis from and under this very power and its acts, and from the common law, that the political and civil rights of the Colonists are derived: And upon those grand pillars of liberty shall my defence be rested. At present therefore, the reader may suppose, that there is not one provincial charter on the continent; he may, if he pleases, imagine all taken away, without fault, without forfeiture, without tryal or notice. All this really happened to some of them in the last century. I would have the reader carry his imagination still further, and suppose a time may come, when instead of a process at common law, the parliament shall give a decisive blow to every charter in America, and declare them all void. Nay it shall also be granted, that 'tis barely possible, the time may come, when the real interest of the whole may require an act of parliament to annihilate all those charters. What could follow from all this, that would shake one of the essential, natural, civil or religious rights of the Colonists? Nothing. They would be men, citizens and british subjects after all. No act of parliament can deprive them of the liberties of such, unless any will contend that an act of parliament can make slaves not only of one, but of two millions of the commonwealth. And if so, why not of the whole? I freely own, that I can find nothing in the laws of my country, that would justify the parliament in making one slave, nor did they ever professedly undertake to make one.

Two or three innocent colony charters have been threatened with destruction an hundred and forty years past. I wish the present enemies of those harmless charters would reflect a moment, and be convinced that an act of parliament that should demolish those bugbears to the foes of liberty, would not reduce the Colonists to a state of absolute slavery. The worst enemies of the charter governments are by no means to be found in England. 'Tis a piece of justice due to Great-Britain to own, they are and have ever been natives of or residents in the colonies. A set of men in America, without honour or love to their country, have been long grasping at powers, which they think unattainable while these charters stand in the way. But they will meet with insurmountable obstacles to their project for enslaving the British colonies, should those, arising from provincial charters be removed. It would indeed seem very hard and severe, for those of the colonists, who have charters, with peculiar priviledges, to loose them. They were given to their ancestors, in consideration of their sufferings and merit, in discovering and settling America. Our fore-fathers were soon worn away in the toils of hard labour on their little plantations, and in war with the Savages. They thought they were earning a sure inheritance for their posterity. Could they imagine it would ever be tho't just to deprive them or theirs of their charter priviledges! Should this ever be the case, there are, thank God, natural, inherent and inseperable rights as men, and as citizens, that would remain after the so much wished for catastrophe, and which, whatever became of charters, can never be abolished *de jure*, if *de facto*, till the general conflagration.* Our rights as men and free born British subjects, give all the Colonists enough to make them very happy in comparison with the subjects of any other prince in the world.

Every British subject born on the continent of America, or in any other of the British dominions, is by the law of God and nature, by the common law, and by act of parliament, (exclusive of all charters from the Crown) entitled to all the natural, essential, inherent and inseparable rights of our fellow subjects in Great-Britain. Among those rights are the following, which it is humbly conceived no man or body of men, not excepting the parliament, justly, equitably and consistently with their own rights and the constitution, can take away.

1st. *That the supreme and subordinate powers of legislation should be free and sacred in the hands where the community have once rightfully placed them.*

2dly. *The supreme national legislative cannot be altered justly 'till the commonwealth is dissolved, nor a subordinate legislative taken away without forfeiture or other good cause.* Nor then can the subjects in the subordinate government be reduced to a state of slavery, and subject to the despotic rule of others. A

---

* The fine defence of the provincial charters by *Jeremy Dummer*, Esq; the late very able and learned agent for the province of the *Massachusetts Bay*, makes it needless to go into a particular consideration of charter priviledges. That piece is unanswerable, but by power and might, and other arguments of that kind.

state has no right to make slaves of the conquered. Even when the subordinate right of legislature is forfeited, and so declared, this cannot affect the natural persons either of those who were invested with it, or the inhabitants,* so far as to deprive them of the rights of subjects and of men—The colonists will have an equitable right notwithstanding any such forfeiture of charter, to be represented in Parliament, or to have some new subordinate legislature among themselves. It would be best if they had both. Deprived however of their common rights as subjects, they cannot lawfully be, while they remain such. A representation in Parliament from the several Colonies, since they are become so large and numerous, as to be called on not to maintain provincial government, civil and military among themselves, for this they have chearfully done, but to contribute towards the support of a national standing army, by reason of the heavy national debt, when they themselves owe a large one, contracted in the common cause, can't be tho't an unreasonable thing, nor if asked, could it be called an immodest request. *Qui sentit commodum sentire debet et onus*, has been tho't a maxim of equity. But that a man should bear a burthen for other people, as well as himself, without a return, never long found a place in any law-book or decrees, but those of the most despotic princes. Besides the equity of an American representation in parliament, a thousand advantages would result from it. It would be the most effectual means of giving those of both countries a thorough knowledge of each others interests; as well as that of the whole, which are inseparable.

Were this representation allowed; instead of the scandalous memorials and depositions that have been sometimes, in days of old, privately cooked up in an inquisitorial manner, by persons of bad minds and wicked views, and sent from America to the several boards, persons of the first reputation among their countrymen, might be on the spot, from the several colonies, truly to represent them. Future ministers need not, like some of their predecessors, have recourse for information in American affairs, to every vagabond stroller, that has run or rid post thro' America, from his creditors, or to people of no

* See Magna Charta, the Bill of Rights. 3 Mod. 159; 2 Salkeld 411; Vaughan 300.

kind of reputation from the colonies; some of whom, at the time of administring their sage advice, have been as ignorant of the state of this country, as of the regions in Jupiter and Saturn.

No representation of the Colonies in parliament alone, would however be equivalent to a subordinate legislative among themselves; nor so well answer the ends of increasing their prosperity and the commerce of Great-Britain. It would be impossible for the parliament to judge so well, of their abilities to bear taxes, impositions on trade, and other duties and burthens, or of the local laws that might be really needful, as a legislative here.

3dly. *No legislative, supreme or subordinate, has a right to make itself arbitrary.*

It would be a most manifest contradiction, for a free legislative, like that of Great-Britain, to make itself arbitrary.

4thly. *The supreme legislative cannot justly assume a power of ruling by extempore arbitrary decrees, but is bound to dispense justice by known settled rules, and by duly authorized independant judges.*

5thly. *The supreme power cannot take from any man any part of his property,* without his consent in *person, or by representation.*

6thly. *The legislature cannot transfer the power of making laws to any other hands.*

These are their bounds, which by God and nature are fixed, hitherto have they a right to come, and no further.

1. *To govern by stated laws.*

2. *Those laws should have no other end ultimately, but the good of the people.*

3. *Taxes are not to be laid on the people, but by their consent in person, or by deputation.*

4. *Their whole power is not transferable.**

These are the first principles of law and justice, and the great barriers of a free state, and of the British constitution in particular. I ask, I want no more—Now let it be shown how 'tis reconcileable with these principles, or to many other fundamental maxims of the British constitution, as well as the natural

* See Locke on Government, B II. C xi.

and civil rights, which by the laws of their country, all British subjects are intitled to, as their best inheritance and birth-right, that all the northern colonies, who are without one representative in the house of Commons, should be taxed by the British parliament.

That the colonists, black and white, born here, are free born British subjects, and entitled to all the essential civil rights of such, is a truth not only manifest from the provincial charters, from the principles of the common law, and acts of parliament; but from the British constitution, which was re-established at the revolution, with a professed design to secure the liberties of all the subjects to all generations.*

In the 12 and 13 of Wm. cited above, the liberties of the subject are spoken of as their best birth-rights—No one ever dreamt, surely, that these liberties were confined to the realm. At that rate, no British subjects in the dominions could, without a manifest contradiction, be declared entitled to all the privileges of subjects born within the realm, to all intents and purposes, which are rightly given foreigners, by parliament, after residing seven years. These expressions of parliament, as well as of the charters, must be vain and empty sounds, unless we are allowed the essential rights of our fellow-subjects in Great-Britain.

Now can there be any liberty, where property is taken away without consent? Can it with any colour of truth, justice or equity, be affirmed, that the northern colonies are represented in parliament? Has this whole continent of near three thousand miles in length, and in which and his other American dominions, his Majesty has, or very soon will have, some millions of as good, loyal and useful subjects, white and black, as any in the three kingdoms, the election of one member of the house of commons?

Is there the least difference, as to the consent of the Colonists, whether taxes and impositions are laid on their trade, and other property, by the crown alone, or by the parliament? As it is agreed on all hands, the Crown alone cannot impose them, we should be justifiable in refusing to pay them, but must and ought to yield obedience to an act of parliament, tho' erroneous, 'till repealed.

---

* See the convention, and acts confirming it.

I can see no reason to doubt, but that the imposition of taxes, whether on trade, or on land, or houses, or ships, on real or personal, fixed or floating property, in the colonies, is absolutely irreconcileable with the rights of the Colonists, as British subjects, and as men. I say men, for in a state of nature, no man can take my property from me, without my consent: If he does, he deprives me of my liberty, and makes me a slave. If such a proceeding is a breach of the law of nature, no law of society can make it just—The very act of taxing, exercised over those who are not represented, appears to me to be depriving them of one of their most essential rights, as freemen; and if continued, seems to be in effect an entire disfranchisement of every civil right. For what one civil right is worth a rush, after a man's property is subject to be taken from him at pleasure, without his consent. If a man is not his *own assessor* in person, or by deputy, his liberty is gone, or lays intirely at the mercy of others.

I think I have heard it said, that when the Dutch are asked why they enslave their colonies, their answer is, that the liberty of Dutchmen is confined to Holland; and that it was never intended for Provincials in America, or any where else. A sentiment this, very worthy of modern Dutchmen; but if their brave and worthy ancestors had entertained such narrow ideas of liberty, seven poor and distressed provinces would never have asserted their rights against the whole Spanish monarchy, of which the present is but a shadow. It is to be hoped, none of our fellow subjects of Britain, great or small, have borrowed this Dutch maxim of plantation politics; if they have, they had better return it from whence it came; indeed they had. Modern Dutch or French maxims of state, never will suit with a British constitution. It is a maxim, that the King can do no wrong; and every good subject is bound to believe his King is not inclined to do any. We are blessed with a prince who has given abundant demonstrations, that in all his actions, he studies the good of his people, and the true glory of his crown, which are inseparable. It would therefore, be the highest degree of impudence and disloyalty to imagine that the King, at the head of his parliament, could have any, but the most pure and perfect intentions of justice, goodness and truth, that human nature is capable of. All this I say and believe of the King and parliament, in all their acts; even in that which so nearly affects the interest of the colonists; and that a most perfect and ready obedience is to be yielded to it, while it remains in force. I will go further, and readily admit, that the intention of the ministry was not only to promote the public good, by this act; but that Mr. Chancellor of the Exchequer had therein a particular view to the "ease, the quiet, and the good will of the Colonies," he having made this declaration more than once. Yet I hold that 'tis possible he may have erred in his kind intentions towards the Colonies, and taken away our fish, and given us a stone. With regard to the parliament, as infallability belongs not to mortals, 'tis possible *they* may have been misinformed and deceived. The power of parliament is uncontroulable, but by themselves, and we must obey. They only can repeal their own acts. There would be an end of all government, if one or a number of subjects or subordinate provinces should take upon them so far to judge of the justice of an act of parliament, as to refuse obedience to it. If there was nothing else to restrain such a step, prudence ought to do it, for forceably resisting the parliament and the King's laws, is high treason. Therefore let the parliament lay what burthens they please on us, we must, it is our duty to submit and patiently bear them, till they will be pleased to relieve us. And tis to be presumed, the wisdom and justice of that august assembly, always will afford us relief by repealing such acts, as through mistake, or other human infirmities, have been suffered to pass, if they can be convinced that their proceedings are not constitutional, or not for the common good.

The parliament may be deceived, they may have been misinformed of facts, and the colonies may in many respects be misrepresented to the King, his parliament, and his ministry. In some instances, I am well assured the colonies have been very strangely misrepresented in England. I have now before me a pamphlet, called the "administration of the colonies," said to be written by a gentleman who formerly commanded in chief in one of them. I suppose this book was designed for public information and use. There are in it many good regulations proposed, which no power can enforce but the parliament. From all which I infer, that if our hands are tied by the passing of an act of parliament, our mouths are not stoped, provided we speak of that transcendent body with decency, as I have endeavoured always to do; and should any thing have escaped me, or hereafter fall from my pen, that bears the least aspect but that of obedience, duty and loyalty to the King & parliament, and the highest respect for the ministry, the candid will impute it to the agony of my heart, rather than to the pravity of my will. If I have one ambitious wish, 'tis to see Great-Britain at the head of the world, and to see my King, under God, the father of mankind. I pretend neither to the spirit of prophecy, nor any uncommon skill in predicting a Crisis, much less to tell when it begins to be "*nascent*" or is fairly midwiv'd into the world. But if I were to fix a meaning to the two first paragraphs of the *administration of the colonies*, tho' I do not collect it from them, I should say the world was at the eve of the highest scene of earthly power and grandeur that has been ever yet displayed to the view of mankind. The cards are shuffling fast thro' all Europe. Who will win the prize is with God. This however I know, *detur digniori*. The next universal monarchy will be favourable to the human race, for it must be founded on the principles of equity, moderation and justice. No country has been more distinguished for these principles than Great-Britain, since the revolution. I take it, every subject has a right to give his sentiments to the public, of the utility or inutility of any act whatsoever, even after it is passed, as well as while it is pending.—The equity and justice of a bill may be questioned, with perfect submission to the legislature. Reasons may be given, why an act ought to be repeal'd, & yet obedience must be yielded to it till that repeal takes place. If the reasons that can be given against an act, are such as plainly demonstrate that it is against *natural* equity, the executive courts will adjudge such act void. It may be questioned by some, tho' I make no doubt of it, whether they are not obliged by their oaths to adjudge such act void. If there is not a right of private judgment to be exercised, so far at least as to petition for a repeal, or to determine the expediency of risking a trial at law, the parliament might make itself arbitrary, which it is conceived it can not by the constitution.—I think every man has a right to examine as freely into the origin, spring and foundation of every power and measure in a commonwealth, as into a piece of curious machinery, or a remarkable phenomenon in nature;

and that it ought to give no more offence to say, the parliament
have erred, or are mistaken, in a matter of fact or of right, than
to say it of a private man, if it is true of both. If the assertion
can be proved with regard to either, it is a kindness done them
to show them the truth. With regard to the public, it is the
duty of every good citizen to point out what he thinks erroneous in the commonwealth.

I have waited years in hopes to see some one friend of the
colonies pleading in publick for them. I have waited in vain.
One priviledge is taken away after another, and where we shall
be landed, God knows, and I trust will protect and provide for
us even should we be driven and persecuted into a more western wilderness, on the score of liberty, civil and religious, as
many of our ancestors were, to these once inhospitable shores
of America. I had formed great expectations from a gentleman,
who published his first volume in quarto on the rights of the
colonies two years since; but, as he foresaw, the state of his
health and affairs have prevented his further progress. The
misfortune is, gentlemen in America, the best qualified in
every respect to state the rights of the colonists, have reasons
that prevent them from engaging: Some of them have good
ones. There are many infinitely better able to serve this cause
than I pretend to be; but from indolence, from timidity, or by
necessary engagements, they are prevented. There has been a
most profound, and I think shameful silence, till it seems almost too late to assert our indisputable rights as men and as
citizens. What must posterity think of us. The trade of the
whole continent taxed by parliament, stamps and other internal duties and taxes as they are called, talked of, and not one
petition to the King and Parliament for relief.

I cannot but observe here, that if the parliament have an
equitable right to tax our trade, 'tis indisputable that they have
as good an one to tax the lands, and every thing else. The taxing trade furnishes one reason why the other should be taxed,
or else the burdens of the province will be unequally born,
upon a supposition that a tax on trade is not a tax on the
whole. But take it either way, there is no foundation for the
distinction some make in England, between an internal and an
external tax on the colonies. By the first is meant a tax on trade,
by the latter a tax on land, and the things on it. A tax on trade is

either a tax of every man in the province, or 'tis not. If 'tis not a tax on the whole, 'tis unequal and unjust, that a heavy burden should be laid on the trade of the colonies, to maintain an army of soldiers, custom-house officers, and fleets of guard-ships; all which, the incomes of both trade and land would not furnish means to support so lately as the last war, when all was at stake, and the colonies were reimbursed in part by parliament. How can it be supposed that all of a sudden the trade of the colonies alone can bear all this terrible burden. The late acquisitions in America, as glorious as they have been, and as beneficial as they are to Great-Britain, are only a security to these colonies against the ravages of the French and Indians. Our trade upon the whole is not, I believe, benefited by them one groat. All the time the French Islands were in our hands, the fine sugars, &c. were all shipped home. None as I have been informed were allowed to be bro't to the colonies. They were too delicious a morsel for a North American palate. If it be said that a tax on the trade of the colonies is an equal and just tax on the whole of the inhabitants: What then becomes of the notable distinction between external and internal taxes? Why may not the parliament lay stamps, land taxes, establish tythes to the church of England, and so indefinitely. I know of no bounds. I do not mention the tythes out of any disrespect to the church of England, which I esteem by far the best *national* church, and to have had as ornaments of it many of the greatest and best men in the world. But to those colonies who in general dissent from a principle of conscience, it would seem a little hard to pay towards the support of a worship, whose modes they cannot conform to.

If an army must be kept up in America, at the expence of the colonies, it would not seem quite so hard if after the parliament had determined the sum to be raised, and apportioned it, to have allowed each colony to assess its quota, and raise it as easily to themselves as might be. But to have the whole levied and collected without our consent is extraordinary. 'Tis allowed even to *tributaries*, and those laid under *military* contribution, to assess and collect the sums demanded. The case of the provinces is certainly likely to be the hardest that can be instanced in story. Will it not equal any thing but down right military execution? Was there ever a tribute imposed even on the conquered? A fleet, an army of soldiers, and another of tax-gatherers kept up, and not a single office either for securing or collecting the duty in the gift of the tributary state.

I am aware it will be objected, that the parliament of *England*, and of Great Britain, since the union, have from early days to this time, made acts to bind if not to tax Ireland: I answer, Ireland is a *conquered* country. I do not, however, lay so much stress on this; for it is my opinion, that a *conquered* country has, upon submission and good behaviour, the same right to be free, under a conqueror, as the rest of his subjects. But the old notion of the *right of conquest*, has been, in most nations, the cause of many severities and heinous breaches of the law of nature: If any such have taken place with regard to *Ireland*, they should form no precedent for the colonies. The subordination and dependency of *Ireland* to Great Britain, is expresly declared by act of parliament, in the reign of G. 1st. The subordination of the *Colonies* to Great Britain, never was doubted, by a Lawyer, if at all; unless perhaps by the author of the administration of the colonies: He indeed seems to make a moot point of it, whether the colony legislative power is as independent "as the legislative Great Britain holds by its constitution, and under the great charter."—The *people* hold under the great charter, as 'tis vulgarly expressed from our law-books: But that the King and parliament should be said to hold under *Magna Charta*, is as new to me, as it is to question whether the colonies are *subordinate* to Great Britain. The provincial legislative is unquestionably subordinate to that of Great Britain. I shall endeavour more fully to explain the nature of that subordination, which has puzzled so many in their enquiries. It is often very difficult for great lovers of power, and great lovers of liberty, neither of whom may have been used to the study of law, in any of its branches, to see the difference between subordination, absolute slavery and subjection, on one side; and liberty, independence and licenciousness, on the other. We should endeavour to find the middle road, and confine ourselves to it. The laws, the proceedings of parliament, and the decisions of the judges, relating to *Ireland*, will reflect light on this subject, rendered intricate only by *art*.

"Ireland being of itself a distinct dominion, and no part of the kingdom of England (as it directly appeareth by many authorities in Calvin's case) was to have PARLIAMENTS holden there as in England." 4 Inst. 349.

Why should not the colonies have, why are they not entitled to their assemblies, or parliaments, at least, as well as a conquered dominion?

"Wales, after the conquest of it, by Edward the first, was annexed to England, jure proprietatis, 12 Ed. 1 by the statute of Rutland only, and after, more really by 27 H. 8. and 34, but at first received laws from England, as Ireland did; but writs proceeded not out of the English chancery, but they had a Chancery of their own, as Ireland hath; was not bound by the laws of England, unnamed until 27 H. 8. no more than Ireland is.

Ireland in nothing differs from it, but having a parliament *gratia Regis* (i. e. upon the old notion of conquest) subject (truly however) to the parliament of England. None doubts Ireland as much conquered as it; *and as much subject to the parliament of England, if it please.*" Vaughan. 300.

A very strong argument arises from this authority, in favour of the *unconquered* plantations. If since Wales was annexed to England, they have had a representation in parliament, as they have to this day; and if the parliament of England does not tax *Ireland*, can it be right they should tax *us*, who have never been *conquered*, but came from England to *colonize*, and have always remained *good subjects* to this day?

I cannot find any instance of a tax laid by the English parliament on *Ireland*. "Sometimes the King of England called his Nobles of Ireland, to come to his parliament of England, &c. and by special words, the parliament of England may bind the subjects of Ireland"—4 *Inst.* 350.—

The following makes it clear to me, the parliament of Great Britain do not tax *Ireland*. "The parliament of Ireland having been prorogued to the month of August *next, before they had provided for the maintenance of the government in that kingdom, a project* was set on foot here to supply that defect, by retrenching the drawbacks upon goods exported thither from England. According to this scheme, the 22d, the house in a grand committee, considered the present laws with respect to drawbacks upon tobaccoes, muslins, and East India silks, carried to Ireland; and came to two resolutions, which were reported the next day, and with an amendment to one of them agreed to by the house, as follows, Viz. 1. That three pence *pr* pound, part of the drawback on tobacco to be exported from Great Britain for Ireland, be taken off.

2. That the said diminution of the drawback do take effect upon all tobacco exported for Ireland, after the 24 of March 1713, and continue until the additional duty of three pence half penny per pound upon tobacco in Ireland, expiring on the said 24th of March, be *regranted*: And ordered a bill to be brought in, upon the said resolutions." Proceedings of House of Commons, Vol. 5. 72.

This was constitutional; there is an infinite difference between taking off British drawbacks, and imposing Irish or other Provincial duties.

"Ireland is considered as a provincial government, subordinate to, but no part of the Realm of England," Mich. 11. G. 2. in case of Otway and Ramsay— "Acts of parliament made here, (i. e. in England) extend not to Ireland, unless particularly named; much less judgments obtained in the courts here; nor is it possible they should, because we have no officers to carry them into execution there." *ib.*

The first part seems to be applicable to the plantations in general, the latter is not; for by reason of charter reservations and particular acts of parliament, some judgments in England may be executed here, as final judgments, before his Majesty in council on a plantation appeal, and so from the admiralty.

It seems to have been disputed in Ireland, so lately as the 6 Geo. 1. Whether any act of the British parliament bound Ireland; or at least it was apprehended, that the undoubted right of the British parliament to bind Ireland, was in danger of being shaken: This, I presume, occasioned the act of that year, which declares, that "the kingdom of Ireland ought to be subordinate unto and dependent upon the Imperial Crown of Great Britain, as being inseparably united thereto. And the King's Majesty, with the consent of the lords and commons of Great Britain in parliament, hath power to make laws to bind the people of Ireland."—This parliamentary power must have some bounds, even as to *Ireland*, as well as the colonies, who are admitted to be subordinate *ab initio* to Great Britain; not as *conquered*, but as *emigrant* subjects. If this act should be said to be a declaration not only of the general, but of the universal power of parliament, and that they may tax Ireland, I ask, Why it has never been done? If it had been done a thousand times, it would be a contradiction to the principles of a free government; and what is worse, destroy all subordination consistent with *freedom*, and reduce the people to *slavery*.

To say the parliament is absolute and arbitrary, is a contradiction. The parliament cannot make 2 and 2, 5: Omnipotency cannot do it. The supreme power in a state, is *jus dicere* only:—*jus dare*, strictly speaking, belongs alone to GOD. Parliaments are in all cases to *declare* what is for the good of the whole; but it is not the *declaration* of parliament that makes it so: There must be in every instance, a higher authority, viz. GOD. Should an act of parliament be against any of *his* natural laws, which are *immutably* true, *their* declaration would be contrary to eternal truth, equity and justice, and consequently void: and so it would be adjudged by the parliament itself, when convinced of their mistake. Upon this great principle, parliaments repeal such acts, as soon as they find they have been mistaken, in having declared them to be for the public good, when in fact they were not so. When such mistake is evident and palpable, as in the instances in the appendix, the judges of the executive courts have declared the act "of a whole parliament void." See here the grandeur of the British constitution! See the wisdom of our ancestors! The supreme *legislative*, and the supreme *executive*, are a perpetual check and balance to each other. If the supreme executive errs, it is informed by the supreme legislative in parliament: If the supreme legislative errs, it is informed by the supreme executive in the King's courts of law.—Here, the King appears, as represented by his judges, in the highest lustre and majesty, as supreme executor of the commonwealth; and he never shines brighter, but on his Throne, at the head of the supreme legislative. This is government! This, is a constitution! to preserve which, either from foreign or domestic foes, has cost oceans of blood and treasure in every age; and the blood and the treasure have upon the whole been well spent. British America, hath been bleeding in this cause from its settlement: We have spent all we could raise, and more; for notwithstanding the parliamentary reimbursements of part, we still remain much in debt. The province of the *Massachusetts*, I believe, has expended more men and money in war since the year 1620, when a few families first landed at Plymouth, in proportion to their ability, than the three Kingdoms together. The same, I believe, may be truly affirmed, of many of the other colonies; tho' the *Massachusetts* has undoubtedly had the heaviest burthen. This may be thought incredible: but materials are collecting; and tho' some are lost, enough may remain, to demonstrate it to the world. I have reason to hope at least, that the public will soon see such proofs exhibited, as will show, that I do not speak quite at random.

Why then is it thought so heinous by the author of the administration of the colonies, and others, that the colonists should aspire after "a one whole legislative power" not independent of, but subordinate to the laws and parliament of Great-Britain?—It is a mistake in this author, to bring so heavy a charge as *high treason* against some of the colonists, which he does in effect in this place,* by representing them as "claiming in fact or indeed, the same full free independent unrestrained power and legislative will, in their several corporations, and under the King's commission, and their respective charters, as the government and legislature of Great-Britain holds by its constitution and under the great charter." No such claim was ever tho't of by any of the colonists. They are all better men and better subjects; and many of them too well versed in the laws of nature and nations, and the law and constitution of Great-Britain, to think they have a right to more than a *provincial subordinate legislative*. All power is of GOD. Next and only subordinate to him, in the present state of the well-formed, beautifully constructed British monarchy, standing where I hope it ever will stand, for the pillars are fixed in judgment, righteousness and truth, is the King and Parliament. Under these, it seems easy to conceive subordinate powers in gradation, till we descend to the legislative of a town council, or even a private social club. These have each "a one whole legislative" subordinate, which, when it don't counteract the laws of any of its superiors, is to be indulged. Even when the laws of subordination are transgressed, the superior does not destroy the subordinate, but will negative its acts, as it may in all cases

* Page 39 of the administration.

when disapproved. This right of negative is essential, and may be inforced: But in no case are the essential rights of the subjects, inhabiting the subordinate dominions, to be destroyed. This would put it in the power of the superior to reduce the inferior to a state of slavery; which cannot be rightfully done, even with *conquered* enemies and *rebels*. After satisfaction and security is obtained of the former, and examples are made of so many of the latter, as the ends of government require, the rest are to be restored to all the essential rights of men and of citizens. This is the great law of nature: and agreeable to this law, is the constant practice of all good and mild governments. This lenity and humanity has no where been carried further than in Great Britain. The Colonies have been so remarkable for loyalty, that there never has been any instance of rebellion or treason in them. This loyalty is in very handsome terms acknowledged by the author of the administration of the colonies. "It has been often suggested that care should be taken in the administration of the plantations, lest, in some future time, these colonies should become independent of the mother country. But perhaps it may be proper on this occasion, nay, it is justice to say it, that if, by becoming independent, is meant a revolt, nothing is further from their nature, their interest, their thoughts. If a defection from the *alliance* of the mother country be suggested, it ought to be, and can be truly said, that their spirit abhors the sense of such; their attachment to the protestant succession in the house of Hanover, will ever stand unshaken; and nothing can eradicate from their hearts their natural and almost mechanical, affection to Great Britain, which they conceive under no other sense, nor call by any other name, than that of *home*. Any such suggestion, therefore, is a false and unjust aspersion on their principles and affections; and can arise from nothing but an intire ignorance of their circumstances."* After all this loyalty, it is a little hard to be charged with claiming, and represented as aspiring after, independency. The inconsistency of this I leave. We have said that the loyalty of the colonies has never been suspected; this must be restricted to a just suspicion. For it seems there have long been groundless suspicions of us in the minds of individuals.

* Administration, p 25 26.

And there have always been those who have endeavoured to magnify these chimerical fears. I find Mr. Dummer complaining of this many years since. "There is, says he, one thing more I have heard often urged against the charter colonies, and indeed tis what one meets with from people of all conditions and qualities, tho' with due respect to their better judgments, I can see neither reason nor colour for it. 'Tis said that their increasing numbers and wealth, joined to their great distance from Britain, will give them an opportunity, in the course of some years, to throw off their dependence on the nation, and declare themselves a free state, if not curb'd in time, by being made *entirely subject to the crown*."*

This jealousy has been so long talked of, that many seem to believe it really well grounded. Not that there is danger of a "revolt", even in the opinion of the *author of the administration*, but that the colonists will by fraud or force, avail themselves, in "fact or in deed", of an independent legislature. This, I think, would be a revolting with a vengeance. What higher revolt can there be, than for a province to assume the right of an independent legislative, or state? I must therefore think this a greater aspersion on the Colonists, than to charge them with a design to revolt, in the sense in which the Gentleman allows they have been abused: It is a more artful and dangerous way of attacking our liberties, than to charge us with being in open rebellion. That could be confuted instantly: but this seeming indirect way of charging the colonies, with a desire of throwing off their dependency, requires more pains to confute it than the other, therefore it has been recurred to. The truth is, Gentlemen have had departments in America, the functions of which they have not been fortunate in executing. The people have by these means been rendered uneasy, at bad Provincial measures. They have been represented as factious, seditious, and inclined to democracy, whenever they have refused passive obedience to provincial mandates, as arbitrary as those of a Turkish Bashaw: I say, Provincial mandates; for to the King and Parliament they have been ever submissive and obedient.

* Defence. 60.

These representations of us, many of the good people of England swallow with as much ease, as they would a bottle-bubble, or any other story of a cock and a bull; and the worst of it is, among some of the most credulous, have been found Stars and Garters. However, they may all rest assured, the Colonists, who do not pretend to understand themselves so well as the people of England; tho' the author of the Administration makes them the fine compliment, to say, they "know their business much better," yet, will never think of independency. Were they inclined to it, they know the blood and the treasure it would cost, if ever effected; and when done, it would be a thousand to one if their liberties did not fall a sacrifice to the victor.

We all think ourselves happy under Great-Britain. We love, esteem and reverence our mother country, and adore our King. And could the choice of independency be offered the colonies, or subjection to Great-Britain upon any terms above absolute slavery, I am convinced they would accept the latter. The ministry, in all future generations may rely on it, that British America will never prove undutiful, till driven to it, as the last fatal resort against ministerial oppression, which will make the wisest mad, and the weakest strong.

These colonies are and always have been, "entirely subject to the crown," in the legal sense of the terms. But if any politician of "tampering activity, of wrong-headed inexperience, misled to be meddling,"* means, by "curbing the colonies in time," and by "being made entirely subject to the crown;" that this subjection should be absolute, and confined to the crown, he had better have suppressed his wishes. This never will nor can be done, without making the colonists vassals of the crown. Subjects they are; their lands they hold of the crown, by common soccage, the freest feudal tennure, by which any hold their lands in England, or any where else. Would these gentlemen carry us back to the state of the Goths and Vandals, and revive all the military tenures and bondage which our fore-fathers could not bear? It may be worth noting here, that few if any instances can be given, where colonies have been

* Administration. 34.

disposed to forsake or disobey a tender mother: But history is full of examples, that armies stationed as guards over provinces, have seized the prey for their general, and given him a crown at the expence of his master. Are all ambitious generals dead? Will no more rise up hereafter? The danger of a standing army in remote provinces is much greater to the metropolis, than at home. Rome found the truth of this assertion, in her Sylla's, her Pompey's and Cæsars; but she found it too late: Eighteen hundred years have roll'd away since her ruin. A continuation of the same liberties that have been enjoyed by the colonists since the revolution, and the same moderation of government exercised towards them, will bind them in perpetual lawful and willing subjection, obedience and love to Great-Britain: She and her colonies will both prosper and flourish: The monarchy will remain in sound health and full vigor at that blessed period, when the proud arbitrary tyrants of the continent shall either unite in the deliverance of the human race, or resign their crowns. Rescued, human nature must and will be, from the general slavery that has so long triumphed over the species. Great-Britain has done much towards it: What a Glory will it be for her to complete the work throughout the world!

The author of the Administration (page 54) "describes" the defects of the "provincial courts," by a "very description," the first trait of which is, "The ignorance of the judges." Whether the description, or the description of the description, are *verily* true, either as applied by Lord Hale, or the Administrator, is left to the reader. I only ask, who makes the judges in the provinces? I know of but two colonies, viz. Connecticut and Rhode-Island, where they are chosen by the people. In all other colonies, they are either immediately appointed by the crown, or by his Majesty's governor, with the advice of what the Administrator calls, the "governor's council of state." And if they are in general such ignorant creatures, as the Administrator describes them, 'tis the misfortune, not the fault, of the people, in the colonies. However, I believe, justice in general, is as well administred in the colonies, as it will be when every thing is devolved upon a court of admiralty, general or provincial. The following is very remarkable. "In those popular governments, and where every executive officer is under a dependence for a temporary, wretched, and I had almost said arbitrary support, on the deputies of the people.*

Why is the temporary support found fault with? Would it be wise to give a governor a salary for a longer time than his political life? As this is quite as uncertain as his natural life, it has been granted annually. So every governor has the chance of one year's salary after he is dead. All the King's officers, are not even in the charter provinces "dependent on the people" for support. The judges of the admiralty, these mirrors of justice, to be trusted, when none of the common law courts are, have all their commissions from home. These, besides other fees, have so much per cent on all they condemn, be it right or wrong, and *this by act of parliament*. Yet so great is their integrity, that it never was suspected that 50 per cent, if allowed, would have any influence on their decrees.

Custom-house officers universally, and Naval-officers, in all but two or three of the colonies, are, I believe, appointed directly from home, or by instruction to the Governor: and take just what they please, for any restraint they are under by the provincial acts. But on whom should a Governor depend for his honorable support, but the people? Is not the King fed from the field, and from the labor of his people? Does not his Majesty himself receive his aids from the free grant of his parliament? Do not all these originate in the house of commons? Did the house of Lords ever originate a grant? Do not our law books inform us that the Lords only assent or dissent, but never so much as propose an amendment, on a money bill? The King can take no more than the Parliament will give him, and yet some of his Governors have tho't it an insufferable hardship, that they could not take what they pleased. To take leave of the administrator, there are in his book some good hints, but a multiplicity of mistakes in fact, and errors in matters of right, which I have not time to mention particularly.

Ireland is a conquered kingdom; and yet have tho't they received very hard measure in some of the prohibitions and restrictions of their trade. But were the colonies ever conquered? Have they not been subject and obedient, and loyal from their settlement? Were not the settlements made under the British laws and

* Administ. 56.

constitution? But if the colonies were all to be considered as conquered, they are entitled to the essential rights of men and citizens. And therefore admitting the right of prohibition, in its
utmost extent and latitude; a right of taxation can never be infer'd
from that. It may be for the good of the whole, that a certain
commodity should be prohibited: But this power should be exercised, with great *moderation* and impartiality, over dominions,
which are not *represented*, in the national parliament. I had
however rather see this carried with a high hand, to the utmost
rigor, than have a tax of one shilling taken from me without my
consent. A people may be very happy, free and easy among themselves, without a particular branch of foreign trade: I am sure
these colonies have the natural means of every manufacture in
Europe, and some that are out of their power to make or produce.
It will scarcely be believed a hundred years hence, that the American manufactures could have been brought to such perfection, as
they will then probably be in, if the present measures are pushed.
One single act of parliament, we find has set people a thinking, in
six months, more than they had done in their whole lives before.
It should be remembred, that the most famous and flourishing
manufactures, of wool, in *France*, were begun by *Lewis* 14, not an
hundred years ago; and they now bid fair to rival the *English*, in
every port abroad. All the manufactures that Great-Britain could
make, would be consumed in America, and in her own plantations, if put on a right footing; for which a greater profit in return
would be made, than she will ever see again for woollen sent to
any part of Europe.

But tho' it be allow'd, that liberty may be enjoy'd in a comfortable measure, where *prohibitions* are laid on the trade of a
kingdom or province; yet if *taxes* are laid on either, *without*
consent, they cannot be said to be free. This barrier of liberty
being once broken down, all is lost. If a shilling in the pound
may be taken from me against my will, why may not twenty
shillings; and if so, why not my liberty or my life? Merchants
were always *particularly* favor'd by the common law—"All
merchants, except enemies, may safely come into *England*,
with their goods and merchandize"—2 Inst. 28.—And why
not as well to the *plantations*? Are they not entitled to all the
British privileges? No, they must be confined in their imports
and exports, to the good of the metropolis. Very well, we have

submitted to this. The act of navigation is a good act, so are all that exclude foreign manufactures from the plantations, and every honest man will readily subscribe to them. Moreover, "Merchant strangers, are also to come into the realm and depart at pleasure; and they are to be friendly entertained." 2 Ri. C. 1. But to promote the manufactures of *England*, 'tis tho't best to shut up the *colonies* in a manner from all the world. Right as to Europe: But for GOD's sake, must we have no trade with other colonies? In some cases the trade betwen *British* colony and colony is prohibited, as in wool, &c. Granting all this to be right, is it not enough? No, duties and taxes must be paid without any *consent* or *representation* in parliament. The common law, that inestimable privilege of a jury, is also taken away in all trials in the colonies, relating to the revenue, if the informers have a mind to go the admiralty; as they ever have done, and ever will do, for very obvious reasons. "It has ever been boasted, says Mr. Dummer in his defence of the charters, as the peculiar privilege of an Englishman, and the security of his property, to be tryed by his country, and the laws of the land: Whereas this admiralty method deprives him of both, as it puts his estate in the disposal of a single person, and makes the civil law the rule of judgment; which tho' it may not properly be called foreign, being the law of nations, yet 'tis what he has not consented to himself, nor his representative for him. A jurisdiction therefore so founded, ought not to extend beyond what *necessity* requires"— "If some bounds are not set to the jurisdiction of the admiralty, beyond which it shall not pass, it may in time, like the element to which it ought to be confin'd, grow outrageous, and overflow the banks of all the other courts of justice." I believe it has never been doubted by one sound, common lawyer of England, whether a court of admiralty ever answer'd many good ends; "the court of King's bench has a power to restrain the court of admiralty in England; and the reasons for such restraining power are as strong in New England as in Great-Britain," and in some respects more so: Yet Mr. Dummer mentions, a clamour that was raised at home by a judge of the admiralty for New England, who complain'd "that the common law courts by granting prohibitions, weaken, and in a manner suppress the authority of this court, and all the good ends for which it was constituted."

Thus we see, that the court of admiralty long ago discover'd, no very friendly disposition towards the common law courts here; and the records of the house of Representatives afford us a notable instance of one, who was expelled the house, of which he had been an unworthy member, for the abusive misrepresentations of the province, by him secretly made.

Trade and traffick, says lord Coke, "is the livelihood of a merchant, the life of the commonwealth, wherein the King and every subject hath interest; for the merchant is the good Bailiff of the realm, to export and vent the native commodities of the realm, and to import and bring in, the necessary commodities for the defence and benefit of the Realm"—2 Inst. 28. reading on Magna Charta. C. 14—And are not the merchants of British America entitled to a livelihood also? Are they not British subjects? Are not an infinity of commodities carried from hence for *the benefit of the realm*, for which in return come an infinity of *trifles*, which we could do without? Manufactures we must go into if our trade is cut off; our country is too cold to go naked in, and we shall soon be unable to make returns to England even for necessaries.

"When any law or custom of parliament is broken, and the crown possessed of a precedent, how difficult a thing is it to restore the subject again to his former freedom and safety?" 2 Inst. *on the confirmation of the great charter*—which provides in these words: "And for so much as divers people of our realm, are in fear, that the aids and tasks which they have given to us before time, towards our wars, and other business of their own grant and good will (howsoever they were made) might *turn to a bondage* to them and their heirs, because they might be at another time found in the rolls, and likewise for the prices taken throughout the realm by our ministers; We have granted for us and our heirs, that we shall not draw such aids, tasks nor prices *into a custom*, for any thing that hath been done heretofore, be it by roll, or any other precedent that may be founden."

By the first chapter of this act, the great charter is declared to be the common law. I would ask, whether we have not reason to fear, that the great aids, freely given by these provinces in the late war, will in like manner turn *to our bondage*, if they are to be kept on and *increased* during a *peace*, for the maintenance of a *standing army* here?—If tis said those aids were given for *our own* immediate defence, and that England spent millions in the same cause; I answer; The names of his present Majesty, and his royal Grand-father, will be ever dear to every loyal British American, for the protection they afforded us, and the salvation, under God, effected by their arms; but with regard to our fellow-subjects of Britain, we never were a whit behind hand with them. The New England Colonies in particular, were not only settled without the least expence to the mother country, but they have all along defended themselves against the frequent incursions of the most inhuman Salvages, perhaps on the face of the whole earth, at *their own* cost: Those more than brutal *men*, spirited and directed by the most inveterate, as well as most powerful enemy of Great Britain, have been constantly annoying our infant settlements for more than a century; spreading terror and desolation, and sometimes depopulating whole villages in a night: yet amidst the fatigues of labor, and the horrors of war and bloodshed, Heaven vouchsaf'd its smiles. Behold, an extensive territory, settled, defended, and secured to his Majesty, I repeat it, *without the least expence to the mother country*, till within twenty years past!— When *Louisbourg* was reduced to his late Majesty, by the valor of his *New-England* subjects, the parliament, it must be own'd, saw meet to refund *part* of the charges: And every one knows the importance of *Louisbourg*, in the consultations of *Aix la Chapple*; but for the loss of our young men, the riches and strength of a country, not indeed slain by the enemy, but overborn by the uncommon hardships of the siege, and their confinement in garrison afterwards, there could be no recompence made.—In the late war, the *northern colonies* not only rais'd their full quota of men, but they went even beyond their ability: they are still deeply in debt, notwithstanding the parliamentary grants, annually made them, *in part* of their expences, in the common, *national, cause*: Had it not been for those grants, they had all been bankrupt long ago; while the *sugar colonies*, have born little or no share in it: They indeed sent a company or two of *Negroes* and *Molattoes*, if this be worth mentioning, to the sieges of Gaudaloupe, Martineco and the Havanna: I do not recollect any thing else that they have done; while the flower of *our* youth were annually pressed by ten thousands into the service, and there treated but little better,

as we have been told, than hewers of wood and drawers of
water. Provincial acts for impressing were obtained, only by
letters of requisition from a secretary of state to a Governor;
requiring him to use his influence to raise men; and sometimes,
more than were asked for or wanted, were pressed, to give a
figure to the Governor, and shew his influence; a remarkable
instance of which might be mentioned. I would further observe, that Great-Britain was as immediately interested in the
late war in America, as the colonies were. Was she not threatned
with an invasion at the same time we were? Has she not an
immense trade to the colonies? The British writers say, more
than half her profitable trade is to *America*: All the profits of
our trade center there, and is little enough to pay for the goods
we import. A prodigious revenue arises to the Crown on
American exports to Great-Britain, which in general is not
murmured at: No manufacture of Europe besides British, can
be lawfully bro't here; and no honest man desires they ever
should, if the laws were put in execution upon all. With regard
to a few Dutch imports that have made such a noise, the truth
is, very little has been or could be run, before the apparatus of
guardships; for the officers of some ports did their duty, while
others may have made a monopoly of smuggling, for a few of
their friends, who probably paid them large contributions; for it
has been observed, that a very small office in the customs in
America has raised a man a fortune sooner than a Government.
The truth is, the acts of trade have been too often evaded; but
by whom? Not by the American merchants in general, but by
some former custom-house officers, their friends and partizans.
I name no man, not being about to turn informer: But it has
been a notorious grievance, that when the King himself cannot
dispense with an act of parliament, there have been custom-house
officers who have practised it for years together, in favor of those
towards whom they were graciously disposed.

But to return to the subject of taxation: I find that "the
lords and commons cannot be charged with any thing for the
defence of the realm, for the safe-guard of the sea, &c. unless
by their *will* in parliament." Ld. Coke, on Magna Charta,
Cap. 30.

"Impositions neither in time of war, or other the greatest
necessity or occasion, that may be, much less in the time of

peace, neither upon foreign or inland commodities, of what nature soever, be they never so superfluous or unnecessary, neither upon merchants, strangers, nor denizens, may be laid by the King's absolute power, without assent of parliament, be it never for so short a time." Viner Prerogative of the King, Ea. 1. cites 2 Molloy. 320. Cap. 12. sec. 1.

"In the reign of Edward 3, the black Prince of Wales having *Aquitain* granted to him, did lay an imposition of fuage or focage *a foco*, upon his subjects of that dukedom, viz. a shilling for every fire, called hearth silver, which was of so great discontentment and odious to them, that it made them revolt. And nothing since this time has been imposed by pretext of any prerogative, upon merchandizes, imported into or exported out of this realm, until Queen Mary's time." 2 Inst. 61.

Nor has any thing of that kind taken place since the revolution. King Charles 1. his ship-money every one has heard of.

It may be said that these authorities will not serve the colonists, because the duties laid on them are by parliament. I acknowledge the difference of fact; but cannot see the great difference in equity, while the colonists are not represented in the house of commons: And therefore with all humble deference I apprehend, that 'till the colonists are so represented, the spirit of all these authorities will argue strongly in their favour. When the parliament shall think fit to allow the colonists a representation in the house of commons, the equity of their taxing the colonies, will be as clear as their power is at present of doing it without, if they please. When Mr. Dummer wrote his defence of the charters, there was a talk of taking them away, by act of parliament. This defence is dedicated to the right honourable the Ld. Carteret, then one of his Majesty's principal secretaries of state, since Earl of Granville. His third proposition is, that "it is not for the interest of the crown to resume the charters, if forfeited." This he proves; as also that it would be more for the interest of Great Britain to enlarge, rather than diminish, the privilege of all the colonists. His last proposition is, that it "seems inconsistent with justice to disfranchise the charter colonies by an act of parliament."

"It seems therefore, says he, a severity without a precedent, that a people, who have the misfortune of being a thousand leagues distant from their sovereign, a misfortune great enough in itself, should, unsummoned, unheard, in one day, be deprived of their valuable privileges, which they and their fathers have enjoyed for near a hundred years." 'Tis true, as he observes, "the legislative power is absolute and unaccountable, and King, lords and commons, may do what they please; but the question here is not about *power*, but *right*" (or rather equity) "and shall not the supreme judicature of all the nation do right"? "One may say, that what the parliament cannot do justly, they cannot do at all. *In maximis minima est licentia*. The higher the power is, the greater caution is to be used in the execution of it; because the sufferer is helpless and without resort." I never heard that this reasoning gave any offence. Why should it? Is it not exactly agreeable to the decisions of parliament and the determinations of the highest executive courts? (See the Appendix.) But if it was thought hard that charter privileges should be taken away by act of parliament, Is it not much harder to be in part, or in whole, disfranchised of rights, that have been always tho't inherent to a British subject, namely, to be free from all taxes, but what he consents to in person, or by his representative? This right, if it could be traced no higher than Magna Charta, is part of the common law, part of a British subjects birthright, and as inherent and perpetual, as the duty of allegiance; both which have been bro't to these colonies, and have been hitherto held sacred and inviolable, and I hope and trust ever will. 'Tis humbly conceived, that the British colonists (except only the conquered, if any) are, by Magna Charta, as well entitled to have a voice in their taxes, as the subjects within the realm. Are we not as really deprived of that right, by the parliament assessing us before we are represented in the house of commons, as if the King should do it by his prerogative? Can it be said with any colour of truth or justice, that we are represented in parliament?

As to the colonists being represented by the provincial agents, I know of no power ever given them, but to appear before his Majesty, and his ministry. Sometimes they have been directed to petition the parliament: But they none of them have, and I hope never will have, a power given them, by the colonists, to act as representatives, and to consent to taxes; and if they should make any concessions to the ministry, especially without order, the provinces could not by that be considered as represented in parliament.

Hibernia habet Parliamenta & faciunt leges et nostra statuta non ligant eos, quia non mittant milites ad Parliamentum. sed personæ eorum sunt subjecti Regis, sicut inhabitantes Calinæ Gasconiæ & Guienæ. 12 Rep. III. cites R. 3. 12.—

"Ireland hath parliaments, and make laws, and our statutes do not bind them, *because they send no Knights to parliament*; but their persons are subjects of the King, as the inhabitants of Guiene, Gascony, &c."

Yet, if specially named, or by general words included as within any of the King's dominions, Ireland, says Ld. Coke, might be bound. 4 Inst. 351.

From all which, it seems plain, that the reason why Ireland and the plantations are not bound, unless named by an Act of Parliament, is, because they are *not represented* in the British parliament. Yet, in special cases, the British parliament has an undoubted right, as well as power, to bind both by their acts. But whether this can be extended to an indefinite taxation of both, is the great question. I conceive the spirit of the British constitution must make an exception of all taxes, until it is tho't fit to unite a dominion to the realm. Such taxation must be considered either as uniting the dominions to the realm, or disfranchising them. If they are united, they will be intitled to a representation, as well as Wales; if they are so taxed without a union, or representation, they are so far disfranchised.

I don't find any thing that looks like a duty on the colonies before the 25th of C. 2. c. 7. imposing a duty on enumerated commodities. The liberty of the subject was little attended to in that reign. If the nation could not fully assert their rights till the revolution, the colonies could not expect to be heard. I look on this act rather as a precedent of power, than of right and equity; if 'tis such, it will not affect my argument. The act appointing a tax on all mariners, of a certain sum per month, to be deducted out of their wages, is not to be compared with this. Mariners are not inhabitants of any part of the dominions: The sea is their element, till they are decrepit, and then the hospital is open for all mariners who are British subjects without exception. The general post-office established thro' the dominions, is for the convenience of trade and commerce: It is not laying any burthen upon it; for besides that it is upon the whole cheaper to correspond in this way than any other, every one is at liberty to send his own letters by a friend. The act of the 6th of his late Majesty, tho' it imposes a *duty* in terms, has been said to be designed for a *prohibition*; which is probable from the sums imposed; and 'tis pity it had not been so expressed, as there is not the least doubt of the just and equitable right of the parliament to lay prohibitions thro' the dominions, when they think the good of the whole requires it. But as has been said, there is an infinite difference between that and the exercise of unlimited power of taxation, over the dominions, without allowing them a representation:—It is said that the duties imposed by the new act will amount to a prohibition: Time only can ascertain this. The utility of this act is so fully examined in the appendix, that I shall add nothing on that head here. It may be said that the colonies ought to bear their proportion of the national burdens: 'Tis just they should, and I think I have proved they have always done it freely and chearfully, and I know no reason to doubt but that they ever will.

Sometimes we have been considered only as the corporations in England: And it may be urged that it is no harder upon us to be taxed by parliament for the general cause than for them, who besides are at the expence of their corporate subordinate government.* I answer, 1. Those corporations are *represented* in parliament. 2. The colonies are and have been at great expence in raising men, building forts, and supporting the King's civil government here. Now I read of no governors and other officers of his Majesty's nomination, that the city of London taxes its inhabitants to support; I know of no forts and garrisons that the city of London has lately built at its own expence, or of any annual levies that they have raised for the King's service and the common cause. These are things very fitting and proper to be done by a subordinate dominion, and tis their duty to do all they are able; but it seems but equal they should be allowed to assess the charges of it themselves. The rules of equity and the principles of the constitution seem to require this. Those who judge of the reciprocal rights that

* See Administration of the Colonies.

subsist between a supreme and subordinate state or dominion, by no higher rules than are applied to a corporation of button-makers, will never have a very comprehensive view of them. Yet sorry am I to say it, many elaborate writers on the *administration of the colonies*, seem to me never to rise higher in their notions, than what might be expected from a secretary to one of the *quorum*. If I should be ranked among this number, I shall have this consolation, that I have fallen into what is called very good company, and among some who have seen very high life below stairs. I agree with the Administrator, that of whatever revenues raised in the colonies, if they must be raised without our consent, "*the first and special appropriation of them ought to be to the paying the Governors, and all the other Crown officers;*" for it would be hard for the Colonists to be obliged to pay them after this. It was on this principle that at the last assembly of this province, I moved to stop every grant to the officers of the Crown; more especially as I know some who have built very much upon the fine salaries they shall receive from the plantation branch of the revenue. Nor can I think it "injustice to the frame of human nature,"* to suppose, if I did not know it, that with similar views several officers of the Crown in some of the colonies have been pushing for such an act for many years. They have obtained their wish, and much good it will do them: But I would not give much for all that will center neat in the exchequer, after deducting the costs attending the execution of it, and the appropriations to the several officers proposed by the Administrator. What will be the unavoidable consequence of all this, suppose another war should happen, and it should be necessary to employ as many provincials in America as in the last? Would it be possible for the colonies, after being burthened in their trade, perhaps after it is ruined, to raise men? Is it probable that they would have spirit enough to exert themselves? If 'tis said the French will never try for America, or if they should, regular troops are only to be employed. I grant our regular troops are the best in the world, and that the experience of the present officers shews that they are capable of every species of American service; yet we should guard against the worst. If another tryal for Canada

* Adm. p. 57.

should take place, which from the known temper of France, we may judge she will bring on the first fair opportunity, it might require 30 or 40,000 regulars to secure his Majesty's just rights. If it should be said, that other American duties must then be levied, besides the impossibility of our being able to pay them, the danger recurs of a large standing army so remote from home. Whereas a good provincial militia, with such occasional succours from the mother country, as exigencies may require, never was, and never will be attended with hazard. The experience of past times will show, that an army of 20 or 30,000 veterans, half 3000 miles from *Rome*, were very apt to proclaim *Cæsars*. The first of the name, the assassin of his country owed his false glory, to stealing the affections of an army from the commonwealth. I hope these hints will not be taken amiss; they seem to occur from the nature of the subject I am upon: They are delivered in pure affection to my King and country, and amount to no reflection on any man. The best army, and the best men, we may hereafter have, may be led into temptation; all I think, is, that a prevention of evil is much easier than a deliverance from it.

The sum of my argument is, That civil government is of God: That the administrators of it were originally the whole people: That they might have devolved it on whom they pleased: That this devolution is fiduciary, for the good of the whole; That by the British constitution, this devolution is on the King, lords and commons, the supreme sacred and uncontroulable legislative power, not only in the realm, but thro' the dominions: That by the abdication, the original compact was broken to pieces: That by the revolution, it was renewed, and more firmly established, and the rights and liberties of the subject in all parts of the dominions, more fully explained and confirmed: That in consequence of this establishment, and the acts of succession and union, his Majesty GEORGE III. is rightful king and sovereign, and with his parliament, the supreme legislative of Great Britain; France and Ireland, and the dominions thereto belonging: That this constitution is the most free one, and by far the best, now existing on earth: That by this constitution, every man in the dominions is a free man: That no parts of his Majesty's dominions can be taxed without their consent: That every part has a right to be represented in

the supreme or some subordinate legislature: That the refusal
of this, would seem to be a contradiction in practice to the
theory of the constitution: That the colonies are subordinate
dominions, and are now in such a state, as to make it best for
the good of the whole, that they should not only be continued
in the enjoyment of subordinate legislation, but be also represented in some proportion to their number and estates, in the
grand legislature of the nation: That this would firmly unite all
parts of the British empire, in the greatest peace and prosperity; and render it invulnerable and perpetual.

The City of *Boston*, at their Annual Meeting in *May*, 1764, made Choice of *Richard Dana, Joseph Green, Nathaniel Bethune, John Ruddock*, Esq'rs; and Mr. *Samuel Adams*, to prepare INSTRUCTIONS for their REPRESENTATIVES.

> The following Instructions were reported by said Committee, and unanimously Voted.

> To *Royal Tyler*, James Otis, Thomas Cushing*, and *Oxenbridge Thacher*, Esq'rs.

GENTLEMEN,

YOUR being chosen by the freeholders and inhabitants of the town of *Boston*, to represent them in the General Assembly the ensuing year, affords you the strongest testimony of that confidence which they place in your integrity and capacity. By this choice they have delegated to you the power of acting in their public concerns in general, as your own Prudence shall direct you; always reserving to themselves the constitutional right of expressing their mind, and giving you such instruction upon particular matters, as they at any time shall judge proper.

We therefore your constituents take this opportunity to declare our just Expectations from you,

That you will constantly use your power and influence in maintaining the invaluable rights and privileges of the province, of which this town is so great a part: As well those rights which are derived to us by the royal charter, as those which being prior to and independent on it, we hold essentially as free-born subjects of Great-Britain;

That you will endeavour, as far as you shall be able, to preserve that independence in the house of representatives, which characterizes a free people; and the want of which may in a great measure prevent the happy effects of a free government: Cultivating as you shall have opportunity, that harmony and union

---

* Now of the honorable Board; in whose room was returned Mr. *Thomas Gray*, Merchant.

there, which is ever desirable to good men, when founded in principles of virtue and public spirit; and guarding against any undue weight which may tend to disadjust that critical balance upon which our happy constitution, and the blessings of it do depend. And for this purpose, we particularly recommend it to you to use your endeavours to have a law passed, whereby the seats of such gentlemen as shall accept of posts of profit from the Crown, or the Governor, while they are members of the house, shall be vacated, agreeable to an act of the British parliament, 'till their constituents shall have the opportunity of re-electing them, if they please, or of returning others in their room.

Being members of the legislative body, you will have a special regard to the morals of this people, which are the basis of public happiness; and endeavour to have such laws made, if any are still wanting, as shall be best adapted to secure them: And we particularly desire you carefully to look into the laws of excise, that if the virtue of the people is endangered by the multiplicity of oaths therein enjoined, or their trade and business is unreasonably impeded or embarrassed thereby, the grievance may be redressed.

As the preservation of morals, as well as property and right, so much depends upon the impartial distribution of justice, agreeable to good and wholesome law: And as the judges of the land do depend upon the free grants of the general assembly for support; it is incumbent upon you at all times to give your voice for their honourable maintenance, so long as they, having in their minds an indifference to all other affairs, shall devote themselves wholly to the duties of their own department, and the further study of the law, by which their customs, precedents, proceedings and determinations are adjusted and limited.

You will remember that this province hath been at a very great expence in carrying on the war; and that it still lies under a very grievous burden of debt: You will therefore use your utmost endeavor to promote public frugality as one means to lessen the publick debt.

You will join in any proposals which may be made for the better cultivating the lands, and improving the husbandry of the province: and as you represent a town which lives by its trade, we expect in a very particular manner, that you make it the object of your attention, to support our commerce in all its just rights, to vindicate it from all unreasonable impositions, and promote its prosperity—Our trade has for a long time laboured under great discouragements; and it is with the deepest concern that we see such further difficulties coming upon it, as will reduce it to the lowest ebb, if not totally obstruct and ruin it. We cannot help expressing our surprize that when so early notice was given by the agent, of the intentions of the ministry, to burthen us with new taxes, so little regard was had to this most interesting matter, that the court was not even call'd together to consult about it 'till the latter end of the year; the consequence of which was, that instructions could not be sent to the agent, tho' sollicited by him, 'till the evil had got beyond an easy remedy.

There is now no room for further delay: We therefore expect that you will use your earliest endeavours in the General Assembly, that such methods may be taken as will effectually prevent these proceedings against us. By a proper representation, we apprehend it may easily be made to appear that such severities will prove detrimental to Great Britain itself; upon which account we have reason to hope that an application, even for a repeal of the act, should it be already pass'd, will be successful. It is the trade of the colonies, that renders them beneficial to the mother country: Our trade, as it is now, and always has been conducted, centers in Great Britain, and in return for her manufactures, affords her more ready cash, beyond any comparison, than can possibly be expected by the most sanguine promoters of these extraordinary methods. We are in short ultimately yielding large supplies to the revenues of the mother country, while we are labouring for a very moderate subsistence for ourselves. But if our trade is to be curtail'd in its most profitable branches, and burdens beyond all possible bearing laid upon that which is suffer'd to remain, we shall be so far from being able to take off the manufactures of Great Britain, that it will be scarce possible for us to earn our bread.—

But what still heightens our apprehensions is, that these unexpected proceedings may be preparatory to new taxations upon us: For if our trade may be taxed, why not our lands? Why not the produce of our lands, and every thing we possess or make use of? This we apprehend annihilates our charter right to govern and tax ourselves—It strikes at our British privileges, which as we have never forfeited them, we hold in common with our fellow subjects who are natives of Britain: If taxes are laid upon us in any shape without our having a legal representation where they are laid, are we not reduc'd from the character of free subjects to the miserable state of tributary slaves?

We therefore earnestly recommend it to you to use your utmost endeavors, to obtain in the general assembly, all necessary instruction and advice to our agent at this most critical juncture; that while he is setting forth the unshaken loyalty of this province and this town—its unrival'd exertion in supporting his Majesty's government and rights in this part of his dominions—its acknowledg'd dependence upon and subordination to Great-Britain; and the ready submission of its merchants to all just and necessary regulations of trade; he may be able in the most humble and pressing manner to remonstrate for us all those rights and privileges which justly belong to us either by charter or birth.

As his Majesty's other northern American colonies are embark'd with us in this most important bottom, we further desire you to use your endeavors, that their weight may be added to that of this province: that by the united application of all who are aggrieved, All may happily obtain redress.

Substance of a Memorial presented the Assembly, in Pursuance of the above Instructions; and by the House voted to be transmitted to JASPER MAUDUIT, Esq; Agent for this Province; to be improved as he may judge proper.

THE publick transactions from William the I. to the revolution, may be considered as one continued struggle between the prince and the people, all tending to that happy establishment, which Great-Britain has since enjoyed.

The absolute rights of Englishmen, as frequently declared in parliament, from Magna Charta, to this time, are the rights of *personal security, personal liberty*, and of *private property*.

The allegiance of British subjects being natural, perpetual and inseparable from their persons, let them be in what country they may; their rights are also natural, inherent and perpetual.

By the laws of nature and of nations, the voice of universal reason, and of God, when a nation takes possession of a desert, uncultivated and uninhabited country, or purchases of Savages, as was the case with far the greatest part of the British settlements; the colonists transplanting themselves, and their posterity, tho' separated from the principal establishment, or mother country, naturally become part of the state with its ancient possessions, and intitled to all the essential rights of the mother country. This is not only confirmed by the practice of the antients, but by the moderns ever since the discovery of America. Frenchmen, Spaniards and Portugals are no greater slaves abroad than at home; and hitherto Britons have been as free on one side of the atlantic as on the other: And it is humbly hoped that his Majesty and the Parliament, will in their wisdom be graciously pleased to continue the colonists in this happy state.

It is presumed, that upon these principles, the colonists have been by their several charters declared natural subjects, and entrusted with the power of making *their own local laws*, not repugnant to the laws of England, and with *the power of taxing themselves.*

This legislative power is subject by the same charter to the King's negative as in Ireland. This effectually secures the *dependence* of the colonies on Great-Britain.—By the *thirteenth* of *George* the *second, chapter the seventh,* even foreigners having lived seven years in any of the colonies, are deemed natives on taking the oaths of allegiance, &c. and are declared by the said act to be his Majesty's natural born subjects of the kingdom of Great-Britain, to all intents, constructions and purposes, as if any of them had been born within the kingdom. The reasons given for this naturalization in the preamble of the act are, "that the increase of the people is the means of advancing the wealth and strength of any nation or country; and that many foreigners and strangers, from the lenity of our government, the purity of our religion, the benefit of our laws, the advantages of our trade, and the security of our *property*, might be induced to come and settle in some of his Majesty's colonies in America; if they were partakers of the advantages and priviledges, which the natural born subjects there enjoy."*

The several acts of parliament and charters declaratory of the rights and liberties of the colonies are but in affirmance of the common law, and law of nature in this point. There are says my Lord Coke, regularly three incidents to subjects born. (1.) Parents under the actual obedience of the King. (2.) That the place of his birth be within the King's dominions. (3.) The time of his birth to be chiefly considered: For he cannot be a subject born of one kingdom, that was born under the allegiance of the King of another kingdom; albeit afterwards the kingdom descends to the King of the other kingdom. See Calvin's case, and the several acts of parliament and decisions on naturalization, from Edward the third to this day. The common law is received and practiced upon here, and in the rest of the colonies; and all antient and modern acts of parliament that can be considered as part of, or in amendment of the common law, together with all such acts of parliament as expressly name the plantations; so that the power of the British parliament is held as sacred and as uncontroulable in the colonies as in England. The question is not upon the general power or right of the parliament, but whether it is not circumscribed within some equitable and reasonable bounds? 'Tis hoped it will not be considered as a new doctrine, that even the authority of the parliament of *Great-Britain* is circumscribed by certain bounds, which if exceeded their acts become those of meer *power* without *right*, and consequently void. The judges of England have declared in favour of these sentiments, when they expressly declare; that *acts of parliament against natural equity are void.* That *acts against the fundamental principles of the British constitution are void.*† This doctrine is agreable to

---

* 13 G. 2. C. 7.

† "A very important question here presents itself. It essentially belongs to the society to make laws both in relation to the manner in which it desires to be governed, and to the conduct of the citizens: This is called the *Legislative Power.* The nation may entrust the exercise of it to the Prince, or to an assembly; or to the assembly and the Prince jointly; who have then a right of making new, and abrogating old laws. It is here demanded whether, if their power extends so far as to the fundamental laws, they may change the constitution of

the law of nature and nations, and to the divine dictates of natural and revealed religion. It is contrary to reason that the supreme power should have right to alter the constitution. This would imply that those who are instructed with Sovereignty by the people, have a right to do as they please. In other

the state? The principles we have laid down lead us to decide this point with certainty, that the authority of these legislators does not extend so far, and that they ought to consider the fundamental laws as sacred, if the nation has not in very express terms given them the power to change them. For the constitution of the state ought to be fixed; and since that was first established by the nation, which afterwards trusted certain persons with the legislative power, the fundamental laws are excepted from their commission. It appears that the society had only resolved to make provision for the state's being always furnished with laws suited to particular conjunctures, and gave the legislature for that purpose, the power of abrogating the ancient civil and political laws, that were not fundamental, and of making new ones: But nothing leads us to think that it was willing to submit the constitution itself to their pleasure.

When a nation takes possession of a distant country, and settles a colony there, that country though separated from the principal establishment, or mother country, naturally becomes a part of the state, equally with its ancient possessions. Whenever the political laws, or treaties make no distinction between them, every thing said of the territory of a nation, ought also to extend to its colonies." D' Vattel.

"An act of parliament made against natural equity, as to make a man judge in his own cause, would be void; For *jura naturæ sunt immutabilia*. Hob 87. Trin. 12. Jac. Day v. Savage S. C. and P. cited Arg. 10. Mod. 115. Hill. 11 Ann. C. B. in the case of Thornby and Fleetwood, "but says, that this must be a clear case, and judges will strain hard rather than interpret an act void, ab initio." *This is granted, but still their authority is not boundless, if subject to the controul of the judges in any case.*

"Holt. Chief Justice thought what Lord Coke says in Doctor Bonham's case a very reasonable and true saying, that if an act of parliament should ordain that the same person should be both party and judge in his own cause, it would be a void act of parliament, and an act of parliament can do no wrong, tho' it may do several things that look pretty odd; for it may discharge one from the allegiance he lives under, and restore to the state of nature; but it cannot make one that lives under a government both judge and party: per Holt. C. J. 12 Mod. 687, 688, Hill. 13 W. 3. B. R. in the case of the city of London v. Wood—It appears in our books, that in several cases the common law shall controul acts of parliament, and sometimes adjudge them to be utterly void; for when an act of parliament is against common *right* and *reason*, or repugnant or impossible to be performed, the common law shall controul it, and adjudge it to be void, and therefore 8 E. 3 30. Thomas Tregor's case upon the statute of W. 2. Cap 38 and Art. Sup. Chart 9. Herle said that sometimes statutes are made contrary to law and right, which the makers of them perceiving will not put them in execution 8 Rep 118 Hill. 7. J. Dr. Bonham's case.

words, that those who are invested with power to protect the people, and support their rights and liberties, have a right to make slaves of them. This is not very remote from a flat contradiction. Should the parliament of Great-Britain follow the example of some other foreign states,* and vote the King absolute and despotic; would such an act of parliament make him so? Would any minister in his senses advise a Prince to accept of such an offer of power? It would be unsafe to accept of such a donation, because the parliament or donors would grant more than was ever in their power lawfully to give. The law of nature never invested them with a power of surrendering their own liberty; and the people certainly never intrusted any body of men with a power to surrender theirs in exchange for slavery.†

* Sweden, Denmark, France, &c.

† "But if the whole state be conquered, if the nation be subdued, in what manner can the victor treat it without transgressing the bounds of justice? What are his rights over the conquest? Some have dared to advance this monstrous principle, that the conqueror is absolute master of his conquest; that he may dispose of it as his property, treat it as he pleases, according to the common expression of *treating a state as a conquered country*; and hence they derive one of the sources of despotic government: But enough of those that reduce men to the state of transferable goods, or use them like beasts of burden, who deliver them up as the property or patrimony of another man. Let us argue on principles countenanced by reason and becoming humanity. The whole right of the conqueror proceeds from the just defence of himself, which contains the support and prosecution of his rights. Thus when he has totally subdued a nation with whom he had been at war, he may without dispute cause justice to be done him, with regard to what gave rise to the war, and require payment for the expence and damage he has sustained; he may according to the exigency of the case impose penalties on it as an example, he may should prudence so dictate disable it from undertaking any pernicious designs for the future. But in securing all these views the mildest means are to be preferred. We are always to remember, that the law of nature permits no injury to be done to an enemy, unless in taking measures necessary for a just defence, and a reasonable security. Some princes have only imposed a tribute on it; others have been satisfied of stripping it of some privileges, dismembring a province, or keeping it in awe by fortresses; others as their quarrel was only with the sovereign in person, have left a nation in the full enjoyment of all its rights, only setting a sovereign over it. But if the conqueror thinks proper to retain the sovereignty of the vanquished state, and has such a right; the manner in which he is to treat the state still flows from the same principles. If the sovereign be only the just object of his complaint, reason declares that by his conquest he acquires only such rights as actually belonged to the dethroned sovereign,

It is now near three hundred years since the continent of North-America was first discovered, and that by British subjects.* Ten generations have passed away thro' infinite toils and bloody conflicts in settling this country. None of those ever dreamed but that they were intitled, at least, to equal priviledges with those of the same rank born within the realm.

British America has been hitherto distinguished from the slavish colonies around about it, as the fortunate Britons have been from most of their neighbours on the continent of Europe. It is for the interest of Great-Britain that her colonies should be ever thus distinguished. Every man must wilfully blind himself that don't see the immense value of our acquisitions in the late war; and that tho' we did not retain all at the conclusion of the peace that we obtained by the sword; yet our gracious Sovereign, at the same time that he has given a divine lesson of equitable moderation to the Princes of the earth, has retained sufficient to make the British arms the dread of the universe, and his name dear to all posterity.

To the freedom of the British constitution, and to their increase of commerce, 'tis owing that our colonies have flourished without diminishing the inhabitants of the mother country; quite contrary to the effects of plantations made by most other nations, which have suffered at home, in order to aggrandize themselves abroad. This is remarkably the case with Spain. The subjects of a free and happy constitution of government, have a thousand advantages to colonize above those who live under despotic princes. We see how the British colonies on the continent, have out-grown those of the French, notwithstanding they have ever engaged the Salvages to keep us back. Their advantages over us in the West-Indies are, among other causes perhaps, partly owing to these, (1.) A capital neglect in former reigns, in suffering them to have a firm possession of so many valuable islands, that we had a better title

---

and on the submission of his people he is to govern it according to the laws of the state. If the people do not voluntarily submit, the state of war subsists." "When a sovereign as pretending to have the absolute disposal of a people whom he has conquered, is for inslaving them, he causes the state of war to subsist between this people & him." Mr. De Vattel. B. 3. C. 10. sec. 201.

* The Cabots discovered the Continent before the Spaniards.

to than they. (2.) The French unable to push their settlements effectually on the continent, have bent their views to the islands, and poured vast numbers into them. (3.) The climate and business of these islands is by nature much better adapted to Frenchmen and to Negroes, than to Britons. (4.) The labour of slaves, black or white, will be ever cheaper than that of freemen, because that of the individuals among the former, will never be worth so much as with the latter; but this difference is more than supplied; by numbers under the advantages abovementioned. The French will ever be able to sell their West-India produce cheaper than our own islanders; and yet while our own islanders can have such a price for theirs, as to grow much richer than the French, or any other of the King's subjects in America, as is the case, and what the northern colonies take from the French, and other foreign islands, centers finally in returns to Great-Britain for her manufactures, to an immense value, and with a vast profit to her: It is contrary to the first principles of policy to clog such a trade with duties, much more to prohibit it, to the risque if not certain destruction of the fishery. It is allowed by the most accurate British writers on commerce, Mr. Postlethwait in particular, who seems to favour the cause of the sugar islands, that one half of the immense commerce of Great-Britain is with her colonies. It is very certain that without the fishery seven eights of this commerce would cease. The fishery is the center of motion, upon which the wheel of all the British commerce in America turns. Without the American trade, would Britain, as a commercial state, make any great figure at this day in Europe? Her trade in woolen and other manufactures, is said to be lessening in all parts of the world, but America, where it is increasing, and capable of infinite increase, from a concurrence of every circumstance in its favour. Here is an extensive territory of different climates, which in time will consume, and be able to pay for as many manufactures as Great-Britain and Ireland can make, if true maxims are persued. The French for reasons already mentioned, can underwork, and consequently undersell the English manufactures of Great-Britain in every market in Europe. But they can send none of their manufactures here; and it is the wish of every honest British American that they never may; 'tis best they never should; we can do better without the manufactures of Europe, save those of Great-Britain, than with them: But without the French West-India produce we cannot; without it our fishery must infallibly be ruined. When that is gone our own islands will very poorly subsist. No British manufactures can be paid for by the colonists. What will follow? One of these two things, both of which it is the interest of Great-Britain to prevent. (1.) The northern colonists must be content to go naked, and turn Savages. Or (2.) Become manufacturers of linnen and woolen, to cloath themselves; which if they cannot carry to the perfection of Europe, will be very destructive to the interests of Great-Britain. The computation has been made, and that within bounds, and it can be demonstrated, that if North-America is only driven to the fatal necessity of manufacturing a suit of the most ordinary linnen or woolen for each inhabitant annually, which may be soon done, when necessity the mother of invention shall operate, Great-Britain & Ireland will loose two millions per annum, besides a diminution of the revenue to nearly the same amount. This may appear paradoxical, but a few years experience of the execution of the sugar act, will sufficiently convince the parliament not only of the inutility, but destructive tendency of it, while calculations may be little attended to. That the trade with the colonies has been of surprizing advantage to Great-Britain, notwithstanding the want of a good regulation is past all doubt. Great-Britain is well known to have increased prodigiously both in numbers and in wealth since she began to colonize. To the growth of the plantations Britain is in a great measure indebted for her present riches and strength. As the wild wastes of America have been turned into pleasant habitations, and flourishing trading towns; so many of the little villages and obscure boroughs in Great-Britain have put on a new face, and suddenly started up, and become fair markets, and manufacturing towns, and opulent cities. London itself, which bids fair to be the metropolis of the world, is five times more populous than it was in the days of Queen Elizabeth. Such are the fruits of the spirit of commerce and liberty. Hence it is manifest how much we all owe to that beautiful form of civil government, under which we have the happiness to live.

It is evidently the interest, and ought to be the care of all those intrusted with the administration of government, to see that every part of the British empire enjoys to the full the rights they are intitled to by the laws, and the advantages which result from their being maintained with impartiality and vigour. This we have seen reduced to practice in the present and preceeding reigns; and have the highest reason from the paternal care and goodness that his Majesty, and the British Parliament, have hitherto been graciously pleased to discover to all his Majesty's dutiful and loyal subjects, and to the colonists in particular, to rest satisfied, that our priviledges will remain sacred and inviolate. The connection between Great-Britain and her colonies is so natural and strong, as to make their mutual happiness depend upon their mutual support. Nothing can tend more to the destruction of both, and to forward the measures of their enemies, than sowing the seeds of jealousy, animosity and dissention between the mother country and the colonies.

A conviction of the truth and importance of these principles, induced Great-Britain during the late war, to carry on so many glorious enterprizes for the defence of the colonies; and those on their part to exert themselves beyond their ability to pay, as is evident from the parliamentary reimbursements.

If the spirit of commerce was attended to, perhaps, duties would be every where decreased, if not annihilated, and prohibitions multiplied. Every branch of trade that hurts a community, should be prohibited for the same reason that a private gentleman would break off commerce with a sharper or an extorsive usurer. 'Tis to no purpose to higgle with such people, you are sure to loose by them. 'Tis exactly so with a nation, if the balance is against them, and they can possibly subsist without the commodity, as they generally can in such cases, a prohibition is the only remedy; for a duty in such case, is like a composition with a thief, that for five shillings in the pound returned, he shall rob you at pleasure; when if the thing is examined to the bottom, you are at five shillings expence in travelling to get back your five shillings, and he is at the same expence in coming to pay it, so he robs you of but ten shillings in the pound, that you thus wisely compound for. To apply this to trade, I believe every duty that was ever imposed on commerce, or in the nature of things can be, will be found to be divided between the state imposing the duty, and the country exported from. This if between the several parts of the same kingdom or dominions of the same Prince, can only tend to embarrass trade, and raise the price of labour above other states, which is of very pernicious consequence to the husbandman, manufacturer, mariner and merchant, the four tribes that support the whole hive. If your duty is upon a commodity of a foreign state, it is either upon the whole useful and gainful, and therefore necessary for the husbandmen, manufacturer, mariner or merchant, as finally bringing a profit to the state by a balance in her favour; or the importation will work a balance against your state. There is no medium that we know of.—If the commodity is of the former kind, it should be prohibited; but if the latter, imported duty free, unless you would raise the price of labour by a duty on necessaries, or make the above wise composition for the importation of commodities you are sure to lose by. The only test of a useful commodity is the gain upon the whole to the state; such should be free; the only test of a pernicious trade is the loss upon the whole, or to the community, this should be prohibited. If therefore it can be demonstrated that the sugar and molasses trade from the northern colonies to the foreign plantations is upon the *whole* a loss to the *community*, by which term is here meant the three kingdoms and the British dominions taken collectively, then and not 'till then should this trade be prohibited. This never has been proved, nor can be; the contrary being certain, to wit, that the nation upon the whole hath been a vast gainer by this trade, in the vend of and pay for its manufactures; and a great loss by a duty upon this trade will finally fall on the British husbandman, manufacturer, mariner & merchant, and consequently the trade of the nation be wounded, and in constant danger of being eat out by those who can undersell her.

The art of underselling, or rather of finding means to undersell, is the grand secret of thrift among commercial states, as well as among individuals of the same state. Should the British sugar islands ever be able to supply Great-Britain and her northern colonies with those articles, it will be time enough to think of a total prohibition; but until that time, both prohibition and duty will be found to be diametrically opposite to the first principles of policy. Such is the extent of this continent, and the increase of its inhabitants, that if every inch of the

British sugar islands was as well cultivated as any part of Jamaica, or Barbadoes, they would not now be able to supply Great-Britain, and the colonies on this continent. But before such further improvements can be supposed to take place in our islands, the demands will be proportionably increased by the increase of the inhabitants on the continent. Hence the reason is plain why the British sugar planters are growing rich, and ever will, because the demand for their produce has and ever will be greater than they can possibly supply, so long as the English hold this continent, and are unrivalled in the fishery.

We have every thing good and great to hope from our gracious Sovereign, his Ministry and his Parliament; and trust that when the services and sufferings of the British American colonies are fully known to the mother country, and the nature and importance of the plantation trade more perfectly understood at home, that the most effectual measures will be taken for perpetuating the British empire in all parts of the world. An empire built upon the principles of justice, moderation and equity, the only principles that can make a state flourishing, and enable it to elude the machinations of its secret and inveterate enemies.

P. S. By ancient and modern gods, p. 51, I mean, all idols, from those of Old Egypt, to the canonized monsters of modern Rome; and by king-craft and priest-craft, civil and ecclesiastic polity, as administred in general till the revolution. I now recollect that I have been credibly informed that the British Sugar colonists are humane towards their slaves, in comparison with the others. Therefore in page 70, let it be read, foreign Sugar-Islanders and foreign Creoles.

FINIS.

[Stephen Hopkins], The Rights of Colonies Examined. Providence, 1765.

Resistance to imperial reforms emerged early and with special intensity in Rhode Island, a colony notorious for its rampant smuggling and extremely democratic or, in the parlance of the day, popular character. With Rhode Island's governor and council being elected annually and the Assembly elected twice a year, the colony was continually racked by something resembling modern party politics. For decades two rival factions vied for control of the government, using every weapon they could, including bribery, name-calling, party trickery, and corruption. So commercially minded were the colony's farmers that between 1710 and 1751 they had pressured the Assembly to pass no less than nine paper money emissions, precipitating Parliament's intervention with the Currency Act of 1751 that forbade the New England colonies from making paper money legal tender. And so jealous of one another were Rhode Islanders that their capital had to be rotated among five different towns.

Stephen Hopkins, governor of Rhode Island and leader of the colony's more popular faction, wrote this pamphlet in November 1764 and published it shortly thereafter with the endorsement of the colony's Assembly. Although Hopkins had no formal schooling, he was a voracious reader, something he was eager to display in his pamphlet. Lacking Otis's sophistication and learning, Hopkins set forth his opposition to the Sugar Act, the new trade regulations, and the possibility of a stamp tax (which had been announced in the text of the Sugar Act) in a much more blunt manner than Otis. Nevertheless, his pamphlet had its own ambiguities. Hopkins admitted that the colonies were dependent on Great Britain, and that it was "the indispensable duty of every good and loyal subject, chearfully to obey" the laws of Parliament. Yet at the same time he insisted that Parliament's taxing of the colonies would be tantamount to turning the Americans into slaves. But what else Parliament could do in dealing with the local affairs of dependent colonies Hopkins left open and unresolved. It never occurred to him, as it had to Otis, that Parliament could be considered to be a court that would correct its own errors. Raising the possibility of colonial representation in Parliament, Hopkins sidestepped that problem, and instead suggested that Americans might simply be kept informed in some way or another about Parliament's intentions toward America. Hopkins's pamphlet was primitive and tentative in many respects, but he was not alone in his uncertainties. Few Americans as yet saw with any clarity how the authority between the colonies and the mother country might be divided.

THE

RIGHTS

OF

COLONIES

EXAMINED.

Published by Authority.

PROVIDENCE:

PRINTED BY *WILLIAM GODDARD*.

M.DCC.LXV.

The Rights of Colonies Examined.

Mid the low murmurs of submissive fear
And mingled rage, my Hambden *rais'd his voice,*
And to the laws appeal'd;——

THOMPSON'S Liberty.

LIBERTY is the greatest blessing that men enjoy, and slavery the heaviest curse that human nature is capable of.—This being so, makes it a matter of the utmost importance to men, which of the two shall be their portion. Absolute Liberty is, perhaps, incompatible with any kind of government.—The safety resulting from society, and the advantage of just and equal laws, hath caused men to forego some part of their natural liberty, and submit to government. This appears to be the most rational account of it's beginning; although, it must be confessed, mankind have by no means been agreed about it: Some have found it's origin in the divine appointment: Others have thought it took it's rise from power: Enthusiasts have dreamed that dominion was founded in grace. Leaving these points to be settled by the descendants of *Filmer, Cromwell,* and *Venner*, we will consider the *British* constitution, as it at present stands, on revolution principles; and from thence endeavour to find the measure of the magistrate's power, and the people's obedience.

This glorious constitution, the best that ever existed among men, will be confessed by all, to be founded by compact, and established by consent of the people. By this most beneficent compact, *British* subjects are to be governed only agreeable to laws to which themselves have some way consented, and are not to be compelled to part with their property, but as it is called for by the authority of such laws: The former is truly liberty; the latter is really to be possessed of property, and to have something that may be called one's own.

On the contrary, those who are governed at the will of another, or of others, and whose property may be taken from them by taxes, or otherwise, without their own consent, and against their will, are in the miserable condition of slaves: "For liberty solely consists in an independancy upon the will of another; and by the name of slave, we understand a man who can neither dispose of his person or goods, but enjoys all at the will of his master;" says *Sidney* on government. These things premised; whether the *British American* colonies on the continent, are justly intituled to like privileges and freedom as their fellow-subjects in *Great-Britain* are, shall be the chief point examined. In discussing this question, we shall make the colonies in *New-England*, with whose rights we are best acquainted, the rule of our reasoning; not in the least doubting but all the others are justly intituled to like rights with them.

New-England was first planted by adventurers, who left *England*, their native country, by permission of King CHARLES the first; and, at their own expence, transported themselves to *America*, with great risque and difficulty settled among savages, and in a very surprising manner formed new colonies in the wilderness. Before their departure, the terms of their freedom, and the relation they should stand in to the mother country, in their emigrant state, were fully settled; they were to remain subject to the King, and dependant on the kingdom of *Great-Britain*. In return, they were to receive protection, and enjoy all the rights and privileges of free-born *Englishmen*.

This is abundantly proved by the charter given to the *Massachusetts* colony, while they were still in *England*, and which they received and brought over with them, as the authentic evidence of the conditions they removed upon. The colonies of *Connecticut* and *Rhode-Island* also, afterwards obtained charters from the crown, granting them the like ample privileges. By all these charters, it is in the most express and solemn manner granted, that these adventurers, and their children after them forever, should have and enjoy all the freedom and liberty that the subjects in *England* enjoy: That they might make laws for their own government, suitable to their circumstances; not repugnant to, but as near as might be, agreeable to the laws of *England*: That they might purchase lands, acquire goods, and use trade for their advantage, and have an absolute property in whatever they justly acquired. These, with many other gracious privileges, were granted them by several kings; and they were to pay as an acknowledgement to the crown, only one fifth part of the ore of gold and silver, that should at any time be found in the said colonies, in lieu of, and full satisfaction for, all dues and demands of the crown and kingdom of *England* upon them.

There is not any thing new or extraordinary in these rights granted to the *British* colonies:—The colonies from all countries, at all times, have enjoyed equal freedom with the mother state. Indeed, there would be found very few people in the world, willing to leave their native country, and go through the fatigue and hardship of planting in a new uncultivated one, for the sake of losing their freedom. They who settle new countries must be poor; and, in course, ought to be free. Advantages, pecuniary or agreeable, are not on the side of emigrants, and surely they must have something in their stead.

To illustrate this, permit us to examine what hath generally been the condition of colonies with respect to their freedom; we will begin with those who went out from the ancient common-wealths of *Greece*, which are the first, perhaps, we have any good account of. *Thucidides*, that grave and judicious historian, says of one of them, "they were not sent out to be slaves, but to be the equals of those who remain behind;" and again, the *Corinthians* gave public notice, "that a new colony was going to *Epidamnus*, into which all that would enter, should have equal and like privileges with those who staid at home." This was uniformly the condition of all the *Grecian* colonies; they went out and settled new countries; they took such forms of government as themselves chose, though it generally nearly resembled that of the mother state, whether democratical or oligarchical. 'Tis true, they were fond to acknowledge their original, and always confessed themselves under obligation to pay a kind of honorary respect to, and shew a filial dependance on, the common-wealth from whence they sprung. *Thucidides* again tells us, that the *Corinthians* complained of the *Corcyreans*, "from whom, though a colony of their own, they had received some contemptuous treatment: for they neither payed them the usual honor on their public solemnities, nor began with a *Corinthian* in the distribution of the sacrifices, which is always done by other colonies." From hence it is plain what kind of dependance the *Greek* colonies were under, and what sort of acknowledgment they owed to the mother state.

If we pass from the *Grecian* to the *Roman* colonies, we shall find them not less free: But this difference may be observed between them, that the *Roman* colonies did not, like the *Grecian*, become separate states, governed by different laws, but always remained a part of the mother state; and all that were free of the colonies, were also free of *Rome*, and had right to an equal suffrage in making all laws, and appointing all officers for the government of the whole common-wealth. For the truth of this, we have the testimony of St. *Paul*, who though born at *Tarsus*, yet assures us he was born free of *Rome*. And *Grotius* gives us the opinion of a *Roman* king, concerning the freedom of colonies: King *Tullius* says, "for our part, we look upon it to be neither truth nor justice, that mother cities ought of necessity and by the law of nature, to rule over their colonies."

When we come down to the latter ages of the world, and consider the colonies planted in the three last centuries, in *America*, from several kingdoms in *Europe*, we shall find them, says *Puffendorf*, very different from the ancient colonies, and gives us an instance in those of the *Spaniards*. Although it be confessed these fall greatly short of enjoying equal freedom with the ancient *Greek* and *Roman* ones; yet it will be said truly, they enjoy equal freedom with their countrymen in *Spain*: but as they are all under the government of an absolute monarch, they have no reason to complain that one enjoys the liberty the other is deprived of. The *French* colonies will be found nearly in the same condition, and for the same reason, because their fellow-subjects in *France* have also lost their liberty. And the question here is not whether all colonies, as compared one with another, enjoy equal liberty, but whether all enjoy as much freedom as the inhabitants of the mother state; and this will hardly be denied in the case of the *Spanish*, *French*, or other modern foreign colonies.

By this it fully appears, that colonies in general, both ancient and modern, have always enjoyed as much freedom as the mother state from which they went out: And will any one suppose the *British* colonies in *America*, are an exception to this general rule? Colonies that came out from a kingdom renowned for liberty; from a constitution founded on compact; from a people, of all the sons of men, the most tenacious of freedom; who left the delights of their native country, parted from their homes, and all their conveniencies, searched out and subdued a foreign country with the most amazing travail and fortitude, to the infinite advantage and emolument of the mother state; that removed on a firm reliance of a solemn compact, and royal promise and grant, that they, and their successors forever, should be free; should be partakers and sharers in all the privileges and advantages of the then *English*, now *British* constitution.

If it were possible a doubt could yet remain, in the most unbelieving mind, that these *British* colonies are not every way justly and fully intituled to equal liberty and freedom with their fellow-subjects in *Europe*, we might shew, that the parliament of *Great-Britain*, have always understood their rights in the same light.

By an act passed in the thirteenth year of the reign of his late majesty King GEORGE the second, intituled an act for naturalizing foreign protestants, *&c.* and by another act, passed in the twentieth year of the same reign, for nearly the same purposes, by both which it is enacted and ordained, "that all foreign protestants, who had inhabited, and resided for the space of seven years, or more, in any of his majesty's colonies in *America*," might, on the conditions therein-mentioned, be naturalized, and thereupon should "be deemed, adjudged and taken to be his majesty's natural born subjects of the kingdom of *Great-Britain*, to all intents, constructions, and purposes, as if they, and every one of them, had been, or were born within the same." No reasonable man will here suppose the parliament intended by these acts to put foreigners, who had been in the colonies only seven years, in a better condition than those who had been born in them, or had removed from *Britain* thither, but only to put these foreigners on an equality with them; and to do this, they are obliged to give them all the rights of natural born subjects of *Great-Britain*.

From what hath been shewn, it will appear beyond a doubt, that the *British* subjects in *America*, have equal rights with those in *Britain*; that they do not hold those rights as a privilege granted them, nor enjoy them as a grace and favor bestowed; but possess them as an inherent indefeasible right; as they, and their ancestors, were free-born subjects, justly and naturally intituled to all the rights and advantages of the *British* constitution.

And the *British* legislative and executive powers have considered the colonies as possessed of these rights, and have always heretofore, in the most tender and parental manner, treated them as their dependant, though free, condition required. The protection promised on the part of the crown, with chearfulness and great gratitude we acknowlege, hath at all times been given to the colonies. The dependance of the colonies to *Great-Britain* hath been fully testified by a constant and ready obedience to all the commands of his present Majesty, and his royal predecessors; both men and money having been raised in them at all times when called for, with as much alacrity and in as large proportions as hath been done in *Great-Britain*, the ability of each considered. It must also be confessed with thankfulness, that the first adventurers and their successors, for one hundred and thirty years, have fully enjoyed all the freedoms and immunities promised on their first removal from *England*.—But here the scene seems to be unhappily changing: —The *British* ministry, whether induced by a jealousy of the colonies, by false informations, or by some alteration in the system of political government, we have no information; whatever hath been the motive, this we are sure of, the parliament in their last session, passed an act, limitting, restricting, and burdening the trade of these colonies, much more than had ever been done before; as also for greatly enlarging the power and jurisdiction of the courts of admiralty in the colonies; and also came to a resolution, that it might be necessary to establish stamp duties, and other internal taxes, to be collected within them. This act and this resolution have caused great uneasiness and consternation among the *British* subjects on the continent of *America*: how much reason there is for it, we will endeavour, in the most modest and plain manner we can, to lay before our readers.

In the first place, let it be considered, that although each of the colonies hath a legislature within itself, to take care of it's interests, and provide for it's peace and internal government, yet there are many things of a more general nature, quite out of the reach of these particular legislatures, which it is necessary should be regulated, ordered and governed. One of this kind is, the commerce of the whole *British* empire, taken collectively, and that of each kingdom and colony in it, as it makes a part of that whole: Indeed, every thing that concerns the proper interest and fit government of the whole common-wealth, of keeping the peace, and subordination of all the parts towards the whole, and one among another, must be considered in this light: Amongst these general concerns, perhaps, money and paper credit, those grand instruments of all commerce, will be found also to have a place. These, with all other matters of a general nature, it is absolutely necessary should have a general power to direct them; some supreme and over-ruling authority, with power to make laws, and form regulations for the good of all, and to compel their execution and observation. It being necessary some such general power should exist somewhere, every man of the least knowledge of the *British* constitution, will be naturally led to look for, and find it in the parliament of *Great-Britain*; that grand and august legislative body, must from the nature of their authority, and the necessity of the thing, be justly vested with this power. Hence, it becomes the indispensable duty of every good and loyal subject, chearfully to obey and patiently submit to all the acts, laws, orders and regulations that may be made and passed by parliament, for directing and governing all these general matters.

Here it may be urged by many, and indeed, with great appearance of reason, that the equity, justice, and beneficence of the *British* constitution, will require, that the separate kingdoms and distant colonies, who are to obey and be governed by these general laws and regulations, ought to be represented, some way or other, in parliament; at least whilst these general matters are under consideration. Whether the colonies will ever be admitted to have representatives in parliament,— whether it be consistent with their distant and dependant state,—and whether if it were admitted, it would be to their advantage,—are questions we will pass by; and observe, that these colonies ought in justice, and for the very evident good of the whole common-wealth, to have notice of every new measure about to be pursued, and new act that is about to be passed, by which their rights, liberties, or interests will be affected: They ought to have such notice, that they may appear and be heard by their agents, by council, or written representation, or by some other equitable and effectual way.

The colonies are at so great a distance from *England*, that the members of parliament can, generally, have but little knowledge of their business, connections and interest, but what is gained from people who have been there; the most of these, have so slight a knowledge themselves, that the informations they can give, are very little to be depended on, though they may pretend to determine with confidence, on matters far above their reach. All such kind of informations are too uncertain to be depended on, in the transacting business of so much consequence, and in which the interests of two millions of free people are so deeply concerned. There is no kind of inconveniency, or mischief, can arise from the colonies having such notice, and being heard in the manner above-mentioned: But, on the contrary, very great mischiefs have already happened to the colonies, and always must be expected, if they are not heard, before things of such importance are determined concerning them.

Had the colonies been fully heard, before the late act had been passed, no reasonable man can suppose it ever would have passed at all, in the manner it now stands; for what good reason can possibly be given for making a law to cramp the trade and ruin the interests of many of the colonies, and at the same time, lessen in a prodigious manner the consumption of the *British* manufactures in them? These are certainly the effects this act must produce; a duty of three pence *per* gallon on foreign melasses, is well known to every man in the least acquainted with it, to be much higher than that article can possibly bear; and therefore must operate as an absolute prohibition. This will put a total stop to our exportation of lumber, horses, flour, and fish, to the *French* and *Dutch* sugar colonies; and if any one supposes we may find a sufficient vent for these articles in the *English* islands in the *West-Indies*, he only verifies what was just now observed, that he wants truer information. Putting an end to the importation of foreign melasses, at the same time puts an end to all the costly distilleries in these colonies, and to the rum trade to the coast of *Africa*, and throws it into the hands of the *French*. With the loss of the foreign melasses trade, the codfishery of the *English*, in *America*, must also be lost, and thrown also into the hands of the *French*. That this is the real state of the whole business, is not fancy; this, nor any part of it, is not exaggeration, but a sober and most melancholy truth.

View this duty of three pence *per* gallon, on foreign melasses, not in the light of a prohibition, but supposing the trade to continue, and the duty to be paid. Heretofore there hath been imported into the colony of *Rhode-Island* only, about one million one hundred and fifty thousand gallons, annually; the duty on this quantity is fourteen thousand three hundred and seventy-five pounds, sterling, to be paid yearly by this little colony; a larger sum than was ever in it at any one time: This money is to be sent away, and never to return; yet the payment is to be repeated every year.—Can this possibly be done? Can a new colony, compelled by necessity to purchase all it's cloathing, furniture, and utensils from *England*, to support the expences of it's own internal government, obliged by it's duty to comply with every call from the crown to raise money on emergencies; after all this, can every man in it pay twenty-four shillings sterling a year, for the duties of a single article only? There is surely no man in his right mind believes this possible. The charging foreign melasses with this high duty, will not affect all the colonies equally, nor any other near so much as this of *Rhode-Island*, whose trade depended much more on foreign melasses, and on distilleries, than that of any others; this must shew that raising money for the general service of the crown, or of the colonies, by such a duty, will be extremely unequal, and therefore unjust. And now taking either alternative; by supposing on one hand, the foreign melasses trade is stopped, and with it the opportunity or ability of the colonies to get money, or on the other, that this trade is continued, and that the colonies get money by it, but all their money is taken from them by paying the duty; can *Britain* be gainer by either? Is it not the chiefest interest of *Britain*, to dispose of and to be paid for her own manufactures? And doth she not find the greatest and best market for them in her own colonies? Will she find an advantage in disabling the colonies to continue their trade with her? Or can she possibly grow rich by their being made poor?

Ministers have great influence, and parliaments have great power;—can either of them change the nature of things, stop all our means of getting money, and yet expect us to purchase and pay for *British* manufactures? The genius of the people in these colonies, is as little turned to manufacturing goods for their own use, as is possible to suppose in any people whatsoever; yet necessity will compel them, either to go naked in this cold country, or to make themselves some sort of cloathing, if it be only of the skins of beasts.

By the same act of parliament, the exportation of all kinds of timber, or lumber, the most natural produce of these new colonies, is greatly incumbered and uselessly embarrassed, and the shipping it to any part of *Europe*, except *Great-Britain*, prohibited: This must greatly affect the linen manufactory in *Ireland*, as that kingdom used to receive great quantities of flax-seed from *America*, many cargoes, being made of that and of barrel staves, were sent thither every year; but, as the staves can no longer be exported thither, the ships carrying only flax-seed casks, without the staves, which used to be intermixed among them, must lose one half of their freight, which will prevent their continuing this trade, to the great injury of *Ireland*, and of the plantations: And what advantage is to accrue to *Great-Britain* by it, must be told by those who can perceive the utility of this measure.

Enlarging the power and jurisdiction of the courts of vice-admiralty in the colonies, is another part of the same act, greatly and justly complained of. Courts of admiralty have long been established in most of the colonies, whose authority were circumscribed within moderate territorial jurisdictions; and these courts have always done the business, necessary to be brought before such courts for trial, in the manner it ought to be done, and in a way only moderately expensive to the subjects; and if seizures were made, or informations exhibited, without reason, or contrary to law, the informer, or seizor, was left to the justice of the common law, there to pay for his folly, or suffer for his temerity. But now this course is quite altered, and a custom-house officer may make a seizure in *Georgia*, of goods ever so legally imported, and carry the trial to *Halifax*, at fifteen hundred miles distance; and thither the owner must follow him to defend his property; and when he comes there, quite beyond the circle of his friends, acquaintance, and correspondents, among total strangers, he must there give bond, and must find sureties to be bound with him in a large sum, before he shall be admitted to claim his own goods; when this is complied with, he hath a trial, and his goods acquitted. If the judge can be prevailed on, (which it is very well known may too easily be done) to certify, there was *only* probable cause for making the seizure, the unhappy owner shall not maintain any action against the illegal seizor, for damages, or obtain any other satisfaction; but he may return to *Georgia* quite ruined, and undone in conformity to an act of parliament. Such unbounded encouragement and protection given to informers, must call to every one's remembrance *Tacitus*'s account of the miserable condition of the *Romans*, in the reign of *Tiberius* their emperor, who let loose and encouraged the informers of that age. Surely if the colonies had been fully heard, before this had been done, the liberties and properties of the *Americans* would not have been so much disregarded.

The resolution of the house of commons, come into during the same session of parliament, asserting their rights to establish stamp duties, and internal taxes, to be collected in the colonies without their own consent, hath much more, and for much more reason, alarmed the *British* subjects in *America*, than any thing that had ever been done before. These resolutions, carried into execution, the colonies cannot help but consider as a manifest violation of their just and long enjoyed rights. For it must be confessed by all men, that they who are taxed at pleasure by others, cannot possibly have any property, can have nothing to be called their own; they who have no property, can have no freedom, but are indeed reduced to the most abject slavery; are in a condition far worse than countries conquered and made tributary; for these have only a fixed sum to pay, which they are left to raise among themselves, in the way that they may think most equal and easy; and having paid the stipulated sum, the debt is discharged, and what is left is their own. This is much more tolerable than to be taxed at the meer will of others, without any bounds, without any stipulation and agreement, contrary to their consent, and against their will. If we are told that those who lay these taxes upon the colonies, are men of the highest character for their wisdom, justice, and integrity, and therefore cannot be supposed to deal hardly, unjustly, or unequally by any; admitting, and really believing that all this is true, it will make no alteration in the nature of the case; for one who is bound to obey the will of another, is as really a slave, though he may have a good master, as if he had a bad one; and this is stronger in politic bodies than in natural ones, as the former have perpetual succession, and remain the same; and although they may have a very good master at one time, they may have a very bad one at another. And indeed, if the people in *America*, are to be taxed by the representatives of the people in *Britain*, their malady is an increasing evil, that must always grow greater by time. Whatever burdens are laid upon the *Americans*, will be so much taken off the *Britons*; and the doing this will soon be extremely popular, and those who put up to be members of the house of commons, must obtain the votes of the people by promising to take more and more of the taxes off them, by putting it on the *Americans*. This must most assuredly be the case, and it will not be in the power even of the parliament to prevent it; the people's private interest will be concerned, and will govern them; they will have such, and only such representatives as will act agreeable to this their interest; and these taxes laid on *Americans*, will be always a part of the supply bill, in which the other branches of the legislature can make no alteration: and in truth, the subjects in the colonies will be taxed at the will and pleasure of their fellow-subjects in *Britain*.—How equitable, and how just this may be, must be left to every impartial man to determine.

But it will be said, that the monies drawn from the colonies by duties, and by taxes, will be laid up and set apart to be used for their future defence: This will not at all alleviate the hardship, but serves only more strongly to mark the servile state of the people. Free people have ever thought, and always will think, that the money necessary for their defence, lies safest in their own hands, until it be wanted immediately for that purpose. To take the money of the *Americans*, which they want continually to use in their trade, and lay it up for their defence, at a thousand leagues distance from them, when the enemies they have to fear, are in their own neighbourhood, hath not the greatest probability of friendship or of prudence.

It is not the judgment of free people only, that money for defending them is safest in their own keeping, but it hath also been the opinion of the best and wisest kings and governors of mankind, in every age of the world, that the wealth of a state was most securely as well as most profitably deposited in the hands of their faithful subjects: *Constantius,* emperor of the *Romans,* though an absolute prince, both practised and praised this method. "*Dioclesian* sent persons on purpose to reproach him with his neglect of the public, and the poverty to which he was reduced by his own fault. *Constantius* heard these reproaches with patience; and, having persuaded those who made them in *Dioclesian*'s name, to stay a few days with him, he sent word to the most wealthy persons in the provinces, that he wanted money, and that they had now an opportunity of shewing whether or no they truly loved their prince. Upon this notice every one strove who should be foremost in carrying to the exchequer all their gold, silver, and valuable effects; so that in a short time *Constantius* from being the poorest, became by far the most wealthy of all the four princes. He then invited the deputies of *Dioclesian* to visit his treasury, desiring them to make a faithful report to their master of the state in which they should find it. They obeyed; and, while they stood gazing on the mighty heaps of gold and silver, *Constantius* told them, that the wealth which they beheld with astonishment, had long since belonged to him; but that he had left it by way of depositum, in the hands of his people: adding, the richest and surest treasure of the prince was the love of his subjects. The deputies were no sooner gone, than the generous prince sent for those who had assisted him in his exigency, commended their zeal, and returned to every one what they had so readily brought into his treasury." *Universal Hist. vol. XV. page* 523.

We are not insensible, that when liberty is in danger, the liberty of complaining is dangerous; yet, a man on a wreck was never denied the liberty of roaring as loud as he could; says Dean *Swift.* And we believe no good reason can be given, why the colonies should not modestly and soberly enquire, what right the parliament of *Great-Britain* have to tax them. We know such enquiries, by a late letter-writer, have been branded with the little epithet of *mushroom policy*; and he insinuates, that for the colonies to pretend to claim any privileges, will draw down the resentment of the parliament on them.—Is the defence of liberty become so contemptible, and pleading for just rights so dangerous? Can the guardians of liberty be thus ludicrous? Can the patrons of freedom be so jealous and so severe?—If the *British* house of commons are rightfully possessed of a power to tax the colonies in *America*, this power must be vested in them by the *British* constitution, as they are one branch of the great legislative body of the nation: As they are the representatives of all the people in *Britain*, they have beyond doubt, all the power such a representation can possibly give; yet, great as this power is, surely it cannot exceed that of their constituents. And can it possibly be shewn, that the people in *Britain* have a sovereign authority over their fellow-subjects in *America*? Yet such is the authority that must be exercised in taking people's estates from them by taxes, or otherwise without their consent. In all aids granted to the crown by the parliament, it is said with the greatest propriety, "We freely give unto your Majesty;" for they give their own money, and the money of those who have intrusted them with a proper power for that purpose: But can they with the same propriety give away the money of the *Americans*, who have never given any such power? Before a thing can be justly given away, the giver must certainly have acquired a property in it; and have the people in *Britain* justly acquired such a property in the goods and estates of the people in these colonies, that they may give them away at pleasure?

In an emperial state, which consists of many separate governments, each of which hath peculiar privileges, and of which kind it is evident the empire of *Great-Britain* is; no single part, though greater than another part, is by that superiority intituled to make laws for, or to tax such lesser part; but all laws, and all taxations, which bind the whole, must be made by the whole: This may be fully verified by the empire of *Germany*, which consists of many states, some powerful, and others weak, yet the powerful never make laws to govern or to tax the little and weak ones, neither is it done by the emperor, but only by the diet, consisting of the representatives of the whole body. Indeed, it must be absurd to suppose, that the common people of *Great-Britain* have a sovereign and absolute authority over their fellow-subjects in *America*, or even any sort of power whatsoever over them; but it will be still more absurd, to suppose they can give a power to their representatives, which they have not themselves. If the house of commons do not receive this authority from their constituents, it will be difficult to tell by what means they obtained it, except it be vested in them by meer superiority and power.

Should it be urged, that the money expended by the mother country, for the defence and protection of *America*, and especially during the late war, must justly intitle her to some retaliation from the colonies; and that the stamp duties and taxes, intended to be raised in them, are only designed for that equitable purpose; if we are permitted to examine how far this may rightfully vest the parliament with the power of taxing the colonies, we shall find this claim to have no sort of equitable foundation. In many of the colonies, especially those in *New-England*, who were planted, as is before observed, not at the charge of the crown or kingdom of *England*, but at the expence of the planters themselves, and were not only planted, but also defended against the savages, and other enemies, in long and cruel wars, which continued for an hundred years, almost without intermission, solely at their own charge: And in the year 1746, when the Duke *D'Anville* came out from *France*, with the most formidable *French* fleet that ever was in the *American* seas, enraged at these colonies for the loss of *Louisbourg*, the year before, and with orders to make an attack on them; even in this greatest exigence, these colonies were left to the protection of heaven, and their own efforts. These colonies having thus planted and defended themselves, and removed all enemies from their borders, were in hopes to enjoy peace, and recruit their state, much exhausted by these long struggles; but they were soon called upon to raise men, and send out to the defence of other colonies, and to make conquests for the crown; they dutifully obeyed the requisition, and with ardor entered into those services, and continued in them until all encroachments were removed, and all *Canada*, and even the *Havana*, conquered. They most chearfully complied with every call of the crown; they rejoiced, yea even exulted, in the prosperity and exaltation of the *British* empire. But these colonies, whose bounds were fixed, and whose borders were before cleared from enemies, by their own fortitude, and at their own expence, reaped no sort of advantage by these conquests; they are not enlarged, have not gained a single acre of land, have no part in the *Indian* or interior trade; the immense tracts of land subdued, and no less immense and profitable commerce acquired, all belong to *Great-Britain*; and not the least share or portion to these colonies, though thousands of their men have lost their lives, and millions of their money have been expended in the purchase of them; for great part of which we are yet in debt, and from which we shall not in many years be able to extricate ourselves. Hard will be the fate, yea cruel the destiny, of these unhappy colonies if the reward they are to receive for all this, is the loss of their freedom; better for them *Canada* still remained *French*, yea far more eligible that it ever should remain so, than that the price of its reduction should be their slavery.

If the colonies are not taxed by parliament, are they therefore exempted from bearing their proper share in the necessary burdens of government? This by no means follows. Do they not support a regular internal government in each colony, as expensive to the people here, as the internal government of *Britain* is to the people there? Have not the colonies here, at all times when called upon by the crown, raised money for the public service, done it as chearfully as the parliament have done on like occasions? Is not this the most easy, the most natural, and most constitutional way of raising money in the colonies? What occasion then to distrust the colonies,—what necessity to fall on an invidious and unconstitutional method, to compel them to do what they have ever done freely? Are not the people in the colonies as loyal and dutiful subjects as any age or nation ever produced,—and are they not as useful to the kingdom, in this remote quarter of the world, as their fellow-subjects are who dwell in *Britain*? The parliament, it is confessed, have power to regulate the trade of the whole empire; and hath it not full power, by this means, to draw all the money and all the wealth of the colonies into the mother country, at pleasure? What motive, after all this, can remain, to induce the parliament to abridge the privileges, and lessen the rights of the most loyal and dutiful subjects; subjects justly intituled to ample freedom, who have long enjoyed, and not abused or forfeited their liberties, who have used them to their own advantage, in dutiful subserviency to the orders and interests of *Great-Britain*? Why should the gentle current of tranquillity, that has so long run with peace through all the *British* states, and flowed with joy and with happiness in all her countries, be at last obstructed, be turned out of its true course, into unusual and winding channels, by which many of those states must be ruined; but none of them can possibly be made more rich or more happy?

Before we conclude, it may be necessary to take notice of the vast difference there is between the raising money in a country by duties, taxes, or otherwise, and employing and laying out the money again in the same country; and raising the like sums of money, by the like means, and sending it away quite out of the country where it is raised. Where the former of these is the case, although the sums raised may be very great, yet that country may support itself under them; for as fast as the money is collected together, it is again scattered abroad, to be used in commerce and every kind of business; and money is not made scarcer by this means, but rather the contrary, as this continual circulation must have a tendency to prevent, in some degree, it's being hoarded. But where the latter method is pursued, the effect will be extremely different; for here, as fast as the money can be collected, 'tis immediately sent out of the country, never to return but by a tedious round of commerce, which at best must take up much time: Here all trade, and every kind of business depending on it, will grow dull, and must languish more and more, until it comes to a final stop at last. If the money raised in *Great-Britain* in the three last years of the late war, and which exceeded forty millions sterling, had been sent out of the kingdom, would not this have nearly ruined the trade of the nation in three years only? Think then, what must be the condition of these miserable colonies, when all the money proposed to be raised in them, by high duties on the importation of divers kinds of goods, by the post-office, by stamp duties, and other taxes, is sent quite away, as fast as it can be collected; and this to be repeated continually, and last forever! Is it possible for colonies under these circumstances to support themselves, to have any money, any trade, or other business, carried on in them? Certainly it is not; nor is there at present, or ever was, any country under heaven, that did, or possibly could support itself under such burdens.

We finally beg leave to assert, that the first planters of these colonies were pious christians; were faithful subjects; who, with a fortitude and perseverance little known, and less considered, settled these wild countries, by GOD's goodness, and their own amazing labours; thereby added a most valuable dependance to the crown of *Great-Britain*; were ever dutifully subservient to her interests; so taught their children, that not one has been disaffected to this day; but all have honestly obeyed every royal command, and chearfully submitted to every constitutional law; have as little inclination as they have ability to throw off their dependancy; have carefully avoided every offensive measure, and every interdicted manufacture; have risqued their lives as they have been ordered, and furnished their money when it has been called for; have never been troublesome or expensive to the mother country; have kept due order, and supported a regular government; have maintained peace, and practised christianity; and in all conditions, and in every relation, have demeaned themselves as loyal, as dutiful, and as faithful subjects ought; and that no kingdom or state hath, or ever had, colonies more quiet, more obedient, or more profitable, than these have ever been.—

May the same divine goodness, that guided the first planters, protected the settlements, inspired kings to be gracious, parliaments to be tender, ever preserve, ever support our present gracious King; give great wisdom to his ministers, and much understanding to his parliaments; perpetuate the sovereignty of the *British* constitution, and the filial dependancy and happiness of all the colonies.

P.

PROVIDENCE, in NEW-ENGLAND,
NOVEMBER 30, 1764.

[Martin Howard Jr.], A Letter from a Gentleman at Halifax, to his Friend in Rhode-Island, Containing Remarks upon a Pamphlet, Entitled, The Rights of Colonies Examined. Newport, 1765.

Martin Howard Jr. was a prominent and well-to-do lawyer closely tied to the Anglican merchant community of Newport, Rhode Island. His pamphlet, a point-by-point response to Hopkins's *Rights of the Colonies Examined*, was one of the first and boldest defenses of British policy and parliamentary authority by an American. But Howard and his Newport clique, which Otis called a "little, dirty, drinking, drabbing, contaminated knot of thieves," were not simply interested in defending the Sugar and Stamp Acts and the new trade regulations, including the new vice-admiralty court in Halifax, Nova Scotia (hence the reference to Halifax in the title of the pamphlet). Frustrated with the popular and faction-ridden politics of Rhode Island, they wanted nothing less than the revocation of Rhode Island's charter and the royalization of this excessively democratic colony. Howard's attempt to rest the jurisdiction of Parliament on the common law was not all that different from Otis's argument in his *Rights of the British Colonies*. But the emerging idea of parliamentary sovereignty—that parliamentary statutes as acts of legislative will trump the traditional rules of the common law—made Howard's position as soft and fluid as Otis's. And Howard's contention that the corporate charter of Rhode Island was merely a gift of the Crown and that the colonists had no rights independent of their charters was bound to raise fear and anger among Rhode Islanders.

In August 1765, before the Stamp Act could be enforced, rioting erupted up and down the continent. Mobs in every colony save Georgia, where a few stamps were briefly distributed, forced the newly appointed stamp agents to resign, effectively nullifying the law. On August 27, 1765, a crowd of protestors in Newport carried through the streets effigies of Howard and several other Newport royalists, including the stamp agent, later suspending the crude figures from gallows erected in front of the courthouse and eventually burning them. When on the following night his house was gutted by another mob, Howard fled to the safety of an English warship, never to return to Rhode Island.

A
LETTER

GENTLEMAN at *Halifax,*

TO HIS

FRIEND in *Rhode-Island,*

CONTAINING

REMARKS UPON A PAMPHLET,

ENTITLED,

THE RIGHTS OF COLONIES

EXAMINED.

NEWPORT:
PRINTED AND SOLD BY S. HALL.   M.DCC.LXV.

A Letter, &c.

MY DEAR SIR,

I THANK you very kindly for the pamphlets and news-papers, you was so obliging as to send me. I will, according to your request, give you a few miscellaneous strictures on that pamplet wrote by Mr. *H—p—s*, your governor, entitled, "The rights of colonies examined."

His honour reminds me of the *Roman* poet.

"Est genus hominum, qui esse primos se omnium rerum volunt, Nec sunt.——"

He seems to give a solemnity to his performance, as if the subject had not been sufficiently handled by any other before him, but I am of opinion he falls very short of Mr. ——, who, though unhappily misled by popular ideas, and at the head of the *tribunitian veto*, yet appears to be a man of knowledge and parts: Whereas *the rights of colonies examined*, is a laboured, ostentatious piece, discovers its author to be totally unacquainted with stile or diction, and eagerly fond to pass upon the world for a man of letters.

I cannot forgive the honourable author in adopting for his motto the three lines from *Thompson*, so little applicable are they to the present times. I might challenge all the sons of discontent and faction, in the *British* dominions, to shew the least similitude between the years one thousand six hundred and forty-one, and one thousand seven hundred and sixty-four. How cruel and invidious is it to insinuate the most distant likeness between the two periods? How much like sedition does it seem, to associate the present transactions of the nation with those of one thousand six hundred and forty-one, which soon after kindled into a civil war, and in the end overturned the *English* constitution?

The honourable author might perhaps flatter himself, that, in future editions of *Thompson*'s liberty, commentators may insert *variæ lectiones* of the text, and the three lines run thus:

> "Mid the low murmurs of submissive fear,
>   And mingled rage, my *H—p—s* rais'd his voice,
>   And to the laws appeal'd."

Or perhaps some future bard may sing the present times, and HE be made the hero of the song. The aptness is easy and striking, and the idea too pleasing to be resisted. *Narcissus*, in contemplating his own image, was turned into a daffodil. Who can think of this, and feel no pity for the pride and weakness of *man that is born of a woman.*

> "So have I seen, on some bright summer's day,
>   A calf of genius, debonnair and gay,
>   Dance on the brink, as if inspired by fame,
>   Fond of the pretty fellow in the stream."
>   LOVE OF FAME, THE UNIVERSAL PASSION.

I would fain hope that his honour's motto is not a true portrait of the general temper and conduct of the *Americans*; I would rather think "*the low murmurs of submissive fear, and mingled rage,*" delineate only a few disappointed traders. It were to be wished that some friend of the colonies would endeavour to remove any unfavourable impressions this, and other pamphlets of the like kind, may have occasioned at home; lest those in power form the general character of the colonies from such notices as these convey, and from thence be inclined to increase their dependance, rather than to emancipate them from the present supposed impositions. Depend upon it, my Friend, a people like the *English*, arrived to the highest pitch of glory and power, the envy and admiration of surrounding slaves, who hold the balance of *Europe* in their hands, and rival in arts and arms every period of ancient or modern story; a nation who, for the defence and safety of *America* only, staked their all in the late war; this people, I say, justly conscious of their dignity, will not patiently be dictated to by those whom they have ever considered as dependant upon them. Happy will it be for the colonies, yea happy for the honourable author, if his pamphlet should meet with nothing more than contempt and neglect; for should it catch the attention of men in power, measures may be taken to stifle in the birth "*the low murmurs of submissive fear*," and crush in embryo "*the mingled rage*," which now so prettily adorns the head of his honour's pamphlet.

However disguised, polished or softened the expression of this pamphlet may seem, yet every one must see, that its professed design is sufficiently prominent throughout, namely, to prove, *that the colonies have rights independant of, and not controulable by, the authority of parliament.* It is upon this dangerous and indiscreet position I shall communicate to you my real sentiments.

To suppose a design of enslaving the colonies by parliament, is too presumptuous; to propagate it in print, is perhaps dangerous. Perplexed between a desire of speaking all he thinks, and the fear of saying too much, the honourable author is obliged to entrench himself in obscurity and inconsistency in several parts of his performance: I shall bring one instance.

In page 131, he says, "It is the indispensible duty of every good and loyal subject chearfully to obey, and patiently submit to, all the laws, orders, *&c.* that may be passed by parliament."

I do not much admire either the spirit or composition of this sentence. Is it the duty *only* of good and loyal subjects to obey? Are the wicked and disloyal subjects absolved from this obligation? else why is this passage so marvellously penned: *Philoleutherus Lipsiensis* would directly pronounce this a figure in rhetorick, called nonsense.—Believe me, my friend, I did not quote this passage to shew my skill in criticism, but to point out a contradiction between it, and another passage in page 138, which runs thus: "It must be absurd to suppose, that the common people of *Great-Britain* have a sovereign and absolute authority over their fellow subjects of *America, or even any sort of power whatsoever over them*; but it will be still more absurd to suppose, they can give a power to their representatives, which they have not themselves," *&c.* Here it is observable, that the first cited passage expresses a full submission to the authority of parliament; the last is as explicit a denial of that authority. The sum of his honour's argument is this: The people of *Great-Britain* have not any sort of power over the *Americans*; the house of commons have no greater authority than the people of *Great-Britain*, who are their constituents; *ergo*, the house of commons *have not any sort of power* *over the* Americans. This is indeed a curious invented syllogism, the sole merit of which is due to the first magistrate of an *English* colony.

I have endeavoured to investigate the true natural relation, if I may so speak, between colonies and their mother state, abstracted from compact or positive institution, but here I can find nothing satisfactory; till this relation is clearly defined upon a rational and natural principle, our reasoning upon the measure of the colonies obedience will be desultory and inconclusive. Every connection in life has its reciprocal duties; we know the relation between a parent and child, husband and wife, master and servant, and from thence are able to deduce their respective obligations; but we have no notices of any such precise natural relation between a mother state and its colonies, and therefore cannot reason with so much certainty upon the power of the one, or the duty of the others. The ancients have transmitted to us nothing that is applicable to the state of modern colonies, because the relation between these is formed by political compact; and the condition of each variant in their original, and from each other. The honourable author has not freed this subject from any of its embarrassments: Vague and diffuse talk of rights and privileges, and ringing the changes upon the words liberty and slavery, only serve to convince us, that words may affect without raising images, or affording any repose to a mind philosophically inquisitive. For my own part, I will shun the walk of metaphysicks in my enquiry, and be content to consider the colonies rights upon the footing of their charters, which are the only plain avenues, that lead to the truth of this matter.

The several *New-England* charters ascertain, define and limit the respective rights and privileges of each colony, and I cannot conceive how it has come to pass that the colonies now claim any other or greater rights than are therein expresly granted to them. I fancy when we speak, or think of the rights of free-born *Englishmen*, we confound those rights which are personal, with those which are political: There is a distinction between these, which ought always to be kept in view.

Our personal rights, comprehending those of life, liberty and estate, are secured to us by the common law, which is every subject's birthright, whether born in *Great-Britain*, on the ocean, or in the colonies; and it is in this sense we are said to enjoy all the rights and privileges of *Englishmen*. The political rights of the colonies, or the powers of government communicated to them, are more limited, and their nature, quality and extent depend altogether upon the patent or charter which first created and instituted them. As individuals, the colonists participate of every blessing the *English* constitution can give them: As corporations created by the crown, they are confined within the primitive views of their institution. Whether therefore their indulgence is scanty or liberal, can be no cause of complaint; for when they accepted of their charters, they tacitly submitted to the terms and conditions of them.

The colonies have no rights independant of their charters, they can claim no greater than those give them, by those the parliamentary jurisdiction over them is not taken away, neither could any grant of the king abridge that jurisdiction, because it is founded upon common law, as I shall presently shew, and was prior to any charter or grant to the colonies: Every *Englishman*, therefore, is subject to this jurisdiction, and it follows him wherever he goes. It is of the essence of government, that there should be a supreme head, and it would be a solecism in politicks to talk of members independant of it.

With regard to the jurisdiction of parliament, I shall endeavour to shew, that it is attached to every *English* subject, wherever he be: And I am led to do this from a clause in page 129 of his honour's pamphlet, where he says, "That the colonies do not hold their rights, as a privilege granted them, nor enjoy them as a grace and favour bestowed; but possess them, as an inherent, indefeasible right." This postulatum cannot be true with regard to political rights, for I have already shewn, that these are derived from your charters, and are held by force of the king's grant; therefore these inherent, indefeasible rights, as his honour calls them, must be personal ones, according to the distinction already made. Permit me to say, that inherent and indefeasible as these rights may be, the jurisdiction of parliament, over every *English* subject, is equally as inherent and indefeasible: That both have grown out of the same stock, and that if we avail ourselves of the one, we must submit to, and acknowlege the other.

It might here be properly enough asked, Are these personal

rights self-existent? Have they no original source? I answer, They are derived from the constitution of *England*, which is the common law; and from the same fountain is also derived the jurisdiction of parliament over us.

But to bring this argument down to the most vulgar apprehension: The common law has established it as a rule or maxim, that the plantations are bound by *British* acts of parliament, if particularly named: And surely no *Englishman*, in his senses, will deny the force of a common law maxim. One cannot but smile at the inconsistency of these inherent, indefeasible men: If one of them has a suit at law, in any part of *New-England*, upon a question of land property, or merchandize, he appeals to the common law, to support his claim, or defeat his adversary; and yet is so profoundly stupid as to say, that an act of parliament does not bind him; when, perhaps, the same page in a law book, which points him out a remedy for a libel, or a slap in the face, would inform him that it does.—In a word, The force of an act of parliament, over the colonies, is predicated upon the common law, the origin and basis of all those inherent rights and privileges which constitute the boast and felicity of a *Briton*.

Can we claim the common law as an inheritance, and at the same time be at liberty to adopt one part of it, and reject the other? Indeed we cannot: The common law, pure and indivisible in its nature and essence, cleaves to us during our lives, and follows us from *Nova Zembla* to *Cape Horn*; And therefore, as the jurisdiction of parliament arises out of, and is supported by it, we may as well renounce our allegiance, or change our nature, as to be exempt from the jurisdiction of parliament: Hence, it is plain to me, that in denying this jurisdiction, we at the same time, take leave of the common law, and thereby, with equal temerity and folly, strip ourselves of every blessing we enjoy as *Englishmen*: A flagrant proof this, that shallow draughts in politicks and legislation confound and distract us, and that an extravagant zeal often defeats its own purposes.

I am aware that the foregoing reasoning will be opposed by the maxim, "That no *Englishman* can be taxed but by his own consent, or by representatives."

It is this dry maxim, taken in a literal sense, and ill understood, that, like the song of *Lillibullero*, has made all the mischief in the colonies: And upon this, the partizans of the colonies rights chiefly rest their cause. I don't despair, however, of convincing you, that this maxim affords but little support to their argument, when rightly examined and explained.

It is the opinion of the house of commons, and may be considered as a law of parliament, that they are the representatives of every *British* subject, wheresoever he be. In this view of the matter then, the aforegoing maxim is fully vindicated in practice, and the whole benefit of it, in substance and effect, extended and applied to the *colonies*. Indeed the maxim must be considered in this latitude, for in a literal sense or construction it ever was, and ever will be, impracticable. Let me ask, is the isle of *Man, Jersey*, or *Guernsey*, represented? What is the value or amount of each man's representation in the kingdom of *Scotland*, which contains near two millions of people, and yet not more than three thousand have votes in the election of members of parliament? But to shew still further, that, in fact and reality, this right of representation is not of that consequence it is generally thought to be, let us take into the argument the moneyed interest of *Britain*, which, though immensely great, has no share in this representation; a worthless freeholder of forty shillings *per annum* can vote for a member of parliament, whereas a merchant, tho' worth one hundred thousand pounds sterling, if it consist only in personal effects, has no vote at all: But yet let no one suppose that the interest of the latter is not equally the object of parliamentary attention with the former. —Let me add one example more: Copyholders in *England* of one thousand pounds sterling *per annum*, whose estates in land are nominally, but not intrinsically, inferior to a freehold, cannot, by law, vote for members of parliament; yet we never hear that these people "*murmur with submissive fear, and mingled rage:*" They don't set up their private humour against the constitution of their country, but submit with chearfulness to those forms of government which providence, in its goodness, has placed them under.

Suppose that this *Utopian* privilege of representation should take place, I question if it would answer any other purpose but to bring an expence upon the colonies, unless you can suppose that a few *American* members could bias the deliberations of the whole *British* legislature. In short, this right of representation is but a phantom, and, if possessed in its full extent, would be of no real advantage to the colonies; they would, like *Ixion*, embrace a cloud in the shape of *Juno*.

In addition to this head, I could further urge the danger of innovations; every change in a constitution, in some degree, weakens its original frame; and hence it is that legislators and statesmen are cautious in admitting them: The goodly building of the *British* constitution will be best secured and perpetuated by adhering to its original principles. Parliaments are not of yesterday, they are as antient as our *Saxon* ancestors. Attendance in parliament was originally a duty arising from a tenure of lands, and grew out of the feudal system; so that the privilege of sitting in it, is territorial, and confined to *Britain* only. Why should the beauty and symmetry of this body be destroyed, and its purity defiled, by the unnatural mixture of representatives from every part of the *British* dominions? *Parthians, Medes, Elamites, and the dwellers of Mesopotamia, &c.* would not, in such a case, speak the same language. What a heterogeneous council would this form? what a monster in government would it be?—In truth, my friend, the matter lies here: The freedom and happiness of every *British* subject depends, not upon his share in elections, but upon the sense and virtue of the *British* parliament, and these depend reciprocally upon the sense and virtue of the whole nation. When virtue and honour are no more, the lovely frame of our constitution will be dissolved. *Britain* may one day be what *Athens* and *Rome* now are; but may heaven long protract the hour!

The jurisdiction of parliament being established, it will follow, that this jurisdiction cannot be apportioned; it is transcendant and entire, and may levy internal taxes as well as regulate trade; there is no essential difference in the rights: A stamp duty is confessedly the most reasonable and equitable that can be devised, yet very far am I from desiring to see it established among us, but I fear the shaft is sped, and it is now too late to prevent the blow.

The examples cited by his honour, with regard to ancient colonies, may shew his reading and erudition, but are of no authority in the present question. I am not enough skilled in the *Grecian* history to correct the proofs drawn from thence, though they amount to very little. If the *Grecian* colonies, as his honour says, "took such forms of government as themselves chose," there is no kind of similitude between them and the *English* colonies, and therefore to name them is nothing to the purpose. The *English* colonies take their forms of government from the crown; hold their privileges upon condition, that they do not abuse them; and hold their lands by the tenure of common socage, which involves in it fealty and obedience to the king: Hence it is plain, his honour's argument is not strengthened by the example of the *Grecian* colonies; for what likeness is there between independant colonies, as those must be, which "took such forms of government as themselves chose," and colonies like ours, which are in a manner feudatory, and holden of a superior.

With regard to the *Roman* colonies, I must beg leave to say, that the honourable author, either ignorantly or wilfully, mistakes the facts: A little more enquiry, or a little more candour, would have convinced him, that the *Roman coloniæ* did not enjoy all the rights of *Roman* citizens; on the contrary, they only used the *Roman* laws and religion, and served in the legions, but had not the right of suffrage, or of bearing honours. In these respects, our *English* colonies exactly resemble them; we enjoy the *English* laws and religion, but have not the right of suffrage, or of bearing honours in *Great-Britain*, and indeed our situation renders it impossible.

If the practice of the ancients was of any authority in this case, I could name examples to justify the enslaving of colonies. The *Carthaginians* were a free people, yet they, to render the *Sardinians* and *Corsicans* more dependant, forbad their planting, sowing, or doing any thing of the like kind, under pain of death, so that they supplied them with necessaries from *Africa*: This was indeed very hard. But there is something extremely weak and inconclusive in recurring to the *Grecian* and *Roman* history for examples to illustrate any particular favourite opinion: If a deference to the ancients should direct the practice of the moderns, we might sell our children to pay our debts, and justify it by the practice of the *Athenians*. We might lend our wives to our friends, and justify it from the Example of *Cato*, among the *Romans*. In a word, my dear Sir, the belly of a sow, pickled, was a high dish in ancient *Rome*; and I imagine, as you advance in the refinements of luxury, this will become a capital part of a *Rhode-Island* feast, so fond you seem of ancient customs and laws.

Instead of wandring in the labyrinth of ancient colonies, I would advise his honour to read the debates in parliament in the year one thousand seven hundred and thirty-three, when Mr. *Partridge*, your agent, petitioned the commons against the then sugar-bill; he will there find more satisfaction upon the subject of colonies, than in *Thucydides's history of the Pelopennesian war*. It was declared in the course of that debate, that the colonists were a part of the people of *Great-Britain*; and, as such, fully represented in that house. The petition then presented by Mr. *Partridge*, was of a very different temper from those now sent home by the colonies; it was extremely modest, and only intimated that the sugar bill, if passed into a law, might be prejudicial to their charter; at the bare mention of this Sir *William Yonge* took fire, and said, "*It looked like aiming at an independency, and disclaiming the jurisdiction of that house, as if* (says he) *this house had not a power to tax the colonies.*" *Mr. Winnington*, with equal warmth, added, "*I hope they have no charter which debars this house from taxing them, as well as any other subject of the nation.*" Here you have the opinion of two of the most eminent members of that time; they spoke the sentiments of the whole house, and these sentiments still continue the same. And from hence you may perceive, how little prospect there is of the colonies gaining any point upon the footing of these new supposititious rights; broaching such opinions will excite the jealousy of the parliament, and you will be looked upon with an evil eye. The promoters of such doctrines are no friends to the colonies, whatever may be their pretensions. Can his honour be so vain as to imagine, that ten thousand such pamphlets as his, will influence the parliament, or that they will be persuaded, by the force of his elocution, to give up their supremacy, and right of taxing the colonies? What purpose then can be served by these pamphlets, but to embitter the minds of a simple, credulous, and hitherto loyal people, and to alienate their affections from *Great-Britain*, their best friend, their protector, and *alma mater*? A different behaviour would be much more prudent and politick. If we have any thing to ask, we should remember that diffidence and modesty will always obtain more from generous minds, than frowardness and impertinence.

The act of the thirteenth of his late majesty, entitled, *An act for naturalizing of foreign protestants*, had better have been omitted by his honour; for if that act is to be the measure of the colonists rights, they will be more circumscribed than he would willingly chuse. In that act, there is a proviso, that no person, who shall become a natural born subject by virtue of that act; should be of the privy council, or a member of either house of parliament, or capable of enjoying, in *Great-Britain* or *Ireland*, any place of trust, civil or military, &c. This statute confirms the distinction I have set up between personal and political rights. After naturalization, foreign protestants are here admitted subjects, to all intents and purposes; that is, to the full enjoyment of those rights which are connected with the person, liberty or estate of *Englishmen*; but by the proviso, they are excluded from bearing offices or honours.

Enlarging the power of the court of admiralty, is much complain'd of by the honourable author. I shall open my mind to you freely on this head.

It is notorious, that smuggling, which an eminent writer calls a crime against the law of nature, had well nigh become established in some of the colonies. Acts of parliament had been uniformly dispensed with by those whose duty it was to execute them; corruption, raised upon the ruins of duty and virtue, had almost grown into a system; courts of admiralty, confined within small territorial jurisdictions, became subject to mercantile influence; and the king's revenue shamefully sacrificed to the venality and perfidiousness of courts and officers.— If, my friend, customs are due to the crown; if illicit commerce is to be put an end to, as ruinous to the welfare of the nation:— If, by reason of the interested views of traders, and the connivance of courts and custom-house officers, these ends could not be compassed or obtained in the common and ordinary way; tell me, what could the government do, but to apply a remedy desperate as the disease? There is, I own, a severity in the method of prosecution, in the new established court of admiralty, under Doctor *S P R Y*, here; but it is a severity we have brought upon ourselves. When every mild expedient, to stop the atrocious and infamous practice of smuggling, has been try'd in vain, the government is justifiable in making laws against it, even like those of *Draco*, which were written in blood. The new instituted court of admiralty, and the power given to the seizer, are doubtless intended to make us more circumspect in our trade, and to confine the merchant, from motives of fear and dread, within the limits of a fair commerce. "The *English* constrain the merchant, but it is in favour of commerce," says the admired *Secondat*. This is the spirit of the new regulations, both with regard to the employing of cutters, and the enlarged power of the admiralty; and both measures are justifiable upon the same principles, as is the late act for preventing murder, which executes and dissects the murderer at surgeons-hall in twenty-four hours after conviction.

But notwithstanding the severity of this act, let me add, that no harm can accrue to the honest and fair trader, so long as the crown fills the admiralty department with an upright judge; such a one is Doctor *S P R Y*, an able civilian, and whose appointments place him above any kind of influence; yet the honourable author of the pamphlet before me, has told us to this effect; That it is very well known this judge *can be prevailed on, very easily*, to certify, upon the acquittal of a seizure, that there was a probable cause for making it.—So shamefully intemperate is his honour's zeal and opposition to every measure adopted by the government at home, that he spares not even private characters, however worthy and respectable. I fear he knows not the high value of a good name, and how dear it is to men of sentiment and honour.

> "He who filches from me my good name,
>   Robs me of that, which not enriches him,
>   But makes me poor indeed."
>   SHAKESPEAR.

To suspect the integrity of others, is not the effusion of a virtuous mind. Those who have been long used to traffick with judges and juries, are, from the depravity of their own hearts, easily led to believe others even as themselves.

This libel upon Doctor *S P R Y*, contained in a pamphlet *published by authority*, may spread over the *British* dominions, and, however false and scandalous it be, yet may leave a shade upon his character which can never be effaced. With what grace, let me ask you, do such reflections as these come from the governor of a colony, where, all the world agree, the law has scarcely yet dawned, and where all your legal rights are decided by the strength of that faction which happens to be uppermost.

I am not enough skilled in trade to know whether the act, so much complained of, will do most good or most harm; and I wish others were as diffident of their knowledge in this particular. To comprehend the general trade of the *British* nation, much exceeds the capacity of any one man in *America*, how great soever he be. Trade is a vast, complicated system, and requires such a depth of genius, and extent of knowledge, to understand it, that little minds, attached to their own sordid interest, and long used to the greatest licentiousness in trade, are, and must be, very incompetent judges of it. Sir *Andrew Freeport* is no inhabitant of *Rhode-Island* colony. For my own part, I am still willing to leave the management of trade with that people, who, according to the same admired author just quoted, "know better than any other people upon earth, how to value at the same time these three great advantages, religion, commerce, and liberty."

Here I would just observe, that, from the intelligence I have gained, the beloved article of melasses is now plentier and cheaper, in all the *New-England* colonies, than when it was avowedly smuggled; and so far is the linen manufacture of *Ireland* from being ruined, as his honour intimates, that never was a greater demand for flax-seed than during the last fall, notwithstanding the clause in the act relating to lumber. How senseless is it to imagine that the prohibiting a few dunnage staves to be carried to *Ireland*, will ruin the manufactures of that kingdom.

Believe me, my Friend, it gives me great pain to see so much ingratitude in the colonies to the mother country, whose arms and money so lately rescued them from a *French* government. I have been told, that some have gone so far as to say, that they would, as things are, prefer such a government to an *English* one.—Heaven knows I have but little malice in my heart, yet, for a moment, I ardently wish that these spurious, unworthy sons of *Britain* could feel the iron rod of a *Spanish* inquisitor, or a *French* farmer of the revenue; it would indeed be a punishment suited to their ingratitude. Here I cannot but call to mind the adder in one of the fables of *Pilpay*, which was preparing to sting the generous traveller who had just rescued him from the flames.

You'l easily perceive, that what I have said is upon the general design of his honour's pamphlet; if he had divided his argument with any precision, I would have followed him with somewhat more of method; The dispute between *Great-Britain* and the colonies consists of two parts; first, the jurisdiction of parliament,—and, secondly, the exercise of that jurisdiction. His honour hath blended these together, and no where marked the division between them: The first I have principally remarked upon: As to the second, it can only turn upon the expediency or utility of those schemes which may, from time to time, be adopted by parliament, relative to the colonies. Under this head, I readily grant, they are at full liberty to remonstrate, petition, write pamphlets and newspapers, without number, to prevent any improper or unreasonable imposition: Nay, I would have them do all this with that spirit of freedom which *Englishmen* always have, and I hope ever will, exert; but let us not use our liberty for a cloak of maliciousness. Indeed I am very sure the loyalty of the colonies has ever been irreproachable; but from the pride of some, and the ignorance of others, the cry against mother country has spread from colony to colony; and it is to be feared, that prejudices and resentments are kindled among them which it will be difficult ever, thoroughly, to sooth or extinguish. It may become necessary for the supreme legislature of the nation to frame some code, and therein adjust the rights of the colonies, with precision and certainty, otherwise *Great-Britain* will always be teazed with new claims about liberty and privileges.

I have no ambition in appearing in print, yet if you think what is here thrown together is fit for the publick eye, you are at liberty to publish it: I the more chearfully acquiesce in this, because it is with real concern I have observed, that, notwithstanding the frequent abuse poured forth in pamphlets and news-papers against the mother country, not one filial pen in

America hath, as yet, been drawn, to my knowledge, in her vindication.

I am, very affectionately,
Your most faithful and obedient servant,

FINIS.

[Thomas Whately], The Regulations Lately Made Concerning the Colonies, and the Taxes Imposed upon Them, Considered. London, 1765.

The Stamp Act, which was approved in the House of Commons on February 27, 1765, and given royal assent on March 22, imposed a tax on legal documents, bonds, deeds, almanacs, newspapers, college diplomas, playing cards, indeed, on nearly every form of paper used in the colonies. Although some of the colonial assemblies had issued stamp taxes, never before had Parliament attempted to impose this kind of internal tax on the colonists. Once the ministry sensed a stirring of colonial opposition to the imperial reforms, a group of able English writers connected with the government set out to explain and justify the new regulations and taxes in a series of pamphlets. The most important and persuasive of these defenses of British policy was the following pamphlet, which was attributed to George Grenville, the prime minister from 1763 to 1765, but which was actually written by Thomas Whately, undersecretary to Grenville at the treasury and the principal drafter of the Stamp Act.

Before offering a justification of his measure, though, Whately devoted much of his lengthy pamphlet to his vision of a well-regulated and prosperous empire. Throughout he demonstrated an extraordinarily detailed knowledge of all aspects of the various colonies, including the value of numerous colonial commodities—from beaver skins to whale fins, rice to hemp. The administration of this "opulent, commercial, thriving" empire required money, and against this backdrop the need for American revenue emerged as the focus of his pamphlet.

Whately conceded that no British subject could be taxed without the consent of his representatives; but since he believed that the colonists were intimately connected to the people of the mother country, being both parts of "one Nation," he readily justified Parliament's extraction of the needed revenue by what the British called "virtual representation." Although the colonists, like many Englishmen in the mother country, did not actually vote for members of Parliament, they were nonetheless virtually represented there, and consequently bound by its laws. The people were represented *not* by the electoral process, that is, by voting, which was incidental to representation, but instead by the mutual interests that members of Parliament were presumed to share with all Britons for whom they spoke—including those, like the colonists, who did not actually vote for them. How the representatives got to the House of Commons was irrelevant to their ability to represent the interests of the nation.

Absurd as this concept of virtual representation seemed to many Americans, it justified the binding of the whole people, in Whately's words, "by the Consent of the Majority of that House, whether their own particular Representatives consented to or opposed the Measures there taken, or whether they had or had not particular Representatives there." It was probably the best justification of majority rule ever made.

THE
REGULATIONS
Lately Made concerning the
COLONIES,
AND THE
TAXES
Impofed upon Them, confidered.

LONDON:

Printed for J. WILKIE, in *St. Paul's Church-Yard* :
and may be had at the Pamphlet-Shops at the *Royal-
Exchange*, and *Charing-Crofs*. 1765.

The Regulations Lately made with Respect to the Colonies Considered.

THE immediate Defence of our Colonies from imminent Danger, was the sole occasion of the last War: Their permanent Security has been effectually obtained by the Peace: And even their Aggrandizement and Improvement have been provided for by the Negotiators of that Treaty, beyond the idea of any former Administration: There have been Ministers ignorant of the Importance of the Colonies; others, have impotently neglected their Concerns; and others again have been diverted by meaner Pursuits from attending to them: But happily for this Country, the Real and Substantial, and those are the Commercial Interests of Great Britain, are now preferred to every other Consideration: And the Trade from whence its greatest Wealth is derived, and upon which its Maritime Power is principally founded, depends upon a wise and proper use of the Colonies: From them we are to expect the Multiplication of Subjects; the Consumption of our Manufactures; the Supply of those Commodities which we want; and the encrease of our Navigation: To encourage their Population and their Culture; to regulate their Commerce; and to cement and perfect the necessary Connection between them and the Mother-Country, should therefore be the principal Objects of a British Minister's care; and many Steps have been lately taken, which by their immediate Operation, or distant Consequences, may materially affect these important Concerns. Every Man who is sincerely interested in whatever is interesting to his Country, will anxiously consider the Propriety of these Measures; will enquire into the Information, and Canvass the Principles upon which they have been adopted; and will be ready to applaud what has been well done; to condemn what has been done amiss; and to suggest any Emendations, Improvements, or Additions, which may lie within his Knowledge, and occur to his Reflection. The following Sheets are written with a View to facilitate such an Examination: They pretend to no more than to collect the several Regulations that have been lately made with respect to the Colonies: To weigh the Reasons upon which each of them appears to have been founded; and to see how far these are supported by Facts, and by Maxims of Trade and of Policy. These Regulations are many; and have been made in the different Departments of our Legislative or Executive Government: They are therefore scattered thro' Proclamations, Statutes, and Orders: But they are all of equal Publick Notoriety; which every Man may know; which every Man ought to know; and which when brought into one View and considered together, will appear to be either crude, incoherent, weak and pernicious Acts of Power, or a well digested consistent, wise and salutary Plan of Colonization and Government.

The new Acquisitions will naturally first attract our Attention: They are vast in extent, and richly productive of the valuable Commodities which belong to their several Climates; but besides these, we derive further Advantages from them on Account of their Situations: The Possession of those in *North America* ensures the safety of the other Colonies there; insomuch, that our only dangerous Neighbours, the *French*, do not think the Pittance that was left them on the Continent, worth Retaining, but by the Cession they are said to have made of *Louisiana* to the *Spaniards*, have avowedly given up for ever those great Objects, for which alone they began the War. The ceded Islands are of almost equal Consequence, for Protecting our own, and for Annoying the Settlements of the *French* and *Spaniards*, if they should be again our Enemies. But the greater the Importance of these Accessions to the *British* Dominion, so much the more Care and Circumspection is requisite in the Dispositions to be made concerning them: And such is the Difference of their Situations and Circumstances, that the same Regulations may be necessary to the one, and fatal to the other.

The Benefit which accrues to the Mother-Country from a Colony on the Continent, principally depends on the Number of its Inhabitants; that of a Plantation in the Islands arises from the Richness of its Commodities: We rely on the former chiefly for the Consumption of our Manufactures: We expect more from the Produce of the latter, for our own Consumption and for Exportation: This Distinction is so strictly true, that tho' the Supply required by the Inhabitants of the *West-Indies* is in value much beyond that which is necessary to the *Americans* in Proportion to their Numbers, yet, that Wealth, that Luxury, and those Circumstances of Climate, which incline them to Extravagance, at the same Time induce them to prefer the finer Productions of other Countries, to the coarse Commodities of our own; for the Manufactures of *Great Britain* are good, rich, and solid, but not delicate; strong without Grace; and rather substantial than elegant: To the plain, the industrious and frugal Republican of *America*, who is content with the Necessaries of Life, these are welcome, because they are useful: but they are not equally acceptable to the *West-Indians*, who think themselves intitled to Superfluities, and whose aristocratical Opulence enables them to demand the Products of the *East-Indies*, and other Countries, more similar in Climate, in Taste, and in Manners, to their own. We are therefore for the most part only Merchants to the one, and sell to them what we ourselves purchase; but we are both Merchants and Manufacturers to the other. The Returns too from each of these Countries, are as different as their Demands: The Products of the Continent are the Earnings of Industry; those of the Islands are the Improvements of Wealth: To an *American* therefore a numerous Family is Substance; but a *West Indian* must depend entirely upon his Capital: He cannot labour himself; he can acquire nothing but by Purchase and Expence. From this Difference of Circumstances it is evident, that the Object of Government with respect to the Acquisitions in *North America*, should be to tempt Inhabitants thither, and to encourage Population; and with respect to the ceded Islands, to enforce the speedy Culture and Improvement of Spots productive of such valuable Commodities, but still requiring a considerable Expence to raise and manage those Commodities. Lands therefore should be granted on easy Terms of Settlement in the one; but sold under strict Conditions of Cultivation in the other.

Agreeably to these Principles, the Governors of *Quebec, East Florida* and *West Florida*, (we are told by his Majesty's Proclamation of the 7th of *October*,) are authorized, *To grant Lands upon such Terms, and under such moderate Quit-Rents, Services, and Acknowledgements, as have been appointed and settled in the other Colonies, and under such other Conditions as shall appear necessary and expedient for the advantage of the Grantees, and the Improvement and Settlement of the said Colonies.* The Experience of a Century has suggested this Mode of Settlement; under the same or similar Terms to these, the whole Continent of *America* has been peopled, and near two Million of Subjects now hold by the Tenure proposed in this Proclamation. No further Encouragment is necessary; for Grants in the New, will always be prefered to the like Grants in the old Colonies: Novelty and Uncertainty attracts Adventurers, who besides ideal Allurements, may depend upon real Advantages; they have their Choice to a great Degree of the Lands they will take up, and the first that are taken up will probably in a few Years become valuable Estates; with these and many other Circumstances of Recommendation, there can be no doubt that the new Colonies, when put upon the same Footing with the other, will be peopled very soon. Many foreign Protestants will go thither. I fear they will be too much resorted to from these Kingdoms, and from *Ireland*, unless Employment can be found at home for those who must else seek it at a distance; but the greatest Supply will be from *America* itself; for such has been the Population of that Country, that many Parts of it can afford to furnish Inhabitants to others. The enterprizing Spirit and Passion for Discovery, which led its first Settlers thither, is not extinct in their Posterity, who are still inclined to rove in quest of new Habitations: They are all bred to the Idea of clearing fresh Lands, and of acquiring to themselves such Estates as their Fathers acquired, by those Means which they have seen so successful in their own Families. In the Provinces which are not yet well settled, this Principle operates within the Provinces themselves; but there are some, in which the greater Part of the Lands near the Sea Coasts and Banks of Rivers, are already occupied; and there the same Principle impels the younger Inhabitants to Migration. If the Colony should at first regret their Departure, the Loss will quickly be repaired by those who are left, and who in a few Years will be able to fill up the Intervals still remaining between the several Settlements; and with respect to the Mother Country, it is certainly very desirable that her People should be spread along every Coast and every River within her Dominions; for the Means of Subsistance will be easier there, than in the interior Parts of the old Colonies: The Settlers will consequently multiply faster, and their Consumption of our Manufactures will in the End be greater; they must apply to Agriculture alone; their Plantations will be open to immediate Access, as well for receiving our Supply, as for returning to us their Produce; and neither the old nor the new Colony, so long as they have Lands given them to cultivate, will have Hands, nor be at leisure to turn to Manufactures: the Connection of both with the Mother-Country is thereby strengthened, and thus our new Acquisitions instead of making the *British* Empire too great and unwieldly; on the contrary, enhance the Value, and secure the Dependance of our former Possessions.

That the granting of Lands in the new Acquisitions upon the same Terms as they are granted in the other Colonies, will alone produce the Effect I have described, is not Matter of Speculation only, but is founded upon constant Experience, brought down to the present Time by very recent Instances. That Part of *Nova Scotia*, which was held by the neutral *French*, has since their Removal been resorted to with an Eagerness hardly conceivable: I am greatly within Compass when I say that it contains already above Ten Thousand Inhabitants, all settled within the Compass of Six or Seven Years; by whose Industry that Province, which so lately was considered as no more than a proper Situation for a Fortress, whose Garrison it could not subsist, will instead of being a desolate Frontier, soon become a flourishing Colony, thronged with a hardy Race of People, who by clearing away the Wood will soften the Rigour of the Climate, and find themselves richly overpaid in the inexhaustible Fertility of the Soil.

It is not Rashness to foretell a similar Progress, in the settlement of our other Acquisitions: Even *Cape Breton*, that barren Appendage to the same Province of *Nova Scotia*, is known now to contain Treasures, which the Ministry have thought so worthy of Attention, as to insert in every Grant a particular Covenant with respect to them. All Coal-Mines are, I understand to be reserved to the Crown; if they were not, the Settlers would be diverted from the Cultivation of Lands, to be Mine Adventurers, led into Enterprizes they would not be able to support, by the tempting promises with which Uncertainty flatters and seduces: On the other hand, these Collieries when reserved to the Crown, may be managed by its Officers, or let to such as are able to make a proper Improvement of them. And there is hardly a doubt of Success in the Undertaking, if it be supported by the Expence it will require: For in many parts of *America*, especially in the Neighbourhood of the Great Towns, a Supply of Fuel is wanting: Such has been the Force and Extent of Cultivation, that Wood is become scarce in Countries, which were an impenetrable Forest not a Century ago; and the General Assemblies have therefore found it necessary to make Provisions for the Preservation of Timber. Coal from *Cape Breton* may on this Account be delivered in many of the Great Towns of *America*, at a cheaper Rate than any other Firing can be bought; and be the Demand ever so great, the Supply from thence will always be equal to it: For the Mines are not Veins; they are Mountains of Coal: Vast Clifts of nothing else stand open and accessible: No Boring is necessary to find it; no Pit need be sunk to come at it; no Fire Engines will be requisite for carrying on the Works: Adequate Capitals only must be had for making the Leading Ways; for providing a sufficient Stock of Carriages, and of Draught Horses or Oxen; and for keeping a large Quantity of Coal always ready to answer the Demands that may be made. These Collieries therefore which do not seem the Objects of Grant, because in the hands of common Settlers they would either be neglected, or prove ruinous to many of the Adventurers, may under proper Management, be at the same time very advantageous and convenient to the most settled Parts of *North America*, a considerable Nursery of Seamen, and a means of subsisting useful Inhabitants in a Climate too inhospitable for much Cultivation.

This Island however, and all the Neighbouring Shores in the Gulph of *St. Laurence*, have another Fund of Wealth in their Fisheries, which will attract Inhabitants without Number, and furnish the Means of Subsistance to all. A Resident Fishery will always overpower one that is carried on from a Distance: The People concerned in it can begin to Fish as soon as the Season permits, and will therefore be the first at Market; and the Merchants who send Ships thither from *Great Britain*, may freight their Vessels outwards, and be sure of a vent for their Cargoes, in the Colonies near to the Fisheries. By this Advantage they will be enabled to dispose of the Return at a cheaper Rate than the *French*, who have no such Colonies to take off their outward-bound Cargo: For the Profit of the *British* will be equal to that of the *French* Merchant upon the whole Voyage, tho' it should be less upon the Fish; the absolute Exclusion therefore of any *French* Settlement from that part of the World, (for I cannot call *Miquelon* and *St. Pierre* Settlements) will make such a difference between the Fisheries of the two Rival Nations, that *Great Britain* must, with respect to supplying other Countries, enjoy almost a Monopoly: And the necessary Consequence will be the Population of all those Coasts, where a Trade so beneficial and encreasing is established. Add to the Cod Fishery that of Whales, which under the Encouragement given to it during the last Sessions of Parliament, will immediately become a considerable Branch of Commerce (as I shall have occasion to shew more at large hereafter;) and there can be no doubt that in a few Years all these Coasts will be flourishing Colonies: The Prospect of their future Prosperity has, we have already seen, raised a Competition for Grants of Lands there: And the general Expectation which this Competition proves, will hasten the Event it presages. Care however must be taken to remove all Obstructions which may arise from Regulations that were established at a time, when these Countries were not in Contemplation: One of these was the Duty upon Whale-fins, which is now taken off by Act of Parliament; another arises from the Act of 15 *Car.* 2. c. 7. s. 6. which wisely prohibits the Importation of any *European* Commodities into the Plantations, unless they have been laden and shipped in *Britain*: But in that Act itself is an Exception of Salt, for the Fisheries of *New England* and *Newfoundland*, upon which the Expence and Delay of bringing the Salt they consume thro' this Country, would have been a heavy Burthen. The Indulgence of carrying it directly from *Europe* has been since extended to *New York* and *Pensylvania*, by 13 *Geo.* 1. c. 5, and by 3 *Geo.* 2. c. 12, and among the Reasons for granting it, which are recited in the Preambles to both those Acts, the Encouragement thereby given to the Fisheries of those Colonies, will, it is said, *be highly beneficial both to the Inhabitants of the said Colonies, and to the Trade of* Great Britain, *and enable the said Inhabitants to purchase more of the* British *Manufactures for their Use, than they are at present able to do.* The same Reasoning surely applies with greater force to our unsettled new

Acquisitions; and therefore the Legislature have had the precaution by an Act of the last Sessions, to provide that *Canada* and the Additions to *Newfoundland* and *Nova Scotia* should be comprehended within the Indulgence allowed to those, who are in the like Circumstances with respect to the Fisheries.

As the Benefits arising from the increase of the Fisheries will spread themselves one way along all the Coasts of our former Colonies, they will in like Manner extend into the new Government of *Quebec*, whose Inhabitants will of course be deeply concerned in so beneficial a Trade, carried on just in their Neighbourhood: The Peltry will be another great Branch of their Commerce; and the Countenance given to one of its most valuable Articles during the last Winter, by taking off the Duty upon Beaver imported here, will be a Means of its increase. I shall reserve for another Place a more particular Account of the Regulation which relates to that Commodity, and only mention it occasionally here, as one Circumstance among many, which will tend to the Improvement of *Quebec*; but there is no Ground for any Anxiety about the Population of this Province: It is already a flourishing Colony, and raises within itself all Kinds of Provisions in great Plenty: It is said that the Inhabitants now amount to ninety Thousand: They will certainly within a short Space of Time be more numerous than they are; and their Demand upon *Great Britain* for a Supply of Manufactures must be immediately very considerable.

It would be Presumption to speak with equal Confidence of the Southern as of the Northern Acquisitions in *America*; they were never frequented by the *English*; we have not that Acquaintance with them, which Conquest has given us with the others, and even their former Possessors were from want of Ability or Inclination, uninformed of their real Value. All Accounts however agree in representing *West Florida* as surprizingly fertile: In its natural State clearer of Wood than any other Part of the Continent, and luxuriantly productive of every Thing else; yielding spontaneously great Variety of Vegetables, abounding with Game and with Cattle, and not only promising, but actually producing Wines, Silk, and Indigo.

With respect to *East Florida*, it has been so much the Subject of Conversation, Ridicule, and Dispute, that it is difficult to form any very certain Ideas concerning it; yet that it is not known to those who depreciate it, is clear, from their Account of it: The Country they say can never be a flourishing Colony, for it is barren, and the greater Part of it is occupied by Tribes of *Indians*, more numerous and more fierce than any other in *America*: The two Circumstances are absolutely inconsistent; for where the *Indians* are numerous, the Country must be fruitful: They who do not cultivate Land, require much for their Subsistance; and if the natural Productions of the Soil are sufficient for such a Consumption, a populous Settlement may depend upon procuring Plenty by Culture. But I believe the Fact to be, that the Eastern Coasts, which alone were formerly visited, are sandy and barren: More recent Accounts however represent the interior Parts of the Country, as quite the Reverse; and at the same Time the *Indians*, who possess it, and who were once numerous, are said to be greatly reduced in their Numbers: The Mulberry and Orange Trees, the Vine, and the Indigo, and Cotton Plants, grow wild in many Parts of the Provinces: These it has in common with *Georgia* and *South Carolina*; but it has one Advantage over them, that being situated between two Seas, and out of the Reach of the bleak Winds, which blow from the *Apalachian* Mountains, it is not subject to that Excess of Cold in Winter, or to those sudden Changes of Weather at all Times of the Year, which, by the frequent Disappointments they occasion, have hitherto retarded the Progress that might have been expected, in the Culture and Management of the tender Plants abovementioned.

Both the *Floridas* are in Climate better adapted to such Cultivation than any other Colony upon the Continent; and I am confident, will be found equal in Soil to the best; to all which must be added, that as the building a Town is one of the first, but at the same Time the most difficult, because the most expensive Step to be taken in a new Settlement, this principal Object is already secured in *East Florida*, which the *Spaniards* have entirely deserted; and thereby have left *St. Augustine*, in which were three Thousand White Inhabitants, ready for the Reception and Accommodation of the *English*.

Mobile in *West-Florida*, tho' not so considerable a Place, is still large enough to obviate the Difficulties, arising from the Want of any Town at all in an Infant Colony; and both will soon increase considerably, by the Resort of those who engage in the contraband Trade with the *Spanish* Settlements, for which these Places are most conveniently situated. Numbers will never be wanting to settle Countries, where immediate Subsistance is from the Fertility of the Soil so certain; and the Prospect of future Wealth is from their valuable Productions, and their lucrative Trade so very flattering; and indeed I have heard some Persons esteem the Lands there so highly, as to think they ought to have been sold: But the Experiment would have been dangerous in Countries so little known, whose staple Commodities cannot be yet ascertained, and where Population is at present the principal Object: Perhaps hereafter it may be a point deserving Consideration, whether the publick should not avail itself of the Value of the Lands it has to dispose of: At present it seems quite sufficient to make this Advantage of those Lands only, which are to be exposed to Sale in the West-Indies: for their Products and their Culture are certain; and they will find Purchasers, which the others probably might not to any sufficient Number.

But I am very glad to see that the future Opulence of the two *Floridas* is so far already in Prospect, as to prevent the Administration from being seduced by the Circumstances of Contiguity, and Resemblance, to unite them under one Government. The Expence of two different Establishments is not to be put in Competition with the Security that results from dividing a Power, which might hereafter become alarming: We have not a better Pledge for the Dependance of the Colonies upon the Mother Country, than that which arises from their being so many distinct Provinces: Unconnected with each other but by their Relation to *Great-Britain*, different in their Manners, opposites in their Principles, and frequently clashing in their Interests and their Views, from Rivalry in Trade and the Jealousy of Neighbourhood, they can never form an Alliance that will be dangerous to the Mother Country; and no one of them is separately formidable: This happy Division was the effect of Accident, but it should be continued throughout by Design: And without promoting Discord or Variance between them, only by taking care that too great a proportion of Territory, People, and Wealth, be not united under one Head, and actuated by the same Motives, the Connection common to all with the Mother Country will be preserved entire, every other Bond of Union will be excluded, and the vast System of *Great Britain* and its Colonies will be permanent and compleat.

Among the Settlers in the new Acquisitions will be many Officers and Soldiers, to whom Lands are offered by his Majesty's Proclamation, in reward for their Services; and who will defend and improve the Countries, which were won by their Valour. But this Bounty is very properly restrained with great Strictness to those *who served there during the late War, who are now reduced or disbanded, and actually residing there, and who shall personally apply to the Governors for the Lands which under those Circumstances they may claim* in the several Proportions assigned them by the Proclamation. Were it extended to all Officers and Soldiers, many might be tempted to leave this Country, which is at all times too thinly peopled, and at present is exhausted by the War: But confined to such as served in *America*, and still continue there, the only Effect of it is to make their Residence comfortable in a Country, where without it they would probably remain.

The Encouragement given to Settlement, is not however indiscriminately extended to the whole Continent of *North-America*, tho' we have now got the Command of the whole. On the contrary, Limits are mark'd beyond which the *British* Colonies are not for the present allow'd to encroach upon the Territories of the *Indians. The Governors of Quebec, East Florida, and West Florida are therefore* strictly forbidden by the Proclamation, *to pass any Patents for Lands beyond the Bounds of their respective Governments, and all the Governors of the other Colonies are in like Manner prohibited from making such Grants of any Lands, beyond the Heads or Sources of any of the Rivers which fall into the Atlantic Ocean, from the West and North West, or of any Lands whatsoever, which not having been ceded by or purchased of the Indians, are reserved to them as their hunting Grounds.* By this prudent Restriction not only one Occasion of Wars equally impolitic and unjust with the Indians, is prevented; but our own Colonists are directed to Settlements of more Importance; nearer to the Sea; and nearer to the Places already well settled: where their Means of Subsistance will be more easy and certain; their Communication with the Mother Country more frequent; and their Dependance upon it more secure; and where they will neither provoke the Indians by their Encroachments, nor tempt them by their exposed and defenceless Situation, to attack them. But another Title to Lands might be set up; That of Purchase from the Indians; which being a Transaction of private Persons only, would be liable to more Abuses, and to greater publick Inconveniencies. Such Purchases are therefore as strictly prohibited as the Grants, and in one Respect the Restraint is carried still further: for even those Lands which lie within the Limits where Settlement is allowed, but which are reserved to the Indians, may not be bought by Individuals; and if the present Possessors should at any Time be inclined to dispose thereof, the Proclamation directs, that *the same shall be purchased only for the Use and in the Name of the Crown, at some public Meeting of the said Indians to be held for that Purpose, by the Governors of the Colonies respectively within which they shall lie*. But none of these Provisions are intended to fix Bounds to the *British* Empire in *America*: The Proclamation does not leave room for the Supposition that the Prohibitions are to be permanent: on the contrary, it declares in express Terms that they are only *for the present, and till his Majesty's Pleasure shall be further known*; for tho' the Circumstances of that Country require them now, yet it may and I doubt not that it will hereafter appear desireable to pass these Boundaries upon many Occasions, and to make Settlements in remote Countries, for particular purposes: but this should always be a Measure of Government, prudently concerted, and cautiously executed; not left to the Decision of a single Governor, and much less to the interested Views of any Individual or Sett of Individuals.

The selfish and inconsiderate Pursuits of private Persons, have already involved the Colonies in many Disputes with the *Indians*; and Objects of much less Importance than the Acquisition of Lands, have been productive of infinite Mischiefs. The itinerant Traders among these ignorant people, have been guilty of such Frauds and Abuses, as to create a general Distrust of our national Faith, and frequently to occasion Animosities for a long time irreconcileable. To guard against such Evils for the Future, by preventing improper Persons from being concerned in that Barter, which is their only Commerce, it is ordered by the same Proclamation, that every Person who

engages in it, shall take out a Licence from the Governor for
that purpose, and give Security to observe such Regulations, as
may from time to time be thought proper for the Benefit of
the *Indian* Trade. The Provision for future Regulations, gives
Reason to hope that some are in view; and indeed many will
be necessary to secure the public tranquility, and to make all
the Advantage that may be made of such an Intercourse, tho'
the want of certain Information, and the late Disturbances in
those Parts, may have hitherto rendered it impossible to establish them; for it is a Work of Delicacy, as an Error once committed cannot easily be retracted; and the Opinion, which
from thence would be conceived of their new Neighbours,
would not soon be removed among these Barbarians: yet now
that they seem inclined to be quiet, I hope the first Opportunity will be taken to put their Trade upon such a Footing, as
will make it a Bond of Union, not a Source of Depredations.

Security both from the Incursions of the *Indians*, and from
the more regular Attacks of other Enemies, will greatly promote the Settlement of the new Colonies; for Planters will
value Property there much higher, and be more sollicitous to
acquire it, when they observe that in the Disposition of the
Forces in *America*, so many Regiments are stationed in *Quebec*
and the *Floridas*: And when they see from the Advertisements
in the public Papers for transporting Cannon and Ordnance
Stores thither, that Measures are taken for putting those Provinces in a State of Defence; but the Circumstance, which will
be the most powerful Inducement to Foreigners to resort
thither, and which *Englishmen* before they embarked would
expect to be certain of, arises from his Majesty's *paternal Care
for the Security of the Liberties and Properties of those who shall
become Inhabitants of those Colonies.* The Freedom and other
Benefits of the *British* Constitution are promised to them, *and
Directions given to the Governors* (as the Proclamation declares)
*in the Letters Patent by which their respective Governments are
constituted, that so soon as the State and Circumstances of the
said Colonies will admit thereof, they shall with the Advice and
Consent of the Members of the Council, summon general Assemblies, in the same Manner as in the other royal Governments;
which Assemblies in concurrence with the Governor and Council,
are to make Laws, as near as may be agreeable to the Laws of*

England, and under such Regulations and Restrictions as are used in the other Colonies.

The Circumstances last mentioned relate equally to the Government of *Grenada*. The same Assurances are given, that a Constitution similar to that of *Great Britain*, shall be formed there; and the same or greater Care is taken to provide for the Security of those Islands; but in every other respect, a Policy, almost opposite to that which is proper for the Acquisitions in *America*, must be observed towards those in the *West Indies*. The characteristic Distinctions, between the two Countries, have been taken Notice of already; and the least Reflection upon those that have been mentioned, will satisfy a very cursory Observer, that more is requisite than merely to provide Inhabitants for the Islands, where Property does not consist so much in Land, as in the Stock that is upon it; Conditions of Culture are annexed to the Sale, and the strongest Pledge a Man can give of his having Substance sufficient for such a Cultivation, is his advancing Part of that Substance on the Speculation of the Profits he may make of it; for a Purchaser certainly thinks himself that he is, and most probably will be found to be equal to the Undertaking; no Precautions could have made Grantees equally responsible to the Public for the due Improvement of such valuable Property. The Objects of Acquisition would have been in reality so great, and in Appearance so much greater, that all Sorts of Impositions, Interest, and Importunity, would have been used, in order to obtain them; and where these had not prevailed, it would still have been impossible to fix the Proportions of the Allotments to the Abilities of the Petitioners; which will now be ascertained to some Degree of Accuracy by the private Interest of every Purchaser, as he must suffer himself if he exceeds the Bounds which his Fortune prescribes to him. But their Numbers would be small, if none were admitted who had not an immediate Command of Money, sufficient to answer all the Demands of such Estates at once: The Buildings, the Negroes, the Cattle, and other Stock which are requisite, will cost more than the Lands themselves; and to enable the Purchaser to furnish themselves with these, it is necessary to relieve them in the Payment of the Purchase Money; Revenue itself is of less Consequence to the Public, even at this Crisis of Distress, than an effectual and speedy Settlement of these important Islands. His Majesty's Proclamation of the 26th of *March*, has therefore declared, that *the Lands shall be sold by publick Auction, and the Purchase-Money shall be paid in different Installments, Twenty* per Cent. *immediately at the time of Sale, Ten* per Cent. *within one Year afterwards, Ten* per Cent. *within the second Year, and Twenty* per Cent. *within every successive Year, until the whole is paid.* But such an Indulgence would be Weakness, if Compliance with the Terms upon which it is granted, were not rigorously enforced; he who is guilty of a Breach of them, justly *forfeits all Right to the Lands*: and on that Condition he receives them.

Another Indulgence is converting part of the Purchase Money into an Annual Quit Rent, the Value of which the Buyers will deduct out of the Purchase Money; and they will thereby have still more of their Capital at Liberty, to answer the Demand upon them, for Clearing and Stocking their Lands. This Charge too is levied with a Lenity perfectly corresponding with the Design of imposing it; it is not to be paid on the whole Lot at once; but is gradually to creep upon it, in proportion as it becomes valuable; the Quit Rents being declared by the Proclamation not to commence till Twelve Months after the time each Acre shall be cleared, in conformity to the Condition of Clearing, which I shall presently have occasion to mention.

But still to enable Men to do Right, is not to oblige them to it: The same Means may also enable them to do Wrong, and then there will be more reason to expect an Abuse, than a proper Application of the Opportunity. Thus the Indulgences shewn to Purchasers with a View to assist them in improving their Lands, might be perverted to a quite contrary Effect, if no further Precautions were taken; for the Money thereby left in their Hands, might be and would be frequently employed only in enlarging their Purchases. All Tendencies to Monopoly are every where pernicious, unless Circumstances make them necessary: But in a new Colony they may be fatal; and must be detrimental: Too many Instances still subsisting of their mischievous Effects occur in several of the Colonies, where large Tracts of Land, which the publick Benefit requires should be cleared and settled, are kept back from Sale by the Proprietors, on the prospect of their daily becoming more and more valuable: And after this Experience it would have been unpardonable, not to have provided against the Evil. The Division of the Lands into Allotments of between One Hundred and Five Hundred Acres, to which Dimensions it appears by the Proclamation they will in general be confined, must be a Means of preventing it: As one of the strongest Temptations to the extending of Territory, the Temptation of Contiguity, will thereby be often removed: Since a cheap Purchase of one Lot, will not at all secure an equally good Bargain for the next. The Prohibition against any one Man's buying more than Three Hundred Acres in *Dominica*, or than Five Hundred in the other Islands, will have a still greater Effect: The Restriction being enforced by the forfeiture of all the Land which he shall Purchase beyond those Numbers, and of the Money he shall have advanced for such Excess; I am not speaking of a few Acres too much, by the Mistake of the Surveyor, and unknown to the Purchaser: These cannot be liable to Forfeiture, for the Crown can never take Advantage of an Error in its own Officer, to subject another person to a Penalty: And such a Penalty can in no Case be extended beyond the subject of the Provision it is intended to enforce; which Provision in the present Case is against exceeding a specified Number of Acres: And the Excess therefore is all that can be affected by the Penalty: But the best Security of all arises from the Conditions of Culture: The Proclamation requires that five Acres in every Hundred be cleared, every Year till half the Lot is thereby brought into a state fit for Cultivation: But as Accidents and Disappointments may sometimes make it difficult to comply with this Condition, the Breach of it is not followed by so rigorous a Punishment as Forfeiture: A pecuniary Penalty of Five Pounds every Year for every Acre that is not cleared within the Term prescribed, is thought sufficient, as, no Man will continue to pay so much annually for unprofitable Lands, which he may make valuable by clearing.

One other Condition is required, which will contribute both to the Improvement and to the Security of the Islanders: *That every Purchaser of cleared Lands shall constantly keep upon his Lot, One White Man, or Two White Women, for every Hundred Acres contained in such Lot; and in default thereof, shall be subject to the Payment of Twenty Pounds per annum for every White Woman, and Forty Pounds for every White Man, that shall be wanting to compleat the Number.* Any one who has the least Acquaintance with the *West Indies*, is apprized of the Advantages arising from White Servants both for Service and for Security. The only Question with me is, whether the Penalty be heavy enough to enforce the Observance of the Condition; for in *Antigua* and *Barbadoes*, where a like Regulation is established under a Penalty of Forty Pounds currency, that Sum has been found to be inadequate: Very few of the Planters have their full Complement; instead of providing all, they pay the Penalty for some, which on every Estate are constantly deficient: And this is now got into so regular a Course, as to become a settled Fund of their Revenue; so that the Penalty instead of enforcing the Law, is perverted into a Mode of Taxation: That imposed by the Proclamation is indeed to be paid in Sterling Money, but whether the difference between that and Currency will be great enough, to make the same Regulation effectual in the one, which for want of being more strongly enforced, has not been observed in the other Colonies, cannot be determined upon Speculation, but must be left to the decision of Time and Experiment.

Yet even if it should compel all the Planters to keep their proper Number of White Servants, that Number would not amount to so many White Inhabitants, as the safety of the Islands require. The Invitation given to poor Settlers by Grants of from Ten to Thirty Acres, will I hope supply the Deficiency; and the Expectation is so far well grounded, that a Policy similar to this has made *Barbadoes* the best peopled Island in all the *West Indies.* The Planters there are excused from keeping White Servants, by making small Grants to such poor Settlers: Two of these are deemed equal to Three White Servants; and by such a Substitution relieve from a Burthen the Estate which they improve. In these ceded Islands the White Servants are retained, and at the same time poor Settlers are invited by the Provision that is made for them: Which is so ample, that they will not long remain meer Cottagers, tho' they may be really poor Settlers in their Beginnings. A small Number of Acres well improved there, is no inconsiderable Property; tho' it will not raise the Possessors above the Rank they were born to, it

will furnish them with all the Comforts and Conveniencies
which are suitable to their Condition, and with many more
than usually belong to it: Some of the Wood they are to clear
will probably be of Value to sell; the rest will suffice to build
their little Tenements, to make their Fences, to furnish them
with a Thousand convenient Accomodations, and to supply all
their moderate Demands. The Products of their small Domains
will not indeed be those by which we are apt too indiscriminately to estimate *West India* Estates: Such Inhabitants as these
must not expect to mimick the Opulence of other Planters; for
the Lands allotted to them will hardly be of those Soils which
are proper for Sugar: But they may raise Coffee, Cocoa, Cotton, Ginger and Tobacco; in process of time perhaps some Indigo; and at all times Provisions: Whatever they raise will all be
their own, whatever Improvements they make will be for the
Benefit of themselves and their Families.

A poor Settler, who has but ten Acres, will find himself
greatly superior to any *English* Labourer; he that has thirty allotted to him, will be equal to many *English* Farmers; and Men
of this Rank in Life having some Stake to lose, and yet being
inured, by their Circumstances, to Hardiness and Labour, will
constitute a Militia, which may be always relied on, to suppress
domestic Disturbances among the Negroes, or to repel foreign
Invasions; but these Lots are to be given to those only who
really mean to reside upon them; the Test of their Intention is
their taking actual Possession themselves, *within three Months
from the Date of the Grant, and continuing to occupy and improve the same, for twelve successive Months.* And that they may
not be induced, by their Poverty, or tempted by an extraordinary Price, to dispose of their Possessions, their Lots are *unalienable by Sale for Seven Years*; this Condition is absolute;
even the Governor cannot dispense with it; but he may, by his
Licence, permit Leases or Mortgages to be made of them; and
such Leases and Mortgages may be made without Licence, in
order to provide for a Child of the poor Settler. As to his Wife
she wants no Provision, till after his Death, and no Restraint is
put upon his Disposition by Will; nor do any of these Restrictions subsist for more than seven Years, in which time, it is to
be hoped, such Settlers will be fixed, and their Lots will be
improved to a Value, which will prevent improper Alienations

of them to their wealthier Neighbours, who, if not check'd by such Precautions, would endeavour to monopolize to themselves, large Tracts of Land, by taking Advantage of the Necessities of these indigent People.

The Lots being thus secured to the Persons for whose Use they are designed, the only remaining Care is to see that they are properly improved; and for this Purpose the Proclamation declares that Conditions are to be inserted in the Grants, that *each Grantee*, being exempted from any Burthens, for four Years, *shall, at the Expiration of that Term, pay a Quit-Rent of Six-pence per Acre, for every Acre then cleared, and a Penalty of two Shillings per Acre, for every Acre of Land uncleared; which said Penalty of two Shillings per Acre, shall be reduced to Six-pence per Acre, as the Land shall be cleared.*

Regulations so wisely adapted to the End of peopling these Islands to a great Degree with white Inhabitants, can hardly miss of their intended Effects. And indeed, their Success is of the utmost Importance; for besides the Advantages, which from thence result, to these in common with all *West India* Islands, it is particularly necessary that Numbers of *English* Protestants should be invited thither, especially to *St. Vincents* and *Dominica*, which would be otherwise more exposed than any Settlements in our Possession; for in the former are still remaining, considerable Tribes of *Carribee Indians*, to the Number, it is supposed, of about four or five Thousand, and who may be troublesome Enemies, if they are not by proper Attention reconciled to their new Neighbours. Both in *St. Vincents* and *Dominica* many *French* have settled; and tho' their Possession is not rightful, because it is contrary to Treaty; yet, since they are allowed to remain there, it is necessary that they should be out-numbered by Inhabitants, who can be more certainly relied on. It is, indeed, a doubted Question, whether their Stay is to be wished; on the one hand, tho' they are an Acquisition of Subjects, yet they are Strangers to our Manners, our Government, and our Religion; and till national Prejudices are removed, cannot be hearty Friends to the Country they now owe Allegiance to: on the other hand, they are there; they have Property; they have Wealth; they are People, and People will be very much wanted; tho' their Titles to their Estates are bad in their Origin, for the King of *France* could not grant where he had not Dominion; and tho' therefore they cannot justly claim, yet they may reasonably desire to retain the Lands, which have been cleared by their Labour, and improved with their Substance; to insist on their Departure, would be driving them to *St. Lucia*, where great Encouragement is given to Settlers; and besides, Humanity revolts at the Idea of expelling from their Habitations, Men hitherto inoffensive, and who may never be pernicious, if time be allowed them to familiarize themselves to the Customs and to adopt the Principles of their present Fellow-subjects. The Experiment at least should be made, and those who are inclined to stay should not be obliged to go, by being immediately and arbitrarily stripped of their Possessions; at the same time they have no Pretence to expect that the Lands they wrongfully occupy, should be given to them, when the *English* can acquire no Property there but by Purchase. They cannot even require to be at once considered as Natives of *Great Britain*, and to be put on such a Footing, that the Government would have no Controul over them, should their Disaffection descend to future Generations. For these Reasons, I presume, it is, that a middle way is taken between confirming them in, and expelling them from their Possessions.

The Proclamation declares that *The Lands which at the time of the Surrender of these Islands were, and still are in the Possession of such* French *Inhabitants, shall be granted to them upon Leases for absolute or renewable Terms, upon certain Conditions, and under proper Restrictions.* By accepting this Offer, they will retain their Property, under a better Title than they can pretend to now. This is alone a Favour; and their subsequent Behaviour may intitle them to greater. What Number will be induced on these Conditions to continue, it is impossible to determine, or even to guess. The two Islands are said to contain now about three Thousand *French* Inhabitants, who employ above nine Thousand Negroes; some will not forsake the Connections to which they have been habituated, and these are certainly not worth retaining; others indifferent to either Form of Government, will tarry where they are; and many will be sensible of the Advantages arising from the Excellence of the *British* Constitution, the Security which a Naval Power gives to its Colonies, and the Wealth of a commercial Nation, extending to all its Dependants; These last will be as valuable Subjects as the Natives of *Great Britain*.

The whole Service of disposing of the Lands in all these Islands, is to be performed by Commissioners appointed for that Purpose. They are to divide each Island into Parishes and Districts, of such Forms and Dimensions, as the Circumstances of natural Boundaries, Contiguity and Convenience require. In every Parish they must trace out a Town, its Streets, its Marketplace, and other public Places, and then parcel out the Ground they shall destine for Habitations, into proper Allotments to build on. To make these still more commodious, a small Field is to be annexed to each, and both together to be sold, if the Land be clear'd, upon Condition to pay the Purchase-money in the same Manner as is prescribed to the Purchasers of Plantations; and a Quit-Rent of one Penny per Foot in Front of each Town Lot, and Six-pence for every Acre of the Field, that accompanies it; if the Land be uncleared, it is to be granted by the Governor, upon Security given to build, to inclose and to fence, within such time as to the Commissioners shall seem reasonable, and to pay the same Quit-Rent as the others. The Commissioners are also to set apart such Spots as shall be deemed proper for Batteries, Forts, and other military Purposes; they are to direct the Highways from one Town to another, and to accommodate every Plantation with easy Means of Access. They are to reserve to the Crown certain Districts of Wood Lands, which by the Damps continually exhaling from them, and the Clouds attracted by them, will furnish a perpetual Supply of Moisture, to all the neighbouring Country, and prevent the Drought to which Places in that Climate, when too much cleared are frequently liable. These Reservations being made, and a suitable Number of Acres also appropriated for the Grants which the Governor is to make to poor Settlers, the Commissioners are to divide the Lands into proper Allotments, and then to advertise, prepare for, and superintend the Sale. They ought to be Men of Knowledge, Abilities, and Confidence, in whom such a Trust is reposed, to contrive for the Accommodation of a future Colony; to fix the Habitations, and to limit the Estates of the Planters; to adjust publick and private Convenience; to mix the poor Settlers with the rich, for their mutual Advantage; to distribute to each his proportion of general Benefit; and to provide for the Cultivation, the Commerce, and the Protection of such an important Dominion. This is to be their liberal, but difficult, and perhaps hazardous Employ; for the Places they are to visit like all others in that Climate which remain in their natural State, must to a certain Degree be unhealthy. *St. Vincents* and *Dominica*, where much is already clear'd, are less so than they were; but *Tobago* is almost totally uncultivated, and the first Persons that go thither would be greatly exposed, if Care were not taken to secure them from the Inclemency of the Climate: It does Honour to the Humanity of those who provided against it, by contracting, as the public Advertisements shew, for one thousand Ton of Shipping to be station'd there for a year, on board of which not only the Surveyors and Commissioners, but all Persons whose Duty calls them thither in a civil or a military Capacity, all who repair thither to view and to purchase the Lands, and in general the first Settlers, may, with the Assistance of the Vessels which must occasionally lie there, be conveniently accommodated; and every Body knows that the Unhealthiness of the Climate is confined to the Land; at Sea, tho' at ever so small a Distance, the Air is always free from the noxious Vapours, which alone occasion that Sickliness and Mortality.

It is another agreeable Circumstance to the Purchasers, that the Commissioners are Gentlemen of such Characters, as leave no Reason to apprehend that the Power reserved to the Crown of revoking their Acts, will ever be exercised, tho' former Abuses suggested such a general Precaution, as a necessary Controul over their Conduct. Under them I doubt not the Sales will be equitably made, and the Public will avail itself of the Fairness of their Proceedings; for his Majesty, besides contributing out of the Duties belonging to him in the new Acquisitions, towards the Support of their civil Establishments, has been graciously pleased to give the Money arising from these Sales to the Use of the Public: No Conjecture can as yet I suppose be form'd of its Amount. Accident, Caprice, Plenty or Scarcity of Money at the Time, and a thousand other Circumstances, will make it greater or less; but at all Events the Purchase Money of so large a Quantity of Land so valuable, cannot be inconsiderable. *Tobago* and *St. Vincents* are reckon'd to be each of them as large as *Barbadoes*, and *Dominica* much larger; Some Parts of *Grenada* too will come to Sale, which were never granted by the King of *France*, or the Grants of which have been forfeited on Failure of complying with the Conditions annexed to them: The whole of the new Acquisitions are together of a greater Extent than all our former Possessions in the *West-Indies*, exclusive of *Jamaica*, and are said to contain between five and six thousand Acres: Of these indeed a great part, particularly in *Dominica*, is mountainous Ground, of little Value for Sale; tho' of inestimable Importance to the adjacent Country, for which it preserves the Seasons, sends forth Rivers, and affords the means of Defence; but still a great Proportion of the whole is as rich a Soil as any in the *West-Indies*, and being fresh Land, it will require less Expence, and at the same Time yield Crops far more luxuriant, than the utmost efforts of Culture can produce from an old Plantation: and tho' it cannot be brought to Perfection as Sugar Land, without a great Stock of Negroes and a considerable Charge in building, in preparing the Ground, and other Articles; yet at a very moderate Expence and in a very short time, it may be made fit for raising Ginger, Cotton, Cocoa, Coffee, Indigo, and other Commodities, which will amply compensate the Purchasers for the Money they may have expended, and will moreover supply them with a Fund for the further Improvement of their Estates, 'till they gradually become thoroughly stock'd, and in every Respect well appointed Sugar Plantations; which the Owners will then find they have acquired for a much less Sum upon the whole, than they must have given for one of equal Income in any other Island; and that Money too advanced at different Times and according to their own Convenience. But besides this general Advantage, each Island has some peculiar Circumstance to recommend it: The Situations of *Grenada* and *Tobago* will give their Inhabitants Opportunities to carry on a most profitable Trade with the *Spanish* Main: The former is besides possessed of two excellent Harbours, capable of containing any Number of Ships of any Burthen, and is never exposed to Hurricanes: It is already so far cultivated as to produce about 10,000 Hogsheads of Sugar, 3,500,000 lb. of Coffee, and 200,000 lb. of Cocoa, besides some Cotton and Indigo.

Tobago is represented as one of the finest Islands in the *West-Indies*, and of such a Surface that a very small if any Part of it is unfit for Cultivation.

St. Vincents is more hilly, but the cultivable Land is excellent, and so much is already clear'd as to yield it is reckon'd about 40000 *l.* annually; yet this is but a very small Proportion of the cultivable Land in the Island. Still more is clear'd in *Dominica*, whose present Produce is valued at near double that Sum; but the most material Advantage is *Prince Rupert's Bay*, which is capable of receiving and sheltering the largest Ships, and which will certainly be the principal Station of the *British* Fleet in all subsequent Wars, on Account of the Situation of the Island. It lies between *Martinico* and *Guadaloupe*, and its Cruisers can always intercept the whole *French* Trade, between those their principal Settlements: It is equally convenient for protecting the *British* Islands against the Depredations of Privateers, or more formidable Attacks: It is itself naturally strong, full of Posts, Defiles, Gullies, Rivers, and Precipices, and particular Attention is shewn in his Majesty's Proclamation to the Peculiarity of its Situation, by directing that the Lots which in the other Islands are in general to contain from one to three hundred, with some few of five hundred Acres, shall in this be for the most Part confined to between fifty and an hundred, but shall never exceed three hundred Acres: By which Provision a greater Number of Whites will be settled there than if the Lands were divided into larger Plantations, and *Dominica* will not only be secure in itself, but formidable both to *Martinico* and *Guadaloupe*. All these Circumstances of Advantage belonging to the ceded Islands in general, and to each in particular being consider'd; and not only unclear'd Lands, but great Quantities which have been clear'd, and belong'd to *French* Inhabitants who have left or will leave them, or to religious Communities, who cannot be allow'd to hold them by Lease or in any Manner whatsoever, being to be sold; his Majesty's gracious Gift to the Public will appear to be an Object worthy of *his* Generosity, and of the Gratitude of his People.

The several Steps above-mention'd with Respect to the Settlement of our new Acquisitions, both in *America* and the *West-Indies*, seem to me to have been so judiciously taken, that in all Probability these Accessions to the *British* Dominion, will in a few Years be peopled, cultivated, and in every Respect in the same Situation as our former Possessions. They will be incorporated into the general System of the *British* Colonies, be affected by the same Circumstances, and the Objects of the same Regulations. Their great Interests too will be the same, and those are also the dearest Interests of *Great Britain*; for to imagine that they can ever be separated, much less that they can stand in Competition, is a narrow, superficial Idea. The *British* Empire in *Europe* and in *America* is still the same Power: Its Subjects in both are still the same People; and all equally participate in the Adversity or Prosperity of the whole. Partial Advantages that opposed the general Good, would finally be detrimental to the Particulars who enjoyed them: The Mother Country would suffer, if she tyrannized over her Colonies: The Colonies would decline, if they distressed their Mother Country; for each is equally important to the other, and mutual Benefits, mutual Necessity cement their Connexion. It is an indisputable Consequence of their being thus one Nation, that they must be govern'd by the same supreme Authority, be subject to one executive Power in the King, to one legislative Power in the Parliament of *Great-Britain*. Their Connexion would otherwise be an Alliance, not a Union; and they would be no longer one State, but a Confederacy of many: Local Purposes may indeed be provided for by local Powers, but general Provisions can only be made by a Council that has general Authority; that Authority vested by indefeasable right in Parliament over all the Subjects of *Great-Britain*, wheresoever resident in the *British* Dominions, and to which it is Rebellion to refuse Obedience, for Parliament has never exempted any from the Submission they owe to it, and no other Power can grant such an Exemption, appears from hence to be founded not only upon just Right, but upon absolute Necessity. It has been accordingly asserted and exercised without Interruption from the Time that the Colonies became Objects of Attention; and must always subsist for the enacting of such Laws as relate to the whole, and even for controuling any particular Acts of local delegated Powers, which may contradict the general Welfare.

The Necessity of such a Superintendance, in order to prevent the Abuse of local tho' legal Authority, was proved by an Instance, which was under the Consideration of Parliament, during the last Sessions. The extravagant Encrease of Paper Money in some Colonies, had ruin'd the Credit of those where it was so multiplied, had embarrassed their Dealings with the neighbouring Provinces, and was destructive to the *British* Merchants who traded to *America*. These Bills were issued from Time to Time, upon Loans, as the Services of the Year, the Exigencies of the Government, or the Pretence of either, required. Funds were at the same time created, sometimes of Land, and sometimes of Taxes, for the Payment not only of the Interest annually, but of the Principal also at the End or during the Continuance of the Terms, for which they were created: But generally the Funds proved deficient, and the Bills consequently sunk in Value: This however was the least of the Evils occasion'd by their Paper Currency: Had their Discount stop'd here, it might have been born, or a Remedy might have been, as it ought to have been, applied, by creating additional Funds; but the contrary Measure was adopted: The Terms were prolong'd, more Bills were issued on Funds deficient already, and the whole Credit was hereby still further depreciated. To force these Bills into Currency, they were made a legal Tender, and that compleated the Mischief. Publick Credit was ruined, for the Payment of its Debts was postponed beyond the Time limited for discharging them; or made in Bills so sunk in Value, as not to be equal to a fifth, or even in some Cases to a tenth, of the Sterling Money advanc'd by the Creditors: Private Transactions were at the same Time equally affected: No Man knew what he should receive upon Payments to be made at any distant Time: All Contracts became uncertain; all Returns in Trade precarious; while the few Persons who concerted these Measures, had frequent Opportunities of making a private Advantage of the publick Calamity. From them who had caused the Evil, a Remedy could not be expected: It was their Influence that had led to *Acts, Orders, Resolutions, and Votes of Assembly, making and declaring such Bills to be legal Tender in Payments of Money.* The Interposition of the Parliament of *Great-Britain* therefore became necessary; it had interfer'd before with Respect to the four *New-England* Governments, and by a salutary Act made in 24 *Geo.* II. *to regulate and restrain Paper Bills in those Colonies,* the Credit of such Bills was retriev'd, and their Currency settled. To check the same Abuses in all the other Colonies, and to diffuse the Benefits of the like Provisions over all the *British* Dominions, an Act was passed during the last Sessions, by which, such Proceedings as have been above-mention'd, are strictly prohibited in all the Colonies, and *every Act, Order, Resolution, or Vote of Assembly which shall be made to prolong the legal Tender of any such Bills now subsisting and current, beyond the Times fixt for discharging the same; or to create or issue Paper Bills of any Kind or Denomination, declaring them to be legal Tender in Payment of any Bargains, Contracts, Debts, Dues, or Demands whatsoever,* is declared to be *null and void.* By which vigorous and seasonable Exertion of supreme Authority, this enormous Abuse will be prevented for the future, and the Bills issued by the Government there, being charged upon adequate Funds, and supported by publick Faith, will preserve their proper Value, during the whole Time of their Circulation; no Person being obliged from henceforth to take depreciated Money in Payment, the Creditors of the publick will receive as much as they advanced, and those to whom Debts are owing on private Transactions will really recover the whole that is due to them.

But without recurring to instances of Misconduct in the general Assemblies of certain Colonies, it is certain that however enlarged their Views may be, however upright their Intentions, yet their Powers must frequently fail in great and extensive Operations; confined as they are within the Limits of their respective Provinces, they can never attempt any Measures, which depend for their Success upon the concurrence of others; much less will they venture to sacrifice their own partial Advantages to the general good, when they cannot be sure that their Concessions will obtain the Ends for which they were intended. The Parliament of *Great Britain* alone can command the Acquiescence of all, and is therefore alone able to devise, conduct, and execute such Measures, as equally relate to all. This Power it has at all times exercised with impartial Sway, and has extended its parental Care to every part of the *British* Dominions; as each has on different Occasions particularly called for its Attention. No Preference, no Privilege, no

Exemption is allowed to any, not even to *Great Britain*, when her particular Interests seem incompatible with this greater System: She has frequently engaged in the Defence of her most distant Dominions, with more alacrity than the Provinces themselves that were immediately attacked: Her Debts have been accumulated by the Protection she has afforded her Colonies in times of War; her Revenues have been freely applied in times of Peace, in Bounties and numberless other Expences for their Encouragement and Support: She has even checked her own Cultivation for the Advancement of theirs, as in the instancy of Tobacco, which because it is a staple Commodity of some of the Colonies, is prohibited to be raised in this Country, except in small Quantities, and for particular purposes. But the Principles are great, the Policy is right, upon which this conduct is founded: The prevalence of these Principles at present is the illustrious Characteristic of the Times: No period of our History can within the same compass boast of so many Measures, with regard to the Colonies, founded upon Knowledge, formed with Judgment, and executed with Vigour, as have distinguished the beginning of his Majesty's Reign. The glorious Peace that ushered it in so auspiciously to his People, is a heap of Concessions forced from our Enemies, in favour of the *British* Plantations. The Tranquility it procured us has been employed in improving the Advantages both of our new and our former Possessions: In the prosecution of which great Work, the true Principles of Commerce have been attended to with so much discernment and care; the Interests of the Mother Country and those of the Colonies have been blended with so much skill; and their Union has been strengthened by so many Bonds of Connection, Obligation and Advantage; that every good Subject, whether in *Europe* or in *America*, must with success and stability to Measures, so wisely, so impartially adapted to the Benefit of all.

The Alteration made in the Duty upon Beaver Skins is one of these Measures, and one that is of great Consequence to a very valuable Article of *American* Produce, and to a considerable Branch of *British* Manufacture: That Commodity is absolutely necessary to the making of fine Hats; no other Material can supply the want of it; and as the Animal is not to be found in any other part of the World but *North America*, the Reduction of *Canada* has given us the entire Monopoly of it. The Acquisition has been made most seasonably for the preservation of the Manufacture of Hats, which had been long declining, and would perhaps in a few Years have been totally lost as an article of Exportation: For our Neighbours can generally underwork us; and if they can be furnished with the raw Materials upon the same Terms, will always be able to undersell us: Yet the Duty upon Beaver was laid on in such a manner, that they were supplied with the Material thro' *Great Britain*, at a cheaper Rate than we could retain it for our own Consumption: Seven-pence was imposed upon every Skin imported from *America*, and a Drawback of Four-pence was allowed upon Exportation: Those that were used here were by this means charged with Three-pence per Skin more, than other Nations paid, when supplied from hence; and the natural Consequence must be the Encouragement of their Manufactory to the prejudice of our own. In fact, the *French* had gradually gained upon us in every Market: The Manufactory was thriving in *Portugal*, and there was great reason to apprehend that it would soon be established in *Spain*, while our own Exportation of Hats was reduced above one half in Ten Years: That this great Diminution was not occasioned by a decrease in the Consumption, but only by a Change of the hands that were to supply it, appeared from the Exports of the Skins being now even greater than the Imports, of which they used to be only one Half, tho' the Imports were encreased from little more than 62,000, in the Year 1750, to above 128,000, in the Year 1763: Smuggling inwards supplied the Excess of the Exports over the Imports, and the number of Skins sent abroad last Year was so large, that had they been made into Hats here, those Hats would have produced to the Nation Sixty or Seventy Thousand Pounds more than the Skins sold for. To remedy these Evils, an Act was passed during the last Sessions, whereby the Duty is transferred from the Importation to the Exportation of Beaver Skins: A Penny only of the former Seven-pence is retained upon those Imported, in order to bring all to a regular Entry, and to be a Check upon the Trade, from whence a Judgment may at any time be formed of the State it is in; And Seven-pence is on the other hand imposed upon every Skin that shall be exported. The Remedy is simple, and therefore the more likely to be effectual; but if the Six-pence which Foreigners must pay for every Skin they use in Addition to its Purchase here, does not turn the Scale in our favour, a still heavier Burthen must be imposed; and the Duty certainly will then, it may now be the means of recovering and improving a considerable Manufacture almost lost; at the same time that a Revenue is raised upon the Consumption of Foreigners, who are absolutely dependant upon us for their Supply; and our Colonies are also relieved in a material Article of their Produce.

The Indulgence shewn to them in taking off the Duty upon Whale Fins, is of still greater Consequence to *America*, and would be thought a Sacrifice of the Interests of *Great-Britain* to those of the Colonies, if she could consider them as distinct and independent of each other. The Whale Fishery has been long the Object of public Attention, and many Provisions have at different Times been made for the Recovery of it from the *Dutch*, for our own Consumption at least, which to our great Disgrace and Detriment, used to be entirely and has even till now been partially supplied from *Holland*. For this Purpose the Rigour of the Act of Navigation was relaxed, and the Trade laid open to all the Inhabitants of *England*, whether Natives or Foreigners, free of Custom by 25 *Car*. II. c. 6. but by the same Act *Fifty Shillings per* Ton is imposed on Whale Fins caught by Ships belonging to the Plantations, unless the same be imported by Ships belonging to *England*, in which Case it is reduced to *Twenty five Shillings per* Ton. This Duty call'd the old Subsidy is no very great Burthen, as a Ton of Whale Bone may fairly be estimated upon an Average at 250 l. but a heavier Imposition of *Three-pence per* Pound weight was laid on by 11 and 12 W. III. c. 21. upon all Whale Fins imported, which entirely ruin'd the Fishery, and made it necessary first by 10 G. I. c. 12. and afterwards by 5 G. II. c. 28, continued by several subsequent Acts, to take off the Duty; but this Relief was confined to such as should be caught in the *Greenland Seas, Davis's Streights, or the Seas adjoining thereto*. The whole Burthen still continued upon the *American* Fishery, which indeed was at that time too inconsiderable an Object to attract the publick Notice, and on the same Account was not included in the Encouragement which was afterwards given to the *Green-*

land Whale Fishery: for the merely freeing it from Duty, being insufficient to establish it, the Assistance of Bounties was applied; first of *Twenty Shillings* for every Ton of Shipping employed therein, by 6 G. II. c. 23, and afterwards of *Forty Shillings per* Ton, by 22 G. II. c. 4. by which Encouragement, the Purposes of all these Endeavours were at last in a great Measure answered, and the *British* Whale Fishery began to cope with the *Dutch*, or at least to intrench on their Monopoly. The Price of Bone has in Consequence thereof been reduced from 700 l. to 250 l. *per* Ton, and that of Oil from 20 l. to 16 *per* Ton. The Oil we procured has generally been equal to our own Consumption, and sometimes foreign Markets have been supplied out of our Abundance; but we have never been able to provide ourselves with a sufficient Quantity of Bone: Between sixty and seventy Ton having still been annually imported from *Holland*, which at the lowest valuation must be reckon'd 16000 l. or 17000 l. *per Annum*. In this State of the Trade the Gulph of *St. Lawrence* becomes Part of the *British* Dominions, and a great Whale-Fishery is discover'd there, which was perhaps unknown to its former Possessors: The Industry of the *Americans* has improv'd it so much, that from 7 *Cwt.* 0 *qrs.* 17 *lb.* of Bone, which was all they imported in 1759, they in 1762 sent hither 335 *C.* 2 *qrs.* 5 *lb.* and in 1763, 1546 *C.* 3 *qrs.* 13 *lb.* and this rapid Progress has been made under the Pressure of a heavy Duty, while at the same Time, the Rival Trade to *Greenland* was supported by a very liberal Bounty. But the Inequality is now removed, and an Act was pass'd during the last Sessions, by which all Duties are taken off from Whale Fins imported from *America*, except the light Charge of the old Subsidy. The Bounty upon the *Greenland* Fishery is indeed continued by another Act 'till the Year 1768, but it will not be long or often demanded; for the *American* Whale Fishery now freed from its Burthen, will soon totally overpower the other, and this Indulgence can therefore only be meant in Favour of the Parties who have hitherto been concerned in the latter, and who are intitled to the Assistance of the Publick to enable them to retire gradually, instead of being forced to an abrupt Determination of a Trade, which was beneficial, tho' it is now become useless to the State. A Year or two more will entirely put an End to it; and that in the Gulph of *St. Lawrence* will immediately furnish as much as was ever brought hither from *Greenland*, and probably far more; so as not only to make any Supply from *Holland* unnecessary, but to enable us in Process of Time to sell at foreign Markets upon cheaper Terms than those who fetch the Commodity from *Greenland* can afford it; for the *American* Whale Fishery being carried on in Seas little encumber'd with Ice, and consequently requiring fewer Precautions in the Construction and Equipment of the Ships, and in the Choice and the Number of the Crew; being open for a much longer Season; and at all Times less liable to Accidents, Disappointments, and Losses than the other; and the Ships employ'd in it having Opportunities to make Returns both Ways in their Voyages; with all these Advantages, it must necessarily in Time prevail over that which has hitherto flourish'd only because there was no other: but whatever may be the Event upon this Speculation, should our own Consumption alone be supplied, even in that confined View it was right to prefer the *American* to the *British* Whale Fishery. Tho' we resign a valuable Branch of Trade in their Favour, a Trade whose Produce may be valued at *Three Hundred Thousand Pounds* a Year, and in which three thousand Seamen, besides a great Number of Shipwrights, and other Artificers were employ'd; yet the Preference is given upon truly national Considerations, when the Inhabitants of *America* and of *Europe* are look'd upon as one People: It then becomes a general Benefit to promote that Fishery which has so many Advantages over the other; and which will maintain itself without the Support of Bounties, the Expence of which was near *Thirty thousand Pounds per Annum*.

Tho' this Accession to the Whale Fishery, that of Seals and Sea Cows, the Monopoly of Beaver, and many other important Branches of Commerce, are particularly Parts of our new Acquisitions, yet the Profits arising from them, and the Benefits resulting from the Encouragement given to them, are by no Means confined to the Inhabitants of the newly acquired Territories: Other Colonies will enjoy an equal, some a greater share: The Beaver, for Instance, is not the Produce of *Canada* alone, and the Vent of it only down the River *St. Laurence*; but the Reduction of *Canada* having open'd our Communication with all the Countries where it is produced; it may now be brought over the Lakes, and down the Rivers, to *New-England*, *New-York*, and perhaps to still more Southern Colonies; whose Merchants will enrich themselves with the Spoils of Desarts, they hardly knew before. The Whale Fishery seems indeed more local, but even that will be carried on by Ships sent from Ports far distant from the Gulph of *St. Laurence*, and a great Part of the Coast of *North-America* will be engaged in so beneficial an Adventure: By them it has been increas'd to its present Extent, for the Inhabitants of the Shores of the Gulph evidently cannot have been sufficient for what has been done already. But even those who are too far removed to be immediately active in the Fishery itself, will be sensible of its Effects, and partake of the Generosity of *Great Britain*. The Profits of the Colonies that are engaged in it, will circulate thro' all the others, from whom they will demand, as their Wealth and their Inhabitants increase, larger Supplies of the Commodities which they do not produce themselves; for hardly any one of the Plantations can pretend to furnish all the Necessaries, none all the Conveniencies of Life; and for the Superfluities, the richest and most fruitful must fetch them from many and from distant Quarters. Each has its several Staple; each its several Delicacies; which by their constant Intercourse are freely communicated from the one to the other; but throng to those Marts, to which large Demands, and quick Returns, or in one Word, Riches invite them. Trade thus diffusing over the whole, the Prosperity of every Part, not only adjacent Provinces, but the most distant, those apparently most opposite, even the *West-Indies* and *North-America*, mutually participate in the Advances they each of them make in their particular Branches of Culture and of Commerce. *Great-Britain* herself enjoys, and both in Trade and in Strength feels herself benefited by the Welfare of every particular Colony. How much more must the Colonies, which are as near in Affinity, and so much nearer in Neighbourhood, interchangeably contribute to the Advantage of each other?

In this View the Indulgence shewn to *Carolina* and *Georgia*, with Respect to the Exportation of Rice, which at first Sight may seem entirely local, if traced thro' all its distant Effects, will appear to be a general Benefit: Rice being an enumerated Commodity could not be carried from the Place of its Growth, unless to some other *British* Plantation, or to the Kingdom of

Great Britain: but the Rigour of this Restriction has been relaxed, and by 3 *Geo.* II. c. 28. and 27 *Geo.* II. c. 18, it is allowed
to be carried directly from the Plantations, to any Part of *Europe* lying Southward of *Cape Finisterre*; the Charge of double
Freight being thus taken off, *Spain* and *Portugal* who used to
bring all their Rice from the *Levant*, receive it now from our
Colonies, and consume 20000 Barrels every Year. The half
Subsidy upon it yields some Revenue; the Bulkiness of the
Commodity employs a great Quantity of Shipping; and the
Demand for it has been one great Means of raising *Carolina*
to its present flourishing Condition. But surely every Reason
that could suggest the granting this Permission with respect to
any part of *Europe*, urges the Propriety of extending it to Foreign Plantations; for tho' Rice be a very desireable Food in
such Climates, it is not absolutely necessary; the want of it may
be supplied by other kinds of Vegetable Provisions: And the
Vent therefore will depend upon the Cheapness. If the Voyage
round by *England* can be saved, and the Commodity thereby
afforded on reasonable Terms, vast Quantities may be disposed
of amongst the foreign Plantations; for in the short time that
Guadalupe and *Martinico* were in our Possession, 14,000
Barrels were consumed there; and an Application was made
last Winter for a Contract to deliver 40,000 Barrels in three
Years at *Cayenne*, which could not be complied with, unless
some Alteration were made in the Law; the *French* too are not
the only Purchasers that may be expected; other Nations will be
desirous of procuring Rice for their Settlements from the same
Quarter, and the Negroes in all these Settlements will take off
the Broken and Mowburnt Rice, which will make the good
Rice cheaper, and is one Advantage that a *West India* Market
for this kind of Provisions has over an *European*. To allow
therefore of its immediate Exportation thither from the places
of its Growth, will be a great Encouragement to a Staple Commodity of two of our Colonies: And the measure is adopted,
not upon Speculation, but on a certainty: We have no Experiment to make; we are only to accept of an Invitation, and a
new Branch of Commerce is obtained: an Improvement will at
the same time be made in the *American* Revenue, for the Act
of the last Sessions which *grants the Liberty of Exporting Rice
from* South-Carolina *and* Georgia *to any part of* America *to the*

Southward of those Provinces, retains the half Subsidy, which amounts to about Seven-pence upon every Hundred Weight of Rice thus exported, and is the same Duty as is paid upon that which is carried directly to the Southward of *Cape Finisterre*, or being brought to *Great Britain*, is Exported from hence to any other Country.

Other Commodities, the Produce of the Colonies, but of still greater and more extensive Importance, both to the Colonies and to *Great Britain*, have this Year received that Encouragement, they stood so much in need of, and so richly deserved: The Bounties upon Hemp and Flax, which were given first by 3 & 4 *Ann.* c. 10. and continued by several other Acts, had been of late Years suffered to drop, and the Act by which they were last given, was expired: The Culture of Hemp did not succeed: Hardly any was Imported; and the Bounty being never called for, fell into Oblivion; but the encrease of the Colonies having enabled them to attend to it again, and annually to raise large Quantities; the Renewal of the Bounty will be a probable means of procuring from thence in Course of Time sufficient for our whole Consumption, tho' it amount at a Medium of the last Ten Years, to more than 300,000*l. per Annum.* To raise so considerable an Article of Naval Stores within ourselves; to shake off our Dependance for a precarious Supply upon other Countries, who by some unexpected fluctuation in political Connections, may become adverse to these Kingdoms, and will then be able to disappoint us in a Time of Crisis, or even to occasion the Distress which they will not relieve; to wrest in short out of the hands of other States, be they ever so friendly, such an undue Influence over all our Operations, is a great object to a Maritime Power: And to procure so extensive a Branch of Trade; is equally interesting to a Commercial People: But when such an Acquisition is in view, *Great Britain* does not morosely grudge to the Colonies the greater share of it: She does not tenaciously adhere to her own Interests alone: On the contrary, she freely gives up the Revenue arising from the Importation of Foreign Hemp: And liberally grants out of her other Revenues the Bounties of *Eight Pounds per Ton for Seven Years, of Six Pounds per Ton for the next Seven Years, and of Four Pounds for another Term of Seven Years more, on Hemp* imported from *America*. The same Bounties on the like

Quantities of Flax imported from thence, are, so far as that
also is a Naval Store, founded upon the same Principles; but
considering Flax as the principal Material in the Manufactory
of Linen, the Encouragement given to the Importation of it
will contribute to another great End, which I shall presently
have occasion to explain more fully, when the Duty upon
Linen, with which it is connected, will, together with the other
Duties which it has been thought expedient to impose, be
particularly considered.

The Circumstances of the Times, the Necessities of this
Country, and the Abilities of the Colonies, concur in requiring
an *American* Revenue; *Great Britain* strained to the utmost of
her Strength, sinks under the Exertion, and will hardly recover
by Rest alone, without the Aid of Remedy: her funded Debt
increased by 65,061,960*l*. 7*s*. 10*d*. for the Expences of the last
War, amounts now, the 1,000,000*l*. Civil List Debt being included, to the enormous Sum of 130,586,968*l*. 4*s*. 0¼. upon
which 4,716,681*l*. 4*s*. 11½. Interest is annually paid: her un-
funded Debt at the End of the War was no less than 9,061,416*l*.
11*s*. 9*d*. of which 2,464,517*l*. 13*s*. 10*d*. is this Year paid off, and
3,483,553*l*. 1*s*. 10*d*. is for the present charged upon the Sinking
Fund; but the whole must be paid, before that Fund can be
applied to the Diminution of the funded Debt: her Peace Establishment is at the same Time increased by the Necessity of
keeping an Army in *America*, of augmenting her Fleet, and of
providing for the many Expences of her additional Dominions.
The whole Annual Revenue that is necessary to answer all
these Demands, amounts to near 3,000,000*l*. and is raised by
many, and some of them burthensome Taxes, which are imposed, not only upon the Luxuries of the Rich, but which all
the Researches of Invention, and all the Resources of Finance,
could not find Means to keep off from the Consumption of
the Poor; and great Part of them are not meer Expedients for
a present Exigency, but are entailed upon our Posterity perhaps
to distant Generations. The whole of this vast Revenue is
raised in *Great Britain*, and is paid by the Inhabitants of *Great
Britain*, expecting such Duties as are levied or retained upon
Exportation to foreign Countries, or to the Colonies, and
which after all Draw-backs and Bounties are allowed, make but
a small Proportion of the whole; and even these, tho' produced

on the Consumption of others, are still a Burthen upon the Trade of *Great-Britain*; while the Colonies in *North America*, near two Million of *British* Subjects, an opulent, commercial, thriving people, and who have been enabled by the Patronage of their Mother Country to extend their Trade and their Cultivation over that fertile Continent, supported by her Wealth, protected by her Power, and blessed with her Laws, contribute to the national Expence by Taxes raised there, no more than seven or eight Hundred Pounds *per Ann.* and the Colonies in the *West-Indies*, where, tho' their Numbers are less, their Riches are greater, have remitted no more than eleven or twelve Hundred Pounds *per Ann.* to *England*: The whole Remittance from all the Colonies at an Average of thirty Years has not amounted to 1900*l.* a year, and to make it still more ridiculous, the Establishment of Officers necessary to collect this 1900*l.* amounts to 7600*l. per Annum.*

There is no Occasion to accompany this Account with any Observations; only to state it, is to prove the Necessity of an additional *American* Revenue; they can certainly bear more; they ought to raise more: The Subjects and the Mode of new Impositions are therefore the only Considerations; but to lay them on Subjects, and in such a Manner as would not be oppressive to those who were to pay them, would not be dangerous, in the delicate Situation of the Colonies, with respect to their Trade, their Improvements, and their Connection with the Mother Country, and would at the same time apply equally to all, in their different Stages of Progress from Infancy to Maturity, was a Measure that required the utmost Caution, Circumspection, and Care: It came under the Deliberation of Parliament the last Winter, and by their Wisdom an Act was passed to be the Foundation of an *American* Revenue, which is formed upon such Principles, that the Increase in the Revenue, which may be expected from it, tho' very considerable, seems the least important Object; so very judicious, so very interesting are the several Provisions of this Act, for the Purposes of Commerce and Colonization.

To encourage the Consumption of our own Produce and our own Manufactures, in preference to those of other Countries, has been at all times an undisputed Maxim of Policy; and for this Purpose, high Duties and even Prohibitions have been laid upon foreign Commodities, while Bounties have been granted on our own. The general Tendency of the Act now before us is to extend the same Principle to the *American*, as is followed in respect to our home Trade and Consumption. One general Clause with this View diminishes the Draw-back allowed on Re-exportation, and enacts that *no Part of the Rate or Duty, commonly called The Old Subsidy, shall be repaid or drawn back, for any foreign Goods of the Growth, Production, or Manufacture of Europe, or the East-Indies, which shall be exported from this Kingdom to any British Colony, Wines, white Callicoes, and Muslins, only excepted,* which are otherwise provided for. In many Articles this will give a Turn in favour of *British* Produce and Manufactures; in some, it may be an Inducement to the Colonies to apply to the Cultivation of Commodities, they may very well raise, but have hitherto neglected; but in none can it be oppressive to retain all the Old Subsidy, the whole of which is a very low Duty, and half of it is retained already; these foreign Commodities will still come much cheaper to the *Americans* than they do to their fellow Subjects here, who pay on almost all of them some, and on many of them very large additional Duties, and indeed can in general afford to pay more. The Revenue too of the Customs here will be increased, from the great Quantity of Goods, upon which this saving of the Draw-back will be made; and tho' it would be tedious to enter into the Detail of the numberless Articles, and the various Rates upon the several Articles that will be affected by it, without which Detail, no exact Calculation can be made of the Produce to be expected from this Duty; yet the general Computation, and which certainly is very moderate, that the Goods imported annually from *Great Britain* into *America*, amount in Value to the Sum of 1,400,000*l.* and that one Third of these are foreign Goods re-exported from hence, make a very low Duty upon so great a Consumption, no contemptible Object; but besides these, it is commonly supposed that foreign Goods to the Amount of 700,000*l.* are annually smuggled into the Colonies, and should the Regulations, I shall presently mention, to have been made for the Prevention of all illicit Trade, have the Effect that is to be wished, to bring the greater Part of these too in the regular Channel thro' *Great Britain*, in which Case the whole Subsidy would be retained on them also, which now yield nothing, then the Amount of this Duty upon all, will really be considerable.

Among the Goods that are the Subjects of this Tax are the foreign Linens, which thereby become less merchantable for this Trade, than the *British*; on the other hand, a rival Manufactory is apprehended in *America* itself, and inhancing the Price of Linens, exported from hence, will, it is said, be a Means of encourageing it. For myself, I own I am under no such Apprehensions, and the Facts that are alledged to support that Opinion, seem to me to prove the contrary. Great Quantities of Linen it is true are made there already; but then the Manufactory is almost confined to *Pensylvania*, and there the weaving Part of it is carried on entirely by the *Germans*, who transport themselves thither in great Numbers every Year, and carry their Mystery with them. For a present Subsistance on their Arrival, they follow the Business they were bred to, but as soon as they get enough to enable them to settle a Piece of Land, (which they soon may, when they can earn Three Shillings and Six-pence *per diem*,) they find farming the more agreeable and more advantageous Employment: they turn to it themselves, and train their Children to that only. A Manufactory thus deserted by those who are engaged in it on the first Opportunity that offers, and dependant upon fortuitous Circumstances for Existence, can never be considered as flourishing and established: Nor is there any Prospect of its being otherwise; for the Extent and Fertility of the Country is so vastly disproportionate to the Number of Inhabitants, that good Lands are in most of the Colonies an easy Acquisition, to those that will clear them, and where Estates may thus be raised by meer Tillage, all Temptations to Manufactures are wanting; Men who can depend upon their Industry alone, will not have recourse to Arts for Subsistance; and a Father, who can enable his Son to provide for himself, by taking up a Piece of uncleared Land for him, as soon as he is of Age to manage it, and till then has his Assistance in cultivating that, which he himself had cleared in his Youth, will think Money and Time both thrown away in teaching him a Business not so good as his own, and by which it will appear to him that his Child is prematurely taken out of his Family. He really can with less Expence set him up in a Farm than in a Trade, and he knows that a Farmer who cultivates improveable Land for his own Advantage, is in a better Situation than a Manufacturer: It is just the Difference between a substantial Yeoman, and a Journeyman Weaver. So long therefore as the *Americans* can get Land at an easy Rate, they will apply to the Cultivation of it in preference to all other Employments: and it is the Glory of the last Peace, that it has furnished them with Territory sufficient to subsist their People in all their Increase to very distant Generations. Still however it may be said all Manufactures in the Colonies are not carried on by Foreigners only; including even those that go from these Kingdoms, who so far may be considered as Foreigners there: Many Natives of *America* it may be urged are amongst them; and it is true; accidental Circumstances engage them, and the Necessities of the Country require them; for there is a certain Degree of Manufacture attendant upon Cultivation, in order to convert to its proper Use the whole of every Production, some Parts of which might otherwise be left a worthless Refuse on the Hands of the Planter. In the Article of Flax, for Instance, which has hitherto been raised in *America* principally to supply the Demand of Flax Seed for sowing, and other Purposes here, the Stalks must be thrown away, if there is no Opportunity to export or to spin them. Hitherto the Exportation has not been found to answer; and therefore the Farmers employ their Families in spinning, when the Rigour or Inclemency of the Season confine them within doors: This is the real Foundation of their Linen Manufactory; They have hitherto proceeded no further than this has carried them; nor is it likely they should soon make a greater Progress; for even in *Pensylvania*, where more Flax is raised and more Weavers are settled, than in any other Province, common Labour is so dear, that if a Farmer cannot spin his own Flax in his own House, and by his own Family, he will not find his Account in putting it out to be spun: if that Expence falls upon him, he can supply himself cheaper with Linen from *England*: So very small is the Advantage of Manufacturing for themselves, and so very confined is such a Manufactory: Materials will never be purposely raised to supply it, it cannot bear the Expence of all its several Branches, if those employed in them are to apply themselves to no other, nor will it ever produce such a Quantity of Merchandize, as to become an Article of

Commerce; yet limited as it is in its Nature, it will probably rather diminish than increase, now that the Parliament has granted a Bounty as above-mentioned on the Importation of Flax: The *American* Planter will no longer complain that his Flax Stalks must be wasted if he does not Manufacture them: but a Vent being opened for them into *Great Britain*, whither he could not afford to send them before, this will probably be found to be the most advantageous Manner of disposing of them.

But there are more cogent Reasons still of a public Consideration against the Attempt to extend such a Manufactory; for tho' the Inhabitants of these Kingdoms and of *America* are equally Subjects of *Great Britain*, yet they serve the State in different Capacities; and if to make unwarrantable Distinctions between them would be Oppression; on the other hand to preserve the Distinctions which the Difference of their Situations has made, is true policy, which has the general Good for its Object: Extent of Country, Fertility of Soil, Cheapness of Land, Variety of Climate, and scarcity of Inhabitants, naturally lead the *Americans* to Cultivation: There are hardly any Productions of the Earth which they cannot raise; including the *West India* Islands I believe there are none: But putting them out of the Case for the present, the Continent alone can produce Provisions for Subsistence, Commodities for Commerce, and the raw Materials for Manufacturers to work with, in much greater Variety, in Quantities immeasurably larger, and on Terms by far more easy than they could be raised in *Great Britain*; here on the contrary, landed Property is very valuable, and but a small proportion of it still remains improveable to any considerable degree, by force of Cultivation only; so that the Occupation of Land is rather a Means of vesting than of acquiring Money. But the Inhabitants of *Great Britain* are more than sufficient for its Cultivation, and must seek for Fortunes, and even for Subsistance in Trade and Manufactures: They have Science, Experience, and Skill, supported by Riches and Credit equal to any undertaking, while a constant Correspondence and easy Intercourse between themselves, and a universal Commerce to all parts of the Globe, enables them to dispose of all they prepare for Merchandize: In every one of these Articles so necessary to Manufactories, they have greatly the Advantage of the *Americans*; and the Basis of all, manual labour, is cheaper here than it is there, so great is their Demand to clear the immense Tracts which still lie waste, and to improve those which they have hitherto been able to cultivate but partially. The Manufactures therefore of *Great Britain* must on all these Accounts be superior in Quality, and lower in price than those of *America*. And the necessary Consequence from the different Circumstances of the two Countries is, that neither can encroach upon the other in the Articles that are particularly adapted to each, without Prejudice to both: Commerce is in many respects common to both; but Lands are wanting in the one for Produce, and hands cannot be found for Manufactories in the other: Should then the *Americans* attempt to extend their Manufactures beyond the point, to which the convenience of the Planter, and the accidental Circumstances of Individuals, will naturally carry them, should they endeavour to establish them as Branches of Commerce, they would immediately raise the price of Labour already extravagantly high; they would draw off their people from their proper Employment in Agriculture; retard the clearing of the Country; check all Improvements of Land; load its produce with an additional Expence; enhance the Value of all the Necessaries of Life; and their success in the End, if they should succeed, would be less Detrimental to their Mother Country, than to themselves. Success however is not to be expected: The Difficulties that will arise from the Circumstances of the Country and the Genius of the People, both naturally adverse to Manufactures, are too great for any Individuals to struggle with; for it will be no easy Task to persuade the *Americans* to forsake the rich Lands that invite their Culture, and promise an ample Recompence for the Labour bestowed upon them; to leave the ways their Fathers trod, and in which themselves were trained; to drop a Business which they already understand, in which they have had a long Experience, and by which all their Family have thriven; in short, to change all their Habits of thinking, and their whole Manner of Life; in order to apply to Arts which they do not know, or know but imperfectly, with a great loss of Time, and at an uncertain Expence, in pursuit of precarious Gain. Yet all this must be effected before regular extensive Mercantile Manufactories can be established in any considerable Numbers in *America*: Those that subsist there now, are of a quite different Nature, arising out of Agriculture itself, as one of its natural Effects, which instead of Checking, encourages its Progress: That of Linens has no other foundation; and when its Extent is fully examined, it will be found not to have passed beyond the Bounds, which such a source would naturally supply. For it is not to be imagined that they manufacture all they do not Import from *Great Britain*: Large Quantities are annually sent thither from the Ports of *Holland* and other Countries on the *German* Ocean, in Ships employed in an illicit Trade with the Colonies. Others are smuggled in by smaller Parcels from the Foreign, particularly from the *Dutch* Islands; and no inconsiderable Quantity is constantly brought by the *Germans* who go to settle there in great Numbers every Year; many of whom have, with them one, two, three, or more, Pieces of Linen, which they find Means to land clandestinely, and dispose of at moderate Prices. These Deductions being made from the Difference between the Exportation from hence, and the Consumption in *America*, the Remainder, which is all that they manufacture themselves, will be found to be much less than is usually supposed.

The Subject is capable of a much larger Discussion than I have Room for; but the Reasons that have been mentioned, may perhaps be sufficent, without urging them any further, or supporting them with others that might be given, to shew that all Attempts to establish Manufactures in *America*, to an Extent that may be alarming to *Great Britain*, must prove abortive in the End; at least, the additional Duty upon Linens affords no Ground for such Apprehensions: it is but half a Subsidy that is imposed, which is too inconsiderable upon the whole to make a material Difference: the Tax it is true, falls unequally, as Linens of very different Prices pay the same Duty, being comprehended under the general Denomination of Narrow *Germans*. This is a Grievance that is equally felt in *Great Britain*, and which I hope will be thought deserving of a Remedy: Could a Line of Distinction be drawn between the finer and coarser Linens, that are now included within the same Description, and such I should think it would not be impossible for Persons engaged in that Trade to draw, I flatter myself that it would be adopted: but in the mean while, the *Americans* have no greater Reason to complain than the *English* of this Disproportion; and as to the actual Duty required of them, they must still consider themselves as favoured, not oppressed, when they reflect that upon the cheapest of these Linens, those on which the Duty is most burthensome, the old Subsidy is but about Three Shillings, and Nine-pence Three Farthings upon a Hundred and Twenty Ells, which is all that they are now to pay, and half of which they paid before; while the several Imposts paid by the *English* for their Consumption upon the same Quantity of the same Linen amounts to about One Pound, One Shilling, and Four-pence, Three Farthings, which is a greater Disproportion of Burthen, than their different Situations and Circumstances require.

Should there, however, be any *Americans* so unreasonable, so rash, as on this Account to engage in the Establishment of Linen Manufactories there, and supposing a Contrariety between the Interests of *Great Britain* and its Colonies, affect to support the one, to the prejudice of the other; they can still proceed in their Attempt no further than the Mother Country will allow: I do not mean to suggest prohibitory Laws; but Laws to which no *American* could form an Objection, would effectually thwart all their Endeavours. It has been already observed, that the only Circumstance which enables the Planter to manufacture Linens cheaper than he can buy them when imported from hence, is because he does not pay for the Spinning; this was the Case under the Duty of half the old Subsidy: Should it for the Sake of Argument be supposed, (tho' I cannot believe,) that the additional half Subsidy will turn the Scale, and enable any Person there, tho' he were to pay for the Spinning of the Flax, to make Linen cheaper than it can be bought; which is the most that can be apprehended; it will always be in the Power of *Great Britain* to reinstate Things where they were, and if the additional Duty has caused an Alteration, the taking off that Duty must necessarily restore the imported Linens to their former Price, which is lower than *American* Manufacturers can afford them for; while on the other Hand, a Bounty upon *American* Flax, imported into *Great Britain*, will give the *British* Manufacturer a still further Advantage over the *American*, and enable him even to purchase his Materials cheaper. Thus by easing the Colonies of a Tax on their Consumption, and by giving Encouragement to their Produce, both which the Mother Country ought upon all Occasions to do, as far as the Exigencies of State will allow, *Great Britain* has it in her Power to disappoint any Establishments of this Kind that are contrary to the general Good; and however Individuals may be affected, the general Assemblies in their respective Provinces will never upon mature Deliberation support the Prosecution of Designs, which have a direct Tendency to hurt the Manufactories of the Mother Country, to check Cultivation in the Colonies, and to lessen the Navigation of both.

The whole Objection, however, against the additional Duty on Linens, applies to the coarser Kinds, upon which alone a Burthen in itself so inconsiderable, can be felt at all: On the finer Kinds, even of the narrow *Germans*, it is not pretended that it is too heavy; much less will there be any Room to cavil at an Increase of Duty upon *French* Lawns and Cambricks, tho' considerably greater than on the other Linens, being instead of Half the Old Subsidy, three Shillings *per* Piece, at thirteen Ells to the Piece. The *Americans* will still pay but about half what used to be paid by the Consumers in this Country, when *French* Cambricks and Lawns were allowed to be worn; and the Principles upon which they have been prohibited here, dictate some Restraint at least on the Consumption of these Commodities in the Colonies, which in effect is laid by the Imposition of a higher Duty upon these than upon other Linens.

The same Observations apply to the prohibited *East India* Goods, the wrought Silks and the painted Callicoes; they are prohibited in order to oblige the Company to import the Silk raw, and the Callicoes white for our own Manufactures. The Indulgence however of wearing them is not taken away from the Colonies, but the Act of the last Sessions lays them under the Discouragement of a Duty of Two Shillings *per* Pound Weight on the wrought Silks, and of Two Shillings and Six-pence *per* Piece on the painted Callicoes. This indeed is a considerable Rise upon the half Subsidy they paid before, which amounted to no more than Four pence Farthing *per* Pound Weight on the former, and Three pence *per* Piece on the latter; but it hardly yet exceeds a Third of the Duty that was charged upon them, while their Consumption was permitted in this Country: Six Shillings *per* Pound on the *East India* wrought Silks, and Three Shillings and Six-pence *per* Piece on the painted Callicoes, together with Fifteen *per Cent.* on the gross Price of the latter, did not check that Consumption so much as the Interests of our own Manufacturers required, and made a Prohibition necessary: for such is the Delicacy and the Beauty of these Commodities, that Persons who pique themselves on Elegance, and can afford to gratify their Taste, will not be detered from the Indulgence, by a much heavier Duty than is now levied on the *American* Consumption. This Consideration solves the Doubt that has been surmised, of the Operation such a Tax may have on the Demand of the Foreign, particularly the *Spanish* Colonies, for *East India* Manufactures: I believe it will have none, or at least no considerable Effect: for there is not a People upon the Globe, to whose Use, to whose Manners, and whose Dispositions, these Commodities are more particularly adapted: No other resemble them so much, as to be easily substituted in their Room; and the advanced Price will not raise them to a Value too extravagant for such Purchasers; but should it be said that the *Dutch* will now be able to furnish them at a cheaper Rate; the Answer is, that the Piece Goods of *India*, have been long imported by our Company in larger Quantities than by any other: that the Concessions made by *France* in the late Treaty of Peace, with respect to the *East India* Trade and Settlements, will in this Branch particularly give us still greater Advantages; and that the *Dutch* therefore must as they actually do provide themselves with the greater Part of their Supply at our *East India* Sales: Upon all that they buy there, they pay a Commission and a Freight, from which the *British* Merchant is free, and which perhaps may be an Equivalent for the Duty: If it is not, the Remedy is obvious, it is but spreading the same Imposition or a Part of it over all Exportation of such Goods, and then the Situations of the *Dutch* and *British* Merchants, with Respect to each other, will again be, just what they have been hitherto. Muslins and White Callicoes, which are not prohibited, are rated by the Act of the last Sessions, but in a different Manner, higher than other Linens; for instead of retaining the additional half Subsidy, a Draw-back of Four Pounds Fifteen Shillings upon every Hundred Pounds of their gross Price at the Sale is retain'd, upon all that are exported to *America*. This is less by almost three Fourths than the Duty paid by the Consumers of the same Commodities in *Britain*; yet under that

Weight the Manufacture of printing Callicoes has flourished, and we may therefore reasonably expect that it will not be oppressed by a Burthen comparatively so light upon printed Callicoes consumed in the Colonies; especially when we consider that the additional Value they acquire by the Manufacture is not taxed, those printed in *England* being construed to be but White Callicoes within the Description of the Acts of Parliament that relate to them: and other Linens which have gone thro' the same Manufacture, and which are now become of such general Use, both for Apparel and Furniture, are free from the Duty on Callicoes.

The Distinction made in this Act of Parliament between the *French* Lawns and Cambricks, the *East India* Callicoes and Muslins which are all high-priced, and other Kinds of Linen which are in general of a lower Value, will I hope justify me in saying, that if a Line could be drawn between the finer and the coarser Linens, which now pass indiscriminately under the Denomination of Narrow *Germans*, it would probably be adopted: if it were, the Duty upon all Kinds of Linens would then be throughout compleatly agreeable to the equitable Maxim of laying Taxes in different Proportions, on the Consumption of the Rich, and on that of the Poor: that while the Indulgencies and Refinements of the one are converted into beneficial Branches of the Public Revenue, the other may with more Chearfulness contribute out of their Pittance the Mite they owe, to the Service of the State they belong to. The Inhabitants of the *West Indies*, whose Opulence, whose Luxury, and I might say, whose Situation leads them into more Extravagance in such Articles, than prevails among the Inhabitants of the Continent, will therefore be more sensibly affected by these Duties, in which the Value is to a certain Degree made the Measure of the Duties; but it is right that throughout all the *British* Dominions, the Necessaries of Life should be less burthened than the Superfluities, and that all his Majesty's Subjects, wheresoever dispersed, should contribute to the publick Revenue, in Proportion to their Abilities, and not to their Numbers.

A Duty upon Wine comes within the same Description of a Tax upon Luxury, but the Regulations made during the last Sessions of Parliament, with respect to the several Sorts of

Wine for the Consumption of *America*, are so different, and
founded upon such peculiar Circumstances, that it is difficult to
say whether in the Event it will prove, that an Imposition has
been laid or taken off from that Commodity. The Wine that
has been hitherto exported from hence to the Colonies, has
been allowed no other Draw-back than on any other Exportation. But the Colonies have always been permitted to import
Wine from the *Madeiras* and the *Azores*, without bringing it
thro' *Great Britain*; the natural Consequence of the Saving
thereby made, both of Freight and of Duty, has been a Preference of these to all others, so that these are become almost
their only Consumption. The Inhabitants of *Madeira* have on
this Account long had a kind of Monopoly of the Wine Trade
to our Colonies, and have taken the Advantages which Mo-
nopolists usually take, of advancing the Price and lowering the
Quality; as the Demand increases with the Population of the
Colonies, the Oppression must be the greater, and it is already
such as to make it necessary to bring the *Madeira* Wines nearer
to a Level with others: with this View a larger Draw-back than
formerly is allowed on all but *French* Wines, exported from
hence to the *West Indies* and *America*; for instead of Eleven
Pounds, Thirteen Shillings and Six-pence *per* Ton Duty which
used to remain, but Three Pounds, Ten Shillings is from
henceforth to be retained here, Ten Shillings is imposed in the
Colonies to make the respective Custom-house Accounts,
Checks upon each other. But while the Duty is lowered on
these, a new one of Seven Pounds *per* Ton is imposed on those
of the *Madeiras*, and other Places from whence Wines may be
lawfully imported into the Colonies. As a Luxury, they ought
in justice, and as a Monopoly, they ought in Policy to be taxed;
but should the Effect of these Regulations be such as may
reasonably be expected, the Price of Wines in general will
rather be lowered than advanced by the Duty upon one Species of them only. Such as are carried from hence will certainly
be cheaper by Seven Pounds, Thirteen Shillings and Six-pence
per Ton, than they used to be; they will for the most Part too
be cheaper than those of the *Madeiras*, their original Price,
and the Duty upon them being so much less, as to over-ballance
the Difference of Freight. The Demand and consequently the
Price of the latter will thereby be lessened: they will be no

longer a Monopoly, because no longer a Necessary, and will therefore be cheaper than they are now; and this Tax upon a Luxury of foreign Growth, co-operating with the Encouragement given to Exportation from hence, will have the still further beneficial Effects of improving at the same time Navigation and Revenue.

Luxuries even of our own Growth do not escape Taxation; Coffee, the Produce of the *British* Plantations, is charged with Seven Shillings the Hundred Weight, and Pimento with an Half-penny *per* Pound. The Duties indeed are light, for it is not meant to prejudice the Consumption of Commodities, of which we must wish to encourage the Cultivation; but only that those who can afford to indulge in such Delicacies, should contribute something to the publick Wants, and ease from heavier Burthens the Necessaries of the Poor: if the Tax went further, it would be pernicious, in loading too much the valuable Produce of some of our Colonies. The Intention of the Legislature appears to have been on the contrary, to encourage the raising of Coffee in our *West India* Islands, by giving it an Advantage over that produced in foreign Plantations, upon every Hundred Weight of which a Duty of Two Pounds Nineteen Shillings and Nine-pence is by the same Act imposed. So great a Difference of Duty upon a Hundred Weight, the prime Cost of which will not exceed Three Pounds, must give a Preference to our own Produce, which is particularly recommended to Public Encouragement, by the Circumstances of being raised with less Expence than Sugar, and therefore within the Reach of the first Settlers in the ceded Islands.

The same Reason holds, and perhaps more strongly, with respect to Indigo, which, if imported from foreign Plantations into any of our Colonies, is by the Act so frequently refered to, charged with a Duty of Six-pence *per* Pound, while our own Produce passes free. Indigo is a Commodity, which particularly attracts our Notice at this Juncture; great Quantities of it used to be raised in our *West India* Islands, but for many Years very little has been produced; and we have been in a great Measure supplied by the *French*. The Reason of this has not been, (as is commonly supposed,) the high Duties that were laid upon it, but the clearing of the Country; for Indigo is a Plant that requires Moisture, which nothing can secure in those torrid

Climates, but the Proximity of Mountains to break the Clouds in their Passage, or of Woods from whence Vapours are continually exhaled, to refresh the Neighbourhood with Showers: as the Woods have been cut away, this Resource has gradually failed, and the Produce of Indigo, which depended upon it, has declined in Proportion. The *West Indians* regret but little the Loss of a Commodity, which has made way for a greater Cultivation of their favourite Produce, Sugar; but the Nation must sensibly feel the Inconvenience of being furnished from other Countries, with so valuable an Article of Commerce, and so necessary a Material of Manufacture.

This Consideration has induced some Planters in *South Carolina* to attempt to raise it there, and they have already succeeded so far as to prove, that the Soil and the Climate agree with the Plant, and that they are acquainted with the Art of extracting the Juice, so as to equal the finest in Quality. The great Losses they sustained by the Captures of their Ships, have a little retarded their Progress: but now that Peace is restored, there is reason to expect that this Cultivation will flourish, and even be extended to *Georgia* and the two *Floridas*, which are rather better adapted to it than *South Carolina*. To make the Indigo they shall raise cheaper than any that can be imported from the *French* Islands into *America*, will facilitate the Attempt to recover this Commodity, and be very serviceable to those Colonies: the ceded Islands too will have their share of the Benefit, as the Certainty of Moisture from the Woodiness of the Country, and the Cheapness of the Culture, will render this a very proper and a very considerable Article of Produce to those who may purchase or settle there.

Another, and that a most important Branch, both of Commerce and of Revenue, I mean the Produce of the Sugar Cane, in its several States of Melasses, Rum and Sugar, has been under the Consideration of Parliament, during the last Winter; and the Degree of Restraint put upon the *French* Trade in this Article, is proportioned to the Stage of Manufacture, in which the Commodity may be at the Time of Importation: Rum is Melasses manufactured: The *French* were unacquainted with the Art, or at least, did not give into the Practice of making Rum, till taught and led to it by our People, while we were in Possession of their Islands: At that Time some Distilleries were set up for this Purpose, which are said to be continued since the Peace; but they can never be of any consequence, if we do not help the Persons concerned in them to dispose of what they produce. *France* will not permit her Colonies to establish a Manufacture that shall interfere with any Branch of her own, and will therefore prevent the making of Rum, so far as it affects the Consumption of her Brandy. There can for this Reason be very little Vent for it, unless by Exportation to our Colonies on the Continent: but hitherto those very Colonies have had the manufacturing of the *French* Melasses; and to permit them now to be brought in any other Shape than as a raw Material, would be very detrimental to the *North America* Distillery: A strict Prohibition is therefore laid on all *Rum or Spirits of the Produce or Manufacture of any of the Colonies or Plantations in* America *not in the Possession or under the Dominion of his Majesty, his Heirs or Successors,* in order to force the *French* to supply the Demands of our Colonies for their Melasses, tho' they can make it into Rum themselves, and tho' the Trade should undergo some Alteration by new Duties and new Regulations.

That Trade was indeed in a Situation that required some Alteration. By 6 *Geo*. II. c. 13. a Duty of Six-pence *per* Gallon was laid upon all foreign Melasses; but such has been the Disregard of all Revenue Laws in *America*, that this has produced hardly any Thing, tho' the Commodity has been imported all the time in great Quantities. Instead of paying the Duty, a regular Course has been fallen into of importing it free of any; and the Expence of such Smuggling has been brought to a Certainty of about Three Half-pence a Gallon; which was a Charge upon the raw Materials before it came to the Manufacturer, amounting to one Fourth of the Duty, and destructive of the whole: under this Charge the Distilleries of *North America* have flourished to a surprizing Degree; and surely it is to be wished that the Burthen now upon the Merchandize, should yield a Revenue to the Publick instead of a Profit to Smugglers, or which is worse, to Officers of the Crown conniving at Smugglers: but it has been said that the excessive high Duty, imposed by the 6 *Geo*. II. was the Cause of the Smuggling, and that nothing will put a Stop to it but reducing the Tax. The Fact is probable; the Legislature seem to have thought that the Load was heavier than the Trade could bear; and have therefore reduced it from Six-pence to Three-pence *per* Gallon: this still is represented by some as too high; and indeed whatever Rate is fixed, will in all Probability be censured by those whom it affects; but so far is certain, that a Duty may always exceed the Expence of Smuggling; for no Man will expose his Character to Reflection, and his Property to Hazards, without the Temptation of Advantages over the fair Trader. And as Three Half-pence *per* Gallon was the Expence of Smuggling, while a general Relaxation of the Laws against it prevailed over all that Continent, now that these Laws are rigorously put into Execution, that Charge will be higher in Proportion to the additional Risque of Seizures; and at the same time the Temptation is less by the Difference between Three-pence and Six-pence. These Reasons concur to prove that a Duty considerably higher than Three Half-pence *per* Gallon may be imposed upon Melasses, without being, by its Excess, an Inducement to Smuggling. The next Question is, what the Trade can bear without being oppressed by it: It certainly can bear more now it is established, than it could in its Beginnings; it has thriven, it has increased, it continues to increase, under a Charge of Three Half-pence *per* Gallon; and as Experience has shewn that it can support such a Burthen, with Ease, the Presumption is from thence alone very strong, that it is equal to a greater without Inconvenience. The additional Charge upon the Commodity, by the Duty of Three-pence, is but Three Half-pence, so much only being the Difference between the former and the present Price of Importation: and as a Gallon of Melasses produces a Gallon of Rum, an Addition of Three Half-pence does not appear to us a severe Tax upon a Gallon of Rum. The cheapest Spirits that are drawn in *England*, pay a Duty of One Shilling and Five-pence Half-penny *per* Gallon to the Publick; and to expect that our fellow Subjects should contribute Three-pence *per* Gallon for their Consumption of the same Commodity, is surely not very unreasonable; so much therefore of the Produce of their Distilleries as is necessary for supplying the Colonies themselves, is certainly not taxed beyond what it ought to be. But it is alledged that the Fishery, the *Guinea*, and the *Indian* Trade cannot support the consequential Rise upon Spirituous Liquors, and that both the

Distilleries and these Branches of Commerce will sink under the Burthen together. The Demand for the Fisheries is not to furnish the *American* Ships only, but to supply those also that are sent for the Purposes of fishing from *Great Britain*, and do not carry out with them sufficient Store of Spirituous Liquors. Whatever Quantity the latter take from the *American* is a Loss to the *British* Distilleries; and if the Effect of this Duty should be to diminish that Quantity, I cannot see any great national Mischief that would attend it, because I cannot admit that any Manufactures should be encouraged in the Colonies, to the Prejudice of those established in the Mother Country. As to the Rum used on board the *American* Ships, that is a Kind of home Consumption; the Duty is but an inconsiderable Addition to the whole Expence of the Trade, and is certainly not too much for it to bear, as the same Trade carried on by Ships from hence, which take in sufficient Store here, does in this Article actually bear a greater; surely the *Americans* have Advantages enough by their Situation with respect to the Fisheries, not to make it necessary to give their Manufactures the Preference to our own, in order to enable them to fish on Terms still so much better. As to the Trade upon the Coast of *Guinea*, that is no longer a Matter of Speculation: the Experiment has been made already of advancing the Price of *American* Rum there, and has succeeded. Their Rum used to be cheaper tho' but a little cheaper than the *British* Spirits on the Coast, but was always greatly prefered by the Natives, not on Account of the Difference of Price, but of its more fiery Quality, which made it more acceptable to the Negroes. The *British* Spirits are sold on the Coast of *Guinea* at about One Shilling and Two-pence Half-penny *per* Gallon; the *American* used to be sold at about One Shilling and Two-pence: but on the Alarm, occasioned last Year by the Establishment of Cutters, to enforce the Collection of the Six-penny Duty, which then subsisted, the *American* Merchants suddenly raised their Price from One Shilling and Two-pence to One Shilling and Six-pence *per* Gallon, and yet preserved the Preference given by the Negroes to their Spirits. The Rise was made on the Presumption that the Six-penny Duty would be levied; at that Time the Reduction to Three-pence was not foreseen, for they never would have required Four-pence of the Consumers to enable them to defray an additional Expence of Three Half-pence only upon the Commodity: they may now lower it again; and fixing the Price of their Rum on the Coast of *Guinea* at Two Shillings and Three-pence Half-penny *per* Gallon, the Profits of the Merchant will be the same as when he sold for Two Shillings and Two pence; and he may depend on the Preference being given to the *American* Spirits, since it was given when they were at Two Shillings and Six-pence and the *British* at Two Shillings and Two-pence Half-penny *per* Gallon. As to the *Indian* Trade the *Americans* have it much more to themselves; there they have no Competitors to apprehend; and the poor Savages are not, I doubt, used to such nice Calculations in their Transactions with us, as to be very sensible to a Difference of Three Half-pence on a Gallon of Rum. I wish they had always been dealt with as fairly as a Rise upon the Commodity will be on the present Occasion; and I should rejoice could I be sure, that they will never have better Grounds to complain of their Traffic with the *English*. Upon examining therefore the several Places of Vent for the Spirituous Liquors made in *America*, there does not seem much Reason to fear any great Detriment to the Distilleries there from this Duty. Something more than mere Apprehensions and general Assertions are necessary to condemn a Tax which appears so proper on so many Accounts; and, unless Experience should prove that it is attended with bad Consequences, or stronger Objections can be made to it than have come to my Knowledge, I cannot join in foreboding Evils that I do not foresee; and which, at the worst, amount to no more than that the Colonies will not be able to manufacture a Material which they purchase of the *French*, upon better Terms than the Inhabitants of *Great Britain* can manufacture *British* Produce. The Colonies may follow the Example of their Mother Country, and distil Spirits from their own Corn. This will be a Consumption of that Commodity in Compensation of the Loss, which it is said they will sustain in the Vent of it to the *French* Islands. But will they lose that or any other Article of Commerce by this Burthen on the Return they receive for them? Are not the Demands of the *French* for Necessaries? Can they now, that they have ceded all *North America*, can they now, tho' they could not before, supply themselves from any other than from our Colonies, with Provisions and with Lumber? Had they no Returns to make, must not they purchase these Necessaries with Money? and can they refuse to make this the Return, as far as it will go, upon our own Terms, since they have no other way to dispose of it? The Trade of the *West India* Islands, whoever they belong to, is always under the Controul of the Nation that is in Possession of *North America*; they depend upon that Continent for the Subsistance of their Inhabitants, and for the Means of disposing of their Produce, as they can no where else procure in any Quantity, or at any tolerable Price, the Casks and other Materials that are necessary for that Purpose. We may reject their Melasses; but they cannot refuse our Provisions and our Lumber; and now that the whole Continent, which produces those Articles, is ceded to *Great-Britain*, the *French* Islands are far more dependant than they were upon her, for their Support and for their Commerce; there is a greater Balance of Trade against them; a larger Proportion of the Profits they make upon their Produce, must be expended in the Purchase of those Necessaries, which *North America* alone can supply; and they are on these and many other Accounts, far less valuable to *France* than they were while she retained her Colonies on the Continent. They will sink still lower in their Value, when the Demands of *North America* shall decrease, as the ceded Islands improve; for the *French* Plantations have hitherto produced Coffee, Cotton, Cocoa, Ginger, Indigo, and Pimento, in greater Quantities than ours: because their Planters are poorer, and their Lands in a lower State of Cultivation. These Articles, exclusive of such of them as may be raised in the *Floridas*, will for the same Reasons be most attended to, by the first Settlers on the ceded Islands; and as soon as they attain to the raising of Sugar, they will again interfere with the *French* in the great Article of Melasses; as it is well known that the Cane yields much larger Quantities of Melasses when planted on fresh Lands; and that the Reason why our Islands do not produce so much as the *French*, is only because the Lands are more exhausted in our than in their Plantations. The Sugar itself, which these Islands will produce, will be a further Diminution of the Demands of our Colonies upon those of the *French*; and the less those Demands are, so much the more must their Plantations be at our Mercy, in such

Articles as we may still have Occasion for from them; while their Want of what we alone can furnish, can never diminish, unless their Colonies decline. The Duty of One Pound Two Shillings on all foreign white or clay'd Sugars, imported into the *British* Colonies, which is imposed by the Act of the last Sessions, cannot be complained of by the *Americans*, so far as their own Consumption is affected by it, since the Inhabitants of *Great Britain* have chearfully submitted their Consumption to the like Regulation, and for the Benefit of the *West India* Plantations, have laid a much higher Duty upon *French* than upon *British* Sugars imported into *Great Britain*: but it is objected to this Tax, that it will hurt the Trade of the *North Americans*, as Carriers of the *French* Sugars to *Europe*; a Trade profitable in itself, and promoting Navigation; on which Accounts it is said, a Drawback of great Part or of the whole of the Duty, should be allowed on Re-exportation. Could this be done without opening Opportunities for the greatest Frauds on the Revenue, it might be proper; but it is well known that no Indulgence to Trade is so much abused to the prejudice, both of the Revenue and of Commerce, as the Allowance of Drawbacks here; and it will be liable to greater Abuses in *America*, unless some more effectual Method than has hitherto been practised, could be found to prevent them: and after all it remains to be proved, that the Object is great enough to justify the dangerous Experiment of making in any Shape an Allowance of a Drawback; the *North Americans* had indeed formerly the Carriage of the *French* Sugars to a considerable Amount; but the *French* have for many Years carried the greater Part themselves. This Duty too, it must be observed, is only on the White and the Clay'd, that is, the manufactured Sugars: the Effect of it may be in some Degree, to induce the *French* to send their Sugars in a lower State of Manufacture to *North America*, and then they will be free of Duty: the Carriage of these is not affected: as to the Carriage of the others, if what is left of that Trade could be retained without exposing the Revenue and the fair Trader to Losses, they ought to be free from, it certainly would be proper to do it; the only Doubt is whether it be possible.

These are the several Duties imposed by Parliament during the last Sessions, upon the Consumption of *America*; and they appear to have been judiciously chosen, not only with a View to the Revenue, which they will produce; but for other, and in my Opinion, greater political Purposes, which each of them will respectively answer; and besides those already mentioned, there is one general Effect that will result from the whole, which will be of the utmost Importance to the Trade of *Great Britain*, and to the Connection between her and her Colonies; tho' the Duties are very low, the Articles on which they are laid are numerous, and comprehend all that have been the Subjects of a contraband Trade, with those Parts of *Europe* which the Colonies are not allowed to trade to. The bringing these to a regular Entry and Account, will be the Means of detecting and of preventing the illicit Proceedings that have hitherto prevailed; and not only support and encourage the *British* Manufactures, but maintain and improve the Commerce and Navigation, both of *Great Britain* and her Colonies, tho' the Merchandize should be the Produce of neither. In other Countries Custom-house Duties are for the most Part, little more than a Branch of the Revenue: In the Colonies they are a political Regulation, and enforce the Observance of those wise Laws to which the great Increase of our Trade and naval Power are principally owing. The Aim of those Laws is to confine the *European* Commerce of the Colonies to the Mother Country: to provide that their most valuable Commodities shall be exported either to *Great Britain* or to *British* Plantations; and to secure the Navigation of all *American* Exports and Imports to *British* Ships and *British* Subjects only. It is the Policy of every Nation to prohibit all foreign Trade with their Plantations: it has been the Policy of this almost as far back as we have had any Colonies worth regarding; the first and great Act of Navigation being nearly co-æval with their Existence as a People; before that Time the *English* of the *West-Indies* were but Adventurers, and the Inhabitants of *North America* were but a few unhappy Fugitives, who had wandered thither to enjoy their civil and religious Liberties, which they were deprived of at home. The Distractions of this Country had indeed increased their Numbers, but they were still separate, weak, necessitous, and truly infant Colonies, nursed by perpetual Supplies from the Mother Country, exposed to every Hazard, sustained with Difficulty, and only beginning to give hopes that they might hereafter be what they now are. Upon this Prospect the Act of Navigation form'd their Dependance into Connection, and gave a Sanction to the Emigration and the Expence occasioned by supporting them; for Colonies are only Settlements made in distant Parts of the World, for the Improvement of Trade; but if they were allowed to transfer the Benefits of their Commerce to any other Country than that from which they came, they would destroy the very Purposes of their Establishment: and it is but an equitable Return for the Accommodation which has been provided for them, and the Emoluments they have received, that they, the Subjects still of the same Country, should continue to act as they must have acted, had they continued its Inhabitants, and that their Produce and their Consumption should be for the Benefit of that Country, in Preference to any other. No Nation would tolerate Colonies upon any other Conditions: It would be suffering themselves to be exhausted, impoverished, and weakened, in support of a People, who might divert their Commerce to the Advantage of another, perhaps of a Rival, and the Mother Country would be ruined by the Prosperity of her Colonies. The Act of Navigation therefore is founded upon Right as well as Policy; the Principles of it have been adopted and confirmed in all our subsequent Laws; the Injunctions it contains have never been departed from, without very cogent Reasons, and then only in a few particular Instances. The Effects of it have been the Increase of our Trade and Navigation; and all Evasions therefore of this, and the other Acts of Trade and Navigation, are destructive of what every Subject of these Kingdoms should pay the utmost Attention to; for tho' Individuals may gain a Profit, tho' Consumers may procure at a cheaper Rate the Commodities they want, by the Breach of these Laws, yet the Interests, I do not mean the Revenue only, but the essential Interests of the Commonweal are thereby sacrificed to private, partial, and trifling Emoluments, uncertain in their Nature, temporary in Duration, and ruinous in the End. Even the Colonies themselves suffer from the Advantages made by some of their Inhabitants; not only in the Distress these iniquitous Practices bring upon their fair Traders; in the Loss of Employment to their Shipping; and in the Perversion of the Industry, and the Depravation of the

Morals of so many of their People; but most materially in depriving their Mother Country (so far as such Practices extend) of those Resources, which the Commerce of her Colonies secured to herself would constantly furnish, for their Benefit and her own; when her Trade and her Manufactures by these Means decline, her people decrease, and her Power and her Revenues diminish; her Efforts must be so much the fainter for general or partial Good, her Ability to raise within herself the Supplies which the Support, the Defence, and the Improvement of her vast Empire require, is so far less; and her Demands for Assistance must consequently be greater upon her Colonies, who can answer those Demands only by oppressing their fair Traders and their honest Consumers. It might not perhaps be difficult to shew that Smuggling has not lower'd the Price upon the whole Consumption of *America* taken together, tho' particular Articles may in some Places and to some Persons have come cheaper. The Effects it has had upon others, that are not so particularly the Object of it, and the general Effects of it upon all Markets, more than counterbalance this Advantage; but these are too many and too great to be discussed at present. It may be sufficient here, just to suggest the Proposition to those who are inclined to examine it, and to support it only with observing, that the salutary Provisions of the Acts of Trade and Navigation, are acknowledged by the most reputable and the most considerate Inhabitants of the Colonies, and that they constantly deplore the little Regard that has been paid to them by their self-interested and inadvertent Countrymen. To them therefore, and to every true Lover of his Country, whatever Part of the *British* Dominions he inhabits, the Act of the last Sessions of Parliament, which, by its general Tendency and particular Provisions, must greatly corroborate those Laws, will be a most welcome Regulation of Commerce. The contraband Trade that is carried on there, is a Subject of the most serious Consideration; and is become a much more alarming Circumstance, than that Increase of Wealth, People, and Territory, which raises Apprehensions in many Persons that the Colonies may break off their Connections with *Great Britain*: That Connection is actually broken already, wherever the Acts of Navigation are disregarded; and for so much of their Trade as is thereby diverted from its proper Channel, they are no longer *British* Colonies, but Colonies of the Countries they trade to. Thither they carry their Produce; from thence they receive their Supply; and Trade and Navigation flourish there, by an illicit Intercourse with the *British* Plantations. The Extent of this Commerce, as it is in its Nature private, cannot be certainly known; but that it is now carried to a dangerous Excess, is an indisputable Fact. Ships are continually passing between our Plantations and *Holland, Hamburg*, and most of the Ports on the *German* Ocean, and in the *Baltic*, all direct Communication, with which, exclusive of the Intervention of *Great Britain*, is illegal. At other Places, which the Ships of the Plantations are allowed to resort to without touching here, for particular Purposes, the Licence is abused, and Commodities not permitted to be sent to our Colonies, but thro' this Country, are immediately carried from thence; and great Quantities of *European* Commodities are besides constantly smuggled from foreign Plantations into ours. The Concurrence of all these several Modes of evading the Acts of Navigation, can alone account for the Demands of the Colonies upon their Mother Country, being vastly disproportioned to their Consumption. The Half Subsidy retained here upon the finer Linens amounts to no more than about 300*l. per Ann.* and yet no one will venture to represent the Linen Manufactory of *North America* to be in so flourishing a State, as to produce all that the Inhabitants use above that small Quantity. The whole annual Export of Wine from hence to the Plantations, falls greatly short of an Hundred Ton; can the *Madeira* and the Western Islands furnish the Rest of their Consumption? The Tea that is sent from hence does not generally exceed One Hundred and Fifty Thousand Pounds weight *per Ann.* tho' by the best Computation that can be made, the Colonies must consume One Million Five Hundred Thousand Pounds Weight in the Year. The *Dutch*, the *French*, the *Swedish*, the *Danish, East India* Companies, supply them with nine tenths of their Consumption, to the Prejudice of the *English* Company, of their Trade and their Navigation. Many other Facts, supported by the concurrent Testimony of all who have ever resided in the Plantations, might be adduced to prove, the great Extent of their illicit Commerce in *European* Commodities, (including those which must be conveyed thro' *Europe* to them,) and justify the common Calculation that the foreign Goods illegally run into the Colonies amount in value to no less than 700000*l. per Annum*, which exceeds by far the Value of those foreign Goods that are conveyed thither thro' *Great Britain*.

The Suppression of so enormous and so dangerous an Evil, is a great Object of State, which has been long, far too long neglected: the Laws that have been made for preventing it, were sunk into Disuse, and the due Execution of them is become obnoxious to those who have been suffered to contemn them with Impunity. That Licentiousness however is now at an End; the Reform that was necessary, has I hear been made among the Officers of the Crown. The Civil, the Military, the naval Powers, appear to have been all exerted, for the same salutary Purposes; and the Legislative Authority has in the great Act, that has been so often mentioned, added Vigour and Effect to the former Laws of Trade and Navigation: the particular Clauses that belong to the immediate Subjects of this Act only, demand the Attention of those who are concerned in the Branches of Trade, which they respectively regulate; but are too numerous and too minute to be enlarged upon at present. It is sufficient to observe, that they are all conducive to the same End with those more general Provisions, which on Account of their extensive Importance, are universally interesting.

The Policy of prohibiting certain enumerated Goods, from being exported out of the Plantations, except to some other *British* Plantation, or to *Great Britain*, was introduced by the first Act of Trade and Navigation, and has been adopted in many subsequent Statutes. The enumerated Commodities were those which appeared at that Time the most important to secure to *British* Traders only; but the great Improvements of the Colonies having produced others equally valuable, and the late Accessions of Territory having given us the Monopoly of some, which we have hitherto only shared with the *French*, the Restraint is upon the same Principles of Policy extended to these also, and Coffee, Pimento, Cocoa Nuts, Whale Fins, Raw Silk, Hides and Skins, Pot and Pearl Ashes, are by the Act of the last Sessions added to the enumerated Commodities, because they are necessary for our own Consumption or Manufactures;

Iron and Lumber, tho' of equal Utility, yet being a great Article of Trade, in foreign Plantations, are allowed to be disposed of there; but are not to be carried to any other Part of *Europe*, except to *Great Britain*.

A Bond has been always required for every Vessel loading enumerated Goods, by which the Parties concerned obliged themselves to comply with the Laws that relate to them; but when non-enumerated Goods only have been shipped, no Security has ever been taken for the proper Disposal of the Returns usually made from the foreign Plantations; and great Quantities of foreign Melasses and Syrups have been clandestinely run into the Colonies, the Importers of which would have been detered from attempting to smuggle, if they had been liable to the Penalties of their Bonds upon Detection. A Bond therefore is by this Act required on the loading of non-enumerated Goods also, with Condition, that if any foreign Melasses or Syrups shall be taken on board in Return, the same shall be brought to *Great Britain*, or to a *British* Plantation, and the Master of the Vessel shall, on his Arrival, make a true Report of his Cargo.

But whether Bond had been given in either of these Cases, or what were the Conditions of it, could not be known at any other Place than the Port from whence the Vessel departed, if the Master of such Vessel were not obliged to take out a Certificate of his having complied with the Law which requires such Security: that Precaution therefore is added with respect both to enumerated and non-enumerated Goods; and it is enforced by making all Vessels liable to Seisure, who shall enter into any *British* Port, or be found within two Leagues of the Shores of the Colonies, without such a Certificate.

And for the further Prevention of the Smuggling of foreign Rum, Sugars, and Melasses, which are great Objects of clandestine Trade, it is provided, that whenever any of those Commodities are shipped, as the Growth of a *British* Plantation, it shall be proved upon Oath that they are so; and a Certificate of such Oath having been taken, shall be given to the Master of the Vessel, who must produce it at the Port of Delivery, or the Goods will be liable to Seizure.

All these Provisions are however but Guards against clandestine Importations: the Goods would be to a Degree in

Safety as soon as they were landed, and might be carried out again along the neighbouring Coasts with Security, if the Vigilance of the Law stopped here. The Danger therefore of an illicit Commerce is continued beyond the first Importation, and the Vent of smuggled Goods is laid under still further Difficulties and Discouragements; for no Merchandize whatever can now be conveyed by Sea from one Colony to another, without a Sufferance, upon which a Cocket is to be made out, particularly specifying the Goods, and the Duties that have been paid thereon, if they are liable to any; and every coasting Vessel not furnished with such a Cocket, may be seized on her Arrival at the Port of her Destination, or if she is met by a Cruizer, within two Leagues of the Shore of any of the Colonies.

These several additional Precautions will certainly contribute very much to the Suppression of that illicit Trade which is carried on by *British* Ships and *British* Subjects; but they do not apply to foreign Vessels, which being already prohibited from entering the Ports of the Colonies, only approach the Coasts, and watch their Opportunities to land their contraband Cargoes. For the Prevention of this Practice, the Provisions of the *British* hovering Acts are extended to *America*, and every foreign Vessel, which shall be found at anchor or hovering within two Leagues of the Shores of any of the Plantations, and shall not depart or proceed on her Voyage to some foreign Port within Forty-eight Hours after Requisition made to depart by a Custom-house Officer, is ordered to be seized, and condemned, whether Bulk shall have been broken or not, the *French* Ships employed in the *Newfoundland* Fishery, within the Limits prescribed to them, only excepted.

But that the necessary Exception, in their Favour, may not be abused, and that the Islands of *St. Pierre* and *Miquelon*, which were granted to the *French*, as a bare Shelter for their Fishermen, and which are in themselves, from their Barrenness and the Smallness of their Extent, fit for that Purpose alone, may not be made Warehouses for supplying the *British* Colonies with *French* Merchandize, to the Prejudice of our Manufactures and Navigation, and the Encouragement of their Fisheries; a vigorous Clause subjects to Forfeiture every *British* Vessel concerned in any Trade whatsoever with these Islands, or hovering on their Coasts, or discovered to have been there.

The Attention of the Legislature has not however been confined to *America*: Frauds practised in *Britain* with a View to a clandestine Trade in the Colonies, have fallen under their Notice; and to prevent them it has been found necessary to regulate the Trade from hence to the Colonies. It has been a common Practice for *British* Ships provided with a Cargo in foreign Countries, which was pretended to be destined for a foreign Plantation, just to touch at some Out-port of this Kingdom, and there to take small Parcels of Goods on board, which they entered for a *British* Colony: Under cover of these, however inconsiderable, they gained Admittance into the *American* Ports, and there Opportunities were not wanting to run the whole Cargoes on shore: This pernicious Contrivance to evade the Law is now defeated, as no Ship can from henceforth be cleared out from any *British* for any *American* Port, unless her whole Cargo be laden here; and all Goods which shall be found on board, and which are not expressly described in the Cocket which the Master is obliged to take, are liable to be seized.

The Power of seizing Ships within certain Distances of the Shore (which as has been seen) is given by this Act in so many Instances, will make the Sea Guard of Cruizers and Cutters which was established before, and has been of singular Use already, still more effectual; To keep up a Body of Seamen fit for Service, and not to keep them in Service, is impracticable: They will not be Seamen long, if active Business is not found for them; and the employing therefore part of that Number which Parliament has thought proper should be maintain'd during the Peace, in the Prevention of Smuggling both here and in the Colonies, conduces at the same time to the great Purpose of supporting a naval Power, to the Improvement of the Revenue, and to the Regulation of Commerce. The Officers and the Men who are engaged in this Duty are encouraged to perform it with Spirit and Alacrity by the Prizes they may expect; and the Check that has hitherto slackened their Vigilance, arising from the Difficulties that attended Prosecutions, and the Uncertainty of the Shares they would entitle themselves to, which were so varied in different Acts of Parliament, that it was become a Science to understand them, is removed by the Act of the last Sessions: The same Forms of

Proceedings being now established for all Prosecutions, and one certain Division being now made of all Seizures. The Custom-house Officers share the Benefits of this Amendment of the Law, and of the several other Facilities given to them in the Execution of their respective Offices; while on the other hand the Performance of their Duty is enforced by additional Penalties on the Breach of it.

These general Regulations and the particular Provisions of the Act in many Instances that required such special Clauses, concurring with the vigorous Measures taken by Government to inforce Obedience to all the Laws; and with the zealous Exertion of the civil, the military, and the naval Powers in the Colonies, as permitted encouraged, or required by Law to assist in the Prevention of Smuggling, give reasonable Ground to hope that that important Object of Policy, of Commerce, and of Revenue, the Suppression of the contraband Trade which has prevailed such a length of time in the Colonies, will in a great measure be attained. As to the Revenue which the new Impositions will produce, I suppose it is very difficult, if not impossible to form any Calculation of its Amount: I will not even hazard a Conjecture upon it, as I cannot presume that I should be right; and I should be sorry to be wrong. Thus far however may be safely affirmed, that Duties so low, and now first laid, will not at present contribute largely to the Exigencies of the Public; for inconsiderable as they are, the Payment of them will be often avoided by Frauds and Subtilties, which no Penetration can foresee, and Experience only can discover and prevent. On the other hand, they will be an improving Revenue; because they are laid upon numerous Articles of general Consumption among an encreasing People; and if not productive of a great Fund immediately, will be at least a wide Foundation for a considerable future Revenue; but upon no Calculation can it be supposed to be equal to the Demand that must be made upon the Colonies; and therefore a further Tax has been proposed; it has been even resolved by a Vote of the House of Commons, that *it may be proper to charge certain Stamp Duties in the Plantations*; and here the Legislature stoped last Sessions out of Tenderness to the Colonies. A Stamp Duty, tho' often used in the Plantations for the Purposes of their own Government, has never been imposed there by Authority of Parliament, and time has been therefore very properly allowed, to enquire whether it will be attended with any Inconveniences, and to provide Expedients of Prevention or Remedy; but I believe the more it is examined, so much the more clearly will it appear, that this Mode of Taxation is the easiest, the most equal and the most certain that can be chosen: The Duty falls chiefly upon Property; but it is spread lightly over a great Variety of Subjects, and lies heavy upon none: The Act executes itself by annulling the Instruments that have not paid the small Sums they are charged with; and the Tax thus supported and secured, is collected by few Officers, without Expence to the Crown, or Oppression on the People.

The Revenue that may be raised by the Duties which have been already, or by these if they should be hereafter imposed, are all equally applied by Parliament, *towards defraying the necessary Expences of defending, protecting, and securing, the British Colonies and Plantations in America*: Not that on the one hand an *American* Revenue might not have been applied to different Purposes; or on the other, that *Great Britain* is to contribute nothing to these: The very Words of the Act of Parliament and of the Resolution of the House of Commons imply, that the whole of the Expence is not to be charged upon the Colonies: They are under no Obligation to provide for this or any other particular national Expence; neither can they claim any Exemption from general Burthens; but being a part of the *British* Dominions, are to share all necessary Services with the rest. This in *America* does indeed first claim their Attention: They are immediately, they are principally concerned in it; and the Inhabitants of their Mother-Country would justly and loudly complain, if after all their Efforts for the Benefit of the Colonies, when every Point is gained, and every wish accomplished, they, and they alone should be called upon still to answer every additional Demand, that the Preservation of these Advantages, and the Protection of the Colonies from future Dangers, may occasion: *Great Britain* has a Right at all Times, she is under a Necessity, upon this Occasion, to demand their Assistance; but still she requires it in the Manner most suitable to their Circumstances; for by appropriating this Revenue towards the Defence and Security of the Provinces where it is raised, the Produce of it is kept in the Country, the People are not deprived of the Circulation of what Cash they have amongst themselves, and thereby the severest Oppression of an *American* Tax, that of draining the Plantations of Money which they can so ill spare, is avoided. What Part they ought to bear of the national Expence, that is necessary for their Protection, must depend upon their Ability, which is not yet sufficiently known: to the whole they are certainly unequal, that would include all the military and all the naval Establishment, all Fortifications which it may be thought proper to erect, the Ordnance and Stores that must be furnished, and the Provisions which it is necessary to supply; but surely a Part of this great Disbursement, a large Proportion at least of some particular Branches of it, cannot be an intolerable Burthen upon such a Number of Subjects, upon a Territory so extensive, and upon the Wealth which they collectively possess. As to the Quota which each Individual must pay, it will be difficult to persuade the Inhabitants of this Country, where the neediest Cottager pays out of his Pittance, however scanty, and how hardly soever earned, our high Duties of Customs and Excise in the Price of all his Consumption; it will be difficult I say, to persuade those who see, who suffer, or who relieve such Oppression; that the *West Indian* out of his Opulence, and the *North American* out of his Competency, can contribute no more than it is now pretended they can afford towards the Expence of Services, the Benefit of which, as a Part of this Nation they share, and as Colonists they peculiarly enjoy. They have indeed their own civil Governments besides to support; but *Great Britain* has her civil Government too; she has also a large Peace Establishment to maintain; and the national Debt, tho' so great a Part, and that the heaviest Part of it has been incurred by a War undertaken for the Protection of the Colonies, lies solely still upon her.

The Reasonableness, and even the Necessity of requiring an *American* Revenue being admitted, the Right of the Mother Country to impose such a Duty upon her Colonies, if duly considered, cannot be questioned: they claim it is true the Privilege, which is common to all *British* Subjects, of being taxed only with their own Consent, given by their Representatives; and may they ever enjoy the Privilege in all its Extent:

May this sacred Pledge of Liberty be preserved inviolate, to
the utmost Verge of our Dominions, and to the latest Page of
our History! but let us not limit the legislative Rights of the
British People to Subjects of Taxation only: No new Law
whatever can bind us that is made without the Concurrence of
our Representatives. The Acts of Trade and Navigation, and all
other Acts that relate either to ourselves or to the Colonies, are
founded upon no other Authority; they are not obligatory if a
Stamp Act is not, and every Argument in support of an Exemption from the Superintendance of the *British* Parliament in
the one Case, is equally applicable to the others. The Constitution knows no Distinction; the Colonies have never attempted to
make one; but have acquiesced under several parliamentary
Taxes. The 6 *Geo.* II. c. 13. which has been already refered to,
lays heavy Duties on all foreign Rum, Sugar, and Melasses,
imported into the *British* Plantations: the Amount of the Impositions has been complained of; the Policy of the Laws has
been objected to; but the Right of making such a Law, has never
been questioned. These however, it may be said, are Duties
upon Imports only, and there some imaginary Line has been
supposed to be drawn; but had it ever existed, it was passed
long before, for by 25 *Charles* II. c. 7. enforced by 7 and 8 *Wil.*
and *Mary*, c. 22. and by 1 *Geo.* I. c. 12. the Exports of the *West
Indian* Islands, not the Merchandize purchased by the Inhabitants, nor the Profits they might make by their Trade, but the
Property they had at the Time, the Produce of their Lands,
was taxed, by the Duties then imposed upon Sugar, Tobacco,
Cotton, Indigo, Ginger, Logwood, Fustick, and Cocoa, exported from one *British* Plantation to another.

It is in vain to call these only Regulations of Trade; the
Trade of *British* Subjects may not be regulated by such Means,
without the Concurrence of their Representatives. Duties laid
for these Purposes, as well as for the Purposes of Revenue, are
still Levies of Money upon the People. The Constitution again
knows no Distinction between Impost Duties and internal
Taxation; and if some speculative Difference should be attempted to be made, it certainly is contradicted by Fact; for an
internal Tax also was laid on the Colonies by the Establishment
of a Post Office there; which, however it may be represented,
will, upon a Perusal of 9 *Anne* c. 10. appear to be essentially a

Tax, and that of the most authoritative Kind; for it is enforced by Provisions, more peculiarly prohibitory and compulsive, than others are usually attended with: The Conveyance of Letters thro' any other Channel is forbidden, by which Restrictions, the Advantage which might be made by public Carriers and others of this Branch of their Business is taken away; and the Passage of Ferries is declared to be free for the Post, the Ferrymen being compellable immediately on Demand to give their Labour without pay, and the Proprietors being obliged to furnish the Means of Passage to the Post without Recompence. These Provisions are indeed very proper, and even necessary; but certainly Money levied by such Methods, the Effect of which is intended to be a Monopoly of the Carriage of Letters to the Officers of this Revenue, and by Means of which the People are forced to pay the Rates imposed upon all their Correspondence, is a public Tax to which they must submit, and not meerly a Price required of them for a private Accommodation. The Act treats this and the *British* Postage upon exactly the same Footing, and expresly calls them both *a Revenue*. The Preamble of it declares, that the new Rates are fixed in the Manner therein specified with a View *to enable her Majesty in some Measure to carry on and finish the War*. The Sum of 700*l. per* Week out of all *the Duties arising from time to time by virtue of this Act is* appropriated for that Purpose, and for other necessary Occasions; the Surplus after other Deductions, was made part of the civil List Revenues; it continued to be thus applied during the Reigns of *George* I. and *George* II. and on his present Majesty's Accession to the Throne, when the Civil List was put upon a different Establishment, the Post Office Revenues were carried with the others *to the aggregate Fund, to be applied to the Uses, to which the said Fund is or shall be applicable*. If all these Circumstances do not constitute a Tax, I do not know what do: the Stamp Duties are not marked with stronger Characters, to entitle them to that Denomination; and with respect to the Application of the Revenue, the Power of the Parliament of *Great Britain* over the Colonies was then held up much higher than it has been upon the present Occasion. The Revenue arising from the Postage in *American* is blended with that of *England*, is applied in Part to the carrying on of a continental War, and other public Purposes; the Remainder of it to the Support of the Civil List; and now the whole of it to the Discharge of the National Debt by Means of the aggregate Fund; all these are Services that are either national or particular to *Great Britain*; but the Stamp Duties and the others that were laid last Year, are appropriated to such Services only as more particularly relate to the Colonies; and surely if the Right of the *British* Parliament to impose the one be acknowledged; that of laying on the other cannot be disputed. The Post-Office has indeed been called a meer Convenience; which therefore the People always chearfully pay for. After what has been said, this Observation requires very little Notice; I will not call the Protection and Security of the Colonies, to which the Duties in question are applied, by so low a Name as a Convenience.

The Instances that have been mentioned prove, that the Right of the Parliament of *Great Britain* to impose Taxes of every Kind on the Colonies, has been always admitted; but were there no Precedents to support the Claim, it would still be incontestable, being founded on the Principles of our Constitution; for the Fact is, that the Inhabitants of the Colonies are represented in Parliament: they do not indeed chuse the Members of that Assembly; neither are Nine Tenths of the People of *Britain* Electors; for the Right of Election is annexed to certain Species of Property, to peculiar Franchises, and to Inhabitancy in some particular Places; but these Descriptions comprehend only a very small Part of the Land, the Property, and the People of this Island: all Copyhold, all Leasehold Estates, under the Crown, under the Church, or under private Persons, tho' for Terms ever so long; all landed Property in short, that is not Freehold, and all monied Property whatsoever are excluded: the Possessors of these have no Votes in the Election of Members of Parliament; Women and Persons under Age be their Property ever so large, and all of it Freehold, have none. The Merchants of *London*, a numerous and respectable Body of Men, whose Opulence exceeds all that *America* could collect; the Proprietors of that vast Accumulation of Wealth, the public Funds; the Inhabitants of *Leeds*, of *Halifax*, of *Birmingham*, and of *Manchester*, Towns that are each of them larger than the Largest in the Plantations; many of less Note that are yet incorporated; and that great Corporation the *East India* Company, whose Rights over the Countries they possess, fall little short of Sovereignty, and whose Trade and whose Fleets are sufficient to constitute them a maritime Power, are all in the same Circumstances; none of them chuse their Representatives; and yet are they not represented in Parliament? Is their vast Property subject to Taxes without their Consent? Are they all arbitrarily bound by Laws to which they have not agreed? The Colonies are in exactly the same Situation: All *British* Subjects are really in the same; none are actually, all are virtually represented in Parliament; for every Member of Parliament sits in the House, not as Representative of his own Constituents, but as one of that august Assembly by which all the Commons of *Great Britain* are represented. Their Rights and their Interests, however his own Borough may be affected by general Dispositions, ought to be the great Objects of his Attention, and the only Rules for his Conduct; and to sacrifice these to a partial Advantage in favour of the Place where he was chosen, would be a Departure from his Duty; if it were otherwise, *Old Sarum* would enjoy Privileges essential to Liberty, which are denied to *Birmingham* and to *Manchester*; but as it is, they and the Colonies and all *British* Subjects whatever, have an equal Share in the general Representation of the Commons of *Great Britain*, and are bound by the Consent of the Majority of that House, whether their own particular Representatives consented to or opposed the Measures there taken, or whether they had or had not particular Representatives there.

The Inhabitants of the Colonies however have by some been supposed to be excepted, because they are represented in their respective Assemblies. So are the Citizens of *London* in their Common Council; and yet so far from excluding them from the national Representation, it does not impeach their Right to chuse Members of Parliament: it is true, that the Powers vested in the Common Council of *London*, are not equal to those which the Assemblies in the Plantations enjoy; but still they are legislative Powers, to be exercised within their District, and over their Citizens; yet not exclusively of the general Superintendance of the great Council of the Nation: The Subjects of a By-law and of an Act of Parliament may possibly be the same; yet it never was imagined that the

Privileges of *London* were incompatible with the Authority of Parliament; and indeed what Contradiction, what Absurdity, does a double Representation imply? What difficulty is there in allowing both, tho' both should even be vested with equal legislative Powers, if the one is to be exercised for local, and the other for general Purposes? and where is the Necessity that the Subordinate Power must derogate from the superior Authority? It would be a singular Objection to a Man's Vote for a Member of Parliament, that being represented in a provincial, he cannot be represented in a national Assembly; and if this is not sufficient Ground for an Objection, neither is it for an Exemption, or for any Pretence of an Exclusion.

The Charter and the proprietary Governments in *America*, are in this Respect, on the same Footing with the Rest. The comprehending them also, both in a provincial and national Representation, is not necessarily attended with any Inconsistency, and nothing contained in their Grants can establish one; for all who took those Grants were *British* Subjects, inhabiting *British* Dominions, and who at the Time of taking, were indisputably under the Authority of Parliament; no other Power can abridge that Authority, or dispense with the Obedience that is due to it: those therefore, to whom the Charters were originally given, could have no Exemption granted to them: and what the Fathers never received, the Children cannot claim as an Inheritance; nor was it ever in Idea that they should; even the Charters themselves, so far from allowing guard against the Supposition.

And after all, does any Friend to the Colonies desire the Exemption? he cannot, if he will reflect but a Moment on the Consequences. We value the Right of being represented in the national Legislature as the dearest Privilege we enjoy; how justly would the Colonies complain, if they alone were deprived of it? They acknowledge Dependance upon their Mother Country; but that Dependance would be Slavery not Connection, if they bore no Part in the Government of the whole: they would then indeed be in a worse Situation than the Inhabitants of *Britain*, for these are all of them virtually, tho' few of them are actually represented in the *House of Commons*; if the Colonies were not, they could not expect that their Interests and their Privileges would be any otherwise considered there, than as subservient to those of *Great Britain*; for to deny the Authority of a Legislature, is to surrender all Claims to a Share in its Councils; and if this were the Tenor of their Charters, a Grant more insidious and more replete with Mischief, could not have been invented: a permanent Title to a Share in national Councils, would be exchanged for a precarious Representation in a provincial Assembly; and a Forfeiture of their Rights would be couched under the Appearance of Privileges; they would be reduced from Equality to Subordination, and be at the same Time deprived of the Benefits, and liable to the Inconveniences, both of Independency and of Connection. Happily for them, this is not their Condition. They are on the contrary a Part, and an important Part of the Commons of *Great Britain*: they are represented in Parliament, in the same Manner as those Inhabitants of *Britain* are, who have not Voices in Elections; and they enjoy, with the Rest of their Fellow-subjects, the inestimable Privilege of not being bound by any Laws, or subject to any Taxes, to which the Majority of the Representatives of the Commons have not consented.

If there really were any Inconsistency between a national and a provincial Legislature, the Consequence would be the Abolition of the latter; for the Advantages that attend it are purely local: the District it is confined to might be governed without it, by means of the national Representatives; and it is unequal to great general Operations; whereas the other is absolutely necessary for the Benefit and Preservation of the whole: But so far are they from being incompatible, that they will be seldom found to interfere with one another: The Parliament will not often have occasion to exercise its Power over the Colonies, except for those Purposes, which the Assemblies cannot provide for. A general Tax is of this Kind; the Necessity for it, the Extent, the Application of it, are Matters which Councils limited in their Views and in their Operations cannot properly judge of; and when therefore the national Council determine these Particulars, it does not encroach on the other, it only exercises a Power which that other does not pretend to, never claimed, or wished, nor can ever be vested with: The latter remains in exactly the same State as it was before, providing for the same Services, by the same Means, and on the same

Subjects; but conscious of its own Inability to answer greater Purposes than those for which it was instituted, it leaves the care of more general Concerns to that higher Legislature, in whose Province alone the Direction of them always was, is, and will be. The Exertion of that Authority which belongs to its universal Superintendance, neither lowers the Dignity, nor depreciates the Usefulness of more limited Powers: They retain all that they ever had, and are really incapable of more.

The Concurrence therefore of the provincial Representatives cannot be necessary in great public Measures to which none but the national Representatives are equal: The Parliament of *Great Britain* not only may but must tax the Colonies, when the public Occasions require a Revenue there: The present Circumstances of the Nation require one now; and a Stamp Act, of which we have had so long an Experience in this, and which is not unknown in that Country, seems an eligible Mode of Taxation. From all these Considerations, and from many others which will occur upon Reflexion and need not be suggested, it must appear *proper to charge certain Stamp Duties in the Plantations to be applied towards defraying the necessary Expences of defending, protecting, and securing the British Colonies and Plantations in America.* This Vote of the House of Commons closed the Measures taken last Year on the Subject of the Colonies: They appear to have been founded upon true Principles of Policy, of Commerce, and of Finance; to be wise with respect to the Mother-Country; just and even beneficial to the Plantations; and therefore it may reasonably be expected that either in their immediate Operations, or in their distant Effects, they will improve the Advantages we possess, confirm the Blessings we enjoy, and promote the public Welfare.

FINIS.

[Daniel Dulany], Considerations on the Propriety of Imposing Taxes in the British Colonies, for the Purpose of Raising a Revenue, by Act of Parliament. [Annapolis], 1765.

Whately's *Regulations Lately Made* was soon joined by other defenses of the Stamp Act, including *The Objections to the Taxation of Our American Colonies . . . Considered* by Soame Jenyns, a poet and former member of the Board of Trade, and *The Claim of the Colonies to an Exemption from Internal Taxes Imposed by Authority of Parliament, Examined* by William Knox, a former colonial official. Americans read these pamphlets with great interest and alarm, knowing that these assertions of parliamentary power had to be answered.

The most formidable among the rejoinders was the following anonymous pamphlet. Its author was Daniel Dulany, son of a prominent and wealthy Maryland family, who had been educated at Cambridge and studied law at Middle Temple in London before returning home to be admitted to the Maryland bar in 1747. Over the next two decades he enjoyed a number of elective and appointive positions in the colony, and in 1765 he was its secretary, commissary general, and a member of the governor's council. In his pamphlet Dulany did not actually repudiate the theory of virtual representation and its claim that certain people from society, if their interests were identical with the rest, could justly speak for the whole. For Dulany, the fallacy in Whately's contention lay not in the inability of the colonists to vote for members of Parliament but rather in the fact that the interests of the English—electors, nonelectors, and representatives alike—were in no way identical with those of the colonists. In other words, he implied that Britons and Americans were not really one people after all.

This pamphlet was quickly reprinted throughout the colonies, and a London edition appeared the following year. Although he later became a Loyalist, in 1765 Daniel Dulany's was one of the most important voices in support of the patriot cause.

CONSIDERATIONS

ON THE

PROPRIETY

OF IMPOSING

TAXES

IN THE

Britiſh COLONIES,

For the Purpoſe of raiſing a REVENUE, by
ACT OF PARLIAMENT.

————*Haud Totum Verba reſignent*
Quod latet arcanâ, non enarrabile, fibrâ.

North-America : Printed by a North-American.
MDCCLXV.

PREFACE.

IT would, now, be an unfashionable Doctrine, whatever the ancient Opinion might be, to affirm that the Constituent can bind his Representative by Instructions; but tho' the obligatory Force of these Instructions is not insisted upon, yet their persuasive Influence, in most Cases, may be; for a Representative, who should act against the explicit Recommendation of his Constituents, would most deservedly forfeit their Regard and all Pretension to their future Confidence.

When it is under Deliberation, whether a new Law shall be Enacted, in which the Electors of *England* are interested, THEY have Notice of it, and an Opportunity of declaring their Sense—THEY may point out every dangerous Tendency, and are not restrained in their Representations, from shewing in the plainest Language, the Injustice or Oppression of it.

When a Law in it's Execution is found to be repugnant to the Genius of Liberty, or productive of Hardships or Inconvenience, THEY may also instruct their Deputies to exert Themselves in procuring a Repeal of it, and in the Exercise of this Right are not constrained to whine in the Style of humble Petitioners.— THEY are exposed to no Danger in explaining their Reasons— THEIR Situation does not become so delicate as to make it prudent, to weaken, by not urging them, with their full Force, and to their utmost Extent. But who are the Representatives of the Colonies? To whom shall THEY send their Instructions, when desirous to obtain the Repeal of a Law striking at the Root and Foundation of every Civil Right, should such an one take Place? Instructions to all the Members who compose the House of Commons would not be proper. To them the Application must be by Petition, in which an unreserved Style would, probably, be deemed Indecency, and strong Expressions Insolence, in which a Claim of Rights may not, perhaps, be explained, or even insinuated, if to impugn, or glance at their Authority whose Relief is supplicated. To soften and deprecate must be the Hope and Endeavour, tho' a guiltless Freeman would, probably, be aukward in ringing all the Changes of *Parce, Precor.*

Under these Circumstances, the Liberty of the Press is of

the most momentous Consequence, for if Truth is not allowed to speak thence in it's genuine Language of Plainness and Simplicity, nor Freedom to vindicate it's Privileges with decent Firmness, we shall have too much Reason to acknowledge his Foresight who predicted, that, "the Constitution of the *British* Government was too excellent to be permament." The Train for the Accomplishment of that Prophecy hath not yet catched in *America*, nor, I trust, been laid.

That there have been Laws extremely unjust and oppressive, the Declarations of subsequent Parliaments, fixing this Stigma upon them, evince; but whilst the Power which introduced them prevailed, it was not prudent to give them their deserved Characters. The Parliament of *Henry* III, or that of *Henry* VI, need not be cited; there are many other Instances, tho' not branded with Epithets so remarkably opprobrious.

In the Opinion of a great Lawyer, an Act of Parliament may be void, and of a great Divine, "all Men have natural, and Freemen legal Rights, which they may justly maintain, and no legislative Authority can deprive them of."

Cases may be imagined in which the Truth of these Positions might, in Theory, be admitted; but in Practice, unless there should be very peculiar Circumstances, such as can't be supposed to exist during the Prevalence of the Power that introduced it, who would rely upon the Authority of Opinions, or the Principles of them, for his Protection against the Penalties of *any* positive Law?

When the Judges were ask'd by *Henry* VIII, Whether a Man might be attainted of High Treason by Parliament, tho' not called to answer, they declared that it was a dangerous Question, and gave the evasive Answer that, "the High Court of Parliament ought to give Examples of Justice to the inferior Courts, none of which could do the like." But tho' it might be dangerous to declare against the Authority of Parliament, we are not bound to acknowledge it's Inerrability, nor precluded from examining the Principles and Consequences of Laws, or from pointing out their Improprieties, and Defects. Upon this Ground I have proceeded in the following Considerations, and shall not be disappointed if they should appear to be too free, or too reserved, to Readers of different Complexions.

VIRGINIA, August 12, 1765.

Considerations, &c.

IN the Constitution of *England*, the Three principal Forms of Government, Monarchy, Aristocracy and Democracy, are blended together in certain Proportions; but each of these Orders, in the Exercise of the legislative Authority, hath its peculiar Department, from which the other are excluded. In this Division, the *Granting of Supplies*, or *Laying Taxes*, is deemed to be the Province of the House of Commons, as the Representative of the People.—All Supplies are supposed to flow from their Gift; and the other Orders are permitted only to assent, or reject generally, not to propose any Modification, Amendment, or partial Alteration of it.

This Observation being considered, it will undeniably appear, that, in framing the late *Stamp Act*, the Commons acted in the Character of Representative of the Colonies. They assumed it as the Principle of that Measure, and the *Propriety* of it must therefore stand, or fall, as the Principle is true, or false: For the Preamble sets forth, That the Commons of *Great Britain* had resolved to *Give and Grant* the several Rates and Duties imposed by the Act; but what Right had the Commons of *Great Britain* to be thus munificent at the Expence of the Commons of *America?*—To give Property, not belonging to the Giver, and without the Consent of the Owner, is such evident and flagrant Injustice, in *ordinary Cases*, that few are hardy enough to avow it; and therefore, when it really happens, the Fact is disguised and varnished over by the most plausible Pretences the Ingenuity of the Giver can suggest.—But it is alledged that there is a *Virtual*, or *implied Representation* of the Colonies springing out of the Constitution of the *British* Government: And it must be confessed on all Hands, that, as the Representation is not actual, it is virtual, or it doth not exist at all; for no third Kind of Representation can be imagined. The Colonies claim the Privilege, which is common to all *British Subjects*, of being taxed *only* with their own Consent given by their Representatives, and all the Advocates for the *Stamp Act* admit this Claim. Whether, therefore, upon the whole Matter, the Imposition of the *Stamp Duties* is a *proper* Exercise of Constitutional Authority, or not, depends upon the single Question, Whether the Commons of *Great Britain* are *virtually* the Representatives of the Commons of *America*, or not.

The Advocates for the Stamp Act admit, in express Terms, that "the Colonies do not chuse Members of Parliament," but They assert that "the Colonies are *virtually* represented in the same Manner with the Non-Electors resident in *Great Britain*."

How have They proved this Position? Where have They defined, or precisely explained what They mean by the Expression, *Virtual Representation*? As it is the very Hinge upon which the Rectitude of the Taxation turns, something more satisfactory than mere Assertion, more solid than a Form of Expression, is necessary; for, how can it be seriously expected, that Men, who think Themselves injuriously affected in their Properties and Privileges, will be convinced and reconciled by a fanciful Phrase, the Meaning of which can't be precisely ascertained by those who use it, or properly applied to the Purpose for which it hath been advanced.

They argue, that "the Right of Election being annexed to certain Species of Property, to Franchises, and Inhabitancy in some particular Places, a very small Part of the Land, the Property, and the People of *England* is comprehended in those Descriptions. All Landed Property, not Freehold, and all Monied Property, are *excluded*. The Merchants of *London*, the Proprietors of the Public Funds, the Inhabitants of *Leeds, Halifax, Birmingham*, and *Manchester*, and that great Corporation of the *East-India* Company, *None of Them* chuse their Representatives, and yet are They all represented in Parliament, and the Colonies being *exactly* in *their* Situation, are represented in the *same* Manner."

Now, this Argument, which is all that their Invention hath been able to supply, is totally defective; for, it consists of Facts not true, and of Conclusions inadmissible.

It is so far from being true, that all the Persons enumerated under the Character of *Non-Electors*, are in that Predicament, that it is indubitably certain there is *no* Species of Property, landed, or monied, which is not possessed by *very many* of the *British Electors*.

I shall undertake to disprove the supposed Similarity of

Situation, whence the same Kind of Representation is deduced of the Inhabitants of the Colonies, and of the *British* Non-Electors; and, if I succeed, the Notion of a *virtual Representation* of the Colonies must fail, which, in Truth, is a mere Cob-web, spread to catch the unwary, and intangle the weak. I would be understood. I am upon a Question of *Propriety*, not of Power; and, though some may be inclined to think it is to little Purpose to discuss the one, when the other is irresistible, yet are They different Considerations; and, at the same Time that I invalidate the Claim upon which it is founded, I may very consistently recommend a Submission to the Law, whilst it endures. I shall say Nothing of the Use I intend by the Discussion; for, if it should not be perceived by the Sequel, there is no Use in it, and, if it should appear then, it need not be premised.

Lessees for Years, Copyholders, Proprietors of the Public Funds, Inhabitants of *Birmingham, Leeds, Halifax,* and *Manchester,* Merchants of the City of *London,* or Members of the Corporation of the *East-India* Company, are, *as such,* under no personal Incapacity to be Electors; for they may acquire the Right of Election, and there are *actually* not only a considerable Number of Electors in each of the Classes of Lessees for Years, *&c.* but in many of them, if not all, even Members of Parliament. The Interests therefore of the Non-Electors, the Electors, and the Representatives, are individually the same; to say nothing of the Connection among Neighbours, Friends, and Relations. The Security of the Non-Electors against Oppression, is, that their Oppression will fall also upon the Electors and the Representatives. The one can't be injured, and the other indemnified.

Further, if the Non-Electors should not be taxed by the *British* Parliament, They would not be taxed *at all*; and it would be iniquitous, as well as a Solecism, in the political System, that They should partake of all the Benefits resulting from the Imposition, and Application of Taxes, and derive an Immunity from the Circumstance of not being qualified to vote. Under this Constitution then, a double or virtual Representation may be reasonably supposed.—The Electors, who are inseparably connected in their Interests with the Non-Electors, may be justly deemed to be the Representatives of the

Non-Electors, at the same Time They exercise their personal Privilege in their Right of Election, and the Members chosen, therefore, the Representatives of both. This is the only rational Explanation of the Expression, *virtual Representation.* None has been advanced by the Assertors of it, and their Meaning can only be inferred from the Instances, by which They endeavour to elucidate it, and no other Meaning can be stated, to which the Instances apply.

It is an essential Principle of the *English* Constitution, that the Subject shall not be taxed without his Consent, which hath not been introduced by any particular Law, but necessarily results from the Nature of that mixed Government; for, without it, the Order of Democracy could not exist.

Parliaments were not formerly so regular in Point of Form as they now are.* Even the Number of Knights for each Shire were not ascertained. The first Writs now extant for their Choice, are 22d *Edward* I, by which, Two, as at this Day, were directed to be chosen for each County; but the King not being satisfied with that Number, other Writs were issued for chusing Two more. This discretionary Power being thought inconvenient, was afterwards restrained by the Statutes of *Richard* II, *Henry* IV, and subsequent Acts.

In earlier Times there was more Simplicity in the Rules of Government, and Men were more solicitous about the Essentials, than the Forms of it. When the Consent of those who were to perform, or pay any Thing extra-feudal, was fairly applied for and obtained, the Manner was little regarded; but, as the People had reason to be jealous of Designs to impose Contributions upon Them without their Consent, it was thought expedient to have Formalities regulated, and fixed, to prevent this Injury to their Rights, not to destroy a Principle, without which, They could not be said to have any Rights at all.

Before the Introduction of those Formalities, which were framed with a View to restrain the Excursions of Power, and to secure the Privileges of the Subject, as the Mode of Proceeding was more simple, so perhaps this Foundation of Consent was more visible than it is at present, wherefore it may be of Use to

* See Treat. Peerage.

adduce some Instances, which directly point out this necessary and essential Principle of *British Liberty.*

The Lords and Commons have separately given Aids and Subsidies to the Crown. In 13th *Edward* III, the Lords granted the Tenth of all the Corn, *&c.* growing upon their Demesnes, the Commons then granting Nothing, nor concerning Themselves with what the Lords thought fit to grant out of their own Estates.—At other Times, the Knights of Shires, separating from the rest of the Commons, and joining with the Lords, have granted a Subsidy, and the Representatives of Cities and Boroughs have likewise granted Subsidies to the Crown separately, as appears by a Writ in 24th *Edward* I, which runs in these Words: *Rex,* &c.—*Cum Comites, Barones, Milites Nobis,* &c. *fecerunt undecimam de omnibus Bonis suis mobilibus, et Cives et Burgenses,* &c. *septimam de omnibus Bonis suis mobilibus,* &c. *nobis curialiter concesserint,* &c.—When an Affair happened, which affected only some Individuals, and called for an Aid to the Crown, it was common for those Individuals *alone* to be summoned; to which Purpose several Writs arc extant. In 35th *Edward* III, there is a Writ (which *Dugdale* has printed in his Collection of Writs of Summons to Parliament) directed to the Earl of *Northampton,* which, after reciting the Confusion the Affairs of *Ireland* were in, and that he, and some other *English* Lords had Possessions in that Kingdom, and were therefore more particularly obliged to the Defence of it, follows in these Words: *Volumus Vobiscum, et cum aliis de eodem Regno (Angliæ scilicet) Terras in dictâ Terrâ habentibus Colloquium habere,* &c.

But, that the Reader may perceive how strictly the Principle of no Persons being Taxed without their Consent, hath been regarded, it is proper to take Notice, that, upon the same Occasion, Writs were likewise directed even to Women, who were Proprietors of Land in *Ireland,* to send their Deputies to consult, and consent to what should be judged necessary to be done on the Occasion; e. g. *Rex,* &c.—*Mariæ,* &c. *Salutem,* &c. *Vobis,* &c. *Mandamus quod aliquem, vel aliquos de quibus confidatis apud Westmon. mittatis ad loquendum nobiscum super dictis Negotiis, et ad faciendum et consentiendum Nomine vestro, super hoc quod ibidem ordinari contigerit.*

A Reflection naturally arises from the Instances cited—When, on a particular Occasion, *some* Individuals *only* were to be taxed, and not the *whole* Community, *their* Consent *only* was called for, and in the last Instance it appears, that they, who upon an Occasion of a general Tax, would have been bound by the Consent of their *virtual Representatives* (for in that Case they would have had no *actual Representatives*) were in an Affair calling for a *particular* Aid from them, *separate* from the rest of the Community, required to send their *particular Deputies.* But how different would be the Principle of a Statute, imposing Duties without *their* Consent who are to pay them, upon the Authority of *their* Gift, who should undertake to give, what doth not belong to them.

That great King, *Edward* I, inserted in his Writs of Summons, as a first Principle of Law, that *quod omnes tangat ab omnibus approbetur,* which by no Torture can be made to signify that their Approbation or Consent *only* is to be required in the Imposition of a Tax, who are to pay *no* Part of it.

The Situation of the Non-Electors in *England*—their Capacity to become Electors—their inseparable Connection with those who are Electors, and their Representatives—their Security against Oppression resulting from this Connection, and the Necessity of imagining a double or virtual Representation, to avoid Iniquity and Absurdity, have been explained—The Inhabitants of the Colonies are, *as such,* incapable of being Electors, the Privilege of Election being exerciseable only in Person, and therefore if *every* Inhabitant of *America* had the requisite Freehold, not *one* could vote, but upon the Supposition of his ceasing to be an Inhabitant of *America,* and becoming a Resident in *Great-Britain,* a Supposition which would be impertinent, because it shifts the Question—Should the Colonies not be taxed by *Parliamentary Impositions,* their respective Legislatures have a regular, adequate, and constitutional Authority to Tax them, and therefore there would not necessarily be an iniquitous and absurd Exemption, from their not being represented by *the House of Commons.*

There is not that intimate and inseparable Relation between the *Electors of* Great-Britain and the *Inhabitants of the Colonies,* which must inevitably involve both in the same Taxation; on the contrary, not a single *actual* Elector in *England,* might be immediately affected by a Taxation in *America,* imposed by a

Statute which would have a general Operation and Effect, upon the Properties of the Inhabitants of the Colonies. The latter might be oppressed in a Thousand Shapes, without any Sympathy, or exciting any Alarm in the former. Moreover, even Acts, oppressive and injurious to the Colonies in an extreme Degree, might become popular in *England*, from the Promise or Expectation, that the very Measures which depressed the Colonies, would give Ease to the Inhabitants of *Great-Britain*. It is indeed true, that the Interests of *England* and the Colonies are allied, and an Injury to the Colonies produced into all it's Consequences, will eventually affect the Mother Country, yet these Consequences being generally remote, are not at once foreseen; they do not immediately alarm the Fears, and engage the Passions of the *English* Electors, the Connection between a Freeholder of *Great Britain*, and a *British American* being deducible only through a Train of Reasoning, which few will take the Trouble, or can have an Opportunity, if they have Capacity, to investigate; wherefore the Relation between the *British-Americans*, and the *English Electors*, is a Knot too infirm to be relied on as a competent Security, especially against the Force of a present, counteracting Expectation of Relief.

If it would have been a just Conclusion, that the *Colonies* being exactly in the *same* Situation with the *Non-Electors* of *England*, are *therefore* represented in the same Manner, it ought to be allowed, that the Reasoning is solid, which, after having evinced a total *Dissimilarity* of Situation, infers that their Representation is *different*.

If the Commons of *Great-Britain* have no Right by the Constitution, to GIVE AND GRANT Property *not* belonging to themselves or others, without their Consent actually or virtually given—If the Claim of the Colonies not to be taxed *without their Consent*, signified by their Representatives, is well founded, if it appears that the Colonies are not actually represented by the Commons of *Great-Britain*, and that the Notion of a double or virtual Representation, doth not with any Propriety apply to the People of *America*; then the Principle of the *Stamp Act*, must be given up as indefensible on the Point of Representation, and the Validity of it rested upon the *Power* which they who framed it, have to carry it into Execution.

"Should the Parliament devise a Tax, to be paid only by those of the People in *Great-Britain*, who are neither Members of either House of Parliament, nor their Electors, such an Act would be unjust and partial," saith the Author of the Claim of the Colonies, *&c.* who yet allows that the "Non-Electors would have a Security against the Weight of such a Tax, should it be imposed, which the Colonies have not, *Viz.* That the Members of Parliament and their Electors, must be relatively affected by it; but the industrious *North-American*, and the opulent *West-Indian* may have their Properties taxed, and no Individual in *Great-Britain* participate with them in the Burden: On the contrary, the Members of Parliament would make their Court to their Constituents most effectually, by multiplying Taxes upon the Subjects of the Colonies."

Is it not amazing that the above Author, *with these Sentiments*, should undertake the Defence of the Stamp Duties, which, by his own Concession, appear to be *more* unjust, and *more* partial than the Tax he supposes, and upon which he bestows, very properly, the Epithets of *unjust* and *partial*?

——*Diluit Helleborum, certó compescere Punctó Nescius Examen.*

But it has been objected, that if the Inhabitants of *America*, because represented in their respective Assemblies, are *therefore* exempted from a *Parliamentary Tax*, then the Citizens of *London*, who are represented in their Common Council, may plead the *same Immunity*. If it were not for the Authority upon which this Objection is urged it might be safely passed over without a particular Answer; but since it hath been introduced with an Appearance of Reliance, and the Opinion which it retails, is said to have been delivered with great Gravity, and pronounced with decisive Confidence, I would not be so wanting in Respect to an eminent Character, as to neglect the Ceremony of a direct Refutation.

But I must observe that, when the Opinion of a Lawyer is taken in a Matter of private Concern, in which he is under no Bias to deceive, a concise Declaration of it may generally suffice; he who applies for it being generally obliged to depend upon his Council's Character of Integrity and Knowledge, not only because the Expence of a methodical and minute Discussion would be too Burthensome, but because the Force of legal Reasoning is not generally understood. But in a Question of Public Concernment, the Opinion of no *Court Lawyer*, however respectable for his Candour and Abilities, ought to weigh more than the Reasons adduced in Support of it. They ought to be explained, they may be examined. Considering his Temptations, Credit ought to be cautiously and diffidently given, to his Assertion of what is his Opinion.—Considering the Consequence of a Decision, not to one Man only, but to Millions that exist and Myriads that may exist, and the exceeding Fallibility of legal Knowledge, nothing short of clear Conviction, after the fullest Explication of the Reasons of the Opinion, and the most accurate and intense Consideration of their Validity, can justify an Acquiescence under it.

On the present Occasion, so immensely important, *Nullius addictus jurare in Verba Magistri*, I shall pin my Faith upon the *Dictum* of no Lawyer in the Universe, and when his *ipse dixit* is authoritatively urged, I shall be at no Pains to repress my Suspicions that his Reasons are concealed, because, if fairly produced and held up to the Light, many Flaws in them would be discovered by a careful Examiner. I have lived long enough to remember many Opinions of *Court Lawyers* upon *American* Affairs; they have been all strongly marked with the same Character; they have been generally very sententious, and the same Observation may be applied to them all—They have all declared *that* to be *legal*, which the Minister for the Time being has deemed to be *expedient*. The Opinion given by a General of the Law in the late War on the Question, Whether Soldiers might be Quartered on Private Houses in *America*, must be pretty generally remembered.

The very learned Gentlemen has, it seems, declared that, "upon mature Deliberation, he has formed his Opinion, that the Colonies are in their Nature, no more than common Corporations, and that the Inhabitants of a Colony are no more entitled to an Exemption from Parliamentary Taxations, because represented in an *American* Assembly, than the Citizens of *London*."

This Opinion may be incontestably just in the Judgment of that accomplished Politician, and elegant Writer, who chuses

to distinguish himself by the Titles of late G—rn—r of the
J—rs—ys, of the M—ss—ch—s—ts B—, and of S—th C—r—
l—a, and who does not chuse to be distinguish'd by the Title
of late *Mâitre d'Hotel* of the late Sir D—v—s O—b—e, or that
exactly fitting, and characteristical Appellation conferred on
him, by an incensed Culprit in an *American* Court of
Star-Chamber, an Appellation rather adapted to signify those
Powers, which are useful in Intrigue, and that lead to Promotion, than expressive of Respect and Dignity*; but having
considered the Subject in the best Manner my very slender and
limited Capacity will allow, neither doth the Opinion of the
one, nor the Approbation of it by the other, influence my
Judgment.

Let a great Man declare a Similitude, and he will soon find a
Polonius to acknowledge, that, "*Yonder Cloud is, by the Mass,
like a Camel indeed*"—or, "*black like an Ouzle*,"—or, "*very
like a Whale*."

The Objection having been Stated, the Answer is obvious
and clear.

The Colonies have a compleat and adequate Legislative Authority, and are not only represented in their Assemblies, but
in *no other Manner*. The Power of making Bye-Laws vested in
the common Council is inadequate and incompleat, being
bounded by a few particular Subjects; and the Common
Council are actually represented too, by having a Choice of
Members to serve in Parliament. How then can the Reason of
the Exemption from internal Parliamentary Taxations, claimed
by the Colonies, apply to the Citizens of *London*?

The Power described in the Provincial Charters is to make
Laws, and in the Exercise of that Power, the Colonies are
bounded by no other Limitations than what result from their
Subordination to, and Dependance upon *Great-Britain*. The
Term *Bye-Laws* is as novel, and improper, when applied to the
Assemblies, as the Expression *Acts of Assembly* would be, if applied to the *Parliament of* Great-Britain, and it is as absurd
and insensible, to call a Colony a common Corporation, because not an independant Kingdom, and the Powers of each to
make Laws and Bye Laws, are limited, tho' not comparable in

* See the Hist. of TOM BRAZEN.

their Extent, and the Variety of their Objects, as it would be to call Lake *Erie*, a *Duck-puddle*, because not the Atlantic Ocean.

Should the Analogy between the *Colonies* and *Corporations* be even admitted for a Moment, in order to see what would be the Consequence of the *Postulatum*, it would only amount to this, The *Colonies* are vested with as compleat Authority to all Intents and Purposes to Tax themselves, as any *English Corporation* is to make a Bye-Law, in any imaginable Instance for any local Purpose whatever, and the *Parliament* doth not make Laws for *Corporations* upon Subjects, in every Respect proper for *Bye-Laws*.

But I don't rest the Matter upon this, or any other Circumstance, however considerable, to prove the Impropriety of a Taxation by the *British* Parliament. I rely upon the Fact, that not one Inhabitant in any Colony is, or can be *actually* or *virtually* represented by the *British House of Commons*, and therefore, that the Stamp Duties are severely imposed.

But it has been alledged, that if the Right to *Give and Grant* the Property of the Colonies by an internal Taxation is denied to the House of Commons, the Subordination or Dependance of the Colonies, and the Superintendence of the *British* Parliament can't be consistently establish'd—That any supposed Line of Distinction between the Two Cases, is but "a whimsical Imagination, a chimerical Speculation against Fact and Experience."—Now, under Favour, I conceive there is more Confidence, than Solidity in this Assertion, and it may be satisfactorily and easily proved, that the Subordination and Dependance of the Colonies may be preserved, and the *supreme Authority* of the Mother-Country be firmly supported, and yet the Principle of Representation, and the Right of the *British* House of Commons flowing from *it*, to *Give and Grant* the Property of the Commons of *America*, be denied.

The Colonies are dependant upon *Great Britain*, and the supreme Authority vested in the King, Lords, and Commons, may justly be exercised to secure, or preserve their Dependance, whenever necessary for that Purpose. This Authority results from, and is implied in the Idea of the Relation subsisting between *England* and her Colonies; for, considering the Nature of human Affections, the Inferior is not to be trusted with providing Regulations to prevent his Rising to an Equality with his Superior. But, though the Right of the Superior to use the proper Means for preserving the Subordination of his Inferior is admitted, yet it does not necessarily follow, that he has a Right to seize the Property of his Inferior when he pleases, or to command him in every Thing, since, in the Degrees of it, there may very well exist a *Dependance* and *Inferiority*, without absolute *Vassalage* and *Slavery*. In what the Superior may *rightfully* controul, or compel, and in what the Inferior ought to be at Liberty to act without Controul or Compulsion, depends upon the Nature of the Dependance, and the Degree of the Subordination; and, these being ascertained, the Measure of Obedience, and Submission, and the Extent of the Authority and Superintendence will be settled. When Powers, compatible with the Relation between the Superior and Inferior, have, by express Compact, been granted to, and accepted by the latter, and have been, after that Compact, repeatedly recognized by the former—When They may be exercised effectually upon every Occasion without any Injury to that Relation, the Authority of the Superior can't properly interpose; for, by the Powers vested in the Inferior, is the Superior limited.

By their Constitutions of Government, the Colonies are impowered to impose internal Taxes. This Power is compatible with their Dependance, and hath been expressly recognized by *British* Ministers and the *British* Parliament, upon many Occasions; and it may be exercised effectually without striking at, or impeaching, in any Respect, the Superintendence of the *British* Parliament. May not then the Line be distinctly and justly drawn between such Acts as are necessary, or proper, for preserving or securing the Dependance of the Colonies, and such as are not necessary or proper for that very important Purpose?

When the Powers were conferred upon the Colonies, They were conferred too as Privileges and Immunities, and accepted as such; or, to speak more properly, the Privileges belonging necessarily to Them as *British* Subjects, were solemnly declared and confirmed by their Charters, and They who settled in *America* under the Encouragement and Faith of these Charters, understood, not only that They *might*, but that it was their *Right* to exercise those Powers without Controul, or Prevention. In some of the Charters the Distinction is expressed, and the strongest Declarations made, and the most solemn Assurances given that the Settlers should not have their Property taxed without their own Consent by their Representatives, though their legislative Authority is limited at the same Time, by the Subordination implied in their Relation, and They are therefore restrained from making Acts of Assembly repugnant to the Laws of *England*, and, had the Distinction not been expressed, the Powers given would have implied it, for, if the Parliament may in any Case interpose, when the Authority of the Colonies is adequate to the Occasion, and not limited by their Subordination to the Mother-Country, it may in every *Case*, which would make *another* Appellation more proper to describe their Condition, than the Name by which their Inhabitants have been usually called, and have Gloried in.

Because the Parliament may, when the Relation between *Great-Britain* and her Colonies calls for an Exertion of her Superintendance, bind the Colonies by Statute, therefore a Parliamentary Interposition in every other Instance, is justifiable, is an Inference that may be denied.

On some Emergencies, the King, by the Constitution, hath an absolute Power to provide for the Safety of the State, to take Care, like a *Roman* Dictator, *ne quid Detrimenti capiat Respublica*, and this Power is not specifically annexed to the Monarchy by any express Law; it necessarily results from the End and Nature of Government, but who would infer from this, that the King, in every Instance, or upon every Occasion, can, upon the Principles of the Constitution, exercise this supreme Power?

The *British Ministers* have, in the most effectual Terms, at different Periods, from the Reign of *Charles* II, to that of the present King, recognized this Distinction in their Requisitions, transmitted to the Colonies to raise and levy Men and Money, by Acts of Assembly; and recently, in the Course of the last War, they were so far from thinking that it was proper for the *British House of Commons* to *Give and Grant* the Property *of the Colonies* to support the military Operations in *America*, upon which not only the immediate Protection of that Part of the *British Dominions*, but the most important Interests, perhaps the ultimate Preservation of *Great Britain* from Destruction, essentially depended; I say, on this great Occasion of the most important, and national Concernment, the *British Ministers* were so far from calling upon *the House of Commons*, in their *peculiar* Department, to *Give and Grant* Property, belonging neither to Themselves, nor their Constituents, that They directly applied to *the Colonies* to tax Themselves, in Virtue of the Authority and Privilege conferred by their Charters, and promised to recommend it to the *British Parliament* to reimburse the Expence They should incur in providing for the general Service.—They made good their Promise; and, if all the Money raised in the Colonies, by Acts of Assembly, in pursuance of the Requisitions of the *British* Ministers, hath not been repaid by Parliament, a very considerable Part of it hath.

Could They, who made the Requisitions I have mentioned, or the Assemblies that complied with them, intend, or imagine the Faith of the *English* Government was to be preserved by a Retribution, at one Time, of the Money disbursed at the Instance, and upon the Credit of the *British Ministry*, enforced and supported by *Royal Assurances*, and by taking it back again at another Time? Is this Method of keeping the Faith of Government to be ranked among the "Improvements which have been made beyond the Idea of former Administrations, concluded by Ministers ignorant of the Importance of the Colonies, or who impotently neglected their Concerns, or were diverted by mean Pursuits, from attending to Them?" Is it absolutely certain, that there never can, at any future Period, arise a Crisis, in which the Exertion of the Colonies may be necessary, or, if there should, that it will bring with it an Oblivion of all former Indirection?—But this is a Subject fitter for silent Meditation, than public Discussion.

There was a Time when Measures of Prevention might have been taken by the Colonies.—There may be a Time when Redress may be obtained—Till then, Prudence, as well as Duty, requires Submission.

It is presumed that it was a notable Service done by *New-England*, when the Militia of that Colony reduced *Cape-Breton*, since it enabled the *British Ministers* to make a Peace less disadvantageous and inglorious than They otherwise must have been constrained to submit to, in the humble State to which they were then reduc'd.—That the general Exertion *of the Colonies* in North-America, during the last War, not only facilitated, but was indispensably requisite to the Success of those Operations by which so many glorious Conquests were atchieved, and that those Conquests have put it in the Power of the present illustrious Ministers to make a Peace upon Terms of so much Glory and Advantage, as to afford an inexhaustible Subject during their Administration, and the Triumph of Toryism, at least, for their ingenious Panegyrists to celebrate.

An *American*, without justly incurring the Imputation of Ingratitude, may doubt, whether some other Motive, besides pure Generosity, did not prompt the *British Nation* to engage in the Defence of the Colonies.—He may be induced to think that the Measures taken for the Protection of the Plantations, were not only connected with the Interests, but even necessary to the Defence of *Great-Britain* herself, because he may have Reason to imagine that *Great-Britain* could not long subsist as an independent Kingdom after the Loss of her Colonies.—He may, without Arrogance, be inclined to claim some Merit from the Exertion of the Colonies, since it enabled *Great-Britain* ultimately to defend herself; I mean that Kind of Merit which arises from Benefits done to others, by the Operation of Measures taken for our own Sakes—a Merit most illustriously display'd in the Generosity of *Great-Britain*, when, with their Co-operation, she protected the Colonies to preserve *herself*.

When an House is in Flames, and the next Neighbour is extremely active, and exerts his Endeavours to extinguish the Fire, which, if not conquered, would catch, and consume his own Dwelling, I don't say, that if the Owner of the House which had been in Flames, should, after the Fire subdued, complaisantly thank his Neighbour generally for his Services, he would be absurdly ceremonious; but, if the Assistant should afterwards boast of his great Generosity, and claim a Right to the Furniture of the House which he had assisted in Saving, upon the Merit of his Zeal and Activity, he would deserve to be put in Mind of the Motive of his Service.

If the Advantages gained by the late *most glorious and succesful War* have been secured by an *adequate* Peace—If the Successes that attended the military Operations of the *British* Arms, were the Effect of the conjunct Efforts of the *British Nation* and her *Colonies*, roused by the Spirit, excited by the Virtue, animated by the Vigour, and conducted by the Wisdom of the ablest Minister that ever served his Country, has there been no Compensation received for the Charges of the War? Are the Colonies entitled to no Credit for it?

When the Design is to oppress the Colonies with Taxes, or calumniate the late patriotic Minister, the *Expences of the War*, and the *Enormity* of the *national Debt* are proclaimed: When the present all-accomplish'd Administration is to be celebrated, then is the immense Value of the new Acquisitions display'd in the brightest Colours, "Acquisitions vast in Extent, richly productive of the valuable Commodities belonging to their several Climates. The Possession of those in *North-America*, ensures the Safety of the other Colonies there, insomuch that our only dangerous Neighbours, the *French*, do not think the Pittance left worth retaining, having, by the Cession of *Louisiana* to the *Spaniards*, avowedly given up for ever those great Objects, for which alone They began the War.—The ceded Islands are almost of equal Advantage, for protecting our own, and annoying the Settlements of the *French* and *Spaniards*, if They should be again our Enemies.—Part of *Nova Scotia*, since the Removal of the neutral *French*, hath been already settled by 10,000 Inhabitants, within the Compass of Six or Seven Years, a Province lately considered as no more than a proper Situation for a Fortress, whose Garrison it could not subsist: Even *Cape-Breton*, that barren Appendage to the Province of *Nova Scotia*, is known now to contain Treasures so worthy of Attention, as to be reserved to the Crown. The Mines there are not Veins; they are Mountains of Coal; vast Clifts of nothing else, stand open, and accessible; no Boring necessary to find it; no Pit necessary to come at it; no Fire-Engines requisite for carrying on the Works. This Island, and all the neighbouring Shores in the Gulph of *St. Laurence*, have another Fund of Wealth in their Fisheries. *Canada* is already a very flourishing Colony, inhabited by 90,000 People, and their Demand on *Great-Britain* for a Supply of Manufactures, must be immediately considerable. The Peltry will be another great Branch of Commerce. *West-Florida* is surprizingly fertile, and luxuriantly productive in its natural State, of every Thing, and not only promising, but actually producing Wines and Silk, and Indigo, *&c. &c.*"

Is no Part of this Description the Ebullition of an exuberant Fancy, and shall we not cast one Glance of Retrospection towards the Man, who, when his Country was despised, and insulted, and sunk into the most abject Condition of Despondence, by inspiring her Sons with that invincible Vigour of Patriotism, with which himself was animated, not only dispelled her Fears, secured her Safety, and retrieved her Honour, but Humbled her Enemies, and tore from them the Resources of their Strength, and the Supports of their Insolence?

Are the Acquisitions of the War retained by the Peace, so inestimably valuable, and ought not the Colonies to have some Consideration that were instrumental in the Successes whence those Acquisitions flowed, and strained every Nerve in the general Service, to that Degree of Exertion, that without it, all the Power of *Great-Britain*, all the amazing Abilities of her Minister, and all the Discipline, and unparallel'd Bravery of her national Troops and Seamen, could not have availed beyond meer Defence, if happily so far? If the War was expensive beyond all former Example, so were the Successes of it beneficial. If the Expences attending the military Operations in *America*, are justly to be charged to the sole Defence of the Colonies, and no Part of it to the Security of *Great-Britain*, or to the Views of extending her Dominions by Conquest, if all the Successes of the War have been atchieved by the national Arms of *Great-Britain* ALONE, without any Assistance, or Co-operation of the Plantations, still ought not the Claim against the Colonies in Equity, to be mitigated upon Reflection of the Advantages derived from Them, and of their Contribution to the national Revenue for a long Course of Years, during which, their Protection put the *British* Nation to very little, if any particular Expence?

If moreover, *Great-Britain* hath an equitable Claim to the Contribution of the Colonies, it ought to be proportioned to their Circumstances, and They might, surely, be indulged with discharging it in the most easy, and satisfactory Manner to Themselves. If Ways and Means convenient, and conciliating would produce their Contribution, as well as oppressive and disgusting Exactions, it is neither consistent with Humanity or Policy, to pursue the latter—A Power may even exist without an actual Exercise of it, and it indicates as little good Sense as good Nature to exercise it, only that the Subjects of it may feel the Rod that Rules Them. Moderation may be observed, and Equity maintained, at the same Time that Superiority is asserted, and Authority vindicated, whatever the Apprehensions of Pusillanimity, or the Insolence of Usurpation may suggest.

What is the annual Sum expected from the Colonies—what Proportion from each—how far do their Abilities extend? These Matters have been, without doubt, precisely ascertained, or easily may be, at a Time "when the real, the substantial, the commercial Interests of *Great-Britain*, are preferred to every other Consideration, and it is so well known, that the Trade whence it's greatest Wealth is derived, and upon which it's maritime Power is principally founded, depends upon a wise and proper Use of the Colonies," which implies, at least, such an Understanding of their Circumstances, as must render it extremely easy, to form a reasonable Estimate of their comparative Wealth, and the Extent of their Abilities. The proportion of each Colony, being so easily ascertainable at this Period of *uncommon* Knowledge of their Affairs, why has the Course observed by *former* Ministers, when Supplies have been expected from *America*, been neglected by the *present*? Why was there not the usual Requisition communicated to the Provincial Assemblies, instead of exacting an uncertain and unequal Sum from each Colony, by a Law abruptly passed, without any previous Default of those who are affected by it?—I shall not call it a Law repugnant to their Genius, cancelling their Charters, infringing the most valuable Rights and Privileges of *British* Subjects, derogatory from the Faith and Honour of Government, unjust and cruel in it's Principles, rigorous and oppressive in the Means provided for it's Execution, and as pernicious in it's Consequences to the Mother Country, as injurious to the Colonies in it's immediate Operation, but I may call it a rigorous and severe Law. It is in vain to attempt a Palliation of this useless Severity, (useless I mean to the Purpose of raising a Revenue) by fallaciously pretending that, as all the Colonies were to be taxed, and the Authority of each is limited, the Interposition of the Parliament became necessary, since Nothing can be less disputable, than that each Colony hath a competent Authority to raise it's Proportion, and consequently nothing is more evident, than that all the Colonies might raise the whole. The Assertion* that the Colonies would have paid no Regard to any Requisitions, is rash and unauthoriz'd, and had the Event actually happened, the Trouble and Loss of Time to the Ministers in making the Experiment, would not have been considerable or detrimental to the Nation, and after it's Failure, an Act of Parliament might still have been made to compel the Contribution, if the Power which hath been exercised is defensible upon the Principles of the *British Constitution*.

A Measure so extreme, could hardly be at once pursued, because the Ministers did not know what to demand, who have made so many Regulations in regard to the Colonies, "founded upon Knowledge, formed with Judgment, and executed with Vigour." Had the Requisitions been communicated, I make no Doubt but They would have been entertained with Respect, and productive of all the Effects that could reasonably have been expected from Them. A petty *American* Assembly would not, in Answer to such Requisitions, have impertinently recommended the Reduction of exorbitant Salaries, the Abatement of extravagant, and the Abolition of illegal Perquisites, the Extinction of useless Places, or the disbanding of undeserving, or ill deserving Pensioners, as a more proper and beneficial Method of relieving the public Burthens, than a new and heavy Imposition upon useful and industrious Subjects.

---

* It is asserted in the Pamphlet entitled, *The Claim of the Colonies, &c.* that *Maryland* availing herself of the Protection of *Virginia* and *Pennsylvania*, contributed *Nothing* to the common Defence. This Writer from a View of some Map of *North-America* imagined, it should seem, that *Virginia* and *Pennsylvania* were settled so as to encompass *Maryland*, but the Truth is, that the Frontiers of *Maryland* were as much exposed, as those of the next Colonies, and the Fact is moreover False, for I have been well informed that *Maryland* contributed near 50,000*l.* and incurred besides a considerable Expence, which is now a Debt upon the Public Journal of that Colony, by putting her Militia into actual Service, and that an unhappy Dispute, attended with a very heavy Provincial Charge on some Topick of Privilege, was the real Cause, why the Grants of *Maryland* were not more liberal. After all, there have been Instances, I speak not of more modern Times, in which the Parsimony of the Parliament hath been complained of, and the Notion of Privilege carried to a great Length by the House of Commons; but these have not been thought solid Reasons for stripping their Constituents of their Rights.

Have great Things been promised for the Ease of the People of *England*, and hath a Measure been fallen upon, that, by putting the Accomplishment of them at a Distance, and keeping Expectation alive, it may contribute to the Prolongation of a Power, which, in the Interim, will find sufficient Opportunities to gratify the Views of Ministerial Avarice or Ambition?

If a Sum had been liquidated, and a precise Demand made, it might, perhaps, have been shewn, if proportioned to the Circumstances of the Colonies, to be of no real Consequence to the Nation; and, if above their Circumstances, that it would, with the Oppression of the Plantations, prove ruinous to the *British* Manufactures; but, whilst Matters are thus vague, and indeterminate, any Attempt to shew that the *Stamp Duties* will be inadequate to the promised Relief, distress the Colonies, and consequently beggar the *British* Manufacturers, may be obviated by saying, that "the Act is in the Nature of an Experiment; if inadequate, other Methods may be superadded; if inconvenient, it may be repealed, as soon as discovered;" and Hints may be thrown out at the same Time, to cherish the Hopes of the Nation, that there are the best Grounds to expect the Measure will be productive of all that can be desired or wished.*

The frugal *Republicans* of *North-America*, (if the *British* Inhabitants there are to be distinguished by a *Nick-Name*, because it implies that They are Enemies to the Government of *England*, and ought therefore to be regarded with a jealous Eye) may be allowed, without derogating from the vast and prodigious knowledge of a Minister, to be acquainted with their own internal Circumstances better than a Stranger, who must depend upon Information; and that too, most frequently, of Men not the most eminent for their Candour, distinguished by their Sagacity, or respectable for their Integrity. Had Requisitions been made, and the Sum demanded been equitable,

---

* It is asserted by the Author of *The Claim of the Colonies, &c.* that the Merchants trading to the several Colonies gave in an Estimate of the Debt due to Them from the Colonies, amounting to 4,000,000*l.* It would have been a real public Service if he had pointed out how this Debt is to be paid under the Oppression of new and heavy Impositions, or what will be the proper Remedy if there should be a Stoppage in the Payment of 4,000,000*l.* a Stagnation of Commerce, and Want of Employment to the *British* Manufacturers.

and proportioned to their Circumstances, They could have fallen upon Ways and Means less oppressive than the *Stamp Duties*. They have frequently taxed Themselves: They have tried various Methods of Taxation: They know, by Experience, the easiest and least expensive.—The Meaning, or Construction of their Levy-Acts is settled: They can be carried into Execution, not only at a small Expence, without exhausting a considerable Part of their Produce by the Multiplication of Officers, and their Support; but without heavy Pains and grievous Penalties, without Oppression of the innocent, giving Countenance to Vexation, and Encouragement to profligate Informers, without the Establishment of arbitrary and *distant* Courts of Admiralty.*

The national Debt is heavy, and it is a popular Scheme to draw from the Colonies a Contribution towards the Relief of the Mother-Country.—The Manner of effecting it is not carefully attended to, or nicely regarded by those who expect to receive the Benefit.—The End is so ardently desired, that, whether the Means might not be more moderate, is not scrupulously examined by Men, who think Themselves in no Danger of Injury or Oppression from their Severity. It is affirmed to those who cannot detect the Fallacy of the Assertion, that Millions have been expended *solely* in the Defence of *America*. They believe it, and thence are easily persuaded that the Claim of a Contribution from the Colonies is just and equitable, and that any Measure necessary to secure it, is right and laudable.—It is represented, that unless the Colonies are stripped of the *Trial by Jury*, and Courts of *Admiralty* are established, in which Judges from *England*, Strangers, without Connection or Interest in *America*, removeable at Pleasure, and supported by liberal Salaries, are to preside; unless Informers are encouraged and favoured, and the accused most rigorously dealt by, that the Tax will be eluded—and these Severities are excus'd on Account of their supposed Necessity. The Colonies are described to be a numerous, flourishing, and opulent

---

* It was formerly held to be a grievous Oppression, that, instead of having Justice at Home, the *English* Subject was drawn to *Rome* by APPEALS, but an *American* is to be drawn from Home, in the FIRST INSTANCE, as well as by Appeals.

People:—It is alledged that They contribute to the national Expence, by Taxes *there* only the pitiful Sum of 1900*l*. per Year, for the Collection of which, an Establishment of Officers, attended with the Expence of 7600*l*. *per Annum*, is necessary.— Upon these Premisses, the Uneasiness of the Colonies, at being forced to bring more into the common Stock, appears to be unreasonable, if not rebellious; and They seem rather to deserve Reprehension and Correction, than Favour and Indulgence.

The Successes of the War were obtained as well by the vigorous Efforts of the *Colonies*, as by the Exertion of *Great-Britain* —The Faith of *Great-Britain* hath been engaged in the most solemn Manner, to re-pay the Colonies the Monies levied by internal Taxations for the Support of the War.—Is it consistent with that Faith to tax Them towards sinking the Debt in Part incurred by that Re-payment? The immense Accession of Territory, and Value of the Acquisitions obtained by the Peace, is the Consequence of the Successes of the War—The Charge of the War is lessened by the Advantages resulting from the Peace—The Colonies, for a long Course of Time, have largely contributed to the public Revenue, and put *Great-Britain* to little or no Expence for their Protection.—If it were equitable to draw from Them a further Contribution, it does not therefore follow, that it is proper to force it from Them, by the harsh and rigorous Methods established by the Stamp-Act; an Act unequal and disproportioned to *their* Circumstances whom it affects; exempting Opulence, crushing Indigence; and tearing from a numerous, loyal, and useful People, the Privileges They had, in their Opinion, earned and merited, and justly held most dear. If They are really in Debt, the Payment of it hath not been refused, it hath not been demanded.—If one Subject, grown giddy with sudden Elevation, should, at any future Period, rashly declare, that the Colonies should be taxed, at all Events, in the most rigorous Manner; and that Millions of industrious and useful Subjects should be grievously oppressed, rather than himself depart from his Character of Pertinacity and Wilfulness, check the Impulse of a tyrannical Disposition, or foregoe the Gratification of his Vanity, in a wanton Display of Power, Submission would be an admirable Virtue indeed, if not the Effect of Impotence.

That the Contribution arising from the *Stamp-Duties* is

disproportioned to *their* Circumstances from whom it is exacted, is manifest; for They will produce in each Colony, a greater, or less Sum, not in Proportion to its Wealth, but to the Multiplicity of Juridical Forms, the Quantity of vacant Land, the Frequency of transferring landed Property, the Extent of Paper Negotiations, the Scarcity of Money, and the Number of Debtors. A larger Sum will be exacted from a Tobacco-Colony than from *Jamaica*; and it will not only be higher in one of the poorest Colonies, and the least able to bear it, than in the richest; but the principal Part of the Revenue will be drawn from the poorest Individuals in the poorest Colonies, from Mortgagors, Obligors, and Defendants. If this be true, does the Act deserve the Encomium of being *a Mode of Taxation the easiest, and the most equal, a Duty upon Property spread lightly over a great Variety of Subjects, and heavy upon none?*

The Commons of Great-Britain, moreover, in their Capacity of *Representative*, not only *Give and Grant* the Property of the *Colonies*; but, in my Construction of the Stamp-Act, (however every Reader may examine and judge for himself,) *Give and Grant* also to certain Officers of the Crown, a Power to tax Them higher still; for these Officers will not, I presume, be called *virtual Representatives* too; and what They shall think fit to levy, by an ingenious Extent of the Fiction, will not be considered as levied with the Consent of the Colonies—The Instances, I believe, are *rare*, in which the Representatives of the People of *England* have delegated to Officers of the Crown, the Power of taxing their Constituents, nor hath any Distinction yet been advanced to prove, that in their Capacity of *virtual Representatives* of the Colonies, the House of Commons not having the same Confidence reposed in Them, ought to proceed upon peculiar Rules. There was a Statute of *Henry* VIII, by which, I think, the King's Proclamations, with the Consent of the Privy Council, were to operate as Laws; and another Statute of *Ric.* II, that the Power of the Two Houses should be vested in Twelve Lords; but these Acts bear *no Resemblance* to the Stamp-Act.

The Stamping Instruments are to be retained in *England*.— Vellum, Parchment, and Paper, are to be sent to *America*, ready stamped.—The first Commissioner of the Treasury, or the Commissioners, or any Three or more of Them, are, by the Act, impowered to set *any* Price upon the Vellum, Parchment and Paper, and the Payment of that Price is secured and enforced by the *same* Pains and Penalties that the Stamp-Duties are.

If the Substitution of an arbitrary Civil Law Court, in the Place of the legal Judicatories, and that deserved Favourite, the Common-Law-Trial by Jury, would not justify the Assertion, that the Stamp-Act hath stripped the Colonies of the Guards and Securities provided by the Constitution against Oppression in the Execution of Laws, I would much less presume to say, the vesting in the Commissioners of the Treasury a Power to tax the Colonies, will amply justify the Assertion, that the Stamp-Act hath not left Them even the Shadow of a Privilege.—It is indeed something difficult to imagine how the Order of Democracy, which is as much a Part of the Constitution, as Monarchy or Aristocracy, can exist when the People are excluded from a Share in the executing, and a Share in the making of Laws; but that is *not* the present Case; and, though I may not be able to answer a specious Objection, formed upon general Principles, I am not obliged to adopt it, 'till I am convinced of its Solidity.

A little Examination will find how unfair and deceptive the Representation is, that the Colonies in *North-America*, "Two Millions of *British* Subjects, an opulent, thriving and commercial People, contribute to the national Expence, no more than 7 or 800*l. per Annum* by Taxes raised *there*;" for tho' it should be acknowledged (which I neither admit nor deny, because I don't know, nor have an Opportunity of coming at the Fact) that the Impositions upon the Inhabitants of the Colonies do not raise *there*, a greater Sum than hath been stated, it doth not follow that, "the Inhabitants of the Colonies are indulged at the Expence of *Great-Britain*, and that the neediest *British Cottager*, who out of his scanty Pittance hardly earned, pays the high Duties of Customs and Excise in the Price of his Consumptions, has Reason to complain," if immense Sums are raised upon the Inhabitants of the Colonies *elsewhere*.

By such Artifices and Sophistry, is Ignorance misled, Credulity deceived, and Prejudices excited. Thus Oppression gains the Credit of Equity, Cruelty passes for Moderation, and

Tyranny for Justice, and the Man who deserves—Reproach, is celebrated by Adulation, and applauded by Delusion for his Wisdom and patriotic Virtues.

The Truth is, that a vast Revenue arises to the *British* Nation from Taxes paid by the Colonies *in* GREAT-BRITAIN, and even *the most ignorant* British *Cottager*, not imposed upon by infamous Misrepresentation, must perceive, that it is of no Consequence to his Ease and Relief, whether the Duties raised upon *America* are paid *there*, and thence afterwards remitted to *Great-Britain*, or paid *at first* upon the produce of the Colonies in *Great-Britain*.

In the Article of Tobacco, for Instance, the Planter pays a Tax upon that Produce of his Land and Labour consumed in *Great-Britain*, more than Six Times the clear Sum received by Him for it, besides the Expences of Freight, Commission and other Charges, and double Freight, Commission and Charges upon the Tobacco re-exported, by which the *British* Merchants, Mariners and other *British* Subjects, are supported—a Tax, at least, equal to what is paid by any Farmer of *Great-Britain*, possessed of the same Degree of Property; and moreover the Planter must contribute to the Support of the expensive internal Government of the Colony, in which He resides.*

Is it objected, that the Duties charged upon Tobacco, fall ultimately upon the Consumers of this Commodity in the consequential Price set upon it? Be it so, and let the Principle be established that all Taxes upon a Commodity, are paid by the Consumers of it, and the Consequence of this Principle be fairly drawn, and equally applied.

The *British* Consumers therefore, ultimately pay the high Duties laid upon Tobacco, in Proportion to the Quantity of that Commodity which They consume—The Colonies therefore, in Proportion to their Consumption of *British* Manufactures, pay also the high Duties of Customs and Excise, with which the Manufacturers are charged in the consequential Price set upon their Consumptions—In their Passage moreover, from the *British* Manufacturers to the *American* Importers, the Commodities go thro' a great many Hands, by which their Costs are enhanced; the Factors, the Carriers, the

* See the Appendix.

Shop-keepers, the Merchants, the Brokers, the Porters, the Watermen, the Mariners, and Others, have their respective Profits, from which They derive their Subsistance, and the Support of their Families, and are enabled to pay the high Duties of Customs and Excise, in the Price of their Consumptions.*

The Policy of the late Regulations of the Colonies is of the same Character with their Justice, and Lenity. The Produce of their Lands, the Earnings of their Industry, and the Gains of their Commerce Center in *Great-Britain*, support the Artificers, the Manufactories, and Navigation of the Nation, and with Them the *British* Land-holders too.

Great-Britain had ALL before, and therefore can have no more from the Colonies; but the Minister, in the pursuit of a "well-digested, consistent, wise and salutary Plan of Colonization and Government, a Plan founded upon the Principles of Policy, Commerce and Finance," chuses to demolish at one Blow, all their Privileges as they have understood Them, that he may raise in *America*, a Part of what was before paid in *Great-Britain*. But if the Execution of it, instead of improving the Advantages already possessed, confirming the Blessings already enjoyed, and promoting the Public Welfare, should happen to distress the Trade, reduce the Navigation, impoverish the Manufacturers, and diminish the Value of the Lands in *Great-Britain*; should it drive the *British* Mechanics and Manufacturers to *America*, by depriving Them of their best Customers at Home, and force the Colonies upon Manufactures, they are disabled from purchasing, other Topics of Eulogy must be discovered by his ingenious Encomiasts, than his Wisdom or his political Atchievements. Upon such an Event, an *American* will have very little Reason to exclaim

> *O! me infelicem, qui nunc demum intelligo*
> *Ut illa mihi profuerint quæ despexeram,*
> *Et illa, quæ laudaram, quantum Luctus habuerint!*

The Right of Exemption from all Taxes *without their Consent*, the Colonies claim as *British* Subjects. They derive this

* See the Appendix.

Right from the Common Law, which their Charters have declared and confirmed, and They conceive that when stripped of this Right, whether by Prerogative or by any other Power, they are at the same Time deprived of every Privilege distinguishing Free-Men from Slaves.

On the other Hand, They acknowledge Themselves to be subordinate to the Mother Country, and that the Authority vested in the supreme Council of the Nation, may be justly exercised to support and preserve that Subordination.

Great and just Encomiums have been bestow'd upon the Constitution of *England*, and their Representative is deservedly the Favourite of the Inhabitants in *Britain*. But it is not because the supreme Council is called *Parliament*, that They boast of their Constitution of Government; for there is no particular magical Influence from the Combination of the Letters which form the Word; it is because They have a Share in that Council, that They appoint the Members who constitute one Branch of it, whose Duty and Interest it is to consult their Benefit, and to assert their Rights, and who are vested with an Authority, to prevent any Measures taking Effect dangerous to their Liberties, or injurious to their Properties.

But the Inhabitants in the Colonies have no Share in this great Council. None of the Members of it are, or can be of their Appointment, or in any Respect dependant upon Them. There is no immediate Connection, on the Contrary, there may be an Opposition of Interest; how puerile then is the Declamation, "what will become of the Colonies Birthright, and the glorious Securities which their Forefathers handed down to Them, if the Authority of the *British* Parliament *to impose Taxes* upon Them should be given up? To deny the Authority of the *British* Legislature, is to surrender all Claim to a Share in it's Councils, and if this were the Tenor of their Charters, a Grant more insidious or replete with Mischief, could not be imagined, a Forfeiture of their Rights would be couched under the Appearance of Privilege, *&c.*"

We claim an Exemption from all *Parliamentary* Impositions, that We may enjoy those Securities of our Rights and Properties, which We are entitled to by the Constitution. For those Securities are derived to the Subject from the Principle *that he is not to be taxed without his own Consent*, and an Inhabitant in

America can give his Consent in no other Manner than in Assembly. It is in the Councils that exist there, and there *only*, that he hath a Share, and whilst He enjoys it, his Rights and Privileges are as well secured as any Elector's in *England*, who hath a Share in the national Councils there; for the Words *Parliament* and *Assembly* are in this Respect, only different Terms to express the same Thing.

But it is argued, that "if the common Law of *England*, is to be brought, as justifying a Claim of Exemption in any Subject of *Great-Britain* from a Parliamentary Tax, it will plead against a Tax imposed by a Provincial Assembly; for as all the Colony Assemblies derive their Authority from the meer Grant of the Crown only, it might be urged that any Tax imposed by Them, is imposed by Authority of the Prerogative of the Crown, and not by full Consent of Parliament. That if this Right in the Crown, is acknowledged to exempt the Subject from the jurisdiction of Parliament in the Case of Taxation, its Power to dispense with Acts of Parliament, or to deprive the same Subject of the Benefit of the Common Law, can't be denied."

One would be inclined to suspect that it is supposed, something else than Reason, may on this Occasion conduce to Persuasion.

The *English* Subjects, who left their *native* Country to settle in the Wilderness of *America*, had the Privileges of *other Englishmen*. They knew their Value, and were desirous of having Them perpetuated to their Posterity. They were aware that, as their Consent whilst They should reside in *America*, could neither be ask'd nor regularly given in the national Legislature, and that if They were to be bound by Laws without Restriction, affecting the Property They should earn by the utmost Hazard and Fatigue, They would lose every other Privilege which They had enjoyed in their native Country, and become meer Tenants at Will dependant upon the Moderation of their Lords and Masters, without any other Security—That as their Settlement was to be made under the Protection of the *English* Government, They knew, that in Consequence of their Relation to the Mother-Country, They and their Posterity would be subordinate to the supreme national Council, and expected that Obedience and Protection would be considered as reciprocal Duties.

Considering Themselves, and being considered in this Light, They entered into a Compact with the Crown, the Basis of which was, *That their Privileges as* English *Subjects, should be effectually secured to Themselves, and transmitted to their Posterity.* And as for this Purpose, precise Declarations and Provisions formed upon the Principles, and according to the Spirit of the *English Constitution* were necessary; CHARTERS were accordingly framed and conferred by the Crown, and accepted by the Settlers, by which all the Doubts and Inconveniencies which might have arisen from the Application of general Principles to a new Subject, were prevented.

By these Charters, founded upon the unalienable Rights of the Subject, and upon the most sacred Compact, the Colonies claim a Right of Exemption from Taxes *not imposed with their Consent.*—They claim it upon the Principles of the Constitution, as once *English*, and now *British* Subjects, upon Principles on which their Compact with the Crown was originally founded.

The Origin of other Governments is covered by the Veil of Antiquity, and is differently traced by the Fancies of different Men; but, of the Colonies, the Evidence of it is as clear and unequivocal as of any other Fact.

By these declaratory Charters the Inhabitants of the Colonies claim an Exemption from *all* Taxes not imposed by their own Consent, and to infer from their Objection to a Taxation, to which their Consent is not, nor can be given, *that They are setting up a Right in the Crown to dispense with Acts of Parliament, and to deprive the* British *Subjects in* America *of the Benefits of the Common Law*, is so extremely absurd, that I should be at a Loss to account for the Appearance of so strange an Argument, were I not apprized of the unworthy Arts employed by the Enemies of the Colonies to excite strong Prejudices against Them in the Minds of their Brethren at Home, and what gross Incongruities prejudiced Men are wont to adopt.

Tho' I am persuaded that this Reasoning hath already been sufficiently refuted, and that no sensible and dispassionate Man can perceive any Force in it, yet I can't help remarking, that it is grounded upon a Principle, which, if it were possible for the Examiner to establish it, would entitle him to the Applause of the Inhabitants in *Great-Britain*, as little as to the Thanks of the Colonies.

From what Source do the Peers of *England* derive their Dignity, and the Share They have in the *British Legislature?* Are there no Places in *England* that derive their Power of chusing Members of Parliament from royal Charters? Will this Writer argue, that the Crown may, by Prerogative, tax the Inhabitants of *Great-Britain*, because the Peers of *England*, and some Representatives of the People, exercise a legislative Authority under Royal Patents and Charters? It must be admitted that all the Members of the House of Commons are freely chosen by the People, and are not afterwards subject to any Influence of the Crown or the Ministry: And are not the Members of the Lower Houses of Assembly as freely chosen also by the People; and, in Fact, as independent as the Members of the House of Commons? If the Truth were confessed, the Objection would not be, *that the Colonies are too dependent upon the Crown*, or that their Claim of Exemption from all Taxes, not imposed by their own Consent, *is founded upon a Principle leading to Slavery*. At one Time, the *North-Americans* are called *Republicans*; at another, *the Assertors of Despotism*. What a strange Animal must a *North-American* appear to be from these Representations to the Generality of *English* Readers, who have never had an Opportunity to admire, that He may be neither black, nor tawny, may speak the *English* Language, and, in other Respects, seem, for all the World, like one of Them!

"The Common Law, the great Charter, the Bill of Rights," are so far from "declaring, with one Voice, that the Inhabitants of the Colonies shall be taxed by no other Authority than that of the *British Parliament*," that They prove the contrary; for the Principle of the Common Law is, *that no Part of their Property shall be drawn from* British *Subjects, without their Consent, given by those whom They depute to represent Them*; and this Principle is enforced by the Declaration of the GREAT CHARTER, and *the Bill of Rights*, neither the one nor the other, introducing any *new* Privilege. In *Great-Britain*, the Consent of the People is given by the House of Commons, and, as Money had been levied there for the Use of the Crown, *by Pretence of Prerogative, without their Consent*, it was properly declared at the Revolution, in Support of the Constitution, and in Vindication of the People's Rights, that the levying of Money, by *Pretence of Prerogative*, without Grant of Parliament, *i. e.* without their

Consent who are to pay it, is illegal, which Declaration was most suitable to the Occasion, and effectually establishes the very Principle contended for by the Colonies.

The Word *Parliament*, having been made use of, the *Letter* of the Declaration is adhered to, and the Consequence drawn, that no *British* Subject can be legally taxed, but by the Authority of the *British Parliament*, against the Spirit and Principle of the Declaration, which was aimed only to check and restrain the *Prerogative*, and to establish the Necessity of obtaining *the Consent* of those on whom Taxes were to be levied. Is not this a new Kind of Logic, to infer from Declarations and Claims, founded upon the necessary and essential Principle of a free Government, that the People ought not to be taxed without their Consent, that therefore the Colonies ought to be taxed by an Authority, in which their Consent is not, nor can be concerned; or, in other Words, to draw an Inference from a Declaration or Claim of Privilege, subversive of the very Principle upon which the Privilege is founded? How aukwardly are the Principles of the Revolution applied by some Men! What Astonishment would the Promoters of that glorious Measure, those Patrons and Friends of Liberty, did They now tread the Stage of this World, express, that a *Word*, by which They meant to assert the Privileges of the Subject, and restrain despotic Power, should be relied upon to demolish the very Principle by which Themselves were animated, and after all their Pains and Hazards to establish the generous Sentiments of Liberty, that those who feel and enjoy the Blessings of their successful Struggles, should not be able to raise a Thought beyond the Ideas affixed to systematic Terms.

It was declared also by the *Bill of Rights*, that the Elections of *Members of Parliment* ought to be free, and the Common Law laid down the same Rule before, which is as applicable to the Election of the Representatives of the Colonies, as of the Commons of *Great-Britain*. But with the Help of the Examiner's Logic, it might be proved from the *Letter* of the *Bill of Rights*, that the Elections *only* of *Members of Parliament* ought to be free; for the Freedom expressed in the Bill of Rights, is as much attached to Elections of Members of Parliament, as the Authority to grant Money is to *the* British *Parliament*, and if the Declaration in the one Case implies a Negative, there is the like Implication in the other. If, moreover, the Common Law, the great Charter, and the Bill of Rights, do really, as the Examiner asserts, with one Voice declare, that the Inhabitants of the Colonies ought to be taxed *only* by the *British* Parliament, it is not consistent with that Character of Vigilance, and Jealousy of their Power, commonly ascribed to the *British Parliament*, that, from their first regular Settlement to the Reign of *Geo.* III, the *American* Assemblies should not only have been suffered, without any Animadversion, without one Resolve, or even a single Motion to restrain Them, to encroach upon the Jurisdiction and Authority of the *British Parliament*; but that the Parliament should never before the late *Stamp-Act*, in one Instance, have imposed an internal Tax upon the Colonies for *the single Purpose of Revenue*, and that, even when Acts of Assembly passed in Consequence of Ministerial inforced by Royal Requisitions have been laid before Them, They should be so far from objecting to their Validity, as actually to recognize the Authority of the Provincial Legislatures, and upon that Foundation superstruct their own Resolves and Acts.

But tho' it hath been admitted, that the *Stamp-Act* is the first Statute that hath imposed an internal Tax upon the Colonies *for the single Purpose of Revenue*, yet the Advocates for that Law contend, that there are many Instances of the Parliament's exercising a supreme legislative Authority over the Colonies, and actually imposing *internal Taxes* upon their Properties—that the Duties upon any Exports or Imports are internal Taxes—That an Impost on a foreign Commodity is as much an internal Tax, as a Duty upon any Production of the Plantations—That no Distinction can be supported between one Kind of Tax and another, an Authority to impose the one extending to the other.

If these Things are really as represented by the Advocates for the *Stamp* Act, why did the *Chancellor of the Exchequer* make it a Question for the Consideration of the House of Commons, whether the Parliament could impose an *internal Tax* in the Colonies or not, for the *single Purpose of Revenue?**

---

* I have presumed to mention this Fact upon the Authority of private Intelligence, as well as of the News Papers, and other Publications, and tho' the Chancellor of the Exchequer is not named, yet the Fact seems in general to be

It appears to me, that there is a clear and necessary Distinction between an Act imposing a Tax for *the single Purpose of Revenue*, and those Acts which have been made for the Regulation of Trade, and have produced some Revenue *in Consequence of their Effect* and Operation as *Regulations of Trade*.

The Colonies claim the Privileges of *British* Subjects—It has been proved to be inconsistent with those Privileges, to tax Them *without their own Consent*, and it hath been demonstrated that a Tax imposed by Parliament, is a Tax *without their Consent*.

The Subordination of the Colonies, and the Authority of the Parliament to preserve it, have been fully acknowledged. Not only the Welfare, but perhaps the Existence of the Mother Country, as an independent Kingdom, may depend upon her Trade and Navigation, and these so far upon her Intercourse with the Colonies, that, if this should be neglected, there would soon be an End to that Commerce, whence her greatest Wealth is derived, and upon which her maritime Power is principally founded. From these Considerations, the Right of the *British Parliament* to regulate the Trade of the Colonies, may be justly deduced; a Denial of it would contradict the Admission of the Subordination, and of the Authority to preserve it, resulting from the Nature of the Relation between the Mother Country and her Colonies. It is a common, and frequently the most proper Method to regulate Trade by Duties on Imports and Exports. The Authority of the Mother Country to regulate the Trade of the Colonies, being unquestionable, what Regulations

referred to in the Postscript to *the excellent Letter concerning Libels, Warrants, Seizure of Papers, and Security of the Peace,* &c. in the following Words: "Otherwise (*i. e.* if it were not right for the Parliament to resolve general Warrants to be illegal) let me ask how that *momentous* Resolution touching an *English* Parliament's Right of taxing the Colonies could be justify'd? It was an independent substantive Resolution, followed by Nothing, (*i. e.* that Session) and yet was a Resolution not only of *extreme Magnitude*, but of the most *general* and *highest legal* Nature, involving in it a Decision of *the first and most fundamental Principles of Liberty, Property, and Government, and well worthy* also, as to the temporary Policy of it, the most *serious* of *all* Consideration. This was resolved too if I am informed right, at the Close of the Night, and the Rising of the House; so that every Body must have taken it as a clear Thing, that They could at any Time come to a Resolution upon any general Point of Law, whenever They should see it *expedient* so to do, *sed Verbum sapienti sat est.*"

are the most proper, are to be of Course submitted to the Determination of the Parliament; and, if an *incidental Revenue*, should be produced by such Regulations; these are not therefore unwarrantable.

A Right to impose an internal Tax on the Colonies, without their Consent *for the single Purpose of Revenue*, is denied, a Right to regulate their Trade without their Consent is admitted. The Imposition of a Duty, may, in some Instances, be the proper Regulation. If the Claims of the Mother Country and the Colonies should seem on such an Occasion to interfere, and the Point of Right to be doubtful, (which I take to be otherwise) it is easy to guess that the Determination will be on the Side of Power, and that the Inferior will be constrained to submit.*

The Writer on the Regulations lately made with Respect to the Colonies, who is said to have been *well informed*, asserts a Fact, which indisputably proves, that the Impositions mentioned, were *only* Regulations of Trade, and can, with no kind of Propriety, be considered in any other Light. The Fact he asserts, is, that "the whole Remittance from all the Taxes in the Colonies, at an Average of Thirty Years, has not amounted to 1900*l.* a Year, and in that Sum, 7 or 800*l. per Annum* only, have been remitted from *North-America*; and that the Establishment of Officers, necessary to collect that Revenue, amounts to 7600*l. per Annum*."

It would be ridiculous indeed to suppose, that the Parliament would raise a Revenue by Taxes in the Colonies to defray Part of the national Expence, the Collection of which Taxes would increase that Expence to a Sum more than three Times the Amount of the Revenue; but, the Impositions being

---

* In the Reign of our great Deliverer, when the *English* and the *Dutch* were at War with *France*, They joined in preventing the Northern Powers from carrying on a Trade with the Enemy. M. *Groning* having formed a Design, to prove the Right of the Northern Powers to a free Trade and Navigation, communicated his Plan to and desired the Opinion of Baron *Puffendorf* upon it, who observed that as the Question had not been settled upon clear and undeniable Principles, and there was a Mixture of Fact and Right, the Confederates might contend that They have a Right to distress the Enemy, and, as the Means to attain that Purpose, to restrain the Trade of the Northern Powers, an Argument that with superior Force wou'd be conclusive.

considered in their true Light, as Regulations of Trade, the Expence arising from an Establishment necessary to carry Them into Execution, is so far from being ridiculous, that it may be wisely incurred.

The Author of the Claim of the Colonies, &c. gives (as hath been observed) the Epithets of *unjust* and *partial*, to a Tax which should be imposed upon the Non-Electors, only in *Britain*; and, in that very Instance, proves, that a Tax upon the Non-Electors in the Colonies, is more unjust and partial, and yet undertakes to defend the Justice of it; and the Writer on the Regulations of the Colonies declares, that it is in vain to call the Acts He has cited as Precedents, by the Name of mere Regulations, notwithstanding He hath irrefragably proved, that They are ridiculous, if considered in any other Light. (See *The Regulation of the Colonies*, &c. Pages 234, 202–3, and *The Claim of the Colonies*, &c. Page 28, 29, 30.)*

Though I conceive that the Distinction which hath been suggested, is sufficiently evident, and that the Argument from Precedents hath been refuted, yet, as there have been two or three Instances particularly enforced and relied upon, I must beg the Reader's Patience whilst I examine Them separately, without undertaking the Task to remove every Incongruity to be found in the Writings of the Enemies of *America* on this Occasion; for it would require an *Hercules* to cleanse the Stable.

The 5th *Geo*. II, it is alledged, "*abrogates so much of the Common Law as relates to Descents of Freeholds in* America, *takes from the Son the Right of Inheritance in the Lands the Crown had granted to the Father*, and his Heirs in absolute Fee, makes them Assets, and applies Them to the Payment of Debts and Accounts contracted by the Father *without the Participation of the Son*; it *sets aside* the Sort of Evidence required by the Common Law, and *establish'd by every Court of Justice in* America, in Proof of a Debt, and enjoins the Admission of an *ex Parte*

---

* A grave Answer to a little pert Pamphlet, called *the Objections to the* Taxation, *&c.* would be too ludicrous. When the Author of it talks of Orders to be observed under Pains and Penalties, he uses the aweful Style of a L——d of T—— but it was too constrained for him to support, and he therefore very naturally relapsed into the Character of a Jack-Pudding. He had very little Reason to apprehend that *Lock, Sidney,* or *Selden*, would be called upon to pull off his—Cap.

Affidavit. The Power of Parliament having been exercised *to take away the Lands of the People in* America, the most *sacred* Part of any Man's Property, and *disposing of Them for the Use of private Persons Inhabitants of* Great-Britain, who can question," says the Examiner, "the Parliament's Right to take away a *small* Part of the Products of those Lands, and apply it to the *public Service?*"

It is very observable, that in applying this Statute, a Language is made use of, which gives the Idea of Violence; and it must be confessed, that great Aggravation of Features, and strong Colouring, were necessary, to make it in any Degree resemble the Impositions of the *Stamp-Act.*

It would be useless, as well as tedious, to point out every Misrepresentation in this Application, since that will be effectually done, by briefly shewing the Effect of the 5th *Geo.* II, and suggesting the Occasion of making that Statute.

Lands, Negroes, *&c.* in the Plantations, are made Assets for the Satisfaction of all Debts owing to his Majesty, or *any of his Subjects*, in like Manner as Real Estates are, by the Law of *England* liable to the Satisfaction of Debts due by Specialty.

If the Creditor resides in *Great-Britain*, the Affidavits of his Witnesses taken there, are to be allowed as Evidence, and to have the same Force their Testimony would have, if given, *vivâ Voce*, in open Court.

The Evidence mentioned in the Statute, prevailed in most, if not all the Colonies, before the Statute, and Lands were also liable to the Satisfaction of all Debts in most Instances, by the Method practised also in the Court of Chancery in *England*, of marshalling Assets. In some of the Colonies, without this Circuity, Lands were immediately liable to simple Contract Debts.

Independent of the Statute, when the Creditor obtains a Judgment against his Debtor, *all* his Lands, *&c.* over which he has a *disposing* Power, are liable, and, since the Statute, only *such* Lands, *&c.* are Assets, as the Debtor had a Power to dispose of. It appears then, that all the Effect of the Statute on this Head, is to subject Real Estates to the Payment of Debts *after* the Death of the Debtor, (for the most Part, the Case before the Statute) which might have been made Subject *before* his Death.

In many of the Colonies, the provincial Creditors of deceased Debtors, were preferred to the *British*, in the same Degree, by Acts of Assembly which carried the Appearance of Partiality; tho' in Fact, the Effect of the Laws of *England* gave Rise to Them; for, upon Bankruptcies in *Great-Britain*, the Steps required by the Statutes to entitle Creditors to a Satisfaction, effectually exclude Colony Creditors in most Cases, and their Distance, when their Debtors die in *Great-Britain*, where Colony Creditors have not standing Agents as the Merchants have in the Plantations, and there happens a Deficiency of Assets, shuts them out likewise from all Chance of Satisfaction in the usual Scramble among Creditors for the Debtor's Estate on such Events.

In some of the Colonies They changed, by Acts of Assembly, certain Species of personal Property, *e. g.* Negroes, into the Nature of real Estates, by making Them descendible; and, by this Alteration of the Common Law, and Confusion of the former Distinction of Property, very considerably diminished the personal Fund, liable to *all* Debts.

As these Circumstances were represented and believed to be great Discouragements to the Trade of the Mother Country, after repeated Requisitions to provide a Remedy in the Colonies, in which the Grievance was most sensibly felt, had been disregarded, the Statute was finally made.

This was, without Doubt, a Subject upon which the Superintendence of the Mother-Country might be justly exercised; it being relative to her Trade and Navigation, upon which her Wealth and her Power depend, and the Preservation of her Superiority, and the Subordination of the Colonies, are secured, and therefore is comprehended in the Distinction.

After citing, and applying this Statute, the Examiner takes Occasion to insult a Gentleman of a most amiable and respectable Character, because he presumed, it seems, to question the Universality of Parliamentary Power, and appears to be so totally occupied in the Business of Defamation, as not to be aware of his running into the most egregious Inconsistencies. If the Examiner is a Lawyer, he has betray'd the most shameful Ignorance; if an Agent, the most infamous Unfaithfulness. Had the *American Chief Justice* acted in *England*, as too many of his Countrymen have done—Had He paid his Court to

Power, by mean Compliances, and endeavoured to recommend Himself, by inventing Accusations against the Colonies,
by representing the Inhabitants in Them, as a refractory, disloyal, and rebellious People, and by proposing Schemes for
their Depression—Had He not firmly maintained his Character of Honour and Probity, we should not have seen this Impeachment of his Understanding; but he left the Task of
Prostitution to the Man of sordid Views,

> *Ille superbos Aditus Regum,*
> *Durasque fores, expers Somni*
> *Colat—*

"Had the Colonies," says the Examiner, "agreed to the Imposition of the Stamp-Duties, a Precedent would have been
established for their being consulted, before any Imposition
upon Them by Parliament would hereafter take Place." He
intimates that They were advised by some of their Agents to
take this Course: If such Advice hath been given, it was weak
or insidious, and the Agents, who recommended the Measure,
ought to be removed for their Incapacity or their Treachery.

How would the Precedent have been established, or, if it
had, what would have been the Advantage? This Conduct
would have admitted, that the Colonies might be taxed at any
Time, and in any Manner, without their Consent; and consequently, would at once have been an effectual Surrender of all
their Privileges as *British* Subjects.

If Precedents were to be regarded, when a Tax in *America*,
for the *single Purpose of Revenue* is required, they are not wanting. Upon such Occasions, the Course hath always, and uniformly been, 'till the Imposition of the Stamp-Duties, to
transmit Requisitions to the Colonies; and, if the Instance
cited by the Examiner, is, in any Degree pertinent, he has
shewn in his Appendix, that the Method of Requisition was *in
that* pursued; for, the Lords of Trade, in their Report, expressly
mention the Refusal of the Colonies to comply with the Requisitions transmitted to them, to remove the Grievance complained of.

The Clause in the Mutiny Act during the late War is also

relied upon, but with how much Propriety, few Words will evince.

The Acts of Assembly of each Colony, could have no obligatory Force beyond the Limits of each; but the Service of the Colony Troops, was not confined within the same Colony in which They were raised; it is therefore evident that the Provincial Legislatures, had not an Authority adequate to the great Object of the military Operations in *America*, which was not merely the Defence of the Plantations, by Measures executed within their Boundaries, but the Enemy was attacked in his own Country, and for this Purpose the *British* and *American* Troops acted conjunctly. On this Occasion it was not only convenient, that the Troops employed in the same Service, should be subject to the same Discipline, but it was indispensably necessary that this Discipline should be established by *Act of Parliament*, the Authority of the *Provincial Legislatures* being deemed to be incompetent. And it is to be remarked, moreover, that the Provincial Troops were raised and paid by the Colonies, and that it was in the Power of their Assemblies, a Power exercised by some of Them, to disband or reduce Them when They pleased, and therefore their supporting and keeping them up, was an effectual Consent to the Act of Parliament; but as hath been shewn, an internal Tax may be as compleatly and adequately laid in every Colony, by the Authority of the *respective Assemblies*, as by the *British Parliament*, and therefore there is not the same Necessity for the Interposition of the Mother Country in this, as in the other Instance, and the Colonies with Reference to the Stamp-Act, are not called upon to do any Act expressive of their Assent to it, nor is it in their Power to hinder it's taking Effect in the fullest Extent.

The Act for *the Establishment of a Post-Office in the Colonies* (9 *Anne*, c. 10,) comes the nearest to the Subject of any Regulation that hath been mentioned; but yet it is materially distinguishable from the Stamp Act. For the same Reason that an Act of Parliament was necessary to secure the Discipline of the Provincial Troops, acting in Conjunction with the *British* Forces during the late War, the Authority of Parliament might be proper for the general Establishment of a regular Post-Office, for as the Laws of each Colony are in their Operation confined within the Limits of each, prohibitory and compulsive Clauses to inforce a general Observance, without which the Establishment would fail, might be eluded. If a Man should maliciously give a Wound in one Colony, and the wounded Person die in another, the Offender could not be convicted of Murder, because the whole Fact constituting that Crime, would not be cognizable in the Colony where the Wound was given, or the Death happened; and the same Principle is applicable to every other inferior Offence, and intimates in what Manner prohibitory Clauses might be evaded. This Matter therefore of the Post-Office, may be referred to the general Superintending Authority of the Mother-Country, the Power of the Provincial Legislatures being too stinted to reach it. In this View, and upon the Consideration of the general Convenience and Accommodation arising from the Establishment, the People of *America* have not complained of it, but if this Instance were more pertinent than it is, it would only prove what hath been too often proved before—When Men do not suspect any Designs to invade their Rights, and subdolous Steps taken to that End, are productive of immediate Convenience without pointing out their destructive Tendency, They are frequently involved in Ruin before they are aware of Danger, or that the Conduct flowing from the Negligence of innocent Intentions, may afford an Handle to Men of different Dispositions, for the Commission of Oppression—Of the Truth of these Observations the Histories of all People who have once been blessed with Freedom, and have lost it, exhibit abundant Examples.

When Instances are urged as an authoritative Reason for adopting a new Measure, They are proved to be more important from this Use of Them, and ought therefore to be reviewed with Accuracy, and canvassed with Strictness. What is proposed ought to be incorporated with what hath been done, and the Result of both stated and considered as a substantive original Question, and if the Measure proposed is incompatible with the constitutional Rights of the Subject, it is so far from being a rational Argument, that Consistency requires an Adoption of the proposed Measure, that, on the contrary, it suggests the strongest Motive for abolishing the Precedent; when therefore an Instance of *Deviation* from the Constitution is pressed as a

Reason for the *Establishment* of a Measure striking at the very Root of all Liberty; tho' the Argument is inconclusive, it ought to be useful.

Wherefore if a sufficient Answer were not given to the Argument drawn from Precedents, by shewing that none of the Instances adduced are applicable, I should have very little Difficulty in denying the Justice of the Principle on which it is founded. What hath been done, if wrongful, confers no Right to repeat it. To justify Oppression and Outrage, by Instances of their Commission, is a Kind of Argument which never can produce Conviction, tho' it may *their* Acquiescence, whom the Terror of greater Evils may restrain from resisting, and thus the Despotism of the East may be supported, and the natural Rights of Mankind be trampled under Feet. The Question of Right, therefore, doth not depend upon Precedents, but on the Principles of the Constitution, and hath been put upon it's proper Point already discussed, whether the Colonies are represented or not, in Parliament.

As the Name of *Hampden* occurred to the Examiner in his Design of casting an oblique Reflection upon the Colonies, it is surprising he did not recollect, that very numerous Precedents have been applied in the Defence of an arbitrary and oppressive Proceeding, destructive of the essential Principle of *English* Liberty. But tho' meer Acts of Power prove no Right, yet the real Opinion entertained of it, may be inferred from Forbearance; for Mankind are generally so fond of Power, that they are oftener tempted to exercise it beyond the Limits of Justice, than induced to set Bounds to it from the pure Consideration of the Rectitude of Forbearance. Wherefore if I had deny'd the Principle of this Kind of Reasoning, without shewing the Defects of the artificial painted Precedents which have been produced, I might still very consistently urge, that, the repeated and uniform Requisitions of the *English* Ministers, as often as Occasions for the *single Purpose of Revenue* have happened, transmitted to the Colonies to tax Themselves by Provincial Acts, and the Acts of Parliament regulating the Trade of the Plantations, as well as of *Ireland*, without one Instance, before the Stamp-Act of a Tax imposed by Parliament upon either, for the *unmixed* Purpose of Revenue prove, that the Imposition of a Tax upon them without their Consent, hath constantly been held to be inconsistent with their Constitutional Rights and Privileges. I have joined *Ireland* with the Colonies, and presume it will hardly be contended that *Ireland*, over which the Courts of Justice in *England* have a superintendant Power, is not, at least, as subject to *Great-Britain* as the Colonies are.

A most extraordinary Reason hath been given, why the Method of Requisition would have been improper, *viz.* that "the Sums raised must be paid into the Exchequer, and if levied by the Provincial Assemblies, the Parliament would have no Right to enquire into the Expenditure of them." This is so extremely futile, that it would be almost absurd to bestow a serious Refutation upon it.

Why must the Sums raised be paid into the Exchequer? If the Intention is to apply them in the Colonies to any internal Purpose, why must they be remitted to *Great-Britain*? If Armies are to be kept up in *America*, to defend the Colonies against *Themselves*, (for it can hardly be imagined that Troops are necessary for their Protection against any foreign Enemy) or are to be employed in the national Service of Cropping the Ears, and Slitting the Nostrils of the Civil Magistrates, as Marks of Distinction,* why must the Money be paid into the Exchequer? Or, if it should be paid into the Exchequer, in order to be applied towards sinking the national Debt, why might not the Parliament enquire into the Application of it? Does the Examiner, in his Idea of the Parliament, figure to himself a Monster with an Hand that can reach to the utmost Verge of the *British* Dominions, and clutch and crush Millions of Subjects at a Gripe; but, when the Object is near, apt to be rendered by some magical Influence, so short, and so feeble, as not to be able to reach the *Exchequer*, or to squeeze the *Chancellor* of it?

We are assured that there never can be any irregular "Attempts of the Prerogative upon our Rights, whilst we are blessed with a Prince of the glorious Line of *Brunswick* upon the Throne of *Great-Britain*." I have all the Confidence in the excellent Dispositions of our present most gracious Sovereign that an *Englishman* ought to have, but I can't penetrate into

---

* See the Narrative of the Outrages committed by the Soldiery, on Mr. Justice *Walker* in *Canada*.

Futurity; and, as the Examiner hath not yet established the Character of a Prophet, I must consider this Assertion rather as a curious Specimen of Lip-Loyalty, I will not call it extravagant Adulation, than as a sober Recommendation, to surrender all those Guards and Securities of Liberty, which the Constitution of a Free Government hath provided; but, if the *British Americans* should ever be reduced to the unhappy Necessity of giving up their Natural Rights, and their Civil Principles, I believe They would as soon make the Surrender to a Prince of the *Line of Brunswick*, as to any other Mortal, or Number of Mortals, in the Universe.

We have seen too a Piece in some of our late News-Papers, all bedawbed with the Lace of Compliment—There is no End to human Ambition! It is perpetually restless, and pushing forward. If a little P—ct—r* is raised to the Title of Excellency, and the Rank of a Kind of Viceroy, there is still a Summit beyond the Eminence to which he hath been elevated, that he is sollicitous to gain.

It hath been truly said, that "it will be no easy Task to persuade the *Americans* to forsake the Culture of their Lands, to leave the Ways their Fathers trod, and in which Themselves were trained, to drop a Business they already understand, in which they have had long Experience, and by which their Families have thriven, to change all their Habits of Thinking, and their Manner of Life, in order to apply to Arts which they do not know, or know but imperfectly, and that where Estates may be easily raised by mere Tillage, the Temptations to Manufacture are wanting, and Men, who can depend upon their Industry alone, will not have Recourse to Arts for Subsistence." But that which Persuasion might not effect, and to which peculiar Circumstances might be adverse, Necessity, and an Alteration of those Circumstances, may accomplish. When the Alternative is proposed, and the one Part of it assures Success, and a comfortable Support by a moderate Application of Industry, familiarized by Use, and rendered easy by Practice; and the other affording only an Experiment of precarious Issue,

---

* A late notable Speech puts me in Mind of the Ingenuity of the Female Disputant, who used to silence Debate, by crying out, *God bless the King and what have you to say to that?*

calling for an Application unexperienced and dreaded, attended with Perplexity, and productive of irksome Anxiety, the Generality of Mankind would not hesitate in chusing the former. But, though it would gain the Preference of Choice, yet, if the Alternative is taken away, and Choice yields to Necessity, the Enterprizing will form Projects, the Judicious improve, the Industrious execute them. Success, in one Instance, will animate the timid to make Trial of the Means which have succeeded under the Direction of others, stimulate the Phlegmatic, and rouse the Indolent—Should the Necessity after a little Time, cease, new Habits may become as strong as the old, and the Alternative would therefore be altered, the Choice be an Act of Deliberation, rather than of blind Impulse; old Prejudices would be greatly abated, if not extinguish'd, new Attachments, perhaps, be formed. From this Change, different Consequences may be conjectured or foretold, and perhaps the most Confident might be disappointed by the Event. It is not so difficult for Men to strike into new Employments and Methods of Life, when impelled by the Urgency of Distress, nor so easy to call them back to their old Manner of Life, and divert them from new Pursuits experienced to be profitable, and *productive of the best Security against Oppression*, as some seem to apprehend.

It is not contended that the Colonies ought to be indulged in a general Liberty of Exporting and Importing every Thing in what Manner they please, but, since they are hindered from making all the Advantages they might do, and what Advantages might they not make, if under no Checks? They have a good Plea against all Rigour and Severity, not absolutely necessary. That *British* Manufactures come dearer, and not so good in Quality to *America*, as formerly, is a very general Complaint, and what Effect it may have, should they still grow dearer and worse in Quality, or the Colonies be rendered less able to consume them, is a Consideration which concerns *Great-Britain*, at least as much as the Colonies. An increase of Price, and falling in the Goodness of Quality, is the usual Effect of Monopolies; there is no Danger of Foreigners taking Advantage of this Circumstance in *America*, whatever they may do in other Countries; but the Industry it may give Rise to in *America*, when other Circumstances concur, is not difficult to be foreseen.

It must be acknowledged, that the Balance of Trade between *Great-Britain* and her Colonies, is considerably against the latter, and that no Gold or Silver Mines have yet been discovered in the old *American* Settlements, or among the *Treasures* of the new Acquisitions. How then is this Balance to be discharged? The former Trade of the Colonies, which enabled them to keep up their Credit with *Great-Britain*, by applying the Balance they gained against Foreigners, is now so fettered with Difficulties, as to be almost prohibited. In order therefore to reduce the Balance against them upon the Trade between the Colonies and *Great-Britain*, this Trade must be contracted, so as to bring the Scales to an Equilibrium, or a Debt will be incurred that can't be paid off, which will distress the Creditor as well as the Debtor, by the Insolvency of the latter. The Income also of the Colonies, which was before invested in their Trade, will be diminished in Proportion to the Produce of the Stamp-Act, and therefore the Amount of that Produce must be drawn out, which will create a further Reduction of the Trade.

I confess that I am one of those who do not perceive the Policy in laying Difficulties and Obstructions upon the gainful Trade of the Colonies with Foreigners, or that it even makes any real Difference to the *English* Nation, whether the Merchants who carry it on with Commodities *Great-Britain* will not purchase, reside in *Philadelphia, New-York* or *Boston, London, Bristol,* or *Liverpool,* when the Balance gained by the *American* Merchant in the Pursuit of that Trade centers in *Great-Britain,* and is applied to the Discharge of a Debt contracted by the Consumption of *British* Manufactures in the Colonies, and in this to the Support of the national Expence.

If in Consequence of the Obstructions, or Regulations as they are called, of their Commerce, and the Imposition of Taxes upon their Properties, the Colonies should only be driven to observe the strictest Maxims of Frugality, the Consequence would rather be disagreeable than hurtful—Should they be forced to use new Methods of Industry, and to have Recourse to Arts for a Supply of Necessaries, the Difficulty in Succeeding would prove less than the Apprehension of Miscarrying, and the Benefit greater than the Hope of it. There are few People of the highest, and even of the middle Rank, but would upon a strict Scrutiny into their ordinary Disbursements, discover some Articles that would admit of Defalcation.

A prudent Man, constrained to abridge his Outgoings, will consider what Articles of Expence may be retrenched or given up, without Distress or Discomfort, and if, after this saving, he still finds that his Expences exceed his Income, he will then consider of what Articles he can provide a Supply by the Application of domestic Industry, or whether some tolerable Substitute may not be fallen upon to answer the Purpose of what he can neither buy, nor hath Skill or Ability to fabricate. He will reflect that the Expedient which is at first but an indifferent Shift, Use and Experience will improve into Convenience, that Practice will confer Knowledge and Skill, and these Facility and Satisfaction, and tho' the Progress should be slow and gradual, Habit will grow with it, and produce Reconcilement and Content.

What are called in *North-America*, Luxuries, ought for the most Part to be ranked among the Comforts and Decencies of Life, but these will not be relinquished, if a Supply of Necessaries may be provided by domestic Industry—For Food, thank GOD, They do not, and for Raiment They need not, depend upon *Great-Britain*.

Any thin Covering in the Summer to preserve Decency, and substantial Cloathing in the Winter to repel the Cold, are sufficient for domestic Servants and Labourers, and these may be provided without any Remora to the Business of Tillage, for there are many Intervals in which it is suspended. There are Times too, when the Employment is so slight as to be rather a moderate Exercise, than a laborious Task, when the Work that is done might be performed by half the Number of Labourers without excessive Exertion, or exhausting Fatigue. There are besides in most Families those, whom the Feebleness of immature Years, or their Sex, at particular Periods, or the Decrepitude of old Age, discharge from the Duties of Tillage. Leather, and Wool, and Cotton, and Flax, are at Hand: How easy then is the necessary Cloathing provided for those whose Station does not require any attention or regard to Fashion, or Elegance; so easy, that many have already gone into this Manufacture without any other Impulse, than the Spirit of Industry, which can't bear Inaction, tho' the Savings on this Head have afterwards been neglected. In this very considerable Branch so little Difficulty is there, that a Beginning is Half the Work. The Path is beaten, there is no Danger of losing the Way, there are Directors to guide every Step. But why should they stop at the Point of cloathing Labourers, why not proceed, when Vigour and Strength will increase with the Progression, to cloath the Planters? When the first Stage is arrived at, the Spirits will be recruited, and the second should be undertaken with Alacrity, since it may be performed with Ease. In this too, the Experiment hath been made and hath succeeded. Let the Manufacture of *America* be the Symbol of Dignity, the Badge of Virtue, and it will soon break the Fetters of Distress. A Garment of Linsey-Wolsey, when made the Distinction of real Patriotism, is more honourable and attractive of Respect and Veneration, than all the Pageantry, and the Robes, and the Plumes, and the Diadem of an Emperor without it. Let the Emulation be not in the Richness and Variety of foreign Productions, but in the Improvement and Perfection of our own—Let it be demonstrated that the Subjects of the *British* Empire in *Europe* and *America* are the same, that the Hardships of the latter will ever recoil upon the former.*

---

* Upon a Surmise that a certain noble L—d, was the Author of some Hardships inflicted upon the Colonies, a reproachful and mischievous Distinction hath been made by some People, between the Natives of *S—t—d*, and of *E—g—d* and *America*, which every judicious Friend of the Colonies must wish to see abolish'd, and an *Union* rather established than Divisions promoted. Every Man who has his all, and the Welfare of his Posterity at Stake, upon the Prosperity of *America*, as he hath an Interest in common with the Natives of it, ought to be considered as an *American*—It is an effectual Way to make Men Adversaries, to call and treat Them as such—Besides, laying aside this Consideration, the Distinction is extremely unjust; for tho' there is too much Reason to believe that some Natives of *America*, and of *E—g—d*, who have resided in the Colonies, have been instrumental in bringing upon Us the Severities We deplore, yet hath it never been even surmised, I speak it to their Honour, that any Native of *S—t—d* residing, or that ever did reside in *America*, had in any Degree a Hand in them. It is much to be feared, if the Breach which a too eager Prosecution of the little Views of Party, hath made among the Inhabitants of a Colony heretofore the most distinguished for Prudence and Unanimity, should not be closed, in Consideration of the general Calamity, that *America* as well as *Denmark*, will furnish an Instance of the excessive Temerity of political Animosity.

In Theory it is supposed that each is equally important to the other, that all partake of the Adversity and Depression of any. The Theory is just, and Time will certainly establish it, but if another Principle should be ever hereafter adopted in Practice, and a Violation deliberate, cruel, ungrateful, and attended with every Circumstance of Provocation, be offered to our fundamental Rights, why should we leave it to the slow Advances of Time (which may be the great Hope and Reliance, probably, of the Authors of the Injury, whose View it may be to accomplish their selfish Purposes in the Interval) to prove what might be demonstrated immediately—Instead of moping, and puling, and whining to excite Compassion; in such a Situation we ought with Spirit, and Vigour, and Alacrity, to bid Defiance to Tyranny, by exposing it's Impotence, by making it as contemptible, as it would be detestable. By a vigorous Application to Manufactures, the Consequence of Oppression in the Colonies to the Inhabitants of *Great-Britain*, would strike Home, and immediately. None would mistake it. Craft and Subtilty would not be able to impose on the most ignorant and credulous; for if any should be so weak of Sight as not to See, they would not be so callous as not to Feel it.—Such Conduct would be the most dutiful and beneficial to the Mother-Country. It would point out the Distemper when the Remedy might be easy, and a Cure at once effected by a simple Alteration of Regimen.

Of this Measure should there be Apprehensions, and Ministerial Orators and Panegyrists endeavour to obviate them by observing, that, "it would always be easy to reinstate Things where they were, and that by easing the Colonies of their Burthens, and giving Encouragement to their Produce; the Establishment of any Manufacture in *America* might be prevented." We should mark well this Reasoning, and avail ourselves of the Instruction given by our Enemies, which would point out to Us the Remedy, and the more speedy the Application of it the better, and that would depend upon ourselves.

Besides the Urgency of such an Occasion (should it happen) there would be another Powerful Inducement to this simple, natural, easy Method—The good or bad Success of one Attempt to oppress, generally produces or prevents future Impositions. In common Life a Tameness in bearing a Deprivation of Part of a Man's Property, encourages Rapacity to seize the rest.

Any Oppression of the Colonies, would intimate an Opinion of them I am persuaded they don't deserve, and their Security as well as Honour ought to engage them to confute. When Contempt is mixed with Injustice, and Insult with Violence, which is the Case when an Injury is done to him who hath the Means of Redress in his Power; if the injured hath one inflammable Grain of Honour in his Breast, his Resentment will invigorate his Pursuit of Reparation, and animate his Efforts to obtain an effectual Security against a Repetition of the Outrage.

If the Case supposed should really happen, the Resentment I should recommend would be a legal, orderly, and prudent Resentment, to be expressed in a zealous and vigorous Industry,* in an immediate Use and unabating Application of the Advantages we derive from our Situation—a Resentment which could not fail to produce Effects as beneficial to the Mother-Country as to the Colonies, and which a Regard to her Welfare as well as our own, ought to inspire us with on such an Occasion.

The General Assemblies would not, I suppose, have it in their Power to encourage by Laws, the Prosecution of this beneficial, this necessary Measure; but they might promote it almost as effectually by their Example. I have in my younger Days seen fine Sights, and been captivated by their dazzling Pomp and glittering Splendor; but the Sight of our Representatives, all adorned in compleat Dresses of their own Leather, and Flax, and Wool, manufactured by the Art and Industry of the Inhabitants of *Virginia*, would excite, not the Gaze of Admiration, the Flutter of an agitated Imagination, or the momentary Amusement of a transient Scene, but a calm, solid, heartfelt Delight. Such a Sight would give Me more Pleasure than the most splendid and magnificent Spectacle the most exquisite Taste ever painted, the richest Fancy ever imagined,

---

* The ingenious Mr. *Hume*, observes in his History of *James* I, that the *English* fine Cloth was in so little Credit even at Home, that the King was obliged to seek Expedients by which he might engage the People of Fashion to wear it, and the Manufacture of fine Linen was totally unknown in the Kingdom— What an Encouragement to Industry! This very penetrating Gentleman also recommends a *mild Government*, as a proper Measure for preserving the Dominion of *England* over her Colonies.

realized to the View—as much more Pleasure as a good Mind would receive from the Contemplation of Virtue, than of Elegance; of the Spirit of Patriotism, than the Ostentation of Opulence.

Not only, "as a Friend to the Colonies," but as an Inhabitant having my All at Stake upon their Welfare I desire an "Exemption from Taxes imposed *without my Consent*, and" I have reflected longer than "a Moment upon the Consequences:"* I value it as one of the dearest Privileges I enjoy: I acknowledge Dependance on *Great-Britain*, but I can perceive a Degree of it without Slavery, and I disown all other. I do not expect that the Interests of the Colonies will be considered by some Men, but in Subserviency to other Regards. The Effects of Luxury, and Venality, and Oppression, Posterity may perhaps experience, and SUFFICIENT FOR THE DAY WILL BE THE EVIL THEREOF.

* See *The Regulations*, &c. Page 238.

APPENDIX.

B Y the 12th *Cha.* II, the Colonies are restrain'd from send-ing the Products enumerated in the Act to *any foreign* Ports.—By the 15th of the same King, they are prohibited from importing Commodities of the Growth or Manufacture of *Europe, except from* GREAT-BRITAIN, saving a few Articles mention'd in this Act.

A Law, which restrains one Part of the Society, from *exporting* it's Products to the most profitable Market, *in favour of another*; or obliges it to *import* the Manufactures of one Country that are dear, instead of those of another that are cheap, is effectually a Tax. For if the profitable *Exportation*, and the *Importation* of the cheaper Commodities were permitted, a Tax equal to such Gain in the former Case, and to the Saving in the latter, wou'd leave that Part of the Society, in the same State and Condition, as if under the Prohibition and Restriction above-mentioned. As for Instance in the Case of *Importation*—Suppose a Country which I will distinguish by the Name of A, can purchase Commodities of the same Kind, and equal Goodness, 20 per Cent cheaper of B, than she can of C;—then it is clear, if A is prohibited from taking these Commodities of B, and obliged to purchase them of C, that A is just in the same State and Condition, as if she were allow'd to purchase the Commodities of B, on paying thereon a Duty of 20 per Cent to C.—This Instance, *mutatis mutandis*, is equally applicable to the Case of *Exportation*. Hence it appears, that the Country favour'd by the Prohibition and Restriction, gains as much thereby, as it wou'd do, if the proportionate Tax were paid to it, upon taking off the Prohibition and Restriction; or, in other Words, the Profit which the one is hinder'd from making, in Consequence of the Prohibition and Restriction, is made by the other, in whose favour they have been introduc'd.

It hath been observed by a well-received Writer on the Subject of Trade, that "a Prohibition acknowledges the Commodities it is laid on, to be good and cheap, otherwise it were needless, and a Prohibition on the Goods of any one

Nation, gives a Monopoly to other Nations, that raise the like."—
Again—"A Prohibition against any one Nation, makes other
Nations, having the like Commodities, take the Advantage and
raise their Price, *and is therefore a Tax*."*

If a Prohibition, extending to one Nation only in favour of
many, confers a Monopoly, and is therefore a Tax; a Prohibition extending to all other Nations in favour of one, is indubitably so.

From *Virginia* and *Maryland* are exported, *communibus
Annis*, 90,000 Hogsheads of Tobacco to *Great-Britain*, of
which it is suppos'd 60,000 are thence re-exported. But these
Colonies not being permitted to send their Tobacco *immedi-
ately* to foreign Markets *distributively*, in proportion to their
Demands, the re-exported Tobacco pays double Freight, double
Insurance, Commission and other Shipping Charges. The whole
Quantity is, moreover, of Course much depreciated, for going
all to *Great-Britain*, the *Home-Market* is overdone, by which
Circumstance, the Quantity requir'd for *Home-Consumption* is
without Doubt purchased cheaper than it wou'd be, if no more
than *that* were imported into *Great-Britain*, and of this Glut
Foreigners, and Purchasers on Speculation also, avail themselves. Besides, a great deal of the Tobacco getting home late,
the rigorous Season hinders it's being re-shipp'd for some
Months, during which, it is dead on hand, and moreover gives
Advantage to Buyers—a Loss to the Planter, which wou'd be
avoided, if the Tobacco cou'd be immediately sent to it's
proper Market.—

The above quoted Author hath computed the Duties, Ex-
cises, *&c.* on Leather, at 50 per Cent; and the Artificial Value
of a Bale of *English* Cloth arising from Taxes, Monopolies and
ill-judg'd Laws at 51 per Cent, by which, he means that every
Hundred Pounds Worth of that Species of Manufacture, includes in that Sum 51*l.* of Taxes. His Computation is, without
Doubt, too low now, Taxes having been increased very considerably since the Time, in which he wrote.

---

* Sir *Matthew Decker.*

	per Cent.
In the gross Sum of the artificial Value, he computed the Amount of the Taxes to be full	31
Monopolies and ill-judged Laws, therefore stand at	20
	51
A Bale of *English* Cloth costing	£. 100
Includes an artificial Value of	51
The artificial Value subtracted, leaves the natural Value	49

But lest the Estimate shou'd be objected to on account of it's including 20 per Cent for Monopolies, *&c.* I will state the artificial Value arising from Taxes, *only* to be 33*l.* 6*s.* 8*d.* which will hardly be objected to, for being too high.

The Colonies, it is suppos'd, take, annually, Manufactures from *Great-Britain*, to the Amount of	£. 2,000,000
Therefore they pay an ANNUAL Tax of	£. 666,666 : 13 : 4
To which must be added Freight, Insurance, Commission and Shipping Charges, amounting at least, to 10 per Cent, the Half of which, as it might be sav'd by back-freight, *&c.* were the Colonies permitted to import *directly* the Manufactures of foreign Countries, is computed at	100,000 : 00 : 0
What may be the Amount from the Restrictions, on all the Enumerated Commodities (except Tobacco) exported from all the Colonies, with Subsidies retain'd and Duties laid, upon the most moderate Computation, may, I suppose, be stated at	150,000 : 00 : 0
	£. 916,666 : 13 : 4

Part of the Commodities sent from *Great-Britain* to the Colonies, is first imported into *Great-Britain* from *foreign*

Countries; but the Estimate is not exceptionable on that Account, for the general Calculation on the advanced Price of *British* Manufactures, is extremely low.—Several of the foreign Commodities receive their Perfection in *Britain*.—All of them are enhanced by the Articles of double Freight, Insurance, Shipping Charges, the Merchant Importer's Commission, the *English* Tradesman a Profit, the Merchant Exporter's Commission, and Subsidies retain'd. If the Colonies were not restrain'd from directly importing foreign Commodities, they would, it is presum'd, pay less for them, even by 50 per Cent, than they do at present.

It hath been already observ'd, that there are shipped from *Virginia* and *Maryland*, annually, at an Average, about 90,000 Hogsheads of Tobacco, 60,000 of which, or upwards, are re-exported from *Great-Britain*, to foreign Markets; but they pay to *Great-Britain*, for the Reasons above explain'd, 3*l.* per Hogshead, *i. e.* the Sum of 3*l.* upon each Hogshead might be saved if the Tobacco might be *immediately* and *distributively* sent to the respective Markets, in Proportion to their Demands; and an equal Sum is paid also to *Great-Britain*, upon the same Rule of Computation, *i. e.* that these Colonies pay what they might save, if not restrain'd. For, tho' the *English* Manufacturer gets the Tobacco he wants, without the double Freight, *&c.* yet he has the Advantage of the Glut, and an Opportunity of buying it as cheap, as it is sold in *Great-Britain* for the foreign Markets, before the Charges of double Freight, *&c.* are incurred, and therefore the Planter gets no more for his Tobacco sold for *Home*, than that which is sold for *Foreign* Consumption, and consequently pays as much for it. For there is great Reason to imagine, that if these Colonies were at Liberty to send their Tobacco *immediately* where they pleas'd, the Market in *England* wou'd be as profitable as those of *France, Holland*, &c.—But when the Tobacco, under the present Regulation, is purchased for Re-Exportation, the Purchaser undoubtedly considers the Expence he is to be at, before it gets to the foreign Market, as Part of the Price of the Commodity, and therefore lowers his Price to the Merchant in Proportion.

The above Sum of 3*l.* for each Hogshead, makes	£. 270,000 : 00 : 0
The Amount of the sundry Impositions and Restrictions before mentioned, brought forward, ...	916,666 : 13 : 4
Total Amount of Taxes to *Great-Britain* . . .	1,186,666 : 13 : 4
Besides the above Amount of Taxes paid to the Mother-Country, the Colonies in *North-America* support their own Civil Establishments, and pay Quit-Rents to the Crown and Proprietaries, to the Amount (supposing 600,000 Taxables, at the moderate Rate of 15*s.* each) of	450,000 : 00 : 0
Total Amount of Taxes paid to our Mother-Country, and the Support of our Civil Establishment, *annually,*	1,636,666 : 13 : 4
Supposing the clear annual Rents of the Lands in *North-America*, (unrestrain'd by Acts of Parliament) wou'd amount to . . .	£. 2,500,000

It appears then, that the whole Tax is upwards of 65 per Cent; and if, therefore, the artificial Value of One Hundred Pounds Worth of *British* Manufacture, (Cloth for Instance) is, according to the above Computation, 33*l.* 6*s.* 8*d.* there was, before the *Stamp-Act*, a Tax paid by the *North-Americans*, near double of that which is paid by the Inhabitants of *England*. If the above Sum of 33*l.* 6*s.* 8*d.* is too low, and ought to be increased, then the Tax on *North-America*, on the Article of Manufactures imported from *Britain*, must also be increased.

It shou'd seem that the Maxim of every Tax upon Labour falling *ultimately* upon the Consumer of its Product, cannot be strictly applied to the Product of the *North-American* Colonies. For, as they are obliged to send their Commodities to some Port in the *British* Dominions, or (where Indulgence is granted to send some of them to other Places) deprived in great Measure of the Benefit of Returns, they are by this Means subjected to dead Freight; and moreover, being confin'd in their Consumption   to   a   particular   Manufacture,   and   the

Commodities they export, being chiefly raw Materials, they have not the Means generally in the Power of other People, by raising the Price of their Labour, to throw their Burthens upon others; but are, for the most Part, obliged, both in their Exports and Imports, to submit to an arbitrary Determination of their Value, though even below first Cost.

The sanguine Genius of one of the *Anti-American* Writers, brings to my Mind the Fable of the Boy and the Hen that laid *Golden Eggs*. He is not content to wait for the Increase of the *Public Revenue*, by that gradual Process and Circulation of Property, which an Attention to the commercial Interests of the Nation hath establish'd, but is at once for tearing away the Embryo, which, in due Time, might be matur'd into Fullness of Size and Vigour; without ever reflecting, that when the Hen is destroy'd by his Violence, there will be no more GOLDEN EGGS.—The following Passage justifies this Observation—

"If we have from the Colonies their ALL already, we only have it (says he) by Trade, and not by Taxes; and surely it is not the same Thing, whether the Wealth be brought into the Public Coffers by Taxes, or coming in by Trade, flows into the Pockets of Individuals, and, by augmenting his Influence with his Wealth, enables the Merchant to plunge us into new Wars and new Debts for his Advantage."*

The Man who thinks the Gains of the Merchant are dangerous, and that the Welfare of the Manufacturers, the Landholders, *&c.* doth not depend upon the Trade and Navigation of *Great-Britain*, is very consistently an Advocate for a Measure which hath a direct Tendency to check them; but whether this Opinion, and very consistent Conduct, might not be more serviceable in some other Employment, than in that of a L—— of T——, is submitted to their Consideration, who are the Judges of Merit, and the Dispensers of its Rewards.

For a Reason, which the above Opinion suggests, I shall subjoin an Estimate of the Duties upon Tobacco consumed in *Great-Britain*, and of the Profit to the Planter on that Tobacco. —The intelligent Reader will not apprehend it to be my Meaning, that the Planter pays out of his Pocket all the Duties

---

* The Objections to the Taxation, *&c.* consider'd.

laid on Tobacco, or be at a Loss to infer, that the Estimate has been made with no other View, than to obviate the Principle others by their Writings seem to adopt.

The old Subsidy is One Penny per Pound, 25 per Cent deducted.

All the other Duties are Seven Pence, and one Third per Pound, 15 per Cent deducted.

An Hogshead of Tobacco, at an Average, contains 952 ℔.

The whole Duties therefore, ... £. 27 : 14 : 0

The Amount of the whole Duties on } £. 831,000 : 00 : 0
  30,000 Hogsheads, is . . . .

The full clear Proceeds of an Hogshead of Tobacco, reckoning 952℔ in each Hogshead, has not, on an Average for some Years past, exceeded 4*l*.* wherefore, on 30,000 Hogsheads, the Planters get 120,000*l.* How much of the above Sum of 831,000*l.* is nett to the Revenue, I shall not undertake to say; but I presume it may be safely asserted, that no Part of this, or any other Public Money, is touch'd by any *Americans,* whether *they have great Powers of Speech* or not; tho' any Gentleman who might be affected by it, is not to be blamed for his Apprehension, that *a sudden Importation* of a certain Commodity, might hurt the *home* Market.

The Sum of the Taxes, paid in *North-America,* will appear enormous to those, who, having been told that these Colonies pay only 7 or 800*l. per Annum,* in Consequence of Taxes laid *there,* might be led, in their Dependence upon *Ministerial Candor,* to believe, that they paid no more *elsewhere;*—but to others, who are better acquainted with the Subject, the Computation will appear too low.—From these Observations it may be infer'd what vast Wealth, in *Taxes only,* the Mother-Country has, in the Course of a Hundred Years, drawn from

---

* See before, P. 301. The attentive Reader will observe, that the nett Proceeds of a Hogshead of Tobacco, at an Average, are 4*l.* and the Taxes 3*l.*—, together, 7*l.*—Quere, How much per Cent does the Tax amount to, which takes from the two wretched Tobacco Colonies, 3*l.* out of every 7*l.*? And how deplorable must their Circumstances appear, when their vast Debt to the Mother-Country, and the annual Burthen of their civil Establishments are added to the Estimate? In these two Colonies there are upwards of 180,000 Taxables.

her Colonies; and how *profoundly well-inform'd* the Writer is, who, with equal Pertinency and Confidence, pronounces, "that it is *now* high Time for *England* to draw some *little* Profit from her Colonies, after the *vast Treasure she has expended on their Settlement.*"

I confess that the above Computations are conjectural, but I believe they are probable. I mean that those, who are best acquainted with the Subject, will think the Charge upon *North-America* is not exaggerated, and which I think very naturally accounts for the enormous Debt she at present labours under to the Mother-Country.

Dr. *Davenant* observes, that, "if ever any Thing great or good be done for the *English* Colonies, Industry must have its due Recompence, and that can't be without Encouragement to it, which, perhaps is only to be brought about by *confirming their Liberties*, and establishing good Discipline among them; —that, as they see they are a Free People, in Point of Government, so they may, by Discipline, be kept free of the Mischiefs that follow Vice and Idleness. And, as great Care should be taken in this Respect, so without Doubt, it is adviseable, that no little Emulation of private Interests of Neighbour Governors, nor that the Petitions of *hungry Courtiers* at home, shou'd prevail to discourage those particular Colonies, who, in a few Years, have raised themselves by their *own Charge, Prudence and Industry*, to the Wealth and Greatness they are now arriv'd at, *without any Expence to the Crown*; upon which Account, any *Innovations*, or *Breach* of their *original Charters*, (besides that it seems a *Breach* of the *Public Faith*) may, peradventure, not tend to the King's Profit." Excellent Observation! but how little it hath been regarded, the present deeply-afflicting Distress of the Inhabitants of *North-America* demonstrates;—a Distress sufficient to drive Men into Despair, who are not animated by the Hope, that—DEUS DABIT HIS QUOQUE FINEM.

THE END.

Richard Bland, An Inquiry into the Rights of the British Colonies, Intended as an Answer to the Regulations Lately Made Concerning the Colonies, and the Taxes Imposed upon Them Considered. In a Letter Addressed to the Author of That Pamphlet. Williamsburg, 1766.

Many Americans were not willing to concede as much as Daniel Dulany to the idea of virtual representation; instead they conceived of an alternative—"actual representation" they called it—more in accord with their own experience. The origins of Parliament's crazy quilt pattern of representation may have been lost in the mists of time, but this was not true of the colonists. When new counties were created in Virginia or new towns in Massachusetts, they had sent delegates to their respective assemblies. Most colonists instinctively believed, as one Pennsylvanian put it, that the people "should be consulted in the most particular manner that can be imagined." Indeed, election for most Americans had become the sole criterion of representation, not just for themselves, but for everyone. "To what purpose," asked James Otis, "is it to ring everlasting changes to the colonists on the cases of Manchester, Birmingham and Sheffield, who return no members? If those now so considerable places are not represented, they ought to be."

Richard Bland was one of the more important planter-aristocrats of Virginia and a long-time and hard-working member of the House of Burgesses. In the following pamphlet he confronted Whately's argument directly and followed the path that Dulany had opened in seeking to clarify the line that presumably existed between the authority of Parliament and the rights of the colonists. Since the English constitution and ancient history offered no help "in fixing the proper Connexion between the Colonies and the Mother Kingdom; . . . we must," said Bland, "have Recourse to the Law of Nature, and those Rights of Mankind which flow from it." And because "*Rights* imply *Equality*," the colonists ought to be treated equally in the empire. Perhaps the Americans were, as English officials sometimes implied, "a distinct People."

In the end, however, Bland drew back from the radical implications of his appeal to nature. Reflecting on Bland's pamphlet in an 1815 letter, Thomas Jefferson identified a curious tension in its argument, one symbolic of the fitful approach of many American writers in the debate: "He would set out with a set of sound principles, pursue them logically till he found them leading to the precipice which he had to leap, start back alarmed, then resume his ground, go over it in another direction, be led by the correctness of his reasoning to the same place and again back about and try other processes to reconcile right and wrong but finally left his reader and himself bewildered between the steady index of the compass in their hand, and the phantasm to which it seemed to point."

AN
INQUIRY

INTO THE

RIGHTS of the BRITISH Colonies,

Intended as an Anſwer to

The Regulations lately made concerning the Colonies, and the Taxes impoſed upon them conſidered.

In a Letter addreſſed to the Author of that Pamphlet.

By *RICHARD BLAND*, of VIRGINIA.

Dedit omnibus Deus pro virili portione ſapientiam, ut et inaudita inveſtigare poſſent et audita perpendere.
LACTANTIUS.

WILLIAMSBURG:
Printed by ALEXANDER PURDIE, & Cᵒ.
MDCCLXVI.

An Inquiry into the Rights
of the British Colonies.

SIR,

I TAKE the Liberty to address you, as the Author of "The Regulations lately made concerning the Colonies, and the Taxes imposed upon them considered." It is not to the Man, whoever you are, that I address myself; but it is to the Author of a Pamphlet which, according to the Light I view it in, endeavours to fix Shackles upon the *American* Colonies: Shackles which, however nicely polished, can by no Means sit easy upon Men who have just Sentiments of their own Rights and Liberties.

You have indeed brought this Trouble upon yourself, for you say that "many Steps have been lately taken by the Ministry to cement and perfect the necessary Connexion between the Colonies and the Mother Kingdom, which every Man who is sincerely interested in what is interesting to his Country will anxiously consider the Propriety of, will inquire into the Information, and canvas the Principles upon which they have been adopted; and will be ready to applaud what has been well done, condemn what has been done amiss, and suggest any Emendations, Improvements, or Additions, which may be within his Knowledge, and occur to his Reflexion."

Encouraged therefore by so candid an Invitation, I have undertaken to examine, with an honest Plainness and Freedom, whether the Ministry, by imposing Taxes upon the Colonies by Authority of Parliament, have pursued a wise and salutary Plan of Government, or whether they have exerted pernicious and destructive Acts of Power.

I pretend not to concern myself with the Regulations lately made to encourage Population in the new Acquisitions: Time can only determine whether the Reasons upon which they have been founded are agreeable to the Maxims of Trade and sound Policy, or not. However, I will venture to observe that if the most powerful Inducement towards peopling those Acquisitions is to arise from the Expectation of a Constitution to be established in them similar to the other Royal Governments in *America*, it must be a strong Circumstance, in my Opinion, against their being settled by *Englishmen*, or even by *Foreigners*, who do not live under the most despotick Government; since, upon your Principles of Colony Government, such a Constitution will not be worth their Acceptance.

The Question is whether the Colonies are represented in the *British* Parliament or not? You affirm it to be an indubitable Fact that they are represented, and from thence you infer a Right in the Parliament to impose Taxes of every Kind upon them. You do not insist upon the *Power*, but upon the *Right* of Parliament to impose Taxes upon the Colonies. This is certainly a very proper Distinction, as *Right* and *Power* have very different Meanings, and convey very different Ideas: For had you told us that the Parliament of *Great Britain* have *Power*, by the Fleets and Armies of the Kingdom, to impose Taxes and to raise Contributions upon the Colonies, I should not have presumed to dispute the Point with you; but as you insist upon the *Right* only, I must beg Leave to differ from you in Opinion, and shall give my Reasons for it.

But I must first recapitulate your Arguments in Support of this Right in the Parliament. You say "the Inhabitants of the Colonies do not indeed choose Members of Parliament, neither are nine Tenths of the People of *Britain* Electors; for the Right of Election is annexed to certain Species of Property, to peculiar Franchises, and to Inhabitancy in some particular Places. But these Descriptions comprehend only a very small Part of the Lands, the Property and People of *Britain*; all Copy-Hold, all Lease-Hold Estates under the Crown, under the Church, or under private Persons, though for Terms ever so long; all landed Property in short that is not Freehold, and all monied Property whatsoever, are excluded. The Possessors of these have no Votes in the Election of Members of Parliament; Women and Persons under Age, be their Property ever so large, and all of it Freehold, have none: The Merchants of *London*, a numerous and respectable Body of Men, whose Opulence exceeds all that *America* can collect; the Proprietors of that vast Accumulation of Wealth, the Publick Funds; the Inhabitants of *Leeds*, of *Halifax*, of *Birmingham*, and of *Manchester*, Towns that are each of them larger than the largest in the Plantations; many of lesser Note, that are incorporated; and that great Corporation the *East India* Company, whose

Rights over the Countries they possess fall very little short of Sovereignty, and whose Trade and whose Fleets are sufficient to constitute them a maritime Power, are all in the same Circumstances: And yet are they not represented in Parliament? Is their vast Property subject to Taxation without their Consent? Are they all arbitrarily bound by Laws to which they have not agreed? The Colonies are exactly in the same Situation; all *British* Subjects are really in the same; none are actually, all are virtually, represented in Parliament: For every Member of Parliament sits in the House not as a Representative of his own Constituents, but as one of that august Assembly by which all the Commons of *Great Britain* are represented."

This is the Sum of what you advance, in all the Pomp of Parliamentary Declamation, to prove that the Colonies are represented in Parliament, and therefore subject to their Taxation; but notwithstanding this Way of reasoning, I cannot comprehend how Men who are excluded from voting at the Election of Members of Parliament can be represented in that Assembly, or how those who are elected do not sit in the House as Representatives of their Constituents. These Assertions appear to me not only paradoxical, but contrary to the fundamental Principles of the *English* Constitution.

To illustrate this important Disquisition, I conceive we must recur to the civil Constitution of *England*, and from thence deduce and ascertain the Rights and Privileges of the People at the first Establishment of the Government, and discover the Alterations that have been made in them from Time to Time; and it is from the Laws of the Kingdom, founded upon the Principles of the Law of Nature, that we are to show the Obligation every Member of the State is under to pay Obedience to its Institutions. From these Principles I shall endeavour to prove that the Inhabitants of *Britain*, who have no Vote in the Election of Members of Parliament, are not represented in that Assembly, and yet that they owe Obedience to the Laws of Parliament; which, as to them, are constitutional, and not arbitrary. As to the Colonies, I shall consider them afterwards.

Now it is a Fact, as certain as History can make it, that the present civil Constitution of *England* derives its Original from those *Saxons* who, coming over to the Assistance of the *Britons* in the Time of their King *Vortigern*, made themselves Masters of the Kingdom, and established a Form of Government in it similar to that they had been accustomed to live under in their native Country;* as similar, at least, as the Difference of their Situation and Circumstances would permit. This Government, like that from whence they came, was founded upon Principles of the most perfect Liberty: The conquered Lands were divided among the Individuals in Proportion to the Rank they held in the Nation;† and every Freeman, that is, every Freeholder, was a Member of their Wittinagemot, or Parliament.‡ The other Part of the Nation, or the Non-Proprietors of Land, were of little Estimation.§ They, as in *Germany*, were either Slaves, mere Hewers of Wood and Drawers of Water, or Freedmen; who, being of foreign Extraction, had been manumitted by their Masters, and were excluded from the high Privilege of having a Share in the Administration of the Commonwealth, unless they became Proprietors of Land (which they might obtain by Purchase or Donation) and in that Case they had a Right to sit with the Freemen, in the Parliament or sovereign Legislature of the State.

How long this Right of being personally present in the Parliament continued, or when the Custom of sending Representatives to this great Council of the Nation, was first introduced, cannot be determined with Precision; but let the Custom of Representation be introduced when it will, it is certain that every Freeman, or, which was the same Thing in the Eye of the Constitution, every Freeholder,¶ had a Right to vote at the Election of Members of Parliament, and therefore might be said, with great Propriety, to be present in that Assembly, either in his own Person or by Representation. This Right of Election in the Freeholders is evident from the Statute 1st *Hen.* 5. Ch. 1st, which limits the Right of Election to those Freeholders only who are resident in the Counties the Day of the Date of the Writ of Election; but yet every resident Freeholder indiscriminately, let his Freehold be ever so small, had a Right to vote at the Election of Knights for his County, so that

---

* *Petyt's Rights of the Com. Brady's Comp. Hist. Rapin. Squire's Inquiry.*

† *Cæsar de Bell. Gall. Tacitus de Germ. C. 28. Temple's Misc.*

‡ *Tacitus de Germ. C. 11.*

§ *Ibid. C. 25.*

¶ 2 *Inst.* 27. 4 *Inst.* 2.

they were actually represented: And this Right of Election continued until it was taken away by the Statute 8th *Hen*. 6. Ch. 7. from those Freeholders who had not a clear Freehold Estate of forty Shillings by the Year at the least.

Now this Statute was deprivative of the Right of those Freeholders who came within the Description of it; but of what did it deprive them, if they were represented notwithstanding their Right of Election was taken from them? The mere Act of voting was nothing, of no Value, if they were represented as constitutionally without it as with it: But when by the fundamental Principles of the Constitution they were to be considered as Members of the Legislature, and as such had a Right to be present in Person, or to send their Procurators or Attornies, and by them to give their Suffrage in the supreme Council of the Nation, this Statute deprived them of an essential Right; a Right without which, by the ancient Constitution of the State, all other Liberties were but a Species of Bondage.

As these Freeholders then were deprived of their Rights to substitute Delegates to Parliament, they could not be represented, but were placed in the same Condition with the Non-Proprietors of Land, who were excluded by the original Constitution from having any Share in the Legislature, but who, notwithstanding such Exclusion, are bound to pay Obedience to the Laws of Parliament, even if they should consist of nine Tenths of the People of *Britain*; but then the Obligation of these Laws does not arise from their being virtually represented in Parliament, but from a quite different Reason.

Men in a State of Nature are absolutely free and independent of one another as to sovereign Jurisdiction,* but when they enter into a Society, and by their own Consent become Members of it, they must submit to the Laws of the Society according to which they agree to be governed; for it is evident, by the very Act of Association, that each Member subjects himself to the Authority of that Body in whom, by common Consent, the legislative Power of the State is placed: But though they must submit to the Laws, so long as they remain Members of the Society, yet they retain so much of their natural Freedom as to have a Right to retire from the Society, to

* *Vattel's Law of Nature. Locke on Civil Govern. Wollaston's Rel. of Nat.*

renounce the Benefits of it, to enter into another Society, and to settle in another Country; for their Engagements to the Society, and their Submission to the publick Authority of the State, do not oblige them to continue in it longer than they find it will conduce to their Happiness, which they have a natural Right to promote. This natural Right remains with every Man, and he cannot justly be deprived of it by any civil Authority. Every Person therefore who is denied his Share in the Legislature of the State to which he had an original Right, and every Person who from his particular Circumstances is excluded from this great Privilege, and refuses to exercise his natural Right of quitting the Country, but remains in it, and continues to exercise the Rights of a Citizen in all other Respects, must be subject to the Laws which by these Acts he *implicitly*, or to use your own Phrase, *virtually* consents to: For Men may subject themselves to Laws, by consenting to them *implicitly*; that is, by conforming to them, by adhering to the Society, and accepting the Benefits of its Constitution, as well, as *explicitly* and directly, in their own Persons, or by their Representatives substituted in their Room.* Thus, if a Man whose Property does not entitle him to be an Elector of Members of Parliament, and therefore cannot be represented, or have any Share in the Legislature, "inherits or takes any Thing by the Laws of the Country to which he has no indubitable Right in Nature, or which, if he has a Right to it, he cannot tell how to get or keep without the Aid of the Laws and the Advantage of Society, then, when he takes this Inheritance, or whatever it is, *with* it he takes and owns the Laws that gave it him. And since the Security he has from the Laws of the Country, in Respect of his Person and Rights, is the *Equivalent* for his Submission to them, he cannot accept *that* Security without being obliged, in Equity, to pay *this* Submission: Nay his very continuing in the Country shows that he either likes the Constitution, or likes it better, notwithstanding the Alteration made in it to his Disadvantage, than any other; or at least thinks it better, in his Circumstances, to conform to it, than to seek any other; that is, he is content to be comprehended in it."

From hence it is evident that the Obligation of the Laws of

* *Wollaston's Rel. of Nat.*

Parliament upon the People of *Britain* who have no Right to be Electors does not arise from their being *virtually* represented, but from a quite different Principle; a Principle of the Law of Nature, true, certain, and universal, applicable to every Sort of Government, and not contrary to the common Understandings of Mankind.

If what you say is a real Fact, that nine Tenths of the People of *Britain* are deprived of the high Privilege of being Electors, it shows a great Defect in the present Constitution, which has departed so much from its original Purity; but never can prove that those People are even *virtually* represented in Parliament. And here give me Leave to observe that it would be a Work worthy of the best patriotick Spirits in the Nation to effectuate an Alteration in this putrid Part of the Constitution; and, by restoring it to its pristine Perfection, prevent any "Order or Rank of the Subjects from imposing upon or binding the rest without their Consent." But, I fear, the Gangrene has taken too deep Hold to be eradicated in these Days of Venality.

But if those People of *Britain* who are excluded from being Electors are not represented in Parliament, the Conclusion is much stronger against the People of the Colonies being represented; who are considered by the *British* Government itself, in every Instance of Parliamentary Legislation, as a distinct People. It has been determined by the Lords of the Privy Council that "Acts of Parliament made in *England* without naming the foreign Plantations will not bind them."* Now what can be the Reason of this Determination, but that the Lords of the Privy Council are of Opinion the Colonies are a distinct People from the Inhabitants of *Britain*, and are not represented in Parliament. If, as you contend, the Colonies are *exactly in the same Situation* with the Subjects in *Britain*, the Laws will in every Instance be equally binding upon them, as upon those Subjects, unless you can discover two Species of *virtual* Representation; the one to respect the Subjects in *Britain*, and always existing in Time of Parliament; the other to respect the Colonies, a mere Non-Entity, if I may be allowed the Term, and never existing but when the Parliament thinks proper to produce it into Being by any particular Act in which

* 2 *Pur. Williams.*

the Colonies happen to be named. But I must examine the Case of the Colonies more distinctly.

It is in vain to search into the civil Constitution of *England* for Directions in fixing the proper Connexion between the Colonies and the Mother Kingdom; I mean what their reciprocal Duties to each other are, and what Obedience is due from the Children to the general Parent. The planting Colonies from *Britain* is but of recent Date, and nothing relative to such Plantation can be collected from the ancient Laws of the Kingdom; neither can we receive any better Information by extending our Inquiry into the History of the Colonies established by the several Nations in the more early Ages of the World. All the Colonies (except those of *Georgia* and *Nova Scotia*) formed from the *English* Nation, in *North America*, were planted in a Manner, and under a Dependence, of which there is not an Instance in all the Colonies of the Ancients; and therefore, I conceive, it must afford a good Degree of Surprise to find an *English* Civilian* giving it as his Sentiment that the *English* Colonies ought to be governed by the *Roman* Laws, and for no better Reason than because the *Spanish* Colonies, as he says, are governed by those Laws. The *Romans* established their Colonies in the Midst of vanquished Nations, upon Principles which best secured their Conquests; the Privileges granted to them were not always the same; their Policy in the Government of their Colonies and the conquered Nations being always directed by arbitrary Principles to the End they aimed at, the subjecting the whole Earth to their Empire. But the Colonies in *North America*, except those planted within the present Century, were founded by *Englishmen*; who, becoming private Adventurers, established themselves, without any Expense to the Nation, in this uncultivated and almost uninhabited Country; so that their Case is plainly distinguishable from that of the *Roman*, or any other Colonies of the ancient World.

As then we can receive no Light from the Laws of the Kingdom, or from ancient History, to direct us in our Inquiry, we must have Recourse to the Law of Nature, and those Rights of Mankind which flow from it.

* *Strahan in his Preface to Domat.*

I have observed before that when Subjects are deprived of their civil Rights, or are dissatisfied with the Place they hold in the Community, they have a natural Right to quit the Society of which they are Members, and to retire into another Country. Now when Men exercise this Right, and withdraw themselves from their Country, they recover their natural Freedom and Independence: The Jurisdiction and Sovereignty of the State they have quitted ceases; and if they unite, and by common Consent take Possession of a new Country, and form themselves into a political Society, they become a sovereign State, independent of the State from which they separated. If then the Subjects of *England* have a natural Right to relinquish their Country, and by retiring from it, and associating together, to form a new political Society and independent State, they must have a Right, by Compact with the Sovereign of the Nation, to remove into a new Country, and to form a civil Establishment upon the Terms of the Compact. In such a Case, the Terms of the Compact must be obligatory and binding upon the Parties; they must be the Magna Charta, the fundamental Principles of Government, to this new Society; and every Infringement of them must be wrong, and may be opposed. It will be necessary then to examine whether any such Compact was entered into between the Sovereign and those *English* Subjects who established themselves in *America*.

You have told us that "before the first and great Act of Navigation the Inhabitants of *North America* were but a few unhappy Fugitives, who had wandered thither to enjoy their civil and religious Liberties, which they were deprived of at Home." If this was true, it is evident, from what has been said upon the Law of Nature, that they have a Right to a civil independent Establishment of their own, and that *Great Britain* has no *Right* to interfere in it. But you have been guilty of a gross Anachronism in your Chronology, and a great Errour in your Account of the first Settlement of the Colonies in *North America*; for it is a notorious Fact that they were not settled by Fugitives from their native Country, but by Men who came over voluntarily, at their own Expense, and under Charters from the Crown, obtained for that Purpose, long before the first and great Act of Navigation.

The first of these Charters was granted to Sir *Walter Raleigh* by Queen *Elizabeth* under her great Seal, and was confirmed by the Parliament of *England* in the Year 1684.* By this Charter the whole Country to be possessed by Sir *Walter Raleigh* was granted to him, his Heirs and Assigns, in perpetual Sovereignty, in as extensive a Manner as the Crown could grant, or had ever granted before to any Person or Persons, with full Power of Legislation, and to establish a civil Government in it as near as conveniently might be agreeable to the Form of the *English* Government and Policy thereof. The Country was to be united to the Realm of *England* in perfect LEAGUE AND AMITY, was to be within the Allegiance of the Crown of *England*, and to be held by Homage, and the Payment of one Fifth of all Gold and Silver Ore, which was reserved for all Services, Duties, and Demands.

Sir *Walter Raleigh*, under this Charter, took Possession of *North America*, upon that Part of the Continent which gave him a Right to the Tract of Country which lies between the twenty fifth Degree of Latitude and the Gulf of *St. Laurence*; but a Variety of Accidents happening in the Course of his Exertions to establish a Colony, and perhaps being overborn by the Expense of so great a Work, he made an Assignment to divers Gentlemen and Merchants of *London*, in the 31st Year of the Queen's Reign, for continuing his Plantation in *America*. These Assignees were not more successful in their Attempts than the Proprietor himself had been; but being animated with the Expectation of mighty Advantages from the Accomplishment of their Undertaking, they, with others, who associated with them, obtained new Charters from King *James* the First, in whom all Sir *Walter Raleigh*'s Rights became vested upon his Attainder; containing the same extensive Jurisdictions, Royalties, Privileges, Franchises, and Pre-eminences, and the same Powers to establish a civil Government in the Colony, as had been granted to Sir *W. Raleigh*, with an express Clause of Exemption for ever from all Taxes or Impositions upon their Import and Export Trade.

Under these Charters the Proprietors effectually prosecuted,

---

* *This Charter is printed at large in Hakluyt's Voyages, P. 725, Folio Edition, Anno* 1589; *and the Substance of it is in the 3d Vol. of Salmon's Mod. Hist. P.* 424.

and happily succeeded, in planting a Colony upon that Part of the Continent which is now called *Virginia*. This Colony, after struggling through immense Difficulties, without receiving the least Assistance from the *English* Government, attained to such a Degree of Perfection that in the Year 1621 a General Assembly, or legislative Authority, was established in the Governour, Council, and House of Burgesses, who were elected by the Freeholders as their Representatives; and they have continued from that Time to exercise the Power of Legislation over the Colony.

But upon the 15th of *July*, 1624, King *James* dissolved the Company by Proclamation, and took the Colony under his immediate Dependence; which occasioned much Confusion, and created mighty Apprehensions in the Colony lest they should be deprived of the Rights and Privileges granted them by the Company, according to the Powers contained in their Charters.

To put an End to this Confusion, and to conciliate the Colony to the new System of Government the Crown intended to establish among them, K. *Charles* the First, upon the Demise of his Father, by Proclamation the 13th of *May*, 1625, declared "that *Virginia* should be immediately dependent upon the Crown; that the Affairs of the Colony should be vested in a Council, consisting of a few Persons of Understanding and Quality, to be subordinate and attendant to the Privy Council in *England*; that he was resolved to establish another Council in *Virginia*, to be subordinate to the Council in *England* for the Colony; and that he would maintain the necessary Officers, Ministers, Forces, Ammunition, and Fortifications thereof, at his own Charge." But this Proclamation had an Effect quite different from what was intended; instead of allaying, it increased the Confusion of the Colony; they now thought their regular Constitution was to be destroyed, and a Prerogative Government established over them; or, as they express themselves in their Remonstrance, that "their Rights and Privileges were to be assaulted." This general Disquietude and Dissatisfaction continued until they received a Letter from the Lords of the Privy Council, dated *July* the 22d, 1634, containing the Royal Assurance and Confirmation that "all their Estates, Trade, Freedom, and Privileges, should be enjoyed by them in as extensive a Manner as they enjoyed them before the recalling the Company's Patent;" whereupon they became reconciled, and began again to exert themselves in the Improvement of the Colony.

Being now in full Possession of the Rights and Privileges of *Englishmen*, which they esteemed more than their Lives, their Affection for the Royal Government grew almost to Enthusiasm; for upon an Attempt to restore the Company's Charter by Authority of Parliament, the General Assembly, upon the 1st of *April*, 1642, drew up a Declaration or Protestation, in the Form of an Act, by which they declared "they never would submit to the Government of any Company or Proprietor, or to so unnatural a Distance as a Company or other Person to interpose between the Crown and the Subjects; that they were born under Monarchy, and would never degenerate from the Condition of their Births by being subject to any other Government; and every Person who should attempt to reduce them under any other Government was declared an Enemy to the Country, and his Estate was to be forfeited." This Act, being presented to the King at his Court at *York, July* 5th, 1644, drew from him a most gracious Answer, under his Royal Signet, in which he gave them the fullest Assurances that they should be always immediately dependent upon the Crown, and that the Form of Government should never be changed. But after the King's Death they gave a more eminent Instance of their Attachment to Royal Government, in their Opposition to the Parliament, and forcing the Parliament Commissioners, who were sent over with a Squadron of Ships of War to take Possession of the Country, into Articles of Surrender, before they would submit to their Obedience. As these Articles reflect no small Honour upon this Infant Colony, and as they are not commonly known, I will give an Abstract of such of them as relate to the present Subject.

1. The Plantation of *Virginia*, and all the Inhabitants thereof, shall be and remain in due Subjection to the Commonwealth of *England*, not as a conquered Country, but as a Country submitting by their own voluntary Act, and shall enjoy such Freedoms and Privileges as belong to the free People of *England*.

2. The General Assembly as formerly shall convene, and transact the Affairs of the Colony.

3. The People of *Virginia* shall have a free Trade, as the People of *England*, to all Places, and with all Nations.

4. *Virginia* shall be free from all Taxes, Customs, and Impositions whatsoever; and none shall be imposed on them without Consent of the General Assembly; and that neither Forts nor Castles be erected, or Garrisons maintained, without their Consent.

Upon this Surrender of the Colony to the Parliament, Sir *W. Berkley*, the Royal Governour, was removed, and three other Governours were successively elected by the House of Burgesses; but in *January* 1659 Sir *William Berkeley* was replaced at the Head of the Government by the People, who unanimously renounced their Obedience to the Parliament, and restored the Royal Authority by proclaiming *Charles* the 2d King of *England, Scotland, France, Ireland*, and *Virginia*; so that he was King in *Virginia* some Time before he had any certain Assurance of being restored to his Throne in *England*.

From this Detail of the Charters, and other Acts of the Crown, under which the first Colony in *North America* was established, it is evident that "the Colonists were not a few unhappy Fugitives who had wandered into a distant Part of the World to enjoy their civil and religious Liberties, which they were deprived of at home," but had a regular Government long before the first Act of Navigation, and were respected as a distinct State, independent, as to their *internal* Government, of the original Kingdom, but united with her, as to their *external* Polity, in the closest and most intimate LEAGUE AND AMITY, under the same Allegiance, and enjoying the Benefits of a reciprocal Intercourse.

But allow me to make a Reflection or two upon the preceding Account of the first Settlement of an *English* Colony in *North America*.

America was no Part of the Kingdom of *England*; it was possessed by a savage People, scattered through the Country, who were not subject to the *English* Dominion, nor owed Obedience to its Laws. This independent Country was settled by *Englishmen* at their own Expense, under particular

Stipulations with the Crown: These Stipulations then must be the sacred Band of Union between *England* and her Colonies, and cannot be infringed without Injustice. But you Object that "no Power can abridge the Authority of Parliament, which has never exempted any from the Submission they owe to it; and no other Power can grant such an Exemption."

I will not dispute the Authority of the Parliament, which is without Doubt supreme within the Body of the Kingdom, and cannot be abridged by any other Power; but may not the King have Prerogatives which he has a Right to exercise without the Consent of Parliament? If he has, perhaps that of granting License to his Subjects to remove into a *new* Country, and to settle therein upon particular Conditions, may be one. If he has no such Prerogative, I cannot discover how the Royal Engagements can be made good, that "the Freedom and other Benefits of the *British* Constitution" shall be secured to those People who shall settle in a new Country under such Engagements; the Freedom, and other Benefits of the *British* Constitution, cannot be secured to a People without they are exempted from being taxed by any Authority but that of their Representatives, chosen by themselves. This is an essential Part of *British* Freedom; but if the King cannot grant such an Exemption, in Right of his Prerogative, the Royal Promises cannot be fulfilled; and all Charters which have been granted by our former Kings, for this Purpose, must be Deceptions upon the Subjects who accepted them, which to say would be a high Reflection upon the Honour of the Crown. But there was a Time when some Parts of *England* itself were exempt from the Laws of Parliament: The Inhabitants of the County Palatine of *Chester* were not subject to such Laws* *ab antiquo*, because they did not send Representatives to Parliament, but had their own *Commune Concilium*; by whose Authority, with the Consent of their Earl, their Laws were made. If this Exemption was not derived originally from the Crown, it must have arisen from that great Principle in the *British* Constitution by which the Freemen in the Nation are not subject to any Laws but such as are made by Representatives elected by themselves to Parliament; so that, in either Case, it is an Instance extremely

* *Petyt's Rights of the Commons. King's Vale Royal of England.*

applicable to the Colonies, who contend for no other Right but that of directing their *internal* Government by Laws made with their own Consent, which has been preserved to them by repeated Acts and Declarations of the Crown.

The Constitution of the Colonies, being established upon the Principles of *British* Liberty, has never been infringed by the immediate Act of the Crown; but the Powers of Government, agreeably to this Constitution, have been constantly declared in the King's Commissions to their Governours, which, as often as they pass the Great Seal, are *new* Declarations and Confirmations of the Rights of the Colonies. Even in the Reign of *Charles* the Second, a Time by no Means favourable to Liberty, these Rights of the Colonies were maintained inviolate; for when it was thought necessary to establish a permanent Revenue for the Support of Government in *Virginia*, the King did not apply to the *English* Parliament, but to the General Assembly, and sent over an Act, under the Great Seal of *England*, by which it was enacted "by the King's Most Excellent Majesty, by and with the Consent of the General Assembly," that two Shillings per Hogshead upon all Tobacco exported, one Shilling and Threepence per Tun upon Shipping, and Sixpence per Poll for every Person imported, not being actually a Mariner in Pay, were to be paid for ever as a Revenue for the Support of the Government in the Colony.

I have taken Notice of this Act, not only because it shows the proper Fountain from whence all Supplies to be raised in the Colonies ought to flow, but also as it affords an Instance that Royalty itself did not disdain formerly to be named as a Part of the Legislature of the Colony; though now, to serve a Purpose destructive of their Rights, and to introduce Principles of Despotism unknown to a free Constitution, the Legislature of the Colonies are degraded even below the Corporation of a petty Borough in *England*.

It must be admitted that after the Restoration the Colonies lost that Liberty of Commerce with foreign Nations they had enjoyed before that Time.

As it became a fundamental Law of the other States of *Europe* to prohibit all foreign Trade with their Colonies, *England* demanded such an exclusive Trade with her Colonies. This was effected by the Act of 25th *Charles* 2d, and some other subsequent Acts; which not only circumscribed the Trade of the Colonies with foreign Nations within very narrow Limits, but imposed Duties upon several Articles of their own Manufactory exported from one Colony to another. These Acts, which imposed severer Restrictions upon the Trade of the Colonies than were imposed upon the Trade of *England*, deprived the Colonies, so far as these Restrictions extended, of the Privileges of *English* Subjects, and constituted an unnatural Difference between Men under the same Allegiance, born equally free, and entitled to the same civil Rights. In this Light did the People of *Virginia* view the Act of 25th *Charles* 2d, when they sent Agents to the *English* Court to represent against "Taxes and Impositions being laid on the Colony by any Authority but that of their General Assembly." The Right of imposing *internal* Duties upon their Trade by Authority of Parliament was then disputed, though you say it was never called into Question; and the Agents sent from *Virginia* upon this Occasion obtained a Declaration from *Charles* 2d the 19th of *April* 1676, under his Privy Seal, that Impositions or "Taxes ought not to be laid upon the Inhabitants and Proprietors of the Colony but by the common Consent of the General Assembly, except such Impositions as the Parliament should lay on the Commodities imported into *England* from the Colony:" And he ordered a Charter to be made out, and to pass the Great Seal, for securing this Right, among others, to the Colony.

But whether the Act of 25th *Charles* 2d, or any of the other Acts, have been complained of as Infringements of the Rights of the Colonies or not, is immaterial; for if a Man of superiour Strength takes my Coat from me, that cannot give him a Right to my Cloak, nor am I obliged to submit to be deprived of all my Estate because I may have given up some Part of it without Complaint. Besides, I have proved irrefragably that the Colonies are not represented in Parliament, and consequently, upon your own Position, that no new Law can bind them that is made without the Concurrence of their Representatives; and if so, then every Act of Parliament that imposes *internal* Taxes upon the Colonies is an Act of *Power*, and not of *Right*. I must speak freely, I am considering a Question which affects the *Rights* of above two Millions of as loyal Subjects as belong to the *British* Crown, and must use Terms adequate to the Importance of it; I say that *Power* abstracted from *Right* cannot give a just Title to Dominion. If a Man invades my Property, he becomes an Aggressor, and puts himself into a State of War with me: I have a Right to oppose this Invader; if I have not Strength to repel him, I must submit, but he acquires no Right to my Estate which he has usurped. Whenever I recover Strength I may renew my Claim, and attempt to regain my Possession; if I am never strong enough, my Son, or his Son, may, when able, recover the natural Right of his Ancestor which has been unjustly taken from him.

I hope I shall not be charged with Insolence, in delivering the Sentiments of an honest Mind with Freedom: I am speaking of the *Rights* of a People; *Rights* imply *Equality* in the Instances to which they belong, and must be treated without Respect to the Dignity of the Persons concerned in them. If "the *British* Empire in *Europe* and in *America* is the same *Power*," if the "Subjects in both are the same People, and all equally participate in the Adversity and Prosperity of the Whole," what Distinctions can the Difference of their Situations make, and why is this Distinction made between them? Why is the Trade of the Colonies more circumscribed than the Trade of *Britain*? And why are Impositions laid upon the one which are not laid upon the other? If the Parliament "have a *Right* to impose Taxes of *every Kind* upon the Colonies," they ought in Justice, as the same People, to have the same Sources to raise them from: Their Commerce ought to be equally free with the Commerce of *Britain*, otherwise it will be loading them with Burthens at the same Time that they are deprived of Strength to sustain them; it will be forcing them to make Bricks without Straw. I acknowledge the Parliament is the sovereign legislative Power of the *British* Nation, and that by a full Exertion of their Power they can deprive the Colonists of the Freedom and other Benefits of the *British* Constitution which have been secured to them by our Kings; they can abrogate all their civil Rights and Liberties; but by what *Right* is it that the Parliament can exercise such a Power over the Colonists, who have as natural a Right to the Liberties and Privileges of *Englishmen* as if they were actually resident within the Kingdom? The Colonies are subordinate to the Authority of

Parliament; subordinate I mean in Degree, but not absolutely
so: For if by a Vote of the *British* Senate the Colonists were to
be delivered up to the Rule of a *French* or *Turkish* Tyranny,
they may refuse Obedience to such a Vote, and may oppose
the Execution of it by Force. Great is the Power of Parliament,
but, great as it is, it cannot, constitutionally, deprive the People
of their *natural* Rights; nor, in Virtue of the same Principle,
can it deprive them of their *civil* Rights, which are founded in
Compact, without their own Consent. There is, I confess, a
considerable Difference between these two Cases as to the
Right of Resistance: In the first, if the Colonists should be
dismembered from the Nation by Act of Parliament, and abandoned to another Power, they have a natural Right to defend
their Liberties by open Force, and may lawfully resist; and, if
they are able, repel the Power to whose Authority they are
abandoned. But in the other, if they are deprived of their civil
Rights, if great and manifest Oppressions are imposed upon
them by the State on which they are dependent, their Remedy
is to lay their Complaints at the Foot of the Throne, and to
suffer patiently rather than disturb the publick Peace, which
nothing but a Denial of Justice can excuse them in breaking.
But if this Justice should be denied, if the most humble and
dutiful Representations should be rejected, nay not even
deigned to be received, what is to be done? To such a Question
Thucydides would make the *Corinthians* reply, that if "a decent
and condescending Behaviour is shown on the Part of the
Colonies, it would be base in the Mother State to press too far
on such Moderation:" And he would make the *Corcyreans*
answer, that "every Colony, whilst used in a proper Manner,
ought to pay Honour and Regard to its Mother State; but,
when treated with Injury and Violence, is become an Alien. They
were not sent out to be the Slaves, but to be the Equals of
those that remain behind."

But, according to your Scheme, the Colonies are to be prohibited from uniting in a Representation of their general
Grievances to the common Sovereign. This Moment "the
British Empire in *Europe* and in *America* is the same Power; its
Subjects in both are the same People; each is equally important
to the other, and mutual Benefits, mutual Necessities, cement
their Connexion." The next Moment "the Colonies are un-

connected with each other, different in their Manners, opposite in their Principles, and clash in their Interests and in their Views, from Rivalry in Trade, and the Jealousy of Neighbourhood. This happy Division, which was effected by Accident, is to be continued throughout by Design; and all Bond of Union between them" is excluded from your vast System. *Divide et impera* is your Maxim in Colony Administration, lest "an Alliance should be formed dangerous to the Mother Country." Ungenerous Insinuation! detestable Thought! abhorrent to every Native of the Colonies! who, by an Uniformity of Conduct, have ever demonstrated the deepest Loyalty to their King, as the Father of his People, and an unshaken Attachment to the Interest of *Great Britain*. But you must entertain a most despicable Opinion of the Understandings of the Colonists to imagine that they will allow Divisions to be fomented between them about inconsiderable Things, when the closest Union becomes necessary to maintain in a constitutional Way their dearest Interests.

Another Writer,* fond of his new System of placing *Great Britain* as the Centre of Attraction to the Colonies, says that "they must be guarded against having or forming any Principle of Coherence with each other above that whereby they cohere in the Centre; having no other Principle of Intercommunication between each other than that by which they are in joint Communication with *Great Britain*, as the common Centre of all. At the same Time that they are each, in their respective Parts and Subordinations, so framed as to be acted by this first Mover, they should always remain incapable of any Coherence, or of so conspiring amongst themselves as to create any other equal Force which might recoil back on this first Mover; nor is it more necessary to preserve the several Governments subordinate within their respective Orbs than it is essential to the Preservation of the Empire to keep them disconnected and independent of each other." But how is this "Principle of Coherence," as this elegant Writer calls it, between the Colonies, to be prevented? The Colonies upon the Continent of *North America* lie united to each other in one Tract of Country, and are equally concerned to maintain their common Liberty. If he

* *The Administration of the Colonies by Governour Pownall.*

will attend then to the Laws of Attraction in natural as well as political Philosophy, he will find that Bodies in Contact, and cemented by mutual Interests, cohere more strongly than those which are at a Distance, and have no common Interests to preserve. But this natural Law is to be destroyed; and the Colonies, whose *real* Interests are the same, and therefore ought to be united in the closest Communication, are to be disjoined, and all Intercommunication between them prevented. But how is this System of Administration to be established? Is it to be done by a military Force, quartered upon private Families? Is it to be done by extending the Jurisdiction of Courts of Admiralty, and thereby depriving the Colonists of legal Trials in the Courts of common Law? Or is it to be done by harassing the Colonists, and giving overbearing Taxgatherers an Opportunity of ruining Men, perhaps better Subjects than themselves, by dragging them from one Colony to another, before Prerogative Judges, exercising a despotick Sway in Inquisitorial Courts? Oppression has produced very great and unexpected Events: The *Helvetick* Confederacy, the States of the *United Netherlands*, are Instances in the Annals of *Europe* of the glorious Actions a petty People, in Comparison, can perform when united in the Cause of Liberty. May the Colonies ever remain under a constitutional Subordination to *Great Britain!* It is their Interest to live under such a Subordination; and it is their Duty, by an Exertion of all their Strength and Abilities, when called upon by their common Sovereign, to advance the Grandeur and the Glory of the Nation. May the Interests of *Great Britain* and her Colonies be ever united, so as that whilst they are retained in a legal and just Dependence no unnatural or unlimited Rule may be exercised over them; but that they may enjoy the Freedom, and other Benefits of the *British* Constitution, to the latest Page in History!

I flatter myself, by what has been said, your Position of a *virtual* Representation is sufficiently refuted; and that there is really no such Representation known in the *British* Constitution, and consequently that the Colonies are not subject to an *internal* Taxation by Authority of Parliament.

I could extend this Inquiry to a much greater Length, by examining into the Policy of the late Acts of Parliament, which impose heavy and severe Taxes, Duties, and Prohibitions, upon the Colonies; I could point out some very disagreeable Consequences, respecting the Trade and Manufactures of *Britain*, which must necessarily result from these Acts; I could prove that the Revenues arising from the Trade of the Colonies, and the Advantage of their Exports to *Great Britain* in the Balance of her Trade with foreign Nations, exceed infinitely all the Expense she has been at, all the Expense she can be at, in their Protection; and perhaps I could show that the Bounties given upon some Articles exported from the Colonies were not intended, primarily, as Instances of Attention to their Interest, but arose as well from the Consideration of the disadvantageous Dependence of *Great Britain* upon other Nations for the principal Articles of her naval Stores, as from her losing Trade for those Articles; I could demonstrate that these Bounties are by no Means adequate to her Savings in such foreign Trade, if the Articles upon which they are given can be procured from the Colonies in Quantities sufficient to answer her Consumption; and that the Excess of these Savings is so much clear Profit to the Nation, upon the Supposition that these Bounties are drawn from it; but, as they will remain in it, and be laid out in its Manufactures and Exports, that the whole Sum which used to be paid to Foreigners for the Purchase of these Articles will be saved to the Nation. I say I could extend my Inquiry, by examining these several Matters; but as the Subject is delicate, and would carry me to a great Length, I shall leave them to the Reader's own Reflection.

The Examination of Doctor Benjamin Franklin, Before an August Assembly, Relating to the Repeal of the Stamp-Act, etc. Philadelphia, 1766.

On June 8, 1765, shortly after news of the passage of the Stamp Act reached Boston, the Massachusetts House of Representatives issued a circular letter to the other colonial assemblies calling upon them to send delegates to a congress in New York "to consider of a general and united, dutiful, loyal and humble, Representation of their Condition to His Majesty and the Parliament; and to implore Relief." In October, twenty-seven delegates from nine colonies met in New York's City Hall (the building later known as Federal Hall) in what one member called "an Assembly of the greatest Ability I ever Yet saw." Although the Stamp Act Congress declared that the colonists owed "all due Subordination to that August Body the Parliament of Great Britain," it also stated that "it is inseparably essential to the Freedom of a People, and the undoubted Right of Englishmen, that no Taxes should be imposed on them, but with their own Consent, given personally, or by their Representatives." And since "the People of these Colonies are not, and from their local Circumstances cannot be, Represented in the House of Commons in Great Britain," that consent could only be given by persons who were chosen by themselves and who served in their respective provincial legislatures.

Meanwhile, in England, George III had replaced Grenville's ministry in July with one headed by Lord Rockingham that was promptly faced with the task of repealing the Stamp Act, now viewed as insupportable in the face of opposition in the colonies and at home. It would not be easy. As Benjamin Franklin explained to Lord Dartmouth, the newly appointed head of the Board of Trade, repeal "will be deem'd a tacit giving up of the Sovereignty of Parliament." Once the British government engaged Parliament as the instrument for reforming the empire, it had raised the stakes to the highest possible level. It is difficult today to appreciate the awe and wonder with which nearly all Englishmen held Parliament in the eighteenth century. Opposing royal power on behalf of liberty was what good Whigs did. But opposing Parliament—the bulwark that stood between the people and monarchical tyranny—was altogether a different matter. As the locus of sovereignty in the British constitution, Parliament was seen by most Englishmen to be beyond challenge. Unlike the American Bill of

Rights, which restrains the entire federal government, including the Congress, the English Bill of Rights placed limits solely on the Crown. Being the creator of the Bill of Rights, Parliament retained the power to rescind these rights: the king could not dispence with or suspend laws, for instance, but Parliament could. Forcing this imposing body to disavow something it had done ran deeply against the grain of Whig thinking.

The Rockingham ministry decided to call upon Franklin, the most famous American in London, to provide cover for Parliament's repeal of the Stamp Act. His three-hour testimony before the House of Commons on February 13, 1766, was effective, and the next month Parliament undid what it had done the previous year. To ease the pain of this humiliating retreat, it accompanied its repeal of the Stamp Act with a Declaratory Act which stated that the Parliament had full authority to bind the colonists "in all Cases whatsoever." If the British government was unable to collect any actual stamp taxes, at least it had made the point that it had the right to.

The EXAMINATION of Doctor BENJAMIN FRANKLIN, *before an* AUGUST ASSEMBLY, *relating to the Repeal of the STAMP-ACT*, &c.

Q. WHAT is your name, and place of abode?

A. Franklin, of Philadelphia.

Q. Do the Americans pay any confiderable taxes among themfelves?

A. Certainly many, and very heavy taxes.

Q. What are the prefent taxes in Pennfylvania, laid by the laws of the Colony?

A. There are taxes on all eftates real and perfonal, a poll tax, a tax on all offices, profeffions, trades and bufineffes, according to their profits; an excife on all wine, rum, and other fpirits; and a duty of Ten Pounds per head on all Negroes imported, with fome other duties.

Q. For what purpofes are thofe taxes laid?

A. For the fupport of the civil and military eftablifhments of the country, and to difcharge the heavy debt contracted in the laft war.

Q. How long are thofe taxes to continue?

A. Thofe for difcharging the debt are to continue till 1772, and longer, if the debt fhould not be then all difcharged. The others muft always continue.

Q. Was it not expected that the debt would have been fooner difcharged?

A. It was, when the peace was made with France and Spain----But a frefh war breaking out with the Indians, a frefh load of debt was incurred, and the taxes, of courfe, continued longer by a new law.

Q. Are not all the people very able to pay thofe taxes?

A. No. The frontier counties, all along the continent, having been frequently ravaged by the enemy, and greatly impoverifhed, are able to pay very little tax. And therefore, in confideration of their diftreffes, our late tax laws do exprefly favour thofe counties, excufing the fufferers; and I fuppofe the fame is done in other governments.

Q. Are not you concerned in the management of the Poft-Office in America?

A. Yes. I am Deputy Poft-Mafter General of North-America.

Q. Don't you think the diftribution of ftamps, by poft, to all the inhabitants, very practicable, if there was no oppofition?

A. The pofts only go along the fea coafts; they do not, except in a few inftances, go back into the country; and if they did, fending for ftamps by poft would occafion an expence of poftage, amounting, in many cafes, to much more than that of the ftamps themfelves.

Q. Are you acquainted with Newfoundland?

A. I never was there.

Q. Do you know whether there are any poft roads on that ifland?

A. I have heard that there are no roads at all; but that the communication between one fettlement and another is by fea only.

Q. Can you difpenfe the ftamps by poft in Canada?

A. There

The Examination of Doctor Benjamin Franklin, before an August Assembly, Relating to the Repeal of the Stamp-Act, &c.

Q. WHAT is your name, and place of abode?

A. Franklin, of Philadelphia.

Q. Do the Americans pay any considerable taxes among themselves?

A. Certainly many, and very heavy taxes.

Q. What are the present taxes in Pennsylvania, laid by the laws of the Colony?

A. There are taxes on all estates real and personal, a poll tax, a tax on all offices, professions, trades and businesses, according to their profits; an excise on all wine, rum, and other spirits; and a duty of Ten Pounds per head on all Negroes imported, with some other duties.

Q. For what purposes are those taxes laid?

A. For the support of the civil and military establishments of the country, and to discharge the heavy debt contracted in the last war.

Q. How long are those taxes to continue?

A. Those for discharging the debt are to continue till 1772, and longer, if the debt should not be then all discharged. The others must always continue.

Q. Was it not expected that the debt would have been sooner discharged?

A. It was, when the peace was made with France and Spain—But a fresh war breaking out with the Indians, a fresh load of debt was incurred, and the taxes, of course, continued longer by a new law.

Q. Are not all the people very able to pay those taxes?

A. No. The frontier counties, all along the continent, having been frequently ravaged by the enemy, and greatly impoverished, are able to pay very little tax. And therefore, in consideration of their distresses, our late tax laws do expresly favour those counties, excusing the sufferers; and I suppose the same is done in other governments.

Q. Are not you concerned in the management of the Post-Office in America?

A. Yes. I am Deputy Post-Master General of North-America.

Q. Don't you think the distribution of stamps, by post, to all the inhabitants, very practicable, if there was no opposition?

A. The posts only go along the sea coasts; they do not, except in a few instances, go back into the country; and if they did, sending for stamps by post would occasion an expence of postage, amounting, in many cases, to much more than that of the stamps themselves.

Q. Are you acquainted with Newfoundland?

A. I never was there.

Q. Do you know whether there are any post roads on that island?

A. I have heard that there are no roads at all; but that the communication between one settlement and another is by sea only.

Q. Can you dispense the stamps by post in Canada?

A. There is only a post between Montreal and Quebec. The inhabitants live so scattered and remote from each other, in that vast country, that posts cannot be supported among them, and therefore they cannot get stamps per post. The English Colonies too, along the frontiers, are very thinly settled.

Q. From the thinness of the back settlements, would not the stamp-act be extreamly inconvenient to the inhabitants, if executed?

A. To be sure it would; as many of the inhabitants could not get stamps when they had occasion for them, without taking long journeys, and spending perhaps Three or Four Pounds, that the Crown might get Sixpence.

Q. Are not the Colonies, from their circumstances, very able to pay the stamp duty?

A. In my opinion, there is not gold and silver enough in the Colonies to pay the stamp duty for one year.

Q. Don't you know that the money arising from the stamps was all to be laid out in America?

A. I know it is appropriated by the act to the American service; but it will be spent in the conquered Colonies, where the soldiers are, not in the Colonies that pay it.

Q. Is there not a ballance of trade due from the Colonies

where the troops are posted, that will bring back the money to the old Colonies?

A. I think not. I believe very little would come back. I know of no trade likely to bring it back. I think it would come from the Colonies where it was spent directly to England; for I have always observed, that in every Colony the more plenty the means of remittance to England, the more goods are sent for, and the more trade with England carried on.

Q. What number of white inhabitants do you think there are in Pennsylvania?

A. I suppose there may be about 160,000.

Q. What number of them are Quakers?

A. Perhaps a third.

Q. What number of Germans?

A. Perhaps another third; but I cannot speak with certainty.

Q. Have any number of the Germans seen service, as soldiers, in Europe?

A. Yes,—many of them, both in Europe and America.

Q. Are they as much dissatisfied with the stamp duty as the English?

A. Yes, and more; and with reason, as their stamps are, in many cases, to be double.

Q. How many white men do you suppose there are in North-America?

A. About 300,000, from sixteen to sixty years of age.

Q. What may be the amount of one year's imports into Pennsylvania from Britain?

A. I have been informed that our merchants compute the imports from Britain to be above 500,000 Pounds.

Q. What may be the amount of the produce of your province exported to Britain?

A. It must be small, as we produce little that is wanted in Britain. I suppose it cannot exceed 40,000 Pounds.

Q. How then do you pay the ballance?

A. The ballance is paid by our produce carried to the West-Indies, and sold in our own islands, or to the French, Spaniards, Danes and Dutch; by the same carried to other colonies in North-America, as to New-England, Nova-Scotia, Newfoundland, Carolina and Georgia; by the same carried to different parts of Europe, as Spain, Portugal and Italy. In all which places we receive either money, bills of exchange, or commodities that suit for remittance to Britain; which, together with all the profits on the industry of our merchants and mariners, arising in those circuitous voyages, and the freights made by their ships, center finally in Britain, to discharge the ballance, and pay for British manufactures continually used in the province, or sold to foreigners by our traders.

Q. Have you heard of any difficulties lately laid on the Spanish trade?

A. Yes, I have heard that it has been greatly obstructed by some new regulations, and by the English men of war and cutters stationed all along the coast in America.

Q. Do you think it right that America should be protected by this country, and pay no part of the expence?

A. That is not the case. The Colonies raised, cloathed and paid, during the last war, near 25000 men, and spent many millions.

Q. Were you not reimbursed by parliament?

A. We were only reimbursed what, in your opinion, we had advanced beyond our proportion, or beyond what might reasonably be expected from us; and it was a very small part of what we spent. Pennsylvania, in particular, disbursed about 500,000 Pounds, and the reimbursements, in the whole, did not exceed 60,000 Pounds.

Q. You have said that you pay heavy taxes in Pennsylvania; what do they amount to in the Pound?

A. The tax on all estates, real and personal, is Eighteen Pence in the Pound, fully rated; and the tax on the profits of trades and professions, with other taxes, do, I suppose, make full Half a Crown in the Pound.

Q. Do you know any thing of the rate of exchange in Pennsylvania, and whether it is fallen lately?

A. It is commonly from 170 to 175. I have heard that it has fallen lately from 175 to 162 and a half, owing, I suppose, to their lessening their orders for goods; and when their debts to this country are paid, I think the exchange will probably be at par.

Q. Do not you think the people of America would submit to pay the stamp duty, if it was moderated?

A. No, never, unless compelled by force of arms.

Q. Are not the taxes in Pennsylvania laid on unequally, in order to burthen the English trade, particularly the tax on professions and business?

A. It is not more burthensome in proportion than the tax on lands. It is intended, and supposed to take an equal proportion of profits.

Q. How is the assembly composed? Of what kinds of people are the members, landholders or traders?

A. It is composed of landholders, merchants and artificers.

Q. Are not the majority landholders?

A. I believe they are.

Q. Do not they, as much as possible, shift the tax off from the land, to ease that, and lay the burthen heavier on trade?

A. I have never understood it so. I never heard such a thing suggested. And indeed an attempt of that kind could answer no purpose. The merchant or trader is always skilled in figures, and ready with his pen and ink. If unequal burthens are laid on his trade, he puts an additional price on his goods; and the consumers, who are chiefly landholders, finally pay the greatest part, if not the whole.

Q. What was the temper of America towards Great-Britain before the year 1763?

A. The best in the world. They submitted willingly to the government of the Crown, and paid, in all their courts, obedience to acts of parliament. Numerous as the people are in the several old provinces, they cost you nothing in forts, citadels, garrisons or armies, to keep them in subjection. They were governed by this country at the expence only of a little pen, ink and paper. They were led by a thread. They had not only a respect, but an affection, for Great-Britain, for its laws, its customs and manners, and even a fondness for its fashions, that greatly increased the commerce. Natives of Britain were always treated with particular regard; to be an Old England-man, was, of itself, a character of some respect, and gave a kind of rank among us.

Q. And what is their temper now?

A. O, very much altered.

Q. Did you ever hear the authority of parliament to make laws for America questioned till lately?

A. The authority of parliament was allowed to be valid in all laws, except such as should lay internal taxes. It was never disputed in laying duties to regulate commerce.

Q. In what proportion hath population increased in America?

A. I think the inhabitants of all the provinces together, taken at a medium, double in about 25 years. But their demand for British manufactures increases much faster, as the consumption is not merely in proportion to their numbers, but grows with the growing abilities of the same numbers to pay for them. In 1723, the whole importation from Britain to Pennsylvania, was but about 15,000 Pounds Sterling; it is now near Half a Million.

Q. In what light did the people of America use to consider the parliament of Great-Britain?

A. They considered the parliament as the great bulwark and security of their liberties and privileges, and always spoke of it with the utmost respect and veneration. Arbitrary ministers, they thought, might possibly, at times, attempt to oppress them; but they relied on it, that the parliament, on application, would always give redress. They remembered, with gratitude, a strong instance of this, when a bill was brought into parliament, with a clause to make royal instructions laws in the Colonies, which the house of commons would not pass, and it was thrown out.

Q. And have they not still the same respect for parliament?

A. No; it is greatly lessened.

Q. To what causes is that owing?

A. To a concurrence of causes; the restraints lately laid on their trade, by which the bringing of foreign gold and silver into the Colonies was prevented; the prohibition of making paper money among themselves; and then demanding a new and heavy tax by stamps; taking away, at the same time, trials by juries, and refusing to receive and hear their humble petitions.

Q. Don't you think they would submit to the stamp-act, if it was modified, the obnoxious parts taken out, and the duty reduced to some particulars, of small moment?

A. No; they will never submit to it.

Q. What do you think is the reason that the people of America increase faster than in England?

A. Because they marry younger, and more generally.

Q. Why so?

A. Because any young couple that are industrious, may easily obtain land of their own, on which they can raise a family.

Q. Are not the lower rank of people more at their ease in America than in England?

A. They may be so, if they are sober and diligent, as they are better paid for their labour.

Q. What is your opinion of a future tax, imposed on the same principle with that of the stamp act; how would the Americans receive it?

A. Just as they do this. They would not pay it.

Q. Have you not heard of the resolutions of this house, and of the house of lords, asserting the right of parliament relating to America, including a power to tax the people there?

A. Yes, I have heard of such resolutions.

Q. What will be the opinion of the Americans on those resolutions?

A. They will think them unconstitutional, and unjust.

Q. Was it an opinion in America before 1763, that the parliament had no right to lay taxes and duties there?

A. I never heard any objection to the right of laying duties to regulate commerce; but a right to lay internal taxes was never supposed to be in parliament, as we are not represented there.

Q. On what do you found your opinion, that the people in America made any such distinction?

A. I know that whenever the subject has occurred in conversation where I have been present, it has appeared to be the opinion of every one, that we could not be taxed in a parliament where we were not represented. But the payment of duties laid by act of parliament, as regulations of commerce, was never disputed.

Q. But can you name any act of assembly, or public act of any of your governments, that made such distinction?

A. I do not know that there was any; I think there was never an occasion to make any such act, till now that you have attempted to tax us; that has occasioned resolutions of assembly, declaring the distinction, in which I think every assembly on the continent, and every member in every assembly, have been unanimous.

Q. What then could occasion conversations on that subject before that time?

A. There was in 1754 a proposition made (I think it came from hence) that in case of a war, which was then apprehended, the governors of the Colonies should meet, and order the levying of troops, building of forts, and taking every other necessary measure for the general defence; and should draw on the treasury here for the sums expended, which were afterwards to be raised in the Colonies by a general tax, to be laid on them by act of parliament. This occasioned a good deal of conversation on the subject, and the general opinion was, that the parliament neither would nor could lay any tax on us, till we were duly represented in parliament, because it was not just, nor agreeable to the nature of an English constitution.

Q. Don't you know there was a time in New-York, when it was under consideration to make an application to parliament to lay taxes on that Colony, upon a deficiency arising from the assembly's refusing or neglecting to raise the necessary supplies for the support of the civil government?

A. I never heard of it.

Q. There was such an application under consideration in New-York; and do you apprehend they could suppose the right of parliament to lay a tax in America was only local, and confined to the case of a deficiency in a particular Colony, by a refusal of its assembly to raise the necessary supplies?

A. They could not suppose such a case, as that the assembly would not raise the necessary supplies to support its own government. An assembly that would refuse it must want common sense, which cannot be supposed. I think there was never any such case at New-York, and that it must be a misrepresentation, or the fact must be misunderstood. I know there have been some attempts, by ministerial instructions from hence, to oblige the assemblies to settle permanent salaries on governors, which they wisely refused to do; but I believe no assembly of New-York, or any other Colony, ever refused duly to support government by proper allowances, from time to time, to public officers.

Q. But in case a governor, acting by instruction, should call on an assembly to raise the necessary supplies, and the assembly should refuse to do it, do you not think it would then be for the good of the people of the colony, as well as necessary to government, that the parliament should tax them?

A. I do not think it would be necessary. If an assembly could possibly be so absurd as to refuse raising the supplies requisite for the maintenance of government among them, they could not long remain in such a situation; the disorders and confusion occasioned by it must soon bring them to reason.

Q. If it should not, ought not the right to be in Great-Britain of applying a remedy?

A. A right only to be used in such a case, I should have no objection to, supposing it to be used merely for the good of the people of the Colony.

Q. But who is to judge of that, Britain or the Colony?

A. Those that feel can best judge.

Q. You say the Colonies have always submitted to external taxes, and object to the right of parliament only in laying internal taxes; now can you shew that there is any kind of difference between the two taxes to the Colony on which they may be laid?

A. I think the difference is very great. An external tax is a duty laid on commodities imported; that duty is added to the first cost, and other charges on the commodity, and when it is offered to sale, makes a part of the price. If the people do not like it at that price, they refuse it; they are not obliged to pay it. But an internal tax is forced from the people without their consent, if not laid by their own representatives. The stamp-act says, we shall have no commerce, make no exchange of property with each other, neither purchase nor grant, nor recover debts; we shall neither marry, nor make our wills, unless we pay such and such sums, and thus it is intended to extort our money from us, or ruin us by the consequences of refusing to pay it.

Q. But supposing the external tax or duty to be laid on the necessaries of life imported into your Colony, will not that be the same thing in its effects as an internal tax?

A. I do not know a single article imported into the Northern Colonies, but what they can either do without, or make themselves.

Q. Don't you think cloth from England absolutely necessary to them?

A. No, by no means absolutely necessary; with industry and good management, that may very well supply themselves with all they want.

Q. Will it not take a long time to establish that manufacture among them? and must they not in the mean while suffer greatly?

A. I think not. They have made a surprising progress already. And I am of opinion, that before their old clothes are worn out, they will have new ones of their own making.

Q. Can they possibly find wool enough in North-America?

A. They have taken steps to increase the wool. They entered into general combinations to eat no more lamb, and very few lambs were killed last year. This course persisted in, will soon make a prodigious difference in the quantity of wool. And the establishing of great manufactories, like those in the clothing towns here, is not necessary, as it is where the business is to be carried on for the purposes of trade. The people will all spin, and work for themselves, in their own houses.

Q. Can there be wool and manufacture enough in one or two years?

A. In three years, I think, there may.

Q. Does not the severity of the winter, in the Northern Colonies, occasion the wool to be of bad quality?

A. No; the wool is very fine and good.

Q. In the more Southern Colonies, as in Virginia; don't you know that the wool is coarse, and only a kind of hair?

A. I don't know it. I never heard it. Yet I have been sometimes in Virginia. I cannot say I ever took particular notice of the wool there, but I believe it is good, though I cannot speak positively of it; but Virginia, and the Colonies south of it, have less occasion for wool; their winters are short, and not very severe, and they can very well clothe themselves with linen and cotton of their own raising for the rest of the year.

Q. Are not the people, in the more Northern Colonies, obliged to fodder their sheep all the winter?

A. In some of the most Northern Colonies they may be obliged to do it some part of the winter.

Q. Considering the resolutions of parliament, as to the right, do you think, if the stamp-act is repealed, that the North Americans will be satisfied?

A. I believe they will.

Q. Why do you think so?

A. I think the resolutions of right will give them very little concern, if they are never attempted to be carried into practice. The Colonies will probably consider themselves in the same situation, in that respect, with Ireland; they know you claim the same right with regard to Ireland, but you never exercise it. And they may believe you never will exercise it in the Colonies, any more than in Ireland, unless on some very extraordinary occasion.

Q. But who are to be the judges of that extraordinary occasion? Is it not the parliament?

A. Though the parliament may judge of the occasion, the people will think it can never exercise such right, till representatives from the Colonies are admitted into parliament, and that whenever the occasion arises, representatives will be ordered.

Q. Did you never hear that Maryland, during the last war, had refused to furnish a quota towards the common defence?

A. Maryland has been much misrepresented in that matter. Maryland, to my knowledge, never refused to contribute, or grant aids to the Crown. The assemblies every year, during the war, voted considerable sums, and formed bills to raise them. The bills were, according to the constitution of that province, sent up to the council, or upper house, for concurrence, that they might be presented to the governor, in order to be enacted into laws. Unhappy disputes between the two houses arising, from the defects of that constitution principally, rendered all the bills but one or two abortive. The proprietary's council rejected them. It is true Maryland did not contribute its proportion, but it was, in my opinion, the fault of the government, not of the people.

Q. Was it not talked of in the other provinces as a proper measure to apply to parliament to compel them?

A. I have heard such discourse; but as it was well known, that the people were not to blame, no such application was ever made, nor any step taken towards it.

Q. Was it not proposed at a public meeting?

A. Not that I know of.

Q. Do you remember the abolishing of the paper currency in New England, by act of assembly?

A. I do remember its being abolished, in the Massachusett's Bay.

Q. Was not Lieutenant Governor Hutchinson principally concerned in that transaction?

A. I have heard so.

Q. Was it not at that time a very unpopular law?

A. I believe it might, though I can say little about it, as I lived at a distance from that province.

Q. Was not the scarcity of gold and silver an argument used against abolishing the paper?

A. I suppose it was.

Q. What is the present opinion there of that law? Is it as unpopular as it was at first?

A. I think it is not.

Q. Have not instructions from hence been sometimes sent over to governors, highly oppressive and unpolitical?

A. Yes.

Q. Have not some governors dispensed with them for that reason?

A. Yes; I have heard so.

Q. Did the Americans ever dispute the controling power of parliament to regulate the commerce?

A. No.

Q. Can any thing less than a military force carry the stamp-act into execution?

A. I do not see how a military force can be applied to that purpose.

Q. Why may it not?

A. Suppose a military force sent into America, they will find nobody in arms; what are they then to do? They cannot force a man to take stamps who chooses to do without them. They will not find a rebellion; they may indeed make one.

Q. If the act is not repealed, what do you think will be the consequences?

A. A total loss of the respect and affection the people of America bear to this country, and of all the commerce that depends on that respect and affection.

Q. How can the commerce be affected?

A. You will find, that if the act is not repealed, they will take very little of your manufactures in a short time.

Q. Is it in their power to do without them?

A. I think they may very well do without them.

Q. Is it their interest not to take them?

A. The goods they take from Britain are either necessaries, mere conveniences, or superfluities. The first, as cloth, &c. with a little industry they can make at home; the second they can do without, till they are able to provide them among themselves; and the last, which are much the greatest part, they will strike off immediately. They are mere articles of fashion, purchased and consumed, because the fashion in a respected country, but will now be detested and rejected. The people have already struck off, by general agreement, the use of all goods fashionable in mournings, and many thousand pounds worth are sent back as unsaleable.

Q. Is it their interest to make cloth at home?

A. I think they may at present get it cheaper from Britain, I mean of the same fineness and neatness of workmanship; but when one considers other circumstances, the restraints on their trade, and the difficulty of making remittances, it is their interest to make every thing.

Q. Suppose an act of internal regulation, connected with a tax, how would they receive it?

A. I think it would be objected to.

Q. Then no regulation with a tax would be submitted to?

A. Their opinion is, that when aids to the Crown are wanted, they are to be asked of the several assemblies, according to the old established usage, who will, as they always have done, grant them freely. And that their money ought not to be given away without their consent, by persons at a distance, unacquainted with their circumstances and abilities. The granting aids to the Crown, is the only means they have of recommending themselves to their sovereign, and they think it extremely hard and unjust, that a body of men, in which they have no representatives, should make a merit to itself of giving and granting what is not its own, but theirs, and deprive them of a right they esteem of the utmost value and importance, as it is the security of all their other rights.

Q. But is not the post-office, which they have long received, a tax as well as a regulation?

A. No; the money paid for the postage of a letter is not of

the nature of a tax; it is merely a quantum meruit for a service done; no person is compellable to pay the money, if he does not chuse to receive the service. A man may still, as before the act, send his letter by a servant, a special messenger, or a friend, if he thinks it cheaper and safer.

Q. But do they not consider the regulations of the post-office, by the act of last year, as a tax?

A. By the regulations of last year the rate of postage was generally abated near thirty per cent. through all America; they certainly cannot consider such abatement as a tax.

Q. If an excise was laid by parliament, which they might likewise avoid paying, by not consuming the articles excised, would they then not object to it?

A. They would certainly object to it, as an excise is unconnected with any service done, and is merely an aid which they think ought to be asked of them, and granted by them, if they are to pay it, and can be granted for them by no others whatsoever, whom they have not impowered for that purpose.

Q. You say they do not object to the right of parliament in laying duties on goods to be paid on their importation; now, is there any kind of difference between a duty on the importation of goods, and an excise on their consumption?

A. Yes; a very material one; an excise, for the reasons I have just mentioned, they think you can have no right to lay within their country. But the sea is yours; you maintain, by your fleets, the safety of navigation in it; and keep it clear of pirates; you may have therefore a natural and equitable right to some toll or duty on merchandizes carried through that part of your dominions, towards defraying the expence you are at in ships to maintain the safety of that carriage.

Q. Does this reasoning hold in the case of a duty laid on the produce of their lands exported? and would they not then object to such a duty?

A. If it tended to make the produce so much dearer abroad as to lessen the demand for it, to be sure they would object to such a duty; not to your right of laying it, but they would complain of it as a burthen, and petition you to lighten it.

Q. Is not the duty paid on the tobacco exported a duty of that kind?

A. That, I think, is only on tobacco carried coastwise from

one Colony to another, and appropriated as a fund for supporting the college at Williamsburgh, in Virginia.

Q. Have not the assemblies in the West-Indies the same natural rights with those in North America?

A. Undoubtedly.

Q. And is there not a tax laid there on their sugars exported?

A. I am not much acquainted with the West-Indies, but the duty of four and a half per cent. on sugars exported, was, I believe, granted by their own assemblies.

Q. How much is the poll-tax in your province laid on unmarried men?

A. It is, I think, Fifteen Shillings, to be paid by every single freeman, upwards of twenty-one years old.

Q. What is the annual amount of all the taxes in Pennsylvania?

A. I suppose about 20,000 Pounds sterling.

Q. Supposing the stamp-act continued, and enforced, do you imagine that ill humour will induce the Americans to give as much for worse manufactures of their own, and use them, preferably to better of ours?

A. Yes, I think so. People will pay as freely to gratify one passion as another, their resentment as their pride.

Q. Would the people at Boston discontinue their trade?

A. The merchants are a very small number, compared with the body of the people, and must discontinue their trade, if nobody will buy their goods.

Q. What are the body of the people in the Colonies?

A. They are farmers, husbandmen or planters.

Q. Would they suffer the produce of their lands to rot?

A. No; but they would not raise so much. They would manufacture more, and plough less.

Q. Would they live without the administration of justice in civil matters, and suffer all the inconveniencies of such a situation for any considerable time, rather than take the stamps, supposing the stamps were protected by a sufficient force, where every one might have them?

A. I think the supposition impracticable, that the stamps should be so protected as that every one might have them. The act requires sub-distributors to be appointed in every county town, district and village, and they would be necessary.

But the principal distributors, who were to have had a considerable profit on the whole, have not thought it worth while to continue in the office, and I think it impossible to find sub-distributors fit to be trusted, who, for the trifling profit that must come to their share, would incur the odium, and run the hazard that would attend it; and if they could be found, I think it impracticable to protect the stamps in so many distant and remote places.

Q. But in places where they could be protected, would not the people use them rather than remain in such a situation, unable to obtain any right, or recover, by law, any debt?

A. It is hard to say what they would do. I can only judge what other people will think, and how they will act, by what I feel within myself. I have a great many debts due to me in America, and I had rather they should remain unrecoverable by any law, than submit to the stamp-act. They will be debts of honour. It is my opinion the people will either continue in that situation, or find some way to extricate themselves, perhaps by generally agreeing to proceed in the courts without stamps.

Q. What do you think a sufficient military force to protect the distribution of the stamps in every part of America?

A. A very great force; I can't say what, if the disposition of America is for a general resistance.

Q. What is the number of men in America able to bear arms, or of disciplined militia?

A. There are, I suppose, at least—

   [*Question objected to. He withdrew. Called in again.*]

Q. Is the American stamp-act an equal tax on that country?

A. I think not.

Q. Why so?

A. The greatest part of the money must arise from law suits for the recovery of debts, and be paid by the lower sort of people, who were too poor easily to pay their debts. It is therefore a heavy tax on the poor, and a tax upon them for being poor.

Q. But will not this increase of expence be a means of lessening the number of law suits?

A. I think not; for as the costs all fall upon the debtor, and are to be paid by him, they would be no discouragement to the creditor to bring his action.

Q. Would it not have the effect of excessive usury?

A. Yes, as an oppression of the debtor.

Q. How many ships are there laden annually in North-America with flax-seed for Ireland?

A. I cannot speak to the number of ships, but I know that in 1752, 10,000 hogsheads of flax-seed, each containing 7 bushels, were exported from Philadelphia to Ireland. I suppose the quantity is greatly increased since that time; and it is understood that the exportation from New York is equal to that from Philadelphia.

Q. What becomes of the flax that grows with that flax-seed?

A. They manufacture some into coarse, and some into a middling kind of linen.

Q. Are there any slitting mills in America?

A. I think there are, but I believe only one at present employed. I suppose they will all be set to work, if the interruption of the trade continues.

Q. Are there any fulling mills there?

A. A great many.

Q. Did you never hear that a great quantity of stockings were contracted for the army during the war, and manufactured in Philadelphia?

A. I have heard so.

Q. If the stamp act should be repealed, would not the Americans think they could oblige the parliament to repeal every external tax law now in force?

A. It is hard to answer questions of what people at such a distance will think.

Q. But what do you imagine they will think were the motives of repealing the act?

A. I suppose they will think that it was repealed from a conviction of its inexpediency; and they will rely upon it, that while the same inexpediency subsists, you will never attempt to make such another.

Q. What do you mean by its inexpediency?

A. I mean its inexpediency on several accounts; the poverty and inability of those who were to pay the tax; the general discontent it has occasioned; and the impracticability of enforcing it.

Q. If the act should be repealed, and the legislature should shew its resentment to the opposers of the stamp-act, would the Colonies acquiesce in the authority of the legislature? What is your opinion they would do?

A. I don't doubt at all, that if the legislature repeal the stamp-act, the Colonies will acquiesce in the authority.

Q. But if the legislature should think fit to ascertain its right to lay taxes, by any act laying a small tax, contrary to their opinion, would they submit to pay the tax?

A. The proceedings of the people in America have been considered too much together. The proceedings of the assemblies have been very different from those of the mobs, and should be distinguished, as having no connection with each other.—The assemblies have only peaceably resolved what they take to be their rights; they have taken no measures for opposition by force; they have not built a fort, raised a man, or provided a grain of ammunition, in order to such opposition. —The ringleaders of riots they think ought to be punished; they would punish them themselves, if they could. Every sober sensible man would wish to see rioters punished, as otherwise peaceable people have no security of person or estate. But as to any internal tax, how small soever, laid by the legislature here on the people there, while they have no representatives in this legislature, I think it will never be submitted to.—They will oppose it to the last.—They do not consider it as at all necessary for you to raise money on them by your taxes, because they are, and always have been, ready to raise money by taxes among themselves, and to grant large sums, equal to their abilities, upon requisition from the Crown.—They have not only granted equal to their abilities, but, during all the last war, they granted far beyond their abilities, and beyond their proportion with this country, you yourselves being judges, to the amount of many hundred thousand pounds, and this they did freely and readily, only on a sort of promise from the secretary of state, that it should be recommended to parliament to make them compensation. It was accordingly recommended to parliament, in the most honourable manner, for them. America has been greatly misrepresented and abused here, in papers, and pamphlets, and speeches, as ungrateful, and unreasonable, and unjust, in having put this nation to immense expence for their defence, and refusing to bear any part of that expence. The Colonies raised, paid and clothed, near 25000 men during the last war, a number equal to those sent from Britain, and far beyond their proportion; they went deeply into debt in doing this, and all their taxes and estates are mortgaged, for many years to come, for discharging that debt. Government here was at that time very sensible of this. The Colonies were recommended to parliament. Every year the King sent down to the house a written message to this purpose, That his Majesty, being highly sensible of the zeal and vigour with which his faithful subjects in North-America had exerted themselves, in defence of his Majesty's just rights and possessions, recommended it to the house to take the same into consideration, and enable him to give them a proper compensation. You will find those messages on your own journals every year of the war to the very last, and you did accordingly give 200,000 Pounds annually to the Crown, to be distributed in such compensation to the Colonies. This is the strongest of all proofs that the Colonies, far from being unwilling to bear a share of the burthen, did exceed their proportion; for if they had done less, or had only equalled their proportion, there would have been no room or reason for compensation.—Indeed the sums reimbursed them, were by no means adequate to the expence they incurred beyond their proportion; but they never murmured at that; they esteemed their Sovereign's approbation of their zeal and fidelity, and the approbation of this house, far beyond any other kind of compensation; therefore there was no occasion for this act, to force money from a willing people; they had not refused giving money for the purposes of the act; no requisition had been made; they were always willing and ready to do what could reasonably be expected from them, and in this light they wish to be considered.

Q. But suppose Great-Britain should be engaged in a war in Europe, would North-America contribute to the support of it?

A. I do think they would, as far as their circumstances would permit. They consider themselves as a part of the British empire, and as having one common interest with it; they may be looked on here as foreigners, but they do not consider themselves as such. They are zealous for the honour and prosperity of this nation, and, while they are well used, will always be ready to support it, as far as their little power goes. In 1739 they were called upon to assist in the expedition against Carthagena, and they sent 3000 men to join your army. It is true Carthagena is in America, but as remote from the Northern Colonies, as if it had been in Europe. They make no distinction of wars, as to their duty of assisting in them. I know the last war is commonly spoke of here as entered into for the defence, or for the sake of the people of America. I think it is quite misunderstood. It began about the limits between Canada and Nova-Scotia, about territories to which the Crown indeed laid claim, but were not claimed by any British Colony; none of the lands had been granted to any Colonist; we had therefore no particular concern or interest in that dispute. As to the Ohio, the contest there began about your right of trading in the Indian country, a right you had by the treaty of Utrecht, which the French infringed; they seized the traders and their goods, which were your manufactures; they took a fort which a company of your merchants, and their factors and correspondents, had erected there, to secure that trade. Braddock was sent with an army to re-take that fort (which was looked on here as another incroachment on the King's territory) and to protect your trade. It was not till after his defeat that the Colonies were attacked. They were before in perfect peace with both French and Indians; the troops were not therefore sent for their defence. The trade with the Indians, though carried on in America, is not an American interest. The people of America are chiefly farmers and planters; scarce any thing that they raise or produce is an article of commerce with the Indians. The Indian trade is a British interest; it is carried on with British manufactures, for the profit of British merchants and manufacturers; therefore the war, as it commenced for the defence of territories of the Crown, the property of no American, and for the defence of a trade purely British, was really a British war—and yet the people of America made no scruple of contributing their utmost towards carrying it on, and bringing it to a happy conclusion.

Q. Do you think then that the taking possession of the King's territorial rights, and strengthening the frontiers, is not an American interest?

A. Not particularly, but conjointly a British and an American interest.

Q. You will not deny that the preceding war, the war with Spain, was entered into for the sake of America; was it not occasioned by captures made in the American seas?

A. Yes; captures of ships carrying on the British trade there, with British manufactures.

Q. Was not the late war with the Indians, since the peace with France, a war for America only?

A. Yes; it was more particularly for America than the former, but it was rather a consequence or remains of the former war, the Indians not having been thoroughly pacified, and the Americans bore by much the greatest share of the expence. It was put an end to by the army under General Bouquet; there were not above 300 regulars in that army, and above 1000 Pennsylvanians.

Q. Is it not necessary to send troops to America, to defend the Americans against the Indians?

A. No, by no means; it never was necessary. They defended themselves when they were but an handful, and the Indians much more numerous. They continually gained ground, and have driven the Indians over the mountains, without any troops sent to their assistance from this country. And can it be thought necessary now to send troops for their defence from those diminished Indian tribes, when the Colonies are become so populous, and so strong? There is not the least occasion for it; they are very able to defend themselves.

Q. Do you say there were no more than 300 regular troops employed in the late Indian war?

A. Not on the Ohio, or the frontiers of Pennsylvania, which was the chief part of the war that affected the Colonies. There were garrisons at Niagara, Fort Detroit, and those remote posts kept for the sake of your trade; I did not reckon them, but I believe that on the whole the number of Americans, or provincial troops, employed in the war, was greater than that of the regulars. I am not certain, but I think so.

Q. Do you think the assemblies have a right to levy money on the subject there, to grant to the Crown?

A. I certainly think so; they have always done it.

Q. Are they acquainted with the declaration of rights? and do they know that, by that statute, money is not to be raised on the subject but by consent of parliament?

A. They are very well acquainted with it.

Q. How then can they think they have a right to levy money for the Crown, or for any other than local purposes?

A. They understand that clause to relate to subjects only within the realm; that no money can be levied on them for the Crown, but by consent of parliament. The Colonies are not supposed to be within the realm; they have assemblies of their own, which are their parliaments, and they are in that respect in the same situation with Ireland. When money is to be raised for the Crown upon the subject in Ireland, or in the Colonies, the consent is given in the parliament of Ireland, or in the assemblies of the Colonies. They think the parliament of Great-Britain cannot properly give that consent till it has representatives from America; for the petition of right expressly says, it is to be by common consent in parliament, and the people of America have no representatives in parliament, to make a part of that common consent.

Q. If the stamp-act should be repealed, and an act should pass, ordering the assemblies of the Colonies to indemnify the sufferers by the riots, would they obey it?

A. That is a question I cannot answer.

Q. Suppose the King should require the Colonies to grant a revenue, and the parliament should be against their doing it, do they think they can grant a revenue to the King, without the consent of the parliament of G Britain?

A. That is a deep question.—As to my own opinion, I should think myself at liberty to do it, and should do it, if I liked the occasion.

Q. When money has been raised in the Colonies upon requisitions, has it not been granted to the King?

A. Yes, always; but the requisitions have generally been for some service expressed, as to raise, clothe and pay troops, and not for money only.

Q. If the act should pass, requiring the American assemblies to make compensation to the sufferers, and they should disobey it, and then the parliament should, by another act, lay an internal tax, would they then obey it?

A. The people will pay no internal tax; and I think an act to oblige the assemblies to make compensation is unnecessary, for I am of opinion, that as soon as the present heats are abated, they will take the matter into consideration, and, if it is right to be done, they will do it of themselves.

Q. Do not letters often come into the post-offices in America, directed to some inland town where no post goes?

A. Yes.

Q. Can any private person take up those letters, and carry them as directed?

A. Yes; any friend of the person may do it, paying the postage that has occurred.

Q. But must he not pay an additional postage for the distance to such inland town?

A. No.

Q. Can the post-master answer delivering the letter, without being paid such additional postage?

A. Certainly he can demand nothing, where he does no service.

Q. Suppose a person, being far from home, finds a letter in a post-office directed to him, and he lives in a place to which the post generally goes, and the letter is directed to that place, will the post-master deliver him the letter, without his paying the postage receivable at the place to which the letter is directed?

A. Yes; the office cannot demand postage for a letter that it does not carry, or farther than it does carry it.

Q. Are not ferrymen in America obliged, by act of parliament, to carry over the posts without pay?

A. Yes.

Q. Is not this a tax on the ferrymen?

A. They do not consider it as such, as they have an advantage from persons travelling with the post.

Q. If the stamp-act should be repealed, and the Crown should make a requisition to the Colonies for a sum of money, would they grant it?

A. I believe they would.

Q. Why do you think so?

A. I can speak for the Colony I live in; I had it in instruction from the assembly to assure the ministry, that as they always had done, so they should always think it their duty to grant such aids to the Crown as were suitable to their circumstances and abilities, whenever called upon for the purpose, in the usual constitutional manner; and I had the honour of communicating this instruction to that honourable gentleman then minister.

Q. Would they do this for a British concern; as suppose a war in some part of Europe, that did not affect them?

A. Yes, for any thing that concerned the general interest. They consider themselves as a part of the whole.

Q. What is the usual constitutional manner of calling on the Colonies for aids?

A. A letter from the secretary of state.

Q. Is this all you mean, a letter from the secretary of state?

A. I mean the usual way of requisition, in a circular letter from the secretary of state, by his Majesty's command, reciting the occasion, and recommending it to the Colonies to grant such aids as became their loyalty, and were suitable to their abilities.

Q. Did the secretary of state ever write for money for the Crown?

A. The requisitions have been to raise, clothe and pay men, which cannot be done without money.

Q. Would they grant money alone, if called on?

A. In my opinion they would, money as well as men, when they have money, or can make it.

Q. If the parliament should repeal the stamp-act, will the assembly of Pennsylvania rescind their resolutions?

A. I think not.

Q. Before there was any thought of the stamp-act, did they wish for a representation in parliament?

A. No.

Q. Don't you know that there is, in the Pennsylvania charter, an express reservation of the right of parliament to lay taxes there?

A. I know there is a clause in the charter, by which the King grants that he will levy no taxes on the inhabitants, unless it be with the consent of the assembly, or by act of parliament.

Q. How then could the assembly of Pennsylvania assert, that laying a tax on them by the stamp-act was an infringement of their rights?

A. They understand it thus; by the same charter, and otherwise, they are intitled to all the privileges and liberties of

Englishmen; they find in the great charters, and the petition and declaration of rights, that one of the privileges of English subjects is, that they are not to be taxed but by their common consent; they have therefore relied upon it, from the first settlement of the province, that the parliament never would, nor could, by colour of that clause in the charter, assume a right of taxing them, till it had qualified itself to exercise such right, by admitting representatives from the people to be taxed, who ought to make a part of that common consent.

Q. Are there any words in the charter that justify that construction?

A. The common rights of Englishmen, as declared by Magna Charta, and the petition of right, all justify it.

Q. Does the distinction between internal and external taxes exist in the words of the charter?

A. No, I believe not.

Q. Then may they not, by the same interpretation, object to the parliament's right of external taxation?

A. They never have hitherto. Many arguments have been lately used here to shew them that there is no difference, and that if you have no right to tax them internally, you have none to tax them externally, or make any other law to bind them. At present they do not reason so, but in time they may possibly be convinced by these arguments.

Q. Do not the resolutions of the Pennsylvania assembly say all taxes?

A. If they do, they mean only internal taxes; the same words have not always the same meaning here and in the Colonies. By taxes they mean internal taxes; by duties they mean customs; these are their ideas of the language.

Q. Have you not seen the resolutions of the Massachusetts Bay assembly?

A. I have.

Q. Do they not say, that neither external nor internal taxes can be laid on them by parliament?

A. I don't know that they do; I believe not.

Q. If the same Colony should say neither tax nor imposition could be laid, does not that province hold the power of parliament can hold neither?

A. I suppose that by the word imposition, they do not

intend to express duties to be laid on goods imported, as regulations of commerce.

Q. What can the Colonies mean then by imposition as distinct from taxes?

A. They may mean many things, as impressing of men, or of carriages, quartering troops on private houses, and the like; there may be great impositions, that are not properly taxes.

Q. Is not the post-office rate an internal tax laid by act of parliament?

A. I have answered that.

Q. Are all parts of the Colonies equally able to pay taxes?

A. No, certainly; the frontier parts, which have been ravaged by the enemy, are greatly disabled by that means, and therefore, in such cases, are usually favoured in our tax laws.

Q. Can we, at this distance, be competent judges of what favours are necessary?

A. The parliament have supposed it, by claiming a right to make tax laws for America; I think it impossible.

Q. Would the repeal of the stamp-act be any discouragement of your manufactures? Will the people that have begun to manufacture decline it?

A. Yes, I think they will; especially if, at the same time, the trade is opened again, so that remittances can be easily made. I have known several instances that make it probable. In the war before last, tobacco being low, and making little remittance, the people of Virginia went generally into family manufactures. Afterwards, when tobacco bore a better price, they returned to the use of British manufactures. So fulling mills were very much difused in the last war in Pennsylvania, because bills were then plenty, and remittances could easily be made to Britain for English cloth and other goods.

Q. If the stamp-act should be repealed, would it induce the assemblies of America to acknowledge the rights of parliament to tax them, and would they erase their resolutions?

A. No, never.

Q. Is there no means of obliging them to erase those resolutions?

A. None that I know of; they will never do it unless compelled by force of arms.

Q. Is there a power on earth that can force them to erase them?

A. No power, how great soever, can force men to change their opinions.

Q. Do they consider the post-office as a tax, or as a regulation?

A. Not as a tax, but as a regulation and conveniency; every assembly encouraged it, and supported it in its infancy, by grants of money, which they would not otherwise have done; and the people have always paid the postage.

Q. When did you receive the instructions you mentioned?

A. I brought them with me, when I came to England, about 15 months since.

Q. When did you communicate that instruction to the minister?

A. Soon after my arrival, while the stamping of America was under consideration, and before the bill was brought in.

Q. Would it be most for the interest of Great-Britain, to employ the hands of Virginia in tobacco, or in manufactures?

A. In tobacco to be sure.

Q. What used to be the pride of the Americans?

A. To indulge in the fashions and manufactures of Great-Britain.

Q. What is now their pride?

A. To wear their old cloaths over again, till they can make new ones.

Withdrew.

The END.

[William Hicks], The Nature and Extent of Parliamentary Power Considered; in Some Remarks upon Mr. Pitt's Speech in the House of Commons, Previous to the Repeal of the Stamp-Act: with an Introduction, Applicable to the Present Situation of the Colonies. Philadelphia, 1768.

On January 14, 1766, William Pitt, the "Great Commoner" and the minister most responsible for Britain's winning the Seven Years War, gave an impassioned speech in Parliament in opposition to the Stamp Act. It ought to be "repealed absolutely, totally, and immediately;" he insisted, because "it was founded on an erroneous principle." Parliament, Pitt said, had no right to take money out of the colonists' pockets. Not only did Pitt defend the Americans' claim that they could not be taxed without their consent, he even rejoiced that they had resisted. Couldn't the British government, he asked, understand the "plain distinction between taxes levied for the purpose of raising a revenue, and duties imposed for the regulation of trade"?

The speech was widely printed in the colonies and made him an American hero all over again. But as William Hicks pointed out in a series of essays originally published in the *Pennsylvania Journal* early in 1768 and reprinted in newspapers in Boston and South Carolina before being collected in this pamphlet, Pitt had revealed "a striking inconsistency" in his speech. While Parliament could not tax the colonies, Pitt had claimed that it had "a right to bind, to restrain America" and that its "legislative power over the colonies is sovereign and supreme." Indeed, Pitt felt Parliament was more than justified in suspending the New York Assembly over its refusal to comply with the Quartering Act of 1765, an action that had deeply troubled leaders throughout the colonies.

How could this inconsistency be understood? Could the colonists really be subordinate to "the two inferior estates of their mother country," that is, to the House of Lords and the House of Commons? Shouldn't they instead be "considered as so many different countries of the same kingdom"? Like many other Americans, Hicks was fumbling to find some way "through the labyrinth of our present dispute." How could Parliament, as Pitt claimed, bind the trade of the colonists, confine their manufactures, and exercise every power whatsoever over them, except tax them? Could Parliament be limited and yet unlimited at the same time? The Great Commoner did not have an answer to these questions, and it seemed no one else did either.

THE

NATURE *and* EXTENT

OF

PARLIAMENTARY POWER

CONSIDERED;

In fome Remarks upon Mr. PITT's SPEECH in
the Houfe of Commons, previous to the
Repeal of the STAMP-ACT:

WITH AN

INTRODUCTION,

Applicable to the prefent SITUATION of the

COLONIES.

By

"*If there be any one fo credulous as not to apprehend the*
" *fatal Confequences of this* FORMIDABLE POWER, *I can-*
" *not but wonder at that Man's fecurity.*"
Demofthenes's 2d Philipic.

PHILADELPHIA, Printed anno M,DCC,LXVIII.

INTRODUCTION.

Number I.

THE following piece was written but a short time before the repeal of the stamp-act; and as the subject of it was of the most general and important nature, the trifling alteration of circumstances which a few months have produced, cannot prevent its being as applicable to the present state of our affairs, as to those disagreeable controversies, in which we have been heretofore unhappily involved. The conciliating spirit which prevaled upon the first intelligence of the stamp-act's being repealed, prevented its publication then; though the author was ever perfectly convinced, the colonies would not long have any reason to flatter themselves, that the repeal of this act was a sacrifice to liberty; or that it proceeded from any thing more than an apprehension of the ill consequences which our brethren of Britain must have felt from the œconomical resolutions which we had formed. Upon examining the debates, previous to the repeal, if any one could have doubted the sense of the legislature, the act for securing the dependence of the colonies, would have reduced it to a sufficient degree of certainty. Indeed, if this act had been more equivocal, the billeting act was explicit enough to have pointed out clearly to every common understanding, their *generous meaning*—A meaning evidenced by such measures as could not but excite the most alarming apprehensions.

In mixt forms of government, where the delicacy of the constitution requires the strictest attention, to the movements of each distinct part, jealous fears frequently intervene, upon the slightest appearance of irregularity. The history of England, alone, will furnish us with facts sufficient to support this assertion; since every man who possesses the smallest share of historical knowledge must certainly have observed, that before any measure of importance could obtain the necessary approbation of the three estates of the kingdom, it first passed a severe and critical examination; lest a superior address in either of the parties interested, should give them some particular advantage—lest a designing minister should extend the prerogative of the crown, or an artful commoner increase the liberty of the subject. A few thousands added to the military list, have alarmed the whole nation; and a body of troops, not equal to those upon the American establishment, have with the most terrible apprehensions, been considered as a formidable army, —so averse have the people of England ever been, to trust their liberties, even with the best of men, that they have chosen to depend upon the precarious aid of subsidiary troops, rather than put arms into the hands of their own countrymen: while there was the least probability that those arms might be employed to the subversion of liberty. This conduct, I only mean to remark as consistent with the genius of liberty: and, though its policy, when critically examined, may not appear altogether unexceptionable, yet will the *jealous caution* which produced it, be ever considered as the grand bulwark of freedom. When I apply myself to consider the situation of the colonists, I cannot but observe that they labour under difficulties peculiar to themselves. They have not only to guard their liberties against the encroachments of the royal prerogative, but even to protect their property against the invasions of their more powerful brethren. The people of England have only one single defence to make for the preservation of their freedom; and, if the system of venality and corruption, which now so generally prevails, does not gradually lead them into a state of slavery, no open violence can ever effect it. Far different is the situation of the divided Americans. Of them every distinct colony has hitherto been considered as a particular plantation of the crown, and been governed by such loose, discretionary powers as were better calculated to support the *despotism* of a minister than the *liberties* of the settlers. They are now considered as dangerous rivals, and their unprotected interests must fall a sacrifice to those of their jealous brethren. An artful, designing minister would naturally endeavour to conciliate the affections of those who more immediately surround the throne, by removing any burthens from their shoulders, and fixing them upon those, by whose murmers and complaints, he could not be so immediately affected. To gratify the desires of his selfish countrymen, and flatter them with the appearance of an *unnatural superiority*; he would willingly subscribe to any acts for the limiting our trade, and restraining our manufactures: But perfectly convinced that the Americans will neither be so stupid as not to perceive the iniquity of these measures, nor so passive as patiently to submit to their being carried into execution, he prudently prepares to support them by means as infamous and oppressive as those which are to be supported. Though our European neighbours are driven from the continent; and, though our savage enemies have long since laid down the hatchet, yet have our careful guardians left us a very considerable body of troops, and are daily sending over fresh supplies—*to protect us from any future dangers*; when it cannot but be evident to every man of common knowledge, that, in our present situation, we are both able and willing to defend our own frontiers, without putting the government to the trouble of transporting troops for that purpose, at such an immense expence. We have now sixteen regiments distributed through the different colonies.—most of them, instead of being a defence to our frontiers, are a burthen to our maritime cities; where they are, by virtue of an act of the British parliament, to be plentifully supplied with necessaries at the expence of the place where they may be quartered; and as the quartering them depends altogether upon the arbitrary will of the commanding officer, he is absolutely vested with a power of oppressing any single colony, which may have been so unfortunate as to have incurred the resentment of those who appointed him.

When the ministry resolved to burthen us with so many troops, it was not thought proper to make the usual requisitions to the different assemblies for the necessary supplies. The power of parliament had met with an unexpected opposition, in their first attempts to enforce the stamp-act. Urged by a prudent attention to their own interests, they had indeed determined to repeal this oppressive act; but, least this extraordinary concession should be considered as an acknowledgement of right, they determined to exert their authority once more in a manner so explicit, as should leave us no room to doubt their meaning.

One act is passed to declare the dependence of the colonies upon the *imperial crown* and *parliament* of *Great-Britain*; and that dependence is immediately proved by a law for billeting soldiers in America, and for obliging those places, in which the commanding officer may think proper to quarter them, to grant certain very ample supplies of necessaries. Upon application to the government of New-York, the general assembly of that province shewed their readiness to comply with every thing that might be required for the accommodation of those troops which had contributed to the valuable acquisitions in America. They framed a law for the purpose, and granted a sufficiency of such articles as they conceived most useful and necessary for the soldiers: They did not indeed comply with every particular contained in the act of parliament—perhaps it might not be in their power. If any thing was to be given by the colonists for the accommodation of the soldiery, surely they were the best judges of their own abilities, as well as of those articles which they could most conveniently procure. If the parliament had thought proper to have ordered porter instead of small beer, and gin instead of rum, they would scarcely have procured a sufficient quantity, had they even sought it with fixt bayonets. Although the inhabitants could not but be alarmed at a requisition supported by the whole legislative authority, yet did they prudently decline taking notice of such an *extraordinary procedure*, and very modestly resolved to comply with the *design* of the act without any immediate referrence to the *act itself.* Some triffling alterations were indeed made in the stipulated allowances; but so inconsiderable were they that I believe the soldiery complained but little of the alteration; and I cannot think that the greatest enemy to America ever imagined that the freemen of New-York, when they used a discretionary power in granting a share of their own private property, for the use of the army, and were hardy enough to deviate, in some minute particulars, from the directions of the British parliament, would ever have excited so violent—so unjustifiable a resentment. A resentment expressed by a proceeding the most unreasonable and unconstitutional—such a proceeding as must prove, beyond all possibility of contradiction, that whatever concessions we may receive from a prudent attachment to their own interest, we can expect nothing from a generous attention to the spirit of their own happy constitution, or from an honest reluctance to invade the natural rights of their fellow subjects.

—Sed comprime motus
Nec tibi quid liceat, sed quid fecissæ decebit
Occurrat, mentemque domet respectus honesti.
CLAUD.

NUMBER II.

MR. PITT has frequently declared that the freemen of Great-Britain have no right to take money out of our pockets, without first obtaining our consent; and yet their representatives in parliament have resolved, without deigning to consult us, that we shall pay a certain sum for furnishing the soldiery with particular necessaries. Unwilling to revive a contest, which had just before been settled so much to our satisfaction, we declined renewing the dispute with regard to the legality of the act. We were contented to receive it as a *reasonable requisition*, though not as *a binding law*; and, consulting our own abilities and convenience, we granted such articles as we thought would answer *the design of the act*. In this conduct, so remarkably temperate, we have incurred the highest displeasure of the British parliament, and are exposed, as a punishment due to our offences, to one of the most general, and severest penalties which the hand of power could inflict. An act has passed to strip us of our legislative power, and render us unable to provide for ourselves in a situation of the most imminent danger; because we have outrageously refused to subscribe to our own ruin. We have modestly avoided controverting a point of the *highest* importance, lest we should draw upon ourselves a charge of *obstinacy* and *malevolence*. We have complied with the *meaning*, though not with the *letter* of the act. We have evidenced the most grateful and complying disposition, and are nevertheless doomed to receive the punishment of the most rebelious opposition. If our every act is thus liable to be misconstrued, and we are patiently to receive such severe chastisement, we must at once renounce the name of free-men, and accommodate ourselves to a state of *abject vassallage*.

We may not, perhaps, just now feel any immediate ill consequences from this restraint upon our legislation; but, when we are to determine upon the propriety or justice of any particular act, we are to consider all the effects which it may probably, or even possibly produce. Suppose (for instance) that our savage neighbours should once more wantonly invade our frontiers— to what a horrid situation should we be reduced! Our lives and fortunes exposed to the attacks of a barbarous enemy, without our being able to raise either men or money for our protection. Can the greatest enemy to America think of our being reduced to a situation so truly distressful, without accusing of the most unnatural severity, those who arrogate to themselves an absolute power of directing and restraining our every action, in such a manner as may best answer their own partial purposes? In this amazing exertion of parliamentary power, the single colony of New-York is not alone concerned. It may hereafter be the fate of every other province, unless they now cordially unite in such an application as may confirm their liberty, or establish their subordination upon some regular principles.

I am no favourer of violent measures. I would endeavour to support our pretensions by force of reasoning, not by force of arms; but yet I would anxiously wish that nothing may intimidate us into an acquiescence with the measures of oppression. We may be compelled to submit, but never to relinquish our claim to the privileges of the free men.

When we complain of the violent proceedings in the late administrations; let us consider the alterations which a century has produced in our constitution. We have now a standing army of one hundred and twenty regiments. Scarce a family of rank but what has some military connections; and even in the house of commons there are too many gentlemen of the sword. No wonder then that we are alarmed with such *spirited resolves*—that execution is to proceed judgment; and that the inhabitants of a colony are regarded as *dependant vassals*, by those who have been accustomed to consider a legion of *free subjects*, as a band of *absolute slaves*—points of honor now take place of points in law, and *Magna-Charta* itself must give way to that *furor militaris* which so universally prevails. The hand which bestows a truncheon can never be guilty of oppression, and the will of an artful minister will become the law of a whole nation.

I am no enemy to the present military establishment, but as I conceive it may influence and endanger our liberties; nor have I any resentment against the inhabitants of that country, which gave birth to my ancestors, but when I consider them as exerting their superior power to reduce their fellow subjects to a state of subordination inconsistent with their natural rights, and not to be reconciled to the spirit of their own constitution. I admire and revere the well regulated government of Great-Britain, and only wish to have our own system established by so excellent a standard.

As a colonist, my most ambitious views extend no further than the rights of a British subject. I can not comprehend how my being born in America should divest me of these; nor can I conceive why the liberty and property of a free-born American should not be protected from every invasion with the same caution, which has ever been exerted to guard the privileges of an englishman. If we are entitled to the liberties of British subjects we ought to enjoy them *unlimited and unrestrained*. If our pretensions to these are without any foundation, why are we left unacquainted with the cause and nature of our subordination. In acts of the greatest solemnity and notoriety, we have been flattered with the title of British subjects—we have received with the blood of our ancestors, the spirit of liberty, and our hearts naturally retain an utter abhorrence of slavery. We have carefully examined those glorious charters, granted to the virtuous resolution of our brave fore-fathers; and the result of our examination can not but inform us—that liberty is only to be supported by a steady opposition to the first advances of arbitrary power. The conduct of the colonists has been most maliciously misrepresented, and they have been stigmatized as *riotous* and *rebellious*, when those who are un-influenced by prejudice, can not but discover that their warmest wishes rise no higher than to a connection, founded upon *natural right*; and that their present resentment could only be excited by the horrid apprehensions of being reduced to a state of *slavish dependance*.

I am not so great a stickler for the independance of the colonies, but I am ready to acknowledge the *necessity* of lodging in some part of the community a *restraining power*, for the regulating and limiting the trade and manufactures of each particular county or colony, in such a manner as might most effectually promote the good of the whole; and I should not obstinately object to the vesting this power in the parliament of Great-Britain, if the violent measures which have lately been carried into execution, did not afford me too much reason to believe, that every concession which might at this time be made from a *principle of necessity*, and a regard to the public utility, would be immediately considered as an acknowledgment of such a *subordination*, as is totally inconsistent with the nature of our constitution. If a laudable motive of moderation, and a generous attention to the welfare and tranquility of the whole community should induce a ready submission to every regulation which the British parliament may think necessary to frame, the ill consequences which may possibly attend such a temperate conduct may draw upon us a charge of *unpardonable negligence*. In a system so complicated as ours, where one power is continually encroaching upon the other, and where the general ballance is so fluctuating and precarious, a spirit of compliance and moderation in the present age, may lay a foundation for the slavery and dependance of future generations; who will have the greatest reason to charge us with having basely betrayed their liberties, by carelessly relaxing from the *rigid scrutiny* which ever ought to be made into matters of national concern.

> *Vos dormitis, nec adhuc mihi videmini intelligere quam nos pateamus.*
>
> Cal. ad Cic.

Number III.

In the pursuit of all political measures, if we are not cautious in preserving the *appearance* of liberty, we may insensibly lose the *reality* itself. As men attentive to our own particular interests, we cannot but discover the many advantages which the colonists would necessarily have over their brethren of Britain, in the course of a *free, uninterrupted commerce*; but, as men of reason and integrity, we do not indulge a wish to enjoy these advantages at the expence of our fellow subjects. We shall ever readily subscribe to such commercial regulations as may enable the inhabitants of Great-Britain and Ireland to meet us at all foreign markets upon an *equal footing*; but WHERE the authority by which these restrictions are to be framed, can with most *safety* and *propriety* be lodged is now the subject of our inquiries.

The boldest advocates for the power of parliament, can not, at this day, without blushing, assert, that it is sovereign and supreme *in every respect whatsoever*. That great man, who is, beyond all contradiction, the best acquainted with the constitution of his own country, and the most sincerely attached to her true interest, never wished to extend the legislative power of Britain, any further, than might be essential to her own preservation; by establishing such regulations as were indispensably necessary to prevent her falling a prey to her rising colonies. As there was an *immediate necessity* of placing this power somewhere, the parliament of Great Britain could urge a claim founded in an *appearance* of reason, and supported by a superiority of strength; and yet, reasonable as this claim appeared to be, it could never be maintained, upon the principles of their own government. The commons of Britain might indeed with great propriety propose regulations for the trade, and restrictions for the manufactures of those by whom they were appointed; but how they can, with any face of equity resolve to extend these regulations and restrictions to those from whom they have received no *delegated power*, is what I cannot easily comprehend. Would they but admit to their general council a certain number of deputies, properly authorized from every colony, to support the interests of their constituents, to explain the nature of their situation, and remonstrate against any acts of oppression, then indeed, whatever commercial regulations they might think proper to form, would be fixed upon a *constitutional basis*, and their authority remain for ever undisputed; as I can never be supposed to mean that it should extend to any other than such matters which immediately relate to commerce; while the *internal policy* of each colony should still be regulated by it's proper representatives, in conjunction with the deputy of the crown? and their liberty should only be restrained and their property fairly disposed of by those who are *legally* vested with that authority. I am very sensible, that to fix a representation in parliament for the purposes of commerce *only*, would be attended with many inconveniencies; but every man who has the cause of liberty, and the interest of his country at heart, would rather accept such a partial, disadvantageous establishment as might immediately be obtained, than submit to such an *unnatural state of subordination*, as must continually keep alive the spirit of contention, and finally involve us in inevitable ruin.

The friends of parliamentary power lose themselves in contemplating the idol they have raised; and to confirm the veneration which they have entertained, they annex to it the idea of *omnipotence* and *infallibility*. It is a received maxim of the law—"*that the king can do no wrong*"; and yet our brave forefathers were not so deluded by this *royal dogma* as to suffer themselves to be stripped of their invaluable rights and privileges by the arbitrary fiat of a wicked Prince; and if *they* were justifiable in their resolute opposition to the unwarrantable encroachments of a power which had been considered as sacred, by a long hereditary succession; how very reasonably may *we* conceive that our conduct will be *strictly defensible* when we unanimously oppose the violent proceedings of a body which we may be said, from day to day, to have fashioned with our own hands. As the original design of delegating power, was, that it might be exercised for the good of the whole community, there cannot be a greater absurdity in politics than to suppose that those whom we have vested with a reasonable and necessary authority, are not accountable to us if they should, by any consideration, be led weakly and wantonly to abuse it. The doctrine of *non resistance* and *passive obedience* to the tyranic will of a wicked Prince has long since been exploded, and those who have endeavoured to inculcate these slavish principles have deservedly been treated with the utmost rigor of the law.* If liberty be the object which we pursue, and slavery the misfortune which we most cautiously avoid, we have as much to apprehend from a corrupt parliament, as from an ambitious king; and he who would patiently submit to the usurpations of the one and resolutely oppose the despotism of the other, only declares, by his conduct, that he would rather be ruled by five hundred tyrants than by one.

The natural right which every man possesses, to restrain, by *every possible method*, the progress of arbitrary, lawless government, is not at this day to be controverted; and, tho' it may be

---

* *Vide Sacheverel's trial.*

insinuated that the too warmly and too frequently pressing this doctrine may excite a spirit of licentiousness, yet, in answer to this, I must beg leave to remark, that the cause of liberty cannot be too carefully cultivated, and that those principles by which it is best supported cannot be too often or too strongly inculcated. Should the parliament of Britain by any act of power, attempt to strip their constituents of some important, unalienable right, would they not meet with as certain and violent opposition, as if the crown, by an exertion of its prerogative should endeavour to divest them of some established privilege. The king of Great-Britain is vested with an extensive, but not an *unlimited authority*; and is himself bound by those laws with the execution of which he is intrusted. The representatives of the nation, in parliament assembled, with justice arrogate to themselves many great and useful powers. They are trustees lawfully appointed for the freemen of Great-Britain— *ne quid detrimenti capiat respublica* is the tenure of their appointment; and, if they should, from any principle of venality or corruption, betray their important trust, no man can doubt but that they are very reasonably accountable to their constituents for every part of their misconduct. Should an act of the British legislature invade the rights of those who cloathed the lawmakers with their legislative power it could only be considered as a breach of trust; but if the same authority should be exerted to deprive us of our most inestimable liberties, we must very properly regard it as an act of violence and oppression. Such violence has lately been offered to the legislature of New-York in particular, and such oppression will with great reason be complained of by the colonies in general, when they more clearly discover the ill tendency of those statutes which have lately been framed under a pretence of regulating our commerce. I cannot think it necessary to enter into a minute examination of every particular statute. The nature and importance of those duties which have been imposed upon such articles as we are under a necessity of importing from Great-Britain *only*, have been very clearly and accurately explained by a late judicious writer.* For my part I have only laboured to impress the *principles* of liberty upon the minds of my countrymen;

* *Author of the Farmer's letters.*

and to draw from those principles such clear and forcible conclusions as might carry with them conviction even to the most prejudiced. I have left the arrangement and consideration of particular facts to those who have more leisure and ability; but if this loose, undigested essay, should, in the most trifling degree, promote the interest of my country, I shall, at any time hereafter, most willingly devote my head, my heart and my hand to the same *glorious purpose*.

> *Te propter colimus leges, animosque ferarum*
> *Exuimus; nitidis quisquis te sensibus hausit*
> *Irruet intrepidus flammis, hiberna secabit*
> *Æquora: consertos hostes superabit inermis.*
> CLAUD.

A CITIZEN.

The Nature and Extent of Parliamentary Power Considered, &c.

"Those laws therefore that I call Leges scriptæ, are such as are usually called statute laws, which are originally reduced into writing, before they are enacted, or receive any binding power; every such law being formally made, as it were, an INDENTURE TRIPARTITE, *between the King, the Lords, and the Commons; for without the concurrent consent of all these three parts no such law is or can be made."*

HALE's Hist. of the Common Law.

NUMBER I.

IT seems to me the distinguishing characteristic of the *English* constitution that no free man shall be restrained in the exercise of his natural liberty, or, in the use of his acquired property but by those regulations to which he has *really* or *virtually* subscribed. Laws which are the result of such a rational and well-digested compact, may bear hard upon some, but they cannot, with propriety, be complained of by any; since every precaution which the wit of man could devise, was necessarily employed for the benefit of the whole united body, after a due attention to the separate interest of each.

The Lords and Commons, with the approbation of the Crown, *agree* to regulate their trade by well-placed restrictions, and settle the establishment of their manufactures in such a manner as shall be most conducive to the public good. In all these disposing and restraining laws the interest of the whole community is consulted, and the spirit of the constitution preserved inviolate.

But, when the Lords and Commons of *England*, by *formal compact* with the Crown, attempt to bind those, who can by no means be considered as parties to their agreement, they discard those noble principles to which they owe the enjoyment of all that is valuable in life, and introduce power in the place of reason to support a system which has its foundation in partial, not in universal good. For, can any thing be more evidently partial, or more inconsistent with the principles of common justice, than that the Lords and Commons of *England* should *give* and *grant** to his Majesty any sum which they may think proper, to be levied, by any mode which they may be pleased to devise, upon his *American* subjects—perhaps for the payment of a subsidy to some Prince of the Empire for the defence of his Majesty's electoral dominions. If the absurdity and injustice of such a procedure is to be discovered by every eye, we shall not be long before we clearly perceive, through all the mists of ingenious sophistry, that, upon the indispensible principles of their own constitution, the Lords and Commons of *England* can no more *covenant* with the Crown for the limiting and restraining our natural liberty than they can *agree* to *give* and *grant* the most valuable of our property to be disposed of for their own private purposes.

The more I consider this maxim, which I have taken from my Lord C. Justice *Hale*, the more sensible am I of its weight and importance. To perceive its full force, it will be necessary to look back to the first dawn of freedom, when the good people of *England*, would no longer submit to have their liberty and property arbitrarily disposed of by the royal fiat. Conscious of their own importance, they, at first, only claimed a privilege of recommending by petition, such measures as they might conceive necessary for the public good. In this humble form did the spirit of liberty first appear, while the power of the crown continued for ages almost unlimited in its extent, and uncontrouled in its operation. But, when an attention to the true interests of the nation, established their manufactures and extended their commerce, the common people readily shook off their servile dependence upon their Lords, and gladly embraced an opportunity of acquiring that affluence of riches which was the firmest foundation of their future liberty. Those, whose situation had lately been that of the most abject vassallage, now suddenly found themselves raised, by their own industry, to the possession of wealth and independence. Proud of such valuable and important acquisitions, they only waited for that information, which was the child of time and experience, to direct their steps in the pursuit of measures

---

* "WHAT PROPERTY HAVE THEY IN THAT WHICH ANOTHER MAY, BY RIGHT, TAKE WHEN HE PLEASES, TO HIMSELF." LOCKE *on Government*.

which were to establish the most solid security for that liberty and property which they had so lately acquired.

Before science extended her happy influence over this rising nation, their progress in the paths of liberty was but slow and irregular—interrupted by events which they were too short sighted to foresee, and obstructed by revolutions which no human prudence could prevent. But, when their acquisition of knowledge, from a careful examination of the past, enabled them not only to regulate the present, but even to penetrate into the remote regions of future contingency, every revolving year furnished them with some opportunity to improve and enlarge their system of liberty. With every assistance which human wisdom could bestow, supported by the experience of ages, they have at last fixed the foundation of their freedom upon such principles as will forever stand the test of the most critical examination. Careful to guard those blessings for which they had so industriously laboured, they established this as a fundamental maxim—that no new regulation could be framed, nor any old law abrogated but by the *general consent* of the nation. Such a consent as must be evidenced by a majority of votes in the different estates of the kingdom—the Lords in their proper persons assenting, while the sense of the common people is known from the voices of their representatives. Can any thing less than infinite wisdom elaborate a system more perfect than that which so effectually secures the happiness of every individual—which admits no law as obligatory but upon those who are *expressly parties*, or have actually subscribed to the obligation?

If these be, as they certainly are, the well digested principles of the *English* constitution, with what appearance of reason can the warmest zealot for the superiority of *Great-Britain* assert, that the legislative power of parliament is *sovereign and supreme?*

Shall the freemen of *New-York* be reduced to a state of subordination, and deprived of those invaluable privileges enjoyed by the inhabitants of that city, which has given a name to their province, because they are unfortunately placed a thousand leagues further from the presence of their sovereign; and, instead of prefering their petitions immediately to the royal ear, can only apply to his deputy for a redress of their grievances, and for the framing such regulations as the infant state of the colony may require? This would be heightening the misfortune of their situation by the most flagrant injustice.

When the emigrants from *Great-Britain* crossed the *Atlantic* to settle the desarts of *America*, they brought with them the spirit of the *English* government. They brought with them the same duties to their sovereign which the freemen of *England* at that time acknowledged; and they very naturally supposed, that, under his direction, they should be allowed to make such regulations as might answer the purposes of their emigration. Ever mindful of their duty and allegiance to their Prince, they cannot easily conceive that they left their brethren the freemen of *England* vested with a *sovereign, supreme power* to restrain their *natural Liberty*,* or to dispose of their acquired property. Removed at an immense distance from the seat of government, they could no longer join the national council; but, as the very spirit of the *English* constitution required it, they naturally applied to their Prince for such protection and assistance, as might raise them to an equality with their brethren of *England*; from whom they only requested their friendly patronage, during the weakness of their infant state.

The formula of their government once settled in some measure to their satisfaction, with the concurrence of those officers appointed by the Crown, the inhabitants of these new settlements, ever faithfully preserving in their memory the principles of that happy government which they had just quitted, totally disclaim all *subordination*† to, and dependence upon, the two

---

* *De plus, le droit de proprietè n'etant que de convention, et d'institution humaine, tout homme peut, a son grè disposer de ce qu'il possede: Mais il n'en est pas de meme des* dons essentiels de la nature, *tels que la vie et la libertè, dont il est permis a chacun de jouir, et* dont il est au moins douteux qu'on ait droit de se depouiller. Rousseau.

Mais quand on pounoit aliener sa libertè comme ses biens, la difference seroit tres grande pour les enfans, qui ne jouissent des biens du pere que par transmission de son droit, au lieu que la libertè etant un don qu'ils tiennent de la nature en qualitè d'Hommes, *leurs parens n'ont eu aucun droit de les en depouiller.* ibid.

† *A subordination not only incompatible with the principles of the* English *constitution, but even not to be reconciled to the* law of nature *if we admit as just the following definition.*

inferior estates of their mother country. Without the power —without the inclination to disturb the tranquility of those to whom they stand so nearly related, they wish to promote an amicable intercourse, founded upon reciprocal interest; without allowing or submitting to any laws, but those which they themselves have made, by *regular agreement* with the deputy of the Crown, properly authorized for that purpose. To suppose the *British* parliament to be vested with a sovereign and supreme legislative power over the colonies, is advancing a supposition inconsistent with the principles of their own constitution; and to assert the *necessity* of subordination from the nature of our situation, without attempting to prove that necessity, is really treating an affair of the utmost importance with too little attention.* Those who may probably be most seriously affected by this doctrine, very naturally require something stronger than general assertions to support it, although those assertions may be advanced by the best and wisest man of the nation.

Perhaps it may not be such an irreconcileable paradox in policy to assert, that the freemen settled in *America* may preserve themselves absolutely independant of their fellow subjects who more immediately surround the throne, and yet discharge, with the strictest fidelity, all their duties to their sovereign. They may not only be loyal and valuable subjects to their Prince, but useful and necessary neighbours to their brethren of *Britain*.

The colonies may, with no great impropriety, be considered as so many different countries of the same kingdom, the nature of whose situation prevents their joining in the general council, and reduces them to a necessity of applying to their Prince for the establishment of such a partial policy as may be the best adapted to their particular circumstances, and, at the same time, the most conducive to the general good. That this partial policy, settled for every distinct part, may not interfere with

---

"*On commence par rechercher les regles, don't, pour* L'Utilité commune *il seroit a propos que les hommes convinssent entre eux; & puis on donne le nom de loi naturelle ala collection de ces regles sans autre preuve* que le bien qu'on trouve qui resulteroit de leur pratique universelle." ROUSSEAU.

*Qui statuit aliquid, parte inaudita altera æquum licet statuerit, haud æquus fuerit. SENEC. Med.

the general welfare of the whole, the restraining power lodged in the Crown will always be able to insure; since we cannot suppose that a wise and just Prince would ever consent to sacrifice the interest and happiness of any one part to the selfish views of another.

As a commercial people, while blessed with the same advantages which the inhabitants of *Great-Britain* enjoy, our interest may sometimes clash with theirs. This is an inconvenience which may, at some future period happen, in the extent of our trade: But shall this *possible inconvenience* be a sufficient authority for stripping us of all the most valuable privileges in society? Shall we be reduced to the most abject state of dependence, because we may possibly become formidable rivals to our jealous brethren, if we are allowed to maintain that equality which we have received from nature, and which we find so firmly supported by the laws of our mother country?

> *Nostri autem magistratus, imperatores que ex hac una re maximam laudem capere studebant*, SI PROVINCIAS, SI SOCIOS EQUITATE ET FIDE DEFENDERENT.
>
> CIC. *de Off.*

NUMBER II.

THERE is no reasoning against those prejudices which are the support of particular interest, or I would ask why my being born in the island of *Great-Britain* should vest me with a power to tie the hands of my *American* neighbour, and then justify me in picking his pocket; although this same *American* should be a loyal subject of the same Prince, and formally declared to be possessed of all the liberties and privileges of a *British* subject? How absurd and unmeaning must this specious declaration appear to one who sees and feels the force of the present violent struggles for reducing us to a state of infamous vassallage.

That right honourable and worthy gentleman who exerted his extensive influence to ward off from the devoted colonies that blow which would have effected their immediate ruin, has been pleased to make these declarations in our favour—"They are the subjects of this kingdom, equally entitled with ourselves to all the *natural rights* of mankind, and the peculiar privileges of *Englishmen*, equally bound by the laws, and equally participating of its constitution. The *Americans* are the sons, not the bastards of *England*." And yet, in the same speech he asserts the authority of *Great-Britain* "over the colonies to be *sovereign* and *supreme* in every circumstance of government and legislation whatsoever." If the latter part of this declaration be by any means reconcileable with the former, I must forfeit all pretensions to reason; since, after the most careful disquisition which I am capable of making, I cannot discover how any inhabitant of the colonies can be said to enjoy the *peculiar privileges* of *Englishmen*, when all that he holds valuable in life must lie at the mercy of that unlimited power, which is so repeatedly said to be *sovereign* and *supreme*. An authority established upon partial principles, and such as must be supported by the force of arms* more than the force of reason, if it is to survive any distant period.

I have the highest veneration for the character and abilities of Mr. *Pitt*, and scarcely dare indulge myself in a train of reasoning, which evidently points out to me the most striking inconsistency in the sense of his speech of *January* last upon *American* affairs. From the best evidence which I am capable of receiving, I cannot but be clearly convinced that our liberty must be only ideal, and our privileges chimerical, while the omnipotence of parliament can "bind our trade, confine our manufactures, and exercise every power whatever except that of taking money out of our pockets without our consent." If this sovereign power, which they so warmly assert, should be once tamely conceded, to what triffling purpose have we exerted ourselves in our glorious opposition to the stamp act. At best, we have but put the evil day afar off—We have not combated the *reality*, but the *mode* of oppression. We have only gained a temporary reprieve, till some future minister, with as little virtue and more abilities than Mr. *G——lle*, shall think proper to employ this unbounded legislative power for the horrid purpose of reducing three millions of people to a state of abject slavery.

---

* *Le contract de government est tellement dissous par le despotisme que le despote n'est le maitre qu'aussi long tems qu'il est le plus fort; et que sitot qu'on peut l'expulser il n'a point a reclamer contre la violence.* ROSSEAU.

If our sovereign lords, the Commons of *England*, have been led, by their absurd jealousy, and envious partiality, under the direction of a rash and impolitic minister, to strike so bold a stroke at both our liberty and property, what danger may we not apprehend from the same selfish principles, when they may be influenced by the deep-laid schemes of some able statesman? Under such pernicious influence the chains of *America* may be forged and riveted on, while her incautious sons are lulled in a state of security. The power of taxation given up to their spirited opposition, the excess of their joy will not suffer them to indulge any gloomy reflections upon that *dangerous reserve* of *legislation*. The present evil averted, the warmth of their sanguine dispositions will not allow them to think that oppression may return at any other time, or in any other form. Their very gratitude and humility prevent their enquiring into a cause of the last importance. In the highest exaltation of heart at a concession scarcely expected, they receive as a matter of *favour* what they demanded as a matter of *right*; and, to avoid an appearance of arrogance in urging any new demands, they neglect the discharge of the most essential duties to themselves and their posterity. Perhaps they will scarcely thank the man who shall endeavour to convince them, that the simple power of legislation may as effectually ruin the colonies as that of taxation.

Let us borrow and improve upon a thought of our greatest enemy. Mr. *G——lle* tells us that *internal* and *external taxes* are the same in *effect*, and differ but in name. Mr. *Pitt* has indeed treated this opinion with so little attention, that he has only answered it by a general assertion—"that there is a plain distinction between taxes levied for the purposes of raising a revenue, and duties imposed for the regulation of trade."

Plain as this distinction is, my most industrious enquiries have not yet led me to it; and I cannot but think with Mr. *G——lle*, that they are the same *in effect*.—The one is precisely determined, while the other is more uncertain and eventual; but, in proportion to the sum raised, the effect will be exactly the same. It is taken for granted that the collection of a stamp duty would drain us of all the specie which we receive as a ballance in our *West-India* trade. If an exorbitant duty laid upon sugar and molasses produces the same effect, in what does the difference consist? By either means the treasury of *England* will be enriched with the whole profit of our labour, and we ourselves shall be reduced to that deplorable state of poverty, of which we have, at this very moment, a most affecting instance. General as the calamity is now become, there are few so uninformed as not to know that the power of legislation has done all this mischief, without any assistance from that of taxation. The severe restrictions imposed upon our trade, have made it impracticable for us to answer every foreign demand, and, at the same time reserve a sufficient stock to keep up that circulation of property so necessary to the well being of society.

Involved in heavy debts, without any prospect of discharging them—in want of the necessaries of life, without the means of acquiring them, the very politic Mr. *G——lle* has furnished us with the most interesting facts to prove the truth of his doctrine. As great an enemy as he may be to the colonies, he has at least kindly bestowed upon them the most irrefragable proof that internal and external taxes are the same in effect; and that they may be as effectually ruined by the powers of legislation as by those of taxation.

When the parliament of *Great-Britain* arrogate to themselves this sovereign jurisdiction over the colonies, I should be glad to know on what principles they found their claim. Do they ground their pretensions on the excellent principles of their own constitution, or is this supremacy a power *virtually inherent* in the name of parliament? A name which should remind them of their original state of humility, when the distinguishing power which they boasted was a privilege of *speaking their mind* and remonstrating their grievances. The Lords indeed may, with some appearance of reason, assert a supreme jurisdiction over the whole body of the nation, as the highest court of judicature: But when an aspiring member of the Commons House confidently declares that he has a power to bind our trade, and restrain our manufactures, I should be glad to know whether he derived this power from the honest freemen his constituents, or whether he acquired it by virtue of his office? From his constituents he could receive no more power than they *naturally possessed*; and, from his office he cannot reasonably be supposed vested with any other authority, than that of deciding upon the formalities, and punctilios annexed to it.

To grasp at a jurisdiction so infinitely extensive, and so little capable of limitation, is expressly declaring, that, from the antiquity of their establishment, they are become sovereigns of the new-discovered world. Upon some such arbitrary principles must they ground their unreasonable pretensions; since no man in his senses will assert that an inhabitant of *Birmingham* or *Manchester* has a *natural right*, after having obtained the consent of the Crown, to restrain, and prevent an industrious settler of the colonies from engaging in those particular manufactures which may interfere with the business of his own profession. Absurd as this assertion is, either this must be maintained, or one full as pregnant with absurdity; since one may with as much reason suppose this *natural superiority* in the freemen of *Great-Britain*, as this *acquired sovereignty* in the collective body of their representatives. Whatever reasons they may devise to support this extraordinary claim, the motives to their usurpation are clearly evinced in that part of Mr. *Pitt's* speech, where he says—"If the legislative power of *Great-Britain* over *America* ceases to be sovereign and supreme, I would advise every gentleman to sell his lands and embark for that country." A jealous fear, that, from the many natural advantages which we possess, we may, in some future age, rival our envious brethren in strength and riches, has urged them to exercise a piece of Ottoman policy, by strangling us in our infancy. When we examine into the nature of those fears which have already proved so fatal to our interest, the slightest examination shews them as contemptible and ill-grounded as were ever entertained by the most selfish of mankind.

Had not this refined policy of our *British Machiavel* interfered, and roused us to attention, we should, in all human probability, have continued for many centuries the faithful drudges of our indulgent mother; and *Great-Britain* would have increased in strength and riches in proportion to the population of her colonies. While our commerce continued unrestrained we should industriously have cultivated every branch of it, that we might be enabled to pay punctually to *Great-Britain*, that ballance which would every year increase; since our attention to the settling an immeasureable extent of

country would effectually prevent our establishing such manufactories as would furnish us with the necessaries of life.

Had I sufficient information to enter into a minute detail of
facts, I believe it would be no difficult matter to prove, that, in
the course of our most successful commerce, *Great-Britain*
receives nine-tenths of the profit; whilst we are humbly contented with being well fed and cloathed as the wages of our
labour.

If this inferiority be the consequence of a reasonable connection, why would they wish to reduce us to a state of abject
dependence? Or, if with the advantages which they already
possess, a fair unlimited trade would bring into their hands all
the specie which we could draw from the *West-Indies*, why
would they wantonly use such detestable measures as they
have lately pursued, to effect the same purpose?

If the present severe system of politics be the result of unreasonable jealousy, I will venture to assert that this very policy
will counteract its own intention. Their distresses first led the
colonists into enquiries concerning the nature of their political
situation, and the justice of the treatment which they had received. That ignorance which had kept them in a state of
peaceable submission fled before their eager researches after
that information which was so essentially necessary to the
preservation of their liberty. Enraged to find, that, while they
had been amused with the specious title of fellow subjects, and
flattered with the rights of *British* freemen, they were in reality
treated as infants in policy, whose every motion was to be directed by the arbitrary will of their jealous parent; when every
such direction evidently tended to reduce the one to an abject
state of dependence, and to raise the other to the most *exalted
superiority*. That both these purposes could easily have been
obtained, by measures artfully managed, is not to be doubted,
since nothing but the most violent oppression could have
roused us from our state of stupefaction to a proper degree of
attention. But when our sensibility was excited by the most
pointed injustice, rage instantly succeeded that tranquility
which had been nourished by our imaginary security. Warmed
with a sense of the injuries which we suffered, neither our
gratitude nor our fear could prevent our asserting those rights,
the possession of which can alone determine us freemen; and,

though we could not but see that superiority of power which could "*crush us to atoms*" yet could we have found even in the modern history of *Europe* so many examples for our encouragement, that we should not have despaired of assistance sufficient to preserve us from the *worst of evils*.

> *Quam vos facillime agitis, quam estis* maxume potentes,
> *dites, fortunati, nobiles, tam maxume vos æquo animo*
> *æqua noscere oportet, si vos voltis perhiberi* probos.
>
> Terent. Adelph.

NUMBER III.

The advocates for the sovereignty of *Great-Britain* enumerate amongst the other obligations by which we are bound, the favours which she has constantly conferred, and the support which we have continually received. If we could reasonably suppose a whole political body, actuated by the same passions which may influence an individual, then, indeed there would be some foundation for our grateful acknowledgements; but when we plainly perceive that the bounties which *Great-Britain* is said so lavishly to have bestowed upon us, are meted out in the common political measure, with an evident intention *finally to promote her own particular benefit*, we can only say that her actions are the result of good policy not of great generosity. As for the support which they have given us in times of danger, if it did not immediately arise from the same motive which has produced their other favours, I am still amazed that it should be even mentioned by those who have lavished so much blood and treasure, for the maintenance of an *imaginary ballance*, or in defending those who never thanked them for their defence.

The most superficial examination must serve to convince us that the battles of *Great-Britain* could no where have been fought with so much advantage as in the woods of *America*; where her troops could be supplied with all the necessaries of life upon the easiest terms, and from whence all the money which they expended immediately returned in immense payments for the extraordinary importations of her manufactures which the exigencies of the war required. Thus were the whole expences of the *American* war very far from lessening the strength or riches of the nation; while her forces, which were not sufficient to make any considerable impression upon the body of her natural enemy, were enabled to lop off one of its most valuable limbs. In effecting this glorious purpose, I will venture to mention the assistance which they received from the provincial troops as an aid of more importance than is generally allowed. I will even take the liberty to assert, that the colonists, in proportion to their *real ability*, did more for the general cause than could reasonably have been expected, if not more than *Great-Britain* herself. This assertion I fancy will gain more credit now than it would have gained some time ago; since the eyes of the world are at last open, and they must, if they are not wilfully blind, plainly discover, that the estimates of our wealth which have been received from ignorant or prejudiced persons, are, in every calculation, grossly erroneous. These misrepresentations, which have been so industriously propagated, are very possibly the offspring of political invention, as they form the best apology for imposing upon us burthens to which we are altogether unequal. The easy faith which every absurd information obtained, and the precipitate measures, which were the consequence of this unreasonable credulity, must sufficiently convince us, that while we are within the reach of parliamentary power, we shall not be suffered to riot in a superfluity of wealth, or to acquire any dangerous degree of strength. Whatever advantages may hereafter present themselves, from an increased population, or a more extended trade, we shall never be able to cultivate them to any valuable purpose; for, howmuch soever we may possess the ability of acquiring wealth and independence, the partial views of our selfish brethren, supported by the sovereignty of Parliament, will most effectually prevent our enjoying such invaluable acquisitions.

If any alteration in our system of agriculture, should furnish us with a sufficiency of the necessary articles for the establishment of the most valuable manufactories, and an increase of population should enable us to carry them on to the greatest advantage, the manufacturers of *Great-Britain*, jealous of such a formidable encroachment, would easily obtain the interposition of our sovereign directors; who would very naturally ordain, that we should export our unwrought materials to be laboured by our more skillful brethren, and dispatch our superfluous inhabitants in search of another vacant world: And, if the extent of our commerce should draw into our hands the wealth of all the *Indies*, the same unlimitted authority would always carefully provide ways and means for conveying the whole into the treasury of *England*. Perhaps some future *G———lle*, refining upon the system of his predecessor, may make the powers of legislation answer the purposes of oppression as effectually as the severest taxation.

The measures which have already been pursued almost give to conjecture the force of conviction; since no man can have been so inattentive to the most interesting facts as not to know that the power of Parliament, exerted in the single instance of restraining our trade, has already reduced us to *inconceivable distress*. Denied the means of acquiring specie sufficient for the purposes of a general circulation, and limitted in the emission of our paper currency, men of considerable real estates become unable to answer the most trifling demands; and, when urged by creditors, perhaps as much perplexed as themselves, their lands are sold by execution for less than half their former value. This, as one of the most striking inconveniences, attending the late unseasonable exertion of parliamentary power, I have selected for observation, from a very extensive catalogue of grievances which it has already produced, and of which we are at this moment most severely sensible. I am led to my choice of this particular fact from a consideration of the fatal consequence by which it may possibly be attended, should the merchants of England immediately demand a rigid payment of the general ballance due to them. It is not an easy matter to conceive how much our property may be affected by so unseasonable a demand; since the calamity would, by a regular connection, extend from the lowest to the highest member of society. But, as it was never my intention to enter into a minute detail of facts, I shall content myself with offering such loose, desultory observations as may serve to direct others in their researches after more particular information upon the most interesting subject. In the further pursuit of this design, I shall just take the liberty to observe upon the resolves of the Commons, of *February* 1766; that the severe censures which they so liberally bestow upon us, are evidently inconsistent with the principles upon which they are supposed to have voted the repeal of the Stamp-act.

From these resolves we may very reasonably suppose that the repeal is more immediately founded upon the *inexpediency* of the act, than upon a conviction that they had exerted an *unconstitutional power*. Had they been willing to allow this act as invasive of an indisputable right, they would not so severely have censured us for our daring opposition, and lavished such praises upon those whose selfish views or slavish principles made them so readily subscribe to the infalibility and omnipotence of Parliament.—A peaceable submission to the first attacks of encroaching power, is altogether incompatible with the genius of liberty; nor could it reasonably be expected, that, in such a sudden and dangerous invasion of our most estimable rights, the form of opposition could be perfectly model'd by the hand of prudence. Violent and precipitate as our measures were, they wanted nothing but success to sanctify them; since the most superficial observer cannot but have discovered, that, in the political world right and wrong are merely *arbitrary modes* totally dependent upon the rise and fall of contending parties.

The people of England very justly dissatisfied with the tyrannic conduct of a weak prince, made the boldest struggles for the support of their languishing liberty. In their first ill-directed efforts under the unfortunate *Monmouth*, the justice of their cause could not save them from the pains and penalties of *open rebellion*: But when a Prince of military abilities gave them his powerful assistance, they suddenly effected the preservation of their freedom and distinguished so important an event by the title of a *glorious revolution*; so much influence has success in rating the merit of our political conduct.

When the Committee of the House resolve, in the most general and expressive terms, that the authority of Parliament over the colonies is *sovereign and supreme in every respect whatever*, there is no reasoning against so formidable a resolution, supported by the power of the whole Kingdom. We can only remark that the same house has heretofore resolved to take under their own particular direction, the rights of the People, the privileges of the Lords, and the sovereignty of the Crown; and, for a long time maintained this unnatural usurpation.

If they did not suffer the passions of the man to influence the judgement of the Senator, they would never treat that as a point of honour which should only be considered as a matter of right.

If, upon a cool, dispassionate enquiry, it may appear that the Commons of Great-Britain, have no *natural or acquired superiority* over the freemen of America, they will certainly do us the justice to acknowledge this very reasonable independence, and not wickedly endeavour to enslave millions to promote the honour and dignity of a few ambitious individuals.

In supporting this doctrine of independence, I have established as an incontrovertible truth, this very accurate definition of my Lord C. J. *Hale*—That every act of Parliament is a *tripartite indenture of agreement between the three estates of the Kingdom.* If this maxim be not disputable, I very humbly conceive that every consequence which I have drawn from it, is fairly and logically deduced; for it cannot, but with the most glaring absurdity, be supposed, that the parties to these political agreements may legally bind those who are not, in any wise privy to them.

The very spirit of the English constitution requires, that general regulations framed for the government of society, must have the sanction of *general approbation*; and, that no man shall be deprived of life, liberty or property, but, by the force of those laws to which he has voluntarily subscribed. These principles once acknowledged as the foundation of English liberty, how can the colonists be said to possess the *natural rights* of *mankind*, or the *peculiar privileges* of *Englishmen*, while they are every day liable to receive laws framed by persons ignorant of their abilities—unacquainted with their necessities, and evidently influenced by partial motives? If my zeal for the good of my country has not greatly clouded my judgment, I still dare so far depend upon the principles which I have established, as to assert, that, while the power of the British Parliament is acknowledged *Sovereign & supreme in every respect whatever*, the liberty of America is no more than a flattering dream, and her privileges delusive shadows.

While I relate matters of fact, from the best evidence which I am capable of receiving, if I have misrepresented them, I lie open to contradiction; and, when I recapitulate the principles from which I have drawn my train of reasoning, I am not so obstinately attached to my own opinion as to be proof against conviction. If I am guilty of any errors in the course of this unconnected performance, they must be attributed to my not having received sufficient information, or to my want of ability in using the materials which I had acquired. I have never wilfully misrepresented a fact, nor designedly drawn from it a falacious consequence. I have not laboured to establish any favourite system, and, with the vanity of a projector, supported it at the expence of my veracity.

But however triffling this performance may appear, both my head and my heart have co-operated in its production, and I really sat down—"to write what I thought, not to think what I should write."

*Ardeo, mihi credite—incredibili quodam amore patriæ—
quod volent denique homines existiment; nemini ego
possum esse bene de republica merenti non amicus.*

CICERO.

A CITIZEN.

FINIS.

No. 4. THURSDAY, *March 10, 1768.*

By

Suo quemque judicio homines odisse aut diligere, et res probare aut improbare debere, non pendere, ex alterius vultu ac nutu, nec alieni momentis animi circumagi.   LIVY.

NOTHING can be more unjustifiable, or indeed more contemptible, than for a man to declare opinions of private characters, or censures of public measures, which are not the result of his own deliberate judgement; but formed under the influence of friendly prejudice. The council of a friend may lead and direct me in my researches after truth; but no man ought to place such boundless confidence in the judgement of another, as to deprive himself of those advantages which he might receive from the exercise of his own reason. Those sentiments which I have taken up on the credit of my friend, may be considered as a body of mercenary troops, with whose strength I am not sufficiently acquainted, and upon whose firmness I can never safely depend; while those opinions which are the laboured production of my own brain, may be regarded as a kind of national militia, known by repeated experience, and trusted with implicit confidence. The partiality which we too frequently shew to the offspring of our own political invention, may sometimes indeed expose us to deserved ridicule; but will not our bigotted attachment to the judgment of those who have gained our confidence, lead us into absurdities as great, and errors much more fatal? Those gentlemen who have generously devoted their pens to the service of their country, and have given such repeated proofs of their extensive abilities, as well as of their *sincere attachment* to the cause of liberty, are justly entitled to our gratitude and applause; but our regard for the *man* should never lead us to adopt the maxims of the *politician*, without the most cautious enquiries into their truth and utility.

When Science had reached her meridian height in Greece, the Athenians, who were the most polite and learned of the Greeks, carried this *dangerous inattention* so far, that they resigned the consideration of all public matters to those few who possessed the art of ingratiating themselves, by tickling their ears with the most elegant orations.—Eloquence then was a talent most cultivated; and measures of the highest importance were less influenced by the unpolished sense of the judicious patriot, than by the fascinating language of the venal orator. Faction, discontent, and at length the total ruin of the common wealth, were the consequences of this unpardonable indolence, and upon the strength of this instance alone, I may venture to assert, that no people can ever continue long in the exercise and enjoyment of liberty, unless they maintain resolution enough *to think for themselves.*

America has never yet seen, and perhaps never will see, any time when this doctrine could be inculcated with greater propriety. The advocates for parliamentary power would stretch it out to a most unlimited extent, while the friends of the colonies have confined their defence to that particular part which was first invaded, and from the loss of which the most fatal effects would immediately ensue. The right of taxation, as it had involv'd in itself every other *disposing authority*, was at first controverted with the greatest warmth; but the success of our opposition produced no more than a temporary remission of an ill tim'd oppressive burthen; guarded with such *salvo jure*, as plainly evinced the principles upon which this concession was made. This *formidable reservation* produced such a spirit of diffidence and timidity, that so far from extending their demands to all the rights of a free people, the modest requisitions of our firmest patriots seem to have reached no further than to the preservation of those privileges most immediately necessary to our welfare. They are fearful of urging all their pretensions to liberty, lest the hand of power should impose some more rigid restraint. They are even industrious in framing reasons to support that branch of parliamentary power, which they very reasonably believe too firmly establish'd to be shaken by any opposition. This is the conduct of an artful politician, not of a steady patriot. To wave one legal demand for the better securing another, may, in the common occurrences of *private life*, be a justifiable piece of policy; but, in matters of *national concern*, where the happiness of a whole community is at stake, compositions of this kind are of the most dangerous nature; and, tho' a superiority of power may justify a peaceable submission, yet nothing can excuse the base relinquishing of our claim to *all the rights of free men*. Let power be lodg'd in the hands of one, or one hundred, it ever was, and ever will be, of an encroaching nature; and, if a selfish motive of *temporary expediency*, should draw from the present inhabitants of the colonies any *unguarded concessions*, they will serve to rivet the chains of slavery upon their wretched posterity.

Sciat regium Majestatem difficilius a summo Fastigio ad medium detrahi, quam a mediis ad Ima præcipitari. LIVY.

If we exert ourselves in a timely opposition to the first advances of an encroaching power, we may reasonably flatter ourselves with a hope of succeeding; but if we supinely wait 'till this usurped authority is confirmed by time, and strengthned by the common arts of usurpation we shall vainly endeavour to check its *irresistible progress*. Common sense, and common experience, most incontestably prove, that too much caution can not be used in determining the nature and extent of all delegated power. The principles upon which such delegation is established, should be carefully guarded against, every doubtful or equivocal construction, and framed upon a plan so clear and simple, as to be easily comprehended by the meanest capacity. This is the peculiar merit and happiness of the English constitution; and to this Great-Britain owes both her present grandeur and her former glory. Enlightened by her example, and flattered with a hope of successfully following her footsteps, shall we not prudently use the same measures to produce the same effect.

The form of the British government, and the nature of our connection with it, are so essentially different from every colonization with which we are acquainted, that we cannot be directed by precedents drawn from any former establishment. Our situation is indeed of the *first impression*, and our conduct must therefore necessarily be regulated by *general constitutional principles*. These principles must lead us through the labyrinth of our present dispute; and by them we shall be enabled to support the most extensive of our demands. Without any great assistance, from the arts of reasoning, we shall very easily discover that those political distinctions which have *even amongst ourselves* too generally prevail'd, are absolutely inconsistent with the spirit of the English government. To deny that the parliament of Great-Britain have any right to dispose of our acquired property, and at the same time to assert their power to restrain our *natural liberty*, is really advancing such a paradox in policy, as I shall never attempt to reconcile.

If the preservation of our liberty is to us a matter of as much importance as the security of our property, from whence can this absurd distinction have arisen? We are told that the power which the parliament of Great-Britain have usurped, to limit our trade and restrain our manufactures, is founded in the very nature of the relation between an infant colony and its parent stock; but no one has ever favoured us with such a definition of this same *parental authority*, as might serve to maintain their *doctrine of dependence*. The advocates for parliamentary power have indeed repeatedly urged this *relative superiority*, to silence the clamours of the discontented colonists; but no one has at any time endeavoured to support these *specious pretensions* by the force of reasoning, or ever attempted to prove, that a British colonist and a Spartan helot, were to be considered in the same light. I will flatter myself that my countrymen are already too well acquainted with the nature and extent of their constitutional rights, to require any more arguments to evince the fatal tendency of that subordination to which our enemies still labour to reduce us. I only wish to convince them, that a concession which most of our own writers appear too ready to make, may be attended with the most dangerous and fatal consequences; and that it cannot, with any appearance of reason, be exacted from us. We have heretofore, with the greatest warmth and unanimity, denied to the parliament of Great-Britain the power of raising money upon us by any *internal tax*, and we boldly remonstrated against the stamp-act, as an act of violence and oppression. How inconsistent then must our conduct appear, if we willingly subscribe to that authority which "*can limit our trade, restrain our manufactures, and bind us in every respect, but that of taking money out of our pockets without our consent;*" since it cannot but be perceived, that this *restraining power* will have as pernicious an effect, both upon our liberty and our property, as any other with which our enemies could wish to curb us. It has repeatedly been alledged, that this restraining authority is essential to the welfare of Great-Britain—that it has grown up with the colonies from their infancy, and is become a necessary ingredient in their constitution. It is readily allowed that such a regulating power ought to be lodged somewhere, for the benefit of the whole community; but when we pay this attention due to the interest of the mother country, let us not be shamefully negligent of our own preservation, by conceding such an extensive, *unlimitted authority* as may at any time be exercised to our own ruin. Under a pretence of regulating our trade we may be stripped of our property; and with an appearance of limitting our manufactures, we may insensibly be robbed of our liberty. To depend for the security of all that is valuable in life, upon that opposition which all mankind have a right to make against acts of violence and oppression, would be expecting relief from a remedy which is too often worse than the disease itself. There cannot indeed be a juster principle in all free governments, than that those who have received any delegated power, are accountable to their constituents for any abuse of their trust: But no man of common sense, can ever consider this *dangerous resource* as a sufficient security against all those mischiefs which so frequently attend the lodging an unlimitted authority in the hands of any individual.

This reservation, which is so reasonably implied in every social compact, should indeed never be totally forgotten; but to rely on *that alone* for safety, and in consequence of this ill-plac'd confidence, to relax from that rigid caution, which distinguish'd the conduct of our prudent ancestors, would most deservedly draw upon us a charge of folly and presumption. Such is the weakness and depravity of human nature, that in every political contract, the welfare of the people should depend as little as possible upon the will and discretion of the magistrate. "*Est sapientis judicis cogitare tantum sibi a populo esse permissum, quantum commissum et creditum sit, et non solum sibi potestatem datam verum etiam Fidem habitam esse miminisse. Cic. pro Cluent.*" In every commission of power, where the utmost force of reason, and every art of political caution have been exerted to guard the interest and happiness of the governed, so imperfect is the state of human knowledge, that something will still depend upon the will of the magistrate. It is therefore essential to the constitution of every free government, that the magistracy should not only be considered as acting by virtue of the *power* which is expressly committed to them, but as bound by the *confidence* necessarily reposed in them, to exercise that power for the general benefit of those from whom they received it. A breach of faith immediately dissolves the political contract, and those who are injur'd, have an indisputable right to use any measures for redress of their grievances; but those, whose judgements are most corrected by an intimate acquaintance with antient and modern history, can very easily discover how little dependence is to be placed on so violent and precarious a remedy.—It is, and ought ever to be preserv'd as a check upon the ambition of our rulers; but let it ever be remember'd, that the safety and happiness of every nation will depend less upon the excellence of their original constitution, than upon their continued care to preserve its principles inviolate. Our political determinations should be govern'd by the same reasoning which constantly influences the prudent dispensation of our establish'd laws, where but very little attention is paid to arguments drawn from a *temporary expediency.* Let us now endeavour to apply what has already been offered, to the purpose for which it was designed, and let us reduce the state of what we at present contend for, to the simplest position. Can we, with any appearance of consistency, boldly deny to the parliament of Great-Britain, a right to dispose of our acquired property, and yet tamely concede a power of restraining our *natural liberty?* Can we explain this paradox to the apprehension of common sense? Or can we reconcile this conduct to the duty which we owe to ourselves and our posterity? Is wealth of more importance to us than freedom, or can we expect to enjoy the one when we have lost the other? Should we not, with great reason, laugh at the folly of that man, who might think to guard his domestic treasure against the invasions of the nightly robber, by carefully shutting up his windows, while his unshut doors offered him an easy passage? And would not this absurdity assume the face of madness, if, in pursuit of his extravagance, he should leave unguarded every passage to his wealth and person, depending altogether for their security upon that opposition which he might justly make to any such illegal attack?

Exposed to artifice which he might never detect, or invaded by a power which he might be unable to resist, we should very reasonably expect that he would fall a sacrifice to his own extravagant presumption.

It has been urged that this power of regulating and restraining our trade, has grown up with the colonies, and is become a part of their constitution. This argument can prove nothing, because it proves too much; since the same mode of reasoning will sanctify all those encroachments upon our liberty which have from time to time been made by the *lawless power* of a wicked minister, or by the envious partiality of a jealous Parliament. Incapable of framing laws for our own government, we willingly received them from the hands of others; and too weak to contend, we patiently submitted to a power which we could not resist: But this conduct, which was the result of an *over ruling necessity*, can never, with any degree of propriety, be urged against our present endeavours to resume and secure the rights and privileges of British subjects. When we come to take a review of that variant, inconsistent form of government which we have receiv'd at different periods of time, from the hands of arbitrary ministers, we cannot but discover numberless deficiencies;—not barely defects in form, but such imperfections as must inevitably destroy the very basis of liberty. Alarm'd with this discovery, do we not very reasonably require that the constitution of the colonies should be regulated by that most excellent model which has been approved by the greatest politicians, and admir'd by all the world. The King of Great-Britain, is King of America, and he may boast of as loyal subjects in his colonies as any in his domestic dominions. Why then are we denied that protection to which every subject is entitled? Or why are the liberties of our more fortunate brethren to be guarded by every precaution which their own prudence could suggest, while the rights of the *neglected Americans*, are not only expos'd to the encroachments of the royal power, but absolutely lie at the mercy of their fellow subjects?

In every government, not regulated by particular charters, we have a council vested with all the legislative and judicial powers of the British Peers; and yet this so important and formidable a body is instantly rais'd by the warmth of ministerial

sunshine, and ceases to exist the moment that is withdrawn.—
our judges too hold their commissions *durante bene Placito*,
and, by the last act of ministerial policy, they are to be rendered
more compleatly independent of the people, and more subject
to the influence of a royal instruction. The Parliament have
devised a method of raising money for the support of government, and that minister who may have the management of
American affairs, may arbitrarily dispose of this supply in such
pensions and salaries as may most effectually advance his own
interest, and reward his numerous dependents. With a constitution so imperfect, and unequal to the support of liberty, how
can we weakly imagine that our legislature shall provide for
our safety by necessary and equitable laws; or that our judges
will secure our property by honest impartial judgements?

Those who are best acquainted with the delicate machinery
of the English government, and who plainly perceive how
precarious and fluctuating its balance is, have ever cautiously
exerted themselves to guard against the most distant appearance of danger. They have gone so far as to consider the power
of creating any additional number of peers, as a dangerous
prerogative; and, in the bill of rights it is expressly declared, as
essential to the preservation of liberty, "that every judge shall
hold his commission *quamdiu se bene gesserit*." Thus will the
history of our mother country, and an examination of its happy
constitution, sufficiently explain to us the dangerous nature of
our present situation, and evidently prove that we cannot be
too early or too urgent in petitioning for the establishment of
such a well digested system of government, as may secure to us
and our posterity all those rights and privileges which our
forefathers heretofore happily enjoyed.

"*Hæc primo paulatim crescere, interdum vindicari; Post,
ubi Contagio, quasi Pestilentia invasit, Civitas immutata,
Imperium ex justissimo atque optimo, crudele intolerandum
factum.*"   Salust. Bell. Catil.

A CITIZEN

[John Dickinson], Letters from a Farmer in Pennsylvania, to the Inhabitants of the British Colonies. Philadelphia, 1768.

In his testimony before the House of Commons Benjamin Franklin had drawn a distinction between "internal" taxes, such as the stamp taxes, and "external" taxes, such as duties levied on imports. Although few colonists had made much of this distinction, the British government seized on it. In 1767 the chancellor of the exchequer, Charles Townshend, admitted that he could not see "any distinction between internal and external taxes; it is a distinction without a difference, it is perfect nonsense." But "since the Americans were pleased to make that distinction," he was "willing to indulge them." Consequently, Parliament went on to levy "external" taxes or duties on colonial imports of lead, glass, paper, and tea, the revenue from which was to be applied to the salaries of royal officials in the colonies, thereby affording them a measure of independence from the colonial assemblies, their traditional paymasters. At the same time the British government decided that the North American colonies had at long last become important enough to require their own ministerial department. Lord Hillsborough, a hard-liner, was appointed the first secretary of the new American department.

The Townshend Duties aroused instant, if sometimes incoherent, opposition in the colonies. It fell to John Dickinson, a wealthy and influential Philadelphia lawyer and former member of the Pennsylvania Assembly, to clarify American thinking about Parliament's rightful authority. His "Letters from a Pennsylvania Farmer," published in the *Pennsylvania Chronicle* beginning on December 2, 1767, were quickly reprinted in other colonial newspapers, and then collected in a pamphlet of which eight editions appeared in America, two in London, one in Dublin, and a French version in Amsterdam. Almost overnight, they made him the most popular patriot in America.

The first two of the Farmer's Letters were published in Boston on December 21, 1767, and on the following day the Boston town meeting, James Otis presiding, instructed its delegates to the Massachusetts House of Representatives to put forward a petition to the King for repeal of the Townshend Acts. The Massachusetts legislature did the town meeting one better, when on February 11, 1768, under the leadership of Samuel Adams, it addressed a Circular Letter to the other colonial assemblies denouncing the new duties as a violation of the principle of no taxation without representation, even as it admitted that "His Majesty's high Court of Parliament is the supreme legislative power over the whole Empire."

In his pamphlet, Dickinson, like nearly all colonists, conceded that Parliament had the right to regulate America's trade, but insisted that it had no right whatsoever to impose taxes on the colonies, whether internal or external. But how to distinguish between duties designed to regulate trade and duties designed to raise revenue? The answer, said Dickinson, lay in the colonists' ability "to discover the intentions of those who rule over them." Suddenly, Americans had turned the imperial debate into an elaborate exercise in the deciphering of British motives—and this at a time when dissembling and deceit were thought to be everywhere in Anglo-American culture. No wonder that Americans in these years became obsessed with British conspiracies designed to deprive them of their liberties.

On February 28, 1768, Massachusetts Governor Francis Bernard forwarded a complete set of the Farmer's Letters to Richard Jackson, a member of Parliament who had formerly served as Massachusetts's colonial agent in London. He warned that if the "System of American Policy," advanced in the Letters, "artfully wrote and . . . universally circulated, should receive no Refutation . . . it will become a Bill of Rights in the Opinion of the Americans."

LETTERS

FROM A

FARMER

IN

PENNSYLVANIA,

TO THE

INHABITANTS

OF THE

BRITISH COLONIES.

PHILADELPHIA:

Printed by DAVID HALL, and WILLIAM SELLERS.
MDCCLXVIII.

Letters from a Farmer, &c.

My dear COUNTRYMEN,

I AM a *Farmer*, settled, after a variety of fortunes, near the banks of the river *Delaware*, in the province of *Pennsylvania*. I received a liberal education, and have been engaged in the busy scenes of life; but am now convinced, that a man may be as happy without bustle, as with it. My farm is small; my servants are few, and good; I have a little money at interest; I wish for no more; my employment in my own affairs is easy; and with a contented grateful mind, undisturbed by worldly hopes or fears, relating to myself, I am compleating the number of days allotted to me by divine goodness.

Being generally master of my time, I spend a good deal of it in a library, which I think the most valuable part of my small estate; and being acquainted with two or three gentlemen of abilities and learning, who honor me with their friendship, I have acquired, I believe, a greater knowledge in history, and the laws and constitution of my country, than is generally attained by men of my class, many of them not being so fortunate as I have been in the opportunities of getting information.

From my infancy I was taught to love *humanity* and *liberty*. Enquiry and experience have since confirmed my reverence for the lessons then given me, by convincing me more fully of their truth and excellence. Benevolence towards mankind, excites wishes for their welfare, and such wishes endear the means of fulfilling them. *These* can be found in liberty only, and therefore her sacred cause ought to be espoused by every man, on every occasion, to the utmost of his power. As a charitable, but poor person does not withhold his *mite*, because he cannot relieve *all* the distresses of the miserable, so should not any honest man suppress his sentiments concerning freedom, however small their influence is likely to be. Perhaps he "may touch some wheel,"* that will have an effect greater than he could reasonably expect.

* POPE.

These being my sentiments, I am encouraged to offer to you, my countrymen, my thoughts on some late transactions, that appear to me to be of the utmost importance to you. Conscious of my own defects, I have waited some time, in expectation of seeing the subject treated by persons much better qualified for the task; but being therein disappointed, and apprehensive that longer delays will be injurious, I venture at length to request the attention of the public, praying, that these lines may be *read* with the same zeal for the happiness of *British America*, with which they were *wrote*.

With a good deal of surprize I have observed, that little notice has been taken of an act of parliament, as injurious in its principle to the liberties of these colonies, as the *Stamp-Act* was: I mean the act for suspending the legislation of *New-York*.

The assembly of that government complied with a former act of parliament, requiring certain provisions to be made for the troops in *America*, in every particular, I think, except the articles of salt, pepper and vinegar. In my opinion they acted imprudently, considering all circumstances, in not complying so far as would have given satisfaction, as several colonies did: But my dislike of their conduct in that instance, has not blinded me so much, that I cannot plainly perceive, that they have been punished in a manner pernicious to *American* freedom, and justly alarming to all the colonies.

If the *British* parliament has a legal authority to issue an order, that we shall furnish a single article for the troops here, and to compel obedience to *that* order, they have the same right to issue an order for us to supply those troops with arms, cloaths, and every necessary; and to compel obedience to *that* order also; in short, to lay *any burthens* they please upon us. What is this but *taxing* us at a *certain sum*, and leaving to us only the *manner* of raising it? How is this mode more tolerable than the *Stamp-Act*? Would that act have appeared more pleasing to *Americans*, if being ordered thereby to raise the sum total of the taxes, the mighty privilege had been left to them, of saying how much should be paid for an instrument of writing on paper, and how much for another on parchment?

An act of parliament, commanding us to do a certain thing, if it has any validity, is a *tax* upon us for the expence that accrues in complying with it; and for this reason, I believe, every colony on the continent, that chose to give a mark of their respect for *Great-Britain*, in complying with the act relating to the troops, cautiously avoided the mention of that act, lest their conduct should be attributed to its supposed obligation.

The matter being thus stated, the assembly of *New-York* either had, or had not, a right to refuse submission to that act. If they had, and I imagine no *American* will say they had not, then the parliament had *no right* to compel them to execute it. If they had not *this right*, they had *no right* to punish them for not executing it; and therefore *no right* to suspend their legislation, which is a punishment. In fact, if the people of *New-York* cannot be legally taxed but by their own representatives, they cannot be legally deprived of the privilege of legislation, only for insisting on that exclusive privilege of taxation. If they may be legally deprived in such a case, of the privilege of legislation, why may they not, with equal reason, be deprived of every other privilege? Or why may not every colony be treated in the same manner, when any of them shall dare to deny their assent to any impositions, that shall be directed? Or what signifies the repeal of the *Stamp-Act*, if these colonies are to lose their *other* privileges, by not tamely surrendering *that* of taxation?

There is one consideration arising from this suspension, which is not generally attended to, but shews its importance very clearly. It was not *necessary* that this suspension should be caused by an act of parliament. The crown might have restrained the governor of *New-York*, even from calling the assembly together, by its prerogative in the royal governments. This step, I suppose, would have been taken, if the conduct of the assembly of *New-York* had been regarded as an act of disobedience *to the crown alone*; but it is regarded as an act of "disobedience to the authority of the BRITISH LEGISLATURE."* This gives the suspension a consequence vastly more affecting. It is a parliamentary assertion of the *supreme authority* of the *British* legislature over these colonies, in *the point of taxation*, and is intended to COMPEL *New-York* into a submission to that authority. It seems therefore to me as much a violation of the liberties of the people of that province, and consequently of all these colonies, as if the parliament had sent a number of

---

* See the act of suspension.

regiments to be quartered upon them till they should comply. For it is evident, that the suspension is meant as a *compulsion*; and the *method* of compelling is totally indifferent. It is indeed probable, that the sight of red coats, and the hearing of drums, would have been most alarming; because people are generally more influenced by their eyes and ears, than by their reason. But whoever seriously considers the matter, must perceive that a dreadful stroke is aimed at the liberty of these colonies. I say, of these colonies; for the cause of *one* is the cause of *all*. If the parliament may lawfully deprive *New-York* of any of *her* rights, it may deprive any, or all the other colonies of *their* rights; and nothing can possibly so much encourage such attempts, as a mutual inattention to the interests of each other. *To divide, and thus to destroy*, is the first political maxim in attacking those, who are powerful by their union. He certainly is not a wise man, who folds his arms, and reposes himself at home, viewing, with unconcern, the flames that have invaded his neighbour's house, without using any endeavours to extinguish them. When Mr. *Hampden*'s ship money cause, for *Three Shillings* and *Four-pence*, was tried, all the people of *England*, with anxious expectation, interested themselves in the important decision; and when the slightest point, touching the freedom of *one* colony, is agitated, I earnestly wish, that *all the rest* may, with equal ardor, support their sister. Very much may be said on this subject; but I hope, more at present is unnecessary.

With concern I have observed, that *two* assemblies of this province have sat and adjourned, without taking any notice of this act. It may perhaps be asked, what would have been proper for them to do? I am by no means fond of inflammatory measures; I detest them. I should be sorry that any thing should be done, which might justly displease our sovereign, or our mother country: But a firm, modest exertion of a free spirit, should never be wanting on public occasions. It appears to me, that it would have been sufficient for the assembly, to have ordered our agents to represent to the King's ministers, their sense of the suspending act, and to pray for its repeal. Thus we should have borne our testimony against it; and might therefore reasonably expect that, on a like occasion, we might receive the same assistance from the other colonies.

> *Concordia res parvæ crescunt.*
> Small things grow great by concord.

A FARMER.

Nov. 5.
The day of King WILLIAM the Third's landing.

LETTER II.

My dear COUNTRYMEN,

THERE is another late act of parliament, which appears to me to be unconstitutional, and as destructive to the liberty of these colonies, as that mentioned in my last letter; that is, the act for granting the duties on paper, glass, *&c.*

The parliament unquestionably possesses a legal authority to *regulate* the trade of *Great-Britain*, and all her colonies. Such an authority is essential to the relation between a mother country and her colonies; and necessary for the common good of all. He, who considers these provinces as states distinct from the *British Empire*, has very slender notions of *justice*, or of their *interests*. We are but parts of a *whole*; and therefore there must exist a power somewhere, to preside, and preserve the connection in due order. This power is lodged in the parliament; and we are as much dependant on *Great-Britain*, as a perfectly free people can be on another.

I have looked over *every statute* relating to these colonies, from their first settlement to this time; and I find every one of them founded on this principle, till the *Stamp-Act* administration.* *All before*, are calculated to regulate trade, and preserve

---

* For the satisfaction of the reader, recitals from the former acts of parliament relating to these colonies are added. By comparing these with the modern acts, he will perceive their great difference in *expression* and *intention*.

The 12th *Cha.* Chap. 18, which forms the foundation of the laws relating to *our* trade, by enacting that certain productions of the colonies should be carried to *England* only, and that no goods shall be imported from the plantations but in ships belonging to *England, Ireland, Wales, Berwick*, or the *Plantations, &c.* begins thus: "*For the increase of shipping, and encouragement of the navigation of this nation*, wherein, under the good providence and protection of *GOD*, the wealth, *safety*, and strength of this kingdom Is so much concerned," *&c.*

The 15th *Cha.* II. Chap. 7, enforcing the same regulation, assigns these

or promote a mutually beneficial intercourse between the several constituent parts of the empire; and though many of them imposed duties on trade, yet those duties were always imposed *with design* to restrain the commerce of one part, that was injurious to another, and thus to promote the general welfare. The raising a revenue thereby was never intended. Thus the King, by his judges in his courts of justice, imposes fines, which all together amount to a very considerable sum, and contribute to the support of government: But this is merely a consequence arising from restrictions, that only meant to keep peace, and prevent confusion; and surely a man would argue very loosely, who should conclude from hence, that the King has a right to

---

reasons for it. "In regard his Majesty's plantations, beyond the seas, are inhabited and peopled by his subjects of this his kingdom of *England; for the maintaining a greater correspondence and kindness between them*, and keeping them in a firmer dependance upon it, and rendering them yet more beneficial and advantageous unto it, *in the further employment and increase of* English *shipping and seamen*, vent of *English* woollen, and other manufactures and commodities, *rendering the navigation to and from the same more safe and cheap*, and making this kingdom a *staple*, not only of the commodities of those plantations, but also of the commodities of other countries and places *for the supplying of them*; and it being the *usage* of other nations to keep their plantations trade to themselves," *&c.*

The 25th *Cha.* II. Chap. 7, made expressly "*for the better securing the plantation trade*," which imposes duties on certain commodities exported from one colony to another, mentions this cause for imposing them: "Whereas by one act, passed in the 12th year of your Majesty's reign, intituled, An act for *encouragement of shipping and navigation*, and by several other laws, passed since that time, it is permitted to ship, *&c.* sugars, tobacco, *&c.* of the growth, *&c.* of any of your Majesty's plantations in *America*, *&c.* from the places of their growth, *&c.* to any other of your Majesty's plantations in those parts, *&c.* and that *without paying custom for the same*, either at the lading or unlading the said commodities, by means whereof the trade and navigation in those commodities, from one plantation to another, is greatly increased, and the inhabitants of divers of those colonies, *not contenting themselves with being supplied with those commodities for their own use, free from all customs* (while the subjects of this your kingdom of *England* have paid great customs and impositions for what of them, hath been spent here) *but, contrary to the express letter of the aforesaid laws, have brought into divers parts of* Europe great quantities thereof, and do also vend great quantities thereof to the shipping of other nations, who bring them into divers parts of *Europe*, to the great hurt and diminution of your Majesty's customs, and of the *trade* and *navigation* of this your kingdom; FOR THE PREVENTION THEREOF, *&c.*

The 7th and 8th *Will.* III. Chap. 22, intituled, "An act for preventing frauds,

levy money in general upon his subjects. Never did the *British* parliament, till the period above mentioned, think of imposing duties in *America*, FOR THE PURPOSE OF RAISING A REVENUE. Mr. *Greenville* first introduced this language, in the preamble

---

and regulating abuses in the plantation trade," recites that, "notwithstanding divers acts, *&c.* great abuses are daily committed, *to the prejudice of the* English *navigation, and the loss of a great part of the plantation trade* to this kingdom, by the *artifice* and *cunning* of ill disposed persons; FOR REMEDY WHEREOF, *&c.* And whereas in some of his Majesty's *American* plantations, a doubt or misconstruction has arisen upon the before mentioned act, made in the 25th year of the reign of King *Charles* II. whereby certain duties are laid upon the commodities therein enumerated (which by law may be transported from one plantation to another, for the supply of each others wants) *as if* the same were, by the payment of those duties in one plantation, discharged from giving the securities intended by the aforesaid acts, made in the 12th, 22d and 23d years of the reign of King *Charles* II. and consequently be at liberty to go to any foreign market in *Europe*," *&c.*

The 6th *Anne*, Chap. 37, reciting the advancement of trade, and encouragement of ships of war, *&c.* grants to the captors the property of all prizes carried into *America*, subject to such customs and duties, as if the same had been first imported into any part of *Great-Britain*, and from thence exported, *&c.*

This was a *gift to persons acting under commissions from the crown*, and therefore it was reasonable that the *terms* prescribed in that gift, should be complied with—more especially as the payment of such duties was intended to give a preference to the productions of *British* colonies, over those of other colonies. However, being found inconvenient to the colonies, about four years afterwards, this act was, *for that reason*, so far repealed, that by another act "all prize goods, imported into any part of *Great-Britain*, from any of the plantations, were made liable to such duties only in *Great-Britain*, as in case they had been of the growth and produce of the plantations."

The 6th *Geo.* II. Chap. 13, which imposes duties on foreign rum, sugar and melasses, imported into the colonies, shews the reasons thus—"Whereas the welfare and prosperity of your Majesty's sugar colonies in *America*, are of the greatest consequence and importance to the *trade, navigation* and *strength* of this kingdom; and whereas the planters of the said sugar colonies, have of late years *fallen into such great discouragements*, that they are unable to improve or carry on the sugar trade, *upon an equal footing* with the foreign sugar colonies, *without some advantage and relief be given to them from* Great-Britain: FOR REMEDY WHEREOF, AND FOR THE GOOD AND WELFARE OF YOUR MAJESTY'S SUBJECTS," *&c.*

The 29th *Geo.* II. Chap. 26, and the 1st *Geo.* III. Chap. 9, which continue the 6th *Geo.* II. Chap. 13, declare, that the said act hath, by experience, been found *useful* and *beneficial*, *&c.* These are all the most considerable statutes relating to the commerce of the colonies; and it is thought to be utterly unnecessary to add any observations to these extracts, to prove that they were all intended *solely as regulations of trade*.

to the 4th of *Geo*. III. Chap. 15, which has these words—"And whereas it is just and necessary that A REVENUE BE RAISED IN YOUR MAJESTY'S SAID DOMINIONS IN AMERICA, *for defraying the expences of defending, protecting, and securing the same*: We your Majesty's most dutiful and loyal subjects, THE COMMONS OF GREAT-BRITAIN, in parliament assembled, being desirous to make some provision in this present session of parliament, TOWARDS RAISING THE SAID REVENUE IN AMERICA, have resolved to GIVE and GRANT unto your Majesty the several rates and duties herein after mentioned," *&c.*

A few months after came the *Stamp-Act*, which reciting this, proceeds in the same strange mode of expression, thus—"And whereas it is just and necessary, that provision be made FOR RAISING A FURTHER REVENUE WITHIN YOUR MAJESTY'S DOMINIONS IN AMERICA, *towards defraying the said expences*, we your Majesty's most dutiful and loyal subjects, the COMMONS OF GREAT-BRITAIN, *&c.* GIVE and GRANT," *&c.* as before.

The last act, granting duties upon paper, *&c.* carefully pursues these modern precedents. The preamble is, "Whereas it is expedient THAT A REVENUE SHOULD BE RAISED IN YOUR MAJESTY'S DOMINIONS IN AMERICA, *for making a more certain and adequate provision for defraying the charge of the administration of justice, and the support of civil government in such provinces, where it shall be found necessary; and towards the further defraying the expences of defending, protecting and securing the said dominions*, we your Majesty's most dutiful and loyal subjects, the COMMONS OF GREAT-BRITAIN, *&c.* GIVE and GRANT," *&c.* as before.

Here we may observe an authority *expresly* claimed and exerted to impose duties on these colonies; not for the regulation of trade; not for the preservation or promotion of a mutually beneficial intercourse between the several constituent parts of the empire, heretofore the *sole objects* of parliamentary institutions; *but for the single purpose of levying money upon us*.

This I call an innovation;* and a most dangerous innovation. It may perhaps be objected, that *Great-Britain* has a right to

---

* "It is worthy observation how quietly subsidies, granted in forms *usual* and *accustomable* (though heavy) are borne; such a power hath use and custom. On the other side, what discontentments and disturbances subsidies *framed in*

lay what duties she pleases upon her exports,* and it makes no difference to us, whether they are paid here or there.

To this I answer. These colonies require many things for their use, which the laws of *Great-Britain* prohibit them from getting any where but from her. Such are paper and glass.

That we may legally be bound to pay any *general* duties on these commodities, relative to the regulation of trade, is granted; but we being *obliged by her laws* to take them from *Great-Britain*, any *special* duties imposed on their exportation *to us only, with intention to raise a revenue from us only*, are as much *taxes* upon us, as those imposed by the *Stamp-Act*.

What is the difference in *substance* and *right*, whether the same sum is raised upon us by the rates mentioned in the *Stamp-Act*, on the *use* of paper, or by these duties, on the *importation* of it. It is only the edition of a former book, shifting a sentence from the *end* to the *beginning*.

Suppose the duties were made payable in *Great-Britain?*

It signifies nothing to us, whether they are to be paid here or there. Had the *Stamp-Act* directed, that all the paper should be landed at *Florida*, and the duties paid there, before it was brought to the *British* colonies, would the act have raised less money upon us, or have been less destructive of our rights? By no means: For as we were under a necessity of using the paper, we should have been under the necessity of paying the duties. Thus, in the present case, a like *necessity* will subject us, if this act continues in force, to the payment of the duties now imposed.

Why was the *Stamp-Act* then so pernicious to freedom? It did not enact, that every man in the colonies *should* buy a

---

a new mould do raise (SUCH AN INBRED HATRED NOVELTY DOTH HATCH) is evident by examples of former times." Lord *Coke*'s 4th Institute, p. 33.

* Some people think that *Great-Britain* has the same right to impose duties on the exports to these colonies, as on the exports to *Spain* and *Portugal, &c.* Such persons attend so much to the idea of exportation, that they entirely drop *that of the connection between the mother country and her colonies.* If *Great-Britain* had always claimed, and exercised an authority to compel *Spain* and *Portugal* to import manufactures from her only, the cases would be parallel: But as she never pretended to such a right, they are at liberty to get them where they please; and if they chuse to take them from her, rather than from other nations, they voluntarily consent to pay the duties imposed on them.

certain quantity of paper—No: It only directed, that no instrument of writing should be valid in law, if not made on stamped paper, &c.

The makers of that act knew full well, that the confusions that would arise from the disuse of writings, would COMPEL the colonies to use the stamped paper, and therefore to pay the taxes imposed. For this reason the *Stamp-Act* was said to be a law THAT WOULD EXECUTE ITSELF. For the very same reason, the last act of parliament, if it is granted to have any force here, WILL EXECUTE ITSELF, and will be attended with the very same consequences to *American* liberty.

Some persons perhaps may say, that this act lays us under no necessity to pay the duties imposed, because we may ourselves manufacture the articles on which they are laid; whereas by the *Stamp-Act* no instrument of writing could be good, unless made on *British* paper, and that too stamped.

Such an objection amounts to no more than this, that the injury resulting to these colonies, from the total disuse of *British* paper and glass, will not be *so afflicting* as that which would have resulted from the total disuse of writing among them; for by that means even the *Stamp-Act* might have been eluded. Why then was it universally detested by them as slavery itself? Because it presented to these devoted provinces nothing but a choice of calamities,* imbittered by indignities, each of which it was unworthy of freemen to bear. But is no injury a violation of right but the *greatest* injury? If the eluding the payment of the taxes imposed by the *Stamp-Act*, would have subjected us to a more dreadful inconvenience, than the eluding the payment of those imposed by the late act; does it therefore follow, that the last is *no violation* of our rights, tho' it is calculated for the same purpose the other was, that is, *to raise money upon us*, WITHOUT OUR CONSENT?

This would be making *right* to consist, not in an exemption from *injury*, but from a certain *degree of injury*.

But the objectors may further say, that we shall suffer no injury at all by the disuse of *British* paper and glass. We might not, if we could make as much as we want. But can any man,

---

* Either the *disuse* of writing, or the payment of *taxes* imposed by others *without our consent*.

acquainted with *America*, believe this possible? I am told there are but two or three *Glass-Houses* on this continent, and but very few *Paper-Mills*; and suppose more should be erected, a long course of years must elapse, before they can be brought to perfection. This continent is a country of planters, farmers, and fishermen; not of manufacturers. The difficulty of establishing particular manufactures in such a country, is almost insuperable. For one manufacture is connected with others in such a manner, that it may be said to be impossible to establish one or two, without establishing several others. The experience of many nations may convince us of this truth.

Inexpressible therefore must be our distresses in evading the late acts, by the disuse of *British* paper and glass. Nor will this be the extent of our misfortune, if we admit the legality of that act.

Great-Britain has prohibited the manufacturing *iron* and *steel* in these colonies, without any objection being made to her *right* of doing it. The *like* right she must have to prohibit any other manufacture among us. Thus she is possessed of an undisputed *precedent* on that point. This authority, she will say, is founded on the *original intention* of settling these colonies; that is, that she should manufacture for them, and that they should supply her with materials. The *equity* of this policy, she will also say, has been universally acknowledged by the colonies, who never have made the least objection to statutes for that purpose; and will further appear by the *mutual benefits* flowing from this usage, ever since the settlement of these colonies.

Our great advocate, Mr. *Pitt*, in his speeches on the debate concerning the repeal of the *Stamp-Act*, acknowledged, that *Great-Britain* could restrain our manufactures. His words are these—"This kingdom, as the supreme governing and legislative power, has ALWAYS bound the colonies by her regulations and RESTRICTIONS in trade, in navigation, in MANUFACTURES—in every thing, *except that of taking their money out of their pockets*, WITHOUT THEIR CONSENT." Again he says, "We may bind their trade, CONFINE THEIR MANUFACTURES, and exercise every power whatever, *except that of taking their money out of their pockets*, WITHOUT THEIR CONSENT."

Here then, my dear countrymen, ROUSE yourselves, and

behold the ruin hanging over your heads. If you ONCE admit, that *Great-Britain* may lay duties upon her exportations to us, *for the purpose of levying money on us only*, she then will have nothing to do, but to lay those duties on the articles which she prohibits us to manufacture—and the tragedy of *American* liberty is finished. We have been prohibited from procuring manufactures, in all cases, any where but from *Great-Britain* (excepting linens, which we are permitted to import directly from *Ireland.*) We have been prohibited, in some cases, from manufacturing for ourselves; and may be prohibited in others. We are therefore exactly in the situation of a city besieged, which is surrounded by the works of the besiegers in every part *but one*. If *that* is closed up, no step can be taken, *but to surrender at discretion*. If *Great-Britain* can order us to come to her for necessaries we want, and can order us to pay what taxes she pleases before we take them away, or when we land them here, we are as abject slaves as *France* and *Poland* can shew in wooden shoes, and with uncombed hair.*

Perhaps the nature of the *necessities* of dependant states, caused by the policy of a governing one, for her own benefit, may be elucidated by a fact mentioned in history. When the *Carthaginians* were possessed of the island of *Sardinia*, they made a decree, that the *Sardinians* should not raise *corn*, nor get it any other way than from the *Carthaginians*. Then, by imposing any duties they would upon it, they drained from the miserable *Sardinians* any sums they pleased; and whenever that oppressed people made the least movement to assert their liberty, their tyrants starved them to death or submission. This may be called the most perfect kind of political necessity.

From what has been said, I think this uncontrovertible conclusion may be deduced, that when a ruling state obliges a dependant state to take certain commodities from her alone, it is implied in the nature of that obligation; is essentially requisite to give it the least degree of justice; and is inseparably united with it, in order to preserve any share of freedom to the dependant state; *that those commodities should never be loaded*

---

* The peasants of *France* wear wooden shoes; and the vassals of *Poland* are remarkable for matted hair, which never can be combed.

with duties, FOR THE SOLE PURPOSE OF LEVYING MONEY ON THE DEPENDANT STATE.

Upon the whole, the single question is, whether the parliament can legally impose duties to be paid *by the people of these colonies only*, FOR THE SOLE PURPOSE OF RAISING A REVENUE, *on commodities which she obliges us to take from her alone*, or, in other words, whether the parliament can legally take money out of our pockets, without our consent. If they can, our boasted liberty is but

> *Vox et præterea nihil.*
> A sound and nothing else.

A FARMER.

LETTER III.

My dear COUNTRYMEN,

I REJOICE to find that my two former letters to you, have been generally received with so much favor by such of you, whose sentiments I have had an opportunity of knowing. Could you look into my heart, you would instantly perceive a zealous attachment to your interests, and a lively resentment of every insult and injury offered to you, to be the motives that have engaged me to address you.

I am no further concerned in any thing affecting *America*, than any one of you; and when liberty leaves it, I can quit it much more conveniently than most of you: But while Divine Providence, that gave me existence in a land of freedom, permits my head to think, my lips to speak, and my hand to move, I shall so highly and gratefully value the blessing received, as to take care, that my silence and inactivity shall not give my implied assent to any act, degrading my brethren and myself from the birthright, wherewith heaven itself "*hath made us free.*" *

Sorry I am to learn, that there are some few persons, who shake their heads with solemn motion, and pretend to wonder, what can be the meaning of these letters. "*Great-Britain,*"

---

* GAL. V. I.

they say, "is too powerful to contend with; she is determined to oppress us; it is in vain to speak of right on one side, when there is power on the other; when we are strong enough to resist, we shall attempt it; but now we are not strong enough, and therefore we had better be quiet; it signifies nothing to convince us that our rights are invaded, when we cannot defend them; and if we should get into riots and tumults about the late act, it will only draw down heavier displeasure upon us."

What can such men design? What do their grave observations amount to, but this—"that these colonies, totally regardless of their liberties, should commit them, with humble resignation, to *chance, time*, and the tender mercies of *ministers*."

Are these men ignorant, that usurpations, which might have been successfully opposed at first, acquire strength by continuance, and thus become irresistible? Do they condemn the conduct of these colonies, concerning the *Stamp-Act?* Or have they forgot its successful issue? Ought the colonies at that time, instead of acting as they did, to have trusted for relief, to the fortuitous events of futurity? If it is needless "to speak of rights" now, it was as needless then. If the behavior of the colonies was prudent and glorious then, and successful too; it will be equally prudent and glorious to act in the same manner now, if our rights are equally invaded, and may be as successful. Therefore it becomes necessary to enquire, whether "our rights *are* invaded." To talk of "defending" them, as if they could be no otherwise "defended" than by arms, is as much out of the way, as if a man having a choice of several roads to reach his journey's end, should prefer the worst, for no other reason, but because it *is* the worst.

As to "riots and tumults," the gentlemen who are so apprehensive of them, are much mistaken, if they think, that grievances cannot be redressed without such assistance.

I will now tell the gentlemen, what is "the meaning of these letters." The meaning of them is, to convince the people of these colonies, that they are at this moment exposed to the most imminent dangers; and to persuade them immediately, vigorously, and unanimously, to exert themselves, in the most firm, but most peaceable manner, for obtaining relief.

The cause of *liberty* is a cause of too much dignity, to be sullied by turbulence and tumult. It ought to be maintained in a manner suitable to her nature. Those who engage in it, should breathe a sedate, yet fervent spirit, animating them to actions of prudence, justice, modesty, bravery, humanity and magnanimity.

To such a wonderful degree were the antient *Spartans*, as brave and free a people as ever existed, inspired by this happy temperature of soul, that rejecting even in their battles the use of trumpets, and other instruments for exciting heat and rage, they marched up to scenes of havock, and horror, with the sound of flutes, to the tunes of which their steps kept pace —"exhibiting," as *Plutarch* says, "at once a terrible and delightful sight, and proceeding with a deliberate valor, full of hope and good assurance, as if some divinity had sensibly assisted them."*

I hope, my dear countrymen, that you will, in every colony, be upon your guard against those, who may at any time endeavor to stir you up, under pretences of patriotism, to any measures disrespectful to our Sovereign and our mother country. Hot, rash, disorderly proceedings, injure the reputation of a people, as to wisdom, valor and virtue, without procuring them the least benefit. I pray GOD, that he may be pleased to inspire you and your posterity, to the latest ages, with a spirit of which I have an idea, that I find a difficulty to express. To express it in the best manner I can, I mean a spirit, that shall so guide you, that it will be impossible to determine whether an *American*'s character is most distinguishable, for his loyalty to his Sovereign, his duty to his mother country, his love of freedom, or his affection for his native soil.

Every government at some time or other falls into wrong measures. These may proceed from mistake or passion. But every such measure does not dissolve the obligation between the governors and the governed. The mistake may be corrected; the passion may subside. It is the duty of the governed to endeavor to rectify the mistake, and to appease the passion. They have not at first any other right, than to represent their grievances, and to pray for redress, unless an emergence is so

* *Plutarch* in the life of *Lycurgus*. Archbishop *Potter*'s Archæologia Græca.

pressing, as not to allow time for receiving an answer to their applications, which rarely happens. If their applications are disregarded, then that kind of *opposition* becomes justifiable, which can be made without breaking the laws, or disturbing the public peace. This consists in the *prevention of the oppressors reaping advantage from their oppressions*, and not in their punishment. For experience may teach them, what reason did not; and harsh methods cannot be proper, till milder ones have failed.

If at length it becomes UNDOUBTED, that an inveterate resolution is formed to annihilate the liberties of the governed, the *English* history affords frequent examples of resistance by force. What particular circumstances will in any future case justify such resistance, can never be ascertained, till they happen. Perhaps it may be allowable to say generally, that it never can be justifiable, until the people are FULLY CONVINCED, that any further submission will be destructive to their happiness.

When the appeal is made to the sword, highly probable is it, that the punishment will exceed the offence; and the calamities attending on war out-weigh those preceding it. These considerations of justice and prudence, will always have great influence with good and wise men.

To these reflections on this subject, it remains to be added, and ought for ever to be remembered, that resistance, in the case of colonies against their mother country, is extremely different from the resistance of a people against their prince. A nation may change their king, or race of kings, and, retaining their antient form of government, be gainers by changing. Thus *Great-Britain*, under the illustrious house of *Brunswick*, a house that seems to flourish for the happiness of mankind, has found a felicity, unknown in the reigns of the *Stewarts*. But if once *we* are separated from our mother country, what new form of government shall we adopt, or where shall we find another *Britain*, to supply our loss? Torn from the body, to which we are united by religion, liberty, laws, affections, relation, language and commerce, we must bleed at every vein.

In truth—the prosperity of these provinces is founded in their dependance on *Great-Britain*; and when she returns to her "old good humour, and her old good nature," as Lord *Clarendon* expresses it, I hope they will always think it their duty and interest, as it most certainly will be, to promote her welfare by all the means in their power.

We cannot act with too much caution in our disputes. Anger produces anger; and differences, that might be accommodated by kind and respectful behavior, may, by imprudence, be enlarged to an incurable rage. In quarrels between countries, as well as in those between individuals, when they have risen to a certain height, the first cause of dissension is no longer remembered, the minds of the parties being wholly engaged in recollecting and resenting the mutual expressions of their dislike. When feuds have reached that fatal point, all considerations of reason and equity vanish; and a blind fury governs, or rather confounds all things. A people no longer regards their interest, but the gratification of their wrath. The sway of the *Cleons* and *Clodius*'s,* the designing and detestable flatterers of the *prevailing passion*, becomes confirmed. Wise and good men in vain oppose the storm, and may think themselves fortunate, if, in attempting to preserve their ungrateful fellow citizens, they do not ruin themselves. Their *prudence* will be called *baseness*; their *moderation* will be called *guilt*; and if their virtue does not lead them to destruction, as that of many other great and excellent persons has done, they may survive to receive from their expiring country the mournful glory of her acknowledgment, that their counsels, if regarded, would have saved her.

The constitutional modes of obtaining relief, are those which I wish to see pursued on the present occasion; that is, by petitions of our assemblies, or where they are not permitted to meet, of the people, to the powers that can afford us relief.

We have an excellent prince, in whose good dispositions towards us we may confide. We have a generous, sensible and humane nation, to whom we may apply. They may be deceived. They may, by artful men, be provoked to anger against us. I cannot believe they will be cruel or unjust; or that their anger will be implacable. Let us behave like dutiful children, who have received unmerited blows from a beloved parent. Let us

---

* *Cleon* was a popular firebrand of *Athens*, and *Clodius* of *Rome*; each of whom plunged his country into the deepest calamities.

complain to our parent; but let our complaints speak at the same time the language of affliction and veneration.

If, however, it shall happen, by an unfortunate course of affairs, that our applications to his Majesty and the parliament for redress, prove ineffectual, let us THEN take *another step*, by withholding from *Great-Britain* all the advantages she has been used to receive from us. THEN let us try, if our ingenuity, industry, and frugality, will not give weight to our remonstrances. Let us all be united with one spirit, in one cause. Let us invent—let us work—let us save—let us, continually, keep up our claim, and incessantly repeat our complaints—But, above all, let us implore the protection of that infinitely good and gracious being, "by whom kings reign, and princes decree justice."*

> *Nil desperandum.*
> Nothing is to be despaired of.

A FARMER.

LETTER IV.

My dear COUNTRYMEN,

AN objection, I hear, has been made against my second letter, which I would willingly clear up before I proceed. "There is," say these objectors, "a material difference between the *Stamp-Act* and the *late act* for laying a duty on paper, *&c.* that justifies the conduct of those who opposed the former, and yet are willing to submit to the latter. The duties imposed by the *Stamp-Act* were *internal* taxes; but the present are *external*, and therefore the parliament may have a right to impose them."

To this I answer, with a total denial of the power of parliament to lay upon these colonies any "*tax*" whatever.

This point, being so important to this, and to succeeding generations, I wish to be clearly understood.

To the word "*tax*," I annex that meaning which the consti-

---

* PROV. viii. 15.

tution and history of *England* require to be annexed to it; that is—that it is *an imposition on the subject, for the sole purpose of levying money.*

In the early ages of our monarchy, certain services were rendered to the crown *for the general good.* These were personal:* But, in process of time, such institutions being found inconvenient, *gifts* and *grants* of their own property were made by the people, under the several names of aids, tallages, tasks, taxes and subsidies, *&c.* These were made, as may be collected even from the names, *for public service* upon "need and necessity."† All these sums were levied upon the people by virtue of their voluntary gift.‡ Their design was to support the *national*

---

* It is very worthy of remark, how watchful our wise ancestors were, lest their *services* should be encreased beyond what the law allowed. No man was bound to go out of the realm to serve the King. Therefore, even in the conquering reign of *Henry the Fifth*, when the martial spirit of the nation was highly enflamed by the heroic courage of their Prince, and by his great success, they still carefully guarded against the establishment of illegal services. "When this point (says Lord Chief Justice *Coke*) concerning maintenance of wars out of *England*, came in question, the COMMONS did make their *continual claim* of their *antient freedom* and *birthright*, as in the first of *Henry the Fifth*, and in the seventh of *Henry the Fifth*, &c. the COMMONS made a PROTEST, that they were not bound to the maintenance of war in *Scotland, Ireland, Calice, France, Normandy*, or other *foreign* parts, and caused their PROTESTS to be entered into the parliament rolls, where they yet remain; which, in effect, agreeth with that which, upon like occasion, was made in the parliament of 25th *Edward* I." 2d *Inst.* p. 528.

† 4th *Inst.* p. 28.

‡ *Reges* Angliæ, *nihil tale, nisi convocatis primis ordinibus, et assentiente populo suscipiunt.* Phil. Comines. 2d *Inst.*

These gifts entirely depending on the pleasure of the donors, were proportioned to the abilities of the several ranks of people who gave, and were regulated by *their* opinion of the public necessities. Thus *Edward* I. had in his 11th year a *thirtieth* from the *laity*, a *twentieth* from the *clergy*; in his 22d year a *tenth* from the *laity*, a *sixth* from *London*, and other corporate towns, *half of their benefices* from the *clergy*; in his 23d year an *eleventh* from the *barons* and others, a *tenth* from the *clergy*, a *seventh* from the *burgesses, &c.* Hume's *Hist. of England*.

The same difference in the grants of the several ranks is observable in other reigns.

In the famous statute *de tallagio non concedendo*, the king enumerates the several *classes*, without whose consent, he and his heirs never should set or levy any tax—"*nullum tallagium, vel auxilium per nos, vel hæredes nostros in regno*

honor and interest. Some of those grants comprehended duties arising from trade; being imposts on merchandizes. These Lord Chief Justice *Coke* classes under "subsidies," and "parliamentary aids." They are also called "customs." But whatever the *name* was, they were always considered as *gifts of the people to the crown, to be employed for public uses.*

Commerce was at a low ebb, and surprizing instances might be produced how little it was attended to for a succession of ages. The terms that have been mentioned, and, among the rest, that of "*tax*," had obtained a national, parliamentary meaning, drawn from the principles of the constitution, long before any *Englishman* thought of *imposition of duties, for the regulation of trade.*

Whenever we speak of "taxes" among *Englishmen*, let us therefore speak of them with reference to the *principles* on which, and the *intentions* with which they have been established. This will give certainty to our expression, and safety to our conduct: But if, when we have in view the liberty of these colonies, we proceed in any other course, we pursue a *Juno** indeed, but shall only catch a cloud.

In the national, parliamentary sense insisted on, the word "tax"[†] was certainly understood by the congress at *New-York*, whose resolves may be said to form the *American* "bill of rights."

The third, fourth, fifth, and sixth resolves, are thus expressed.

III. "That it is *inseparably essential to the freedom of a people,*

---

nostro ponatur seu levetur, sine voluntate et assensu archiepiscoporum, episcoporum, comitum, baronum, militum, burgensium, et aliorum liberorum com. de regno nostro." 34th *Edward* I.

Lord Chief Justice *Coke*, in his comment on these words, says—"for the quieting of the *commons*, and for a *perpetual and constant law for ever after*, both in this AND OTHER LIKE CASES, this act was made." These words are *plain*, WITHOUT ANY SCRUPLE, *absolute*, WITHOUT ANY SAVING." 2d *Coke*'s Inst. p. 532, 533. Little did the venerable judge imagine, that "*other* LIKE *cases*" would happen, in which the spirit of this law would be despised by *Englishmen*, the posterity of those who made it.

* The Goddess of *Empire*, in the Heathen Mythology; according to an antient fable, *Ixion* pursued her, but she escaped in a cloud.

† In this sense *Montesquieu* uses the word "tax," in his 13th book of *Spirit of Laws*.

and the *undoubted right* of *Englishmen*, that NO TAX* be imposed on them, *but with their own consent*, given personally, or by their representatives."

IV. "That the people of the colonies are not, and from their local circumstances, cannot be represented in the house of commons in *Great-Britain*."

V. "That the only representatives of the people of the colonies, are the persons chosen therein by themselves; and that NO TAXES ever have been, or can be constitutionally imposed on them, but by their respective legislatures."

VI. "That all *supplies to the crown*, being free gifts of the people, it is *unreasonable, and inconsistent with the principles and spirit of the* British *constitution*, for the people of *Great-Britain* to grant to his Majesty *the property of the colonies*."

Here is no distinction made between *internal* and *external* taxes. It is evident from the short reasoning thrown into these resolves, that every imposition "to grant to his Majesty *the property of the colonies*," was thought a "tax;" and that every such imposition, if laid any other way, than "with their consent, given personally, or by their representatives," was not only "unreasonable, and inconsistent with the principles and spirit of the *British* constitution," but destructive "to the freedom of a people."

This language is clear and important. A "TAX" means an imposition to raise money. Such persons therefore as speak of *internal* and *external* "TAXES," I pray may pardon me, if I object to that expression, as applied to the privileges and interests of these colonies. There may be *internal* and *external* IMPOSITIONS, founded on *different principles*, and having *different tendencies*; every "tax" being an imposition, tho' every imposition is not a "tax." But *all taxes* are founded on the *same principle*; and have the *same tendency*.

External impositions, for the regulation of our trade, do not "grant to his Majesty *the property of the colonies*." They only

---

* The rough draught of the resolves of the congress at *New-York* are now in my hands, and from some notes on that draught, and other particular reasons, I am satisfied, that the congress understood the word "tax" in the sense here contended for.

prevent the colonies acquiring property, in things not necessary, in a manner judged to be injurious to the welfare of the whole empire. But the last statute respecting us, "grants to his Majesty *the property of the colonies,*" by laying duties on the manufactures of *Great-Britain* which they MUST take, and which she settled them, on purpose that they SHOULD take.

What *tax** can be more *internal* than this? Here is money

---

* It seems to be evident, that Mr. *Pitt,* in his defence of *America,* during the debate concerning the repeal of the *Stamp-Act,* by "*internal* taxes," meant any duties "for the purpose of raising a revenue;" and by "*external* taxes," meant duties imposed "for the regulation of trade." His expressions are these—"If the gentleman does not understand the difference between *internal* and *external* taxes, I cannot help it; but there is a plain distinction between taxes levied FOR THE PURPOSES OF RAISING A REVENUE, and duties imposed FOR THE REGULATION OF TRADE, for the accommodation of the subject; altho', in the consequences, some revenue might incidentally arise from the latter."

These words were in Mr. *Pitt*'s reply to Mr. *Greenville,* who said he could not understand the difference between external and internal taxes.

In every other part of his speeches on that occasion, his words confirm this construction of his expressions. The following extracts will shew how positive and general were his assertions of our right.

"It is my opinion that this kingdom has NO RIGHT to lay A TAX upon the colonies."—"The *Americans* are the SONS, not the BASTARDS of *England.* TAXATION is NO PART of the *governing* or *legislative* power".—"The *taxes* are a voluntary *gift* and *grant* of the *commons* ALONE. In LEGISLATION the THREE estates of the realm are ALIKE concerned, but the concurrence of the PEERS and the CROWN to a TAX, is only necessary to close with the FORM of a law. The GIFT *and* GRANT is of the COMMONS ALONE." —"*The distinction between* LEGISLATION *and* TAXATION *is essentially necessary to liberty.*"—"The COMMONS of *America,* represented in their several assemblies, have ever been in possession of the exercise of this their constitutional right, of GIVING and GRANTING their OWN MONEY. *They would have been SLAVES, if they had not enjoyed it.*" "The idea of a *virtual* representation of *America* in this house, is the most contemptible idea that ever entered into the head of man.—It does not deserve a serious refutation."

He afterwards shews the unreasonableness of *Great-Britain* taxing *America,* thus—"When I had the honor of serving his Majesty, I availed myself of the means of information, which I derived from my office, I SPEAK THEREFORE FROM KNOWLEDGE. My materials were good. I was at pains to *collect,* to *digest,* to *consider* them; and *I will be bold to affirm,* that the profit to *Great-Britain* from the trade of the colonies, through all its branches, is TWO MILLIONS A YEAR. *This* is the fund that carried you triumphantly through the last war. The estates that were rented at two thousand pounds a year, threescore years ago, are three thousand pounds at present. Those estates sold then from fifteen to eighteen years purchase; the same may now be sold for thirty. YOU drawn, *without their consent*, from a society, who have constantly enjoyed a constitutional mode of raising all money among themselves. The payment of this *tax* they have no possible method of avoiding; as they cannot do without the commodities on which it is laid, and they cannot manufacture these commodities themselves. Besides, if this unhappy country should be so lucky as to elude this act, by getting parchment enough, in the place of paper, or by reviving the antient method of writing on wax and bark, and by inventing something to serve instead of glass, her ingenuity would stand her in little stead; for then the parliament would have nothing to do but to prohibit such manufactures, or to lay a tax on *hats* and *woollen cloths*, which they have already prohibited the colonies *from supplying each other with*; or on instruments and tools of *steel* and *iron*, which they have prohibited the provincials *from manufacturing at all*:*And then, what little gold and silver they have, must be torn from their hands, or they will not be able, in a short time, to get an ax,† for cutting their firewood, nor a plough, for raising their food. In what respect, therefore, I beg leave to ask, is the late act preferable to the *Stamp-Act*, or more consistent with the liberties of the colonies? For my own part, I regard them both with equal apprehension; and think they ought to be in the same manner opposed.

OWE THIS TO AMERICA. THIS IS THE PRICE THAT AMERICA PAYS YOU FOR HER PROTECTION."—"I dare not say how much higher these profits may be augmented."—"Upon the whole, I will beg leave to tell the house what is really my opinion; it is, that the *Stamp-Act* be repealed absolutely, totally, and immediately. That the reason for the repeal be assigned, because it was founded on an ERRONEOUS PRINCIPLE."

* "And that *pig* and *bar iron*, made in his Majesty's colonies in *America*, may be FURTHER MANUFACTURED IN THIS KINGDOM, be it further enacted by the authority aforesaid, that from and after the twenty-fourth day of *June*, 1750, no *mill*, or *other engine*, for *slitting* or *rolling* of iron, or any *plating forge*, to work with a *tilt hammer*, or any *furnace* for *making steel*, shall be erected; or, after such erection, continued IN ANY OF HIS MAJESTY'S COLONIES IN AMERICA." 23d *George* II. Chap. 29, Sect. 9.

† Tho' these particulars are mentioned as being absolutely necessary, yet perhaps they are not more so than glass in our severe winters, to keep out the cold from our houses; or than paper, without which such inexpressible confusions must ensue.

*Habemus quidem senatus consultum,—tanquam gladium
    in vagina repositum.*

We have a statute, laid up for future use, like a sword in
    the scabbard.

                                              A FARMER.

                          LETTER V.

My dear COUNTRYMEN,

PERHAPS the objection to the late act, imposing duties upon
paper, *&c.* might have been safely rested on the argument
drawn from the universal conduct of parliaments and ministers, from the first existence of these colonies, to the administration of Mr. *Greenville.*

What but the indisputable, the acknowledged exclusive right
of the colonies to tax themselves, could be the reason, that in
this long period of more than one hundred and fifty years, no
statute was ever passed for the sole purpose of raising a revenue
on the colonies? And how clear, how cogent must that reason
be, to which every parliament, and every minister, for so long
a time submitted, without a single attempt to innovate?

England, in part of that course of years, and *Great-Britain,*
in other parts, was engaged in several fierce and expensive
wars; troubled with some tumultuous and bold parliaments;
governed by many daring and wicked ministers; yet none of
them ever ventured to touch the *Palladium* of *American* liberty. Ambition, avarice, faction, tyranny, all revered it. Whenever it was necessary to raise money on the colonies, the
requisitions of the crown were made, and dutifully complied
with. The parliament, from time to time, regulated their trade,
and that of the rest of the empire, to preserve their dependence, and the connection of the whole in good order.

The people of *Great-Britain,* in support of their privileges,
boast much of their antiquity. It is true they are antient; yet it
may well be questioned, if there is a single privilege of a *British*
subject, supported by longer, more solemn, or more uninterrupted testimony, than the exclusive right of taxation in these
colonies. The people of *Great-Britain* consider that kingdom
as the sovereign of these colonies, and would now annex to

that sovereignty a prerogative never heard of before. How would they bear this, was the case their own? What would they think of a *new* prerogative claimed by the crown? We may guess what their conduct would be, from the transports of passion into which they fell about the late embargo, tho' laid to relieve the most emergent necessities of state, admitting of no delay; and for which there were numerous precedents. Let our liberties be treated with the same tenderness, and it is all we desire.

Explicit as the conduct of parliaments, for so many ages, is, to prove that no money can be levied on these colonies by parliament, for the purpose of raising a revenue, yet it is not the only evidence in our favor.

Every one of the most material arguments against the legality of the *Stamp-Act*, operates with equal force against the act now objected to; but as they are well known, it seems unnecessary to repeat them here.

This general one only shall be considered at present: That tho' these colonies are dependent on *Great-Britain*; and tho' she has a legal power to make laws for preserving that dependence; yet it is not necessary for this purpose, nor essential to the relation between a mother country and her colonies, as was eagerly contended by the advocates for the *Stamp-Act*, that she should raise money on them without their consent.

Colonies were formerly planted by warlike nations, to keep their enemies in awe; to relieve their country, overburthened with inhabitants; or to discharge a number of discontented and troublesome citizens. But in more modern ages, the spirit of violence being, in some measure, if the expression may be allowed, sheathed in commerce, colonies have been settled by the nations of *Europe* for the purposes of trade. These purposes were to be attained, by the colonies raising for their mother country those things which she did not produce herself; and by supplying themselves from her with things they wanted. These were the *national objects* in the commencement of our colonies, and have been uniformly so in their promotion.

To answer these grand purposes, perfect liberty was known to be necessary; all history proving, that trade and freedom are nearly related to each other. By a due regard to this wise and just plan, the infant colonies, exposed in the unknown climates and unexplored wildernesses of this new world, lived, grew, and flourished.

The parent country, with undeviating prudence and virtue, attentive to the first principles of colonization, drew to herself the benefits she might reasonably expect, and preserved to her children the blessings, on which those benefits were founded. She made laws, obliging her colonies to carry to her all those products which she wanted for her own use; and all those raw materials which she chose herself to work up. Besides this restriction, she forbad them to procure *manufactures* from any other part of the globe, or even the *products* of *European* countries, which alone could rival her, without being first brought to her. In short, by a variety of laws, she regulated their trade in such a manner as she thought most conducive to their mutual advantage, and her own welfare. A power was reserved to the crown of *repealing* any laws that should be enacted: The *executive* authority of government was also lodged in the crown, and its representatives; and an *appeal* was secured to the crown from all judgments in the administration of justice.

For all these powers, established by the mother country over the colonies; for all these immense emoluments derived by her from them; for all their difficulties and distresses in fixing themselves, what was the recompence made them? A communication of her rights in general, and particularly of that great one, the foundation of all the rest—that their property, acquired with so much pain and hazard, should be disposed of by none but themselves*—or, to use the beautiful and emphatic language of the sacred scriptures, "that they should sit *every man* under his vine, and under his fig-tree, and NONE SHOULD MAKE THEM AFRAID."†

Can any man of candor and knowledge deny, that these institutions form an affinity between *Great-Britain* and her colonies, that sufficiently secures their dependence upon her? Or that for her to levy taxes upon them, is to reverse the nature of things? Or that she can pursue such a measure, without reducing them to a state of vassalage?

---

* "The power of *taxing themselves*, was the privilege of which the *English* were, WITH REASON, *particularly jealous.*" *Hume's Hist. of England.*
† MIC. iv. 4.

If any person cannot conceive the supremacy of *Great-Britain* to exist, without the power of laying taxes to levy money upon us, the history of the colonies, and of *Great-Britain*, since their settlement, will prove the contrary. He will there find the amazing advantages arising to her from them—the constant exercise of her supremacy—and their filial submission to it, without a single rebellion, or even the thought of one, from their first emigration to this moment—And all these things have happened, without one instance of *Great-Britain*'s laying taxes to levy money upon them.

How many *British authors** have demonstrated, that the present wealth, power and glory of their country, are founded upon these colonies? As constantly as streams tend to the ocean, have they been pouring the fruits of all their labors into

---

* It has been said in the House of Commons, when complaints have been made of the decay of trade to any part of *Europe*, "That such things were not worth regard, as *Great-Britain* was possessed of colonies that could consume more of her manufactures than she was able to supply them with."

"As the case now stands, we shall shew that the *plantations* are a spring of *wealth* to this nation, that they *work* for us, that their TREASURE CENTERS ALL HERE, and that the laws have tied them fast enough to us; so that it must be through our own fault and mismanagement, if they become independent of *England*." DAVENANT *on the Plantation Trade.*

"It is better that the islands should be supplied from the Northern Colonies than from *England*; for this reason, the provisions we might send to *Barbados, Jamaica, &c.* would be *unimproved* product of the earth, as grain of all kinds, or such product where there is little got by the improvement, as malt, salt beef and pork; indeed the exportation of salt fish thither would be more advantageous, but the goods which we send to the *Northern Colonies*, are such, whose *improvement* may be justly said, one with another, to be near *four fifths* of the value of the *whole commodity*, as apparel, houshold furniture, and many other things." *Idem.*

"*New-England* is the most prejudicial plantation to the kingdom of *England*; and yet, to do right to that most industrious *English* colony, I must confess, that though we lose by their unlimited trade with other foreign plantations, yet we are very great gainers by their direct trade to and from *Old England*. Our yearly exportations of *English* manufactures, malt and other goods, from hence thither, amounting, in my opinion, to *ten times* the value of what is imported from thence; which calculation I do not make at random, but upon *mature consideration*, and, peradventure, upon *as much experience in this very trade*, as any other person will pretend to; and therefore, whenever reformation of our correspondency in trade with that people shall be thought on, it will, in my poor judgment, require GREAT TENDERNESS, and VERY SERIOUS CIRCUMSPECTION." *Sir* JOSIAH CHILD's *Discourse on Trade.*

their mother's lap. Good heaven! and shall a total oblivion of former tendernesses and blessings, be spread over the minds of a good and wise nation, by the sordid arts of intriguing men, who, covering their selfish projects under pretences of public good, first enrage their countrymen into a frenzy of passion,

---

"Our plantations spend mostly our *English* manufactures, and those *of all sorts almost imaginable*, in *egregious quantities*, and employ near *two thirds of all our* English *shipping*; so that we have *more people* in *England*, by reason of our plantations in *America*." *Idem.*

Sir JOSIAH CHILD says, in another part of his work, "That not more than fifty families are maintained in *England* by the refining of sugar." From whence, and from what *Davenant* says, it is plain, that the advantages here said to be derived from the plantations by *England*, must be meant chiefly of the continental colonies.

"I shall sum up my whole remarks on our *American* colonies, with this observation, that as they are a certain annual revenue of SEVERAL MILLIONS STERLING to their mother country, they ought carefully to be protected, duly encouraged, and every opportunity that presents, improved for their increment and advantage, as every one they can possibly reap, must at last return to us with interest." BEAWES*'s Lex Merc. Red.*

"We may safely advance, that our trade and navigation are greatly encreased by our colonies, and that they really are a source of treasure and naval power to this kingdom, since THEY WORK FOR US, and THEIR TREASURE CENTERS HERE. Before their settlement, our manufactures were few, and those but indifferent; the number of *English* merchants very small, and the whole shipping of the nation much inferior to what now belongs to the Northern Colonies only. *These are certain facts.* But since their establishment, our condition has altered for the better, almost to a degree beyond credibility.—Our MANUFACTURES are prodigiously encreased, chiefly by the demand for them in the plantations, where they AT LEAST TAKE OFF ONE HALF, and supply us with many valuable commodities for exportation, which is as great an emolument to the mother kingdom, as to the plantations themselves." POSTLETHWAYT*'s Univ. Dict. of Trade and Commerce.*

"Most of the nations of *Europe* have interfered with us, more or less, in divers of our staple manufactures, within half a century, not only in our woollen, but in our lead and tin manufactures, as well as our fisheries." POSTLETHWAYT, *ibid.*

"The inhabitants of our colonies, by carrying on a trade with their *foreign neighbours*, do not only occasion *a greater quantity of the goods and merchandizes of* Europe *being sent from hence to them*, and a greater quantity of the product of *America* to be sent from them hither, *which would otherwise be carried from, and brought to* Europe *by foreigners*, but an increase of the seamen and navigation in those parts, which is of great strength and security, as well as of great advantage to our plantations in general. And though *some of our colonies* are not only for preventing the *importations of all goods of the same species*

and then advance their own influence and interest, by gratifying the passion, which they themselves have basely excited.

Hitherto *Great-Britain* has been contented with her prosperity. Moderation has been the rule of her conduct. But now, a generous humane people, that so often has protected the liberty of *strangers*, is inflamed into an attempt to tear a privilege from her own children, which, if executed, must, in their opinion, sink them into slaves: AND FOR WHAT? For a pernicious power, not necessary to her, as her own experience may convince her; but horribly dreadful and detestable to them.

It seems extremely probable, that when cool, dispassionate

---

they produce, but suffer particular planters to *keep great runs of land in their possession uncultivated*, with design to prevent new settlements, whereby they imagine the prices of their commodities may be affected; yet if it be considered, that the markets of *Great-Britain* depend on the markets of ALL *Europe in general*, and that the *European* markets *in general* depend on the proportion between the *annual consumption* and the *whole quantity* of each species *annually produced* by ALL *nations*; it must follow, that whether we or foreigners are the producers, *carriers*, importers and exporters of *American* produce, yet their respective prices in *each colony* (the difference of freight, customs and importations considered) will always bear proportion to the *general consumption* of the *whole quantity* of each sort, *produced in all colonies*, and *in all parts*, allowing only for the usual contingencies that trade and commerce, agriculture and manufactures, are liable to in all countries." POSTLETHWAYT, *ibid.*

"It is certain, that from the very time Sir *Walter Raleigh*, the father of our *English* colonies, and his associates, first projected these establishments, there have been persons who have found an interest, in *misrepresenting*, or lessening the value of them—The attempts were called chimerical and dangerous. Afterwards many malignant suggestions were made about sacrificing so many *Englishmen* to the obstinate desire of settling colonies in countries which then produced very little advantage. But as these difficulties were gradually surmounted, those complaints vanished. No sooner were *these lamentations* over, but *others* arose in their stead; when it could be no longer said, that the colonies were *useless*, it was alledged that they were not *useful enough* to their mother country; that while we were loaded with taxes, they were absolutely free; that the *planters* lived like *princes*, while the inhabitants of *England* laboured hard for a tolerable subsistence." POSTLETHWAYT, *ibid.*

"Before the settlement of these colonies," says *Postlethwayt*, "our manufactures were few, and those but indifferent. In those days we had not only our naval stores, but our ships from our neighbours. *Germany* furnished us with all things made of metal, even to nails. Wine, paper, linens, and a thousand other things, came from *France*. *Portugal* supplied us with sugar; all the products of *America* were poured into us from *Spain*; and the *Venetians* and *Genoese* retailed to us the commodities of the *East-Indies*, at their own price."

posterity, shall consider the affectionate intercourse, the reciprocal benefits, and the unsuspecting confidence, that have subsisted between these colonies and their parent country, for such a length of time, they will execrate, with the bitterest curses, the infamous memory of those men, whose pestilential ambition unnecessarily, wantonly, cruelly, first opened the sources of civil discord between them; first turned their love into jealousy; and first taught these provinces, filled with grief and anxiety, to enquire—

> *Mens ubi materna est?*
> Where is maternal affection?

A FARMER.

"If it be asked, whether foreigners, for what goods they take of us, do not pay on *that consumption* a great portion of our taxes? It is admitted they do." POSTLETHWAYT'*s Great-Britain's True System.*

"If we are afraid that one day or other the colonies will revolt, and set up for themselves, as some seem to apprehend, let us not *drive* them to a *necessity* to *feel* themselves independent of us; as they *will* do, the moment they perceive that *THEY CAN BE SUPPLIED WITH ALL THINGS FROM WITHIN THEMSELVES*, and do not need our assistance. If we would keep them still dependent upon their mother country, and, in some respects, *subservient* to her *views* and welfare; let us make it their INTEREST always to be so." TUCKER *on Trade.*

"Our colonies, while they have *English* blood in their veins, and have relations in *England*, and WHILE THEY CAN GET BY TRADING WITH US, the *stronger* and *greater they* grow, the *more* this *crown* and *kingdom* will *get* by them; and nothing but such an arbitrary power as shall make them desperate, can bring them to rebel." DAVENANT *on the Plantation Trade.*

"The Northern colonies are not upon the same footing as those of the South; and having a worse soil to improve, they must find the recompence some other way, which only can be in property and dominion: Upon which score, any INNOVATIONS in the form of government there, should be cautiously examined, for fear of entering upon measures, by which the industry of the inhabitants be quite discouraged. 'Tis ALWAYS UNFORTUNATE for a people, either by CONSENT, or upon COMPULSION, to depart from their PRIMITIVE INSTITUTIONS, and THOSE FUNDAMENTALS, by which they were FIRST UNITED TOGETHER." *Idem.*

The most effectual way of *uniting* the colonies, is to make it their common interest to oppose the designs and attempts of *Great-Britain.*

"All wise states will well consider how to preserve the advantages arising from colonies, and avoid the evils. And I conceive that there can be but TWO ways

LETTER VI.

My dear COUNTRYMEN,

IT may perhaps be objected against the arguments that have been offered to the public, concerning the legal power of the parliament, "that it has always exercised the power of imposing duties, for the purposes of raising a revenue on the productions of these colonies carried to *Great-Britain*, which may be called a tax on them." To this objection I answer, that this is no violation of the rights of the colonies, it being implied in the relation between them and *Great-Britain*, that they should not

---

in nature to hinder them from throwing off their dependence; *one*, to keep it out of their *power*, and the *other*, out of their *will*. The *first* must be by *force*; and the *latter*, by *using them well*, and keeping them employed in such productions, and making such manufactures, as will support themselves and families comfortably, *and procure them wealth too*, and at least not prejudice their mother country.

"*Force* can never be used effectually to answer the end, *without destroying the colonies themselves.* Liberty and encouragement are necessary to carry people thither, and to keep them together when they are there; and violence will hinder both. Any body of troops, considerable enough to awe them, and keep them in subjection, under the direction too of a needy governor, often sent thither to make his fortune, and at such a distance from any application for redress, will soon put an end to all planting, and leave the country to the soldiers alone, and if it did not, *would eat up all the profit of the colony.* For this reason, arbitrary countries have not been equally successful in planting colonies with free ones; and what they have done in that kind, has either been by force, at a vast expence, or *by departing from the nature of their government*, and *giving such privileges to planters* as were *denied to their other subjects.* And I dare say, that a few prudent laws, and a little prudent conduct, would soon give us far the greatest share of the riches of all *America*, perhaps drive many of other nations out of it, or into our colonies for shelter.

"There are *so many exigencies* in all states, *so many foreign wars*, and *domestic disturbances*, that these colonies CAN NEVER WANT OPPORTUNITIES, if they watch for them, *to do what they shall find their interest to do;* and therefore we ought to take all the precautions in our power, that it shall never be *their interest* to act against that of their native country; an evil which can no otherwise be averted, than by keeping them *fully employed* in such trades *as will increase their own*, as well as our wealth; for it is much to be feared, if we do not find employment for *them*, they may find it for *us*; the interest of the mother country, is always to keep them dependent, and so employed; and it requires all her address to do it; and it is certainly more *easily* and *effectually* done by *gentle* and *insensible* methods, than by *power* alone." CATO'*s Letters.*

carry such commodities to other nations, as should enable them to interfere with the mother country. The imposition of duties on these commodities, when brought to her, is only a consequence of her parental right; and if the point is thoroughly examined, the duties will be found to be laid on the people of the mother country. Whatever they are, they must proportionably raise the price of the goods, and consequently must be paid by the consumers. In this light they were considered by the parliament in the 25th *Charles* II. Chap. 7, Sect. 2, which says, that the productions of the plantations were carried from one to another free from all customs, "while the subjects of this your kingdom of *England* have paid *great customs and impositions for what of them have been* SPENT HERE," *&c.*

Besides, if *Great-Britain* exports these commodities again, the duties will injure her own trade, so that she cannot hurt us, without plainly and immediately hurting herself; and this is our check against her acting arbitrarily in this respect.

It* may be perhaps further objected, "that it being granted

---

* If any one should observe that no opposition has been made to the legality of the 4th *Geo.* III. Chap. 15, which is the FIRST act of parliament that ever imposed duties on the importations into *America*, for the *expressed* purpose of raising a revenue there; I answer—First, That tho' the act expresly mentions the raising a revenue in *America*, yet it seems that it had as much in view the "improving and securing the trade between the same and *Great-Britain*," which words are part of its title: And the preamble says, "Whereas it is expedient that new provisions and regulations should be established for improving the revenue of this kingdom, and *for extending and securing the navigation and commerce between* Great-Britain *and your Majesty's dominions in* America, which by the peace have been so happily extended and enlarged," *&c.* Secondly, *All* the duties mentioned in that act are imposed solely on the *productions and manufactures of foreign countries*, and not a single duty laid on any production or manufacture of our mother country. Thirdly, The authority of the provincial assemblies is not therein so plainly *attacked* as by the last act, which makes provision for defraying the charges of the "administration of justice," and "the support of civil government." Fourthly, That it being *doubtful*, whether the intention of the 4th *Geo.* III. Chap. 15, was not as much *to regulate trade*, as *to raise a revenue*, the minds of the people here were wholly engrossed by the terror of the *Stamp-Act*, then impending over them, about the intention of which there could be *no doubt.*

These reasons so far distinguish the 4th *Geo.* III. Chap. 15, from the last act, that it is not to be wondered at, that the first should have been submitted to, tho' the *last* should excite the most universal and spirited opposition. For *this* that statutes made for regulating trade, are binding upon us, it will be difficult for any persons, but the makers of the laws, to determine, which of them are made for the regulating of trade, and which for raising a revenue; and that from hence may arise confusion."

To this I answer, that the objection is of no force in the present case, or such as resemble it; because the act now in question, is formed *expresly* FOR THE SOLE PURPOSE OF RAIS- ING A REVENUE.

However, supposing the design of parliament had not been *expressed*, the objection seems to me of no weight, with regard to the influence which those who may make it, might expect it ought to have on the conduct of these colonies.

It is true, that *impositions for raising a revenue*, may be hereafter called *regulations of trade*: But names will not change the nature of things. Indeed we ought firmly to believe, what is an undoubted truth, confirmed by the unhappy experience of many states heretofore free, that UNLESS THE MOST WATCH- FUL ATTENTION BE EXERTED, A NEW SERVITUDE MAY BE SLIPPED UPON US, UNDER THE SANCTION OF USUAL AND RE- SPECTABLE TERMS.

Thus the *Cæsars* ruined the *Roman* liberty, under the titles of *tribunicial* and *dictatorial* authorities—old and venerable dignities, known in the most flourishing times of freedom. In imitation of the same policy, *James* II. when he *meant* to estab- lish popery, *talked* of liberty of conscience, the most sacred of all liberties; and had thereby almost deceived the Dissenters into destruction.

All artful rulers, who strive to extend their power beyond its just limits, endeavor to give to their attempts as much sem- blance of legality as possible. Those who succeed them may venture to go a little further; for each new encroachment will be strengthened by a former. "That which is now supported

---

will be found, on the strictest examination, to be, in the *principle* on which it is founded, and in the *consequences* that must attend it, if possible, more de- structive than the *Stamp-Act*. It is, to speak plainly, a *prodigy* in our laws; not having one *British* feature.

by examples, growing old, will become an example itself,"* and thus support fresh usurpations.

A free people therefore can never be too quick in observing, nor too firm in opposing the beginnings of *alteration* either in *form* or *reality*, respecting institutions formed for their security. The first kind of alteration leads to the last: Yet, on the other hand, nothing is more certain, than that the *forms* of liberty may be retained, when the *substance* is gone. In government, as well as in religion, "The *letter* killeth, but the *spirit* giveth life."†

I will beg leave to enforce this remark by a few instances. The crown, by the constitution, has the prerogative of creating peers. The existence of that order, in due number and dignity, is essential to the constitution; and if the crown did not exercise that prerogative, the peerage must have long since decreased so much as to have lost its proper influence. Suppose a prince, for some unjust purposes, should, from time to time, advance so many needy, profligate wretches to that rank, that all the independence of the house of lords should be destroyed; there would then be a manifest violation of the constitution, *under the appearance of using legal prerogative.*

The house of commons claims the privilege of forming all money bills, and will not suffer either of the other branches of the legislature to add to, or alter them; contending that their power simply extends to an acceptance or rejection of them. This privilege appears to be just: But under pretence of this just privilege, the house of commons has claimed a licence of tacking to money bills, clauses relating to things of a totally different kind, and thus forcing them in a manner on the king and lords. This seems to be an abuse of that privilege, and it may be vastly more abused. Suppose a future house, influenced by some displaced, discontented demagogues—in a time of danger, should tack to a money bill, something so injurious to the king and peers, that they would not assent to it, and yet the commons should obstinately insist on it; the whole kingdom would be exposed to ruin by them, *under the appearance of maintaining a valuable privilege.*

* TACITUS.
† 2 COR. iii. 6.

In these cases it might be difficult for a while to determine, whether the king intended to exercise his prerogative in a constitutional manner or not; or whether the commons insisted on their demand factiously, or for the public good: But surely the conduct of the crown, or of the house, would in time sufficiently explain itself.

Ought not the PEOPLE therefore to watch? to observe facts? to search into causes? to investigate designs? And have they not a right of JUDGING from the evidence before them, on no slighter points than their *liberty* and *happiness*? It would be less than trifling, wherever a *British* government is established, to make use of any arguments to prove such a right. It is sufficient to remind the reader of the day, on the anniversary of which the first of these letters is dated.

I will now apply what has been said to the present question.

The *nature* of any impositions laid by parliament on these colonies, must determine the *design* in laying them. It may not be easy in every instance to discover that design. Wherever it is doubtful, I think submission cannot be dangerous; nay, it must be right; for, in my opinion, there is no privilege these colonies claim, which they ought in *duty* and *prudence* more earnestly to maintain and defend, than the authority of the *British* parliament to regulate the trade of all her dominions. Without this authority, the benefits she enjoys from our commerce, must be lost to her: The blessings we enjoy from our dependence upon her, must be lost to us. Her strength must decay; her glory vanish; and she cannot suffer without our partaking in her misfortune. *Let us therefore cherish her interests as our own, and give her every thing, that it becomes* FREEMEN *to give or to receive.*

The *nature* of any impositions she may lay upon us may, in general, be known, by considering how far they relate to the preserving, in due order, the connection between the several parts of the *British* empire. One thing we may be assured of, which is this—Whenever she imposes duties on commodities, to be paid only upon their exportation from *Great-Britain* to these colonies, it is not a regulation of trade, but a design to raise a revenue upon us. Other instances may happen, which it may not be necessary at present to dwell on. I hope these colonies will never, to their latest existence, want understanding sufficient to discover the intentions of those who rule over them, nor the resolution necessary for asserting their interests. They will always have the same rights, that all free states have, of judging when their privileges are invaded, and of using all prudent measures for preserving them.

> *Quocirca vivite fortes*
> *Fortiaque adversis opponite pectora rebus.*
> Wherefore keep up your spirits, and gallantly oppose
> this adverse course of affairs.

A FARMER.

LETTER VII.

My dear COUNTRYMEN,

THIS letter is intended more particularly for such of you, whose employments in life may have prevented your attending to the consideration of some points that are of great and public importance: For many such persons there must be even in these colonies, where the inhabitants in general are more intelligent than any other people whatever, as has been remarked by strangers, and it seems with reason.

Some of you, perhaps, filled, as I know your breasts are, with loyalty to our most excellent Prince, and with love to our dear mother country, may feel yourselves inclined, by the affections of your hearts, to approve every action of those whom you so much venerate and esteem. A prejudice thus flowing from goodness of disposition, is amiable indeed. I wish it could be indulged without danger. Did I think this possible, the error should have been adopted, and not opposed by me. But in truth, all men are subject to the frailties of nature; and therefore whatever regard we entertain for the *persons* of those who govern us, we should always remember that their conduct, as *rulers*, may be influenced by human infirmities.

When any laws, injurious to these colonies, are passed, we cannot suppose, that any injury was intended us by his Majesty, or the Lords. For the assent of the crown and peers to laws, seems, as far as I am able to judge, to have been vested in them, more for their own security, than for any other purpose.

On the other hand, it is the particular business of the people, to enquire and discover what regulations are useful for themselves, and to digest and present them in the form of bills, to the other orders, to have them enacted into laws. Where these laws are to bind *themselves*, it may be expected that the house of commons will very carefully consider them: But when they are making laws that are not designed to bind *themselves*, we cannot imagine that their deliberations will be as cautious and scrupulous,* as in their own case.

I am told, that there is a wonderful address frequently used in carrying points in the house of commons, by persons experienced in these affairs.—That opportunities are watched—and

---

* Many remarkable instances might be produced of the extraordinary inattention with which bills of great importance, concerning these colonies, have passed in parliament; which is owing, as it is supposed, to the bills being brought in by the persons who have points to carry, so artfully framed, that it is not easy for the members in general, in the haste of business, to discover their tendency.

The following instances shew the truth of this remark. When Mr. *Greenville*, in the violence of reformation, formed the 4th *Geo.* III. Chap. 15th, for regulating the *American* trade, the word "*Ireland*" was dropt in the clause relating to our iron and lumber, so that we could send these articles to no part of *Europe*, but to *Great-Britain*. This was so unreasonable a restriction, and so contrary to the sentiments of the legislature for many years before, that it is surprizing it should not have been taken notice of in the house. However the bill passed into a law. But when the matter was explained, this restriction was taken off by a subsequent act. I cannot positively say how long after the taking off this restriction, as I have not the act, but I think, in less than 18 months, another act of parliament passed, in which the word "*Ireland*" was left out, just as it had been before. The matter being a second time explained, was a second time regulated.

Now if it be considered, that the omission mentioned struck off with ONE word SO VERY GREAT A PART OF OUR TRADE, it must appear *remarkable*; and equally so is the method, by which *Rice* became an enumerated commodity.

"The enumeration was obtained (says Mr. *Gee*[a]) by one *Cole*, a Captain of a ship, employed by a company then trading to *Carolina*; for several ships going from *England* thither, and purchasing rice for *Portugal*, prevented *the aforesaid Captain* of a loading. Upon his coming home, he possessed one Mr. *Lowndes*, a member of parliament (*who was very frequently employed to prepare bills*) with an opinion, that carrying rice directly to *Portugal*, was a prejudice to the trade of *England*, and PRIVATELY got a clause into an act, to make it an enumerated commodity; *by which means he secured a freight to himself.* BUT THE CONSEQUENCE PROVED A VAST LOSS TO THE NATION."

---

[a] *Gee* on Trade, page 32.

sometimes votes are passed, that if all the members had been present, would have been rejected by a great majority. Certain it is, that when a powerful and artful man has determined on any measure against these colonies, he has always succeeded in his attempt. Perhaps therefore it will be proper for us, whenever any oppressive act affecting us is passed, to attribute it to the inattention of the members of the house of commons, and to the malevolence or ambition of some factious great man, rather than to any other cause.

Now I do verily believe, that the late act of parliament, imposing duties on paper, *&c.* was formed by Mr. *Greenville*, and his party, because it is evidently a part of that plan, by which he endeavoured to render himself POPULAR at home; and I do also believe, that not one half of the members of the house of commons, even of those who heard it read, did perceive how destructive it was to *American* freedom. For this reason, as it is usual in *Great-Britain*, to consider the King's speech as the speech of the ministry, it may be right here to consider this act as the act of a *party*—perhaps I should speak more properly, if I was to use another term.

There are two ways of laying taxes. One is, by imposing a certain sum on particular kinds of property, to be paid by the *user* or *consumer*, or by rating the *person* at a certain sum. The other is, by imposing a certain sum on particular kinds of property, to be paid by the *seller*.

When a man pays the first sort of tax, he *knows with certainty* that he pays so much money *for a tax.* The *consideration* for which he pays it, is remote, and, it may be, does not occur to him. He is sensible too, that he is *commanded and obliged* to pay it *as a tax*; and therefore people are apt to be displeased with this sort of tax.

The other sort of tax is submitted to in a very different manner. The purchaser of any article, very seldom reflects that

---

I find that this clause, "PRIVATELY got into an act," FOR THE BENEFIT OF CAPTAIN COLE, to the "VAST LOSS OF THE NATION," is foisted into the 3d and 4th *Ann*, Chap. 5th, intituled, "An act for granting to her Majesty a further subsidy on wines and merchandizes imported," with which it has no more connection, than with 34th *Edward* I. the 34th and 35th of *Henry* VIII. and the 25th of *Charles* II. WHICH PROVIDE, THAT NO PERSON SHALL BE TAXED BUT BY HIMSELF OR HIS REPRESENTATIVE.

the seller raises his price, so as to indemnify himself for the tax *he* has paid. He knows that the prices of things are continually fluctuating, and if he thinks about the tax, he thinks at the same time, in all probability, that he *might* have paid as much, if the article he buys had not been taxed. He gets something *visible* and *agreeable* for his money; and tax and price are so confounded together, that he cannot separate, or does not chuse to take the trouble of separating them.

This mode of taxation therefore is the mode suited to arbitrary and oppressive governments. The love of liberty is so natural to the human heart, that unfeeling tyrants think themselves obliged to accommodate their schemes as much as they can to the appearance of justice and reason, and to deceive those whom they resolve to destroy, or oppress, by presenting to them a miserable picture of freedom, when the inestimable original is lost.

This policy did not escape the cruel and rapacious *NERO*. That monster, apprehensive that his crimes might endanger his authority and life, thought proper to do some popular acts, to secure the obedience of his subjects. Among other things, says *Tacitus*, "he remitted the twenty-fifth part of the price on the sale of slaves, but rather in *shew* than *reality*; for the *seller* being ordered to pay it, it became part of the price to the *buyer*."*

This is the reflection of the judicious *Historian*; but the deluded *people* gave their infamous Emperor full credit for his false generosity. Other nations have been treated in the same manner the *Romans* were. The honest, industrious *Germans*, who are settled in different parts of this continent, can inform us, that it was this sort of tax that drove them from their native land to our woods, at that time the seats of perfect and undisturbed freedom.

Their Princes, enflamed by the lust of power, and the lust of avarice, two furies that the more they are gorged, the more hungry they grow, transgressed the bounds they ought, in regard to themselves, to have observed. To keep up the deception in the minds of subjects, "there must be," says a very learned author,[†] "some proportion between the impost and the value of the commodity; wherefore there ought not to be

---

* *Tacitus*'s *Ann.* Book 13, §. 31.
[†] *Montesquieu*'s *Spirit of Laws*, Book 13, Chap. 8.

an excessive duty upon merchandizes of little value. There are countries in which the duty exceeds seventeen or eighteen times the value of the commodity. In this case the Prince removes the illusion. His subjects plainly see they are dealt with in an unreasonable manner, which renders them most exquisitely sensible of their slavish situation." From hence it appears, that subjects may be ground down into misery by this sort of taxation, as well as by the former. They will be as much impoverished, if their money is taken from them in this way as in the other; and that it will be taken, may be more evident, by attending to a few more considerations.

The merchant or importer, who pays the duty at first, will not consent to be so much money out of pocket. He therefore proportionably raises the price of his goods. It may then be said to be a contest between him and the person offering to buy, who shall lose the duty. This must be decided by the nature of the commodities, and the purchaser's demand for them. If they are mere luxuries, he is at liberty to do as he pleases, and if he buys, he does it voluntarily: But if they are absolute *necessaries*, or *conveniences*, which use and custom have made requisite for the comfort of life, and which he is not permitted, by the power imposing the duty, *to get elsewhere*, there the seller has a plain advantage, and the buyer *must* pay the duty. In fact, the seller is nothing less than a collector of the tax for the power that imposed it. If these duties then are extended to the necessaries and conveniences of life in general, and enormously encreased, the people must at length become indeed "most exquisitely sensible of their slavish situation." Their happiness therefore entirely depends on the moderation of those who have authority to impose the duties.

I shall now apply these observations to the late act of parliament. Certain duties are thereby imposed on paper and glass, imported into these colonies. By the laws of *Great-Britain* we are prohibited to get these articles from any other part of the world. We cannot at present, nor for many years to come, tho' we should apply ourselves to these manufactures with the utmost industry, make enough ourselves for our own use. That paper and glass are not only convenient, but absolutely necessary for us, I imagine very few will contend. Some perhaps, who think mankind grew wicked and luxurious, as soon as they found out another way of communicating their sentiments than by speech, and another way of dwelling than in caves, may advance so whimsical an opinion. But I presume no body will take the unnecessary trouble of refuting them.

From these remarks I think it evident, that we *must* use paper and glass; that what we use, *must* be *British*; and that we *must* pay the duties imposed, unless those who sell these articles, are so generous as to make us presents of the duties they pay.

Some persons may think this act of no consequence, because the duties are so *small*. A fatal error. *That* is the very circumstance most alarming to me. For I am convinced, that the authors of this law would never have obtained an act to raise so trifling a sum as it must do, had they not intended by *it* to establish a *precedent* for future use. To console ourselves with the *smallness* of the duties, is to walk deliberately into the snare that is set for us, praising the *neatness* of the workmanship. Suppose the duties imposed by the late act could be paid by these distressed colonies with the utmost ease, and that the purposes to which they are to be applied, were the most reasonable and equitable that can be conceived, the contrary of which I hope to demonstrate before these letters are concluded; yet even in such a supposed case, these colonies ought to regard the act with abhorrence. For WHO ARE A FREE PEOPLE? Not *those*, over whom government is reasonably and equitably exercised, but *those*, who live under a government so *constitutionally checked and controuled*, that proper provision is made against its being otherwise exercised.

The late act is founded on the destruction of this constitutional security. If the parliament have a right to lay a duty of Four Shillings and Eight-pence on a hundred weight of glass, or a ream of paper, they have a right to lay a duty of any other sum on either. They may raise the duty, as the author before quoted says has been done in some countries, till it "exceeds seventeen or eighteen times the value of the commodity." In short, if they have a right *to* levy a tax of *one penny* upon us, they have a right to levy a *million* upon us: For where does their right stop? At any given number of Pence, Shillings or Pounds? To attempt to limit their right, after granting it to exist at all, is as contrary to reason—as granting it to exist at all, is contrary to justice. If *they* have any right to tax *us*—then,

whether *our own money* shall continue in *our own pockets* or
not, depends no longer on *us*, but on *them*. "There is nothing
which" we "can call our own; or, to use the words of Mr.
Locke—WHAT PROPERTY HAVE" WE "IN THAT, WHICH ANOTHER
MAY, BY RIGHT, TAKE, WHEN HE PLEASES, TO HIMSELF?"*

These duties, which will inevitably be levied upon us—which
are now levying upon us—are *expresly* laid FOR THE SOLE PUR-
POSE OF TAKING MONEY. This is the true definition of "*taxes.*"
They are therefore *taxes*. This money is to be taken from *us*. We
are therefore *taxed. Those* who are *taxed* without their own
consent, expressed by themselves or their representatives, are
slaves. We are taxed without our own consent, expressed by
ourselves or our representatives. *We* are therefore—SLAVES.[†]

---

* Lord *Cambden*'s speech.

[†] "It is my opinion, that this kingdom has no right to lay A TAX upon the colonies."—"The *Americans* are the SONS, not the BASTARDS of *England.*"—"The
distinction between LEGISLATION and TAXATION is essentially necessary to
liberty."—"The COMMONS of *America*, represented in their several assemblies,
have ever been in possession of this their constitutional right, of GIVING AND
GRANTING THEIR OWN MONEY. They would have been *SLAVES*, if they had
not enjoyed it." "The idea of a *virtual representation* of *America* in this house,
is the most contemptible idea, that ever entered into the head of man.—It
does not deserve a serious refutation." *Mr. Pitt's speech on the* Stamp-Act.

That great and excellent man Lord *Cambden*, maintains the same opinion.
His speech in the house of peers, on the declaratory bill of the sovereignty of
Great-Britain over the colonies, has lately appeared in our papers. The following extracts so perfectly agree with, and confirm the sentiments avowed in
these letters, that it is hoped the inserting them in this note will be excused.

"As the affair is of the *utmost importance*, and in its consequences may
involve the *fate of kingdoms*, I took the strictest review of my arguments; I
reexamined all my authorities; fully determined, if I found myself mistaken,
publickly to own my mistake, and give up my opinion: But my searches have
more and more convinced me, that the *British* parliament have *NO RIGHT
TO TAX* the *Americans.*"—"Nor is the doctrine new; it is as old as the constitution; it grew up with it; indeed it is its support."—"TAXATION and REP-
RESENTATION are inseparably united. *GOD* hath joined them: No *British*
parliament can separate them: To endeavour to do it, is to stab our vitals."

"My position is this—I repeat it—I will maintain it to my last hour—
TAXATION and REPRESENTATION are inseparable—this position is founded on
the laws of nature; it is more, it is itself AN ETERNAL LAW OF NATURE; for
whatever is a man's own, is absolutely his own; NO MAN HATH A RIGHT TO
TAKE IT FROM HIM WITHOUT HIS CONSENT, either expressed by himself or
representative; *whoever attempts to do it, attempts an injury*; WHOEVER DOES

Miserabile vulgus.
A miserable tribe.

A FARMER.

LETTER VIII.

My dear COUNTRYMEN,

IN my opinion, a dangerous example is set in the last act relating to these colonies. The power of parliament to levy money upon us for raising a revenue, is therein *avowed* and *exerted*. Regarding the act on this single principle, I must again repeat, and I think it my duty to repeat, that to me it appears to be *unconstitutional.*

No man, who considers the conduct of the parliament since the repeal of the *Stamp-Act*, and the disposition of many people at home, can doubt, that the chief object of attention there, is, to use Mr. *Greenville*'s expression, "providing that the DE-PENDENCE and OBEDIENCE of the colonies be asserted and maintained."

IT, *COMMITS A ROBBERY*; HE THROWS DOWN THE DISTINCTION BETWEEN LIBERTY AND SLAVERY."—"There is not a *blade of grass*, in the most obscure corner of the kingdom, which is not, which was not ever *represented*, since the constitution began: There is not a *blade of grass*, which, when taxed, *was not taxed by the consent of the proprietor.*" "The forefathers of the *Americans* did not leave their native country, and subject themselves to every danger and distress, TO BE REDUCED TO A STATE OF SLAVERY. They did not give up their rights: They looked for protection, and *not for* CHAINS, from their mother country. By her they expected to be defended in the possession of their property, and not to be deprived of it: For should the present power continue, THERE IS NOTHING WHICH THEY CAN CALL THEIR OWN; or, to use the words of Mr. *Locke*, "*WHAT PROPERTY HAVE THEY IN THAT, WHICH ANOTHER MAY, BY RIGHT, TAKE, WHEN HE PLEASES, TO HIMSELF?*"

It is impossible to read this speech, and Mr. *Pitt*'s, and not be charmed with the generous zeal for the rights of mankind that glows in every sentence. These great and good men, animated by the subject they speak upon, seem to rise above all the former glorious exertions of their abilities. A foreigner might be tempted to think they are *Americans*, asserting, with all the ardor of patriotism, and all the anxiety of apprehension, the cause of their native land—and not *Britons*, striving to stop their mistaken countrymen from oppressing others. Their reasoning is not only just—it is, as Mr. *Hume* says of the eloquence of *Demosthenes*, "vehement." It is disdain, anger, boldness, freedom, involved in a continual stream of argument.

Under the influence of this notion, instantly on repealing the *Stamp-Act*, an act passed, declaring the power of parliament to bind these colonies *in all cases whatever*. This however was only planting a barren tree, that cast a *shade* indeed over the colonies, but yielded no *fruit*. It being determined to enforce the authority on which the *Stamp-Act* was founded, the parliament having never renounced the right, as Mr. *Pitt* advised them to do; and it being thought proper to disguise that authority in such a manner, as not again to alarm the colonies; some little time was required to find a method, by which both these points should be united. At last the ingenuity of Mr. *Greenville* and his party accomplished the matter, as it was thought, in "an act for granting certain duties in the *British* colonies and plantations in *America*, for allowing drawbacks," *&c.* which is the title of the act laying duties on paper, *&c.*

The parliament having several times before imposed duties to be paid in *America*, IT WAS EXPECTED, NO DOUBT, THAT THE REPETITION OF SUCH A MEASURE WOULD BE PASSED OVER, AS AN USUAL THING. But to have done this, without expresly "asserting and maintaining" the power of parliament to take our money without our consent, and to apply it as they please, would not have been, in Mr. *Greenville*'s opinion, sufficiently declarative of its supremacy, nor sufficiently depressive of *American* freedom.

Therefore it is, that in this memorable act we find it *expresly* "provided," that money shall be levied upon us without our consent, for PURPOSES, that render it, *if possible*, more dreadful than the *Stamp-Act*.

That act, alarming as it was, declared, the money thereby to be raised, should be applied "towards defraying the expences of defending, protecting and securing the *British* colonies and plantations in *America*." And it is evident from the whole act, that by the word "*British*," were intended colonies and plantations *settled by* British *people*, and not generally, *those subject to the* British *crown*. That act therefore seemed to have something gentle and kind in its intention, and to aim only at *our own welfare*: But the act now objected to, imposes duties upon the *British* colonies, "to defray the expences of defending, protecting and securing *his Majesty's* DOMINIONS *in* America."

What a *change* of words! What an *incomputable addition* to the expences intended by the *Stamp-Act!* "*His Majesty's* DOMINIONS" comprehend not only *the* British *colonies*, but also *the conquered provinces of* Canada *and* Florida, *and the* British *garrisons of* Nova-Scotia; for *these* do not deserve the name of *colonies*.

What justice is there in making US pay for "defending, protecting and securing" THESE PLACES? What benefit *can* WE, or *have* WE ever derived *from them?* None of them was conquered *for* US; nor will "be defended, protected or secured" *for* US.

In fact, however advantageous the subduing or keeping any of these countries may be to *Great-Britain*, the acquisition is greatly injurious to these colonies. Our chief property consists in *lands*. These would have been of much greater value, if such prodigious additions had not been made to the *British* territories on this continent. The natural increase of our own people, if confined within the colonies, would have raised the value still higher and higher every fifteen or twenty years: Besides, we should have lived more compactly together, and have been therefore more able to resist any enemy. But now the inhabitants will be thinly scattered over an immense region, as those who want settlements, will chuse to make new ones, rather than pay great prices for old ones.

These are the consequences to the colonies, of the hearty assistance they gave to *Great-Britain* in the late war—a war *undertaken solely for her own benefit.* The objects of it were, the securing to herself the rich tracts of land on the back of these colonies, with the *Indian* trade; and *Nova-Scotia*, with the fishery. *These, and much more, has that kingdom gained*; but the *inferior animals*, that hunted with the *lion*, have been amply rewarded for all the sweat and blood their loyalty cost them, by the honor of having sweated and bled in such company.

I will not go so far as to say, that *Canada* and *Nova-Scotia* are curbs on *New-England*; the *chain of forts* through the back woods, on the *Middle Provinces*; and *Florida*, on the *rest*: But I will venture to say, that if the products of *Canada, Nova-Scotia,* and *Florida,* deserve any consideration, the two first of them are only rivals of our Northern Colonies, and the other of our Southern.

It has been said, that without the conquest of these countries, the colonies could not have been "protected, defended and secured." If that is true, it may with as much propriety be

said, that *Great-Britain* could not have been "defended, protected and secured," without that conquest: For the colonies
are parts of her empire, which it *as much* concerns *her* as *them*
to keep out of the hands of any other power.

But these colonies, when they were much weaker, defended
themselves, before this Conquest was made; and could again
do it, against any that might properly be called *their* Enemies.
If *France* and *Spain* indeed should attack them, *as members of
the* British *empire*, perhaps they might be distressed; but it
would be in a *British* quarrel.

The largest account I have seen of the number of people in
Canada, does not make them exceed 90,000. *Florida* can
hardly be said to have any inhabitants. It is computed that
there are in our colonies 3,000,000. *Our* force therefore must
increase with a disproportion to the growth of *their* strength,
that would render us very safe.

This being the state of the case, I cannot think it just that
these colonies, labouring under so many misfortunes, should
be loaded with *taxes*, to maintain countries, not only not useful, but hurtful to them. The support of *Canada* and *Florida*
cost yearly, it is said, half a million sterling. From hence, we
may make some guess of the load that is to be laid *upon* US; for
WE are not only to "defend, protect and secure" *them*, but also
to make "an adequate provision for defraying the charge of the
administration of justice, and the support of civil government,
in such provinces where it shall be found necessary."

Not one of the provinces of *Canada, Nova-Scotia*, or *Florida*, has ever defrayed *these expences within itself*: And if the
duties imposed by the last statute are collected, *all of them together*, according to the best information I can get, will not pay
one quarter as much as Pennsylvania *alone*. So that the *British
colonies* are to be drained of the rewards of their labor, to
cherish the scorching sands of *Florida*, and the icy rocks of
Canada and *Nova-Scotia*, which never will return to us one
farthing that we send to them.

Great-Britain—I mean, the ministry in *Great-Britain*, has
cantoned *Canada* and *Florida* out into *five* or *six* governments,
and may form *as many more*. There now are *fourteen* or *fifteen*
regiments on this continent; and there soon may be *as many*

more. To make "an adequate provision" FOR ALL THESE EX-PENCES, is, no doubt, to be the *inheritance* of the colonies.

Can any man believe that the duties upon paper, &c. are the *last* that will be laid for these purposes? It is in vain to hope, that because it is imprudent to lay duties on the exportation of manufactures from a mother country to colonies, as it may promote manufactures among them, that this consideration will prevent such a measure.

Ambitious, artful men have made it popular, and whatever injustice or destruction will attend it in the opinion of the colonists, at home it will be thought just and salutary.*

The people of *Great-Britain* will be told, and have been told, that *they* are sinking under an immense debt—that great part of this debt has been contracted in defending the colonies —that *these* are so ungrateful and undutiful, that they will not contribute one mite to its payment—nor even to the support of the army now kept up for their "defence and security"— that they are rolling in wealth, and are of so bold and republican a spirit, that they are aiming at independence—that the only way to retain them in "obedience," is to keep a strict watch over them, and to draw off part of their riches in *taxes*— and that every burden laid upon *them*, is taking off so much from *Great-Britain*.—These assertions will be generally believed, and the people will be persuaded that they cannot be too angry with their colonies, as that anger will be profitable to themselves.

In truth, *Great-Britain* alone receives any benefit from *Canada*, *Nova-Scotia* and *Florida*; and therefore she alone ought to maintain them. The old maxim of the law is drawn from reason and justice, and never could be more properly applied, than in this case.

Qui sentit commodum, sentire debet et onus.
They who feel the benefit, ought to feel the burden.

A FARMER.

* "So *credulous*, as well as *obstinate*, are the people in believing *every thing*, which flatters their *prevailing passion*." Hume's *Hist. of England.*

LETTER IX.

My dear COUNTRYMEN,

I HAVE made some observations on the PURPOSES for which money is to be levied upon us by the late act of parliament. I shall now offer to your consideration some further reflections on that subject: And, unless I am greatly mistaken, if these purposes are accomplished according to the *expressed* intention of the act, they will be found effectually to *supersede* that authority in our respective assemblies, which is essential to liberty. The question is not, whether some branches shall be lopt off—The axe is laid to the root of the tree; and the whole body must infallibly perish, if we remain idle spectators of the work.

No free people ever existed, or can ever exist, without keeping, to use a common, but strong expression, "the purse strings," in their own hands. Where this is the case, *they* have a *constitutional check* upon the administration, which may thereby be brought into order *without violence*: But where such a power is not lodged in the *people*, oppression proceeds uncontrouled in its career, till the governed, transported into rage, seek redress in the midst of blood and confusion.

The elegant and ingenious Mr. *Hume*, speaking of the *Anglo Norman* government, says—"Princes and Ministers were too ignorant, to be themselves sensible of the advantage attending an equitable administration, and there was no established council or *assembly*, WHICH COULD PROTECT THE PEOPLE, and BY WITHDRAWING SUPPLIES, regularly and PEACEABLY admonish the king of his duty, and ENSURE THE EXECUTION OF THE LAWS."

Thus this great man, whose political reflections are so much admired, makes *this power* one of the foundations of liberty.

The *English* history abounds with instances, proving that *this* is the proper and successful way to obtain redress of grievances. How often have kings and ministers endeavored to throw off this legal curb upon them, by attempting to raise money by a variety of inventions, under pretence of law, without having recourse to parliament? And how often have they been brought to reason, and peaceably obliged to do justice, by the exertion of this constitutional authority of the people, vested in their representatives?

The inhabitants of these colonies have, on numberless occasions, reaped the benefit of this authority *lodged in their assemblies.*

It has been for a long time, and now is, a constant instruction to all governors, *to obtain a* PERMANENT *support for the offices of government.* But as the author of "the administration of the colonies" says, "this order of the crown is generally, if not universally, rejected by the legislatures of the colonies."

They perfectly know *how much* their grievances would be regarded, if they had *no other* method of engaging attention, than by *complaining.* Those who rule, are extremely apt to think well of the constructions made by themselves in support of their own power. *These* are frequently erroneous, and pernicious to those they govern. Dry remonstrances, to shew that such constructions are wrong and oppressive, carry very little weight with them, in the opinion of persons who gratify their own inclinations in making these constructions. *They* CANNOT understand the reasoning that opposes *their* power and desires. But let it be made *their interest* to understand such reasoning —and a *wonderful light* is instantly thrown upon the matter; and then, rejected remonstrances become as clear as "proofs of holy writ."*

The three most important articles that our assemblies, or any legislatures can provide for, are, First—the defence of the society: Secondly—the administration of justice: And thirdly—the support of civil government.

Nothing can properly regulate the expence of making provision for these occasions, but the *necessities* of the society; its *abilities*; the *conveniency* of the modes of levying money in it; the *manner* in which the laws have been executed; and the *conduct* of the officers of government: *All which* are circumstances, that *cannot* possibly be properly *known*, but by the society itself; or if they should be known, *will not* probably be properly *considered* but by that society.

If money be raised upon us by *others*, without our consent, for our "defence," those who are the judges in *levying* it, must also be the judges in *applying* it. Of consequence the money *said* to be taken from us for our defence, *may be employed* to

* SHAKESPEARE.

our injury. We may be chained in by a line of fortifications—obliged to pay for the building and maintaining them—and be told, that they are for our defence. With what face can we dispute the fact, after having granted that those who *apply* the money, had a right to *levy* it? For surely, it is much easier for their wisdom to understand how to apply it in the best manner, than how to levy it in the best manner. Besides, the *right of levying* is of infinitely more consequence, than *that of applying*. The people of *England*, who would burst out into fury, if the crown should attempt to *levy* money by its own authority, have always assigned to the crown the *application* of money.

As to "the administration of justice"—the judges ought, in a well regulated state, to be equally independent of the executive and legislative powers. Thus in *England*, judges hold their commissions from the crown "*during good behavior*," and have salaries, suitable to their dignity, *settled* on them by parliament. The purity of the courts of law since this establishment, is a proof of the wisdom with which it was made.

But in these colonies, how fruitless has been every attempt to have the judges appointed "*during good behavior?*" Yet whoever considers the matter will soon perceive, that *such commissions* are beyond all comparison more necessary in these colonies, than they were in *England*.

The chief danger to the subject *there*, arose from the arbitrary *designs of the crown*; but *here*, the time may come, when we may have to contend with the *designs of the crown, and of a mighty kingdom*. What then must be our chance, when the laws of life and death are to be spoken by judges totally dependent on *that crown*, and *that kingdom*—sent over perhaps *from thence*—filled with *British prejudices*—and *backed by a* STANDING *army*—supported out of OUR OWN pockets, to "assert and maintain" OUR OWN "dependence and obedience."

But supposing that through the extreme lenity that will prevail in the government *through all future ages*, these colonies will never behold any thing like the campaign of chief justice *Jeffereys*, yet what innumerable acts of injustice may be committed, and how fatally may the principles of liberty be sapped, by a succession of judges *utterly independent of the people?* Before such judges, the supple wretches, who cheerfully join in avowing sentiments inconsistent with freedom, will always meet with smiles; while the honest and brave men, who disdain to sacrifice their native land to their own advantage, but on every occasion boldly vindicate her cause, will constantly be regarded with frowns.

There are two other considerations relating to this head, that deserve the most serious attention.

By the late act, the officers of the customs are "impowered to enter into any HOUSE, warehouse, shop, cellar, or other place, in the *British* colonies or plantations in *America*, to search for or seize prohibited or unaccustomed goods," *&c.* on "writs granted by the superior or supreme court of justice, having jurisdiction within such colony or plantation respectively."

If we only reflect, that the judges of these courts are to be *during pleasure*—that they are to have "*adequate provision*" made for them, which is to continue *during their complaisant behavior*—that they may be *strangers* to these colonies—what an engine of oppression may this authority be in such hands?

I am well aware, that writs of this kind may be granted at home, under the seal of the court of exchequer: But I know also, that the greatest asserters of the rights of *Englishmen* have always strenuously contended, that *such a power* was dangerous to freedom, and expresly contrary to the common law, which ever regarded a man's *house* as his castle, or a place of perfect security.

If such power was in the least degree dangerous *there*, it must be utterly destructive to liberty *here*. For the people there have two securities against the undue exercise of this power by the crown, which are wanting with us, if the late act takes place. In the first place, if any injustice is done *there*, the person injured may bring his action against the offender, and have it tried before INDEPENDENT JUDGES, who are NO PARTIES IN COMMITTING THE INJURY.* *Here* he must have it tried before DEPENDENT JUDGES, being the men WHO GRANTED THE WRIT.

To say, that the cause is to be tried by a jury, can never reconcile men who have any idea of freedom, to *such a power.* For we know that sheriffs in almost every colony on this continent, are totally dependent on the crown; and packing of juries has

---

* The writs for searching houses in *England*, are to be granted "under the seal of the court of exchequer," according to the statute—and that seal is kept by the chancellor of the exchequer. *4th Inst. p.* 104.

been frequently practised even in the capital of the *British* empire. Even if juries are well inclined, we have too many instances of the influence of over-bearing unjust judges upon them. The brave and wise men who accomplished the revolution, thought the *independency of judges* essential to freedom.

The other security which the people have at home, but which we shall want here, is this.

If this power is abused *there*, the parliament, the grand resource of the oppressed people, is ready to afford relief. Redress of grievances must precede grants of money. But what regard can *we* expect to have paid to our assemblies, when they will not hold even the puny privilege of *French* parliaments—that of registering, before they are put in execution, the edicts that take away our money.

The second consideration above hinted at, is this. There is a *confusion* in our laws, that is quite unknown in *Great-Britain*. As this cannot be described in a more clear or exact manner, than has been done by the ingenious author of the history of *New-York*, I beg leave to use his words. "The state of our laws opens a door to much controversy. The *uncertainty*, with respect to them, RENDERS PROPERTY PRECARIOUS, and GREATLY EXPOSES US TO THE ARBITRARY DECISION OF BAD JUDGES. The common law of *England* is generally received, together with such statutes as were enacted before we had a legislature of our own; but our courts EXERCISE A SOVEREIGN AUTHORITY, in determining *what parts of the common and statute law* ought to be extended: For it must be admitted, that the *difference of circumstances* necessarily requires us, in some cases, *to* REJECT *the determination of both*. In many instances, they have also extended even acts of parliament, passed since we had a distinct legislature, *which is greatly adding to our confusion*. The practice of our courts is no less *uncertain* than the law. Some of the *English* rules are adopted, others rejected. Two things therefore seem to be ABSOLUTELY NECESSARY for the PUBLIC SECURITY. First, the passing an act for settling the extent of the *English* laws. Secondly, that the courts ordain a general sett of rules for the regulation of the practice."

How easy it will be, under this "state of our laws," for an artful judge, to act in the most arbitrary manner, and yet cover his conduct under specious pretences; and how difficult it will be for the injured people to obtain relief, may be readily perceived. We may take a voyage of 3000 miles to complain; and after the trouble and hazard we have undergone, we may be told, that the collection of the revenue, and maintenance of the prerogative, must not be discouraged—and if the misbehavior is so gross as to admit of no justification, it may be said, that it was an error in judgment only, arising from the confusion of our laws, and the zeal of the King's servants to do their duty.

If the commissions of judges are *during the pleasure of the crown*, yet if their salaries are *during the pleasure of the people*, there will be *some check* upon their conduct. Few men will consent to draw on themselves the hatred and contempt of those among whom they live, for the empty honor of being judges. It is the sordid love of gain, that tempts men to turn their backs on virtue, and pay their homage where they ought not.

As to the third particular, "the support of civil government,"—few words will be sufficient. Every man of the least understanding must know, that the *executive* power may be exercised in a manner so disagreeable and harrassing to the people, that it is absolutely requisite, that *they* should be enabled by the gentlest method which human policy has yet been ingenious enough to invent, that is, *by shutting their hands*, to "ADMONISH" (as Mr. *Hume* says) certain persons "OF THEIR DUTY."

What shall we now think when, upon looking into the late act, we find the assemblies of these provinces thereby stript of their authority *on these several heads?* The *declared* intention of the act is, "that a revenue should be raised IN HIS MAJESTY'S DOMINIONS IN AMERICA, for making a more certain and adequate provision *for defraying the charge of* THE ADMINISTRATION OF JUSTICE, and *the support of* CIVIL GOVERNMENT in such provinces where it shall be found necessary, and *towards further defraying the expences of* DEFENDING, PROTECTING AND SECURING THE SAID DOMINIONS."

Let the reader pause here one moment—and reflect—whether the colony in which *he* lives, has not made such "certain and adequate provision" *for these purposes*, as is *by the colony judged suitable to its abilities, and all other circumstances.* Then let him reflect—whether if this act takes place, money is not to be raised on *that* colony *without its consent*, to make "provision" *for these purposes*, which *it does not judge to be suitable to its*

abilities, and all other circumstances. Lastly, let him reflect—
whether the people of that country are not in a state of the
most abject slavery, *whose property may be taken from them*
under the notion of right, *when they have refused to give it.*

For my part, I think I have good reason for vindicating the
honor of the assemblies on this continent, by publicly asserting, that THEY *have made as "certain and adequate provision"
for the purposes abovementioned, as they ought to have made,* and
that it should not be presumed, that they will not do it hereafter. Why then should *these most important trusts* be wrested
out of their hands? Why should they not now be permitted to
enjoy that authority, which they have exercised from the first
settlement of these colonies? Why should they be scandalized
by this innovation, when their respective provinces are now,
and will be, for several years, laboring under loads of debt,
imposed on them for the very purpose now spoken of? Why
should all the inhabitants of these colonies be, with the utmost
indignity, treated as a herd of despicable stupid wretches, so
utterly void of common sense, that they will not even make
"adequate provision" for the "administration of justice, and
the support of civil government" among them, or for their
own "defence"—though without such "provision" every people
must inevitably be overwhelmed with anarchy and destruction?
Is it possible to form an idea of a slavery more *compleat*, more
miserable, more *disgraceful*, than that of a people, where *justice
is administered, government exercised*, and a *standing army
maintained*, AT THE EXPENCE OF THE PEOPLE, and yet WITH-
OUT THE LEAST DEPENDENCE UPON THEM? If we can find no
relief from this infamous situation, it will be fortunate for us, if
Mr. *Greenville*, setting his fertile fancy again at work, can, as by
one exertion of it he has stript us of our *property* and *liberty*, by
another deprive us of so much of our *understanding*; that, un-
conscious of what we *have been* or *are*, and ungoaded by tor-
menting reflections, we may bow down our necks, with all the
stupid serenity of servitude, to any drudgery, which our lords
and masters shall please to command.

When the charges of the "administration of justice," the
"support of civil government," and the expences of "defending, protecting and securing" us, are provided for, I should be
glad to know, upon *what occasions* the crown will ever call our

assemblies together. Some few of them may meet of their own accord, by virtue of their charters. But what will they have to do, when they are met? To what shadows will they be reduced? The men, whose deliberations heretofore had an influence on every matter relating to the *liberty* and *happiness* of themselves and their constituents, and whose authority in domestic affairs at least, might well be compared to that of *Roman* senators, will *now* find their deliberations of no more consequence, than those of *constables*. They may *perhaps* be allowed to make laws *for the yoking of hogs*, or *pounding of stray cattle*. Their influence will hardly be permitted to extend *so high*, as the *keeping roads in repair*, as *that business* may more properly be executed by those who receive the public cash.

One most memorable example in history is so applicable to the point now insisted on, that it will form a just conclusion of the observations that have been made.

Spain was once *free*. Their *Cortes* resembled our parliaments. No *money* could be raised on the subject, *without their consent*. One of their Kings having received a grant from them, to maintain a war against the *Moors*, desired, that if the sum which they had given, should not be sufficient, he might be allowed, *for that emergency only*, to raise more money *without assembling the Cortes*. The request was violently opposed by the best and wisest men in the assembly. It was, however, complied with by the votes of a majority; and this single concession was a PRECEDENT for other concessions of the like kind, until at last the crown obtained a general power of raising money, in cases of necessity. From that period the *Cortes* ceased to be *useful*,—the *people* ceased to be *free*.

> *Venienti occurrite morbo.*
> Oppose a disease at its beginning.

A FARMER.

LETTER X.

My dear COUNTRYMEN,

THE consequences, mentioned in the last letter, will not be the utmost limits of our *misery* and *infamy*, if the late act is acknowledged to be binding upon us. We feel too sensibly, that *any ministerial measures** relating to these colonies, are soon carried successfully through the parliament. Certain prejudices operate there so strongly against us, that it may be justly questioned, whether *all* the provinces united, will ever be able effectually to call to an account before the parliament, any minister who shall abuse the power by the late act given to the crown in *America*. He may divide the spoils torn from us in what manner he pleases, *and we shall have no way of making him responsible*. If he should order, that every *governor* shall have a yearly salary of 5000 l. sterling; every *chief justice* of 3000 l; every inferior officer in proportion; and should then reward the most profligate, ignorant, or needy dependents on himself or his friends, with places of the greatest trust, because they were of the greatest profit, this would be called an arrangement in consequence of the "adequate provision for defraying the charge of the administration of justice, and the support of the civil government:" And if the taxes should prove at any time insufficient to answer all the expences of the numberless offices, which ministers may please to create, surely the members of the house of commons will be so "*modest*," as not to "contradict a minister" who shall tell them, it is become necessary to lay a new tax upon the colonies, for the laudable purposes of defraying the charges of the "administration of justice, and support of civil government" among them. Thus, in fact, we shall be taxed by ministers.[†] In short, it will be in

* "The gentleman must not wonder he was not contradicted, when, as *minister*, he asserted the right of parliament to tax *America*. I know not how it is, but there is a MODESTY in this house, *which does not choose to contradict a minister*. I wish gentlemen would get the better of this *modesty*. IF THEY DO NOT, PERHAPS THE COLLECTIVE BODY MAY BEGIN TO ABATE OF ITS RESPECT FOR THE REPRESENTATIVE." *Mr.* Pitt*'s Speech.*

† "Within this act (*statute de tallagio non concedendo*) are all *new* offices erected with *new* fees, or *old* offices with *new* fees, for that is a tallaga put upon the subject, which cannot be done without common assent by act of parliament. And this doth notably appear by a petition in parliament in anno 13 *H.* IV. where the commons complain, that an office was erected for measurage of cloths and canvas, with a new fee for the same, by colour of the king's letters patents, and pray that these letters patents may be revoked, for that the king could erect no offices with new fees to be taken of the people, who may not so be charged but by parliament." *2d Inst. p.* 533.

their power to settle upon us any CIVIL, ECCLESIASTICAL, or MILTARY establishment, which they choose.

We may perceive, by the example of *Ireland*, how eager ministers are to seize upon any settled revenue, and apply it in supporting their own power. Happy are the men, and *happy the people who grow wise by the misfortunes of others*. Earnestly, my dear countrymen, do I beseech the author of all good gifts, that you may grow wise in this manner; and if I may be allowed to take such a liberty, I beg leave to recommend to you in general, as the best method of attaining this wisdom, diligently to study the histories of other countries. You will there find all the arts, that can possibly be practised by cunning rulers, or false patriots among yourselves, so fully delineated, that, changing names, the account would serve for your own times.

It is pretty well known on this continent, that *Ireland* has, with a regular consistency of injustice, been cruelly treated by ministers in the article of *pensions*; but there are some alarming circumstances relating to that subject, which I wish to have better known among us.*

* An enquiry into the legality of pensions on the *Irish* establishment, by *Alexander M'Aulay*, Esq; one of the King's council, *&c.*

Mr. *M'Aulay* concludes his piece in the following beautiful manner. "If any *pensions* have been obtained on that establishment, TO SERVE THE CORRUPT PURPOSES OF AMBITIOUS MEN.—If his Majesty's revenues of *Ireland* have been employed in pensions, TO DEBAUCH HIS MAJESTY'S SUBJECTS of both kingdoms.—If the treasure of *Ireland* has been expended in pensions, FOR CORRUPTING MEN OF THAT KINGDOM TO BETRAY THEIR COUNTRY; and men of the neighbouring kingdom, to betray both.—If *Irish* pensions have been procured, TO SUPPORT GAMESTERS AND GAMING-HOUSES; promoting a vice which threatens national ruin.—If pensions have been purloined out of the national treasure of *Ireland*, under the MASK OF SALARIES ANNEXED TO PUBLIC OFFICES, USELESS TO THE NATION; newly invented, FOR THE PURPOSES OF CORRUPTION.—If *Ireland*, just beginning to recover from the devastations of massacre and rebellion, be obstructed in the progress of her cure, BY SWARMS OF PENSIONARY VULTURES PREYING ON HER VITALS.—If, by squandering the national substance of *Ireland*, in a LICENTIOUS, UNBOUNDED PROFUSION OF PENSIONS, instead of employing it in nourishing and improving her infant *agriculture, trade* and *manufactures*, or in *enlightening* and *reforming* her *poor, ignorant, deluded, miserable natives* (by nature most amiable, most valuable, most worthy of public attention)—If, *by such abuse of the national substance, sloth* and *nastiness, cold* and *hunger, nakedness* and *wretchedness, popery, depopulation* and *barbarism*, still maintain their ground; *still deform a country, abounding with all the riches of nature*, yet hitherto destined to beggary.—If SUCH PENSIONS be

The revenue of the crown there arises principally from the Excise granted "*for pay of the army, and defraying other* PUBLIC *charges, in defence and preservation of the kingdom*"—from the tonnage and additional poundage granted "*for protecting the trade of the kingdom at sea, and augmenting the* PUBLIC *revenue*" —from the hearth money granted—as a "PUBLIC *revenue, for* PUBLIC *charges and expences.*" There are some other branches of the revenue, concerning which there is not any *express* appropriation of them for PUBLIC *service*, but which were plainly *so intended.*

Of *these* branches of the revenue the crown is only *trustee* for the public. They are unalienable. They are inapplicable to any other purposes, but those for which they were established; and therefore are not *legally* chargeable with pensions.

There is another kind of revenue, which is a private revenue. This is not limited to any public uses; but the crown has the same property in it, that any person has in his estate. This does not amount, at the most, to *Fifteen Thousand Pounds* a year, probably not to *Seven*, and is the only revenue, that can be *legally* charged with pensions.

If ministers were accustomed to regard the rights or happiness of the people, the pensions in *Ireland* would not exceed the sum just mentioned: But long since have they exceeded that limit; and in *December* 1765, a motion was made in the house of commons in that kingdom, to address his Majesty on the great increase of pensions on the *Irish* establishment, amounting to the sum of 158,685 l.—in the last two years.

Attempts have been made to gloss over these gross encroachments, by this specious argument—"That expending a competent part of the PUBLIC REVENUE in pensions, from a principle of charity or generosity, adds to the dignity of the crown; and is *therefore* useful to the PUBLIC." To give this argument any weight, it must appear, that the pensions proceed from "*charity* or *generosity* only"—and that it "adds to the dignity of the crown," *to act directly contrary to law.*—

From this conduct towards *Ireland*, in open violation of law,

---

found on the *Irish* establishment; let such be cut off: And let the perfidious advisers be branded with indelible characters of public infamy; adequate, if possible, to the dishonor of their crime."

we may easily foresee what *we* may expect, when a minister will have the *whole revenue* of *America* in his own hands, to be disposed of at his own pleasure: For *all* the monies raised by the late act are to be "*applied* by virtue of warrants under the sign manual, countersigned by the high treasurer, or any three of the commissioners of the treasury." The "RESIDUE" indeed is to be "paid into the receipt of the exchequer, and to be disposed of by parliament." So that a minister will have nothing to do, but to take care, that there shall be no "residue," and he is superior to all controul.

Besides the burden of *pensions* in *Ireland*, which have enormously encreased within these few years, almost all the *offices* in that poor kingdom, have been, since the commencement of the present century, and now are bestowed upon *strangers*. For tho' the merit of persons born there, justly raises them to places of high trust when they go abroad, as all *Europe* can witness, yet he is an uncommonly lucky *Irishman*, who can get a good post *in his* NATIVE *country*.

When I consider the manner in which that island has been uniformly depressed for so many years past,* with this pernicious

---

* In *Charles* the second's time, the house of commons, influenced by some factious demagogues, were resolved to prohibit the importation of *Irish* cattle into *England*. Among other arguments in favor of *Ireland* it was insisted —"That by cutting off almost entirely the trade between the kingdoms, ALL THE NATURAL BANDS OF UNION WERE DISSOLVED, and nothing remained to keep the *Irish* in their duty, but *force* and *violence*."

"The king (says Mr. *Hume*, in his history of *England*) was so convinced of the justness of these reasons, that he used all his interest to oppose the bill, and he openly declared, that he could not give his assent to it with a safe conscience. But the commons were resolute in their purpose."—"And the spirit of TYRANNY, *of which* NATIONS *are as susceptible as* INDIVIDUALS, had animated the *English* extremely TO EXERT THEIR SUPERIORITY *over their dependent state*. No affair could be conducted with greater violence than this by the commons. They even went so far in the preamble of the bill, as to declare the importation of *Irish* cattle to be a NUSANCE. By this expression they gave scope to their *passion*, and at the same time *barred the king's prerogative*, by which he might think himself intitled to dispense with a law, SO FULL OF INJUSTICE AND BAD POLICY. The lords expunged the word, but as the king was sensible that no supply would be given by the commons, unless they were gratified in all their PREJUDICES, he was obliged both to employ his interest with the peers, to make the bill pass, and to give the royal assent to it. He could not, however, forbear expressing his displeasure, at the jealousy entertained against him, and at the intention which the commons discovered, of retrenching his prerogative.

particularity *of their parliament continuing as long as the crown pleases,** I am astonished to observe *such a love of liberty* still animating that LOYAL and GENEROUS nation; and nothing can raise higher my idea of the INTEGRITY and PUBLIC SPIRIT† of a people,

---

THIS LAW BROUGHT GREAT DISTRESS FOR SOME TIME UPON IRELAND, BUT IT HAS OCCASIONED THEIR APPLYING WITH GREATER INDUSTRY TO MANUFACTURES, AND HAS PROVED IN THE ISSUE BENEFICIAL TO THAT KINGDOM."

Perhaps the *same reason* occasioned the "barring the king's prerogative" in the late act suspending the legislation of *New-York*.

This we may be assured of, that WE are as dear to his *Majesty*, as the people of *Great-Britain* are. WE are his *subjects* as well as they, and *as faithful subjects*; and his Majesty has given too many, too constant proofs of his piety and virtue, for any man to think it possible, that *such a prince* can make any unjust distinction between *such subjects*. It makes no difference to his Majesty, whether supplies are raised in *Great-Britain*, or *America*; but it makes *some* difference to the commons of that kingdom.

To speak plainly, as becomes an honest man on such important occasions, all our misfortunes are owing to a LUST OF POWER in men of *abilities* and *influence*. This prompts them to seek POPULARITY by *expedients* profitable to themselves, though ever so destructive to their country.

Such is the accursed nature of lawless ambition, and yet—What heart but melts at the thought!—Such false, detestable PATRIOTS, in *every state*, have led their blind, confiding country, shouting their applauses, into the jaws of *shame* and *ruin*. May the wisdom and goodness of the people of *Great-Britain*, save them from the usual fate of nations.

"—MENTEM MORTALIA TANGUNT."

* The last *Irish* parliament continued 33 years, during all the late King's reign. The present parliament there has continued from the beginning of this reign, and probably will continue till this reign ends.

† I am informed, that within these few years, a petition was presented to the house of commons, setting forth, "that herrings were imported into *Ireland* from some foreign parts of the north so cheap, as to discourage the *British* herring fishery, and therefore praying that some remedy might be applied in that behalf by parliament."—

That upon this petition, the house came to a resolution, to impose a duty of Two Shillings sterling on every barrel of foreign herrings imported into *Ireland*; but afterwards dropt the affair, FOR FEAR OF ENGAGING IN A DISPUTE WITH IRELAND ABOUT THE RIGHT OF TAXING HER.

So much higher was the opinion, which the house entertained of the spirit of *Ireland*, than of that of these colonies.

I find, in the last *English* papers, that the resolution and firmness with which the people of *Ireland* have lately asserted their freedom, have been so alarming in *Great-Britain*, that the Lord Lieutenant, in his speech on the 20th of last *October*, "recommended to that parliament, that such provision may be made for securing the judges in the enjoyment of their *offices* and *appointments*, DURING THEIR GOOD BEHAVIOR, as shall be thought most expedient."

who have preserved the sacred fire of freedom from being extinguished, tho' the altar on which it burnt, has been overturned.

In the same manner shall we unquestionably be treated, as soon as the late taxes laid upon us, shall make posts in the "government," and the "administration of justice" *here*, worth the attention of persons of influence in *Great-Britain*. We know enough already to satisfy us of this truth. But this will not be the worst part of our case.

The *principals*, in all great offices, will reside in *England*, making some paltry allowance to deputies for doing the business *here*. Let any man consider what an exhausting drain this must be upon us, when ministers are possessed of the power of creating what posts they please, and of affixing to such posts what salaries they please, and he must be convinced how destructive the late act will be. The injured kingdom lately mentioned, can tell us the mischiefs of ABSENTEES; and we may perceive already the same disposition taking place with us. The government of *New-York* has been exercised by a deputy. That of *Virginia* is now held so; and we know of a number of secretaryships, collectorships, and other offices, held in the same manner.

True it is, that if the people of *Great-Britain* were not too much blinded by the passions, that have been artfully excited in their breasts, against their dutiful children the colonists, these considerations would be nearly as alarming to them as to us. The influence of the crown was thought by wise men, many years ago, too great, by reason of the multitude of pensions and places bestowed by it. These have been vastly encreased since,* and perhaps it would be no difficult matter to prove that the people have decreased.

What an important concession is thus obtained, by making demands becoming freemen, with a courage and perseverance becoming Freemen!

* One of the reasons urged by that great and honest statesman, Sir *William Temple*, to *Charles* the Second, in his famous remonstrance, to dissuade him from aiming at arbitrary power, was, that the King "had few offices to bestow." *Hume*'s Hist. of *England*.

"Tho' the wings of prerogative have been clipt, the influence of the crown is greater than ever it was in any period of our history. For when we consider in how many boroughs the government has the votes at command; when we consider the vast body of persons employed in the collection of the revenue, in every part of the kingdom, the inconceivable number of placemen, and candidates for places in the customs, in the excise, in the post-office, in the

Surely therefore, those who wish the welfare of their country, ought seriously to reflect, what may be the consequence of such a new creation of offices, in the disposal of the crown. The *army*, the *administration of justice*, and the *civil government* here, with such salaries as the crown shall please to annex, will extend *ministerial influence* as much beyond its former bounds, as the late war did the *British* dominions.

But whatever the people of *Great-Britain* may think on this occasion, I hope the people of these colonies will unanimously join in this sentiment, that the late act of parliament is injurious to their liberty, and that this sentiment will unite them in a firm opposition to it, in the same manner as the dread of the *Stamp-Act* did.

Some persons may imagine the sums to be raised by it, are but small, and therefore may be inclined to acquiesce under it. A conduct more dangerous to freedom, as before has been observed, can never be adopted. Nothing is wanted at home but a PRECEDENT,* the force of which shall be established, by the tacit submission of the colonies. With what zeal was the statute erecting the post-office, and another relating to the recovery of debts in *America*, urged and tortured, as *precedents* in support of the *Stamp-Act*, tho' wholly inapplicable. If the parliament succeeds in this attempt, other statutes will impose other duties. Instead of

---

dock-yards, in the ordnance, in the salt-office, in the stamps, in the navy and victualling offices, and in a variety of other departments; when we consider again the extensive influence of the money corporations, subscription jobbers and contractors, the endless dependencies created by the obligations conferred on the bulk of the gentlemens families throughout the kingdom, who have relations preferred in our navy and numerous standing army; when I say, we consider how wide, how binding a dependence on the crown is created by the above enumerated particulars, and the great, the enormous weight and influence which the crown derives from this extensive dependence upon its favor and power, any lord in waiting, any lord of the bed-chamber, any man may be appointed minister."

A doctrine to this effect is said to have been the advice of L— H——. *Late News Paper.*

* "Here may be observed, that when any ancient law or custom of parliament is broken, and the crown possessed of a *precedent*, how *difficult a thing it is to restore the subject again to his* FORMER FREEDOM *and* SAFETY." 2*d Coke's Inst. p.* 529.

"It is not almost credible to *foresee*, when any maxim or *fundamental law* of this realm is altered (as elsewhere *hath* been observed) what *dangerous inconveniencies* do follow." 4*th Coke's Inst. p.* 41.

taxing ourselves, as we have been accustomed to do, from the first settlement of these provinces, all our usual taxes will be converted into parliamentary taxes on our importations; and thus the parliament will levy upon us such sums of money as they chuse to take, *without any other* LIMITATION, *than their* PLEASURE.

We know how much labor and care have been bestowed by these colonies, in laying taxes in such a manner, that they should be most *easy* to the people, by being laid on the proper articles; most *equal*, by being proportioned to every man's circumstances; and *cheapest*, by the method directed for collecting them.

But *parliamentary taxes* will be laid on us, without any consideration, whether there is any *easier* mode. The *only point* regarded will be, the *certainty of levying the taxes*, and not the *convenience* of the people on whom they are to be levied; and therefore all statutes on this head will be such as will be most likely, according to the favorite phrase, "*to execute themselves.*"

Taxes in every free state have been, and ought to be, as exactly *proportioned as is possible to the abilities of those who are to pay them*. They cannot otherwise be *just*. Even a *Hottentot* would comprehend the *unreasonableness* of making a poor man pay as much for "defending" the property of a rich man, as the rich man pays himself.

Let any person look into the late act of parliament, and he will immediately perceive, that the immense estates of Lord *Fairfax*, Lord *Baltimore*, and our *Proprietaries*,* which are amongst his Majesty's other "DOMINIONS" to be "defended, protected and secured" by the act, will not pay a *single farthing* for the duties thereby imposed, except Lord *Fairfax* wants some of his windows glazed; Lord *Baltimore* and our *Proprietaries* are quite secure, as they live in *England*.

I mention these particular cases, as striking instances how far the late act is a deviation from *that principle of justice*, which has so constantly distinguished our own laws on this continent, and ought to be regarded in all laws.

---

* *Maryland* and *Pennsylvania* have been engaged in the warmest disputes, in order to obtain an equal and just taxation of their Proprietors estates: But this late act of parliament does more for those Proprietors, than they themselves would venture to demand. It *totally exempts* them from taxation—tho' their vast estates are to be "secured" by the taxes of other people.

The third consideration with our continental assemblies in laying taxes, has been the *method* of collecting them. This has been done by a few officers, with moderate allowances, under the inspection of the respective assemblies. *No more was raised from the subject*, than was used for the intended purposes. But by the late act, a minister may appoint *as many officers as he pleases* for collecting the taxes; may assign them *what salaries he thinks* "adequate;" and they are subject to *no inspection but his own*.

In short, if the late act of parliament takes effect, these colonies must dwindle down into "COMMON CORPORATIONS," as their enemies, in the debates concerning the repeal of the *Stamp-Act, strenuously insisted they were*; and it seems not improbable that some future historian may thus record our fall.

"The eighth year of this reign was distinguished by *a very memorable event*, the *American* colonies then submitting, for the *FIRST* time, to be *taxed* by the *British* parliament. An attempt of this kind had been made about two years before, but was defeated by the vigorous exertions of the several provinces, in defence of their liberties. Their behavior on that occasion rendered their name very celebrated *for a short time* all over *Europe*; all states being extremely attentive to a dispute between *Great-Britain*, and so considerable a part of her dominions. For as she was thought to be grown too powerful, by the successful conclusion of the late war she had been engaged in, it was hoped by many, that as it had happened before to other kingdoms, civil discords would afford opportunities of revenging all the injuries supposed to be received from her. However, the cause of dissension was removed, by a repeal of the statute that had given offence. This affair rendered the SUBMISSIVE CONDUCT of the colonies so soon after, the more extraordinary; there being *no difference* between the mode of taxation which they opposed, and that to which they submitted, but this, that by the first, they were to be continually *reminded* that they *were taxed*, by certain marks *stamped* on every piece of paper or parchment they used. The authors of *that statute* triumphed greatly on this conduct of the colonies, and insisted, that if the people of *Great-Britain* had persisted in enforcing it, the *Americans* would have been, in a few months, *so fatigued with the efforts of patriotism*, that they would have yielded obedience.

"Certain it is, that tho' they had before their eyes *so many illustrious examples* in their mother country, of the *constant success* attending *firmness* and *perseverance*, in opposition to dangerous encroachments on liberty, yet they quietly gave up a point of the LAST IMPORTANCE. From thence the decline of their freedom began, and its decay was extremely rapid; for as *money* was always raised upon them by the parliament, their *assemblies* grew immediately *useless*, and in a short time *contemptible*: And in less than one hundred years, the people sunk down into that *tameness* and *supineness* of spirit, by which they still continue to be distinguished."

> *Et majores vestros & posteros cogitate.*
> Remember your ancestors and your posterity.

A FARMER.

LETTER XI.

My dear COUNTRYMEN,

I HAVE several times, in the course of these letters, mentioned the late act of parliament, as being the *foundation* of future measures injurious to these colonies; and the belief of this truth I wish to prevail, because I think it necessary to our safety.

A perpetual *jealousy*, respecting liberty, is absolutely requisite in all free states. The very texture of their constitution, in *mixt* governments, demands it. For the *cautions* with which power is *distributed* among the several orders, *imply*, that *each* has that share which is proper for the general welfare, and therefore that any further acquisition must be pernicious. *Machiavel* employs a whole chapter in his discourses,* to prove that a state, to be long lived, must be frequently corrected, and reduced to its first principles. But of all states that have existed, there never was any, in which this jealousy could be more proper than in these colonies. For the government here is not only *mixt*, but *dependent*, which circumstance occasions *a peculiarity in its form*, of a very delicate nature.

Two reasons induce me to desire, that this spirit of apprehension may be always kept up among us, in its utmost vigilance.

---

* *Machiavel's Discourses—Book* 3. *Chap.* I.

The first is this—that as the happiness of these provinces indu-bitably consists in their connection with *Great-Britain*, any separation between them is less likely to be occasioned by civil discords, if every disgusting measure is opposed *singly*, and *while it is new*: For in this manner of proceeding, every such measure is most likely to be rectified. On the other hand, oppressions and dissatisfactions being permitted to accumulate—*if ever* the governed throw off the load, *they will do more*. A people does not reform with moderation. The rights of the subject there-fore cannot be *too often* considered, explained or asserted: And whoever attempts to do this, shews himself, whatever may be the rash and peevish reflections of pretended wisdom, and pretended duty, a friend to *those* who injudiciously exercise their power, as well as to *them*, over whom it is so exercised.

Had all the points of prerogative claimed by *Charles* the First, been separately contested and settled in preceding reigns, his fate would in all probability have been very different; and the people would have been content with that liberty which is compatible with regal authority.* But he thought, it would be as dangerous for him to give up the powers which at any time had been by usurpation exercised by the crown, as those that were legally vested in it. This produced an equal excess on the part of the people. For when their passions were excited by *multiplied* grievances, they thought it would be as dangerous for them to allow the powers that were legally vested in the crown, as those which at any time had been by usurpation exer-cised by it. Acts, that might *by themselves* have been upon many considerations excused or extenuated, derived a contagious malignancy and odium from other acts, with which they were connected. They were not regarded according to the simple force of each, but as parts of a system of oppression. Every one therefore, however small in itself, became alarming, as an addi-

---

*The author is sensible, that this is putting the gentlest construction on *Charles*'s conduct; and that is one reason why he chooses it. Allowances ought to be made for the errors of those men, who are acknowledged to have been possessed of many virtues. The education of this unhappy prince, and his con-fidence in men not so good or wise as himself, had probably *filled* him with mistaken notions of his own authority, and of the consequences that would attend concessions of any kind to a people, who were represented to him, as aiming at too much power.

tional evidence of tyrannical designs. It was in vain for prudent and moderate men to insist, that there was no necessity to abolish royalty. Nothing less than the utter destruction of monarchy, could satisfy those who *had* suffered, and thought they had reason to believe, they always *should* suffer under it.

The consequences of these mutual distrusts are well known: But there is no other people mentioned in history, that I recollect, who have been so constantly watchful of their liberty, and so successful in their struggles for it, as the *English*. This consideration leads me to the second reason, why I "desire that the spirit of apprehension may be always kept up among us in its utmost vigilance."

The first principles of government are to be looked for in human nature. Some of the best writers have asserted, and it seems with good reason, that "government is founded on *opinion*." *

Custom undoubtedly has a mighty force in producing *opinion*, and reigns in nothing more arbitrarily than in public affairs. It gradually reconciles us to objects even of dread and detestation; and I cannot but think these lines of Mr. *Pope* as applicable to vice in *politics*, as to vice in *ethics*.—

> "Vice is a monster of so horrid mien,
>   As to be hated, needs but to be seen;
>   Yet *seen too oft*, familiar with her face,
>   We first *endure*, then *pity*, then *embrace*."

When an act injurious to freedom has been *once* done, and the people *bear* it, the *repetition* of it is most likely to meet with

---

* "OPINION is of two kinds, *viz. opinion* of INTEREST, and *opinion* of RIGHT. By *opinion* of *interest*, I chiefly understand, *the sense of the public advantage which is reaped from government*; together with the persuasion, that the particular government which is established, is *equally advantageous* with any other, *that could be easily settled*."

"*Right* is of two kinds, *right* to *power*, and *right* to *property*. What prevalence *opinion* of the first kind has over mankind, may easily be understood, by observing the attachment which all nations have to their antient government, and even to those names which have had the sanction of antiquity. *Antiquity always begets the opinion of right*."—"It is sufficiently understood, that the *opinion* of *right* to *property*, is of the greatest moment in all matters of government." *Hume's Essays*.

submission. For as the *mischief* of the one was found to be tolerable, they will hope that of the second will prove so too; and they will not regard the *infamy* of the last, because they are stained with that of the first.

Indeed nations, in general, are not apt to *think* until they *feel*; and therefore nations in general have lost their liberty: For as violations of the rights of the *governed*, are commonly not only *specious*, but *small* at the beginning,* they spread over the multitude in such a manner, as to touch individuals but slightly. Thus they are disregarded.[†] The power or profit that arises from these violations, *centering in few persons*, is to them considerable. For this reason the *governors* having in view their particular purposes, successively preserve an uniformity of conduct for attaining them. They regularly encrease the first injuries, till at length the inattentive people are compelled to perceive the heaviness of their burthens.—They begin to complain and enquire—but too late. They find their oppressors so strengthened by success, and themselves so entangled in examples of express authority on the part of their rulers, and of tacit recognition on their own part, that they are quite confounded: For millions entertain no other idea of the *legality* of power, than that it is founded on the *exercise* of power. They voluntarily fasten their chains, by adopting a pusillanimous *opinion*, "that there will be too much *danger* in attempting a remedy,"—or another *opinion* no less fatal,—"that the government has a *right* to treat them as it does." They then seek a wretched relief for their minds, by persuading themselves, that to yield their *obedience*, is to discharge their *duty*. The deplorable *poverty of*

---

* Omnia mala exempla ex bonis initiis orta sunt. SALLUST. *Bell. Cat. S.* 50.

[†] "The *republic* is always *attacked* with greater vigor, than it is *defended*: For the *audacious* and *profligate*, prompted by their natural enmity to it, are *easily impelled* to act by the *least nod* of their *leaders*: Whereas the HONEST, I know not why, are generally *slow* and *unwilling* to stir; and *neglecting* always the *BEGINNINGS of things*, are *never roused* to exert themselves, but by the *last necessity*: So that through IRRESOLUTION and DELAY, when they would be glad to compound at last for their QUIET, at the expence even of their HONOR, they *commonly lose them* BOTH." CICERO's *Orat. for* SEXTIUS.

Such were the sentiments of this great and excellent man, whose vast abilities, and the calamities of his country during his time, enabled him, by mournful experience, to form a just judgment on the conduct of the friends and enemies of liberty.

spirit, that prostrates all the dignity bestowed by divine providence on our nature—*of course succeeds.*

From these reflections I conclude, that every free state
should incessantly watch, and instantly take alarm on any addition being made to the power exercised over them. Innumerable instances might be produced to shew, from what slight
beginnings the most extensive consequences have flowed: But
I shall select two only from the history of *England*.

Henry the Seventh was the *first* monarch of that kingdom,
who established a STANDING BODY OF ARMED MEN. This was a
band of *fifty* archers, called yeomen of the guard: And this institution, notwithstanding the smallness of the number, was,
to prevent discontent, "disguised under pretence of majesty
and grandeur."* In 1684 the standing forces were so much
augmented, that *Rapin* says—"The king, in order to make his
people *fully sensible of their new slavery*, affected to muster his
troops, which amounted to 4000 well armed and disciplined
men." I think our army, at this time, consists of more than
seventy regiments.

The method of taxing by EXCISE was first introduced amidst
the convulsions of the civil wars. Extreme necessity was pretended for it, and its short continuance promised. After the
restoration, an excise upon *beer, ale* and *other liquors*, was
granted to the king,† one half in fee, the other for life, as an
equivalent for the *court of wards*. Upon *James* the Second's
accession, the parliament gave him the first *excise*,‡ with an additional duty on *wine, tobacco*, and some *other* things. Since the
revolution it has been extended to salt, candles, leather, hides,
hops, soap, paper, paste-boards, mill-boards, scale-boards,
vellum, parchment, starch, silks, calicoes, linens, stuffs, printed,
stained, *&c.* wire, wrought plate, coffee, tea, chocolate, *&c.*

Thus a *standing army* and *excise* have, from their first slender
origins, tho' always *hated*, always *feared*, always *opposed*, at
length swelled up to their vast present bulk.

These facts are sufficient to support what I have said. 'Tis
true, that all the mischiefs apprehended by our ancestors from

* *Rapin*'s History of *England*.
† 12 *Char*. II. Chap. 23 and 24.
‡ 1 *James* II. Chap. 1 and 4.

a *standing army* and *excise*, have not *yet happened*: But it does
not follow from thence, that they *will not happen*. The inside of
a house may catch fire, and the most valuable apartments be
ruined, before the flames burst out. The question in these cases
is not, what evil *has actually attended* particular measures—but,
what evil, in the nature of things, *is likely to attend* them. Certain
circumstances may for some time delay effects, that *were reasonably expected*, and that *must ensue*. There was a long period, after
the *Romans* had prorogued his command to *Q. Publilius Philo*,*
before *that example* destroyed their liberty. All our kings, from
the revolution to the present reign, have been *foreigners*. Their
ministers generally continued but a short time in authority;[†] and
they themselves were *mild* and *virtuous* princes.

A bold, *ambitious* prince, possessed of *great abilities*, firmly
fixed in his throne *by descent*, served by *ministers like himself*,
and rendered either *venerable* or *terrible* by the *glory of his
successes*, may execute what his predecessors did not dare to
attempt. *Henry* the Fourth tottered in his seat during his
whole reign. *Henry the* Fifth drew the strength of that kingdom into *France*, to carry on his wars there, and left the *commons* at home, *protesting*, "that the people were not bound to
serve out of the realm."

It is true, that a strong spirit of liberty subsists at present in
Great-Britain, but what reliance is to be placed in the *temper* of
a people, when the prince is possessed of an unconstitutional
power, our own history can sufficiently inform us. When *Charles*
the Second had strengthened himself by the return of the garrison of *Tangier*, "*England* (says *Rapin*) saw on a sudden an
amazing revolution; saw herself *stripped of all her rights and*

---

* In the year of the city 428, "Duo singularia hæc ci viro primum contigere;
prorogatio imperii non ante in ullo facta, et acto honore triumphus." *Liv. B.*
8. *Chap.* 23. 26.

"Had the rest of the *Roman* citizens imitated the example of *L. Quintius*,
who refused to have his consulship continued to him, they had never admitted
that custom of proroguing of magistrates, and then the prolongation of their
commands in the army had never been introduced, *which very thing was at
length the ruin of that commonwealth.*" *Machiavel's Discourses, B.* 3. *Chap.* 24.
[†] I dont know but it may be said, with a good deal of reason, that a quick rota-
tion of ministers is very desirable in *Great-Britain*. A minister there has a vast
store of materials to work with. *Long administrations* are rather favorable to
the *reputation* of a people abroad, than to their *liberty*.

privileges, excepting such as the king should vouchsafe to grant her: And what is *more astonishing*, the *English* themselves *delivered up* these very rights and privileges to *Charles* the Second, which they had so *passionately*, and, if I may say it, *furiously* defended against the designs of *Charles* the First." This happened only *thirty-six* years after this last prince had been beheaded.

Some persons are of opinion, that liberty is not violated, but by such *open* acts of force; but they seem to be greatly mistaken. I could mention a period within these forty years, when almost as great a change of disposition was produced by the SECRET measures of a *long* administration, as by *Charles*'s violence. Liberty, perhaps, is never exposed to so much danger, as when the people believe there is the least; for it may be subverted, and yet they not think so.

Public disgusting acts are seldom practised by the ambitious, at the beginning of their designs. Such conduct *silences* and *discourages* the weak, and the wicked, who would otherwise have been their *advocates* or *accomplices*. It is of great consequence, to allow those who, upon any account, are inclined to favor them, something specious to *say* in their defence. Their power may be fully established, tho' it would not be safe for them to do *whatever they please*. For there are things, which, at some times, even *slaves* will not bear. *Julius Cæsar*, and *Oliver Cromwell*, did not dare to assume the title of *king*. The *Grand Seignor* dares not lay a *new tax*. The king of *France* dares not be a *protestant*. Certain popular points may be left untouched, and yet freedom be extinguished. The commonalty of *Venice* imagine themselves free, because they are permitted to do what they ought not. But I quit a subject, that would lead me too far from my purpose.

By the late act of parliament, taxes are to be levied upon us, for "defraying the charge of the *administration of justice*—the support of *civil government*—and the expences of *defending* his Majesty's dominions in *America*."

If any man doubts what ought to be the conduct of these colonies on this occasion, I would ask him these questions.

Has not the parliament *expresly* AVOWED their INTENTION of raising money from us FOR CERTAIN PURPOSES? Is not this scheme *popular* in *Great-Britain*? Will the taxes, imposed by the late act, *answer those purposes*? If it will, must it not take an *immense sum* from us? If it will not, *is it to be expected*, that the parliament will not *fully execute* their INTENTION when it is *pleasing at home*, and *not opposed here?* Must not this be done by imposing NEW *taxes?* Will not every addition, thus made to our taxes, be an addition to the power of the *British* legislature, *by increasing the number of officers* employed in the collection? Will not every additional tax therefore render it *more difficult* to abrogate any of them? When a branch of revenue is once established, does it not appear to many people *invidious* and *undutiful*, to attempt to abolish it? If taxes, sufficient to *accomplish the* INTENTION of the parliament, are imposed by the parliament, *what taxes will remain* to be imposed by our assemblies? If *no material taxes remain* to be imposed by them, what must become of *them*, and the *people* they represent?

"If any person considers these things, and yet thinks our liberties are in no danger, I wonder at that person's security."*

One other argument is to be added, which, by itself, I hope, will be sufficient to convince the most incredulous man on this continent, that the late act of parliament is *only* designed to be a PRECEDENT, whereon the future vassalage of these colonies may be established.

Every duty thereby laid on articles of *British* manufacture, is laid on some commodity, upon the exportation of which from *Great-Britain*, a *drawback* is payable. Those *drawbacks*, in most of the articles, are *exactly double* to the *duties* given by the late act. The parliament therefore might, in *half a dozen lines*, have raised MUCH MORE MONEY, only by *stopping the drawbacks* in the hands of the officers at home, on exportation to these colonies, than by this solemn imposition of taxes upon us, to be collected here. Probably, the artful contrivers of this act formed it in this manner, in order to reserve to themselves, in case of any objections being made to it, this specious pretence —"that the drawbacks are gifts to the colonies, and that the late act only lessens those gifts." But the truth is, that the drawbacks are intended for the encouragement and promotion of *British* manufactures and commerce, and are allowed on exportation to *any foreign parts*, as well as on exportation to these provinces. Besides, care has been taken to slide into the act, some articles on which there are no drawbacks. However,

* Demosthenes's 2d Philippic.

the *whole duties* laid by the late act on *all* the articles therein specified are *so small*, that they will not amount to *as much* as the *drawbacks* which are allowed on *part* of them only. If therefore, *the sum to be obtained by the late act*, had been the *sole object* in forming it, there would not have been any occasion for "the COMMONS of *Great-Britain*, to GIVE and GRANT to his Majesty RATES and DUTIES for *raising a revenue* IN *his Majesty's dominions in* America, for making a more certain and adequate provision for defraying the charges of the administration of justice, the support of civil government, and the expence of defending the said dominions;"—nor would there have been any occasion for an expensive board of commissioners,* and all the other new charges to which we are made liable.

Upon the whole, for my part, I regard the late act as an *experiment made of our disposition*. It is a bird sent out over the waters, to discover, whether the waves, that lately agitated this part of the world with such violence, are yet *subsided*. If *this adventurer* gets footing here, we shall quickly find it to be of the kind described by the poet.†—

> "*Infelix vates.*"
> A direful foreteller of future calamities.

A FARMER.

---

* The expence of this board, I am informed, is between Four and Five Thousand Pounds Sterling a year. The establishment of officers, for collecting the revenue in *America*, amounted before to Seven Thousand Six Hundred Pounds *per annum*; and yet, says the author of "The regulation of the colonies," "the whole remittance from *all* the taxes in the colonies, at an average of *thirty years*, has not amounted to One Thousand Nine Hundred Pounds a year, and in that sum Seven or Eight Hundred Pounds *per annum* only, have been remitted from *North-America*."

The smallness of the revenue arising from the duties in *America*, demonstrates that they were intended only as REGULATIONS OF TRADE: And can any person be so blind to truth, so dull of apprehension in a matter of unspeakable importance to his country, as to imagine, that the board of commissioners lately established at such a charge, is instituted to assist in collecting One Thousand Nine Hundred Pounds a year, or the trifling duties imposed by the late act? Surely every man on this continent must perceive, that they are established for the care of a NEW SYSTEM OF REVENUE, which is but now begun.

† "Dira cælæno," *&c. Virgil, Æneid* 3.

LETTER XII.

My dear COUNTRYMEN,

SOME states have lost their liberty by *particular accidents*: But this calamity is generally owing to the *decay of virtue*. A *people* is travelling fast to destruction, when *individuals* consider *their* interests as distinct from *those of the public*. Such notions are fatal to their country, and to themselves. Yet how many are there, so *weak* and *sordid* as to *think* they perform *all the offices of life*, if they earnestly endeavor to encrease their own *wealth, power*, and *credit*, without the least regard for their society, under the protection of which they live; who, if they can make an *immediate profit to themselves*, by lending their assistance to those, whose projects plainly tend to the injury of their country, rejoice in their *dexterity*, and believe themselves entitled to the character of *able politicians*. Miserable men! Of whom it is hard to say, whether they ought to be most the objects of *pity* or *contempt*: But whose opinions are certainly as *detestable*, as their practices are *destructive*.

Tho' I always reflect, with a high pleasure, on the integrity and understanding of my countrymen, which, joined with a pure and humble devotion to the great and gracious author of every blessing they enjoy, will, I hope, ensure to them, and their posterity, all temporal and eternal happiness; yet when I consider, that in every age and country there have been bad men, my heart, at this threatening period, is so full of apprehension, as not to permit me to believe, but that there may be some on this continent, *against whom you ought to be upon your guard* *—Men, who either hold, or expect to hold certain ad-

---

* It is not intended, by these words, to throw any reflection upon gentlemen, because they are possessed of offices: For many of them are certainly men of virtue, and lovers of their country. But supposed obligations of *gratitude*, and *honor* may induce them to be silent. Whether these obligations *ought to be* regarded or not, is not so much to be considered by others, in the judgment they form of these gentlemen, as whether *they think* they ought to be regarded. Perhaps, therefore, we shall act in the properest manner towards them, if we neither *reproach* not *imitate* them. The persons meant in this letter, are the *base spirited wretches*, who may endeavor to *distinguish themselves*, by their sordid zeal in defending and promoting measures, which *they know, beyond all question*, to be *destructive* to the *just rights* and *true interests* of their country.

vantages, by setting examples of servility to their countrymen.
—Men, who trained to the employment, or self taught by a
natural versatility of genius, serve as decoys for drawing the
innocent and unwary into snares. It is not to be doubted but
that such men will diligently bestir themselves on this and every
like occasion, to spread the infection of their meanness as far as
they can. On the plans *they* have adopted, this is *their* course.
This is the method to recommend themselves to their *patrons.*

From *them* we shall learn, how *pleasant* and *profitable* a
thing it is, to be for our SUBMISSIVE behavior *well spoken of* at
St. James's, or *St. Stephen's*; at *Guildhall*, or the *Royal Exchange*.
Specious fallacies will be drest up with all the arts of delusion,

---

It is scarcely possible to speak of *these men* with any degree of *patience*—It is
scarcely possible to speak of them with any degree of *propriety*—For no words
can truly describe their *guilt* and *meanness*—But every honest bosom, on their
being mentioned, will *feel* what cannot be *expressed.*

If their wickedness did not blind them, they might perceive along the coast
of these colonies, many men, remarkable instances of wrecked ambition, who,
after *distinguishing themselves* in the support of the *Stamp-Act*, by a coura-
geous contempt of their country, and of justice, have been left to linger out
their miserable existence, without a government, collectorship, secretaryship,
or any other commission, to console them *as well as it could*, for loss of virtue
and reputation—while numberless offices have been bestowed in these colonies on people from *Great-Britain*, and new ones are continually invented, to
be thus bestowed. As a *few great prizes* are put into a lottery to TEMPT *multitudes to lose*, so *here* and *there* an *American* has been raised to a good post.—
   "*Apparent* rari nantes *in gurgite vasto.*"
Mr. *Greenville*, indeed, in order to recommend the *Stamp-Act*, had the *un-
equalled* generosity, to pour down a golden shower of offices upon *Americans*;
and yet these *ungrateful* colonies did not thank Mr. *Greenville* for shewing his
kindness to their countrymen, nor *them* for accepting it. How must that great
statesman have been surprized, to find, that the unpolished colonies could not
be reconciled to *infamy* by *treachery?* Such a *bountiful* disposition towards
us never appeared in any minister before him, and probably never will appear
again: For it is *evident*, that *such a system* of policy is to be established on
this continent, as, in a short time, is to render it utterly unnecessary to use
the least *art* in order to *conciliate* our approbation of any measures. Some of
our countrymen may be employed to *fix* chains upon us, but *they* will never
be permitted to *hold* them afterwards. So that the utmost, that any of them
can expect, is only a *temporary provision*, that *may* expire in their own time;
but which, they may *be assured*, will preclude their children from having any
consideration paid to *them*. NATIVES of *America* must sink into total NEGLECT
and CONTEMPT, the moment that THEIR COUNTRY loses the constitutional
powers she now possesses.

to persuade one colony *to distinguish herself from another*, by unbecoming condescensions, *which will serve the ambitious purposes of great men* at home, and therefore will be thought by them *to entitle their assistants in obtaining them* to considerable rewards.

Our fears will be excited. Our hopes will be awakened. It will be insinuated to us, with a plausible affectation of *wisdom* and *concern*, how *prudent* it is to please the *powerful*—how *dangerous* to provoke them—and then comes in the perpetual incantation that freezes up every generous purpose of the soul in cold, inactive expectation—"that if there is any request to be made, compliance will obtain a favorable attention."

Our *vigilance* and our *union* are *success* and *safety*. Our *negligence* and our *division* are *distress* and *death*. They are *worse*—They are *shame* and *slavery*. Let us equally shun the benumbing stillness of *overweening sloth*, and the feverish activity of that *ill informed zeal*, which busies itself in maintaining *little, mean* and *narrow* opinions. Let us, with a truly wise *generosity* and *charity*, banish and discourage all *illiberal distinctions*, which may arise from differences in *situation*, forms of *government*, or modes of *religion*. Let us consider ourselves as MEN—FREEMEN—CHRISTIAN FREEMEN—*separated from the rest of the world*, and *firmly bound together* by the *same rights, interests* and *dangers*. Let *these* keep our attention inflexibly fixed on the GREAT OBJECTS, which we must CONTINUALLY REGARD, in order to *preserve those rights*, to *promote those interests*, and to *avert those dangers*.

Let these *truths* be indelibly impressed on our minds—*that we cannot be* HAPPY, *without being* FREE—that we cannot be free, *without being secure in our property*—that *we* cannot be secure in our property, *if, without our consent, others may, as by right, take it away*—that *taxes imposed on us by parliament*, do thus take it away—that *duties laid for the sole purpose of raising money*, are taxes—that *attempts* to lay such duties *should be instantly and firmly opposed*—that this opposition can never be effectual, *unless it is the united effort of these provinces* —that therefore BENEVOLENCE *of temper towards each other*, and UNANIMITY *of counsels*, are essential to the welfare of the whole —and lastly, that for this reason, every man amongst us, who in any manner would encourage either *dissension, diffidence*, or *indifference*, between these colonies, is an enemy to *himself*, and to *his country*.

The belief of these truths, I verily think, my countrymen, is indispensably necessary to your happiness. I beseech you, therefore, "teach them diligently unto your children, and talk of them when you sit in your houses, and when you walk by the way, and when you lie down, and when you rise up."*

What have these colonies to *ask*, while they continue free? Or what have they to *dread*, but insidious attempts to subvert their freedom? *Their prosperity* does not depend on *ministerial favors doled* out to *particular* provinces. *They* form *one* political body, of which *each colony* is a *member*. *Their happiness* is founded on *their constitution*; and is to be promoted, by preserving that constitution in unabated vigor, *throughout every part*. A spot, a speck of decay, however small the limb on which it appears, and however remote it may seem from the vitals, should be alarming. We have *all the rights* requisite for our prosperity. The *legal authority* of *Great-Britain* may indeed lay hard restrictions upon us; but, like the spear of *Telephus*, it will cure as well as wound. Her unkindness will instruct and compel us, after some time, to discover, in our *industry* and *frugality*, surprising remedies—*if our rights continue unviolated*: For as long as the *products* of our *labor*, and the *rewards* of our *care*, can properly be called *our own*, so long it will be worth our while to be *industrious* and *frugal*. But if when we plow —sow—reap—gather—and thresh—we find, that we plow— sow—reap—gather—and thresh *for others*, whose PLEASURE is to be the SOLE LIMITATION *how much* they shall *take*, and *how much* they shall *leave*, WHY should we repeat the unprofitable toil? *Horses* and *oxen* are content with *that portion of the fruits of their work*, which their *owners* assign them, in order to keep them strong enough to raise successive crops; but even *these beasts* will not submit to draw for their *masters*, until they are *subdued* by *whips* and *goads*.

Let us take care of our *rights*, and we *therein* take care of *our prosperity*. "SLAVERY IS EVER PRECEDED BY SLEEP."† *Individuals* may be *dependent* on ministers, if they please. STATES SHOULD SCORN IT;—and if *you* are not wanting *to yourselves*, you will have a *proper regard* paid *you* by *those*, to

* Deuteron. vi. 7.
† *Montesquieu*'s Spirit of Laws, Book 14, Chap. 13.

whom if you are not *respectable*, you will be *contemptible*.
But—if *we have already forgot* the *reasons* that urged us, with
unexampled unanimity, to exert ourselves two years ago—if
our zeal for the public good is *worn out* before the *homespun
cloaths*, which it caused us to have made—if *our resolutions* are
so faint, as by our present conduct to *condemn* our own late
successful example—if *we are not affected* by any reverence for
the memory of our ancestors, who transmitted to us that freedom in which they had been blest—if *we are not animated* by
any regard for posterity, to whom, by the most sacred obligations, we are bound to deliver down the invaluable inheritance
—THEN, indeed, any *minister*—or any *tool* of a minister—or
any *creature* of a tool of a minister—or any *lower instrument* *
of administration,[†] if lower there be, is a *personage* whom it
may be dangerous to offend.

---

* "Instrumenta regni." *Tacitus*'s Ann. *Book* 12, § 66.

[†] If any person shall imagine that he discovers, in these letters, the least dislike
of the dependence of these colonies on *Great-Britain*, I beg that such person
will not form any judgment on *particular expressions*, but will consider the
tenor of all the letters taken together. In that case, I flatter myself, that every
unprejudiced reader will be *convinced*, that the true interests of *Great-Britain*
are as dear to me, as they ought to be to every good subject.

If I am an *Enthusiast* in any thing, it is in my zeal for the *perpetual dependence* of these colonies on their mother country.—A dependence founded
on *mutual benefits*, the continuance of which can be secured only by *mutual
affections*. Therefore it is, that with extreme apprehension I view the smallest seeds of discontent, which are unwarily scattered abroad. *Fifty* or *Sixty*
years will make astonishing alterations in these colonies; and this consideration
should render it the business of *Great-Britain* more and more to cultivate our
good dispositions towards her: But the misfortune is, that those *great men*,
who are wrestling for power at home, think themselves very slightly interested
in the prosperity of their country *Fifty* or *Sixty* years hence, but are deeply concerned in blowing up a popular clamor for supposed *immediate advantages*.

For my part, I regard *Great-Britain* as a *Bulwark*, happily fixed between
these colonies and the powerful nations of *Europe*. That kingdom remaining
safe, we, under its protection, enjoying peace, may diffuse the blessings of
religion, science, and liberty, thro' remote wildernesses. It is therefore incontestably our *duty*, and our *interest*, to support the strength of *Great-Britain*.
When confiding in that strength, she begins to forget from whence it arose,
it will be an easy thing to shew the source. She may readily be reminded of
the loud alarm spread among her merchants and tradesmen, by the universal
association of these colonies, at the time of the *Stamp-Act*, not to import any
of her MANUFACTURES.

In the year 1718, the *Russians* and *Swedes* entered into an agreement, not to

I shall be extremely sorry, if any man mistakes my meaning in any thing I have said. Officers employed by the crown, are, while according to the laws they conduct themselves, entitled to legal obedience, and sincere respect. These it is a duty to render them; and these no good or prudent person will withhold. But when these officers, thro' rashness or design, desire to enlarge their authority beyond its due limits, and expect improper concessions to be made to them, from regard for the employments they bear, their attempts should be considered as equal injuries to the crown and people, and should be courageously and constantly opposed. To suffer our ideas to be confounded by *names* on such occasions, would certainly be an *inexcusable weakness*, and probably an *irremediable error*.

We have reason to believe, that several of his Majesty's present ministers are good men, and friends to our country; and it seems not unlikely, that by a particular concurrence of events, we have been treated a little more severely than they wished we should be. *They* might not think it prudent to stem a torrent. But what is the difference to *us*, whether arbitrary acts take their rise from ministers, or are permitted by them? Ought any point to be allowed to a good minister, that should be denied to a bad one?* The mortality of ministers, is a very frail mortality. A —— may succeed a *Shelburne*—A —— may succeed a *Conway*.

---

suffer *Great-Britain* to export any NAVAL STORES from their dominions but in *Russian* or *Swedish* ships, and at their own prices. *Great-Britain* was distressed. *Pitch* and *tar* rose to *Three Pounds* a barrel. At length she thought of getting these articles from the colonies; and the attempt succeeding, they fell down to *Fifteen Shillings*. In the year 1756, *Great-Britain* was threatened with an invasion. An easterly wind blowing for six weeks, she could not MAN her fleet, and the whole nation was thrown into the utmost consternation. The wind changed. The *American* ships arrived. The fleet sailed in ten or fifteen days. There are some other reflections on this subject, worthy of the most deliberate attention of the *British* parliament; but they are of such a nature, that I do not choose to mention them publicly. I thought it my duty, in the year 1765, while the *Stamp-Act* was in suspence, to write my sentiments to a gentleman of great influence at home, who afterwards distinguished himself, by espousing our cause, in the debates concerning the repeal of that act.

* Ubi imperium ad ignaros aut minus bonos pervenit; *novum illud exemplum*, ab dignis & idoneis, ad indignos & non idoneos *transfertur. Sall.* Bell. Cat. § 50.

We find a new kind of minister lately spoken of at home—
"THE MINISTER OF THE HOUSE OF COMMONS." The term
seems to have peculiar propriety when referred to these colonies, *with a different meaning annexed to it*, from that in which
it is taken there. By the word "minister" we may understand
not only a *servant of the crown*, but a *man of influence* among
the commons, who regard themselves as having a share in the
sovereignty over us. The "minister OF the house" may, in a point
respecting the colonies, be so strong, that the minister of the
crown *in* the house, if he is a distinct person, may not choose,
even where his sentiments are favorable to us, to come to a
pitched battle upon our account. For tho' I have the highest
opinion of the deference of the house for the King's minister,
yet he may be so good natured, as not to put it to the test,
except it be for the mere and immediate profit of his master or
himself.

But whatever kind of *minister* he is, that attempts to innovate *a single iota* in the privileges of these colonies, him I hope
you will *undauntedly oppose*; and that you will never suffer
yourselves to be either *cheated* or *frightened* into any *unworthy
obsequiousness*. On such emergencies you may surely, without
presumption, believe, that ALMIGHTY GOD himself will
look down upon your righteous contest with gracious approbation. You will be a "*band of brothers*," cemented by the
dearest ties,—and strengthened with inconceivable supplies of
force and constancy, by that sympathetic ardor, which animates
good men, confederated in a good cause. Your *honor* and *welfare* will be, as they now are, most intimately concerned; and
besides—*you are assigned by divine providence*, in the appointed
order of things, the *protectors of unborn ages*, whose *fate* depends upon your *virtue*. Whether *they* shall arise the *generous*
and *indisputable heirs* of the noblest patrimonies, or the *das-
tardly* and *hereditary drudges* of imperious task-masters, YOU
MUST DETERMINE.

To discharge this double duty to *yourselves*, and to your *posterity*, you have nothing to do, but to call forth into use the *good
sense* and *spirit* of which you are possessed. You have nothing to
do, but to conduct your affairs *peaceably—prudently—firmly—
jointly*. By *these means* you will support the character of *freemen*,
without losing that of *faithful subjects*—a good character in

any government—one of the best under a *British* government. —You will *prove*, that *Americans* have that true *magnanimity* of soul, that can resent injuries, without falling into rage; and that tho' your devotion to *Great-Britain* is the most affectionate, yet you can make PROPER DISTINCTIONS, and know what you owe *to yourselves*, as well as *to her*—You will, at the same time that you advance your *interests*, advance your *reputation*—You will convince the world of the *justice of your demands*, and the *purity of your intentions.*—While all mankind must, with unceasing applauses, confess, that YOU indeed DESERVE liberty, who so *well understand* it, so *passionately love* it, so *temperately enjoy* it, and so *wisely, bravely*, and *virtuously assert, maintain*, and *defend* it.

> "*Certe ego libertatem, quæ mihi a parente meo tradita est, experiar: Verum id frustra an ob rem faciam, in vestra manu situm est, quirites.*"
>
> For my part, I am resolved to contend for the liberty delivered down to me by my ancestors; but whether I shall do it effectually or not, depends on you, my countrymen.
>
> "How little soever one is able to write, yet when the liberties of one's country are threatened, it is still more difficult to be silent."

A FARMER.

Is there not the strongest probability, that if the universal sense of these colonies is immediately expressed by RESOLVES of the assemblies, in support of their rights, by INSTRUCTIONS to their agents on the subject, and by PETITIONS to the crown and parliament for redress, these measures will have the same success now, that they had in the time of the *Stamp-Act*.

The END.

[Allan Ramsay], Thoughts on the Origin and Nature of Government. Occasioned by the Late Disputes Between Great Britain and Her American Colonies: Written in the Year 1766. London, 1769.

By the 1760s there were not many Britons left who were willing to voice publicly the older seventeenth-century Tory beliefs in absolute monarchy, indefeasible hereditary succession, and passive obedience. Since the defeat of Charles Edward Stuart at Culloden in 1745 the Jacobite claim to the throne had lost nearly all of its credibility. With the accession of George III in 1760 the Hanoverian grip on the English throne at last seemed secure. All the leading politicians continued to claim to be good Whigs. Nevertheless, George III welcomed many Tory gentry to court, and Toryism experienced something of a revival upon his accession; indeed, there seemed to be enough Toryism in the court to frighten Whigs like Edmund Burke into believing that the absolutist authority of the Stuarts was being restored.

A pamphlet like this one by Allan Ramsay would have done nothing to allay those fears. Although this Scottish painter considered himself to be "an absolute Whig," his poet father had been a Jacobite and he himself was close to Lord Bute and George III. Indeed, he produced many portraits of the king and queen and became a great favorite at court, being appointed in 1767 as Principal Painter in Ordinary to the king.

Ramsay wrote this pamphlet—probably as contrary to the American position as any written—in 1766 but did not publish it until late in 1768 (so late that it bears a 1769 publication date). It is full of Toryish sentiments about hierarchy and the inevitability of the division between master and servant, patron and client, and king and subject. Not only was this relation between superior and inferior "of natural and of divine appointment," but, according to Ramsay, the right of determining what the inferior owed the superior had to rest with the superior. "In all disputes between the governing and the governed, concerning the limits of authority and obedience, the governing part must, of necessity, be both judge and party." With such premises, it was not surprising that Ramsay found American claims to be absurd—not just absurd but without "any degree of firmness and consistency," changing day by day as the mood suited them. Perhaps it is also not surprising that he predicted that the imperial dispute would necessarily have to be settled by force.

THOUGHTS

ON THE

ORIGIN and NATURE

OF

GOVERNMENT.

Occaſioned by
The late Diſputes between GREAT BRITAIN
and her AMERICAN COLONIES:

Written in the Year 1766.

————VICTOR*que volentes*
Per populos dat jura.————

VIRG.

LONDON:

Printed for T. BECKET and P. A. DE HONDT, in
the Strand. MDCCLXIX.

Thoughts on Government.

THE question which has been for some time agitated, *Whether the legislative power of Great Britain has a right to tax its American colonies?* is of all questions the most important that was ever debated in this country. Those who compare it to that which was discussed at the Revolution, do not sufficient justice to its importance; for it is not concerning the forms of our constitution, or the share which this or that man, or this or that family, should have in the supreme government; but whether there should be any supreme government at all, and whether this, which is now a great and independent state, should, all at once, fall from its greatness, and perhaps cease to be reckoned amongst the least.

But although I mean in the following sheets to defend the rights of government, and to shew the Americans, and those of this country who encourage them, the unreasonableness of their late claims and pretensions, yet I do not mean to become advocate for those now entrusted with the administration of government, nor for those to whom they succeeded in that important talk. On the contrary, I cannot help considering those claims, and the indecent manner in which they have been urged, as something very much to their disadvantage. Government cannot to so great a degree cease to be respected, without raising a just suspicion of its having, some how or other, ceased to be respectable: and, to apply to political virtue what has been said by a lady of great wit, with regard to the virtue of her own sex, we must be allowed

> In part to doubt the *state* that has been tried;
> They come too near who come to be denied.*

Whatever may have given encouragement to such an attack, I am heartily sorry for it: but the attack being now made, it becomes the duty of every man who wishes well to this flourishing empire, the prosperity, the very existence of which depend upon the union of all its parts under one head, to repel

* See Dodsley's Collection, vol. I.

the attack by all the means which law, justice, and good sense authorise.

I doubt not but this my attempt to discover what is true and what is useful, however weak and insufficient, will be generally acceptable. I do not expect it will be universally so. There is no calamity which can be supposed to befall any country, except that of being totally swallowed up by an earthquake, which may not be advantageous, and possibly desirable to some of the individuals in it. CÆSAR, whose pride and ambition were so unbounded as to make him profess that he would rather be the first man in a miserable village than be the second in Rome, would not, in all probability, have scrupled to have adopted such measures as might have reduced that noble city to an equality with the most miserable village, rather than suffer any man in it to be his superior.

To such I do not mean to address any part of this paper. I know that any attempt to reason men out of their passions and supposed interest, is but so much ink thrown away. I only write for those, who, without ambition or resentment, suffer themselves to be enflamed by the ambition and resentment of others; and are made, by false reasoning, the promoters of interests the very reverse of their own.

The great difficulty attending this American controversy is, that the question changes upon us from day to day; and what would be a compleat answer one week, by the next is nothing at all to the purpose. Were the dispute betwixt England and America to stand upon the same ground that it did on the 14th of January* before two o'clock; were the colonists still to argue from the validity of their charters, and of the advantages resulting to them from thence; the laws of England might have been appealed to, and the constitution of England might have been investigated, in the practice of parliaments, from Magna Carta down to this day: but when acts of parliament

---

* The first day of the last session of parliament, when Mr. PITT came unexpectedly to London, and, in a debate upon the words of an address to his Majesty, took occasion to declare, as his opinion, *that the stamp duty laid upon the Americans the year before was unconstitutional and illegal, having been imposed without their own consent*: an opinion, however, that was not altogether new, it having appeared before in several American pamphlets.

are openly derided, and the authority of the supreme legisla-ture branded with the odious appellation of *force*, we are called upon to go somewhat deeper in our reasoning, and to inquire, in what this legislative authority itself is founded.

But before I endeavour to establish any thing of my own, it is neccessary to take notice of a principle frequently laid down upon this and former occasions, as a sure foundation for polit-ical reasoning; and that is, *That all men in their natural state are free and independent*: but if we are to judge of the nature of man, as we do of the nature of other existences, by experi-ence, there can be no foundation more unsound. No history of the past, no observation of the present time, can be brought to countenance such a *natural state*; nor were men ever known to exist in it, except for a few minutes, like fishes out of the water, in great agonies, terror and convulsions. This principle of equal right to liberty, which can hardly be separated from that of an equal right to property, has never been *actually* ac-knowledged by any but the very lowest class of men; who have been easily persuaded to embrace so flattering a doctrine from the mouth of a WAT TYLER or JACK CADE, and in consequence of it, for it leads to nothing else, have cut the throats and seized the goods of their masters.

The position, however, being established, this farther has been added to it, *that all the rights of government are derived from a voluntary social contract, by which each man gives up, as it were into a common stock, a small portion of this natural lib-erty, in order to form a sovereign power for the protection of the whole, and of every individual.* But unfortunately, as no such state of independence was ever known to exist, no such volun-tary contract was ever known to be entered into; so that if the legality of government depended upon it, it follows, that there never existed a legal government in any part of the globe.

Such are the idle dreams of metaphysicians, uncountenanced by fact and experience; and the more dangerous that, like other dreams, they carry, upon certain occasions, some con-fused resemblance of reality.

The rights of government are built upon something much more certain and permanent than any *voluntary* human con-tract, real or imaginary; for they are built upon the weakness and necessities of mankind. THE NATURAL WEAKNESS OF MAN IN A SOLITARY STATE, PROMPTS HIM TO FLY FOR PROTECTION TO WHOEVER IS ABLE TO AFFORD IT, THAT IS TO SOME ONE MORE POWERFUL, THAN HIMSELF; WHILE THE MORE POWERFUL STANDING EQUALLY IN NEED OF HIS SERVICE, READILY RECEIVES IT IN RETURN FOR THE PROTECTION HE GIVES. This is the true nature of that contract, which pervades every part of the social world, and which is to be seen at all times, in every empire, republic, city and family, or indeed where-ever two or three are met together. From this is derived all the relations of master and servant, patron and client, king and subject; and every project in public and private life which does not proceed upon this reciprocal obligation of protection and service, will be for ever abortive, or fatal to the projector.

Amongst the many philosophical heads which have speculated upon the origin of that right which one man in society has been found to claim to the service of another, some have derived it from victory in war, which giving, as they say, a right to the conqueror of taking away the life of the vanquished, gives him *à fortiori* a right to his service.* But this is endeavouring to establish a right that is doubtful, by the help of one that is at least equally so; for what proof is there that one man has a natural right to kill another? The two great marks by which we judge any act to be natural, are, the general instinct or desire to perform it, and the general utility arising from the performance. But no natural desire appears in man to imbrue his hands in the blood of his fellow creatures, nor is there any utility naturally arising from it; for nothing can be of less use than a man, when killed. I believe it will be found that the process is the very reverse of what those learned gentlemen have represented, and that any right which it is supposed one man may occasionally acquire of killing another, arises from a right previously conceived to his service. For in the great volume of nature's laws it appears to be thus written: THAT EVERY MAN IN SOCIETY SHALL RANK HIMSELF AMONGST THE RULING OR THE RULED, AS IT SHALL BEST SUIT HIS CIRCUMSTANCES AND ABILITIES; ALL EQUALITY AND INDEPENDENCE BEING BY

* See Grotius De jure belli et pacis, lib. 3. cap. 4.

THE LAW OF NATURE STRICTLY FORBIDDEN: AND IT IS FARTHER DECLARED BY THE SAME AUTHORITY, THAT WHOSOEVER IS NOT ABLE TO COMMAND, NOR WILLING TO OBEY, SHALL FORFEIT HIS LIVING OR HIS LIFE: And it is probably by this law that all are condemned to die who fall in battle; it being only a compleat victory which determines who are exempted from the fatal sentence; by shewing who are able to command, and who are willing to obey.

These are truths not drawn from sophistical reasoning, and juggling with ill-defined words; but from plain sense and observation. By an appeal to universal experience we may prove that the relation between master and servant is of natural and of divine appointment, just as we should prove, if any body were so senseless as to doubt it, that the sun and moon were so. That which chiefly wants to be ascertained is, what is the nature and what the limits of the servitude that is due to the master, or, what it is he has a right to exact from his servant. And here necessity, the foundation of all my reasoning, obliges me to pronounce, that the sole determination of that right rests with the superior; because, if that is not allowed, it cannot under God reside any where; and so the union, which we suppose so necessary in society, and which comes alone from the whole body being actuated by one mind, must of course be dissolved.

I have hitherto spoken of society as if composed of one individual master and one individual servant: and as the whole law of government, that is the reciprocal obligation of protection and obedience, is made more intelligible by this simplicity, I shall often treat of it in that form. There are a great many specific differences in the various combinations of larger societies, but with regard to the great principle, the first example will apply to them all. Let the number of men who compose the society be ever so great, there is an absolute necessity in order to their remaining one society, that they be separated into two parts, with this distinction; that the governing part, always the least numerous, must act and be considered as one body, actuated by one mind; while the other, from whose great number unanimity is not to be expected, and for whose situations unanimity is not necessary, ought never to be considered as one body, but as so many separate persons. The individual governing to the many individuals governed, is as the brain to the members of the human body. Be the brain ever so foolish, all wisdom must be allowed there to reside; and every motion of a limb, without its dictates, is only a convulsion and a sure mark of a distempered state. In short there must exist in every society a ruling power, whose will, from the necessity of things, must be allowed the measure of its own rights, and of those of its subjects.

"Is there then no bounds, no stay to this absolute power? Has it a right to do what it pleases? Has it a right to do wrong?"—No certainly; for that would be admitting an absurdity, a right of doing what ought never to be done. We must distinguish betwixt a right (*jus*) and right (*rectum*) which, from a poverty in the English language have often added embarrassment to this subject. No act of power can turn what is wrong into what is right. But right and wrong cannot decide themselves; they are the objects of human judgment, and must be decided by some body or other: and let what rules soever be laid down for the better decision, the rules and the subject will at last become matter of opinion. But private opinion cannot possibly be admitted; for, all being equally entitled, no man would suffer what he called his rights to be decided by any other private opinion than his own. This is, however, the state of man in those dreadful moments, when the bonds of rule, order and society are dissolved; a state of war and confusion, which some writers have been so senseless as to call a *state of nature*, while it is only a state of distemper and misery.

The end and intention of government is to prevent private opinion from ever taking place, except in matters of private concern. All the duties which one man owes to another, or which each man owes to the whole, must be marked out and decided by some tribunal to which all men must equally submit; and which, having judged, can make its judgments effectual; without which there can be no decision. After this it is needless to say that the right of making and executing all laws, the right of clearing all doubts about the lives, properties and privileges of all the members of the society, must be vested absolutely in the Supreme governing power, and that from it there can be no appeal. A law without a penalty is no more than an advice; and a penalty without a power to inflict it would be ridiculous: and this is so consonant to common sense and common language, that there is probably no language in the world in which to *prevail* and *to give law* are not synonomous.

In all societies which are made up of more than two individuals, there are two sorts of laws. One of these is what is framed as a rule for deciding the claims of the individuals of the society, and their duty both with respect to one another, and to the state, in matters of private right. This may be called the *civil law*, and is generally, and with great propriety delegated to inferior judges by the Supreme power ever ready at hand to support their decisions, except where they admit of an appeal to itself. The other, which may be called the *law of government* or *suprema lex*, is that by which all pretensions of right between governor and governed, in matters of government, are tried. With regard to this law, the ruleing and the ruled are exactly in the state of a society made up of two single persons: the law cannot be exactly defined; nor can the execution of it be delegated to the discretion of any body. What concerns the *safety of the whole* can never be committed to the arbitration of any of the subordinate parts; so that in all disputes betwixt the governing and the governed, concerning the limits of authority and obedience, the governing part must, of necessity, be both judge and party.

To enquire whether this may not be attended with great inconveniencies and oppression, would be extremely useless. The enquiry is cut short, by barely affirming, that it was always so, that it cannot be otherwise, and that those who are desirous of partaking the advantages arising from law and government must accept of them upon those terms, since upon no other can they be obtained.

"Are there then no natural rights of mankind independent of the despotic will of their rulers?" There certainly are a great many such rights; rights established by the laws of God and nature, of equal authority with the rights of government, which extend no farther than to the framing of such laws for particular societies, as are, in respect of the laws of nature, to be considered only as *bye laws*: and if the terms I have used seem to intimate any thing to the contrary, it is full time that those terms were explained. When I speak of *service* due at the will of the master, I desire to be understood of such service only as, according to the common sense, and universal practice of every age and country, one man in society may lawfully receive at the hands of another: and when I speak of the uncontroulable right in the ruler of making and executing *laws*, I would be understood to mean such laws only as are not repugnant to the laws of nature. A man by becoming an obedient subject does not cease to be a man, and as such has certainly rights which no human power can infringe without committing an act of lawless tyranny and oppression! The difficulty lies in distinguishing those constant, universal, and indefeasible rights of the species, from the ever fluctuating rights of the individuals, of which alone I have been hitherto treating; and it were to be wished, that amongst the many who now write about these rights, there were some one or other who would give himself the trouble of telling us what he imagines them to be. To give a detail of them might perhaps be tedious, but not to subject myself to the same reflection, I will venture to give one general rule, formed upon the reciprocal obligations of protection and service, and supported by experience and observation upon the actual conduct and sentiments of men, by which the rights of government may be, with respect to the natural rights of mankind, in great measure, limited and defined.

WHATEVER ACT OF POWER IS EXERTED AGAINST THE SUBJECT MANIFESTLY NOT NECESSARY, OR NOT TENDING TO THE SUPPORT OR SAFETY OF GOVERNMENT, THAT IS TO THE PROTECTION OF THE WHOLE, IS, BY THE LAWS OF GOD AND NATURE, DECLARED ILLEGAL, AND A BREACH OF THE NATURAL COMPACT BETWEEN THE RULER AND THE RULED. Millions of treasure may be squandered away, thousands of lives may be sacrificed, to very little purpose, in one morning's battle; and yet the bond between ruler and subject continue firm and unbroken; while the smallest injury done by Government to the meanest peasant, where no necessity of state can be rationally alledged, is sufficient to throw the whole into confusion.

The Almighty seems to have said to every ruler or body of rulers upon investing them with their authority, TAKE AND

PRESERVE THIS POWER, WHICH THE PEACE AND HAPPINESS OF MANKIND REQUIRE TO BE ENTRUSTED WITH SOME BODY OR OTHER; AND TAKE CARE TO USE IT IN SUCH MANNER AS *ne quid detrimenti capiat respublica*, FOR IT IS FOR THAT END, AND FOR THAT ALONE, THAT YOU ARE ENTRUSTED WITH IT. THE TASK I IMPOSE IS DIFFICULT, AND FROM WEAKNESS OF UNDERSTANDING, OR VIOLENCE OF PASSION, YOU WILL COMMIT MANY ERRORS IN THE PERFORMANCE OF IT: BUT GO ON BOLDLY, BE NOT DISCOURAGED, FOR NONE OF THOSE ERRORS SHALL BE IMPUTED TO YOU AS CRIMES, IF YOU CAN FORGIVE YOURSELF, ALL MEN SHALL FORGIVE YOU. BUT BEWARE HOW YOU SUFFER THIS POWER, BY WHICH ALONE YOU CAN PROTECT YOURSELF OR MY PEOPLE, TO BE DIMINISHED; AND BEWARE OF EMPLOYING IT FOR ANY OTHER PURPOSE BUT THAT OF SUPPORTING YOURSELF AND PRESERVING ORDER; FOR ALL SUCH TRANSGRESSIONS WILL BE ACCOUNTED AS CRIMES, AND WILL BE PUNISHED IN YOU AS YOU WOULD PUNISH THE LOWEST CRIMINAL.

From an inattention to these great commands have arisen all the disorders and revolutions in government with which history acquaints us: for instance,

The ravishing of men's wives and daughters was never supposed necessary for the support of Government; and therefore produced the downfall of the regal and decemviral governments of ancient Rome.

The putting a father under the cruel necessity of shooting at an apple upon his son's head, could never be supposed necessary for the support of government, and therefore this piece of wanton insolence put an end to the Austrian rule in Switzerland.

The forcing men, under severe penalties, to profess this or that speculative opinion in matters of eternal salvation, contrary to what they believe true, could never be supposed by any but ideots, necessary for the support of government; and we all know what the foolish attempt occasioned to the Spanish dominion in the Low Countries, and to the regal authority of the STEWARTS in Great Britain.

Do you ask who has a right to judge what acts of power are against nature, and what are not? I answer, no body. The immediate impulse of every man's feelings stands in the stead of all judgment in such cases; and when the passions of men are all raised by one motive, and all pointed to one end, they require no leader to give them unity of mind and uniformity of conduct; while those whose proper office it is to wield the sword in defence of government, partaking of the common feelings, either desert their employers, or, by a dubious and feeble assistance, serve to render their ruin more compleat.

But, of all the transgressions or neglects of nature's laws, none have been so fatal to rulers as that breach of the original compact, in being unwilling or unable to give that *protection*, to which the duty of *obedience* must be ever subsequent or secondary. In forming that social compact, which is the foundation of all my reasoning, the proposal is not, *If you will be obedient I will be powerfull*, for that would be too absurd to deserve any notice; but it is, *If you are powerfull I will be obedient*; and this being the order of the conditions, the first not being forthcoming, the second becomes void and null of itself. For in the whole Code of nature there is no law more distinctly expressed than this:

> *Ne liceat facere id quod quis vitiabit agendo*
> *Publica lex hominum naturaque continet hoc fas*
> *Ut teneat vetitos inscitia debilis actus.* *

Which means, when applied to government, that THEY ONLY HAVE, BY NATURE, A RIGHT TO RULE WHO ARE QUALIFIED FOR IT, it being high treason against nature for the weak to pretend to govern the strong, the foolish the wise, the ignorant the skilful, the fearful the bold, or the poor the rich. To retain the rights of government, without the powers from whence those rights were originally derived, is the greatest of crimes against society; and which, society and its divine guardian never fail to punish, according to the degree of the offence, that is, according to the inconveniencies and dangers to which society is exposed by such ineffectual pretensions.

Such are the laws which will ever supersede all laws of human contrivance, and which being broken, by any ruler or rulers, the original compact is dissolved, and no farther allegiance

* Persius sat. 5.

due. But what have those laws of nature to do with the present controversy between the British government and its subjects of America? *The original compact*, it is said, *has been broken.* When? By what means? Whose ass has been stolen, whose wife has been ravished, whose conscience has been constrained, by act of parliament? What protection has been required from the legislature of Great Britain, that has not been willingly and manfully afforded? None. *We are taxed*, say the Americans, *contrary to right, for we are taxed without our own consent.* Were they fairly to tell us upon what they found this pretended right, of laying burthens upon themselves according to their own pleasure and conveniency, it would be no hard task to combat it; but when we have got fast hold of what we suppose the main argument, and are ready to squeeze it to death, it immediately flips like an eel through our fingers. *It is*, at one time, *by the law of nature.* When you ask them to quote the page, or shew them some law of nature which speaks the very reverse, *it is* then *by the constitution of Britain.* There when they are shewn that the solemn declarations of the legislature, and the constant practice, wherever it was necessary, speak against them, they declare themselves against all those solemn declarations and practices, telling us, *That what has been done, if wrongfully done, confers no right to repeat it*, and back again they go to *their* laws of nature, or to the flimsy hypothesis of some scholastic writer to new-model nature and the constitution of England, so as to make them more favourable to their pretensions. For my part I know of no human authority to which I dare appeal, except to acts of Parliament; and, if they could be admitted, there would be soon an end of the controversy; as the present parliament has as unquestionable an authority as any of the former parliaments; and the Stamp Act itself of as much authority as any former act which could be quoted to authorise it.

It being therefore, useless to deduce any argument from an authority, the disclaiming of which furnishes the very question in debate, I will return once more to my general plan, and enquire what is the true nature of levying taxes, and whether it differs, as has been often asserted by the Americans, from the other rights of legislation.

To take up this in a plain, easy, and regular way, let us return to the point from whence we set out. In a state consisting of one individual ruler, and one individual subject, like that of ROBINSON CRUSOE and his man FRIDAY, the service of one of these in return for the protection of the other, can be only personal; and the mode, as well as the quantity, of this service must be left, as has been shewn before, to the discretion of the superior; whose will must serve for all the different sorts of law, either with regard to public or private rights, which the nature of that simple society can possibly admit. But, in a numerous society, it would be extremely inconvenient, not to say absurd, that all the subjects should be personally employed in the public service; as such employment must necessarily hinder them from providing for their own support. Nor is such a generality of personal service any more needful than it is possible; as a very few of a numerous community are sufficient to do all that is required for the defence and protection of the whole. But as all are equally liable, and the letting the whole labour fall upon a few, would be unjust and ruinous, it became necessary that each man in the community should contribute a certain portion of the product of his private industry, for the maintenance of those, who being occupied in fulfilling the general obligation, of serving or assisting the protecting power, have not sufficient leisure to provide subsistance for themselves. In short, a TAX, in whatever mode it may appear, is but another word for SERVICE; and as that enters essentially into the very Being of government; whatever concerns the appointing, regulating, or rendering it effectual, becomes the most important part of legislation; and which, from the nature of things, no inferior part of administration, much less the subjects, have the least right to meddle with, except under the supreme authority. Were the supreme authority to resign this power of the purse into the hands of any other part of the society, such a resignation would amount to an abdication of the government; and that part which became invested with the power of levying money, would be, *ipso facto*, supreme. These I give as fundamental principles of government, and do not desire them to be admitted if they are not found to be in fact universally true. Point me out but one single instance of a state where a right was acknowledged in any, but the supreme

power, of imposing or with-holding taxes, and I shall immediately give up all that is contained in these reasonings as false;
they being entirely grounded upon a principle that does not
admit of such a possibility.

What then becomes of the notion, *That people ought not to
be taxed but by their own consent?* I cannot tell; let those look to
the proposition who advance it. I can only say that any set of
people who are masters of their own purses, are masters of their
own services, they are their own masters, and subject to no
body. If ever such people had engaged themselves in a compact
of service and protection, such compact subsists for them no
longer; they are perfectly independent, and any verbal acknowledgement of superiority from them, after the *actual* acknowledgement is thus withdrawn, is no better than a piece of
mockery. In short, from those who are really subjects such
consent never was nor ever can be asked. It will be said *that the
people of England consent to their own taxation by their representatives.* But this is nothing but a vulgar misapprehension; the
consent of the people being no more required in England,
upon such occasions, than it is in Turkey: and, indeed, if the
principles of Government which I have laid down as general,
are not equally true, and equally, *in fact*, admitted in England
and in Turkey, I shall no longer acknowledge them as principles. The sole difference is that the supreme power happens to
be differently constituted in those two different states, but
when constituted, it equally assumes the right of imposing
taxes upon the people without their consent. The people of
England, or certain classes of them, have a right by election to
constitute the third part of the legislative power for seven
years; and it would make no difference in my argument if they
constituted the whole for that term: but from the day of election, the people have no more share in the legislation than
those of Turkey, and the strings of their purses are equally resigned into the hands of their rulers. It may be perhaps said,
that if these members of parliament abuse the confidence that
is put in them, the people may at the end of seven years elect
others in their stead. But this does not in the least affect the
present question, which is not what is to happen after the supreme legislative power is dissolved; but what happens while it
actually subsists. When a parliament is dissolved, the people

must proceed to the election either of the same or other Members; but whoever they elect will have the same unlimited power with their predecessors; and, although the persons may be changed, the constitution of the government and the rights of the governors and the governed are perpetual, and are no more changed along with the Members of parliament, than they are in Turkey, when one Sultan, in that military democracy, is deposed by his constituents the Janizaries, and another set up in his place. So far from the consent or opinion of the people of England being more particularly necessary in this species of legislation than in any other, that all who know any thing of the practice of parliament, must know that it is a constant rule not to admit any petition, however humbly conceived, against any bill in deliberation for levying money, while this priviledge is allowed upon almost every other occasion.*

In order to shew in its utmost extent, and unembarrassed by any accidental circumstances, the frivolousness of the vulgar notion that the people of England keep the possession of their own purses, and give their consent to their own taxation by their representatives; I have supposed that every ditcher in the country, and every chimney-sweeper in town gives his vote for electing Members of the House of Commons, Peers of the realm, and if you please, the King likewise, for the space of seven years; and have shewn, that with all these suppositions, they would be taxed without their own consent, as much as if they lived under the Great Turk. After this it may seem superfluous and foreign to my purpose, to shew that this supposed *representation*, even with regard to the House of Commons, is very far from being true, and that the word *Virtual*, which has been clapped in, to supply this defect, has no meaning at all; but as this subject has furnished, and may still furnish matter for dispute, I cannot let it pass without some animadversion.

The first parliaments in England after the Norman conquest,

---

* There are instances of petitions having been received, as in the case of the excise upon wine and tobacco, in 1733, and of the excise upon cyder, in 1763, which may be urged in contradiction to what is here asserted. But those petitions were not admitted as against the taxes themselves, but only as against the mode of collecting them.

were composed of these only who held lands *in capite* under the crown. They were few in number; being according to Dooms-day book not above 700, and might have all been assembled together in one place without any inconveniency.

By the time of King JOHN, the number of freeholders or tenants *in capite* was greatly increased, but that principle of their all having a right to be summoned to parliament, which we suppose to have been the original constitution, still subsisted; for thus we read in KING JOHN's Magna Carta: *and for holding the common Council of the kingdom for assessing aids or for imposing scutages, we will cause to be summoned Archbishops, Bishops, Abbots, Earls, and greater Barons, separately, by our letters; and we will cause to be summoned, in general, by our sheriffs and bailiffs, all those who hold of us* in capite. This is the full account of the members of parliament according to Magna Carta, which, as it is understood to be a declaration of the common law of the land, and of the liberties of Englishmen in the best times, free from any abuses that might have been before introduced, we may rely upon this description as the genuine constitution of parliament at the time. But here is no *representation*: every man who came to parliament, either by particular or general summons, came of his own right, as the peers do to this day; nor could the word or idea of a *representative* be known amongst them.

There is reason to believe that the clause for calling by general summons the smaller barons or freeholders to parliament was inserted into Magna Carta by the particular will of King JOHN,* in order to break and counteract the power of the greater Barons, who were at that time very troublesome to the crown. Accordingly, in the Magna Carta of the first year of his son HENRY the III, the whole clause concerning the constitution of parliament is omitted, and instead of it is inserted a sort of notice *that this matter was by the advice of his Bishops and great Lords reserved for more mature consideration*. But although there was a Magna Carta granted in the 16th, and

---

* See the preliminary articles presented by the Barons to King John, compared with his Magna Carta, in the appendix to an *Essay on the constitution of England*, second edition, printed for T. Becket and P. A. de Hondt, London, 1766.

another in the 18th of this King's reign; there is no farther mention made of it. Whether it was that the great Barons prevailed too much during this unhappy reign, to permit the smaller to take any share with them in the legislative power, or whether their great number made their assembling impracticable, is what our ancient historians do not sufficiently inform us. But towards the end of this reign the smaller freeholders were ordered to chuse and send commissioners from each shire, to represent in parliament all those who were absent.

Here was a change in the form of parliament, but none in the principle. The knights commissioners represented the freeholders only, who, whether present or absent, held the same place in the state as under King JOHN's Magna Carta.

This method, however, of election, in order to carry on with more conveniency, what was in itself ancient and constitutional, gave hint for producing what was of a newer kind. There was one great acknowledged and constitutional power in the ancient kings of England, without which it would have been impossible to have preserved the government from being entirely aristocratical, and that was, the power of chusing who should come to parliament and who should not; or, at least, of adding what new members of parliament they thought fit. Almost at the same time that it was found useful to summon the smaller freeholders to appear by their commissioners; the King, by his letters patent, erected a few, we shall say, for distinctness, one borough, of those which were of his own domain, and particularly dependent upon him, into a body corporate; and gave it, amongst other priviledges, that of chusing something equivalent to a baron to fit in parliament. But this elected baron represented nothing but his own townsmen; and if he assisted in taking the money out of the purses of other towns, which he certainly did, he must have done it by some other right than that of representing them. And although this one baron was multiplied in the course of time to a great number, yet with regard to those who do not chuse them, they all stand upon the same footing with the first. But some of those barons are of no more ancient standing than the reign of King CHARLES the II. and some of the most opulent towns of England send none to this day; yet it never came into any bodies head to fancy that the money levied from them for the publick service, was illegally and unconstitutionally levied.

But to return to my freeholders. Were I to stop my history of Representation here, my reader might possibly go off with an opinion, that it was a fundamental principle of the English constitution, that every freeholder should sit in parliament, either in person, or in the person of one whom he had concurred in chusing. But this was not the ancient idea of this matter. The freeholders sate in parliament as the POWERS OF THE STATE, and when they ceased to be powerful, they ceased to be qualified. This is manifest in the act of parliament of the 8th Henry the VI. for restricting the number of voting freeholders to those who were possessed of 40 *shillings a-year at the least*; the preamble of which runs thus: *Whereas the election of knights of the shires to come to parliament of our Lord the King, in many counties of the realm of England, have now, of late, been made by very great outrageous and excessive number of people dwelling within the same counties of the realm of England, of the which most part was of people of small substance, and of no value, whereof every of them pretended a voice equivalent, as to such elections to be made, with the most worthy Knights and Esquires dwelling within the same counties; whereby manslaughter, riots, batteries, and divisions among the gentlemen and other people of the same counties shall very likely rise and be, unless convenient and due remedy be provided in this behalf.* *

---

* By several circumstances to be learnt from ancient records, it appears that sending or being sent to parliament was reckoned, if not a burthen, at least a priviledge very little worth the contesting with those who thought fit to claim it. For this reason the law was for some ages very loose and uncertain, as well with regard to the number of the representatives, as with regard to the number and quality of their electors, while a variety of other privileges, which now appear to us of much less consequence, were most jealously guarded by express statutes. There is no room to doubt but that the constituents of the Great Council or parliament were originally no other than the king's immediate vassals; but after the smaller sort of them came to be represented by a few persons elected at meetings called by the sheriff in the county town, others who held their lands, by free tenures, under other Lords, and who had been used to attend the county-courts upon other occasions, were, by degrees, under the common title of freeholders, jumbled amongst the King's tenants in the election of the county member. Nor would probably this growing abuse

This act was very wisely intended to give a stability to the constitution, which, by a constant increase of the constituents, was gradually changing; but unhappily by supposing a stability in the value of money, it produced an effect the very reverse of what was intended. By the most moderate calculation, a piece of land which was then worth two pounds *per annum*, would be now worth twenty, so that there is a possibility of there being now ten legal voters for a knight of the shire for one that there was in the time of Henry the VI. But although these are legal voters by the letter of the law, they are not so by the spirit of the ancient constitution, which plainly intended to lop off nine out of ten of them; and consequently no argument can be drawn from their present multiplicity, with regard to the necessity of all freeholders being represented.

I pass over the labourers, the farmers, and even the copy-holders of land, who have no vote in chusing those who impose taxes upon them; I pass over the many inhabitants, even of those towns which send members, who have no vote in chusing those members, or in chusing those who chuse them, and hasten to examine what is called a *virtual representation*, by which all those notorious deficiencies in the real one are to be patched up.

It is said that all the lands of England, being divided amongst the freeholders, they become by that means the *virtual representatives* of all those who live upon these lands; and by that *virtual representation*, have a right of giving laws to the whole,

---

have been attended to, even in the reign of Henry the VI. as parliamenteering was still an unprofitable trade, had it not been productive of those dangerous tumults related in the above preamble.

In Scotland, where the laws and constitution, formed anciently upon the model of those of England, have not undergone the same changes, the King's tenants *in capite* are alone capable of electing, or being elected, Knights of the shires. They, though few in number, are the only persons represented in parliament; and by a peculiar attention of the law of Scotland to their qualifications, they are, in great measure, the same class of men, who, by the ancient constitutions both of England and Scotland, were alone entitled to be consulted in any act of legislation. Estimating the present rents of Scotland at only the double of their ancient valuation in the Exchequer rolls; one elector of a county member must hold, by a royal charter, as great a quantity of land as would qualify thirty-three voters in England, upon a like occasion.

and to which the whole, by a sort of tacit or *virtual compact*, give their consent.

If this is a principle of government, it will be true in every application of it, and if it is not found true in every application, I would advise those who use it to lay it aside as a principle, and to look out for something else that will better bear this necessary test.

The freeholders, as ordered to be summoned to parliament by King JOHN's Magna Carta, were, it seems, the *virtual representatives* of every man in the kingdom. We do not know precisely what their number was, and the knowledge is certainly not at all necessary for verifying the principle of *virtual representation*, which will be equally true, whether their number be great or small. They were possibly at that time two or three thousand. Suppose they had been only seven hundred, as in the 20th year of the Conqueror, or suppose them seventy, or if peradventure they had been only seven, then these seven must be acknowledged to be the *virtual representatives* of the whole. What signifies so much higling: let us come to the matter at once, and suppose all the lands held by one freeholder; as is actually the case in Turkey. Then is the GRAND SIGNOR *virtual representative* of all the people of Turkey, their universal knight of the shire, and, in a most parliamentary manner, levies what taxes he pleases upon them, by *their own consent*.

I would not here be thought to mean any reflection upon the GRAND SIGNOR or his rights; I am not, thank God, so great a bigot to the form of government under which I was born and bred, as to look upon any other form with contempt or abhorrence. Far from it. While that great prince exercises his rights for the order, peace, and happiness of his people, he is the good and faithful servant of the truly sovereign power, and merits the respect of all men, whether they receive any benefit from his superintendency or not. What I find ridiculous in this process, and what would never enter into the head of the most senseless Mussulman, is, that he should enjoy these extended rights over his people by the unintelligible and useless fiction of being their *virtual representative*.

I have taken a great deal of pains to shew that the notion of people consenting to their own taxation is contrary to the nature of government, and unsupported by any fact. I have been at pains to shew that the notion of the legislative power acting by virtue of representation, is no principle in the British constitution; and I have finished by shewing that the words *virtual representation*, either mean nothing at all, or mean a great deal more than those who use them would be willing to admit: and yet, after all my pains, my American antagonists are as much out of my reach as before.

The truth is, that having heard them so often repeat that they were Englishmen, entitled to all the rights of Englishmen, so as to be taxed, like Englishmen, *by their own consent*: I was misled to believe that they wanted to be represented, like other Englishmen, in the British parliament. But upon a closer examination, I find they have no such meaning. *Each American colony*, say they, *has a parliament of its own, though we have hitherto called them only assemblies: each has its house of Commons chosen by the people, and which has alone the right of raising money from them; each has its council or house of peers; and each has its King, to wit, his Majesty King* GEORGE *the* III. *who, as he cannot preside in so many parliaments at once, is represented in each by his Excellency the Governor. We did not*, say they, *sail the wide Atlantic Ocean, to leave the free constitution of England behind us; no, we carried it along with us, and—*

There cannot be imagined a question more important for the safety and happiness of mankind in general, than that which is the subject of these sheets, and yet there is perhaps no question, the solution of which requires less learning and subtlety, nor any, which is more within the compass of a plain and sound understanding. The principles upon which it is to be discussed are universal, comprehensive, and applicable to every possible case; and every opposition to them is immediately reducible to a falsity in point of fact, or an absurdity in point of reasoning. If there is found any difficulty in applying them to the present case of America, it arises only from this, that the Americans are either not able or not willing to tell us with any degree of firmness and consistency, what they are, and what they would be at. One moment they desire no more than what belongs to every British subject; the next they refuse to be taxed like other British subjects, and each colony requires a parliament of its own. At one time they acknowledge their subjection to Great Britain; and almost in the same breath, endeavour to prove that each petty colony has a right to be her equal. One moment they bar all considerations of force from being admitted in deciding the rights of sovereigns and subjects, and the next endeavour to establish what they call their rights by a variety of outrages, such as were never imputed to any established government of the most arbitrary kind. At one time an American claims the rights of an Englishman; if these are not sufficient, he drops them, and claims the rights of an Irishman; and, when those do not fully answer his purpose, he expects to be put upon the footing of a Hanoverian.

To support, by turns, this variety of contradictory pretensions, a variety of principles no less contradictory, are by turns produced. First they try to found the extraordinary privileges they claim upon *birth-right*; but when they are shewn that by *birth* they had no *right* to desert their native country, they drop the birth-right, and bring forth their *charters*. When they are shewn that these charters are no other than what are given to every common corporation and trading company, they then cease to be charters, and become all at once *compacts*. At one time it is the love of liberty that made them take shelter in those distant climes, from the *tyranny of prerogative*; yet when we ask them with whom they made those *compacts* just mentioned; they tell us, with a King JAMES or a King CHARLES. How must the great shades of ALGERNOON SIDNEY and JOHN LOCK exclaim, how must they rage in their independent mansions, to hear that there should be *Englishmen* who pretend to read and admire their writings, and yet understand them so little as to own that they had entered into a *compact*, or as these patriots would call it, a *conspiracy*, with a King, in order to obtain a dispensation from the laws of the land, and the authority of parliament!

The assertion that these charters are not charters, but *Pacta conventa*, is brim-full of absurdity. For, passing over the manifest illegality already hinted, of one part of the sovereign power dispensing with the authority of the whole; the whole sovereign power could not, by the nature of things, enter into any indefeasible compact of that sort. Nor is this more to be considered as matter of reasoning than as matter of language. *Sovereignty* admits of no degrees, it is always *supreme*, and to level it, is, in effect, to destroy it; I mean with regard to those who suffer it to be levelled: for, as to sovereignty itself, it is unsusceptible of destruction; and, like the sun, only sets in one place, that it may rise, with full splendour, in another. *Pacta conventa* cannot, with any propriety, subsist, but amongst parties independent of one another; nor are they then of much significance, unless there be, at the same time, some despotick power provided, for explaining any difficulty that might arise concerning the several conditions of the agreement, and for enforcing the observance of them. Without such an effectual arbitrator, a covenant between two independent powers, is no other than a Treaty, which is no longer to be relied on than while it suits with the conveniency of both the parties to observe it. In case of any misunderstanding, there lies no appeal but to the God of battles, whose decision only suspends the suit till a future term, when the party that was cast may find the means of entering a new action.

But enough of these abstractions. One good example of a real covenant between two sovereign states will give more light into the nature of *Pacta conventa* in general, and may perhaps contribute more to elucidate the particular subject of this paper, than a thousand pages of general reasoning and description.

Since the creation of the world there never was a more voluntary, more deliberate, more legal, and more solemn paction than that which was made by the union of the two ancient and independent kingdoms of England and Scotland; nor any whose articles had a better title to be religiously observed. But immutability in human affairs is contrary to the nature of them, and every attempt to produce it, is an attempt to counteract the providence of God by the wisdom of man.

In this solemn paction there was one article absolutely necessary for binding and cementing the whole, according to the general intention of the covenanting parties; but which at the same time threw every other particular article loose. I mean that article which settled the constitution of the British parliament, and gave it as absolute and supreme an authority, to decide in all the concerns of the now united kingdom, as the several parliaments had in those kingdoms when separate. To this uncontroulable power was entrusted, amongst other things, the guardianship of the other articles of the union, with the sole right of explaining their meaning and intention, in case any doubt should arise concerning them; without reserving to any man, or any number of men, the least right to rejudge their judgments. To actuate this great body, and to procure a perfect and lasting union, such a directing soul was absolutely necessary; and that such has been the idea always conceived of it, by the wisdom of the united nation, will appear by the following instance.

In the year 1725, an act passed in the British parliament for extending the malt-tax to Scotland, where a malt-tax was as new as a stamp-tax was last year in America. This innovation had been objected to on a former occasion,* by many of the Scottish peers and members of parliament, supported by others, who, for the sake of opposing the administration, pretended to take a share in their grievances, and joined with them in declaring this tax a breach of the articles of the Union, which, they said, parliament had no right to infringe, it being upon those *Pacta conventa* that the authority of the British parliament itself was established; and that they being broken, the *original compact* was dissolved. In answer to this it had been said; that nothing was meant against the Union or its articles, but that it was apprehended the tax proposed was entirely within the spirit and intention of those articles; and whether it was or was not, could only be determined by the majority of both houses with his Majesty's concurrence. It was accordingly voted a legal as well as expedient mode of taxation.

But many of the people in Scotland judging in this matter very differently from their rulers; declared the tax to be illegal, and swore they never would consent to the payment of it; never considering that their pretensions to infallibility were no better founded than those of the British parliament, and that their pretensions to authority were much worse. Nor did they content themselves with this verbal denunciation, but when the officers attempted to levy the tax, they put them to flight with blows and insulting language; at the same time pulling down the houses, destroying the furniture; and threatning the

* In the year 1713.

lives of such of their countrymen as had concurred in passing the Act. What would our American friends have advised government to do in this case? To repeal the Act, because the Scotch mob pronounced it illegal; or to try by pamphlets, or by repeated letters in the Daily Gazetteer, to convince them they were in the wrong? No, this folly and outrage was treated in a manner much more consistent with the nature and dignity of parliament, which requires from subjects obedience, and not reasoning. There were sent to Glasgow, where the pretended standard of liberty was set up, some companies of foot, and some troops of dragoons, with a sensible and spirited officer at their head, who, *pulveris exigui jactu*, soon brought those mistaken reasoners to a better understanding concerning the rights of the supreme legislature, than all the eloquence of CICERO or MANSFIELD, without such an accompaniment, could have effected.

This the gentlemen of America will say is *club law*. I will not dispute it. They may call it by what name they please, but there never was a question of supremacy decided by any other sort of law. Those who try to separate law from force, attempt impiously to put those asunder whom God has been pleased to join; and as the reasonings of such men are never correspondent to any facts that have gone before; so are their own actions never correspondent to their reasonings. Is it to argument or club law, to which the *respectable populace* of Boston and Rhode-island trust the justice of their cause? Is it argument to demolish the houses or destroy the goods of those who differ from them in opinion; or is it argument to carry them to *the tree of liberty*, and there oblige them to take God to witness to sentiments not their own, for fear of being immediately put to death? These are outrages which none but the most ignorant and distempered imaginations could ever dread from any kind of established government, and yet are committed by those, who, in the very height of their riots, complain of cruel and arbitrary exertions of power in the mild government of Great Britain, under the most just and humane of Kings.

In the course of this enquiry I have often used the word *Colony*, in speaking of those parts of the British empire which lie on the other side of the Atlantick ocean, and have done so

in compliance with the present mode of America, upon a supposition that the essence of things being known, the terms to
express them become matters of indifference. But this, I acknowledge, is a very ill grounded supposition, and to proceed
upon it extremely dangerous: for nothing is more serviceable
to the cause of falsehood than the admission of improper
terms, which, though at first admitted only as counters, having
received a currency, will be afterwards tendered to us as sterling coin. By virtue of this heathen word *colony*, the example of
Roman colonies has been urged in favour of American claims;
and when these have not been found perfectly favourable to
independency, recourse has been had to Greek colonies, which,
indeed, had little other relation to their mother-country, than
a sort of cousinship, such as the Jews, in the time of the Maccabees, claimed with the Lacedemonians; claimed when they
stood in need of their assistance, and perhaps was never mentioned by them either before or since. But all this parade of
Greek and Roman learning comes to nothing, when we are
informed that the districts in question are not properly *colonies*
either in word or in deed. Their most ancient English and legal
name is *plantations*, and they have always been, in fact, *provinces*, governed by a lieutenant or governor, sent by the King
of Great Britain, and recalled by him at pleasure. Nor are they
entitled to participate of those many advantages which they
enjoy as Englishmen by virtue of their British descent, but from
a much more solid and rational principle, their being faithful
subjects of Great Britain; since the same advantages are by law
expressly communicated to such of them as were born in
Westphalia and the Palatinate, and who never set foot upon
British ground till they meet with it on the other side of the
Atlantic. In these and in many other respects they are widely
different from either Greek or Roman colonies; so that whoever is really acquainted with the affairs of those ancient nations, must without difficulty perceive, that the Americans
have preferred the word *Colony*, for the sake of assuming along
with it a degree of independency, which from the words *plantation* or *province*; could not be so easily derived.

The plain truth is, that those countries, let them be called
plantations, settlements, colonies, or by what other name they
will, are, from their nature and situation, only subordinate

parts in the empire of Britain, and such they would necessarily continue, though perhaps in a much lower degree, under some other powerful European state, in case their more safe and honourable tie, with what they are still pleased to call, their *Mother Country*, should happen to be dissolved.

I shall therefore conclude with saying, that the separation of Great Britain from her American appertinencies would be destructive of the prosperity and liberty of both. If so, it seems to follow that till such time as New England is strong enough to protect Old England, and the seat of the British empire is transferred from London to Boston, there is an absolute necessity that the right of giving law to America, should continue to be vested in Great Britain. That it is the interest of Great Britain to protect and cherish her American provinces instead of oppressing them, is an undeniable truth; and it is, perhaps, no less true, that some farther attention, and some farther means of communication, are still wanting to that desirable end: but let every true friend to Britain and to all her connexions stand forth in defence of her great legislative uncontroulable power, without which no union, and of course no safety, can be expected.

FINIS.

[Silas Downer], A Discourse, Delivered in Providence, in the Colony of Rhode-Island, upon the 25th. Day of July, 1768. At the Dedication of the Tree of Liberty, from the Summer House in the Tree. Providence, 1768.

The imperial relationship was now seriously fraying. In April 1768 Lord Hillsborough, the head of the newly created American Department, responded to the Massachusetts Circular Letter with a circular letter of his own, directing the governors of each colony to persuade their colonial assemblies to ignore the "dangerous & factious" Massachusetts Letter upon pain of being dissolved. At the same time Hillsborough ordered the Massachusetts House of Representatives to rescind its letter. When the House refused by a vote of ninety-two to seventeen (thereby enshrining the number "ninety-two" in patriot slogans and rituals), Governor Bernard dissolved the Massachusetts legislature.

In Rhode Island things were calmer, but only because this corporate colony without a royal governor was too small and insignificant to capture the attention of officials three thousand miles away. In July 1768 the people of Providence gathered to witness the dedication of a Liberty Tree and an address by one of the Sons of Liberty, Silas Downer, a Harvard graduate and one of the few highly educated men in the colony. It was probably a good thing that the colony was beneath Hillsborough's notice, for Downer's *Discourse* was possibly the most radical pamphlet yet to have appeared in the rapidly intensifying imperial debate.

Sons of Liberty, Liberty Trees, Liberty Poles—liberty was everywhere in the colonists' protests. In fact, liberty was central to the very being of an Englishman. No people in the world had ever made so much of it. Unlike the poor enslaved French, the English told themselves, they had no standing army, no lettres de cachet; instead they had trial by jury, freedom of speech and conscience, guaranteed rights to travel and trade. Even the young prince of Wales, before he became George III, had shared in this celebration of liberty. "The pride, the glory of Britain, and the direct end of its constitution," said the future king, "is political liberty."

No American provincial could have put it better. Indeed, colonists like Downer so often raised the "dreadful expectation of certain slavery" flowing from the British actions because slavery was precisely the opposite of liberty. And slavery was what Downer believed the Declaratory Act portended. Unlike many colonists who had tended to ignore this act, Downer at once grasped its frightening logic. Far from being able to legislate for the colonies "in all cases whatsoever," Parliament, said Downer, lacked "any lawful right to make *any laws whatsoever* to bind us." Instead, Downer claimed that the colonial assemblies were "our own parliaments," which were "*compleat*" in themselves; they alone could pass laws affecting the people in each colony. Downer even implied that the only thing tying the colonies to Great Britain was their allegiance to the king.

A

DISCOURSE,

DELIVERED in PROVIDENCE,

IN THE

COLONY of RHODE-ISLAND,

upon the 25th. Day of July, 1768.

AT

The DEDICATION of the

TREE of LIBERTY,

From the Summer Houſe in the TREE.

By a SON of LIBERTY.

PROVIDENCE:

PRINTED AND SOLD BY JOHN WATERMAN,
AT HIS PRINTING OFFICE, AT THE PAPER-MILL.
M.DCC.LXVIII.

A Discourse, Delivered at the Dedication of the Tree of Liberty, in Providence.

Dearly beloved Countrymen.

WE His Majesty's subjects, who live remote from the throne, and are inhabitants of a new world, are here met together to dedicate the *Tree of Liberty*. On this occasion we chearfully recognize our allegiance to our sovereign Lord, *George* the third, King of *Great-Britain*, and supreme Lord of these dominions, but utterly deny any other dependence on the inhabitants of that island, than what is mutual and reciprocal between all mankind.—It is good for us to be here, to confirm one another in the principles of liberty, and to renew our obligations to contend earnestly therefor.

Our forefathers, with the permission of their sovereign, emigrated from *England*, to avoid the unnatural oppressions which then took place in that country. They endured all sorts of miseries and hardships, before they could establish any tolerable footing in the new world. It was then hoped and expected that the blessings of freedom would be the inheritance of their posterity, which they preferred to every other temporal consideration. With the extremest toil, difficulty, and danger, our great and noble ancestors founded in *America* a number of colonies under the allegiance of the crown of *England*. They forfeited not the privileges of *Englishmen* by removing themselves hither, but brought with them every right, which they could or ought to have enjoyed had they abided in *England*.— They had fierce and dreadful wars with savages, who often poured their whole force on the infant plantations, but under every difficulty and discouragement, by the good providence of GOD they multiplied exceedingly, and flourished, without receiving any protection or assistance from *England*. They were free from impositions. Their kings were well disposed to them, and their fellow subjects in *Great-Britain* had not then gaped after *Naboth*'s vineyard. Never were people so happy as our forefathers, after they had brought the land to a state of inhabitancy, and procured peace with the natives. They sat every man under his own vine, and under his own fig-tree. They had but few wants; and luxury, extravagance, and debauchery, were known only by the names, as the things signified thereby had not then arrived from the old world. The public worship of GOD, and the education of children and youth, were never more encouraged in any part of the globe. The laws which they made for the general advantage were exactly carried into execution. In fine, no country ever experienced more perfect felicity. Religion, learning, and a pure administration of justice were exceeding conspicuous, and kept even pace with the population of the country.

When we view this country in its extent and variety of climates, soils, and produce, we ought to be exceeding thankful to divine goodness in bestowing it upon our forefathers, and giving it as an heritage for their children.—We may call it the promised land, a good land and a large—a land of hills and vallies, of rivers, brooks, and springs of water—a land of milk and honey, and wherein we may eat bread to the full. A land whose stones are iron, the most useful material in all nature, and of other choice mines and minerals; and a land whose rivers and adjacent seas are stored with the best of fish. In a word, no part of the habitable world can boast of so many natural advantages as this northern part of *America*.

But what will all these things avail us, if we be deprived of that liberty which the GOD of nature hath given us. View the miserable condition of the poor wretches, who inhabit countries once the most fertile and happy in the world, where the blessings of liberty have been removed by the hand of arbitrary power. Religion, learning, arts, and industry, vanished at the deformed appearance of tyranny. Those countries are depopulated, and the scarce and thin inhabitants are fast fixed in chains and slavery. They have nothing which they can call their own; even their lives are at the absolute disposal of the monsters who have usurped dominion over them.

The dreadful scenes of massacre and bloodshed, the cruel tortures and brutal barbarities, which have been committed on the image of GOD, with all the horrible miseries which have overflowed a great part of the globe, have proceeded from wicked and ambitious men, who usurped an absolute dominion over their fellows. If this country should experience such a shocking change in their affairs, or if despotic sway should succeed the fair enjoyment of liberty, I should prefer a life of freedom in *Nova-Zembla, Greenland*, or in the most frozen regions in the world, even where the use of fire is unknown, rather than to live here to be tyrannized over by any of the human race.

Government is necessary. It was instituted to secure to individuals that natural liberty, which no human creature hath a right to deprive them of. For which end the people have given power unto the rulers to use as there may be occasion for the good of the whole community, and not that the civil magistrate, who is only the peoples trustee, should make use of it for the hurt of the governed. If a commander of a fortress, appointed to make defence against the approaches of an enemy, should breech about his guns and fire upon his own town, he would commence tyrant, and ought to be treated as an enemy to mankind.

The ends of civil government have been well answered in *America*, and justice duly administred in general, while we were governed by laws of our own make, and consented to by the Crown. It is of the very essence of the *British* constitution, that the people shall not be governed by laws, in the making of which they had no hand, or have their monies taken away without their own consent. This privilege is *inherent*, and cannot be *granted* by any but the Almighty. It is a natural right which no creature can *give*, or hath a right to take away. The great charter of liberties, commonly called *Magna Charta*, doth not *give* the privileges therein mentioned, nor doth our *Charters*, but must be considered as only declaratory of our rights, and in affirmance of them. The formation of legislatures was the first object of attention in the colonies. They all recognized the King of *Great-Britain*, and a government in each was erected, as like to that in *England*, as the nature of the country, and local circumstances, would admit. Assemblies or parliaments were instituted, wherein were present the King by his substitutes, with a council of great men, and the people, by their representatives. Our distant situation from *Great-Britain*, and other attendant circumstances, make it impossible for us to be represented in the parliament of that country, or to be governed from thence. The exigencies of state often require the immediate hand of government; and confusion and misrule would ensue if government was not topical. From hence it will follow that our legislatures were *compleat*, and that the parliamentary authority of *Great-Britain* cannot be extended over us without involving the greatest contradiction: For if we are to be controuled by their parliament, our own will be useless. In short, I cannot be perswaded that the parliament of *Great-Britain* have any lawful right to make *any laws whatsoever* to bind us, because there can be no fountain from whence such right can flow. It is universally agreed amongst us that they cannot tax us, because we are not represented there. Many other acts of legislation may affect us as nearly as taking away our monies. There are many kinds of property as dear to us as our money, and in which we may be greatly injured by allowing them a power in, or to direct about. Suppose the parliament of *Great-Britain* should undertake to prohibit us from walking in the streets and highways on certain saints days, or from being abroad after a certain time in the evening, or (to come nearer to the matter) to restrain us from working up and manufacturing materials of our own growth, would not our liberty and property be as much affected by such regulations as by a tax act? It is the very spirit of the constitution that the King's subjects shall not be governed by laws, in the making of which they had no share; and this principle is the great barrier against tyranny and oppression. If this bulwark be thrown down, nothing will remain to us but a dreadful expectation of certain slavery. If any acts of the *British* parliament are found suitable and commensurate to the nature of the country, they may be introduced, or adopted, by special acts of our own parliaments, which would be equivalent to making them anew; and without such introduction or adoption, our allowance of the validity or force of *any* act of the *English* or *British* parliament in these dominions of the King, must and will operate as a concession on our part, that our fellow subjects in another country can choose a sett of men among themselves, and impower them to make laws to bind us, as well in the matter of taxes as in every other case. It hath been fully proved, and is a point not to be controverted, that in our constitution the having of property, especially a landed estate, entitles the subject to a share in government and framing of laws. The *Americans* have such property and estate, but are not, and never can be represented in the *British* parliament. It is therefore clear that that assembly cannot pass *any* laws to bind us, but that we must be governed by our own parliaments, in which we can be in person, or by representation.

But of late a new system of politics hath been adopted in *Great-Britain*, and the *common people* there claim a sovereignty over us although they be only fellow subjects. The more I consider the nature and tendency of this claim, the more I tremble for the liberties of my country: For although it hath been unanswerably proved that they have no more power over us than we have over them, yet relying on the powerful logic of guns and cutlery ware, they cease not to make laws injurious to us; and whenever we expostulate with them for so doing, all the return is a discharge of threats and menaces.

It is now an established principle in *Great-Britain*, that we are subject to the *people* of that country, in the same manner as they are subject to the Crown. They expressly call us their subjects. The language of every paultry scribler, even of those who pretend friendship for us in some things, is after this lordly stile, *our colonies—our western dominions—our plantations—our islands—our subjects in America—our authority—our government* —with many more of the like imperious expressions. Strange doctrine that we should be the subjects of subjects, and liable to be controuled at their will! It is enough to break every measure of patience, that fellow subjects should assume such power over us. They are so possessed with the vision of the plenitude of their power, that they call us rebels and traitors for denying their authority. If the King was an absolute monarch and rule us according to his absolute will and pleasure, as some kings in *Europe* do their subjects, it would not be in any degree so humiliating and debasing, as to be governed by one part of the Kings subjects who are but equals. From every part of the conduct of the administration, from the acts, votes, and resolutions of the parliament, and from all the political writings in that country, and libels on *America*, this appears to be their claim, which I think may be said to be an invasion of the rights of the King, and an unwarrantable combination against the liberties of his subjects in *America*.

Let us now attend a little to the conduct of that country towards us, and see if it be possible to doubt of their principles. In the 9th. of *Anne*, the post-office act was made, which is a tax act, and which annually draws great sums of money from us. It is true that such an establishment would have been of great use, but then the regulation ought to have been made among ourselves. And it is a clear point to me that let it be ever so much to the advantage of this country, the parliament had no more right to interfere, than they have to form such an establishment in the electorate of *Hanover*, the King's *German* dominions.

They have prohibited us from purchasing any kind of goods or manufactures of *Europe* except from *Great-Britain*, and from selling any of our own goods or manufactures to foreigners, a few inconsiderable articles excepted, under pain of confiscation of vessel and cargo, and other heavy penalties. If they were indeed our sovereign lords and masters, as they pretend to be, such regulations would be in open violation of the laws of nature. But what adds to this grievance is, that in the trade between us they can set their own prices both on our and their commodities, which is in effect a tax, and of which they have availed themselves: And moreover, duties are laid on divers enumerated articles on their import, for the express purpose of a revenue. They freely give and grant away our monies without our consent, under the specious pretence of defending, protecting, and securing *America*, and for the charges of the administration of justice here, when in fact, we are not indebted to them one farthing for any defence or protection from the first planting the country to this moment, but on the contrary, a balance is due to us for our exertions in the general cause; and besides, the advantages which have accrued to them in their trade with us hath put millions in their pockets. As to the administration of justice, no country in the world can boast of a purer one than this, the charges of which have been always chearfully provided for and paid without their interposition. There is reason to fear that if the *British* people undertake the business of the administration of justice amongst us it will be worse for us, as it may cause an introduction of their fashionable corruptions, whereby our pure streams of justice will be tainted and polluted. But in truth, by the administration of justice is meant the keeping up an idle sett of officers to rob us of our money, to keep us down and humble, and to frighten us out of our undoubted rights.

And here it may be proper to mention the grievances of the

custom house. Trade is the natural right of all men, but it is so restrained, perplexed and fettered, that the officers of the customs, where there happens a judge of admiralty to their purpose, can seize and get condemned any vessel or goods they see fit. They will seize a vessel without shewing any other cause than their arbitrary will, and keep her a long time without exhibiting any libel, during all which time, the owner knows not on what account she is seized, and when the trial comes on, he is utterly deprived of one by a jury, contrary to the usages among our fellow subjects in *Britain*, and perhaps all his fortune is determinable by a single, base, and infamous tool of a violent, corrupt, and wicked administration. Besides, these officers, who seem to be born with long claws, like eagles, exact most exorbitant fees, even from small coasting vessels, who pass along shore and carry from plantation to plantation, bread, meat, firewood, and other necessaries, and without the intervention of which the country would labour under great inconveniencies, directly contrary to the true intent and meaning of one of the acts of trade, by which they pretend to govern themselves, such vessels by that act not being obliged to have so much as a register. It is well known that their design in getting into office is to enrich themselves by fleecing the merchants, and it is thought that very few have any regard to the interest of the Crown, which is only a pretence they make in order to accomplish their avaricious purposes.

The *common people* of *Great-Britain* very liberally give and grant away the property of the *Americans* without their consent, which if yielded to by us must fix us in the lowest bottom of slavery: For if they can take away one penny from us against our wills, they can take all. If they have such power over our properties they must have a proportionable power over our persons; and from hence it will follow, that they can demand and take away our lives, whensoever it shall be agreeable to their sovereign wills and pleasure.

This claim of the commons to a sovereignty over us, is founded by them on their being the *Mother Country*. It is true that the first emigrations were from *England*; but upon the whole, more settlers have come from *Ireland, Germany*, and other parts of *Europe*, than from *England*. But if every soul came from *England*, it would not give them any title to sovereignty or even to superiority. One spot of ground will not be sufficient for all: As places fill up, mankind must disperse, and go where they can find a settlement; and being born free, must carry with them their freedom and independence on their fellows, go where they will. Would it not be thought strange if the commonalty of the *Massachusetts-Bay* should require our obedience, because this colony was first settled from that dominion? By the best accounts, *Britain* was peopled from *Gaul*, now called *France*, wherefore according to their principles the parliaments of *France* have a right to govern them. If this doctrine of the maternal authority of one country over another be a little examined, it will be found to be the greatest absurdity that ever entered into the head of a politician—In the time of *Nimrod*, all mankind lived together on the plains of *Shinar*, from whence they were dispersed at the building of *Babel*. From that dispersion all the empires, kingdoms, and states in the world are derived. That this doctrine may be fully exposed, let us suppose a few *Turks* or *Arabs* to be the present inhabitants of the plains of *Shinar*, and that they should demand the obedience of every kingdom, state, and country in the world, on account of their being the *Mother Country*, would it be one jot more ridiculous than the claim made by the parliament of *Great-Britain* to rule and reign over us? It is to be hoped that in future, the words *Mother Country* will not be so frequently in our mouths, as they are only sounds without meaning.

Another grievance to be considered, is the alarming attempt of the people of *Old England* to restrain our manufactures. This country abounds in iron, yet there is an act of parliament, passed in the late King's reign to restrain us from manufacturing it into plates and rods by mill-work, the last of which forms are absolutely necessary for the making of nails, the most useful article in a new country that can be conceived.—Be astonished all the world, that the people of a country who call themselves Christians and a civilized nation, should imagine that any principles of police will be a sufficient excuse, for their prohibiting their fellow subjects in a distant part of the earth from making use of the blessings of the GOD of nature! There would be just as much reason to prohibit us from spinning our wool and flax, or making up our cloaths. Such prohibitions are infractions on the natural rights of men, and are utterly void.

They have undertook, at the distance of three thousand miles, to regulate and limit our trade with the natives round about us, and from whom our lands were purchased—a trade which we opened ourselves, and which we ought to enjoy unrestricted. Further, we are prohibited by a people, who never set foot here from making any more purchases from the *Indians*, and even of settling those which we have made. The truth is, they intend to take into their own hands the whole of the back lands, witness the patents of immense tracts continually sollicited, and making out to their own people. The consequence will be shocking, and we ought to be greatly alarmed at such a procedure. All new countries ought to be free to settlers; but instead thereof every settler on these patent lands, and their descendants forever, will be as compleat slaves to their landlords, as the common people of *Poland* are to their lords.

A standing army in time of profound peace is cantoned and quartered about the country to awe and intimidate the people—Men of war and cutters are in every port, to the great distress of trade. In time of war we had no station ships, but were obliged to protect our trade, but now in time of full peace, when there are none to make us afraid we are visited with the plague of men of war, who commit all manner of disorders and irregularities; and behave in as hostile a manner as if they were open and declared enemies. In open defiance of civility, and the laws of *Great-Britain*, which they profess to be governed by, they violently seize and forcibly carry on board their ships the persons of the King's loving subjects. What think ye my brethren, of a military government in each town? —Unless we exert ourselves in opposition to their plan of subjecting us, we shall all have soldiers quartered about upon us, who will take the absolute command of our families. Centry boxes will be set up in all the streets and passages, and none of us will be able to pass, without being brought too by a soldier with his fixed bayonet, and giving him a satisfactory account of ourselves and business. Perhaps it will be ordered that we shall put out fire and candle at eight of the clock at night, for fear of conspiracy. From which fearful calamities may the GOD of our fathers deliver us!

But after all, nothing which has yet happened ought to alarm us more then their suspending government here, because our parliaments or assemblies (who ought to be free) do not in their votes and resolutions please the populace of *Great-Britain*. Suppose a parcel of mercenary troops in *England* should go to the parliament house, and order the members to vote as they directed under pain of dissolution, how much liberty would be left to them? In short, this dissolving of government upon such pretences as are formed, leaves not the semblance of liberty to the people.—We all ought to resent the treatment which the *Massachusetts-Bay* hath had, as their case may soon come to be our own.

We are constantly belied and misrepresented to our gracious sovereign, by the officers who are sent hither, and others who are in the cabal of ruining this country. They are the persons who ought to be called rebels and traitors, as their conduct is superlatively injurious to the King and his faithful subjects.

Many other grievances might be enumerated, but the time would fail.—Upon the whole, the conduct of *Great-Britain* shews that they have formed a plan to subject us so effectually to their absolute commands, that even the freedom of speech will be taken from us. This plan they are executing as fast as they can; and almost every day produces some effect of it. We are insulted and menaced only for petitioning. Our prayers are prevented from reaching the royal ear, and our humble supplications to the throne are wickedly and maliciously represented as so many marks of faction and disloyalty. If they can once make us afraid to speak or write, their purpose will be finished. —Then farewel liberty.—Then those, who were crouded in narrow limits in *England* will take possession of our extended and fertile fields, and set us to work for them.

Wherefore, dearly beloved, let us with unconquerable resolution maintain and defend that liberty wherewith GOD hath made us free. As the total subjection of a people arises generally from gradual encroachments, it will be our indispensible duty manfully to oppose every invasion of our rights in the beginning. Let nothing discourage us from this duty to ourselves and our posterity. Our fathers sought and found freedom in the wilderness; they cloathed themselves with the skins of wild beasts, and lodged under trees and among bushes; but in that state they were happy because they were free—Should these our noble ancestors arise from the dead, and find their posterity trucking away that liberty, which they purchased at so dear a rate, for the mean trifles and frivolous merchandize of *Great-Britain*, they would return to the grave with a holy indignation against us. In this day of danger let us exert every talent, and try every lawful mean, for the preservation of our liberties. It is thought that nothing will be of more avail, in our present distressed situation, than to stop our imports from *Britain*. By such a measure this little colony would save more than 173,000 pounds, lawful money, in one year, besides the advantages which would arise from the industry of the inhabitants being directed to the raising of wool and flax, and the establishment of manufactures. Such a measure might distress the manufacturers and poor people in *England*, but that would be their misfortune. Charity begins at home, and we ought primarily to consult our own interest; and besides, a little distress might bring the people of that country to a better temper, and a sense of their injustice towards us. No nation or people in the world ever made any figure, who were dependent on any other country for their food or cloathing. Let us then in justice to ourselves and our children, break off a trade so pernicious to our interest, and which is likely to swallow up both our estates and liberties.—A trade which hath nourished the people, in idleness and dissipation—We cannot, we will not, betray the trust reposed in us by our ancestors, by giving up the least of our liberties—We will be freemen, or we will die— we cannot endure the thought of being governed by subjects, and we make no doubt but the Almighty will look down upon our righteous contest with gracious approbation. We cannot bear the reflection that this country should be yielded to them who never had any hand in subduing it. Let our whole conduct shew that we know what is due to ourselves. Let us act prudently, peaceably, firmly, and jointly. Let us break off all trade and commerce with a people who would enslave us, as the only means to prevent our ruin. May we strengthen the hands of the civil government here, and have all our exertions tempered with the principles of peace and order, and may we by precept and example encourage the practice of virtue and morality, without which no person can be happy.

It only remains now, that we dedicate the *Tree of Liberty*.

WE do therefore, in the name and behalf of all the true SONS *of* LIBERTY *in* America, Great-Britain, Ireland, Corsica, *or wheresoever they are dispersed throughout the world*, dedicate *and* solemnly devote *this tree, to be a* TREE of LIBERTY.— *May all our councils and deliberations under it's venerable branches be guided by wisdom, and directed to the support and maintenance of that liberty, which our renowned forefathers sought out and found under trees and in the wilderness.—May it long flourish, and may the* SONS *of* LIBERTY *often repair hither, to confirm and strengthen each other.—When they look towards this sacred* ELM, *may they be penetrated with a sense of their duty to themselves, their country, and their posterity:—And may they, like the house of* David, *grow stronger and stronger, while their enemies, like the house of* Saul, *grow weaker and weaker.* AMEN.

An Inquiry into the Nature and Causes of the Present Disputes Between the British Colonies in America and Their Mother-Country; and Their Reciprocal Claims and Just Rights Impartially Examined, and Fairly Stated. London, 1769.

Not all Englishmen writing on the imperial issues took the hard line that Ramsay had. The anonymous English author of this pamphlet, published around the same time as Ramsay's, appeared on the surface to be very sympathetic to the American cause, so much so that he was sure that he would "seem to be an advocate for the Americans." Indeed, well into the nineteenth century the pamphlet was mistakenly attributed to Benjamin Franklin. (As it happens, the margins of Franklin's personal copy are filled with critical comments.)

The pamphleteer began by focusing on the genius of the English constitution, which was the pride of Englishmen everywhere and admired by enlightened liberals throughout Europe. Even the members of the Stamp Act Congress had gloried in "having been born under the most perfect form of government." What made the constitution perfect was the fact that all three estates of English society—the king, lords, and people—literally constituted the government, as the Crown, the House of Lords, and the House of Commons. In this way the constitution, expressed in political terms as "the king in Parliament," embodied the three simple categories of politics—monarchy, aristocracy, and democracy—that theorists had talked about for centuries. By balancing and mixing these three simple forms of government in their constitution, Englishmen, it seemed, had concretely achieved what political philosophers from antiquity on had only dreamed of.

Having established the genius of the English government, the author proceeded to uncover the central paradox of the imperial debate: it was the constitution itself that was the source of the controversy with America. This proved an intriguing point and one that Americans themselves came to appreciate—since in the end they would claim to be revolting not against the English constitution but on behalf of it.

AN
INQUIRY
INTO THE
NATURE AND CAUSES
OF THE
PRESENT DISPUTES
BETWEEN THE
BRITISH COLONIES
IN
AMERICA
AND THEIR
MOTHER-COUNTRY;

And their reciprocal Claims and juſt Rights
impartially examined, and fairly ſtated.

QUID NOSTRAM CONCENTUM DIVIDAT, AUDI.

HOR.

LONDON.
Printed for J. WILKIE, in St. Paul's Church-yard.
M.DCC.LXIX.

An Inquiry into the Nature and Causes, &c.

THE disputes at present subsisting between our Colonies in America and their Mother Country, are as weighty and important in their nature, as they are alarming and formidable in their effects, and of so long standing, that every true friend to either cannot help ardently wishing they were amicably adjusted and fairly determined. If the following remarks upon this subject, wherein I shall endeavour to place it in a new, and, I presume, a clear point of view, will any way contribute to this end, it will give me real pleasure; although to conceive the most distant expectations of success from any thing that can be said upon it, will perhaps be a much stronger argument of my benevolence and good wishes, than of my prudence or sagacity. For in a cause wherein the interests of mankind are so nearly concerned, and their passions and prejudices so deeply engaged, as the present, to suppose that the *still voice* of reason and of truth stands any great chance to be heard, would indicate no small inexperience of the world. But, on the other hand, to suppose that a whole nation, however generally under the above unhappy predicaments, is altogether void of candour and ingenuity, would no less indicate the same inexperience, or else, what is much worse, a great deal of self-depravity.

Peace, harmony and friendship, especially between kingdoms, and more emphatically still between the different parts and members of the same kingdom, are certainly objects of the highest consequence, never to be despaired of, and always to be preserved and cultivated with the utmost application. Whoever promotes these deserves well of his country, and whoever disturbs or acts in opposition to them, is an enemy to it. And even in the pursuit of liberty itself, the most valuable of blessings in this world, certain measures are to be observed; and decency, as it generally is, not wholly to be forgotten or trampled on. For by this means matters are very often pushed on to extremities, which might otherwise be very honourably and equitably adjusted.

To discuss this subject as it stands upon the footing of charters and statute laws, is what I do not at present intend. For this has been already very copiously and solemnly done, by persons no less distinguished for their abilities than station, with equal precision and judgment. But, in my humble opinion, they did not allow themselves, in handling it, the latitude it would have admitted of, nor consider it in some points of view, which it seems to require. But this perhaps was then beside their purpose, and, as the case was then circumstanced, not altogether necessary; although to me, in the present state of things, a more ample discussion of it appears indispensible.

Charters may be again explained, statutes enacted, and parliamentary declarations made fifty times over, and yet the public grievances still remain, if their true cause is not well understood. I do not say that this is really the case at present; but I think the fundamentals of legislation, in what has been hitherto said upon the subject, have not been properly attended to, nor examined. To supply this defect, therefore, is what I propose in the sequel; not to point out what measures we are authorized to take, in virtue of charters, statutes and parliamentary declarations, or even of received customs, but rather to inquire what in this matter ought to be done, and what prudence and sound policy dictate, upon the footing of the most approved maxims, and true principles of Legislation.

We live in an age when the sciences, in every kind, are arrived at a perfection unknown to former times; it is therefore but reasonable to expect that our public and most solemn acts should be proportionably dignified with authentic marks of these boasted improvements. But the misfortune is, where our interest is concerned, we meet with such a narrowness both of thinking and acting upon every occasion, as is far from distinguishing us from the most barbarous period of antiquity, or at least from ages that were almost perfect strangers to our present advantages. If this were not the case, the national spirit of Great Britain would appear quite different in regard to the matter in debate, from what we now find it. And her infant colonies would observe a more obliging and dutiful demeanor towards her, than they seem at present inclined to do. But directly to the point.

The following essay shall be founded upon the three following inquiries; First, Whether the colonies should not be allowed to enjoy the same political privileges and advantages with the mother-country? Secondly, Whether the frame and model of the

British constitution is such, as practically to admit thereof in respect of America? And Thirdly, Whether, in case that should be found impracticable, such a form of government should not be established there, as shall appear most unexceptionable, and will best secure to the colonies their just rights and natural liberties?

The affirmative, in regard to the first of these queries, requires, one would think, no proof. And yet it is, I believe, what a great majority among us would be very unwilling to admit of in fact, whatever they might pretend to. Colonies we are apt to consider in the light of factories, who are only to contribute to our wealth and aggrandisement, and are wholly to be regulated and controuled by ourselves, in such manner as we think will best answer our present designs and purposes. But herein we are certainly mistaken. The increase of dominions and subjects, should only be a proportionable increase of wealth and power to the whole empire, and not the aggrandisement of one part of it at the expence of the other. A large empire, well connected, and equitably governed, has indeed many advantages; not only as it is best able to defend itself against injuries and encroachments from its neighbours, and as it affords a more ample supply of the necessaries and conveniences of life within its own boundaries, but also upon many other accounts, too tedious here to enumerate. But if the different countries or nations which form it, are distinguished, from no reasonable, or, as it often happens, from the most unjust motives, with a partiality in the laws by which they are governed, divisions and murmurings, if not actual rebellions, are evidently unavoidable. The more extensive such an empire is, the weaker it is. For the divisions and parties in it are the more numerous, and consequently its dissolution will be the more signal and speedy.

An empire therefore should pay equal attention to all its parts; and, if there is any difference, the most distant demand the greatest, at least in point of policy, if not of justice. For abuses, more or less, will inevitably creep into all governments; and it is in the remotest provinces they generally harbour with most impunity. And as these provinces are always the first to revolt, when an opportunity offers, frequently after a series of ill usage; they therefore most certainly ought not to be the last attended to, or worst regulated.

Kingdoms and empires are often styled bodies politic, intimating that every part or member thereof should be so connected together, to form the whole, as we see they are in natural bodies. The same attention and impartiality which is invariably observed in guarding or guiding the latter, should no less invariably be exercised towards the former. And it is from hence they derive their harmony, strength and vigour. And one cannot help wishing there were the same involuntary sympathy between the several members of bodies politic, as there is between those of natural ones, since moral equity has generally so little force to produce it.

It is therefore wholly the effect of the illiberal notions, and partial views of government here complained of, that the trade and manufactures of different provinces are laid under the restraints we often see them. And, in short, from the same unhappy source, spring most of the inequitable laws and inhibitions, to which colonies and the more remote parts of an empire are frequently subjected. It would require but a small share of knowledge in the nature of trade and manufactures, fully to prove, and even demonstrate that, in general, they should lie under as few restrictions as possible, and, for the same reasons, should be freely allowed to retire and settle in whatever provinces of the empire they may be carried on to most advantage. But this is a maxim which would be almost universally contested, if not absolutely rejected in England, as often at least as her interest should seem to come into competition with that of her colonies. But why they should be denied or envied the natural advantages of their situation, I cannot see. If Britain herself is not immediately thereby benefited, the British empire, which ought to be considered as the same thing, most evidently is. But we are continually, in this matter, mistaking our true point of interest. Instead of seeking to collect into this island the specie of the whole empire, every channel should be laid open to diffuse it equally throughout it, which would naturally, in a short time, divest the colonies of their present superiority, in the article of cheapness, over their mother-country. But while money is accumulating in England, in a proportion beyond that of its neighbour nations, our trade must inevitably decline. And it is the French, and not our colonies, that we ought to be jealous of. But this may be thought rather a digression, though I cannot view it altogether in that light, if it helps, as I presume it does, to point out the folly and injustice of not treating all the parts and provinces of an empire, with the exactest impartiality.

This, upon the foot of nature, is undeniable. For why should not the Americans, though born in another part of the globe, be entitled, while subject to the same government, to all the privileges, indulgences and advantages, which are considered as the birth-right of those who first breathe the air in Great Britain? To dispute or deny this would be equally ridiculous and absurd. And in point of policy, as well as equity, I can discover no reason why they should be abridged of any of them. And even if their loyalty was, upon good grounds, suspected, whatever vigilance or severity might become necessary, they ought to be only such as should be agreeable to the practice of England, upon like occasions; but the current of the laws should not be diverted, or made to run opposite to the spirit and fundamentals of our constitution. To accumulate proofs, in support of what I here assert, may justly be deemed unnecessary, and therefore I shall immediately proceed to my second proposition, which was, To inquire whether the frame and model of the British constitution is such, as practically to admit of securing to the colonies the same political rights and privileges with the mother-country.

This to me appears a very material inquiry, although it seems but very little attended to, if not wholly overlooked. That it is the nature of some governments not to admit of an enlargement of dominions, is clear beyond all doubt. Of this the Spartan constitution, in particular, is a noted instance. The design of Lycurgus in framing it, was only that it should maintain its own independency amongst the states of Greece, without in the least aiming at the reduction of any of its neighbours. And this end, so long as it was preserved inviolable, it very effectually answered. And not only so, but it gave the Spartans, while contented with their original limits, a kind of superiority over their neighbours, which, when they attempted to extend them, they were not able to preserve. It was, in its fundamental principles, notwithstanding whatever might be vicious or defective in it, one of the freest and most perfect forms of government in all antiquity. It was composed of the three estates, not unlike that of Great Britain at present; only the constitution of the Ephori, whose power was not very different from that of the Tribunes at Rome, was annexed to it about an hundred and thirty years after it was first founded by Lycurgus.

But, as free and perfect as it was within itself, it was the most illiberal in the world for an extension of empire. Nothing could be more impracticable, upon the plan and principles of it. Nor could it ever be attempted without actual violation of so material a part thereof, as brought on, at length, its final ruin and dissolution, together with the absolute reduction and conquest of that once brave and heroic people.

Nor was the Athenian constitution much better calculated for this purpose. By a very impolitic decree, ascribed to Pericles, it was rendered, in its views and nature, perfectly confined. For by this decree it was declared, that none should be held for natural and true Athenians, but such as had both Athenian fathers and mothers. Through this fatal measure the state was not only extremely weakened at home, above one quarter of the citizens being thereby excluded, but was likewise quite disabled from annexing or incorporating any of its conquests; and was therefore obliged to hold them only upon the footing of allies, or of tributary provinces. And the consequence of this was, as might have been easily foreseen, that all of them, in their turn, seized the first opportunity that offered, to assert their liberty and independence. So long as they were distinct people, they had still different and distinct views, which could only have been contracted by an actual union with the Athenian commonwealth. And this, in all probability, if it had been seasonably effected, and the nature of the constitution had admitted of it, would have rendered her sovereignty over them lasting and permanent. This very capital error was likewise common to the Thebans, and all the Grecian states.

But the Roman government was of a genius more liberal and comprehensive. The colonies and conquests of this wonderful empire, were, to a considerable extent, naturalized and incorporated, and had their proper share of weight in the legislature. This constitution, it is true, when first founded by Romulus, was extremely defective and imperfect, as consisting only of two estates, the popular one being wholly excluded. In length of time, however, it became so much improved, by the addition of the third estate, and other alterations, as to admit, when arrived at the highest pitch of perfection, of as much freedom and liberty, as perhaps almost any form of government that we read of in ancient history.

This constitution, notwithstanding, however excellent in itself, could not operate with the same vigour, and to as good purpose beyond a certain sphere. The more distant provinces, how much soever of the Roman laws and customs they might adopt, or were actually introduced and established among them could not possibly enjoy all the privileges and advantages of a citizen of Rome. It was in Italy alone that the people, with the tribunes at their head, could arrest the consuls, confirm or abolish the decrees of the senate, deliberate of peace and war, and decide alliances, treaties of peace, and conventions with foreign states and princes. This was a power which could not possibly, in the nature of things, be vested in different provinces. Nor could it, with any propriety or convenience, fall to the share of any other, than that only where the seat of empire was fixed. And yet it was upon the full enjoyment and exercise of this prerogative, that their freedom and liberty must in a great measure depend. Besides, it was in Italy alone they were sole masters and arbiters of rewards and punishments, and could fix pecuniary mulcts upon such as had been possessed of the highest employments. And, above all, it was here alone they had the sole right of condemning Roman citizens capitally.

In the provinces and more remote parts of the empire, the governors and presidents were invested with large and extensive powers, which they very often most shamefully abused. And though in many of them the taxes, levied by the Romans, were frequently much less than had been raised in them in the time of their independence, yet we find them sometimes demanded and collected by these and other superior officers, in a manner extremely unequal and irregular. These practices, however, were by no means warrantable upon the principles of the constitution, which in its frame and model had abundantly guarded against all oppressions of this nature.

For, ever since the reign of Servius Tullius, their sixth and last king but one, they had established among them a regular and equitable method of raising and collecting taxes, which they called a *census*, or enrolment, whereby they were required upon oath to register their estates, according to their value in money, and likewise their names, quality, and employment, together with the name of their parents, their own age, and the names of their wives and children. To this they were also required to add the number of their servants or slaves, specifying the work or service they were employed in; an exact estimate of the true value and profits of all which was to be made out, and finally settled by the censors. And it was agreeably to the amount of this estimate the taxes were to be raised and collected.

This form of levying taxes, which was the ancient and constitutional one, was likewise the same that was usually observed in the provinces. But an order of the senate, or edict of the emperor, were the measure of these levies: and sometimes even the base will and direction of the president. The people's consent for this purpose was not at all thought requisite; nor were they herein ever consulted. The Roman liberty could here be but little boasted of. It was not their prerogative, nor yet their privilege to make laws, but humbly to obey. And whenever they thought themselves injured or aggrieved, they could only prefer their complaints to the senate. For it was only from the senate, and not from themselves, they could hope for redress. They were notwithstanding, in general, governed with great equity and moderation; and complaints of this kind were much fewer, than might have been expected from so large and extensive an empire.

They were not however considered as aliens to the commonwealth, but as the children and friends of the republic. And they were allowed, upon the whole, perhaps the best conditions which the nature of their government would admit of. Offices and preferments, both civil and military, were alike open to all; and none were precluded the highest dignities in the state. Rome and her provinces were in this respect upon a level: for to secure them from revolting, they rightly judged it the best means to take into their service the most active and ambitious therein, and to reward the most deserving with suitable preferment. Thus both the Gauls, in particular, were filled with consular families. And in this conduct indeed, both their justice and their policy, it must be acknowledged, were equally conspicuous. The wise maxim of uniting and incorporating, as much as possible, all parts of the empire, which they had received from Romulus, they ever afterwards continued. And to this may be justly imputed, in a great measure, the stability and duration of it, whereof they themselves were perfectly sensible.

These few, succinct and cursory remarks, upon the nature of the Grecian governments, may serve to shew us that some constitutions are of that kind, as to render colonization or any extension of empire, in a manner, wholly impracticable: and those also upon that of the Roman, to convince us, that even the most liberal and comprehensive form thereof, cannot operate with equal vigour beyond a certain sphere. For all the privileges and prerogatives of the citizens of Rome, could not possibly, in the nature of things, be vested in the provinces, without an actual subversion of the state. For all governments must be drawn to some certain point wherein the whole is to centre. Supreme power and authority must not, cannot reside equally every where throughout an empire. For this would rather suppose absolute confusion and anarchy, than any imaginable mode of government. However, as in all free states supreme authority is derived from, so it ultimately resides in, the people.

For the laws by which they are governed must necessarily derive their very existence from them, through the medium of their representatives; kings and princes being only the chief magistrates chosen and appointed to superintend the execution of those laws, whereby they themselves are no less bound than their subjects. Now the bottom on which a free government is founded, is in its nature just as extensive as the utmost limits of the empire itself, from the several parts whereof one only supreme assembly of representatives, for making laws, can regularly be formed. If we admit more such assemblies than one, the power and authority of all but one must necessarily be abridged, and brought in subordination to one only as supreme. For if each assembly, in this case, were absolute, they would, it is evident, form not one only, but so many different governments perfectly independent of one another. These are, I grant, obvious and known truths; but known truths are not always as generally so as they ought to be, much less are they as duly weighed and considered. And obvious as they are, it was necessary for me in this place to premise them, in order to set my argument in a just and proper light.

Now that of Great Britain being exactly the kind of government I have been here speaking of, the absolute impracticability of vesting the American assemblies with an authority, in all respects equal to that of the mother country, without actually dismembering the British empire must naturally occur to every one. For all government is founded alike in a subordination as well as union of all its constituent parts; of which notwithstanding none can be justly excluded its natural and due weight in regulating, as it necessarily has in forming the whole. Thus although the British parliament may indeed with propriety make laws for Britain, yet it cannot with the same propriety exercise the like power with respect to America, while those parts of our dominions are not fairly represented in it. Nor, on the other hand, can our colonies make laws for themselves in their own assemblies, without thereby actually declaring themselves independent states, unless what they enact is only of force, so long as it is not inhibited or reversed by the parliament of Great Britain. And while their power stands thus limited by a superior authority, whereof they themselves have no share, they cannot be considered as a free people. For they are subject to laws and regulations not of their own making, which is the very definition of slavery. That they may notwithstanding be governed with equity, and treated with mildness, in a degree not at all inferior to England, is very possible, and on some accounts, by no means improbable; yet still, upon the above footing, their constitutional rights and liberties must be precarious and uncertain.

And here I cannot help making this remark, that the more free a constitution is in its nature, the less extensive it is in its views. For the larger the empire, the more numerous and unwieldy the democratic branch of it necessarily becomes. And therefore where divers remote and distant countries are united under one government, an equal and fair representation becomes almost impracticable, or, at best, extremely inconvenient.

But inconveniences, arising purely from extent of dominions, where they all lie contiguous upon a continent, are nothing comparable to those where they are divided and parted by seas, especially wide oceans like that between us and America. A parliament or diet might be convened from all parts of Germany, for example, at any particular city therein, without any extreme difficulty, even on a few weeks notice, notwithstanding the vast extent of that country. Nor, should we suppose France also annexed thereto, would the thing be at all impracticable. But should we carry our supposition much farther, the inconveniences attending such long journeys would be very great, although not interrupted by water. This, however, would not be nearly so difficult as to convene a parliament partly from Europe and partly from America, which yet, in the present case, is certainly necessary to render government equal to all the subjects of the British crown. For the nature of our constitution is evidently such as absolutely requires a general and impartial representation; which, notwithstanding, cannot be supposed to exist, so long as American members are not admitted to sit in the British senate. Hence therefore appears the stubbornness and inflexibility, if I may so call it, of the genius of our constitution, although in itself the most complete and perfect of any in the whole world.

An arbitrary or military government would have laboured under no difficulties of this kind at all. France would have ruled over the whole continent of North-America, with more ease and less ceremony, than we can over one single province of it. A few brief and succinct forms, together with a good standing army there, would have readily done the business. But the English constitution is quite of another nature, and proclaims to all a liberty and freedom unknown in other countries. And it is this peculiar excellence of it, which constitutes the genuine and true cause from whence the present difficulties in adjusting the rights and privileges of our colonies arise. To point out, therefore, the most effectual and consistent means, for compromising the disputes and differences resulting from these difficulties, is what we should next attempt, but that I must first proceed, agreeably to the order I have laid down, to inquire, in the third place, whether, although it should be found impracticable, from the nature of our constitution, to admit the Americans to the full possession of all the prerogatives and privileges of Englishmen in the mother country, they should not be allowed such a form of government, as will best secure to them their just rights and natural liberties?

But this very inquiry will possibly appear quite unnecessary, if not absurd to many; yet I cannot help thinking it much more absurd, to hold that the British parliament, as it now stands, hath an undeniable right to make laws for North-America. Were people considerate and impartial enough to make this inquiry for themselves, it would certainly be quite needless for me to make it here for them. For barely to put the question, one might reasonably expect, to most men, a sufficient answer to it. Indeed to maintain this position, that it is just and equitable for one half of a kingdom, to hold the other half in chains, is what, I believe, few among us are hardy enough openly to attempt, although three parts in four, perhaps, of the whole island, are very forward to embrace tenets and maxims scarcely more liberal. And it is not unlikely but most of those, if not all, who are strenuous advocates for one side of the question in England, would immediately veer about, and espouse quite the opposite in America. Besides, what would they say, were it put in supposition that the seat of empire were shifted over and fixed in America, and England was to be governed upon the footing of a colony? it is very easy to conceive, I think, what in this case would be their language. And justice requires that we should do by others, as we would, in similar circumstances, be done by ourselves. Nay, is it not, let me ask, most egregious folly, so loudly to condemn the Stuart family, who would have governed England without a parliament, when at the same time we would, almost all of us, govern America, upon principles not at all more justifiable?

And though they were tied down by their charters to the most servile and dependent state imaginable, it would, I think, be extremely ungenerous now to make that an argument for continuing them upon the same footing. For in my opinion the question should be, not how low we can depress them, but how high we can raise them without making them absolute or independent, and consistently with our rights of sovereignty over them. This certainly is by far the most liberal and Christian way, both of thinking and acting in this matter. And whatever is so, is ultimately the most politic. For the most lasting empires are always founded in principles the most agreeable to justice. And their dissolution is as invariably the consequence of a deviation therefrom, either in mode or practice. But those founded in violence and oppression are seldom durable. Besides, it can never be deemed a wise measure by men of the least thought or reflection, to make slaves of the Americans, were it a thing ever so practicable. So large a body of men, at the devotion of a wicked minister, would be very formidable to England. And a people long habituated to servitude, and in whom the love of liberty as well as all sense of the just value of it, was extinguished, would certainly be the most proper instruments to reduce others to the like condition. In some things indeed we seem jealous of our liberty, and even of what we apprehend has the most distant tendency to undermine it, almost to a degree of enthusiasm; and yet in others our apprehensions on this head are perfectly dormant. Where prejudice, passion, or seeming interest are concerned, we are no longer Englishmen, wise, circumspect, just and generous, but the blind dupes of our own folly; of which our conduct, upon the present occasion, is too glaring an instance. But to return—

Now as some truths are so clear and obvious, that to go about to prove them, is only taking pains to render them suspected, or, what is worse, if possible to obscure them. Among these the object of the present inquiry should, I think, be considered; I shall therefore change the state of it, and proceed to examine in the sequel, what that form of government is which will best answer the purposes above specified. But, in the first place, I must beg leave to observe that, in my opinion, the Americans found their complaints upon a narrower bottom, than the nature of the subject would admit of. For the only grievance they seem to be sensible of, is the right of taxation, claimed over them by the British parliament. This certainly is a very important branch of legislation, and may be called one of the three principal objects of government. For to this number these may in some sort be reduced, *the security of person, property, and religion*, and whoever, therefore, claims a right to dispose of any one's property, without his consent either directly or indirectly, claims at the same time a right to rob him of the protection of government in one of its principal objects, and indeed consequentially in two. For an unlimited power to dispose of a person's goods may, through wantonness or cruelty, be exercised to that degree of severity, as actually to cause both him and his family to perish. And though government itself, which yet necessarily is absolute, should claim such an authority, under the above predicaments, it would evidently be a government founded in injustice. Hence then it appears what alarming consequences a right of imposing taxes involves in it. Can it therefore surprise any one that the colonies should be jealous of this right? or rather would it not be much more surprising, were they not jealous of it?

However, a right of legislation in general over them, they certainly may with equal justice and propriety dispute, so long as they continue unrepresented in our parliament, or some other way are not admitted to a due share of power, in making those laws to which they are subject. For people may be harassed or injured an infinite number of ways besides only in the article of taxing them. But this not being the case at present, their complaints seem to be wholly confined to this one article. To this therefore I shall entirely confine my subsequent inquiries, and more especially since it is not improbable, if a point so very material could be adjusted to mutual satisfaction, but it would be less difficult to settle any other that should ever come to be disputed.

That every government should support itself, is a truth too obvious to be contested. And that England has an undeniable right to consider America as part of her dominions, is a fact, I presume, which can never be questioned. For few empires can produce as just a claim to half their provinces, as that of England to her's in America. I will only observe at present, that it was England, in some sense, which at first gave them being (excepting only that part of them which was ceded to us by the French) and ever since has defended them with her arms, and governed them with her laws. It is therefore but just and equitable that they should, in return, contribute a reasonable proportion for the support of that government, by which they are protected. This they have not as yet the effrontery openly to deny. But the manner of levying such supplies is the subject in debate.

Now all the ways of raising them, which at present occur to

me, are chiefly four; though each of these may perhaps be variously modeled. The first is by a requisition, made by the king and his council, of a certain sum by them fixed, to be raised in each province, in such manner as their own assemblies shall think fit. The second is by a like requisition made by parliament, and to be raised in like manner. The third is by a tax imposed in the British parliament, upon its present footing. And the fourth is by the same authority in conjunction with a general representation therein of the Americans.

The first of these, however acquiesced in on the part of the colonies, is, in my opinion, by far the most exceptionable. For if only a few men, who constitute the ministry, have a right to appoint what sums they shall raise, and their requisition is to be indispensibly complied with, they must evidently in this case be wholly subject to ministerial government, and of course to ministerial tyranny. And that such a requisition should without reserve be complied with, is altogether obvious. For should the Americans be allowed herein a discretionary power, they will in fact be perfectly independent, and the sovereignty of England over them will be only a nominal one: because if they are at liberty to chuse what sums to raise, as well as the manner of raising them, it is scarcely to be doubted but their allowance will be found extremely short. And it is evident they may, upon this footing, absolutely refuse to pay any taxes at all. And if so, it would be much better for England, if it were consistent with her safety, to disclaim all further connection with them, than to continue her protection to them wholly at her own expence. However, should such a requisition as I have here described be acquiesced in, I know no reason we have to object to it.

The second method I took notice of, was by a like requisition made by the British parliament, and to be raised and collected in such manner as the provincial assemblies shall like best. This method, however inadequate upon the whole, appears to me much preferable to the former, as in so large a body of men, both justice and the true interest of the empire are more likely to be duly regarded; and therefore they may reasonably expect the burden will be more equitably laid upon them. Besides, it is not improbable but some who have property among them may sit in this assembly. And it may farther be observed, that their proceedings are not quite so rapid and precipitate as those of the privy-council, so that should it be found unnecessary, they will have more time to petition or make remonstrances. For this privilege, the least which a subject can enjoy, is not to be denied them, however an ultimate compliance may be insisted on as indispensable. And it is likewise, let me add, much more probable that their ability to pay taxes, and the true state of their finances, will be better understood, as well as their petitions and remonstrances more solemnly canvassed: on all which accounts, and several others not mentioned, I cannot help giving it much the preference to the former, although I cannot pretend to recommend either.

And of the impropriety of the third method above pointed out, the Americans seem abundantly sensible, as appears from their conduct on occasion of the late *stamp-act*, the repeal whereof looks somewhat like an acknowledgement of the same thing on the part of the British parliament. For if that act was in itself just and equitable, though in its circumstances not quite convenient, means might have been easily discovered to remove these difficulties, without a total repeal of it. For if it was only oppressive, as imposing too heavy a tax, or productive in its consequences of some unnecessary trouble; to these surely proper remedies might have been applied, and yet its essence still preserved. But here the chief stress of the complaints made against it was not laid; but the inequitableness of it in its full extent, is what the colonies principally objected to it. The British parliament, they urged, exercised an authority they had naturally and constitutionally no right to. And a law, deriving its existence from such an authority, must necessarily, in respect of those it is imposed upon, be inequitable and arbitrary. And this the parliament, in repealing it, notwithstanding all their declarations and resolutions to the contrary, seem tacitly to have acknowledged. But this still is the grand point in debate, which I fear cannot be very easily adjusted. That there are a great many persons of integrity, worth, and character on both sides of the question, cannot be doubted. But the misfortune is, they are not all quite so cool and dispassionate in their inquiries as might be wished. Moral truth, upon which justice is founded, is generally obvious to the meanest capacity, and never lies more out of sight, than when concealed by prejudice or passion. And to have their judgments biassed by either of these, or both, is what falls sometimes to the lot of all men; and is therefore what all men ought to be the more ready to excuse or pardon in each other.

My own sentiments, touching this point, are sufficiently evident from what I have already said upon it. And whoever considers it with the same impartiality and disinterestedness, will not, I believe, find himself in the result widely to differ from me. For, as to my opinion herein, I would obtrude it upon no one, but only desire it may be fairly examined, and as fairly confuted before it is rejected or condemned. And if I seem to be an advocate for the Americans, it is for no other reason but purely because I think myself an advocate for truth. For surely I stand as unconnected, with respect to that people, as any man in the kingdom. I know of no other interest to influence me in this cause, but the interest of humanity. And the question with me is not so much what the rights of the Americans are in particular, as what the just and natural rights of all mankind are? and liberty in the utmost latitude that government can secure it, is the undoubted birthright, my reason tells me, of every man, till he has forfeited it. And this forfeiture, on the part of a whole nation, it is quite impossible to incur. For at least children, whereof all nations in part are composed, while too young to violate any law, must necessarily be exempted. Besides, to suppose, that of those grown to maturity none at all, or only few are innocent, is to put a case so extravagant, as not to be paralleled in history, if I am not mistaken.

But to think that any people can be free, while subject to laws they are no way consulted in making, is such an absurdity as few, I believe, in their own case, would not readily discover: and common honesty requires that we should as readily acknowledge in the case of others. Let us, though but for a moment, consider ourselves Americans, and I more than presume we shall be of this opinion. For as nothing will better assist us to view each side of the question in the strongest light, so nothing will better assist us in forming an impartial judgment of it. Nor, again, is it at all more rational to maintain that that people are represented in the British parliament as it now stands. An equal representation, indeed, is a thing scarcely practicable, and what England herself cannot boast of; but the

Americans cannot properly be said to have the smallest share in it. The weight their trade and commerce with us may give them, deserves not to be mentioned on this occasion. For that is no more than what any country in Europe, in some degree might have. And who durst say, that Holland, for instance, is represented in England?

But those who maintain our right of legislation over them, do it chiefly, if not wholly, I suppose, because they see the necessity there is, in order to an unity of government, that such a right should be vested in us. An unity of government, it is true, is necessary to an unity of empire. But besides that this perhaps may be otherwise effected, than at the expence of the just birth-right of our fellow-creatures; yet were it only to be accomplished by such a violation, I am perfectly at a loss how to demonstrate the equity of such a procedure, unless it can be fully proved that the safety of the state can be secured by no other means. For nothing less can justify it. And the present case, I think, includes no such extremity. For whatever reasons we have to consider the retention of our sovereignty over them as indispensable; yet with me it is by no means a maxim, that we cannot otherwise secure that sovereignty, than at the expence of their natural rights. And if this may be really done, it most certainly ought. For I see no reason why conscience, truth and justice should be less regarded in national acts than private ones. And I do not at all think myself the only casuist that would argue in this manner. Nor is the practice of other states, on similar occasions, nor yet our own of whatever standing, by any means sufficient to justify an action in itself wrong. And surely to claim and exercise an authority we have naturally no right to, is an action in itself as wrong as any, I think, that we can put in supposition. But this, I presume, in general, will be granted, and yet perhaps denied in the particular case before us. Our right of legislation over the Americans, unrepresented as they are, is the point in question. This right is asserted by most, doubted of by some, and wholly disclaimed by a few. But to put the matter in a stronger light, the question, I think, should be, Whether we have a general right of making slaves, or not? the affirmative of it I solemnly protest against, although I should be reputed for it the very worst politician that ever presumed to make his sentiments public.

But, on the other hand, it must be confessed, that under governments, in themselves very imperfect, justice may be duly administered, and order preserved. For, were not this the case, there would be little either of justice or order in the world. And the Americans may be treated with as much equity, and even tenderness, by the parliament of Great Britain, as by their own assembles. This, at least, is possible, although perhaps not very probable. Besides, our distance from them is such, as must inevitably disqualify us to be altogether as good judges of what grievances they may labour under, or of what supplies they can afford to raise, as they themselves. It is every one's own feelings can best inform him wherein he is aggrieved or distressed. And this is the case of every nation, as well as of every individual; and therefore none should be excluded a proper share in their own government.

And it may be further observed, that the dissolution of an empire, is not always to be considered as inevitable, where some parts thereof are possessed of a power, by no means consistent with that unity of government I have been speaking of. Nay it is possible that such a power may never be found productive of any great inconvenience. To this purpose the case of Ireland, as forming a part of the English dominions, may be readily instanced. For the power of parliament in that kingdom, to reject and throw out money-bills, as well as their very extensive authority on other accounts, must certainly be acknowledged as not quite consistent with this unity. Here, most undoubtedly, is a great defect in point of theory; and yet the inconveniences arising therefrom, in practice, have been hitherto by no means considerable. Nor can it be denied but most governments, in some respect or other, are extremely defective, although perhaps not very many in the particular now mentioned; as despotic ones, which are by far the most numerous, are seldom exceptionable on this account. But the truth of the matter is, it is not so much the best form of government, as the most exact and regular administration of justice, that most effectually fastens together the different parts of an empire, whereon the stability and duration of it must ever necessarily depend. And it is seldom that the people abuse the power they are possessed of to their ruin, but only when they have received very heavy provocations to enrage them, from the excesses of their governors. And the most perfect model of government in the world, where according to it justice is not duly administered, is no security against the outrages of the people.

But, after all, it must be confessed, that the most perfect form thereof is ever the most eligible. For the rights of mankind can never be too well guarded. And it is under this sort of government they certainly stand the best chance to be least invaded. I know no reason therefore why we should think so very hard of the Americans, only because they are so strenuous to have theirs established upon this footing, and because they are so unwilling to submit to the mode of taxation here proposed, which several, even among ourselves, have not the highest opinion of.

I could therefore most heartily wish, that the fourth and last above-mentioned, was as convenient and practicable, as it is just and equitable. To convene indeed our colonial representatives at London, would certainly be attended with very great, though I dare not say quite insurmountable, difficulties. To the equity of this measure the Americans themselves, I presume, could have nothing fairly to object. However, it would not be extremely easy perhaps to settle the number of members to be sent by each province. But yet this business, I make no doubt, might in time be adjusted. But the inconveniences, arising from the distance they lie from us, are perpetual, various and complicated. As to those, indeed, which attend only the chusing a new parliament, they may perhaps, by proper means, be considerably lessened, although not wholly removed. It is true, if our parliaments were annual, as they ought to be, they would rather increase; but even then they might, I believe, be in a great measure remedied. But should the king, at any time, be disposed to dissolve his parliament, and convene a new one, as hath been often done, only on a few weeks notice, this, upon the above footing, could not be effected. And yet, I believe, a variety of cases might occur, wherein this may be proper, if not necessary.

But were the duration or dissolution of parliaments fixed wholly to stated times, a thing, by the bye, not at all to be wished for, the difficulties upon these occasions would not certainly be quite insuperable. The method however of examining and deciding contested elections when necessary, must undoubtedly, with respect to America, be set, in a great measure, upon a different footing from that at present practised in this kingdom. But to sketch out a plan for removing these or the like difficulties, is not within my present design, as it is not in the least, at this time, probable, that an American representation will ever be convened in England. But there are other difficulties, which, in my opinion, form a much more considerable objection to this scheme; that whenever the colonies shall have occasion to have a recourse to parliament, for their intervention in more particular provincial business, as from the nature of things they often must, their distance from it will render it in a manner impracticable. They will be almost wholly excluded the benefit of private acts, by reason of the immoderate expence, both of time and money they must be at to procure them. And yet applications to parliament for such purposes may often become necessary. Besides, there may be an infinite number of occasions, respecting matters of a more public nature, such as the repairing of high-ways, making rivers navigable, and cutting canals, with a variety of other things of the like kind, wherein recourse must be had to parliament, and yet the expence be supported chiefly, if not wholly, by private persons. But in either case it will be a considerable burden, and as considerable an objection to all undertakings of that sort. And the delays in business occasioned by such long voyages, as those from America to England, must greatly retard it, and no less discourage those who are concerned in it. Besides, when at any time it should become necessary, as it often happens, to produce witnesses, in support or prosecution of any cause, America lies at such a distance as scarcely to admit of it. Therefore, upon all these, and many other very similar accounts, I can only consider this scheme as barely practicable. However, should the Americans prefer it to any other, as it is an establishment they have, I think, an undoubted right to, I know not how we can, in conscience, debar them of it. But if they could be otherwise satisfied, with any conditions that we can safely grant them, this mode of compromise, which may be justly termed the *dernier resort*, may as well be waived, as it cannot be effected, it is evident, without immense trouble.

And now, since each of the methods above proposed, is pregnant, as we have seen, with a variety of difficulties, hardships and inconveniences, it may here be asked, what measure then upon the whole is most eligible, and fittest to be pursued on the present occasion? But to give a plain and decisive answer to this question, is, perhaps, the greatest difficulty of all. And though I may not be able rightly to solve it, I cannot consider the above remarks as wholly useless, if they only serve to point out, and convince the public of this very difficulty by a proper explanation of it, and so dispose them, at least, to be a little less censorious towards all parties concerned in this very intricate business. For it really is, in my opinion, as arduous and important a question, as ever the English government was engaged in. And if they should be divided in their sentiments upon it, and uncertain what measures to adopt and follow, it cannot be matter of just wonder or censure.

But it must be confessed that in all our transactions with the world, the temper and dispositions of those we have to deal with, is generally the best index to point out the measures most proper to be pursued upon any occasion. But that they should never be in themselves unjust, I need not here observe; and the truest policy, I am very certain, is ever founded in the soundest morality. Besides, the Americans, as they must inevitably lie under some very considerable inconveniences, have, I think, if they are not permitted to be represented in our senate, a right of chusing what mode of government they should best like, provided it be not inconsistent with the sovereignty of England over them. For what England seems chiefly to have a right to dictate is, that they shall continue in subjection to her, and form a part of her dominions, upon the footing of her own laws and constitution. The one, I think, she has a right to command; and the other they have a right to claim. But if less rigid terms are agreed or consented to on either side, it must be considered as matter of favour and indulgence. As for example, if England should grant the Americans the same conditions as the Irish now enjoy, in respect to the article of levying taxes, it should be deemed only as matter of grace, to be resumed at pleasure. And custom, of however long a standing, can never convert it into matter of undeniable claim. And again, should the Americans consent to be taxed in the British parliament upon its present footing, it is such a submission as cannot be equitably insisted on, they having always a right to be represented in the assembly they are taxed by, or which forms the popular branch of their legislature.

These appear to me to be true limits of right and equity on either side. And here may easily be found a criterion, whereby to judge of the claims and concessions of both parties. To be placed upon a level with the rest of the subjects of the British crown, is the utmost the colonies can challenge. And to refuse them this, is more, I believe, than can be rightly justified upon the principles of common honesty. But supposing this were quite impracticable, and either party must necessarily make abatement, several reasons, and very plausible if not solid ones, may be urged, why this should be done on the part of the colonies. For although the common rights of mankind should, with the utmost tenderness, be preserved inviolate: yet there may be occasions whereon they may be fairly and justifiably abridged. Indeed something of this kind, with respect to individuals, is congenial to the very essence of all government. For every member of a regular society is supposed voluntarily, for the sake of the common good thereof, to resign some portion of the rights and privileges wherewith nature has invested him, into the hands of those, who may be expected to use them with more impartiality and discretion. Thus every man is naturally constituted sole judge in his own cause; a prerogative which yet government permits no one to exercise, as it would be destructive of the very existence of it, as well as of that of society. In the same manner and for the same reasons, the Americans might be justly divested of some portion of their natural claims, if government cannot be supported upon more equitable terms, or at least if it should be dangerous to England, to allow them the enjoyment of a more unlimited power. I do not say that we have a right to subjugate any people, only because they are troublesome; but if they are truly dangerous we certainly have. Nor yet is it at all warrantable to abridge the just liberties of any country we may possess ourselves of, merely because we cannot otherwise maintain our sovereignty over it, unless our safety were actually at stake, and absolutely required it.

But the case, perhaps, may be in some degree altered, when such country is planted by our own natives, and especially at our own expence; or indeed by any people whatever, who were previously well informed of the nature of the grant, and the terms whereon they were to occupy it. Thus they who first migrated from England to settle in America well knew, I presume, they were still to continue the subjects of the same government. And if their charters were not so explicit as they should have been, in regard to some particulars they believed they had a right to; yet still they could only claim the most favourable conditions the nature of things would admit of. They knew they were not to be independant: but if they were really more strictly tied down by them than there now seemed to be occasion for, I fairly confess, that ought to be no argument, in my opinion, for debarring them of better terms. For no one, I imagine, would doubt, if their charters granted them an inconsistent power, but they might be justly cancelled, as no government can be supposed to alienate prerogatives necessary to its safe existence. Therefore equity, at least, would dictate to us the like procedure in the opposite case, it being just as reasonable to abolish all unnecessary limitations on the one hand, as it would be to augment and multiply them on the other. However, a right of sovereignty in this case, we may undeniably claim and vindicate: and though we might safely grant them absolute independency, yet whatever generosity might suggest, justice does not seem to require it; notwithstanding the terms of submission might be somewhat hard. But this, in acquisitions of another nature, would not, perhaps, be quite so defensible.

Now, our title and pretensions to all our American provinces are of that sort that seem fairly to justify our asserting and preserving our sovereignty over them, although at the expence of some portion of their natural prerogatives. They partly consist of our own plantations, and partly of the conquests we have made from a nation, in whose hands it would have been dangerous for us to have them continued. In both which cases we have the most unexceptionable right to keep them upon such a footing as will best consist with, and support our government. And had we, indeed, the generosity to declare them independent, as finding that our keeping them must inevitably superinduce a necessity of abridging their natural liberty, yet this would not be consistent with our safety. They would immediately fall a prey to the French, and, of course, would be such a weight in their scale, as might contribute not a little to endanger, if not overturn the liberty of all Europe. For it would help to give them the mastery of the seas, which seems to be the only thing that more peculiarly humbles, and keeps them within their present bounds. Our very being, therefore, at least as a free people, depends upon our retention of them: nor is it the interest of any one nation whatever, who have the French for their neighbours, that it should be otherwise. Much less then is it the interest of the Americans themselves, as they would soon be made sensible of the difference of the two governments. The Gallic yoke they would experience to their cost, is not so easily borne. They are now treated as children; their complaints are heard, and grievances redressed; but then they would be treated rather as slaves, having the swords of their masters perpetually held at their throats, if they should presume to offer half the indignities to the officers of the French crown, which they have often, with impunity, done to those of the British.

At present they enjoy, in general, the full benefit of the English laws and constitution. Nay, they have assemblies of their own to redress their grievances, and regulate their polity. Therein they exercise an authority little inferior to that of the British parliament. And indeed what they seem to struggle for is, to be set upon a footing equal to it. And if that should be done, what marks of sovereignty will they allow us to enjoy? What sort of claim will they indulge us with? Only, I suppose, a mere titular one. And, if so, would they then expect that we should still protect them with our forces by sea and land? Or will they themselves maintain an army and navy sufficient for that purpose? This they certainly at present are not able to do, if they were not sheltered by the wings of Great Britain. And to contribute a reasonable proportion for this purpose is all we require of them. This, indeed, they will say, perhaps, they are not unwilling to do, if they are allowed to do it as an act of their own; nor should that privilege, in my opinion, be refused them, if they are not permitted to be represented in England: for this alternative should certainly be left to their option: and for such a measure I have been all along an advocate. For as the inconveniences, arising from such a representation must almost wholly fall to their share, it is what we may with the less reluctance grant, as we can with the less propriety refuse them: nor is there any reason to apprehend that they should be at all formidable to England, as their number might be properly limited, as those of Scotland were at the union.

But here I am arguing upon a supposition of the absolute impracticability of this measure. Upon this view of the point in question, I still insist that the Americans, no less than the English, should contribute a due proportion for the support of government; yet this again they may possibly affirm that they actually do. But here, in order to an impartial decision of this case, we want a proper criterion to judge by: for an exact estimate can scarcely be made of what expence their protection stands in to Great Britain. Besides, we can certainly afford to protect them at less expence than they could afford to protect themselves, were they either so many independant states, or only one general community. For the same forces it would be necessary for us to keep on foot, upon our own proper account, may serve in a great measure to guard them likewise. However, it is not a very inconsiderable addition thereto we are obliged to make, merely for their defence. And this, at least, they ought to maintain. But if they should argue that these forces may be safely reduced, and consequently the expence of supporting them; this is little to the purpose. For though their remonstrances, upon all occasions, should be candidly heard, and duly regarded, yet, in the last result, England is still to form her own judgment, and is not to be dictated to by her colonies: for should that be the case, it is no longer England, but her colonies, that govern. And, besides, they are justly chargeable with a certain portion of the *civil list*; for this most indubitably constitutes a part of government. How this article, at present, is managed in England, is not now my business to inquire: but certain it is, that in all regal governments it is indispensable, unless an equivalent provision is otherwise made, for the king's maintenance and private charges, by an allotment in lands, or some such other property; which, by the bye, would give him such a weight in the state, over and above that necessarily resulting from his prerogatives, as in the estimate of many, perhaps, were scarcely to be wished for. And even in commonwealths the pomp of government, if I may so call it, is unavoidably attended with expences, and not inconsiderable, of a similar nature. It is therefore but reasonable that the colonies, as they are part of the state, should bear their share of these, as the necessary charges of it. Were they obliged to do so, I see no reason they should justly have to complain.

The immense taxes which England pays are known to all. It is not indeed very easy to calculate what proportion of a man's labour, or how much of his wages should be considered in this light; but certainly it is extremely large. America, however, is not in a condition to pay the taxes that England does, as not having the same advantages; yet surely if an Englishman works one day in the week, let us suppose, for the public; an American, I should imagine, may afford to work on the same account, at least one day in a fortnight. There are obvious reasons for a considerable lenity in favour of the Americans; because an infant colony, circumstanced as ours is, lies under many disadvantages. For they have land to clear, houses to build, roads to make, fences to erect, trees to plant; and, in short, everything that can be imagined for converting a wilderness into a habitable country. And besides, all this is to be done in opposition to a variety of difficulties, which, though each by itself may seem scarcely to merit notice, yet taken collectively, are by no means inconsiderable. Tools and engines, for instance, are seldom so conveniently fabricated there, as in a country antiently inhabited, wherein generally artificers, in all the more necessary branches are commodiously situated. The distance of their residence likewise, as it often happens, from the spot they cultivate, is another impediment to their dispatch of business. But it would be endless to enumerate them all. This, however, is by no means the universal state of our plantations. In many parts they are little, perhaps, or nothing at all inferior in respect of these conveniences, to the mother-country. Yet after all, if it appears right to us to extend our colonies, it ought to appear no less right to us to give them all due encouragement. And one way of doing this, most certainly is, not to be over-rigorous in taxing them. For heavy taxes are heavy oppressions, although, as far as they are absolutely necessary, however burdensome, they scarcely deserve the appellation; for their being necessary is sufficient to justify them. Yet they should not be wantonly accumulated, as nothing more emphatically depresses a state, or discourages improvements. In Molesworth's history of Denmark, I think, it is said, that in a certain northern province of that kingdom, the lands were so highly charged, that the peasants petitioned the king's acceptance of them fully and wholly to himself, rather than pay the taxes imposed upon them; which, however, he did not care to do, as well knowing they could not possibly be of any use to him, any farther than they were cultivated. And thus any country may be equally distressed by excessive taxes.

How far this would have been really the case, in respect of America, if the late *stamp-act* had taken place, is more than I can tell. It was indeed complained of as enormous, although it was not here the capital objection against it was grounded. But this, perhaps, is not quite clear. For although, on the one hand, the English may be considered rather as incompetent judges; all that the Americans are pleased to say on the other is scarcely to be admitted always for fact, especially in a matter where interest may justly be supposed to have so much influence. Yet it must be granted, that they know best the state of their own finances, and what taxes they can afford to pay; in the imposing whereof there are some circumstances which merit attention, that, in regard to the act above-mentioned, may not perhaps have been properly considered. And, in particular, due respect should be had, to the difference of the value of money in both countries. Of this difference I do not pretend to be a perfect master, although it may be easily ascertained. Indeed what quantity of specie they have circulating among them I know not; but from a variety of circumstances, I have reason to conclude they are, in this point, by no means upon a level with England. And therefore it is possible that six-pence additional duty upon any article among them, may be equal to a much larger sum with us. But, admitting the difference were only as one to ten, or even less; yet I still think that, in cafes of this nature, it is a consideration that should not be left wholly unregarded.

But there is an advantage to be derived from this very difference, were the point carried to all the nicety it would admit of. For were it really material, a proportionable reduction might be made in the pay of the forces stationed in that country;—but this is a saving I would by no means recommend. It would, on many accounts, be cruel to attempt it, unless it were only among the provincials. But even among them, it is probable it would prove a measure highly imprudent, if not worse; for I know of no greater folly than to render, as it might, any part of our forces disaffected,—But, to proceed.

Whatever lenity her colonies may be entitled to from England, whether on the above accounts or any other, it is very certain that England is entitled to a great deal of gratitude from her colonies. They cannot be ignorant that if it had not been for the English they must have been long since swallowed up by the French; and what their condition must then have been, they may easily judge. That the late war was chiefly kindled, and carried on upon their account, can scarcely be denied: and the many millions of debt which we have thereby contracted, as well as the immense number of lives therein sacrificed, are not matters of so very little moment as not to deserve to be considered. But they will object, perhaps, that all this while it was our own safety and benefit we had ultimately in view. Yet this very objection, it is not impossible to convert into an argument in our favour. For if it were only or chiefly our own ends we had in view, and they, knowing that, joined with us in the same cause, is it not an evident proof how favourable an opinion they, at that time, entertained of them? If then our views were really unjust, why did they co-operate in support of them? But if they were just, why will they now go about to frustrate them, by the steps they seem to take to shake off our sovereignty? For if this should happen, these views will be abundantly defeated: and our peace and safety, instead of being secured, will become even more precarious than ever. For as soon as they are no longer dependant upon England, they may be assured they will immediately become dependant upon France. And their weight in that scale is what all Europe besides have reason to dread.

But could they really support their own independancy, we are by no means sure whose friends they would be in case of a rupture. And whatever reasons there might exist to dispose them in our favour, in preference to the French; yet how far these would operate, no one can pretend to say. For we have seen the Dutch, very lately, siding with the French, their inveterate enemies, from whom they have every thing to fear, against the English their ancient allies; to whom in some degree they owe their very being. And this alone is sufficient reason for us to be jealous of our sovereignty.

But evident it is, that, whatever benefit England might propose to herself in the prosecution of the late war, the colonies themselves have been incomparably the principal gainers by it. Now they enjoy a peace and tranquillity, which they scarcely ever knew before. And if they have any thing to fear, it is chiefly from the Indians, their neighbours, whose outrages they have often too justly provoked. And the diligence wherewith our government has protected them from insults and rapine, as well from that as every other quarter, seems, in theory at least, to demand some degree of gratitude. But as I have all along in the former part of this essay, allowed and defended the justice of their claims, it may here be queried, wherein then are they to be condemned? It is not indeed for their jealousy of their rights and liberties, but for their riotous and seditious manner of asserting them. Besides, England, on her part, has much to say on this occasion, to justify her conduct. She is conscious she has a right of sovereignty over them, which perhaps may not be quite so easy to maintain, when the point in dispute is given up. And this sovereignty she well knows to be a matter of the last consequence for her to support. Nor am I very clear how much less she has at stake, in the decision, than the Americans themselves; only it is probable that they would be the first sufferers, should their connection with her cease. And therefore she may well be jealous in her turn, and as tenacious of her prerogatives. For she has a right, and a weighty one, to assert, as well as they. And if she had not thought proper to center almost all her care, as she has done, upon making the late peace, in procuring them a safe establishment, and to sacrifice to it in a manner every other object, she might, at least, expect from them a more decent and dutiful demeanor. Firmness and outrage are two very different things; and they might easily have shewn the former without being guilty of the latter. Nor would they have been at all, I would hope, the less likely to be heard for it in the British parliament. And it seldom happens that any one fares the better for his insolence.

But if they should think it their interest to set us wholly at defiance, and were able thereby to secure some points, which England might rather chuse to give up than contest, yet I can hardly consider it as the most consummate prudence. For if their insolence should continue to increase, as it seems to do, in proportion to her concessions to them, and nothing less than absolute independency should content them, it will probably force her upon quite other measures; and they themselves will be the first, that shall have cause most signally to repent of their conduct. For should matters on all sides, as I hope they never will, be carried to extremities, I cannot take upon me to say but England may yet produce both a ministry and a parliament that would rather share them once more with the French, than totally relinquish her present pretensions, from a very just conviction that such a step would be much more politic than to suffer them to throw themselves wholly into the arms of that nation; and such a measure, under such circumstances, would be abundantly defensible, however aukward it may sound at the first mention. But I hope they will never be so egregiously infatuated as to render it inevitable; for if they do, they may very soon find themselves again involved in the same scenes of bloodshed and horror, out of which they have but lately emerged. But such an event is dreadful even to think of at a distance: nor is it by any means grateful to me to suggest the idea of it to the imagination, but that, if duly and seasonably reflected on, it may dispose them to more temper and moderation, without which it is impossible for them to act with reason and propriety.

It would not be amiss, perhaps, to ask them, what bounds they would be content to fix to their claims and demands upon us, as hitherto they seem to be at a loss where to stop. And it is but very lately they were pleased to make distinctions and describe barriers, which they have since not thought fit to admit of. It was only their own produce they then objected to our right of taxing; but now, our's likewise, it seems, is entitled to the same exemption in their ports. All this, for my own part, I have candour enough to grant, under the predicaments I have more than once mentioned. For the positions I advance are, First, that the Americans, no less than the English, have a right to be represented in the assembly they not only are taxed by, but wherein the laws in general they are governed by are enacted: Secondly, that the legislative power of every kingdom or empire, should center in one supreme assembly: Thirdly, that, as a consequence of both these positions, the Americans should be allowed, if they should chuse it, to be represented in the British senate: and, Fourthly, that in case that should be found impracticable, they should be allowed such an establishment, in subordination to the sovereignty of England, as should appear most favourable to their rights and liberties. This is the system, and these are the principles I have all along argued upon and supported; but, that they will be objected to by some of both parties, I can easily foresee. However, I think they are in themselves just, which to me is sufficient. And, certain it is, that, in order to a right understanding in this debate, it were much to be wished that some fixed principles were on all sides agreed to and established, whereupon to ground the whole superstructure of their subsequent reasoning. But this is only to be wished, and not to be expected in cases of this nature; nor, indeed, were they actually adjusted, would it probably much mend the matter. For it is not unusual to see people, as interest inclines them, draw quite opposite conclusions from the same premises; or, what is still worse, if possible, what is granted at one time, is totally disavowed or denied at another, as seems to be the case of the *New Englanders* in particular, in relation to the business abovementioned.

And I must freely own, that whatever opinion I may have of their right, I certainly have not quite as favourable a one of their conduct, which often is neither consistent nor prudent. If they are really willing we should exercise any acts of sovereignty among them at all, the imposition they have so riotously resisted, might not improperly, perhaps, have been allowed better quarter; for it could have occasioned no further hardship than was voluntary, they having it always wholly left to their own choice to buy the commodities so charged, or not. Had they quietly submitted to an imposition of this nature, while they were allowed the full enjoyment of their more important privileges, it would, not improbably, have proved such a compromise of matters, as they might never have had cause to be sorry for. Of this, however, I have but little to say, only that I am very certain the resistance they have made to it was absolutely inconsistent with the demeanor usually expected from subjects towards their governors. Less tumultuous proceedings would, undoubtedly, in most mens opinions, have been deemed much more becoming: and our government, I should humbly hope, would have paid full as favourable an attention to their just remonstrances.

But unless the reciprocal claims and rights, on both sides, are more duly regarded, and better established, little else than disorder and confusion are to be expected; and if they are not seasonably put a stop to, it is impossible to foresee what may be the issue. The proper bounds and limits of these should therefore be fairly adjusted, as the most direct means to redress grievances, and to introduce harmony and good intelligence. And were that done as it ought, we might then hope that the colonies, on the one hand, should no longer have cause to complain of incroachments on their liberties, on the part of the English, nor yet the English, on the other, to complain of the unequal payment of taxes on the part of the colonies; both being equally obliged to do justice by each other. And this, were it only attempted with that temper and coolness that would permit people to distinguish right from wrong, might be totally effected; although indeed, from the untoward nature of things, not with all the impartiality and exactness one could wish. Nor should mere custom, nor any charter or law in being, be allowed any great weight in the decision of this point; for truth and justice, whereon government should ever be founded, and not in power, are prior to all these, and therefore ought chiefly, if not solely, to be consulted. Prudence, however, which includes nothing thereto contrary, should no doubt be duly regarded: for upon all occasions, not only what is in itself just, but also what on each in particular is directly proper, should always be done. And in the determination of this point, prudence seems principally concerned; the dictates whereof more especially should be attended to, in framing our conduct in regard to what I am here going to mention, I mean the possibility, or rather probability there is, that the Americans may insist upon the same rights, privileges, and exemptions as are allowed the Irish, because of the similarity, if not identity, of their connections with us. Hence it may be thought hard, perhaps, that in a case, in appearance circumstanced so much alike, our conduct should not be alike too. Indeed were this real fact, there might still exist very solid reasons for a difference of conduct; but the truth is, their case, in my humble opinion, is, on some accounts, far from being so very similar. I will say nothing of our original claim to either country, but that it is full as good as the world in general, in matters of this kind, can produce. But if any distinction were to be made, most certainly, of the two nations, the Americans are least entitled to any lenity on that score; and yet I believe most people are of opinion, they have been hitherto, by far, the most favoured.

But, in matters of this nature, England seems to have a discretionary power, which, however, she has no just power to exercise inequitably, as I hope she never will; and the terms she may think safe and proper to grant the Irish, she may judge full as dangerous and imprudent to grant the Americans: for as they lie at such a distance from us, they may have it much more in their power to create disturbances with impunity; because, long before we could send among them any considerable number of forces, they might do a great deal of mischief, if not actually overturn all order and government. But this is not so very exactly the case with respect to Ireland, which lies almost contiguous to us. These, and several other reasons might be offered, why the same measures, in regard to both nations, might not be altogether alike convenient and adviseable. I do not, however, deliver it as my fixed opinion, that they should be placed upon a less advantageous footing than the Irish, if their conduct doth not evidently render that unsafe. But I only mention these as obvious arguments why such seeming partiality may possibly, in fact, be no more than what strict justice admits, and sound policy requires. Rigorous measures I certainly am no advocate for, in matters of government more particularly, excepting only when they become altogether indispensable: for nothing less than absolute necessity can justify them.

And if the Americans, at this time, would, in any tolerable

proportion, contribute their quota of taxes, and otherwise should demean themselves as dutiful and loyal subjects, I am not the only person, I suppose, that would chuse rather to suffer their antient establishment, however imperfect, to remain undisturbed, than oblige them to any innovations, at the expence of an open rupture. But government, however, is not to be trampled on; and a proper degree of firmness is no way inconsistent with the most perfect lenity. Yet while we expect every thing from them, we ought carefully to see that we, on our part, are not wanting. Whatever justice is due to us, is due to them too. If they ought to support the expence of government, as well as we, they ought also, as well as we, to enjoy the full benefit of that government; and, if we insist upon the former, they, in their turn, may justly insist upon the latter.

And the utmost of their claim, upon this ground, can amount only to a proper representation in the British senate. This, I believe, if they are to obey the laws enacted there, they have a clear right and title to, unless it can be fairly proved they are unworthy the same privileges and advantages, as we of this nation enjoy. But this, I presume, cannot very easily be made to appear; and therefore I conclude this claim to be good. But if they should wave it, as impracticable, it would not, I conceive, be improper to grant them the benefit of their own assemblies, upon their present footing, allowing their acts to be only of force, while not declared otherwise in that superior one of Great Britain. Hereby an union of government might perfectly be preserved, and the colonies, at the same time, allowed all the advantages the nature of their situation would admit of. But, if nothing less than absolute independency should content them, I am ready, for the most important reasons, to join in whatever measures shall appear most justifiable and proper for frustrating their views, and asserting our own claims; for England must either maintain her sovereignty, or hazard her safety.

With these brief observations, I shall at once close this short essay, and take leave of my reader, to whom, I presume, my sentiments in general, upon this subject, will appear, if not altogether just, yet perfectly humane, liberal, and friendly to the common interests of mankind. For I am not conscious to have advanced a single position throughout the whole of a different tendency. However, if I should be found to be mistaken, I desire no better quarter than the humane reader may think I merit.

FINIS.

[John Joachim Zubly], An Humble Enquiry into the Nature of the Dependency of the American Colonies upon the Parliament of Great-Britain, and the Right of Parliament to Lay Taxes on the Said Colonies. By a Freeholder of South-Carolina. Charleston, 1769.

John Joachim Zubly was a Swiss-born pastor who migrated to the North American colonies in 1744, settling first in South Carolina and then in 1760 moving on to Georgia, where he became the first minister of the Presbyterian Church in Savannah. An outspoken critic of British policy, Zubly wrote a number of pamphlets on behalf of the patriot cause, the most important of which follows. While offering a detailed analysis of the empire and its various parts, including Scotland, Ireland, and the North American colonies, Zubly expressed much of the same confusion over the relationship of the colonies to Parliament that other Americans had. "Every part of the British empire is bound to support and promote the advantage of the whole," he declared; nevertheless, every part of the empire had "a different degree of dependency on the mother state" and could not be equitably taxed by a House of Commons that represented only England and Scotland.

Zubly set forth one of the most explicit explanations of actual representation made by the colonists. "Every representative in Parliament," he said, "is not a representative for the whole nation, but only for the particular place for which he hath been chosen." And that "representation arises entirely from the free election of the people." Election, in other words, and not some mutuality of interests, was the sole criterion of representation. And since the Americans did not elect anyone to the House of Commons, that body had no right to tax them. Yet Zubly conceded that the colonists had "a profound veneration for the British Parliament, they look on upon it as the great palladium of the British liberties." And he wanted the dependency of the colonies on the mother country to remain "as full and firm as ever." Confronted with the prospect of independence, which he deeply rejected, Zubly could only propose that the colonies "freely and chearfully" give requisitions in place of taxes to Great Britain— hardly a solution that would satisfy most Americans.

A N

HUMBLE ENQUIRY

I N T O

The NATURE of the DEPENDENCY of the *AMERICAN* COLONIES upon the PAR-LIAMENT of *GREAT-BRITAIN*,

A N D

The RIGHT of PARLIAMENT to lay TAXES on the ſaid COLONIES.

By a FREEHOLDER of *SOUTH-CAROLINA.*

A Houſe divided against itſelf cannot ſtand.

When people heard ſhip money demanded *as a right*, and found it by ſworn judges of the law adjudged ſo, upon ſuch grounds and reaſons as every ſtander-by was able to ſwear was not law, and ſo had loſt the pleaſure and delight of be-ing kind and dutiful to the King, and, inſtead of GIVING, were required to PAY, and by a logick that left no man any thing that he might call his own, they no more looked upon it as the caſe of one man, but the caſe of the kingdom, nor as an impoſition laid upon them by the King, but by the judges, which they thought themſelves bound in publick juſtice not to ſubmit to. It was an obſer-vation long ago of *Thucydides*, "That men are much more paſſionate for injuſtice " than for violence, becauſe (ſaith he) the one proceeding as from an equal ſeems " rapine, when the other proceeding from a ſtranger is but the effect of neceſſity." —When they ſaw reaſon of ſtate urged as elements of law, judges as ſharp-ſighted as ſecretaries of ſtate, judgment of law grounded upon matter of fact of which there was neither enquiry nor proof, and no reaſon given for the payment but what included all the eſtates of the ſtanders by, they had no reaſon to hope that doctrine, or the promoters of it, would be contained within any bounds; and it is no wonder that they who had ſo little reaſon to be pleaſed with their own condi-tion were no leſs ſolicitous for, or apprehenſive of the inconveniences that might attend any alteration.—*Hiſtory of the long Rebellion, vol.* I . *p.* 70, 71.

PRINTED in the YEAR M,DCC,LXIX.

[Price Twelve Shillings and Sixpence.]

An Humble Enquiry, &c.

THOUGH few or none claim infallibility in express terms, yet it is very difficult ever to persuade some men they are mistaken. We generally have so good an opinion of our own understanding, that insensibly we take it for granted those that do not think as we do must needs be in the wrong. When disputes are once heightened by personal prejudice, or the bitterness of party, it becomes so much the more difficult to the disputants themselves to see their mistakes, and even to bystanders the truth appears wrapped up in a cloud, and through the fog and dust of argument becomes almost imperceptible.

These remarks I believe will particularly hold good in the subject now in agitation between *Great-Britain* and her colonies, a subject however of too serious a nature to be given up to prejudice, or to be decided by the rage of party. Every argument *pro* or *con* deserves to be most carefully weighed, and he that sets the whole in the clearest light does the publick no inconsiderable service, and that whether it be by pointing out the justice of the *American* claims to *Great-Britain*, or setting such constitutional arguments before the *Americans* as must either leave obstinacy inexcusable, or will dispose loyal and reasonable men to a chearful acquiescence.

The argument on which the *Americans* seem to lay the greatest stress is, they say that it is a principle of the *British* constitution, that no *Englishman* ought to be taxed but by his own consent, given either by himself or his representative. I find it admitted by such as disapprove the *American* claims, that no man is bound by any law to which he hath not given his consent either in person or by a representative. Perhaps these two propositions are not perfectly equivalent; however it seems clear, that he that holds that no man is bound BY ANY LAW to which he has not personally or by a representative consented, must also admit, that no man is bound by any law that lays a tax on him without his consent given by himself or representative. What is true of ALL laws in general must also hold true of EVERY law in particular. If no law can operate upon any man that hath not in the above manner given his assent to it, certainly no such law can be binding upon whole communities, or any considerable part of the whole nation. In the spirit of the above principle, it seems essential to law, that it be assented to by such on whom it is afterwards to operate. To suppose, therefore, that a law is binding upon such as have not given their assent, is to suppose (I argue upon that principle) a law may be valid and binding at the same time it is confessedly destitute of the very essential point to make it so; and if the assent of those that are to be governed by the law is not necessary or essential to the making of it, then representation is a mere superfluous thing, no better than an excrescence in the legislative power, which therefore at any convenient time may be lopped off at pleasure, and without the least danger to the constitution; the governed then have no part in the legislation at all, the will of those in power, whoever they be, is the supreme and sole law, and what hath been above asserted to be a constitutional principle seems to me to fall to the ground without remedy to all intents and purposes.

Supposing, on the other hand, that principle, as is asserted to be constitutional, then to me, as is further asserted, it seems to be of the very nature of it, that it be general and hold in all cases. This it does not only clearly imply, but also fully and strongly express; but yet if so, it would also seem that no man, or no people, in no case, or by no power whatever, can be bound to pay a tax to which they have not consented either personally or by their representatives. Every constitutional principle must be general and hold in all cases, and I may add in all places too, for it is usually said that the liberties of an *Englishman* follow him to the end of the world, much more then must they follow him over all the *British* dominions; this is so true, that by an express law, the children of *British* parents, though born in a foreign dominion, are just as much entitled to all *British* liberties as those who have been born within the realm.

An inference may possibly hence be drawn, that if so, the *British* colonies are subject to none of the acts of the *British* Parliament, (*scil.* because they never assented to them neither in person nor by representative) and therefore must be considered as independent of the legal or parliamentary power of *Great-Britain*. I confess I should be sorry to see *America* independent of *Great-Britain*, and if any of the arguments the *Americans* make use of imply an independency on the mother state, I should shrewdly suspect there must be some fallacy couched under an otherwise specious appearance. The sum and strength of this inference I conceive lies thus: The *British* legislature must be the supreme power in all the *British* dominions, and if so, all the *British* dominions ought to pay obedience in all cases to all the laws in which they are mentioned that may be enacted by the *British* Parliament, and to refuse obedience in any such case is to declare themselves an independent people.

I freely own I have not heard any thing stronger said in favour of taxation by the *British* Parliament, and I think this argument is highly deserving the most serious consideration. Every good man would wish to hear the voice of dispassionate reason before he forms his judgment in any debate. Vulgar prejudices may sway vulgar minds, but a wise man is neither carried away by the torrent of power, nor the blast of popularity. I would endeavour therefore to consider this argument with all the candour and impartiality I am capable of; I would do it with a mind open to conviction, and with steadiness sufficient to follow truth wherever she may lead me.

To have a clear view how far this argument may affect the present question between *Great-Britain* and her colonies, it will be necessary carefully to state the relation which they bear to one another; without this we shall never have a precise and determinate idea of the matter. The argument I think is made up of two propositions, *viz.*

The Parliament of *Great-Britain* is the supreme legislature in all the *British* empire.

All the *British* dominions therefore ought to pay obedience thereto in all cases and to all the laws in which they are mentioned, and to refuse obedience to any such is to declare themselves an independent people.

Before I proceed to take a distinct view of each of these propositions, I repeat, that they are said to be built upon a constitutional principle, and that this principle must be general and hold in all cases; this must undoubtedly be admitted, for what enters into the very essence of the constitution must doubtless operate as far as the constitution itself. Let us now proceed to consider every part of these two propositions distinctly, and this must infallibly lead us to form a sound judgment of the whole.

The kingdom of GREAT-BRITAIN consists of two parts, north and south, or *England* and *Scotland*, united since 1707 into one kingdom, under the name of *Great-Britain*. This union hath not been so full and absolute, as to put both kingdoms in all respects upon a perfect equality; but tho' the legislature is the same, yet the laws and the administration of justice are not the same in every instance. The same legislature making laws that affect only the one or the other of these kingdoms, and even laws made to be binding upon both, do not affect both alike, of which the difference in raising the supplies by land tax is a very full and striking proof, this could not be the case if the union between the two kingdoms was so entire and absolute, as for instance between *England* and the principality of *Wales*.

The BRITISH EMPIRE is a more extensive word, and should not be confounded with the kingdom of *Great-Britain*; it consists of *England, Scotland, Ireland*, the Islands of *Man, Jersey, Guernsey, Gibraltar*, and *Minorca, &c.* in the *Mediterranean; Senegal, &c.* in *Africa; Bombay, &c.* in the *East-Indies*; and the Islands and Colonies in *North-America, &c.* As *England*, strictly so called, is at the head of this great body, it is called the mother country; all the settled inhabitants of this vast empire are called *Englishmen*, but individuals, from the place of their nativity or residence, are called *English, Scotch, Irish, Welch, Americans, &c.*

Scotland and *Ireland* were originally distinct kingdoms and nations, but the colonies in *America*, being settled upon lands discovered by the *English*, under charters from the crown of *England*, were always considered as a part of the *English* nation, and of the *British* empire, and looked upon as dependent upon *England*; I mean, that before the union of the two kingdoms, (and very few colonies have been settled since) they depended on *England* only, and even now I suppose are rather considered as a dependance upon *England* than of the two kingdoms united under the name of *Great-Britain*. Were it not for the union, which incorporates the two kingdoms, the colonies never would have depended on that part of *Britain* called *Scotland*, and by the terms of the union I apprehend *England* has not given up or brought her colonies under the dominion of *Scotland*, but tho' dependent on *Great-Britain*, they still remain what they always were, *English* colonies.

All the inhabitants of the *British* empire together form the BRITISH NATION, and that the *British* Parliament is the supreme power and legislature in the *British* nation I never heard doubted.

By the *English* constitution, which is that which prevails over the whole empire, all *Englishmen*, or all that make up the *British* empire, are entitled to certain privileges indefeasible, unalienable, and of which they can never be deprived, but by the taking away of that constitution which gives them these privileges. I have observed that the *British* empire is made up of different kingdoms and nations, but it is not the original constitution of *Scotland* or *Ireland*, but of *England*, which extends and communicates its privileges to the whole empire. This is an undeniable principle, and ought never to be lost out of sight, if we would form a sound judgment on the question now to be considered.

From the consideration above admitted, that the *British* Parliament is the supreme legislative power in the whole *British* empire, the following conclusion has been drawn; the colonies (and the same I suppose is meant of all the *British* empire, of which the colonies are a part) are bound by and subject to all the laws of the *British* Parliament in which they are mentioned, or are subject to none of any kind whatsoever.

Before this can be properly discussed, it must be observed, that *Great-Britain* has not only a Parliament, which is the supreme legislature, but also a constitution, and that the now Parliament derives its authority and power from the constitution, and not the constitution from the Parliament. It may also be very fairly inferred hence, that the liberties of *Englishmen* arise from and depend on the *English* constitution, which is permanent and ever the same, whereas the individuals which compose the Parliament are changed at least once every seven years, and always at the demise of a king.

The Parliament of *Great-Britain* is the supreme legislature in the *British* empire. It must be so either absolutely or agreeable to the constitution; if absolutely, it can alter the constitution whenever it sees fit; if absolutely, it is not bound by the constitution, nor any thing else; if agreeable to the constitution, then it can no more make laws, which are against the constitution, or the unalterable privileges of *British* subjects, than it can alter the constitution itself. Supposing a Parliament, under some of the arbitrary reigns of the last century, should have made a law, that for the future the king's warrant should be sufficient to lay a tax on the subject, or to oblige him to pay ship money, it would have been an act of the supreme legislature, but it may safely be doubted, whether the nation would have thought it constitutional. I conclude therefore, that the power of Parliament, and of every branch of it, has its bounds assigned by the constitution.

If the power of the Parliament is limited by the constitution, it may not be improper next to enquire, whether the power of the *British* Parliament affects all the subjects of the *British* empire in the same manner.

If the power of the *British* Parliament affects all the subjects of the *British* empire in the same manner, it follows, that all the laws made by the *British* Parliament are binding alike upon all those over whom this power extends, or in other words, that all the subjects of the *British* empire are bound not only by those laws in which they are expressly mentioned, but every law by the Parliament made, for what need is there to mention every individual of those for whom the law is made in general, every subject therefore of the *British* empire, upon this supposition, must be bound by every law of the *British* Parliament, unless expressly excepted.

Those that hold the subjects of *Great-Britain*, living without *England* or *Scotland*, are bound by every law in which they are mentioned, seem also clearly to hold, that the same persons are not bound by such laws in which they are not mentioned. Thus the alternative, that the subjects of the *British* empire must be subject to all or none of the laws of the *British* Parliament, is limited even by those who plead for an universal submission. He that is only bound to obey some laws, cannot be said to be bound by all laws, as, on the contrary, he that is bound to obey all laws, is excused in none.

I suppose, before the union with *Scotland*, none would have scrupled to call the *English* Parliament the supreme legislature of all the *British* empire, though *Scotland* was still an independent kingdom, and by the union *Scotland* and its Parliament was not swallowed up and absorbed by *England* and its Parliament, but united with the kingdom, and the Parliaments also of the two kingdoms united in one general legislature. The ecclesiastical laws and constitution also of each kingdom remains as it was before, *i. e.* entirely different from each other.

Perhaps it may not be amiss to conceive, that the authority of the *British* Parliament extends over the whole *British* nation, though the different respective subjects are not altogether alike affected by its laws: That, with regard to national trade, the power of making it most beneficial to the head and every branch of the empire is vested in the *British* Parliament, as the supreme power in the nation, and that all the *British* subjects every where have a right to be ruled by the known principles of their common constitution.

Next, it may be proper to take a nearer view how far, and in what manner, the acts of Parliament operate upon the different subjects of the *British* empire.

ENGLAND doubtless is the first and primary object of the *British* Parliament, and therefore all laws immediately affect every resident in *England*; and of the king himself it has been said, *Rex Angliæ in regno suo non habet superiorem nisi Deum & legem.* Proceedings at law I take to be the same in *England* and *England*'s dependencies.

SCOTLAND is united with *England*, and therefore there is a different operation of the laws that subsisted before and those that have been made since the union, and even these do not affect *Scotland* as of themselves; but in consequence of and in the terms of the union between the two nations, the union makes no alteration in proceedings at law, nor does it take away any private property.

IRELAND is a distinct kingdom, and hath been conquered from the native *Irish* two or three times by the *English*; it hath nevertheless a Parliament of its own, and is a part of the *British* empire. It will best appear how far the *British* Parliament think *Ireland* dependent upon *Great-Britain*, by inserting, *A Bill for the better securing of the Dependency of* Ireland. The act was as follows: Whereas attempts have lately been made to shake off the subjection of *Ireland* unto, and dependence upon the imperial crown of this realm, which will be of dangerous consequence to *Great-Britain* and *Ireland*. And whereas the House of Lords in *Ireland*, in order thereto, have, of late, against law, assumed to themselves a power and jurisdiction to examine, correct and amend, the judgment and decrees of the courts of justice in the kingdom of *Ireland*; therefore, for the better securing of the dependency of *Ireland* upon the crown of *Great-Britain*, may it please your Majesty, that it may be enacted, and it is hereby declared and enacted, by the King's most excellent Majesty, by and with the advice and consent of the Lords Spiritual and Temporal, and Commons, in this present Parliament assembled, and by the authority of the same, That the said kingdom of *Ireland* hath been, is, and of right ought to be, subordinate unto, and dependent upon the imperial crown of *Great-Britain*, as being inseparably united and annexed thereunto, and that the King's Majesty, by and with the advice and consent of the Lords Spiritual and Temporal, and Commons of *Great-Britain*, in Parliament assembled, had, hath, and of right ought to have, full power and authority to make laws and statutes of sufficient force and validity to bind the people and kingdom of *Ireland*.

And be it farther enacted, by the authority aforesaid, That the House of Lords of *Ireland* have not, nor of right ought to have, any jurisdiction to judge of, affirm, or reverse any judgment, sentence, or decree, given or made in any court within the said kingdom, and that all proceedings before the House of Lords upon any such judgment, sentence, or decree, are, and are hereby declared to be utterly null and void to all intents and purposes whatsoever.

The occasion of this bill was an appeal brought 1719 from the House of Peers in *Ireland* to the House of Peers in *England*. A PITT was the first that spoke against it in the House of Commons, because, as he said, in his opinion it seemed calculated for no other purpose than to encrease the power of the *British* House of Peers, which in his opinion was already but too great. The Duke of *Leeds* protested against it in the House of Lords, and gave fifteen reasons to support the claim of the House of Peers in *Ireland*. The bill however passed, though Mr. *Hungerford*, Lord *Molesworth*, Lord *Tyrconel*, and other members, endeavoured to shew, that *Ireland* was ever independent with respect to courts of judicature. Some proposals have several years ago been made to incorporate *Ireland* with *Great-Britain*, but without any effect.

The Islands of *Guernsey* and *Jersey*, though in ecclesiastical matters considered as a part of *Hampshire*, are under the direction of an Assembly called the Convention of the States of *Jersey, &c.* The *Isle of Man* hath lately been annexed to the crown, but their own *Manks* laws still obtain in the island.

The *British* colonies and islands in *America* are not the least important part of the *British* empire; that these owe a constitutional dependence to the *British* Parliament I never heard they denied; though of late they have frequently been charged with it, these charges have not been grounded upon any declaration of theirs of the kind, their very petitioning, petitions and resolutions, manifestly speaking the very reverse; but their aversion to certain new duties, laid upon them for the sole purpose of raising a revenue, have been made a handle of against them, and they have as good as been charged, that they declare themselves an independent people. These insinuations the *Americans* are apt to look upon as being neither very fair nor very friendly; however at present I would only consider what kind of dependence is expected from the *American* colonies. An act of Parliament has fixed that of *Ireland*; a later act of the same power hath also fixed that of *America*, though, as will appear from the comparison, not altogether on the same footing. The act is entitled, *An Act for the better securing the Dependency of his Majesty's Dominions in* America *upon the Crown and Parliament of* Great-Britain, and runs thus:

Whereas several of the Houses of Representatives in his Majesty's colonies and plantations in *America* have of late, against law, claimed to themselves, or to the General Assemblies of the same, the sole and exclusive right of imposing duties and taxes upon his Majesty's subjects in the said colonies and plantations, and, in pursuance of such claim, passed certain votes, resolutions and orders, derogatory to the legislative authority of Parliament, and inconsistent with the dependency of the said colonies and plantations upon the crown of *Great-Britain*, may it therefore please your most excellent Majesty, that it may be declared, and be it declared, by the King's most excellent Majesty, by and with the advice and consent of the Lords Spiritual and Temporal, and Commons, in the present Parliament assembled, and by the authority of the same, That the said colonies and plantations in *America* have been, are, and of right ought to be, subordinate unto and dependent upon the imperial crown and Parliament of *Great-Britain*, and that the King's Majesty, by and with the advice and consent of the Lords Spiritual and Temporal, and Commons, of *Great-Britain*, in Parliament assembled, had, hath, and of right ought to have, full power and authority to make laws and statutes of sufficient force and validity to bind the colonies and people of *America*, subjects of the crown of *Great-Britain*, in all cases whatsoever.

And be it further declared and enacted, by the authority aforesaid, That all resolutions, votes, orders and proceedings, in any of the said colonies or plantations, whereby the power and authority of the Parliament of *Great-Britain* to make laws and statutes as aforesaid is denied, or drawn into question, are, and are hereby declared to be utterly null and void to all intents and purposes whatsoever.

This is the standard of dependence which the Parliament of *Great-Britain* hath fixed for the *British* colonies on the 18th of *March*, 1766. The Stamp Act was repealed the same day, and the opinion of several noblemen who protested against that repeal was, "that this declaratory bill cannot possibly obviate the growing mischiefs in *America*, where it may seem calculated only to deceive the people of *Great-Britain*, by holding forth a delusive and nugatory affirmance of the legislative right of *Great-Britain*, whilst the enacting part of it does no more than abrogate the resolutions of the House of Representatives in the *North-American* colonies, which have not in themselves the least colour of authority, and declares that which is apparently and certainly criminal only null and void." I presume I may venture to affirm, that in and by this act, the Parliament did not mean to set aside the constitution, infringe the liberties of *British* subjects, or to vindicate unto themselves an authority which it had not before, was known to have, and would always have had, though this act had never been made. I also find, that, in order to overset any act, law, resolution, or proceeding, of the colony Assemblies, nothing seems necessary, but that the Parliament should declare it null and void to all intents and purposes whatsoever. And it seems pretty clear, that the same power that can disannul any act by a simple declaration, with one single stroke more, can also annihilate the body that made it.

The remark already made, that though all the different parts of the *British* empire are in a state of dependence upon the Parliament of *Great-Britain*, yet that the nature and degree of dependence is not exactly alike in the respective different parts of the same, will receive new strength and light, if we compare the act for better securing the dependency of *Ireland* with that for better securing the dependency of the colonies. Both acts, though at different times, have been made by the same authority, and for a similar purpose, and none can better tell us what kind and degree of dependency the Parliament expects and requires of its dependents than the Parliament itself.

The *Irish* is entitled in very general words, for the better securing the dependency of *Ireland*.

The title of the *American* law is more explicit; *Ireland*'s dependency is mentioned, but the dependency of the *Americans* is more clearly expressed, and said to be upon the crown and Parliament of *Great-Britain*. *America* seems to owe two dependencies, one to the crown, and one to the Parliament.

The preamble of the *Irish* bill brings no less a charge than an attempt to shake off subjection unto and dependence upon the imperial crown of *Great-Britain*.

The preamble of the *American* bill brings no such accusation, but only, that the *Americans* have claimed an exclusive right to lay on taxes on his Majesty's subjects within the colonies, and passed votes and resolutions derogatory to the legislative power of Parliament, and inconsistent with the dependency of the said colonies and plantations upon the crown (the word and Parliament is not made use of in this place) of *Great-Britain*. The principal differences between these bills seems to me to lie in this, that *Ireland* is said to be subject to and dependent only on the crown of *Great-Britain*, whereas *America* throughout is declared subject, at least dependent and subordinate, not only to the crown, but also to the Parliament of *Great-Britain*, and then *Ireland* is only declared dependent upon, and subordinate to, in very gentle terms, whereas the right of making laws to bind the *Americans* is expressed in these very strong, most extensive terms, IN ALL CASES WHATSOEVER.

Time was when the dependency of the colonies upon *England* was spoke of exactly in the terms made use of for *Ireland*; the charter of this province saith, "our pleasure is, that the tenants and inhabitants of the said province be subject IMMEDIATELY to the crown of *England*, as depending thereof forever;" but by the late law all *America* is said to be dependent on crown and Parliament. This alteration seems to me by no means immaterial, but to imply a change both in the subjection expected from the colony and in the authority to which the colony owes dependency and subordination. In Parliament, King, Lords, and Commons, constitute the supreme power; but as each of these has its own distinct unalienable right, and incommunicable prerogatives, rights, or privileges, so I cannot but conceive dependency upon the crown and dependency upon crown and Parliament are things not exactly alike. If (as asserted in the charter) the colonies at some time or other were only dependent on the crown, and now are subordinate unto and dependent upon crown and Parliament, it should seem both the authority on which they depend, and the nature of their dependency, hath undergone some alteration; neither doth this appear to me a trifling alteration, and it seems to me at least if so it must needs make some alteration in the system of government and obedience.

Hitherto all appeals from the colonies, after passing thro' chancery in *America*, have been made to the King in council; this I conceive must have been in consequence of the dependency of the colonies immediately upon the crown; but perhaps for the future appeals will not be carried to the King in council, but to the King and Parliament.

The crown has hitherto had a right of a negative upon all *American* laws, and they were obliged to be passed in *America* with a saving clause; but if, as is asserted in the declaratory bill, the King has a right and power to make laws to bind the *Americans, by and with the advice and consent of the Lords Spiritual and Temporal, and Commons of* Great-Britain, *assembled in Parliament*, then probably the same authority must also concur to repeal the laws made in *America*, whereas the crown hitherto repealed any law made in *America* without asking or waiting for the consent of Lords and Commons.

It appears also, by a late act suspending the Assembly of *New-York*, that the parliamentary authority also extends to suspend, which is but another word for proroguing or dissolving (or annihilating) Assemblies; all which has hitherto been done by the crown without the interfering of Parliament: But that the crown hath a right of proroguing or dissolving the Parliament itself by its own authority I suppose will not be denied. I cannot dismiss this subject without observing, that even the declaratory bill speaks of the Assemblies in *America* as Houses of Representatives. If it is allowed that they are represented in *America*, unless they are represented doubly, they cannot be represented any where else; this strikes at the root of virtual representation, and if representation is the basis of taxation, they cannot be taxed but where they are represented, unless they are doubly taxed, as well as doubly represented.

It is evident upon the whole, that a much greater degree of dependency and subordination is expected of *America* than of *Ireland*, though, by the way, *Ireland*, in the preamble of their bill, is charged with much greater guilt than *America*; nay, the words in ALL CASES WHATSOEVER are so exceeding extensive, that, in process of time, even hewing of wood, and drawing of water, might be argued to be included in them.

It was necessary to state the authority claimed by Parliament over *America* as clear and full as possible; with regard to the *Americans* it must be owned, when they profess to owe dependency and subordination to the *British* Parliament, they do not mean so extensive and absolute a dependency as here seems to be claimed, but that they think themselves in a constitutional manner dependent upon and in subordination to the crown and Parliament of *Great-Britain*, even those votes, resolutions, and proceedings, which are disannulled by the House of Commons and the declaratory bill, most fully and chearfully declare.

It has indeed been said, that unless they are subject to all the *British* acts in which they are mentioned, they are subject to none of any kind whatsoever, and consequently to be considered as independent of the legal and parliamentary power of

Great-Britain; but I should think it might be as fairly and safely concluded, that while the *Americans* declare themselves subject to any one law of the *British* legislature, it cannot be said they declare themselves independent, or not subject to any law whatever.

In so delicate and important a matter, may I be permitted to observe, that the measure of power and of obedience in every country must be determined by the standard of its constitution. The dispute seems to lie between the Parliament and colonies; the Parliament will certainly be the sitting judges; I will not take upon me to say that the *Americans* may not look upon Parliament as judge and party; however, it is very possible for a judge to give a most righteous sentence, even where he himself is deeply interested, but they that are sufferers by the sentence will ever be apt to wish that he had not been party as well as judge.

From what hath been said hitherto, the due and constitutional authority of the *British* Parliament appears clear, and it does not less so I hope, that the subordination to and dependency on the *British* Parliament is not exactly the same in all the respective parts of that extensive empire; perhaps this will appear with still greater evidence by taking a particular view of the subject of taxation.

Any unlimited power and authority may lay on the subjects any tax it pleaseth; the subjects in that case themselves are mere property, and doubtless their substance and labour must be at their disposal who have the disposal of their persons. This is the case in arbitrary governments; but the *British* empire is an empire of freemen, no power is absolute but that of the laws, and, as hath been asserted, of such laws to which they that are bound by them have themselves consented.

Did the power and authority of the *British* Parliament in point of taxation extend in the same manner over all its dependencies, *e. g.* the same over *Scotland* as over *England*, over *Ireland* in the same manner as over *Scotland*, over *Guernsey* and *Jersey* as over *Ireland*, *&c.* then the very same act which lays a general tax would lay it also at the same time upon all over whom that authority extends. The laws of every legislature are supposed to extend to and be made over all within their jurisdiction, unless they are expressly excepted. Thus an excise law extends to all the *British* kingdom, because it is a publick law; but acts have frequently been made to lay on a penny *Scots* on beer, which, being for a local purpose, cannot operate on the whole kingdom. The same I believe may be said with regard to the method of recovering small debts; it seems absurd to say, that any supreme legislature makes an unlimited law which at the same time is designed not to be binding upon the greatest part of the subjects within that empire. Was it ever known that the land tax being laid on the whole united kingdom, the bishoprick of *Durham*, and the manor of *East-Greenwich*, were not also supposed to be included? and if any part within the immediate jurisdiction, and equally dependent on the same legislature, should be designed to be excused from, or not liable to pay a general tax, would it not be absolutely necessary that such a place should be expressly excepted? If, because *America* is a part of the *British* empire, it is as much so, or in the same manner is a part of it, as is the bishoprick of *Durham*, or the manor of *East-Greenwich*, nothing can be plainer than that it must be affected by every tax that is laid just in the same manner and proportion as is the bishoprick of *Durham*, or manor of *East-Greenwich*. This hath not been the case, nor thought to be the case hitherto. *Ireland* and *America* have not been called upon to pay the *British* land tax, malt tax, nor indeed any tax in which they have not been expressly mentioned; the reason of which I presume must be, either that the *British* Parliament did not look upon them as any part of the kingdom of *Great-Britain*, or else did not think them liable to any tax in which they were not expressly mentioned. If any subjects of the *British* empire are not liable to any or every tax laid on by the *British* Parliament, it must be either because they are not liable by the constitution, (as not being represented) or because they are excused by the favour of Parliament; if they are not liable by the privileges of the constitution, their not being compelled to pay is no favour, the contrary would be oppression and an anticonstitutional act; if they have been hitherto excused by the lenity of the *British* Parliament, it must be owned the Parliament bore harder on those who were made to pay those taxes than on those who by their lenity only were excused.

The noble Lords who protested against the repeal of the Stamp

Act observe, "it appears to us, that a most essential part of that authority, (*sc.* the whole legislative authority of *Great-Britain*, without any distinction or reserve whatsoever) the power of legislation, cannot be properly, equitably, or impartially exercised, if it does not extend itself to all the members of the state in proportion to their respective abilities, but suffers a part to be exempt from a due share of those burdens which the publick exigencies require to be imposed upon the whole: A partiality which is directly and manifestly repugnant to the trust reposed by the people in every legislature, and destructive of that confidence on which all government is founded."

If in the opinion of these Noblemen, therefore, it is partiality to suffer any part of the state to be exempt from a due share of those burdens which the publick exigencies require should be imposed upon the WHOLE, it would also seem to be a species of partiality, to lay a burden on ANY PART of the state which the other parts of the same state are not equally bound to bear. Partial burdens, or partial exemptions, would doubtless affect those that are burdened or exempted in a very different manner; but if not extending alike to the whole, must still be looked upon as partial. And if this partiality is inconsistent with the trust *reposed BY THE PEOPLE in every legislature*, it would also seem that the legislature could not lay any burdens but as entrusted by the people who chose them to be their representatives and a part of the legislature. We may hence also learn what is to be expected, if every other part of the *British* empire, *England* and *Scotland* only excepted, have hitherto been exempted from the taxes paid in *England*, which it must be owned are very heavy, by mere favour; or, as some seem to express it, "*flagrant partiality and injustice*;" their being indulged time immemorial will not be deemed a sufficient plea to excuse them always, but with an impartial hand the very same taxes that now obtain in *Great-Britain* will be laid upon *Ireland, America, Jersey, Guernsey*, the *Mediterranean, African* and *East-India* settlements, and, in short, on every individual part of the *British* empire. Whether a design to do this be not ripening apace I will not take upon me to say, but whenever it does, it must make some alteration in the policy of the mother and infant state, nay in the system of the whole *British* empire.

There are several parts of the *British* empire that pay no tax at all; this I take to be the case of *Gibraltar, Minorca, New-foundland, East-Florida*, and all the *African* and *East-India* settlements, *&c.* The reason is, that all these places have no legislature of their own, and consequently none to give or dispose of their property; had these places been taxed by Parliament, there might however this reason been given, that having no representatives within themselves, and having never contributed any thing to the publick burdens, though they all receive protection, perhaps greater than the *American* colonies, the Parliament supplied that defect; but this cannot be urged against the colonies, who both have legislatures, and also contributed to the publick burdens, and that so liberally, that even the crown and Parliament thought they had exerted themselves beyond their abilities, and for several years gave them some compensation. I may mention those parts of the *British* empire as striking instances, that where there is no representation, taxation hath not been thought of, and yet *Newfoundland*, which is not taxed at all, is certainly as much represented in Parliament as all the colonies, which are designed to be doubly taxed.

By the constitution taxes are in the nature of a free gift of the subjects to the crown; regulations of trade are measures to secure and improve the trade of the whole nation. There is no doubt but regulations may be made to ruin as well as to improve trade; yet without regulations trade cannot subsist, but must suffer and sink; and it seems no where more proper to lodge the power of making these regulations than in the highest court of the empire; yet a man may trade or not, he may buy or let it alone; if merchandizes are rated so high that they will not suit him to purchase, though it may be an inconvenience, yet there is no law to compel him to buy; to rate the necessaries of life, without which a man cannot well do, beyond their real value, and hinder him at the same time from purchasing them reasonably of others, is scarce consistent with freedom; but when duties are laid on merchandizes not to regulate trade, but for the express and sole purpose of raising a revenue, they are to all intents and purposes equal to any tax, but they can by no means be called the free gift of those who never helped to make the law, but, as far as in them lay, ever looked upon it as an unconstitutional grievance.

If taxes are a free GIFT of the people to the crown, then the crown hath no right to them but what is derived from the GIVERS. It may be absolutely necessary that the subject should give, but still he that is to give must be supposed the judge both of that necessity, and how much he may be able and ought to give upon every necessary occasion. No man can give what is not his own, and therefore the constitution hath placed this right to judge of the necessity, and of what is to be given, in the Commons as the representatives of all those who are to give, in vesting a right in them to give publick supplies to the crown; it did not, could not mean to invest them with any power to give what neither belongs to them, nor those whom they represent; and therefore, as no man constitutionally "owes obedience to any law to which he has not assented either in person or by his representative;" much less doth the constitution oblige any man to part with his property, but freely and by his own consent; what those who are representatives are not willing to give, no power in *Great-Britain* hath any right violently to take, and for a man to have his property took from him under pretence of a law that is not constitutional, would not be much better than to have it took from him against the express consent of those whom he constitutionally made his representatives.

It is held a maxim, that in government a proportion ought to be observed between the share in the legislature and the burden to be borne. The *Americans* pretend to no share in the legislature of *Great-Britain* at all, but they hope they have never forfeited their share in the constitution.

Every government supposes rule and protection from the governors, support and obedience from those that are governed; from these duly tempered arises the prerogative of the crown and the liberty of the subject; but he that has not a right to his own hath no property, and he that must part with his property by laws against his consent, or the consent of the majority of the people, has no liberty. The *British* constitution is made to secure liberty and property; whatever takes away these takes away the constitution itself, and cannot be constitutional.

To form a clear judgment on the power of taxation, it must be enquired on what right that power is grounded. It is a fundamental maxim of *English* law, that there is a contract between the crown and subjects; if so, the crown cannot lay on any tax, or any other burden, on the subject, but agreeable to the original contract by authority of Parliament; neither can the Lords properly concur, or the Commons frame a tax bill for any other purpose but the support of the crown and government, consistent with the original contract between that and the people.

All subjects are dependent on and subordinate to the government under which they live. An *Englishman* in *France* must observe the laws of *France*; but it cannot be said that the dependency and subordination in *England* is the same as dependency and subordination in *France*. In governments where the will of the sovereign is the supreme law, the subjects have nothing to give, their ALL is in the disposal of the government; there subjects pay, but having nothing of their own cannot give; but in *England* the Commons GIVE and GRANT. This implies both a free and voluntary act, and that they give nothing but their own property.

Though every part of the *British* empire is bound to support and promote the advantage of the whole, it is by no means necessary that this should be done by a tax indiscriminately laid on the whole; it seems sufficient that every part should contribute to the support of the whole as it may be best able, and as may best suit with the common constitution.

I have before observed the different degree of dependency on the mother state; I shall now review the same again, with a particular regard to imposing or paying taxes, and if a material difference hath always obtained in this respect, it will confirm my assertion, that every branch of the *British* empire is not affected by the tax laws of *Great-Britain* in the self same manner.

The Parliament has a right to tax, but this right is not inherent in the members of it as men; I mean, the members of Parliament are not (like the Senate of *Venice*) so many rulers who have each of them a native and inherent right to be the rulers of the people of *England*, or even their representatives; they do not meet together as a court of proprietors to consider their common interest, and agree with one another what tax they will lay on those over whom they bear rule, or whom they represent, but they only exercise that right which nature hath placed in the people in general, and which, as it cannot conveniently be exercised by the whole people, THESE have lodged in some of their body chosen from among themselves, and by themselves, for that purpose, and empowered for a time only to transact the affairs of the whole, and to agree in their behalf on such supplies as it may be necessary to furnish unto the crown for the support of its dignity, and the necessities and protection of the people.

It would be absurd to say, that the crown hath a right to lay on a tax, for as taxes are granted to the crown, so in this case the crown would make a grant to itself, and hence the bill of rights expressly asserts, that *the levying of money for or to the use of the crown, by pretence of prerogative, without grant of Parliament, for a longer time or in any other manner than the same is or shall be granted, is illegal*; hence also there is a material difference between money bills and all other laws. The King and Lords cannot make any amendment in money bills, as the House of Lords frequently doth in all others, but must accept or refuse them such as they are offered by the Commons, the constitutional reason of which is very obvious, it is the people only that give, and therefore giving must be the sole act of those by whom the givers are represented. The crown cannot take till it is given, and they that give cannot give but on their own behalf, and of those whom they represent; nay even then they cannot give but in a constitutional manner; they cannot give the property of those they represent without giving their own also exactly in the same proportion; every bill must be equally binding upon ALL whom they represent, and upon every one that is a representative.

Every representative in Parliament is not a representative for the whole nation, but only for the particular place for which he hath been chosen. If any are chosen for a plurality of places, they can make their election only for one of them. The electors of *Middlesex* cannot chuse a representative but for *Middlesex*, and as the right of sitting depends entirely upon the election, it seems clear to demonstration, that no member can represent any but those by whom he hath been elected; if not elected he cannot represent them, and of course not consent to any thing in their behalf. While *Great-Britain*'s representatives do not sit assembled in Parliament, no tax whatever can be laid by any power on *Great-Britain*'s inhabitants; it is plain therefore, that without representation there can be no taxation. If representation arises entirely from the free election of the people, it is plain that the elected are not representatives in their own right, but by virtue of their election; and it is not less so, that the electors cannot confer any right on those whom they elect but what is inherent in themselves; the electors of *London* cannot confer or give any right to their members to lay a tax on *Westminster*, but the election made of them doubtless empowers them to agree to or differ from any measures they think agreeable or disagreeable to their constituents, or the kingdom in general. If the representatives have no right but what they derive from their electors and election, and if the electors have no right to elect any representatives but for themselves, and if the right of sitting in the House of Commons arises only from the election of those designed to be representatives, it is undeniable, that the power of taxation in the House of Commons cannot extend any further than to those who have delegated them for that purpose; and if none of the electors in *England* could give a power to those whom they elected to represent or tax any other part of his Majesty's dominions except themselves, it must follow, that when the Commons are met, they represent no other place or part of his Majesty's dominions, and cannot give away the property but of those who have given them a power so to do by choosing them their representatives.

The Parliament hath the sole right to lay on taxes, and, as hath been observed in Parliament, 'tis not the King and Lords that GIVE and GRANT, but this is the sole act of the Commons. The Commons have the right to do so either from the crown or people, or it is a right inherent in themselves. It cannot be inherent in themselves, for they are not born representatives, but are so by election, and that not for life, but only for a certain time; neither can they derive it from the crown, else the liberty and property of the subject must be entirely in the disposal and possession of the crown; but if they hold it entirely from the people, they cannot hold it from any other people but those who have chosen them to be their representatives, and it should seem they cannot extend their power of taxing beyond the limits of time and place, nor indeed for any other purpose but that for which they have been chosen. As the Commons in Parliament cannot lay any tax but what they must pay themselves, and falls equally on the whole kingdom of *England*, so, by a fundamental law, they cannot lay but such a part of the general tax on some part of the united kingdom. The principality of *Wales* was never taxed by Parliament till it was incorporated and represented, and, poor as it is, it pays now considerably larger than *Scotland*, which is as big again. When *England* is taxed two millions in the land tax, no more is paid in *Scotland* than 48,000*l*. and yet to lay a higher land tax on *North Britain* the *British* Parliament cannot, it cannot without breaking the union, that is, a fundamental law of the kingdom. All the right it hath to tax *Scotland* arises from and must be executed in the terms of the union.*

The Islands of *Guernsey, &c.* are not taxed by the *British* Parliament at all, they still have their own States, and I never heard that the *British* Parliament ever offered to hinder them to lay on their own taxes, or to lay on additional ones, where they are not represented.

Ireland is a conquered kingdom, the greater part of its inhabitants *Papists*, who in *England* pay double tax. The *Romans* always made a difference between their colonies and their conquests, and as reasonable, allowed greater and indeed all common liberties to the former. *Ireland* hath been conquered twice again upon the natives since its first conquest, nevertheless it hitherto had its own legislature; if the Parliament of *Great-Britain* claims a right to tax them, they never yet have made use of the right, and seeing for ages past they enjoyed

---

* While *Scotland* was yet a separate kingdom, it was once debated in Parliament, whether a subsidy should first be granted, or overtures for liberty first be considered; when the Queen's Ministry insisted on the former, a member urged, that it was now plain the nation was to expect no return for their expence and toil, but to be put to the charge of a subsidy, and to lay down their necks under the yoke of slavery, *&c.* Another member said, that he insisted for having a vote upon the question which had been put: That he found as the liberties of the nation were suppressed, so the privileges of Parliament were like to be torn from them, but that he would rather venture his life than that it should be so, and should chuse rather *to die a freeman* than *live a slave*. Some pressed for the vote, adding that if there was no other way of obtaining so natural and undeniable a privilege of the Parliament, *they would demand it with their swords in their hands*.

See Annals of Queen *Anne* 1703, page 76. These were no *American* speakers.

the privilege of having their own property disposed of by representatives in a Parliament of their own, it is very natural to suppose, that they think themselves entitled to these things, and the more so, because, in the very bill that determines their dependency, they are not said to be dependent on the *British* Parliament, nor yet on crown and Parliament, but only on the crown of *Great-Britain*.

I would now proceed to take a distinct view of the point in debate between *Great-Britain* and her colonies.

It seems to be a prevailing opinion in *Great-Britain*, that the Parliament hath a right to tax the *Americans*, and that, unless they have so, *America* would be independent of *Great-Britain*.

And it seems to be a prevailing opinion in *America*, that to be taxed without their consent, and where they are not and cannot be represented, would deprive them of the rights of *Englishmen*, nay, in time, with the loss of the constitution, would deprive them of liberty and property altogether.

It is easily seen, that this is a very interesting subject, the consequences in each case very important, though in neither so alarming and dangerous to *Britain* as to *America*. With regard to *Great-Britain*, if it should not prove so as is claimed, the consequence can only be this, that then no tax can be laid, or revenue be raised, on the *Americans*, but where they are represented, and in a manner which they think consistent with their natural rights as men, and with their civil and constitutional liberties as *Britons*. The dependency of *America* upon *Great-Britain* will be as full and firm as ever, and they will chearfully comply with the requisitions of the crown in a constitutional manner. The question is not, whether the *Americans* will withdraw their subordination, or refuse their assistance, but, whether they themselves shall give their own property, where they are legally represented, or, whether the Parliament of *Great-Britain*, which does not represent them, shall take their property, and dispose of it in the same manner as they do theirs whom in Parliament they actually represent. The *Americans* do not plead for a right to withhold, but freely and chearfully to give. If 100,000*l.* are to be raised, the question is not, shall they be raised or no? but shall the Parliament levy so much upon the *Americans*, and order them to pay it, as a gift and grant of the Commons of *Great-Britain* to the King? or, shall the *Americans* also have an opportunity to shew their loyalty and readiness to serve the King by freely granting it to the King themselves? It is not to be denied the *Americans* apprehend, that if any power, no matter what the name, where they are not represented, hath a right to lay a tax on them at pleasure, all their liberty and property is at an end, and they are upon a level with the meanest slaves.

England will not lose a shilling in point of property; the rights and privileges of the good people of *Britain* will not be in the least affected, supposing the claim of the *Americans* just and to take place; whereas every thing dreadful appears in view to the *Americans* if it should turn out otherwise. The crown cannot lose; the *Americans* are as willing to comply with every constitutional requisition as the *British* Parliament itself can possibly be. The Parliament cannot lose, it will still have all the power and authority it hitherto had, and ought to have had, and when every branch of the legislature, and every member of the *British* empire, has a true regard to reciprocal duty, prerogative and privilege, the happiness of the whole is best likely to be secured and promoted.

The *Americans* most solemnly disclaim every thought, and the very idea of independency; they are sometimes afraid they are charged with a desire of it, not because this appears to be the real case, but to set their arguments in an invidious light, and to make them appear odious in the sight of their mother country. This is not a dispute about a punctilio, the difference in the consequence is amazingly great; supposing *America* is not taxed where not represented, and supposing things are left upon the same footing in which with manifest advantage to *Britain* and *America* they have been ever since *Britain* had colonies, neither the trade nor authority of *Britain* suffers the least diminution, but the mischief to the colonies is beyond all expression, if the contrary should take place. If they are not to raise their own taxes, all their Assemblies become useless in a moment, all their respective legislatures are annihilated at a stroke; an act passed by persons, most of whom probably never saw, nor cared much for *America*, may destroy all the acts they ever passed, may lay every burden upon them under which they are not expected immediately to sink, and all their civil and religious liberties, for which their forefathers went into this wilderness, and, under the smiles of Heaven, turned it into a garden, and of immense consequence to the mother country, will, or may be at an end at once. Probably the present Parliament or generation would never carry matters to this length, but who knows what might be done in the next? The first settlers of the *American* wilds never expected that would come to pass what we have seen already. It seems as if some evil genius had prevailed of late; had these new duties been laid on payable in *England*, at least the expence of a Board of Commissioners, and of the swarms of new officers, might have been prevented; but it looks as though some men wished that *America* might not only be borne hard upon, but also be made to know and feel that their liberty and property lay at the mercy of others, and that they must not flatter themselves to enjoy them any longer than the good pleasure of some who would willingly take away what *they* never did give. I have endeavoured candidly to state the question, let us now endeavour to view the claim made on each side as calmly and impartially as possible.

'Tis said the *British* Parliament hath a right to tax the *Americans*. If this proposition is incontrovertible, it must certainly be built on such a basis and such clear principles as will be sufficient to dispose loyal and reasonable men chearfully to acquiesce in it. There are some points in government which perhaps are best never touched upon, but when any question once becomes the subject of publick debate, strength of reason is the sole authority that with men of reason can determine the matter.

If the Parliament of *Great-Britain* have a right to tax the *Americans*, it must either be the same right in virtue of which they have a right to tax *Great-Britain*, and be vested in them by the same power, or it must be a distinct right either inherent in themselves, or vested in them by some other power.

The right of the Commons of *Great-Britain* to lay on taxes arises, as I conceive, from their having been chosen by the people who are to pay these taxes to act in their behalf and as their representatives. There may be other qualifications necessary, that a man be a *Briton* born, subject of the King, possessed of a certain estate, *&c.* but none is so absolutely necessary as election. He that hath been a representative had a right to refuse or concur in any tax bill whilst a member, but if he is not chosen again in a following Parliament, he hath no right whatever to meddle in the matter; this proves that the power is originally in the people, and the legislative capacity of the whole House, and of every member, depends upon their free election, and is of force no longer than for the time for which they have been elected; this being elapsed, the trust reposed in them entirely ceases, it absolutely returns to the body of the people; in that interval during which the people are unrepresented, any power their representatives might have is entirely and solely in the people themselves, no tax can be laid on, nor any law to bind the people be formed, for this plain reason, because there are no persons qualified for the purpose. The people have not representatives assigned, but chuse them, and being so chosen, the rights of the people reside now in them, and they may, but not before, act in their behalf. Now, when the crown issues writs of election, it is not to empower the electors to chuse representatives for *America*, nor yet for all *Great-Britain*, but only for some certain place specified in the writ; and when the electors of *Great-Britain* chuse representatives, their meaning also is not to chuse representatives for their fellow subjects in *America*, or any where else, but for themselves. In *Great-Britain English* electors cannot elect in behalf of *Scotland*, and *Scotch* electors cannot in behalf of *England*; and for the same reason neither *Scotch* nor *English* can elect any for *America*. These electors do not represent the *Americans*, nor are they their proxies to vote in members in their behalf; neither can *British* electors give any instructions to *British* representatives, or invest them with any power to dispose of the rights and property of any of their fellow subjects without the kingdom of *Great-Britain*. It seems not unreasonable then to conclude, that the right which the elected acquire by their election to pass tax laws binding upon their electors does not at the same time give them a right to represent and lay on taxes on those who never invested them with any such power, and by whom they neither were nor could be elected. If the *Americans* themselves are not received as voters in the bishoprick of *Durham*, manor of *East Greenwich*, or any place mentioned in their charters, and the same liberty and privileges with those places therein secured unto them, if they are not allowed to chuse any representatives for themselves in the House of Commons, it seems natural, that what they have no right to do themselves, none can have a right to do for them, and so no body can chuse or send a representative for them to any place where they are not allowed to sit or be represented. If so, the electors of *Great-Britain* never in fact elected representatives for *America*, nor could these electors possibly convey any power to give away property where they have no property themselves. The electors do not represent *America*, neither their representatives by them elected; the electors cannot dispose of the property of *America*, therefore they cannot give a power so to do unto others. In *England* there can be no taxation without representation, and no representation without election; but it is undeniable that the representatives of *Great-Britain* are not elected by nor for the *Americans*, and therefore cannot represent them; and so, if the Parliament of *Great-Britain* has a right to tax *America*, that right cannot possibly be grounded on the consideration that the people of *Great-Britain* have chosen them their representatives, without which choice they would be no Parliament at all.

If the Parliament of *Great-Britain* has a right to tax the *Americans* distinct from the right which they derive from their electors, and which they exercise as the representatives of the people of *Great-Britain*, then this right they must hold either from the crown, or from the *Americans*, or else it must be a native inherent right in themselves, at least a consequence of their being representatives of the people of *Great-Britain*.

It is plain that the colonies have been settled by authority and under the sanction of the crown, but as the crown did not reserve unto itself a right to rule over them without their own Assemblies, but on the contrary established legislatures among them, as it did not reserve a right to lay taxes on them in a manner which, were the experiment made in *England*, might be thought unconstitutional, so neither do I find that a reserve of that kind was made by the crown in favour of the Parliament, on the contrary, by the charters all the inhabitants were promised the enjoyment of the same and all privileges of his Majesty's liege subjects in *England*, of which doubtless not to be taxed where they are not represented is one of the principal. As to any right that might accrue to Parliament from any act or surrender of the *Americans*, I believe it hath never been thought of; they have a profound veneration for the *British* Parliament, they look upon it as the great palladium of the *British* liberties, but still they are not there represented, they have had their own legislatures and representatives for ages past, and as a body cannot be more than in one place at once, they think they cannot be legally represented in more than one legislative body, but also think, that by the laws of *England Protestants* ought not to be doubly taxed, or, what they think worse, taxed in two places.

If therefore this right of taxing the *Americans* resides in the Commons of *Great Britain* at all, it must be an inherent right in themselves, or at least in consequence of their being representatives of the people of *Great-Britain*. The act for better securing the dependency of the colonies, which I have inserted at large, evidently seems to tend this way. That the colonies were thought at the disposal of Parliament one might be led to think, because by that act, from the simple authority of the crown, which they were till then subject to by their charters, they were now declared to be subordinate to and dependent (on the joint authority) of crown and Parliament. Yet, concerning this act, I would only observe, that however it may determine the case from that day, it cannot be the ground on which the subordination of the colonies originally WAS or now can be built; for it declares not only, that the colonies ARE AND OUGHT TO BE, but also that they ALWAYS HAVE BEEN, subject to crown and Parliament. A law binds after it is made, it cannot bind before it exists, and so surely it cannot be said, that the colonies have *always* been bound by a law which is above a hundred years posterior to them in point of existence. It is also a little difficult to reconcile this law with prior charters; our *Carolina* charter makes our province subject immediately to the crown, and near a hundred years after a law is made to declare, that this was not and must not be the case, but that the *Americans* always were and ought to be subject to crown and Parliament. Perhaps this hath not been so seriously considered as it may hereafter, but neither this nor any law can be supposed to be binding *ex post facto*, or contrary to our fundamental constitution. *Montesquieu* observes, that the *British* constitution (which God preserve) will be lost, whenever the legislative power shall be more corrupted than the executive part of the legislature.

And after all, in this very law, the *Americans* are allowed to be represented in their own Assemblies, and to lay on duties and taxes, though not exclusively; but whether *America*, or any part of the *British* empire, should be liable to have taxes imposed on them by different legislatures, and whether these would not frequently clash with one another to the detriment of crown and subjects, I leave others duly to consider.

It is said, if *America* cannot be taxed by the *British* Parliament, then it would be independent of *Great-Britain*. This is now a very popular cry, and it is well if many join in it only because they know no better. This is not, will not, cannot be the case. *America* confessedly hath not been thus taxed since it was settled; but no body in *Britain* or *America* ever dreamed that *America* was independent. In *England* the people cannot be taxed when the Parliament does not sit, or when it is dissolved; are they then therefore independent. *Scotland* cannot be taxed in the same degree as *England*; is it therefore independent? *Ireland* and *Jersey* have their own legislatures, and so tax themselves; will you call them independent? All those parts of the *British* empire that have no Assemblies pay no taxes at all, neither among themselves, nor to *Great-Britain*; but it will not therefore be said, that they are independent. The Parliament itself claims a right to refuse supplies till their grievances are heard and redressed, this is looked upon as a constitutional remedy against any encroachments by the crown, and hath very often been made use of in former reigns, and yet the Parliament neither claimed nor were charged with a desire of independency. Those who so freely charge with a desire of independency, and even treason and rebellion, would do well to consider, that this charge, heinous as it is, reflects greater disgrace on those who unjustly make it, than on those on whom it is unjustly made. A man of honour would not easily forgive himself whenever he should discover that he made so rash a charge against two millions of people, as innocent, loyal, and well affected to their King and country, as any of his fellow subjects or himself possibly can be. There never was an *American Jacobite*, the very air of *America* is death to such monsters, never any grew there, and if any are transported, or import themselves, loss of speech always attends them. The loyalty of the *Americans* to their King hath not only been ever untainted, it hath never been as much as suspected. There is a difference between independency and uneasiness. In the late reign, the people in *England* were uneasy at the *Jew* Bill, and it was rapidly repealed; in the present, the Cyder Act was an odious measure, and immediately altered, and that without any disgrace or diminution of parliamentary authority. If there hath been any appearance of riot in *America*, perhaps it may hereafter appear at whose instigation, the law was ever open, and even overbearing odious Custom-House Officers might have been redressed, if they had thought fit to apply for a legal rather than a military remedy. In *England* it is possible Majesty itself hath met with indignities which have not been shewn in *America* even to those men to whom the nation in general is indebted for the present uneasiness, and it is not improbable, that, after all that hath been said and done, the *Americans* will be found an exception to the general rule, that oppression makes even a wise man mad: An ancient rule, the truth of which hath been experienced in *England* oftener than in *America*. The opinion of the *Americans* is, that to be taxed where they are not represented would deprive them of the rights of *Englishmen*, nay, in time, with the loss of the constitution, might and must deprive them of liberty and property altogether. These it must be owned are gloomy apprehensions; two millions of people are so thoroughly prepossessed with them, that even their children unborn may feel the parents impressions; should there be any real ground for them, the *Americans* can hardly be blamed; they sit uneasy under them; they can no more help their uneasiness, than deny the blood which glows in their veins, or be angry with the milk that was their first nourishment. This is not a dark abstruse point, but seems plain and essential to the very being of liberty. The sole question is, Is it, or is it not, the right of an *Englishman* not to be taxed where he is not represented? Can you be tired of being represented, O *Britons!* Is it consistent with the constitution you so justly boast of to be thus taxed? Then representation is not essential to your constitution, and sooner or later you will either give it up or be deprived of it. A borough that does not exist shall send two representatives, a single country, neither the largest nor richest, shall send forty-four members, and two millions of souls, and an extent of land of eighteen hundred miles in length, shall have taxes laid on them by such as never were nearer to them than one thousand leagues, and whose interest it may be to lay heavy burdens on them in order to lighten their own. And are these, who are thus taxed, unrepresented, unheard and unknown, *Englishmen*, and taxed by *Englishmen*? Do these enjoy what the charters most solemnly ensure them, the same and all the privileges of the subjects born and resident within the realm? I must doubt it.

Let those who make light of *American* grievances give a plain answer to this plain question, Are the colonies to be taxed by Parliament represented in Parliament? if they are, by whom, or since when? if not, once more, Is it, or is it not, the right of *Britons* not to be taxed where not represented? Here the whole matter hinges, and surely the question is not so impertinent but a civil answer might be given before a mother sends fire and sword into her own bowels. When constitutional liberty is once lost, the transit is very short to the loss of property; the same power that may deprive of the one may also deprive of the other, and with equal justice; those that have not liberty enough to keep their property in reality have no property to keep. Some that look no further build right upon power, and insist the Parliament can do so. If power is all that is meant very like it may, so it may alter the constitution. If a stately tree should take umbrage at some diminutive shrubs, it can fall upon and crush them, but it cannot fall upon them without tearing up its own roots; it can crush those within reach, but its own branches will take off the weight of the impression, permit the shrubs to send forth new shoots, while there is no greater probability that the envious oak will return to its former stand and vigour. *C'est une chose a bien considerer*, (this ought to be well considered first) said *Moliere's Malade imaginaire*, when his quack proposed to him to have one of his arms cut off, because it took some of the nourishment which in that case would center in the other, and make it so much the stronger. If every Assembly in *America* is suspended, the consequence must be, that the people are without their usual legislature, and in that case nothing short of a miracle seems capable to prevent an anarchy and general confusion.

No power can alter the nature of things, that which is wrong cannot be right, and oppression will never be productive of the love and smiles of those that feel it.

The Parliament can crush the *Americans*, but it can also, and with infinitely greater certainty and ease, conciliate their affections, have the ultimate gain of all their labours, and by only continuing them the privileges of *Britons*, that is, by only doing as they would be done by, diffuse the blessings of love and concord throughout the whole empire, and to the latest posterity; and which of these two is the most eligible, it is NOW for you, O *Britons!* to consider, and in considering it, *majores vestros cogitate & posteres*, think on your ancestors and your posterity.

Those whom God hath joined together, (Great-Britain *and* America, *Liberty and Loyalty*) *let no man put asunder: And may peace and prosperity ever attend this happy union.*

FEB. 1, 1769.

[William Knox], The Controversy Between Great Britain and Her Colonies Reviewed; the Several Pleas of the Colonies, in Support of Their Right to All the Liberties and Privileges of British Subjects, and to Exemption from the Legislative Authority of Parliament, Stated and Considered; and the Nature of Their Connection with, and Dependence on, Great Britain, Shewn, upon the Evidence of Historical Facts and Authentic Records. London, 1769.

William Knox was one of the many sub-ministers in the British bureaucracy who for decades had sought to reform the empire but had been stymied by Whig politicians reluctant to enhance the Crown's power. Now with the instability of politics at the ministerial level in the 1760s, they at long last had an opportunity to make their voices heard. Although Knox wrote several pamphlets in defense of imperial policies, this one had the distinction of busting the imperial debate wide open. By the time the air cleared the controversy had come to rest on new ground. In 1765 the main issue had been representation —to what extent could the colonists be considered represented in Parliament? After the appearance of Knox's pamphlet the central issue of sovereignty could no longer be avoided—where and with whom did the final, supreme, indivisible authority in the empire lie?

Sovereignty was the most important doctrine in eighteenth-century English political and legal culture. It had developed gradually out of the seventeenth-century debates until by the middle of the eighteenth century it had come to dominate most English constitutional thinking. As the famous English jurist William Blackstone declared in his *Commentaries on the Laws of England* (1765), all governments had to have one final, supreme, irresistible, and absolute law-making authority. In Great Britain that authority, that sovereignty, lay in Parliament. Its power was uncontrollable except by itself. It could determine the succession to the crown. It could alter the established religion of the land. It could even change the constitution of the realm. "It can, in short," wrote Blackstone, "do every thing that is not naturally impossible."

Although other British polemicists had invoked this doctrine of parliamentary sovereignty, Knox exploited it more fully than anyone before. He was merciless in mocking the colonists' "absurdities and contradictions" in accepting Parliament's right to regulate their trade but not its right to tax them. Could they not understand that parliamentary sovereignty was indivisible? If Parliament even "in one instance" was as supreme over the colonists as over the people of England, then, said Knox, the Americans were members "of the same community with the people of England." But if Parliament's authority over the colonists was denied "in any particular," then it must be denied in "all instances" and the union between the mother country and its colonies must be dissolved. "There is no alternative: either the Colonies are a part of the community of Great Britain, or they are in a state of nature with respect to her, and in no case can be subject to the jurisdiction of that legislative power which represents her community, which is the British parliament."

This bold assertion of the logic of sovereignty now compelled many Americans to rethink their position.

THE
CONTROVERSY
BETWEEN
Great Britain and her Colonies
REVIEWED;

THE SEVERAL PLEAS OF THE COLONIES,
In Support of their Right to all the Liberties
and Privileges of BRITISH Subjects, and to
Exemption from the Legiſlative Authority of
Parliament,

STATED AND CONSIDERED;

AND

The Nature of their Connection with, and
Dependence on, GREAT BRITAIN,

SHEWN,

UPON THE EVIDENCE OF
HISTORICAL FACTS
AND
AUTHENTIC RECORDS.

LONDON:
Printed for J. ALMON, oppoſite Burlington-Houſe, in
Piccadilly.   MDCCLXIX.

A Review of the Controversy Between Great Britain and Her Colonies.

"HE that goeth about to persuade a multitude, that they are not so well governed as they ought to be (says the learned and judicious *Hooker*) shall never want attentive and favourable hearers; because such as openly reprove supposed disorders of state, are taken for principal friends to the common benefit of all, and for men that carry singular freedom of mind. Under this fair and plausible colour, whatsoever they utter passeth for good and current. That which wanteth in the weight of their speech is supplied by the aptness of mens minds to accept and believe it. Whereas, on the other side, if we maintain things that are established, we have to strive with a number of heavy prejudices, deeply rooted in the hearts of men, who think that herein we serve the time, and speak in favour of the present state, because thereby we either hold or seek preferment." Hence it is that the grossest absurdities pass for irrefragable arguments in the mouth of a popular declaimer, whilst the clearest deductions of reason, on the side of authority, are termed delusive sophistry, and the artful chicane of a courtier. Hence it is also that so few men of talents are willing to hazard their reputation on the success of their arguments in defence of government, or to become volunteers in the cause of truth, whilst calumny and falshood are propagated amongst the people against their rulers without contradiction, and even sometimes with the indolent acquiescence of men of enlightened understandings and candid hearts. Yet surely the task of asserting the rights of government, maintaining the authority of the supreme power over the whole community, of calling back the misguided multitude from factious combinations, and persuading them to unite in promoting the public happiness, by yielding a chearful obedience to the laws, and cherishing a zealous attachment to our excellent constitution, ought not to be left to the panegyrists of ministers, to those only who "hold or seek preferment." Is it the duty of the hirelings of an administration only, to inform the people of the extent of their rights, and to exhort them to their duty? To expose the malevolent designs, and detect the artifices of their seducers? To

617

point out to them the dangers which beset them, and the fatal consequences which hang over them? To shew to them the hazard they run of losing their substantial liberty, by pursuing the *ignus fatuus* which they have been deluded to follow? Shall we see our fellow-subjects in the Colonies intoxicated with a fond conceit of their own importance, and charmed by the flattering whispers of independency, forsaking the *guide of their youth*, the sure stay of all their liberties, and the protector of all their rights and possessions, the parliament of Great Britain; and throwing themselves into the arms of prerogative, and putting all their confidence in the good pleasure of the crown? Is the British empire to be suffered to be rent in pieces, and each member of it exposed to become a prey to its powerful neighbour, from a vain imagination that there is no supreme power in the state, which has authority to command the strength, the riches, and the swords of all the subjects of the realm, to defend every part of its dominions, and to protect the rights and possessions of every individual who lives under it? Are we to fold our hands, and submit ourselves to the pressure of these calamities, because the followers of a minister do not think the cause of their patron concerned, or his stability endangered, or because the shafts of calumny and detraction are ready to be launched against whoever is hardy enough to endeavour to stop the madness of the people?

Far be it from me to wish to be thought insensible to the good or ill opinion of my countrymen; but as I consider it to be my duty to promote their welfare to the utmost of my poor ability, I will *shew them my opinion*, whether they may reward or censure me for my endeavours.—On this principle, and actuated by these motives, it is, that, unawed by the terrors which rise before me, I adventure upon my present undertaking; and I set down to review the American controversy, with the single, and I hope honest, purpose of bringing back my fellow-subjects in the Colonies to a just sense of their duty to the supreme legislative power, by exposing to them the fallacies by which they have been deluded, and exploring the dangers which the paths wherein they are now bewildered must unavoidably lead them into.

The several pleas which have been urged by those who have distinguished themselves in this controversy, on behalf of the

Colonies, may be comprehended under these two general heads:

The title of the inhabitants in the Colonies to all the rights, liberties, and privileges of Englishmen;—and their claim to exemption from the jurisdiction of parliament.

It should seem to be of the utmost importance to the Colonies, that the former plea was established before they adduced any proofs in support of the latter; for, should they fail in the one, nothing could be more fatal to their freedom, and consequently to their prosperity, than their succeeding in the other.

If they should unhappily be able to demonstrate, that the Colonies are no part of the British state; that they are the king's domain, and not annexed to the realm; that the inhabitants are not British subjects, nor within the jurisdiction of parliament; they can have no title to such privileges and immunities as the people of England derive under acts of parliament, nor to any other of those rights which are peculiar to British subjects within the realm. What would then be their situation it behoves them well to consider; and before they reject the authority of parliament, they ought seriously and dispassionately to weigh the consequences, and be very well assured, that whilst they are labouring to free themselves from the present inconveniencies, which the jurisdiction of parliament subjects them to, they do not, by avoiding them, run into difficulties much more embarrassing, and expose themselves to hardships much more intolerable. They ought to reflect, that whatever may be their condition, they cannot apply to parliament to better it. If they reject the jurisdiction of parliament, they must not in any case sue for its interposition in their behalf. Whatever grievances they may have to complain of, they must seek redress from the grace of the crown alone; for, should they petition parliament to do them right, they themselves have authorized the crown to tell parliament, as the secretary of state to James the First did the house of commons, "America is not annexed to the realm, nor within the jurisdiction of parliament, you have therefore no right to interfere."

Such being the case, we are therefore to expect to find the strongest efforts of the colony advocates directed to this point. We may indeed look for the clearest evidence, the most convincing arguments, and even demonstrative proofs of their right to these privileges, independent of acts of parliament, since we see them so eager to preclude parliament from the power of conveying to them any privilege whatever. Let us then see on what they found their title.

In May 1765, the house of burgesses in Virginia resolved, "That the first adventurers and settlers of this his majesty's colony and dominion of Virginia, brought with them and transmitted to their posterity, and all other his majesty's subjects since inhabiting in this his majesty's said colony, all the liberties, privileges, franchises, and immunities, that have at any time been held and enjoyed, and possessed by the people of Great-Britain."

This resolution is adopted by the assembly of Maryland, and repeated in the very same words: and as the assembly of Virginia has been said to have hung out the standard for American liberty, and the other Colonies have little more merit than that of following their leader, I must confess I expected to have found a *much clearer* proof of the truth of the proposition contained in their resolution than I am able to collect from the terms in which it is expressed. They tell us indeed "That the *first adventurers* in the reign of James the First, *brought with them, and transmitted to their posterity*, &c. all the liberties, privileges, franchises, and immunities, that the people of Great-Britain have at *any time* (since as well as before) enjoyed and possessed." But in what sort of *menstruum, nucleous*, or *embryo*, it was that they carried with them to Virginia, in the reign of James the First, the *habeas corpus* act, which the people of England did not enjoy or possess till the reign of Charles the Second; or the bill of rights, which they did not enjoy till the reign of William and Mary; the acts for altering the succession and the limitation of the crown, and many others passed in that and the subsequent reigns; as they have not condescended to inform their friends in England, so they can only expect us to admire their profound logical skill, and must content themselves with the more *rational applause* of their countrymen, who they may have more fully instructed.

The assembly of Pennsylvania, by their resolutions in the same year, declare, "That the inhabitants of this province *are intitled* to all the liberties, rights, and privileges of his majesty's subjects in Great-Britain, or *elsewhere*; and that the constitution of government in this province is founded on the *natural rights* of mankind, and the *noble principles* of English liberty, and therefore *is* or *ought* to be *perfectly free*."

This resolution asserts in like manner, as do the resolutions of Virginia and Maryland, that the people of that colony *are intitled* to all the rights of British subjects; but it does not pretend that the *first settlers* carried them there: neither does it found their claim to them upon the royal charter to the proprietor, or upon the laws of Great-Britain, but upon the "natural rights of mankind, and the noble principles of English liberty."

That *the natural rights of mankind* should give any people a right to all the liberties and privileges of Englishmen, is, I believe, a doctrine unknown to all civilians, except the assembly of Pennsylvania. It is indeed a most benevolent doctrine; for if it be established, it will render the blessings which British subjects enjoy under their excellent constitution universal to all people, at least to all those who live under any constitution of government which is founded upon the natural rights of mankind, in whatever part of the world they may inhabit, or whoever may be their sovereign. The native Indians in North America, the Hottentots at the Cape of Good Hope, the Tartars, Arabs, Cafres, and Groenlanders, will all have an equal title to the liberties and rights of Englishmen, with the people of Pennsylvania; for all their constitutions of government are founded on the *natural rights* of mankind.

The *noble principle of English liberty* is, however, another and more peculiar foundation for the constitution of the government in Pennsylvania; but where to find these *noble principles* of English liberty, except it be in the laws of the land, I confess I am ignorant: and if the assembly of Pennsylvania got them *elsewhere*, it would have been kind in them to have informed the world whence they had them, that other nations might have drawn from the same precious fountain. But, not to press too hard upon such tender ground, the consequence of their discovering these nobles principles, and of having founded their constitution of government upon them, it seems is, that "the constitution of government in Pennsylvania *is* or *ought* to be *perfectly free*."

To be *perfectly free* is, I apprehend, to be in a state of nature absolutely independent of, and uncontrolable by, any other, in all cases whatever: and when applied to states, is the most complete definition of equality and independency that can be given. It excludes all possibility of a superior or paramount, and furnishes us with a full idea of supreme and unlimited jurisdiction. No law of another state can have force within that territory, nor can the inhabitants be amenable to any foreign judicature. No act whatever of the British parliament is or ought to be therefore of force in Pennsylvania, otherways the government of that *country* (I must not henceforth call it *province*, for that term implies dependence) cannot be, as it *is* or *ought to be*, perfectly free. The act of the 7th and 8th of king William, which declares, that "all laws, bye-laws, usages, and customs, which shall be in practice in any of the Plantations, repugnant to any law made or to be made in this kingdom relative to the said Plantations, shall be void and of none effect," is plainly inconsistent with this *perfect freedom* of the Pennsylvania constitution of government, and therefore it *is not*, or *ought* not to be, of force: neither indeed *ought* the act of the 5th of George the Second, which makes the lands in America assets for the payment of debts, nor any other of the several acts of parliament which relate to the Plantations, to be executed within the jurisdiction of the government of Pennsylvania. Had the *Examiner of the Claim of the Colonies* been acquainted with this resolution when he wrote his pamphlet, he probably would not have given so much offence to the author of *The Considerations on the Propriety of imposing Taxes*, as that gentleman has taken, at his producing acts of parliament in evidence of the right of parliament to dispose of the property of the people in Pennsylvania and the other American Colonies, for that resolution abrogates them all alike. None of them *is* or *ought* to be of force within that government; and instead of censuring the chief justice for denying the authority of one act of parliament, when he admitted the authority of so many others, he would have blamed him for having admitted the authority of any, perhaps have accused him in so doing of denying the *perfect freedom of the constitution of the government of Pennsylvania*. We now see the reason of the assertion in the former part of this resolution: "that the constitution of the government is founded on the natural rights of mankind;" and the inference drawn therefrom, that all mankind have a natural right to the liberties, privileges, &c. of British subjects: for if that be not the case, it will be impossible for the people of Pennsylvania to have any right to such of them as are contained in acts of parliament, because those acts *cannot*, or at least *ought not*, as we have seen, to have any force there.

The assembly of Massachusets Bay support their claim to all the rights and privileges of British subjects by the following resolutions, entered upon their journals the 29th of October 1765.

"RESOLVED, That there are certain essential rights of the *British constitution* of government, which are founded in the *law of God* and *nature*, and are the *common rights of mankind*: Therefore,

RESOLVED, That the inhabitants of this province are un-alienably intitled to those *essential rights* in *common with all men*.

RESOLVED, That his majesty's subjects in America are in *reason* and *common sense* intitled to the *same extent* of liberty with his majesty's subjects in Britain.

RESOLVED, That by the declaration of *the royal charter* of this province, the inhabitants are intitled to all *the rights, liberties*, and *immunities* of free and natural-born subjects of Great-Britain, to all intents, purposes, and constructions whatever.

RESOLVED, That the inhabitants of this province appear to be intitled to *all the rights aforementioned*, by an *act of parliament* the 13th of George the Second.

RESOLVED, That *those rights* do belong to the inhabitants of this province upon *principles of common justice*."

Here we see that the *law of God and Nature*, the *common rights of mankind, reason and common sense*, the *royal charter*, an *act of parliament*, and *common justice*, are all so many pillars on which the assembly of Massachusets found their claim to the rights and privileges of British subjects; and where the props are so numerous, it will be hard indeed if none of them prove strong enough to support the building. Far be it from me to deny to the inhabitants of Massachusets a participation in and of *such rights and privileges* as British subjects are inti-tled to in *common with all* mankind, or such as we derive from the *laws of God* or *Nature*. *Such rights* they are certainly intitled to, as they are men, and as they are Christians; but all men, and all Christians, are not intitled to the rights and privileges of every *particular society of which they are not members or subjects.* Every society has rights and privileges peculiar to those who compose that society; and when we treat of the rights and privileges of the members of that society, we must be understood to mean *such privileges* as are *peculiar* to that society, and not such as are the common rights and privileges of all Christian men. When therefore we are discussing the *rights and privileges of British subjects*, we must confine our enquiries to such rights as a natural-born subject of the British society or state is intitled to, and to which an *alien*, or one who is not a member of that society, has no claim. The laws of *God* or of *Nature*, or the *common rights* of mankind, cannot therefore give the inhabitants of Massachusets any title to the *peculiar* privileges of British subjects, if they are not also members of the British community or state. The laws of God and of nature, and the common rights of mankind, would indeed equally serve to support their claim to the rights and privileges of Dutchmen, Frenchmen, Italians, or of any other Christian society or state, as to justify their pretensions to the rights and privileges of British subjects.

Reason and common sense are much fitter to be employed in proving the goodness of a title, than to be set up themselves as a title. *Reason* and *common sense* are faculties of the mind, by which the truth or falshood of any proposition is tried, but they are not in themselves either principles or propositions; when therefore we shall have tried and examined the several propositions on which the colony assemblies found their claim to all the rights and privileges of British subjects, we shall then see whether they are intitled to them *in reason and common sense*, or not.

A *royal charter*, it must be allowed, conveys a clear title to whatever it is in the right or prerogative of the crown to grant; but it is not the prerogative of the crown to make free denizens of aliens; that is, to bestow on *foreigners* the rights and privileges of natural-born subjects.—Every act of parliament for naturalizing a foreigner is a proof that it is not. The king of England, or any other king, may grant to any people who are their subjects rights and privileges *similar* to those enjoyed by the people of Great Britain; but no authority, other than the supreme legislature of Great Britain, can incorporate any individual or people into the British community, or make them partakers of the rights and privileges of British subjects. If the inhabitants of Massachusets are not therefore the natural born subjects of the realm of Great Britain, and a part of the British community, the king cannot by any act of his alone naturalize them, or give them a title to the rights and privileges of British subjects.

An *act of parliament* is indeed a sufficient authority to convey to any people who acknowledge its supremacy, the rights and privileges of British subjects; but I little expected to have seen an act of parliament appealed to by the assembly of Massachusets, as having conveyed to them any rights or privileges, when at the same time they are denying that parliament has any jurisdiction over them whatever. But it seems parliament has a right to *benefit* the colonies, but not to *bind* them: it may *give* them *bounties*, but it must not *impose burdens*. Its power over the colonies is somewhat like that allowed by the deists to the Almighty over his creatures, he may reward them with eternal happiness if he pleases, but he must not punish them on any account. Parliament however, I am afraid, will not be content with such a power, and I would not advise the Colonies to rely too much upon its good nature; for if it should find itself to have been *mistaken* in ranking the inhabitants in the Colonies among the subjects of the realm, and that it has granted the privileges and immunities of British subjects to those who are not of the British community, and disavow its authority over them; there might be danger of its recalling that grant, and declaring by another act of parliament, that the rights and privileges of British subjects shall not extend to the Colonies. Even the *principles of common justice*, which is the last pillar of the Massachusets assemblies title, would demand this of parliament; for it is the highest *injustice* that those who will not share in the burdens of the community, nor be bound by its laws, should partake of its benefits, and enjoy its privileges in common with those who are its members.

The assembly of New York introduce their resolutions of the 18th of December, 1765, with a declaration of "their faith and allegiance to his majesty king George the Third, and of *their submission to the supreme legislative power*," undertaking at the same time to shew "that the rights claimed by them, are *in no manner inconsistent with either*." Had the subsequent resolutions been conceived in the same spirit with this introduction, I should have been happy in applauding the wisdom of the assembly at New York, and have proposed their example for the instruction and imitation of all the other Colonies. God forbid that any of the inhabitants of the Colonies should be deprived of any "right which is consistent with their faith and allegiance to the king, and *their submission to the supreme legislative power*." To intitle them to all *such rights*, it is sufficient that they acknowledge themselves to be *subjects of the realm*, and that the supreme legislature admits them so to be; the resolution therefore which would be the plain consequent of this introduction is simply this, that the people of New York are *British subjects*, and thence intitled to all the rights, privileges, and immunities of their fellow subjects the people of England. But instead of this explicit declaration, that assembly resolves, "That *they* (the people of that Colony) owe obedience to all acts of parliament *not inconsistent with the essential rights and liberties of Englishmen*, and are intitled to the same rights and liberties which his majesty's *English subjects*, both *within* and *without* the realm, have ever enjoyed."

I would not be thought to find fault without reason; and yet if I do not *seek occasion* for offence in this resolution, I am sure I shall not find any; for who would wish that the people of New York, any more than the people of England, should pay obedience to any act of parliament which *is inconsistent with the rights and liberties of Englishmen*? and notwithstanding I may not be convinced of their title, yet as I sincerely desire that they may partake of all the rights and liberties which his majesty's *English subjects within* the realm enjoy; so do I most freely give them all the rights and liberties which his *English subjects without* the realm have ever enjoyed, although I profess I do not very well know what it is I am yielding when I say so, for I really am ignorant who his majesty's *English subjects without the realm* are, or what are the rights and liberties which they enjoy. I shall therefore leave this assembly in full possession of their resolutions, and only extract two other of them, which I shall hereafter have occasion to take notice of.

"RESOLVED, That it involves the greatest inconsistency with the known principles of the English constitution, to suppose that the honourable house of commons of Great Britain can, without divesting the inhabitants of this colony of their most essential rights, grant to the crown their, or any part of their estates for any purpose whatsoever.

RESOLVED, That from the first settlement of the Colonies, it has been the *sense of the government at home, that such grants could not be constitutionally made*, and therefore applications for the support of government, and other public exigencies, have *always* been made to the representatives of the people of this colony."

I come now to what Mr. Dickenson calls the American declaration of rights, which are the resolutions of the committees from the several Colony assemblies, which met at New York, 19 October, 1765. and here we may expect to find the separate and irregular claims of each Colony consolidated and reduced into system and consistency. Their resolutions are as follow:

"That his majesty's subjects in these Colonies owe the same allegiance to the crown of Great Britain that is owing from his subjects *born within the realm*, and *all due subordination* to that *august body*, the parliament of Great Britain.

That his majesty's *liege* subjects in these Colonies *are intitled* to all the *inherent rights* and liberties of his natural-born subjects within the kingdom of Great Britain."

In their petition to the house of commons they thus express themselves: "It is from and under the English constitution we derive all our civil and religious rites and liberties; we glory in being subjects of the best of kings, and having been born under the most perfect form of government." Further: "We esteem our connexions with and *dependence* on Great Britain as one of our greatest blessings; and apprehend the latter will appear to be sufficiently secure, when it is considered that the *inhabitants* in the Colonies have the most unbounded affection for his majesty's person, family, and government, as well as for the mother country, and that *their subordination* to the parliament is universally acknowledged."

A plain English reader of these resolutions and petitions would be apt to imagine these committees had, in effect, given up the point, and had fairly acknowledged the supreme authority of parliament over the Colonies; and that, as we all meant the same thing on both sides the water, it was not worth while to quarrel about the manner of expressing it. This the committees expected; and their skill in framing their resolutions and petitions would have been thrown away, if their manner of expressing themselves had not excited in the reader ideas much more extensive than the strict, even *English*, meaning of the term would justify.

What Englishman could desire more of the Colonies than *due obedience* to that august body, the parliament of Great Britain? But what is *due obedience* is a matter in which they and the people of England differ exceedingly; and the committees chose to reserve to the colonies *their own construction* of the terms, while they hoped the people of England would be led to believe they agreed with them in theirs.

An Englishman conceives due obedience to parliament to mean lawful obedience, or obedience to an act of parliament. The Colonies conceive the parliament to have no right to make laws for them; and due obedience to parliament is therefore, in their apprehension, no obedience at all. An Englishman, without treason, though perhaps not without mental falshood, may swear to pay all *due obedience* to the king of France; because, as he conceives that king to have no *right* to his obedience as an Englishman, he promises to pay him none. Where there is no right to require obedience, there can be none due; and to deny the right to the demand, and profess to pay what is due, is contemptible chicane.

The title of *August Body*, which they give the parliament, is another subterfuge for *seeming* to respect its authority, whilst they *mean* to disavow it. An august body it certainly is, and *foreigners* frequently call it so; but the subjects of the realm know it by another title, that of supreme legislature. That title would however have implied obedience to its laws in those who gave it; but the committees, not intending to acknowledge such obedience, avoided giving it that title which is only proper from subjects, and gave it one which implied no relation or dependence on it, and yet carried so much the appearance of respect, that it might be mistaken to mean it.

The distinction they mark in their resolutions between the

people of America and the people of England, by terming the one *his majesty's liege subjects in the Colonies*, and the other, his *natural-born* subjects, or his subjects *born within the realm*, plainly, though indirectly, declares it to be their opinion, that the people in the Colonies, are not the king's *natural-born subjects*, or his subjects *born within the realm*. They cannot therefore claim the rights and privileges of Englishmen, from their being British subjects in common with the people of England, or the subjects born within the realm; and yet no other title to those rights do any of them pretend, than that such are the rights and privileges of Englishmen or British subjects. For they go on to resolve, "That it is inseparably essential to the freedom of a people, and the undoubted right of *Englishmen*, that no taxes be imposed on them but with their own consent, given personally, or by their representatives. That trial by jury is the inherent and invaluable right of every *British subject* in these Colonies." Also, "that it is the right of the *British subjects* in these Colonies to petition the king or either house of parliament." This is all very true and very sensible; but who those *Englishmen* or *British subjects* in the Colonies are, to whom, and *to whom only*, these rights belong, cannot easily be discovered. They cannot be the inhabitants of the Colonies, or those who have been born there; for the former resolutions say, that the Colonies are *not within the British realm*, nor that the people who are born there are the *natural-born subjects* of the king, *born within the realm*.

Having thus seen upon what sort of foundations the different colony assemblies build their several titles to the rights and privileges of Englishmen, and that each superstructure, at the approach of reason, vanishes like—*the baseless fabric of a vision.* —I will not fatigue the reader with a discussion of the arguments introduced by the colony advocates in support of the assemblies resolutions. Whatever they can urge in behalf of the Colonies claim to the rights and privileges of Englishmen, whilst they deny that they are subjects of the realm, or natural-born British subjects, and that the Colonies are within the realm, must be obnoxious to the same charges of inconsistency and absurdity to which the assemblies resolutions are so palpably liable; and the simplest of my countrymen can easily detect the most artful American sophister, by insisting upon his answering this plain question: Are the people in the Colonies British subjects, or are they aliens or foreigners?

The assemblies and their advocates, aware of this dangerous dilemma, have never directly and explicitly declared, as the reader must have observed, that they are, or that they are not, British subjects; that is, subjects of the British state or community. They avoid that declaration by every artifice and subterfuge that words can supply them with. They are at one time "Englishmen," at another "the children, and not the bastards of Britons:" they are "free Britons;" "the king of Great Britain's *liege* subjects;" "they owe the same fealty and allegiance to his majesty that is due to him from his subjects in Great Britain," and numberless other equivocal professions, which serve to elude the main question; at the same time, as if under each character they had defined their condition to be that of British subjects, they boldly draw the consequence, *that they are intitled to all the rights and privileges of natural-born subjects in common with the people of England.* That they cannot however maintain their title to those rights upon any other ground, than that of their being British subjects, born and inhabiting within the realm, is, I think, sufficiently evident; and therefore, that they may fail in proving that they are not British subjects, and that the Colonies lie without the realm, is the most friendly wish I can give them. How far they have succeeded in the fatal attempt, must be the subject of our next enquiry.

And here we shall perceive, that however cautious the Colonies have been in admitting that they are British subjects in any sense whatever, that they do not nevertheless, *as yet*, reject the authority of parliament to bind them in any case, save in the article of taxation; and, against even this right in parliament, they do not urge that they are not British subjects, and consequently not within the jurisdiction of the supreme British legislature, because that plea would involve every other right of jurisdiction in the decision of that question; and it is the artifice of the managers on behalf of the Colonies, to avoid general questions, and to keep back and conceal consequences, lest the unsuspecting people of England should too soon catch the alarm, and resolve to withstand their first attempts at independency.

When the repeal of the stamp-act was their object, a distinction was set up between internal and external taxes; they pretended not to dispute the right of parliament to impose external taxes, or port duties, upon the Colonies, whatever were the purposes of parliament in laying them on, or however productive of revenue they might be. Nay, Doctor Franklin tells the house of commons, that "they have a *natural and equitable* right to some *toll* or *duty* upon merchandizes carried through that part of their dominions, viz. the American seas, *towards defraying the expence they are at in ships to maintain the safety of that carriage.*" This, however, was only the language for 1765 and 1766, but when parliament seemed to adopt the distinction, and waiving for the present the exercise of its right to impose internal taxes, imposed certain duties on merchandizes imported into the Colonies, and carried through those seas which the parliament was told were *theirs*: the distinction between internal and external taxes is rejected by the colony advocates, and a new one devised between taxes for *the regulation of trade*, and taxes for the *purpose of revenue*.

This new distinction, however, between taxes for the regulation of trade, and taxes for the purpose of revenue, as far as it respects the right of parliament to impose the one, but not the other, is, of all absurdities, the most ridiculous that ever was contended for. It is saying, in other words, that parliament has a right to impose a *heavy tax*, but not a *small one*. It may lay one so grievous, that no body can afford to pay it; but it has no authority to impose one which may be easily borne: nay, in the instances referred to by Mr. Dickenson in his Farmer's Letters, it should seem to mean that parliament has no right to *reduce* a tax which it has had a legal right to impose in a manner *extremely burdensome*. The right of Parliament to charge foreign molasses with a duty of six-pence a gallon was unquestionable; but, for parliament to *reduce* the six-pence to three-pence, is a violent usurpation of unconstitutional authority, and an infringement of the rights and privileges of the people in the Colonies. The reduction of the duty upon black teas too was another intolerable grievance: whilst they carried out with them a duty of one shilling a pound, paid at the East-India Company's sales, which, by the ordinary increase of charges, amounted to near eighteen pence when the teas arrived in

America, things went on very well; but when parliament took off that shilling, and instead thereof laid on a duty of three pence, to be paid on importation of the tea into the Colonies, which precluded all increase of charges, then were the Colonies undone. Even the late duties upon oils and colours, &c. it seems, have become grievous from their being *no duties at all*; for Mr. Dickenson tells us, in his eleventh letter, that the drawbacks which are allowed upon their exportation from England, amount to more money than all the duties together which are laid upon them on their arrival in the Colonies will produce. I believe it is the first time that the Colonies of any state, have complained of the injustice of the mother-country in laying taxes upon them which were not *sufficiently heavy*; nor was it ever before discovered, that the proper means to redress the grievances of any people, were to increase their taxes. And yet this is certainly the case in the present instance between Great Britain and her Colonies; for, if parliament had augmented the duties upon foreign molasses, instead of reducing them, or had it laid on another shilling upon black teas exported to the Colonies, instead of taking one off, the right to do so would have been admitted. But (says Mr. Dickenson) the heavy tax would have operated as a prohibition, which is a *regulation of trade*; the light tax is intended to *be paid*, and is laid for the *purpose of revenue*.

It is the *purpose of parliament* in laying the tax, which, it seems, gives it the right of laying it. Curious reasoning this!— Now, should it happen, that parliament was at any time mistaken in its purpose, and that a tax which it imposed with an intention that no body should pay it, that is, that it should operate as a prohibition, should really turn out to be such a tax as the commodity on which it was charged could bear, and the people in the Colonies were willing to purchase it at the price the tax had raised it to, what should we do then? If the tax be paid it then becomes a revenue tax, and no longer a prohibitory one; and is thenceforward a grievance, and an infringement of the rights of the Colonies. On the other hand, suppose parliament should be mistaken in a tax it laid for the purpose of revenue, and it turned out a prohibition, would the tax then become a constitutional one?

Nevertheless, say the colony advocates, the essential distinction between the two sorts of taxes will subsist *in the purpose* for which the tax is laid, no matter how it may operate; and for this essential distinction we are referred to our old statutes. Let the reasoning of parliament in the preamble to the 15th of Charles the Second, chap. the seventh, be the measure of this distinction, and then we shall see where the boundary line is to be drawn.

In regard, says this statute, "that his majesty's plantations, &c. beyond the seas, are *inhabited and peopled by his subjects of this his kingdom of England*, for the maintaining a greater correspondence and kindness between them, *and keeping them in a firmer dependence upon it*, and rendering them yet more *beneficial and advantageous to it*, in the further employment and increase of *English* shipping and seamen, *vent of English woollen, and other manufactures and commodities*, rendering the navigation to and from the same more safe and *cheap*, and making *this kingdom* a staple, not only of *the commodities of those plantations*, but also of the commodities of *other countries and places*; for the supplying of them, be it enacted, &c." These several purposes are therefore to be deemed regulations of trade; and to whatever tax or duty which may be imposed with any of those purposes, the Colonies ought to submit, notwithstanding a revenue should incidentally arise from them. Be it so. One purpose, then it appears, is, "the making the colonies a vent for British manufactures." Now if the British manufacturers are heavily taxed, and the American manufacturer pays no taxes, or very small ones, the British manufactures must come much dearer to the consumer in the Colonies than American manufactures, and consequently the British manufactures will not sell there, and the Colonies will no longer be a vent for them. To prevent which, there can be no means so evident or effectual, as taking off taxes from the British manufacturers and laying them on the American manufacturer. With this view, and with this purpose, of "securing a vent for the British manufactures," an act of parliament, laying a poll-tax upon all manufacturers of linen or wool, or a heavy tax upon all kinds of manufactures which should be made in the Colonies, would be extremely proper. For this purpose also, all materials for manufactures should be taxed, unless exported to Great Britain; as should all tools and instruments for manufacturing. The encouragement of *English* navigation like-wise opens another vein for drawing off the *life-blood* of the Colonies, as they call their money. Tonnage duties upon all ships and vessels built in the Colonies; duties upon all materials for ship-building, of the product of the Colonies, or imported there; and, in short, there is scarcely a tax, internal or external, which the people in England are liable to, that might not be imposed on the Colonies, for some of these purposes. Besides, if we enter thoroughly into the matter, we shall find that it is always an argument of the want of finance ability in the minis-ter who proposes any tax which is not intended to operate beneficially as a regulation, as well as to produce revenue.

A land-tax is a judicious regulation, inasmuch as it excites the land owner to cultivate and improve his lands; and with this very view, taxes are laid upon unimproved lands in Amer-ica, by the colony assemblies. Thus our East-India duties are many of them calculated to promote our own manufactures, as well as to raise a revenue. Thus the duties upon French goods were imposed with a view to check the trade of France, to en-courage our own manufactures, and, at the same time, to raise a fund for defraying the public expences. So likewise are a multitude of our taxes upon articles of luxury and of extrava-gance in our home consumption; so likewise are the taxes upon many of our exports, to prevent the manufacture of our raw materials abroad, and to encourage it at home. The double tax upon the Roman Catholics was laid with a view to weaken that interest, as well as to raise a revenue; and it was considered and urged as the strongest motive for laying on the British stamp duties upon licences to keep ale-houses, to sell wine and spirituous liquors, and even those upon all law-proceedings, and upon the admission of attorneys, and many others, that those duties would greatly operate to discourage and diminish what was wished to be checked, as well as produce a public revenue.

Upon this principle, even the stamp-act in America might have been considered as a regulation; for it was intended like-wise to prevent or detect the forgery of deeds, wills, or other instruments; to discourage, by a high duty, the grant of large quantities of land to one person; to make all law proceedings and instruments in the English language, and thence incite the foreign subjects to learn it; to discourage a spirit of unnecessary litigation in the Colonies; to prevent disorders which frequently happen from tippling-houses in remote places, and from selling spirituous liquors to the Indians in the woods; to make the entries and clearances of ships more regular; and to prevent false cockets, and several things of the like nature.

This boasted distinction between taxes for the regulation of trade, and taxes for the purpose of revenue, we therefore see is without a difference, and will in no sort serve to protect the Colonies from parliamentary internal and external taxation, however it may serve for a pretence, under which to strip parliament of all jurisdiction over the Colonies.

I have indeed thought of a distinction which would suit the Colonies purposes much better, and which, I believe, is what they mean, by the difference between taxes for the purpose of revenue, and taxes as regulations of trade, if they chose to speak it out, which is that between the imposing taxes and collecting them. They would acknowledge, with all their hearts, a right in parliament to do the one, provided it never attempted to do the other. It is this *new invention* of *collecting taxes* that makes them burdensome to the Colonies, and an infringement of their rights and privileges;—and herein it is that Mr. Grenville's administration has proved the æra of the Colonies loss of liberty.

The duty of six pence a gallon upon foreign molasses, which had been laid thirty years before Mr. Grenville was first commissioner of the treasury, was no grievance, *because it had never been collected*; but when that gentleman reduced the duty to three pence, all liberty was at an end—for he took measures for the Colonies to pay the three pence.

For *this invention* of collecting taxes, and making them productive of revenue, it is, that this gentleman has been considered by some of the heated advocates of the Colonies as the determined, implacable enemy of their liberties; that he has been pursued by them, and their partizans, on this side the water, with the bitterest malevolence. Yet, notwithstanding these calumnies, those who know his public declarations, and his private sentiments, can testify, that he never entertained a thought of resenting the harsh and unjust treatment he met with from them, much less did he ever wish to deprive the

Colonies of any privilege which the British constitution gave them a right to, or their safety, and that of Great Britain, would permit them to enjoy. Many gentlemen in the Colonies authentically know, that such are his private dispositions; nor can they or the people of Great Britain be ignorant, that he has frequently manifested them in the most public and solemn manner. When the parliamentary right of taxation has been questioned, have they not heard him declare in these terms, "That to such a surrender of the legislative authority I can never be a party, as I think it the highest species of treason against the constitution and sovereign authority of this kingdom, to deprive it of one-fourth part of its subjects: but tho' I cannot adopt nor approve of such a plan, yet I can submit to it; and having done my duty to the utmost, by endeavouring to convince the king, the parliament, and the people, of the unhappy consequences of such a measure, I shall wait the event till experience has given conviction one way or the other; and so far am I from thinking, if I had the power, that I have a right to carry matters to extremity, as it is supposed I would, in order to inforce my own opinions in contradiction to theirs, upon a subject of such infinite importance to the whole, that if I were to see the king, the parliament, and the people, ready to run into extremes on that side, which in the course of things seems to me highly probable, I would employ all the means in my power to prevent it, and to suggest temperate measures as long as they were practicable; being fully persuaded, that whatever blame there is, it is owing to those in England who have weakly or wickedly misled the subjects in America, and not to the Colonies themselves, who have done no more than any other people would have done, to whom an immunity from taxes had been holden forth, and who have been encouraged as they have been." But not to enter further into this matter, and to return from this digression, which justice to so distinguished a character, and the desire of undeceiving my fellow-subjects in the Colonies led me into, let us enquire whether this tax could have operated as a regulation of trade, or fulfilled any purpose of parliament in imposing it, if it were not collected.

The purpose of parliament in imposing the tax, as the statute expresses it, was to give a preference to the molasses of the

British islands, or, in other words, to raise the price of foreign molasses so high, that the molasses of our own islands could be afforded cheaper, or at least at the same price. Now, unless this tax was collected, this purpose could not be effected; and if it was collected, and the same quantity of foreign molasses was imported, as has been imported since the tax was reduced to three pence, the revenue which should have arisen from this regulation tax would have been double the sum of what the tax of three pence imposed for the purpose of revenue produced, which would have been a most notable proof of the difference in this distinction. But suppose the tax of six pence a gallon was too heavy for the foreign commodity to bear, and that the molasses of the British islands only was imported, as cheaper than the foreign with the duty, the duty then operates as a prohibition upon foreign molasses; and what is the consequence? The people in the Colonies are obliged to purchase the molasses of the British islands at the price they can afford to sell it for, or at which they chuse to part with it. Now, as it comes dearer than the foreign molasses would, if there were no duty, the difference of price between what the Colonies paid for foreign molasses before the Duty, and that which they paid for the molasses of the British islands since the duty, is a tax taken out of the pockets of the people in the Colonies by act of parliament, and put into the pockets of the planters in the British islands. Are these then the sort of taxes which parliament has a right to impose upon the Colonies? Does the purpose of the tax, being for enriching the sugar planters in the British islands at the expence of the Colonies on the Continent, make it more palatable to the Colonies, than if it were for the general service of protecting and securing themselves? And after all, is it the privilege of being taxed by parliament for the benefit of individuals in other parts of the British empire, and an exemption from taxes for the general good, that the Colonies are contending for?

Perhaps it may be thought that I have spent more time and taken more pains in exposing the absurdities contained in this extravagant doctrine, of a right in parliament to impose taxes as regulations of trade, but not to impose any for the purpose of revenue, than the importance of it merited, or the authority by which it is supported intitled it to; for it would be so very easy for parliament to draw from the Colonies whatever revenue it thought fit to require, under the description of taxes *for the regulation of trade*, that, *merely* for the *purpose of revenue*, it might never be requisite for parliament to impose any taxes whatever on the Colonies, and therefore the right of doing so *on that account* is not worth enquiring into. But whatever impeaches the jurisdiction of parliament over the Colonies, however insignificant in itself, becomes of importance from its consequences; for if the authority of the legislative be not in one instance equally supreme over the Colonies as it is over the people of England, then are not the Colonies of the same community with the people of England. All distinctions destroy this union; and if it can be shewn in any particular to be dissolved, it must be so in all instances whatever. There is no alternative: either the Colonies are a part of the community of Great Britain, or they are in a state of nature with respect to her, and in no case can be subject to the jurisdiction of that legislative power which represents her community, which is the British parliament.

However faint any line of partition may be attempted to be drawn between the people in England and the people in the Colonies, it is not to be endured, if we would preserve the union between them as one community, and the supremacy of parliament over all as the representative of that community.

If the Farmer's Letters were indeed to be considered as mere speculative essays upon civil government, neither the justness or elegance of the composition, the knowledge of the subject handled, or the constitutional learning displayed in them, would give them much authority, or intitle them to the notice I have taken of them; but their purpose being to excite resentment in the Colonies against their parent country, and to push them on to a separation from her, tenderness for my deluded fellow-subjects engaged me to expose the fallacies and absurdities attempted to be imposed upon them for demonstrative truths; with the same view, I shall now select a few out of the many inconsistencies and self-contradictions of that writer. "If (says he in his first letter) the British parliament has a legal authority to order that we shall furnish *a single article* for the troops here, and to compel obedience to that order, they have the same right to order us to supply those troops with arms, cloaths, and every necessary; and to compel obedience to that order also: in short, *to lay any burdens they please upon us.* Again, an act of parliament, *commanding us to do a certain thing*, if it has any validity, is *a tax upon us* for the expence that accrues in complying with it." In another place in the same letter he says, "If Great Britain can order us *to come to her for necessaries we want*, and can order us to pay what taxes she pleases *before we take them away*, or when we land them here, we are as abject slaves as France and Poland can shew in wooden shoes and with uncombed hair."

"Let us (says he in his twelfth letter) consider ourselves as men, freemen, christian-freemen, *separated from the rest of the world*, and firmly bound together by the same rights, interests, and dangers." "What (continues he) have these Colonies to ask while they continue free? or what have they to dread, but insidious attempts to subvert their freedom? *They form one political body of which each colony is a member.*"

If we take the sense of these several passages together, we shall find that the exercise of sovereign authority over the Colonies is connected so intimately with the right of taxation, that the one cannot subsist without the other in any case whatsoever. The impressing waggons or boats for the transportation of troops or their baggage; the quartering them even upon public houses; their trampling down a man's fences in their march, or encamping upon his grounds; their passage over ferries or toll-bridges—are all taxes, it seems; for in all these cases, *something* is furnished to the troops, or something is done by them, or something is commanded to be done for them, from whence *some expence will accrue to the people in the Colonies*. And if parliament has no right to require any of these things to be done, without the consent of the Colonies, it can have no right to keep up any troops in the Colonies, or to march them through the country without their consent, which is repugnant to every idea of sovereignty on the one part, and of dependence on the other; besides, there can be neither restraints nor regulations of trade but what must fall within some of these descriptions of taxes. To oblige a planter to carry his products to a port of entry, when a vessel can take them in at his own landing-place, nay, to oblige a merchant to ship his goods from the customhouse-quay, when another wharf is more convenient to him, is to *command the planter and mer-chant to do certain things from whence expence will accrue.* The fees paid the officers of the customs for entries and clearances, are also expences charged upon the Colonies, and consequently taxes. Confining the Colonies to purchase commodities or manufactures in Great Britain, when they could purchase them at a cheaper rate elsewhere, is taxing them in this way of rea-soning; obliging the Colonies to sell their products in Great Britain, or to land them there before they carry them to an-other market, is likewise a tax upon them—for in all these cases, they are *commanded to do something from whence expence accrues.*

All the taxes which are paid by the people in England, inas-much as they serve to raise the price of labour or materials, and thereby raise the price of manufactures, are all taxes upon the people of the Colonies, who are obliged to purchase those manufactures at our prices, and may not get them from other countries.

It would be endless to trace this doctrine of taxes through all its consequences. I have already gone far enough to shew, that upon Mr. Dickenson's principles, where they cannot be imposed, there can be neither restraints upon trade, nor exer-cise of sovereign authority; and that if Great Britain does not possess the right of taxing the Colonies, she has no right to exercise any jurisdiction over them; but that the Colonies are, as Mr. Dickenson says they are, of themselves, "a distinct com-munity, or one political body of which each colony is a mem-ber, separated from the rest of the world," and especially from Great Britain. Yet notwithstanding, these are clearly the conse-quences which must follow from his premise; and that such are the consequences the Colonies mean should follow from them; yet Mr. Dickenson, not caring to discover the whole of their purpose so fully at present, in the beginning of his second let-ter, thus expresses himself: "The parliament unquestionably possess *a legal authority to regulate the trade of* Great Britain *and all her Colonies*: such an authority is essential to the rela-tion between a mother country and her Colonies, and neces-sary for the common good of all. He who considers these provinces, as *states distinct from the British empire*, has very slender notions of justice, or of their interests: we *are but parts of a whole*, and therefore *there must exist a power somewhere to preside and preserve the connection in due order; this power is lodged in the parliament."* Again, in the same letter, he says, "that we (the Colonies) may be legally bound, by act of parliament, *to pay any general duties* on these commodities, that is, paper and glass &c. relative to the regulation of trade, *is granted."* How it comes to pass that these general duties *do not occasion an expence to the people who pay them*, Mr. Dickenson has not told us, or in what manner the parliament of Great Britain can exercise its *legal authority* to regulate the trade of the Colonies, and preside *over the whole, and preserve the connection in due order*, without a power of commanding the Colonies *to furnish a single article* for such part of the national forces, as it may, for these purposes, be thought fit to station among them; or what sort of regulations of trade parliament can devise, from the observance of which no expence will accrue to the Colonies, are matters which he has not thought proper to explain.

But these are not all the difficulties which occur in this extraordinary performance. The definition of a tax, says this writer, in his fourth letter, is, that it is an *imposition on the subject, for the* SOLE PURPOSE *of levying money.* All taxes whatever, therefore, which are not imposed with *this sole purpose*, are no taxes at all; and neither the imposing or the levying the tax, can therefore be the grievance, but *the purpose for which it is granted*, or the use to which it is applied. But in his ninth letter, he changes his opinion; for, says he, "if money be raised upon us by others, without our consent, for our defence, those who are the judges in *levying it*, must also be the judges in *applying it.* With what face can we dispute the fact, after having granted, that those who *apply* the money had a right *to levy it?* Besides," he goes on, "*the right of levying is of infinitely more consequence than that of applying."* The reference he makes to the practise in England, in order to elucidate his reasoning in this particular, is an equal proof of his knowledge of the constitution of this country, and of his qualifications as a critic upon its government. "The people of England, says he, who would burst out into fury, if the crown should attempt to levy money by its own authority, *have always assigned to the crown the application of money."*

Perhaps all these seeming absurdities and contradictions would be reconciled or obviated, if we rightly understood the account he gives us in the first page of his second letter, of the connection between Great Britain and her Colonies; and it is a pity his learned editor has not given the public a dissertation upon that most ingenious and instructive passage. "We are," that is, the Colonies are, says he "as *much dependent* on Great Britain, as a *perfectly free* people can be on another."

But the main objection, and on which all the other objections made by the Colonies against the right of parliament to impose taxes upon them, is founded, remains to be examined. "They tell us, that it is the true principle of government, that no man should pay a tax to which he does not consent, either in his own person, or by his representative chosen by him; that the Colonies are not represented in the British parliament, and therefore cannot be taxed by it."

This doctrine, that taxation and representation upon the true principles of government must go together, is so well calculated to captivate the multitude in this country, and so flattering to the Americans, as it intirely abrogates the authority of parliament to tax the Colonies; that it is not surprizing it has found partizans in Great Britain, and has been universally adopted in America, without much enquiry or examination into its foundation, in reason or fact. And yet, if it be applied, as in the instance before us, to an actual or *a distinct* representation of *all those who are taxed*, and no other will serve the purpose of the Colonies, it is not true of any government now existing, nor, I believe, of any which ever did exist. In this sense it neither is nor ever was true in Great Britain! It is not true in any of the charter or royal governments in America: it is not true in the province of Massachusets Bay, in which, by the last history of it, there appears not only to be a multitude of individuals, but even forty townships of freeholders now taxed, who have no distinct representatives: so far therefore is this doctrine of distinct representation and taxation from going together, "being joined by God himself; founded in the eternal law of nature; having grown up with the constitution of England;" that it never existed, either in England, or any other country in the world.

The origin of parliament in England lies hid indeed in the obscurity of antiquity; we only know, that antecedent to the times which our histories run back to, the great men of the realm, who held their lands *in capite* from the crown, together with the king, composed the supreme legislature. The consent of those who held their lands of the crown was therefore necessary, from time immemorial, to give being to every law, by which the people of England were bound. But it cannot be said, that these tenants *in capite* were then the representatives of the *people* of England, in any other sense of the term, than the lords of parliament may now be said to be *their representatives*. And when, from the frequent forfeitures of the great tenants, and the parcelling out their lands among the successive kings favorites; from the granting away the patrimony of the crown to sundry individuals, and from a variety of other causes, the tenants *in capite* became too numerous for all to assemble in parliament, and many of them were too poor to bear the charge of an attendance there; the device of sending a *few* of their body, as representatives of the whole of these lesser tenants, was hit upon. Yet, even these *deputies of the lesser tenants* were not the distinct representatives of the *people* of England; *they* distinctly represented those only who in themselves had a right to a share in the legislature, *and by whom* they were *deputed* or *elected*.

In Doctor Robertson's celebrated history of Scotland, we have a full account of a similar transaction in that kingdom, where the constitution was the same with the ancient constitution of England; and a copy of the petition of the lesser tenants to parliament, for leave to send representatives, is there given in the appendix. But a still more recent instance to the same purpose is to be met with in the treaty of union between the two kingdoms. We there see the peers of Scotland, all of whom had an unquestionable right to a personal share in the legislature of that kingdom, relinquishing their individual right, and taking up with a right of sending sixteen of their body as representatives of the whole to the parliament of Great Britain. It is not pretended that these sixteen peers of Scotland are the distinct representatives of the *people* of Scotland, from their being elected by the peers of Scotland; and why should the knights of shires in that kingdom or in England be called the distinct representatives of the *people* of Scotland or of England, because they are elected by the *freeholders* in each kingdom? They distinctly represent those who elect them, and who have a right by the constitution to be distinctly represented, and they distinctly represent no one else; nor are the members sent to parliament by boroughs and corporations, more properly the distinct representatives of the people of Great Britain, than are the knights of the shires. All the corporations and boroughs who elect members for parliament, do it by virtue of a charter for that purpose from the crown, or by prescription, which, in law, presupposes a grant or charter beyond time of memory. The kings of England for many centuries constantly exercised the right of creating corporations, with the power of chusing members to parliament, and vested that power in many or in a few at their discretion; some of these, particularly the two universities, were incorporated for that purpose so late as the reign of James the First; and, unless it is restrained by the act of union of the two kingdoms, I do not know that this power has ever been taken away.

This right in corporations of electing representatives to parliament, is therefore clearly derived from the grant of the crown; and the members of the corporation exercise that right, because the corporation *holds of the crown*. A corporation seems to be analogous to a great barony or county, held *in capite* from the crown, the tenant for the whole of which had a right to a personal share in the legislative; but the crown choosing to divide the lands among a number of individuals, the whole right to a seat in the legislative assembly cannot be claimed by any one individual, it being the common or joint right of all the members. But they can by their election unite the right of the whole body in such person as they depute to represent their body. Hence does it appear, that the representatives sent to parliament by corporations, are the *distinct* representatives only of those who are members of the several corporations; that is, of such as partake of these grants from the crown, and hold under them: for to say, that representatives chosen by perhaps twelve men, or the majority of twelve, which is seven, incorporated by the crown for that purpose, are the *actual* or *distinct* representatives of the whole people, is to confound all ideas of language or things.

How then can it be said, that taxes imposed by a house of commons, constituted, as we have seen, by the freeholders in counties and members of corporations, are given by the consent of the majority of the people, or their deputies, at the time being.

It is, moreover, worthy of remark, that these members sent to parliament by the freeholders and corporations, are not called the *representatives of the people*, but the *commons in parliament*. They are so styled in all the old writs and records; they are so styled to this day in every act of parliament; and they act not only for their own particular communities, by whom they are severally elected, but each of them for the community of the whole.

The subjects of Great Britain are not, however, without their representatives, though the members who compose the House of Commons cannot be said to be distinctly so. Neither are they bound by laws, nor is their money taken from them without their own consent given by their representatives. *The King, Lords, and Commons are their representatives*; for to them it is that they have *delegated* their individual rights over their lives, liberties, and property; and so long as they approve of that form of government, and continue under it, so long do they consent to whatever is done by those they have intrusted with their rights.

"Laws they are not (says Hooker) which public approbation hath not made so. But *approbation not only they give*, who personally declare their assent by voice, sign, or act, but also *when others* do it in their names, by *right originally at the least derived from them*. And to be commanded *we do consent*, when that *society whereof we are part* hath at any time before *consented*, without revoking the same after by the like universal agreement." And Mr. Locke, who followed this learned investigator of the rights of mankind, in his answer to Sir Robert Filmer, after having shewn that the origin of all power is from the people only; that every form of government, whether a democracy, an oligarchy, an elective or hereditary monarchy, is nothing more than a trust delegated by the society to the person or persons so appointed, lays it down as a fundamental maxim in all governments: "That the *legislative* is the joint power of every member of the society, given up to that person or assembly which is legislator; and that even the *executive*, when vested in a single person, is to be *considered as the representative of the commonwealth*." And he then adds; "Nobody doubts but an *express consent* of any man entering into society, makes him a perfect member of that society, a subject of that government. The difficulty is what ought to be looked upon as a *tacit consent*; and to this I say, that every man that hath "any *possessions or enjoyment of any part of the dominions of any government, doth thereby give his tacit consent, and is as far forth obliged to obedience to the laws of that government during such enjoyment, as any one under it*."

Upon this principle, the king and the two houses of parliament, are by our constitution *representatives* of the legislative, as the king alone is of the executive power of the commonwealth; and, upon this principle, every subject of Great Britain, when he is taxed by parliament, is taxed by his own consent, for he is then taxed by consent of those whom the society has impowered to act for the whole; and every member of the community must therefore subscribe his tacit consent to all such taxes as may be imposed, or other legislative acts that may be done by those whom the society has appointed, as long as the form of government subsists. This is the *British constitution*; and if the British subjects in America still continue to be part of our community, it follows that they also are represented by the British legislative, and equally bound by its laws.

That the first inhabitants of the Colonies were part of the British community, and bound to obey its legislative power in all respects, as any other subjects at *the time of the establishment* of those Colonies, will not be denied. How then has that obedience been altered or released? Those Colonies were all created by charters or temporary authorities, from the executive power of this community, except in the cases of Jamaica, New York, and the late acquisitions of Quebec, the Ceded Islands, and the Two Floridas, which were conquests made by this community upon foreign powers, and such of their subjects as remained were incorporated with us under our laws and obedience. And it cannot, we have seen, be pretended, that this obedience has been altered or released by charters or authorities from the executive power; for, on the contrary, the obedience to the laws of Great Britain, *without any restriction*, is expresly reserved in every one of them, and particularly the right of taxation is mentioned and reserved to the parliament of Great Britain by the charter of Pennsylvania, in which colony Mr. Dickenson wrote his Farmer's Letters.

But suppose it had been otherwise; can it be contended, that the executive power of the crown, can, by any grant or authority, alter or annul the legislative power in the article of taxation, or any other? Will those who contend that this right of taxation belongs only to, and can only be exercised by the deputies of the people, contend at the same time for a right in the crown or executive to annul or restrain the legislative power, partly composed as it is of these deputies, in that very article of taxation? If they do, let them hear Mr. Locke in reply. He will tell them, that "even the *legislative power itself* cannot transfer the power of making laws to any other hands; for it being but a delegated power from the people, they who have it cannot pass it over to others." He says, moreover, that "all obedience, which, by the most solemn ties any one can be obliged to pay, ultimately terminates in this supreme power, the legislative, and is directed by those laws which it enacts; nor can any oaths to any foreign power whatsoever, *or any domestic subordinate power*, discharge any member of the society from his obedience to the legislative, acting pursuant to their trust; nor oblige him to any obedience contrary to the laws so enacted, or farther than they do allow; it being ridiculous to imagine, one can be tied *ultimately* to obey any power in the society which is not supreme." He says in another place; "there can be but one supreme power, which is the legislative, to which all the rest are and must be subordinate."

It is however pretended, that the lands in America lying without the realm, and appertaining to the king only, their possessors cannot from those circumstances be subject to the jurisdiction of parliament, whose authority is necessarily confined within the limits of the realm. This plea, it is presumed, cannot be made by the inhabitants of such lands as were conquered by the forces of the British state from foreign powers, or ceded to Great Britain by treaty. Those conquests or cessions are surely the dominions of the crown of Great Britain, not the private property of the king, which have thus been acquired by the efforts, the blood, and treasure of the community; and indeed Mr. Dickenson puts these out of the question in all that he says of the rights of the Colonies.

But does the discovery of countries by the subjects of the British state, or the cession of them by the natives, make those countries more particularly the private property of the king, than would the conquest of them by force of arms from a foreign prince, or the acquisition of them by treaty? The difference only lies in the change of the term, the *Crown* for that of the *King*; but that change has been made without authority, either of reason or fact. The kings of England never had personally, nor ever claimed to have any property in the lands in the Colonies. Those of them who carried their claims of prerogative the highest, never pretended to have any other title to those lands than what they derived from their possession of the crown of England, and they granted them under *that title* to their present possessors, or their ancestors; for all grants of lands in the Colonies have been made under the great seal of England, or by authority derived under the great seal of England, which is the same thing, from the first discovery of America to this day.

No man, at least no lawyer, will pretend, that the great seal of England is the private seal of the king. It is the seal of the state, and distinguishes the acts of the state from the private acts of the king; now, had the kings of England claimed to hold the lands in the Colonies as *their own private estate*, they would have granted them of their *own private authority*, and passed them under their own private seal, and not under the great seal of England. The very nature of the grant or charter is therefore an undeniable proof, that the lands in the Colonies are, and always have been, the possessions or dominions of the crown of England, and not the private personal property of the kings of England. And it is an equally undeniable consequence, that those who hold those lands under such grants or charters, or by whatever title which derives its authority originally or immediately under the great seal of England, *hold them of the crown of England, and as part and parcel of the realm*; for the crown's estate must necessarily be within the realm, since it is the estate or dominions of the crown (though not of the king) which make the realm. What then are the quit-rents which are paid by the possessors of lands in the Colonies to the crown, or to those who derive under the crown, but a tax imposed by authority of the great seal of England on such who should take possession of those lands, not only as an acknowledgment of their fealty and allegiance, *but for the purpose of revenue?*

Those quit-rents are a part of the *unappropriated* revenue of the state, and, *as such*, become the property of the crown *without account.* But it is not the private property of the king; for the king cannot alienate it, or give it away from the successor to the crown, for a longer term than he can alienate or give away other *unappropriated* revenues arising in England.

The lands in all the Colonies having therefore been clearly shewn to be part of the dominions of Great Britain, and the possessors of them to hold them under authorities and titles derived from the British state, Mr. Locke would require no other proof of the right of the legislative power of Great Britain to the obedience of the possessors of those lands; for, speaking of the manner by which a man tacitly makes himself a subject of any country or government, he says:

"It is commonly supposed, that a father could oblige his posterity to that government of which he himself was a subject, and that his compact held them; whereas it *being only a necessary condition annexed to the land, and the inheritance of an estate which is under that government*, reaches only those who *will take it on that condition*, and so is no natural tie or engagement, but a *voluntary submission*; for every man's children, being by nature as free as himself, or any of his ancestors ever were, may, whilst they are in that freedom, choose what society they will join themselves to, what commonwealth they will put themselves under; but *if they will enjoy the inheritance of their ancestors, they must take it on the same terms their ancestors had it, and submit to all the conditions annexed to such a possession.*" "Whoever (says he in another place) by inheritance, *purchase, permission*, or *otherways*, enjoys any part of the land so annexed to, and under the government of, that commonwealth, must take it with the condition it is under; that is, of *submitting to the government* of the *commonwealth under whose jurisdiction it is, as far forth as any subject of it.*"

I have quoted these passages from Mr. Locke's Treatise upon Civil Government, because his opinions in this treatise have been principally relied on as the foundation of many extravagant and absurd propositions which he never meant to encourage; and because I have the highest regard in general for the good sense and free spirit of that excellent work, written to defend the natural rights of men, and particularly the principles of our constitution, when they were attacked both by force and fraud: although, at the same time, there are some passages in it, which probably the temper and fashion of that age drew from him, in which I can by no means agree with him, especially when he defines prerogative to be "a power in the prince to act according to *discretion* for the public good, without the prescription of the law, and sometimes even against it;" and when he endeavours to prove that the executive power, by the just prerogative of the prince, hath "a right to regulate, not by old custom, but by true reason, the number of members in all places that have a right to be distinctly represented; because this would be manifestly for the good of the people, and therefore is, and always will be, just prerogative."

The first of these propositions evidently sets up a dispensing power in the prince over the laws, when properly exercised: and by the latter, "the prince by his own authority might vary the measures of representation, and those places which have a just right to be represented, which before had none; and by the same reason, those cease to have a right, and be too inconsiderable for such a privilege which before had it." Such an alteration of the constitution, and depriving many boroughs of the right to be distinctly represented, which they now enjoy, however advantageous it might be to the people of England that the members who compose the house of commons should be fairly and equally chosen, could not be lawfully made by the prerogative of the prince, in whom, by our constitution, no such power is vested; and whose prerogative is as much ascertained and restrained by the laws, as the rights and properties of the subject. I mean not by this to throw any blame upon Mr. Locke, but merely to shew, that in a work of this extent there must be some inaccuracies and errors, and that it is not an infallible guide in all cases. He is not however to be charged with the opinions imputed to him by some late ignorant commentators, upon certain passages in this treatise, who have made him speak a language in the latter part of his eleventh chapter directly contradictory to the whole tenor of his work. His words are: "The supreme power cannot take from any man *any part of his property* without his *own consent*; for the preservation of property being the end of government, and that for which men enter into society, it necessarily supposes and requires that the *people* should have property, without which they must be supposed to lose that by entering into society which was the end for which they entered into it—too gross an absurdity for any man to own. Men therefore in society having property, they have such a right to the goods *which by the law of the community are theirs*, that no body hath a right to take their substance, or any part of it, from them, without their *own consent*: without this they have no property at all; for I have no property in that which another can by right take from me, when he pleases, against my consent. Hence it is a mistake to think, that the supreme legislative power of any commonwealth can *do what it will, and dispose of the estates of the subjects arbitrarily,* or *take any part of them at pleasure.*" Again: "The prince or senate, however it may have power to make laws for the regulating of property between the subjects, one amongst another, yet can never have a power *to take to themselves* the whole, or any part of the subject's property, without their own consent; for this would be in effect, to leave them no property at all."

That Mr. Locke in these passages means no more than, that the supreme legislative has no right to take the property of any individual of the community, and apply it to his or their own *private use or purpose*, if not sufficiently evident from the expressions themselves, must appear so from the instance by which he explains them: "Neither the serjeant (says he) that could command a soldier to march up to the mouth of a cannon, or stand in a breach where he is almost sure to perish, can command that soldier *to give him* one penny of his money; nor the general that can condemn him to death for deserting his post, or for not obeying the most desperate orders, can yet, with all his absolute power of life and death, *dispose of one farthing of that soldier's estate, or seize one jot of his goods.*"

Every one knows, that in all armies that ever had pay, the officers *punished* the soldiers by stoppages and pecuniary mulcts; and in so doing, *took the money out of the soldiers pockets*, but then they did it not *for their own private emolument*; they did it for the *public benefit*, and under authority of the supreme legislature. Mr. Locke could therefore never have produced *this instance* in proof of the supreme legislative power having no right to take any part of the property of any man, and apply it for the public service: what he clearly means is this, that the king, lords, and commons of Great Britain have no right to pass an act, *vesting in themselves* the property of the people of Great Britain; nor in the most absolute countries, has the prince a right to seize on, and take away, the property of his subjects, and apply it to his *own use*, without the express consent of the proprietor; such a power not being within the authority vested in them by the community at their first institution; their power having been given them as a trust to be exercised for the general good, and for general purposes. But he never meant to question, or deny the right of the supreme legislative power, acting pursuant to their trust, to dispose of any part of the property of the people for the public safety and advantage. "For (he says) this *arbitrary* disposing of the estates of the subjects, is not much to be feared in governments where the legislative consists wholly, or in part, in assemblies which are variable; whose members, upon the dissolution of the assembly, are subjects under the common laws of their country equally with the rest." What! are no taxes to be levied by such sort of legislative assemblies for the public service? Is that Mr. Locke's meaning? No surely:—but the members of such legislative assemblies, will be careful not to strip their fellow-subjects of their property, to vest it *in themselves*, because they must know that the time will shortly come, when they shall be in the same predicament; and the members who may succeed them in the legislative assembly, would strip them in their turn, and plead their example as a precedent.

But what puts Mr. Locke's meaning in these passages out of all question, is what he says in his eighth chapter of the beginning of civil societies: "That every man, when he at first incorporates himself into any commonwealth, he, by his uniting himself thereunto, *annexes also, and submits to the community, those possessions* which he has or shall acquire, that do not already belong to any other government: for it would be a direct contradiction for any one to enter into society with others, for the *securing and regulating of property*, and yet to suppose *his land, whose property is to be regulated by the laws of the society,* should *be exempt from the jurisdiction of that government to which he himself, the proprietor of the land, is a subject.* By the same act therefore, whereby any one unites his person, which was before free to any commonwealth, by the same he unites his *possessions,* which were before free to it also; and they become, both of them, *person and possession, subject to the government and dominion of that commonwealth as long as it hath a being.*"

Can any words more strongly express the right of the supreme legislature to tax or dispose of the property of the subject for *public purposes,* than do these last quoted? And those who would draw from any other more loose or general expressions of Mr. Locke, any argument to exempt the property of any subject from taxes imposed by the supreme legislative for the *public service,* must impute to him such inconsistencies as Mr. Locke was incapable of, and charge him with contradictions which ought to destroy his credit, both as an honest man and a clear reasoner.

I have given this doctrine of representation and taxation, going together, so full a discussion, because it is the most important of all the pleas set up by the colony advocates, in support of their claim of exemption from the jurisdiction of parliament, and that which has had most influence on the minds of such of the people of England as have taken part with them in this unhappy contest.

I might indeed have brought it to a much speedier conclusion, and have exposed the absurdity and impracticability of the doctrine, from the *very principles* upon which its promulgers would establish it. They say; "That no man ought to be taxed, but by his *own consent;*" or, in other words, "that the consent of those who *pay the taxes* is necessary to their being constitutionally imposed. That *this consent* must be given by the people *themselves who pay the taxes,* or by *their* distinct representatives chosen by them." And these, they say, are the rights of Englishmen. Now, if these be the rights of Englishmen, I will undertake to say, there is scarce a session of parliament passes in which they are not most notoriously violated, and if parliament did not do so, it could lay no taxes whatever.

When the tax was laid upon hops, did the people who were to pay the tax, viz. the hop-growers, consent to it, either by themselves or their distinct representatives? Did the people in the cyder counties, or their distinct representatives, consent to the tax upon cyder? Is the land-tax kept up at three shillings with the consent of all the land-owners in the kingdom, or that of all the knights of shires, their distinct representatives? What tax is it indeed to which those who pay it, or their distinct representatives, have all consented?—But if this actual and distinct consent of the taxed, or of their distinct representatives, be constitutionally necessary to their being taxed; by consequence, whenever such consent is *not given*, no tax can be constitutionally imposed. If this be the case, he must be a patriot indeed who pays any tax whatever, since he can so easily discharge himself from it, by only saying he does not choose to pay it. I should be glad to see a calculation of the public revenue of Great Britain, or of any other country which could be raised *in this way*, no one paying towards it who did not do so by his own consent; or the consent of those he actually appointed to be his distinct representatives. But the most curious part of the argument has not yet been considered; for it will follow from this doctrine, that the minority will in all cases controul the majority: nay, every individual member of parliament will have the power to stop the proceedings of all the others. For whoever says, *he is against any tax*, neither himself, nor the people whom he distinctly represents, can be liable to pay such tax; because they do not, either by themselves, or their distinct representatives, consent to it.

This, however, is not our meaning, say these admirable expounders of the rights of Englishmen. Then be so good to tell us, in defined terms, what it is you mean? Is it your meaning that no taxes can be imposed, but by the consent of the majority of the people who pay them, or by the consent of the majority of their distinct representatives? The *minority* then may constitutionally be made to pay taxes to which they do not consent, either by themselves or their distinct representatives. So that *almost half* the people of Great Britain may, it seems, be taxed without either their own or their distinct representatives consent. Now, why may not the people in the Colonies, who do not amount to near that number, be taxed also without their own consent, or the consent of distinct representatives elected by themselves?—One step farther, and we are got back to where we set out from.

The consent, you will perhaps say, of the majority of the distinct representatives of the people, of *necessity* involves the consent of the whole. So then it is necessary that the people should submit to pay taxes, to which neither themselves nor their distinct representatives do consent; and the whole meaning of this ingenious argument may be summed up in these few plain words:—That a people may constitutionally be taxed by those whom the constitution has vested with the power to impose taxes, which is the supreme legislature; and that every man who consents to that constitution or government, who is possessed of property under it, and enjoys its protection, consents to all taxes imposed by it, inasmuch as he *consents* to the authority by which they are imposed; and this conclusion will hold equally good when applied to the people in the Colonies, as it does for the people in Great Britain.

But although we have thus got within the circle of these magicians, yet, in respect to the issue of the dispute between us, the breaking the charm of this doctrine has not brought us one jot nearer to our purpose of a reconciliation with the Colonies. Neither indeed would it be advanced by leaving them in possession of it; for should we admit, either upon principles of right in the Colonies, or of justice or expediency in Great Britain, that the Colonies ought to send members to parliament, the Colonies are ready to tell us, nay, they have told us so already, that they will not accept of our offer: for it is impossible for them, they say, to be represented in the British parliament.

Thus, whilst they exclaim against parliament for taxing them when they are not represented, they *candidly* declare they will not have representatives, lest they should be taxed—like froward children, they cry for that which they are determined to refuse, if it should be offered them. The truth however is, that they are determined to get rid of the jurisdiction of parliament *in all cases whatsoever*, if they can; and they therefore refuse to send members to that assembly, lest they should preclude themselves of this plea against all its legislative acts—*that they are done without their consent*; which, it must be confessed, holds equally good against *all laws*, as against taxes. For it is undoubtedly a principle of the British constitution, "*that no man shall be bound by any law to which he does not give his consent*," of equal efficacy with that of his not being taxed, but by his own consent. In what manner however *that consent* is given, we have already seen; and the futility and falacy of the pretence, that it cannot be given but by *distinct* representatives, elected by those who pay taxes, or are bound by laws, have been sufficiently exposed.

The colony advocates however, not caring to develope their whole purpose *at present*, tell us, that by refusing to accept our offer of representatives, they only mean to avoid giving parliament a pretence for taxing them, which they say it is not necessary for parliament to do, as they have assemblies of their own in each Colony, who are the representatives of the people; and who, being acquainted with their circumstances, can best judge what taxes they can bear, and what sums they ought to contribute to the public occasions, whenever his majesty shall call upon them for their aid.

The colony assemblies are indeed *but seven-and-twenty*, and perhaps it might happen, that they should all agree in opinion upon some *one point*; but I much fear that point would not be—*to lay taxes upon themselves*. There is much more reason to apprehend it might be as we have seen—*not to do so*. Mankind are in general apt enough to agree to *keep* their money, but not so frequently of one mind when the proposition is to *part* with it. But to take the matter on its fairest side, let us suppose these *twenty-seven states* all equally disposed to shew regard to his majesty's requisition—*provided they think the occasion fitting*. Upon what occasion then shall his majesty call upon them? Not to settle a permanent revenue for support of their own civil establishments; for he has already made requisitions to many of them, without end, for that purpose, and always without effect; and those few who have complied *most heartily regret it*. Shall it be for support of the military establishment kept up in time of peace? The continental Colonies tell us, "they don't want our troops; and if we keep any among them we must pay them." Shall it be for a fund to give presents to the Indians? The islands say, "they have nothing to do with the Indians. Those who have the benefit of their trade, and live upon their lands, ought to give them presents." Shall it be for discharge of the public debt? One and all will tell us, "that is the affair of Great Britain alone." Suppose then a war breaks out; the Indians attack the back settlers in Virginia—what will Carolina contribute for defence of that province? "Just as much as she has ever done." What will the Islands give? Exactly the same. Suppose the Barbary states quarrel with us; the fishing colonies, and the rice and sugar colonies, suffer by their depredations on the ships bound to Portugal and the Streights —what would Pennsylvania, Maryland, and Virginia, do in the matter? A war in Germany becomes the occasion of the requisition; rice, sugar, and tobacco all go thither, but no fish—why then should New England, Nova Scotia, or Quebec, give any thing? If it was for support of the Italian states, these colonies might indeed contribute something, as they buy their fish; but if that were the occasion, would Pennsylvania, Virginia, or Carolina do so?

The defence of our possessions in the East would be equally obnoxious to them all; and the preservation of our African trade and settlements, is an abomination to the middle and northern Colonies. A war with France might possibly occasion them to bestir themselves a little, but then it would be for *their own immediate defence*. For as they are all accessible to a naval force, they would with good reason apprehend themselves in danger, in case of a war with a maritime power.—Such was the late war, and such was their conduct in it; for so long as the continent of America was the theatre of war, the Islands did not contribute one single shilling for the defence of their Sister-colonies; and it was not until they apprehended an attack upon that province, that the assembly of South Carolina thought of raising troops; and the regiment they did raise in 1757, they confined to *act within the province*; and so soon as their apprehensions for their own safety subsided, they reduced it: nor was it until the Cherokees attacked their frontiers, in 1760, that they again took up arms.

I have thus far followed the Colonies in their own paths; and, instead of exposing the absurdity of their idea of a *polypus* government, where a head sprouts out of every joint, I have endeavoured to make the best of it, and even in that view shewn it to be monstrous and impracticable. Little less so indeed than it would be. In England, where there are but *fifty-two counties*, should the crown make requisitions to each of their *grand juries*, who have authority to assess money *for local purposes* upon the respective inhabitants, as well as the colony assemblies, instead of applying to parliament, to provide for the exigencies of the state? and what sort of public revenue or credit we should then have, is easily to be imagined.

Indeed, to do justice to the candour of the New York assembly, they give strong intimation of its being their opinion, that the raising a revenue for *general purposes*, by grants from the several colony assemblies, is impracticable; and that either it must be done by parliament, or cannot be done at all. For in one of their resolutions, the 18th of December, 1765, they say, "*That the impracticability of inducing the Colonies to grant aids* in an equal manner proportioned to their several abilities, does by no means induce a necessity of divesting the Colonies of their essential rights."

What then is to be done? Are the Colonies to pay nothing in *any way* to the public charges? and is the island of Great Britain to pay all? "No," say the colony advocates, "that is not the case; for we contribute towards the revenue raised in Great Britain, by purchasing your manufactures with the taxes upon them, when we could buy them cheaper at other markets; we lay out all the money we have or can procure with you; and what can you desire more of us?" How travelling improves the genius, and sharpens the wit! If the ancestors of the inhabitants of the Colonies had remained in England to this day, I question much if they would have once thought of telling parliament, that they ought not to tax them, because they laid out all their money in the purchase of British products or manufactures; and yet they might certainly have made that plea as truly at least in the one case, as they do in the other.

What county in England is it, whose inhabitants don't lay out their money in the purchase of the products or manufactures of Great Britain and yet I never heard that they did not all *pay taxes notwithstanding*: and as avarice is certainly not the vice of the age, were all taxes to be taken off the people of England, there can be little doubt but our trade, both foreign and domestic, would be greatly increased thereby, perhaps full as much as our whole trade to America is worth. The misfortune, however, is that we cannot do what we wish in all cases; for such are the circumstances of the times, that a fleet and army must be maintained for the defence of the state, and even for the protection of the trade both of the Colonies and of Great Britain. This cannot be done without revenue, and a revenue cannot be raised without taxes. The question then is not, whether *it would not be better for our trade that we laid no taxes upon either people*, upon the inhabitants of Great Britain, or of America? But whether, *since taxes are absolutely necessary*, they should not be *equally imposed upon all the subjects who derive safety and benefit from the force maintained by the revenue they produce*? Whenever therefore the people in the Colonies are refused by Great Britain, the protection of their fleets and armies, *then*, and *not till then*, may the Colonies complain that they are taxed for their maintenance.

In the course of this discussion of the Colonies pleas, I have occasionally taken notice of their charters from the crown which they once held forth, as having conveyed to them all the rights and privileges of Englishmen, and exemptions from taxes imposed by parliament; but as all those charters reserved the authority of parliament, either in general or special terms, and the secret purpose of the Colonies *now* being to get rid by piece-meal of all parliamentary jurisdiction whatever, their advocates have not of *late* relied much upon their charter rights; on the contrary, when the reservations in their charters have been urged against them, they appeal to acts of parliament, as a superior authority for limiting and expounding the expressions in their charters. Dr. Franklin, in his examination before the House of Commons, says, "he knows there is a clause in the Pennsylvania charter, by which the king grants that he will levy no taxes on the inhabitants, unless it be with the consent of the assembly, or by *act of parliament*; but that they *understand it* thus: By the same charter, *and otherways*, they are intitled to all the privileges and liberties of Englishmen. They find in the *great charter*, and the *petition and declaration of rights*, that one of the privileges of English subjects is, that they are not to be taxed but by their *common consent*; they have there-fore relied upon it from the first settlement of the province, that the parliament never *would*, nor *could*, by *colour of that clause* in the charter, assume a right of taxing them, till it *had qualified itself* to exercise such right by admitting representa-tives from the people taxed." Such being the case, I shall spend no more time in examining their colony charters, but proceed to enquire, by what means the great charter and the bill of rights can be brought to support their claim of exemption from taxes imposed by the authority of parliament.

The great charter granted by king John in 1215, says, "That the king engages not to impose any taxes without summoning the archbishops, the abbots, the earls, the greater barons, and the tenants *in capite*." The 17th of Edward the 2d is more explicit. It says, "that *whatever concerns the estate of the realm and the peo-ple*, shall be treated of in parliament by the king, with the con-sent of the prelates, earls, barons and commonalty of the realm as hath been customary heretofore." The statute of the 15th of Edward the second declares, "that the statute of Magna Charta, Charta Foresta, and the other statutes, were made by the king and his predecessors, the peers, and the commons of the realm."

The bill of rights assented to by king William, among other things, declares, "That the pretended power of suspending laws, or the execution of laws by regal authority, without con-sent of parliament, is illegal." "That the levying money *for, or to the use of the crown*, by pretence of prerogative, *without grant of parliament* for longer time, or in other manner than the same is, or shall be granted, is illegal."

It should seem to be the English meaning of these several declarations, that the right of imposing taxes, and of exercising all other legislative powers, was in the three estates of the realm, which is the parliament only; and that all taxes which should be imposed, and all acts which should be done by any other authority, were illegal. But as Dr. Franklin says, "the *same words* have not always the *same meaning* in America that they have in England;" and it is therefore incumbent on us to look for the American meaning of the several expressions con-tained in these declarations; and for this purpose, the ingenious author of the *Considerations on the Propriety*, &c. has provided us with a very curious glossary. This gentleman tells us, that by these expressions which we understand to be declaratory of the right of parliament to impose taxes and make laws, parliament really meant to say, *that it had no such powers whatever, at least* in respect to the Colonies, but that those powers belonged to the colony assemblies only. His words are, "the common law, the great charter, and the bill of rights, are so far from declaring with one voice, that the inhabitants of the Colonies shall be taxed by no other authority than that of the British parliament, *that they prove the contrary*; for the *principle* of the common law is, that no part of their property shall be drawn from British subjects, without *their consent* given by those *they depute to represent them*; and this principle is inforced by the declaration of the great charter, and the bill of rights." "In Great Britain, says he, *the consent of the people is given by the House of Commons*, and as money had been levied *there* for the use of the crown, by pretence of prerogative without *their* consent, it was properly declared at the Revolution, that the levying of money by pretence of prerogative without grant of parliament, i. e. *without their consent who are to pay it*, is illegal." He goes on, "the *word parliament* having been made use of, the *letter* of the declaration is adhered to, and the consequence drawn, that no British subject can be legally taxed but by the authority of the British parliament against the *spirit and principle* of the declaration, which was aimed only to check and restrain the prerogative, and to establish the necessity of obtaining *the consent of those on whom taxes were to be levied*."

Here we perceive, that the *word parliament* means, in respect to Great Britain, the *House of Commons*; that the *consent of parliament to impose a tax*, means the *consent of those who are to pay the tax*; that the word *parliament*, instead of meaning the king, the prelates, earls, barons, the tenants *in capite*, or the commonalty of the realm, as Magna Charta, &c. define it, means in respect to the Colonies, the house of burgesses in Virginia, and the other colony assemblies.

I will not affront the reader's understanding, by making any further comment on this curious performance, which it is said operated so forcibly on the minds of some extraordinary persons in this country, as to lead them to adopt the cause of the Colonies, and to justify their resistance of acts of parliament.

Neither will I further investigate the various arguments of the several colony advocates, in support of their claim to exemption from the jurisdiction of parliament: I have shewn the main branches to be unsound, and the lesser, which sprout from them, must of course wither and decay.

I shall here stop my researches into the political history of the Colonies, and of the conduct which has been held by parliament and ministry towards them. And let me now ask the advocates for their independency, upon which period of this history it is, that they would fix, as the epocha of the Colonies emancipation from the sovereign authority of the supreme legislature of the realm, or where will they carry us for those pretended rights and privileges which exempt them from its jurisdiction? We have sought for them in the "Dog's Ear'd statute books," but we found them not; we have looked for them in the conduct of a long series of ministers; and in the opinions of the truly learned and great lawyers, that were of council to our kings, in the past ages, and lo, they are not there. Where then shall we hope to meet with them? In the rancorous and malignant heart of a superannuated politician, pining with envy, at seeing the skilful hand of an able finance minister, employed in healing the wounds his rash and wasteful ambition had given his country; in the *factious* brain of an ignorant *man of the law*.

And, "*are these thy gods, O Israel?*" Was it by the miserable sophistry, or the unintelligible jargon, of an extravagant or futile declaimer, that you my fellow-subjects in the Colonies, have been deluded into the absurd and vain attempt of exchanging the mild and equal government of the laws of England, for prerogative mandates: of seeking to inlarge your liberties, by disfranchising yourselves of the rights of British subjects. Where would your madness carry you? or at what point will your frenzy suffer you to stop? Will you renounce your claim to the title and privileges of Englishmen, and cut yourselves off from the protection and benefits peculiar to the subjects of the British state? Will you relinquish the fishery, and restore it to the inhabitants of the deserted western coasts of England? Will you expose your trading ships to the depredations of the Barbary Corsairs, or subject your products to the heavy and prohibitory impositions of rapacious ministers in foreign countries? Will you exclude your ships from British ports, and throw away the lucrative employment of transporting British merchandise, to the revival of the expiring English trade of ship-building? Will you subject yourselves to the aliens duties on all your products imported into Great Britain, and deprive yourselves of the most advantageous market in Europe for the sale of your commodities, and from which you draw so *large a balance*, with which to improve your lands, build your houses, and purchase slaves?* Will you debar yourselves of that unbounded credit, which the generous spirited merchants of England have given you, even to the amount of double your whole capital, and by the use of which you have arrived at your present opulent condition, insomuch, that instead of your arrogant boast, that London has risen out of the Colonies, it may truly be said, that the Colonies have sprung from the Royal Exchange of London? If you be content to carry your paracidial designs at the hazard of these consequences to *yourselves*, be at least so candid and grateful to your mother country, as to declare yourselves in plain terms independent of her, that *her* friends may in time provide for her safety, and make use of the present interval of war, to cicatrise her amputated body. Or if you do not mean to push matters to this extremity, if regard for your own interest shall make you still seek a union with her; be so fair as to say upon what terms you mean to live with her? Do you mean to share in all the benefits of her

* It is one of the impudent artifices of the Colony advocates, to endeavour to persuade the people of England, that *they* get all the people in the Colonies can scrape together by their labour and traffic with all the world, and that it all goes in payment of the *balance due from* the Colonies to Great Britain. Whereas the truth is, that Great Britain imports to a much greater amount from the Colonies, than she exports to them, and the balance in favour of the Colonies, in their trade with her, is that on which most of them live and raise their fortunes.

The exports to the Colonies in 1765, and 1766, and imports from them in those years stand thus:

In 1765	Imports 3,549,070	Ex. 3,334,980	Bal. 214,090
1766	3,987,675	3,320,954	666,721
Balance in favour of the Colonies in those two years			880,811

people, and to bear none of their burdens? Is she to *pay all* and you to *enjoy all*? Are your lands to be cultivated, because their products are untaxed, and her's to lie deserted from the excessive weight of taxes upon every species of vegitation? Are your manufactures to rival her's in every market, from your manufacturers being exempt from taxes, whilst British manufacturers pay taxes upon every thing they consume? Is Britain to impoverish her people, by subsisting a vast military force at *her sole expence*, to guard the seas for your ships to pass thereon in safety? Is she to take every measure to compel her people to desert her, and seek an assylum from taxes in your happier climates, and thus raise your empire on the ruin of her own? Surely you will not be so unreasonable, to expect these things at her hands? Say then, what is it you propose? Which of her laws are to be abrogated, or must she cancel them all? Will you acknowledge the authority of her legislature *in any instance?* Or will you allow her to be your sovereign in nothing? Do not trifle with her, by starting one objection after another, till you prevail on her to whittle down her authority, so that it shall become neither of use to herself or you; but tell her what it is you are willing to *suffer her to retain*, as well as what it is you *choose she should give up?* Name but the thing you will agree to, and you may then hope to find attention to your complaints? But do not flatter yourselves, that she is yet so despicable as to be terrified by your threats, or so ignorant of your affairs, as to imagine you can carry them into execution. There is a spirit rising in this country, which will make you to know its strength and your own weakness, that will convince you of its authority and of your dependence.

I have honestly endeavoured to call you back to your duty, by shewing you the weakness of the ground you stand upon, and the fatal consequences which hang over you. If you do not avail yourselves of the information I have given you, perhaps the people of England may be led by it to conceive more justly of their *Rights*, and of your *Intentions*, than they have hitherto done; and may compel you to submit, if they unhappily find no argument, but force can induce you to obey. It is time indeed for my countrymen to bestir themselves, and to vindicate the honour of the state, and the rights of its legislature—for will not posterity learn with amazement, that the Commons of

Great Britain, in the first parliament of George the Third, with this cloud of evidence before their eyes, seemed to doubt of the authority of the legislature to bind the Colonies, and left it to their successors to *carry into execution* those rights of parliament, which they had scarcely sufficient courage to *declare*. They will indeed find two protests in the Lords Journals, which will shew them, that there were then men in parliament who had ability to discern, and firmness to assert their own, and the people of England's rights, at that disgraceful æra. But the history of those times will inform them, however unwillingly the feelings of the historian may suffer him to record the dishonour of his country, that those great statesmen were not then the servants of the crown, and that those to whom the King had intrusted his ministry, were directed, in their measures, by *the very men* who had fomented and countenanced, by their public and private writings and discourses, resistance in the Colonies to acts of parliament. They will be told, perhaps, how truly posterity must judge, that the majority of that House of Commons were the followers of every minister, and the tools of every faction, that could possess themselves of the power to dispense places and pensions among their dependants; that they were reproached with their servility, even by those whom they most meanly flattered. They will hear, that the lawful authority of the sovereign, had been debased and insulted by the sworn servants of the crown, whose immediate duty it was to support it. If they can give credit to such representations, they will cease to be astonished at the repeal of a law by the same parliament, which enacted it for no better a reason, than that the Colonies declared they would not obey it. But they will gladly turn from these gloomy reflections, and place their hopes in the wisdom and vigor of the new House of Commons, which they will be told, was freely chosen by the people in 1768. They will flatter themselves, that that House of Commons eagerly seized the first fit occasion for vindicating its honour, and restoring the sinking dignity of parliament to its former lustre. They will hope to find those who had been misled by the artful misrepresentations of the Colony advocates, making haste to repair to their country the cruel injuries they had done her. They will expect to see a well considered plan proposed, for healing the unhappy breach between Great

Britain and her Colonies, and that such temperate and effectual measures were adopted, and so firmly pursued, that before the revolt became general, and discrimination impossible, the mass of the people were restrained from rebellion, by the wisdom and spirit of their councils. They will persuade themselves, that the people of England, and the trading part especially, *whose property and commercial interests so much depend upon the power of parliament to bind the Colonies*, set aside every smaller consideration, and private concern, and united as one man in support of their common rights, and in the furtherance of measures for bringing back the Colonies to their duty.

The journals of parliament in the present session will shew how well founded were their hopes.

Edward Bancroft, Remarks on the Review of the Controversy Between Great Britain and Her Colonies. In Which the Errors of Its Author Are Exposed, and the Claims of the Colonies Vindicated, upon the Evidence of Historical Facts and Authentic Records. New London, 1771.

When this pamphlet was first published anonymously in London in 1769, England was experiencing rioting and disorder that surpassed anything going on in Massachusetts. Mob violence in London was in fact recurrent throughout the 1760s, and it reached a peak at the end of the decade. At the center of this popular tumult was John Wilkes, one of the greatest demagogues in English history. Born the son of a distiller in 1725, Wilkes was an impoverished journalist with a seedy reputation when, with the patronage of Lord Temple, he became a member of Parliament in 1757. Six years later he was imprisoned for publishing a libel against the king in No. 45 of his newspaper, the *North Briton*, and the House of Commons ordered the offending issue publicly burned. Freed by virtue of his immunity as a member of Parliament, Wilkes later fled to France, and the English courts declared him an outlaw. He returned to England in 1768 and was several times elected to the House of Commons, but each time Parliament denied him his seat. Huge London crowds, composed of shopkeepers, tradesmen, petty merchants, and others deprived of a substantial role in English politics, took to the streets in tumultuous riots crying, "Wilkes and Liberty."

This emerging English radicalism could not help but intensify the imperial controversy. A vocal supporter of colonial rights, Wilkes quickly became an American hero. The colonists named towns and children after him, raised money for his cause, and made the "No. 45" a libertarian symbol of their common fight against tyranny. Such divisions within the English political class helped convince the colonists that their struggle with Parliament was part of a larger contest in which not only their liberties but those of all British subjects were at stake.

Like his friend Benjamin Franklin, Massachusetts-born Edward Bancroft was no admirer of mobs and the disorder they brought. Also like Franklin, he was keen to find a way of holding the empire together. Six years before he wrote this pamphlet, a nineteen-year-old Bancroft had run away to sea and spent several years in Surinam before in turn migrating to London in 1767 to study medicine. The same year his *Remarks* appeared he published *The Natural History of Guiana*, which established his scholarly reputation and led to his election to the Royal Society. In 1776 he would be recruited as a spy for the American commissioners in Paris, but in fact he became a double agent, spying much more effectively for the British while serving as secretary to the American legation in France.

In the pages that follow his loyalties seem firmly rooted in the land of his birth. Bancroft's pamphlet, which was republished, now with his byline, in New London, Connecticut, in 1771, directly confronted the dilemma that Knox had posed for the colonists—that Americans were either totally under Parliament's authority or totally outside of it, which to Knox meant they could no longer be British subjects. Based on a detailed survey of their seventeenth-century crown-chartered origins, Bancroft argued that the colonies were distinct states existing outside the realm and thus outside of all parliamentary authority, while at the same time the colonists remained within the British Empire by virtue of their common allegiance to the king. This ingenious solution to the problem of sovereignty posed by Knox was so attractive to the colonists that one scholar has claimed that Bancroft's pamphlet "became the most influential patriot text of the early 1770s." But the idea that Americans would tie themselves solely to the king was deeply perplexing to British Whigs. Lord North, for one, accused the Americans of using the language of "Toryism."

REMARKS

ON THE

REVIEW of the CONTROVERSY

BETWEEN

GREAT BRITAIN and her COLONIES.

IN WHICH

The ERRORS of its AUTHOR are expofed,

AND

The CLAIMS of the COLONIES vindicated,

Upon the EVIDENCE of

Hiftorical FACTS and authentic RECORDS.

To which is fubjoined,
A PROPOSAL for terminating the prefent unhappy DISPUTE
with the COLONIES;
Recovering their COMMERCE;
Reconciling their AFFECTION;
Securing their RIGHTS;
And eftablifhing their DEPENDENCE on a juft and
permanent BASIS.

Humbly fubmitted to the Confideration of the BRITISH LEGISLATURE.

By EDWARD BANCROFT.

Confilia qui dant prava cautis hominibus,
Et perdunt operam et deridentur turpiter.
PHOEDR. Fab. xxv.

LONDON: Printed in the Year 1769.
NEW-LONDON, in NEW-ENGLAND:
Re-printed and Sold by T. GREEN. M,DCC,LXXI.

Remarks on the Review of the Controversy Between Great Britain and Her Colonies.

THE Right Honourable *George Grenville* succeeded to the Treasury, on its Abdication by Lord *Bute*; and eager to display the Abilities of a Financier, undertook to provide new Resources for national and ministerial Exigencies, by Commerical Regulations; an extension of Excise in *Great-Britain*; and a Tax on the Colonies. An unprecedented Naval Establishment was formed to aid in Collection of the Customs; the Vigour of Commerce was depressed, and a most valuable Branch of Trade exterminated in *America*: The odious Cyder and Stamp Acts also received Existence, and were received with universal Opposition; whilst their common Parent, from another Cause, was happily divested of every public Employment. Incessant have been his Endeavours, and various his Expedients, since that Æra, for the Recovery of Power; among which that of writing himself into Office is not the least considerable. The Public has seen his ministerial Conduct and Capacity applauded without Modesty or Truth, not only in Prose, but Verse,* not only in the Daily Papers, but in Volumes, written either by himself or Dependants, for no other Purpose. The most considerable of these Performances are, *The Present State of the Nation*, and *The Controversy between Great Britain and her Colonies reviewed*, both apparently written by the same Persons. In the former, the Authors endeavour to convey an Eulogium on Mr. *Grenville*'s political Conduct; present an exaggerated Idea of those Miseries in which the Nation is involved by the preposterous Measures of the present Ministry; and by suggesting the Necessity of a Change, to make Way for their Patron's Return to his pristine Power. The latter has been written more especially to obviate the many Objections which have been justly made to Mr. *Grenville*'s Return to Office, on Account of the Difficulties in which the Nation has been already involved by his *American* Measures. Through both these Performances have ultimately the same End in View, they have

---

* See an Ode on the present Period of Time, with a Letter addressed to the Right Hon. *George Grenville*. 4to.

been very differently received by the Ministry. The former was naturally condemned; but the latter, conveying no direct Censure on the present Administration, and aiming only to justify Mr. *Grenville*'s former Conduct, by vindicating that national Supremacy over the Colonies, which those in Power have somewhat intemperately supported, has received the concurrent Support of Ministerial, and *Grenvillian* Approbation. It is this Performance that is the Subject of my present Observations. A Performance undertaken with many Advantages, and executed with laboured Fallacy, Art, and Sophistry, for the *laudable* Purpose of encouraging the People of *Great Britain* to oppress their *American* Brethren; and of persuading the Inhabitants of the Colonies, in Opposition to the Feelings of Nature, and the Dictates of Common Sense, to relinquish those Rights, which alone constitute the Distinctions between Freedom and Slavery.—To oppose a Design so malevolent is the Duty of every Individual, but more especially of every uncorrupt *British American*, not yet converted to a Patricide by a lucrative Office, or ministerial Dependance.—"On this Principle, and actuated by these Motives, it is, that, unawed by the Terrors that rise before me, I adventure upon my present undertaking, and set down to expose *The Review of the American Controversy*, with the single, and, I hope, honest Purpose," of vindicating the Right of my Fellow Subjects in that Country in which I received my Being, and of exposing the Fallacy of those Arguments which have been urged against them by the Author, or rather Authors, of the Work before me.—I cannot, indeed, investigate the Nature of those Terrors which these Gentlemen foresaw, as attendant on their Attempt to vindicate that national Sovereignty over the Colonies, which a British Parliament has solemnly asserted (Terrors of which they have expressed lively and affecting Ideas, in the Words I have just recited,) as Reason seems to suggest more Danger in an Undertaking, in some Degree repugnant to the Sovereignty thus asserted. I flatter myself, however, that, as the Colonies are denied every Species of Representation in the British Legislature, I may be allowed, in this Manner, to expose the Grievance attending the present Exercise of Parliamentary Authority over them, who have no better Method of Justification; provided it be done with that Decency, Moderation, and Justice, which I hope will characterize my present Observations.

The Pleas urged by the Advocates for the Colonies, our Authors have reduced to the two following general Heads: "The Title of the Inhabitants in the Colonies to all the Rights, Liberties and Privileges of *Englishmen*; and their Claim to Exemption from the Jurisdiction of Parliament." But the latter of these Claims, of Exemption from the Jurisdiction of Parliament, was never exhibited by any Advocate for the Colonies, and is a perfect Non-entity, which our Authors have imposed on the Publick, to obtain an Opportunity of combatting Errors of their own Creation, and of *sagaciously* demonstrating the obvious Absurdity of claiming the Privileges of *British* Subjects, and at the same Time denying the Jurisdiction of the *British* Legislature.—The Colonies do not deny the Authority of Parliament in any Particular, except that of arbitrarily taking away their Property, actually acquired through all the Restraints which Parliament has opposed to the Acquisition. Had they therefore, imputed to the Colonies a Claim of Exemption from the *Taxation*, instead of "*Jurisdiction*" of Parliament, they would have acted with more Justice.

Having thus erroneously stated the Claims of the Colonies, our Author (for I shall hereafter mention them in the Singular Number, as they mention themselves,) proceeds to shew the Danger they must incur from Prerogative, should they succeed in vindicating their *imputed* Claim of Exemption from Parliamentary Authority, without first proving their Title to the Rights, Liberties, and Privileges of *Englishmen*: To determine the Justice of this Title in the Colonies, he examines the Resolves of their several Assemblies, subsequent to the late Stamp-Act, and in the Course of his Examination rejects every Fact alledged by them in Support of their Claim to the Rights and Privileges of *Englishmen*. The Law of God and Nature, the natural Rights of Mankind, a Royal Charter, an Act of Parliament, common Justice, &c. are all with him of no Avail; and he exults in the flattering Idea, of having proved the Contents of the *American* Resolves to be inconsistent and absurd. It is not my Intention to enter into a particular Vindication of the Resolutions of these Assemblies; it will be sufficient for me to observe, that the Absurdity he has imputed to them, is wholly imaginary, and arises solely from his having imposed on them a Claim of Exemption from Parliamentary Jurisdiction, which they never exhibited. I could wish, however, that our Author had explained the Principles on which the British Nation founds its Title to the Constitution it now enjoys; since he has rejected those alledged by the *American* Assemblies. I do not mean the Title of an *Englishman* to the Privileges of an *English* Subject, but of the Nation collectively to its Constitution.—I am sufficiently aware of the Impropriety of claiming the Rights belonging to the Members of a State, without yielding Obedience to its Legislative Authority; but will venture, notwithstanding, to affirm, that if the Colonies should be found without the Jurisdiction of the British Parliament, their Title to Rights and Privileges, similar to those of British Subjects, is founded on Principles as valid, and just, as those which support the Right of the British Nation to its present Constitution. The first Settlers in the *American* Colonies, at the Time of their Migration, besides their natural Right to Freedom, were constitutionally intitled to all the Rights, Privileges, and Immunities of *Englishmen*; and the Security and Perpetuation of these, or similar Privileges, was, in forming the Constitution of the Colonies, expresly stipulated, between the King and People, and confirmed by the Faith of Royal Charters; fundamental, and consequently indefeasible Acts, equally binding on the Prince and Subjects; and I will venture to assert, that neither *Great Britain*, nor any other Nation, has a better Title to its Constitution, than that of the Colonies. Whether the Clauses in their Charters, which expresly convey to their Inhabitants, and their "Children and Posterity which shall be born there, all the Privileges, Liberties, Franchises, and Immunities of free Denizens, and natural Subjects, within any of" his Majesty's "Dominions, to all Intents and Purposes, as if they had been abiding and born within" his "Realm of *England*, *&c.*" was intended to secure them the Enjoyment of these Privileges in Quality of English Subjects, or only to confirm to them Privileges similar to those of English Subjects, is of little Importance: Our Author, indeed, denies the Right of the King to grant Foreigners the Privileges of natural Subjects; but he will not deny the King's Right to grant the Inhabitants of the

Colonies without the Realm, Privileges perfectly similar to those of *Englishmen*; and these will satisfy us in *America*, as well as the very identical ones; and whenever we chuse to return within the Realm, if our Royal Charters cannot render us *Englishmen*, perhaps it may be expedient to avail ourselves of the Act of the 13th of *George* the Second, which is abundantly sufficient for that Purpose. Our Author has, indeed, objected to this, as inconsistent, in the Assembly of the *Massachusetts*; but let him not object it to me as such. Ludicrous as he may think it, I assert, that Parliament may have a "*Right to benefit, but not bind,*" a State, and to "*give Bounties, but not impose Burthens.*" It may give the People of *Holland*, who live within the Realm, the Privileges of natural Subjects, but not tax them when in their own Country. The Rights of the Colonies being thus secured, whether within or without the Realm, all those alarming Apprehensions of Danger from our falling into the Hands of Prerogative, which our Author, and some others equally *notorious* for their Affection to the Colonies, and sollicitous for the Preservation of their Rights, profess to entertain, and good naturedly, though somewhat officiously, disclose, appear to have no just Foundation. A King inclined to Despotism might, indeed, invade the Rights of the Colonies, in Spite of those Compacts and Charters, by which they have been solemnly confirmed: But the same King might, with equal Justice and Facility, infringe the Conditions of the Great Charter of *English* Liberty; and from the Corruption which at present universally prevails in this Kingdom, I doubt not but it might be effected with more Impunity than in the Colonies; so that if they should ever be deemed distinct States, I doubt not but their Liberties would be at least as secure from the Encroachments of Prerogative, as those of *Great Britain*.

The next Subject of our Author's Enquiry is, Whether the Colonies ought to be considered as distinct independent States, or mere British Corporations, within the Realm and Jurisdiction of Parliament: And in several Parts of his Review, he endeavours to support the latter Conclusions, though by very delusive Arguments and unfair Representations. Shall I controvert this Conclusion, and expose the Fallacy on which it is founded; or shall I tacitly assent thereto?—The Colonies do not declare themselves distinct States, independent to the

British Parliament; nor do I really know whether they would chuse to be considered as such. The present Ministry, indeed, appear sollicitous to have them deemed as Parts of the Realm, and already adequately and constitutionally represented in its Legislative Assembly, in which not one Member is elected by, or dependent on them. But as this, if admitted, must reduce them to a State of Slavery, as positive and abject as any that ever was imposed on any People, and as I cannot so far divest myself of Patriotism as to be unconcerned for the Fate of my native Country; I shall endeavour to expose the Fallacy of this ministerial Position, so injurious to the Colonies, by fairly explaining the Terms, Principles, and Designs of their Settlement; and the Degree and Mode of Connection, which was intended, and ought to subsist, between them and their Parent Country. To effect this, it will be necessary to review their Political History, the Charters on which they were settled, the Circumstances attending their Settlement, and the Conduct of the King and Parliament towards them since that Æra; which will afford an Opportunity of exposing the Fallacy and Partiality of our Author's Extracts from the Charters of the several Colonies, and the Acts of Parliament relating to them.—As the original Constitution of the Colonies, and their Connection with this Kingdom, is of Importance in determining the present Controversy, and as our Author has treated it in various Forms, and in different Parts of his Work, I shall beg Leave to refute his Arguments, under one general Head, without regarding the Order (if it may be so called) in which he has disposed them.

"The first Charter granted by the Crown of *England* for the Purpose of Colonization, is" *not* "that granted by King *James* the First, to the two *Virginia* Companies, dated *April* the 10th, 1606," as our Author asserts, "those which precede it" *not* "having been granted for the Purpose of *Discovery*" only, but of *Colonization* also; the first Patent ever granted by the English Crown for planting Colonies, being that from Queen *Elizabeth* to Sir *Walter Raleigh*, investing him with all such Territories in *America* as he should Discover and *Plant*, between the 33d and 40th Degrees of *North* Latitude, of which the following is an Abstract.

"*Elizabeth*, by the Grace of God, &c.—Know ye, that of our

special Grace and mere Motion, we have given and granted, and by these Presents, for Us, our Heirs and Successors, do give and grant, to our trusty and well-beloved *Walter Raleigh*, Esq; and to his Heirs and Assigns for ever, free Liberty at all Times for ever hereafter, to Discover and View such remote, *Heathen*, and barbarous Lands and Territories, not actually possessed of any *Christian* Prince, or inhabited by *Christian* People, as to him and them shall seem good, and the same to have, hold, occupy, and enjoy, to him, his Heirs and Assigns, for ever, with all *Prerogatives, Jurisdictions, Royalties, Privileges*, and *Franchises* thereunto belonging, by *Sea* or Land: And the said *Walter Raleigh*, his Heirs and Assigns, are hereby impowred to *build* and *fortify* on such Land, *&c.* at their Discretion.

And we do likewise impower the said *Walter Raleigh*, his Heirs and Assigns, to take and lead in the said Voyage, or to inhabit there, as many of our Subjects as shall willingly accompany him or them, with sufficient Shipping and Necessaries for their Transportation.

And further, the said *Walter Raleigh*, his Heirs and Assigns, shall hold, occupy, and enjoy, all such Lands and Countries so to be discovered and possessed; and the Cities, Towns, Castles, and Villages in the same, with the *Royalties, Franchises*, and *Jurisdictions* thereof, with full Power, *&c.* reserving to Us, our Heirs and Successors, the fifth Part of all Gold and Silver Ore that shall be acquired or got in such Countries; and the same shall be holden of Us, our Heirs and Successors, by *Homage*, and the Payment of the said fifth Part, *&c.* in Lieu of all Services.

And moreover, we do, by these Presents, grant, That the said *Walter Raleigh*, his Heirs, and Assigns, may encounter, expulse, and resist all such Persons as shall, without his or their Consent, attempt to inhabit in the said Countries, *&c.*

And we do further grant to the said *Walter Raleigh*, his Heirs and Assigns, full Power and Authority to correct, punish, pardon, and govern, as well in Cases Capital as Criminal and Civil, all such of our Subjects as shall adventure themselves in the said Voyages, or inhabit such Lands or Countries according to such Laws and Statutes as shall be established by him and them, for the better Government of the said People; so as such Laws be as agreeable to the Laws of *England* as may be, and be not contrary to the Christian Faith, and so as the said People remain subject to the Crown of *England*.

Witness Ourself at *Westminster*, the 25th of *March*, 1584, and in the Twenty-sixth Year of our Reign."

As our Author chuses to consider the Colonies as unalienable from the Realm by the Crown, and as this is the first Royal Grant of *American* Territory to English Subjects, it may not be improper to consider the Title on which it is founded. The Pope was the first who assumed Authority to dispose of the Countries of Infidels, and that by his Apostolic Succession; and to this all *Christian* Princes submitted, when the East was granted to *Portugal*, and the West to *Spain*. But his Right in this Particular being afterwards questioned, every *European* Prince assumed the same Authority, and liberally granted away the Dominion and Property of *Pagan* Countries; judging, undoubtedly, that *Christianity* could alone give a Title to the Enjoyment of this World, or the next. And however ridiculous this may now appear, it is evident, that Queen *Elizabeth*'s Grant was founded on no other Title, even from the Patent itself; because, had she been vested with any Right to those Countries, which was not common to all *Christian* Princes, the Reservation in Favour of any *Christian* Sovereigns, by whom those Countries might be possessed, would never have been inserted. And, indeed, it was impossible the Queen could have had any other Title to the Territory in question, unless it was derived from *Sebastian Cabot*'s Discovery of the Northern Continent of *America*, near one Hundred Years before. But Discovery, (at best a very slender Title,) when unattended with Possession or Occupancy, (which alone could give it any Validity,) during the long Interval that succeeded, and especially when the Property of the discovered Country was already vested in its natural Proprietors and Inhabitants, certainly could afford but a very indifferent Right: Nor does it appear, that *Cabot* ever discovered the Country which was granted by this Patent. But however valid the Queen's Title to the Lands then granted in *America* might be, it was vested in herself only; and no Person will affirm, that the Nation had any Claims thereto, or that that Part of *America*, situated between the 33d and 40th Degrees of North Latitude, was then annexed to the Realm; and I believe it will be difficult to prove, that it has been since united thereto, or indeed, that any Power, after it had been legally granted to others, could annex it to the Realm without *their* Consent. If therefore the Crown, by Discovery or otherwise, acquired a Title to any Part of *America*, it belonged to the Crown alone, and could be for ever alienated from the Realm, either to Subjects or Foreigners, at the Pleasure of the Crown. As it is an indisputable Maxim, that every Acquisition of foreign Territory is at the King's absolute Disposal, and after being thus alienated from the Realm, cannot be again united to it, without Consent of its Proprietors. Whether the Territory of the Colonies has been in this Manner alienated, their several Charters will best determine. As to Queen *Elizabeth*'s Charter to Sir *Walter Raleigh*, it was a modified Grant of the Sovereignty of that Country, with all the Privileges necessary to constitute a distinct State, to be held of the Crown by Homage, *&c.* the Queen divesting herself of all Share in the Legislative and Executive Authority, prescribing, however, for her own Security, a Model for its Constitution, as agreeable as might be to that of *England*; for that this was the End of the Limitation therein contained, relative to its Laws, will fully appear hereafter. This Charter, after many unsuccessful Attempts to settle a Colony in *Virginia*, being forfeited by Sir *Walter Raleigh*'s Attainder, King James the First, by Letters Patent, dated the 10th of *April*, 1606, in the Fourth Year of his Reign, created the two *Virginia* Companies, authorizing them to plant Colonies in *America*, between the thirty-fourth and forty-fifth Degree of North Latitude; granting them for that Purpose, "all the Lands, Woods, Soil, Grounds, Havens, Ports, Rivers, Mines, Minerals, Marshes, Commodities, Fishings, Hereditaments, Jurisdictions, *&c.* within the same," and authorizing them to "inhabit and remain there, and also build and fortify within the same;" declaring that no other of his Subjects should "be permitted or suffered to inhabit or plant therein," without their Licence. The Colonies, when planted, were to be governed each by a Council of thirteen Persons, agreeable to such Laws, Ordinances, &c. as should be transmitted to them by his Majesty, under his Sign Manual or Privy Seal, and were authorized to "establish and cause to be made a *Coin* to pass current there, of such Metal, and in such Form, as the said several Councils there shall limit and appoint:" His Majesty therein declaring, that all his Subjects inhabiting the said Colonies, or their Children born therein, should "have and enjoy all Liberties, Franchises, and Immunities, within any of his other Dominions," to all Intents and Purposes, "as if they had been abiding and born within this his Realm of *England*:" A Declaration which (with others of a similar Nature in every *America* Charter) expressly implies, that the Colonies were not intended to be within the Realm of *England*. A Council was likewise established here, similar to the Privy Council of *England* and *Ireland*, for the superior Direction of these Colonies; and the Exercise of the Power it was vested with would have been incompatible with any other Constitution than that of distinct States. Through the Whole of this Charter, the Colonies are considered as being without the Realm, and not the least Provision is made therein for their Dependance, either on the Laws or Legislature of *England*, which are not even named in the Patents. In 1609, a second Charter was granted to the Treasurer and Company of *Virginia*, to enlarge and explain their Privileges, by which they were erected into "one Body or Commonalty perpetual," and vested with the Property of that Country and the Islands lying within one Hundred Miles of the Shores of both Seas, with all their Commodities, Jurisdictions, Royalties, &c. to be holden of the King, his Heirs and Successors, as of his Manor of *East Greenwich*, in free and common Soccage, paying only one fifth of all Gold and Silver Ore to be obtained therein, in Lieu of all Manner of Services; vesting in the Council for the said Company, first appointed by the King, and afterwards chosen by themselves, with the Approbation of the Lord Chancellor, "full Power and Authority to make, ordain, and establish all Manner of Orders, Laws, Directions, Instructions, Forms, and Ceremonies of Government and Magistracy, fit and necessary for, and concerning the Government of, the said Colony, and the same to abrogate, revoke, or change at all Times, not only within the Precincts of the said Colony, but also on the Seas in going or coming to or from the said Colony," without any Reservation for securing their Dependance on the Laws, or Parliament of this Kingdom, which are here likewise nameless.

It is likewise especially provided, that the said Company, "and every of them, their Factors, and Assigns, shall be free of all Subsidies and Customs in *Virginia*, for the Space of one-and-twenty Years, *and from all Taxes and Impositions for ever*, upon any Goods or Merchandizes at any Time or Times hereafter, either upon Importation thither, or Exportation from thence." —The third Charter from the King, dated *March* 12, 1611–12, grants to the Treasurer and Company of *Virginia*, all Islands lying in the Sea, and within Three Hundred Miles of *Virginia*, to be held in the same Manner, and with the same Privileges, as the rest of that Province; and especially ordains, that there shall be four Times in each Year, "for ever, one great, general, and solemn Assembly, which four Assemblies shall be stiled and called the Four Great and General Courts of the Council and Company of Adventurers of *Virginia*: In all and every of which said Great and General Courts, so assembled, our Will and Pleasure is, and we do, for Us, our Heirs and Successors, for ever, give and grant to the said Treasurer and Company, or the greater Number of them so assembled, that they shall and may have full Power and Authority, from Time to Time, and at all Times hereafter, to elect and chuse discreet Persons to be of our said Council for the first Colony of *Virginia*, and to nominate and appoint such Officers as they shall think fit and requisite, for the Government, managing, ordering and dispatching of the Affairs of the said Company, and shall likewise have full Power and Authority to ordain and make such Laws and Ordinances for the Good and Welfare of the said Plantation, as to them, from Time to Time, shall be thought requisite and meet, *so always as the same be not contrary to the Laws and Statutes of this our Realm of England*."

This is the first Instance in which King *James* the First ever divested himself of all Share in the Legislative and Executive Authority of any *American* Colony: And here, for the first Time, we find him adding a Clause for limiting the Power of Legislation therein, to a Conformity with the Laws of *England*, similar to that contained in Queen *Elizabeth*'s Charter to Sir *Walter Raleigh*, which, though properly omitted in the preceding Charter, in which the King had reserved to himself a Power of restraining their Legislation, was now become necessary for limiting those Laws which he could never afterwards revise or repeal, to the end that the Authority, thus solemnly granted, might not be perverted to his own Disadvantage; and to prevent this, by prescribing a Form and Model for their Civil Constitution, over which the Royal Prerogative could afterwards have no Power, he wisely inserted the aforesaid Clause; and for the same cogent Reason it was afterwards copied into the Charters of *Massachusetts Bay, Maryland, &c.* with some Variations; as that their Laws should "be consonant to Reason, and not repugnant or contrary, but as near as conveniently may be, agreeable to the Laws, Statutes, and Rights of this our Kingdom of *England*;" a Mode of Expression which alone proves, that the Clause was not inserted to bind the Colonies to obey Acts of Parliament, but only to limit and modulate their Government and Laws upon Principles conformable to the Constitution of *England*: And agreeable to this, we find, that the Government of *Virginia*, upon the Arrival of Sir *George Yardly*, soon after this Patent had been obtained, was new modelled, that it might "resemble the *British* Constitution composed of two Houses of Parliament and a Sovereign: The Number of the Council was increased, intending this Body should represent the House of Lords, while the House of Commons was composed of Burgesses assembled from every Plantation and Settlement in the Country." *Mod. Univers. Hist.* It would, indeed, have been absurd and unnecessary to invest the Colonies with the Power of Legislation, if the Laws of *England* were to extend thither. Besides, the Limitation in Question is very insufficient to authorize any such Extension, as their Laws might be very dissimilar, but not repugnant to the Laws of *England*. And we find that Crimes which, in this Kingdom, are punishable with Death, in some of the Colonies have only a pecuniary Punishment, *et vice versa*; the Laws of *England*, in general, never having had any Force in *America*; and the Lords of Council having determined, "that Acts of Parliament not naming the Colonies, shall not bind them:" And if the Clause of Limitation does not give Validity to all Acts of Parliament in *America*, without Discrimination, it certainly does not to any particular ones. But natural and obvious as this Construction must appear, the Opponents to the Colonies will by no Means admit of it, having singled out this restraining Clause as sufficient to authorize the Extension of Parliamentary Taxation to *America*; and our Author asserts, that the Colonies cannot pretend that their Obedience to Parliamentary Authority "has been altered or released by Charters, or Authorities, from the Executive Power; for, on the contrary, Obedience to the Laws of *Great Britain*, without any Restriction, is expressly reserved in every one of them." Thus we see the Sense of this restraining Clause, which has been Copied into all the Charters, perverted, and Conclusions boldly drawn therefrom, unwarrantable by Reason or Justice. How, then, is the true Intent and Meaning of this Clause, for limiting the Legislative Acts of the Colonies, to be discovered? *James* and *Charles*, by whom (after *Elizabeth*) this Clause was primarily inserted in the *American* Charters, and whose Conduct, in this Particular, was the Example followed in adding it to the subsequent Charters for Colonization, are long since dead, and unable to give the desired Explanation. If, however, it should be found that these Monarchs, by any Acts of theirs, had clearly and indubitably explained their Intention relative to the Clause in Question, it would be all that can possibly be expected or required; and I flatter myself that an Explanation of this Nature would receive the Assent of the most prejudiced Person on this Subject, even of Mr. *Grenville* himself; and at the present Æra, when Posts of Honour and Profit are prostituted as Rewards to those, who, by Artifice and Sophistry, are most successful in subverting the Claims of the Colonies, I am particularly happy in reciting Facts which discover the Intention of the Clause in Question, or at least prove beyond Contradiction, that it was not inserted to render the Colonies subject to Parliamentary Authority, or render the Laws of *England* valid in *America*. The Charter which provides that the Laws of *Virginia* shall not be contrary to the Laws and Statutes of *England*, bears Date the 12th of *March*, 1612; and on the 25th of *April*, 1621, soon after the Constitution of *Virginia* had received that Form it has ever since retained, when a Bill was proposed in the House of Commons for granting to the Subjects of *England* free Liberty of Fishing on the Coast of *America*, the House was told by the Secretary of State, from his Majesty, that *America* was not annexed to the Realm, and that it was not fitting that Parliament should make Laws for those Countries; and though the House was uncommonly sollicitous for this Bill, and often offered it for the Royal Assent, it was always refused by the Crown, for those very just and cogent Reasons. And the King's Successor, *Charles* the First, by whom the *Plymouth, Massachusetts,* and *Maryland* Charters were soon after granted, when the same Bill was again offered, refused it the Royal Assent, declaring, at the same time, that it was "unnecessary; that the Colonies were without the Realm and Jurisdiction of Parliament, and that the Privy Council would take order in Matters relating to them;" though a little after, when the *Maryland* Charter was granted, he reserved to the Subjects of *England* the same Right of Fishing upon the Coast of that Province, which was intended to be secured by the Bill that was denied the Royal Assent; which abundantly proves, that the King did not refuse the Bill for any secret Reasons, but only because he thought it might afford a Precedent for an unwarrantable Extension of Parliamentary Jurisdiction. Will any Person, who is informed of these Facts, believe that those Kings who repeatedly denied their Assent to every Act relating to *America*, because it was without the Realm and Jurisdiction of Parliament, could have inserted the Clause in Question, to render *Virginia, Massachusetts Bay, Maryland. &c.* subject to the Authority of Parliament? Or that the Colonies were not by them considered as distinct States, not dependent on the Authority of the English Legislature? And yet, if this should be granted, and if the Crown (as is evident) have a Right to constitute distinct States in *America*; and if the Colonies, according to the Royal Intention and Construction, were so constituted, and if they were peopled and planted on this Principle and Condition, it will follow, as a necessary Consequence, that no Power on Earth could afterwards unite them to the Realm of *England*, or subject them to the Authority of its Parliament, without their own special Consent, given in the same formal and solemn Manner as was done by the Kingdom of *Scotland*, at its Union with *England*; and that every Act of Parliament, which has hitherto bound them is an Infringement of their Rights.

The Settlement of *New-England* followed that of *Virginia*, and was occasioned by a noble Disdain of civil and religious Tyranny, the very Object for which it was solely undertaken being an Emancipation from the Authority of Parliament, and those Grievances which they suffered under the Laws of *England*; an Object for which they had before retired to foreign Countries, particularly *Holland*; where they remained till Sir *Robert Naunton*, then Secretary of State, convinced his Majesty of the Impolicy of unpeopling his own Dominions, by religious Oppression, for the Benefit of his Neighbours, and obtained Leave for the *Puritans* to settle in *America*, for which they embarked in *Holland*, having previously treated with the *Virginia* Company for a Tract of Land near *Hudson*'s River. But upon their Arrival in *America*, they found themselves at *Cape Cod*, where the Season of the Year obliged them to land, though it was without the Limits of the *Virginia* Company's Patent, and their future Settlement, consequently, could not be held by them from any *European* Prince or State. In this Situation they considered themselves as having reverted to their native Freedom; but being desirous still to continue under the Allegiance and Protection of their former Sovereign, they executed the following Instrument, which was signed by all the Heads of Families.

"In the Name of God, Amen! We, whose Names are underwritten, the loyal Subjects of our dread Sovereign Lord King *James*, by the Grace of God of *Great Britain, France*, and *Ireland*, King, Defender of the Faith, *&c.* having undertaken, for the Glory of God and the Advancement of the *Christian* Faith, and the Honour of our King and Country, a Voyage to plant the first Colony in the Northern Parts of *Virginia*, do, by these Presents, solemnly and mutually, in the Presence of God and one another, *covenant and combine ourselves together into a Civil Body Politick for our better ordering and Preservation, and Furtherance of the Ends aforesaid, and by Virtue hereof, to enact, constitute, and frame such just and equal Laws, Ordinances, Acts, Constitutions, and Officers, from Time to Time, as shall be thought most meet and convenient, for the general Good of the Colony, unto which we promise all due Submission and Obedience.*

> In Witness whereof we have hereunto subscribed our
> Names, at *Cape Cod*, *Nov.* the 11th, 1620."

This was the Constitution of the Colony of *New Plymouth*,
the Inhabitants acquiring a most equitable Title to their Lands
by Purchase and Cession from its natural Proprietors, the *Indian* Tribes. King *James*, however, soon after their Embarka-
tion for *America*, had established a Council at *Plymouth*, in the
Country of *Devon*, "for the planting, ruling, ordering, and
governing of *New-England* in *America*," and granting to "them,
their Successors and Assigns, all that Part of *America* lying and
being in Breadth from forty Degrees of Northerly Latitude
from the *Equinoctial* Line, to the forty-eighth Degree of the
said Northerly Latitude, inclusively; and in Length, of and
within all the Breadth aforesaid, throughout all the main Lands
from Sea to Sea, together with all the firm Lands, Soils, Grounds,
Havens, Ports, Rivers, Waters, Fishings, Mines, Minerals, precious
Stones, Quarries, and all and singular other Commodities, Jurisdictions, Royalties, Privileges, Franchises, and Pre-eminences,
both within the said Track of Land upon the Main, and also
within the Islands and Seas adjacent," to be holden of his said
Majesty, his Heirs and Successors, as of his Manor of *East-
Greenwich*, in free and common Soccage, yielding and paying
to, *&c.* the fifth Part of all Gold and Silver Ore to be obtained
therein, "for and in Respect of all and all Manner of Duties
Demands, and Services." To this Grant was likewise added
the sole and exclusive Power of Legislation, and of electing
and constituting all Officers of Government, both Civil and
Military, together with Authority to coin Money, make War
and Peace with the *Indians*, and all other Privileges necessary
for their distinct and independent Government: And the Colony of *New Plymouth* falling within this Grant, the Inhabitants,
a few Years after, purchased the entire Right of the Patentees
to that Part of the Country, with all their Rights, Privileges,
and Immunities. "Thus the Colony became a Kind of Republick by Patent from King *James* I. whereby they were
enabled to chuse a Governor, Council, and General Court,
who should have full Power of making and executing all Laws,
which should be judged necessary for the Publick Good, the

Sovereignty being still reserved to the Crown of *England*."— *Neal's History of New-England*.

The Colony of *Massachusetts* was settled for the same End, and from the same Motives, as that of *New-Plymouth*; first under the Sanction of a Patent from the Council established at *Plymouth*, and the next Year by a Charter from King *Charles* the First, bearing Date the 4th of *March*, in the Fourth Year of his Reign, whereby the Adventurers and Inhabitants were created "one Body Politick and Corporate in Fact and Name, by the Name of the Governor and Company of the *Massachusetts Bay* in *New England*," and invested with Powers, Liberties, and Privileges, similar to those of the Colony of *New-Plymouth*. Before this, however, King *James* had, by a Proclamation, dated the 15th of *July*, 1624, dissolved the *Virginia* Company, and received the Colony into his own immediate Dependence; which alarmed its Inhabitants, and produced a Remonstrance from them to the Throne, in which they expressed their Apprehensions of "Designs formed against their Rights and Privileges." To quiet these, the Lords of Council, in a Letter, dated the 22d of *July*, 1634, assured them from his Majesty, "That all their Estates, Trade, Freedom, and Privileges, should be enjoyed by them in as extensive a Manner as they enjoyed them before the Recall of the Company's Patent;" and their former Constitution and Laws were accordingly established and confirmed.

The Charter of *Maryland*, which followed that of the *Massachusetts Bay*, was granted to *Cecilius* Baron of *Baltimore*, by *Charles* the First, in the Eighth Year of his Reign, and invests the said Lord *Baltimore*, his Heirs and Assigns, with the Territory and Country of *Maryland*, and Islands adjacent, together with all their "Commodities, Jurisdictions, Privileges, Prerogatives, Royal Rights, *&c. &c.* of what Kind soever, as well by Sea as by Land:" In the fullest and most ample Manner constituting and appointing the "said Lord *Baltimore*, his Heirs and Assigns, true and absolute Lords and Proprietaries of the said Country, and of all the Premises aforesaid; saving always the Faith and Allegiance, and Sovereign Dominion, due to *Himself*, his Heirs, and Successors, to be holden of the Kings of *England* as of their Castle of *Windsor*, in free and common Soccage, *by Fealty only*, and not *in Capite*, or by Knights

Service, yielding and paying, therefore, to the said King, his Heirs, and Successors, two *Indian* Arrows of those Parts, to be delivered at his said Castle of *Windsor*, every Year, the second *Tuesday* in *Easter* Week; and also the fifth Part of all Gold or Silver Ore within the Limits aforesaid, which shall from Time to Time happen to be found. Granting also for himself, his Heirs and Successors, full and absolute Power to the said Lord *Baltimore*, his Heirs, *&c.* for the good and happy Government of the said Country, to ordain, make, enact, and, under his or their Seals, to publish any Laws *whatsoever*, appertaining either to the publick State of the said Province, or to the private Utility of particular Persons, according to their best Discretion, by and with the Advice, Assent, and Approbation of the Freemen of the said Province, or the greater Part of them, or of their Delegates or Deputies, whom, for the enacting of the said Laws, when and as often as need shall require, we will, that the said now Lord *Baltimore*, and his Heirs, shall assemble, in such Sort and Form, as to him and them shall seem best; and the said Laws duly to execute upon all People within the said Province or Limits thereof, for the time being, or that shall be constituted under the Government and Power of him or them, either sailing towards *Maryland*, or returning from thence towards *England*, or any other of our Dominions, by Imposition of Penalties, Imprisonment, or other Punishment; yea, if it shall be needful, and that the Quality of the Offence require it, by taking away Members, or Life, either by him the said now Lord *Baltimore*, and his Heirs, or by his or their Deputies, Lieutenants, Judges, Justices, Magistrates, Officers, and Ministers, to be ordained and appointed according to the Tenor and true Intention of these Presents: And likewise to appoint and establish any Judges, Justices, Magistrates, and Offices whatsoever, at *Sea* and *Land*, for what Cause soever, and with what Power soever, and in such Form, as to the said now Lord *Baltimore*, or his Heirs, shall seem most convenient: Also to remit, release, pardon, and abolish, whether before Judgment or after, all Crimes and Offences whatsoever against the said Laws, and to do all and every other *Thing or Things which unto the complete Establishment of Justice unto Courts, Prætories, and Tribunals, Forms of Judicature, and Manners of Proceedings do belong*, although in these Presents express

Mention be not made thereof; and by Judges by them delegated, to award Process, hold Pleas, and determine in all the said Courts and Tribunals, all Actions, Suits, and Causes whatsoever, as well criminal as civil, personal, real, mixed and pretorial; which Laws, so as aforesaid, to be punished, our Pleasure is, and so we enjoin, require, and command, shall be most absolute and available in Law, and that all the liege People and Subjects of us, our Heirs and Successors, do observe and keep the same inviolably in those Parts, so far as they concern them, under the Pains therein expressed, or to be expressed; provided nevertheless, that the said Laws be consonant to Reason, and be not repugnant, or contrary, but as near as conveniently may be, agreeable to the Laws, Statutes, and Rights of this our Kingdom of *England*." (A Limitation very expedient, for the Reasons which I have before recited.) Granting also to the said Lord *Baltimore, &c.* full Power and Authority to "build and fortify Castles, and other Places of Strength, for the publick and their own private Defence;" ordaining, that the said Country should be of his Allegiance, and its Inhabitants, Denizens and Lieges of the said King, *&c.* of their Kingdoms of *England* and *Ireland*; and empowering "the said Lord *Baltimore*, his Heirs, *&c.* or their Captains, or other Officers, to levy, muster, and train, all Sorts of Men, of what Condition, or wheresoever born, within the said Province, and to make War, and pursue their Enemies, as well by Sea as by Land, even without the Limits of the said Province, and to vanquish and take them, and to put them to Death by the Law of War, or save them, at their Pleasure," and to exercise the Law Martial upon all offending Persons, and "to confer Favours, Rewards, and Honours, upon such of the Inhabitants within the said Province as shall deserve the same; and invest them with what Titles and Dignities soever he or they shall think fit;"—and "to erect and incorporate Boroughs and Cities with convenient Privileges and Immunities." Authorizing the said Lord Proprietor, his Heirs, *&c.* "to make and constitute, within the said Province, and the Isles and Islets aforesaid, such and so many Sea Ports, Harbours, *&c.* with such Rights, Jurisdictions, Liberties, and Privileges, as to him or them shall seem most expedient." Granting for himself, his Heirs and Successors, "unto the said Lord *Baltimore*, his Heirs and Assigns, that he the said

Lord *Baltimore, &c. may, from Time to Time, for ever*, have and enjoy the Customs and Subsidies within the said Ports, Harbours, *&c.* within the Province aforesaid, payable or due for Merchandizes and Wares, there to be laden and unladen; the said Subsidies and Customs to be reasonably assessed, (upon any Occasion,) by themselves and the People there as aforesaid, to whom we give Power by these Presents, for us, our Heirs and Successors, upon just Cause, and in due Proportion, to assess and impose the same."

To this is added the following Covenant between the King and Inhabitants of the said Province, by which they are formally and positively exempted from every Species of Foreign Taxation: *viz.*

"And further our Pleasure is, and by these Presents, for us, our Heirs and Successors, we do covenant and grant to and with the said now Lord *Baltimore*, and his Heirs and Assigns, that we, our Heirs and Successors, shall at no Time hereafter set or make, or cause to be set or made, any Imposition, Custom, or other Taxation, Rate, or Contribution whatsoever, in and upon the Dwellers and Inhabitants of the aforesaid Province, for their Lands, Tenements, Goods, or Chattels, within the said Province, or to be laden or unladen within the Ports or Harbours of the said Province. And our Will and Pleasure is, and for us, our Heirs and Successors, we charge and command, that this our Declaration, shall henceforward, from Time to Time, be received and allowed before all our Courts, and before all the Judges of us, our Heirs and Successors, for a sufficient and lawful Discharge, Payment, and Acquittance; commanding all and singular our Officers, and Ministers of us, our Heirs and Successors, and enjoining them, upon Pain of our high Displeasure, that they do not presume, at any Time, to attempt any Thing to the contrary of the Premises, or that they do in any Sort withstand the same; but that they be, at all Times, aiding and assisting, as fitting, unto the said now Lord *Baltimore*, and his Heirs, and to the Inhabitants and Merchants of *Maryland* aforesaid, their Ministers, Servants, Factors, and Assigns, in the full Use and Fruition of the Benefit of this our Charter."

Whoever considers these, and various other Privileges, too numerous to recite, which have been granted to the Province of *Maryland* in this Charter, by which the King divests himself, his Heirs, *&c.* of all Share in the Legislative and Executive Authorities of Government within the said Province, and formally exempts its Inhabitants from foreign Taxation, alienating to the Lord Proprietor, *&c.* all Customs, Duties, Subsidies, *&c.* collected in any of its Ports or Harbours, with all the Prerogatives and Privileges necessary to a distinct and sovereign State, will easily perceive, that their Exercise and enjoyment must have been incompatible with a Subjection to Parliamentary Authority; that in Reality, the Constitution of *Maryland* was not capable of, or intended for, any such Subjection, and that no Provision for any Species of Legislative Dependance, in that, or any former Colony, to this Kingdom, was made; as I have already sufficiently proved, that the Clauses in their Charters, which prescribe a Similitude between their Laws, and those of *England*, imply no such Dependance, since the Kings by whom they were inserted, ever declared them to be without the Realm of *England*, and Jurisdiction of its Parliament. I know it has been asserted, that the Clause of Exemption from foreign Impositions in the *Maryland* Charter, was not designed to preclude Parliamentary Taxation, but only to secure the Inhabitants from Impositions by the King's Prerogative; and indeed this is more than probable, as the Extension of Parliamentary Taxation to *America* was then so little thought of, that a Clause to prevent it would have been deemed as unnecessary, as was the Law against Paricides at *Rome*. But that the King meant to reserve to his Parliament a Right of taxing the Colonies, will hardly be believed, by one who knows that he considered them as without the Jurisdiction of that Parliament; nor will it appear probable, that he would, in that Case, have granted to the Lord Proprietor all Duties, Customs, and Subsidies raised in that Province, and vested the Right of raising them solely in the Legislature of the Province itself. Besides, if the *English* Parliament had a Right of taxing the Province, its Inhabitants must, of Necessity, have been *English* Subjects, and therefore could not have been taxed by Prerogative, so that the whole Clause in that Case must have been destitute of Use, Sense, or Meaning, and consequently never would have been inserted; neither could the Inhabitants of *Massachusetts Bay, New Plymouth, &c.* after their Charters were vacated by a Judgment in the Court of Chancery, in the 39th Year of *Charles* the Second, if they had been considered as *English* Subjects, have been taxed by Sir *Edmund Andros*, the King's Governor, and a Council of three or four Persons appointed by the King, without the Consent of any Assembly or Parliament of the People, which was evidently repugnant to the Great Charter of King *John*, in which the King engages, "not to impose any Taxes without summoning the Archbishops, the Abbots, the Earls, the greater Barons, and the Tenants *in Capite*." And if the *English* Parliament was then the Legislative Power of the Colonies, and their Constitutional Representative, as our Author asserts, its Interposition in Behalf of the injured Inhabitants of those Colonies was a Duty necessarily incumbent on them, as the Guardians and Protectors of the Rights of *English* Subjects, though it never was discharged towards those Colonies, nor did they, notwithstanding their frequent Remonstrances, ever obtain any Relief, until they procured it for themselves, by imprisoning the King's Governor, and restoring their original Form of Government, a Measure which afterwards received King *William*'s Approbation. To this let me add, that when King *William* afterwards applied to the Judges, to know whether he might lawfully appoint a Governor for the Colony of *Massachusetts Bay*, (its Charter being then vacated) they declared, that without entering into the Merits of those Complaints on which the Charter had been cancelled, it having been vacated by a Judgment in Chancery, "the King might, by his Prerogative, put the Inhabitants of that Colony under whatever Form of Government he pleased." Which clearly proves, that the Judges did not then think those Colonists to be *English* Subjects, because the King, in that Case, could not, by his Prerogative, "put them under whatever Form of Government he pleased." By *English* Subjects, at present, I mean no more, than Persons obliged to obey Acts of an *English* Parliament; because that Obligation is necessarily connected with a Right to the Enjoyment of all the Privileges of *Englishmen*.

But to return from this Digression. We have now examined the most important of all the *American* Charters granted before the Restoration, and indeed all of them that merit Attention, and these abundantly prove, that the Colonies were not then considered as annexed to the Realm of *England*, or subject to its Laws. In what State then shall we consider them?

I have already proved, that whatever Right *Elizabeth, James,* and *Charles* had to the Lands they granted in *America*, it was vested solely in themselves, either personally, or as Sovereigns of this Realm. The latter Conclusion appears most favourable to our Author's Purpose, at least he has argued strongly in its Support; and as I am not disposed to maintain an unnecessary Dispute, I will assent to it; as I well know he can infer no other Consequence therefrom, than that the Territory of *America* being the Property of the Crown, until it is alienated therefrom, must attend the Succession of the Crown, as an Appendage thereto; and this, if it be necessary, will serve to explain the Reason why the Colonies, being without the Realm, have yet invariably continued within the Allegiance of the *English* Crown, notwithstanding its different Revolutions: An Explanation that will sufficiently expose the Impropriety of our Author's Question where he asks the Colonies, "What King it is they profess themselves the loyal Subjects of?" Adding, "It cannot be his present most gracious Majesty, *George* the Third, King of *Great Britain*, for his Title is founded on an Act of Parliament; and they will not surely acknowledge that Parliament can give them a King, which is of all others the highest Act of Sovereignty, when they deny it to have the Power to tax or bind them in any other Case, although they must see, that if they reject Parliamentary Authority, they make themselves to be still the Subjects of the abjured *Stuart* Race."

Had our Author been acquainted with the History of the Colonies, he would have known, that they have ever recognized and proclaimed the rightful Kings of *England*: That in *Virginia Charles* the Second was proclaimed King of *England, Scotland, France, Ireland,* and VIRGINIA, (that Colony then considering itself a distinct State,) long before his Restoration; and that he actually reigned in that Colony a considerable Time before he was King in *England*; and that in the *Massachusetts Bay* the Prince and Princess of *Orange* were Proclaimed, before it was known that they were invested with Sovereignty in *England*. But the Allegiance of the Colonies to the Succession of the *English* Crown, whether that is governed by lineal Descent or Acts of Parliament, is especially provided for by Clauses for that Purpose in their Charters as *James* and *Charles*, though they did not consider the Colonies as annexed to the Realm, intended, nevertheless to connect them to it, by securing their Subjection to the same Sovereign.

Let me now return to the Title of *Elizabeth, James,* and *Charles*, to the Lands in *America*, which, whether more or less valid, was, as I have already declared, vested in themselves only, either personally or as Possessors of the *English* Crown, and that when they granted the Territory of *Virginia, New England, Maryland, &c.* they were constitutionally authorized to dispose of it either to Foreigners or Subjects, in any Manner whatsoever; it being an unquestionable Truth, that the Kings of *England* may constitutionally alienate for ever from the Crown and Realm, without Consent of Parliament, any Acquisition of Foreign Territory, whether by Cession, Conquest, or Discovery, not being already with the Royal Assent formally annexed to the Realm. This is a Proposition so universally acknowledged, that not one of the many Proofs that may be alledged in its Support is necessary; and I am sure that our Author, however he might endeavour to evade the Question, will never deny the Validity of the several Grants of Territory from the Crown to the Colonies; how then will he be able to defend his unwarrantable Conclusions, (Pages 652 and 653.) to prove that the Lands in *America* were originally within the Realm and Jurisdiction of Parliament? Can any thing, which is at the sole and absolute Disposal of the King, be the Property of the Nation, and under the Controul of its Parliament? Inconsistent Absurdity! Nor is our Author's long Quotation from Mr. *Locke* (Page 653.) at all pertinent to the Subject.—It indeed argues, that he who receives an Inheritance in "a Commonwealth, must take it with the Condition it is under, that is, of submitting to the Government of the Commonwealth, under whose Jurisdiction it is, as far forth as any Subject of it." But has this Assertion of Mr. *Locke* the least Tendency to prove, that those who received the Lands in *America* should submit to the Government of a Commonwealth, or Kingdom, to which these Lands were never annexed? Impossible!

Thus, then, the Validity of the several Grants of Territory from the Crown to the Colonies is indisputable: The King's

Right of emancipating their Inhabitants from the Jurisdiction of Parliament, and of erecting them into distinct States, remains next to be considered; and this our Author, among other Opponents to the Colonies, has denied, and endeavoured to support his Denial by the most fallacious, and sometimes impertinent Arguments; such are those from Page 650 to 653.—"That the first Inhabitants of the Colonies were part of the *British* Community, and bound to obey its Legislative Power, in all Respects, as any other Subjects, at the Time of the Establishments of these Colonies," I will not deny; but he certainly proposes a very unnecessary and improper Question, in asking whether "the Executive Power of the Crown can, by any Grant or Authority, alter or annul the Legislative Power in the Article of Taxation, or any other?" Nor is Mr. *Locke*'s Assertion, that "even the Legislative Power itself cannot transfer the Power of making Laws to any other Hands; for it being but a delegated Power from the People, they who have it cannot pass it over to others," at all applicable to the present Subject. Mr. *Locke* therein justly observes, that the Parliament cannot transfer to others its Authority of making Laws over those by whom this Authority has been delegated to itself; but no where even insinuates, that the Parliament, after having constantly recognized and assented to the King's Prerogative Right of permitting his Subjects to withdraw themselves from the Realm, and the Jurisdiction of its Laws, cannot permit them to enter into a second Community, and throw off their Subjection to the first. On the contrary, Mr. *Locke* repeatedly declares, that a Man, by being born in a State, is thereby under no Obligation to continue therein; that all Men, being by Nature free, have a Right "to choose what Society they will join themselves to, and what Commonwealth they will put themselves under." This being the Case, and the first Inhabitants of our Colonies having a just Right to separate themselves, and the King a Constitutional Right to permit them to separate themselves, from the Community, and having granted them an Accession of foreign Territory, which he had a legal right to alienate for ever from the Crown and Realm, even to Foreigners, what Law or Principle in the *English* Constitution, forbids their retiring to the Territories so granted in *America*, and there, by the Consent of their Sovereign, becoming distinct

States, on the Terms and Privileges stipulated between their King and themselves? Whoever places the Settlement of the Colonies in this just Point of View, will immediately discover the Fallacy of all those Arguments which have been objected to the Power of the Crown, in granting their Inhabitants an Emancipation from the Authority of Parliament.—As long as they continued within the Realm as a collective Part of its Inhabitants, and received Protection from its Laws and Government, no Power whatever could possibly exempt them from Obedience to its Legislative Authority: But this Obligation to Obedience necessarily depended on the Term of their Continuance within the Community, and naturally ceased on their Separation from it; and though the King's Prerogative extends, indiscriminately, to all States owing him Allegiance, yet the Legislative Power of each State, if the People have any Share therein, is necessarily confined within the State itself, it being repugnant to the Laws of Nature and Nations for the Subjects of one State to exercise Jurisdiction over those of another: The People being allowed to participate the Legislative Authority, thereby to preserve their own Freedom, not invade that of others. This our Author admits, when he acknowledges, that "it may be pretended that the Lands in *America*, lying without the Realm, and appertaining to the King only, their Possessors cannot, from those Circumstances, be subject to the Jurisdiction of Parliament, *whose Authority is confined within the Limits of the Realm*." He indeed presumes, that this Plea "cannot be made by the Inhabitants of such Lands as were conquered by the Forces of the *British* State from foreign Powers, or ceded to *Great Britain* by Treaty: Those Conquests or Cessions (says he) are surely the Dominions of the Crown of *Great Britain*, not the private Property of the King." But in this he is likewise mistaken, nor did Mr. *Dickenson* mean to "put these intirely out of the Question, in all that he says about the Rights of the Colonies." And whatever Opinion our Author may entertain of this Subject, it is an indisputable Fact that no Territory, acquired either by Conquest or Cession, is thereby rendered a Part of the Realm, but remains at the absolute Disposal of the King, till by the Royal Assent it is formally annexed to the Kingdom; and of this the late Act of Parliament for rendering *Gibraltar* unalienable from *Great Britain*, by the Crown, is a sufficient Proof; and our Author, I am very sure, will not pretend that the Nation could, by Discovery, acquire a better Title to the Country in *America*, than by Cession or Conquest. He, however, endeavours to prove, that the Territory possessed by the Colonists in *America*, was originally the Property not of the King, personally, but of the Crown of *England*, and from thence infers, that they must necessarily be a Part of the Realm: This, however, is a very unwarrantable Inference, as the holding a Country under the *English* Crown, by no Means renders it a Part of the Kingdom; to prove this, I need only instance the *Isle of Man*, which was granted to Sir *John Stanly*, and his Heirs, by *Henry* the Fourth, and has been held as a Dependence from the Crown, by a *Tenure* similar to that of the Colonies, (in every Respect material to the present Question,) though it never was considered as Part of the Realm, or subjected to its Laws, until the late Change made in its Constitution, *by Consent of its King.*

Thus have I abundantly demonstrated the Right of the Crown to grant the Colonists the Constitution and Privileges of distinct States; and whether this Constitution and these Privileges have been granted them, let the Facts, which I already have, and shall hereafter recite, declare. But before I proceed farther in the political History of the Colonies, it is proper for me to consider some Facts and Arguments, which have been alledged by our Author, to prove that they were not originally deemed distinct States by the King and Nation.

The Debates of the House of Commons, of *May* 1614, *February* 1620, and *April* 1621, related only to the Expediency of encouraging or discouraging the Importation and Use of Tobacco in *England*, and tended in no respect to extend the Authority of Parliament to *America*; and the Fishing Bill, brought into the House the 25th of *April*, 1621, was only an Attempt in the Commons to secure to the Subjects of this Kingdom the Privilege of Fishing on the Coasts of *America*, which the King deemed an Infringement of the Privileges he had before granted the Colonies; for which Reason, joined to the Consideration of their being without the Realm, and Jurisdiction of its Parliament, he refused the Royal Assent thereto, as did his Successor for the same Reasons. And whoever will peruse the various Debates on this Subject, will discover, that the principal Arguments were confined to the Expediency, rather than the Right, of granting free Liberty of Fishing in *America* to the King's *English* Subjects, with the necessary Incidents of drying Fish, and using Wood, which (as was asserted) would be of no Detriment to the Colonies, because of no Value there, declaring it a Hardship on the *English* to be prohibited Fishing in *America*, while the *French* and *Dutch* were allowed to do it; observing, that the *English* formerly enjoyed that Liberty, but that the Colonists then obliged them "to compound for Places, or took away their Salt, or exacted great Sums, and even fired Ordnance at them." To these Assertions, however, it was objected, that the Fishermen injured the Colonies, and that they were not Objects of Parliamentary Legislation. The Secretary of State in particular declared, that though he never would strain the Prerogative against the Good of the Commonwealth, yet that it was "not fit to make any Laws here for those Countries, they not being annexed to the *Crown*;" (and if this was then the Case, I believe it will be difficult for our Author to prove them the Domains of the Crown, much less the Dominions of the Nation.) In answer to these Objections, against the *Right of Parliament*, nothing material was urged by the Advocates for the Bill: Mr. *Brooke*, indeed, very sagaciously alledged, that "if the King gave his Assent to the Bill, it would controul the Patent;" but he did not pretend, or even seem to think, that the King's Act in that particular would acquire any additional Force from the Authority of the Lords and Commons. Sir *Edward Cooke* also represented the Clause in Sir *Francis Gorges*'s *American* Patent, declaring, "That no Subject of *England* should visit the Coast upon Forfeiture of Ship and Goods," as a Grievance, because, says he, "this is to make a Monopoly of the Sea, which is wont to be free," and that the exclusive Grant of Liberty to pack and dry Fish on that Coast, was likewise attempting a Monopoly of "the Wind and Sun." But the Man, who from these Debates will discover Proofs in Support of the Right of Parliament to legislate for the Colonies, must certainly discover what has no Existence.

As to the Act of the Commonwealth Parliament, which our Author has alledged against the Colonies, I shall only observe, that it is by no Means strange that an Assembly, which had usurped the Right of the King and Lords, should also infringe the Rights of the People of *Virginia* and the *West Indies*, who had denied, and at the same time actually resisted, its Authority: But when that Assembly declared, that these Colonies had, "ever since the Planting thereof, been, and ought to be, subject to such Laws, Orders, and Regulations as are or shall be made by the Parliament of *England*;" and it is known that at that time no Laws ever had been made by the Parliament of *England* for the Colonies, this Declaration will doubtless appear somewhat ludicrous.—But the Degree of Dependance, which this Parliament thought it had a Right to exact from these Colonies, will best appear, by the Treaty concluded between *Virginia* and the Commissioners of Parliament, who were sent with an Armament to reduce it to Obedience to the Commonwealth.—The Articles of this Treaty were as follow:

First, "The Plantation of *Virginia*, and all the Inhabitants thereof, shall be and remain in due Subjection to the Commonwealth of *England*; not as a conquered Country, but as a Country submitting by their own voluntary Act; and shall enjoy such Freedoms and Privileges as belong to the free People of *England*."

Second, "The General Assembly, as formerly, shall convene and transact the Affairs of the Colony."

Third, "The People of *Virginia* shall have a free Trade, as the People of *England*, to all Places and Nations."

Fourth, "Virginia shall be free from all Taxes, Customs, and Impositions whatsoever; and none shall be imposed upon them without Consent of their General Assembly; and that neither Forts nor Castles be erected, nor Garrisons maintained without their Consent."

These Conditions will likewise serve to convey a just Idea of the Rights and Privileges to which the Inhabitants of *Virginia* then thought themselves intitled: And though the Dependance imposed on them by these Articles was little more than nominal, they were so far from thinking these Privileges any considerable Acquisition, that in *January* 1659, they restored Sir *William Berkley*, proclaiming "*Charles* the Second, King of *England, Scotland, France, Ireland*, and Virginia," some Time before his Restoration to *England*.

These are the most important Occurrences in the Political History of the Colonies preceding the 12th Year of the Reign

of *Charles* the Second, an Æra which produced the first Act of
Parliament of any Kind, that ever was extended to *America*,
since the Settlement of *British* Colonies in that Quarter of the
Globe. This Act was, indeed, passed for the wisest and best of
Purposes, that of increasing the *English* Trade and Navigation,
by prohibiting the Importation into, and Exportation of, all
Goods and Commodities out of "any Lands, Islands, Plantations or Territories to his Majesty belonging, or in his Possession, or which may hereafter belong unto, or be in Possession
of, his Majesty, his Heirs and Successors, in *Asia, Africa*, and
America, except in Ships belonging to the People of *England*
or *Ireland*, or the said Lands, Islands, and Plantations," and
navigated by the Inhabitants of these several Places. It is however to be lamented, that the then Parliament had not thought
proper to discover, for the Information of Posterity, the Source
from whence it derived the Right of making Laws, not only for
all Countries under his Majesty's Dominion in *Asia, Africa*,
and *America*, but for all Countries which hereafter may belong
to, or be in the Possession of "his Heirs and Successors," as it
must doubtless have been new and hitherto undiscovered;
since, however extensive the King's Prerogative may be over
his foreign Subjects, the *English* Constitution has made no
Provision for this Species of National, External Legislation, the
Power of Parliament being originally confined to the Limits of
the Realm, and the Nation collectively, of which it was the
Representing and Legislative Assembly. How far the Parliament, of which I am now speaking, departed from the primitive Spirit of our Constitution, let others judge:—But certain it
is, that future Kings of *Great-Britain* may acquire Territories
which Parliamentary Authority ought not to controul; and yet
this Act will necessarily bind them, if situated either in *Asia,
Africa*, or *America*, as it now would *Hanover*, had not the
Word *Europe* been omitted in the Act as unnecessary, from the
apparent Improbability of the King's making any future Acquisitions of *European* Territory, which might not be comprehended within the Kingdoms of *England* or *Ireland*. But how
the Parliament, at that Time, acquired a Right of Legislating
for the Colonies in *America*, is to me inconceivable.—
*Virginia, Massachusetts Bay, New Plymouth, Maryland, Con-
necticut, New Haven, New Hampshire*, and the Province of

Main, were then the only Colonies held under the *English* Crown on the Continent of *America*; and in all these the People enjoyed the sole Legislative and Executive Powers of Government, (*Virginia* excepted,) they having all been settled on the Faith of Charters, granted either by *James* or *Charles* the First, who, according to their own Construction, had constituted them distinct States, and such they had been reputed till the 12th of *Charles* the Second: How then could the Parliament of *England*, after the Colonies had been thus constitutionally alienated from the Realm, and settled on the Faith of those fundamental and indefeasible Stipulations by which they were so alienated, make Laws for their Government, consistent with the Principles of Justice? Were the Colonies previously united to the Kingdom? Or could any Authority whatever unite them to it, without their formal and express Consent? The Answers to these Questions are obvious, and will sufficiently demonstrate, that though a Right of Legislating for the Colonies was then assumed by Parliament, it would have been difficult to support the Assumption by Law or Equity.

The Rectitude and Utility of a Measure tending to encrease the *English* Shipping and Navigation, was doubtless obvious; and as some of the King's Settlements in *Africa, &c.* were mere Factories without Legislative Power, and as in others it might have been tedious, and perhaps impracticable, to obtain the Consent of their several Assemblies to this Law, the Legislature of this Kingdom was, perhaps, from these Considerations, encouraged to exercise a Power, (in that particular Instance,) evidently tending to the general Good; or, at least, if these were not the Motives to this Law, perhaps they were not less exceptionable.

Two Years afterwards, that is, in the 14th Year of *Charles* the Second, the Colonies of *Connecticut*, and *New Haven*, petitioned his Majesty to unite them into one Colony, by a new Charter. The King was by that Time, become jealous of his Prerogative in the Colonies; but by the wise Interposition of the Earl of *Clarendon*, then Lord Chancellor, his Majesty granted the Charter, with Privileges in Effect as extensive as any that had ever been granted to any Colony; securing to himself their Allegiance only, without the smallest Share in the

Legislative and Executive Powers of Government; and the
next Year *Rhode-Island* and *Providence* Plantations obtained
from the King a Charter, with Privileges in every Respect similar to those granted the Colony of *Connecticut.*

I have not hitherto interrupted the Course of my Observations, to remark on our Author's very fallacious, partial, and
unfair Extracts from the Charters of the several Colonies,
which must be obvious to any one, who will compare them
with their Originals, or even with those Passages which I have
faithfully recited from them. How he will reconcile an Attempt
to impose on his Readers, by such Artifices, with the Principles
of common Honesty, is best known to himself; certain I am,
however, that his Purpose ought to be much better than it
appears, to justify the use of such low and ungenerous Means
for its Execution.

Our Author's erroneous Account of the *Connecticut* and
Rhode-Island Charters, (without recurring to those of *Virginia, Maryland, &c.*) will furnish a sufficient Instance of that
Fallacy which I have just censured, and at the same Time afford
the Reader a just Idea of that Degree of Credit which ought to
be reposed in his Assertions, as well as of the "*Honesty of his
Purpose,*" in reviewing the *American* Controversy. "The Charters, (says he,) dated in the 14th Year of *Charles* the Second,
which were granted to the Inhabitants of *Connecticut,* and
Rhode-Island, are simply Charters of Incorporation, erecting
the respective Inhabitants in those Places into a Corporate
Body, and empowering them to do Corporate Acts, in like
Manner as other Corporations in *England* are empowered to
do:" And in Support of this very erroneous Assertion, he recites a single Clause extracted from those Charters, and then
sagaciously adds, "The Man who thinks the Terms of this
Clause of the *Connecticut* and *Rhode Island* Charters, descrip-
tive of, or applicable to, a Sovereign State, or Supreme Legislature, deserves not that any sober Argument should be held
with him."

But whatever Degree of Truth there may be in this Conclusion, I will venture to affirm, that if he had recited those
Clauses in these Charters which are most pertinent to the
Controversy, there is no Man deserving a sober Argument who
would have compared the Colonies of *Connecticut* and *Rhode*

Island, to simple *English* Corporations. That I may not unnecessarily extend these Observations, I shall offer the Reader an Account of the Constitution of these Colonies, as presented to the House of Lords in January 1734, rather than transcribe the different Clauses of the Charters themselves, which would require a greater Extent.

"*Connecticut* and *Rhode Island* (say the Commissioners,) are Charter Governments, where almost the whole Power of the Crown is delegated to the People, who make an Annual Election of their Assembly, their Councils, and their Governors, likewise to the Majority of which Assemblies, Councils, and Governors respectively, being Collective Bodies, the Power of making Laws is granted; and as their Charters are worded, they can and do make Laws even without the Governor's Assent, no negative Voice being reserved to them as Governors in said Charters.—These Colonies have the Power of making Laws for their better Government and Support, and are not under any Obligation, by their respective Constitutions, to return authentic Copies of their Laws to the Crown for Approbation and Disallowance, or to give any Account of their Proceedings; nor are their Laws repealable by the Crown, but the Validity of them depends on their not being contrary, but, as near as may be, agreeable to the Laws of *England*."

To this Account of the Constitution of these Colonies, many other important Privileges might have been added by the Commissioners of Trade and Plantations, (whose Impartiality, I presume, no Person will suspect:) These, however, are not necessary, as the smallest Knowledge of the present State of *Connecticut* and *Rhode Island*, will abundantly demonstrate, that their internal Constitution is perfectly distinct and independent; all the Authority of their Governments being vested in the People, or the Officers elected by them, no Civil or Military Officer, in these Colonies, having the smallest Dependence on the Crown; not even their Troops are subject to the King's Authority, as they have repeatedly refused Obedience to his Generals, particularly when King *William* appointed *Benjamin Fletcher*, Esq; Governor of *New-York*, to command them; a Refusal which their Charters amply justified.

As to our Author's Remarks, that the King, in the Charters of *Connecticut* and *Rhode Island*, "expresly admits that these

Colonies were then within the Realm of *England*, or annexed to it, by using these Words, *As other our liege People of this our Realm of* England, *or any other Corporation within the same*," I shall observe, that the indeterminate Application of the Word *other*, in this Particular, might have furnished some Pretext for this Remark, could it be supposed that he was ignorant of several other Clauses in these Charters, which entirely preclude the Sense he has attempted to impose thereon. In each of these Charters, the King expresly covenants, that "All and every the Subjects of us, our Heirs, *&c*. who shall go to inhabit within the said Colony, and every of their Children, which shall happen to be born there, *&c*. shall have and enjoy all the Liberties and Immunities of free and natural Subjects, within any of the Dominions of us, our Heirs, and Successors, to all Intents, Constructions, and Purposes whatsoever, as if they and every of them were born within the Realm of *England*." And in the Preamble to the Charter of *Rhode-Island*, the King expresses, that its Inhabitants "did, by the Consent of our Royal Progenitors, transport themselves out of this Kingdom of *England* into *America*." But numerous Clauses to this Effect, are found in the Charters of all the Colonies, and in every Publick Act relating to them; and even without these, which are perfectly incompatible with the Sense of our Author's Remark, there are too many Instances of the vague, and even improper Use of the Word *other*, in the *American* Charters, to warrant the Conclusion he has drawn, from its Application to the present Instance. Thus in the third *Virginia* Charter, Art. XI. is the following Expression, "All such, and so many of our loving Subjects, or any *other* Strangers, that will," *&c*. from which, however, no Person will infer, that the King's loving Subjects are Strangers, though this Conclusion would be justifiable, as that contained in our Author's Remark. To this let me add the following Extract from the *Connecticut* and *Rhode Island* Charters, (for in both it is exactly the same,) which abundantly proves that the King then not only deemed these Colonies, without the Realm, but was sensible, that he had retained but little more than a nominal Sovereignty over them, and that he could no otherwise punish any Crimes or Misdemeanors committed by them, than by withdrawing his Protection from them, or putting them out of his Allegiance.—"We do hereby declare to all *Christian* Kings, Princes, and States, that if any Persons, which shall hereafter be of the said Company, or Plantation, or any other, by Appointment of the said Governor and Company, for the Time being, shall at any Time or Times hereafter, rob or spoil, by Sea or by Land, or do any Hurt, Violence, or unlawful Hostility, to any of the Subjects of us, our Heirs, or Successors, or any of the Subjects of any Prince or State, being then in League with us, our Heirs, or Successors, upon Complaint of such Injury done to any such Prince or State, or their Subjects, we, our Heirs, or Successors, will make open Proclamation within any Parts of this our Realm of *England*, fit for that Purpose, that the Person or Persons committing any such Robbery or Spoil, shall, within the Time limited by such Proclamation, make full Restitution, or Satisfaction, for all Injuries done or committed, so as the said Prince, or others, so complaining, may be fully satisfied and contented; and if the said Person or Persons, who shall commit any such Robbery or Spoil, shall not make Satisfaction accordingly, within such Time so to be limited; that then it shall and may be lawful for us, our Heirs, and Successors, to put such Person or Persons out of our Allegiance and Protection; and that it shall and may be lawful and free for all Princes and others, to prosecute with Hostilities, such Offenders and every of them, their and every of their Procurers, Aiders and Abettors, and Counsellors in that Behalf."

To conceive the Expediency of this Clause, it is necessary to inform the Reader, that at that Æra the final Determination of all Judicial Appeals, in all the *American* Colonies, had been invariably vested in their several Assemblies, as being their supreme Legislatures, no Appeals having been ever made to the King in Council. Lord *Colepepper*, indeed, when Governor of *Virginia* some Years afterwards, and meditating a Claim to the Propriety of the Northern Neck in that Province, found that his Project would not succeed whilst the *Dernier Resort* in Judicial Proceedings continued in the General Assembly; and artfully created a Disagreement on this Subject, between the Council and House of Burgesses, which he soon after grosly misrepresented, and engaged his Majesty to direct all final Appeals in the Colonies for the future to himself in Council. But however legal this Measure might be in *Virginia*, (a Royal

Government,) it was a manifest Violation of the Rights of all the then Chartered Colonies, and such it has been generally deemed in them; and though, in several Instances, Individuals have submitted to this Regulation, yet those who have the Administration of national Concerns must know, (if their Knowledge is as extensive as it ought to be,) that unless the Executive Authority in the Chartered Colonies, such as *Connecticut* and *Rhode Island*, is willing to adopt the Judgment of the King in Council, relative to Appeals from them, (to which there is no Obligation,) the King has no Way to put it in Execution, nor can he punish their Refusal except by putting them out of his Allegiance, agreeable to the Clause in the Charters last recited; which nevertheless does not warrant his Majesty to take Cognizance of any Disputes between the respective Inhabitants in each of these Colonies. But even the Alteration of Appeals from the *American* Assemblies to the King abundantly proves that the Peers of *England* were not then considered as Peers of *America*, and that the Colonies were not considered as Parts of the Realm, since in that Case, the final Decision of all Judicial Causes in the Colonies must necessarily have been made by the *English* House of Lords.*

The next Year, that is, in the 15th of *Charles* the Second, the Territory of *Carolina* was erected into a Principality; and by a Royal Patent, dated the 24th of *March*, 1663, granted to eight Lords Proprietors, with all its Rights, Privileges, Prerogatives, Royalties, *&c.* with all the Legislative and Executive Powers of Government exclusively, with the Powers of creating Nobility, *&c.* This Principality was to be governed by a Palatine, chosen for Life out of the eight Proprietaries, and succeeded by the eldest of the surviving Lords Proprietaries. The Form of Government was settled by a solemn Compact between the People and the Proprietaries, called the Fundamental Constitutions, and consisting of One Hundred and Twenty Articles, which, it was declared, should "be and remain the sacred and unalterable Form and Rule of Government in *Carolina* for ever." By these

* The Practice of transporting Felons to the Colonies likewise proves their being without the Realm; as the End and Design of this Punishment is to banish them from the Community they have offended, and from the Benefit and Protection of those Laws they have transgressed.

Constitutions, the Legislative Authority of Government was vested in the Parliament of that Country: The Upper House of which consisted of the Proprietors, or their Deputies, the Governor, and the Nobility, as the Landgraves, *&c.* and the Lower House, of the Commons, or Delegates of the People; the Palatine, as Sovereign, either granting or refusing his Assent. The Palatine was likewise President of a Court, composed by himself and three other Proprietaries, in whom was vested the Execution of all the Powers of the Charter. Besides this were the Chief Justice's Court, the High Constable's Court, Chancellor's Court, Treasurer's Court, Chamberlain's Court, and High Steward's Court: The great Officers of State, in Titles, Numbers, and Power, resembling those of this Realm: And so fully convinced were the Proprietaries of *Carolina* of their Authority to form that Country into distinct independent States, and so tenacious of this Authority, that they constantly disputed even the King's Right to create Courts of Vice Admiralty therein, though for the Decision of Misdemeanors committed without the Limits of their Charter, appointing an Admiral of their own for that Purpose: And when *Joseph Morton*, the eldest Langrave of that Province, was elected Governor, he was charged with "a Breach of the Trust reposed in him, by the true and absolute Lords and Proprietaries, in accepting of a Commission from King *William*, to be Judge of the Admiralty in that Province, when he had, at the same Time, a Commission from the Lords Proprietaries for the same Office;" and this Charge appeared so weighty, that he was, in Consequence thereof, set aside from the Government. These Particulars, I flatter myself, will be deemed sufficient to prove, that the original Constitution and Government of *Carolina*, was that of a distinct, independent State.

The fifteenth Year of *Charles* the Second likewise produced an Act of Parliament, naming the Colonies, and establishing further Regulations, "for the Employment and further Increase of *English* Shipping, and Seamen, Vent of *English* Woollen, and other Manufactures, and rendering the Navigation to and from the same, (the Colonies,) more safe and cheap." The Justice of this Act, doubtless, depends on the same equitable Principles, as those which authorized the preceding Act of Navigation; but as the Legislature did not think proper to explain their Nature and Origin, I have never been able to discover them.

The ensuing Act, of the 25th of *Charles* the Second, was the first that ever imposed Taxes on the Colonies, for any Purpose: And these, as the Preamble to the Act itself declares, were for the Regulation of Trade, and were confined solely to the Exportation of those Commodities, on which they were imposed, not to *England*, but to Foreigners, and to other Colonies: And in those Articles, where the Duties were heavy, were evidently intended to operate as Prohibitions, and in other Particulars to prevent Foreigners having these Commodities at a cheaper Price than the People of *England*; and not to produce a Revenue, because (besides the Tenor of the Preamble,) the Produce of these Impositions was applied to no Service, and from thence was evidently not intended as a Supply for any.

This Act was an Extension of that Power, which the Parliament of *England*, by I know not what Right, had assumed and exercised in the two preceding Acts, for regulating the Commerce of the Colonies, and the Duties thereby imposed were considered as Auxilaries in effecting this Purpose. But whatever Idea the Legislature of this Kingdom might entertain of its Right of imposing Taxes on the Colonies, even for Commercial Purposes, it is certain that the Colonies themselves protested against this first Exercise of it; and this, with the preceding Acts of Parliament, were the principal, if not only Cause, of that general Insurrection in *Virginia*, which, soon after followed under Colonel *Bacon*; for when Sir *William Berkley*, the Governor of that Province, was compelled to fly from the Place of his usual Residence, and retire to *Accomack*, instead of that friendly Reception which he had promised himself from the known Attachment of the Inhabitants to him, even they began to make Terms for a Redress of those Grievances they suffered by Acts, of the Parliament of *England*; and when, after *Bacon*'s Death, this Insurrection subsided, the Province sent Agents to *England*, to remonstrate "*against Taxes and Impositions being laid on the Colony, by any Authority but that of the General Assembly.*" This Remonstrance produced a Declaration from King *Charles* the Second, under the Privy Seal, and dated the 19th of *April*, 1676, affirming, that "*Taxes ought not to be laid upon the Proprietors and Inhabitants of the*

Colony, but by the common Consent of the General Assembly; except such Impositions as the Parliament should lay on the Commodities imported into *England* from the Colony." This Declaration was subsequent to the Act of the 25th of *Charles* the Second, and is a farther Proof, that the Duties thereby imposed on the Colonies, were considered merely as Commercial Regulations, and not as Taxes: and this is farther confirmed, by the subsequent Conduct of that Monarch, who, when a permanent Revenue for the Support of *Virginia* was wanting, did not attempt to procure it by Parliamentary Authority, but, conscious of the Justice of the Declaration I have just recited, framed in *England* an Act for this Purpose, and in 1679 sent it to *Virginia* by Lord *Colepepper*, Governor of that Province, desiring it might be passed into a Law, as it accordingly was, and "*Enacted by the King's most excellent Majesty, by and with the Consent of the General Assembly of the Colony of* Virginia," that a Duty of Two Shillings *per* Hogshead for every Hogshead of Tobacco exported out of that Colony; a Rate of Fifteen-pence per Ton for every Ship upon each Return of her Voyage, whether empty or full; and a Duty of Six-pence *per* Poll for every Passenger going into that Country to remain, whether bond or free, should be granted to his Majesty for ever, as a Revenue for the Support of his Government in that Colony.

Let me here desire the Reader to observe the Terms in which this Law was expressed, and the Authority by which it was enacted, and then candidly ask himself, whether he imagines that King *Charles*, if he had deemed the Colonies to be mere *English* Corporations, as our Author would have them, he would have condescended to be named as a Part of their Legislature: Whether the Terms and mode of Expression are pertinent to any other than a distinct Sovereign State, and whether, if the King had deemed *Virginia* a Part of the Realm, and subject to Taxation by Parliamentary Authority, he could have joined himself with any other Persons in that Colony in raising Money from the Inhabitants, without violating the fundamental Principles of the *British* Constitution? Would he not, in so doing, have levied Money from the People without Consent of Parliament, contrary to the Great Charter, of King *John*, and the Bill and Declaration of Rights?—I am confident, and I insist, that if the Inhabitants of the Colonies are *British*

Subjects, and subject to the Authority of a *British* Parliament, the King cannot lawfully join himself with any other Authority than the Lords and Commons of *Great Britain* in imposing Taxes on them, because *British* Subjects cannot be constitutionally taxed by any other Authority; and that if the late Acts of Parliament, imposing Duties upon the Importation of *British* Commodities into the Colonies, are just, every other Act for Levying Money, for or to the Use of the Crown in the Colonies, which has received the Assent of the King or his Governors, is unwarrantable: because this double Taxation for the Service of Government is incompatible with the Privileges of a *Briton*, and as a *British American* I protest against it.

But notwithstanding the Remonstrances of the Colonies against the Act of 25th of *Charles* the Second, and the Royal Declaration in their Favour, it was not totally repealed till some Years after, and the Colonies, then in their Infant State, found that Opposition could have but little Effect on the Measures of a great Nation, and experienced (as they have since done) that the Arguments of the strongest are always the best; even in the Charter of *Pennsylvania*, which did not precede this Act, as our Author asserts, but was subsequent to it, the King, after granting almost all the Rights and Privileges contained in that of *Maryland*, and copying *Verbatim* from that Charter the Clause of Exemption from Taxation, adds, "except by the Proprietary, or Chief Governor, or Assembly, or by *Act of Parliament in England*;" an Exception, as far as it concerns the *English* Parliament, perfectly singular, having never been found in any preceding or subsequent *American* Charter, and is eventually very absurd, by rendering the whole Clause of Exemption useless and without Meaning, for the Reasons which I have before given. Those Ministers, however, who were the Authors of the Act of the 25th of *Charles* the Second, thought it necessary, after having thereby imposed Duties on the Colonies, to make a reservation for them in this Charter, which was granted soon after; and chose thus to act with Uniformity, tho' not without Absurdity. In this Particular, however, they were never imitated; for in the next *American* Charter, which was granted to the Province of *Massachusetts Bay* by *William* and *Mary* (its old one having been cancelled by a Judgment in Chancery) we find, that the Power "to levy proportionable and reasonable Assessments, Rates, and Taxes, for our Service, in the necessary Defence and Support of our Government of our said Province or Territory, and the Protection and Preservation of the Inhabitants there," is vested in the General Court, or Assembly of that Province, without any Provision for the Exercise of this Authority by Parliament; and that it was then understood that no such Authority could be exercised by the Parliament of *England*, will be evident from the following Transaction.

In 1691, when the new Charter of *Massachusetts Bay* was granted, the Agents thought it so inadequate to the Deserts and Expectations of the Inhabitants of that Province, that they debated whether it was their Duty to accept it, or stand a Trial at Law for reversing the Judgment against the former Charter. The Majority, however, after consulting the most able Lawyers and Politicians, resolved to accept it; and, for their own Justification, declared the Reasons of their Conduct, by an Instrument executed by the Majority of them, and containing five Articles, from the last of which I will offer the following Extract, as conveying a just Idea of what they then understood to be the Constitutional Rights and Privileges of that Province. "The Colony, say these Gentlemen, is now made a Province, and the General Court has, with the King's Approbation, as much Power in *New-England*, as the King and Parliament have in *England*. They have all *English* Privileges and Liberties, and can be touched by no Law, and by no Tax, but of their own making: All the Liberties of their Religion are for ever secured, &c."

The Patent for *Georgia* is the last of the *American* Charters, and of the least Importance in the present Controversy, though our Author's Extracts from it are much more extensive than from any other. In Answer to his Remarks thereon, I shall only observe, that this Charter is of recent Date, and was procured for a Herd of impoverished Wretches, who were to be transported to, and settled in, *America*, by the charitable Contributions of others; and Pity it is, that the Promoters of that Settlement destroyed all the Merit of their Benefactions, by ungenerously depriving the Objects of their Charity of those Rights which alone constitute the Distinctions between Freedom and Slavery. But the little Progress which that Settlement made in that State, and the Change in its Constitution, which has since been found necessary, have abundantly demonstrated, what common Sense ought to have before suggested, that Population, Riches, Arts and Sciences, are the natural and peculiar Fruits of Liberty.

After the 25th of *Charles* the Second, several other Acts succeeded for regulating the Trade and Policy of the Colonies, though no Act, from that Æra to the Conclusion of the late War, ever extended Taxation to *America*, unless the Establishment of the Post-Office there be considered as such. Our Author, indeed, gives us the Plan of an Act for compelling the Province of *New-York* to afford a Supply for the Support of Government, which, as he tells us, was projected by the Ministry in the Reign of Queen *Anne*, though never brought into either House of Parliament; and this he urges against the Assembly of *New-York*, as "a direct Contradiction to their Assertion, that from the first Settlement of the Colonies, it has been the Sense of the Government at Home, that such Grants (Supplies) could not be constitutionally made by Parliament:" If, however, the Sense of the Ministry is, by the Assembly of *New-York*, to be deemed the Sense of Government, and treated as such, *the Sense of Government* will doubtless appear very precarious, often inconsistent, and sometimes absurd. He might, however, have cited, in the Province of *Massachusetts Bay*, an Instance in which the Ministry, by two Governors, *Burnet* and *Belcher*, successively demanded, peremptorily, from the Assembly of that Province, a settled Salary for the Governor's Support, threatning, in Case of a Refusal, to obtain it by Authority of Parliament: This the Legislature of that Province, conscious and tenacious of the Rights of its Inhabitants, as peremptorily refused to comply with, and the Ministry gave over the Demand, without attempting the Execution of their former Threats. But the Caprice of a Minister is of no great Importance either to support or destroy the Rights of a People, which rest on a more firm and permanent Basis; and I shall therefore conclude my Observations on this Particular.

After this Review of the most important Transactions relating to the most ancient of our Colonies, I flatter myself it will appear indisputable, that in their first Settlement, they were constituted distinct States, independent to the Parliament of

England, because I have sufficiently demonstrated that *James* and *Charles*, by whose Authority they were settled, had a Constitutional Right to grant the first Settlers their Title to the Territories in *America*, with all the Powers of distinct Legislation and Government; and that these Monarchs exercised that Right, will appear sufficiently evident, from the Tenor of the Charters themselves, confirmed and explained by their subsequent Conduct and Declarations, than which nothing more was necessary to constitute the Independency of the Colonies, since if their first Inhabitants received and settled those Countries, on the Terms of independent Legislation and Government, made by those who had a legal Right to grant these Terms, it is self-evident that no Power whatever could afterwards unite them to the Realm of *England*, without their formal and express Consent, which has never been given, nor have they ever been considered as within this Kingdom. It will likewise appear, that from the Æra of the first Discovery of *America*, to the 12th of *Charles* the Second, no Act of Parliament had ever been extended to the Colonies, because they were "not within the Realm or Jurisdiction of Parliament." At that Time it will be found, that the Legislature of *England* first exercised its Authority in the Colonies, for regulating their Trade, and afterwards for directing their exterior Policy, but, at best, on a very obscure, I will not say, no *Right*. If, however, it should be agreed, that the Colonies were never annexed to the Realm, or within the Jurisdiction of its Parliament, it will require no great Sagacity to determine how far their Submission to these Acts, in their Infant State, can preclude their future Claims to the Right of their original Constitution.* It will likewise appear, that, from the Discovery of *America*, to the Æra of *Grenvillian* Administration, the only Act of Parliament that can, with Justice, be said to have imposed Duties, or Taxes, on the Colonies for any Purpose, it that of the 25th of *Charles* the Second; and that this was never designed to raise Money for any national Service, or establish a Precedent for Taxing the Colonies on any future Occasion, has been already abundantly proved by the Nature of the Act, the Tenor of its

---

* Quod ab initio injustum est, nullum potest habere juris effectum. *Grot. de Jur. Bel. & Pac.*

Preamble, the subsequent Declaration of the King in answer to the *Virginia* Remonstrance, and the Measures he pursued afterwards for obtaining a Revenue for the Support of Government in that Colony, not by Authority of Parliament, but the Consent of the General Assembly of the Province. And as even this Act was deemed an Infringement of the Rights of the Colonies, and as such became the Subject of Remonstrances to the Throne, which were countenanced by the King, no Person will pretend, that it can authorize the *British* Legislature to prescribe for the Right of Taxing the Colonies.—I am, however, uncertain, whether by thus exposing the Title of the Colonies to the Privileges of distinct States, I am acting for their Service, or agreeable to their Wishes, as they do not, at present, dispute the Power exercised by *Great Britain*, in binding them by political and commercial Regulations; it is, however, but just, that those, who, not content with the Exercise of this Power, ungenerously endeavour, from this Concession of the Colonies, to infer a Right of taking away their Property at Pleasure, should know the very slender Foundation that supports even the Power from whence this Inference is deduced.—If, however, I could believe it possible to unite *Great Britain* and the Colonies, equally and justly, in a legislative Capacity, and overcome those insuperable Obstacles which Nature has interposed to this Union, I would endeavour to promote it by every honest Expedient, as the surest Method of securing their Stability and Happiness, instead of citing Facts to prove the Right of the latter to the Privileges of distinct Legislation and Government; but as I cannot believe this practicable, and as I well know, that it is incompatible with their Freedom, and repugnant to the Spirit of the *British* Constitution, to live in Subjection to the Laws of an Assembly in which they have no Representation, I have thought it my Duty thus to explain their original State and Constitution.

I shall not contend with our Author concerning the Difference between internal and external Taxation, or between Taxes for the Purpose of a Revenue, and those for the Regulation of Trade; as I am convinced, that a Power of imposing Duties, even for commercial Regulations, ought not to be vested in any other Person, or Assembly of Persons, than those who have a Right of Taxing for every Purpose; because, under specious Pretences, it may be perverted to an intolerable Grievance; and yet the Conduct of this Nation towards *Ireland* and the Colonies, since its Departure from the Spirit of its original Constitution, by assuming a Power of exercising Foreign Legislation, has afforded Cause to believe the real Existence of this Distinction; and perhaps Duties imposed merely to restrain Commerce, and not to procure a Revenue, cannot be deemed Taxes with any Propriety; at least the apparent Difference is so plausible, that it can afford no Cause for Surprize, if the Colonies were deluded by it, and reluctantly submitted to the Act of the 25th of *Charles* the Second, though they afterwards universally resisted the Stamp Act. But if this be not the Case, it is still a most unnatural Perversion of Reason and Argument in our Author, to infer a Right of universal Taxation over the Colonies, by proving the Non Entity of this Difference, as the just and obvious Inference therefrom would operate against every Kind of Imposition for any Purpose.

Our Author observes, that the Colonies do not, "as yet, reject the Authority of Parliament to bind them in any Case, save in the Article of Taxation," but treats their Concession in this Particular, as inconsistent with their other Claims; alledging, that they must be subject to the Authority of Parliament in every Respect, or else in none; and perhaps there may be some Justice in this Observation, since in most Countries Legislation and Taxation have been invariably united in the same Person or Persons; and yet the History and Constitution of *England* afford many Precedents to the contrary. A Bill of Supply is not simply a Law, but a Free Gift from the People, by their Delegates, the Commons of the Realm; and the House of Peers, though an equal Part of the Supreme Legislature, and equally authorized to originate all other Bills, are in the former excluded from that Privilege, nor allowed to make any Addition or Change whatever therein. The Peers are, indeed, allowed simply to give or refuse their Assent to a Money Bill, because they are precluded from the Right of Suffrage for Members of the House of Commons, and unrepresented therein, so that without this Privilege, they would necessarily suffer a Deprivation of one of the most important Rights enjoyed by all other Freeholders in the Realm, that of giving their Property by themselves, or their Representatives. And by the 19th of *Henry* the Seventh, it appears, that the King does not give the Royal Assent, but the Royal Thanks, to Bills of Supply; all which renders it evident, that, by the *English* Constitution, the Right of Taxation is not necessarily vested in the Supreme Legislature of the Nation, but that all Pecuniary Grants to the Crown are properly Acts of the People, giving their Sovereign a Part of their Property, either personally, or by Delegation. And agreeable to this is Mr. *Locke*'s Maxim, that "The Prince, or Senate, however it may have power to make Laws, for the Regulation of Property between the Subjects one amongst another, yet can never have a Power to take to themselves the Whole or any Part of the Subjects Property, without their own Consent; because that would be, in Effect, to leave them no Property at all." Nor is the Practice of the *British* Parliament, in imposing Taxes upon the People, at all repugnant to this Maxim, whatever our Author may have advanced to the contrary; because though Bills of Supply are originated by the Commons, assented to by the Lords, and complimented with the Royal Thanks, yet this is not done in a Legislative Capacity, as the Lords and Commons do but make a pecuniary Donation to the Crown, the former in Behalf of themselves, and the latter as the Representatives of the People.

This may be easily demonstrated, by many Facts in the Political History of *England*. Thus it appears, that while the House of Commons anciently granted the Crown Supplies from those Counties, Cities, and Boroughs which they represented, other Parts of the Realm, which had no Representation therein, such as the Principality of *Wales*, the Counties Palatine of *Chester*, &c. were allowed to tax themselves, in a Mode adapted to the peculiar Circumstances of their distinct Situation: And when the Commons afterwards assumed the Power of granting Supplies for those Places, the King, deeming the Measure repugnant to the Principles of the Constitution, suspended the Collection of those Grants, till an equal Representation was allowed them. To this may be added, that the Clergy, though bound to obey the general Laws of the Realm, were antiently allowed to tax themselves. *Ireland*, likewise, has invariably yielded Obedience to the Laws of this Kingdom, for regulating its Policy and Commerce; and yet there is no *Irishman*, who would not think the *British* Legislature committed a most unjust and oppressive Act in imposing a Land Tax of One Penny *per* Pound on his Estate, though our Author acknowledges that this Tax would be as just as any whatever; and I flatter myself, that the Colonies have as equitable and rational Pretensions to an Exemption from Taxation, by an Assembly in which they have no Delegate, as the People of *Ireland*, which is in Reality a conquered Country, brought into Subjection by *Henry* the Second, *Jure Gladii*, and submitting on this express Condition, "The People and Kingdom of *Ireland* shall be governed by the same mild Laws, as those which govern the People of *England*." It is likewise to be remembered, that when King *Charles* the Second, disgusted with the *New-England* Colonies, on Account of their former Attachment to the Commonwealth, brought Writs of *Scire Facias* against their Charters, under various Pretences, the principal Offence, for which Judgment was given in Chancery against the *Massachusetts-Bay*, was, as our Author confesses, that the Colony had undertaken to raise Money for the Support and Defence of Government, for which there was no particular Authority in its Charter, although it contained ample Power of Legislation, by an Act which the Colonies were alone authorized to believe, that the Right of making Laws, and that of imposing Taxes, are not necessarily vested in the same Body; they being, by the *British* Constitution, distinct and separate Acts; the former of which is to be exercised by the supreme Legislature, and the latter by the People, or their Delegates only.—This, and the preceding Instances, therefore, will sufficiently justify the Colonies from that Absurdity with which our Author charges their Conduct, in acknowledging the Supremacy of Parliament, and yet denying its Right of Taxation.

I flatter myself, that I have now satisfactorily proved, that the most ancient of our Colonies were, agreeable to the express Acts and declared Intentions of the King, lawfully constituted distinct States, and that having been settled on these fundamental and indefeasible Conditions, no Power could afterwards unite them to the Realm, or subject them to the Jurisdiction of Parliament, without their express Consent: I have likewise shewn, that if, rather than avail themselves of their Right to the Privileges of distinct Legislation and Government, they prefer a limited Dependence on the *British* Parliament, that this Dependence does not necessarily divest them of their exclusive Right to grant their own Property; and it now remains for me to prove, that they cannot be divested of this Right, and in their present State made subject to Parliamentary Impositions, without being deprived of the most important of those Privileges which are enjoyed by the Subjects of *Great Britain* in general, and even reduced to a State of actual Slavery. This, notwithstanding all the Art and Sophistry with which our Author endeavours to perplex the Subject, is a Task easily executed, even without deducing the Constitution from its *Saxon* Origin, where every one, who had any Landed Property, however small, was instituted to a personal Suffrage in the Supreme Legislative Assembly, or Parliament: I shall not take upon myself a distinct Refutation of all the fallacious Sophisms introduced by our Author, in his Enquiry into the Right of Election and Representation; they are specious, but repugnant to the Ideas which the Nation has invariably entertained of its Constitution, inconsistent with the Notion of a popular Assembly, and with the Transactions of Parliament, and tending to confound the Opinion which *Britons* universally entertain of the superior Advantage of their Government, and the Regularity of its Operation; neither shall I controvert his Conclusion, that the "Right in Corporations of electing Representatives to Parliament, is derived from the Grant of the Crown, and the Members exercise that Right, because the Corporation holds of the Crown;" and that the Commons distinctly represent "those only who in themselves had a Right to a Share in the Legislature, and by whom they were deputed or elected."

The great *Sidney*, however, has given a much better Account of this Matter: "In the Counties, (says he,) which make up the Body of the Nation, all Freeholders have their Votes; these are properly *Cives*, Members of the Commonwealth, in Distinction from those who are only *Incolæ*, or Inhabitants, Villains, *&c*. These, in the Beginning of the *Saxons* Reign in *England*, composed the *Micklegemots*, and when they grew to be so numerous, that one Place could not contain them, or so far dispersed, that, without Trouble and Danger, they could not leave their Habitations, they deputed such as should represent them: When the Nation came to be more polished, to inhabit Cities and Towns, and to set up several Arts and Trades, those, who exercised them, were thought to be as useful to the Commonwealth, as the Freeholders in the Country, and to deserve the same Privileges. But, it not being reasonable that every one should, in this Case, do what he pleased, it was thought fit, that the King, with his Council, (which always consisted of the *Proceres et Magnates Regni,*) should judge what Numbers of Men, and what Places deserved to be made Corporations, or Bodies Politic, and to enjoy those Privileges; by which he did not confer upon them any Thing that was his; but, according to the Trust reposed in him, did dispense out of the Public Stock, Parcels of what he received from the whole Nation. That which renders this most plain and safe is, that Men, chosen in this Manner to serve in Parliament, do not act by themselves, but in Conjunction with others, who are sent thither by Prescription; not by a Power derived from Kings, but from those who choose them."

This is perfectly true, and it is the happy Privilege of all *British* Subjects, whose Property and Condition create in them a permanent Attachment to the Realm, and a Sollicitude for its Welfare, to share in that Legislation by which they are governed, either personally or by Representation. It is not, however, with Propriety, that our Author declares, that "the King, Lords, and Commons, are their Representatives;" since, as *Sidney* declares, "The House of Peers, as it is constituted, act for themselves, and are chosen by Kings." How far the Sovereign is, by the *British* Constitution, vested with the Legislative Authority, let others determine; his Assent is, indeed, necessary to give Validity to Laws, yet by his Coronation Oath he is obliged to assent to "*such Laws as the People choose.*" (*Quas Vulgus elegerit.*)

These Observations I have thought pertinent to the present Subject, as tending to ascertain the Rights of individual *Britons*, which is all that seems necessary to determine the Legality of exercising Parliamentary Legislation for the Colonies, if they are within the Realm, as is now pretended, because even our Author does not deny their Inhabitants all the Privileges and Immunities of *British* Subjects, well knowing that such Denial would be repugnant to the *British* Constitution, which places all Subjects, whose Condition is similar, on the same Level of Liberty, and intitles them all to equal Rights and

Privileges. In ascertaining this Particular, it is not sufficient to examine what are the Privileges which are common to every *British* Subject; and because the Rabble of the Kingdom are not intitled to the Right of Suffrage for Members of the House of Commons, from thence to infer, that the Inhabitants of the Colonies, whether possessed of Freeholds or not, ought to be indiscriminately denied that Right, and thereby confounded with those whom the Ancient Laws of the Realm have denominated *Villains*. On the contrary, let us examine the Privileges which belong to *British* Freeholders, and afterwards compare them to those which will remain to the Freeholders in the Colonies, when subjected to the Authority of the *British* Legislature in their present unrepresented State; from whence it will be easily discovered, how far the Operation of the late Acts of Parliament, for raising a Revenue in *America*, is compatible with their Rights as *British* Subjects; possessed of that Share and Species of Property, which, by the Laws of the Realm, entitle them to participate its Legislative Authority. This will determine the present Controversy with unerring Justice; and, on this firm and equitable Basis, the simplest of my Country-men may encounter even a *Grenville*, a *Knox*, or a *Mauduit*. I shall, therefore, proceed to explain the most important of the Rights of *British* Freeholders, as far as they are necessary to the present Controversy, on the Authority of the late Earl of *Bath*, who declares it to be the unquestionable Privilege of a Free-holder, "to assent to all those Laws, by which he is governed, and that his Life, Liberty, and Property, cannot be taken from him, but according to those Laws." "So that a Freeholder," (says Mr. *Addison*,) "is but one Remove from a Legislator; for such is the Nature of our happy constitution, that the Bulk of the People virtually give their Approbation to every thing they are bound to obey."

Is it necessary for me to ask, How many Removes the *American* Freeholders are from *British* Legislators? Whether they assent to those Acts of Parliament by which their Property is given to the Crown, or whether it can be supposed, without confounding all Ideas of Language and Things, that in their present State they give any other Assent to those Acts, than what is given by the Inhabitants of *France*, or *Spain*, unless the universal Opposition of the People, and the Protests and

Resolves of the *American* Assemblies against these Acts, and the Authority by which they have been enacted, can, by some strange Expedient, be construed into *Consent*.

Our Author, however, pretends, in Opposition to the Idea that every *Briton* entertains of the *British* Constitution, and contrary to the Assertion of the Author of the *Considerations on the Propriety of Taxing the Colonies*, that it is *not* "the Principle of the Common Law, that no Part of their Property shall be drawn from *British* Subjects without their Consent, given by those they depute to represent them;" and recites several Passages from the Great Charter of King *John*, and the Statutes of the 15th and 17th of *Edw*. II. which he thinks are favourable to his Opinion. It is, however, both absurd and unjust, in the present System of Things, to confine, to the strict Sense of Words, the Meaning of those ancient Acts, which were adapted to the then State of the Constitution, but little altered from its Feudal Institution, when Parliaments were chiefly composed of potent Barons, whose Number, Wealth, and Power at that Æra justly gave them a much greater Share in the Legislature, then is enjoyed by the House of Peers, since the Alteration which has been progressively induced, by the Transition of Property into the Hands of the People, their Enfranchisement from the Vassalage of their Barons, and Papal Authority, together with the Operation of Commerce, Arts, and Sciences. All this is evident from the present Nature of Parliamentary Transactions; and though, by the Great Charter, *&c.* the House of Commons is no where intitled to the sole Privilege of originating Bills of Supply, yet, since the Change which I have just mentioned, it has claimed and exercised that Right, as the Representative of those by whom the Burthen of all Supplies is principally supported. Nor need I any other Arguments in Opposition to our Author, than those alledged by the Commons, in Support of their Claim to the sole Right of originating and modifying all Pecuniary Grants to the Crown, and which abundantly prove it to be a fundamental Principle of the Constitution, that all who, by the Circumstances of their Religion and Property, are intitled to the Privileges of Citizens of the State, shall be taxed only by themselves or their Representatives; and that the Privilege of introducing and modifying all Acts, for granting Pecuniary Supplies, shall be the sole Privilege of those who represent the greatest Number of those who are to provide the Means of such Supplies: And, strange as it may appear, it is nevertheless undoubtedly true, that those Members of the late House of Commons, who originated the Bills for granting his Majesty certain *Stamp*, and other Duties, in the Colonies, whose Inhabitants they did not represent, and of which neither they nor their Constituents paid any Part, were convinced of the Truth and Justice of these very Arguments, so repugnant to a Measure of that Nature.

But the Impropriety, Prolixity, and Diffusion of our Author's Arguments, to invalidate the Claim of the Colonies to Special Representation in Parliament, previous to the Imposition of Taxes by its Authority, would render a distinct Refutation of them as tedious as it is unnecessary, since I flatter myself that I shall be able, with more Brevity, to expose their Fallacy, by a few, just, and natural Conclusions, from as many Propositions of acknowledged and indisputable Truth.

First, then, the Power of Legislation is by the *British* Constitution, vested in the King, Lords, and Commons of the Realm (the latter being delegated from those Counties, Cities, Boroughs, *&c.* which, by Law, are intitled to participate the Authority of making Laws.)

Secondly, If the Inhabitants of the Colonies are not *British* Subjects, they are necessarily not within the Jurisdiction of the *British* Legislature.

Thirdly, If they are *British* Subjects, they are necessarily intitled to all the Rights, Privileges, and Immunities, which belong to *British* Subjects of the same Condition, Class, or Denomination.

Fourthly, By the Constitution and Laws of the Realm, every *British* Subject, possessed of a Freehold of the yearly Value of Forty Shillings, besides the Right he may have of Voting for the Delegates from Cities, Boroughs, *&c.* is entitled to a Suffrage for the Representatives of the County in which his Freehold is situated.

This being true, it necessarily follows, that if the Colonies are within the Realm and Jurisdiction of its Parliament, every Individual among their Inhabitants, who is possessed of a Freehold of Forty Shillings *per Annum*, is thereby intitled to an actual Representation in the *British* House of Commons;

and till that Representation is granted, he will be denied one of the most important Rights of a *British* Freeholder, and the Parliament will not be qualified to exercise Jurisdiction over him. This brings the Dispute, between *Great Britain* and the Colonies, to a short, but final Conclusion: A Conclusion that necessarily precludes all future Controversy, and incontestibly demonstrates the Fallacy and Injustice of all those Sophistical Arguments, by which Ministerial and *Grenvillian* Partizans have attempted to involve the Rights of the Colonies in Perplexity and Error. It will now appear absurd to alledge, that the Colonies are not intitled to a distinct Representation in Parliament, because all the Inhabitants of *Great Britain* are not distinctly represented.—I well know that a Mode of Representation, established in those Ages when Land was almost the only Species of Local Property in *England*, must necessarily be unequal, at a Time when Arts, Manufactures, and Commerce, have derived a Flow of Wealth of a different Species; but because *Britons*, residing here, are but unequally or imperfectly represented, shall *Britons*, residing in *America* be wholly unrepresented? We do not ask a better Representation than our Fellow Subjects in *Great Britain*; we ask but the same; we only desire that our Land may be represented by Knights, and our Monied Property by Citizens and Burgesses, in that Assembly which grants this Property to others; 'tis this alone that can make us a free People, and enable us to use the Language of the great *Sidney*:* When speaking of the Rights of *Englishman*, "*Asiatic* Slaves (says he) usually pay such Tributes as are imposed on them. We owe none but what we freely give. None is or can be imposed on us, unless by ourselves: We measure our Grants according to our Will, or the present Occasion, for our own Safety.—The Happiness of those who enjoy the like Liberty, and the shameful Misery they lie under, who have suffered themselves to be forced or cheated out of it, may persuade, and the Justice of the Cause encourage us, to think nothing too dear to be hazarded in Defence of it." And if this is denied us, if the House of Commons, in which we have no Delegates, assumes (in Opposition to those just and cogent Arguments urged against the Peers by a former House) the

---

* Discourses on Government.

Privilege of originating and modifying Bills for granting away our Property; the unrepresented *American* Freeholder will not only be deprived of the Rights belonging to the Freeholders of *Great Britain*, Rights, for which *English* Patriots have bled, and *English* Monarchs been dethroned, but even reduced to a State much worse even than that of the unrepresented Rabble of this Kingdom; for immense is the Difference between a Nation but imperfectly represented, and a People who have no Representation.

The unrepresented Inhabitants of *Great Britain* are secured in Life and Property, because they pay no Tax, and are governed by no Law, which does not equally affect the Legislators themselves and their Constituents: A Circumstance from which they acquire an effectual Barrier against Oppression; which the *Americans* are so far from enjoying, that every Motive and Suggestion of Interest must operate to their Disadvantage; because the Acts, which impose Taxes on them, are not general, but partial; and instead of burthening those by whom they are made, tend to exonerate the Legislators and their Constituents, the People of *Great Britain*, in Proportion to the increased Weight of the Burthens imposed on the Colonies. Every Restraint, therefore, which affords Security to the unrepresented Inhabitants of *Great Britain*, is either removed or converted into a *Stimulus* to Oppression; and every Temptation which Interest (the most universal and prevalent of all Passions) can suggest, must operate against them.* In a State like this, what Security can they have against Oppression, or what Incitements to industry, when the arbitrary Will of a *British* Parliament, over which they can have no Influence or Restraint, and whose Interest it is to oppress them, is to be the precarious *Tenure* of their Property.

---

* "The Legislative Power, (says *Sidney*,) is not to be trusted in the Hands of any who are not bound to obey the Laws they make. This is the Case with our Parliament, they may make unjust Laws, *&c.* yet they must bear the Burthen as much as others, and when they die the Teeth of their Children will be set on Edge by the sour Grapes they have eaten." This Circumstance he deems of the highest Importance for the Security of Liberty "because the Hazard of being ruined by those who must perish with us is not so much to be feared, as by those who may enrich and strengthen themselves by our Destruction," as may happen from the Exercise of Parliamentary Authority over the Colonies.

This, however, is not all that constitutes the Inequality in the Situation of the Colonies.—Those Inhabitants of *Great Britain*, who have no Suffrages at the Elections of the Representatives for Counties, Cities, *&c.* are yet far from being destitute of Influence; they are connected with the Electors, by Parentage, Relation, Friendship, Commerce, Employment, Dependance, *&c.* and the Interest they derive from these Connections, when exerted, is far from producing an inconsiderable Effect on the Event of every Election. Thus the Influence of the *London* Merchants, (who, in general, are not Liverymen,) on these Occasions, is well known; and even the Applause or Censure of the Rabble is far from being insignificant. But how dissimilar is the Case of the Colonies, unknown to, and unconnected with, either the Representing or Represented? and subject to a Foreign Power, which they have neither delegated nor intrusted, and which will benefit those, by whom it is exercised, in Proportion to its frequent and oppressive Use? What Degree of Freedom is compatible with a State like this? or what can they enjoy therein but Slavery, more wretched and abject than that of the *Spartan Helotes*? These were the Labourers, the Servants, the Slaves of their Masters, who could know their Burthens, and estimate their Ability to support them: Could see their Sufferings, hear their Groans, be affected by their Misery, relent, and alleviate the Weight of Oppression. The Colonies, on the contrary, would be the Slaves of those to whom they are unknown, and from whom they are widely separated. The Commons, who originate their Taxes, the Lords who assent to them, and the King, by whom they are thanked for granting the Property of others, must be Strangers to their Persons and Circumstances, at least they can have but little Knowledge of their Debility, their Wants and Sufferings, but what is derived from the precarious, and perhaps corrupt Representations, of Officers and Placemen, who, distinguishing their own Fortune from that of the State, and, ready to sacrifice the State to their own Advancement, may be, and perhaps have already been, by Interest or Malevolence, prompted to the most injurious Representations of the People among whom they reside.

And let me now ask any Man, whose Mind is not callous to the Sensations of Justice or Humanity, if a State like this is

compatible with the Enjoyment of those Rights which constitute the Freedom and Happiness of *British* Subjects; or of the
Terms of those solemn Compacts, on the Faith of which our
Progenitors abandoned their native Country, and all its en-
dearing Connections, and encountered the Toils and Dangers
which inseparably attend the Settlement of a wild, inhospitable
Desert; by which the King's Dominions have been widely extended, and the National Commerce and Power so immensely
increased? And is Slavery the Reward which Gratitude or Justice prescribe for Services like these? If not, why are we calum-
niated for endeavouring to resist it? *Britons* revere the Fortitude
and Virtue of their Ancestors, who have fought, bled, and died
in the Cause of Freedom, and preserved and transmitted to
their Posterity, the glorious Franchises of *English* Subjects:
And shall we, descended from the same Progenitors, and Heirs
to the same Right, be insulted with every Species of Detraction, and even intimidated by a Military Force to compel us to
relinquish these Rights, and to intail Slavery on our Posterity,
who, with the Groans of Oppression, would blend Execrations
on the Pusillanimity of their Parents.

If our Cause is just, Resistance is a Virtue; and if *Britons* are
the Aggressors, our Fortitude is laudable; and if Force may be
used in subverting our Rights, what may not be done in their
Defence?* "Allegiance, says *Sidney*, signifies no more than
such an Obedience as the Law requires." Can it, then, oblige a
People to submit to that which is repugnant to the fundamental and indefeasible Rights of their Government and Constitution? I flatter myself, however, that a Nation, distinguished for
its Love of Freedom and Justice, will recover from its Delusion,
and recoil at the Inhumanity of reducing to Slavery those who,
by Descent and Compact, are intitled to all the Blessings of
Liberty, and who have merited so much from the *British* Nation. Can there be one uncorrupt *Briton*, who reflects on the
Blessings of that Freedom he enjoys, who would even wish to
see his *American* Brethren deprived of those Rights, without
which they can have no Security for their Lives or Estates,

---

* Justa piaque sunt arma (says *Pontius*, the *Samnite*) quibus necessaria, et necessaria quibus nulla nisi in armis spes est salutis. *Tit. Liv. Lib.* 8.

much less become an Instrument in effecting a Purpose so unjust and inhuman?

But if the Suggestions of Gratitude, Humanity, and Justice, are of no Avail in the present Contest, I hope the People of *Great Britain* will not be inattentive to the Dictates of true Policy, and national Interest, which are in every Respect contrary to an Infringement of the Rights of my Countrymen. As for the late Acts of Parliament, imposing Duties on *British* Commodities imported into the Colonies, which have more immediately occasioned this Controversy, their direct Repugnance to Equity, and the Principles of Commerce, is so obvious, that every *British* Subject may justly declare, with the ingenious Author of the Case of *Great Britain* and *America*, "That they are so impolitic, that we should reject them, tho' Justice did not condemn them; that they are so unjust, that we should reject them, were they ever so politic." And I can, with the most perfect Truth declare, that if I wished to see the Colonies formed into distinct States, without the least Connection or Dependence on *Great Britain*, I should not only oppose the Repeal of those Acts, but wish the Duties imposed by them, might be extended to every Commercial Article of *British* Manufacture, as the most effectual Expedient from promoting the Independence of my Countrymen, since nothing but a Sense of Injuries, and that Spirit of Resentment which Parliamentary Taxation has already inspired, can sufficiently repress their growing Luxury and extravagant Consumption of *British* Commodities, and promote Industry, Frugality, and Manufactures among them.

I cannot however, so far divest myself of an affectionate Attachment to the Land of my Progenitors, as to be unconcerned for its Welfare: With Anxiety I reflect on that Effeminacy, Luxury, and Corruption, which extend to all Orders of Men in this Kingdom, and which, unless Causes fail of their usual Effects, must induce a Decline of Empire; these, however, may yet be overcome, and the Danger averted. The State, supported by the Youth, Health and Vigour of her Colonies, may yet recover its pristine Integrity and Power, and both they, and the Parent Country, increase and prosper mutually, blessing and blessed by their Political Union. But this Union, necessary to the Being of the State, can never be permanent, unless formed on the Basis of Equity and mutual Advantage, and connected by the Ties of reciprocal Affection.

Let *Britons* divest themselves of all Regard for the Rights of the People of *America*, and of every Sentiment of Humanity, Gratitude, and Justice, and attend only to their own partial Interest, and they will find, that even that rightly pursued, will direct them to fix the Constitution of the Colonies on the Pillars of Freedom; to secure their Connection and Friendship, by making it their Interest to continue in Union and Friendship with *Great Britain*, and attach them to the Government, by making it impossible for them to obtain a better: They were planted, and have flourished, under the benign Influence of Freedom, and the Enthusiasm of Liberty glows in their Minds; if it be continued to them, no future Increase of Numbers, or Power, no favourable Concurrence of Circumstances, will ever engage them to a Change of Government, because no Change can be for their Advantage.* But if, on the contrary, they are made subject to the despotic Power of those whom they have neither delegated nor entrusted, and over whom they have no restraining Influence, and if their Life and Property depends on the arbitrary Exercise of this Power, whether it be lodged in a single Person, or many Hundreds, their total Loss of Freedom will be too palpable, and their Slavery too real, too feeling, not to urge them to improve every Occasion which may be favourable to a Change of Government, because no Change can be for the worse.

How soon their Increase of Numbers will be sufficient to resist the Power of *Great Britain*, is what I will not determine: Their Force, opposed to this Kingdom, is an Idea that excites Pain and Horror: And though I frequently reflect with Pleasure on their future Increase of Numbers, Wealth, and Power, they are only pleasing when I consider them as employed for the common Happiness and Glory of *Great Britain* and her Colonies. I am therefore unwilling to mention the future Increase of the latter, lest it should be imagined I do it with a

---

* "Being taught by Reason and Experience (says *Sidney*) that Nations delight in the Peace and Justice of a good Government, Kings will never fear a general Insurrection, while they take Care it be rightly administred."

Desire to intimidate those, who have the Administration of the Affairs of State, from the Pursuit of those Measures which the Interest of *Great Britain* may require. This, however, is by no means my Intention: I would rather prevail by the more amiable Motives of Justice and Humanity, if happily an Attention to these might have any Influence in the present Contest. A prudential Regard ought, however, to be had to the future Increase of the Colonies, of which many in this Kingdom have conceived but very inadequate Ideas,* and which, perhaps, in a few Years, may produce a People too numerous to continue Victims of Oppression, and too brave not to assert their just and constitutional Rights; and if this should ever happen, that Distance, which separates this Kingdom from the Colonies, might be converted to a very important Instrument for establishing the Independence of the latter. And perhaps it might never be consistent with the Safety of this Kingdom to unpeople itself, by converting its Inhabitants into Armies, and employing them on such distant and *laudable* Expeditions.

The Certainty of the Increase of the Colonies, and the Possibility of their hostile Disposition towards this Kingdom, demonstrate the Necessity, of conciliating Measures. The Time must come, when their Friendship or Enmity will be of the utmost Importance to the very Being of the State; and it is then that the Conduct of those in Power will be either

---

* In *Connecticut*, a Colony that has but little immediate Communication with *Great Britain*, and where no transported Felons are ever permitted to land, the Number of Inhabitants had doubled the last seventeen Years preceding the Commencement of the late War, and during that Time had not been at all augmented by Importation from *Europe*, or at least the acquisition of Foreigners thereby, from various Discouragements, had not been more than sufficient to compensate the Diminution of Numbers sustained by the Emigration of native Inhabitants to less populous Colonies; from whence it will appear, that in *Pennsylvania, Maryland, Virginia. &c.* to which there is a constant accession of foreign Inhabitants, their Increase must exceed Dr. *Franklin*'s Estimation: Nor is this at all extraordinary.—"Wherever a Place is found (says the celebrated Baron *de Montesquieu*,) in which two Persons can live commodiously, there they marry: Nature has a sufficient Propensity to it when unrestrained by the Difficulty of Subsistence. A rising People increase and multiply extremely, because with them it would be a great Inconveniency to live in Celibacy, and none to have many Children: The contrary of which is the Case when a Nation is formed." *The Spirit of Laws*, Vol. ii.

applauded or execrated, as it has tended to secure or alienate their Affections. But if, on the contrary, the Colonies were ever to continue in their present Mediocrity, unable to resist the Force of *Great Britain*; even then, whatever Species of Government might be established for them, I will venture to affirm, that the more it might be allied to Freedom, the more advantageous to this Kingdom would those become, who might live under it. If they were governed in Moderation and Justice, they would prove the Strength and Support of the State; but if by Force, they would be its Weakness. Nor could rapacious Tyranny extort half the Sums from them by Taxes, which they would voluntarily contribute, in a State of Freedom, for the Protection and Support of a good Government. Had the People of *New England*, during the late War, when, besides fighting against the common Enemy, they alone expended near three Millions in the public Service, been a disaffected People, could all the Efforts of Despotism have obtained Half the Sum from them?

It is abundantly evident, from every Transaction in the Colonies, that not the Populace only, but even their Legislative Assemblies, together with the whole Body of the People, unanimously consider Parliamentary Taxation as an Infringement of their most important Rights; nor will the Presence of Troops to intimidate, or the Resolution of a Minister to compel them to Submission, whether manifested by official Letters, or echoed from the Mouth of a K——, or converted to P———tary *Resolves*, convince them of its Justice; but every Shilling, which is obtained from them in this Manner, will realize their Ideas of lost Freedom, in a Manner so feeling, as necessarily to alienate their Affections from this Kingdom, and render them a disgusted, disaffected People; and when this happens, Force alone can secure their Dependence; and their Dependence, when it can only be secured by Force, will never afford any Advantage to *Great Britain* during its Continuance; and its Continuance will not be for ever.

These are important Truths, which, abstracted from all Regard to Equity, ought to determine the Conduct of those, on whom the Government of the State depends; and from them let me ask whether the Revenue, produced by the late Impositions on the Colonies, which are the immediate Objects of the present Controversy, is more than sufficient to defray the incidental Charges of the additional Officers employed in collecting it? And whether the Surplus is an adequate Exchange for the Affection of the Colonies, which has been thereby well nigh alienated from their Parent Country? But the Impolicy of Measures, tending to discourage *British* Manufactures, and promote those of the Colonies, must be obvious even to those by whom they are apparently abetted: And unfavourable as the Disposition of the present Ministry to the Colonies appears, I am yet persuaded, they would promote the Repeal of the late Acts, but for an imaginary Necessity of supporting the *Dignity of Government*. But let the Wise and Just determine, whether the true Dignity of Government is best supported by an indiscriminate Adherence to every Act, without Regard to its Justice, or by a magnanimous Avowal of Errors, and a voluntary Renunciation of those Measures which may be found repugnant to Equity, and true Policy. That "the Glory of Kings, is to reform themselves whatever they may have been prompted to act contrary to Justice," was a favourite Maxim with that Prince, to whom *France* decreed the Name of Wise.

These Observations, I flatter myself, will sufficiently demonstrate the Utility, and even Necessity, of removing the late, and desisting from all future Impositions on the Colonies, at least, till they are united to *Great Britain* in a Civil Capacity, and allowed to participate that Authority, by which they are governed. This is evidently prescribed, both by Policy and Justice, and Prudence will dictate the Expedience of doing it, before the Controversy is irreconcileable, or the Affection of the Colonies irrecoverably alienated, and whilst the Conduct of the Legislature can be attributed to a Regard for Justice.

As to our Author's Account of Mr. *Grenville*'s Disposition towards the Colonies, I wish it may be just: I never was among those, who approved that Virulence with which he has been treated by some, and yet willing as I am to believe any thing in his Favour, that is not repugnant to known Truths, without regarding the Stamp Act, there are other Causes for my Incredulity on this Subject; such, for Instance, was the projected Clause in an Act of Parliament, intended to have been carried into a Law, to impower the Officers of the King's Troops in *America*, to quarter their Soldiers in the Houses of any of the

Inhabitants, thereby subjecting them to a Species of Military Tyranny, incompatible with the least Share of Civil Freedom, and unknown in this Kingdom; repugnant to its Constitution, and similar to that exercised by *Lewis* the Fourteenth, in persecuting the *Protestants* of *France*. Did Mr. *Grenville*, in this Attempt, preserve a proper Tenderness for the Rights of the Colonies; or was his Conduct therein consonant to his professed Desire to secure to them the Rights of *British* Subjects inviolate? Surely not! I hope, however, he is, by this Time, not only sensible to the Grievance of this his former Attempt, but to the Injustice of subjecting the Colonies to Parliamentary Taxation in their present unrepresented and distinct State, and that he will have the generous Magnanimity to renounce his former Measures; and whenever this shall happen, I promise, in Behalf of my Countrymen, that they will obliterate every Idea that may have been conceived to his Disadvantage.

Our Author declaims much on the supposed Impracticability of engaging the Colonies to act in due Concert for the general Good, unless by Parliamentary Authority: But whatever Degree of Justice there may be in this Supposition, though it may suggest the Utility of modifying their Government on a Plan more extensively useful, yet, as the assembly of *New-York* has justly resolved, it can "by no Means induce a Necessity of divesting the Colonies of their essential Rights."

It is a melancholly Reflection, that a Character the most respectable for Learning, Probity, and Honour, is no Security against those invidious Aspersions, which our Author has directed against Dr. *Franklin*, who will doubtless, think it unnecessary to descend to vindicate himself from such unmerited Censure, since every judicious Person, who impartially peruses the several Addresses from the Assemblies of the *Massachusetts Bay* and *Virginia*, and unbiassed by those unwarrantable Inferences which our Author has made from them, with all the Confidence of apparent Truth, considers, that these Representations were extorted from the Colonies by Letters from the King's Ministers, urging them to take Arms, and repel the *French* from their Encroachment on the King's Territories, will easily perceive, that they neither militate against Dr. *Franklin's* Testimony to the Great Council of the Nation, nor authorize those unfavourable Conclusions which he has unwarrantably drawn, and basely aggravated, by a pretended Tenderness for his Character. The Colonies well knew, that by attempting the Repulsion of the *French*, they should involve themselves, unassisted by *Great Britain*, in an Offensive War, not only with the *Canadians*, but with *France* also, whose Troops would be sent against them on that Account. They reflected on the Importance of their former Services, and their very sparing Rewards, and considered it as a Duty incumbent on *Great Britain* to participate the Expence of defending the King's uncultivated Territory in *America*, usurped by *France*, and not situated within the Limits of any Colony; and when they were authorized to expect this, they, at his Majesty's Desire, undertook to repel the *French* from their usurped Possessions in *America* near two Years before the Commencement of the last War; which abundantly proves, that their Danger from the Superiority of the *French*, or their own Debility, was not so imminent, as necessarily to involve *Great Britain* in a War with *France*.

As to Governor *Shirley*'s Proposal, to assess the Colonies, in proportionate Sums, for their own Defence, during the late War, by Authority of Parliament, it is not strange that a Servant of the Crown should form a Plan of this Nature; but to give it any Degree of Pertinence or Validity, in the present Contest, our Author should have been able to tell his Readers, that the Colonies themselves approved it: But unluckily, neither they nor the Parliament of *Great Britain*, if I may judge from their Conduct, thought it at that Time just or expedient.

Our Author asserts, that "*Great Britain* imports to a much greater Amount from the Colonies than the Exports to them; and the Balance in Favour of the Colonies, in their Trade with her, is that on which most of them live, and raise their Fortunes." This, however, to say no worse, is a most erroneous Assertion, as may be easily demonstrated by known Facts and Common Sense, without the unnecessary Trouble of recurring to Custom-House Entries, which are ever uncertain as to the real Amount of *British* Commodities exported. To support his Assertion, our Author states the Imports and Exports between *Great Britain* and *America* in 1765 and 1766, chusing those Years, in which the Exports were unusually small, from the Disgust which his Patron's Stamp Act had excited in *America*; and as the Exports to the Colonies were, in those two Years, less than the Imports, by 880,811 *l.* (if the Entries of the Custom-House may be credited,) it serves to convey some Idea of the Loss *Great Britain* has already, and may hereafter sustain, by that unhappy Scheme of Taxing the Colonies.

It is an indisputable Truth, that any Nation which imports, from another, Commodities of greater Value, than those exported thereto, must necessarily be in Debt to the latter. This Kingdom, however, neither is, nor ever was, in Debt to the Colonies: They, on the contrary, owe *Great Britain* very considerable Sums, on Account of the Deficiency in the Value of those Commodities they send hither, even though they maintain a circuitous Commerce with almost all the Nations of *Europe* and *America*, and ransack *Spain, Portugal, Holland,* the *English, French, Spanish, Dutch,* and *Danish* Plantations in *America*, to acquire Bills of Exchange and Money, for the Payment of *British* Commodities. Is not this a Truth universally known; and does it not directly falsify our Author's Assertion? It is indeed true, that the *British West India* Islands send more to *Great Britain* than they receive from her; but the Balance in their Favour, instead of being carried out of the Nation, eventually becomes a Free Gift to the People of *Great Britain*, being squandered away by those numerous *West-Indian* Families, who either visit or reside in this Kingdom; this is evident, because no Money is ever carried from hence to any Part of *America*, in Return for its Produce. To this let me add, that all the Commodities exported from hence to *Africa*, and used in the Slave Trade, ought to be considered as sent to *America*, because the Slaves, for which they are exchanged, are sold in the Colonies, and paid for in Money, Bills, or Commodities remitted hither; from all which it is evident, that the Trade of the Colonies is, of all others, the most fruitful Source of Wealth and Power to this Kingdom; its Streams are, indeed, at present, unhappily diminished, and a Perseverance in the present Measures may, perhaps, in a little Time, make them cease to flow.

I have purposely avoided any Observations on the many Absurdities, which our Author has unjustly imputed to the Colonies, thereby to give their Claims a ridiculous Appearance, and procure an Opportunity of introducing his own Witticisms. These are contemptible Artifices, unworthy of Notice. I shall likewise pass over the fallacious Declamation with which he finishes his Review; its Impertinence will be sufficiently obvious, if my preceding Observations have produced that Conviction, which, I flatter myself, their Truth and Importance merit. Menacing the Colonies, he tells them, "There is a Spirit rising in this Country, which will make you know its Strength, and your own Weakness; that will convince you of its Authority, and of your Dependence." By this *tremendous* Spirit, I presume he means that Temerity, which has impelled our present Ministers to brave the Resentment of an injured People, and insolently trample under Foot the common Rights of *Britons* and *Americans*, without Discrimination. But, stripped of that Confidence and Power they have abused, in a little Time they will be taught by painful Experience, the Extent of their Misconduct. Happy! thrice happy will it be, for *Great Britain* and the Colonies, if this Æra shall arrive before an incongruous intemperate Ministry has irrefragably confirmed their unhappy Disagreement, or irrecoverably destroyed that mutual Affection, which forms the strongest and most permanent Union between them, and exposed us to all the Miseries arising from Civil Discord.

Having now demonstrated the Impolicy and Injustice of the Measures lately adopted for governing the Colonies, I hope I shall not incur the Charge of Presumption, by offering to the Publick a Plan for determining the Nature of their Dependence and Connection to *Great Britain*, ascertaining the Extents of their Rights, and fixing their Constitution on an equitable and permanent Basis. This, though of the highest Utility, has never been attempted by any of those numerous Writers, who have been employed in the present Controversy between *Great Britain* and the Colonies; and I am too sensible of the Difficulty that must attend its Execution, to flatter myself that the Plan which I shall propose, will be found unexceptionable, or incapable of Improvement by others: On the contrary, I shall have accomplished my Purpose, if the Attention of the Publick may, by this Attempt, be attracted to an Object of the utmost Importance, and the Legislature engaged to establish the Government and Dependence of the Colonies on the Principles of Justice and mutual Advantage.

"The present Session of Parliament should determine upon some permanent System in this Point; *Great Britain* should fix the Pretensions which she will never relinquish, and the Colonies should have certain Information of those Claims which they must submit to. Until such a System be resolved on, there will be Irresolution on one Side, and Repugnance on the other, and no System can be stable that is not founded upon Equity and Wisdom."*—That determined Opposition to Parliamentary Taxation, which has universally arisen in the Colonies, is now suspended, by the Hopes of obtaining Relief from the Wisdom and Justice of the *British* Legislature; but if, contrary to their Expectation, the present Session of Parliament should elapse, without this happy Effect, and their Petitions be dismissed with no other Determination than that contained in the Resolutions and Addresses of the L—ds and C——ns, who that is sollicitous for the Welfare of the State, and acquainted with the Temper and Designs of the Colonies, but must fear, that their present Tranquility will suffer an unhappy Interruption the ensuing Summer?

I have already declared, that if it could be thought practicable to unite the Colonies to *Great Britain* in a Civil Capacity, and on an equal Basis of Freedom, I should wish my Countrymen to participate the Happiness of *British* Laws and Government: But the Distance which Nature has interposed, creates insuperable Obstacles to this Union. The Expence and Inconvenience which must attend a Representation from a Country so remote; the little Advantage it could produce to a People, who, from their Situation, could have no Opportunity of knowing or directing the Conduct of their Delegates; the Insufficiency and Imperfection of Laws, made by Persons unacquainted with the State of those for whom they are made; and the frequent Necessity of present and immediate Legislation, joined to the great Delay and Expence that would necessarily attend all private Bills, are such important Difficulties, as must render Government, in these Circumstances, a Grievance to them, rather than a Benefit. To this let me add, that the Executive Authority, unconstrained by the Legislative Power of the Colonies, would become oppressive, and the People of *America*,

* *Case of Great Britain and America.*

deprived of their Assemblies, would become Victims to the Tyranny and Rapacity of every haughty, avaricious, or needy Governor, disposed to avail himself of the Advantages deducible from their Distance, and his own Connection and Interest with those in Power. To these might be added, many other Obstacles of a similar Nature, which are sufficiently known, and abundantly prove the Impracticability of an *American* Representation in Parliament, without which the Colonies cannot be united to *Great Britain* in a Civil Capacity, and yet continue to enjoy those Privileges, which constitute the Happiness of *British* Liberty. *From hence, the Necessity of a distinct Government for the Colonies will appear.* But as the *British* Legislature will, perhaps, never consent to emancipate them from every Kind and Degree of Subjection to itself, I hope my Countrymen, to avoid the Evils of Civil Discord, and Enmity with their Parent Country, will relinquish some of those Rights which are enjoyed by the Subjects of *Great Britain*, for the Preservation of those which are of more Importance; for the Security of their Lives, and *acquired* Property; and as they cannot be united to *Great Britain* in a Civil Capacity, let them unite to her in a Commercial one; and forming with this Kingdom, and its other Dependencies, one Commercial Empire, submit their Trade to the absolute Government of the *British* Parliament, (without desiring a Representation therein,) to be restrained and directed by its Laws for the general Good.

This Submission, I know, will deprive them of many Advantages for the Improvement of their Property, and leave them a less Share of Freedom, and fewer Privileges, than are enjoyed by *British* Subjects: But let them offer this Sacrifice, as a Tribute to their Parent Country, and the Advantages resulting from their Connection and Intercourse with it; and let *Great Britain*, on the other hand, be content with these Concessions, as abundantly sufficient to secure the Dependence of the Colonies. A Power over the Trade of a People, affects the Merchants, the Landholders, and the Manufacturers; it may command a Stagnation of their Property, and diminish its Value, by preventing its Increase; it may deprive them of the Sea, the common Benefit of Mankind, and render their Strength, Labour, and Ingenuity, of but little Value: And surely a Power more extensive cannot be desired by those who do not wish to deprive us of every Degree of Freedom; and let not *Britons* wish for more. Let them, for their own Advantage, leave us the intire Disposal of that Property, which we may be permitted to acquire through all these Restraints, and not discourage our Industry, when it must ultimately benefit themselves. *Let the* British *Legislature disclaim all Right of taxing us, even for regulating our Commerce, because, as I have already observed, that Right, under specious Pretences, may be perverted to the Purpose of raising a Revenue.* Whenever, therefore, a Trade is prejudical to the Parent Country, instead of restraining it by Duties, let it be prohibited by Laws, and let Penalties be annexed to the Breach of them. Let the Colonies enjoy the Right of manufacturing the Produce of their own Lands, because this is a Right necessary for the Preservation of Life, and conferred with it on all Mankind; but let *Great Britain* have Power to restrain the Exportation of these Manufactures to the Detriment of her own Commerce. Let the Colonies, in their own distinct internal Government, continue to obey such Laws only as shall be made by their respective Assemblies; but as in War, and a Variety of other Occasions, they will have one common Interest, and ought to act equally and with Unanimity for their general Good, let them be united in a general Political League and Confederation, for their common Government, and mutual Support and Defence: And for managing, directing, and ordering all Affairs concerning the whole Confederation, let a certain Number of Commissioners be chosen, by the Assembly of each Colony, and authorized to hear and determine all Affairs of War or Peace, and of Aids, Supplies, Pecuniary Grants, and all other Things which are proper Concomitants or Consequences of such Union or Confederation, for Amity, general Government and Defence, without intermeddling in any Affairs or Concerns appertaining to the distinct internal Government of any Colony, which is ever to be preserved inviolate.—The Number of Commissioners from each Colony might depend on the Discretion of the said Colony, but their Voices ought to be limited, according to the Number and Wealth of the Inhabitants in the Colony from whence they are delegated. These Commissioners to be annually elected, and assembled at stated Times, or on particular Occasions, by some one of the King's Governors, or other Person to be appointed by his Majesty for that Purpose, and authorized to give the Royal Assent to any Acts of the said Assembly, which Assent shall be necessary to give them Validity; and all Acts which shall be made or done by the Majority of Voices so assembled, and assented to by the King's Deputy, shall be absolutely binding on the several Confederated Colonies, to all Intents and Purposes, as if they had been made or done by their respective Assemblies; and all pecuniary Aids and Supplies, which may be granted for any just Purpose, by the assembled Delegates from the Confederated Colonies, shall be raised or levied by their respective Assemblies in just Proportion, according to the Wealth and Number of Inhabitants in each Colony, in such Manner, and from such Objects, as to each shall appear most eligible. But to prevent the Evils which may arise from Corruption, or breach of Trust, let the Delegates be made responsible for their Conduct, and obliged to act in Conformity to such Instructions as they may receive from the Assemblies by whom they are chosen, which Instructions they shall desire upon any Affairs of an extraordinary Nature or unusual Importance. And if the Part which the Confederated Colonies may take in all the Wars in which *Great-Britain* may be engaged, and the Expences they may thereby incur, as well as in defending themselves against their *Indian* Enemies, joined to the Benefit which this Kingdom may derive from the Power of confining their Commerce to the Channels of its own Interest, should not be found sufficient to defray the necessary Charges of their Government and Protection, let his Majesty require the proper Aids and Supplies from the Assembly of the united Colonies, instead of attempting to procure it by Authority of Parliament. This will afford them the pleasing Opportunity of demonstrating their Affection and Loyalty to their Sovereign, and preserve to them the important Privilege of granting their own Property, which is enjoyed by every other Part of the *British* Empire: And surely the Liberality of their former Grants, for the public Service, is a sufficient Earnest of their future good Conduct, and proves that they well deserve this Privilege.

In all Causes between any of the Inhabitants of any Colony, let final Appeals be made, not to the King in Council, but to the General Assembly of the Colony, as was invariably practised, till that Alteration, which Lord *Colepepper* procured, for a private and lucrative Purpose. Till then the Legislature of each Colony had been its Supreme Court of Chancery; and sure none could better administer the Laws than those by whom they are made. It is, besides, a real Grievance on the Inhabitants of the Colonies, to be rendered amenable to a Foreign Judicature, from the Verdict of their Equals and Neighbours, who, from their Situation and Connection, are, of all others, the best qualified to judge rightly. Does it not deprive them of the important Privilege of a Trial by their Peers?

In all Disputes between two or more Colonies, let the Matter be finally determined by the General Assembly of the Confederates; and in any Difference between the Colonies and any other of his Majesty's Subjects, or Allies, let the Decision be made by the King in Council.

Our Author has declaimed much on the Impracticability of engaging the Colonies, in their present State, to act with Unanimity, and in Concert for the general Good, which he considers as a Fact that requires and justifies the Exercise of Parliamentary Authority, for governing them. But I have already proved, that this Authority, when exercised over their Property, is incompatible with the Enjoyment of their Rights; and I flatter myself, that every one will discover, that it will be rendered perfectly unnecessary by the Confederation that I have now proposed, which will both secure them against all the Inconveniencies arising from Want of Union, Harmony, and Alacrity, and effectually preserve to them all the Rights of Property; and, indeed, this seems the only Expedient for effecting these important Purposes.—A similar Union and Confederation was formed, in 1640, between the four *New-England* Colonies, and subsisted for many Years, to their mutual Advantage.

These may serve as the Outlines of a Plan for establishing the Government and Dependence of the Colonies; and, as such, I shall presume to offer them to the Consideration of those who are entrusted with the Administration of National Concerns, to be improved, amended, and afterwards proposed to the Assemblies of the Colonies, as the Conditions of a voluntary Compact, and an everlasting Union between the King's *British* and *American* Subjects; and to give all possible Validity to this Compact, let it be assented to by the King, the Parliament, and the General Assemblies of the Colonies.—But in settling the Terms of this Union, let *Britons* act with Moderation, and attend to the Dictates of true Policy; let them consider, they are forming a Compact with a People, whose future Increase will hereafter necessarily put it in their Power to break its Conditions with Impunity; and that the only effectual Expedient to guard against this Event, and discharge their Duty to their Country and Posterity, is to act with such Justice, Moderation, and even Indulgence, towards the Colonies, that, however they may hereafter have the Power, they may never have the Inclination, to violate the Conditions of their Connection and Dependence on *Great Britain*; and on this Subject I can, with Justice, adopt the Language of the Ambassador of the *Privernates*, who, when questioned by the *Roman* Senate concerning a Peace he was sent to sollicit, answered, "If the Terms you grant us be good, the Treaty will be observed by us faithfully and perpetually; if bad, it will soon be broken."* Convinced of the Truth and sound Policy contained in this Answer, and its obvious Application to the Colonies, *Great Britain* will govern them with Lenity, even in her Commercial Capacity: Before she expects them to participate her Burthens, she will make them able; and instead of governing their Commerce, on those confined Principles that influenced a late Ministry, she will allow them every Degree of Freedom compatible with her own Trade, and by happy Experience will soon discover, what due Observation might, before this, have taught, that the best Way of Taxing them, is by conferring Benefits on them, which will naturally revert to the Donors, with Increase, or at least may always be made to do so, by the Commercial Policy and Superintendency of the *British* Legislature, mildly exercised, over a loyal and grateful People. This is the utmost Extent of Taxation that one People can exercise over another: This is the Policy by which *Britain* can alone govern the East and the West; and this that Wisdom which alone can heal the Wounds of Publick Credit, and support the Weight of a tottering Empire.

These are Reflections which I would wish to convey to the Mind of every *Briton*.—They are the real Sentiments of one,

---

* "Si bonam dederitis fidam et perpetuam, si malam haud diuturnam."

who is sollicitous for the common Welfare of this Kingdom and the Colonies, and has bestowed some Attention on the present Subject.—If, in the preceding Observations, he has advanced any thing disconsonant to Reason or Truth, it has been done without his Knowledge or Design; and he flatters himself, that the Rectitude and Integrity of his Intention, in this Undertaking, will plead in Excuse for those Errors to which every Person is, in some Degrees, exposed, from the Imbecillity of human Reason.

FINIS.

Joseph Warren, An Oration Delivered March 5th, 1772. At the Request of the Inhabitants of the Town of Boston; to Commemorate the Bloody Tragedy of the Fifth of March, 1770. Boston, 1772.

The reforms accompanying the Townshend Duties had created three new vice-admiralty courts in Boston, Philadelphia, and Charleston to supplement the one in Halifax. To oversee these institutions of trade enforcement, Parliament had also established a new American Board of Customs located in Boston. This was scarcely the best place to put it, for Boston—in fact the entire colony of Massachusetts—was seething. Attacked by mobs, customs officials in Boston found it impossible to enforce the new trade regulations, and they pleaded for military support. When a British warship arrived in Boston in June 1768, emboldened customs officials promptly seized John Hancock's ship *Liberty* for violating the trade laws. This set off one of the fiercest riots in Boston's history.

Following Governor Bernard's dissolution of the Massachusetts assembly, Boston's town meeting had ordered the town's inhabitants to arm and called upon all the towns in the colony to send delegates to an extra-legal convention. Lord Hillsborough, secretary of state for American affairs, concluded that all order had broken down in Massachusetts, and he sent two regiments to Boston. By 1769 there were nearly four thousand armed redcoats in the crowded seaport of fifteen thousand inhabitants. Since the colonists shared the traditional English fear of standing armies, relations between the townspeople and soldiers rapidly deteriorated. On March 5, 1770, a party of eight British soldiers fired on a threatening crowd and killed five civilians.

This "Boston Massacre," as it was called, immediately aroused American passions and inspired some of the most sensational rhetoric of the period. That fall, John Adams and Josiah Quincy as co-counsels successfully defended the soldiers against the charge of murder. As Quincy told his father, he and Adams had taken the case only after the leading patriots, including Samuel Adams, John Hancock, and Dr. Joseph Warren, had urged them to do so.

Boston began commemorating the incident with an annual oration, an observance that would continue until independence, when it was replaced by orations celebrating the Fourth of July. Warren, who was called on to deliver the oration in 1772, had become a prominent radical in 1767 when he published in the *Boston Gazette* under the pseudonym of "A True Patriot" a series of protests against the Townshend Acts. They were so incendiary that Governor Bernard sought to have him prosecuted for libel. Warren would be asked to deliver the Massacre oration once again in 1775, just three months before he was killed at the battle of Bunker Hill. The second time he delivered the oration while wearing a Roman toga—a vivid sign of the republicanism that was by then fast approaching.

A N

ORATION

DELIVERED

MARCH 5th, 1772.

AT THE

REQUEST OF THE INHABITANTS

OF THE

TOWN OF *BOSTON;*

TO

COMMEMORATE THE BLOODY TRAGEDY

OF THE

FIFTH OF *March*, 1770.

BY

Dr. JOSEPH WARREN.

Quis talia fando,
Myrmidonum, Dolopumve, aut duri miles Ulyſſei,
Temperet a lacrymis.   VIRGIL.

BOSTON:

Printed by EDES and GILL, by Order of the Town of BOSTON.
1772.

*At a Meeting of the Freeholders and other Inhabitants of
the Town of* BOSTON, *duly qualified and legally assembled in* Faneuil-Hall, *and from thence adjourn'd to the*
Old South Meeting-House, *on* Thursday *the 5th Day of*
March, Anno Domini, 1772.

Voted Unanimously,
THAT the Moderator *Richard Dana,* Esq; the Honorable *John
Hancock,* Esq; Mr. *Samuel Adams, Joseph Jackson,* Esq; Mr.
Henderson Inches, Mr. *David Jeffries,* and Mr. *William Molineux,* be and hereby are appointed a Committee to return
the Thanks of this Town to *Joseph Warren,* Esq; for the Oration
just now delivered by him at their Request, in Commemora-
tion of the horrid Massacre perpetrated on the Evening of the
5th of *March,* 1770, by a Party of Soldiers of the XXIXth Regiment; and to desire a Copy thereof for the Press.   *Attest,*
William Cooper, *Town-Clerk.*

GENTLEMEN,
THE generous Candor of my Fellow-Citizens prevails on me to
give a Copy of what was Yesterday delivered, for the Press.
I am, Gentlemen, with much Respect,
Your most humble Servant,
JOSEPH WARREN.
March 6, 1772.

An Oration.

WHEN we turn over the historic page, and trace the rise
and fall of states and empires; the mighty revolutions
which have so often varied the face of the world strike our
minds with solemn surprize, and we are naturally led to endeavor to search out the causes of such astonishing changes.

That Man is formed for *social life,* is an observation which
upon our first enquiry presents itself immediately to our view,
and our reason approves that wise and generous principle
which actuated the first founders of civil government; an institution which hath its origin in the *weakness* of individuals, and

hath for its end, the *strength and security* of all: And so long as the means of effecting this important end, are thoroughly known and religiously attended to, Government is one of the richest Blessings to mankind, and ought to be held in the highest veneration.

In young and new-formed communities, the grand design of this institution is most generally understood, and most strictly regarded; the motives which urged to the social compact cannot be at once forgotten, and *that* equality which is remembered to have subsisted so lately among them, prevents those who are cloathed with authority from attempting to invade the freedom of their Brethren; or if such an attempt is made, it prevents the community from suffering the offender to go unpunished: Every member feels it to be his interest, and knows it to be his duty, to preserve inviolate the constitution on which the public safety depends,* and is equally ready to assist the *Magistrate* in the execution of the laws, and the *subject* in defence of his right; and so long as this noble attachment to a constitution, founded on free and benevolent principles exists in full vigor in any state, *that* state must be flourishing and happy.

It was *this* noble attachment to a free constitution, which raised ancient Rome from the smallest beginnings to that bright summit of happiness and glory to which she arrived; and it was the loss of *this* which plunged her from *that* summit into the black gulph of infamy and slavery. It was *this* attachment which inspired her senators with wisdom; it was *this* which glowed in the breasts of her heroes; it was *this* which guarded her liberties, and extended her dominions, gave peace at home and commanded respect abroad: And when *this* decayed, her magistrates lost their reverence for justice and the laws, and degenerated into tyrants and oppressors—her senators forgetful of their dignity, and seduced by base corruption, betrayed their country—her soldiers regardless of their relation to the community, and urged *only* by the hopes of plunder and rapine, unfeelingly committed the most flagrant enormities; and hired to the trade of death, with relentless fury they perpe-

---

* Omnes ordines ad conservandam rempublicam, mente, voluntate, studio, virtute, voce, consentiunt. Cicero.

trated the most cruel murders, whereby the streets of imperial Rome were drenched with her *noblest* blood—Thus *this empress* of the world lost her dominions abroad, and her inhabitants dissolute in their manners, at length became contented *slaves*; and she stands to this day, the scorn and derision of nations, and a monument of this eternal truth, that PUBLIC HAPPINESS DEPENDS ON A VIRTUOUS AND UNSHAKEN ATTACHMENT TO A FREE CONSTITUTION.

It was *this* attachment to a constitution, founded on free and benevolent principles, which inspired the first settlers of this country:—They saw with grief the daring outrages committed on the free constitution of their native land—they knew that nothing but a civil war could at that time restore it's pristine purity. So hard was it to resolve to embrue their hands in the *blood* of their brethren, that they chose rather to quit their fair possessions and seek another habitation in a distant clime —When they came to this new world, which they fairly purchased of the Indian natives, the only rightful proprietors, they cultivated the then barren soil by their incessant labor, and defended their dear-bought possessions with the fortitude of the christian, and the bravery of the hero.

After various struggles, which during the tyrannic reigns of the house of STUART, were constantly kept up between right and wrong, between liberty and slavery, the connection between Great-Britain and this Colony was settled in the reign of King William and Queen Mary by a compact, the conditions of which were expressed in a Charter; by which all the liberties and immunities of BRITISH SUBJECTS were confirmed to this Province, as fully and as absolutely as they possibly could be by any human instrument which can be devised. And it is undeniably true, that the greatest and most important right of a British subject is, that *he shall be governed by no laws but those to which he either in person or by his representative hath given his consent*: And this I will venture to assert, is the grand basis of British freedom; it is interwoven with the constitution; and whenever this is lost, the constitution must be destroyed.

The *British constitution* (of which ours is a copy) is a happy compound of the three forms (under some of which all governments may be ranged) viz. Monarchy, Aristocracy, and Democracy: Of these three the *British Legislature* is composed, and without the consent of each branch, nothing can carry with it the force of a law: In most cases, either the aristocratic or the democratic branch may propose a law, and submit it to the deliberation of the other two; but, when a law is to be passed for raising a tax, that law can originate only in the democratic branch, which is the House of Commons in Britain, and the House of Representatives here—The reason is obvious: They, and their constituents are to pay much the largest part of it, but as the aristrocratic branch, which in Britain, is the House of Lords, and in this province, the Council, are also to pay some part, THEIR consent is necessary; and as the monarchic branch, which in Britain is the King, and with us, either the King in person, or the Governor whom he shall be pleased to appoint to act in his stead, is supposed to have a just sense of his own *interest*, which is *that* of all the subjects in general, HIS consent is also necessary, and when the consent of these three branches is obtained, the taxation is most certainly legal.

Let us now allow ourselves a few moments to examine the *late acts of the British parliament for taxing America*—Let us with candor judge whether they are constitutionally binding upon us:—If they are, IN THE NAME OF JUSTICE let us submit to them, without one murmuring word.

First, I would ask whether the members of the British House of Commons are the Democracy of this Province? if they are, they are either the people of this province, or are elected by the people of this province, to represent them, and have therefore a constitutional right to originate a Bill for taxing them: It is most certain they are neither; and therefore nothing done by *them* can be said to be done by the democratic branch of our constitution. I would next ask, whether the Lords who compose the aristocratic branch of the British legislature, are Peers of America? I never heard it was (even in these extraordinary times) so much as pretended, and if they are not, certainly no act of *theirs* can be said to be the act of the aristocratic branch of our constitution. The power of the monarchic branch we with pleasure acknowledge, resides in the King, who may act either in person or by his representative; and I freely confess that I can see no reason why a PROCLAMATION *for raising money in America* issued by the King's *sole* authority, would not be equally consistent with our constitution, and therefore equally binding upon us with the *late acts of the British parliament for taxing us*; for it is plain, that if there is any validity in *those acts*, it must arise altogether from the monarchical branch of the legislature: And I further think that it would be at least as equitable; for I do not conceive it to be of the least importance to us by *whom* our property is taken away, so long as it is taken without our consent; and I am very much at a loss to know by what figure of rhetoric, the inhabitants of this province can be called FREE SUBJECTS, when they are obliged to obey implicitly, such laws as are made for them by men three thousand miles off, whom they know not, and whom they never have impowered to act for them; or how they can be said to have PROPERTY, when a body of men over whom they have not the least controul, and who are not in any way accountable to them, shall oblige them to deliver up any part, or the whole of their substance, without even asking their consent: And yet, whoever pretends that the late acts of the British parliament for taxing America ought to be deemed binding upon us, must admit at once that we are absolute SLAVES, and have no property of our own; or else that we may be FREE-MEN, and at the same time under a necessity of obeying the *arbitrary commands of those* over whom we have no controul or influence; and that we may HAVE PROPERTY OF OUR OWN, which is entirely at the disposal of another. Such gross absurdities, I believe will not be relished in this enlightened age: And it can be no matter of wonder that the people quickly perceived, and seriously complained of the inroads which these acts must unavoidably make upon their *Liberty*, and of the hazard to which their *whole property* is by *them* exposed; for, if they may be taxed without their consent even the smallest trifle, they may also without their consent be deprived of every thing they possess, although never so valuable, never so dear. Certainly it never entered the hearts of our ancestors, that after so many dangers in this then desolate wilderness, their hard-earned property should be at the disposal of the British parliament; and as it was soon found that this taxation could not be supported by reason and argument, it seemed necessary that one act of oppression should be enforced by another, and therefore, contrary to our just rights as possessing, or at least having a just title to possess, all the *liberties* and IMMUNITIES of British subjects, a standing army was established among us in time of peace; and evidently for the purpose of effecting *that*, which it was one principal design of the founders of the constitution to prevent, (when they declared a standing army in time of peace to be AGAINST LAW) namely, for the enforcement of obedience to acts which upon fair examination appeared to be unjust and unconstitutional.

The ruinous consequences of standing armies to free communities may be seen in the histories of SYRACUSE, ROME, and many other once flourishing STATES; some of which have now scarce a name! Their baneful influence is most suddenly felt, when they are placed in populous cities; for, by a corruption of morals, the public happiness is immediately affected; and that this is one of the effects of quartering troops in a populous city, is a truth, to which many a mourning parent, many a lost, despairing child in this metropolis, must bear a very melancholy testimony.—Soldiers are also taught to consider arms as the only arbiters by which every dispute is to be decided between contending states;—they are instructed *implicitly* to obey their commanders, without enquiring into the justice of the cause they are engaged to support: Hence it is, that they are ever to be dreaded as the ready engines of tyranny and oppression.— And it is too observable that they are prone to introduce the same mode of decision in the disputes of individuals, and from thence have often arisen great animosities between *them* and *the inhabitants*, who whilst in a naked defenceless state, are frequently insulted and abused by an armed soldiery. And this will be more especially the case, when the troops are informed, that the intention of their being stationed in any city, is to OVERAWE THE INHABITANTS. That, *this* was the avowed design of stationing an armed force in this town, is sufficiently known; and WE, my fellow-citizens have seen, WE have felt the tragical effects!—THE FATAL FIFTH OF MARCH 1770, CAN NEVER BE FORGOTTEN—The horrors of THAT DREADFUL NIGHT are but too deeply impressed on our hearts—Language is too feeble to paint the emotions of our souls, when our streets were stained with the BLOOD OF OUR BRETHREN,—when our ears were wounded by the groans of the *dying*, and our eyes were tormented with the sight of the mangled bodies of the *dead*.— When our alarmed imagination presented to our view our

houses wrapt in flames,—our children subjected to the barbarous caprice of the raging soldiery—our beauteous virgins exposed to all the insolence of unbridled passion,—our virtuous
wives endeared to us by every tender tie, falling a sacrifice to
that worse than brutal violence, and perhaps like the famed
LUCRETIA, distracted with anguish and despair, ending their
wretched lives by their own fair hands.—When we beheld the
authors of our distress parading in our streets, or drawn up in
regular *battalia*, as though in a hostile city; our hearts beat to
arms; we snatched our weapons, almost resolved by one decisive stroke, to avenge the death of our SLAUGHTERED BRETH-
REN, and to secure from future danger, all that we held most
dear: But propitious heaven forbad the bloody carnage, and
saved the threatned victims of our too keen resentment, not by
their discipline, not by their regular array,—no, it was royal
GEORGE's livery that proved their shield—it was that which
turned the pointed engines of destruction from their breasts.*
The thoughts of vengeance were soon buried in our inbred
affection to Great-Britain, and calm reason dictated a method
of removing the troops more mild than an immediate recourse
to the sword. With united efforts you urged the immediate
departure of the troops from the town—you urged it, with a
resolution which ensured success—you obtained your wishes,
and the removal of the troops was effected, without one drop
of *their blood* being shed by the inhabitants!

The immediate actors in the tragedy of THAT NIGHT were
surrendered to justice.—It is not mine to say how far they
were guilty! they have been tried by the country and AC-
QUITTED of murder! And they are not to be again arraigned
at an earthly bar: But, surely the men who have promiscuously
scattered *death* amidst the *innocent* inhabitants of a populous
city, ought to see well to it, that they be prepared to stand at
the bar of an OMNISCIENT JUDGE! And all who contrived or
encouraged the stationing troops in this place, have reasons of

* I have the strongest reason to believe that I have mentioned the only circumstance, which saved the troops from destruction. It was then, and now is,
the opinion of those who were best acquainted with the state of affairs at that
time, that had thrice that number of troops, belonging to any power at open
war with us, been in this town in the same exposed condition, scarce a man
would have lived to have seen the morning light.

eternal importance, to reflect with deep contrition on their base designs, and humbly to repent of their impious machinations.

The infatuation which hath seemed for a number of years to prevail in the British councils with regard to us, is truly astonishing! What can be proposed by the repeated attacks made upon our freedom, I really cannot surmise; even leaving justice and humanity out of the question, I do not know one single advantage which can arise to the British nation, from our being enslaved:—I know not of any gains, which can be wrung from us by oppression, which they may not obtain from us by our own consent in the smooth channel of commerce: We wish the wealth and prosperity of *Britain*; we contribute largely to both.—Doth what we contribute lose all its value, because it is done voluntarily? The amazing increase of riches to *Britain*, the great rise of the value of her lands, the flourishing state of her navy; are striking proofs of the advantages derived to her, from her commerce with the Colonies; and it is our earnest desire that she may still continue to enjoy the same emoluments, until her streets are paved with AMERICAN GOLD; only, let us have the pleasure of calling it our own, whilst it is in our hands;—but this it seems is too great a favor—we are to be governed by the *absolute commands of others, our property is to be taken away without our consent*—if we complain, our complaints are treated with contempt; if we assert our rights, that assertion is deemed insolence; if we humbly offer to submit the matter to the impartial decision of reason, the SWORD is judged the most proper argument to silence our murmurs!— But, this cannot long be the case—surely, the *British* nation will not suffer the reputation of their justice, and their honor, to be thus sported away by a *capricious ministry*; no, they will in a short time open their eyes to their true interest: They nourish in their own breasts a noble love of Liberty, they hold her dear, and they know that all who have once possessed her charms had rather die than suffer her to be torn from their embraces—They are also sensible that *Britain* is so deeply interested in the prosperity of the colonies, that she must eventually feel every wound given to their freedom; they cannot be ignorant that more dependence may be placed on the affections of a BROTHER, than on the forced services of a SLAVE—They must approve your efforts for the preservation of your rights; from a sympathy of soul they must pray for your success: And I doubt not but they will e'er long exert themselves effectually to redress your grievances. Even in the dissolute reign of king CHARLES II, when the house of *Commons* impeached the Earl of Clarendon of high treason, the first article on which they founded their accusation was, that "*he had designed a standing army to be raised, and to govern the kingdom thereby.*" And the eighth article was, that "*he had introduced an arbitrary government into his Majesty's plantations*".—A terrifying example, to those who are now forging *chains* for this COUNTRY!

You have my friends and countrymen often frustrated the designs of your enemies, by your unanimity and fortitude: It was your union and determined spirit which expelled those troops, who polluted your streets with INNOCENT BLOOD.— You have appointed this anniversary as a standing memorial of the BLOODY CONSEQUENCES OF PLACING AN ARMED FORCE IN A POPULOUS CITY, and of your deliverance from the dangers which then seemed to hang over your heads; and I am confident that you never will betray the least want of spirit when called upon to guard your freedom.—None but they who set a just value upon the blessings of Liberty are worthy to enjoy her—Your illustrious fathers were her zealous votaries—when the blasting frowns of tyranny drove her from public view, they clasped her in their arms, they cherished her in their generous bosoms, they brought her safe over the rough ocean, and fixed her seat in this then dreary wilderness; they nursed her infant age with the most tender care; for her sake, they patiently bore the severest hardships; for her support, they underwent the most rugged toils: In her defence, they boldly encountered the most alarming dangers; neither the ravenous beasts that ranged the woods for prey; nor the more furious savages of the wilderness; could damp their ardor!—Whilst with one hand, they broke the stubborn glebe; with the other, they grasped their weapons, ever ready to protect her from danger.—No sacrifice, not even their own blood, was esteemed too rich a libation for her altar! God prospered their valour, they preserved her brilliancy unsullied, they enjoyed her whilst they lived, and dying, bequeathed the dear inheritance, to your care. And as they left you this glorious legacy, they have undoubtedly transmitted to you, some portion of their noble spirit, to inspire you with virtue to merit her, and courage to preserve her; you surely cannot, with such examples before your eyes, as every page of the history of this country affords,* suffer your liberties to be ravished from you by lawless force, or cajoled away by flattery and fraud.

The voice of your Fathers blood cries to you from the ground; MY SONS, SCORN TO BE SLAVES! In vain we met the frowns of tyrants—In vain, we left our native land—In vain, we crossed the boisterous ocean, found a new world, and prepared it for the happy residence of LIBERTY—In vain, we toiled—In vain, we fought—We bled in vain, if you, our offspring want valour to repel the assaults of her invaders!—Stain not the glory of your worthy ancestors, but like them resolve, never to part with your birth-right; be wise in your deliberations, and determined in your exertions for the preservation of your liberties.—Follow not the dictates of passion, but enlist yourselves under the sacred banner of reason: Use every method in your power to secure your rights: At least prevent the curses of posterity from being heaped upon your memories.

If you with united zeal and fortitude oppose the torrent of oppression; if you feel the true fire of patriotism burning in your breasts; if you from your souls despise the most gaudy dress that slavery can wear; if you really prefer the lonely cottage (whilst blest with liberty) to gilded palaces surrounded with the ensigns of slavery; you may have the fullest assurance that tyranny with her whole accursed train will hide their hideous heads in confusion, shame and despair—If you perform your part, you must have the strongest confidence, that THE SAME ALMIGHTY BEING who protected your pious and venerable fore-fathers—who enabled them to turn a barren wilderness into a fruitful field, who so often *made bare his arm* for their salvation, will still be mindful of you their offspring.

May THIS ALMIGHTY BEING graciously preside in all our councils.—May he direct us to such measures as he himself shall approve, and be pleased to bless.—May we ever be a people favored of GOD.—May our land be a land of Liberty,

---

* At simul heroum laudes, et facta parentis
Jam legere, et quæ sit poteris cognoscere virtus.   VIRG.

the seat of virtue, the asylum of the oppressed, *a name and a praise in the whole earth*, until the last shock of time shall bury the empires of the world in one common undistinguished ruin!

FINIS.

The Votes and Proceedings of the Freeholders and Other Inhabitants of the Town of Boston, in Town Meeting Assembled, According to Law. Boston, [1772].

This pamphlet, which soon came to be known as the "Boston pamphlet," was one of the most important in the period leading up to the final dissolution of the empire. As a straightforward and unembellished summary of American rights and grievances as perceived by its Boston authors in 1772, it was neither gracefully written nor full of learned allusions, and it made no new theoretical contribution to the imperial debate. Unlike most of the pamphlets, it was not written by a single person, nor was it primarily designed to convince the Tories or the English of the justice of the American Whig cause. Instead, it was written by a committee of twenty-one persons appointed by the town of Boston, and, in violation of all proper constitutional protocol, it explicitly solicited the sentiments of the people in the other towns of Massachusetts on the issues raised in the pamphlet.

In spite of its lack of originality, its mixed authorship, and its inconsistencies of tone and character, the *Votes and Proceedings* became crucially significant both as an intellectual document and as a powerful political event in its own right. Not only did it anticipate the Declaration of Independence in its statement of rights and grievances, but it also inspired the towns of Massachusetts to create committees of correspondence throughout the colony—producing a model of networking that soon spread to the other American colonies. These committees of correspondence, John Adams would later recall, were "purely an American invention," "an Engine" that helped to bring about the American Revolution and subsequent revolutions elsewhere.

Throughout 1773 the bulk of Massachusetts' two hundred and sixty towns responded to Boston's request. The outpouring of popular sentiments was extraordinary. Some of the outlying towns, aware that they lacked the sophistication of "the Metropolis," were willing to follow the lead of Boston. But most of the replies revealed an independent awareness of political matters that went beyond anything ever expressed in the colony before. When English officials later learned of these popular expressions of Massachusetts opinion, which they found "full of the most extravagant absurdities," their only response was to mock them. In their arrogance they failed to appreciate the extent to which Massachusetts was already primed for rebellion.

759

THE

VOTES and PROCEEDINGS

OF THE

FREEHOLDERS and other INHABITANTS

OF THE

Town of BOSTON,

In Town Meeting assembled,

ACCORDING TO LAW.

[*Published by Order of the Town.*]

To which is prefixed,
As Introductory, an attested Copy of a Vote
of the Town at a preceeding Meeting.

BOSTON:

PRINTED BY EDES and GILL, IN QUEEN-STREET,
AND T. AND J. FLEET, IN CORNHILL.

At a Meeting of the Freeholders and other Inhabitants of the Town of Boston, *duly warned, and legally assembled, in* Faneuil-*Hall, on Wednesday the* 28th *of* October, 1772; *and from thence continued by Adjournments to Monday the* 2d *of* November *following.*

It was moved,

That a Committee of Correspondence be appointed, to consist of Twenty-one Persons, "to state the Rights of the Colonists, and of this Province in particular, as Men, as Christians, and as Subjects; to Communicate and Publish the same to the several Towns in this Province, and to the World, as the Sense of this Town, with the Infringements and Violations thereof that have been, or from Time to Time may be made; also requesting of each Town a free Communication of their Sentiments on this Subject."

Whereupon the following Gentlemen were nominated and appointed for the Purposes aforesaid, to make Report to the Town as soon as may be, viz. The Hon. *James Otis,* Esq; Mr. *Samuel Adams,* Dr. *Joseph Warren,* Dr. *Benjamin Church,* Mr. *William Dennie,* Mr. *William Greenleaf, Joseph Greenleaf,* Esq; Dr. *Thomas Young,* Mr. *William Powell,* Mr. *Nathaniel Appleton,* Mr. *Oliver Wendell,* Mr. *John Sweetser, Josiah Quincy,* Esq; Capt. *John Bradford, Richard Boynton,* Esq; Captain *William Mackay,* Major *Nathaniel Barber,* Deacon *Caleb Davis,* Mr. *Alexander Hill,* Mr. *William Molineux,* and Mr. *Robert Pierpont.*

A true Copy,

Attest.

WILLIAM COOPER, *Town-Clerk.*

At a Meeting of the Freeholders and other Inhabitants of the Town of BOSTON, *duly warned and assembled in* Faneuil-*Hall according to Law, on Friday the* 20th *of* November, 1772; *then and there to receive and act upon the Report of a Committee appointed at a former Meeting on the* 2d *of the same Month, and such other Things as might properly come under the Consideration of the Town.*

The Honorable JOHN HANCOCK, *Esq*;

Being unanimously chosen Moderator,

The Chairman of said Committee acquainted him that he
was ready to make Report, and read the same as follows.

THE Committee appointed by the Town the second Instant "to state the Rights of the Colonists and of this Province in particular, as Men, as Christians, and as Subjects; to communicate and publish the same to the several Towns in this Province and to the World, as the Sense of this Town, with the Infringements and Violations thereof that have been, or from Time to Time may be made. Also requesting of each Town a free Communication of their Sentiments on this Subject,"— beg Leave to report.

First, A State of the Rights of the Colonists and of this Province in particular.

Secondly, A Lift of the Infringements and Violations of those Rights.

Thirdly, A Letter of Correspondence with the other Towns.

I. NATURAL RIGHTS OF THE COLONISTS AS MEN.

Among the natural Rights of the Colonists are these: First, a Right to *Life*; secondly, to *Liberty*; thirdly, to *Property*; together with the Right to support and defend them in the best Manner they can. These are evident Branches of, rather than Deductions from the Duty of Self-Preservation, commonly called the first Law of Nature.

All Men have a Right to remain in a State of Nature as long as they please: And in Case of intollerable Oppression, civil or religious, to leave the Society they belong to, and enter into another.

When Men enter into Society, it is by voluntary Consent; and they have a Right to demand and insist upon the Performance of such Conditions and previous Limitations as form an equitable *original Compact*.

Every natural Right, not expresly given up, or from the Nature of a social Compact necessarily ceded, remains.

All positive and civil Laws, should conform as far as possible, to the Law of natural Reason and Equity.

As neither Reason requires, nor Religion permits the contrary, every Man living in or out of a State of civil Society, has a Right peaceably and quietly to worship GOD, according to the Dictates of his Conscience.

"*Just and true Liberty, equal and impartial Liberty*" in Matters spiritual and temporal, is a Thing that all Men are clearly entitled to, by the eternal and immutable Laws of GOD and Nature, as well as by the Law of Nations, and all well grounded municipal Laws, which must have their Foundation in the former.

In Regard to Religion, mutual Toleration in the different Professions thereof, is what all good and candid Minds in all Ages have ever practiced; and both by Precept and Example inculcated on Mankind: And it is now generally agreed among Christians, that this Spirit of Toleration, in the fullest Extent consistent, with the Being of Civil Society, "is the chief characteristical Mark of the true Church."* Insomuch that Mr. Lock has asserted, and proved beyond the Possibility of Contradiction on any solid Ground, that such Toleration ought to be extended to all whose Doctrines are not subversive of Society. The only Sects which he thinks ought to be, and which by all wise Laws are excluded from such Toleration, are those who teach Doctrines subversive of the civil Government under which they live. The Roman Catholicks or Papists are excluded, by Reason of such Doctrines as these, "that Princes excommunicated may be deposed, and those they call *Hereticks* may be destroyed without Mercy; besides their recognizing the Pope in so absolute a Manner, in Subversion of Government, by introducing as far as possible into the States, under whose Protection they enjoy Life, Liberty and Property, that Solecism in Politicks, *Imperium in Imperio*,† leading directly to the worst Anarchy and Confusion, civil Discord, War and Bloodshed.

* See Lock's Letters on Toleration.
† A Government within a Government.

The natural Liberty of Man, by entering into Society, is abridg'd or restrain'd so far only as is necessary for the great End of Society, the best Good of the Whole.

In the State of Nature, every Man is, under GOD, Judge, and sole Judge, of his own Rights and of the Injuries done him: By entering into Society, he agrees to an *Arbiter* or indifferent Judge between him and his Neighbours; but he no more renounces his original Right, than by taking a Cause out of the ordinary Course of Law, and leaving the Decision to Referees or indifferent Arbitrators. In the last Case he must pay the Referees for Time and Trouble; he should also be willing to pay his just Quota for the Support of Government, the Law and the Constitution; the End of which is to furnish indifferent and impartial Judges in all Cases that may happen, whether civil, ecclesiastical, marine or military.

"The *natural* Liberty of Man is to be free from any superior Power on Earth, and not to be under the Will or legislative Authority of Man; but only to have the Law of Nature for his Rule."*

In the State of Nature, Men may, as the *Patriarchs* did, employ hired Servants for the Defence of their Lives, Liberties and Property; and they should pay them reasonable Wages. *Government* was instituted for the Purposes of common Defence; and those who hold the Reins of Government have an equitable natural Right to an honorable Support from the same Principle "that the Labourer is worthy of his Hire": But then the same Community which they serve, ought to be the Assessors of their Pay: Governors have no Right to seek and take what they please; by this, instead of being content with the Station assigned them, that of honorable Servants of the Society, they would soon become absolute *Masters, Despots* and *Tyrants.* Hence as a private Man has a Right to say, what Wages he will give in his private Affairs, so has a Community to determine what *they* will give and grant of their Substance, for the Administration of publick Affairs. And in both Cases, more are ready generally to offer their Service at the proposed and stipulated Price, than are able and willing to perform their Duty.

* Locke on Government.

In short, it is the greatest Absurdity to suppose it in the Power of one or any Number of Men, at the entering into Society, to renounce their essential natural Rights, or the Means of preserving those Rights; when the grand End of civil Government from the very Nature of its Institution, is for the Support, Protection and Defence of those very Rights: The principal of which as is before observed, are *Life, Liberty* and *Property*. If Men through Fear, Fraud or Mistake, should *in Terms* renounce or give up any essential natural Right, the eternal Law of Reason and the grand End of Society, would absolutely vacate such Renunciation; the Right to Freedom being *the Gift of* GOD ALMIGHTY, it is not in the Power of Man to alienate this Gift, and voluntarily become a Slave.

II. THE RIGHTS OF THE COLONISTS AS CHRISTIANS.

These may be best understood by reading and carefully studying the Institutes of the great Lawgiver and Head of the Christian Church: which are to be found clearly written and promulgated in the *New-Testament*.

By the Act of the British Parliament commonly called the Toleration Act, every Subject in England, expect Papists, &c. was restored to, and re-established in, his natural Right to worship GOD according to the Dictates of his own Conscience. And by the Charter of this Province, it is granted, ordain'd and establish'd (that is declared as an original Right) that there shall be Liberty of Conscience allow'd in the Worship of GOD, to all Christians except Papists, inhabiting, or which shall inhabit or be resident within said Province or Territory.* Magna Charta itself is in Substance but a constrain'd Declaration, or Proclamation and Promulgation, in the Name of King, Lords, and Commons, of the Sense the latter had, of their original, inherent, indefeasible natural Rights;† as also those of free Citizens equally perdurable with the other. That great Author, that great Jurist, and even that Court Writer Mr. Justice *Blackstone* holds, that this Recognition was justly obtain'd of King

---

* Sec 1 Wm. and Mary, St. 2. C. 18. and Massachusetts Charter.
† Lord Coke's Inst. Blackstone's Commentaries, V. I, pa. 122. the Bill of Rights and the Act of Settlement.

John Sword in Hand: And peradventure it must be one Day Sword in Hand again rescued and preserv'd from total Destruction and Oblivion.

III. THE RIGHTS OF THE COLONISTS AS SUBJECTS.

A Commonwealth or State is a Body politick or civil Society of Men, united together to promote their mutual Safety, and Prosperity, by Means of their Union.*

The *absolute Rights* of Englishmen, and all Freemen in or out of civil Society, are principally, *personal Security*, *personal Liberty* and *private Property*.

All Persons born in the British American Colonies, are, by the Laws of GOD and Nature, and by the common Law of England, *exclusive of all Charters* from *the Crown*, well entitled, and by Acts of the British Parliament are declared to be entitled, to all the natural, essential, inherent and inseperable Rights, Liberties and Privileges of Subjects born in Great-Britain, or within the Realm. Among those Rights are the following; which no Man, or Body of Men, consistently with their own Rights as Men and Citizens, or Members of Society, can for themselves give up, or take away from others.

First, "The first fundamental positive Law of all Commonwealths or States, is the establishing the Legislative Power: As the first fundamental *natural* Law also, which is to govern even the Legislative Power itself, is the Preservation of the Society."†

Secondly, The Legislative has no Right to absolute arbitrary Power over the Lives and Fortunes of the People: Nor can Mortals assume a Prerogative, not only too high for Men, but for Angels; and therefore reserv'd for the Exercise of the *Deity* alone.

"The Legislative cannot justly *assume* to itself a Power to rule by extempore arbitrary Decrees; but it is bound to see that Justice is dispensed, and that the Rights of the Subjects be decided, by promulgated, standing and known Laws, and authorized *independent Judges*;" that is, Independent as far as

---

* See Locke and Vatel.
† Locke on Government. Salus Populi suprema Lex esto.

possible, of Prince and People. "*There should be one Rule of Justice for Rich and Poor; for the Favourite at Court, and the Countryman at the Plough.*"*

Thirdly, The Supreme Power cannot justly take from any Man, any Part of his Property without his Consent, in Person or by his Representative.

These are some of the first Principles of natural Law and Justice, and the great Barriers of all Free States, and of the British Constitution in particular. It is utterly irreconcileable to these Principles, and to many other fundamental Maxims of the common Law, common Sense and Reason, that a British House of Commons, should have a Right, at Pleasure, to give and grant the Property of the Colonists. That these Colonists are well entitled to all the essential Rights, Liberties and Privileges of Men and Freemen, born in Britain, is manifest, not only from the Colony Charters in general, but Acts of the British Parliament. The Statute of the 13th of Geo. 2. c. 7. naturalizes even Foreigners after seven Years Residence. The Words of the Massachusetts-Charter are these, "And further our Will and Pleasure is, and we do hereby for Us, our Heirs and Successors, grant, establish and ordain, that all and every of the Subjects of Us, our Heirs and Successors, which shall go to and inhabit within our said Province or Territory and every of their Children which shall happen to be born there, or on the Seas in going thither, or returning from thence, shall have and enjoy all Liberties and Immunities of free and natural Subjects within any of the Dominions of Us, our Heirs and Successors, to all Intents, Constructions and Purposes whatsoever, as if they and every of them were born within this our Realm of England." Now what Liberty can there be, where Property is taken away without Consent? Can it be said with any Colour of Truth and Justice, that this Continent of three Thousand Miles in Length, and of a Breadth as yet unexplored, in which however, it is supposed, there are five Millions of People, has the least Voice, Vote, or Influence in the Decisions of the British Parliament? Have they, all together, any more Right or Power to return a single Member to that House of

* Locke.

Commons, who have, not inadvertently, but deliberately assumed a Power to dispose of their Lives,* Liberties and Properties, than to chuse an Emperor of China! Had the Colonists a Right to return Members to the British Parliament, it would only be hurtful; as from their local Situation and Circumstances, it is impossible they should be ever truly and properly represented there. The Inhabitants of this Country, in all Probability, in a few Years, will be more numerous, than those of Great Britain and Ireland together: Yet it is absurdly expected, by the Promoters of the present Measures, that these, with their Posterity to all Generations, should be easy, while their Property shall be disposed of by a House of Commons at Three Thousand Miles distance from them; and who cannot be supposed to have the least Care or Concern for their real Interest: Who have not only no natural Care for their Interest, but must be *in effect* bribed against it; as every Burden they lay on the Colonists is so much saved or gain'd to themselves. Hitherto many of the Colonists have been free from Quit Rents; but if the Breath of a British House of Commons, can originate an Act for taking away all our Money, our Lands will go next; or be subject to Rack Rents from haughty and relentless Landlords who will ride at ease, while we are trodden in the Dirt. The Colonists have been branded with the odious Names of Traitors and Rebels only for complaining of their Grievances: How long such Treatment will, or ought to be born, is submitted.

A List of Infringements and Violations of Rights.

WE cannot help thinking, that an Enumeration of some of the most open Infringements of our Rights, will by every candid Person be judged sufficient to justify whatever Measures have been already taken, or may be thought proper to be taken, in order to obtain a Redress of the Grievances under which we labour. Among many others, we humbly conceive, that the following will not fail to excite the Attention of all

---

* See the Act of the last Session relating to the King's Dock-Yards.

who consider themselves interested in the Happiness and Freedom of Mankind in general, and of this Continent and Province in particular.

1st. The British Parliament have assumed the Powers of Legislation for the Colonists in all Cases whatsoever, without obtaining the Consent of the Inhabitants, which is ever essentially necessary to the rightful Establishment of such a Legislative.

2dly. They have exerted that assumed Power, in raising a Revenue in the Colonies without their Consent; thereby depriving them of that Right which every Man has to keep his own Earnings in his own Hands until he shall, in Person, or by his Representative, think fit to part with the Whole or any Portion of it. This Infringement is the more extraordinary, when we consider the laudable Care which the British House of Commons have taken, to reserve intirely and absolutely to themselves the Powers of giving and granting Money. They not only insist on originating every Money Bill in their own House, but will not even allow the House of Lords to make an Amendment in these Bills. So tenacious are they of this Privilege, so jealous of any Infringement of the sole and absolute Right the People have to dispose of their own Money. And what renders this Infringement the more grievous is, that what of our Earnings still remains in our Hands is in a great measure deprived of it's Value, so long as the British Parliament continue to claim and exercise this Power of taxing us; for we cannot justly call that *our* Property, which *others* may, when they please take away from us against our Will.

In this respect we are treated with less Decency and Regard than the Romans shewed even to the Provinces which they had conquered. *They* only determined upon the Sum which each should furnish, and left every Province to raise it in the Manner most easy and convenient to themselves.

3dly. A Number of new Officers, unknown in the Charter of this Province, have been appointed to superintend this Revenue; whereas by our Charter, the Great and General Court or Assembly of this Province, has the sole Right of appointing all Civil Officers, excepting only such Officers, the election and constitution of whom is, in said Charter, expressly excepted; among whom these Officers are not included.

4thly. These Officers are by their Commissions invested

with Powers altogether unconstitutional, and entirely destructive to that Security which we have a right to enjoy; and to the
last degree dangerous, not only to our property, but to our
lives: For the Commissioners of his Majesty's Customs in
America, or any three of them, are by their Commission impowered, "by writing under their hands and seals to constitute
and appoint inferior Officers in all and singular the Port within
the Limits of their Commissions." Each of these petty officers
so made is intrusted with Power more absolute and arbitrary
than ought to be lodged in the hands of any Man or Body of
Men whatsoever; for in the Commission aforementioned, his
Majesty gives and grants unto his said Commissioners, or any
three of them, and to all and every the Collectors, Deputy-
Collectors, Ministers, Servants, and all other Officers serving
and attending in all and every the Ports & other Places within
the Limits of their Commission, full Power and Authority,
from time to time, at their or any of their Wills and Pleasures,
as well by Night as by Day, to enter and go on board any Ship,
Boat, or other Vessel, riding, lying, or being within, or coming
into, any Port, Harbour, Creek or Haven, within the limits of
their Commission; and also in the day-time to go into any
House, Shop, Cellar, or any other Place, where any Goods,
Wares or Merchandizes lie concealed, or are *suspected* to lie
concealed, whereof the customs and other duties, have not
been, or shall not be, duly paid and truly satisfied, answered or
paid unto the Collectors, Deputy-Collectors, Ministers, Servants, and other Officers respectively, or otherwise agreed for;
and the said House, Shop, Warehouse, Cellar, and other Place
to search and survey, and all and every the Boxes, Trunks,
Chests and Packs then and there found to break open."

Thus our Houses, and even our Bed-Chambers, are exposed
to be ransacked, our Boxes, Trunks and Chests broke open,
ravaged and plundered, by Wretches, whom no prudent Man
would venture to employ even as menial Servants; whenever
they are pleased to say they *suspect* there are in the House,
Wares, &c. for which the Duties have not been paid. Flagrant
instances of the wanton exercise of this Power, have frequently
happened in this and other seaport Towns. By this we are cut
off from that domestic security which renders the Lives of the
most unhappy in some measure agreeable. These Officers may

under color of Law and the cloak of a general warrant, break through the sacred Rights of the *Domicil*, ransack Mens Houses, destroy their Securities, carry off their Property, and with little Danger to themselves commit the most horrid Murders.

And we complain of it as a further Grievance, that notwithstanding by the Charter of this Province, the Governor and the Great and General Court or Assembly of this province or Territory, for the time being, shall have full power and authority, from time to time, to make, ordain and establish all manner of wholesome and reasonable Laws, Orders, Statutes, and Ordinances, Directions and Instructions, and that if the same shall not within the term of three years after presenting the same to his Majesty in Privy Council be disallowed, they shall be and continue in full force and effect, until the same shall be repealed by the Great and General Assembly of this province: Yet the Parliament of Great-Britain have rendered, or attempted to render, null and void, a Law of this province, made and passed in the Reign of his late Majesty George the First, intituled, "An Act stating the Fees of the Custom-House Officers within this province," and by meer dint of power, in violation of the Charter aforesaid, established other and exorbitant Fees, for the same Officers; any Law, of the province, to the contrary notwithstanding.

5thly. Fleets and Armies have been introduced to support these unconstitutional Officers in collecting and managing this unconstitutional Revenue; and Troops have been quartered in this Metropolis for that purpose. Introducing and quartering Standing Armies in a free Country in times of Peace, without the consent of the People either by themselves or by their Representatives, is, and always has been deemed, a violation of their Rights as Freemen; and of the Charter or Compact made between the King of Great Britain and the People of this Province, whereby all the Rights of British Subjects are confirmed to us.

6thly. The Revenue arising from this Tax unconstitutionally laid, and committed to the management of Persons arbitrarily appointed and supported by an armed Force quartered in a free City, has been in part applied to the most destructive purposes. It is absolutely necessary in a mixt Government, like that of this Province, that a due proportion or balance of Power should be established among the several Branches of the Legislative. Our Ancestors received from King William and Queen Mary a Charter, by which it was understood by both Parties in the contract, that such a proportion or balance was fixed; and therefore every thing which renders any one Branch of the Legislative more independent of the other two than it was originally designed, is an alteration of the Constitution as settled by the Charter; and as it has been, until the establishment of this Revenue, the constant practice of the general Assembly to provide for the support of Government, so it is an essential part of our Constitution, as it is a necessary means of preserving an *Equilibrium*, without which we cannot continue a free State.

In particular it has always been held, that the dependence of the Governor of this Province upon the General Assembly for his support, was necessary for the preservation of this *Equilibrium*; nevertheless his Majesty has been pleased to apply Fifteen Hundred Pounds Sterling annually, out of the American Revenue, for the support of the Governor of this Province independent of the Assembly; whereby the ancient connection between him and this People is weakened, the Confidence in the Governor lessened, the Equilibrium destroyed, and the Constitution essentially altered.

And we look upon it highly probable, from the best intelligence we have been able to obtain, that not only our Governor and Lieutenant Governor, but the Judges of the Superior Court of Judicature, as also the King's Attorney and Solicitor General are to receive their Support from this grievous tribute. This will, if accomplish'd, compleat our Slavery: For if Taxes are to be raised from us by the Parliament of Great Britain without our consent, and the Men on whose opinions and decisions our Properties, Liberties, and Lives, in a great measure depend, receive their Support from the Revenues arising from these Taxes, we cannot, when we think on the depravity of mankind, avoid looking with horror on the danger to which we are exposed! The British Parliament have shewn their wisdom in making the Judges there as independent as possible both on the Prince and People, both for place and support: But our Judges hold their commissions only during pleasure;

the granting them Salaries out of this Revenue is rendering them dependent on the Crown for their support. The King, upon his first accession to the Throne, for giving the last Hand to the independency of the Judges in England, not only upon himself but his successors, by recommending and consenting to an Act of Parliament, by which the Judges are continued in office, notwithstanding the demise of the King, which vacates all other Commission, was applauded by the whole Nation. How alarming therefore must it be to the inhabitants of this province, to find so wide a difference made between the subjects in Britain and America, as the rendering the Judges here altogether dependent on the Crown for their support.

7thly. We find ourselves greatly oppressed by Instructions sent to our Governor from the Court of Great Britain; whereby the first branch of our legislature is made meerly a ministerial Engine. And the Province has already felt such effects from these instructions, as we think, justly intitle us to say, that they threaten an entire destruction of our Liberties; and must soon, if not check'd, render every branch of our government a useless burthen upon the people. We shall point out some of the alarming effects of these instructions which have already taken place.

In consequence of instructions, the Governor has called and adjourned our General Assemblies to a place highly inconvenient to the Members and greatly disadvantageous to the interest of the province, even against his own declared Intention.

In consequence of instructions, the Assembly has been prorogued from time to time, when the important concerns of the Province required their meeting.

In obedience to instructions the General Assembly was Anno 1768 dissolved by Governor Bernard, because they would not consent to *rescind* the Resolution of a *former* House, and thereby sacrifice the Rights of their Constituents.

By an Instruction, the honorable his Majesty's Council are forbid to meet and transact matters of publick concern as a council of advice to the Governor, unless called by the Governor; and if they should from a zealous regard to the Interest of the province so meet at any time, the Governor is ordered to negative them at the next Election of Councellors. And although by the Charter of this province the Great and General Court have full power and authority to impose Taxes upon the Estates and persons of all and every the proprietors and inhabitants of this province, yet the Governor has been forbidden to give his consent to an act imposing a Tax for the necessary support of government, unless such persons as were pointed out in the said instruction, were exempted from paying their just proportion of said Tax.

His Excellency has also pleaded instructions for giving up the provincial Fortress, Castle William, into the hands of Troops, over whom he had declared he had no controul (and that at a time when they were menacing the slaughter of the inhabitants of the town, and our streets were stain'd with the blood which they had barbarously shed.) Thus our Governor, appointed and paid from Great-Britain with Money forced from us, is made an instrument of totally preventing, or at least of rendering futile, every attempt of the other two branches of our Legislative in favour of a distressed and wronged people: And lest the complaints naturally occasioned by such oppression should excite compassion in the royal Breast, and induce his Majesty seriously to set about relieving us from the cruel Bondage and Insults which we, his loyal Subjects, have so long suffered, the Governor is forbidden to consent to the payment of an Agent to represent our grievances at the Court of Great Britain, unless he, the Governor, consent to his Election; and we very well know what *the Man must be* to whose appointment a Governor, in such circumstances, will consent.

While we are mentioning the Infringements of the Rights of this Colony in particular by means of Instructions, we cannot help calling to remembrance the late unexampled Suspension of the Legislative of a Sister Colony, *New-York*, by force of an Instruction, until they should comply with an arbitrary act of the British Parliament, for quartering Troops, designed, by military execution, to enforce the raising of a tribute.

8thly. The extending the power of the Courts of Vice-Admiralty to so enormous a degree, as deprives the people in the colonies, in a great measure, of their inestimable right to trials *by Juries*; which has ever been justly considered as the grand Bulwark and Security of English property.

This alone is sufficient to rouse our jealousy: And we are

again obliged to take notice of the remarkable contrast, which the British parliament have been pleased to exhibit between the Subjects in Great-Britain and the Colonies. In the same Statute, by which they give up to the decision of one dependent interested Judge of Admiralty the estates and properties of the Colonists, they expressly guard the estates and properties of the People of Great-Britain; For all forfeitures and penalties inflicted by the statute of the fourth of George the third, or any other Act of Parliament relative to the Trade of the Colonies, may be sued for in any Court of Admiralty in the Colonies; but all penalties and forfeitures which shall be incurred in Great-Britain, may be sued for in any of his Majesty's Courts of Record in Westminster, or in the Court of Exchequer in Scotland, respectively. Thus our Birthrights are taken from us; and that too with every mark of indignity, insult and contempt. We may be harrassed and dragged from one part of the Continent to the other (which some of our Brethren here and in the country towns already have been) and finally be deprived of our whole property, by the arbitrary determination of one biassed, capricious Judge of the Admiralty.

9thly. The restraining us from erecting Slitting-Mills for manufacturing our Iron the natural produce of this Country, is an Infringement of that Right with which God and Nature have invested us, to make use of our skill and industry in procuring the necessaries and conveniencies of Life. And we look upon the Restraint laid upon the Manufacture and Transportation of Hats to be altogether unreasonable and grievous. Although by the Charter all Havens, Rivers, Ports, Waters, &c. are expressly granted the Inhabitants of the Province and their Successors, to their only proper use and behoof forever, yet the British Parliament passed an act, whereby they restrain us from carrying our Wool, the produce of our own Farms, even over a Ferry; whereby the Inhabitants have often been put to the expence of carrying a Bag of Wool near an hundred miles by land, when passing over a River or Water of one quarter of a mile, of which the province are the absolute proprietors, would have prevented all that trouble.

10thly. The Act passed in the last Session of the British Parliament, intituled, *An Act for the better preserving his Majesty's*

Dock-Yards, Magazines, Ships, Ammunition and Stores, is, as we apprehend, a violent Infringement of our Rights. By this Act, any one of us may be taken from his Family, and carried to any part of Great-Britain, there to be tried, whenever it shall be pretended that he has been concerned in burning or otherwise destroying any Boat or Vessel, or any Materials for building, &c. any naval or victualling Store, &c. belonging to his Majesty. For by this Act all Persons in the Realm, or in any of the Places thereto belonging (under which Denomination we know the Colonies are meant to be included) may be indicted or tried either in any County or Shire within this Realm, in like manner and form as if the Offence had been committed in said County, as his Majesty and his Successors may deem most expedient. Thus we are not only deprived of our grand Right to *Trial by our Peers in the Vicinity,* but any person suspected, or pretended to be suspected, may be hurried to Great-Britain, to take his Trial in any County the King or his Successors shall please to direct; where, innocent or guilty, he is in great danger of being condemned; and whether condemned or acquitted, he will probably be ruined by the Expence attending the Trial, and his long Absence from his Family and Business; and we have the strongest reason to apprehend that we shall soon experience the fatal Effects of this Act, as about the Year 1769, the British Parliament passed Resolves for taking up a number of persons in the Colonies and carrying them to Great-Britain for trial, pretending that they were authorised so to do by a Statute passed in the Reign of Henry the Eighth in which they say the Colonies were included, although the Act was passed long before any Colonies were settled, or even in contemplation.

11thly. As our Ancestors came over to this Country that they might not only enjoy their civil but their religious Rights, and particularly desired to be freed from the Prelates, who in those times cruelly persecuted all who differed in sentiment from the established Church; we cannot see without concern, the various attempts which have been made, and are now making, to establish an American Episcopate. Our Episcopal brethren of the Colonies do enjoy, and rightfully ought ever to enjoy, the free exercise of their Religion; but as an American Episcopate is by no means essential to that free exercise of their Religion, we cannot help fearing that they who are so warmly contending for such an Establishment, have Views altogether inconsistent with the universal and peaceful enjoyment of our Christian privileges: And doing or attempting to do any thing which has even the remotest tendency to endanger this Enjoyment, is justly looked upon a great Grievance, and also an Infringement of our Rights; which is not barely to exercise, but peaceably and securely to enjoy, that Liberty with which CHRIST hath made us free.

And we are further of Opinion, that no Power on Earth can justly give either temporal or spiritual Jurisdiction within this Province, except the Great & General Court. We think therefore that every design for establishing the Jurisdiction of a Bishop in this Province, is a design both against our civil and religious Rights: And we are well informed, that the more candid & judicious of our Brethren of the Church of England in this and the other Colonies, both Clergy and Laity, conceive of the establishing an American Episcopate both unnecessary and unreasonable.

12thly. Another Grievance under which we labour is, The frequent Alteration of the Bounds of the Colonies by Decisions before the King and Council, explanatory of former Grants and Charters. This not only subjects Men to live under a Constitution to which they have not consented, which in itself is a great Grievance; but moreover under Color, that the *Right of Soil* is affected by such Declarations, some Governors, or Ministers, or both in Conjunction, have pretended to grant in Consequence of a Mandamus many Thousands of Acres of vacant and appropriated Lands near a Century past, and rendered valuable by the Labors of the present Cultivators and their Ancestors. There are very notable Instances of Settlers, who having first purchased the Soil of the Natives, have at considerable Expence obtained Confirmation of Title from this Province; and, on being transfer'd to the Jurisdiction of the Province of *New-Hampshire*, have been put to the Trouble and Cost of a new Grant or Confirmation from thence; and after all this, there has been a third Declaration of the Royal Will, that they shou'd thenceforth be considered as pertaining to the Province of *New-York*. The Troubles, Expences and Dangers which Hundreds have been put to on such Occasions, cannot here be recited; but so much may be said, that they have been most cruelly harrassed, and even threatened with a military Force, to dragoon them into a Compliance with the most unreasonable Demands.

A Letter of Correspondence, to the Other Towns.

BOSTON, *November* 20, 1772.

GENTLEMEN,

WE, the Freeholders and other Inhabitants of *Boston*, in Town-Meeting duly assembled, according to Law, apprehending there is abundant Reason to be alarmed that the Plan of *Despotism*, which the Enemies of our invaluable Rights have concerted, is rapidly hastening to a completion, can no longer conceal our impatience under a constant, unremitted, uniform Aim to inslave us, or confide in an Administration which threatens us with certain and inevitable destruction. But, when in Addition to the repeated Inroads made upon the Rights and Liberties of the Colonists, and of those in this Province in particular, we reflect on the late extraordinary Measure in affixing Stipends, or Salaries from the Crown to the Offices of the Judges of the Superior Court of Judicature, making them not only intirely independent of the People, whose Lives and Fortunes are so much in their Power, but absolutely dependent on the Crown, (which may hereafter be worn by a *Tyrant*) both for their Appointment and Support, we cannot but be extremely alarm'd at the mischievous Tendency of this Innovation; which, in our Opinion is directly contrary to the Spirit of the British Constitution, pregnant with innumerable Evils, & hath a direct Tendency to deprive us of every thing valuable as Men, as Christians, and as Subjects, entitled, by the Royal Charter, to all the Rights, Liberties and Privileges of native Britons. Such being the critical State of this Province, we think it our Duty on this truly distressing Occasion, to ask you, What can withstand the Attacks of mere Power? What can preserve the Liberties of the Subject, when the Barriers of the Constitution are taken away? The Town of *Boston*, consulting on the Matter above-mentioned, thought proper to make Application to the Governor by a Committee; requesting his Excellency to communicate such Intelligence as he might have received, relative to the Report of the Judges having their Support independent of the Grants of this Province, a Copy of which you have herewith in Paper No. 1.* To which we received as Answer the Paper No. 2.† The Town on further Deliberation, thought it adviseable to refer the Matter to the Great and General Assembly; and accordingly in a second Address, as No. 3.‡ they requested his Excellency that the General Court might convene at the Time to which they then stood prorogued; to which the Town received the Reply as in No. 4.§ in which we are acquainted with his Intentions further to prorogue the General Assembly, which has since taken Place. Thus, Gentlemen, it is evident his Excellency declines giving the least Satisfaction as to the Matter in Request. The Affair being of public Concernment, the Town of *Boston* thought it necessary to consult with their Brethren throughout the Province; and for this Purpose appointed a Committee, to communicate with our Fellow Sufferers, respecting this recent Instance of Oppression, as well as the many other Violations of our Rights under which we have groaned for several Years past—This Committee have briefly recapitulated the sense we have of our invaluable Rights as Men, as Christians, and as Subjects; and wherein we conceive those Rights to have been violated, which we are desirous may be laid before your Town, that the Subject may be weighed as its Importance requires, and the collected wisdom of the whole People, as far as possible, be obtained, on a deliberation of such great and lasting moment as to Involve in it the Fate of all our Posterity.—Great Pains has been taken to perswade the British Administration to think, that the good People of this Province in general are quiet and undisturbed at the late Measures; and that any Uneasiness that appears, arises only

* See Appendix, No. 1.
† See Appendix, No. 2.
‡ See Appendix, No. 3.
§ See Appendix, No. 4.

from a few factious designing and disaffected Men. This renders it the more necessary, that the sense of the People should be explicitly declared.—A free Communication of your Sentiments to this Town, of our common Danger, is earnestly solicited and will be gratefully received. If you concur with us in Opinion, that our Rights are properly stated, and that the several Acts of Parliament, and Measures of Administration, pointed out by us, are subversive of these Rights, you will doubtless think it of the utmost Importance that we stand firm as one Man, to recover and support them; and to take such Measures, by directing our Representatives, or otherwise, as your Wisdom and Fortitude shall dictate, to rescue from impending Ruin our happy and glorious Constitution. But if it should be the general Voice of this Province, that the Rights, as we have stated them, do not belong to us; or, that the several Measures of Administration in the British Court, are no Violations of these Rights; or, that if they are thus violated or infringed, they are not worth contending for, or resolutely maintaining;—should this be the general Voice of the Province, we must be resigned to our wretched Fate; but shall forever lament the Extinction of that generous Ardor for Civil and Religious Liberty, which in the Face of every Danger, and even Death itself, induced our Fathers, to forsake the Bosom of their Native Country, and begin a Settlement on bare Creation.—But we trust this cannot be the Case: We are sure your Wisdom, your Regard to Yourselves and the rising Generation, cannot suffer you to doze, or set supinely indifferent, on the brink of Destruction, while the Iron Hand of Oppression is daily tearing the choicest Fruit from the fair Tree of Liberty, planted by our worthy Predecessors, at the Expence of their Treasure, and abundantly water'd with their Blood.—It is an observation of an eminent Patriot, that a People long inured to Hardships, loose by Degrees the very notions of Liberty; they look upon themselves, as Creatures *at Mercy*, and that all Impositions laid on, by Superior Hands, are legal and obligatory.—But thank Heaven this is not yet verified in *America!* We have yet some Share of public Virtue remaining: We are not afraid of Poverty, but disdain Slavery. —The Fate of Nations is so precarious, and Revolutions in

States so often take Place at an unexpected Moment, when the Hand of Power, by Fraud or Flattery, has secured every Avenue of Retreat, and the Minds of the Subject debased to its Purpose, that it becomes every Well-Wisher to his Country, while it has any Remains of Freedom, to keep an Eagle Eye upon every Inovation and Stretch of Power, in those that have the Rule over us. A recent Instance of this we have in the late Revolutions in *Sweden*; by which the Prince, once subject to the Laws of the State, has been able of a sudden, to declare himself an absolute Monarch. The Sweeds were once a free, martial and valiant People: Their Minds are now so debased, that they even rejoice at being subject to the Caprice and arbitrary Power of a Tyrant, and kiss their Chains. It makes us shudder to think, the late Measures of Administration may be productive of the like Catastrophe; which Heaven forbid!—Let us consider Brethren, we are strugling for our best Birth Rights and Inheritance; which being infringed, renders all our Blessings precarious in their Enjoyments, and consequently trifling in their Value. Let us disappoint the Men, who are raising themselves on the Ruin of this Country. Let us convince every Invader of our Freedom, that we will be as free as the Constitution our Fathers recognized, will justify.

The foregoing Report was twice read distinctly, and amended in the Meeting. And then the Question was put, Whether the same be accepted? *And passed in the Affirmative*, Nem. Con.

A true Copy,
Attest.
WILLIAM COOPER, *Town-Clerk.*

Upon a Motion made, *Voted*, That the foregoing Proceedings be attested by the Town-Clerk, and printed in a Pamphlet; and that the Committee be desired to dispose of *Six Hundred* Copies thereof to the Selectmen of the Towns in the Province, and such other Gentlemen as they shall think fit.

Voted, That the Town-Clerk be directed to sign the foregoing

Letter, and forward as many of the same to the Selectmen of each Town in this Province, as the Committee shall judge proper, and direct.

A true Copy,
Attest.
WILLIAM COOPER, *Town-Clerk*.

APPENDIX.

THE MESSAGE OF THE TOWN OF BOSTON
TO THE GOVERNOR.

May it please your Excellency,

THE Freeholders and other Inhabitants of the Town of *Boston*, legally assembled in *Faneuil-Hall*, beg Leave to acquaint your Excellency, that a Report has prevailed, which they have reason to apprehend is well grounded, that Stipends are affixed to the Offices of the Judges of the Superior Court of Judicature, &c. of this Province, whereby they are become Independent of the Grants of the General Assembly for their Support; contrary to ancient and invariable Usage. This Report has spread an Alarm among all considerate persons who have heard of it in Town and Country; being viewed, as tending rapidly to compleat the System of their Slavery; which originated in the House of Commons of Great-Britain, assuming a Power and Authority, to give and grant the Monies of the Colonists without their Consent, and against their repeated Remonstrances. And, as the Judges hold their Places during Pleasure, this Establishment appears big with fatal Evils, so obvious that it is needless to trespass on your Excellency's Time in mentioning them.

It is therefore the humble and earnest Request of the Town, that your Excellency would be pleased to inform them, Whether you have received any such Advice, relating to a Matter so deeply interesting to the Inhabitants of this Province, which gives you Assurance that such an Establishment has been, or is likely, to be made.

(NO. II.)
THE GOVERNOR'S ANSWER TO THE
FOREGOING MESSAGE.

GENTLEMEN,

IT *is by no Means proper for me to lay before the Inhabitants of any Town whatsoever, in Consequence of their Votes and Proceedings in a Town-Meeting, any Part of my Correspondence as*

Governor of the Province, or to acquaint them whether I have or have not received any Advices relating to the public Affairs of the Government. This Reason alone, if your Address to me had been in other Respects unexceptionable, would have been sufficient to restrain me from complying with your Desire.

I shall always be ready to gratify the Inhabitants of the Town of Boston, *upon every regular Application to me on Business of public Concernment to the Town, as far as I shall have it in my Power consistent with Fidelity to the Trust which his Majesty has reposed in me.*

T. HUTCHINSON.

Province-House, 30 Oct. 1772.

To the Inhabitants of the Town of Boston *in Town-Meeting assembled at* Faneuil-Hall.

(NO. III.)

THE PETITION OF THE TOWN TO THE GOVERNOR.

The PETITION of the Freeholders and other Inhabitants of the Town of *Boston*, legally assembled by Adjournment in *Faneuil-Hall*, on Friday October 30, 1772.

Humbly sheweth,

THAT your Petitioners are *still* greatly alarmed at the Report which has been prevalent of late, viz. That Stipends are affixed to the Offices of the Judges of the Superior Court of Judicature of this Province, by Order of the Crown, for their Support.

Such an Establishment is contrary, not only to the plain and obvious Sense of the Charter of this Province, but also to some of the fundamental Principles of the Common Law; to the Benefit of which, all British Subjects, wherever dispersed throughout the British Empire, are indubitably intitled.

Such a Jealousy have the Subjects of England for their Rights, Liberties and Privileges, and so tender a Regard has been shown to them by his Majesty, that notwithstanding the Provision made at the Revolution, that the Judges of the King's Superior Courts of Law there, should hold their Commissions, not at Pleasure, but during good Behaviour, and since that Time for their Support, His Majesty, among other the first Acts of his Reign, was graciously pleased to recommend it to Parliament, and an Act passed, that their Commissions should not cease at the Demise of the King; whereby every thing possible in human Wisdom seems to have been done, to establish an Impartiality in their Decisions not only between Subject and Subject, but between the Crown and the Subject.—Of how much greater Importance must it be to preserve from the least supposeable Bias, the Judges of a Court, invested by the Laws of this Province, which have been approved of by Majesty, with Powers as fully and amply to all Intents and Purposes whatsoever, as the Courts of King's-Bench, Common Pleas and Exchequer, within his Majesty's Kingdom of England have, or ought to have?

Your Excellency will allow your Petitioners, with due Submission to repeat, that this Establishment appears to them pregnant with such fatal Evils, as that the most distant thought of its taking Effect, fills their Minds with Dread and Horror.

These Sir, are the Sentiments and Apprehensions of this Metropolis: Expressed however, with due Defference to the Sentiments of the Province, with which your Petitioners are anxiously sollicitous of being made acquainted.

It is therefore their earnest and humble Request, that your Excellency would be pleased to allow the General Assembly to meet at the Time to which it now stands prorogued; in order, that in that *Constitutional* Body, with whom it is to inquire into Grievances and Redress them, the joint Wisdom of the Province may be employed, in deliberating and determining on a Matter so important and alarming.

(NO. IV.)

THE GOVERNOR'S ANSWER TO THE
FOREGOING PETITION.

GENTLEMEN,
THE Royal Charter reserves to the Governor full Power and Authority, from time to time, as he shall judge necessary, to adjourn, prorogue and dissolve the General Assembly.

In the Exercise of this Power, both as to Time and Place, I have always been governed by a Regard to his Majesty's Service and to the Interest of the Province.

It did not appear to me necessary for those Purposes that the Assembly should meet at the Time to which it now stands prorogued, and, before I was informed of your Address, I had determined to prorogue it to a further Time.

The Reasons which you have advanced have not altered my Opinion.

If, notwithstanding, in Compliance with your Petition, I should alter my Determination and meet the Assembly, contrary to my own Judgment, at such Time as you judge necessary, I should, in Effect, yield to you the Exercise of that Part of the Prerogative, and should be unable to justify my Conduct to the King.

There would, moreover, be danger of encouraging the Inhabitants of the other Towns in the Province to assemble, from time to time, in order to consider of the Necessity or Expediency of a Session of the General Assembly, or to debate and transact other Matters which the Law that authorizes Towns to assemble does not make the Business of a Town-Meeting.

T. HUTCHINSON.

Province-House, Nov. 2. 1772.
To the Inhabitants of the Town of Boston *in Town-Meeting assembled at* Faneuil-Hall.

This Reply having been read several Times and duly considered; it was moved, and the Question accordingly put— Whether the same be Satisfactory to the Town, which passed in the Negative, *Nem. Con.*

And thereupon RESOLVED as the Opinion of the Inhabitants of this Town, That they have, ever had, and ought to have, a Right to Petition the King or his Representative for the Redress of such Grievances as they feel, or for preventing of such as they have Reason to apprehend; and to Communicate their Sentiments to other Towns.

Attest.

WILLIAM COOPER, *Town-Clerk.*

CHRONOLOGY

BIOGRAPHICAL NOTES

NOTE ON THE TEXTS

NOTES

INDEX

A Chronology of the First British Empire

1497   Sponsored by the English king, Henry VII (r. 1485–1509), Venetian Giovanni Caboto (John Cabot) sails across the North Atlantic and makes landfall in eastern Canada. Cabot's discovery of this "newe founde lande" becomes the basis for English claims to all of North America.

1533   Amid the controversy with Rome over his divorce from Catherine of Aragon, Henry VIII (1509–47) effects passage in Parliament of an Act in Restraint of Appeals, which declares "that this realm of England is an empire, and so hath been accepted in the world, governed by one supreme head and King having the dignity and royal estate of the imperial crown of the same, unto whom a body politic, compact of all sorts and degrees of people divided in terms and by names of spirituality and temporality, be bounded and owe to bear next to God a natural and humble obedience." Henry's eventual break with Rome and the subsequent flowering of Protestantism in England during the short reign of his son, Edward VI (1547–53), will introduce a religious dimension to England's long struggle for empire with Europe's Catholic powers, France and Spain.

1541   Henry VIII is declared King of Ireland by the Irish Parliament, a body that represents the island's minority population of Anglo-Norman descent, those living within the Pale, a swath of territory in the east that encompasses Dublin. For much of the remainder of the century the Tudor monarchs will attempt to subdue the rest of Ireland through various colonization efforts and military adventures, developing strategies and ideologies that will inform English colonization in the New World.

1559   England loses Calais, the last vestige of its dynastic claims on the Continent.

1562   With backing from London merchants and the court of Queen Elizabeth I (1558–1603), John Hawkins makes the first of three voyages carrying enslaved people from Africa to Spanish America. When this trade is halted by the Spanish, Hawkins, Francis Drake, and other seafarers turn to privateering expeditions against Spain's New World possessions.

1565   Spain establishes the first permanent European settlement in North America at St. Augustine in Florida.

1584   Walter Raleigh receives a royal patent from the queen for the exploration and settlement of North America. His principal venture, a settlement at Roanoke Island in North Carolina's Outer Banks, ends in failure.

1588   The successful defense of the kingdom against a major invasion force (the Spanish Armada) boosts English pride and confidence on the world stage.

1600   The East India Company, a joint-stock venture, is formed by a group of London merchants in an effort to break Portugal's monopoly on trade with Asia.

1603   With the death of Elizabeth, her cousin, James VI of Scotland, succeeds to the English throne as James I (1603–25). The first of the Stuart monarchs tries to unite the two mostly Protestant kingdoms—one presbyterian and the other episcopal—but meets with resistance from the English Parliament, notwithstanding his assurance that his motivation "in seeking union is only to advance the greatness of your empire seated here in England." Despite Parliament's concerns, James styles himself King of Great Britain.

1604   Confronted with a nearly bankrupt government in England after years of war with Spain, James concludes a peace and announces a ban on privateering, a pivot that frees resources for renewed attempts to establish overseas plantations.

1605   A group of English Catholics, disappointed by the failure of the new king (whose wife is Catholic) to relax legal and political restrictions on followers of the old faith, conspires to blow up the Houses of Parliament when James is present to open the session. The so-called Gunpowder Plot is discovered before it can be put into effect and Guy Fawkes and his fellow conspirators are arrested, tried, and executed. November 5, the day the plot is uncovered, is proclaimed "the joyful day of deliverance" by an act of Parliament and "Guy Fawkes Day," as it will become known, is long commemorated throughout the empire as a reminder of the nefarious specter of "popery."

1606　Under a royal patent North American settlement rights are granted to two joint-stock companies made up of merchants and investors, one based in London, the other in Plymouth, which are to be governed by a council in London appointed by the king. The charter states that subjects who emigrate to or are born in a colony "shall have and enjoy all Liberties, Franchises and Immunities . . . as if they had been abiding and born within this our Realm of England," a principle that will be echoed in subsequent colonial charters.

1607　An expedition sent by the London Company establishes the first permanent English settlement in North America, on Jamestown Island, in Virginia.

1608　Samuel de Champlain establishes a settlement at Quebec, the genesis of what will be the colony of New France. Essentially a series of trading posts for the fur trade, New France grows slowly along the St. Lawrence River, its success dependent on good relations with the region's native inhabitants. English merchants establish the first trading post or "factory" in India.

1609　In the wake of a long conflict with the Gaelic chieftains of Ireland (the Nine Years' War), James initiates a program encouraging Protestants from England and Scotland to establish plantations, organized principally through guilds and corporations, on confiscated Catholic land in Ulster.

1612　England establishes permanent settlement on Bermuda and the island is later incorporated under the Virginia Company's charter. In Virginia, John Rolfe begins to experiment with the cultivation of tobacco, a labor-intensive crop that will quickly become the colony's staple commodity.

1619　After imposing increasingly harsh legal codes in response to persistent starvation and disorder in Virginia, the Company promises to reform the colony and reaffirms the settlers' claims to the rights of Englishmen, including a representative assembly. The first General Assembly of Virginia accordingly meets at Jamestown in July. The Company also grants a community of English Separatists living in Leiden (the Pilgrims) permission to settle in the northern part of its Virginia claim. In August, Dutch slave traders sell twenty Africans—the first known to have reached English America—into servitude at Jamestown. By the end of the century over half a million unfree people will have crossed the Atlantic to the English colonies, including 350,000 African slaves and 200,000 indentured servants.

1620   The Pilgrims land on Cape Cod and decide to establish a colony at Plymouth, beyond the Virginia Company's northern boundary. Outside any organized jurisdiction, the settlers enter into a formal agreement, the Mayflower Compact, which serves as the basis for the colony's government. Plymouth remains autonomous until absorbed into Massachusetts in 1691.

1621   Sir Edwin Sandys, one of the founders of the Virginia Company and chair of a parliamentary committee investigating England's flagging trade and bullion scarcity, proposes a bill to establish a monopoly for Virginia tobacco in the English market. Jealously guarding his prerogative powers, the king announces his opposition to the measure, as he will another seeking to regulate access to colonial fisheries, insisting that the administration of overseas plantations is not subject to parliamentary oversight because the colonies are not annexed to the Crown, that is, they are not part of the realm of England, but rather the personal property of the monarch.

1622   John Mason and Ferdinando Gorges receive royal grants to the territory between the Merrimack and Sagadahoc (Kennebec) rivers, and settlement begins along the Piscataqua River, the site of present-day Portsmouth, New Hampshire, the following year. These and other settlements further north along the Maine coast will fall into the orbit of the Massachusetts Bay Colony government.

1623   In Indonesia, ten English traders are put to death by authorities of the Dutch East India Company, which has established control of the Spice Islands. The incident strengthens the Dutch hold on the region, and encourages the English to focus instead on India.

1624   Virginia becomes a royal colony after a commission appointed by the king dissolves the Company for chronic mismanagement. The Dutch West India Company establishes the New Netherland colony, with settlements along the Hudson River. Like New France, it grows slowly. The first permanent English settlement in the Caribbean is established on St. Kitts. Nearly a score of additional settlements will follow, though many are subsequently destroyed by the Spanish, who claim all the Caribbean. In addition to St. Kitts, the most successful English colonies in the region are Barbados (1627), Nevis (1628), Montserrat and Antigua (1632), the Bahamas (1647), and Jamaica (conquered from Spain in 1655). Of the more than 200,000 English who migrate to the New World between 1630 and 1660, more than half travel to these small West Indian colonies, where the lucrative sugar trade promises fast wealth to those who can survive the harsh conditions and unhealthful climate.

1625   With the death of James I, his son becomes Charles I (1625–49). The new king presides over a deteriorating economy, as English trade suffers from the disruption of Continental markets resulting from the Thirty Years' War, and a fractured English Church; religious non-conformists (Puritans) who believe the national church to be insufficiently reformed resist the imposition of uniformity in worship and vestments by an increasingly active episcopacy under the leadership of Charles's advisor William Laud, who will become the archbishop of Canterbury in 1633.

1628   Having failed in the early years of his reign to secure sufficient funds to support the army from Parliament, Charles resorts to martial law and the forcible quartering of troops in private homes. These and other actions provoke Parliament to issue the Petition of Right, which seeks to define the proper limits on prerogative. Edward Coke, the petition's principal architect, observes that "the prerogative is like a river without which men cannot live, but if it swell too high it may lose its own channel." Charles accepts the petition in exchange for much-needed subsidies.

1629   Initially conceived as a commercial venture, the Massachusetts Bay Company is chartered by the king and granted rights to an area north of the Plymouth colony. Led by John Winthrop, a majority group of the company's shareholders determine to use the grant to create a refuge for Puritans facing persecution in England. Charles dissolves Parliament in the wake of recurring conflicts over his financial and religious policies. He will not call another for eleven years, a period that will become known as the "Personal Rule."

1630   Large groups of migrants, most of them Puritans, establish settlements at Boston and ten other sites in the Massachusetts Bay Colony. By 1641, some 20,000 men, women, and children will have made the crossing, in what will become known as the Great Migration. Leading the first wave, John Winthrop brings with him the Company's charter—which is missing the standard clause requiring administrative meetings to be held in England—affording him and the Company's other leaders considerable latitude in setting up their holy commonwealth. The charter's provision for a General Court of shareholders, responsible for electing a governor and a board of assistants, serves as the basis for what becomes by 1644 the colony's bicameral representative assembly.

1632   In a move away from joint-stock ventures as the principal mode of overseas colonization, Charles grants Cecilius Calvert, 2nd Baron Baltimore, a royal charter to found a colony in a large tract of land north of the Potomac River. Under the terms of the grant, Baltimore, as Lord Proprietor, is exempt from royal taxation and granted the power to appoint all sheriffs and judges and to create a local nobility. Settlement in the new colony of Maryland, named for the queen consort, Henrietta Maria, and conceived in part as a refuge for English Catholics, begins two years later.

1635   Expelled from Massachusetts, Roger Williams, a Puritan minister with Separatist leanings, relocates to the south, where on land purchased from Narragansett Indians he founds a colony called Providence Plantation. Other settlements by those seeking freedom of worship are founded along Narragansett Bay, and in 1644 Williams secures a parliamentary patent uniting the towns into a single colony.

1635–37 Dissatisfied with church government in the Bay Colony and seeking economic opportunities in the fertile Connecticut River Valley, groups of Puritans move to the southwest, establishing the Saybrook, Connecticut, and New Haven colonies. Saybrook will merge with the larger Connecticut colony in 1644, New Haven in 1664. Among the financial devices Charles exploits to raise revenues during the Personal Rule is "ship money," a traditional rate charged to the gentry in coastal counties for naval defense in times of emergency, now extended to those in inland communities in times of peace. Several gentlemen resist this novelty, which they say opens the door for the king to tax his people at his pleasure and without their consent. Among them is John Hampden, a wealthy member of Parliament who forces the case to trial before King's Bench. Hampden loses the decision, but the case proves a Pyrrhic victory for the king, who suffers badly in popular opinion.

1638   The Swedish West India Company establishes a series of fur trading posts along the lower Delaware River, genesis of the short-lived colony of New Sweden, which will be annexed by the more powerful New Netherland colony in 1655.

1639–40   In need of money to pay the English army he has dispatched to Scotland to impose religious conformity on his northern kingdom (the First Bishops' War), Charles summons and then promptly dissolves the so-called Short Parliament, because it will not appropriate funds without major restrictions on his prerogative powers. When Scottish forces overrun northern England (the Second Bishops' War), Charles summons the so-called Long Parliament into session. It will sit for the better part of a decade and contains a vocal Puritan bloc that quickly moves to impeach the king's advisors, including Archbishop Laud, and launch a legislative campaign against prerogative monarchy.

1641   Rebellion breaks out in Ireland, as the Catholic majority there seeks to capitalize on the disorder in England. Massachusetts leaders promulgate a legal code, the Body of Liberties, which guarantees freedom of speech, jury trials, and the right to counsel, among other provisions.

1642   The English Civil War begins when Charles, unable to dissolve a defiant Parliament, raises his standard against parliamentary forces.

1643   Royalist forces in Ireland reach a truce with Catholic insurgents, releasing manpower to fight the parliamentary army in England. For its part, Parliament enters into an alliance with the Scots. Massachusetts, Plymouth, Connecticut, and New Haven form a military alliance called the United Colonies of New England, or the New England Confederation, in order to combat threats from Dutch and Indian communities bordering their settlements.

1645–46   Parliament reforms its army, removing it from the control of county elites. The officer corps of the resulting "New Model Army," including second in command Oliver Cromwell, is more uniformly Puritan in outlook. After a series of military defeats, Charles surrenders to a Scottish army and is eventually transferred to Parliament's custody.

1648   Cromwell conclusively defeats a resurgent Scottish-Royalist army. In London, he directs officers of the New Model Army to prevent some 180 members of Parliament from taking their seats, and arrest forty more. The resultant staunchly Puritan "Rump Parliament" proceeds to abolish the monarchy, calling it "unnecessary, burdensome, and dangerous to the liberty, safety and public interest of the people." The House of Lords is similarly abolished soon thereafter and England is declared a "Commonwealth and Free State" under the rule of a unicameral Parliament, with the government entrusted to a Council of State chaired by Cromwell.

1649   Charles is charged with high treason and put on trial. Found guilty, he is beheaded on January 30. Cromwell launches a retributive assault on Ireland. Large numbers of Royalist officers and sympathizers go into exile; many of the aristocratic families who will come to dominate Virginia trace their foundation in America to this Cavalier exodus.

1651   In exchange for guarantees of religious tolerance to the Scots, the eldest son of Charles I is crowned King of Scotland. Charles II leads an army into England to recover his father's throne, but is defeated by Cromwell and goes into exile abroad. The Rump Parliament passes the first of what will become known as Navigation Acts; it stipulates that no goods may be imported into "this Commonwealth of England, or into Ireland, or any lands, islands, plantations, or territories to this Commonwealth belonging, or in their possession," except on English ships or on ships of the country where the commodity being transported was grown or produced. Though the act is neutral in its language, it is evidently aimed at the Dutch and their extensive carrying trade and it further polarizes relations between the two countries, whose far-flung traders compete for markets around the globe. (The resulting Anglo-

Dutch War of 1652–54 is the first of several naval conflicts which will be fought between the two states before century's end.) Parliament justifies its regulation of the colonies' trade with a muscular assertion of its authority: "Colonies and Plantations, which were planted at the Cost, and settled by the People, and by Authority of this Nation, which are and ought to be subordinate to, and dependent upon England; and hath ever since the Planting thereof been, and ought to be subject to such Laws, Orders and Regulations as are or shall be made by the Parliament of England."

1653   Cromwell declares himself Lord Protector of the Commonwealth, assuming powers akin to a monarch.

1658   On his death Cromwell is succeeded by his son Richard, but financial crisis cripples the Commonwealth. Negotiations begin for the restoration of the Stuart dynasty.

1660   Charles II (1649–85) is officially restored to the English throne on May 29. The Restoration Parliament re-enacts the Navigation Act of 1651, and goes further, enumerating certain colonial commodities, including sugar, tobacco, and cotton, which must be shipped directly to England. The Crown's administration of colonial affairs is delegated to the newly created secretary of state for the Southern Department, whose portfolio also includes southern England, Wales, Ireland, and southern Europe.

1663   Parliament passes another Navigation Act providing administrative machinery to enforce the existing trade regulations. The Company of Royal Adventurers Trading to Africa (renamed the Royal African Company in 1672) is chartered by Charles and granted a monopoly on trade with that continent. The Company acquires slaves in Africa in return for cloths and other manufactured goods from England and exchanges them in the West Indies and the American colonies for sugar, tobacco, and other staples for sale in the English market, a circuit that becomes known as the Atlantic triangular trade. Charles also makes a grant of a large swath of land between Virginia and Spanish Florida to a group of eight courtiers, including Anthony Ashley Cooper, later the Earl of Shaftsbury. These Lords Proprietors name their colony Carolina in honor of the king and offer fifty-acre grants to attract settlers. In 1669 Shaftsbury's secretary, John Locke, drafts the Fundamental Constitutions of Carolina, an intricate charter mixing liberal and quasi-feudal elements that bears little resemblance to the highly competitive, slave-based society that will develop. The king also grants a liberal charter to the colony of Rhode Island and the Providence Plantations, including provision for an elected governor. New France is made a royal province by Louis XIV, who takes measures to stimulate migration to the sparsely populated colony.

1664   Amid rising hostilities which will lead to the Second Anglo-Dutch War (1665–67), an English naval force conquers New Netherland. Charles II names his brother James, the Duke of York, proprietor of the new province, which is renamed New York. Though provision is made in the new colony's charter for a representative assembly, the proprietor will not call one into being until 1682; of all the Restoration colonies New York will come closest to realizing the proprietors' ideal of a hierarchical, feudalistic society in which they could profit from settlers' rents. The southern section of the grant includes the territories that will become the colonies of New Jersey and Delaware, which James will re-grant to various proprietors. New Jersey will be divided into two halves in 1676: West Jersey will be settled predominantly by Quakers, East Jersey by Anglicans and Scotch Presbyterians. The three counties of the Delaware region will be governed by a deputy from New York until 1682, when they will be absorbed into Pennsylvania.

1670   A group of English merchants and investors forms the Hudson's Bay Company and the Crown grants it a monopoly on the fur trade in the Hudson Bay watershed, comprising much of present-day Canada.

1672   Concerned about smuggling, especially of tobacco, Parliament passes a third Navigation Act, this time requiring a bond on enumerated articles brought into England.

1673   Aimed at Catholics and Nonconformists, the Test Act imposes legal penalties on public officials who refuse to swear an oath of allegiance recognizing the monarch as the head of the Church of England and to subscribe to a declaration denying the Catholic doctrine of transubstantiation. The Duke of York resigns his post as lord high admiral rather than swear the oath, thereby publicly revealing his conversion to Catholicism, which has occurred some years earlier.

1674   In keeping with the Restoration policy of placing military men as colonial governors, the Duke of York appoints Edmund Andros, a distinguished veteran of the Dutch wars, to be governor of New York. By 1680 more than 60 percent of American colonists are subject to such "governors general."

1676   As settlement in Virginia presses westward and meets stiffening resistance from the region's Indians, who have twice before, in 1622 and 1644, launched major uprisings threatening the existence of the colony, a group of up-country settlers led by Nathaniel Bacon demand a policy of armed expansion from the colony's leadership in the east. Unable to command the votes of the colonial assembly (the House of Burgesses) at Jamestown, Bacon and his followers—newly established planters with relatively small holdings, and indentured servants, both white and black—stage a coup and force the royal governor, William Berkeley, to flee. Bacon's Rebellion does not long outlast its namesake, who succumbs to dysentery within a month of putting the colonial capitol to torch, and the planter elite promptly reestablishes control. But the episode is emblematic of a persistent friction between backcountry settlers and coastal power centers, often involving relations with Indians, which will recur in many colonies throughout the colonial period.

1679   Exasperated by resistance to royal authority in Puritan Massachusetts, where the Navigation Acts are largely ignored, Charles II carves out a new royal colony, New Hampshire, from its territory. The province of Maine will remain part of Massachusetts until 1820.

1679–81   Mounting fears about Catholics at court, stoked by the so-called Popish Plot to kill the king a year earlier, provoke a parliamentary inquiry that reveals compromising correspondence between the Duke of York's secretary and the French court. Charles II dissolves the Parliament and calls a new election, the first since 1661. At the same time the expiration of the Licensing Act unleashes a torrent of propagandistic literature on a scale unseen since the early 1640s. In this heated atmosphere two political coalitions —each given their lasting name by their adversaries—take shape: Whigs (the term was originally applied to Scottish rebels) favor a bill to formally exclude the Duke of York from the succession; Tories (Irish cattle brigands) defend royal prerogative and warn against a repeat of the disorders of the Civil War. After the election Charles II quickly dissolves the new parliament, which again favors exclusion, and summons a third, this time to meet in Oxford, away from the Whig power center in London. Finally, Charles II secures a secret subsidy from Louis XIV of France that frees him from financial dependence on Parliament, and he once more dissolves the body, ending the Exclusion Crisis.

1681 Repaying a debt owed to Penn's father, Charles grants to William Penn the last large unallocated tract of American territory at his disposal. Penn, sole proprietor of the new colony of Pennsylvania, is a Quaker, a member of one of the more radical sects born amid the tumult of the Civil War. Penn's First Frame of Government (1682) establishes civil liberties, an elected assembly, and an appointed governor representing the proprietor. With its guarantees of religious liberty and easy access to land, Pennsylvania will attract large numbers of migrants from Europe, including some 100,000 Germans by 1775. Penn grants the three Lower Counties (Delaware) their own assembly in 1704.

1684 In an effort to exercise greater control over Massachusetts, the Crown issues a *quo warranto* writ for its 1629 charter, and dispatches commissioners to ensure compliance. Massachusetts becomes a royal colony, though the incumbent governor and General Court continue to govern until 1686.

1685 With the death of Charles II, who converts to Catholicism on his deathbed, his brother, the Duke of York, ascends to the throne as James II (1685–89). Charles's illegitimate son, James Scott, the Duke of Monmouth, a Protestant, challenges his uncle for the throne. His West Country rebellion is put down at the battle of Sedgemoor and he is executed for treason. In the ensuing "Bloody Assizes" presided over by George Jeffreys, lord chief justice of the King's Bench, scores of Monmouth's followers are tried and executed and some eight hundred are transported to Barbados.

1686–88 Continuing the project of streamlining the administration of the colonies begun under his brother, James II consolidates the territories of Connecticut, Rhode Island,

Plymouth, Massachusetts, and New Hampshire into the Dominion of New England and appoints Edmund Andros as its governor. In 1688, New York and East and West Jersey are added to the territory, which Andros governs from Boston, where the introduction of Anglicanism, together with the governor's arbitrary manner, makes the Dominion intensely unpopular.

1688–89   Popular opinion in England is inflamed when James II's second wife, Mary of Modena, also a Catholic, gives birth to a son. The child raises the specter of a Catholic succession and is denounced as a fraud. Whig leaders who favor the succession of James's eldest daughter, Mary, a Protestant and wife of the Dutch prince William of Orange, leader of the Protestant coalition arrayed against the forces of Louis XIV, appeal to the couple to claim the throne. On November 5 (Guy Fawkes Day) William lands a large multinational force at Torbay in the southwest of England, and as English nobles and officers defect to his standard, James II flees into exile in France. William III (1689–1702) and Mary II (1689–94) are proclaimed joint monarchs on February 13, 1689. (The following month James II lands in Ireland with a large French army, and quickly secures control of most of the island.) The Glorious Revolution, as it is called, imposes new limitations on the monarchy: Parliament enacts a Bill of Rights that prohibits the keeping of a standing army or the levying of taxes without its consent and defines the terms of the royal succession, definitively excluding Catholics from the throne.

The Revolution also spawns a series of "rebellions" in the American colonies, where popular leaders capitalize on the instability to overthrow colonial structures that had been established under the Stuarts, especially the Dominion of New England, or that are associated with Catholicism, as is the proprietary government of Maryland. Connecticut and Rhode Island are restored to the status they had prior to the Dominion and New Hampshire, New York, and New Jersey are reconstituted as royal colonies. Ascension to the English throne greatly strengthens William's hand in his contest with France as England and Scotland join the League of Augsburg in opposition to Louis XIV and become embroiled in the Nine Years' War (1688–97). The conflict is known as King William's War in North America, the first of several that will be fought over the next seventy years between the English colonies, especially in New England, and New France and its Indian allies.

1690   William defeats James at the battle of the Boyne in Ireland in July, and in a little over a year completes the re-conquest of the island. The Irish Parliament introduces a comprehensive series of penal laws that will effectively bar Catholics from public life throughout the eighteenth century.

1691   Massachusetts and Maryland are granted new royal charters. In royal colonies the form of government is established by the royal governor's commission from the king. This generally provides for a legislature composed of a council appointed by the Crown and an elected assembly or house of representatives that, together with the governor (who wields a veto), is empowered to make laws for the colony, with the stipulation that any such laws may be nullified by the Crown if found contrary to those of England.

1696   Administration of the colonies, previously the domain of ad hoc committees of the Privy Council, is formalized with William's appointment of the Lords Commissioners of Trade and Foreign Plantations, an eight-member committee commonly known as the Board of Trade. Among other functions, the Board funnels information received from the colonies to the secretary of the Southern Department and relays his instructions to the colonial governors.

1698   A year after English weavers, dyers, and linen drapers, threatened by its importation of Indian cloth, attacked the East India Company's London headquarters, and amid growing criticism of the Company's monopoly from English merchants, Parliament establishes a new East India Company to rival the existing one. It also ends the monopoly of the Royal African Company, greatly expanding the slave trade. French settlements are established near the mouth of the Mississippi, reinforcing France's claim to the vast territory of Louisiana, which extends to Canada in an arc around the English colonies.

1700   Between 377,000 and 397,000 individuals have emigrated from the British Isles to America over the course of the seventeenth century, the overwhelming majority from England and Wales. In the first eighty years of the eighteenth century 270,000 more will make the crossing.

Seventy percent of these emigrants will come from Scotland and Ireland.

1701   In the Act of Settlement, Parliament makes provision for succession in the event of the deaths of William and his heir presumptive, Princess Anne, both of whom are childless. (Queen Mary died in 1694.) The crown will revert to the nearest Protestant claimant, in this case Sophia, Elector of Hanover, twelfth child of Elizabeth, daughter of James I and wife of Frederick V, the Elector Palatine.

1702   With the death of William III, his sister-in-law Anne (1702–14), the last of the Stuarts, assumes the throne. After a brief interlude war resumes among the European powers, this time over control of the Spanish throne. The War of the Spanish Succession (1701–14) reignites conflict in North America, where it is known as Queen Anne's War (1702–13).

1704–5 The Scottish Parliament passes the Act of Security, stipulating that it will not accept the Hanoverian succession unless Scotland's constitutional, economic, and religious liberties are secured. The English Parliament retaliates with the Aliens Act, which categorizes Scots as foreign nationals and bars them from trade in England or its colonies. Troubled, however, by the looming threat of rebellion in Scotland, where the Stuarts retain popular support, especially in the Highlands, the English include a suspending clause in the Aliens Act to be triggered if the Scottish Parliament appoints commissioners to treat for union between the two kingdoms.

1707   The Act of Union formally combines England and Scotland into Great Britain, guaranteeing the Hanoverian succession over the unified realm. The Scottish Parliament is dissolved, but the Scots receive forty-five seats in the House of Commons and sixteen in the House of Lords in the British Parliament at Westminster. The Scots also gain legal access to the empire's extensive overseas markets and Scottish merchants will figure prominently in Britain's colonial trade, especially in the tobacco-growing colonies in America.

1709   The rival East India Companies are consolidated into the United East India Company, which receives a grant of £3 million from the Crown.

1710   Parliament incorporates the existing colonial postal services within that of Great Britain and Ireland.

1713   The Treaty of Utrecht, ending the War of the Spanish Succession, confirms Spanish authority in South America and awards Great Britain the asiento, an exclusive thirty-year contract to supply slaves to the Spanish colonies. The monopoly is in turn granted to the South Sea Company, a joint-stock venture, in exchange for its taking on government debt accumulated during the war. Under the terms of the treaty Britain also gains Gibraltar and Minorca from Spain, greatly enhancing its naval position in the Mediterranean, and Acadia (present-day New Brunswick and Nova Scotia excepting Cape Breton Island) and Newfoundland from France, strengthening its control of the valuable North Atlantic fishing banks.

1714   Queen Anne dies on August 1. Sophia of Hanover having died in the spring, Sophia's eldest son becomes George I (1714–27), King of Great Britain and Ireland. The new king, who does not speak English, retains his title as Elector of Hanover and will spend much of his reign in the German territory. The shift of power embodied by Parliament's control of the royal succession accelerates a transition, begun with the Glorious Revolution, to a cabinet-style government, in which crown authority is controlled by a group of ministers which must maintain majority support in Parliament to be effective. At the same time the royal negative, the prerogative right to refuse assent to parliamentary measures, falls into disuse.

1715   Having engineered the succession, Whigs win a convincing victory in parliamentary elections over the Tories, who object to the deviation from hereditary rule. Whigs will remain politically ascendant for the next fifty years, as Tories are marginalized at the Hanoverian court. In Scotland, embittered supporters of the deposed Stuarts (Jacobites) rise in an ill-fated and underfunded rebellion in support of James II's son James Francis Edward Stuart, "The Old Pretender" to his Whig detractors. Maryland reverts to proprietary control when Benedict Calvert, 4th Baron Baltimore, converts to Protestantism.

1718   The Transportation Act allows for penal transportation to British colonies. Some 50,000 convicts will be brought to America by 1775. Large-scale migration of Scots and

Irish-born Presbyterians from Ulster to America also begins. As many as 200,000 Scots-Irish will cross the Atlantic by 1775, more than two-thirds of those in the decade from 1765 to 1775; most will pass through colonial ports and into the hinterlands, especially the backcountries of Pennsylvania, Virginia, and the Carolinas.

1720   In order to settle a constitutional dispute provoked by jurisdictional claims made by the Irish House of Lords, Parliament passes an "Act for the better securing the Dependency of the Kingdom of Ireland upon the Crown of Great Britain," sometimes called the Irish Declaratory Act, asserting its "full power and authority to make laws and statutes of sufficient validity to bind the Kingdom and people of Ireland." Bolstered by rumors of the vast riches to be had in overseas trade and by the implied endorsement of the government, which continues to exchange debt for company stock, shares in the South Sea Company soar to more than ten times their initial value. When investor confidence in the Company begins to wane in July and a sell-off begins, the stock quickly plummets in value, and the South Sea Bubble bursts.

1721   Parliamentary investigations of the Bubble lead to impeachment or resignation of several cabinet ministers and Robert Walpole assumes the post of chancellor of the Exchequer. He emerges as a driving force in the cabinet, and from his leadership position in the House of Commons, he will control the government for the next twenty years, effectively inaugurating the position of prime minister.

1727   George II (1727–60) succeeds to the throne on the death of his father. Walpole remains in the premiership and extends the Whig ministry's control over Parliament through the use of crown patronage.

1729   Indian wars in the province of Carolina having exposed divisions between the colony's northern and southern sections and the weakness of proprietary rule in both, the Crown buys out the Proprietors' heirs and creates the separate royal colonies of North Carolina and South Carolina.

1732   Parliament grants a twenty-one-year charter to a group of trustees led by James Oglethorpe to found a colony between South Carolina and Spanish Florida. Conceived in part as a refuge for debtors, and established with an idealistic legal code that bans slavery and alcohol, the new colony of Georgia does not attract settlers and is eventually converted to a royal colony in 1752.

1733   In an effort to establish a monopoly within the empire for the sugar cane growers of Britain's West Indian colonies, Parliament passes the Molasses Act, imposing a prohibitory tax of six pence per gallon on all foreign molasses entering British America. But because the British West Indies produce far too little molasses to meet the demand on the American mainland, where it is distilled into rum, the act is widely flouted by smuggling.

1740   Parliament passes the Plantation or Naturalization Act, stipulating that foreign-born Protestants residing in any of the American colonies for a period of seven years who swear allegiance to the king and to "the true faith of a Christian . . . should be deemed, adjudged, and taken to be his Majesty's natural born subjects of this kingdom."

1744–48 During King George's War, the North American theater of the War of Austrian Succession (1740–48), New England forces capture the French fortress at Louisbourg on Cape Breton Island. Subsequent attempts to organize an intercolonial invasion of Canada fail, and frontier settlements from Maine to New York face depredations from the French and their Indian allies. The Treaty of Aix-la-Chapelle ending the war returns Louisbourg to the French in exchange for concessions in India, angering American colonists. The Earl of Halifax assumes the presidency of the Board of Trade, and will exercise a steady hand on colonial affairs until his resignation in 1761.

1745–46 From the Jacobite stronghold of the Scottish Highlands, Charles Edward Stuart, grandson of James II, mounts an invasion of England that advances as far as Derby before turning back for want of support from the French. His forces are finally defeated at Culloden in the Highlands, and the fractious region is subjected to harsh reprisals that effectively end the Jacobite threat for good.

1750   In an influential, widely reprinted sermon entitled *A Discourse Concerning Unlimited Submission*, Boston minister Jonathan Mayhew uses the occasion of the anniversary of the execution of Charles I (who has become memorialized as a martyr in the Church of England) to make the case for resistance "made in defence of the natural and legal rights of the people, against the unnatural and illegal encroachments of arbitrary power."

1751   Responding to protests from English merchants who object to the use of public bills of credit issued by the colonial assemblies in New England to pay private debts, Parliament passes an act prohibiting the use of such bills as legal tender and restricting further such currency emissions.

1754   Competing claims by Virginia, Pennsylvania, and France to the Ohio River Valley, which is also contested by various Indian tribes, spark a conflict that ignites the French and Indian War (1754–63), the last of the North American colonial wars between Britain and France. Delegates from seven colonies north of Virginia meet in Albany to lay plans for collective defense. The delegates endorse a Plan of Union proposed by Benjamin Franklin of Pennsylvania and Thomas Hutchinson of Massachusetts which would create an intercolonial Grand Council to regulate Indian affairs, resolve territorial disputes between colonies, and provide for coordinated military action. The Grand Council would be empowered to requisition funds from the colonies according to an agreed-upon formula to fulfill its aims. The Albany Plan of Union comes to naught when the colonial assemblies reject or ignore it, and look instead to the British government to take the lead in the management of the conflict, which in 1756 will expand into the global Seven Years' War.

1755   British influence in the Ohio Valley suffers a major setback when, on July 9, a large force of British regulars and colonial volunteers under General Edward Braddock are ambushed by French and Indian forces near Fort Duquesne and routed. Other expeditions against French fortresses at Niagara and Crown Point are also unsuccessful. Only in Nova Scotia are key French posts taken, precipitating the forced expulsion of some five to seven thousand French Canadians (Acadians) who refuse to swear an oath of allegiance.

1757   Although Anglo-Americans outnumber the population of New France by more than twenty to one, French forces under commander in chief Louis Joseph Montcalm maintain the offensive initiative, and friction hinders a coordinated response from the British colonies. Franklin, who as

a leader in the Pennsylvania Assembly has been pressing
for the revocation of the Penn family's proprietary exemption from land taxes, accepts the Assembly's nomination
to serve as its agent in London. He will remain in England
for most of the next eighteen years, eventually serving as
agent for Georgia, New Jersey, and Massachusetts as well
as Pennsylvania, which he will seek to have converted into
a royal colony. William Pitt, as secretary of state for the
Southern Department, assumes a leading role in the Whig
ministry of the Duke of Newcastle, directing the war effort
("I know that I can save this country and that no one else
can"). Newcastle had previously served for twenty-four
years in the Southern Department and he and Pitt share a
conviction that the key to victory in North America is the
effective mobilization of colonial soldiers. Pitt proposes to
reimburse colonial governments for the cost of raising and
maintaining provincial troops.

1758   The colonies muster 21,000 troops in response to Pitt's
offer, enabling new commander in chief General Jeffery
Amherst to mount successful attacks against Fort Duquesne,
renamed Fort Pitt (Pittsburgh), and Louisbourg, turning
the tide of the conflict in North America. In Virginia, in
order to relieve taxpayers in the wake of droughts which
have led to short crops, the House of Burgesses passes the
second of the so-called Twopenny Acts, temporary measures permitting the commutation of payments to the
colony's established Anglican clergy at a rate of two pence
per pound of tobacco, the traditional medium of exchange.
Because these acts are designed to deal with an exigent
situation, they do not contain the standard suspending
clause required under the colony's charter, which stipulates that all acts are in abeyance until approved by the
Crown. The colony's Anglican ministers appeal to London
for redress.

1759   Anglo-American forces drive the French from northern
New York in a campaign that culminates in the capture of
the fortress city of Quebec on September 18. This triumph,
coupled with decisive British victories on land and sea in
Europe, prompts many in the empire to christen this the
Annus Mirabilis. On August 10, after hearings before the
Board of Trade, the Privy Council disallows the Twopenny
Acts (which in any case have already expired) and repri-

mands Virginia's royal governor for having signed the 1758 measure. This doctrinaire interpretation of the charter is viewed by many Americans as a threat to their traditional self-government of internal affairs. The Council at the same time declines to award the ministers back pay for the period the law was in effect, opening the way for a series of lawsuits in Virginia known as the Parsons' Cause, in which Patrick Henry will rise to prominence.

1760   In southern India, forces of the British East India Company score a victory over those of the French, opening the way to its control of the region. Organized French resistance in North America ends with the British capture of Montreal on September 8 and Detroit on September 15. George II dies suddenly on October 25 and is succeeded by his twenty-two-year-old grandson, George III (1760–1820), whose father, Frederick, Prince of Wales, had died in 1751. The new king, the first of the Hanoverians to speak English as his primary language, resolves to take a more active leadership role than either of his predecessors.

1761   In February, in arguments before the Massachusetts Superior Court, presided over by Chief Justice Thomas Hutchinson, Boston lawyer James Otis challenges the constitutionality of general writs of assistance (search warrants) which, in furtherance of the Navigation Acts, authorize customs officers to search any ship or building they suspect contains contraband goods, and to demand the assistance of local law enforcement in conducting the searches. After the death of George II, Massachusetts customs officials had petitioned the court to renew their writs, which expire six months following the death of the sovereign in whose name they are issued. Otis, the advocate general of the Boston vice-admiralty court, has resigned his position in order to appear before the superior court on behalf of Boston merchants challenging the petition. Otis loses the case, but of his impassioned attack on what he considers arbitrary power, John Adams, who is present in the courtroom, later recalls: "Then and there the child Independence was born." In March, George III installs his longtime tutor John Stuart, 3rd Earl of Bute, a Scotsman and a Tory, as secretary of state for the Northern Department. The king is determined on peace, and Pitt, under pressure to conclude negotiations contrary to his desire to further Britain's gains by declaring war on Spain, resigns in October.

1762   Having stated the year before that he would oppose "any alteration, that may be proposed of the present Constitution, or receiv'd usage and practice, with regard either to Scotland, Ireland, or our Settlements in America," Newcastle falls out with Bute and resigns in May and Bute becomes the prime minister. Despite long-standing English antipathy for standing armies, the king and his new advisors make provisions for the maintenance of a peacetime army in North America, concluding that only such a force can preserve order among the many restive parts of the now greatly expanded empire. The annual cost of maintaining ten regiments in North America is more than £300,000. This, coupled with the reimbursement to the colonial assemblies of their war-related expenses, inflames opinion against Americans among taxpayers in Britain, where hopes for a peace dividend evaporate in the face of a national debt that has nearly doubled in less than a decade.

1763   As negotiations proceed toward a formal end to the Seven Years' War, the British press debates the merits of retaining the rich sugar islands of Guadeloupe and Martinique captured from the French, and returning Canada to the French, but the government finally decides to relinquish the islands. The Treaty of Paris, signed on February 10, formalizes British control of the North American continent from the Gulf of Mexico to Hudson Bay. Fearing that this uncontested hegemony will accelerate colonial encroachment on their lands, and angered by their treatment at the hands of General Amherst, Indians in the Ohio Valley rise up in May under the leadership of an Ottawa leader and destroy all British posts in the region except Fort Pitt and Detroit. Confronted with Pontiac's Rebellion, as this uprising becomes known, as well as a welter of conflicting and competing colonial claims to western lands, George III issues on October 7 a proclamation barring colonial settlement beyond, roughly, the Appalachian ridge line. The proclamation also establishes royal colonies in Quebec and East and West Florida, which the Crown hopes will serve as alternative sites for expansion. Meanwhile, Bute's decision to retire in April in the face of vehement attacks from the press, much of it, like John Wilkes's scandalous newspaper *North Briton*, fueled by anti-Scot bigotry, elevates George Grenville, First Lord of the Treasury, to the premiership. Grenville faces an early confidence vote when opposition forces led by Newcastle and Pitt challenge the Crown's use of general warrants to silence the press criticism, but prevails, largely owing to the support of the Scottish bloc in Parliament.

1764   In January, armed Pennsylvania frontiersmen, known as the Paxton Boys, march to Philadelphia to remonstrate against the colonial government, which they feel has been inattentive to their security amid the ongoing hostilities related to Pontiac's Rebellion. In London, on March 9, Grenville proposes a revision of the 1733 Molasses Act to make it more productive of revenue. The rationale for the proposed bill is made clear in its text: "it is just and necessary, that a revenue be raised, in your Majesty's said dominions in America, for defraying the expenses of defending, protecting, and securing the same." At the same time Grenville introduces complicated new regulations designed to further combat smuggling by funneling colonial trade to or through British ports and by creating a vice-admiralty court in Halifax, Nova Scotia, where customs violators can be prosecuted without obstruction from sympathetic colonial juries. In his remarks Grenville suggests the possibility of a further revenue measure, a stamp tax. Parliament passes the American Revenue Act, better known as the Sugar Act, on April 5. Parliament also passes a Currency Act extending the provisions of the 1751 act (which in the interest of harmony the British government had not enforced during the war) to the colonies south of New England. By year's end, petitions protesting Parliament's actions are endorsed by the assemblies of Massachusetts, Rhode Island, Connecticut, New York, Pennsylvania, Virginia, North Carolina, and South Carolina.

1765   By forestalling to the next parliamentary session action on a stamp tax—which, rather than regulating trade through an *external* duty, will impose an *internal* tax on the paper used in the colonies for newspapers, almanacs, pamphlets, broadsides, and legal and commercial documents—Grenville intends to provide the colonies an opportunity to suggest alternative measures for raising revenues to defray the costs of maintaining British forces in North America. However, no official requests are made to the colonial assemblies or to the colonial governors, through the Board of Trade or otherwise, and no alternatives are forthcoming. At a last-minute meeting on February 2 with Grenville, four colonial agents, including Franklin, present petitions from their assemblies protesting the proposed measure, but the House of Commons, in keeping with its traditional practice, refuses to hear appeals related to a money bill. The ministry presses ahead with the measure in the Commons, insisting, in the words of a government spokesperson, on "the important point it establishes, the right of Parliament to lay an internal tax on the colonies. We wonder here that it was ever doubted. There is not a single member of Parliament that will dispute it." By a large majority the Commons passes the Stamp Act on February 27; it receives the royal assent on March 22 and is scheduled to go into effect on November 1. On May 15, Parliament passes the Quartering Act, requiring colonial assemblies, in the absence of barracks, to provide for the billeting of His Majesty's troops in private buildings, taverns, and inns at the colonies' expense.

News of the Stamp Act's passage reaches America in April and the Virginia House of Burgesses on May 30 adopts a series of resolves introduced by Patrick Henry, among them "that the Taxation of the People by themselves, or by Persons chosen by themselves to represent them . . . is the distinguishing Characteristick of *British* Freedom." On June 8, the Massachusetts House of Representatives issues a circular letter to the other colonial assemblies calling upon them to send delegates to a congress in New York "to consider of a general and united, dutiful, loyal and humble, Representation of their Condition to His Majesty and the Parliament; and to implore Relief." Popular protests against the Stamp Act occur throughout the colonies during the summer. In Boston—where active opponents of the Stamp Act will adopt the name "Sons of Liberty" by the end of the year—mobs loot the homes of Andrew Oliver, a prominent merchant who had been appointed stamp distributor for Massachusetts, on August 14, and of Lieutenant Governor Thomas Hutchinson (Oliver's brother-in-law) on August 26. Similar actions follow in other colonial ports, and by the end of October all but two of the stamp distributors, those for North Carolina and Georgia, resign in the face of intimidation and violence. The holdouts will not give way until November and January respectively, but the act is essentially nullified before the date it is scheduled to take effect. The Stamp Act Congress, comprising twenty-seven delegates from nine colonies, meets in New York's City Hall, October 7–25, and issues a Declaration of the Rights and Grievances of the Colonies calling for repeal.

1766   The Grenville ministry having been dismissed in July 1765 for reasons unrelated to the American controversy, the new administration of Lord Rockingham engineers repeal of the Stamp Act on March 18; at the same time Parliament passes the Declaratory Act, which asserts its authority to legislate for the colonies "in all cases whatsoever." On June 6, in a bid to further calm tensions, Parliament passes a Revenue Act, further reducing the duty on molasses from three pence per gallon to just one. In July, Pitt, whose health is poor and who no longer commands a large following in the Commons, assumes the premiership once more when Rockingham is dismissed, again for reasons unrelated to the colonial dispute. Pitt is elevated to the peerage as the Earl of Chatham, and governs from the House of Lords. In New York, in defiance of the Quartering Act, the Assembly refuses to fully fund a request for provisions submitted by General Thomas Gage, commander of British forces in North America, who maintains his headquarters in New York City. Chatham alienates many in his cabinet when he launches an investigation into the financial management of the East India Company and calls for the transferal to the Crown of its territorial holdings in India, which have grown extensive. Before he can implement his plan, Chatham's gout forces him to retire to Bath in December.

1767   In the absence of strong leadership from Chatham, Charles Townshend, chancellor of the Exchequer, emerges as the driving force in the ministry. On May 13, seizing on the distinction between internal and external taxation that has emerged from the Stamp Act controversy, he proposes duties on lead, glass, paper, tea, and other goods imported into the colonies. The ministry also proposes the New

York Restraining Act, suspending the New York Assembly until it complies with the Quartering Act. After negotiations with the East India Company (of which Townshend is a shareholder), the ministry also proposes the Indemnity Act, which lowers taxes on Company tea imported to England and allows a drawback on the export of tea to Ireland and the British colonies in America in exchange for an annual payment to the Exchequer and the right to retain its territory in India. To streamline enforcement of the new duties, the ministry further proposes to establish a board of customs commissioners to be based in Boston, where resistance to customs regulations is most pronounced, along with three new admiralty courts in Philadelphia, Charleston, and Boston, to supplement the one previously established in Halifax. Passed by the House of Commons on July 2, the Townshend Acts renew tensions in America. In June, on receiving news of the proposed suspension, the New York Assembly quickly passes an act fulfilling the terms of the Quartering Act. Townshend dies on September 4 and is replaced by Frederick North (called Lord North as a courtesy title).

1768   On February 11, the Massachusetts House of Representatives adopts a petition, written by Samuel Adams, protesting the Townshend Acts. After the protest is circulated to the other colonial assemblies, Massachusetts governor Francis Bernard dissolves the General Court, prompting further popular unrest. In response to the mounting crisis, the British government creates a third secretary of state responsible specifically for colonial administration. The Earl of Hillsborough, a hardliner on American affairs who had been president of the Board of Trade, assumes the post and quickly runs afoul of colonial leaders with his imperious response to the Massachusetts Circular Letter. Demonstrations in Boston in March lead the harried customs commissioners to request that troops be sent to Boston to maintain order. Contrary to Hillsborough's orders, the Massachusetts House—by a vote of 92–17, enshrining the number 92 in patriot political discourse—refuses to rescind its resolutions, and several other colonial assemblies issue similar statements. In May the British warship *Romney* arrives in Boston. Further harassment of customs officials follows the seizure in June of John Hancock's sloop *Liberty* on suspicion of smuggling. In late summer, merchants in Boston and New York adopt agreements to cease importing most goods from Britain until the Townshend duties are repealed. The first British troops land in Boston on October 1.

1769   Debate on American affairs resumes in the House of Commons as the ministry successfully moves a motion for an address to the king pledging the nation to support all measures necessary "to maintain entire and inviolate the supreme authority of the Legislature of Great Britain over every part of the British empire." Premised on the idea that the disorder in Massachusetts has been produced by a small number of rabble-rousers, among the measures contemplated is the extension to the colonies of a treason law from the reign of Henry VIII, enabling the Crown to bring the ringleaders to England for trial. The idea is never implemented, but it nonetheless provokes considerable anger in America. In February merchants in Philadelphia adopt a non-importation agreement similar to those in Boston and New York. Other colonies follow suit, and in May the Virginia House of Burgesses passes resolves again denying Parliament's right to tax colonies. When the royal governor promptly dissolves the House, the Burgesses reconvene at a nearby tavern and adopt non-importation. British manufacturers and traders begin to agitate for repeal of the Townshend duties. Hillsborough sends a circular letter to the colonial governors in May announcing that the cabinet has decided to propose repeal of the duties in the next session of Parliament.

1770   Long-simmering tensions in Boston erupt when on March 5 British soldiers under Captain Thomas Preston open fire on an angry, taunting crowd, killing five Boston residents. In the aftermath, facing the prospect of what he calls a "general insurrection" among Bostonians, Massachusetts's acting governor Thomas Hutchinson arranges to have British troops removed to Castle William in Boston Harbor to avoid further clashes. On April 12 Parliament votes to repeal most of the Townshend duties, retaining only the duty on tea, which the cabinet of Lord North, who has succeeded to head of the Treasury and prime minister in January, preserves by a five-to-four vote in order to maintain the principle of parliamentary sovereignty. In late autumn, John Adams leads the defense at the trials of Captain Preston and eight of his soldiers charged in the "Boston Massacre." Preston and his men are acquitted save for two, who are convicted of manslaughter and branded on the thumb. Repeal of the Townshend duties results in the collapse of the non-importation movement in the colonies and a general easing of tensions with the mother country.

1771   As the imperial controversy absorbs the major port cities in the colonies, persistent frictions on the frontier flare in the contested borderlands between New York and New Hampshire, where the Green Mountain Boys have become a de facto government, and in western North Carolina, where bands of self-appointed "Regulators" disrupt the mechanisms of a provincial government they believe to be corrupt and unconcerned with their interests. The Regulator Movement culminates on May 16 at the battle of Alamance, when the royal governor and twelve hundred militia defeat a force of two thousand poorly organized Regulators.

1772   On June 9, citizens of Providence burn the *Gaspee*, a British revenue schooner, when it runs aground in Narragansett Bay. A special royal commission is appointed to investigate the incident but cannot gather the names of anyone to punish. In his June 22 judgment in the *Somersett* case, Lord Mansfield, chief justice of the King's Bench, rules that no positive law in England permits a slave-owner to forcibly send a slave overseas. Interpretation of his decision by other judges will make slavery legally unenforceable in Britain, eventually resulting in de facto emancipation there. While the case has no effect as a matter of law in the colonies, it does complicate the recurrent American appeals to natural liberty and the rights of Englishmen in their dispute with Parliament. In July, in one of his last acts as secretary of state for the Colonies, Hillsborough issues an order that the salaries of the judges of the Massachusetts Superior Court be paid by the Crown, instead of the General Court, an inflammatory move designed to insulate the judges from the influence of popular opinion.

1773   In March, the Virginia House of Burgesses elects a standing Committee of Correspondence to communicate and coordinate with other assemblies. Other colonial legislatures follow suit over the course of the year. With the East India Company approaching insolvency, Parliament in May passes the Regulating Act, establishing a new governing structure for the Company, and the Tea Act, granting it a monopoly on the sale of tea in the colonies. The first of three ships carrying East India Company tea arrives in Boston on November 28. Duty is payable upon off-loading, which must by law be accomplished within twenty days of docking, but which Boston mobs prevent. Governor Hutchinson refuses entreaties to allow the ships to depart with their cargo, which defuses similar situations in other colonial ports, and as the deadline approaches a large crowd boards the ships on December 16 and dumps 342 chests of tea, worth an estimated £10,000, into the harbor.

1774 News of the destruction of the East India Company's tea reaches London on January 19. In response to the Boston Tea Party, Parliament passes four measures that become known as the Coercive Acts, but which American patriots will call the Intolerable Acts. The Boston Port Act closes Boston's harbor, effective June 1, until "peace and obedience to the laws" are restored in the town and its people pay for the destroyed tea. The Massachusetts Government Act abrogates Massachusetts's 1691 royal charter by removing power of appointing the governor's council from the elected assembly and giving it to the king. It also gives the royal governor power to appoint (or nominate, for the king's assent) all provincial judges and sheriffs, makes the sheriffs responsible for choosing jury panels, and severely restricts town meetings. The Administration of Justice Act allows trials of those accused of committing capital crimes while enforcing the law or collecting revenue to be removed to Britain or Nova Scotia. The Quartering Act allows quartering of troops in occupied dwellings throughout the colonies. (The Quebec Act, which establishes civil government for Quebec without an elected legislature, grants the Roman Catholic Church the right to collect tithes, and potentially extends the province's borders to the Mississippi and Ohio rivers, is viewed as a hostile measure by many colonists, and comes to be regarded as one of the Intolerable Acts.) General Thomas Gage, commander in chief of British forces in North America, is commissioned as royal governor of Massachusetts and arrives in Boston on May 13; British troops begin landing in the city in mid-June. Unable to enforce the law outside of Boston, Gage begins fortifying the city on September 3.

 The Coercive Acts electrify public opinion in America, and calls for an intercolonial congress to propose common measures of resistance are made in Providence, Philadelphia, New York, and Williamsburg, Virginia, in May. The First Continental Congress opens in Philadelphia on September 5 and is eventually attended by fifty-six delegates. On September 17 it endorses the Suffolk County Resolves, recently adopted by a convention in Massachusetts, which declare that no obedience is due the Coercive Acts and advocate measures of resistance, including the formation of a provincial congress, nonpayment of taxes, the boycott of British goods, and weekly militia training. On October 14 Congress adopts a series of declarations and resolves that denounce the Coercive Acts and Quebec Act as "impolitic, unjust, and cruel, as well as unconstitutional"; call for the repeal of several other laws passed since 1763; protest the dissolution of elected assemblies and the royal appointment of colonial councils; and condemn the keeping of a standing army in the colonies in peacetime, without the consent of colonial legislatures, as "against law." Congress votes on October 18 to create the Continental Association, modeled on the Virginia Association formed in early August. Its articles pledge the colonies to discontinue the slave trade and cease importing goods from Great Britain, Ireland, and the East and West Indies after December 1, 1774; to cease consuming British goods after March 1, 1775; and, if necessary, to cease all exports (excluding rice) to Britain, Ireland, and the West Indies after September 10, 1775. The Association is to be enforced by elected town, city, and county committees, which will punish violators by publicity and boycott. After preparing addresses to the British people and to the king, Congress calls on the people of the colonies to elect deputies to provincial congresses, which in turn will elect delegates to a second congress, called for May 10, 1775. Congress adjourns October 26. By the end of the year, provincial congresses or conventions have been formed in eight colonies.

1775   On February 9 Parliament declares Massachusetts to be in rebellion. The House of Commons endorses on February 27 a conciliatory proposal by the North ministry, under which Parliament would refrain from laying revenue taxes upon the colonies if the colonial assemblies agree to levy their own taxes to support imperial defense. General Gage receives orders from the ministry on April 14 (written January 27 but not dispatched until March 13) directing him to use force against the Massachusetts rebels. The Revolutionary War begins when a British force attempts to destroy military supplies at Concord, leading to fighting with militia at Lexington, Concord, and along the road back to Boston on April 19. Massachusetts forces thereafter begin a siege of Boston.

The Second Continental Congress meets in Philadelphia on May 10, with representatives from every state except Georgia present. The Massachusetts Provincial Congress asks Congress for advice on establishing a government during the conflict with Great Britain. Congress responds on June 9 by recommending that the colony elect a new assembly and council to govern itself until the Crown agrees to abide by the 1691 charter (the new Massachusetts legislature meets in late July, with the council serving as the executive). Congress votes on June 14 to form a Continental army. John Adams nominates Virginia delegate George Washington as its commander, and he is unanimously approved on June 15, just two days before the battle of Bunker Hill is fought at Charlestown, Massachusetts (Washington assumes command in Cambridge, Massachusetts, on July 3). To finance the army, Congress votes on June 22 to issue $2 million in paper money not backed by specie and pledges that the "12 Confederated Colonies" will redeem the issue.

On July 5 Congress approves the Olive Branch Petition, a conciliatory message to George III drafted by John Dickinson, and on July 6 adopts the Declaration of the Causes and Necessities of Taking Up Arms, drafted by Thomas Jefferson and rewritten by Dickinson. The Declaration disavows any intention to establish American independence, but asserts that colonists are "resolved to die freemen rather than to live slaves" and states that "foreign assistance is undoubtedly attainable" for the colonial cause. Congress appoints commissioners to negotiate with Indians on July 19; establishes a post office department headed by Benjamin Franklin on July 26; and rejects Lord North's proposal for conciliation on July 31, before adjourning on August 2. George III rejects the Olive Branch Petition and on August 23 proclaims the American colonies to be in rebellion (news which reaches Congress on November 9).

Congress begins organizing a navy in October, appoints on November 29 a five-member Committee of Correspondence to establish contact with foreign supporters (which becomes the Committee for Foreign Affairs on April 17, 1777), and on December 6 disavows allegiance to Parliament. British rule continues to collapse throughout the thirteen colonies in the autumn and winter. George III signs the Prohibitory Act on December 23, closing off commerce with America and making American ships and crews subject to seizure by the Royal Navy.

1776   Congress votes on March 3 to send Silas Deane to Europe to buy military supplies. The British garrison evacuates Boston on March 17 and sails to Nova Scotia. South Carolina's Provincial Congress adopts a plan of government on March 26. Congress opens American ports to all nations except Britain on April 6. North Carolina's Provincial Congress authorizes its delegates on April 12 to vote in Congress for independence, while reserving for North Carolina the "sole and exclusive right" of forming its own constitution and laws.

At the urging of his foreign minister the Comte de Vergennes, Louis XVI of France authorizes clandestine support of the American insurgents on May 2. (After his arrival in Paris on July 7, Silas Deane will work with Vergennes and Pierre de Beaumarchais in arranging covert shipments of arms, supplies, and money, an effort soon joined in by Spain.) Rhode Island's legislature disavows allegiance to George III on May 4. Under the leadership of John Adams and Richard Henry Lee, Congress recommends on May 10 that each of the "United Colonies" form a government and on May 15 calls for royal authority in the colonies to be "totally suppressed." On May 15 the Virginia convention (successor to the convention called by the assembly after its dissolution by Lord Dunmore in 1774) instructs its delegates in Congress to propose a declaration of independence and the formation of a confederation; it also appoints a committee to prepare a declaration of rights and constitution for Virginia. Following these instructions, Richard Henry Lee submits a resolution in Congress on June 7, declaring that "these United Colonies are, and of right ought to be, free and independent States," urging the formation of foreign alliances, and recommending the preparation and transmission of "a plan of confederation" to the colonies for their approval. John Dickinson, James Wilson, Robert R. Livingston, and others argue that an immediate declaration of independence would be premature. Congress postpones decision and refers the resolution on independence to a committee of five (Franklin, John Adams, Livingston, Jefferson, and Roger Sherman) on June 11; Jefferson begins drafting a declaration. On June 12 a resolution to form an American confederation is submitted to a committee of thirteen, consisting of one representative from each colony; its chairman, John Dickinson, begins drafting a confederation plan. On July 1 Congress resumes debate on Lee's independence resolution and approves it on July 2, severing all political ties with Great Britain. After revising Jefferson's draft (changes include the deletion of a passage condemning the slave trade), Congress adopts the Declaration of Independence on July 4.

The Revolutionary War, which with the addition of France, Spain, and the Dutch Republic as belligerents becomes the global War of American Independence, lasts eight years and costs the British at least £80 million. Over its course some 60,000 Loyalists leave America and resettle in other parts of the empire, taking roughly 15,000 slaves with them. In the Treaty of Paris, which formally ends the war in 1783, Great Britain recognizes the independence of the United States with borders extending north to the Great Lakes, west to the Mississippi, and south to the 31st parallel. In doing so it acknowledges the loss of a million square miles of its empire and the allegiance of over two and a half million subjects.

Biographical Notes

EDWARD BANCROFT (January 20, 1745–September 8, 1821) Born in Westfield, Massachusetts, the son of a farmer. Practiced medicine in Dutch Guiana, 1763–66. Moved to England in 1767. Studied at St. Bartholomew's Hospital, London. Published *An Essay on the Natural History of Guiana* (1769), *Remarks on the Review of The Controversy between Great Britain and Her Colonies* (1769), and a deistic novel, *The History of Charles Wentworth, Esq.* (1770). Visited Dutch Guiana in 1770. Became friends with Benjamin Franklin and Joseph Priestley. Studied dyeing and calico printing. Contributed to *The Monthly Review*, 1774–77. Became paid British agent in February 1777. Moved to Paris in April 1777, where he served as unofficial secretary to the American legation while spying on Franklin and his fellow envoys Silas Deane, Arthur Lee, and (later) John Adams. Returned to England in June 1783. Visited the United States, September 1783–84. Continued study of the chemistry of dyes. Published *Experimental Researches Concerning the Philosophy of Permanent Colours* (1794). Died in Margate, Kent.

FRANCIS BERNARD (July 1712–June 6, 1779) Born in Brightwell, Berkshire, the son of an Anglican minister. Educated at St. Peter's College, Westminster, and Christ Church, Oxford. Studied law at the Middle Temple, London, and was admitted to the bar in 1737. Practiced law in Lincolnshire until 1758, when he was appointed governor of New Jersey. Appointed governor of Massachusetts in 1760. Enforced Stamp Act and Townshend Acts in the face of widespread colonial resistance. Dissolved the Massachusetts General Court (legislature) in 1768 after it circulated a protest against Townshend Acts to other colonial assemblies. Requested that British troops be sent to Boston to protect customs commissioners against harassment. Granted baronetcy in 1769. Resigned governorship after *Boston Gazette* published letters in which he advocated that the provincial council be appointed by the Crown. Sailed for England in August 1769. Published *Select Letters on the Trade and Government of America*, written 1763–68, in 1774. Died in Aylesbury, Buckinghamshire.

RICHARD BLAND (May 6, 1710–October 26, 1776) Born in Prince George County, Virginia, the son of a planter. Studied at the College of William and Mary. Inherited family plantations and purchased additional land. Served in the House of Burgesses, 1742–74. Admitted to the bar in 1746. Published *A Letter to the Clergy of Virginia* (1760), asserting the power of the general assembly to set salaries for the colony's clergy; *The Colonel Dismounted: or the Rector Vindicated* (1764), a satirical dialogue defending the legislative and taxing powers of the assembly; and *An Inquiry into the Rights of the British Colonies* (1766). Served as a delegate to the First and Second Continental Congresses, 1774 and 1775; in the Virginia Convention, 1775–76; on the Committee of Safety, 1775–76; and in the House of Delegates, 1776. Helped draft the Virginia Constitution. Died in Williamsburg, Virginia.

JOHN DICKINSON (November 8, 1732–February 14, 1808) Born on family estate in Talbot County, Maryland. Family moved to Kent County, Delaware, in 1740. Studied law in London, 1753–57, and was admitted to the Pennsylvania bar in 1760. Served in the Delaware Assembly, 1760–61, and the Pennsylvania Assembly, 1762–65 and 1770–76. Delegate to the Stamp Act Congress, 1765. Published *Letters from a Farmer in Pennsylvania* (1767–68), a defense of colonial rights. Delegate to the First Continental Congress, 1774, and the Second Continental Congress, 1775–76. Voted against declaring independence; drafted the Articles of Confederation in 1776. Delegate to Congress from Delaware, 1779–80. Served as president of Delaware, 1781–82, and as president of the Pennsylvania supreme executive council, 1782–85. Delegate from Delaware to the Constitutional Convention in 1787. Died in Wilmington, Delaware.

SILAS DOWNER (July 16, 1729–December 15, 1785) Born in Norwich, Connecticut, the son of a farmer. Graduated from Harvard in 1750. Established legal practice in Providence, Rhode Island. Joined the Provincial Committee of Correspondence and the Rhode Island Sons of Liberty in 1766. Served as acting attorney general of Rhode Island in 1766 and helped revise the colony's laws in 1767. Published *A Discourse, Delivered in Providence, in the Colony of Rhode-Island, upon the 25th. Day of July, 1768. At the Dedication of the Tree of Liberty* (1768). Attended the First Continental Congress as clerk of the Rhode Island delegation. Served as clerk to the Rhode Island Council of War during the War of Independence. Died in Roxbury, Massachusetts.

DANIEL DULANY (June 28, 1722–March 17, 1797) Born in Annapolis, Maryland, the son of a lawyer and land speculator. Educated at Eton College and Clare College, Cambridge. Studied law at the Middle Temple, London, and was called to the English bar in 1746. Returned to Maryland in 1747 to practice law. Served in the lower house of the Maryland Assembly, 1751–54 and 1756–57, and on the governor's council, 1757–61 and 1763–74. Visited England, 1761–63 and 1771–72. Published *Considerations on the Propriety of Imposing Taxes in the British Colonies, for the Purpose of Raising a Revenue* (1765). Engaged in newspaper exchange with Charles Carroll of Carrollton in 1773 in which Dulany defended the power of the governor to set officials' fees. Retired to his estate near Baltimore in 1776 and remained there until 1781, when most of his property was confiscated as punishment for his alleged loyalism. Died in Baltimore.

BENJAMIN FRANKLIN (January 17, 1706–April 17, 1790) Born in Boston, the son of a candle and soap maker. Learned printing trade in Boston and London. Settled in Philadelphia in 1726 and bought *The Pennsylvania Gazette* in 1729. Published *Poor Richard's Almanack*, 1732–57. Founded the American Philosophical Society in 1743. Member of the Pennsylvania Assembly, 1751–64. Proposed plan for colonial union in 1754. Elected to the Royal Society in 1756 after conducting series of experiments with electricity. Represented Pennsylvania Assembly in London, 1757–62. Returned to London as Pennsylvania agent in 1764, and by 1770 was also representing Georgia, New Jersey, and Massachusetts. Returned to Philadelphia on May 5, 1775. Served as delegate to the Second Continental Congress, 1775–76. Appointed diplomatic commissioner by Congress on September 26, 1776, and arrived in France on December 3, 1776. Negotiated treaty of alliance with France, 1778, and peace treaty with Britain, 1782. Returned to United States in September 1785. Served as president of the Pennsylvania supreme executive council, 1785–88. Delegate to the Constitutional Convention, 1788. Died in Philadelphia.

WILLIAM HICKS (March 10, 1735–May 25, 1772) Born on Long Island, New York. Admitted to Pennsylvania bar in 1768. Published *The Nature and Extent of Parliamentary Power Considered* (1768). Practiced law in Bucks County. Appointed to Pennsylvania governor's council in 1771. Died in Philadelphia.

STEPHEN HOPKINS (March 7, 1707–July 13, 1785) Born in Providence, Rhode Island, the son of a farmer. After working as farmer and surveyor in Scituate, moved to Providence in 1742 and became a successful merchant and shipbuilder. Served in the Rhode Island house of representatives, 1732–52, 1770–75, 1777–79; as chief justice of the superior court, 1751–55, 1755–56, and 1770–75; and as governor of Rhode Island, 1755–56, 1758–61, 1763–64, and 1767. Attended the Albany Congress, 1754. Helped found the *Providence Gazette*, 1762. Served as the first chancellor of the College of Rhode Island (later Brown University), 1764–85. Published *The Rights of Colonies Examined* (1765). Delegate to the First Continental Congress, 1774, and the Second, 1775–76. Served on the Rhode Island Council of War, 1776–78. Died in Providence.

MARTIN HOWARD (1725?–November 1781) Possibly born in Newport,

Rhode Island, where he later read and practiced law. Published *A Letter from a Gentleman at Halifax, to His Friend in Rhode-Island, Containing Remarks upon a Pamphlet, Entitled, The Rights of Colonies Examined* (1765) and subsequent defenses of same. Sailed to England after his house was ransacked on August 28, 1765, by rioters protesting the Stamp Act. Appointed chief justice of North Carolina in 1766. Became member of the governor's council in 1770. Retired to plantation in Craven County at outbreak of Revolutionary War. Left North Carolina in 1777 after refusing to swear loyalty oath in support of the new state government. Sailed to England in 1778. Died in Chelsea, Middlesex.

WILLIAM KNOX (1732–August 25, 1810) Born in Monaghan, Ireland, the son of a physician. Attended Trinity College. Appointed provost marshal of Georgia in 1756 and served 1757–62. Moved to London in 1762, where he served as colonial agent for Georgia until 1765. Published *The Claim of the Colonies to an Exemption from Internal Taxes Imposed by Authority of Parliament, Examined* (1765), a defense of the constitutionality of the Stamp Act that led to his dismissal by the Georgia Assembly; *The Present State of the Nation* (1768); and *The Controversy between Great Britain and Her Colonies Reviewed* (1769). Appointed undersecretary in the American Department in 1770. Published *The Justice and Policy of the Late Act of Parliament for . . . the Province of Quebec* (1774) and *The Interest of the Merchants and Manufacturers of Great Britain* (1774), a defense of the Coercive Acts. Lost government position in 1782 when the new Rockingham ministry abolished the American Department. Published pamphlet in 1790 defending the slave trade. Died in Ealing, Middlesex.

JAMES OTIS (February 5, 1725–May 23, 1783) Born in West Barnstable, Massachusetts, the son of a lawyer. Graduated from Harvard in 1743 and was admitted to the bar in 1748. Began successful law practice and was appointed crown advocate general of the Boston vice-admiralty court in 1756. Resigned position to argue case before the Massachusetts Superior Court challenging the legality of writs of assistance (general search warrants) issued to royal customs officers; after hearing the case in February 1761 the court upheld the writs. Served in the Massachusetts House of Representatives, 1761–70. Published a series of pamphlets, 1762–65, including *The Rights of the British Colonies Asserted*, defending colonial rights and protesting the Sugar and Stamp acts. Helped organize the Stamp Act Congress in 1765 and the non-importation movement launched in response to the Townshend Acts in 1767. Suffered from mental instability that worsened after he was struck on the head by an English customs officer during a brawl in 1769. Won election to the legislature in 1771, but was soon declared mentally incompetent and placed in the care of his family. Killed by lightning in Andover, Massachusetts.

ALLAN RAMSAY (October 2, 1713–August 10, 1784) Born in Edinburgh, the son of a bookseller. Studied painting in Edinburgh, London, and Italy. Moved to London in 1738 and became successful portrait painter. Published essays *On Ridicule* (1753), *Concerning the Affair of Elizabeth Canning* (1753), *On the Naturalization of Foreigners* (1754) and *A Dialogue on Taste* (1755). Formed friendship with David Hume. Visited Italy, 1754–57. Returned to London in 1757. Painted coronation portraits of George III and Queen Charlotte. Published *An Essay on the Constitution of England* (1765), *Thoughts on the Origin and Nature of Government. Occasioned by the Late Disputes between Great Britain and Her American Colonies* (1768), *An Enquiry into the Rights of the East India Company* (1772), and *A Plan of the Government of Bengal* (1772). Suffered injury to his right arm in 1773 that ended painting career. Visited Italy, 1775–77. Published *Letters on the Present Disturbances in Great Britain and her American Provinces* (1777), *A Succinct Review of the American Contest* (1778), *A Letter to Edmund Burke* (1780), and *Observations on the Riot Act* (1781). Returned to Italy, 1782–84. Died at Dover.

JOSEPH WARREN (May 30, 1741–June 17, 1775) Born in Roxbury, Massachusetts, the son of a farmer. Graduated from Harvard College in 1759. Established medical practice in Boston in 1763. Successfully operated inoculation clinic during smallpox epidemic in 1764. Began contributing pseudonymous letters to the *Boston Gazette* in 1765 in opposition to the Stamp Act and, later, the Townshend Acts. Became active member of the Sons of Liberty. Cowrote pamphlet *A Short Narrative of the Horrid Massacre in Boston* (1770) with James Bowdoin and Samuel Pemberton. Published *An Oration Delivered March 5th, 1772. At the Request of the Inhabitants of the Town of Boston; to Commemorate the Bloody Tragedy of the Fifth of March, 1770* (1772). Helped found the Boston Committee of Correspondence in 1772. Attended Suffolk County Convention in September 1774 and helped draft resolves advocating resistance to the Coercive Acts. Elected to Massachusetts Provincial Congress and became member of the Massachusetts Committee of Safety. Delivered Boston Massacre oration for second time on March 5, 1775. Sent Paul Revere and William Dawes to warn patriots in Lexington of British military expedition from Boston on night of April 18. Elected president of the Provincial Congress on April 23. Killed at battle of Bunker Hill while serving as volunteer with the Massachusetts militia.

THOMAS WHATELY (August 1728–May 26, 1772) Born in Epsom, Surrey, the son of a merchant and banker. Educated at Clare College, Cambridge. Studied law at the Middle Temple, London, and called to the bar in 1751. Member of Parliament for Ludgershall, 1761–68, and

Castle Rising, 1768–72. Became private secretary to George Grenville in 1762 and secretary to the Treasury after Grenville became prime minister in 1763. Played leading role in drafting the American Revenue Act (Sugar Act) of 1764 and the Stamp Act of 1765. Published *Remarks on the Budget* (1765) and *The Regulations Lately Made Concerning the Colonies, and the Taxes Imposed upon Them, Considered* (1765). Went into opposition after Grenville was dismissed in July 1765. Opposed the repeal of the Stamp Act in 1766. Published *Considerations on the Trade and Finance of this Kingdom* (1766), a defense of the Grenville ministry, and *Observations on Modern Gardening* (1770). Returned to office as a supporter of the North ministry, serving on the Board of Trade, 1771–72, and as undersecretary of the Northern Department, 1771–72. Died in Epsom. His unfinished study of Macbeth and Richard III was posthumously published as *Remarks on some of the Characters of Shakespeare* (1785).

JOHN JOACHIM ZUBLY (August 27, 1724–July 23, 1781) Born Hans Joachim Zublin in St. Gall, Switzerland, the son of a weaver. Ordained in the German Reformed Church in London in 1744. Immigrated to South Carolina, where he became pastor of the Wappetaw Independent Congregational Church in Wando Neck. Accepted position as pastor of the Independent Presbyterian Church in Savannah, Georgia, 1760. Published sermons: *The Real Christians Hope in Death* (1756); *The Wise Shining as the Brightness of the Firmament* (1770), on the death of George Whitefield; *The Nature of that Faith, without which It is Impossible to Please God* (1772); and *The Faithful Minister's Course Finished* (1773); as well as political pamphlets: *The Stamp-Act Repealed* (1766); *An Humble Enquiry Into the Nature of the Dependency of the American Colonies Upon the Parliament of Great-Britain* (1769); *Letter to the Reverend Samuel Frink* (1770), an attack on the Anglican establishment in Georgia; *Calm and Respectful Thoughts on the Negative of the Crown on a Speaker* (1772); and *The Law of Liberty* (1775). Attended Second Georgia Provincial Congress in July 1775. Delegate in the fall of 1775 to the Second Continental Congress, where he opposed independence. Resigned after he was discovered corresponding with Sir James Wright, the royal governor of Georgia. In 1777 the new state government confiscated his property and banished him from the state. Published *To the Grand Jury of the County of Chatham* (1777), a protest against his treatment. Returned from South Carolina to Savannah after its capture by the British in 1779. Published series of letters in the *Royal Georgia Gazette* in 1780 denouncing supporters of American independence. Died in Savannah.

Note on the Texts

This volume, the first of a two-volume set, collects nineteen pamphlets from the political debate triggered by Parliament's imposition, starting in 1764, of new taxes and regulations on Britain's North American colonies. It traces the main lines of a polemical exchange about the colonies—their origins and history, their governance, and their rights and obligations—that developed into a deeper contest about the nature of the British constitution. Spanning 1764 to 1772, it includes works written both by Americans and Britons, though the increasingly interconnected character of the empire in this period can make such distinctions misleading. These texts were part of a lively transatlantic discourse in which pamphlets published in Boston or Philadelphia soon appeared in London and were quickly reprinted, and vice versa, triggering further rounds of pamphleteering. Printers and booksellers, often themselves political partisans, played a crucial role in this rapid-fire exchange by preparing the works for publication, advertising them in newspapers, distributing them to subscribers and other book buyers, and posting copies to vendors in other locales. Though print runs for political pamphlets could be relatively small, often as few as five hundred copies, their reach was multiplied many times over by being made available in coffeehouses, clubs, and other gathering places and by extensive republication in part or in full in newspapers and periodical digests. The circulation of pamphlets built and reinforced ties among like-minded readers in the different colonies, encouraging the coalescence of shared convictions about the imperial relationship and exposing the ideological fissures that were ultimately to upend the traditional structures of authority in the colonies and break the imperial bonds.

What follows is a brief account of the publication history of each of the pamphlets collected here, along with some details about its reception and influence. These works ranged from as few as sixteen to as many as 262 pages in length. Normally published in either octavo or quarto format, they varied from roughly 6 to 9½ inches in height, resulting in shapes that were rectangular if octavo or, if quarto, somewhat more square. Most of these pamphlets have not been published in full in modern editions. Among the exceptions are Pamphlets 3, 4, 5, and 7, which were collected in Bernard Bailyn, *Pamphlets of the American Revolution, 1750–1776* (Cambridge, MA: The Belknap Press of Harvard University Press, 1965), I: 1750–1765, the first volume of what was projected to be a four-volume edition.

Two bibliographies by Thomas Randolph Adams (1921–2008), the longtime librarian of the John Carter Brown Library at Brown University, are indispensable guides to this literature: *American Independence: The Growth of an Idea; A Bibliographical Study of the American Political Pamphlets Printed Between 1764 and 1776 Dealing with the Dispute Between Great Britain and Her Colonies* (Providence, RI: Brown University Press, 1965) and *The American Controversy: A Bibliographical Study of the British Pamphlets About the American Disputes, 1764–1783* (2 vols., Providence, RI: Brown University Press, 1980).

1: *Thoughts on a Question of Importance Proposed to the Public* (1765)

This anonymous forty-eight-page pamphlet was published by James Dixwell, a printer and bookseller active in the Westminster section of London from 1752 to 1788. Judging from notices, it was issued sometime in the early spring of 1765. A review in the April issue of *The Critical Review, or Annals of Literature*, a generally Tory publication that had been edited by Tobias Smollett from 1756 to 1763, criticized "the aukward pertness of this writer, and his miserable deficiency in that kind of knowledge requisite for the subject he undertakes," but nonetheless admitted that "his question deserves consideration." "A little attention to, or acquaintance with, the history of the late general peace and the last war," the review went on, "would have been more service to him than all his classical knowledge or French reading; . . . The immense territory acquired by the late peace was connected with other causes than the rage for extending dominion; for it was in a manner forced upon Great Britain. Whatever speculative notions this author may entertain, it was her duty and capital interest to vindicate the rights and possessions of her American colonists; and it was evident, from the very principles on which the war was founded and conducted, that this could not be done, while a restless, ambitious, enterprizing people, in the neighborhood, had it in their power every hour to attack, alarm, rob, and murder them." The reviewer concluded with the hope "that the British government, while they are consulting the welfare of our colonies, ought to consult likewise the means of keeping them in a dutiful obedience on their mother country. This great and salutary end, however, never can be answered by such publications as that before us." The Whig *Monthly Review, or Literary Journal* for April pronounced the author "not a first rate writer, nor does he pretend to any skill in mercantile affairs; but he is a thinking, rational man; and what he offers to the consideration of the public, being solely intended for their advantage, most certainly deserves their serious consideration." A French edition was published in 1768. This volume prints the complete text of the Dixwell edition.

2: Francis Bernard, "Principles of Law and Polity" (1764/1774)

Though written and privately circulated in June 1764, Francis Bernard's "Principles of Law and Polity" was not published until early 1774, when it was included in *Select Letters on the Trade and Government of America; and the Principles of Law and Polity, Applied to the American Colonies Written by Governor Bernard in the Years 1763, 4, 5, 6, 7, and 8,* a 137-page pamphlet published by the London printers William Bowyer and John Nichols. Bowyer was printer to the Royal Society and the Society of Antiquities, and in 1771 he became president of the Stationers' Company, one of the royally chartered professional guilds of London. Nichols apprenticed with Bowyer and succeeded him on Bowyer's death in 1777, becoming a leading antiquarian and, in 1788, editor of the *Gentlemen's Magazine.* Sometime during the spring a second edition was issued by the London bookseller Thomas Payne with additional material and an expanded title: *To which are added The Petition of the Assembly of Massachuset's Bay against the Governor, his Answer thereto, and the Order of the King in Council thereon.* It was recommended in *The Monthly Review* for May 1774: "those who wish to acquire a competent idea of the principles of American law and policy, will meet with a great degree of satisfaction in the perusal of this pamphlet; which deserves to be distinguished from the rubbish with which every political question that arises in this land of statesmen is usually overwhelmed." That same month *The Critical Review* lamented that "the political affairs of our American colonies are at present so much embroiled, and the minds of the colonists so much prejudiced, that these Letters will probably meet with a less candid reception on the other side of the water than is there due. If (as there seems no reason to doubt of it) the letters now published are genuine copies of those written by governor Bernard, that gentleman was really much less an enemy to the cause of the Americans than has been represented, and the publication of them will of course be of advantage to his reputation." The Payne edition was reprinted in Boston by the bookselling firm of Edward Cox and Edward Berry and advertised for sale on October 27, 1774. (Cox and Berry had moved to Massachusetts from London in 1766 and used their contacts in the metropolis to arrange the publication of Phillis Wheatley's poetry there in 1773. They relocated to New York after the war began.) This volume prints "The Principles of Law and Polity" from the Bowyer and Nichols edition of the *Select Letters.*

3: James Otis, *The Rights of the British Colonies Asserted* (1764)

Advertised as "this day published" in the July 23, 1764, edition of the *Boston Evening Post,* James Otis's pamphlet was issued in an eighty-page edition by the Boston printers Benjamin Edes and John Gill, proprietors since 1755 of the *Boston Gazette and Country Journal*, organ of the patriot movement in Massachusetts. It was republished in a 120-page edition by the London bookseller and journalist John Almon (a protégé of Lord Temple and confidant of John Wilkie) in late 1764 and reviewed in the February 1765 issue of *The Monthly Review*: "A very zealous defence of the colonies, tending to prove, that every man in the British dominions is constitutionally a free man; that no parts of his Majesty's dominions can constitutionally be taxed without their own consent; and that every part has a right to be represented in the supreme, or some subordinate legislature. In fine, that they should not only be continued in the enjoyment of subordinate legislation, but be also represented, in proportion to their number and estates, in the grand national legislation;—which, the Author avers, and we think with good reason, would firmly unite all parts of the British empire, in peace and prosperity, and render it invulnerable and perpetual.—There are many things in this tract, that (however warmly the Author may write) deserve to be very coolly and seriously consider'd." Two more British editions were released in 1766, and that same year Almon included the pamphlet in his *Collection of the Most Interesting Tracts Lately Published in England and America, on the Subjects of Taxing the American Colonies.* The present volume prints the complete text of the Edes and Gill edition.

4: [Stephen Hopkins], *The Rights of Colonies Examined* (1765)

In November 1764, Rhode Island governor Stephen Hopkins summoned the colony's legislature into special session to address the onerous new regulations imposed by the Sugar Act and warn the legislators that a cabal of influential men in the colony was appealing to the Crown to revoke Rhode Island's charter and install a royal government. In December 1764, the Assembly issued an order to publish a pamphlet the governor had written outlining these concerns and it was duly printed on December 22, without attribution, in a twenty-four-page edition by the Providence printer William Goddard, publisher since 1762 of the town's first newspaper, the *Providence Gazette*. Its title page indicates simply that it was "Printed by Authority." A second edition, printed shortly after, replaced this assertion with a passage from scripture (2 Corinthians 12:14): "For the children ought not to lay up for the parents, but the parents for the children." In January and February of 1765, Hopkins's pamphlet was reprinted in the *Pennsylvania Journal, New York Mercury,* and *South Carolina Gazette*. Almon issued it in a forty-eight-page edition in 1766 entitled *The Grievances of the American Colonies Candidly Examined* and included it in the *Collection of the Most Interesting Tracts*. The London edition of the pamphlet was digested in the January 1766 edition of *The Gentleman's and London Magazine*, whose editors, perhaps because of its somewhat less than sure-handed style, presumed it "the work of many." *The Monthly Review* found the pamphlet a "modest yet pathetic recital of the hardships laid on our American brethren." This volume prints the complete text of the first Goddard edition.

5: [Martin Howard Jr.], *A Letter from a Gentleman at Halifax* (1765)

Hopkins's pamphlet was answered in short order by Martin Howard Jr.'s anonymous *Letter*, published in a twenty-two-page edition by Samuel Hall, printer of the *Newport Mercury* in Newport, Rhode Island. It was advertised for sale on February 13, 1765, in the February 11 edition of the *Mercury*. It in turn prompted a response by James Otis the following month in a pamphlet entitled *A Vindication of the British Colonies Against the Aspersions of the Halifax Gentleman* (Boston: Edes and Gill), to which Howard replied with *A Defense of the Letter from a Gentleman at Halifax*, again published by Hall. Otis finally closed out the exchange in May with *Brief Remarks on the Defence of the Halifax Libel*. The present volume prints the complete text of the Hall edition of Howard's *Letter*.

6: [Thomas Whately], *The Regulations Lately Made Concerning the Colonies* (1765)

This 114-page pamphlet, printed and sold by John Wilkie, treasurer of the London Stationers' Company and publisher of the *London Chronicle*, appeared in January 1765. Its authorship was much disputed. A "third" edition (no copies of a second edition have been found) was released in 1775, also from Wilkie, with "By the Late Right Hon. George Grenville" on the title page, and many readers did indeed attribute the work to the former prime minister and architect of the Stamp Act. Whately resolved the matter for historians in an August 14, 1766, letter to John Temple, the surveyor general of customs in Boston: "I remember you once mention'd to me a pamphlet call'd *The Regulations lately made in ye Colonies & the Taxes imposed upon them Consider'd*. I was guilty of writing that same pamphlet, & you see I abide by my principles by my acknowledging that work which I never own'd till lately." *The Regulations Lately Made* was extracted in the *London Chronicle* for February 21–23, 1765, and reviewed in the February issue of *The Monthly Review*: "The sensible Author of this elaborate performance endeavours to shew, that as the immediate defence of our colonies was the sole cause of the last war, so has their permanent security been effectually obtained by the peace. . . . The following sheets were written with a view to facilitate such an examination [of imperial policy]: they pretend to no more than to collect the several regulations lately made with respect to the colonies, to weigh the reasons upon which each of them appears to have been founded, and to see how far these are supported by facts, and by maxims of trade and policy. These regulations are many, and have been made in the different departments of our legislative or executive government; but they are all of equal public notoriety; which every man may know, or ought to know; and which are here, therefore, brought into one view. . . . The perusal of this tract, therefore, though a ministerial production, cannot be too earnestly recommended to a great commercial nation, abounding with provincial settlements in almost every part of the globe." *The Critical Review* was even more complimentary of "this masterly performance," calling it "an accurate and excellent vindication of the ministry's conduct with regard to our American settlements, . . . calculated to remove all apprehensions of their aspiring to be independent upon their mother-country. No sensible British American, let his notions of liberty and independency be ever so high, can read this pamphlet without being convinced of the folly and impracticability of his countrymen ever having an interest separate from that of Great Britain." The pamphlet's reception in America would prove otherwise. Extracts of Whatley's *Regulations* were published in the April 11, 1765, edition of the *Massachusetts Gazette and Boston Weekly News-Letter* and the April 22 *Newport Mercury*, and two strident rebuttals (pamphlets 7 and 8 below) soon appeared. This volume prints the complete text of the first Wilkie edition.

7: [Daniel Dulany], *Considerations on the Propriety of Imposing Taxes in the British Colonies* (1765)

The October 10, 1765, edition of the *Maryland Gazette* announced that this fifty-five-page pamphlet was to be for sale "next Monday." Its publisher, identified simply as "a North-American" on the title page, was Jonas Green of Annapolis, public printer to the province since 1740. Green reissued it in a second edition that same month, with another printing in November, and reprints quickly appeared in New York (advertised for sale in the October 31 *New-York Gazette*), Boston (advertised in the January 30, 1766, *Massachusetts Gazette*), and London, in two editions by Almon. *The Critical Review* for January 1766 was not impressed with "These Considerations, which evidently flow from the pen of a red-hot American." Its brief notice read as follows: "The author trumpets forth the services of the North-Americans during the last two wars; the provisions of the Great Charter are shewn to extend to America; the hardships of those colonies are delineated;

and this *patriot* vehemently enters his protest, desiring an exemption from taxes imposed '*without his consent.*'" *The Monthly Review* (also for January) was somewhat more measured: "This is a . . . strenuous champion for the colonies. . . . He denies the parliament's right of taxing the colonists, internally; and he enters pretty deeply into the argument. The zeal of this patriotic North-American sometimes carries him rather too far in his reflections on the mother country; but we think such warmth the more excusable, as it may be an indication of the Writer's honesty, whatever may be said of his prudence. In his preface he sensibly apologizes for 'the plainness, simplicity, and freedom' of his manner; and, indeed, we think with him, that a *decent firmness*, in a good cause, is to be preferred to a softer and more delicate style, which sometimes may serve only to enervate the argument, for want of urging it with its full force. On the whole, there are many important considerations in this tract; which, therefore, must be ranked among the most material of those pieces which have appeared on behalf of our American brethren." The present volume prints the complete text of the first Green edition.

8: Richard Bland, *An Inquiry into the Rights of the British Colonies* (1766)

Bland's pamphlet was issued in March 1766 in a thirty-one-page edition by Alexander Purdie, publisher with John Dixon of *The Virginia Gazette*. It was reprinted in full in London in the January 1769 issue of the *Political Register and Impartial Review of New Books* and Almon issued an edition shortly thereafter. In 1773 it was included in the first volume of Almon's four-volume *Collection of Tracts on the Subjects of Taxing the British Colonies in America, and Regulating Their Trade*. The present volume prints the complete text of the Purdie edition.

9: *The Examination of Doctor Benjamin Franklin* (1766)

Benjamin Franklin's February 13, 1766, testimony about the Stamp Act before the House of Commons (sitting in the Committee of the Whole) was recorded by the body's clerk, Thomas Tyrwhitt, and/or his assistant, John Hatsell. Though Parliament prohibited the publication of unauthorized reports of its debates and proceedings, newspaper publishers often had sources that enabled them to circumvent this restriction. The London printer William Strahan, a friend of Franklin, used such sources to secure a copy of the transcript of Franklin's testimony. As he explained in a May 10 letter transmitting the transcript to the Philadelphia printer David Hall, Franklin's former partner and publisher of the *Pennsylvania Gazette*, he did so with "great Difficulty, and with some Expense. . . . If you determine to print it either in a Pamphlet by itself, or in your Paper (the former I think the best way) do not say as taken by the Clerk of the House; that would be highly improper, and might bring my Friend, who favoured me with it, into an ugly Scrape. You need only call it, An Examination before a Great Assembly, or by some such General Title. . . . If you do print it, however, in any Shape, pray send me a Dozen Copies of it, directed to Dr. F. to save Postage." Strahan added for emphasis that "to this very Examination, more than any thing else, you are indebted to the *speedy* and *total* Repeal of the odious law." Hall and his new partner William Sellers published the transcript as a sixteen-page pamphlet in September 1766. Because of the restrictions on such publications, it appeared without a title page or publisher's imprint, the House of Commons was referred to generically as "an August Assembly" in the title, and the names of Franklin's interrogators were withheld. Hall's edition was reprinted that same month in a nearly identical setting by the New York printer James Parker, another Franklin associate. In October it was issued in a twenty-three-page edition by the Boston firm of Thomas and John Fleet, publishers of the *Boston Evening-Post*. In December it appeared in Williamsburg in a thirty-three-page edition by printer William Rind, publisher of a rival newspaper to Dixon's also called, confusingly, *The Virginia Gazette*. Around the same time a German-language edition, forty-three pages in length, was published in Philadelphia by Henry Miller (Hessian-born Johann Heinrich Müller), yet another printer who had worked for Franklin in the past. Almon released the first British edition in the summer of 1767, again without a title page, using the Hall and Sellers edition but replacing "August Assembly" with "Honourable Assembly." A second edition, this time with a title page and Almon's imprint, appeared shortly after. Extracts ran in the *London Chronicle*, July 4–7, and *The Gentleman's Magazine* for July. On August 8, 1767, Franklin wrote to Joseph Galloway that "our Friends here have thought that a Publication of my Examination here might answer some of the above Purposes, by removing Prejudices, refuting Falshoods, and demonstrating our Merits with regard to the Country. It is accordingly printed and has had a great Run." Franklin sent copies of the Almon edition to various friends, and in at least one case he added annotations in which he identified many of his questioners by name from memory. These notes, which are incorporated into the Notes in the present volume, are reproduced in *The Papers of Benjamin Franklin*, Leonard W. Labaree et al., eds. (New Haven and London: Yale University Press, 1969), XIII, 129–59, and are used here by permission. This volume prints the complete text of the Hall and Sellers edition.

10: [William Hicks], *The Nature and Extent of Parliamentary Power Considered* (1768)

William Pitt's January 14, 1766, speech in the House of Commons in favor of repealing the Stamp Act was first made public in a pamphlet simply called *Political Debates*. To deflect scrutiny by the authorities, its title page bore the following faux imprint: "A PARIS, Chez J. W. Imprimeur, Rue du Colombier Fauxbourg St. Germain, à l'Hotel de Saxe." The text of this pamphlet was reprinted in the April 1766 issue of *The Gentleman's Magazine*. Another version of Pitt's speech was published in a pamphlet entitled *The Speech of Mr. P—— and Several Others, in a Certain August Assembly*. Pitt's remarks were widely reprinted in colonial newspapers and broadsides, and even in some almanacs (for instance the *South Carolina & Georgia Almanack* for 1767). William Hicks responded to the speech in a series of six essays published in the *Pennsylvania Journal* between January 21 and February 25, 1768. These essays were reprinted in the *Boston Evening Post*, February 15–March 21, and the *South Carolina Gazette*, March 28–April 11. They were collected and issued as a thirty-two-page pamphlet in Philadelphia sometime that spring, most likely by the father-son firm of William and Thomas Bradford, publishers of the *Pennsylvania Journal*. An edition "reprinted from the Pennsylvania Journal" was issued by New York printer John Holt and advertised in the July 7, 1768, edition of Holt's newspaper, the *New-York Journal*. This volume prints the complete text of the Philadelphia edition of Hicks's pamphlet.

11: [John Dickinson], *Letters from a Farmer in Pennsylvania* (1768)

These twelve highly influential letters first appeared in the *Pennsylvania Chronicle* between November 30, 1767, and February 8, 1768, and within the next month or so nineteen of the twenty-three English-language newspapers in the colonies reprinted some or all of them. The Philadelphia firm of Hall and Sellers collected them in a closely printed, seventy-one-page pamphlet published in March, with a second edition following a month later. More editions soon appeared in Boston (one by Edes and Gill, another by the Tory printers John Mein and John Fleeming), New York (Holt), London (Almon), and Dublin. In a March 13 letter to his son William Temple Franklin, Benjamin Franklin recounted a recent meeting with Lord Hillsborough, secretary of state for the colonies, who "mentioned the Farmer's letters to me, said he had read them, that they were well written, and he believed he could guess who was the author, looking in my face at the same time as if he thought it was me. He censured the doctrines as extremely wild." Almon's London edition includes a preface,

"The British Editor to the Reader" (dated May 8, 1768), attributed to Franklin:

> When I consider our fellow-subjects in *America* as *rational creatures*, I cannot but wonder, that during the present wide difference of sentiments in the two countries, concerning the power of parliament in laying taxes and duties on *America*, no application has been made to their *understandings*, no able and learned pen among us has been employed in *convincing* them that they are in the wrong; proving clearly, that by the established law of nations, or by the terms of their original constitution, they are taxable by our parliament, *though they have no representative in it.*
>
> On the contrary, whenever there is any news of discontent in *America,* the cry is, "Send over an army or a fleet, and reduce the dogs to *reason.*"
>
> It is said of choleric people, that with them there is *but a word, and a blow.*
>
> I hope *Britain* is not so choleric, and will never be so angry with her colonies as to *strike* them: But that if she should ever think it *may be* necessary, she will at least let the word go before the *blow*, and reason with them.
>
> To do this clearly, and with the most probability of success, by removing their *prejudices*, and rectifying their *misapprehensions* (if they are such) it will be necessary to learn what those prejudices and misapprehensions are; and before we can either refute or admit their reasons or arguments, we should certainly know them.
>
> It is to that end I have handed the following letters (lately published in *America*) to the press here. They were occasioned by the act made (since the repeal of the Stamp-act) for raising a revenue in *America* by duties on glass, paper, etc.
>
> The Author is a gentleman of repute in that country for his knowledge of its affairs, and, it is said, speaks the general sentiments of the inhabitants. How far those sentiments are right or wrong, I do not pretend at present to judge. I wish to see first, what can be said on the other side of the question. I hope this publication will produce a full answer, if we can make one. If it does, this publication will have had its use. No offense to government is intended by it; and it is hoped none will be taken.

The Monthly Review (July 1768) found the *Letters* to be "a calm yet full inquiry into the right of the British Parliament, lately assumed, to tax the American colonies; the unconstitutional nature of which attempt is maintained in a well-connected chain of close and manly reasoning." It concluded that "if *reason* is to decide between us and our colonies, in the affairs here controverted, our Author, whose name the advertisements inform us is Dickenson (of Pennsylvania), will not perhaps easily meet with a satisfactory refutation." Dickinson's authorship was indeed soon widely known, and when the Bradfords published a third edition of the *Letters* in Philadelphia in the autumn of 1768, some copies featured an engraved portrait of Dickinson. An edition published by William Rind in Williamsburg in 1769 paired the Farmer's Letters with another series, called the Monitor's Letters, by Arthur Lee, and introduced the combined edition with a preface attributed to Lee's brother Richard Henry Lee. It reads in part:

It may perhaps seem strange to slight consideration, that these LET-TERS which have already passed through all *America*, should now a second time be produced before the Public in their present form. But a little further reflection will shew the UTILITY of this WORK. The sacred cause of liberty is of too great consequence, and the necessity of freedom for the security of human happiness too obvious, not to render every precaution wise, that tends to prevent the introduction of slavery. Notwithstanding therefore, these letters have been already published, yet here, they have been seen only in the Gazettes, which, from the uncertainty of their dispersion, and the length of time passing between the reception of newspapers in the country, may probably have prevented much of the benefit to be derived from a collective, uninterrupted view of the manly reasoning, the timely information, and the true constitutional principles of liberty with which these letters every where abound. Whoever considers again that the nature of men in authority is inclined rather to commit two errors than to retract one (see Clarendon's History of the Rebellion), will not be surprised to see the *Stamp-Act* followed by a Bill of Right, declaring the power of Parliament to bind us in all cases whatsoever; and this act followed again by another, imposing a duty on paper, paint, glass, etc. imported into these colonies. But however unbounded may be the wish of power to extend itself, however unwilling it may be to acknowledge mistakes, 'tis surely the duty of every wise and worthy *American*, who at once wishes the prosperity of the Mother country and the colonies, to point out all invasions of the public liberty, and to shew the proper methods of obtaining redress. This has been done by the Authors of the following LETTERS with a force and spirit becoming freemen, *English* freemen, contending for our just and legal possession of property and freedom. A possession that has its foundation on the clearest principles of the law of nature, the most evident declarations of the *English* constitution, the plainest contract made between the Crown and our forefathers, and all these sealed and sanctified by the usage of near two hundred years. *American* rights thus resting on the best and strongest ground, it behoves all her inhabitants with united heads, hearts, and hands, to guard the sacred deposit committed by their fathers to their care, as well to bless posterity as to secure the happiness of the present generation. In vain 'tis for some few (and very few I hope they are) who, governed either by base principles of fear, or led by vile hope of gain, the reward of prostituted virtue, to say, "your rights are indeed invaded, but *Great-Britain* is too strong. What can we do against superior strength?" Let these evil designing men remember what the highest authority has told us, "that the race is not always to the swift, nor the battle to the strong."

That same year there appeared a French-language edition of the *Letters* bearing an Amsterdam imprint. The present volume prints the complete text of the first Hall and Sellers edition.

12: [Allan Ramsay], *Thoughts on the Origin and Nature of Government* (1768)

As indicated on its title page, Allan Ramsay wrote this tract in 1766. It may perhaps have been the response to Dickinson's *Letters* that encouraged him to bring the work to press late in 1768. It was released in a sixty-four-page edition by the London publishers Thomas Becket and Peter Abraham de Hondt. *The Monthly Review* (January 1769) was scathing: "To enter into a discussion of arguments with this writer, would be a meer prostitution of reasoning, and doing him an honour he by no means deserves. A man who resolves all *right* and *law*, into *power* . . . will scarcely surprise his readers when he winds up his argument to the following point [the review quotes here from the pamphlet; see page 513, lines 19–24, in this volume]. As it is by no means probable, or to be wished, that Britons, or British Americans, will ever subscribe to our author's ideas, or incline to be thus laughed out of their constitution; he may stand a better chance by publishing his future thoughts on government at Morocco, under the emperor's *imprimatur*." *The Critical Review* (January 1769) observed that "this writer falls into the very error he wishes to explode, we mean that of system in government. . . . His truths, he tells us, are not drawn from sophistical reasoning and juggling with ill defined words, but from plain sense and observation. We cannot help thinking, that nothing is so uncommon as plain sense; for though it is what every rational creature boasts of, scarcely any two agree upon its meaning." For all that, it concluded that "this performance, though manifestly weak and purblind in its outset, acquires vigour and penetration in its progress, and ends with many shrewd and sensible observations." *The London Magazine* (February 1769) concluded simply that "this author is more of a philosopher than a politician, and answers many things which may be right enough in theory, but which we think rather impossible to be introduced into practice." Franklin made extensive marginal comments in his copy of this pamphlet. These are reproduced in *The Papers of Benjamin Franklin*, William B. Willcox et al., eds. (New Haven and London: Yale University Press, 1972), XVI, 304–26, and selections from them have been incorporated into the Notes in the present volume. This volume prints the complete text of the Becket and de Hondt edition.

13: [Silas Downer], *A Discourse . . . at the Dedication of the Tree of Liberty* (1769)

This volume prints the complete text of this pamphlet, which was published in a sixteen-page edition in the summer of 1768 by the Providence printer and bookseller John Waterman. Though the full text of the pamphlet does not appear to have been reprinted in colonial newspapers, an account of the July 25 Liberty Tree ceremony, including Downer's brief dedication (see page 536), ran in *The Providence Gazette, and Country Journal* (July 30); the *Essex Gazette*, of Salem, Massachusetts (August 2); *The New-Hampshire Gazette, and Historical Chronicle* of Portsmouth (August 5); and *The Connecticut Journal, and New-Haven Post-Boy* (August 12).

14: *An Inquiry into the Nature and Causes of the Present Disputes* (1769)

Though it carries a 1769 imprint, a notice in the November 19 *London Chronicle* suggests that this anonymous seventy-six-page pamphlet was published by Wilkie in November 1768. An excerpt was published the following month in the *Chronicle*, and a second edition was issued sometime in 1769. In its December 1768 issue, *The Monthly Review* offered lengthy extracts from the *Inquiry*, calling it a "dispassionate, somewhat prolix, discussion of a question, which, as the author observes, is as arduous and important as ever the English government was engaged in." *The London Magazine* for December found that the "author of this pamphlet is not without moderation, and says, that the Americans should either be allowed a representation in the parliament of Great Britain, or that they should be indulged with an internal legislation of their own, subject however to the control of the mother country." Sometime in 1770 Franklin made extensive marginal comments in his copy of this pamphlet. These are reproduced in *The Papers of Benjamin Franklin*, William B. Willcox et al., eds. (New Haven and London: Yale University Press, 1973), XVII, 317–48, and selections from them have been incorporated into the Notes in the present volume. This volume prints the complete text of the first Wilkie edition.

15: [John Joachim Zubly], *An Humble Enquiry into the Nature of the Dependency of the American Colonies* (1769)

This pamphlet was issued in a twenty-six-page edition in the late spring of 1769 in Charleston, South Carolina, presumably by Peter Timothy, publisher of the *South Carolina Gazette*, where the pamphlet was advertised on June 5. Zubly was identified as the author by Henry Miller, publisher of *Der wöchentliche Philadelphische Staatsbote*, in the October 20, 1775, edition of that paper. (Miller had learned the printer's trade in Switzerland, where his father had been born, and became associated with the Swiss-born Zubly in 1775 when the latter came to Philadelphia to represent Georgia in the Second Continental Congress.) A second edition of the *Humble Enquiry*, now titled *Great Britain's Right to Tax Her Colonies, Placed in the Clearest Light*, was published in London late in 1774 by the printer James Delegal. (Miller served as its principal distributor in America in 1775.) *The Critical Review* took notice of this edition in its November 1774 issue: "Whether the author of this pamphlet be really a Swiss, or it is only ascribed to a native of that country, as being a lover of public liberty, we shall leave undetermined. Admitting him to be such, we find nothing in the honest Helvetian's arguments which places the subject in a clearer light than before. Suffice it to say, that he is an advocate for the independency of America with respect to taxation." The current volume prints the complete text of the South Carolina edition of the *Humble Enquiry*.

16: [William Knox], *The Controversy Between Great Britain and Her Colonies Reviewed* (1769)

John Almon published *The Controversy . . . Reviewed* in a 262-page edition early in 1769. Its authorship was itself controversial, attributed variously to George Grenville, Thomas Whately, Israel Mauduit, John Mein, and William Knox. The true authorship is indicated in a memo from Knox to Lord Dartmouth, in which Knox, referring to himself in the third person, reported that the pamphlet had been printed "at the author's risk. A large number of Copies were struck off in expectation that the Government would have distributed them in the Colonies but not one having been purchased by the Government for that purpose, he was obliged to compound with Almon for the loss by assigning him all that were on hand, the profits of what had been sold and paying him in [£28] Cash." The text of the pamphlet runs to 207 pages, most of the last hundred of which are given over to extracts from what are called in the pamphlet's full title "Authentic Records"—various laws, colonial charters, addresses, speeches, and petitions purporting to demonstrate that Americans had always been subject to parliamentary authority and had consistently acknowledged as much in the past. To this text Knox added a fifty-five-page appendix presenting extracts from the Journals of the House of Commons, colonial resolutions, and other related documents. *The Monthly Review* for February 1769 found the pamphlet "a very close and shrewd examination . . . deserving the mature consideration of both parties involved in the present unhappy contest; for if the Americans have nothing satisfactory to offer to invalidate the positive evidences here brought in opposition to their claims of exemption from parliamentary authority, many will undoubtedly hesitate in opinion as to the real merits of their opposition." Editions of *The Controversy . . . Reviewed* soon appeared in Dublin and Boston (printed by Mein and Fleeming), and in 1773 it was included by Almon in *A Collection of Tracts on the Subjects of Taxing the British Colonies in America, and Regulating Their Trade.* The current volume does not reproduce Knox's lengthy historical extracts or his appendix. It prints pages [1]–106 and 200–207 of the first Almon edition.

17: Edward Bancroft, *Remarks on the Review of the Controversy Between Great Britain and Her Colonies* (1769/1771)

This pamphlet, which responds directly to Knox's, was first published without ascription in London by Becket and de Hondt. *The Monthly Review* (July 1769) felt it had been written "by an able hand; who by attending to the obvious import of words in the charters of the principal colonies, and the general tenor of those transactions wherein they have been concerned, clearly proves them to be distinct dependencies, not included within the realm of England, but having constitutions framed after the same model." After presenting lengthy excerpts, *The Monthly Review* offered the following judicious conclusion: "The political constitution of a people is a complicated system, seldom the result of any regular formed plan, but the growth of long experience, of which no reference to *past* time can afford a compleat idea; and the distracted measures of the long parliament in the last century, with the uneasiness caused by the late schemes of American taxation, will shew the danger of attempting sudden alterations, and violent innovations in government." *The Critical Review* (August 1769) was more spirited: "The author has advanced nothing that is new, or that has not been again and again answered; and till the writers for the American secession, for so we may call it, can prove that ever the authority of legislation subsisted or can subsist without the power of taxation, their professions of loyalty to their king, and affection for their mother-country, must be considered by all men of sense and knowledge as mere flummery and declamation." A second edition of the pamphlet was published in New London, Connecticut, in 1771, this time with Edward Bancroft identified as the author on the title page. This 130-page edition was the work of Timothy Green, a member of the third generation of a family of printers who owned and operated most of the presses in the colony. This volume prints the complete text of the Green edition.

18: Joseph Warren, *An Oration Delivered March 5th, 1772* (1772)

This volume prints the complete text of the first edition of this eighteen-page pamphlet, which was published by Edes and Gill in March 1772. A second edition appeared in April.

19: *The Votes and Proceedings of . . . the Town of Boston* (1772)

The Boston Committee of Correspondence convened for the first time on November 3, 1772, and a subcommittee prepared a statement of rights, principally authored by Samuel Adams, and a list of grievances. The Boston selectmen approved these statements at a town meeting on November 20 and ordered that they be published along with a letter to the other towns in Massachusetts and an exchange with Governor Hutchinson concerning the salaries of judges, the issue that had provoked Boston to action. The resulting pamphlet, generally known as the Boston Pamphlet, was jointly issued in a forty-seven-page edition by the Boston firms of Edes and Gill and Thomas and John Fleet. Six hundred copies were printed and provision made for delivery to each of the towns and districts in the Bay Colony, to every selectman and clergyman in Boston, and to "such other gentlemen as the committee shall think fit." Tory critics like "Q.E.D." in the *Boston Weekly News-Letter* (November 12) derided the project, predicting that "it is very certain that it is an exceeding busy Time in the Country, all hands being employed in picking Apples, making Cyder and gathering in the Harvest, so that upon the whole it looks very likely that this political Manœuvre will be frustrated." In the event, more than a hundred towns found time to respond in support of Boston. On November 28 Thomas Cushing, speaker of the Massachusetts House of Representatives, dispatched a copy of the pamphlet to Franklin in London, who received it in February and promptly had it printed in an edition to which he contributed a "Preface of the British Editor." It reads in part:

> All Accounts of the Discontent so general in our Colonies, have of late Years been industriously smothered, and concealed here; it seeming to suit the Views of the American Minister [Hillsborough] to have it understood, that by his great Abilities all Faction was subdued, all Opposition suppressed, and the whole Country quieted. That the true State of Affairs there may be known, and the true Causes of that Discontent well understood, the following Piece (not the Production of a Private Writer, but the unanimous Act of a large American City) lately printed in New-England, is republished here. This Nation, and the other Nations of Europe, may thereby learn with more Certainty the Grounds of a Dissension, that possibly may, sooner or later, have Consequences interesting to them all.

Franklin sent the copies of this printing back to America, where they were circulating by May. Finally, in June, he arranged for the public release of a London edition, published by Wilkie. This was noticed in the July issues of *The Scots Magazine* and *The Monthly Review*, prompting in the latter a mournful wish "that things could be restored to the same situation in which they were before" the passage of the Stamp Act. Another edition of the pamphlet was published in Dublin in 1773. The current volume publishes the complete text of the Edes and Gill, Fleet and Fleet edition.

This volume presents the texts of the editions chosen for inclusion here without change, except in the following respects. Typographical errors have been corrected, and errata listed in the original sources have been incorporated. Instances of inverted letters, a common error in typesetting during this period, have been silently corrected. The use of quotation marks to begin every line of a quoted passage, a convention of the time, has been dispensed with, though the inclusion of the identification of the speaker within the quotation marks, also conventional, has been retained. In those instances where a sentence clearly ends, but without terminal punctuation, a period has been added. Footnote symbols, which in the eighteenth century often preceded the text or quotation being noted, have been moved to conform to modern usage. Spelling, punctuation, capitalization, and italicization are often expressive features, and they have not altered, even when inconsistent or irregular. Each pamphlet reflects the style of its author and publisher, and no effort has been made to standardize their use of italics for proper names and large and small capitals for emphasis. With the exception of facsimile title pages, this edition does not attempt to reproduce nontextual features of typographical design or such features of eighteenth-century typography as the long "s". The following is a list of typographical errors corrected in this edition, cited by page and line number: 19.20, Corn?; 20.17, Applicacation; 23.14, Phsiycians; 53.7, *enthusiam,*; 54.36, unletered; 54.37, Olargarchy; 56.37, *irrestible.**; 65.3, Chap. 9.; 70.9, face.; 72.6, vertue.; 73.7, unqestionable.; 76.38, 3 Mod. 152;; 78.34, parliament.; 83.13, believe,,; 85.29, 3 *Inst.*; 96.12, Realm—2; 96.13, C. 15; 97.12, dircted; 100.31, prorogative?; 101.4, *Parliamentum.*; 101.16, the the; 104.12, Cesars.; 106.2, Meet- in; 110.26, *ninth,*; 113.33, perferred.; 113.37, stiping; 115.3, (3); 117.14, jealously,; 148.27, admimiration; 148.28, surrrounding; 156.37, *mater.*; 157.36, disease:; 158.5, doubtlese; 169.4–5, Commmodities; 169.11–12, aristrocratical; 173.24, 17 *Car.*; 186.26, *cancertain*; 187.18, built;; 188.40, *St. Vincent's*; 189.4, Failute; 194.36, Pruduce,; 200.21, *Guardalupe*; 209.7, *Brieain*; 210.34, *America*; 211.23, Linens,; 214.2, Circustances,; 223.34, unphappy; 225.38, whereever;

226.28, furnished; 233.10, the the; 235.33, constitue; 237.32, Representaton; 254.19, *partial.*; 267.3, Temselves; 274.19, denied.; 281.5, Page; 299.8, substracted,; 302.13, the the; 351.21, for for; 367.29, slighest; 367.34, of three; 367.35, least; 367.36, least; 374.24, suscribe; 374.27, sensibly; 376.29, *trial,*; 377.23, ligislature; 383.22, surrounded; 383.26, *Britain*; 383.27, impropeiety,; 385.4, *Great-Britain* over; 390.19, lavishily; 396.33, utility:; 397.32, paliamentary; 398.1, basely relinquishing our; 402.7, of of; 402.19, goverment; 402.22, deficiences;; 402.22–23, imperperfections; 413.8, TERE; 417.31, *Coke's* 2d; 428.27, *assinsu*; 526.36, overflowed great; 527.9, of whole; 531.16, bread meat; 542.40, mother-county; 545.21, proopsition,; 551.38, impraciable,; 557.26, exrravagant; 561.39, waved,; 565.9, themn:; 573.39, probabily; 585.2, happiness, I; 610.33, essenttial; 611.32, *Ce'st*; 625.34, parment; 626.33, liberrties; 627.38, Englsh; 632.18, melasses; 633.5, eleventh,; 637.11, pnce; 637.15, melasses;; 641.11, *the the whole,*; 644.1, district; 645.26, heriditary; 658.3, impractible.; 660.39, declerations;; 661.33, definite; 662.5, whither; 672.20, witten; 678.7–8, unaliable; 680.9, Dominions, to; 685.2, Rights,; 689.7, leige; 691.17, decleared; 693.11–12, thereform,; 701.26, Assembles; 706.35, ever,"; 707.28, Govvrnment; 714.4, Parliment,; 722.19, King Lords,; 722.22, Laws,); 724.8, imprefectly; 726.7, Deseat; 730.34, it; 734.13, *Holland* the; 735.2, Impertience; 737.39, Strength Labour,; 749.38, conservamdam; 778.2, Infringemen; 778.39, Episopate; 782.19, mantaining; 782.29, tearing the the.

Notes

In the notes below, the reference numbers denote page and line of this volume (the line count includes headings, but not rule lines). No note is made for material included in the eleventh edition of *Merriam-Webster's Collegiate Dictionary*, except for certain cases where common words and terms have specific historical meanings or inflections. Biblical quotations and allusions are keyed to the King James Version; references to Shakespeare to *The Riverside Shakespeare*, ed. G. Blackmore Evans (Boston: Houghton Mifflin, 1974). For further historical background and references to other studies, see Bernard Bailyn, *Pamphlets of the American Revolution, 1750–1776* (Cambridge, MA: The Belknap Press of Harvard University Press, 1965), I: 1750–1765; Jack P. Greene, *The Constitutional Origins of the American Revolution* (New York: Cambridge University Press, 2010); Merrill Jensen, *The Founding of a Nation: A History of the American Revolution, 1763–1776* (New York: Oxford University Press, 1968); Robert Middlekauff, *The Glorious Cause: The American Revolution, 1763–1789* (New York: Oxford University Press, 1982); Edmund S. and Helen M. Morgan, *The Stamp Act Crisis: Prologue to Revolution* (Chapel Hill: University of North Carolina Press, 1953); and Gordon S. Wood, *The American Revolution: A History* (New York: Modern Library, 2002).

INTRODUCTION

xvi.4–6 "a mighty empire . . . to none."] Jonathan Mayhew, *Two Discourses Delivered October 25th. 1759. Being the Day Appointed by Authority to be Observed as a Day of Public Thanksgiving, for the Success of His Majesty's Arms, More Particularly in the Reduction of Quebec, the Capital of Canada* (Boston, 1759).

xviii.32–34 "to preserve . . . their privileges."] Arthur Dobbs (1689–1765), governor of North Carolina, 1754–64, quoted in George Chalmers, *An Introduction to the History of the Revolt of the American Colonies* (Boston, 1845).

xxi.40–xxii.1 "his blood full of prerogative,"] James Boswell, *The Life of Samuel Johnson, LL.D.* (2 vols., London, 1791), II, 481.

xxii.29 "salutary neglect"] In Pamphlet 35 in the companion to this volume, *The American Revolution: Writings from the Pamphlet Debate 1773–1776*.

I: THOUGHTS ON A QUESTION OF IMPORTANCE

1.2 "Cato,"] Evoking the Roman statesman (95–46 B.C.) known for his moral integrity and opposition to corruption, this pseudonym was often used in eighteenth-century Anglo-American political writings, most famously by the radical Whigs John Trenchard (1662–1723) and Thomas Gordon (d. 1750).

1.20–21 "none of the spirit . . . appeared."] Thomas Hutchinson to the Earl of Dartmouth, December 14, 1773.

5.5 repeated Victories] The Grenville ministry (April 1763–July 1765) triumphed over a divided opposition in a series of votes in the parliamentary session that opened on January 10, 1765, including the defeat of proposals to declare general warrants illegal (January 29) and to postpone consideration of a stamp tax on the American colonies (February 27).

5.8 Court of Judicature] The House of Lords functioned as the kingdom's highest appellate court during this period.

6.9–10 violent Clamours against the late Peace.] Reflecting the king's strong desire for a lasting peace with France, the Bute ministry (May 1762–April 1763) had pressed hard to conclude negotiations ending the Seven Years' War. Consequently, some in Parliament and in the British press thought that the Treaty of Paris made excessive, even treasonous, concessions to the defeated enemy.

9.8–9 did not keep the whole Island of Cuba] The British took Havana after a two-month siege in the summer of 1762. In the peace treaty of 1763, Cuba was restored to Spain as an equivalent for the British keeping the Floridas.

10.39 Sir William Johnson] Born in Ireland to a family of English descent, Johnson (1715–1774) moved to New York in 1738 to oversee the Mohawk Valley estate of an uncle. There he learned Indian languages and customs, forming close ties to native leaders that enabled him to profit greatly by trade and land acquisition. He was appointed superintendent of Indian affairs for the northern colonies in 1756 and awarded a baronetcy after the Seven Years' War.

11.9 Appius Clausus] According to Livy, Appius Claudius led a faction of the Sabines, a tribe the Roman republic had defeated in 505 B.C., that elected to move to Rome rather than renew fighting. Granted citizenship and allocated land, the group became known as the Old Claudian tribe. Appius quickly rose to power in the Roman senate, becoming consul in 495 B.C.

11.16 Luxury] In the eighteenth century this word retained its Latin root sense of vicious indulgence, connoting degeneration and corruption as well as sumptuous living. It was, in a medical metaphor common in this period, the principal source of disease in the body politic.

12.17 Havannah Expedition] Over six thousand British troops perished from disease during and after the successful two-month siege of Havana in the summer of 1762, more than had died in all of North America during the Seven Years' War.

14.28–29 Baron Montesquieu] Charles-Louis de Secondat, Baron de La Brède et de Montesquieu (1689–1755), French political thinker whose *De l'esprit des loix* (1748; *The Spirit of the Laws*, 1750) was one of the most influential works of political theory in both the French- and English-speaking worlds of the eighteenth century.

15.34   says a late eminent Author] Though unspecified, this may be another reference to *The Spirit of the Laws*, which includes a chapter "On the Spirit of Commerce" (Bk. XX, ch. 2), in which Montesquieu observes that "if the spirit of commerce unites nations, it does not in the same manner unite individuals. We see that in countries where the people move only by the spirit of commerce, they make a traffic of all the humane, all the moral virtues; the most trifling things, those which humanity would demand, are there done, or there given, only for money. The spirit of trade produces in the mind of a man a certain sense of exact justice, opposite, on the one hand, to robbery, and on the other to those moral virtues which forbid our always adhering rigidly to the rules of private interest, and suffer us to neglect this for the advantage of others."

17.36   αχμη] Ancient Greek: literally acme, here vigorous spirit, exalted state.

18.16–17   Restrictions we have . . . Ireland under] Including Poyning's Law of 1494, which required the prior approval in London of all bills brought before the Irish Parliament, and the Irish Declaratory Act of 1720 (see Chronology). Ireland became a touchstone for many writers in the imperial debate of the 1760s, its constitutional relationship to Great Britain seen as similar in many respects to that of the North American colonies.

19.32–33   an Assertion . . . (David Hume)] The celebrated Scottish philosopher (1711–1776) wrote extensively on economic matters. This would seem to be a reference to the essay "Of the Jealousy of Trade," one of the *Essays, Moral, Political, and Literary*, in which he writes: "Nothing is more usual, among states which have made some advances in commerce, than to look on the progress of their neighbours with a suspicious eye, to consider all trading states as their rivals, and to suppose that it is impossible for any of them to flourish, but at their expense. In opposition to this narrow and malignant opinion, I will venture to assert, that the encrease of riches and commerce in any one nation, instead of hurting, commonly promotes the riches and commerce of all its neighbours; and that a state can scarcely carry its trade and industry very far, where all the surrounding states are buried in ignorance, sloth, and barbarism."

22.25–26   Dr. Burnet says somewhere] Scottish theologian Gilbert Burnet (1643–1715), who became the Bishop of Salisbury in 1689, was the author of a number of historical works, including the one likely referred to here, *Bishop Burnet's History of His Own Time*. First published in two volumes, 1724–34, and reissued in five in 1753, it spanned from the Restoration to the reign of Queen Anne.

22.26–27   the Revolution] The Glorious Revolution of 1688–89. See Chronology.

22.27   upon the Tapis] That is, under consideration. The figure of speech was derived from the use of small tapestries (tapis) as coverings for council tables.

2: FRANCIS BERNARD, PRINCIPLES OF LAW AND POLITY

32.2–3   *Wales, Chester*, and *Durham* have been, and *Ireland* may be] Wales had been represented in Parliament since 1535. Chester and Durham were known as palatine counties, having been established in the eleventh century as semi-autonomous buffer states on the western (Welsh) and northern (Scottish) borders of England. Chester maintained its own parliament until it was absorbed into England and granted representation at Westminster in 1543. Durham gained its first representative in Parliament in 1654, but did not gain statutory confirmation of its representation until 1672. Not until 1801, with the passage of the Act of Union, would Ireland be allocated seats in the British Parliament.

33.6   avoided] Obsolete: voided.

35.25–26   independent Civil List] *Civil list* was the term applied to the annual grant made to pay the expenses of crown officials. The fact that many royal governors, including Bernard as governor of Massachusetts Bay, had to wrangle with their legislatures for their own salaries and those of other royal officials was a source of continual frustration; many imperial reformers called for such salaries to be paid by Britain directly.

37.28   If the Charters can be pleaded] Although the seventeenth-century charters that the Crown had granted to individuals and groups to settle colonies had been documents that *created* power, by the 1760s in the eyes of most colonists they had become defensive documents that *limited* power; in effect, rudimentary written constitutions.

38.16   to make the governments large and respectable] Bernard's suggestion here harks back to the ill-fated Dominion of New England (see Chronology for 1686–88).

38.23   The want of such a third Legislative power] Governor's councils, the advisory bodies that functioned as the upper houses of the colonial assemblies, were widely regarded as the colonial counterpart of the House of Lords in a proper mixed constitution. Imperial bureaucrats like Bernard much lamented the weakness of these councils, which stemmed from the absence in America of an aristocracy that was clearly distinguishable from other colonial elites.

3: JAMES OTIS, THE RIGHTS OF THE BRITISH COLONIES ASSERTED

41.27–31   "universally approved" . . . constitutional liberty."] As reported in the April 8, 1765, edition of the *Boston Evening-Post*, copying an advertisement "from a late London paper."

43.7–10   *Hæc omnis . . . condant.*] Virgil, *Aeneid*, XI.320–24: "Those mountains fill'd with firs, that lower land, / If you consent, the Trojan shall command, / Call'd into part of what is ours; and there, / On terms agreed, the common country share. / There let'em build and settle, if they please." (John Dryden translation.)

45.27–28 Questions like the following] These are Otis's rhetorical questions, not quotations.

47.3–4 Locke's . . . De Vattel's] John Locke's *Two Treatises of Government* . . . *the Latter . . . an Essay Concerning the True Original, Extent, and End of Civil-Government* (1689) and Emmerich de Vattel's *Le droit des gens; ou, Principes de la loi naturelle, Appliqués à la conduite et aux affaires des nations et des souverains* (1758; *The Law of Nations; or, Principles of the Law of Nature, Applied to the Conduct and Affairs of Nations and Sovereigns*, 1759).

48.3 W. 3.] William III.

48.15 an election of a king of the Romans] The Holy Roman Empire was an elective monarchy and the King of the Romans was the designation for the heir apparent to imperial throne, who was chosen by a small group of German princes known as the Electors. The last such election had occurred in Frankfurt on March 27, 1764, and one of the nine electors was George III, King of Great Britain and Elector of Hanover.

49.19–20 *Harrington . . . Oceana*] James Harrington (1611–1677), English political theorist of classical republicanism and author of *The Commonwealth of Oceana* (1656).

49.23 musquash] Muskrat.

50.17–18 whose rain falls on the just and the unjust] Cf. Matthew 5:45.

51.5–8 "in the last age . . . absolute power"] Locke, *First Treatise of Government*, ch. i, sect. 3.

51.8–11 "slavery is so vile . . . plead for it:"] From the opening passage of Locke's *First Treatise*.

51.18–19 *Salus populi suprema lex esto*] Latin: Let the good of the people be the supreme law. A well-known maxim from Roman antiquity—first coined in this form by Cicero in *De Legibus* (On the Laws)—commonly cited in patriot writings.

51.26–27 "*idolatry*, begotten by *flattery*, on the body of *pride*"] Cf. Bernard de Mandeville, *The Fable of the Bees: or, Private Vices, Public Benefits* (1714): "the nearer we search into human Nature, the more we shall be convinced, that the Moral Virtues are the Political Offspring which Flattery begot upon Pride."

51.32–33 *Dii majorum . . . gentium*] Latin: The classes of major and minor gods; or, as Otis has it in his postscript, "ancient and modern gods."

53.20 *Nimrod*] Great-grandson of Noah and the proverbial first king, mentioned in Genesis 10:8.

54.17–18 *Sic volo, . . . voluntas*] Juvenal, *Satires*, VI.221: Thus I wish, thus I decree, let my desire serve for reason.

56.10–11 infallible prediction of *Harrington*] Made in *Oceana*: "The first of these Nations (which, if you stay her leisure, will in my mind be *France*) that recovers the health of antient Prudence, shall certainly govern the World."

56.39 See Mr. Locke . . . Government.] In the *Second Treatise*, ch. xix, sect. 225: "*Revolutions happen* not upon every little Mismanagement in publick Affairs. *Great Mistakes* in the ruling part, many wrong and inconvenient Laws, and all the *Slips* of human Frailty, will be *borne by the People* without Mutiny or Murmur. But if a long train of Abuses, Prevarications and Artifices, all tending the same way, make the Design visible to the People, and they cannot but feel, what they lie under, and see, whither they are going; 'tis not to be wonder'd, that they should then rouze themselves, and endeavour to put the Rule into such hands, which may secure to them the Ends for which Government was at first erected." (Quotation from fifth edition, published in London in 1728, the first known to have circulated in America.)

57.13 W & M. sess. I. C. I.] Citations to parliamentary statutes are made with an abbreviation that designates, in order, the year of the current reign (called the regnal year), the session of Parliament (indicated only if, as in the current case, there was more than one in that year), the chapter (a sequential ordering of public acts passed in a session), and in many cases, though not here, the section of the act being specifically cited. Thus Otis is referring here to the first act of the first session of Parliament under the newly installed monarchs William and Mary in 1689. To take another example, the Stamp Act was the twelfth public measure passed in the fifth year of the reign of George III. Its eighth section, which stipulated (for the benefit of non-English-speaking British subjects in Quebec and the Caribbean) that the stamp tax would not be inflated on papers printed in a foreign language, is cited as 5 Geo. III, cap. 12, sect. 8 or, in a common further abbreviation, 5 G 3 c. 12 s. 8.

63.1 *non obstante*] Latin: notwithstanding; in English law, the act of the king by which he dispenses with the law or authorizes its violation.

63.14 *quamdiu se bene gesserint*] Latin: as long as they conduct themselves properly.

63.29 passage from Mr. Locke.] Cobbled from the *Second Treatise*, ch. xiii, sect. 149 and ch. xix, sects. 211–12, 222.

66.1–2 two provinces and two colonies] That is, the royal colonies, or provinces, of Massachusetts and New Hampshire, and the chartered colonies of Connecticut and Rhode Island.

66.27 *Grotius* and *Pufendorf*] Hugo Grotius (1583–1645), Dutch jurist who helped lay the foundations for international law. Samuel von Pufendorf (1632–1694), German jurist and political thinker, articulated seminal theories about natural law.

66.31–35 "The learned . . . with *Grotius*."] In the second chapter of the first book of *Du contrat social* (1762; *A Treatise on the Social Contract*, 1764),

Jean-Jacques Rousseau included in a footnote the first quotation, which took from the "Manuscript Treatise on the Interests of France, by the Marquis d'A." He followed with the observation that Otis includes here as the second quotation. The work in question, by René Louis de Voyer, Marquis d'Argenson, was subsequently published in 1764 as *Considérations sur le gouvernement ancient et présent de la France, comparé avec celui des autre états.*

67.5   *Grotius* B. 3. C. 1. sec. 21] Grotius's *De Jure Belli ac Pacis* (1625; *The Laws of War and Peace*, 1654). Many subsequent English translations were entitled *The Rights of War and Peace.*

67.8–9   *mundiburgium*] Glossed as follows in a footnote in a 1738 edition of Grotius's work: "the term, according to some, is derived from the old Teutonic *Munto, to defend* or *protect*, and *Burde, charge* or *burthen.*"

67.14   *so long as the colony was well treated.*"] Otis has added this clause.

67.20   Dion. Hali] Referring to *Roman Antiquities*, a work from the first century B.C. by the Greek historian Dionysius of Halicarnassus.

67.24–40   "Colonies . . . commonwealth."] From Pufendorf's *De Jure Naturae et Gentium* (1672; *Of the Law of Nature and Nations*, 1703).

68.9   Dr. Strahan says] William Strahan, LL.D., in the preface to *The Civil Law and Its Natural Order, Together with the Publick Law . . . With Additional Remarks on Some Material Differences Between the Civil Law and the Law of England*, his 1722 translation of Jean Donat's *Les lois civiles dans leur ordre naturel* (1698). This Strahan was not the famous printer and friend of Benjamin Franklin.

68.20–21   the learned treatise of Solorzanus] *De Indiarum Jure* (1629–39), an important analysis of Spanish colonial law by Juan de Solorzano Pereira (1575–1655), judge of the high court at Lima.

69.37–70.1   Montesquieu has humorously given] In an ironic defense of slavery in *The Spirit of the Laws*, Bk. XV, ch. 5.

70.29   says Mr. Locke] In the *Second Treatise*, ch. ii, sect. 4 and ch. iv, sect. 22.

72.28   fields of St. Germains] James II lived in exile at Saint-Germain-en-Laye in France until his death in 1701.

73.12–16   "that the King . . . thereof"] Quoting from the Act for the Security of Her Majesty's Person and Government, and of the Succession to the Crown of Great Britain in the Protestant Line, also known as the Succession to the Crown Act of 1707.

73.36   formally declared as to Ireland] In the Irish Declaratory Act of 1720.

75.35   The fine defence . . . *Dummer*] Jeremiah Dummer (1681–1739), Harvard 1699, was agent in London for Massachusetts, 1710–21, and Connecticut, 1712–30, and author of *A Defence of the New-England Charters* (London,

1721), which John Adams considered "one of our most classical American productions." Dummer's pamphlet concludes on a dramatic note: "Burnt Houses may rise again out of their Ashes, and even more Beautiful than Before, but 'tis to be fear'd that Liberty *once lost, is lost for ever.*"

76.19   *Qui sentit . . . et onus*] Latin: He who enjoys the benefit ought also to bear the burden. A maxim of contract law dating at least to the fifteenth century, and favored by Sir Edward Coke (1552–1634) and other English jurists.

76.38–39   See Magna Charta . . . Vaughan 300.] In addition to the Magna Carta (1215) and the Bill of Rights (1689), Otis cites three cases, each from a different legal compendium, dealing with the question of conquest in colonial law. 3 Mod. 159 (*Modern Reports, Being a Collection of Several Special Cases Argued and Adjudged in the Court of the King & Queen's Bench*, 12 vols., London, 1682–1738) refers to *Wytham v. Dutton* (1688), a case from Barbados in which the court rejected the defendant's claim that "the King is not restrained by the laws of England to govern that island by any particular law whatsoever, and therefore not by the common law," because it and other islands in the West Indies "were gotten by conquest or by some of his subjects going in search of some prize, and planting themselves there." 2 Salkeld 411 (William Salkeld, *Reports of Cases Adjudged in the Court of King's Bench*, 2 vols., London, 1717) refers to *Blankard v. Galdy* (1694), in which the court ruled that the municipal laws of England do not extend to Jamaica, finding instead that "the laws by which the people were governed before the conquest of the island, do bind them till new laws are given, and Acts of Parliament made here since the conquest do not bind them unless they are particularly named." Vaughn 300 (Edward Vaughan, ed., *The Reports and Arguments of the Learned Judge, Sir John Vaughan, Kt., Late Chief Justice of the Court of Common-Pleas . . .* , London, 1677) refers to *Craw v. Ramsey* (1670), a naturalization case originating in Ireland that reaffirmed the then-prevailing legal distinction between those territories, like Ireland and the American colonies, that were dominions of the *Crown* of England and therefore subject to parliamentary authority and Scotland which, as the personal dominion of the *King* of England, was not.

78.3   the northern colonies] That is, the North American continental colonies, as distinct from those in the British West Indies.

78.39   See the convention, and acts confirming it.] Otis points to the major legislative events of the Glorious Revolution: the Convention Parliament of January–February 1689, the irregular body that formally transferred the crown to William and Mary and began the remodeling of the English constitution with the issuance of a Declaration of Right, which was later codified in December 1689 as the Bill of Rights; and the 1701 Act of Settlement, described in the Chronology.

80.7   "ease, . . . of the Colonies,"] On March 13, 1764, Jasper Mauduit, agent for Massachusetts, 1762–65, forwarded a copy of Parliament's resolutions to the colony's House of Representatives. In his cover he noted that George Grenville, who led the ministry as chancellor of the Exchequer, had used the language Otis quotes here: "the Stamp Duty you will see, is deferr'd till next Year. I mean the actual laying it: Mr. Grenville being willing to give the Provinces their option to raise that or some equivalent tax, Desirous as he express'd himself to consult the Ease, the Quiet, and the Good Will of the Colonies."

80.10   taken away our fish, and given us a stone.] Cf. Luke 11:11.

80.33–34   a pamphlet] *The Administration of the Colonies* (London, 1764) by Thomas Pownall (1722–1805). This first edition was published anonymously, but subsequent editions—there would be four more before the decade was out—bore Pownall's name.

81.12   the first two paragraphs] Quoted from in the headnote to Pamphlet 2 in this volume. Pownall's reference there to "revolution" was struck from subsequent editions of his treatise.

81.18   *detur digniori.*] Latin: let it be given to the more worthy.

82.16–17   volume in quarto . . . two years since] *Coloniæ Anglicanæ Illustratæ: or, The Acquest of Dominion, and the Plantation of Colonies Made by the English in America, With the Rights of the Colonies Examined, Stated, and Illustrated. Part I* (London, 1762), a pamphlet by William Bollan (1710–1782).

84.5   since the union] See Chronology for 1707.

84.21–22   "as the legislative . . . the great charter."] From Pownall, *Administration of the Colonies.*

84.39–85.2   "Ireland being . . . as in England."] From Sir Edward Coke, *The Fourth Part of the Institutes of the Laws of England* (1644).

85.7   jure propietatis] Latin: by right of property.

86.9–10   Proceedings of the House of Commons] *The History and Proceedings of the House of Commons from the Restoration to the Present Time* (14 vols., London, 1742–44).

86.14–20   "Ireland is considered . . . execution there."] From the findings in re *Otway v. Ramsay*, tried before the King's Bench during the Michaelmas term of the eleventh year of the reign of George II.

86.30   the act of that year] See note 73.36.

87.9–10   *jus dicere . . . jus dare*] Latin: to declare the law and to make the law.

89.30   *home.*] Otis silently cut two sentences that followed here in *The Administration of the Colonies*, perhaps because they are more practical and less patriotic in tone: "Besides, the merchants are, and must ever be, in great measure allied with those of Great Britain: their very support consists in this alliance. The liberty and religion of the British colonies are incompatible with either French or Spanish government; and they know full well, that they could hope for neither liberty nor protection under a Dutch one; no circumstances of trade could tempt them thus to certain ruin."

91.4–5   Stars and Garters] Astonished.

92.8   Sylla's] Lucius Cornelius Sulla (c. 138–78 B.C.), the last general before Julius Caesar to be granted the title of dictator of the Roman republic.

92.24   a "very description,"] In characterizing the defects of the colonial courts Pownall explicitly echoed similar complaints made about the English county courts by Lord Chief Justice Matthew Hale (1609–1676) in his posthumously published *History and Analysis of the Common Law of England* (1713).

95.4–5   "Merchant strangers . . . friendly entertained."] From a 1378 statute, the first of the reign of Richard II.

95.9–16   In some cases . . . obvious reasons.] Otis alludes here to provisions of the Woollen Act of 1699—a protectionist measure primarily aimed against Ireland but which also prohibited Americans from engaging in intercolonial trade in wool and woolens—and of various Navigation Acts, which directed legal proceedings for customs and other trade violations to admiralty courts, where single judges, not juries, rendered the final decisions.

97.21–25   When *Louisbourg* was reduced . . . *Aix la Chapple*] See Chronology for 1744–48.

97.39   *our* youth were annually pressed] Although impressment for the navy was legal in Britain, its legality in the colonies was questionable. An act of 1708 had declared America out of bounds for press gangs, but the Crown believed the law had expired in 1714. In 1747, Boston experienced a major anti-impressment riot.

99.5–6   Viner Prerogative . . . sec. 1.] Referring to the legal compendium *A General Abridgment of Law and Equity Alphabetically Digested* . . . (23 vols., Aldershot, 1741–51) by Charles Viner. Otis cites section E.a.1, "Prerogative of the King," from Vol. XVI, in which Viner refers to Charles Molloy's 1676 work *De Jure Maritimo et Navali: or, A Treatise of Affairs Maritime and of Commerce.*

99.16   King Charles I. his ship-money] See Chronology for 1635–37.

99.30   Ld. Carteret] John Carteret, 2nd Earl Granville (1690–1763), was secretary of state for the Northern Department, 1742–44.

100.9   *In maximis minima est licentia.*] Paraphrasing a speech by Julius Caesar in Sallust's *De bellum Catilinae* (c. 44–40 B.C.)

101.2–4   *Hibernia* . . . 12 Rep. III. cites R. 3. 12.—] The Latin is from the *Merchants of Waterford Case* (1484) in Year Book 2 Richard III, 12, plea 26, which Otis copied from *The Twelfth Part of the Reports of Sir Edward Coke, Kt.* (London, 1658). Year Books were the collected law reports of medieval England, regularly published from 1268 to 1535.

101.7–10 "Ireland . . . Gascony, &c."] The question of Parliament's authority over Ireland had been very controversial, but by the eighteenth century most jurists assumed that all acts of Parliament bound Ireland. The provinces of Gascony and Guyenne in the southwest of France had been under the suzerainty of the kings of England from the twelfth through the mid-fifteenth centuries.

101.28 25th of C. 2. c. 7] An Act for the Encouragement of the Greenland and Eastland Trades, and for Better Securing the Plantation Trade (1672), the third of the four major Navigation Acts passed by Parliament in the seventeenth century.

102.4–5 The act of the 6th of his late Majesty] The Molasses Act of 1733. (See Chronology.)

106.5–6 INSTRUCTIONS for their REPRESENTATIVES.] Drafted by Samuel Adams.

106.34 the honorable Board] The Governor's Council, the upper chamber of the Massachusetts legislature (the General Court), whose twenty-eight members were selected annually by the House of Representatives, subject to gubernatorial veto.

107.7–9 the seats . . . shall be vacated] In addition to the annual struggle over salaries for crown officials, plural office-holding was a recurring source of friction in colonial politics, particularly when it was perceived to be an intrusion on the independence of the legislature. Beyond simply cronyism and nepotism, such consolidation of power suggested to its critics the emergence of something like a court party in the colonies. In Massachusetts, much animus was directed at the interrelated Hutchinson and Oliver clans, who between them held a number of key positions. Listing them all in his diary on August 15, 1765, the day after the home of Andrew Oliver, the man charged with implementing the Stamp Act in Massachusetts, had been ransacked by an angry mob, John Adams asked, "Is not this amazing ascendancy of one Family, Foundation sufficient on which to erect a Tyranny? Is it not enough to excite Jealousies among the People?"

109.25 Substance of a Memorial] This is likely the work of Otis himself.

110.25–26 the *thirteenth* of *George* the *second, chapter the seventh*] The Naturalization Act of 1740. (See Chronology.)

111.6 says my Lord Coke] In *The Seventh Part of the Reports of Sir Edward Coke, Kt.* (London, 1727).

112.23 D' Vattel.] The first two paragraphs of this long footnote are quotations from Emmerich de Vattel's *Law of Nations*, Bk. I, ch. iii, sect. 34, and ch. xviii, sect. 210.

112.25 *jura naturæ sunt immutabilia.*] Latin: the laws of nature are immutable.

112.25–27 Hob 87. . . . Fleetwood] Legal citations drawn from various casebooks referring to Sir Henry Hobart's judgment in *Day v. Savage* (1614, in the Trinity term of 12 James I); Sir Thomas Powys's plea in *Thornby, On the Demise of the Dutchess of Hamilton, v. Fleetwood* (1712); Sir John Holt's decision in *City of London v. Wood* (1701); and Coke's opinion in *Dr. Bonham's Case* (1610), from the eighth part of his *Reports*. S. C. and P. means for the same case and point. *Arg.* is short for *arguendo*, a Latin legal term meaning for the sake of argument.

115.21 Mr. Postlethwait] Malachy Postlethwayt (c. 1707–1767), *Britain's Commercial Interest Explained and Improved* . . . (2 vols., London, 1757).

4: [STEPHEN HOPKINS], THE RIGHTS OF COLONIES EXAMINED

125.3–5 *Mid the low . . . appeal'd*] James Thomson, *Liberty, A Poem* (1735–36), IV.1012–14. This four-part epic, which traces the course of liberty from ancient Greece and Rome to the Glorious Revolution, appealed to patriots because of its passionate protests against corruption. This particular quotation refers to Hampden's famous stance against royal prerogative in the Ship Money case.

125.19–20 *Filmer, Cromwell, and Venner*] Sir Robert Filmer (c. 1588–1653), English political theorist whose posthumously published work *Patriarcha* (1680) propounded the divine right of kings (Locke answered Filmer directly in the *First Treatise*); Oliver Cromwell (1599–1658) led parliamentary forces in the English Civil War and was Lord Protector of the Commonwealth; Thomas Venner, a wine cooper who had emigrated to New England in 1637 and returned to London in 1651, joining the radical republican underground of the Interregnum. He led the Fifth Monarchy Men, a millenarian Puritan sect that rose in rebellion in the name of "King Jesus" in 1657 and again in 1661, when he was executed.

125.21 on revolution principles] That is, the settlement forged in the Glorious Revolution of 1688–89.

126.3 says *Sidney*] Algernon Sidney (1623–1683), an influential republican theorist executed for treason against the government of Charles II. The text of his then-unpublished *Discourses Concerning Government*—Hopkins quotes here from ch. i, sect. 5, which is entitled "To depend upon the will of a man is slavery"—was used as evidence against him at his trial. Published posthumously in 1698, the work became very important to eighteenth-century radical Whigs.

127.17 *Thucidides*] There follow three passages from *The History of the Peloponnesian War*, trans. William Smith (London, 1753).

128.9 *Grotius* gives us] In *The Laws of War and Peace*.

128.17 says *Puffendorf*] In *The Law of Nature and of Nations*. It has been suggested that Hopkins was led to Thucydides, Grotius, and Pufendorf by his reading of Otis's *Rights of the British Colonies*, where references to the same passages may be found.

133.6–7   about one million . . . annually] Hopkins's numbers are intriguing since *officially* only 53,708 gallons of foreign molasses were imported into New England as a whole in 1763 and 93,314 gallons in 1764, amounts far short of the figures he gives for Rhode Island alone. This suggests that most of the molasses imported into the colony to feed the thriving rum industry was smuggled.

134.9   greatly incumbered . . . embarrassed] The twenty-eighth section of the Sugar Act stipulated that "no iron, nor any sort of wood, commonly called Lumber," could be exported from the British colonies without a bond or surety for double the value of the goods and that "said goods shall not be landed in any part of Europe except Great Britain." Bonds were forfeit if compliance was not certified by customs officials within eighteen months for shipments to Britain, six months for shipments to other British colonies in America, and twelve months for "any other place in America, Africa, or Asia."

135.10–11   *Tacitus*'s account . . . of the *Romans*] In the *Annals*, Bk. IV, ch. 30.

137.28–29   *Universal Hist.*] Published in various editions over the course of the eighteenth century, *An Universal History, From the Earliest Account of Time* was a highly ambitious multivolume work—twenty-three volumes in folio and sixty-four in octavo when completed in 1784—compiled by a committee of writers that included, for a time, the novelist Tobias Smollett.

137.32–33   says Dean *Swift.*] Cf. Jonathan Swift, *The Drapier's Letters*, IV: "For those who have used *Power* to cramp *Liberty*, have gone so far as to resent even the *Liberty of Complaining*; although a Man upon the Rack, was never known to be refused the Liberty of *roaring* as loud as he thought fit."

137.36   a late letter-writer] Possibly a reference to John Huske (1724–1773), a New Hampshire–born member of Parliament, who wrote a letter to a committee of merchants in Boston (where he had been in trade before moving to England in 1748) that was published in the November 2, 1764, edition of the *New-London Gazette*. In the letter Huske pledged to support the colonial cause in Parliament while cautioning the Bostonians that "the necessity in the opinion of administration of establishing either the stamp duty, or some other inland tax seems partly to arise from the indiscreet conversation of some Americans, who deny the rights of Kings, Lords and Commons, to impose such a tax on America," adding that "as I had never, in the 24 years I resided in America, nor in any conversation I have since had with the gentlemen from that country, heard such an impolitic and dangerous opinion, I was, I confess, much astonished. It was not without great difficulty that I remov'd the prejudices conceiv'd against the northern colonies from such erroneous and alarming doctrine," which Huske later referred to as "this mushroom policy," by which he may have meant to suggest that it had sprung up quickly and in the dark, or was rootless and full of holes.

139.19–20   the Duke *D'Anville* came out from *France*] In 1746, when an expedition against Quebec was being planned, news arrived in the colonies that an enormous French fleet commanded by the Duc d'Anville intended to reconquer Louisbourg and ravage the New England coast. Because of bad weather, epidemic disease, and d'Anville's inexperience, however, the French venture failed.

5: [MARTIN HOWARD JR.], A LETTER FROM A GENTLEMAN

143.11–12   "little, dirty . . . knot of thieves,"] From [James Otis], *Brief Remarks on the Defence of the Halifax Libel, on the British-American-Colonies* (Boston, 1765).

147.10–11   *"Est genus . . . Nec sunt.——"*] From Terence, *The Eunuch*, II.iii.16–17: "There are a Sort of Men, who wou'd fain appear at the Head of ev'ry Thing, and are not so." Translation from Thomas Cooke, *Terence's Comedies, Translated into English* (2 vols., London, 1749).

147.14   Mr.——] Otis, in his *Rights of the British Colonies Examined*.

147.16   *tribunitian veto*] Howard likens Rhode Island's popular party, which he regards as little more than a demagogic faction, to the *tribuni plebis* of the Roman republic, popularly elected officials who had the power to veto actions taken by magistrates and in other ways intervene legally on behalf of the people (plebians).

147.35   *variæ lectiones*] Latin: variant readings.

148.9   *man that is born of a woman.*] Cf. Job 14.1.

148.10–13   "So I have seen, . . . in the stream."] From Edward Young, *Love of Fame the Universal Passion. In Seven Characteristical Satyrs* (London, 1728), satire II. This popular work was published in its twelfth edition in 1762.

149.24   *Philoleutherus Lipsiensis*] *Philoleutherus* (or *Phileleutherus*) *Lipsiensis* was the pseudonym of English critic and classicist Richard Bentley (1662–1742).

152.26   *Nova Zembla* to *Cape Horn*] That is, from pole to pole. An archipelago in the Russian arctic, Nova Zembla was first encountered by western European explorers in the mid-sixteenth century as an impediment in their quest for a northeast passage to China.

152.40   the song of *Lillibullero*] A song satirizing the Earl of Tyrconnel, whom James II had dispatched to Ireland as Lord Deputy, 1686–87. Written by Thomas Earl of Wharton with music, likely adapted from a traditional tune, credited to Henry Purcell, it became a popular marching song in the Williamite war in Ireland (1689–91). Bishop Burnet, in his memoirs (see note 22.25–26), described its influence in much the spirit that Howard displays here: "A foolish ballad was made at that time treating the Papists, and chiefly the *Irish*, in a very ridiculous manner, which had a burden [refrain], said to be *Irish* words, *lero lero lilibullero*, that made an impression on the Army that cannot be imagined by those who saw it not. The whole Army, and at last all people both in city and country, were singing it perpetually. And perhaps never had so slight a thing so great an effect." According to Macaulay, Wharton is said to have "afterwards boasted that he had sung a King out of three Kingdoms."

153.21–27 freeholder . . . Copyholders] Under the feudal land tenure system still operative in the eighteenth century, freeholders were individuals who owned their land outright, as distinct from copyholders, whose title to the land was conditional on the exchange of specified services to the manorial lord.

154.3 like *Ixion*, . . . in the shape of *Juno*.] A Thessalonian king condemned for murdering his father-in-law, Ixion was rescued by Zeus and brought to Olympus. There, he attempted to seduce Hera (Juno), who reported this affront to her husband. To confirm Ixion's temerity, an angry Zeus sent a cloud in Hera's form to visit him; Ixion impregnated it, thereby begetting Centaurus, father of the race of Centaurs.

156.6 Mr. *Partridge*] Merchant Richard Partridge (1681–1759) was colonial agent for Rhode Island from 1715 until his death. He also represented Connecticut, New Jersey, New York, and Pennsylvania at various times.

156.14 the sugar bill] The Molasses Act of 1733. The remarks by William Yonge and Thomas Winnington are drawn from extracts of the parliamentary debate on this measure, originally published in *The London Magazine* for October 1733 and reprinted in the January 14, 1765, edition of the *Newport Mercury*.

157.38 Doctor *S P R Υ*] On October 9, 1764, the new court of vice-admiralty for all of America opened at Halifax, Nova Scotia, William Spry, LL.D., presiding. Much of the "severity" that Howard refers to was a function of the distance of Halifax from the major colonial ports, which made mounting a defense extremely difficult, and to the absence of juries, a privilege Howard clearly believes had been abused in the colonial courts.

158.3 *Draco*] Athenian lawgiver whose code (621 B.C.) was proverbially harsh, hence draconian.

158.9 says the admired *Secondat*.] Montesquieu, in *The Spirit of the Laws*, Bk. XX, ch. 7.

158.18–19 whose appointments . . . influence] Spry, who was married to William Pitt's sister, was perhaps not as isolated from the web of patronage that defined eighteenth-century English politics as Howard suggests.

158.29–31 "He who filches . . . poor indeed."] *Othello*, III.iii.159–61.

159.17–18 Sir *Andrew Freeport*] Fictional merchant from *The Spectator*, the influential daily periodical (1711–12, 1714) published by Joseph Addison (1672–1719) and Sir Richard Steele (c. 1672–1729). One of a group of representative types who made up the "Spectator Club," Freeport was a departure from typical literary and dramatic portrayals of merchants as greedy and dishonest, possessing instead a broad-minded and worldly-wise character Howard contrasts here with the selfishness and provincial shortsightedness of Hopkins and the popular party.

159.21–23 "know better . . . and liberty."] Montesquieu, *The Spirit of the Laws*, Bk. XX, ch. 7.

160.4 the fables of *Pilpay*] Ancient fables of Indian and Arabic origin, first translated into English in 1570. In "The Man and the Adder," to which Howard refers here, the adder, justifying his determination to bite the hand that has just rescued him, explains to the man that "I shall do no more than what yourselves do every Day; that is to say, retaliate good Deeds with wicked Actions, and requisite Benefits with Ingratitude."

6: [THOMAS WHATELY], THE REGULATIONS LATELY MADE

169.35–36 his Majesty's Proclamation of the 7th of *October*] Though best known for its provision barring British colonists from moving westward beyond the Appalachians, the Proclamation of 1763 also extended generous land grants in Canada and the Floridas in order to entice them to move both north and south and to populate the empire's newly acquired territories.

171.17–18 That Part of *Nova Scotia*, . . . their Removal] A reference to the Acadians, who had been recognized as neutral subjects in the British colony of Nova Scotia until their forced expulsion during the Seven Years' War.

172.14 Clifts] Variant of *clefts*; both words were often confounded with *cliff* in the eighteenth century.

172.16 Fire Engines] Steam-powered pumps used to extract water from deep mines.

173.5 *Miquelon* and *St. Pierre*] Though France ceded all its territory in North America to Britain in the Treaty of Paris (1763), it retained these small islands situated off the southern coast of Newfoundland, near the Grand Banks, as well as fishing rights in the area. They remain a French territory today.

173.24 17 *Car*. 2. c. 7. s. 6.] An Act for the Encouragement of Trade, better known as the Navigation Act of 1663. Though he was in exile until 1660, Charles II's regnal years are measured from the date of the execution of his father in 1649.

173.32–33 13 *Geo*. 1. c. 5 . . . 3 *Geo*. 2. c. 12] The Importation Acts of 1726 and 1729.

174.32 *West Florida*] Encompassing the Gulf coast between the Mississippi and Apalachicola rivers and extending north to a line near the present-day cities of Jackson, Mississippi, and Montgomery, Alabama.

174.38   *East Florida*] Comprising the remainder of the present-day state of Florida.

181.2   His Majesty's Proclamation of the 26th of *March*] Of 1764, providing for the sale by auction of newly acquired crown lands in the West Indies (Grenada, the Grenadines, Dominica, St. Vincent, and Tobago).

192.3–4   The extravagant Encrease . . . some Colonies] The excessive printing of rapidly depreciating paper money and its use in attempting to pay off commercial debts, especially in the colony of Virginia, prompted vigorous protests from British creditors. These creditors pressured Parliament to pass the Currency Act of 1764 forbidding the colonies from designating paper money legal tender. This measure extended the reach of a similar 1751 act, which had targeted only New England, to all the colonies, including those like Pennsylvania that had been more responsible in the management of their paper emissions.

192.10–11   sometimes of Land] Public land banks were established by many colonies in the eighteenth century (South Carolina had the first in 1712; nine other colonies followed suit by 1737) as a means of infusing liquidity into their specie-starved economies. The banks loaned paper money to individuals who put up collateral in the form of real estate. The Crown generally viewed such measures unfavorably and in 1720, chastened by the experience of the South Sea Bubble (see Chronology), it instructed royal governors to suspend the operation of land banks pending review in the Privy Council, though many continued to function until 1740. Massachusetts investors established a short-lived private land bank in 1741, only to have it invalidated by Parliament's Act for Restraining and Preventing Several Unwarrantable Schemes and Undertakings in His Majesty's Colonies and Plantations in America.

192.35–37   *Acts, Orders,* . . . *of Money.*] From the Currency Act of 1764, the act "passed during the last Sessions" to which Whately refers on the following page.

192.40   24 *Geo.* II] The Currency Act of 1751.

197.21–22   7 *Cwt.* 0 *qrs.* 17 *lb.*] Cwt. is the abbreviation for a hundredweight, or centum weight, the equivalent of 112 lbs. A hundredweight is made up of four quarters (qrs.), each equal to two stones. This particular measurement then comes to 801 lbs., though because units of measurement were not standardized in this period such a figure is at best approximate.

197.27–28   an Act was pass'd during the last Sessions] Passed in response to a petition from English hatters, this measure was typical of the regulatory calibrations undertaken to address trade imbalances in a mercantilist system. Whately likely prepared the text of this act, as well as the one referred to at 200.38–39.

198.31   Sea Cows] Walruses.

200.4   *Cape Finisterre*] This cape, the northern- and westernmost point in

Spain, was often used in British trade regulations as a line of demarcation between northern European and Mediterranean markets or customs zones, with Spain and Portugal included in the latter.

200.21   *Guadalupe* and *Martinico* were in our Possession] Captured by Britain during the Seven Years' War in 1759 and 1762, respectively, the valuable sugar islands of Guadeloupe and Martinique were restored to France in the Treaty of Paris in exchange for the cessation of its claims in North America.

200.29   Mowburnt] Damaged in harvest.

202.16   Civil List Debt] Resulting from expenditures funding the royal household and all civil service salaries and pensions (see note 35.25–26). George III considerably expanded the civil list during his reign, creating places and pensions for his supporters in Parliament or their family members.

202.21–22   the Sinking Fund] A financial mechanism first employed in 1710 by Robert Walpole, then first lord of the Treasury and chancellor of the Exchequer, this was a dedicated fund supported by a special tax designed to reduce (sink) Britain's long-term debt. As tax proceeds reduced the principal, the interest savings were in theory to be returned to the fund, hastening the final retirement of the debt. In practice, the fund proved irresistible to Treasury officials, who frequently raided it for other purposes.

204.2–3   the Act now before us] The Sugar Act.

204.35–36   annually smuggled into the Colonies] Following the Molasses Act of 1733 the illegal importation of foreign molasses for making rum rapidly increased. Indeed, smuggling of all sorts and avoidance of the several Navigation Acts became more and more common. Customs officials were regularly bribed and corruption became so endemic that the officials began settling for a certain percentage of the legal duties. By the eve of the Revolution a large proportion of the northern colonial economy was based on the systematic violation of the law.

209.25–26   all Attempts . . . alarming to *Great Britain*] In order to ensure that large-scale manufacturing would be confined to the mother country, the British government had discouraged the manufacture of certain goods in the colonies. The Woollen Act (see note 95.9–16) had prohibited the export of American wool or woolen products from one colony to another, and the Hat Act (1732) had banned the export of American-made hats from the colony in which they were manufactured. In 1750, Parliament prohibited the manufacture of specific textiles and in the Iron Act outlawed the erection of slitting, plating, or steel mills in the colonies.

212.21–22   Concessions made . . . to the *East India* Trade] In the Treaty of Paris, France renounced all conquests it had made in India and the East Indies since 1749.

223.30–31   the first and great Act of Navigation] See Chronology for 1651.

223.36–37   The Distractions of this Country] The tumultuous decades of the Civil Wars and Interregnum had prompted waves first of Puritan and then of Royalist emigration to the colonies.

226.9   the *German* Ocean] The North Sea.

231.36–37   *it may be proper . . . in the Plantations*] From a resolution moved by Grenville in the Commons on March 10, 1764. The colonial governors were informed of the resolution in a circular letter dated August 11, 1764, from the Earl of Halifax, secretary of state for the Southern Department.

234.37–39   an internal Tax . . . Post Office] This was a false analogy for most Americans. See for instance Daniel Dulany's response in Pamphlet 7, pages 285–86 in this volume.

237.19   *Old Sarum*] This once-flourishing medieval city in Wiltshire was abandoned when its cathedral was relocated to Salisbury in the thirteenth century, becoming the most notorious of the so-called rotten boroughs, de-populated communities that nonetheless retained customary representation in Parliament. It still had two MPs in 1830 when the *Times* of London reported that the borough "consists at present of a large circular mound of earth, sur-mounted in the centre by a smaller mound. Some bushes grow upon the top, and a flourishing crop of wheat and barley occupies the situation of the former rampart, but there is no house nor vestige of a house." The rottenness of such boroughs was accentuated by the lack of representation of rapidly growing population centers in new industrial cities like Manchester and Birmingham.

7: [DANIEL DULANY], CONSIDERATIONS ON IMPOSING TAXES

243.10–11   *Haud Totum . . . fibrâ.*] From Persius, *Satires*, V.28–29: "Let not my Words shew all; The hidden Mischief cannot be express'd." As translated in the New York edition of Dulany's pamphlet, advertised for sale there shortly after the first publication in Annapolis. Unless otherwise indicated, the transla-tions from Latin in the notes that follow come from this New York edition.

245.36   *Parce, Precor.*] Ibid., VI.172: "O spare, I beseech you."

246.16   a great Lawyer] Coke, in his comments on Dr. Bonham's Case (1610), had maintained that "in many Cases, the Common Law will controll Acts of Parliament, and sometimes adjudge them to be utterly void." *The Eighth Part of the Reports of Sir Edward Coke, Kt.* (London, 1727).

246.17   a great Divine] Whig controversialist Benjamin Hoadly (1676–1761) was the Bishop of Bangor when he was quoted to similar effect by Archibald Hutcheson in his speech against the repeal of the Triennial Act before the House of Commons on April 24, 1716. The source of the original quota-tion is unknown, but Hutcheson's speech was oft reprinted, including in *Eight Speeches Made in Parliament, on Several Important Occasions. Recommended to the Electors of Great-Britain, as a Seasonable Preparative for the Ensuing Elec-tions* (London, 1733).

246.29–31   "the High Court . . . do the like."] From Coke's *Fourth Institutes.*

248.4   The Advocates for the Stamp Act] Referring principally to the author of *The Regulations Lately Made*, from which Dulany paraphrases in this and the two following paragraphs.

250.39   See Treat. Peerage.] Possibly Arthur Collins, *The Peerage of England; Containing a Genealogical and Historical Account of All the Peers of England*, a large reference work first published in London in 1717. A third edition, in six volumes, was issued in London in 1756.

251.13–16   *Cum Comites, . . . concesserint*, &c.—] Latin: "*The earls, barons, and knights, having given unto us in parliament, the eleventh part, and the citizens and burgesses the seventh part of their goods and chattels, &c.*"

251.20–21   *Dugdale* has printed . . . Parliament)] Sir William Dugdale (1605–1686), *A Perfect Copy of All Summons of the Nobility to the Great Councils and Parliaments of this Realm, from the XLIX. of King Henry the IIId. until These Present Times* (London, 1685).

251.26–28   *Volumus . . . habere*, &c.] Latin: "*We will confer with you, and others of the same kingdom (viz.* England*) possessed of lands in the said country.*"

251.36–39   *Mandamus . . . contigerit.*] Latin: "*We command you to send to* Westminster, *some person or persons, whom you may confide in, to confer with us, on the abovesaid affair, and to do and assent, in your name, to whatever shall be there decreed.*"

252.14–15   *quod omnes . . . approbetur*] A maxim of ancient Roman law: "*what concerns all, must be approved by all.*"

254.4–5   the Author of the Claim of the Colonies] William Knox, imperial bureaucrat and anonymous author of *The Claim of the Colonies to an Exemption from Internal Taxes Imposed by Authority of Parliament, Examined* (London, 1765). Knox is also the author of Pamphlet 16 in this volume.

254.20–21   *Diliut Helleborum . . . Examen.*] From Persius, *Satires*, V.100–101, translated in the New York edition of this pamphlet as "*He infuses a dangerous drug, without skill to know the proper point between its good and ill effects.*"

255.16–17   *Nullius addictus . . . Magistri*] From Horace's *Epistles*, I.i.14, translated in the New York edition as "*unused to swear on any master's word.*"

255.28–31   The Opinion given . . . generally remembered.] Asked by the Privy Council in 1755 to assess the legitimacy of colonial concerns about quartering troops during the Seven Years' War (the Pennsylvania Assembly, controlled by pacifist Quakers, had lodged a formal complaint), William Murray (1705–1793), the British attorney general (who the following year was elevated to Lord Chief Justice of the King's Bench as the 1st Earl of Mansfield), had concluded that "propositions true in the mother country, and rightly asserted in the reigns of Charles the First and Charles the Second, in times of peace, when soldiers were kept up without consent of Parliament," did not necessarily extend to colonies, and "that the application of such propositions to a colony in time of war in the case of troops raised for their protection by the authority of the Parliament of Great Britain, made the first time by an assembly, many of whom plead what they call conscience for not making or assisting military operations to resist the enemy, should not be allowed to stand as law."

255.32   The very learned Gentleman] The author of *The Regulations Lately Made*.

255.40   that accomplished Politician, and elegant Writer] Thomas Pownall, by now the acknowledged author of *The Administration of the Colonies*.

256.4   *Mâitre d'Hotel* of the late Sir *D—v—s O—b—e*] The title page of the second edition of Pownall's *Administration* had rather grandiosely identified the author as "Late Governor and Commander in Chief of his Majesty's Provinces, Messachusets-Bay [sic] and South-Carolina, and Lieutenant-Governor of New-Jersey." Pownall had first come to America in 1753 in the more humble position of private secretary to Sir Danvers Osborne, the newly appointed governor of New York, who hanged himself within a week of his arrival, leaving the ambitious young bureaucrat temporarily without a sponsor in the colonies. Pownall quickly cultivated new ties, however, and in 1755 was appointed lieutenant governor of New Jersey, with hopes of succeeding the aged incumbent governor, who uncooperatively lived on to 1757. That year he became governor instead of Massachusetts, serving for three years. Though appointed governor of South Carolina in 1760, Pownall had never actually assumed the post.

256.15–17   "*Yonder Cloud is, . . . like a Whale.*"] *Hamlet*, III.ii.361–65.

256.39   See the Hist. of TOM BRAZEN.] Pownall's meteoric rise in the colonial administration and his reputation for vanity and self-aggrandizement made him an easy target for critics. Dulany refers here to *Proposals for Printing by Subscription, The History of the Publick Life and Distinguished Actions of Vice-Admiral Sir Thomas Brazen* (Boston, 1760), a mock prospectus satirizing Pownall's administration in Massachusetts written by Samuel Waterhouse under the pseudonym of Thomas Thumb.

257.23–25   "a whimsical Imagination, . . . and Experience."] If this is a quotation, the source is unclear, though both "whimsical imagination" and "chimerical speculations" are phrases favored by Hume.

259.21–22   *ne quid . . . Respublica*] Latin, from the decree administered by the Roman Senate to consuls in time of emergency: "[Let the consuls see to it] that the commonwealth suffer no harm."

260.11–12   a very considerable Part of it hath.] On January 28, 1766, a few months after Dulany published his pamphlet, the Board of Trade released a report itemizing the colonies' contributions to the war effort and the amounts Parliament had reimbursed each. Massachusetts, with the highest expenses, £818,000, received the largest sum, £351,994; Maryland (£39,000) and Georgia (£1,820) received none. Expenses for all colonies totaled £2,568,248; reimbursements, £1,068,769.

260.20–24   "Improvements . . . to Them?"] Paraphrasing *The Regulations Lately Made.* See page 167 in this volume.

260.35   when the Militia . . . reduced *Cape-Breton*] See Chronology for 1744–48.

262.1–2   the ablest Minister that ever served his Country] William Pitt, who had become a national hero guiding the British war effort as leader of the House of Commons, was especially esteemed in the colonies, not least for his role in organizing the reimbursement scheme. He is also the "late patriotic Minister" referred to at 262.6.

262.10–39   "Acquisitions . . . *&c. &c.*"] Paraphrasing *The Regulations Lately Made.* See pages 168, 171–72, and 174 in this volume.

264.9–14   "when the real . . . the Colonies,"] Ibid., page 167.

265.2   The Assertion*] Dulany here defends his colony from an insinuation made in *The Claim of the Colonies.* Maryland had in fact been backward in contributions to the war effort, largely because of a lengthy dispute between the House of Delegates and the Council over the proper method of supporting paper emissions. Numerous attempts to fund appropriations with a tax on licenses for ordinaries (taverns) were stymied, resulting in modest total war expenditures of roughly £40,000, far less than Pennsylvania's or Virginia's. Benjamin Franklin was asked about Maryland's putative dereliction during his testimony before Parliament (see Pamphlet 9, page 345, in this volume).

265.13–14   "founded upon Knowledge, . . . with Vigour."] From *The Regulations Lately Made.* See page 194 in this volume.

266.23   The frugal *Republicans* of *North-America*] Whately deploys this "*Nick-Name*" in *The Regulations Lately Made*, ibid., 169.

267.37   drawn to *Rome* by APPEALS] English bishops and prelates had long complained about the delays and inconveniences involved in the referral of ecclesiastical cases to Rome for final settlement when the practice was outlawed in 1533 by the Act in Restraint of Appeals, one of the pillars of the Henrician reformation. (See Chronology.)

268.4   the Expence of 7600*l. per Annum*] This figure is cited in *The Regulations Lately Made.* See page 203 in this volume.

269.13–16   *a Mode of Taxation . . . upon none?*] Ibid., 232.

269.32–33   There was a Statute of *Henry* VIII] An Act that Proclamations Made by the King Shall be Obeyed (1539), which established a mechanism by which royal proclamations, when signed by twelve councilors, would have the force of law "as though they were made by act of parliament." It proved impractical and unnecessary and was repealed in 1547.

270.24–27   "Two Millions . . . raised *there*;"] From *The Regulations Lately Made*. See page 203 in this volume.

270.32–36   "the Inhabitants of the Colonies . . . Reason to complain,"] Ibid., 233.

272.15–17   "well-digested, . . . and Finance,"] Ibid., 168, 240. Dulany's attribution of this quote to "the Minister" reflects the widespread assumption that George Grenville was the author of *The Regulations Lately Made*. (See Note on the Texts.)

272.32–34   *O! me infelicem, . . . habuerint!*] From "The Stag at the Stream" by the Roman fabulist Phaedrus, translated in the New York edition of Dulany's *Considerations* as "*O! unhappy I, who now at length am sensible / How the things I had despised were of advantage to me, / And how much mourning they caused, which I had so much approved!*"

273.27–30   "what will become . . . given up?] Paraphrasing *The Claim of the Colonies*.

273.30–35   To deny . . . Privilege, &*c*."] From *The Regulations Lately Made*. See page 239 in this volume.

274.8–19   "if the common Law . . . can't be denied."] Paraphrasing *The Claim of the Colonies*.

276.25–28   "The Common Law, . . . *British Parliament*,"] Ibid.

276.37–38   it was properly declared at the Revolution] See Chronology for 1688–89.

278.2–3   the Examiner] The author of *The Claim of the Colonies . . . Examined*.

278.33   the *Chancellor of the Exchequer*] Grenville.

279.28–29   Postscript to . . . *the Peace*, &c.] In the quotation following from *A Postscript to the Letter, on Libels, Warrants, &c. in Answer to a Postscript in the Defence of the Majority, and Another Pamphlet, Entitled, Considerations on the Legality of General Warrants* (second edition, London, 1765), the parenthetical glosses are Dulany's.

279.41   *sed Verbum sapienti sat est*."] Translated in the New York edition as "*but a word is enough to the wise*."

280.16   who is said to have been *well informed*,] The author of *The Regulations Lately Made* was called "the judicious and well-informed writer" in *The Claim of the Colonies*.

280.31   the Reign of our great Deliverer] William III. This footnote refers to the 1689 declaration of England and Holland, made during the War of the League of Augsburg, that their naval forces would seize any nation's vessels trading with France. John Gröning, in his *Navigatio Libra* (1693), denounced this violation of neutral shipping, but, as Dulany indicates, Pufendorf (see note 66.27) suggested that perhaps England and Holland had a legitimate right to distress France's trade.

281.15   Pages 234, 202–3] In this volume.

281.25   The 5th *Geo.* II] An Act for the More Easy Recovery of Debts in His Majesty's Plantations and Colonies in America (1732).

281.34   a little pert Pamphlet] *The Objections to the Taxation of Our American Colonies, by the Legislature of Great Britain, Briefly Consider'd* (London, 1765), an anonymous pamphlet by English poet Soame Jenyns, a former member of the Board of Trade (hence "L[or]d of T[rade]"). In it Jenyns writes: "I am well aware that I shall hear *Lock, Sidney, Seldon,* and many other great Names quoted, to prove that every Englishman, whether he has a Right to vote for a Representative, or not, is still represented in the *British* Parliament; in which opinion they all agree: . . . but then I will ask one Question, and on that I will rest the whole Merits of the Cause: Why does not this imaginary Representation extend to *America* as well as over the whole Island of *Great Britain*? If it can travel three hundred Miles, why not three thousand?"

283.31–32   the Examiner takes Occasion to insult a Gentleman] It is not clear which "*American Chief Justice*" Dulany believes Knox to have been attacking. The passage in question from *The Claim of the Colonies* appears to be generic, not ad hominem.

284.9–11   *Ille superbos . . . Colat*—] Seneca, *Hercules Furens,* ll. 164–66, translated in the New York edition as "*Let such a one, without taking sleep, / Attend the proud levees, and haughty gates / Of kings*—."

286.20   subdolous] Obsolete: crafty, cunning, sly.

287.19   the Name of *Hampden* occurred to the Examiner] Knox posed the following questions in *The Claim of the Colonies*: "Can the crown grant an exemption to any subject of Great Britain, from the jurisdiction of parliament? Will any descendant of the associates of Pym or Hamden, avow it for his opinion that the crown can do so?" Throughout the imperial debate, British Whigs like Knox sounded this incredulous tone whenever Americans, especially the sons of Puritan New England—John Pym and John Hampden were leading Puritan parliamentarians during the English Civil War—looked to the Crown for protection against Parliament. In the eyes of most Britons, the conflict between the king's prerogative (as exercised by the Crown) and the subjects' rights (as defended by Parliament) underlay all English politics since at least Magna Carta. The Glorious Revolution, and the development of the concept of the King-in-Parliament, was presumed to have settled the conflict and created an ideal balance in Britain between the two principal contestants.

288.32   We are assured] In *The Claim of the Colonies.*

288.34   the glorious Line of *Brunswick*] The House of Hanover, rulers also of the Duchy of Brunswick-Lunëburg.

288.38–39   See the Narrative . . . in *Canada.*] Referring to an incident in Montreal on December 6, 1764, when a group of soldiers broke into the house of Thomas Walker and cut off his right ear. Walker, a justice of the peace, had been trying to address abuses arising from the billeting of troops. Accounts of the assault circulated in colonial newspapers in the spring and summer of 1765. A more detailed narrative entitled *The Trial of Daniel Disney . . . upon an Indictment . . . for a Burglary and Felony, in Breaking and Entering Mr. Thomas Walker's House . . . with an Intention to Murder . . .* was published in Quebec in 1767 and reprinted in New York the following year.

289.15   little P—ct—r*] Protector, a reference to the quasi-kingship of Oliver Cromwell.

289.19–29   "it will be no easy Task . . . for Subsistence."] Paraphrasing *The Regulations Lately Made.* See pages 208 and 205 in this volume.

292.25   Remora] Obsolete: hindrance, from the Latin for delay. The family of suckerfish (*Echeneidae*) was so named because they were believed capable of delaying ships by adhering to their hulls.

293.13   Linsey-Wolsey] Linsey-woolsey, a course fabric of cotton or linen woven with wool.

294.27–31   "it would always . . . be prevented."] Paraphrasing *The Regulations Lately Made.* See page 210 in this volume.

295.34   History of *James* I] The first volume of David Hume, *The History of Great Britain under the House of Stuart* (2 vols., Edinburgh, 1754–57).

296.15–16   SUFFICIENT FOR THE DAY . . . THEREOF.] Matthew 6:34.

297.2   By the 12th *Cha.* II, . . . By the 15th] The Navigation Acts of 1660 and 1663.

297.33   a well-received Writer] Sir Matthew Decker (1679–1749), a merchant who had been both an MP and a director of the East India Company. The quotations that follow are paraphrases from Decker's anonymously published *An Essay on the Causes of the Decline of the Foreign Trade, Consequently of the Value of the Lands of Britain, and on the Means to Restore Both* (London, 1744). The italics are Dulany's.

298.9–10   *communibus Annis*] Latin: in an average year.

304.1   *profoundly well-inform'd . . .* Writer] Dulany's reference at 280.16 suggests that he is again referring to Whately here.

304.12–29   "if ever any Thing . . . the King's Profit."] From *Discourses on the Publick Revenues, and the Trade of England. In Two Parts* (1698), by

Charles Davenant, LL.D. (1656–1714), inspector general of imports and exports from 1705 until his death.

304.33   DEUS . . . FINEM.] From Virgil, *Aeneid*, I.199, translated in the New York edition as "*God shall also put an End to these.*"

8: RICHARD BLAND, AN INQUIRY INTO THE RIGHTS

305.15–16   "should be consulted . . . imagined."] From an anonymous Philadelphia pamphlet of June 1774 entitled *Reflections on Appointing Delegates to the General Congress.*

305.18–22   "To what purpose . . . ought to be."] From [James Otis], *Considerations on Behalf of the Colonists in a Letter to a Noble Lord* (London, 1765).

306.1–8   "He would set out . . . to point."] Thomas Jefferson to William Wirt, August 5, 1815.

307.11–12   *Dedit omnibus . . . perpendere.*] From Lactantius, *Institutiones Divinae*, Bk. II, ch. viii: "God hath given to all men such a degree of understanding, as may enable them to search out new truths, and examine old ones." Translation from *A Letter from the Revered Sir Harry Trelawny, Bart. A. B. to the Reverend Thomas Alcock* (London, 1780).

309.14–23   "many Steps . . . to his Reflexion."] Cf. page 167 in this volume.

310.20–311.12   "the Inhabitants of the Colonies . . . are represented."] Ibid., pages 236–37.

312.29–30   1st *Hen.* 5 Ch. 1st] Passed in 1413, the first year of the reign of Henry V.

312.35   *Petyt's Rights . . . Squire's Inquiry.*] William Petyt, *The Antient Right of the Commons of England Asserted* (1680); Robert Brady, *A Complete History of England* (1685); Paul de Rapin-Thoyras, *Histoire D'Angleterre* (10 vols., 1723–27, *The History of England, as well Ecclesiastical as Civil*, 15 vols., 1728–32); Samuel Squire, *An Enquiry into the Foundation of the English Constitution; or, An Historical Essay upon the Anglo-Saxon Government both in Germany and England* (1745, expanded edition, 1753).

312.36   *Cæsar de Bell. . . . Temple's Misc.*] Julius Caesar, *Commentarii de Bello Gallico* (Commentaries on the Gallic War); Tacitus, *de Origine et Situ Germanorum* (On the Origins and Situation of Germania), ch. 28; Sir William Temple, *Miscellanea. The First Part* (1705), especially "An Essay upon the Original and Nature of Government, Written in the Year 1672."

312.39   2 *Inst.* 27. 4 *Inst.* 2.] The second and fourth parts of Coke's *Institutes.*

313.2–3   8th *Hen.* 6. Ch. 7.] Enacted in 1429 and operative until passage of the Representation of the People Act in 1918.

313.39   *Vattel's Law . . . Wollaston's Rel. of Nat.*] For Vattel and Locke see note 47.3–4. William Wollaston, *The Religion of Nature Delineated* (London, 1722).

315.15–17 "Order or Rank . . . without their Consent."] If this is a quotation, its source is not known.

315.39 2 *Pur. Williams.*] William Peere Williams, ed., *Reports of Cases Argued and Determined in the High Court of Chancery* (2 vols., London, 1740).

316.39 *Strahan in his Preface to Domat.*] See note 68.9.

317.25–29 "before the first . . . at Home."] Paraphrasing *The Regulations Lately Made.* See page 223 in this volume.

318.37 *Hakluyt's Voyages*] Richard Hakluyt, *The Principall Navigations, Voiages and Discoveries of the English Nation* (1589).

318.38 *Salmon's Mod. Hist.*] Bland cites the third edition of Thomas Salmon, *Modern History: or, the Present State of All Nations* (3 vols., London, 1744–46).

321.10–11 Sir *W. Berkley*] Sir William Berkeley (1605–1677) was Virginia's longest-serving governor, in office from 1642 to 1652 and again from 1660 until his death. During his tenure Berkeley encouraged the development of the Virginia Assembly into a mature legislative body reflecting the will of the colony's planter elite, to whom he offered significant local autonomy in exchange for a free hand in Virginia's external affairs. He was staunchly loyal to the House of Stuart, having been knighted by Charles I in 1639.

321.22–25 "the Colonists . . . at home,"] From *The Regulations Lately Made.* See page 223 in this volume.

322.4–6 "no Power can . . . an Exemption."] Ibid., 238.

322.15–16 "the Freedom and . . . Constitution"] Ibid., 179.

322.29–30 County Palatine of *Chester*] See note 32.2–3.

322.30 *ab antiquo*] Latin: from ancient times.

322.32 *Commune Concilium*] Latin: Common Council, or parliament.

322.39 *King's Vale Royal*] Daniel King, *The Vale-Royal of England, or, The County Palatine of Chester Illustrated* (1656).

323.17 sent over an Act] One of three measures drafted by the Privy Council that Thomas, Lord Culpeper (1635–1689), brought with him to Virginia when he assumed the governorship in person in 1680. (Culpeper had been appointed to the post in 1677, but like most governors of the Old Dominion had been content to be an absentee until being pressured by the Crown to make the transit.) The other two offered a free and general pardon after Bacon's Rebellion (see Chronology for 1676) and provided for a more generous naturalization process. The clause Bland quotes is found in all three acts.

323.40   the Act of 25th *Charles* 2d] See note 101.28.

324.13–14   "Taxes and Impositions . . . Assembly."] Quoting from the petition Virginia's colonial agents delivered to the Privy Council's committee for foreign plantations at Whitehall on November 19, 1675. The royal charter confirming Virginia's "immediate dependence upon the crown of England"— as opposed to the Parliament, whose jurisdiction the Virginians wished to limit only to "any imposition that may be laid . . . on the commodities which come" from the colony—was dated October 10, 1676.

325.17–20   "the *British* Empire . . . of the Whole,"] From *The Regulations Lately Made*. See page 191 in this volume.

325.24–25   "have a *Right* . . . upon the Colonies,"] Ibid., 236.

326.25   *Thucydides* would make the *Corinthians* reply] Thucydides makes extensive use of speeches in his *History of the Peloponnesian War*, including by the Corinthian and Corcyrean envoys to Athens and Sparta.

326.36–327.6   "the *British* Empire . . . Union between them"] Bland counterpoises two passages from *The Regulations Lately Made*. See pages 191 and 176–77 in this volume.

327.7–8   "an Alliance . . . to the Mother Country."] Ibid., 176.

328.19–22   The *Helvetick* Confederacy, . . . Cause of Liberty] Two examples —savored by eighteenth-century Whigs, especially in America—of small federated states facing off against powerful and despotic adversaries: first, from the fifteenth century, the stalwart resistance (personified by the legendary folk hero William Tell) of the confederation of Swiss cantons and city states against the Habsburgs; and second, the long Dutch revolt against Spanish rule in the sixteenth and seventeenth centuries.

9: THE EXAMINATION OF FRANKLIN

331.13–14   "an Assembly . . . ever Yet saw."] Delaware delegate Caesar Rodney (1728–1784), in an October 20, 1765, letter to his brother Thomas.

335.4   Q. WHAT is your name, and place of abode?] Franklin sent copies of this pamphlet to various friends, and in at least one case he added annotations that identified many of his questioners by name. These notes reveal what many critical readers of the *Examination* had suspected, that a certain degree of orchestration with sympathetic MPs had enabled Franklin to make his points in prepared answers. But of the 174 questions in the *Examination*, more than half are identified as coming from members of the former Grenville ministry, the architects of the Stamp Act, or some other "Adversary." These questions Franklin had to parry in real time, on his feet. This first question, he noted, was one of "form; askd of everyone that is examin'd."

335.6–30   Q. Do the Americans pay . . . those taxes?] Franklin noted that these questions were from James Hewitt (1712–1789), "Member from

Coventry, a Friend of ours and were designd to draw out the Answers that follow, being the Substance of what I had before said to him on the subject, to remove a common Prejudice, that the Colonies paid no Taxes, and that their Governments were supported by burthening the People here." "Friend" was a common designation for a fellow partisan in eighteenth-century English politics. Its use often traced the sinews of patronage that made up the body politic, as for instance the "King's Friends," the large block of placemen and pensioners that supported George III's more active role in government.

336.1–26   Q. Are not you concerned . . . if executed?] These questions were posed by John Huske (see note 137.36), as were those from 337.9 to 338.9. According to Franklin's notes, Huske's "Questions about the Germans and about the Number of People were intended to make the Opposition to the stamp Act in America appear more formidable. He ask'd some others here that the Clerk has omitted, particularly one I remember. There had been a considerable Party in the House for saving the Honour and Right of Parliament by retaining the Act, and yet making it tolerable to America, by reducing it to a stamp on Commissions for Profitable Offices and on Cards and Dice. I had in conversation with many of them objected to this, as it would require an Establishment for the Distributors, which would be a great Expence for that the stamps would not be sufficient to pay them, and so the Odium and Contention would be kept up for nothing. The Notion of Amending however still continued, and one of the most active of the Members for promoting it, told me he was sure, I could if I would assist them to amend the Act in such a manner as that America should have little or no Objection to it. I must confess, says I, I have thought of one Amendment, that if you will make it, the Act may remain and yet the Americans will be quieted. 'Tis a very small Amendment, too, 'tis only a Change of a single Word. Ay! says he what is that? It is says I, in that Clause where it is said that from and after the first day of November *One* read *Two*, and then all the rest of the Act may stand as it does: I believe it will give nobody in America any Uneasiness. Mr. Huske had heard of this, and desiring to bring out the same Answer in the House askd me, Whether I could not propose a small Amendment that would make the Act palatable? But as I thought the Answer He wanted too light and ludicrous for the House, I evaded the Question."

338.13–26   Q. Do you think it right . . . in the Pound?] Franklin: "I think these were by Mr. Greenville [George Grenville], but am not certain."

338.31–32   the rate of exchange in Pennsylvania] That is, between the Pennsylvania currency and pound sterling, commonly during this period 170 to 175 Pennsylvania currency to 100 pounds sterling, as Franklin indicates.

339.1–13   Q. Are not the taxes . . . heavier on trade?] Questions from Robert Nugent (1709–1788), MP for Bristol, "who was against us" (Franklin).

339.21–340.24   Q. What was the temper of America . . . respect for parliament?] Franklin noted that these five questions were from "Mr. Cooper and other Friends." Grey Cooper (c. 1726–1801), MP for Rochester and secretary to the Treasury, 1765–82, was a "fast friend" of Franklin's.

340.1   except . . . internal taxes.] With this clause Franklin opened up a can of worms for his fellow Americans, very few of whom accepted the distinction between internal and external taxes he appears to draw here. Franklin later hedges when the distinction is revisited at 359.17–24.

340.32   refusing to receive . . . humble petitions.] As for instance Parliament's recent handling of the petitions of the Stamp Act Congress. The latter's memorial to the House of Lords was deemed inappropriate in form and withheld from consideration. Its petition to the Commons was presented to the House on January 27, 1766, and though William Pitt urged its acceptance in a strong speech, the Rockingham ministry opposed the motion to receive because the petition challenged Parliament's authority to tax the colonies. The House supported the ministry without a division (that is, by a clearly decisive voice vote).

340.37–341.5   Q. What do you think . . . than in England?] Questions "by Mr. Nugent again, who I suppose intended to infer that the Poor People in America were better able to pay Taxes than the Poor in England" (Franklin).

341.8–17   Q. What is your opinion . . . on those resolutions?] Questions from George Prescott (c. 1711–1790), MP for Stockbridge, whom Franklin described as "an Adversary." His second question refers to resolutions declaring Parliament's legislative authority over the colonies which had been introduced in both houses on February 3, ten days before Franklin's appearance.

342.15–19   Q. Don't you know . . . of the civil government?] Nathaniel Ryder (1735–1803), MP for Tiverton, who took notes during Franklin's testimony, attributed this question and the two following to Jeremiah Dyson (c. 1722–1776), MP for Yarmouth (Isle of Wight), an opponent of repeal. The episode Dyson refers to here was described as follows in the supporting material attached to *The Controversy Between Great Britain and Her Colonies Reviewed* (Pamphlet 16 in this volume): "Grants which had been made by [the New York] assembly for several years before, for the support of government, were discontinued in the year 1710; and upon the representation of the then governor of that Province, of the assembly's refusal to renew the grant, the Whig Ministers immediately resolved to bring in a bill into parliament, for imposing all the taxes which had been discontinued." For William Knox, the ministry spokesperson who wrote *The Controversy Reviewed*, this "furnishes a strong proof of the attention which the great ministers, of that time, gave to the Colony proceedings; and of *their opinion* of the right of parliament to tax them; and the subsequent conduct of the assembly of New York, is also an evidence of the just conceptions they then had of the authority of parliament, and of their wisdom in obviating the necessity for its interposition, *by imposing the tax themselves.*"

343.15–346.10   Q. You say the Colonies . . . abolishing the paper?] Nineteen questions "chiefly by the former Ministry" (Franklin).

345.17–18   Q. Did you never hear that Maryland, . . . towards the common defence?] See note 265.2.

345.39–40   Q. Do you remember . . . act of assembly?] Thomas Hutchinson was speaker of the Massachusetts House of Representatives in 1749 when he engineered a bill to use the parliamentary reimbursement for the expedition to Cape Breton (£183,649) to redeem the colony's paper money for silver.

346.15–25   Q. Have not instructions . . . stamp-act into execution?] Four questions "by Friends" (Franklin).

346.28   Q. Why may it not?] Franklin: "by one of the late Ministry."

346.33–34   Q. If the act is not repealed, . . . consequences?] Franklin: "by Mr. Cooper."

346.38–347.24   Q. How can the commerce . . . be submitted to?] Franklin noted that these six questions were posed "by some of the late Ministry."

347.12–13   the use of all goods fashionable in mournings] It was customary during this period in both Britain and British North America, but perhaps nowhere more so than in New England, for families to make a gift of mourning gloves or scarves to those attending the funeral of a deceased loved one. The discontinuance of this expensive practice, to which Franklin alludes here, afforded an indication of what might be achieved through coordinated non-consumption.

347.38–348.7   Q. But is not the post-office, . . . as a tax?] Two questions about the colonial postal service posed by Grenville. Franklin, writing as "The Colonist's Advocate," elaborated on the answer he provides here in a letter (the third in a series) he published in the London *Public Advertiser* on January 11, 1770: "The Post-Office, say the Grenvillians, is, in Effect, a Tax upon America, which they have never complained of. The advancing of so frivolous an Apology for their Injustice and Oppression, shews the Difficulty they find in patching up an indefensible Cause. They might as well have drawn a Defence of their Policy from the establishing of Tolls at Turnpikes. Will any Man of common Sense attempt to force a Comparison between a Regulation evidently for the Benefit of the Colonies, and of our Merchants trading with them, and whose Effect is a saving of Money to the Colonists, and a Scheme, whose declared Intention is, to take from them their Property, and to increase the Revenue at their Expence, and contrary to their Inclination?"

348.1   quantum meruit] Latin: literally, as much as one is entitled to. In contract law, the proper value for services rendered.

348.11–349.6   Q. If an excise was laid . . . on their sugars exported?] Franklin noted that these six questions were asked "by some of the late Ministry." According to Nathaniel Ryder's notes, the last three were from Welbore Ellis (1713–1802), MP for Aylesbury, and secretary at war, 1762–65.

349.10–15   Q. How much is the poll-tax . . . in Pennsylvania?] Franklin noted that these two questions were asked "by some Friend, I think sir Geo.

Saville." Sir George Saville, Bart. (1726–1784), MP for Yorkshire; a leading member of the opposition during the Grenville ministry, he nonetheless declined to join the Rockingham administration.

349.17–350.11 Q. Supposing the stamp-act continued, . . . by law, any debt?] Franklin noted that these six questions were posed "by several of the late Ministry."

350.20–351.11 Q. What do you think a sufficient military force . . . with that flax-seed?] Eight questions "by Friends" (Franklin).

350.27 *He withdrew.*] Franklin, that is.

351.14–22 Q. Are there any slitting mills . . . in Philadelphia?] Three questions asked by Anthony Bacon (c. 1717–1786), MP for Aylesbury, a London merchant who claimed to have opposed the Stamp Act. He inquires about two industrial operations seen as leading indicators of the potential for self-sufficiency in the colonies: slitting mills, which processed iron into rods for making nails, and fulling mills, which were used to clean cloth by beating it with fuller's earth, a fine-grained substance that naturally absorbs oils and other discoloring agents.

351.24–35 Q. If the stamp act should be repealed, . . . by its inexpediency?] Franklin noted that these three questions were posed "by some of the late Ministry."

351.40–352.3 Q. If the act should be repealed, . . . they would do?] Franklin noted that this question was asked "by an Adversary," the next "by a Friend."

353.33–354.38 Q. But suppose Great-Britain . . . is not an American interest?] Two questions by Charles Townshend (1725–1767), MP for Harwich, who was then paymaster general and who would become chancellor of the Exchequer in August 1766.

354.2 the expedition against Carthagena] A major two-year military effort in the war with Spain (the War of Jenkin's Ear), in which a large but incompetently led British expeditionary force failed to take the crucial South American outpost, which possessed perhaps the best harbor on the Spanish main.

354.12–13 we had therefore . . . in that dispute.] Franklin is being less than candid here. As he was very well aware, the Ohio Company, a land speculation company organized in 1747 by a group of Virginia planters, was deeply implicated in the tensions that gave rise to conflict in the Ohio Valley, as was his own colony of Pennsylvania.

354.19 Braddock was sent with an army] See Chronology for 1755.

355.1–3 Q. You will not deny . . . the American seas?] This is Robert Nugent again.

355.6–7 Q. Was not the late war . . . for America only?] Asked by Grenville. For Pontiac's Rebellion, see Chronology for 1763.

355.12 General Bouquet] Swiss-born Henry Bouquet (1719–1766) was still a colonel when he led an expedition in 1764 into the Ohio Valley to suppress Pontiac's Rebellion.

355.15–16 Q. Is it not necessary . . . against the Indians?] Asked by "one of the late Ministry" (Franklin).

355.26–27 Q. Do you say . . . the late Indian war?] Grenville again.

355.35–356.3 Q. Do you think the assemblies . . . for any other than local purposes?] Franklin noted that these questions were posed "by Mr. Welbore Ellis late Secry. at War."

355.38 Q. Are they acquainted with the declaration of rights?] A highly provocative question for any good Whig, for whom the Bill of Rights of 1689 was mother's milk.

357.4–28 Q. Do not letters often come . . . on the ferrymen?] Franklin noted that these seven questions came from "some of the late Ministry, intending to prove that Postage was demanded where no service was done, and therefore it was a Tax."

357.31–33 Q. If the stamp-act should be repealed, . . . would they grant it?] A question "by a Friend, I forget who" (Franklin).

357.36–37 I had it in instructions from the assembly] Franklin brought these instructions from the Pennsylvania Assembly, dated November 1, 1764, with him when he sailed for England six days later to become the colony's agent in London. The "honourable gentleman then minister" was Grenville.

358.5–6 Q. Would they do this . . . that did not affect them?] Asked by Charles Townshend.

358.9–358.28 Q. What is the usual . . . representation in parliament?] Franklin noted that these six questions were posed "by some of the late Ministry."

358.30–359.26 Q. Don't you know . . . all taxes?] Franklin noted that these six questions were posed by "Mr. Prescot and Others of the same."

359.31–360.4 Q. Have you not seen . . . as distinct from taxes?] Four questions from Townshend.

360.11 Q. Are all parts . . . able to pay taxes?] Franklin: "By a Friend: I think Sir Geo. Savile."

360.19–21 Q. Would the repeal . . . decline it?] Franklin: "By some Friend."

360.32–34 Q. If the stamp-act . . . erase their resolutions?] Franklin recalled that this and the next question were asked "by an Adversary."

361.1–2 Q. Is there a power . . . to erase them?] Franklin: "by a Friend, I think."

361.5–15   Q. Do they consider . . . to the minister?] Three questions from "a Friend" (Franklin).

361.18–24   Q. Would it be most . . . their pride?] Three questions from "another Friend" (Franklin).

361.27   *Withdrew.*] Franklin added the following postscript to his notes on the *Examination*: "Mr. Nugent made a violent speech next day upon this Examination. In which he said 'We have often experienced Austrian Ingratitude, and yet we assisted Portugal. We experienced Porteguese Ingratitude, and yet we assisted America. But what is Austrian Ingratitude, what is the Ingratitude of Portugal compared to this of America? We have fought, bled and Ruin'd ourselves, to conquer for them; and now they come and tell us to our Noses, even at the Bar of this House, that they are not obliged to us! &c. &c.' But his Clamour was very little minded."

10: [WILLIAM HICKS], NATURE OF PARLIAMENTARY POWER

365.14–16   "*If there be . . . Man's security.*"] The Second Philippic, delivered 344–43 B.C. by the Greek statesman and orator Demosthenes (384–322 B.C.), was a vehement attack on Philip, king of Macedon, for violating the peace.

367.21   the billeting act] The Quartering Act of 1765 (see Chronology).

368.20–21   The people of England . . . their freedom] That is, against the encroachment of royal power, through the vigilance of Parliament, against which the colonists must now also be on guard.

369.19   plentifully supplied with necessaries] Under the terms of the Quartering Act the colonies were also required to supply the troops with certain provisions, including firewood, candles, rum, and beer.

370.3–4   Upon application to the government of New-York] Many of the British troops in America were quartered in New York, especially around the Albany area. Although the Redcoats had been used in June 1766 to put down an uprising of tenant farmers in the Hudson Valley, the New York Assembly showed no gratitude and instead refused to comply with all of the provisions of the Quartering Act. When the New York governor sent a copy of the act to the Assembly, it declined even to acknowledge the statute's existence.

371.1–3   —*Sed comprime . . . honesti.*] From C. Claudian, *Panegyricus De Quarto Consulatu Honorii Augusti* (Panegyric on the Fourth Consulship of the Emperor Honorius): "Thou, the first Sallies in thy Bosom quell, / Nor e'er be thy Concern what 'tis Thou canst, / But what Thou ought'st to do: and the Regard / Of what is just, let always rule thy Will." Translation from Henry Baker, *Medulla Poetarum Romanorum: or, The Most Beautiful and Instructive Passages of the Roman Poets. . . . with Translations of the Same in English Verse* (London, 1737).

371.21–22 An act . . . to strip us of our legislative power] New York's refusal to acknowledge the binding effect of a parliamentary statute pertaining
to the army infuriated William Pitt, now Lord Chatham, head of the new
ministry (in office July 1766–October 1768) that had replaced the Rockingham
Whigs. In June 1767, Parliament passed an act suspending all legislative functions of the New York Assembly until it fully complied with all the requirements of the Quartering Act.

372.34 *furor militaris*] Latin: military fever.

374.22–23 *Vos dormitis . . . nos pateamus.*] From a letter from Caelius to
Cicero, 48 B.C., in Cicero, *Epistolarum ad Familiares* (Letters to Friends):
"You are asleep, and do not know how exposed we are here."

376.39 *Vide Sacheverel's trial.*] In 1710 the Oxford High Church clergyman Henry Sacheverell (1674–1724) was tried for sedition in the House of
Lords for his inflammatory sermons on behalf of the Tory principle of non-
resistance to established authority. The verdict resulted in his suspension
from preaching for three years and the burning of the offending sermons.
This made him a martyr in the eyes of the populace, precipitating riots and
attacks on religious dissenters and resulting in a Tory triumph in the elections of 1710. Hicks refers here to the published trial transcripts, *The Tryal of
Dr. Henry Sacheverell, Before the House of Peers, for High Crimes and Misdemeanors* (London, 1710).

377.17 *ne quid . . . respublica*] See note 259.21–22.

377.36–37 a late judicious writer.*] John Dickinson (see Pamphlet II in this
volume).

378.9–12 *Te propter . . . inermis.*] From C. Claudian, *Panegyricus De Consulatu Fl. Mallii Theodori* (Panegyric on the Consulship of Flavius Mallius
Theodorus), addressing Justice: "For thy sake only We the laws revere: / To
humanize the Mind, and thence expel / All brutal Passions, 'tis to Thee we
owe. / Whose upright Soul Thee deeply has imbib'd, / Fearless thro' Flames
shall rush: thro' Northern Storms / Shall sail undaunted: and a Host of Foes
/ Shall overthrow, unarmed, and alone." Translation from Baker, *Medulla Poetarum Romanorum*.

379.3–9 "*Those laws . . . can be made.*"] From *The History and Analysis of
the Common Law of England* (see note 92.24).

380.38 LOCKE *on Government.*] *Second Treatise*, sect. 140.

382.33 ROSSEAU.] Hicks provides here three passages (interrupted by another
footnote) from Rousseau, *Discours sur l'origine et les fondemens de l'inegalité
parmi les hommes* (Amsterdam, 1755). They are translated in the first English
edition, *A Discourse upon the Origin and Foundation of Inequality among
Mankind* (London, 1761), as follows:

Besides, the Right of Property being of mere Human Convention and Institution, every Man may dispose as he pleases of what he possesses: But the Case is otherwise with regard to the essential Gifts of Nature, such as Life and Liberty, which every Man is permitted to enjoy, and of which it is doubtful at least whether any Man has a right to divest himself.

But tho' we could transfer our Liberty as we do our Substance, the Difference would be very great with regard to our Children, who enjoy our Substance but by a Cession of our Right; whereas Liberty being a Blessing, which as Men they hold from Nature, their Parents have no Right to strip them of it.

The Writers of these Books set out by examining, what Rules it would be proper, for their common Interest, Men should agree to among themselves; and then, without further Ceremony, they proceed to give the Name of natural Law to a Collection of these Rules, without any other Proof of such a Collection's deserving that Name, than the Advantage they find would result from an universal Compliance with it.

383.40 SENEC. Med.] A proverbial phrase from Seneca's *Medea*, ll. 199–200: "Who passes Judgment, e'er both Sides are heard, / Tho' right his Sentence prove, is yet unjust." Translation from Baker, *Medulla Poetarum Romanorum*.

384.17–19 *Nostri autem . . .* DEFENDERENT.] From Cicero, *De officiis*, Bk. II, ch. viii: "[O]ur Officers and Commanders made it their greatest Glory to defend their Provinces, and assist their Allies, with Justice and Fidelity." Translation from Thomas Cockman, *Tully's Three Books of Offices, in English* (seventh edition, London, 1753).

384.32 That right honourable and worthy gentleman] Pitt, from whose January 14, 1766, speech in the House of Commons Hicks paraphrases in this paragraph and passim.

385.33 Mr. *G——lle*] Grenville.

385.37–39 *Le contract . . . la violence.*] Another passage from Rousseau's *Discours sur l'origine et les fondemens de l'inegalité*, translated in the 1761 English edition as "the Contract of Government is so much dissolved by Despotism, that the Despot is no longer Master than he continues the strongest, and that, as soon as his Slaves can expel him, they may do it without his having the least Right to complain of their using him ill."

388.26 a piece of Ottoman policy] Along with polygamy, sodomy, and ritual murder, infanticide was a common component of lurid portrayals of "Mahometan" court culture in early modern Europe.

388.31 our *British Machiavel*] Grenville is here likened to the Italian political philosopher for favoring expediency over morality.

390.2   "*crush us to atoms*"] From Pitt's speech: "A great deal has been said without doors of the power, of the strength of America. It is a topic that ought to be cautiously meddled with. In a good cause, on a sound bottom, the force of this country can crush America to atoms. . . . But on this ground, on the Stamp Act, . . . in such a cause, your success would be hazardous."

390.6–8   *Quam vos* . . . probos.] From Terence, *Adelphoe* (The Brothers), III.vi: "The more You live at Ease, the more you're blest / With Pow'r, and Wealth, Preferment, and a Name, / So much the stricter must be your Regard / For Honesty and Justice, if you wish/ To have the World believe you Men of Honour." Translation from Baker, *Medulla Poetarum Romanorum*.

392.39–40   resolves . . . of *February* 1766] In addition to passing the Declaratory Act, the House of Commons in February 1766 endorsed a series of resolves affirming that the riots in America had violated the law, that the colonial assemblies had supported the riots, that victims of the riots ought to be compensated, and that those who had complied with the Stamp Act in the face of popular intimidation would have the protection of Parliament.

393.25–26   the unfortunate *Monmouth* . . . *open rebellion*] See Chronology for 1685.

393.27   a Prince of military abilities] William of Orange.

394.12–13   this very accurate definition of my Lord C. J. *Hale*] Hicks presents Chief Justice Hale's definition more fully in the epigraph on page 379 in this volume.

395.13–14   "to write what I thought . . . I should write."] In his preface to the popular *Love Elegies* of James Hammond (1710–1742)—which were written in 1732, first published shortly after Hammond's death in 1742, and in their sixth edition by 1768—Lord Chesterfield wrote of the author that "he sat down to write what he thought, not to think what he should write."

395.15–17   *Ardeo, mihi* . . . *non amicus.*] From Cicero, *De Provinciis Consularibus* (A Speech Concerning the Consular Provinces): "I am consumed, believe me, with the fire . . . of a surpassing love for my country. . . . In fact, let men think what they will, for me it is impossible not to be the friend of one who renders good service to the State." Translation from R. Gardner, *Cicero: Pro Caelio, De Provinciis Consularibus, Pro Balbo* (Cambridge, MA: Harvard University Press, 1937).

396.3–5   *Suo quemque* . . . *circumagi.*] From Livy, *Ab Urbe Condita Libri* (Chapters [in the History of Rome] from the City's Founding), Bk. XXXIX, ch. 5: "One's own heart and reason ought to regulate his love or hatred, approbation or condemnation of actions: one ought not to depend upon the looks and nods of others." Translation from John Henry Freese et al., *The Roman History by Titus Livius* (6 vols., London, 1744).

397.22   *salvo jure*] Latin: literally, without prejudice to the right. More broadly, a provision that a given arrangement or agreement will not be binding where it would interfere with a specified right or obligation. In this case, Hicks is referring to Parliament's claim to jurisdiction over the colonies.

398.8–9 *Sciat regium . . . præcipitari.*] From Livy, *Ab Urbe Condita*, Bk. XXXVII, ch. 45: "['The king, by delaying to make peace while he has it in his power, will make it when his fortune is worse. If he hesitates,] let him reflect, that it is more difficult to reduce a king from the summit of power to a middle fortune, than to precipitate him from that to the lowest.'" Translation from *The Roman History by Titus Livius.*

399.35–37 "*can limit . . . without our consent;*"] Echoing language, again, from Pitt's speech.

400.33–36 "*Est sapientis judicis . . .* pro Cluent."] From Cicero, *Oratio Pro Cluentio* (A Speech in Defense of Aulus Cluentius): "For it is the part of a wise judge, to think that he has just the power permitted to him by the [Roman] people, which is committed and entrusted to him; and to remember that not only is power given to him, but also that confidence is placed in him." Translation from C. D. Yonge, *The Orations of Marcus Tullius Cicero* (London, 1856).

403.2 *durante bene Placito*] Latin: as long as it pleases [the prince]. In 1701 Parliament had passed the Act of Settlement, which, among other things, had declared that judges would no longer serve *durante bene placito* but rather *quamdiu se bene gesserint* ("as long as they conduct themselves properly"); that is, with a life tenure (see page 63 of this volume). But this aspect of the revolutionary settlement was explicitly denied to the colonies in 1761, when the Privy Council instructed royal governors to desist from issuing judicial commissions that were not revocable at the pleasure of the king, a move that provoked considerable protests from Americans who feared that it would compromise the ability of their judges to act independently of crown control. Parliament went further with the Townshend Acts of 1767, the "last act of ministerial policy" referred to here, levying new colonial duties with the proceeds to be used to pay the salaries of colonial governors and judges, which were traditionally granted by the colonial assemblies.

403.31–34 "*Hæc primo . . . factum.*"] From Sallust, *Bellum Catilinae* (The War with Catiline), sec. 10: "These vices grew up but slowly for some time, and were now and then punished. But the infection at last carrying all before it like the plague, the state was hugely altered, and the government, from being the most just, and the best that ever was, became cruel and intolerable." Translation from John Clarke, *Bellum Catilinarium et Jugurthimum . . . i.e. The History of the Wars of Catiline and Jugurtha, by Sallust* (London, 1734).

11: [JOHN DICKINSON], LETTERS FROM A FARMER IN PENNSYLVANIA

405.10–12 "any distinction . . . perfect nonsense."] As quoted in a February 12, 1767, letter from William Samuel Johnson, Connecticut's agent in

London, to William Pitkin, the colony's governor, 1766–69. According to Johnson, Townshend had made this declaration in the House of Commons "a few days past, upon an accidental mention of America," and having done so looked up and "added with emotion, 'I speak this aloud, that all you who are in the galleries may hear me.'"

405.12–13   "since the Americans . . . indulge them."] As quoted in a May 16, 1767, letter from Johnson to Pitkin.

409.4   I AM a *Farmer*] Dickinson's pseudonym could not have been more disingenuous. Far from being a retired farmer freed from the busy scenes of life by virtue of income from interest on money out on loan—a posture designed to establish his disinterestedness for the reader—he was a wealthy Philadelphia lawyer very much in the midst of political affairs. (See Biographical Notes.)

409.36   POPE] Cf. *An Essay on Man* (1734), Epistle I, ll. 57–60: "So man, who here seems principal alone, / Perhaps acts second to some sphere unknown, / Touches some wheel, or verges to some goal; / 'Tis but a part we see, and not a whole."

410.14   the act for suspending . . . *New-York.*] See note 371.21–22.

413.1   *Concordia res parvæ crescunt.*] From Sallust, *Bellum Iugurthinum* (The War with Jugurtha).

413.5   The day of . . . landing.] See Chronology for 1688–89.

413.30   The 12th *Cha.* Chap. 18] The Navigation Act of 1660.

413.33   *Berwick*] Until the Act of Union in 1707, the town of Berwick-upon-Tweed was disputed between England and Scotland, a status that required the specific reference here. Both it and Wales were statutorily integrated into England by Parliament in 1746.

413.38   The 15th *Cha.* II. Chap. 7] The Navigation Act of 1663.

414.24   The 25th *Cha.* II. Chap. 7] The Navigation Act of 1672.

414.44   The 7th and 8th *Will.* III. Chap. 22] The Navigation Act of 1696.

415.18   The 6th *Anne*, Chap. 37] An Act for the Encouragement of Trade to America (1707).

415.31   The 6th *Geo.* II. Chap. 13] The Molasses Act of 1733.

415.41   The 29th *Geo.* II. Chap. 26, and the 1st *Geo.* III. Chap. 9] Supplemental trade regulations of 1756 and 1760.

416.1   the 4th of *Geo.* III. Chap. 15] The Sugar Act of 1763.

417.31   Lord *Coke*'s 4th Institute, p. 33.] The parenthetical asides in this quotation from the first chapter of Coke's *Fourth Institutes* are in the original, though the indications of emphasis (as in almost all of the quotations in the *Letters*) are Dickinson's.

421.10   *Vox et præterea nihil.*] From Plutarch, *Apophthegmata Laconia* (Sayings of the Spartans). In *Plutarch's Morals: Translated from the Greek by Several Hands* (London, 1704), the apothegm is rendered thus: "Another pulling a Nightingale, and finding but a very small Body, said, *Thou art Voice and nothing else.*"

423.37   emergence] Emergency.

423.38   *Plutarch . . . Potter*'s Archæologia Græca.] Dickinson has paraphrased an excerpt from Plutarch's *The Life of Lycurgus* contained in *Archælogia Græca: or, the Antiquities of Greece* (eighth edition, London, 1764), a documentary history of ancient Greece, first published in 1697–98, by John Potter (c. 1674–1747), Archbishop of Canterbury, 1737–47.

424.32–36   if once *we* are separated . . . bleed at every vein.] This was precisely why Dickinson could not accept the Declaration of Independence in 1776. Though he did not become a Loyalist, his refusal to sign the Declaration would cost him much of the goodwill he had engendered among his countrymen as the "Pennsylvania Farmer."

424.39   "old good humour, and her old good nature,"] From a speech by Edward Hyde, 1st Earl of Clarendon (1609–1674), Lord Chancellor under the newly restored Charles II, delivered before the House of Lords on September 13, 1660, which Dickinson likely took from the twenty-second volume of *The Parliamentary or Constitutional History of England* (second edition, London, 1763).

426.15   *Nil desperandum.*] From Horace, *Odes*, I.vii.27.

427.23   *Calice*] The French port of Calais was an English possession from 1347 until 1558.

427.29–30   *Reges* Angliæ . . . 2d *Inst.*] Dickinson here cites Coke's reference ("hear what a stranger truly writeth," Coke says) to the memoirs of the Burgundian and French diplomat Philippe de Commynes (1447–1511); the Latin reads: "For the kings of England [have] nothing of the kind [revenue], without calling together and receiving the assent of the first ranks of the people."

427.37–38   *Hume*'s *Hist. of England.*] David Hume, *The History of England, from the Invasion of Julius Cæsar to the Revolution in 1688* (8 vols., London, 1767), II, 335.

427.41   the famous statute *de tallagio non concedendo*] Which held that "no Tallage or Aid shall be taken or levied by us or our Heirs in our Realm, without the good Will and Assent of Archbishops, Bishops, Earls, Barons, Knights, Burgesses, and other Freemen of the Land." This statute became so famous in part because it was quoted in the 1628 Petition of Right (see Chronology), which Coke himself had played a decisive role in shaping. Translation from *The Statutes at Large from Magna Charta, to the End of the Reign of King Henry the Sixth* (London, 1763).

428.22–24   the congress at *New-York* . . . "bill of rights."] In addition to the petitions to the King and House of Commons and memorial to the House of Lords (see note 340.32), the Stamp Act Congress (October 7–24, 1765) had issued a declaration of fourteen resolves, which Dickinson here likens to the English Bill of Rights of 1689.

428.37–38   according to an antient fable] Cf. note 154.3.

430.17   Greenville] As Dickinson spells Grenville's name throughout.

431.37   23d *George* II. Chap. 29, Sect. 9.] Commonly referred to as the Iron Act of 1750.

432.1–2   *Habemus quidem* . . . *repositum.*] Dickinson was likely led to this quote, a slightly altered version of a passage from Cicero's *Oratio in L. Catilinam* (Oration Against Lucius Catiline), by Coke, who includes it in the fourteenth chapter of his discussion of the Magna Carta in the *Second Institutes.*

432.20–21   England, . . . in other parts] That is, before and after the Act of Union of 1707.

433.5   the late embargo] In September 1766, when Parliament was not in session, the Crown had acted to suspend the exportation of all grain from British ports in an emergency response to grain riots throughout the kingdom. Though the Chatham ministry had supported the measure, the use of royal prerogative without prior parliamentary approval set off a heated constitutional debate.

435.23   DAVENANT *on the Plantation Trade.*] Charles Davenant, *Discourses on the Publick Revenues, and the Trade of England. In Two Parts* (London, 1698).

435.44   *Sir* JOSIAH CHILD's *Discourse on Trade.*] *A New Discourse of Trade* (fourth edition, London, 1745?) by Sir Josiah Child (1630–1699), a merchant, economist, and politician who had been a governor of the East India Company.

436.7   *egregious*] Child used this word in a now archaic sense of *prodigious.*

436.10   in another part of his work] Child's 1669 tract "The Nature of Plantations, and Their Consequences to Great Britain, Seriously Considered."

436.20   BEAWES's *Lex Merc. Red.*] Wyndham Beawes, *Lex Mercatoria Rediviva: or, the Merchant's Directory* (London, 1752).

436.32–33   POSTLETHWAYT's *Univ. Dict. of Trade and Commerce.*] Malachy Postlethwayt, *The Universal Dictionary of Trade and Commerce, Translated from the French of the Celebrated Monsieur Savary, Inspector-General of the Manufactures for the King, at the Custom-House of Paris: with Large Additions and Improvements . . . Which More Particularly Accommodate the Same to the Trade and Navigation of These Kingdoms . . .* (second edition, London, 1757).

438.10   *Mens ubi maternal est?*] Ovid, *Metamorphoses*, Bk. VIII, l. 499.

438.15   POSTLETHWAYT'*s Great-Britain's True System.*] Published in London in 1757.

438.22–23   TUCKER *on Trade.*] *A Brief Essay on the Advantages and Disadvantages Which Respectively Attend France and Great Britain, with Regard to Trade* (third edition, London, 1753) by Welsh churchman and economist Josiah Tucker (1713–1799), who became Dean of Gloucester in 1758.

439.44   CATO'*s Letters.*] *Cato's Letters: or, Essays on Liberty, Civil and Religious, and Other Important Subjects* by radical Whigs John Trenchard and Thomas Gordon. Initially published from 1720 to 1723 in London and later collected and republished in many editions under this title (most recently in a four-volume London edition of 1755), *Cato's Letters* was one of the most important influences on the thinking of the American Revolutionaries.

440.9   25th *Charles* II Chap. 7, Sect. 2] The Navigation Act of 1672 (see note 101.28).

440.18   It*] Dickinson attaches a footnote here discussing the Sugar Act of 1763.

442.38   TACITUS.] An apothegm from the eleventh book of Tacitus's *Annals*. After the death of John Trenchard in 1723, Thomas Gordon turned to translating and writing commentaries on the Roman historians Tacitus and Sallust, whose works provided cautionary tales for eighteenth-century Whigs. His *Works of Tacitus; with Political Discourses upon that Author*, first published in 1728, was especially important for many American patriots. Dickinson's copy of the five-volume third edition of 1753, now in the collection of the Library Company of Philadelphia, is thoroughly dog-eared; he quotes here from volume 2, page 21.

443.13–14   the day, . . . letter is dated.] See page 413 in this volume.

444.6–7   *Quocirca vivite . . . rebus.*] Horace, *Satires*, II.ii.135–36.

445.44   *Gee* on Trade] Dickinson quotes in this footnote from the fourth edition of *The Trade and Navigation of Great Britain Considered* (London, 1738) by Joshua Gee (1667–1730), a London merchant who had been involved in a 1718 scheme to colonize Nova Scotia. On March 8, 1775, during parliamentary debate on Lord North's measures against the colonies, Lord Clare recalled Gee as "a great friend to America, though no patriot, a man who had written better on trade than any other man living, and who knew more of America."

446.38–39   34th *Edward* I. . . . the 25th of *Charles* II.] Referring to acts by which Wales and the Counties Palatine of Chester and Durham were granted representation in Parliament. See note 32.2–3.

450.14   Lord *Cambden*'s speech.] Dickinson quotes here and at greater length in the next footnote from a March 1766 speech in the House of Lords by Charles Pratt, 1st Earl Camden (1714–1794), chief justice of the Common Pleas and political ally of Lord Chatham. Camden took a bold stance in his remarks, not only supporting the American position on the Stamp Act but breaking with Chatham by opposing the Declaratory Act. His speech was published in the September 1767 issue of the *Political Register* and reprinted in at least half a dozen colonial newspapers in December 1767 and January 1768. When republished in the February 1768 edition of *The London Magazine*, it appeared under the running head *No Taxation without Representation*, though Camden nowhere used the famous phrase that would become a defining slogan of the American Revolution.

451.1 *Miserabile vulgus.*] Virgil, *Aeneid*, II.798.

451.38 as Mr. *Hume* says] A reference to Hume's essay "Of Eloquence," which had been most recently collected in *Essays and Treatises on Several Subjects . . . in four volumes* (London, 1760).

455.32 *Qui sentit . . . et onus.*] See note 76.19.

456.22–28 "Princes and . . . EXECUTION OF THE LAWS."] Hume, *The History of England*, II, 127.

457.21–22 "proofs of holy writ."*] *Othello*, III.iii.324.

458.1 chained in by a line of fortifications] Dickinson would elaborate on this point in a footnote in his 1774 pamphlet, *An Essay on the Constitutional Power of Great-Britain over the Colonies in America*: "The *probability* of this measure taking place, is confirmed by the CANADA bill [the Quebec Act], a political device so extraordinary, as to excite surprise even in those colonists who live in the year 1774. By this bill, it is said, the *legislative* power is lodged in the governor and a few men, not less than 17 nor more than 23, appointed and removeable by the crown; and the government becomes wholly military.—*Trials by jury* are abolished, though multitudes of *English* subjects settled there on the encouragement given by the king's proclamation in 1763—the *French* laws are *restored*, and ALL THE COUNTRY ON THE BACK OF THESE COLONIES is added to *Canada*, and PUT UNDER THE SAME MILITARY GOVERNMENT. This is indeed to be '*chained in*.'"

458.35–36 the campaign of chief justice *Jeffereys*] See Chronology for 1685.

459.18 at home] That is, in Britain. Like Dulany and other American writers, Dickinson consistently referred to the mother country as home.

460.4–5 the revolution, . . . *independency of judges*] See note 403.2.

460.19–37 "The state . . . of the practice."] From William Smith (1728–1793), *The History of the Province of New-York, from the First Discovery to the Year M.DCC.XXXII* (London, 1757). New York's last colonial chief justice, Smith tried to remain neutral in 1776 but eventually became a Loyalist in British-occupied New York. After a brief sojourn in England, he returned to North America as Chief Justice of Quebec (later Lower Canada).

463.30   *Venienti occurrite morbo.*] Persius, *Satires*, III.64.

465.5–6   Happy are the men, . . . *misfortunes of others.*] Dickinson would
again employ this proverb in an October 26, 1774, Address of Congress to the
Inhabitants of Quebec, which he drafted, referring to it there as "an observation of antiquity." Its American provenance dates at least to William Bradford's
History of Plimouth Plantation, which reproduces a 1622 letter from ship captain John Huddleston recalling "The old rule which I learned when I went
to schoole . . . That is, Hapie is he whom other mens harmes doth make to
beware."

465.20–21   An enquiry . . . by *Alexander M'Aulay*] Dickinson here quotes
from the concluding paragraph of Alexander McAulay, *An Inquiry into the Legality of Pensions on the Irish Establishment* (London, 1763). The proliferation
of pensions in Ireland and absenteeism among landlords and civil officials were
recurring and related complaints during this period. In *A Short but True History of the Rise, Progress, and Happy Suppression, of Several Late Insurrections
Commonly Called Rebellions in Ireland* (Dublin, 1760), Irish pamphleteer
James Digges La Touche lamented that his country was "obliged to support
a large national, civil, and military Establishment, with a numberless Band of
strange Pensioners, English, Scots, German, as well as Irish."

467.21   In *Charles* the second's time] In 1666 the House of Commons, responding to pressure from English cattle farmers chafing at competition from
Irish imports, banned the trade with the Irish Cattle Act. They did so despite
vocal opposition in the House of Lords from peers with Irish estates or who
were involved in the resale of imported cattle in England. Dickinson quotes
here from Hume's account of the bill's passage in *The History of England*.

468.26   "—MENTEM MORTALIA TANGUNT."] Virgil, *Aeneid*, I.462: "[Ev'n
here Compassion reigns, and] human Minds / Are touch'd with human
Mis'ry". Translation from Joseph Trapp, *The Aeneid of Virgil, Translated into
Blank Verse* (London, 1718).

468.43   the Lord Lieutenant, in his speech] A reference to an October 20,
1767, speech before the Irish Parliament by George Townshend (1724–1807),
the newly arrived Lord Lieutenant. After a long period of non-resident vice-
roys, Townshend had been appointed to the post by his younger brother
Charles, the prime mover in the Chatham ministry, in hopes of establishing
firmer and more direct royal control over the Irish Parliament. Toward that
end, he undertook a charm offensive in his inaugural address, promising to
support reforms of judicial tenure, the pension list, and the duration of parliaments, among other long-standing Irish grievances. As it happened, the concession regarding judicial tenure was short-lived, for the Irish bill to enact
it was returned from England with a revision effectively allowing the British
Parliament to remove Irish judges at will, greatly angering the Irish MPs and
undercutting any hopes of a rapprochement under Townshend's leadership.

469.17–19   The government of *New-York* . . . is now held so] Cadwallader

NOTES

893

Colden (1688–1776), lieutenant governor of New York from 1760 to 1776, was several times acting governor during his long tenure, including in 1765, when he was burnt in effigy in New York City during protests against the Stamp Act. Though Virginia was Britain's largest and most important North American colony, its governors almost never travelled there, instead allowing deputies to govern in their place. Lieutenant Governor Francis Fauquier (1703–1768) was Virginia's acting governor at the time Dickinson wrote the *Farmer's Letters*.

469.32–33 Sir *William Temple*, . . . in his famous remonstrance] Statesman and essayist William Temple (1628–1699), whose 1674 remarks to Charles II are mentioned in Hume's *The History of England*. The long quotation that follows is drawn from "An impartial Account of a late interesting Conference, with the several Particulars previous and subsequent," an unattributed contribution to *The Political Register* for August 1767—the "*Late News Paper*" mentioned at 470.35–36—where it appears in a footnote. The first portion of the passage, from the beginning to "the above enumerated particulars," is in turn a quotation from an anonymous pamphlet entitled *Seasonable Hints from an Honest Man on the Present Important Crisis of a New Reign and a New Parliament* (London, 1761). That pamphlet is attributed to John Douglas (1721–1807) and is thought to be one of several political tracts he wrote at the direction of his patron, the retired Whig statesman the Earl of Bath. The remainder of the quotation, and the line that follows, with its veiled reference to Lord Holland, a former paymaster general widely alleged to have been corrupt, were written by the unnamed author of the *Political Register* article.

473.4 of the LAST IMPORTANCE.] Today we would say "of the first importance."

473.11 *Et majores . . . cogitate.*] From Tacitus, *Agricola*, ch. 32.

473.25–26 *Machiavel* . . . in his discourses,*] Machiavelli's works, including the famous *Discourses*, were published in numerous English translations in the eighteenth century, most recently in a two-volume collection of 1762. Dickinson had more than one edition in his personal library.

475.15–16 "government is founded on *opinion*."*] This is Dickinson's distillation of the essay "Of the First Principles of Government" in Hume, *Essays and Treatises on Several Subjects . . . in four volumes* (London, 1760), I, 47–48, from which he quotes at length in the footnote.

475.22–25 "Vice is a monster . . . then *embrace*."] Pope, *Essay on Man*, Epistle II, ll. 217–220; Dickinson has "horrid" here instead of Pope's "frightful."

476.29 Omnia mala . . . orta sunt.] From Sallust, *Bellum Catilinae*, sect. 50: "All ill examples had their rise from harmless beginnings." Translation from John Clarke, *Bellum Catilinarium et Jugurthimum . . . i.e. The History of the Wars of Catiline and Jugurtha, by Sallust* (London, 1734).

476.37 CICERO's *Orat. for* SEXTIUS.] Dickinson drew this translation of Cicero's *Oratio Pro Sextius* (A Speech in Defense of Publius Setius), sect. 47, from Conyers Middleton, *The History of the Life of Marcus Tullius Cicero* (fifth edition, London, 1755).

477.37   *Rapin*'s History of *England.*] See note 312.35.

478.21–22   "that the people . . . of the realm."] By the reign of Henry IV (1399–1413) it had become accepted that troops assembled under commissions of array (royal grants to officers to form military units in the counties) were not obliged to serve outside the realm, or even beyond the borders of their respective counties. Such commissions, which had fallen into disuse by the end of the sixteenth century, were revived by Charles I in 1642, in response to Parliament's assumption of control of armed forces with the Militia Ordinance.

478.28   *Tangier*] This city on the African side of the Strait of Gibraltar was an English possession from 1661 to 1684.

478.30–31   "Duo singularia . . . honore triumphus."] From the eighth book of Livy's history of Rome: "A double unprecedented honor was conferred on this man: for he was continued in his authority beyond the usual time, which had never been done to any person before him, and obtained a triumph after his honorable command was expired." Translation from *The Roman History by Titus Livius* (London, 1744).

479.11   SECRET measures of a *long* administration] Whigs like Dickinson believed that the apparent stability of the long Walpole ministry (1721–42) had been a function of a systematic corruption of the constitution, with the executive using subtle methods, principally patronage, to undermine the independence of the legislature.

480.14–15   "If any person . . . person's security."*] See note 365.14–16.

481.26–27   "The regulation of the colonies,"] Whately's *Regulations Lately Made*. See page 203 in this volume.

481.39   "Dira cælæno,"] Virgil, *Aeneid*, III.245–46. The "direful foreteller" is Celaeno ("So says Celaeno"), one of the Harpies who predicts Aeneas's coming journeys.

483.11   *St. James*'s, . . . *Royal Exchange*] Four loci of British power in London: the royal palace; the royal chapel, where the House of Commons sat until 1834; and the administrative and trading centers, respectively, of the City of London, the metropolis's financial hub.

483.27   "*Apparent* rari nantes *in gurgite vasto*."] Virgil, *Aeneid*, I.117, describing the aftermath of shipwreck: "A few appear here and there swimming in the vast abyss." The phrase was proverbial, suggesting rarity.

484.10–11   "that if there is . . . favorable attention."] The exact source of this "perpetual incantation" is not known, though it captures the tone of royal instructions to colonial governors.

485.17   the spear of *Telephus*] In Greek mythology Telephus, son of Hercules, finding that a wound suffered in combat with Achilles during the Trojan War would not heal, consulted an oracle who told him, "he that wounded shall also heal." It was Odysseus who deduced that this referred not to Achilles but to his spear, some rust from which, when applied to the wound, did indeed prove curative.

487.23–24   A —— may succeed . . . a *Conway.*] American Whigs had been cheered by the elevation in the Chatham ministry of William Petty, 2nd Earl of Shelburne (1737–1805), and Henry Seymour Conway (1721–1795)—both advocates of a conciliatory policy toward the colonies—as, respectively, the secretaries of state for the Southern and Northern departments. But Dickinson's note of caution was prescient, as both would leave office in 1768: Conway resigned in January to return to the military, and Shelburne would be dismissed in October.

487.36–37   to write my sentiments to a gentleman of great influence at home] Dickinson wrote to William Pitt on December 21, 1765.

487.39–40   Ubi imperium . . . idoneos *transfertur.*] From Sallust, *Bellum Catilinae*, sect. 50: "But when power comes into the hands of ignorant or wicked men, the precedent set is transferred from deserving and proper objects to such as are not so." Translation from John Clarke, *Bellum Catilinarium et Jugurthimum . . . i.e. The History of the Wars of Catiline and Jugurtha, by Sallust* (London, 1734).

488.1   a new kind of minister] Dickinson is expressing concern that the king's chief minister was increasingly viewed as more beholden to the House of Commons than to the Crown. This was indeed an important moment in the development of ministerial responsibility to Parliament, one celebrated by English Whigs at home. But for the colonists, suffering, as they felt, from assertions of parliamentary sovereignty, it could only be regarded as a dangerous turn. Later, when Americans came to write their new state constitutions in 1776, they prohibited this kind of identity between the legislature and the executive; it was what they meant by separation of powers, which has prevented the development of parliamentary cabinet government in America.

488.24   "*band of brothers,*"] *Henry V*, IV.iii.63.

489.14–16   "*Certe ego . . . quirites.*"] From Sallust, *Bellum Iugurthinum* (The War with Jugurtha), sect. 33.

489.20–22   "How little . . . to be silent."] From Jeremiah Dummer, *A Defence of the New-England Charters.*

12: [ALLAN RAMSAY], ORIGIN AND NATURE OF GOVERNMENT

493.10–11   VICTOR *que . . . dat jura.*] Virgil, *Georgics*, IV.561–62: "[While great Caesar thundered in war by deep Euphrates] and gave a victor's laws unto willing nations." Translation from H. Rushton Fairclough, *Virgil: Eclogues, Georgics, Aeneid I–IV* (Cambridge: Harvard University Press, 1935).

495.28–29   In part to doubt . . . to be denied.] Ramsay adapts to political purpose a couplet from Lady Mary Wortley Montagu's poem "The Lady's Resolve," which was anthologized in Robert Dodsley, *A Collection of Poems in Four Volumes, by Several Hands* (third edition, London, 1755). The original reads, "In part she is to blame that has been try'd; / He comes too near, that comes to be deny'd."

495.34   the union of all its parts under one head] Franklin wrote extensive comments in the margins of his copy of this pamphlet, including here, where he asserted that "if such an Union be necessary to G.B. let her endeavour to obtain it by fair Means. It cannot be forced." Of the pamphlet as a whole he noted at the end: "This Writer is concise, lively, and elegant in his Language, but his reasonings are too refin'd and Paradoxical to make Impression on the Understanding or convince the Minds of his Readers. And his main Fact on which they are founded [that there is no such thing as a social contract] is a Mistake."

497.20   a WAT TYLER or JACK CADE] Two figures from English history associated with popular uprisings triggered by high taxes and prices: Wat Tyler, leader of the Peasants' Revolt of 1381, and Jack Cade, leader of a 1450 rebellion against Henry VI.

497.33   Such are the idle dreams of metaphysicians] Franklin: "This is only your dream."

498.38   See Grotius] See note 67.5.

499.19–20   the sole determination of that right rests with the superior] Franklin: "That is, He that is strongest may do what he pleases with those that are weaker. A most Equitable Law of Nature indeed."

500.30   taking place] That is, from having undue weight or influence.

503.3–4   *ne quid . . . respublica*] See note 259.21–22.

503.19–20   all the disorders and revolutions] Ramsay follows with a litany of self-destructive abuses of power, some more legendary than others: the abduction of Verginia (c. 450 B.C.) by the Roman patrician Appius Claudius (for his father, see note 11.9) was said to have brought about the overthrow of the Decemvirate, just as, according to Livy, the rape of Lucretia (c. 500 B.C.) had led to the end of the Roman monarchy; the popular fourteenth-century Swiss tale of William Tell who was forced by Austrian authorities to shoot an apple off his son's head (see note 328.19–22); and the wars of religion spawned by the Protestant Reformation, exemplified in their unprofitable excesses by the long Spanish effort to suppress the Dutch revolt and the English Civil War.

504.19–21   *Ne liceat . . . debilis actus.**] Persius, *Satires,* V.97–99: "[Even Reason itself opposes you, it whispers you in the Ear,] That no person ought to attempt any thing which is to be the worse for his undertaking it. The Laws of Man, and Nature forbid Ignorance to meddle with what is beyond its Power." Translation from *The Satires of Persius, Translated into English by Thomas Sheridan* (London, 1777).

507.20   than it is in Turkey] For eighteenth-century Anglo-Americans and Europeans the Ottoman Empire epitomized absolutism (see also note 388.26).

508.29–30   the word *Virtual*, . . . has no meaning at all] Franklin: "Thus the English change their Ground as well as the American! We were once told much of this *virtual* representation."

508.35   excise upon wine . . . in 1763] Ramsay refers here to the Molasses Act of 1733 and to the Excise Bill of 1763, better known as the Cider Act. Proposed by the Bute administration but finally passed by Parliament under the Grenville ministry, this measure included a controversial tax of four shillings per hogshead of cider. It provoked resistance in England's cider-producing regions, particularly in the West Country, similar to that in America against the Stamp Act, with confrontations between producers and excise-men and petitions against (and a lively pamphlet debate about) the government's use of general warrants to search and seize.

509.1   *in capite*] Latin: literally, in chief; in feudal law, holding land immediately of the king or lord.

509.37–38   an *Essay on the constitution of England*] Anonymous pamphlet written by Ramsay, first published in 1765.

511.3–4   my history of Representation] Ramsay's account of the development of representation in England is reasonably accurate, though it was not until 1553 in the case of *Wimbish* v. *Taillebois* that Chief Justice Edward Montague (d. 1557) clearly set forth a rudimentary notion of representation in order to justify Parliament's taking of private property in apparent violation of the common law. Parliament, declared Montague, could not really take property since it was itself "nothing but a court." Instead, the legal owners of the property, or the "feoffees to uses," were themselves the donors, "for when a gift is made by parliament every person in the realm is privy to it and assents to it. . . . For if it should be adjudged the gift of any other, then parliament would do a wrong to the feoffees, in taking a thing from them and making another a donor to it." It would be another century or more before Parliament finally shed such complicated legal fictions, the last vestiges of its origins as a court, and became a modern legislature.

511.9   sate] Archaic: sat.

511.11–12   the act of . . . 8th Henry the VI.] See note 313.2–3.

515.33–34   *Pacta conventa*] Latin: Articles of agreement, as between states.

517.11–12   In the year 1725 . . . malt-tax to Scotland] By the terms of the 1707 Act of Union, which made most taxes uniform throughout Great Britain, Scotland was exempted from a preexisting English tax on malt that had been imposed to pay for the war against France. When, with the end of the war in

1713, Parliament voted to extend the tax to Scotland, where malt was vital to the production of whiskey, a group of Scottish peers and MPs called for the dissolution of the Union. The tax proved not very productive and in December 1724, Parliament revisited the issue by substituting a duty of sixpence a barrel on beer, thereby precipitating serious riots the following year in several Scottish cities. Brewers went on strike and mobs destroyed the homes of Scottish MPs who had been pressured by Walpole to support the tax. Eight people died in rioting before, as Ramsay approvingly notes, the troops were called in.

518.12 *pulveris exigui jactu*] From a passage on warring bees in Virgil, *Georgics*, IV.87: "[These storms of passion, these conflicts so fierce,] by the tossing of a little dust [are quelled and laid to rest.]" Translation from Fairclough, *Virgil: Eclogues, Georgics, Aeneid I–IV*, 203.

518.15 MANSFIELD] Ramsay equates the Lord Chief Justice of the King's Bench (see note 255.28–31) with the Roman orator known for his formidable powers of persuasion.

519.14–15 the Jews, . . . with the Lacedemonians] The first book of the Maccabees (composed c. 135 B.C. and considered canonical scripture by the Catholic and Orthodox churches) several times mentions an alliance between the Jewish kingdom and the inhabitants of Sparta (Lacedaemon), who were thought to share a common descent from Abraham.

13: [SILAS DOWNER], DISCOURSE AT THE TREE OF LIBERTY

523.9 TREE of LIBERTY] From Sherwood Forest, to the oak tree that had served as the emblem of Jack Cade's rebellion (see note 497.20), to the trees displayed on flags and coins in colonial Massachusetts, old trees had had symbolic significance in England and the American colonies long before August 14, 1765, when one of the great elms on Deacon Jacob Elliott's plot on Washington Street in Boston was christened the Liberty Tree, the first of many so designated during the course of the American Revolution. Connoting defiance, strength, and permanence, such trees also served as easily recognized sites where large crowds could gather and shelter for public meetings. Where such a tree was not well situated, colonists might set up a liberty pole to serve similar functions, as New Yorkers did on May 21, 1766, to celebrate repeal of the Stamp Act, in that case erecting a tall ship's mast with a sign reading "George 3rd, Pitt—and Liberty."

525.34 *Naboth*'s vineyard.] When Naboth the Jezreelite refused to sell a vineyard coveted by Ahab, king of Samaria, Jezebel, Ahab's wife, plotted his disgrace and murder in order to secure the property. See 1 Kings 21.

525.36–37 They sat . . . his own fig tree.] Recurring imagery in the Hebrew Scriptures, as at Micah 4:4, 1 Kings 4:25, 2 Kings 18:31, Isaiah 36:16, and elsewhere.

527.1 *Nova-Zembla*] See note 152.26.

531.38–39   more settlers . . . than from *England.*] It is estimated that by 1760, 30 percent of New Englanders had come from somewhere other than England. In the middle colonies, where there were large numbers of German, Scottish, Scots-Irish, and Irish immigrants, that number rose to 55 to 70 percent, and in the southern colonies, where Africans were very numerous, to 55 to 65 percent.

532.4–5   on their fellows] That is, on their persons.

532.14–15   the plains of *Shinar*] A site in ancient Mesopotamia mentioned several times in the Hebrew Scriptures, associated with Babylonia.

533.17   the common people of *Poland* are to their lords.] The inequality of Polish society was notorious. In a 1772 essay (*Considerations sur le gouvernement de la Pologne*) Rousseau famously described the Polish nation as being "composed of three orders: the nobles, who are everything; the burghers, who are nothing; and the peasants, who are less than nothing."

534.12–13   the treatment . . . *Massachusetts-Bay* hath had] See Chronology for 1768.

536.3   we dedicate the *Tree of Liberty.*] At the age of eighty-one, Providence resident Samuel Thurber recorded the following boyhood memory of the Providence Liberty Tree: It was "the largest elm tree I ever saw. A flight of steps was erected, leading perhaps twenty feet up to where three or four limbs set out. There, a convenient seat was fixed for, say, ten or twelve people to sit in and enjoy themselves in the shade." It was from this "summer house" that Downer gave his speech, after which, while the dignitaries on the platform laid their hands on the tree, he read the dedication that follows in the text.

536.5   Corsica] Personified by its charismatic leader, General Pascal Paoli (1725–1807), the long Corsican struggle against first Genoese and later French rule captured the imagination of many in the Anglo-American world. In the October 13, 1768, edition of the *New-York Journal* it was reported that "the brave Paoli, being asked how long he would hold out, should the French assist the Genoese against Corsica, replied, *Till Death;—for Life is not worth keeping, unless we can preserve too our Liberty.*"

14: NATURE AND CAUSES OF PRESENT DISPUTES

539.15   QUID NOSTRAM . . . AUDI.] From Horace, *Epistolarum*, I.xiv.31: "Now hear, from whence our Sentiments divide." Translation from Philip Francis, *The Epistles and Art of Poetry of Horace. In Latin and English* (London, 1746).

541.16   *still voice*] Cf. 1 Kings 19:12.

542.16   in the sequel] That is, in the following.

546.2–3   the constitution of the Ephori] A body of five magistrates (established in the eighth century B.C.) initially designed to govern in the absence of the kings of Sparta, but which in time came to exercise supervisory authority over them.

547.39   Servius Tullius] A legendary figure thought to have reigned in the sixth century B.C.

548.39   both the Gauls] Though Caesar famously begins his *History of the Gallic Wars* by observing that "all Gaul is divided into three parts," the author is likely referring here to just the two largest Roman provinces: Gallia Belgica and Gallia Celtica.

551.40–552.1   they should not be allowed such a form of government] Franklin made extensive marginal notes in his copy of this pamphlet. They appear to have been written in 1770 and many of them have the immediacy of dialogue, as in his response to this assertion: "They have it already. All the Difficulties have arisen from the British Parliament's Attempting to deprive them of it."

554.25–27   that England . . . I presume, which can never be questioned.] Franklin: "You do indeed *presume* too much. America *is not* part of the Dominions *of England*, but of *the King's* Dominion. England is a Dominion itself, and has no Dominions."

560.19–21   To the equity . . . fairly to object.] Though James Otis had raised the possibility of American representation in Parliament (before quickly dropping it) and Franklin had several times floated the idea, they were unusual in this regard. Almost all other American patriots, including the delegates to the Stamp Act Congress, did indeed object, dismissing the idea of American representation in Parliament out of hand.

561.39   *dernier resort*] French: the last resort.

563.38–39   maintain our sovereignty over it] Franklin: "I am quite sick of this our Sovereignty."

568.4   Molesworth's history of Denmark] *An Account of Denmark, as it was in the Year 1692*, by Robert Lord Viscount Molesworth (1656–1725), was first published in 1694 and in its sixth edition in 1752.

570.3   the Dutch, very lately, siding with the French] As it entered a period of fiscal retrenchment after the Peace of 1763, and as the focus of its foreign policy was increasingly distracted by the embarrassing crisis with its American colonies, Britain's commitment to maintain a strong presence on the Continent and in the Mediterranean (where the acquisition of Corsica by the French in the Treaty of Versailles of May 1768 was seen as a significant blow to British power and prestige) was questioned by allies and adversaries alike. Especially in doubt was the system of triangular alliances with Holland and Austria that had effectively erected a barrier against French encroachment into the Low Countries for most of the eighteenth century. In this climate, Étienne François, duc de Choiseul (1719–1785), France's chief minister, was able to detach both Holland and Portugal from their traditional alliances with

Britain, diplomatic spadework that would pave the way, a decade later, for the emergence of the anti-British League of Armed Neutrality during the War of American Independence.

570.21 their riotous and seditious manner] Franklin: "Do you Englishmen then pretend to censure the Colonies for Riots? Look at home!!! I have seen within a Year, Riots in the Country about Corn, Riots about Elections, Riots about Workhouses, Riots of Colliers, Riots of Weavers, Riots of Coalheavers, Riots of Sawyers, Riots of Sailors, Riots of Wilkites [see page 663 in this volume], Riots of Government Chairmen, Riots of Smugglers in which Customhouse Officers and Excisemen have been murdered, the King's armed Vessels and Troops fired at; &c &c &c. In America if one Mob rises and breaks a few Windows, or tars and feathers a single rascally Informer, it is called REBELLION: Troops and Fleets must be sent, and military Execution talk'd of as the decentest Thing in the World. Here indeed one would think Riots part of the Mode of Government."

571.15 share them once more with the French] Franklin: "We have been often threaten'd with this wise Measure of returning Canada to France. Do it when you please. Had the French Power, which you were 5 Years subduing with 25000 Regulars, and 25000 of us to help you, continu'd at our Backs, ready to support and assist us whenever we might think proper to resist your Oppressions, you would never have thought of a Stamp Act for us; you would not have dared to use us as you have done. If it be so politic a Measure to have Enemies at hand to keep (as the Notion is) your Subjects in Obedience; then give Part of Ireland to the French to plant [line missing] another French Colony in the Highlands to keep rebellious Scotland in order. Plant another on Tower hill [in London] to restrain your own Mobs. There never was a Notion more ridiculous. Don't you see the Advantage you have now if you preserve our Connection? The 50000 Men, and the Fleet employ'd in America during the last War, is now so much Strength at Liberty to be employ'd elsewhere."

573.40–574.1 the same rights, . . . allowed the Irish] Some British officials did raise Ireland as a model for the colonies' relationship with Great Britain. Although Parliament clearly claimed sovereignty over Ireland, it had been cautious in the exercise of it. At the end of the American Revolution, in 1782–83, the Irish Parliament gained greater autonomy. Then, two years after the Irish rebellion of 1798, Acts of Union by the two parliaments created the United Kingdom of Great Britain and Ireland, with the Irish closing their parliament and being granted over a hundred members in the U.K. House of Commons.

15: [JOHN JOACHIM ZUBLY], AN HUMBLE ENQUIRY

579.11 *A House divided . . . cannot stand.*] Cf. Mark 3:25.

579.30 *History of the long Rebellion*] *The History of the Rebellion and Civil Wars in England, Begun in the Year 1641* by the Earl of Clarendon (see note 424.39) was a popular work published in numerous multivolume editions over the course of the eighteenth century.

582.36   *scil.*] Latin abbreviation for *scilicet*: namely; that is to say.

587.24–25   *Rex Angliæ . . . legem.*] A maxim adapted from Henry de Bracton in *De Legibus et Consuetudinibus Angliae* (London, 1640): "The King of England has no superior in his kingdom except God and the law." *Bracton on the Laws and Customs of England*, translated by Samuel E. Thorne (Cambridge, MA: Harvard University Press, 1968–1977).

588.33   A PITT] John Pitt (1698–1754), Member for Old Sarum (see note 237.19) and uncle of William Pitt. Zubly drew this account of the debate from volume 6 of *The History and Proceedings of the House of Commons from the Restoration to the Present Time*.

589.8–9   The *Isle of Man . . . Manks* laws] Concerned about its use as a base of operations for smugglers plying the Irish Sea, George Grenville engineered the annexation of the Isle of Man (it had been the private possession first of the Stanley family and later of the dukes of Athol) to the Crown in a bill passed on May 10, 1765. The island's people are known as the Manx.

589.27–29   *An Act . . . Parliament of* Great-Britain] The Declaratory Act of 1766.

590.25–33   "that this declaratory . . . null and void."] Thirty-three dissenting members of the House of Lords published a *Protest against the Bill to repeal the American Stamp Act, of Last Session* (Paris [i.e. London], 1766). This quote is from a follow-up pamphlet: *Second Protest, with a List of the Voters Against the Bill to Repeal the American Stamp Act, of Last Session* (Paris [i.e. London], 1766).

592.6   this province] South Carolina.

593.3–4   a late act suspending the Assembly of *New-York*] See note 371.21–22.

593.13   unless they are represented doubly] The conventional wisdom that Zubly expresses here, that the people "cannot be legally represented in more than one body" (as he says later at 608.7–8), would be challenged in the late 1770s and 1780s as Americans struggled to justify the senates, or upper houses, in their new Revolutionary state constitutions. Ultimately, the federalist system they created would be premised on the unprecedented idea that the people could in fact be represented doubly, indeed many times over; that all parts of the federal and state governments—including senators and executives—were as representative as the so-called houses of representatives.

595.2   a penny *Scots*] The Scottish pound had only a twelfth of the silver content of an English pound, making it worth only twenty English pence. A shilling Scots, in turn, was worth a single English penny, and a penny Scots was equivalent to a third of an English farthing.

595.9–10   the bishoprick of *Durham*, and the manor of *East-Greenwich*] Two locales that had historically enjoyed exemptions from parliamentary authority.

For the former, see note 32.2–3. The latter, a royal estate located some four miles below London Bridge, was conventionally invoked in legal documents of the era, including in most of the colonial charters, as a model of property held directly by the king.

599.34 the Senate of *Venice*] In the waning days of its existence during this period, the republic of Venice operated under a highly restrictive frame of government older than any of the royal houses of Europe. Citizenship in the republic was conferred only to members of the Venetian senate, or Great Council, which was founded in 1172. Membership in the senate, in turn, was confined to a small number of noble families, those whose names were enrolled in the Golden Book of 1315. So controlled was access to the senate over the centuries that the number of eligible families actually fell from 240 in 1367 to just 111 in 1796, the year before the body dissolved itself and the republic fell.

600.30–32 Every representative . . . for which he hath been chosen.] This is as clear a statement of the American conception of actual representation as was ever made, and one that directly contradicted the prevailing British idea of representation, which Edmund Burke would articulate in his Speech to the Electors of Bristol in 1774. Parliament, according to Burke, was "not a *congress* of ambassadors from different and hostile interests; which interests each must maintain, as an agent and advocate, against other agents and advocates; but parliament is a *deliberative* assembly of *one* nation, with *one* interest, that of the whole; where, not local purposes, not local prejudices, ought to guide, but the general good, resulting from the general reason of whole." For Britons, the electoral process was incidental to representation; but for Americans, as Zubly's pamphlet demonstrates, election was the sole criterion of representation.

602.7 as big again.] Twice as large.

602.41 See Annals of Queen *Anne* 1703] [Abel Boyer], *The History of the Reign of Queen Anne, Digested into Annals. Year the Second* (London, 1704).

608.39 *Montesquieu* observes] In *The Spirit of the Laws*, Bk. XI, ch. 6.

610.5 the *Jew* Bill] Introduced in the House of Lords by the Earl of Halifax on April 3, 1753, this measure opened naturalization to "persons professing the Jewish Religion . . . without receiving the Sacrament of the Lord's Supper." It passed the Lords on April 16 and the Commons on May 22. Though its provisions would apply to a relatively small number of privileged and well-connected individuals—naturalization in each case still required a private act of Parliament—the act provoked a furious popular response. Sermons and pamphlets protesting the measures flew off London's presses, and Jewish peddlers were harassed in the streets (one was murdered). When Parliament reconvened in November 1753 it quickly voted to repeal the bill.

610.6 Cyder Act] See note 508.35.

611.25 so it may alter the constitution.] In a 1774 London reprint of this pamphlet entitled *Great Britain's Right to Tax Her Colonies. Placed in the Clearest Light, by a Swiss*, this sentence is followed by "and yet all the power of the house of *Austria* could not re-conquer a handful of *Swiss*."

611.33–34 *Moliere's Malade imaginaire*] *The Imaginary Invalid*, a three-act comedy by Molière that premiered in Paris in 1673.

16: [WILLIAM KNOX], THE CONTROVERSY REVIEWED

617.3–17 "He that goeth . . . seek preferment."] Knox begins with the opening lines of the first book of *Of the Lawes of Ecclesiastical Polity* (1594), an influential work by the English theologian Richard Hooker (1554?–1600). Composed of eight books, five of which were published at the end of the sixteenth century with three others published posthumously, this work staked out a middle ground in the religious controversies of the Elizabethan era. Hooker's moderation led to his often being labeled "judicious."

618.4 *ignus fatuus*] *Ignis fatuus*: an illusion or false hope.

619.27–29 If they reject . . . in their behalf.] Knox raises here the awesome possibility of the Americans' denying the authority of Parliament, the historic bulwark of the people's liberty, something no good British Whig could contemplate with equanimity. What if the Crown once again became tyrannical? If the colonists were outside Parliament's authority, what institution was capable of defending their rights? These were the kinds of questions bewildered British Whigs were asking.

619.34–36 "America is not . . . to interfere."] See Chronology for 1621.

620.3–4 Let us then see . . . their title.] After this sentence the author inserted the following footnote:

> To free the text from the embarrassment of long quotations, and to prevent the reader's attention from being carried off to other objects, I have here inserted only such of the several assemblies resolutions as have relation to the subject of the present enquiry. But in justice to the assemblies, I have given entire copies of their resolutions in the appendix.

This volume does not reproduce Knox's appendix.

620.5 the house of burgesses in Virginia resolved] The Virginia Resolves were the first and most important of the colonial responses to the Stamp Act. They were published, in slightly differing versions, in the June 24, 1765, edition of the *Newport Mercury* and the July 4, 1765, *Maryland Gazette*.

620.37 The assembly of Pennsylvania, by their resolutions] The Pennsylvania Resolves were issued on September 21, 1765.

621.21–23 The native Indians . . . and Groenlanders] Reflecting racial prejudices typical of his era, Knox offers here a litany of "savage" peoples presumed incapable of supporting the liberties of Englishmen: American Indians; Hottentots, a derogative term, derived from the Dutch, for the Khoekhoe people of South Africa; the Tartars, a term vaguely applied to the many peoples of Central Asia; Arabs; Cafres, another epithet for Africans, this one derived from the Arabic word for non-believer (kafir); and Greenlanders, here standing in for all Eskimo peoples.

622.12–13 The act of the 7th and 8th of king William] An Act for Preventing Frauds and Regulating Abuses in the Plantation Trade (1695).

622.20 the 5th of George the Second] An Act for the More Easy Recovery of Debts in His Majesty's Plantations and Colonies in America (1732).

622.24 the *Examiner of . . . the Colonies*] Knox himself (see note 254.4–5).

622.27 *The Considerations . . . imposing Taxes*] Pamphlet 7 in this volume.

623.26–27 an *act of parliament* the 13th of George the Second.] The Naturalization Act of 1740. (See Chronology.)

627.13–14 Mr. Dickenson calls . . . declaration of rights] On page 428 in this volume.

629.30 *the baseless fabric of a vision.*] Cf. *The Tempest*, IV.i, 141.

631.6–7 Doctor Franklin tells the . . . commons] In Pamphlet 9. See page 348 in this volume.

633.4–5 the 15th of Charles the Second] See note 173.24.

634.25–26 The double tax upon the Roman Catholics] Described under the heading "Papists taxed" in an eighteenth-century legal dictionary: "*Papists* or reputed *Papists*, who refuse to take the *Oaths* 1 *W.* & *M.* are to pay double to the Land-Tax, &*c.* Stat. 8 *W.* 3. *c.* 6. And a *Tax* of 100,000*l.* for the Year 1723. was laid on the Lands of all *Papists*, over and above the double *Taxes*, towards reimbursing the Publick the Charges occasioned by the late Conspiracies." From *A New Law-Dictionary* (first published 1729; sixth edition, London, 1750) by legal scholar and literary critic Giles Jacob (1686–1744), who was immortalized as one of the dunces in Pope's *Dunciad*.

636.9–32 "That to such . . . as they have been."] Knox quotes from a letter, dated July 15, 1768, addressed to him from Grenville.

642.31–32 by the last history of it] Knox may be referring to William Douglass, *A Summary, Historical and Political, of the First Planting, Progressive Improvements, and Present State of the British Settlements in North-America* (2 vols., London, 1760), I, 489–90: "Lately (by instruction to the governor, or otherways, I am not certain) this province [Massachusetts-Bay] hath constituted townships, with all town or corporation privileges, excepting that of deputing representatives to the general assembly; though the charter expressly says, that they all may send representatives: it is true, that the multiplying of townships, especially by subdividing old large well-regulated townships, into many small jangling townships, has been, not many years ago, practised with particular views; but has occasioned an INCONVENIENT number of representatives. . . . [Yet this] seems to be inconsistent with that privilege essential to the constitution of Great-Britain, *viz.* that all freeholders of 40*s. per annum* income, and others legally qualified are to be represented in the legislature and taxation."

643.25   Doctor Robertson's celebrated history of Scotland] First published in 1759, the two-volume *History of Scotland During the Reigns of Queen Mary and of King James VI* by William Robertson (1721–1793), minister in the Church of Scotland and principal of the University of Edinburgh, was in its fifth edition in 1769.

645.25–32   "Laws they are not . . . like universal agreement."] Hooker, *Of the Laws of Ecclesiastical Polity*, Bk. I, sect. 10.

645.39–646.11   "That the *legislative . . . as any one under it.*"] These two quotes pull together language from three passages in Locke's *Second Treatise*: the first, from ch. xi, sect. 135, and ch. xii, sect. 151; the second, from ch. vii, sect. 119. The emphases are Knox's.

647.15–18   "even the *legislative . . .* over to others."] Ibid., ch. xi, sect. 141.

647.18–28   "all obedience, . . . is not supreme."] Ibid., ch. xi, sect. 134.

647.28–30   "there can be . . . subordinate."] Ibid., ch. xiii, sect. 149.

649.19–31   "It is commonly supposed, . . . *such a possession.*"] Ibid., ch. vi, sect. 73.

649.32–37   "Whoever . . . *as any subject of it.*"] Ibid., ch. viii, sect. 120.

650.10–13   "a power in the prince . . . even against it;"] Ibid., ch. xiv, sect. 160.

650.15–19   "a right to regulate, . . . just prerogative."] Ibid., ch. xiii, sect. 158.

650.22–26   "the prince by his own authority . . . before had it."] Ibid.

651.3–19   "The supreme power . . . *at pleasure.*"] Ibid., ch. xi, sect. 138.

651.20–25   "The prince or senate, . . . no property at all."] Ibid., ch. xi, sect. 139.

651.31–38   "Neither the serjeant . . . *of his goods.*"] Ibid.

652.20–25   "For (he says) . . . equally with the rest."] Ibid., ch. xi, sect. 138.

652.36–653.11   "That every man, . . . *hath a being.*"] Ibid., ch. viii, sect. 120.

656.23   *but seven-and-twenty*] Including those of Britain's Canadian and Caribbean colonies.

657.12   the Streights] The Strait of Gibraltar.

659.33–660.6   "he knows there is . . . people taxed."] See pages 358–59 in this volume.

660.20 Charta Foresta] A complementary charter (1217) to the Magna Carta, so named because it dealt with rights related to the use of royal forests.

661.6–27 "the common law . . . *taxes were to be levied.*"] Three passages from Dulany's *Considerations.* See pages 276–77 in this volume.

662.20 a superannuated politician] Though he was only sixty-one years old in 1769, the Earl of Chatham suffered from gout and episodes of mental instability, afflictions that often kept him away from London and rendered him something of a non-entity in the ministry (July 1766–October 1768) that bore his name. As this aspersion makes clear, Pitt's vocal support for the colonies during the Stamp Act crisis had earned him the lasting enmity of Knox and other members of the imperial administration. But for all that, the Great Commoner remained a national icon. This passage was removed from later printings of the first edition and replaced with the more anodyne "In extravagant declamations and unfounded arguments. In the weak artifices of party, and in the studied misrepresentations of designing and interested men."

662.21–22 an able finance minister] Frederick, Lord North (1713–1792), became chancellor of the Exchequer in December 1767, filling the vacancy left by the death of Townshend in September. The following month, after Conway resigned (see note 487.23–24), Lord North became Leader of the Commons as well. (North's title was merely honorific, since he was not yet a peer.) The confidence he engendered in these roles led to his becoming prime minister in 1770.

662.23–24 an ignorant *man of the law.*] Lord Camden (see note 450.14).

662.25 "*are these thy gods, O Israel?*"] Cf. Exodus 32:4.

663.24 cicatrise] Heal, allow to scar over.

665.6 two protests in the Lords Journals] These were later published as pamphlets. See note 590.25–33.

665.12–13 not then servants of the crown] That is, they were not in the government.

17: [EDWARD BANCROFT], REMARKS ON THE REVIEW

668.20 one scholar has claimed] Eric Nelson, *The Royalist Revolution: Monarchy and the American Founding* (Cambridge, MA: The Belknap Press of Harvard University Press, 2014), 43.

669.23–24 Confilia qui . . . turpiter.] From the twenty-fifth fable of Phaedrus, "The Dog and the Crocodile": "They who give ill advice to Men of Caution, lose their Labour, and shamefully expose themselves to Laughter." Translation from *The Fables of Phaedrus, Translated into English Prose* (London, 1745).

671.13–15 whilst their common Parent, . . . divested of every public

Employment.] Grenville was dismissed in July 1765 for reasons unrelated to the American controversy. He remained in the Commons until his death in 1770, but never again held office.

671.24–25   both apparently written by the same Persons.] Like *The Controversy . . . Reviewed*, *The Present State of the Nation: Particularly with Respect to Its Trade, Finances, &c. &c. Addressed to the King and both Houses of Parliament* (London, 1768) was at first ascribed to Grenville or, as Bancroft sometimes seems to, to a team of writers working at his direction, but is now believed to have been the work of William Knox.

671.36–37   an Ode on . . . the Right Hon. *George Grenville.*] The immodesty, if not the untruthfulness, of this anonymous 1769 paean may be gauged with a sampling of two stanzas:

> Come then, my GRENVILLE, come away,
> 'Tis criminal to lose a Day,
>   With Talents bright as thine:
> Let Indolence, on beds of Flow'rs,
> Consume the weary, lagging Hours,
>   Action's Thy nobler Line.
>
> Like Quintus, at his Country's call,
> Haste to avert a Nation's Fall,
>   Thy Absence signs its Fate:
> Felt by the Senate's loud Applause,
> Thy Manly Truths shall plead its Cause,
>   Thy Counsels make it Great.

672.19–23   "On this Principle . . . honest Purpose,"] Paraphrasing *The Controversy . . . Reviewed*. See page 618 in this volume.

675.6   the Act of the 13th of *George* the Second] The Naturalization Act of 1740.

675.10–12   "*Right to benefit, . . . impose Burthens.*"] Paraphrasing *The Controversy . . . Reviewed*. See page 625 in this volume.

676.28–32   "The first Charter . . . of *Discovery*"] Bancroft quotes here from the latter section of *The Controversy . . . Reviewed*, not reproduced in this volume, in which Knox presents lengthy extracts from colonial charters and other documents to substantiate his arguments.

678.10–14   The Pope was the first . . . West to *Spain.*] In 1493 Pope Alexander VI issued a series of bulls designating all lands to the east of a pole-to-pole line running 100 leagues west of the Azores to Portugal, and all lands to the west of the line to Spain, an arrangement further codified (and modified) by the two powers in the Treaty of Tordesillas (1494).

682.20   Sir *George Yardly*] Captain George Yeardley (c.1577–1627), who arrived in Virginia in 1610 and later served as deputy governor, 1616–17, and governor, 1618–21.

682.21–27 "resemble the *British* . . . in the Country."] From volume four-teen of *The Modern Part of the Universal History. Compiled from Original Writers* (16 vols., London, 1763). See also note 137.28–29.

682.37–38 "that Acts . . . shall not bind them."] See note 315.39.

683.7–11 "has been altered . . . every one of them."] Paraphrasing *The Controversy . . . Reviewed*. See pages 646–47 in this volume.

683.39–684.1 when a Bill was proposed . . . Liberty of Fishing] See Chronology for 1621.

685.6 an Emancipation from the Authority of Parliament] It is unlikely that many of New England's first settlers would have agreed with this character-ization. To the extent they looked for motives for their migration beyond the ties of kinship and community, they would probably have identified an aggressive episcopal hierarchy, supported and encouraged by an activist king and court, as the principal impetus. Indeed, the height of the Puritan exo-dus to New England occurred during precisely that period (1629–40) when Charles I tried to govern England without Parliament, the so-called Personal Rule.

685.9–10 Sir *Robert Naunton*] Naunton (c. 1563–1635), a staunch Protestant, was a secretary of state from 1618 to 1623.

685.13 Leave for the *Puritans*] Bancroft is referring here to the Leiden Sepa-ratists, better known in American history as the Pilgrims. See Chronology for 1619.

685.24 the following Instrument] The Mayflower Compact.

686.34–687.1 "Thus the Colony . . . of *England*."] From the first volume of Daniel Neal, *The History of New-England . . . In Two Volumes* (London, 1720).

691.26 Law against Paricides at *Rome*.] According to *A Complete Dictionary of the Greek and Roman Antiquities* (London, 1700), "the *Romans* made no Law against Parricides, because they did not think there could be a Man so wicked as to kill his Parents."

692.3 Sir *Edmund Andros*] An English officer and administrator (1637–1714) who played a major role in the implementation of James II's plan for colonial consolidation. He was governor of the Dominion of New-England from De-cember 1686 to April 1689, when he was arrested by Boston leaders embold-ened by news of the Glorious Revolution in the mother country (see Chronology for 1688–89).

693.18–27 "What King it is . . . *Stuart* Race."] Bancroft quotes here from the latter section of Knox's *The Controversy . . . Reviewed*, not reproduced in this volume.

693.36 the Prince and Princess of *Orange*] William and Mary.

697.27–30   The Debates . . . Tobacco in *England*] See Chronology for 1621.

698.16–17   "not fit to make . . . the *Crown*;"] Sir. George Calvert (1579–1632), the 1st Baron Baltimore after 1625, was a secretary of state from 1619 to 1625. This quote and those that follow from Christopher Brooke (c. 1566–1628), MP for York, and Sir Edward Coke are drawn from "*Extracts from the* JOURNALS *of the* HOUSE *of* COMMONS," the first entry in Knox's appendix to *The Controversy . . . Reviewed*.

699.3   when that Assembly declared] In An Act for Prohibiting Trade with the Barbadoes, Virginia, Bermuda and Antego, passed by the Rump Parliament on October 3, 1650.

700.1–2   the first Act . . . of any Kind] The Navigation Act of 1660.

701.4   (*Virginia* excepted,)] As a royal colony, Virginia's governors were appointed by the Crown.

703.7–23   "*Connecticut* . . . the Laws of *England*."] Bancroft may have taken this excerpt from the Board of Trade's report to the House of Lords from John Huddlestone Wynne, *A General History of the British Empire in America . . . In Two Volumes* (London, 1770).

703.36–37   when King *William* . . . to command them] In 1693, during King William's War, the Crown authorized Fletcher, whose colony was bearing the brunt of the fighting, to take command of the forces of neighboring Connecticut and Rhode Island, but when he traveled to Hartford on October 26, 1693, to enforce the commission he was rebuffed and personally threatened by leaders of the Connecticut militia.

705.31   Lord *Colepepper*] See note 323.17. Charles I had granted Culpeper's father a large swath of land in northern Virginia, the so-called Northern Neck, between the Potomac and Rappahannock Rivers, and much of his son's energy in office was directed at finally making good on the family's claim. Ultimately it would fall to the family of his son-in-law, Thomas Fairfax.

707.20–21   *Joseph Morton*] Morton was governor of South Carolina from October 1682 to August 1684, and then again from October 1685 to November 1686.

707.33   an Act of Parliament] The Navigation Act of 1663.

708.25–26   the principal, if not only Cause] Again, Bancroft shades the matter significantly. Bacon's Rebellion had at least as much to do with friction between Virginia's Tidewater planters and upcountry settlers over Indian policy as it did with the Navigation Acts.

711.11   the Agents thought it so inadequate] When Puritan minister Increase Mather (1639–1723), who led the Massachusetts delegation sent to London to secure a new charter, lost his cool in a session with the Privy Council and declared that "I would sooner part with my life than consent to . . . any thing else that did infringe any Liberty or Privilege of Right belonging to my Countrey," he was sharply rebuked by a member of the council who said that "they did not think the *Agents* of *New-England* were *Plenipotentiaries* from another Sovereign State."

712.11   the Plan of an Act] See note 342.15–19.

713.38   Quod ab initio . . . juris effectum.] This passage from book 3 of Hugo Grotius's *De Jure Belli ac Pacis* (see note 67.5) is also cited in a 1750 edition of Algernon Sidney's *Discourses Concerning Government*, where it is translated "that which is unjust in the beginning, can never have the effect of justice."

715.18–20   "as yet, reject . . . Taxation,"] From *The Controversy . . . Reviewed*. See page 630 in this volume.

716.8   Mr. *Locke*'s Maxim] See note 651.20–25.

717.8   *Jure Gladii*] Latin: By the right of the sword.

718.23–28   "Right in Corporations . . . or elected."] Two passages from *The Controversy . . . Reviewed*. See pages 644 and 643 in this volume.

718.30–719.16   "In the Counties, . . . who choose them."] From Sidney, *Discourses*, ch. iii, sect. 38. The Latin phrase at 719.6 means "nobles and great men of the realm."

719.24–25   "The House of Peers, . . . chosen by Kings."] Ibid., ch. iii, sect. 44.

720.21   *Mauduit*.] Israel Mauduit (1708–1787), political pamphleteer and brother of the former Massachusetts agent Jasper Mauduit. His most recent contribution to the imperial debate, published in London in December 1768, was *A Short View of the History of the Colony of Massachusetts Bay, with Respect to Their Original Charter and Constitution*.

720.26–28   "to assent to all . . . those Laws."] From the "Freeholder's Political Catechism," an unattributed work published in the September 22, 1733, edition of *The Craftsman*, an anti-Walpole periodical produced by William Pulteney (1684–1764, the Earl of Bath after 1742) and Henry St. John, Viscount Bolingbroke (1678–1751). It was reprinted in the March 25, 1769, edition of *The North Briton*, John Wilkes's paper, with the following preamble: "At a time when our most valuable privileges, especially that of chusing our own representatives in parliament, are invaded in the most open and barefaced manner, by a set of arbitrary and despotic ministers, we thought we could not present our readers with any thing more immediately useful, than the following extract from the *Freeholder's Political Catechism*; a little piece by the late Earl of Bath, then William Pultney, esq. and containing a short but judicious summary of the duty, as well as rights, of every English Freeholder." The work has been variously attributed to Bath and Bolingbroke.

720.28–32   "So that a Freeholder, . . . to obey."] A quotation from the December 23, 1715, issue of *The Freeholder*, the first of a series of essays that Addison published at the height of the Jacobite Rebellion.

721.7–10   "the Principle . . . to represent them;"] See pages 276 and 661 in this volume.

723.27–35   "*Asiatic* Slaves . . . Defence of it."] From Sidney, *Discourses*, ch. iii, sect. 8.

724.32–40   "The Legislative Power, . . . over the Colonies.] In this footnote Bancroft offers paraphrases of two passages from Sidney's *Discourses*, ch. iii, sect. 45. The first includes an allusion to Jeremiah 31:29–30.

725.10   are not Liveryman] That is, they are not members of one of London's Livery Companies, guild organizations which during this period retained the exclusive right to elect the four MPs that represented the City of London in Parliament.

726.24–25   "Allegiance, . . . as the Law requires."] From Sidney, *Discourses*, ch. iii, sect. 36.

726.37–38   Justa piaque . . . est salutis.] From Livy, *Ab Urbe Condita Libri*, Bk. IX, ch. 1. The same passage appears in Sidney's *Discourses* (ch. iii, sect. 40), where it is translated "those arms were just and pious that were necessary, and necessary when there was no hope of safety by any other way."

727.14–16   "That they are so . . . politic."] From *The Case of Great Britain and America, Addressed to the King, and Both Houses of Parliament* (London, 1769), an anonymous pamphlet variously attributed to Gervase Parker Bushe (1744–1793), a member of the Irish Parliament, and George B. Butler of New York.

728.37–39   "Being taught . . . they take Care it be rightly administered."] From Sidney, *Discourses*, ch. iii, sect. 36.

729.34–35   Dr. *Franklin*'s Estimation] In "Observations Concerning the Increase of Mankind, Peopling of Countries, &c.," an essay written in 1751 and first published in 1754 as an appendix to another pamphlet, Franklin posited the population of the American colonies "must at least be doubled every 20 years." Franklin included the essay in the fourth edition of his *Experiments and Observations on Electricity* (London, 1769), ensuring it a broad circulation and wide influence, including on the work of the political economist Thomas Malthus.

730.26–27   Mouth of a K——, . . . P——tary *Resolves*] Bancroft resorts here to dashes, which along with ellipses, blank spaces, and other typographical tricks were used to shield authors from accusations of libel or, in this case, treason, since he is discussing resistance to royal and parliamentary authority.

731.17–19   "the Glory of Kings, . . . to Justice,"] Bancroft may have drawn this maxim, attributed to Charles V ("le Sage") of France, from the December 1765 issue of *The London Magazine: Or, Gentleman's Monthly Intelligencer*, where it is introduced with much the same language.

731.38   Clause in an Act of Parliament] After passing the Stamp Act, Parliament approved amendments to the Mutiny Bill providing for the quartering of troops stationed in America at public houses or barracks at the expense of the colonial governments. If such public housing was inadequate, the act stipulated that then "and upon no other account" the governor and council of the affected colonies might appoint agents to identify "such and so many uninhabited houses, outhouses, barns, and other buildings, as shall be necessary." This measure seems to have been mainly the brainchild of the Earl of Halifax, secretary of state for the Southern Department, and Welbore Ellis, the secretary at War. Grenville, for his part, thought it ill-advised, "by far the most likely . . . to create difficulties and uneasiness, and therefore [it] ought certainly to be thoroughly weighed and considered before any step is taken in it." He further reminded the king that "the quartering of soldiers upon the people against their wills is declared by the petition of right to be contrary to law."

732.23–24   "by no Means . . . essential Rights."] From the New York Resolves against the Stamp Act, issued December 18, 1765.

733.18   Governor *Shirley*'s Proposal] In a January 5, 1756, letter to the Board of Trade, William Shirley (1694–1771), governor of Massachusetts, 1741–49 and 1753–56, proposed a variety of measures, including a stamp duty, to raise a colonial revenue. He suggested "for the general Satisfaction of the People in each Colony, it would be advisable to leave it to their Choice to raise the Sum assessed upon them according to their own discretion."

733.27   Our Author asserts] See the footnote on page 663 in this volume.

735.5–8   "There is a Spirit . . . of your Dependence."] See page 664 in this volume.

740.1–2   Lord *Colepepper* . . . lucrative Purpose.] See note 705.31.

741.14–15   the *Privernates* . . . answered] As recorded in Livy's *History of Rome*, Bk. VIII, ch. 21.

18: JOSEPH WARREN, BOSTON MASSACRE ORATION

745.15–17   Quis talia . . . a lacrymis.] Virgil, *Aeneid*, II.6–8: "What Myrmidon or Dolopian, or soldier of stern Ulysses, could in telling such a tale refrain from tears?" Translation from Fairclough, *Virgil: Eclogues, Georgics, Aeneid I–IV*, 295.

748.38–39   Omnes ordines . . . consentiunt.] From Cicero, *Orations against Catiline*, IV, sect. 9: "All ranks support the preservation of the republic with heart and will, with zeal and virtue, and with their voices."

752.36–753.3   our streets were stained . . . our beauteous virgins exposed]

This kind of heated language, which can strike the modern ear as sensational and luridly exaggerated, was a conventional aspect of eighteenth-century rhetoric.

753.5   that worse than brutal violence] Rape. For Lucretia, see note 503.19–20.

754.3–4   The infatuation . . . with regard to us, is truly astonishing!] One of the reasons Samuel Adams and the other patriot leaders urged two such top-notch attorneys as John Adams and Josiah Quincy to defend the soldiers in the trial was their concern for the reputation of Boston in the empire.

756.32   *made bare his arm*] Cf. Isaiah 52:10.

756.38–39   At simul heroum . . . cognoscere virtus.] Virgil, *Eclogues*, IV. 26–27: "But soon as thou canst read of the glories of heroes and thy father's deeds, and canst know what valour is." Translation from Fairclough, *Virgil: Eclogues, Georgics, Aeneid I–IV*.

757.1–2   *a name and a praise in the whole earth*] Cf. Zephaniah 3:20.

19: THE VOTES AND PROCEEDINGS

759.26–27   "purely an American Invention"] John Adams to Thomas Digges, March 14, 1780.

759.27   "an Engine"] John Adams to Dr. Jedidiah Morse, December 22, 1815.

759.37   "full of the most extravagant absurdities,"] From a January 29, 1774, speech before the Privy Council by Solicitor General Alexander Wedderburn (1733–1805), concerning the theft and unauthorized publication of letters from Thomas Hutchinson and other Massachusetts officials to Thomas Whatley. For more on this episode, see Pamphlet 39 in the companion to this volume, *The American Revolution: Writings from the Pamphlet Debate 1773–1776*.

765.37   See Lock's Letters on Toleration.] First published in 1689.

766.39   Locke on Government.] From the *Second Treatise*, ch. iv, sect. 22.

767.35   1 Wm. and Mary, St. 2. C. 18.] The footnote here refers the reader to An Act for Exempting their Majesties Protestant Subjects Dissenting from the Church of England from the Penalties of Certain Laws, better known as the Act of Toleration of 1689, and to the Massachusetts charter of 1691.

768.21–769.3   "The first fundamental . . . *at the Plough*."] Paraphrasing the *Second Treatise*, ch. xi.

770.35   See the Act . . . Dock-Yards.] The Dockyards, &c. Protection Act of 1772 made arson in the King's naval yards punishable by death. It would remain so, statutorily, even after the abolition of the death penalty in the United Kingdom in 1965.

773.20–21   "An Act stating . . . within this province,"] Passed by the Massachusetts legislature in 1716.

775.24–25   to a place highly inconvenient] In June 1769, Lord Hillsborough had ordered Francis Bernard to remove the Massachusetts General Court from its traditional meeting place in Boston in order to isolate it from the influence of the town's "licentious and unrestrained Mob." After Bernard's return to England later that year, Thomas Hutchinson, the lieutenant governor, received somewhat ambiguous instructions from Hillsborough to maintain the change at his discretion. He chose to do so, despite vigorous protests from the legislators.

782.32   an observation of an eminent Patriot] From the opening passages of Jonathan Swift, *The Drapier's Letters*, IV.

783.27   Nem. Con.] Latin abbreviation for *nemine contradicente*: with no one dissenting; unanimously.

Index

Acadians, 171

Accomack, Virginia, 708

Act for Prohibiting Trade with the Barbadoes, Virginia, Bermuda and Antego (1650), 699

Act for the More Easy Recovery of Debts in His Majesty's Plantations and Colonies in America (1732; 5 George II, chap. 7), 281–82, 622

Act in Restraint of Appeals (1533; 24 Henry VIII, chap. 12), 267

Act of Settlement (1701; 12 & 13 William III, chap. 2), 63, 78

Act of Toleration (1689; 1 William III and Mary II, chap. 18), 767

Act of Union (1707; 6 Anne, chap. 11), 432, 516–17, 566, 584–87, 602, 684–85

Act Stating the Fees of the Custom-House Officers (1716; Massachusetts provincial law), 773

Act that Proclamations Made by the King Shall Be Obeyed (1539; 31 Henry VIII, chap. 8), 269

Adams, John, xiii, 743, 759

Adams, Samuel, 106, 405, 743, 747, 763

Addison, Joseph, 720

Admiralty, courts of, 69, 92–96, 130, 134–35, 143, 157–58, 267, 328, 531, 743, 776–77

Africa, 21, 70, 132, 155, 218–20, 584, 597, 621, 657, 700–1, 734

Agriculture, 349, 391, 409, 437; as basis of American colonies, 10–11, 23, 171, 208, 354, 419; in southern colonies, 174–76, 221, 262; in West Indies, 184, 189–90, 207, 221

Alexander VI (pope), 678

Americans, as different from British, 241, 305

Amherst, Jeffrey, xx

Amsterdam, Netherlands, 405

Andros, Edmund, 692

Anglicans (Church of England), 83, 143, 778–79

Annapolis, Maryland, 241

Anne, Queen, xviii, 61, 63, 73, 602, 712

Antigua, 183

Anville, Jean-Baptiste d', 139

Appalachian Mountains, xv, xix–xx, 175, 177

Appleton, Nathaniel, 763

Aquitaine, 99

Arabs, 532, 621

Argenson, marquis d' (René-Louis de Voyer), 66

Aristocracy, xx, 250–51, 402; in American colonies, 38, 706; and Magna Carta, 510, 660–61, 721; as one principal form of government, 54, 247, 270, 442, 444, 537, 749–50; relationship to monarchy, 442, 444, 510

Army, British, 12, 83–84, 103, 179, 202, 310, 439, 518, 565, 574, 659, 726, 773, 776, 780; Boston Massacre, 743, 747, 752–53, 755, 776; expense of maintaining, 232–33, 259–60, 267–68, 288, 336–37, 339, 370, 390–91, 410–11, 416, 452, 454, 638–40, 656–57, 664; land granted to soldiers, 177; quartering of, 59, 255, 328, 360, 369–70, 533, 569, 639, 731–32, 752, 773, 776; in Seven Years' War, xxi, 177, 255, 285, 351, 353–55, 390–91

Asia, 700, 723

Assemblies, colonial, xiii, xviii, 37, 179, 193, 237, 305, 331, 405–6, 457, 463, 521, 534, 559, 593, 597, 611, 624, 629–30, 661, 673–74, 721, 730, 737; authority of, 456, 550, 565, 590, 607; as complete in themselves, 522, 527–28; and expense of maintaining British troops, 369; and manufacturing, 295, 324; militia raised by, 347, 425, 489, 706; petitions by, 285; proposed confederacy between colonies and Great Britain, 738–41; and Stamp Act Congress, 627; support of

British policy, 341–43, 360–61;
taxation by, 34–36, 163, 274, 288,
349, 352, 355–56, 450, 472, 514, 555,
563, 589, 604, 607, 609, 634, 656;
and trade, 323–24. *See also
individual colonies*
Athens, 154–55, 396, 425
Austria, 503
Azores, 214

Bacon's Rebellion, 708
Baltic Sea, 226
Baltimore, Baron (George Calvert),
471, 687–91, 698
Bancroft, Edward: *Remarks on the
Review of the Controversy between
Great Britain and Her Colonies*,
667–742
Bankruptcy, 283
Barbados, 65, 119, 183, 189, 435
Barbary states, 657, 663
Barber, Nathaniel, 763
Barrington, William, 25
Bath, Earl of (William Pulteney), 720
Beaver skins, 163, 174, 194–96, 198
Beawes, Wyndham, 436
Belcher, Jonathan, 712
Bentley, Richard, 149
Berkeley, William, 321, 699, 708
Bermuda, 65
Bernard, Francis, 406, 521, 743–44;
"Principles of Law and Polity,"
25–39
Bethune, Nathaniel, 106
Bill of Rights, British (1689; I William
III and Mary II, chap. 2), xviii, 58–
62, 76, 78, 276–78, 332, 355–56, 359,
620, 659–61, 709, 767
Birmingham, England, 236–37, 248–
49, 305, 310, 388
Blackstone, William, 613, 767
Bland, Richard: *An Inquiry into the
Rights of the British Colonies*, 305–29
Blankard vs. Galdy, 76
Board of Trade, xvii, xx, xxii, 25, 241,
331
Bollan, William, 82
Bombay, India, 584
Bonham's Case, 42, 112
Boston, Massachusetts, xvi, 25, 41, 291,
331, 363, 518, 520; British army in,

743, 747, 752, 755; Governor
Hutchinson's message to, 785–88;
letters of correspondence from, 780–
81; petition for repeal of Townshend
Acts, 405; Town Meeting, 106–7,
109, 759, 763; trade of, 349
Boston Massacre, 743–44, 747, 752–53,
755, 776
"Boston Pamphlet," 759–88
Bouquet, Henry, 355
Boyer, Abel, 602
Boynton, Richard, 763
Bracton, Henry de, 587
Braddock, Edward, 354
Bradford, John, 763
Brady, Robert, 312
Brazen, Thomas, 256
Bristol, England, 291
Britons, ancient, 311
Brooke, Christopher, 698
Brunswick, Germany, xv, 424
Bunker Hill, battle of, 744
Burke, Edmund, xxii, 491
Burnet, Gilbert, 22
Burnet, William, 712
Bute, Earl of (John Stuart), xxi–xxii,
491, 671

Cabot, John and Sebastian, 114, 678
Cade, Jack, 497
Caelius, 374
Caesar, Julius, 56, 92, 312, 459–60,
496
Calico cloth, 204, 211–13
Calvin's Case, 85, 111
Camden, Earl of (Charles Pratt), 450
Canada, 73, 103, 140, 179, 288, 316,
336, 455, 657; commodities from,
171–72, 262; expulsion of Acadians,
171, 262; fisheries of, 172–74, 197–
99, 262; furs from, 174, 195; land in,
169–70, 177; new British possessions
in, xv, 1, 453, 646; in Seven Years'
War, xx, 97, 139, 260, 354, 454, 733;
and trade, 172–74, 337. *See also
individual provinces*
Cape Breton, 97, 171–72, 260, 262
Cape Cod, 685–86
Cape Finisterre, 200
Cape of Good Hope, 621
Caribs, 185

Cartagena, New Granada (Colombia), 354

Carthage, 21, 155, 420

Case of Great Britain and America, Addressed to the King, and Both Houses of Parliament, 727, 736

Castle William (Boston), 776

Catholics, xv, 59, 68–69, 267, 441, 602, 634, 765, 767

Cato, 155

"Cato": *Thoughts on a Question of Importance*, 1–23

Cato's Letters, 440

Cattle, 174, 180, 463, 467

Cayenne, 200

Chancery, courts of, 46, 85, 282, 592, 717

Charles I, 319–20, 683–84, 687, 693, 701, 713; and exploration of New England, 126; and liberty, 479, 515; prerogative claims of, 474; and ship-money, 99; and Virginia's dependence on Crown, 319–20, 694

Charles II, 259, 324, 467, 477, 510, 620, 692, 700–2, 706–10, 713; antipathy toward New England, 717; arbitrary power of, 469; dissolute reign of, 755; as king in Virginia, 321, 693, 699; and liberty, 323, 478–79

Charles V (France), 731

Charleston, South Carolina, 743

Charlotte, Queen, 491

Charta de Foresta, 660

Charters, colonial, xvi, 37, 151, 238–39, 322, 373, 463, 496, 564, 592, 606–8, 668, 713, 768, 697; authority of, 150, 256, 258, 260, 273, 275–76, 515, 527, 542, 611, 717; of Connecticut, 66, 126, 150, 700–6; of Georgia, 711–12; of Maryland, 682, 684, 687–91, 702, 710; of Massachusetts, 66, 75, 106, 108–9, 150, 620, 623, 759; of Massachusetts (1629), 126, 682, 684, 687, 691–92, 717, 779; of Massachusetts (1691), 710–12, 749–50, 767, 769, 771, 773–74, 776–77, 786–88; of New Hampshire, 66, 150, 700; Otis on, 66, 72, 74–75, 78, 88, 90, 93, 95, 99, 106, 108–11; of Pennsylvania, 358–59, 620–22, 647, 659–60, 710; of Plymouth, 150, 684–87, 691; of Rhode Island, 66, 126,

143, 150, 156, 702–6; royal, requisites of, 276, 623–24, 642, 646, 673–76; of South Carolina, 608, 706–7; of Virginia, 317–21, 324, 676–84, 687, 702, 704

Cherokees, 657

Chester, England, 32, 322, 716

Chesterfield, Earl of (Philip Stanhope), 395

Child, Josiah, 435–36

Christianity, 142, 484, 532, 552, 624, 677–78, 685, 705, 763–65, 767–68, 779–81

Church, Benjamin, 763

Church of England. *See* Anglicans

Cicero, 374, 384, 395, 400, 432, 476, 518, 748

Cider Act (1763; 3 George III, chap. 12), 508, 610, 671, 731

Circular letters: from the Boston Town Meeting, 764, 780–88; from the Crown, 358, 521; from the Massachusetts assembly, 331, 405–6, 521

City of London vs. Wood, 112

Civil list, 35, 235–36, 566

Civil War, English, 147

Clarendon, Earl of (Edward Hyde), 424, 579, 701, 755

Claudian, 371, 378

Claudius, Appius, 11

Cleon, 425

Clodius, 425

Clothing: British-made, 298–99, 301, 343, 347, 360; colonial manufacturing of, 292–93, 295, 344, 347, 361, 533, 535

Coal mining, 171–72, 262

Cocoa, 184, 189, 221, 227, 234

Cod, 173

Coffee, 184, 189, 215, 221, 227

Coke, Edward, 94, 96, 98, 101, 246, 416–17, 427–28, 459, 464, 470, 698, 767; on Bonham's Case, 42, 112; on Calvin's Case, 85, 111

College of William and Mary, 349

Collins, Arthur, 250

Colonial agents, 75, 100, 156, 406, 412, 489, 711, 776

Colonial Trade Act (1729; 3 George II, chap. 28), 200

Colonial Trade Act (1760; 1 George III, chap. 9), 415

Colonies, 65–66; administration of, 81; in ancient Greece and Rome, 519, 546, 549; aspirations for independence, 88–91, 662–63; assistance in Seven Years' War, xv–xvi, 139, 260–63, 268, 569–70; British defense of, 33–34, 97, 117, 194, 261–68, 369, 371–72, 416, 452–62, 520, 565–69, 657–63; civil rights of, 72–105; commodities from, 167–69, 189, 194–202, 204, 291–92, 297–304, 663; compared with municiple corporations, 102–3, 151, 256–57, 675, 702–4, 709; corporate, xvi–xvii, 143, 521; and debt from Seven Years' War, xv, 97, 107, 117, 139, 259–63, 266, 268, 335, 353, 569; dependent on Great Britain, 130, 177–78, 238, 256–59, 276, 292, 296, 316, 331, 399, 424–25, 432–34, 577, 584, 589–93, 599, 603, 608–9, 627, 642, 664, 681, 717–18, 727, 735, 737, 741; disadvantages of, 11–13, 23, 567; distance from Great Britain, 90, 99, 132, 347, 351, 360, 518, 521, 525, 550–51, 559, 561, 574, 729, 736, 770; and Glorious Revolution, 47–48; government of, xvi, 1, 25, 92–93, 121, 150; grievances of colonists, 770–80; infringement of rights of, 770–80; interests of, 241, 245, 253, 264, 328, 353; land grants in, 169–71, 173, 177, 183–85, 189; legislative authority to raise own taxes, 34–37, 163, 256, 259, 264–65, 267–68, 274, 287–88, 349, 352, 355–56, 369, 450, 472, 514, 555, 563, 589, 604, 607, 609, 634; limits of settlement, 177–79; Parliamentary reforms of, xxii, 25–26, 30, 38–39, 41, 121, 613; petitions to monarch, 347, 381, 405, 425–26, 489, 556, 562, 619, 706; petitions to Parliament, 100, 156, 340, 342, 425–26, 489, 556, 619; population of, xix, 11, 65, 132, 167, 169–71, 174, 185, 199, 203, 214, 309, 337, 340–41, 355, 391, 454; property in, 373, 386, 429–30, 462, 528, 597, 603–7, 610–11, 673, 737–38, 751, 754, 777; proposed confederacy with Great Britain, 738–41; proprietary, xvi–xvii, 39, 68, 471; as provinces, 519; reimbursed by Parliament, 83, 87, 97, 117, 139, 338, 352–53; rights of, 66–105, 620–30, 659, 662, 667, 719–20, 726–28, 732, 740, 754, 756, 759, 763–64, 767–70, 780–83; royal grants establishing, xvi–xvii, 11–12, 32–33, 37, 68, 151, 238–39; sovereignty of, 569–70; subordinate to Parliament, 80, 84, 88–89, 105, 131, 256–59, 273, 279, 325–32, 363, 369, 372–83, 413, 424, 519–20, 550, 591–94, 599, 608, 627; suffrage in, 305; union of, 439, 484, 486; whale fishery of, 196–99. *See also* Assemblies, colonial; Charters, colonial; Governors, colonial; Manufacturing; Representation; Taxation; Trade; *and individual colonies*

Commerce. *See* Trade

Committees of correspondence, 759, 763, 781

Commodities, from colonies, 167–69, 189, 194–204, 271, 291–92, 297–304, 663. *See also individual commodities*

Common law, 42, 69, 134, 460, 509; and colonial rights, 74–75, 78, 273–78, 281, 283, 769; courts of, 93, 328; and juries, 95, 270; and Magna Carta, 96, 100, 509; and power of Parliament, 111–12, 143, 150–52; and trade, 94

Commonwealth, English, 320–21, 717

Commonwealths, as political entities, 53, 56, 63, 67, 74–75, 81–82, 87, 96, 104, 127, 131, 312, 567, 646, 649, 694–95, 698, 768

Compact, original, 45–50, 53, 56, 104, 317, 497, 502, 504–5, 598–99, 764–65

Competency, as colonial trait, 169, 233, 254, 266

Connecticut, 729; charter of, 66, 126, 150, 700–6; as corporate colony, xvii, 66; judges in, 92

Consent, 313, 315, 317, 326, 381; express/tacit, 46, 314, 646, 652; of Parliament, 355–56

Constantine, 137

Constitution, British, 17, 19, 69, 153, 180, 314, 385, 425, 485, 496, 613, 638, 643, 726, 732; and Act of Union, 516; alterations to, 112, 154, and colonies, 105, 114, 129, 131, 138, 140, 151, 234, 236, 275, 287–88, 305, 316, 327, 358, 374, 399–400, 543, 565, 593–94, 627, 674, 697, 700, 709–12, 714, 721, 729; and commerce, 114, 375; common law basis of, 152, 273–74; and English Civil War, 147; extends to all of empire, 551, 582–87, 589; fundamental principles of, 111, 265, 311, 545; genius of, 51, 56, 186, 246, 398, 401, 537; and law of nature, 505, 642, 769; legislative and executive power in, 38, 81, 84, 87–88, 104, 112, 381, 383, 456, 608–9, 676, 719, 722; and liberty, 41, 73, 125, 128, 179, 286–87, 289, 313, 322–23, 325, 328, 379–80, 382, 393–94, 403, 413, 550–51, 598, 603, 611, 636, 714, 719, 749, 783; monarchy, aristocracy and democracy in, 247, 259, 270, 331, 442–43, 478, 510–12, 749–50; and natural rights, 326, 370; and property, 253, 382, 394, 598, 718, 721; and representation, 249, 315, 342, 514, 562, 644, 646, 650, 654–56, 722; and settlement of America, 679–80, 682, 695, 697, 700, 709–12, 714, 716; sovereignty of, 142; spirit of, 780; and standing army, 752, 773; and taxation, 77–78, 101–2, 104, 138, 140, 236, 250, 276, 288, 426–29, 431, 450–51, 527–28, 581, 595, 597–600, 607, 610, 632, 717, 721, 750; and trade, 402, 631–32

Constitution, Scottish, 512, 643

Constitutions, of ancient Greece and Rome, 545–49, 748–49

Constitutions, colonial. See Charters, colonial

Contract, political, 400–1

Contract, social. See Original compact

Conway, Henry Seymour, 487

Cooper, William, 747, 763, 783–84, 788

Corcyrea, 127, 326

Corinth, 127, 326

Corinthians (biblical book), 442

Corn, 19, 220, 251

Corporations, 88, 102–3, 151, 256–57, 644–45, 675, 702–4, 709, 718–19

Corruption, xvii, 64, 121, 157, 376–77, 531, 675

Corsica, 155, 536

Cotton, 175, 184, 189, 221, 234, 292

Craw vs. Ramsey, 76

Creoles, 70, 119

Cromwell, Oliver, 125, 289, 479

Crown, British: appointment of public officers by, 382–83; colonial petitions to, 347, 381, 405, 425–26, 489, 556, 592, 619, 706; commission of judges by, 63, 403, 414, 461, 787; despotism of, 113, 331, 474–75, 515, 749; grants of land by, 32–33, 648–49; relationship to Parliament, 32–33, 88, 93, 322, 331–32, 356, 379, 443, 446, 627, 751; represented in colonies by royal governors, xvi–xvii, 92–93, 514, 738–39, 750. See also Monarchy and individual monarchs

Cuba, xv, 9, 12, 97, 139

Culloden, battle of, 491

Culpeper, John, 705, 709, 740

Currency Act (1751; 24 George II, chap. 53), 192–93

Currency Act (1764; 4 George III, chap. 34), 121, 192–93

Cushing, Thomas, 106

Custom-house officers, 83, 93, 98, 134, 157, 229, 610, 772–73

Customs Act (1763; 4 George III, chap. 9), 197, 777

Dana, Richard, 106, 747

Dartmouth, Earl of (William Legge), 331

Davenant, Charles, 304, 435–36, 439

Davis, Caleb, 763

Day vs. Savadge, 112

Debt: of colonies, from Seven Years' War, xv, 97, 107, 117, 139, 259–60, 262–63, 266, 268, 335, 353, 733; of colonists, 281–83, 350–51, 387, 470; of Great Britain, from Seven Years' War, xx–xxi, 76, 97, 107, 117, 202, 233, 236, 267, 335, 569–70; and paper money, 192–93

Decker, Matthew, 298

Declaration of Resolves (Stamp Act Congress), 428–29, 627

Declaratory Act (1766; 6 George III, chap. 12), 332, 450, 522, 589, 593

Defoe, Daniel, 506

Delaware River, 409

Democracy, 50, 53–54, 90, 143, 508; in ancient Greece, 127; and House of Commons, 19, 750; as one principal form of government, 54, 247, 250, 270, 537, 550, 749–50

Demosthenes, 365, 451, 480

Denmark, 61, 63, 113, 226, 293, 337, 568, 734

Dennie, William, 763

Despotism: of the Crown, 113, 331, 474–75, 515, 749; of Parliament, 323, 368

Deuteronomy (biblical book), 485

Dickinson, John, 377, 627, 631–32, 638–42, 647–48, 696; *Letters from a Farmer in Pennsylvania*, 405–89

Diocletian, 137

Dionysius of Halicarnassus, 67

Dissenters, 441

Dobbs, Arthur, xviii

Dockyards Protection Act (1772; 12 George III, chap. 24), 766, 770, 777–78

Dodsley, Robert, 495

Domat, Jean, 68

Domesday Book, 509

Dominica, xv, 182, 185, 188–90

Douglas, John, 469–70

Douglass, William, 642

Downer, Silas: *Discourse at the Tree of Liberty*, 521–36

Draco, 158

Dublin, Ireland, 405

Dugdale, William, 251

Dulany, Daniel, 305, 622, 661; *Considerations on the Propriety of Imposing Taxes*, 241–304

Dummer, Jeremiah: *Defence of the New-England Charters*, 75, 90, 95, 99, 489

Dunkirk, France, xv, 21

Durham, England, 32, 595, 606

Duties. *See* Taxation

East Florida, xv, 169–70, 174–77, 179, 216, 221, 417, 453–55, 597, 646

East Greenwich, royal manor of, 595, 606, 680, 686

East India Company, 226, 237, 248–49, 310–11, 631, 634

East Indies, 22, 85, 169, 204, 209, 211–13, 392, 437, 584, 596–97

Edward, the Black Prince, 99

Edward I, 85, 250, 252, 427–28

Edward III, 99, 111

Egypt, ancient, 119

Elections, 163–64, 236, 239, 248–50, 252–54, 274, 276–77, 305, 310–14, 319

Elizabeth, I, 116, 318, 676–79, 681, 683, 693–94

Emigration to America, xix, 1, 10, 126–27, 170, 205, 209, 337, 382, 525, 531, 564, 577, 674, 749, 756

England, xii, 21, 65, 293, 321, 427, 512, 658; constitutional status of, 516, 566, 584–87, 594, 596, 602, 606, 609, 684–85; economy of, xix–xx; emigrants from, 531; Parliament of, 84–85. *See also* Great Britain

Epidamnus, 127

Equality, 55, 557, 584, 662; between colonies and Great Britain, 129, 305, 325, 374, 382, 385, 391, 550–51, 563, 719, 725; natural, 48, 69, 384, 497–98, 500

Equity, natural, 46, 57, 81, 111–12

Ethiopia, 70

Exchequer, 80, 278, 287, 405, 459, 467, 512, 777, 787

Excise tax, 348, 477–78

Executive power, 130, 461, 736; embodied in monarch, 19, 87, 191, 259, 332, 377, 434, 474, 491, 646–47, 695; judges independent of, 458; and settlement of America, 681, 691, 701–2, 706; supreme, 53–56, 87

Factions, 90, 121, 143, 147, 581

Fairfax, Thomas, 471

Faneuil Hall (Boston), 747, 763, 785–88

Feudalism, 91, 155, 250

Filmer, Robert, 125, 645

Fisheries, 21, 115–16, 172–74, 218–19, 229, 262, 419, 436, 662, 684, 697–98

Flanders, 18

Flax, 201–2, 205–7, 210, 292, 295, 351, 533, 535

Fletcher, Benjamin, 703

Florida. *See* East Florida; West Florida

Fort Detroit, 355

Fort Duquesne, 354

Fort Niagara, 355

France, xviii, 57, 61–62, 104, 159–60, 280, 321, 326, 420, 427, 478–79, 521, 551, 565, 571, 624, 639, 657, 667–68, 685, 693, 699, 720, 731–32, 734; absolute monarchy in, 50, 113, 599, 628; cession of Louisiana to Spain, xv, 168, 262; colonial government of, 68, 79, 110, 128; and colonial wars, xv, xx, 1, 18–19, 83, 97, 103–4, 139–40, 335, 354–55, 454, 554, 569–70, 733; fisheries of, 173, 229, 698; former West Indies islands, 185–86, 189–90, 221; manufacturing in, 94, 115; parliaments of, 460, 532; settlers expelled from Nova Scotia, 171, 262; trade of, 21, 41, 94, 115, 132, 172–73, 190, 195, 200, 211–17, 220–22, 226–27, 300, 337, 437, 544

Franklin, Benjamin, xix, 1, 450, 537, 631, 659–61, 667, 729, 732; *Examination Relating to the Repeal of the Stamp Act*, 331–61

Freedom. *See* Liberty

Freehold, 106, 236, 248, 253, 281, 310, 312–13, 319, 510–11, 577, 642, 644, 715, 718–24, 747, 759, 780, 786

French and Indian War. *See* Seven Years' War

Frontier: defense of, xxi, 354–55, 369, 372, 390, 657; formation of colonies on, 126, 274, 534–36, 605; and Proclamation of 1763, xx, 169, 177–79; settlement on, 335–36, 360, 533; as wilderness, 1, 82, 434, 486, 751, 755

Fundamental Constitutions of Carolina, 706–7

Fur trade, xvi, 163, 174, 194–96, 198, 227

Fustic, 234

Galatians (biblical book), 421

Gascony, 101

Gaul, 532, 548

Gee, Joshua, 445

Genoa, Italy, 437

George I, xviii, xxi–xxii, 73, 84, 235, 773

George II, xviii, xxi, 97, 129, 235, 468

George III, 7, 48, 73, 104, 110, 194, 235, 259, 278, 288, 353, 468, 496, 514, 517–18, 530, 534, 667, 693, 753, 786–88; colonial petitions to, 405; colonial respect for, xv, 50, 91, 97, 402, 412, 423, 444, 525, 610, 625; involvement in politics, xxi–xxii, 163, 331, 491, 521, 560, 776

Georgia, 134–35, 143, 175, 216, 316, 337, 577; charter of, 711–12; rice from, 199–200

Germany, xv, 19, 46, 48, 312, 447, 519, 530, 551, 657; emigrants from, 205, 209, 337, 531; trade of, 211, 213, 226, 437

Gibraltar, 584, 597, 657, 696

Ginger, 184, 189, 221, 234

Glasgow, Scotland, 518

Glass, 405, 413, 417–19, 431, 448–49

Glorious Revolution, xviii, 22, 47, 56, 65–66, 78, 81, 92, 104, 109, 119, 125, 276–77, 393, 460, 495, 661, 786

Gold, 8–9, 291, 318, 346

Goldsmith, Oliver, 1

Gorges, Francis, 698

Goths, 91

Government, 50, 495; civil, 53, 104, 457, 461–64, 470, 481, 527, 535, 638, 747; law of, 501–2; origins of, 45–65, 497–505; purpose of, 52, 54; and representation, 31, 33, 36, 55; self-, xiii, 19

Governors, colonial, 150, 342, 346, 439, 457, 560, 573; and impressment, 98; and land acquisition, 177, 779; in Maryland, 345; in Massachusetts, 1, 25, 346, 406, 521, 743–53, 773–76, 785–88; in New York, 411, 703; in Rhode Island, 121, 521; royal, enforcing authority of the Crown, xvi–xvii, 92–93, 514, 738–39, 750; salaries, 93, 464; and trade with Indians, 178–79; in Virginia, 321, 682, 699, 708

Grants: colonial, xvi–xvii, 11–12, 32–33, 37, 68, 151, 238–39, 648–49, 679; of land, 32–33, 169–71, 173, 177, 183–85, 189

Granville, Earl of (John Carteret), 99

Gray, Thomas, 106

Great Britain, 367–68, 373, 424, 542; abdication of James II, 47–48, 56, 58–59; colonial wars of, xv–xvi, xx–xxi, 1, 18–19, 83, 97, 139; defense of colonies, 33–34, 97, 117, 194, 261, 263, 265, 267–68, 335, 338, 342, 369, 371–72, 416, 452–55, 457–58, 461–62, 520, 565–66, 569, 657, 659, 662; depopulation of, 6, 11–12; fisheries of, 173; government bureaucracy in, xvi–xvii, 25–26; interests of, 241, 245, 253, 264, 327, 353, 400; proposed confederacy with American colonies, 738–41; suffrage in, 236, 239, 248–50, 252–54, 274, 276–77, 305, 310–13; taxation in, xx, 33, 98, 141, 270, 276, 567, 595–96, 658–59, 664, 724; whale fishery of, 196–99. See also Manufacturing; Trade

Great Lakes, 199

Greece, ancient, 67–68, 127–28, 150, 154–56, 396–97, 399, 423, 425, 519, 545–46, 549, 725

Green, Joseph, 106

Greenland, 101, 196–98, 621

Greenland Fishery Act (1731; 5 George II, chap. 28), 196

Greenleaf, Joseph, 763

Greenleaf, William, 763

Grenada, xv, 180, 189

Grenville, George, 80, 163, 272, 278, 331, 385–87, 392, 415, 430, 432, 445–46, 451–52, 462, 483, 635–36, 671–72, 683, 713, 720, 723, 731–33

Groning, John, 280

Grotius, Hugo, 66–67, 128, 498, 713

Guadeloupe, 1, 97, 190, 200

Guernsey, 153, 584, 589, 594, 596, 602

Guinea, 218–20

Gulf of St. Lawrence, 172, 197–99, 262, 318

Hakluyt, Richard, 318

Hale, Matthew, 92, 379–80, 394

Halifax, Earl of (George Montagu Dunk), xx, 25

Halifax, England, 236, 248–49, 310

Halifax, Nova Scotia, 134, 143, 147, 743

Hamburg, Germany, 226

Hampden, John, 125, 287, 412

Hampshire, England, 589

Hancock, John, 743, 747, 764

Hanover, Electorate of, xv, 530, 700

Hanoverians, xviii, xxi, 73, 89, 288–89, 424, 491, 515

Harrington, James, 49, 56

Hat Act (1732; 5 George II, chap. 22), 209

Hats, manufacture of, 194–95

Havana, Cuba, xv, 12, 97, 139

Hemp, 163, 201

Henry II, 717

Henry III, 246, 509

Henry IV, 250, 478, 697

Henry V, 427, 478

Henry VI, 246, 511–12

Henry VII, 477

Henry VIII, 246, 269, 778

Hicks, William: *The Nature and Extent of Parliamentary Power Considered*, 363–403

Hill, Alexander, 763

Hillsborough, Earl of (Wills Hill), 25, 405, 470, 521, 743

Hoadley, Benjamin, 246

Hobart, Henry, 112

Holt, John, 112

Holy Roman Empire, 48

Hooker, Richard, 617, 645

Hopkins, Stephen: *The Rights of Colonies Examined*, 121–42; responses to, 143, 147–48

Horace, 255, 426, 444, 539

House of Burgesses. *See* Virginia

House of Representatives. *See* Massachusetts

Howard, Martin, Jr.: *Letter from a Gentleman at Halifax*, 143–61

Hudson River, 685

Hume, David, 19, 295, 427, 434, 451, 455–56, 461, 467, 469, 475
Hungerford, Wilson, 588
Huske, John, 137; questions Franklin, 336
Hutchinson, Thomas, 1, 346, 773–76, 785–88

Importation Act (1726; 13 George I, chap. 5), 173
Importation Act (1729; 3 George II, chap. 12), 173
Impressment, 97–98, 360
Inches, Henderson, 747
Independency, 84, 239, 577, 593, 630, 675, 729; absolute, 564, 575, 622; colonists' aspirations for, 88–91, 662–63; criticism of, 520, 569, 604, 609–10, 618; declarations of, 564, 583, 589, 594
India, xv, 212, 584, 597
Indians, 9–10, 65, 68, 116, 175, 185, 321, 621, 648, 678; hostilities with, xix–xx, 1, 75, 83, 97, 114, 139, 372, 686, 739, 755; land purchased from, 110, 177, 749, 779; peace with, xx, 369, 525, 686; Pontiac's Rebellion, 335, 355; in Seven Years' War, 354–55, 570; trade with, 178–79, 218, 220, 354–55, 453, 533, 635, 657
Indigo, 174–75, 189, 215–16, 221, 234, 262
Inquiry into the Nature and Causes of the Present Disputes between the British Colonies in America and Their Mother-Country, 537–76
Inquisition, 69, 160
Ireland, 57, 61–62, 73, 104, 157, 287–88, 321, 374, 427, 515, 536, 680, 685, 689, 693, 699–700, 770; constitutional status of, 84–87, 110, 345, 356, 559, 562, 574, 577, 584–85, 587–89, 591–96, 602; emigrants from, 170, 531; and Glorious Revolution, 47–48; land ownership in, 251; manufacturing in, 115–16, 134, 159, 351, 420; parliament of, 468, 587–88, 609; peers in, 588; pensions in, 465–69; representation in Parliament, 32, 101; taxation of, 84–87, 711–13; trade with, 18, 93, 420, 445

Irish Declaratory Act (1720; 6 George I, chap. 5), 73, 86, 587
Iron, 228, 419, 431, 445, 532, 777
Iron Act (1750; 23 George II, chap. 29), 209, 431
Isaiah (biblical book), 756
Isle of Man, 153, 584, 589, 697
Israelites, ancient, 766
Italy, 337, 547, 624, 657; trade of, 437

Jackson, Joseph, 747
Jackson, Richard, 406
Jacobites, xviii, 491, 609
Jamaica, 65, 71, 189, 269, 435, 646
James I, 295, 318–19, 515, 619–20, 644, 676, 679–83, 685–87, 693–94, 701, 713
James II, xviii, 47–48, 56–59, 72, 441, 477
Jefferson, Thomas, xiii, 305–6
Jeffreys, George, 458
Jeffries, David, 747
Jenyns, Soame: *Objections to the Taxation of Our American Colonies*, 241, 281, 302–4
Jersey, 153, 584, 589, 594, 596, 609
Jews, 519, 610
John, King, 509–10, 513, 660, 692, 709, 721, 767–68
Johnson, Samuel, xxi–xxii, 1
Johnson, William, 10
Johnson, William Samuel, 405
Judges: of admiralty courts, 92–93, 267, 328, 531; commissioned by the Crown, 63, 403, 414, 461, 787; independence of, 77, 87, 458–60, 768, 774–75, 780–81, 785–86; power of, 460; and role of House of Lords, 402
Juries, 61, 95, 267, 270, 328, 340, 459–60, 521, 778
Justice: administration of, 457–58, 461–62, 464, 470, 481, 526, 530, 584; natural, 57
Juvenal, 54

King, Daniel, 322
King George's War, 97
King William's War, 702
Knox, William: *The Controversy between Great Britain and Her Colonies*

Reviewed, 613–66; responses to, 668, 671–73, 675–76, 678, 693, 695, 697, 704, 715, 717, 720, 730–33; *Claim of the Colonies to an Exemption from Internal Taxes*, 241, 254, 265–66, 278

Lactantius, 307

Land: in Canada, 169–70, 177; cheapness of, 13, 176; grants of, 32–33, 169–71, 173, 177, 183–85, 189, 779; seizure of, 282; and suffrage, 236, 248, 310; taxes on, 269, 335, 338–39, 634, 654, 717; in West Indies, 176, 180–90

Law: canon, 68; civil, 270, 501–2; fundamentals of, 598–99; of government, 501–2; of nations, 47, 66, 95, 110, 112, 765; of nature, 46–47, 49, 51–53, 66, 69–71, 79, 110–13, 157, 305, 311, 316–17, 328, 499–505, 696, 764–66, 768–69; unjust and oppressive, 246, 341, 406, 444–45, 460. *See also* Common law

Lawyers, 254–55, 662

Lead, 405

Leather, 292, 295, 298

Leeds, England, 236, 248–49, 310

Legislative power, 31, 38, 110, 247, 371, 497, 507, 596, 608–9, 720, 736; embodied in Parliament, 19, 87, 191, 313, 331–32, 363, 375, 377, 381, 510, 572, 591, 614, 638, 660, 695–96, 724, 771; judges independent of, 402–3, 458; for making fundamental laws, 111–12, 647, 764; over policies, 363, 383, 385–87, 495, 591, 646, 649, 660; and settlement of America, 701–2, 706; as supreme, 53–56, 63–64, 87, 100, 104, 383, 626, 651–52

Levant, 200

Lexington, battle of, xiii

Liberty: absolute, 125; in ancient Greece and Rome, 546–48; and arbitrary power, 57, 373; and British constitution, 41, 73, 125, 128, 179, 286–87, 289, 313, 322–23, 325, 328, 379–80, 382, 394, 403, 413, 550–51, 598, 603, 611, 636, 714, 719, 749, 783; and civil rights, 78–79, 603; and colonial assemblies/charters, 620–23, 626–27, 659; colonial compared with British, 128–30, 373, 619, 736; and emigration to America, 127, 317; freedom of conscience (religion), 74, 82, 317, 321, 441, 521, 553, 604, 767, 778–79, 782; freedom of the press, 749–50; freedom of speech, 60, 137–38, 521, 534; and independent judges, 458–60; infringement by Parliamentary power, 376–77, 394, 402, 410–11, 413, 417–18, 420, 422, 431–32, 446, 451, 456, 463, 470, 485; natural, 46, 48, 64, 69–71, 113, 125, 379–82, 399–401, 447, 497, 527, 543, 552, 565, 674, 764–70; and property, 64, 109, 125–26, 135, 150, 373, 386, 394, 462, 484, 598, 603, 605–6, 610–11, 720, 738, 751, 764, 767–68; protected by Parliament, 340, 608; and royal power, 331, 368, 376–77, 474, 478–79, 515; in Scotland, 602; and taxation, 428–29, 431, 484, 573, 635, 741; and trade, 94, 375, 385–86, 402, 433, 535, 597

Liberty (ship), 743

Liberty poles, 521

Liberty trees, 518, 521, 525, 536, 782

"Lillibullero" (song), 152

Linen, 85, 116, 134, 159, 202, 205–7, 209–13, 226, 295, 351, 420, 437, 633

Liverpool, England, 291

Livy, 396, 398, 478, 726, 741

Locke, John, 67, 281, 515; *First Treatise on Government*, 47, 51, 313; *Letters Concerning Toleration*, 765; *Second Treatise on Government*, 47, 52, 56, 63–65, 70, 77, 313, 380, 450–51, 645–47, 649–53, 694–96, 716, 766, 768–69

London, England, xviii, 2, 6, 16, 112, 291, 318, 332, 406, 427, 483, 496, 560, 663, 668; as capital of empire, 460, 520; mob violence in, 667; pamphlets published in, 1, 25, 41, 163, 241, 405, 491, 537, 577, 613, 667; population of, 116; representation of, 236–38, 248–49, 254, 310, 601, 725; taxation in, 102

Louis XIV, 94, 732

Louisbourg, fortress of, 97, 139

Louisiana, xv, 168, 262
Lowndes, Richard, 445
Loyalists, 241
Loyalty, 18, 65, 72–73, 78, 89, 91, 109, 121, 140, 149, 185, 289, 327
Lucretia, 753
Lumber, 134, 159, 221, 228, 234, 445
Luxury goods, xx, 11, 14, 155, 169, 202, 213–15, 292, 296
Lycurgus, 423, 545–46

Maccabees, 519
Machiavelli, Niccolò, 388, 473, 478
Mackay, William, 763
Madeira wine, 214–15, 226
Magna Carta, 72, 76, 84, 96, 98, 100, 109, 276, 278, 317, 359, 372, 496, 509–10, 513, 527, 659–61, 675, 692, 709, 721
Maine (province), 700–1
Majority rule, 47, 54, 164, 239, 241, 381, 644–45, 654–55
Malt, 517–18, 595
Manchester, England, 236–37, 248–49, 305, 310, 388
Manila, Philippines, xv
Mansfield, Earl of (William Murray), 255, 518
Manufacturing, 11; in colonies, 1, 12–14, 94, 96, 171, 205–13, 226, 292–95, 324, 343–44, 347, 349, 351, 360–61, 363, 368, 375, 385, 387–88, 391–92, 419–20, 431, 448, 455, 533, 535, 544, 633–34, 727, 738, 777; in France, 94, 115; in Great Britain, xvi, 95, 98, 108, 115–16, 132–34, 167–69, 171, 173–74, 194–96, 203, 206–13, 262, 266, 271–72, 290–91, 299, 301, 329, 338, 340, 343, 346–47, 349, 354, 360–61, 390, 419–20, 430, 434–37, 440, 449, 455, 480, 486, 530, 532, 633–34, 658, 664, 727, 731, 738; in Ireland, 115–16, 134, 159, 351, 420
Martinique, 1, 97, 190, 200
Mary I, 99
Mary II, xviii, 47, 57–58, 61–62, 72, 620, 693, 710, 749, 774
Maryland, 65, 241, 265, 657, 694, 700, 729; Assembly, 345, 620–21; charter of, 682, 684, 687–91, 702, 710;

governors, 345; as proprietary colony, xvii, 471; tobacco from, 298, 300
Massachusetts, 41, 66, 73, 256, 532, 642, 667, 693–94, 700; Boston Massacre, 743–44, 747, 752–53, 755, 776; and "Boston Pamphlet," 759, 764; charter of 1629, 126, 682, 684, 687, 691–92, 717, 779; charter of 1691, 710–12, 749–50, 767, 769, 771, 773–74, 776–77, 786–88; charters, in general, 66, 75, 106, 108–9, 150, 623, 759; committees of correspondence in, 780–88; and expense of colonial wars, 88, 107, 733; governors of, 1, 25, 346, 406, 521, 743–44, 773–76, 785–88; Governor's Council, 106; House of Representatives, 106–9, 305, 331, 345, 359, 405, 521, 534, 623–25, 675, 712, 732, 743, 771, 773–75, 781, 785–88; paper money in, 346
Master-servant relationship, 491, 498–99
Mather, Increase, 711
Matthew (gospel), 296, 579
Mauduit, Israel, 720
Mauduit, Jasper, 109
Mayflower Compact, 685–86
Mayhew, Jonathan, xvi
McAulay, Alexander, 465–66
Mediterranean Sea, xv, 21, 584, 596
Mexico, 15
Micah (biblical book), 434
Micklegemot (Saxon assembly), 718
Middlesex, England, 600
Militia, xv, xxi, 104, 184, 260, 265, 285, 338, 350, 353, 355, 730
Mining, 171–72, 262, 291
Minorca, xv, 584, 597
Minority rights, 654
Mississippi River, xv
Mobile, West Florida, 175
Molasses, 41, 118, 132–33, 216–18, 221, 228, 234, 415, 632, 635–37
Molasses Act (1733; 6 George II, chap. 13), 102, 156, 204, 217, 234, 415, 508, 635–37
Molesworth, Robert, 568, 588
Molière (Jean-Baptiste Poquelin), 611
Molineux, William, 747, 763
Molloy, Charles, 99

Monarchy, 46, 55, 81, 369, 424, 452, 531, 605, 607, 647, 719; absolute, 19, 50–51, 91, 331, 376, 458–59, 491; arbitrary power of, 469; and civil/political rights of colonists, 78–80, 126, 527; colonies dependent on, 592; and colonists' right to settle in America, 317; divine right of, 50–51, 491, 499; executive power embodied in, 19, 87, 191, 259, 332, 377, 434, 474, 491, 646–47, 695; following Glorious Revolution, 56–63, 620; and infringement of liberty, 331, 368, 376–77, 474, 478–79, 515; lawful authority of, 665; as one principal form of government, 54, 247, 270, 442, 444, 537, 749–50; relationship to aristocracy, 442, 444, 510; restraining power of, 384; right to repeal laws, 434; right to tax subjects, 414–15, 427, 429–30, 432–33, 598–601; sovereignty of, 31, 393, 513, 693–94, 704. *See also* Crown, British *and individual monarchs*

Money: paper, 121, 131, 192–93, 340, 345–46; and suffrage, 236, 248, 310

Monmouth, Duke of (James Scott), 393

Monopolies, 290, 298–99

Montagu, Mary Wortley, 495

Montesquieu, baron de (Charles-Louis de Secondat), 14, 69–70, 158, 428, 447, 485, 608, 729

Montreal, Canada, 336

Moore, Henry, 411

Moors, 463

Morton, Joseph, 707

Muslims, 513

Muslin cloth, 204, 212–13

Mutiny Acts, 284–85, 731

Naturalization, 78, 110, 129, 157

Naturalization Act (1739; 13 George II, chap. 7), 110–11, 157, 623, 675, 769

Naunton, Robert, 685

Naval stores, 201–2, 233, 329, 437, 487, 778

Navigation Acts, xvi–xvii, xx–xxi, 95, 196, 204, 223–31, 317, 321, 700, 708;
of 1651, 413–14; of 1660 (12 Charles II, chap. 18), 297, 414–15; of 1663 (15 Charles II, chap. 7), 173, 297, 413–14, 633, 707; of 1672 (25 Charles II, chap. 7), 101, 234, 323–24, 414–15, 439–40, 709–10, 712–15; of 1695 (7 & 8 William III and Mary II, chap. 22), 234, 414–15, 622

Navy, British, xv, 12, 25, 83–84, 93, 186, 190, 202, 230–33, 263, 310, 320, 338, 348, 439, 470, 487, 565, 659, 664, 743, 773

Neal, Daniel, 686–87

Negroes, 65, 78, 97, 219, 657, 734; enslavement of, 69–70, 115, 119, 180, 184, 186, 189, 200, 282–83, 335, 663

Nero, 447

Netherlands, 280, 558, 570, 624, 675, 685, 734; colonial government of, 79; fisheries of, 698; independence from Spain, 328, 503; trade of, 21–22, 98, 132, 209, 212, 226, 300, 337; whale fishery of, 196–98

New England, 65, 95, 126, 520, 572, 657, 711, 740; common law in, 152; fisheries of, 173, 199; industriousness of, 435; manufacturing in, 13; militia of, 260; paper money in, 121, 345–46; during Restoration, 717; settlement of, 685–87, 694; in Seven Years' War, 97, 730; trade of, 159, 337. *See also individual colonies*

Newfoundland, 21, 173–74, 229, 336–37, 597

New Hampshire, 779; charter of, 66, 150, 700

New Haven (colony), 700–1

New Jersey, 256

New London, Connecticut, 667–68

New Orleans, Louisiana, xv

Newport, Rhode Island, 143

Newspapers, xiii, 1, 13, 21, 147, 160, 289, 352, 363, 671; tax on, 163, 278

New York, 65, 460, 469, 646, 779; Assembly, 342, 363, 370, 372, 377, 381, 410–12, 468, 593, 625–26, 658, 712, 732, 776; fisheries of, 173, 199; governors of, 411, 703

New York City, 291, 331, 351, 381, 428–29, 627

New York Resolves (1765), 732
New York Restraining Act (1767; 7
    George III, chap. 59), 363, 371–72,
    377, 410–12, 468, 593
Nimrod, 53
Non-resistance, 376
Normandy, France, 427
Normans, 72, 456, 508
Northampton, Earl of, 251
North Carolina, 65, 337, 445, 657
North Sea, 209, 226
Nottingham, England, 13
Nova Scotia, 97, 171–72, 174, 260, 262,
    316, 337, 354, 453–55, 657

Ohio River, 354–55
Old Sarum, England, 237
Old South Meeting-House, 747
Oligarchy, xxi, 54–55, 127
Oranges, 175
Original compact, 45–50, 53, 56, 104,
    317, 497, 502, 504–5, 598–99, 764–
    65
Osborne, Danvers, 256
Otis, James, 121, 143, 305, 405, 763;
    The Rights of the British Colonies, 41–
    119
Ottoman Empire, 90, 326, 388, 507–8,
    513, 532
Otway vs. Ramsay, 86
Ovid, 438

Pamphlets, role of, xiii, 147, 156, 160,
    163, 309, 352, 496, 577, 613, 671
Papacy, 45, 68–69, 119, 678, 765
Paper/paper goods, 163, 235, 269–70,
    405, 413, 417–19, 426, 431–32, 437,
    446, 448–49, 452
Paper money, 121, 131, 192–93, 340,
    345–46
Paris, France, 668
Parliament, British, 5–6, 19, 110, 537,
    571, 618, 667; and accession of
    William and Mary, 57–63; and Bill of
    Rights, xviii, 60–62, 76, 332; colonial
    petitions to, 100, 156, 340, 342, 425–
    26, 489, 556, 592, 619, 627; and
    colonial reforms, xiii, xxii, 25–26, 30,
    38–39, 41, 121, 613, 743; colonial
    respect for, 340, 577, 608; colonies
    subordinate to, 80, 84, 88–89, 105,
131, 256–59, 273, 279, 325–28, 331–32,
363, 369, 372–77, 382–83, 413, 424,
519–20, 550, 592–94, 599, 608, 627;
duration of, 560–61; early,
representation in, 508–12, 643–44;
election of members to, 236, 239,
248–50, 252–54, 274, 276–77, 310–
15, 510, 561, 577, 601, 606, 644–45,
665, 676, 715, 718, 720, 750, 769;
Franklin's testimony before, 332, 335–
61; and George III, xxi–xxii, 331;
House of Lords against repeal of
Stamp Act, 590, 595–96; and
infringement of liberty, 376–77, 394,
402, 410–11, 413, 417–18, 420, 422,
431–33, 446, 451, 456, 463, 470,
485; and interests of Great Britain,
241, 245, 264; judicial power of
House of Lords, 402; legislative
power embodied in, 19, 87, 191, 313,
331–32, 363, 375, 377, 381, 510, 572,
591, 614, 638, 660, 695–96, 724,
771; money bills formed in House of
Commons, 442, 508, 559, 600, 715,
771; passage of Stamp Act, 163, 230,
247, 278; power of House of Lords,
19; and protection of liberty, 340,
608; reimbursement of colonies, 83,
87, 97, 117, 139, 338, 352–53;
relationship to the Crown, 32–33, 88,
93, 322, 331–32, 356, 379, 443, 446,
627, 751; repeal of Stamp Act, 331–32,
363, 367, 393; and seizure of
property, 282; self-correction of, 80,
82, 87, 121; supremacy of, 73, 80, 87,
105, 112, 156, 385, 387, 394, 435, 516–
18, 583, 585–86, 613–14, 625–28, 630,
638, 643, 651–53, 662, 715–18, 769;
suspension of New York Assembly,
363, 372, 377, 410–12, 468, 593;
unjust and oppressive laws of, 246,
341, 406, 444–45, 460; virtual
representation in, 163–64, 237–38,
241, 247–50, 252–53, 269, 305, 313,
315, 328, 430, 450, 508, 512–14
Parliament, Irish, 468, 587–88, 609
Parliament, Saxon, 312
Parliament, Spanish, 463
Parliament Act (1689; 1 William III and
    Mary II, chap. 1), 57–58
Partridge, Richard, 156

Patriotism, 57, 263, 271, 293, 296, 315, 423, 472, 724

Patriots, American, 241, 405, 521, 577, 668, 676, 743, 756

Paul (apostle), 128

Peloponnesian War, 156

Pennsylvania, 265, 305, 349, 355, 360, 409, 657, 729; Assembly, 339, 357–58, 405, 412, 460, 620–21; charter of, 358–59, 621, 647, 659–60, 710; fisheries of, 173; linen manufacturing in, 205–6; as proprietary colony, xvii, 471; taxes in, 335, 337–40, 349, 454

Pennsylvania Chronicle, 405

Pennsylvania Journal, 363

Pennsylvania Resolves (1765), 620

Pensions, 465–69

Pericles, 454

Persius, 254, 463, 504

Peru, 15

Petitions: to the Crown, 347, 381, 405, 425–26, 489, 556, 592, 619, 706; to Parliament, 100, 156, 340, 342, 425–26, 489, 556, 592, 619, 627

Petyt, William, 312, 322

Phaedrus, 272, 669

Philadelphia, Pennsylvania, 291, 331, 335, 351, 363, 405, 743

Philo, Quintus Publilius, 478

Pierpont, Robert, 763

Pilgrims (Separatists), 685–87

Pilpay, 160

Pimento, 215, 221, 227

Pirates, 663

Pitt, John, 588

Pitt, William (later Earl of Chatham), xv, 262, 371, 386; speeches against Stamp Act, 363, 385, 388, 390, 399, 419, 430–31, 450–52, 464, 487, 496

Plutarch, 421, 423

Plymouth (colony), 88, 696; charter of, 150, 684–87, 691

Poland, 420, 533, 639

Poll tax, 335, 349

Pompey the Great (Gnaeus Pompeius Magnus), 92

Pontiac's Rebellion, 335, 355

Pontius the Samnite, 726

Pope, Alexander, 409, 475

Portugal, 15, 110, 195, 200, 337, 417, 437, 445, 657, 678, 734

Postlethwayt, Malachy, 115, 436–38

Post office, 101–2, 141, 234–36, 285–86, 336, 347–48, 357, 360–61, 470, 529–30, 712

Post Office Act (1710; 9 Anne, chap. 10), 234, 285, 529

Poverty, 16, 215, 233, 270–71, 335, 350–51

Powell, William, 763

Power, 475–77, 511, 543; absolute, 31, 51, 54, 57, 59, 64, 87, 113, 259, 372, 385, 491, 500, 507, 513; arbitrary, 72, 77, 87, 90, 267, 270, 373, 376, 389, 403, 458–59, 469, 751, 755, 768, 776, 779; delegated, 191, 375–76, 398, 400, 645, 647, 695; and formation of government, 45, 49; of God, 50–51; judicial, 402–4, 458–62; master-servant relationship, 491, 498–99; versus right, 100, 310, 324. *See also* Executive power; Legislative power

Pownall, John, 25

Pownall, Thomas, 255, 327, 457; *Administration of the Colonies*, 25, 80–81, 84, 88–93, 102–3

Powys, Thomas, 112

Press, freedom of the, 245–46

Privy Council, 26, 157, 269, 315, 319, 680, 773

Proclamation of 1763, on limits of settlement, xx, 169, 177–79

Proclamation of 1764, on West Indies settlement, 181–86, 190

Property, 325, 724, 776; of colonists, 373, 386, 429–30, 462, 528, 597, 603–7, 610–11, 673, 737–38, 751, 754, 777; and formation of government, 45, 48–49; and liberty, 64, 109, 125–26, 135, 150, 373, 386, 394, 462, 484, 598, 603, 605–6, 610–11, 720, 738, 751, 764, 767–68; Locke on, 651–53; rights of, 109, 126, 135, 380–82, 394, 450–51, 475, 484, 497, 553–54, 598, 622, 718–21, 764–70; seizure of, 77, 79, 282–83; and suffrage, 236, 248, 310–11, 314; and taxation, 125, 135, 138

Protestants, xv, xviii, 58–60, 73, 129, 157, 170, 185, 441, 479, 732. *See also individual sects*

Proverbs (biblical book), 426

Providence, Rhode Island, 121, 142, 521
Public credit, 192–93
Public land banks, 192
Pufendorf, Samuel, 66, 128, 280
Puritans, 685, 687

Quakers, 337
Quartering Act (1765; 5 George III, chap. 33), 363, 367, 369–70
Quartering of soldiers, 59, 255, 328, 360, 363, 367, 369–70, 533, 569, 639, 731–32, 752, 773, 776
Quebec, xv, xx, 169–70, 174, 177, 179, 336, 646, 657
Quincy, Josiah, 743, 763
Quit rents, 181, 185, 187, 648–49, 770

Raleigh, Walter, 317–18, 437, 676–77, 679, 681
Ramsay, Allan, 537; *Thoughts on the Origin and Nature of Government*, 491–520
Rapin-Thoyras, Paul de, 312, 477–78
Rebellion, 38, 88–90, 191, 346, 371, 373, 393, 503, 537, 543, 571, 609, 666, 708, 747, 759, 770, 782–83
Reform, imperial, xiii, xxii, 25–26, 30, 38–39, 41, 121, 613, 743
Religion, freedom of, 74, 82, 317, 321, 441, 521, 553, 604, 767, 778–79, 782
Representation, 31, 33, 55, 85, 136, 152, 245, 257, 271, 650, 715, 718–22; actual, 252–53, 305, 577, 600, 644; in early Parliaments, 508–12; of London, 236–38, 248–49, 254, 310, 601, 725; in Scotland, 153, 643–44; and taxation, 163, 233–34, 236–37, 239–40, 247–48, 254, 405, 411, 429, 528–29, 565–66; virtual, 163–64, 237–38, 241, 247–50, 252–53, 269, 305, 313, 315, 328, 430, 450, 508, 512–14, 593
Representation of Chester Act (1543; 34 & 35 Henry VIII), 446
Representation of Durham Act (1672; 25 Charles II), 446
Republicanism, xiii, 169, 266, 276, 744
Revenue. *See* Taxation
Revolutionary War, xiii, 744, 759
Rhode Island, 156, 159, 518; Assembly, 121; charter of, 66, 126, 143, 150, 156, 702–6; as corporate colony, xvii, 66,

143, 521; democracy in, 143; factional politics in, 121, 143; governors of, 121, 521; judges in, 92; and molasses trade, 133
Rice, xvi, 163, 199–201, 445
Richard II, 250, 269
Rights, 422, 475; civil, 72–105, 245–46, 275–76, 288–89, 317, 321, 326, 515, 543, 550, 552, 572–73, 603–4, 778, 782; of colonists, 620–30, 659, 662, 667, 719–20, 726–28, 732, 740, 754, 756, 759, 763–64, 767–70, 780–83; infringement of, 770–80; natural, 41–42, 46, 53, 66–72, 75, 77–78, 287–89, 305, 314, 316–17, 326, 349, 370, 373, 376, 384, 388, 394, 498–501, 531, 557–58, 603, 621–24, 650, 674, 764–70; political, 72–105, 151; and power, 100, 310, 324; property, 109, 126, 135, 380–82, 394, 450–51, 475, 484, 497, 553–54, 598, 622, 714–17, 764–70; religious, 74, 82, 317, 321, 441, 521, 553, 604, 767, 778–79, 782
Riots, 143, 352, 356, 422, 518, 610, 667, 743
Robertson, William, 643
Rockingham, Marquis of (Charles Watson-Wentworth), 331–32
Rodney, Caesar, 331
Rome, ancient, xv, 10–11, 56, 67–68, 104, 127–28, 135, 137, 150, 154–55, 259, 316, 425, 441, 447, 463, 478, 496, 503, 519, 546–49, 691, 741, 744, 748–49, 752–53, 771
Rome, Italy, 119
Romulus, 546, 549
Rousseau, Jean-Jacques, 66, 382–83, 385
Ruddock, John, 106
Rum, 41, 132–33, 216–20, 228, 234, 335, 415
Russia, 486–87

Sabines, 11
Sacheverell, Henry, 376
St. Augustine, East Florida, 175
St. Lawrence River, 198
St. Lucia, 186
St. Pierre et Miquelon, 173, 229
St. Vincent and the Grenadines, xv, 185, 188, 190
Salkeld, William, 76

Sallust, 403, 413, 476, 487, 489
Sardinia, 155, 420
Savannah, Georgia, 577
Saxons, 154, 311–12, 718
Scotland, xxi, 47, 57, 293, 321, 427, 693, 699, 777; constitution of, 512; constitutional status of, 516, 566, 577, 584–87, 594–96, 602, 606, 609, 684–85; economy of, xix–xx; liberty in, 602; peers in, 517, 643; representation in, 153, 643–44; taxation in, 517–18. *See also* Great Britain
Seal skins, 198
Selden, John, 281
Seneca, 284, 383
Senegal, xv, 584
Separatists (Pilgrims), 685–87
Servant-master relationship, 491, 498–99
Servants, white, 183
Servius Tullius, 67, 128, 547
Seven Years' War, xvi, 18, 141, 167, 235, 261, 284, 345, 352, 363, 729; British army in, xv, xxi, 177, 255, 285, 351, 353–55, 390–91; colonial debt from, xv, 97, 107, 117, 139, 259–60, 262–63, 266, 268, 335, 353, 733; colonial manufacturing during, 360; colonial militia in, xv, xxi, 260, 285, 338, 353, 355, 730; Great Britain's war debt from, xx–xxi, 76, 97, 107, 117, 202, 233, 236, 267, 335, 569–70; Indians in, 354–55, 570; territory acquired, xv, xx–xxi, 1, 7, 9, 11–12, 23, 83, 168, 268, 309, 354, 453–54, 470, 554, 646
Shakespeare, William, 158, 256, 457, 488, 629
Sheffield, England, 305
Shelburne, Earl of (William Petty), 487
Shipping, xvi, xix, 198, 436, 487, 633–35, 663, 772, 778; seizure of vessels, 228–31
Shirley, William, 733
Sidney, Algernon, 126, 281, 515, 718–19, 723–24, 726, 728
Silk, xx, 85, 174–75, 211, 227, 262
Silver, 8, 291, 318, 346
Slavery: in ancient Rome, 447, 548, 725, 748; of Negroes, 69–70, 115, 119, 180, 184, 186, 189, 200, 282–83,

335, 663; as political condition, 46, 51, 56, 64, 71, 74–76, 79, 84, 87, 89, 91–92, 109–10, 113–14, 121, 125–27, 135–36, 140, 148–50, 155, 238, 258, 273, 276, 296, 326, 368, 373–74, 376, 385, 394, 398, 420, 430, 448, 450–51, 462, 479, 485, 521–22, 531, 533, 535, 550, 565, 676, 711, 718, 723, 726, 728, 749, 751, 754, 756, 767, 780, 782, 785; in West Indies, 70, 115, 180, 184, 186, 189, 200
Slave trade, 21, 70, 218–20, 657, 734
Smith, William, 460
Smuggling, xvii, xx, 41, 98, 121, 157–59, 176, 195, 209, 217–18, 225–31
Solorzano Pereira, Juan de, 68
Sons of Liberty, 521, 536
South Carolina, 65, 175, 216, 256, 337, 363, 577, 592; Assembly, 657; charter of, 608, 706–7; indigo from, 246; rice from, 199–200, 445
Southern Department, xvii, xxii, 25
Sovereignty, xiii, 71, 497, 513, 515, 679, 709; of colonies, 569–70; of constitution, 142; of monarch, 31, 393, 513, 693–94, 704; of nations, 516; of Parliament, 31–33, 143, 363, 375, 381–83, 385–88, 390–94, 397, 399, 405, 432–33, 450, 460, 488, 529–32, 558, 563–64, 570, 572, 575, 613–14, 636, 639–40, 662, 668, 672, 693; of the people, 51, 112, 138
Spain, 70, 335, 355, 720, 734; absolute monarchy in, 79; cession of Louisiana from France, xv, 168, 262; colonial government of, 68, 110, 114, 128, 316; as colonial power, 8–9, 15, 454, 678; Dutch independence from, 328, 503; Inquisition in, 69, 160; parliament of, 463; trade of, 16, 176, 189, 195, 200, 212, 337–38, 417, 437
Sparta, 399, 423, 519, 545–46, 725
Speech, freedom of, 60, 137–38, 521, 534
Spices, 22
Spies, 668
Spry, William, 157–58
Squire, Samuel, 312
Stamp Act (1765; 5 George III, chap. 12), xxi, 25, 517, 673; British defense of, 154, 203, 231–36, 240–41, 505,

634; colonial opposition to, 143, 163, 241, 247–48, 253–54, 257, 266–70, 278, 282, 284–85, 287, 301, 369, 385–86, 671, 715, 722, 733; Dickinson's views on, 410, 413, 416–19, 422, 426, 433, 440–41, 453, 470, 483, 486–87; Franklin's views on, 336–38, 340–41, 343–44, 346, 349–52, 356–58, 360–61; Pitt's speeches against, 363, 385, 388, 390, 399, 419, 430–31, 450–52, 464, 487, 496; proposed, 121, 130, 135, 139, 141; repeal of, 331–32, 350, 360, 363, 367, 393, 411, 430–31, 450–52, 472, 496, 556, 568, 590, 595–96, 631, 665, 731

Stamp Act Congress, 331, 340, 428–29, 537, 627

Stamp agents, 143, 284

Standing army, 59–60, 76, 92, 96, 104, 288, 372, 470, 477–78, 521, 533–34, 743, 752, 755, 773

Stanley, John, 697

State of nature, 47–48, 69, 313, 497–500, 614, 621, 638, 766

Steel, 419

Strahan, William, 68, 316

Strait of Gibraltar, 657

Stuart, Charles Edward, 491

Stuarts, xvii–xviii, 72, 424, 491, 503, 552, 693, 749

Succession to the Crown Act (1707; 6 Anne, chap. 7), 73

Suffrage. See Elections

Sugar, xvi, 1, 41, 70, 83, 97, 115, 118, 132, 184, 189, 215–16, 221–22, 228, 234, 349, 414–15, 436–37

Sugar Act (1764; 4 George III, chap. 15), 41, 116, 121, 132, 134, 143, 204, 416, 440

Sulla, Lucius Cornelius, 92

Surinam, 667

Sweden, 113, 226, 486–87, 783

Sweetser, John, 763

Swift, Jonathan, 137, 782

Switzerland, 328, 503, 577

Syracuse, 752

Tacitus, 135, 441–42, 447, 473, 486

Tangier, Morocco, 478

Tariffs, 41

Tarsus, 128

Tartars, 621

Taxation, 446–47, 477, 506; in ancient Greece and Rome, 547–48; of beaver skins, 195–96; of cider, 508; of coffee, 215; by colonial assemblies, 34–37, 163, 274, 288, 349, 352, 355–56, 450, 472, 514, 555, 563, 589, 604, 607, 609, 634; for defense of colonies, 163, 194, 230–36, 240, 335, 338, 342, 345, 369, 371–72, 416, 452–55, 457–58, 520, 565–66, 569, 657, 659, 733; excise, 348, 477–78; expense of maintaining troops as, 410–11, 416; external/internal, 34–35, 82–83, 130, 135, 154, 163, 256–58, 278, 324, 328, 340–41, 343, 351–52, 356, 359–60, 386, 405–6, 426, 429–30, 631, 634, 714; of glass, 405, 413, 417–19, 431, 448–49; in Great Britain, xx, 33, 98, 141, 270, 276, 567, 595–96, 658–59, 724; of hemp and flax, 201–2, 205–7, 210; of imported slaves, 335; of indigo, 215–16; of Ireland, 84–87; of land, 269, 335, 338–39, 634, 654, 713; of lead, 405; of linen, 202, 205–7, 209–13, 633; of malt, 517–18, 595; of paper/paper goods, 163, 235, 269–70, 405, 413, 417–19, 426, 431–32, 437, 446, 448–49, 452; Parliamentary authority for, 508–14, 517–18, 553–56, 571–72, 577, 583, 594–95, 599–611, 614, 630–31, 635–37, 639–41, 646–47, 653, 660–61, 683, 691, 693, 695, 709–11, 714–15, 717, 722, 725, 727, 730, 732, 736, 750–51, 771, 785; and representation, 163, 233–34, 236–37, 239–40, 247–48, 254, 406, 411, 528–29, 565–66; of rice, 199–201; of sugar, molasses and rum, 216–22, 234, 335, 349, 414–15, 632, 635–37; of tea, 405, 631–32; of tobacco, 271–72, 298–303, 348–49, 414, 508; of trade, 163, 202–5, 215, 222–23, 234, 240, 297–304, 318, 321, 323–25, 340–41, 343, 348, 363, 377, 386, 399–400, 402, 405–6, 413–15, 417–21, 428–32, 438–41, 443, 448–52, 455, 714–15, 733–34, 738, 741; of whale fins, 196–98; of wine, 213–15, 335, 508, 634; of wool, 633. See also individual acts

Tea, xx, 226, 405, 631–32

Temple, William, 312, 469, 667

Terence, 147, 390

Territory, acquisition of, xv, xx–xxi, 1,
    7, 9, 11–12, 23, 83, 268, 309, 354,
    453–54, 470, 554

Thacher, Oxenbridge, 106

Thebes, 546

Thomson, James, 125, 147–48

Thornby vs. Fleetwood, 112

Thucydides, 67, 127, 156, 326, 579

Tiberius, 135

Tobacco, xvi, 85–86, 184, 194, 234,
    269, 271–72, 298–303, 323, 348–49,
    360–61, 414, 508, 697

Tobago, xv, 188–90

Tories, xvii–xviii, xxi, 261, 491, 668, 759

Townshend, Charles, 405

Townshend Acts (1767), 405–6, 422,
    426, 431, 433, 456, 459, 464, 470–
    73, 479, 481, 743–44

Trade, 433; in ancient times, 21;
    balance of, 15, 19; deficits, xx; and
    fisheries, 173; of France, 21, 41, 94,
    115, 132, 172–73, 190, 195, 200, 211–
    17, 220–22, 226–27, 300, 437, 544;
    free, 16, 321, 323, 663; of Germany,
    211, 213, 226, 437; importance to
    British empire, 167; with Indians,
    178–79, 218, 220, 354–55, 453, 533,
    635, 657; with Ireland, 420, 445; of
    Italy, 437; laws/principles relating
    to, 17–20; as natural right, 531; of
    Netherlands, 21–22, 98, 132, 209,
    212, 226, 300; and smuggling, xvii,
    xx, 41, 98, 121, 157–59, 176, 195, 209,
    217–18, 225–31; of Spain, 16, 176,
    189, 195, 200, 212, 417, 437; taxation
    of, 163, 202–5, 215, 222–23, 234,
    240, 297–304, 318, 321, 323–25,
    340–41, 343, 348, 363, 377, 386,
    399–400, 402, 405–6, 413–15, 417–
    21, 428–32, 438–41, 443, 448–52,
    455, 714–15, 733–34, 738, 741. See also
    individual acts

Treasury, British, xvii, 269–70, 342

Treaty of Aix-la-Chapelle (1748), 97

Treaty of Paris (1763), xv, xx, 1, 7, 18,
    167, 212, 260, 263, 335, 355

Treaty of Tordesillas (1494), 678

Treaty of Utrecht (1713), 354

Tregor's Case, 112

Trial by jury, 61, 267, 270, 328, 340,
    459–60, 521, 778

Tucker, Josiah, 438

Turks. See Ottoman Empire

Tyler, Royal, 106

Tyler, Wat, 497

Tyranny. See Despotism

Tyrconnell, Earl of (George
    Carpenter), 588

Tyre, 21

Vandals, 91

Vattel, Emmerich de, 47, 112–14, 313,
    768

Vaughan, John, 76, 85

Venice, Italy, 437, 479, 599

Venner, Thomas, 125

Viner, Charles, 99

Virgil, 43, 304, 451, 468, 481–82, 493,
    518, 745, 756

Virginia, 65, 246, 265, 469, 657, 685,
    693–94, 700–1, 729; Bacon's
    Rebellion, 708; charter of, 317–21,
    324, 676–84, 702, 704; governors
    of, 321, 682, 699, 708; House of
    Burgesses, 305, 319–21, 323–24, 620,
    661, 681, 699, 705, 709, 714, 732;
    tobacco from, 298, 300, 360–61;
    trade deficit of, xx; wool from, 295,
    344

Virginia Company, 676, 679–81, 685,
    687

Virginia Resolves (1765), 620

Vortigern, 311

Votes and Proceedings of the Freeholders
    and Other Inhabitants of the Town of
    Boston, 759–88

Wales, 32, 85, 101, 716; constitutional
    status of, 584, 602. See also Great
    Britain

Walker, Thomas, 288

Walrus skins, 198

War of Jenkins' Ear, 355, 360

War Office, xvii

Warren, Joseph, 763; An Oration
    Delivered March 5th, 1772, 739–53

Washington, George, xx

Wealth, 12, 15, 51, 110, 116, 137, 140,
    167, 169, 185–86, 199, 225, 233, 236,

262, 264, 269–70, 279, 283, 310, 391, 543, 728

Wedderburn, Alexander, 759

Wendell, Oliver, 763

West Florida, xv, 169–70, 174–77, 179, 216, 221, 262, 417, 453–55, 646

West Indies, 8, 12, 16, 65, 97, 199, 209, 392, 657, 699; agriculture in, 184, 189–90, 207, 221; land in, 176, 180–90; lifestyle in, 168–69, 213, 233, 254; molasses from, 41, 118, 132–33, 216–18, 221, 637; new British possessions in, xv, 1, 9, 168, 646; slavery in, 70, 115, 180, 184, 186, 189, 200; and trade, 83, 114–16, 118–19, 132–33, 203, 214–23, 337, 349, 386, 389, 435, 637, 734. *See also individual islands*

Westphalia, 519

Whale fishery, 163, 173, 196–99, 227

Whately, Thomas, 25, 241, 246, 255, 280–81, 283–84, 287, 289, 294, 296, 305, 307, 309–11, 317, 321–22, 325–26; *The Regulations Lately Made Concerning the Colonies*, 163–240

Whigs, xvii–xviii, xxi, 331–32, 491, 613, 668, 759

Wilderness. *See* Frontier

Wilkes, John, 667

William I, 109, 513

William III, xviii, 47–48, 57–59, 61–63, 72, 280, 393, 413, 620, 660, 692–93, 703, 707, 710, 749, 774

Williams, William Peere, 315

Williamsburg, Virginia, 305, 349

Windsor Castle, 687–88

Wine, 174–75, 204, 213–15, 226, 262, 335, 437, 446, 508, 634

Winnington, Thomas, 156

Wirt, William, 306

Wittinagemot (Saxon parliament), 312

Wollaston, William, 313–14

Women, 46, 236, 251, 310

Wool, 18, 94–95, 115–16, 292, 295, 344, 414, 532, 535, 633, 777

Woollen Act (1699; 11 William III, chap. 13), 95, 209

Wytham vs. Dutton, 76

Yeardley, George, 682

Yonge, William, 156

York, England, 320

Young, Edward, 148

Young, Thomas, 763

Zephaniah (biblical book), 757

Zubly, John Joachim: *An Humble Enquiry into the Nature of the Dependency of the American Colonies upon the Parliament of Great-Britain*, 577–612

*This book is set in 10 point ITC Galliard Pro, a
face designed for digital composition by Matthew Carter
and based on the sixteenth-century face Granjon. The paper
is acid-free lightweight opaque and meets the requirements
for permanence of the American National Standards Institute.
The binding material is Brillianta, a woven rayon cloth made
by Van Heek–Scholco Textielfabrieken, Holland.
Composition by Dedicated Book Services. Printing and
binding by Edwards Brothers Malloy, Ann Arbor.
Designed by Bruce Campbell.*

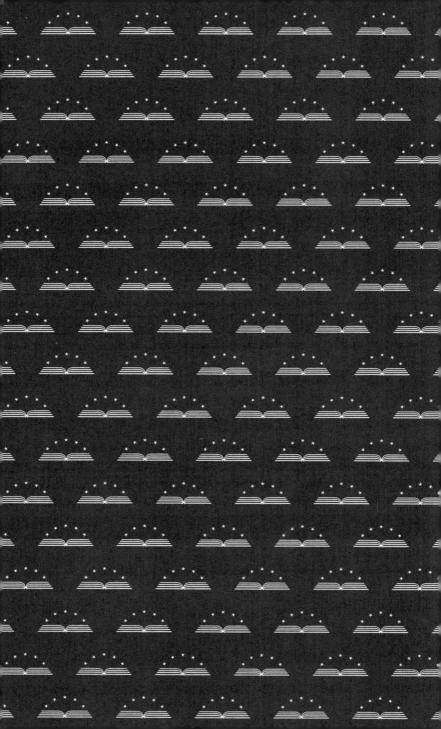